HALSBURY'S
Laws of England

FOURTH EDITION
REISSUE

LORD HAILSHAM OF ST. MARYLEBONE

Lord High Chancellor of Great Britain
1970–74 and 1979–87

Volume 8(1)

BUTTERWORTHS

LONDON   1996

UNITED KINGDOM	Butterworths, a Division of Reed Elsevier (UK) Ltd Halsbury House, 35 Chancery Lane, **London** WC2A 1EL and 4 Hill Street, **Edinburgh** EH2 3JZ
AUSTRALIA	Butterworths, **Sydney, Melbourne, Brisbane, Adelaide, Perth, Canberra** and **Hobart**
CANADA	Butterworths Canada Ltd, **Toronto** and **Vancouver**
HONG KONG	Butterworths Asia, **Hong Kong**
IRELAND	Butterworth (Ireland) Ltd, **Dublin**
MALAYSIA	Malayan Law Journal Sdn Bhd, **Kuala Lumpur**
NEW ZEALAND	Butterworths of New Zealand Ltd, **Wellington** and **Auckland**
SINGAPORE	Butterworths Asia, **Singapore**
SOUTH AFRICA	Butterworth Publishers (Pty) Ltd, **Durban**
USA	Michie, **Charlottesville**, Virginia

FIRST EDITION

Published in 31 volumes between 1907 and 1917 under the Editorship of the Rt. Hon. the Earl of Halsbury, Lord High Chancellor of Great Britain, 1885–86, 1886–92 and 1895–1905

SECOND EDITION

Published in 37 volumes between 1931 and 1942 under the Editorship of the Rt. Hon. the Viscount Hailsham, Lord High Chancellor of Great Britain, 1928–29 and 1935–38

THIRD EDITION

Published in 43 volumes between 1952 and 1964 under the Editorship of the Rt. Hon. the Viscount Simonds, Lord High Chancellor of Great Britain, 1951–54

FOURTH EDITION

Published in 56 volumes between 1973 and 1987 under the Editorship of the Rt. Hon. Lord Hailsham of St. Marylebone, Lord High Chancellor of Great Britain, 1970–74 and 1979–87

ISBN   (complete set, standard binding) 0 406 03400 1
(this volume, standard binding) 0 406 052085

Typeset by Thomson Litho Ltd, East Kilbride, Scotland
Printed and bound in Great Britain by
Butler & Tanner Ltd, Frome

Editor in Chief

THE RIGHT HONOURABLE

LORD HAILSHAM OF ST. MARYLEBONE

LORD HIGH CHANCELLOR OF GREAT BRITAIN

1970–74 and 1979–87

Editors of this Volume

SIMON HETHERINGTON, LL.B.

CAROL MARSH, M.A., LL.B.

Managing Editor (Commissioning)

DEBORAH SAUNDERS, B.A.
OF GRAY'S INN, BARRISTER

Editorial Staff

CLAIRE MASSON, M.A.,
A SOLICITOR OF THE SUPREME COURT

HEON STEVENSON, B.A.
OF GRAY'S INN, BARRISTER

Administrative Manager

SARAH L. HORNSBY, Dip. Pub.

Indexer

B. BURKE, B.Sc.

General Editor

DAVID HAY, M.A., LL.M.
OF THE INNER TEMPLE, BARRISTER

Publisher

JAMES BOWMAN, LL.B.
A SOLICITOR OF THE SUPREME COURT

The titles in Volume 8(1) have been contributed by:

COMPULSORY
ACQUISITION OF LAND

Advisory Editor
THE HON. SIR ROBERT CARNWATH,
C.V.O., M.A., LL.B.; one of the Justices of
Her Majesty's High Court of Justice

Consultant Editor and Contributor
JOSEPH HARPER, B.A., LL.M., of Gray's
Inn; one of Her Majesty's Counsel

Contributors
DAVID HANDS of the Inner Temple;
one of Her Majesty's Counsel

THE RT. HON. LORD KINGSLAND,
P.C., T.D., D.Phil; one of Her Majesty's
Counsel

JOHN FURBER, M.A., of the Inner
Temple; one of Her Majesty's Counsel

EIAN CAWS, B.A., of the Inner Temple,
Barrister

CHRISTOPHER LEWSLEY, B.Sc., Ph.D.,
C.Eng., M.I.Struct.E., of Lincoln's Inn,
Barrister

JONATHAN KARAS, M.A., of the Middle
Temple, Barrister

DAVID FORSDICK, B.A., of Gray's Inn,
Barrister

CONFIDENCE AND
DATA PROTECTION

A. H. HUDSON, M.A., LL.B., Ph.D., of
Lincoln's Inn, Barrister; Emeritus Professor of
Common Law, University of Liverpool

NORMAN PALMER, B.C.L., M.A., of
Gray's Inn, Barrister; Rowe & Maw Professor
of Commercial Law, University College
London

CONFLICT OF LAWS

DAVID McCLEAN, C.B.E., D.C.L.,
of Gray's Inn; one of Her Majesty's Counsel;
Pro-Vice-Chancellor and Professor of Law,
University of Sheffield

ADRIAN BRIGGS, B.C.L., M.A., of the
Middle Temple, Barrister; Fellow and Tutor
in Law, St Edmund Hall, Oxford

TABLE OF CONTENTS

CONFIDENCE AND DATA PROTECTION

CONFLICT OF LAWS

REFERENCES AND
ABBREVIATIONS

ACT	Australian Capital Territory
A-G	Attorney General
Adv-Gen	Advocate General
affd	affirmed
affg	affirming
Alta	Alberta
App	Appendix
art	article
Aust	Australia
B	Baron
BC	British Columbia
BYIL	British Yearbook of International Law
C	Command Paper (of a series published before 1900)
c	chapter number of an Act
CA	Court of Appeal
CAC	Central Arbitration Committee
CA in Ch	Court of Appeal in Chancery
CB	Chief Baron
CCA	Court of Criminal Appeal
CC Fees Order 1982	County Court Fees Order 1982 (SI 1982/1706) as subsequently amended (see the current County Court Practice)
CCR	County Court Rules 1981 (SI 1981/1687) as subsequently amended (see the current County Court Practice)
CCR	Court for Crown Cases Reserved
C-MAC	Courts-Martial Appeal Court
CO	Crown Office
COD	Crown Office Digest
Can	Canada
Cd	Command Paper (of the series published 1900–18)
Cf	compare
ch	chapter
cl	clause
Cm	Command Paper (of the series published 1986 to date)
Cmd	Command Paper (of the series published 1919–56)
Cmnd	Command Paper (of the series published 1956–86)
Comr	Commissioner
Corpn	Corporation

Court Forms (2nd Edn)...............	Atkin's Encyclopaedia of Court Forms in Civil Proceedings, 2nd Edn. See note 2, p *16* post
Court Funds Rules 1987	Court Funds Rules 1987 (SI 1987/821) as subsequently amended (see the current Supreme Court Practice and County Court Practice)
DC......................................	Divisional Court
DPP...................................	Director of Public Prosecutions
EAT	Employment Appeal Tribunal
EC......................................	European Community
ECJ....................................	Court of Justice of the European Community
ECSC	European Coal and Steel Community
EEC....................................	European Economic Community
EFTA..................................	European Free Trade Association
EMLR	Entertainment and Media Law Reports
Edn.....................................	Edition
Euratom	European Atomic Energy Community
Ex Ch	Court of Exchequer Chamber
ex p	ex parte
Fed.....................................	Federal
Forms & Precedents (5th Edn)......	Encyclopaedia of Forms and Precedents other than Court Forms, 5th Edn. See note 2, p *16* post
GLC	Greater London Council
HC......................................	High Court
HL	House of Lords
H of C	House of Commons
ILPr....................................	International Litigation Procedure
IRC.....................................	Inland Revenue Commissioners
Ir..	Ireland
J...	Justice
JA.......................................	Judge of Appeal
JC.......................................	Justiciary Cases
Kan.....................................	Kansas
LA......................................	Lord Advocate
LC......................................	Lord Chancellor
LCC	London County Council
LCJ.....................................	Lord Chief Justice
LJ	Lord Justice of Appeal
LoN.....................................	League of Nations
MR	Master of the Rolls
Man.....................................	Manitoba
n	note
NB	New Brunswick
NI	Northern Ireland
NS.......................................	Nova Scotia
NSW	New South Wales
NZ......................................	New Zealand
Nfld....................................	Newfoundland

OJ	The Official Journal of the European Community published by the Office for Official Publications of the European Community
Ont	Ontario
P	President
PC	Judicial Committee of the Privy Council
PEI	Prince Edward Island
QBD	Queen's Bench Division of the High Court
Qld	Queensland
Que	Quebec
r	rule
RDC	Rural District Council
RFL	Reports of Family Law (Canada)
RPC	Restrictive Practices Court
RSC	Rules of the Supreme Court 1965 (SI 1965/1776) as subsequently amended (see the current Supreme Court Practice)
reg	regulation
Res	Resolution
revsd	reversed
Rly	Railway
s	section
SA	South Africa
S Aust	South Australia
SC	Supreme Court
SC Fees Order 1980	Supreme Court Fees Order 1980 (SI 1980/821) as subsequently amended (see the current Supreme Court Practice)
SI	Statutory Instruments published by authority
SR & O	Statutory Rules and Orders published by authority
SR & O Rev 1904	Revised Edition comprising all Public and General Statutory Rules and Orders in force on 31 December 1903
SR & O Rev 1948	Revised Edition comprising all Public and General Statutory Rules and Orders and Statutory Instruments in force on 31 December 1948
SRNI	Statutory Rules of Northern Ireland
Sask	Saskatchewan
Sch	Schedule
Sess	Session
TS	Treaty Series
Tas	Tasmania
UDC	Urban District Council
UN	United Nations
V-C	Vice-Chancellor
Vict	Victoria
W Aust	Western Australia

NOTE 1. A general list of the abbreviations of law reports and other sources used in this work can be found in vol 54 (Reissue) Consolidated Table of Cases at p *v* et seq.

NOTE 2. Where references are made to other publications, the volume number precedes and the page number follows the name of the publication; eg the reference '12 Forms & Precedents (5th Edn) 44' refers to volume 12 of the Encyclopaedia of Forms and Precedents, page 44.

NOTE 3. An English statute is cited by short title or, where there is no short title, by regnal year and chapter number together with the name by which it is commonly known or a description of its subject matter and date. In the case of a foreign statute, the mode of citation generally follows the style of citation in use in the country concerned with the addition, where necessary, of the name of the country in parentheses.

NOTE 4. A statutory instrument is cited by short title, if any, followed by the year and number, or, if unnumbered, the date.

TABLE OF STATUTES

TABLE OF STATUTORY
INSTRUMENTS

Reference should be made to the Supreme Court Practice for the
Rules of the Supreme Court.

TABLE OF
EUROPEAN COMMUNITY
LEGISLATION

TABLE OF OTHER TREATIES AND CONVENTIONS

TABLE OF
CODES OF CONDUCT
AND GUIDANCE

TABLE OF CASES

PARA

PARA

E

PARA

G

PARA

O

PARA

Decisions of the European Court of Justice are listed below numerically.
These decisions are also included in the preceding alphabetical list.

COMPULSORY ACQUISITION OF LAND

1. POWERS TO ACQUIRE LAND

(1) NATURE OF COMPULSORY PURCHASE

1. Compulsory purchase and requisitioning. Where land or an interest in land is purchased or taken under statutory powers[1] without the agreement of the owner[2] it is said to have been compulsorily acquired[3], but where there is statutory power to take mere possession of the land without the acquisition of any estate or interest in it apart from the possession, it is said to have been requisitioned. Statutes giving requisitioning powers are usually named so as to indicate the limitation of the power given[4].

1 See eg the Lands Clauses Consolidation Act 1845 s 18; the Compulsory Purchase Act 1965 s 5 (as amended); and para 100 post.
2 Even where there is power to acquire land compulsorily the acquisition may be effected by agreement. As to when an acquisition amounts to one by agreement, and when it amounts to compulsory purchase, see para 93 et seq post.
3 Where, however, there is a purchase of the whole or any part of any statutory undertaking under any enactment in that behalf prescribing the terms on which the purchase is to be effected, the provisions of the Land Compensation Act 1961 as to compulsory acquisitions of land are excluded (s 36(1))); and transfers of industries to public ownership did not amount to a compulsory purchase or sale (*John Hudson & Co Ltd v Kirkness (Inspector of Taxes)* [1954] 1 All ER 29, [1954] 1 WLR 40, CA; affd sub nom *Kirkness (Inspector of Taxes) v John Hudson & Co Ltd* [1955] AC 696, [1955] 2 All ER 345, HL). For the purposes of the Land Compensation Act 1961 s 36, 'statutory undertaking' means an undertaking established under any enactment: s 36(2). 'Enactment' includes an enactment in any local or private Act of Parliament and an order, rule, regulation, byelaw or scheme made under an Act of Parliament (s 39(1)); and references in the Land Compensation Act 1961 to any enactment are to be construed as references to that enactment as amended by or under any other enactment (s 39(9)).
4 See eg the Requisitioned Land and War Works Act 1945; and the Requisitioned Land and War Works Act 1948. Such powers of requisitioning are usually for the defence of the realm, and in earlier days were found in the Defence Acts 1842–1935. See further WAR AND EMERGENCY.

2. Nature of power of compulsory acquisition. A statutory power to acquire or take land compulsorily is usually a power to take the whole land and the interests in it, but a statute may specifically authorise the purchase of a stratum of the land[1] or the creation and taking of a leasehold interest[2] or an easement[3] or some statutory right over the land[4].

Where a power is given to purchase or otherwise acquire land or a right over it, provision is invariably made for the payment of compensation or purchase money for the interests in the land purchased or made subject to the right[5]. Persons without such interests in the land, for example persons entitled to the benefit of a right of way or other easement over the acquired land or to the benefit of a restrictive covenant with respect to the land or the benefit of maintaining statutory works on it, will receive no compensation or purchase money and will continue to enjoy their rights after the acquisition until the acquiring authority does some act in pursuance of the statutory purchase adversely affecting the right of way, easement, covenant or statutory right, whereupon a right to compensation may arise[6].

Whether the statutory purpose giving rise to the acquisition may be effected notwithstanding the possibility of injury to the rights of other persons will depend upon the construction of the statutory power[7]; and the persons entitled to a right of way, easement, covenant or statutory right will have no remedy for any injury they suffer unless provision is made for compensation for that injury[8]. Any compensation provided for is given in lieu of the right of action those persons would have had but for the statutory authorisation[9], although there is also a statutory right to compensation for injury by statutory works which would not have given rise to any cause of action[10].

Some statutes anticipate that injury to such rights is inevitable, and give special power to extinguish rights of way over the acquired land[11] and deal with the rights of statutory undertakers with apparatus on and rights over the land[12].

The principal subject of this title is the general law and procedure concerning compulsory powers to acquire ownership of land or of an existing interest in land, and the compensation or purchase money payable by reason of the exercise of those powers[13].

1 See paras 30–32 post.
2 See eg the Agriculture Act 1947 s 93 (as amended); and AGRICULTURE vol 1(2) (Reissue) para 964.
3 See eg the Civil Aviation Act 1982 s 44 (as amended); and AVIATION vol 2 (Reissue) para 1119 et seq; the Highways Act 1980 s 250 (as amended); and HIGHWAYS vol 21 (Reissue) para 808. Without specific authorisation, easements may be acquired by agreement only: see para 31 post.
4 See eg ibid s 250 (as amended); and HIGHWAYS vol 21 (Reissue) para 808.
5 See para 197 et seq post.
6 See paras 353–354 post.
7 See para 335 post.
8 See *Caledonian Rly Co v Walker's Trustees* (1882) 7 App Cas 259 at 293, HL; and para 335 post.
9 See para 355 post.
10 See the Land Compensation Act 1973 Pt I (ss 1–19) (as amended); and para 359 et seq post.
11 See eg the Town and Country Planning Act 1990 ss 247–248, 271–273; and HIGHWAYS vol 21 (Reissue) para 156 et seq, TOWN AND COUNTRY PLANNING vol 46 (Reissue) para 834 et seq; the Acquisition of Land Act 1981 s 32 (as amended); and HIGHWAYS vol 21 (Reissue) para 171. See also para 334 post. As to the procedures to be followed see the Highways Act 1980 ss 118–119A, Sch 6 (as amended); and HIGHWAYS vol 21 (Reissue) para 307 et seq.
12 See para 334 post.
13 Powers of acquisition specific to the subjects of particular classes of legislation are considered in detail in the titles of this work appropriate to those subjects. Many of these powers apply to a greater or lesser extent the general provisions discussed in this title: see eg the Electricity Act 1989 s 10(1), Sch 3 (as amended); and FUEL AND ENERGY vol 19(2) (Reissue) para 985.

(2) ACQUIRING AUTHORITIES

3. Acquisition by royal prerogative or by government department. The right to take land or affect injuriously some or all of the rights of ownership in land, whether by the taking of those rights or their curtailment, was originally a prerogative right enjoyed by the sovereign power in the state[1], but even in time of war and where land is required only temporarily the executive prefers to act under statutory authority[2].

In normal times ministers or government departments requiring land are given statutory power to purchase it which is similar to the powers given to local authorities and other public bodies[3].

1 The sovereign power of Parliament is unrestricted, and there is no need to rely on any doctrine of state necessity: see CONSTITUTIONAL LAW.
2 This is normally so even in times of national emergency: eg statutes conferring powers to requisition, as under the Emergency Powers (Defence) Act 1940 (repealed). Such powers are wider and more comprehensive than the prerogative powers: see eg *A-G v De Keyser's Royal Hotel Ltd* [1920] AC 508, HL. In exceptional cases the old prerogative power is still exercised, subject however to compensation: see *Burmah Oil Co (Burma Trading) Ltd v Lord Advocate* [1965] AC 75, [1964] 2 All ER 348, HL.
3 See para 59 et seq post.

4. Acquisition by public bodies requiring land for statutory purposes. Where a person or statutory body is given statutory power to carry out works or to give effect to some other statutory purpose, and the ownership of land is necessary for that purpose, the person or body, if he or it has no or insufficient land for the purpose, will require power to purchase or otherwise acquire land by agreement or, in default of agreement, compulsorily[1], unless power is given to do works on the land without acquiring it by purchase or otherwise[2].

The need for land is usually for immediate requirements for the statutory purpose, and statutory power is given accordingly[3], but in some cases power has been given to acquire land in advance of requirements[4].

The purposes for which powers of acquisition are given may be specifically defined by statute[5] as, for example, in private Acts authorising a railway project. In public general Acts, however, it is normal for those purposes to be defined in general terms[6], leaving it to a compulsory purchase order to define the particular project[7].

1 As to statutory powers to acquire land see para 5 et seq post; as to the right to purchase money or compensation see paras 103, 197 et seq post.
2 As to such powers and the right to compensation see para 5 post.
3 As to the time for the exercise of statutory powers see paras 101, 328 post.
4 As to such powers see para 24 note 1 post.
5 As to the purposes of a compulsory acquisition see para 24 post.
6 See eg the Town and Country Planning Act 1990 s 226; and TOWN AND COUNTRY PLANNING vol 46 (Reissue) para 760.
7 See para 6 post.

5. Power to purchase or power to take for use. Where a statute gives a power to purchase land it is implicit that the acquiring authority is to pay the purchase price, even if not expressly stated. The statute will define the acquisition procedure[1] and the matters to be taken into account in assessing the purchase price[2]. The same applies if the statute gives power to purchase a right in or over land without any necessity to purchase the land itself[3]. Where, however, a statute gives power merely to take over the use of land, purchase money will not be payable[4], and whether or not compensation is payable is a question of statutory construction[5]. Persons with no right to purchase money or compensation for an interest on a compulsory purchase may have a right to payments for disturbance when displaced from land[6], or voluntary payments may be made[7].

Where a statute merely gives power to execute works in or over land, purchase money is not payable; but in such cases the statute may make provision for a right to compensation for the injurious affection of the land. If the statute does not do so, no right to compensation will arise[8]. Even if there is provision for the vesting of the works themselves, on completion, in the authority empowered to do the works, this is merely a statutory transfer of the right to use the land for the purposes of the works, so long as those purposes exist, and is not a purchase of the land[9]. There is no need to purchase land for the execution of works where the statute gives sufficient power to execute the works without purchasing the land[10].

A statute may give powers to execute works on a highway in which there is already sufficient property vested in the authority to justify the use of the highway for the works, and so no purchase of the land will be necessary[11].

The statutory transfer of an undertaking is not a compulsory acquisition of land, even though the land owned by the undertaking is also transferred[12].

1 Ie a notice to treat, inviting claims to the purchase money or compensation: see para 100 et seq post.

2 See para 233 et seq post.
3 See para 30 et seq post.
4 Eg upon requisitioning. Thus there is no ownership enabling the requisitioning authority to grant a tenancy: see *Southgate Borough Council v Watson* [1944] KB 541, [1944] 1 All ER 603, CA; *Minister of Agriculture and Fisheries v Matthews* [1950] 1 KB 148, [1949] 2 All ER 724.
5 See *Rockingham Sisters of Charity v R* [1922] 2 AC 315 at 322, PC. Nevertheless, an intention to take away a subject's property without compensation must be clear: see *Central Control Board (Liquor Traffic) v Cannon Brewery Co Ltd* [1919] AC 744, HL. For an example see the Opencast Coal Act 1958 s 4 (amended by the Acquisition of Land Act 1981 s 34(1), Sch 4 para 11) (compulsory rights orders); and MINES.
6 See the Land Compensation Act 1973 ss 37, 38 (as amended); and paras 314–315 post.
7 See ibid s 37(5); and para 314 post.
8 See paras 335, 353 et seq post. Similarly, if the works cause injury to land on which they are not executed there will be no right to compensation unless such a right is provided: see paras 335, 353 et seq post; and see note 9 infra.
9 For an example of a power to execute works over the land without involving the acquisition of land see local authorities' former powers under the Public Health Act 1936 s 15(1)(b) (repealed) to construct a public sewer in, on or over any land. 'Land' included buildings (Interpretation Act 1889 s 3 (repealed: see now the Interpretation Act 1978 s 5, Sch 1); *Hutton v Esher UDC* [1974] Ch 167, [1973] 2 All ER 1123, CA), so the power included power, where necessary, to demolish buildings: *Hutton v Esher UDC* supra. Although, when completed, the public sewer itself (ie not merely the materials of which it was made but also the space it occupied: *Taylor v Oldham Corpn* (1876) 4 ChD 395 at 411) would vest in the local authority under the Public Health Act 1936 s 20 (repealed), no purchase of land was involved but only the right of any person who had sustained damage through the exercise of the power to full compensation from the local authority. See now the Water Industry Act 1991 ss 159, 180, Sch 12 (as amended); and WATER.
10 See *Roderick v Aston Local Board* (1877) 5 ChD 328, CA; *London and North Western Rly Co v Westminster Corpn* [1904] 1 Ch 759, CA.
11 See *London and North Western Rly Co v Westminster Corpn* [1904] 1 Ch 759 at 765–766, CA, in relation to the former vesting of the subsoil of London streets sufficient for the construction of public conveniences under the Public Health (London) Act 1936 s 113(2) (repealed). See also *Escott v Newport Corpn* [1904] 2 KB 369, where there was power to erect poles in a street and so interfere with the subsoil, and it was held that there was no need to purchase land for the purpose but only a right to compensation for any injury caused.
12 See the Land Compensation Act 1961 s 36(1); and para 1 ante. See also *John Hudson & Co Ltd v Kirkness (Inspector of Taxes)* [1954] 1 All ER 29, [1954] 1 WLR 40, CA; affd sub nom *Kirkness (Inspector of Taxes) v John Hudson & Co Ltd* [1955] AC 696, [1955] 2 All ER 345, HL.

(3) THE EMPOWERING ENACTMENTS

6. The legislation. Up to the middle of the nineteenth century the power to acquire land was usually given by local or private Act, identifying the particular land to be acquired and providing for the procedure for the acquisition, for compensation and for conveyance[1], but the Lands Clauses Consolidation Act 1845[2] was enacted to provide a uniform acquisition procedure which would be incorporated in the special Act which authorised the specific acquisition[3].

Later it became necessary for local authorities and other public bodies to have a continuous general power to acquire land in the discharge of their functions, so various public general Acts were passed giving general acquisition powers, some of which allowed an acquiring authority to purchase any land for its purposes without any further authorisation[4] but most of which provided that the powers of compulsory acquisition could only be exercised with regard to specific land by a provisional order which usually had to be confirmed by Parliament[5]. Modern statutes authorising compulsory acquisition normally require a compulsory purchase order (as opposed to a provisional order), to be confirmed by a government department[6]; and confirmation by Parliament is required only in the case of the acquisition of special land[7]. A uniform compulsory purchase order procedure was provided by the Acquisition of Land (Authorisation Procedure) Act 1946, which incorporated many of the provisions of the Lands Clauses Consolidation Act 1845 now re-enacted in the Compulsory Purchase Act 1965[8]. The Act of 1946 has been applied by a vast number of modern Acts authorising compulsory acquisition and has been consolidated in the Acquisition of Land Act 1981[9].

1 As to powers under local Acts see para 7 post.
2 See para 11 et seq post. Many of the provisions of the Lands Clauses Consolidation Act 1845 were incorporated in the Acquisition of Land (Authorisation Procedure) Act 1946 s 1, Sch 2 (repealed) but are now re-enacted in the Compulsory Purchase Act 1965: see para 15 post.
3 Ie unless specifically excluded.
4 See para 22 post.
5 This was known as the 'provisional order procedure'. See further para 9 post.
6 The public general Act confers the power of compulsory purchase for particular purposes. The acquiring authority, acting under the public general power, submits a compulsory purchase order to the confirming authority for confirmation. The confirming authority can confirm, refuse or vary the order. Most compulsory acquisitions now occur under the procedure which is, in most cases, governed by the Acquisition of Land Act 1981: see para 33 et seq post.
7 See paras 56, 59 et seq post.
8 See paras 11 et seq, 33 et seq post.
9 See para 33 note 2 post.

7. Acquisition under local Act. Where a power to acquire land compulsorily is necessary for the carrying out of some undertaking, and there are no available powers under existing statutes, it will be necessary to promote a local or private Bill. The procedure is regulated by parliamentary standing orders, under which, when power is sought to acquire land compulsorily, the promoters of the Bill must give notice by public advertisement and by personal service on the persons likely to be affected, and must deposit plans with books of reference showing the land proposed to be acquired and the names of the owners, lessees and occupiers of the land[1].

When passed, the Act, which will be classed as a local and personal Act in the statute book[2], authorises the compulsory acquisition of such of the land so shown as is required for the purposes of the undertaking[3]. Among local and personal Acts a few instances will be found in which land not specifically described has been authorised to be acquired from time to time as required[4].

1 As to the procedure on the promotion of private Bills see PARLIAMENT.
2 As to local and personal Acts see STATUTES vol 44(1) (Reissue) paras 1213–1214.
3 As to the incorporation of the Lands Clauses Acts or the Compulsory Purchase Act 1965 see paras 11, 15 post; as to the time for the exercise of the powers see para 101 post.
4 See eg the Metropolitan Paving Act 1817 ss 80–96 (repealed), under which land could be taken as occasion required for the purpose of widening and improving London streets. This means of compulsory acquisition is likely to be more rarely used in future because of the procedures contained in the Transport and Works Act 1992: see para 10 post.

8. Acquisition under public general Act. Some public general Acts authorise the acquisition of specific land where the land is required for a special purpose[1] and the body or person authorised may proceed directly to acquire the land in accordance with the provisions of the Act. Other public general Acts have given a general power to take limited quantities of land for particular purposes without the land being specified in the Act, in which case the land is only identified when the purchase is negotiated or a notice to treat is given[2].

It is, however, now customary for public general Acts to give power to take land for particular purposes[3] without specifying the land but to provide for a further authorisation procedure after the land required for the particular purpose has been decided upon. The authorisation may be by provisional order[4] or compulsory purchase order[5].

1 See eg the Land Registry (New Buildings) Act 1900 (repealed); and the Public Works (Festival of Britain) Act 1949 (repealed). See also the Roosevelt Memorial Act 1946, which provided for the compulsory extinguishment of private rights over Grosvenor Square and its maintenance as a public garden.
2 See eg the Admiralty (Signal Stations) Act 1815 (repealed); the Customs Consolidation Act 1853 ss 33–345 (repealed); and the Coastguard Act 1925 s 1(3) (repealed). Under those Acts, the acquiring authority could compulsorily acquire land without any further authorisation.
3 Ie to establish the principle that land may be compulsorily acquired for such purposes.
4 See para 9 post.
5 See para 33 et seq post.

9. Provisional order authorisation. Where a statute confers power in general terms on authorities or undertakers, or classes of authorities or undertakers, to take land for specified purposes without specifying the land to be taken and requiring specific authority by provisional order to take any specified land[1], the acquiring authority or undertakers must, by means of advertisements and notices served on owners, lessees and occupiers of the land in question, give notice of their intention to petition the authority having power to make the order. This authority is usually a government department. The petition must contain full particulars and supporting evidence showing that the provisions of the particular empowering Act have been complied with.

The authority empowered to make the order must then consider the petition and may be required to direct the holding of a public local inquiry to hear objections to the making of the order[2]. If the authority is then satisfied that power to take the land should be given, a provisional order is made and a Bill submitted to Parliament to confirm the order, which does not have effect until so confirmed.

If a petition is presented against a Bill to confirm an order whilst the Bill is pending in either House of Parliament, the petitioner may appear before the select committee to which the Bill is referred and oppose the order as in the case of a private Bill[3].

This procedure has been almost totally replaced by the procedures for the making of compulsory purchase orders[4] and the procedures set out in the Transport and Works Act 1992[5]; and it now applies to very few compulsory acquisitions.

1 For examples of this procedure see the Acts referred to in note 2 infra.
2 The actual procedure depends on the particular Act under which the provisional order is made, and slight variations exist. Under the Military Lands Act 1892 s 2(7)(b), eg, a public local inquiry must be held unless the petition is dismissed; whereas under the Light Railways Act 1896 s 7(3) (repealed subject to transitional provisions), there was no requirement of a public local inquiry to consider objections.
3 See eg the Military Lands Act 1892 s 2(10). The procedure in Parliament on provisional orders and private Bills is provided by the standing orders of each House: see PARLIAMENT.
4 See para 33 et seq post.
5 See para 10 post.

10. Compulsory acquisition under the Transport and Works Act 1992. Under the Transport and Works Act 1992, a new procedure has been introduced for authorising the construction of works such as tramways and railways and associated compulsory acquisition of land. The Secretary of State may make works orders by statutory instrument authorising the construction of railways, tramways, inland water-ways and associated infrastructure[1]. The works order may provide for the compulsory acquisition of land and the creation and extinguishment of rights over land[2].

An application for a works order is made to the Secretary of State after the requirements for advertising the application have been complied with[3]. If objections are validly made and not withdrawn by the local authority for the area or by an owner, lessee or occupier[4], the Secretary of State must hold a public inquiry or a hearing[5]. The Secretary of State has power to approve a works order with or without modifications[6] and any person aggrieved[7] may challenge the Secretary of State's decision in the High Court[8].

A works order will be subject to special parliamentary procedure[9] where a compulsory purchase order would be subject to such a procedure under the Acquisition of Land Act 1981[10].

 1 See the Transport and Works Act 1992 ss 1–3; and RAILWAYS. See also the explanatory notes to the Transport and Works Act 1992 (Commencement No 3 and Transitional Provisions) Order 1992, SI 1992/2784. The Secretary of State here concerned is the Secretary of State for Transport.
 2 See the Transport and Works Act 1992 s 5, Sch 1; and RAILWAYS.
 3 See ibid s 6; the Transport and Works Act 1992 (Applications and Objections Procedure) Rules 1992, SI 1992/2902; and RAILWAYS. The requirements include advertising the application in the London Gazette and a local newspaper, display of notices on the site and service of notices on all owners, lessees and occupiers of the land proposed to be compulsorily acquired: see rr 9, 10.
 4 As to objections see the Transport and Works Act 1992 s 10; and RAILWAYS.
 5 See ibid s 11. Rules as to the conduct of the inquiry or hearing are contained in the Transport and Works (Inquiries Procedure) Rules 1992, SI 1992/2817, made under the Tribunals and Inquiries Act 1992 s 9: see generally RAILWAYS.
 6 See the Transport and Works Act 1992 s 13; and RAILWAYS.
 7 For the meaning of 'person aggrieved' see ADMINISTRATIVE LAW vol 1(1) (Reissue) para 56. See also para 85 note 1 post.
 8 See the Transport and Works Act 1992 s 22; and RAILWAYS.
 9 As to special parliamentary procedure see para 78 post.
10 Transport and Works Act 1992 s 12(1). See the Acquisition of Land Act 1981 ss 18, 19, 28, Sch 3 (as amended); and paras 76–77, 79 et seq post.

(4) INCORPORATION OF ACTS IN EMPOWERING ENACTMENTS

(i) Incorporation of Lands Clauses Acts in Empowering Enactments

11. Incorporation of Lands Clauses Acts in local Acts as special Act. Before the Lands Clauses Acts 1845 to 1895[1], empowering or special Acts authorising works of a public nature provided their own mode of acquisition, compensation and completion of purchase of land. Parliament then deemed it expedient, in the Lands Clauses Consolidation Act 1845, to comprise in one general Act the various provisions usually found in statutes relative to the acquisition of land required for works of a public nature and the compensation to be made, so as to avoid the necessity of repeating these provisions in each empowering Act, and so as to ensure greater uniformity in the provisions themselves[2].

The Lands Clauses Acts apply to every undertaking of a public nature[3] authorised by any Act passed after 8 May 1845[4] which empowers the purchase or taking of lands for that undertaking[5], and they are incorporated with that empowering Act, whether expressly mentioned or not[6], and all their clauses and provisions apply to the undertaking, so far as they are applicable[7], unless they are expressly varied or excepted by that

Act[8]. Where an Act passed before 8 May 1845 authorises an undertaking, and that Act is varied by a subsequent Act which provides for the taking of other lands for the same undertaking, the Lands Clauses Acts apply to the whole undertaking[9] so far as applicable[10].

The Lands Clauses Acts, as well as the clauses and provisions of every other Act which is incorporated with the empowering enactment, are to be construed together[11] as forming one Act called 'the special Act'[12].

1 Ie the Lands Clauses Consolidation Act 1845; the Lands Clauses Consolidation Acts Amendment Act 1860; the Lands Clauses Consolidation Act 1869 (repealed); the Lands Clauses (Umpire) Act 1883 (repealed); and the Lands Clauses (Taxation of Costs) Act 1895 (repealed): see the Interpretation Act 1978 s 5, Sch 1; and STATUTES vol 44(1) (Reissue) para 1229. The Lands Clauses Consolidation Act 1845 was extensively amended by the Compulsory Purchase Act 1965 s 39(4), Sch 8.

2 See the Lands Clauses Consolidation Act 1845 preamble; and *Metropolitan District Rly Co v Sharpe* (1880) 5 App Cas 425 at 440, HL. The provisions of the 1845 Act as to compensation and the assessment of it are affected by the Land Compensation Act 1961, and the jurisdiction for assessment was transferred to the Lands Tribunal by the Lands Tribunal Act 1949, with minor exceptions: see paras 200, 203 et seq post.

3 They do not apply to matters sanctioned by private estate Acts: *Wale v Westminster Palace Hotel Co* (1860) 8 CBNS 276; *Re Sion College, ex p London Corpn* (1887) 57 LT 743, CA.

4 Ie the date of the passing of the Lands Clauses Consolidation Act 1845.

5 Ibid s 1.

6 It is, however, usual to incorporate the Lands Clauses Acts in express terms. For examples of application of those Acts see the Coast Protection Act 1949 s 27(3) (amended by the Acquisition of Land Act 1981 s 34, Sch 4 para 1); the London Underground (Victoria) Act 1991 ss 3(1)(a), 14; and the London Underground Act 1992 ss 3(1)(a), 6(3), 22(3)(a), 24. For an example of a power of incorporation by subordinate instrument see the Harbours Act 1964 s 14(3), s 16(6) (as amended); and PORTS AND HARBOURS vol 36 paras 479, 422 respectively. The Lands Clauses Acts may be partially incorporated; as to the interpretation of such a provision in an empowering enactment see *R v London Corpn* (1867) LR 2 QB 292; *Ferrar v London Sewers Comrs* (1869) LR 4 Exch 227, Ex Ch; distinguishing *Broadbent v Imperial Gas Co* (1857) 7 De GM & G 436 at 447–448 (affd without this point being taken sub nom *Imperial Gas Light and Coke Co v Broadbent* (1859) 7 HL Cas 600); *Dungey v London Corpn* (1869) 38 LJCP 298. The Lands Clauses Consolidation Act 1845 s 5, which formerly gave guidance on such interpretation, was repealed by the Statute Law (Repeals) Act 1993 s 1(1), Sch 1 Pt XIV. For an example of the partial application of the Lands Clauses Acts see the Compulsory Purchase Act 1965 s 37(3), applying the Lands Clauses Consolidation Act 1845 ss 127–132 (sale of superfluous land) in relation to land acquired in pursuance of a compulsory purchase order under the Pipe-lines Act 1962 s 11. See further para 378 et seq post; and RAILWAYS.

7 See *Re Cherry's Settled Estates* (1862) 31 LJ Ch 351; *Re Westminster Estate of the Parish of St Sepulchre, ex p Vicar of St Sepulchre* (1864) 4 De GJ & Sm 232; *Re Spitalfields Schools and Comrs of Woods and Forests* (1870) LR 10 Eq 671; *Re Wood's Estate, ex p Works and Buildings Comrs* (1886) 31 ChD 607 at 617–618, CA; *Re Mills' Estate, ex p Works and Public Buildings Comrs* (1886) 34 ChD 24, CA.

8 Lands Clauses Consolidation Act 1845 s 1; *Central Control Board (Liquor Traffic) v Cannon Brewery Co Ltd* [1919] AC 744, HL. The Lands Clauses Acts are no longer incorporated in relation to compulsory purchases in accordance with the procedure provided by the Acquisition of Land Act 1981, but the Compulsory Purchase Act 1965 Pt I (ss 1–32) (as amended), re-enacting the Lands Clauses Acts in relation to compulsory purchase orders, applies instead: see para 15 et seq post. For examples of the exclusion of the Lands Clauses Acts see the Channel Tunnel Act 1987 s 37(6); the London Underground Act 1992 s 24(3); the Cardiff Bay Barrage Act 1993 s 4(5); and the Croydon Tramlink Act 1994 s 5(3).

9 *Lancashire and Yorkshire Rly Co v Evans* (1851) 15 Beav 322; *Re London and Birmingham Rly Co's Act 1833, Re London and North Western Rly Co's Act 1846, ex p Eton College* (1850) 20 LJ Ch 1.

10 Eg the Lands Clauses Consolidation Act 1845 s 16 (subscription of capital: see para 99 post) may not be applicable to the extension of a previously authorised undertaking: *Weld v South Western Rly Co* (1863) 32 Beav 340; *R v Great Western Rly Co* (1852) 1 E & B 253.

11 See para 12 post.

12 See the Lands Clauses Consolidation Act 1845 ss 1, 2.

12. Construction together of special Act and Lands Clauses Acts. When incorporated the special Act[1] and the Lands Clauses Acts[2] are construed together as forming one Act[3].

In construing the special Act and the provisions of the Lands Clauses Acts together, questions have arisen as to the extent to which the former has varied the latter. The general rule of construction when two Acts are to be construed as one is that every part of each of them must be construed as if it had been contained in the one Act unless there is some manifest discrepancy making it necessary to hold that the later Act has to some extent modified something found in the earlier Act[4]. The Lands Clauses Acts are to be followed unless the special Act by express words or necessary intendment varies or excepts them[5]. A variation showing that a provision is inapplicable will have the same effect as an express variation[6].

Where the special Act makes provisions as to a particular subject matter which differ from the corresponding provisions in the Lands Clauses Acts, but do not cover the whole of those provisions in the Lands Clauses Acts, the provisions not covered will apply[7].

Difficulties of construction have also arisen owing to words used in special Acts to include clauses differing from the statutory headings[8]. In such cases effect must be given to the words of the special Act[9], but slight variations may not be material[10]. The effect to be given to these introductory headings in construing the sections ranged under them is not governed by any general rule. They may be referred to in order to determine the sense of any doubtful expression in a section[11].

1 For the meaning of 'the special Act' see para 11 ante.
2 As to the Lands Clauses Acts see para 11 note 1 ante.
3 Lands Clauses Consolidation Act 1845 s 1.
4 *Canada Southern Rly Co v International Bridge Co* (1883) 8 App Cas 723 at 727, PC; *Hart v Hudson Bros Ltd* [1928] 2 KB 629, DC; *Phillips v Parnaby* [1934] 2 KB 299, DC; and see further STATUTES vol 44(1) (Reissue) para 1485.
5 *R v London Corpn* (1867) LR 2 QB 292 at 295 per Blackburn J (in delivering the judgment of the court); *Weld v South Western Rly Co* (1863) 32 Beav 340. For applications of the rule see *Ex p Rayner* (1878) 3 QBD 446; *Metropolitan District Rly Co v Sharpe* (1880) 5 App Cas 425, HL.
6 *Metropolitan District Rly Co v Sharpe* (1880) 5 App Cas 425 at 441, HL, per Lord Blackburn.
7 *Re Westminster Estate of the Parish of St Sepulchre, ex p Vicar of St Sepulchre* (1864) 4 De GJ & Sm 232; *R v St Luke's, Chelsea* (1871) LR 7 QB 148, Ex Ch; and see the cases cited in para 355 notes 2–3 post.
8 As to the incorporation or exclusion of clauses contained in the Lands Clauses Acts see para 11 ante.
9 *Broadbent v Imperial Gas Co* (1857) 7 De GM & G 436 at 447 per Lord Cranworth; *Kirby v Harrogate School Board* [1896] 1 Ch 437 at 448, CA.
10 *R v London Corpn* (1867) LR 2 QB 292.
11 *Hammersmith and City Rly Co v Brand* (1869) LR 4 HL 171 at 203 per Lord Chelmsford; *Eastern Counties and London and Blackwall Rly Cos v Marriage* (1860) 9 HL Cas 32; and cf *Bryan v Child* (1850) 5 Exch 368; *Latham v Lafone* (1867) LR 2 Exch 115 at 123; *Lang v Kerr, Anderson & Co* (1878) 3 App Cas 529 at 536, HL; *Union SS Co of New Zealand v Melbourne Harbour Trust Comrs* (1884) 9 App Cas 365, PC, decided under other statutes.

13. Construction of definitions in Lands Clauses Acts. In construing the Lands Clauses Acts[1] certain words have defined meanings. 'Prescribed' means prescribed or provided for in the special Act[2], and the sentence in which that word occurs is construed as if, instead of the word 'prescribed', the expression 'prescribed for that purpose in the special Act' had been used[3]. 'The works' or 'the undertaking' means the works or undertaking, of whatever nature, authorised by the special Act to be executed, and is not confined to the execution of works and undertakings of a purely physical nature[4]; and 'the promoters of the undertaking' means the parties, whether a company, undertakers, commissioners, trustees, corporations or private persons, empowered by the special Act to execute those works or undertakings[5]. Those parties are referred to below as 'the undertakers'.

Certain other words and expressions have meanings assigned to them which apply both in the Land Clauses Acts and in the special Act, unless there is something either in the subject or context repugnant to such construction[6]. 'Lands' extends to messuages, lands, tenements and hereditaments of any tenure[7]. As used in several sections it includes incorporeal hereditaments, but in others it does not[8]; it may include an option to purchase land but will not include such an option unless otherwise provided[9]. The definition does not, however, apply so as to permit the compulsory acquisition of part only of the land by taking a stratum or part only of the interest in the land, or by requiring a lease, easement or right over the land unless specially provided, or the acquiring or taking of an interest against the land[10].

In provisions where notice is required to be given to the owner of any land, or where the authority or consent of any such owner is required to some act, 'owner' means any person or corporation who would be entitled under the Lands Clauses Acts or the special Act to sell and convey the land to the undertakers[11].

Provision is also made for the construction of expressions relating to number, gender and time[12].

1 As to the Lands Clauses Acts see para 11 note 1 ante.
2 For the meaning of 'the special Act' see para 11 ante.
3 Lands Clauses Consolidation Act 1845 s 2.
4 Ibid s 2; and see *Central Control Board (Liquor Traffic) v Cannon Brewery Co Ltd* [1919] AC 744, HL, where the expression was held to include the control of the liquor traffic.
5 Lands Clauses Consolidation Act 1845 s 2.
6 Ibid s 3. For examples of repugnancy see *Clark v London School Board* (1874) 9 Ch App 120; *Worsley v South Devon Rly Co* (1851) 16 QB 539.
7 Lands Clauses Consolidation Act 1845 s 3. 'Lease' includes an agreement for a lease: s 3.
8 *Great Western Rly Co v Swindon and Cheltenham Rly Co* (1884) 9 App Cas 787 at 800 et seq, HL, per Lord Watson, and at 808 per Lord Bramwell; *R v Cambrian Rly Co* (1871) LR 6 QB 422 at 427 per Cockburn CJ, and at 431 per Blackburn J, which was overruled on another point in *Hopkins v Great Northern Rly Co* (1877) 2 QBD 224, CA; *Hill v Midland Rly Co* (1882) 21 ChD 143; *Pinchin v London and Blackwall Rly Co* (1854) 5 De GM & G 851, 24 LJ Ch 417; *Re Brewer* (1875) 1 ChD 409, CA.
9 *Oppenheimer v Minister of Transport* [1942] 1 KB 242, [1941] 3 All ER 485, where an option to purchase land was held to be 'lands or an interest therein' within the meaning of the Lands Clauses Consolidation Act 1845 s 49 (repealed).
10 See paras 30–32 post.
11 Lands Clauses Consolidation Act 1845 s 3.
12 Words importing the singular number only include the plural number and words importing the plural number only include the singular number; words importing the masculine gender only include females; and 'month' means a calendar month: ibid s 3.

14. Access to special Act. All persons interested in the special Act[1] must be able to have access to it[2]. For this purpose a company[3] must, at all times after the expiration of six months from the passing of the special Act, keep a Queen's printers' copy of it in its principal office of business; and where the undertaking is such that the works[4] are not confined to one town or place, as in the case of a railway or canal, it must also, within those six months, deposit another such copy of the special Act in the office of each of the clerks of the county councils of the several counties into which the works extend[5]. Failure on the part of the company to keep or deposit the copies of the Act renders it liable to a fine not exceeding level 2 on the standard scale[6].

The clerks of the councils are required to receive, and they and the company must retain, these copies, and permit all persons interested to inspect the Act at all reasonable hours, and make copies of or extracts from it, on payment for every inspection, and a further sum for every hour during which the inspection continues after the first hour[7]. Failure to comply with these provisions entails a penalty on summary conviction not exceeding level 1 on the standard scale[8].

1   For the meaning of 'the special Act' see para 11 ante.
2   See the Lands Clauses Consolidation Act 1845 ss 150, 151 (as amended); and the text and notes 3–8 infra. These sections are not generally incorporated where the power to acquire is derived from a public general Act, and they are not re-enacted in the Compulsory Purchase Act 1965 in relation to compulsory purchase orders, which may be otherwise inspected: see para 36 post.
3   The expression 'company' is used in the Lands Clauses Consolidation Act 1845 ss 150, 151 (as amended), and not 'the promoters of the undertaking', as in other sections: see para 13 ante.
4   For the meaning of 'the works' see para 13 text to note 4 ante.
5   Lands Clauses Consolidation Act 1845 s 150; Courts Act 1971 s 56(1), Sch 8 Pt I para 1(2).
6   Lands Clauses Consolidation Act 1845 s 151 (amended by virtue of the Criminal Law Act 1977 s 31; and the Criminal Justice Act 1982 ss 38, 46). The 'standard scale' means the standard scale of maximum fines for summary offences as set out in the Criminal Justice Act 1982 s 37(2) (as substituted): Interpretation Act 1978 s 5, Sch 1 (amended by the Criminal Justice Act 1988 s 170(1), Sch 15 para 58(a)). See CRIMINAL LAW vol 11(2) (Reissue) para 808; and MAGISTRATES. At the date at which this volume states the law, the standard scale is as follows: level 1, £200; level 2, £500; level 3, £1,000; level 4, £2,500; level 5, £5,000: Criminal Justice Act 1982 s 37(2) (substituted by the Criminal Justice Act 1991 s 17(1)). As to the determination of the amount of the fine actually imposed, as distinct from the level on the standard scale which it may not exceed, see the Criminal Justice Act 1991 s 18 (substituted by the Criminal Justice Act 1993 s 65); and MAGISTRATES. Appeal lies to the Crown Court: Lands Clauses Consolidation Act 1845 s 146 (amended by the Courts Act 1971 s 56(2), Sch 9 Pt I).
7   Lands Clauses Consolidation Act 1845 s 150; Local Government Act 1972 s 228(5).
8   Ibid s 228(7) (amended by virtue of the Criminal Justice Act 1982 ss 38, 46).

(ii) Application of Compulsory Purchase Act 1965 to Acquisitions Authorised by Compulsory Purchase Orders

15. Application of Compulsory Purchase Act 1965. Part I of the Compulsory Purchase Act 1965[1], which re-enacts various provisions of the Lands Clauses Acts[2], applies to any compulsory purchase to which the provisions of Part II of the Acquisition of Land Act 1981[3] apply or to which Schedule 1 to that Act applies, that is, authorisations of purchase by a compulsory purchase order under the 1981 Act[4].

1   Ie the Compulsory Purchase Act 1965 Pt I (ss 1–32) (as amended): see para 92 et seq post.
2   As to the Lands Clauses Acts see para 11 note 1 ante.
3   Ie the Acquisition of Land Act 1981 Pt II (ss 10–15) (as amended): see para 34 et seq post.
4   Compulsory Purchase Act 1965 s 1(1) (substituted by the Acquisition of Land Act 1981 s 34, Sch 4 para 14(1), (2)). Subject to exceptions and modifications, the Compulsory Purchase Act 1965 Pt I (as amended) is also applied by s 37 (as amended) to compulsory purchase orders under the Pipe-lines Act 1962 s 11 (see RAILWAYS) made after 1 January 1966: see the Compulsory Purchase Act 1965 s 37(1), (4) (s 37(1) amended by the Acquisition of Land Act 1981 Sch 4 para 14(7)). For those purposes, the Compulsory Purchase Act 1965 s 11(1), (2) (as amended) (see paras 123, 129 post), s 30 (as substituted) (see para 102 post) and s 31 (as amended) (see para 150 post) do not apply: s 37(2). As to the application of the 1965 Act see also the Channel Tunnel Act 1987 s 37(4), (5).

16. Construction of Compulsory Purchase Act 1965 with empowering enactment as special Act. In construing Part I of the Compulsory Purchase Act 1965[1], the enactment under which the purchase is authorised and the compulsory purchase order[2] are to be deemed to be the special Act[3].

1   Ie the Compulsory Purchase Act 1965 Pt I (ss 1–32) (as amended): see para 92 et seq post.
2   For these purposes, 'compulsory purchase order' has the same meaning as in the Acquisition of Land Act 1981 (see para 34 note 1 post): Compulsory Purchase Act 1965 s 1(1)(b) (substituted by the Acquisition of Land Act 1981 s 34(1), Sch 4 para 14(1), (2)).

3 Compulsory Purchase Act 1965 s 1(2) (amended by the Acquisition of Land Act 1981 s 34(3), Sch 6 Pt I). For the purposes of the Compulsory Purchase Act 1965 Pt I (as amended) as applied by s 37 (as amended) (see para 15 note 4 ante), 'the special Act' means the Pipe-lines Act 1962 together with the compulsory purchase order under s 11: Compulsory Purchase Act 1965 s 37(1). See further RAILWAYS. Compare the meaning of 'the special Act' in para 11 ante. As to the effect of the construction of the Acquisition of Land Act 1981 and the empowering enactment see para 12 ante. No provision is made for access to the special Act, but the compulsory purchase order may be inspected: see para 58 post.

(iii) Incorporation of Railways Clauses Consolidation Act 1845

17. Incorporation in local Acts and compulsory purchase orders of provisions excluding minerals. A local Act may incorporate the provisions of the Railways Clauses Consolidation Act 1845 giving power to exclude minerals from the purchase of land[1] and restricting the working of minerals[2]. Otherwise minerals must be purchased as included in the land to be acquired[3].

In the case also of acquisitions of land authorised by a compulsory purchase order to which the Acquisition of Land Act 1981 applies[4] there is express power to incorporate in the order the provisions of the 1845 Act referred to above[5]. Otherwise minerals must be purchased as included in the land to be acquired[6].

1 Ie the Railways Clauses Consolidation Act 1845 s 77: see MINES vol 31 para 73.
2 Ie ibid ss 78–85: see MINES vol 31 para 80 et seq.
3 See para 32 post.
4 See para 33 post.
5 See the Acquisition of Land Act 1981 s 3, Sch 2 paras 1–5; and MINES.
6 See para 32 post.

(iv) Application of Land Compensation Act 1961

18. Application of Land Compensation Act 1961 where land is authorised to be acquired compulsorily. Where by or under any statute, whether passed before or after 22 June 1961[1], land[2] is authorised to be acquired compulsorily, any question of disputed compensation is to be referred to the Lands Tribunal[3] and is to be determined by it in accordance with the provisions of the Land Compensation Act 1961[4] which provide, inter alia, rules for the assessment of compensation[5] and the matters to be taken into account[6].

1 Ie the date the Land Compensation Act 1961 was passed.
2 For these purposes, 'land' means any corporeal hereditament, including a building, and includes any interest or right in or over land and any right to water; and 'building' includes any structure or erection and any part of a building as so defined, but does not include plant or machinery comprised in a building: ibid s 39(1).
3 As to references to the Lands Tribunal see ibid ss 2–4 (as amended); and paras 198–199, 218 et seq post.
4 Ibid s 1.
5 See ibid ss 5–22 (as amended); and para 234 et seq post.
6 See ibid ss 31–39 (as amended); and paras 120, 203, 243 et seq post. See also *Taylor v North West Water Ltd* [1995] RVR 83, Lands Tribunal.

19. Application to the Crown. The Land Compensation Act 1961 applies in relation to the acquisition of interests in land[1], whether compulsorily or by agreement, by government departments, being authorities possessing compulsory purchase powers[2], as it applies in relation to the acquisition of interests in land by such authorities which are not government departments[3].

1 For the meaning of 'land' see para 18 note 2 ante.
2 For the meaning of 'authority possessing compulsory purchase powers' see para 244 note 6 post.
3 Land Compensation Act 1961 s 33.

20. Special provision in relation to ecclesiastical property in England. Where the fee simple of any ecclesiastical property[1] in England is in abeyance, it is treated for the purposes of the Land Compensation Act 1961 as being vested in the Church Commissioners[2].

1 For these purposes, 'ecclesiastical property' means land belonging to any ecclesiastical benefice, or being or forming part of a church subject to the jurisdiction of a bishop of any diocese or the site of such a church, or being or forming part of a burial ground subject to such jurisdiction: Land Compensation Act 1961 s 34(2). For the meaning of 'land' see para 18 note 2 ante.
2 Ibid s 34(1).

(5) LAND SUBJECT TO ACQUISITION

(i) In general

21. In general. The land which may be acquired may be unspecified in the empowering enactment or special Act[1] except as to general area[2], it may be specified in it by plans or sections[3] or it may await specification by a compulsory purchase order authorising the acquisition of defined land for the purposes of the empowering enactment[4].

1 For the meaning of 'special Act' see paras 11, 16 ante.
2 See para 22 post.
3 See para 23 post.
4 See paras 16 ante, 35 post.

22. Land unspecified in special Act. Many special Acts[1] give compulsory powers of purchase over a large area, but provide that only so much of that land may be taken as is actually required[2]. Such a power does not extend to inalienable lands unless it is extended by special provision or necessary implication[3]. In any case the power will be limited to acquisition for the authorised purposes[4].

1 For the meaning of 'special Act' see paras 11, 16 ante.
2 See eg the Coastguard Act 1925 s 1(2); and the Defence Acts 1842–1935.
3 *R v Minister of Health, ex p Villiers* [1936] 2 KB 29 at 44, [1936] 1 All ER 817 at 823, DC; but see now para 28 post. As to the exclusion and protection of certain land see para 27 et seq post.
4 See para 24 post.

23. Land specifically described in special Act. Special Acts[1] commonly authorise land to be taken by providing that, for the purposes of the Act, the undertakers may enter upon, take, and use the land delineated and described in the deposited plans and books of reference or any of them[2].

The plans and books of reference are only binding to the extent to which they are incorporated and referred to in the special Act, and only for the purpose in regard to which that Act refers to them[3]. Representations on the plans as to the position, extent or nature of the works proposed to be constructed are not binding on the undertakers unless the representations are incorporated in the Act, even though the effect of the representations may have prevented the landowner from opposing the Bill when before Parliament[4]. In the same way, notices given before the promotion of the Bill as to the extent of land proposed to be taken will not prevent the undertakers from taking a greater quantity if the Act in fact authorises it[5]. Conversely, undertakers cannot execute works shown on the deposited plans unless power to do so is expressly given in the special Act[6].

Before the undertakers can take land under a clause in the above form it must appear that the land in question is delineated on the plans[7]. Land within the limits of deviation is considered to be delineated, even though all the outside boundaries are not shown[8]. Land partly within and partly outside these limits may be held not to be delineated if only some of its boundaries are shown. In disputes of this nature the question turns upon whether, upon looking at the plans, the landowner can reasonably be deemed to have had notice that his land might be required, and the answer in each particular case will depend upon the size and nature of the particular close of land and the extent to which the boundaries are indicated[9]. Land outside the limits of deviation may, of course, be taken if properly delineated and required[10].

1 For the meaning of 'special Act' see paras 11, 16 ante.
2 Provision for the correction of errors and omissions in deposited plans and books of reference is commonly made in a special Act or enactments incorporated with it. A provision of this nature usually requires notice to be given to the owners, occupiers or lessees affected, a certificate of two justices that the error or omission arose from a mistake and the deposit of the certificate or copy of it with the appropriate officer of the local authority: see eg the Railways Clauses Consolidation Act 1845 s 7.
3 *North British Rly Co v Tod* (1846) 12 Cl & Fin 722, HL; *Beardmer v London and North Western Rly Co* (1849) 1 Mac & G 112 at 114 per Lord Cottenham; *Taff Vale Rly Co v Cardiff Rly Co* [1917] 1 Ch 299, CA.
4 See the cases cited in note 3 supra; and *Breynton v London and North Western Rly Co* (1846) 10 Beav 238; *R v Caledonian Rly Co* (1850) 16 QB 19; *Ware v Regent's Canal Co* (1858) 3 De G & J 212; *A-G v Great Eastern Rly Co* (1872) 7 Ch App 475; affd (1873) LR 6 HL 367.
5 *Re Huddersfield Corpn and Jacomb* (1874) 10 Ch App 92. The accidental omission of the names of persons interested in land from the book of reference will not prevent the land from being taken: *Kemp v West End of London and Crystal Palace Rly Co* (1855) 1 K & J 681.
6 *A-G v Great Northern Rly Co* (1850) 4 De G & Sm 75 (further proceedings 15 Jur 387); *R v Wycombe Rly Co* (1867) LR 2 QB 310 at 319 per Cockburn CJ.
7 *Dowling v Pontypool, Caerleon and Newport Rly Co* (1874) LR 18 Eq 714.
8 *Wrigley v Lancashire and Yorkshire Rly Co* (1863) 9 Jur NS 710; *Dowling v Pontypool, Caerleon and Newport Rly Co* (1874) LR 18 Eq 714. The purpose for which limits of deviation are introduced into plans is to allow a certain latitude in the construction of the centre line of the works authorised, and they are not intended in themselves to define the area within which land may be taken: see *Finck v London and South-Western Rly Co* (1890) 44 ChD 330 at 347, 351, 353, CA; *Doe d Payne v Bristol and Exeter Rly Co* (1840) 6 M & W 320; *Cardiff Rly Co v Taff Vale Rly Co* [1905] 2 Ch 289.
9 See the cases cited in note 8 supra; and *Protheroe v Tottenham and Forest Gate Rly Co* [1891] 3 Ch 278, CA; *Coats v Caledonian Rly Co* (1904) 6 F 1042.
10 *Crawford v Chester and Holyhead Rly Co* (1847) 11 Jur 917; *Finck v London and South-Western Rly Co* (1890) 44 ChD 330, CA.

24. Land only for purposes authorised. The Act which confers the power of taking land must be considered in order to ascertain the purposes for which the land may be taken[1]. These purposes may include the execution of works, in which case land may be taken for all the works, of whatsoever nature, authorised to be executed[2].

All undertakers, whether local authorities or companies formed for trade, can take land only for those purposes for which the legislature has invested them with the power; if they attempt to take it for any collateral object, the court will restrain them by injunction[3]; and they may not take land and at the same time agree not to use it for the statutory purposes[4].

If there is any doubt as to the powers to take land, the Act will be construed in favour of the landowner[5], but in the case of local authorities carrying out public improvements, the interest of the public as well as of the landowner will be considered in construing a doubtful provision[6].

If the purposes for which the land is required are legitimate, the undertakers are the persons to determine which portion of the land is required[7]. In coming to a determination they must act honestly and in good faith with a view to using the land for the authorised purpose, and not for any sinister or collateral purposes[8]. It is immaterial that the works might be carried out in another way which might cause less inconvenience[9], and the fact that under their statutory powers the undertakers could have taken other land instead of the land taken, which would have been less harmful to the plaintiff, cannot be used to found an action for damages for negligence[10].

Undertakers of particular classes of undertaking have been authorised to purchase land for what are called extraordinary purposes, which seem to be purposes for which it was not foreseen, at the time of the passing of the special Act, that land would, of necessity, be required[11]. Land for these purposes can only be acquired by agreement, and the quantity of the land as well as the purposes for which it may be purchased are generally specified in the special Act[12].

Undertakers may sell the land so acquired and purchase other land for the same purposes, and, so long as the amount held does not exceed the prescribed[13] quantity, they may deal with the land as an ordinary proprietor may do[14]. Land acquired for extraordinary purposes is not subject to the provisions relating to superfluous land[15].

1 *Simpson v South Staffordshire Waterworks Co* (1865) 34 LJ Ch 380 at 387 per Lord Westbury; see also *Palmer v Minister of Housing and Local Government and Romford Corpn* (1952) 3 P & CR 165, CA (claim that acquisition was in advance of requirements where there was no such power). There is no power to acquire land in advance of requirements unless specially authorised by statute; for examples of such authority see the Housing Act 1985 s 17(4); the Local Government Act 1972 s 120(2). As to acquisitions for collateral objects see the text and notes 3–4 infra.

2 See the definitions of 'the undertaking' and 'the works' in the Lands Clauses Consolidation Act 1845 s 2 (see para 13 ante); and the Compulsory Purchase Act 1965 s 1(4) (see para 92 note 3 post). Thus, in the case of a railway, these would ordinarily include not only the line itself but also stations, warehouses, offices, yards and other conveniences (*Cother v Midland Rly Co* (1848) 5 Ry & Can Cas 187 at 193–194 per Lord Cottenham; *Sadd v Maldon, Witham and Braintree Rly Co* (1851) 6 Exch 143; cf *Boland v Canadian National Rly Co* [1927] AC 198, PC, where a subway was held not to be a part of a railway undertaking); and in the case of a dock there would be included quays, wharves and warehouses (*London Association of Shipowners and Brokers v London and India Docks Joint Committee* [1892] 3 Ch 242 at 249–250, CA, per Lindley LJ); but in the case of a tramway, where land was authorised to be acquired only for the construction of buildings 'necessary for the working of the tramway', it was held that dwellings and a recreation ground for the use of the company's inspectors were not included (*West India Electric Co Ltd v Kingston Corpn* [1914] AC 986, PC).

3 See *Meravale Builders Ltd v Secretary of State for the Environment* (1978) 36 P & CR 87 (land acquired for housing; authority not entitled to build road other than for access). See also *Galloway v London Corpn* (1886) LR 1 HL 34 at 43 per Lord Cranworth; *Marquess of Clanricarde v Congested Districts Board for Ireland* (1914) 79 JP 481, HL; *Sydney Municipal Council v Campbell* [1925] AC 338, PC; and see other cases cited in note 5 infra. Thus, a railway company having the ordinary powers of constructing a railway was restrained from taking land in order to obtain materials with which to make an embankment (*Bentinck v Norfolk Estuary Co* (1857) 26 LJ Ch 404; *Eversfield v Mid-Sussex Rly Co* (1858) 3 De G & J 286; *Lund v Midland Rly Co* (1865) 34 LJ Ch 276), or in order to carry out an agreement with a landowner (*Vane v Cockermouth, Keswick and Penrith Rly Co* (1865) 13 WR 1015; *Lord Carington v Wycombe Rly Co* (1868) 3 Ch App 377 at 381, 385). The undertakers may take land in order to make accommodation works for adjoining owners and occupiers, where such works are required to be made: see the Railways Clauses Consolidation Act 1845 s 68; and *Wilkinson v Hull etc Rly and Dock Co* (1882) 20 ChD 323, CA; *Lord*

Beauchamp v Great Western Rly Co (1868) 3 Ch App 745; and cf *Dodd v Salisbury and Yeovil Rly Co* (1859) 1 Giff 158. When a field is authorised to be taken by a water company in order to make a tunnel, and only part is required, the company cannot take the whole field and use the remainder for sinking wells and erecting pumping machinery: *Simpson v South Staffordshire Waterworks Co* (1865) 34 LJ Ch 380; *Cardiff Corpn v Cardiff Waterworks Co* (1859) 5 Jur NS 953; see also *Simpsons Motor Sales (London) Ltd v Hendon Corpn* [1964] AC 1088, [1963] 2 All ER 484, HL (where the purposes of use became vague, but no determination to use outside authorised purposes); *Capital Investments Ltd v Wednesfield UDC* [1965] Ch 774, [1964] 1 All ER 655 (change of intention, but within the authorised powers). Local authorities authorised to take land to widen a street cannot under that power take land merely to alter the level of the street (*Lynch v London Sewers Comrs* (1886) 32 ChD 72, CA), and they cannot take it for purposes of resale unless power is given to them by the special Act (*Gard v London Sewers Comrs* (1885) 28 ChD 486, CA); see also *JL Denman & Co Ltd v Westminster Corpn, JC Cording & Co Ltd v Westminster Corpn* [1906] 1 Ch 464; *Fernley v Limehouse Board of Works* (1899) 68 LJ Ch 344.

4 *Ayr Harbour Trustees v Oswald* (1883) 8 App Cas 623, HL; *Re Heywood's Conveyance, Cheshire Lines Committee v Liverpool Corpn* [1938] 2 All ER 230.

5 *Webb v Manchester and Leeds Rly Co* (1839) 4 My & Cr 116 at 120 per Lord Cottenham; *Lee v Milner* (1837) 2 Y & C Ex 611; *Gray v Liverpool and Bury Rly Co* (1846) 9 Beav 391; *Re London and Birmingham Rly Co's Act 1833, Re London and North Western Rly Co's Act 1846, ex p Eton College* (1850) 20 LJ Ch 1; *Simpson v South Staffordshire Waterworks Co* (1865) 34 LJ Ch 380; *Cardiff Corpn v Cardiff Waterworks Co* (1859) 5 Jur NS 953; and see *Gildart v Gladstone* (1809) 11 East 675 at 685; *Scales v Pickering* (1828) 4 Bing 448. However, the court will not allow persons to avail themselves of omissions in the powers given to the undertakers in order to make exorbitant claims: *Bell v Hull and Selby Rly Co* (1840) 1 Ry & Can Cas 616.

6 *Galloway v London Corpn* (1866) LR 1 HL 34; *Quinton v Bristol Corpn* (1874) LR 17 Eq 524; *Rolls v London School Board* (1884) 27 ChD 639 at 642; *North London Rly Co v Metropolitan Board of Works* (1859) 28 LJ Ch 909; *Batson v London School Board* (1903) 67 JP 457.

7 *Stockton and Darlington Rly Co v Brown* (1860) 9 HL Cas 246; *Webb v Manchester and Leeds Rly Co* (1839) 4 My & Cr 116.

8 See the cases cited in note 7 supra; and *Flower v London, Brighton and South Coast Rly Co* (1865) 34 LJ Ch 540; *Kemp v South Eastern Rly Co* (1872) 7 Ch App 364; *Errington v Metropolitan District Rly Co* (1882) 19 ChD 559, CA; *Marquess of Clanricarde v Congested Districts Board for Ireland* (1914) 79 JP 481, HL; *Sydney Municipal Council v Campbell* [1925] AC 338, PC. As to the evidence necessary see the cases cited supra. If the purpose is apparently legitimate, the burden of proving the contrary will lie upon the landowner: *Marquess of Clanricarde v Congested Districts Board for Ireland* supra. The same principles are applicable when undertakers are authorised to interfere with lands, eg in laying sewers or water mains: *Earl of Derby v Bury Improvement Comrs* (1869) LR 4 Exch 222 at 225, Ex Ch, per Willes J; *Lewis v Weston-super-Mare Local Board* (1888) 40 ChD 55.

9 See the cases cited in note 7 supra; and *London, Brighton and South Coast Rly Co v Truman* (1885) 11 App Cas 45, HL; *R v Pease* (1832) 4 B & Ad 30; *Lamb v North London Rly Co* (1869) 4 Ch App 522.

10 See *Tutin v Northallerton RDC* (1947) 91 Sol Jo 383, when the principle enunciated by Lord Atkinson in *Lagan Navigation Co v Lambeg Bleaching, Dyeing and Finishing Co Ltd* [1927] AC 226 at 243, HL, that if statutory powers might as well be exercised in a manner hurtful or innocuous to third parties, the person exercising them would be negligent if he chose the former, both being available, was held inapplicable to the taking of land under statutory powers.

11 See *Hooper v Bourne* (1877) 3 QBD 258 at 272, CA, per Bramwell LJ; affd (1880) 5 App Cas 1, HL.

12 See the Markets and Fairs Clauses Act 1847 s 9; the Harbours, Docks, and Piers Clauses Act 1847 s 20. As to the purchase of such land see the Lands Clauses Consolidation Act 1845 s 12; and para 93 et seq post. It may be land included within the limits of deviation: *Hooper v Bourne* (1877) 3 QBD 258, CA; affd (1880) 5 App Cas 1, HL. For the meaning of 'special Act' see paras 11, 16 ante.

13 Undertakers may not purchase more than the prescribed quantity of land from any party under a legal disability, or enabled only to sell under powers conferred by the special Act or the Lands Clauses Acts; if they purchase the prescribed quantity of land from such a party and afterwards sell the whole or part of it, that party cannot sell other land to them in lieu of the land sold: see the Land Clauses Consolidation Act 1845 s 14. As to the Lands Clauses Acts see para 11 note 1 ante; and for the persons enabled to sell by the Lands Clauses Acts see para 96 post.

14 See the Lands Clauses Consolidation Act 1845 s 13; and *City of Glasgow Union Rly Co v Caledonian Rly Co* (1871) LR 2 Sc & Div 160 at 165, HL, per Lord Westbury. Where the land sold was purchased by the undertakers subject to a restrictive covenant which was ultra vires the undertakers, the covenant did not bind the purchaser to whom the promoters sold the land in question: *Re South Eastern Rly Co and Wiffin's Contract* [1907] 2 Ch 366, as explained in *Stourcliffe Estates Co Ltd v Bournemouth Corpn* [1910] 2 Ch 12, CA.

15 *City of Glasgow Union Rly Co v Caledonian Rly Co* (1871) LR 2 Sc & Div 160, HL; *Hooper v Bourne* (1877) 3 QBD 258, CA. For the provisions relating to superfluous land see para 377 et seq post.

25. Land for whole undertaking only; reimbursement and exchange. Land may not be taken where there is no intention, or no ability, to complete the whole undertaking[1]; nor may land be taken for the purpose of going beyond the statutory powers[2].

If the special Act[3] clearly authorises the land to be taken for the actual works only, a local authority or other public body will be restrained from taking more than is actually necessary for the works[4], but if it appears to be the Act's intention that the authority or body be allowed to reimburse itself, it will be at liberty to take all the land delineated on the plans[5].

A power to acquire land to be given in exchange for the land acquired is given in some special Acts[6] to facilitate the acquisition of land such as commons and open spaces when land is required to be given in exchange as a condition of acquisition[7].

1 See *Agar v Regent's Canal Co* (1814) 1 Swan 250n; *Cohen v Wilkinson* (1849) 1 Mac & G 481.
2 *Simpson v South Staffordshire Waterworks Co* (1865) 34 LJ Ch 380; *Cardiff Corpn v Cardiff Waterworks Co* (1859) 5 Jur NS 953; *Colman v Eastern Counties Rly Co* (1846) 10 Beav 1.
3 For the meaning of 'special Act' see paras 11, 16 ante.
4 *Donaldson v South Shields Corpn* (1899) 68 LJ Ch 162, CA; *JL Denman & Co Ltd v Westminster Corpn, JC Cording & Co Ltd v Westminster Corpn* [1906] 1 Ch 464; *Fernley v Limehouse Board of Works* (1899) 68 LJ Ch 344; see also *Rolls v London School Board* (1884) 27 ChD 639.
5 *Galloway v London Corpn* (1866) LR 1 HL 34; *Quinton v Bristol Corpn* (1874) LR 17 Eq 524.
6 See eg the Highways Act 1980 s 239(5); and HIGHWAYS vol 21 (Reissue) para 800.
7 See paras 29, 77, 82 post.

26. Compulsory purchase orders comprising ancient monuments. The Secretary of State may compulsorily acquire ancient monuments[1] for the purposes of securing their preservation[2].

1 For the meaning of 'ancient monument' see the Ancient Monuments and Archaeological Areas Act 1979 s 61(12); and OPEN SPACES vol 34 para 566.
2 See ibid s 10 (as amended); and OPEN SPACES. The Acquisition of Land Act 1981 applies to any such compulsory acquisition: see the Ancient Monuments and Archaeological Areas Act 1979 s 10(2) (amended by the Acquisition of Land Act 1981 s 34, Sch 4 para 1, Sch 6 Pt I).

(ii) Exclusion and Protection of Certain Land

27. In general. Some Acts expressly exempt from compulsory acquisition land such as parks, gardens or land of local authorities or other bodies; the enactment may be one giving only a general power of compulsory acquisition[1] or one providing for land otherwise to be specified for acquisition in a compulsory purchase order[2].

Further protection is given generally in the process of acquisition by the right afforded to an owner, part only of whose property is required, to insist upon the whole property being taken[3].

1 See eg the restrictions imposed on the compulsory acquisition of land for allotments in the Land Settlement (Facilities) Act 1919 s 16 (as amended); and ALLOTMENTS vol 2 (Reissue) para 24.
2 As to the making and confirmation of compulsory purchase orders see para 34 et seq post.
3 See paras 105–114 post.

28. Inalienable land. Where the power to acquire compulsorily was only a general power, there was formerly no power to acquire compulsorily land made inalienable by statute; only if express power was given to acquire that land could it be so acquired[1]. Now, however, except in so far as any express provision of any such enactment restricts the exercise of the power, any power conferred by or under the Acquisition of Land Act 1981, the Acquisition of Land (Authorisation Procedure) Act 1946 or any enactment passed before the commencement of the 1946 Act[2] to purchase land[3] compulsorily is exercisable notwithstanding any other enactment providing that the land is to be inalienable[4].

Some protection from acquisition is provided both for land which is inalienable, and for certain other categories of land, by the statutory provisions relating to special parliamentary procedure[5].

1 Cf *R v Minister of Health, ex p Villiers* [1936] 2 KB 29 at 44–45, [1936] 1 All ER 817 at 823–824, DC.
2 The Acquisition of Land (Authorisation Procedure) Act 1946 (repealed) came into force on 18 April 1946.
3 For these purposes, 'land' includes messuages, tenements and hereditaments, and in relation to compulsory purchase under any enactment, includes anything falling within any definition of the expression in that enactment: Acquisition of Land Act 1981 s 7(1). For the meaning of 'compulsory purchase' see para 34 note 1 post.
4 Acquisition of Land Act 1981 s 9. This gives general power to take inalienable land under Acts passed before 1946 but not under Acts passed after then unless deemed to have been passed before the Acquisition of Land (Authorisation Procedure) Act 1946 (repealed). The New Towns Act 1981 is deemed to have been passed before the commencement of the Acquisition of Land Act 1981 for these purposes: see the New Towns Act 1981 s 72(2) (amended by the Acquisition of Land Act 1981 s 34(1), Sch 4 para 33); and TOWN AND COUNTRY PLANNING vol 46 (Reissue) paras 1104 note 6, 1105 note 10.
5 See para 76 et seq post.

29. Commons, open spaces, local authority land etc. Where commons are specified for acquisition in the empowering enactment they may be acquired under the terms of that Act, but where there is only a general authority to acquire land under the Lands Clauses Acts[1] or any Act incorporating those Acts, acquisition will be invalid unless made by any government department or made with the consent of the Secretary of State[2]. Where commons[3], open spaces[4] or fuel or field garden allotments[5] are authorised to be purchased by a compulsory purchase order to which the Acquisition of Land Act 1981 applies[6] the order will be subject to special parliamentary procedure[7] unless the Secretary of State is satisfied:

(1) that there has been or will be given in exchange for such land[8] other land, not being less in area and being equally advantageous to the persons, if any, entitled to rights of common or other rights, and to the public, and that the land given in exchange has been or will be vested in the persons in whom the land purchased was vested, and subject to the like rights, trusts and incidents as attach to the land purchased[9]; or

(2) that the land is being purchased in order to secure its preservation or improve its management[10]; or

(3) that the land does not exceed 250 square yards in extent or is required for the widening or drainage of an existing highway or partly for the widening and partly for the drainage of such a highway and that the giving in exchange of other land is unnecessary, whether in the interests of the persons, if any, entitled to rights of common or other rights or in the interests of the public[11],

and certifies accordingly[12].

Land belonging to local authorities, statutory undertakers or the National Trust and held inalienably which is included in such a compulsory purchase order may also be entitled to the protection of special parliamentary procedure[13].

These provisions are modified in their application to compulsory rights orders under the Opencast Coal Act 1958[14] and do not apply in relation to the compulsory purchase of a right to store gas in an underground gas storage[15] or of any right[16] as respects wells, boreholes and shafts in a storage area or protective area[17].

1 As to the Lands Clauses Acts see para 11 note 1 ante.
2 See the Commons Act 1899 s 22(1), Sch 1 (as amended); and COMMONS vol 6 (Reissue) para 603.
3 'Common' includes any land subject to be inclosed under the Inclosure Acts 1845 to 1882, and any town or village green: Acquisition of Land Act 1981 s 19(4). As to the meaning of 'the Inclosure Acts 1845 to 1882' see COMMONS vol 6 (Reissue) para 708 note 2.
4 'Open space' means any land laid out as a public garden, or used for the purposes of public recreation, or land being a disused burial ground: Acquisition of Land Act 1981 s 19(4).
5 'Fuel or field garden allotment' means any allotment set out as a fuel allotment, or a field garden allotment, under an Inclosure Act: Acquisition of Land Act 1981 s 19(4) See further ALLOTMENTS vol 2 (Reissue) para 65 et seq.
6 See para 34 et seq post. For the meaning of 'compulsory purchase order' see para 34 note 1 post.
7 As to special parliamentary procedure see para 78 post.
8 For the meaning of 'land' see para 28 note 3 ante.
9 Acquisition of Land Act 1981 s 19(1)(a).
10 Ibid s 19(1)(aa) (added by the Planning and Compensation Act 1991 s 70, Sch 15 para 12(1)(a)).
11 Acquisition of Land Act 1981 s 19(1)(b).
12 Ibid s 19(1). Subject to s 24 (court's powers to quash certificate: see para 87 post), the certificate becomes operative on the date on which notice of giving it is first published in accordance with the statutory provisions: s 26(2). As to publication of notice of intention to give the certificate and the right to make objections see para 77 post. Power to acquire compulsorily land to be given in exchange is conferred by some Acts: see eg the Highways Act 1980 s 239(5); and HIGHWAYS vol 21 (Reissue) para 800. The court has jurisdiction to hear a challenge on substantive as well as purely procedural grounds to a certificate under the Acquisition of Land Act 1981 s 19 (as amended) that equally advantageous land is being provided: *Greenwich London Borough Council v Secretary of State for the Environment and Secretary of State for Transport, Yates v Secretary of State for the Environment and Secretary of State for Transport* [1994] JPL 607. As to the acquisition of new rights over commons etc see para 82 post.
13 See paras 76, 81 post.
14 See the Acquisition of Land Act 1981 s 29(7); and para 83 post.
15 Ie a right under the Gas Act 1965 s 12(1) (as amended): see FUEL AND ENERGY vol 19(1) (Reissue) para 689.
16 Ie any right under ibid s 13(2) or (3) (as amended): see FUEL AND ENERGY vol 19(1) (Reissue) para 690.
17 See the Acquisition of Land Act 1981 s 30(3); and para 84 post.

(iii) Power to Acquire Leases, Strata or Easements Only

30. Existing interests, easements and rights. Where powers are given by statute to acquire land compulsorily, the whole interest must be acquired notwithstanding the definition of 'land' in the empowering enactment as including easements or rights over land, unless special provision is made, and there is no power to require and acquire an easement, right or lease only[1]. So also, unless special provision is made, the whole land must be acquired, and there is no power to require and acquire only a stratum or section of the land[2].

Where there are interests against the land acquired[3], such as a right of way or some other easement or a restrictive covenant enjoyed by the owner of other land, the acquiring authority has no obligation or power, in the absence of express power, to acquire those rights compulsorily[4] and, if the authority interferes with the rights, the owners who have the benefit of the rights are not entitled to a notice to treat for the acquisition of the land to be taken, but are entitled only to compensation for the injury[5].

If the land acquired has attached to it the benefit of a right of way or other easement with respect to other land, that benefit will pass to the acquiring authority on the conveyance of the land acquired[6].

A local authority[7] may by means of a compulsory purchase order acquire such new rights over land[8] as may be specified in the order[9]. New rights over land may also be acquired by certain other authorities and undertakers[10].

1 See para 31 post; and see *Sovmots Investments Ltd v Secretary of State for the Environment, Brompton Securities Ltd v Secretary of State for the Environment* [1977] QB 411, [1976] 3 All ER 720, CA; revsd on other grounds [1979] AC 144, [1977] 2 All ER 385, HL.
2 See para 32 post. Unless entry is required leases for more than a year need not be purchased but may be allowed to expire or to become interests of less than a year: see para 180 post. If entered upon and by mistake omitted to be purchased they may be dealt with as explained in para 132 post. Interests for a year or less may be allowed to expire or be terminated by notice to quit or notice requiring possession: see para 181 post.
3 See *Thicknesse v Lancaster Canal Co* (1838) 4 M & W 472.
4 See eg the National Parks and Access to the Countryside Act 1949 ss 103(6), 114(1) (as amended); and OPEN SPACES vol 34 para 465.
5 *Macey v Metropolitan Board of Works* (1864) 33 LJ Ch 377; *Clark v London School Board* (1874) 9 Ch App 120; *Duke of Bedford v Dawson* (1875) LR 20 Eq 353; *Badham v Marris* (1881) 52 LJ Ch 237n; *Swainston v Finn and Metropolitan Board of Works* (1883) 52 LJ Ch 235; *Bush v Trowbridge Waterworks Co* (1875) LR 19 Eq 291 (affd 10 Ch App 459); *London School Board v Smith* [1895] WN 37; *Thicknesse v Lancaster Canal Co* (1838) 4 M & W 472. See further paras 354–355 post. The owner of such a right is not entitled to notice of a compulsory purchase order: see para 37 note 3 post. Instead of providing for compensation for injury to a right of way, some statutes provide for its extinguishment subject to compensation: see para 334 post.
6 See para 139 post.
7 For these purposes, 'local authority' means a county council, a district council, a London borough council, the Common Council of the City of London, the Council of the Isles of Scilly, a police authority established under the Police Act 1964 s 3 (as substituted) and a joint authority established by the Local Government Act 1985 Pt IV (ss 23–42) (as amended): Local Government (Miscellaneous Provisions) Act 1976 s 44(1) (definition substituted by the Local Government Act 1985 s 84, Sch 14 para 53(b); amended by s 102(2), Sch 17; the Education Reform Act 1988 s 237(2), Sch 13 Pt I; and by the Police and Magistrates' Courts Act 1994 s 43, Sch 4 para 18). The Broads Authority is treated as a local authority for these purposes: see the Local Government (Miscellaneous Provisions) Act 1976 s 44(1A) (added by the Norfolk and Suffolk Broads Act 1988 s 21, Sch 6 para 15). No prospective amendment to these provisions appears, however, to have been made to reflect the changes to local government in Wales made by the Local Government (Wales) Act 1994.
8 For the meaning of 'land' see para 28 note 3 ante.
9 See the Local Government (Miscellaneous Provisions) Act 1976 s 13 (as amended); the Acquisition of Land Act 1981 s 28(b); and LOCAL GOVERNMENT vol 28 para 1219.
10 See ibid s 28, Sch 3 (as amended); and para 79 et seq post.

31. Whole interest in land to be purchased unless power to create and purchase lease, easements or rights only.

There is no power to create and take an interest in land such as a lease without acquiring the freehold or other interests unless specific power to do so is given in the special Act[1]; nor is there power to create and purchase an easement without purchasing the land unless special provision is made[2] or in either case the owner agrees[3].

1 *Great Western Rly Co v Swindon and Cheltenham Rly Co* (1884) 9 App Cas 787 at 798, 800–801, HL, per Lord Watson. For examples of such a specific power see the Small Holdings and Allotments Act 1908 s 39 (as amended); and ALLOTMENTS vol 2 (Reissue) para 18; the Agriculture Act 1947 s 83; and AGRICULTURE vol 1(2) (Reissue) para 962. For the meaning of 'special Act' see paras 11, 16 ante.
2 *Hill v Midland Rly Co* (1882) 21 ChD 143 at 147; *Great Western Rly Co v Swindon and Cheltenham Rly Co* (1884) 9 App Cas 787 at 802, HL; *Ramsden v Manchester, South Junction and Altrincham Rly Co* (1848) 1 Exch 723; *Sparrow v Oxford, Worcester and Wolverhampton Rly Co* (1852) 2 De GM & G 94 at 108 per Lord Cranworth; and see *Falkner v Somerset and Dorset Rly Co* (1873) LR 16 Eq 458. For examples of

powers to acquire easements or rights over land by creating them see the National Parks and Access to the Countryside Act 1949 ss 103(6), 114(1) (as amended); and OPEN SPACES vol 34 para 465; the Highways Act 1980 s 250 (as amended); and HIGHWAYS vol 21 (Reissue) para 808.

3   *Pinchin v London and Blackwall Rly Co* (1854) 5 De GM & G 851 at 862, 24 LJ Ch 417 at 420 per Lord Cranworth LC; *Re Metropolitan District Rly Co and Cosh* (1880) 13 ChD 607 at 616, CA, per Jessel MR; *Re London School Board and Foster* (1903) 87 LT 700, CA.

32. Whole land to be purchased unless power to acquire or exclude strata. The acquiring authority[1] cannot acquire compulsorily a stratum of land or appropriate and use the subsoil, as for the purpose of making a tunnel, but must acquire the entire land[2] unless there is specific power to acquire a stratum or easement or right through the land or the owner agrees[3]. Thus the minerals must also be purchased unless there is power to exclude them from purchase[4].

1   For the meaning of 'acquiring authority' see para 34 note 2 post.
2   *Errington v Metropolitan District Rly Co* (1882) 19 ChD 559, CA; *Great Western Rly Co v Swindon and Cheltenham Rly Co* (1884) 9 App Cas 787 at 800, HL; *Farmer v Waterloo and City Rly Co* [1895] 1 Ch 527; *Ramsden v Manchester, South Junction and Altrincham Rly Co* (1848) 1 Exch 723; *Goodson v Richardson* (1874) 9 Ch App 221. Power to appropriate and use subsoil is equivalent to power to take it: *Metropolitan Rly Co v Fowler* [1893] AC 416 at 426, HL, per Lord Watson.
3   *Great Western Rly Co v Swindon and Cheltenham Rly Co* (1884) 9 App Cas 787 at 801, HL. See also the cases cited in para 31 note 3 ante.
4   In the case of acquisitions authorised by compulsory purchase orders to which the Acquisition of Land Act 1981 applies (see para 33 post), power is given by s 3, Sch 2 para 1 (amended by the Coal Industry Act 1994 s 67(1), Sch 9 para 27(3) as from the restructuring date appointed under ss 7(1), 68(2)) to incorporate with the compulsory purchase order the Acquisition of Land Act 1981 Sch 2 Pt II (para 2) (which re-enacts the Railway Clauses Consolidation Act 1845 s 77 (exclusion of minerals from the purchase of the land)), or the Acquisition of Land Act 1981 Sch 2 Pts II, III (paras 2–9 (as amended)) (which together re-enact the Railways Clauses Consolidation Act 1845 ss 78–85 (restricting the working of minerals)): see further MINES.

(6) COMPULSORY PURCHASE ORDERS

(i) In general

33. Application and incorporation of Acquisition of Land Act 1981. In respect of most compulsory acquisitions, the procedures for the making and confirmation of compulsory purchase orders contained in the Acquisition of Land Act 1981 are applied[1]. Since 1946, the procedure now contained in the Acquisition of Land Act 1981 and previously enacted in the Acquisition of Land (Authorisation Procedure) Act 1946 has been incorporated in a host of enactments[2] conferring powers of compulsory acquisition on ministers of the Crown, local authorities[3] and a variety of public bodies including statutory undertakers[4].

The Acquisition of Land Act 1981 prescribes a standard procedure for use where land is to be acquired compulsorily by public authorities, but its procedures only apply where this is specifically required[5]. The provisions of the Act apply to compulsory acquisitions under most, but not all[6], public general Acts in force at the time of its commencement[7] and also to compulsory acquisitions under the enabling Acts specified in the 1981 Act[8]. Most, but not all, Acts authorising compulsory acquisition passed since the commencement of the 1981 Act have incorporated the procedures in that Act and the procedures therein contained now apply to most compulsory acquisitions by public authorities[9]. The procedures in the 1981 Act do not apply to Acts in which the

1981 Act is not specifically incorporated[10] and under certain empowering enactments, the procedures in the 1981 Act have been incorporated in a varied form[11].

1 The procedure for the making and confirmation of compulsory purchase orders under various Acts conferring powers of compulsory acquisition differed in many respects until the Acquisition of Land (Authorisation Procedure) Act 1946 (repealed) provided a uniform procedure for the making of compulsory purchase orders for the acquisition of land by local authorities under powers conferred by public enactments (with limited exceptions) in force immediately before the passing of that Act. It not only repealed most of the previous provisions in those enactments relating to compulsory purchase orders but also substituted authorisation by compulsory purchase order for authorisation by provisional order in other Acts: see the Acquisition of Land (Authorisation Procedure) Act 1946 s 10(3), Sch 6 (repealed). The 1946 Act could also be applied to acquisitions by a local authority under a local Act similarly in force where the local Act conferred a power to authorise compulsory acquisition: see the Acquisition of Land (Authorisation Procedure) Act 1946 s 7 (repealed).
2 See eg the Agriculture Act 1947 s 92(1) (as amended); and AGRICULTURE vol 1(2) (Reissue) para 863; the Ancient Monuments and Archaeological Areas Act 1979 s 10 (as amended); and OPEN SPACES; the Electricity Act 1989 s 10(1), Sch 3 para 5; and FUEL AND ENERGY vol 19(2) (Reissue) paras 983, 985; and the Water Industry Act 1991 s 155(4); and WATER.
3 For the meaning of 'local authority' see para 34 note 2 post.
4 For the meaning of 'statutory undertaker' see para 38 note 8 post.
5 See the Acquisition of Land Act 1981 s 1(1). The Acquisition of Land Act 1981 may apply by virtue of any other enactment, whether or not passed or made before the 1981 Act; and 'enactment' includes any statutory instrument: s 1(3). Apart from the Acts set out in s 1(2) (as amended) (see note 8 infra), the specific statutory provision applying the Act will normally be found in the enabling Act: see the examples cited in note 2 supra.
6 See eg the Pipe-lines Act 1962 ss 11–14 (as amended); and RAILWAYS vol 38 para 1077 et seq; the Forestry Act 1967 s 40 (as amended); and FORESTRY vol 19(1) (Reissue) paras 22–23; and the New Towns Act 1981 ss 10–16 (as amended); and TOWN AND COUNTRY PLANNING vol 46 (Reissue) para 1104 et seq.
7 Acquisition of Land Act 1981 s 1(1), Sch 5 para 5. The commencement date was 30 January 1982: s 35(2).
8 See ibid s 1(1)(b). The enactments so specified are (1) the Metropolitan Police Act 1886 s 2 (as amended); (2) the Military Lands Act 1892 s 1(3) (as amended); (3) the Small Holdings and Allotments Act 1908 ss 25(1), 39(1) (as amended); (4) the Development and Road Improvement Funds Act 1909 s 5(1) (repealed) as it applied to acquisition by local authorities (as defined in the Acquisition of Land Act 1981 s 7(1) (as amended) (see para 34 note 2 post) or by the Secretary of State; (5) the Small Holdings and Allotments Act 1926 s 4 (as amended); and (6) the Education Act 1944 s 90(1) (as amended): Acquisition of Land Act 1981 s 1(2) (amended by the Water Act 1989 s 190(3), Sch 27 Pt I). The Acquisition of Land Act 1981 does not extend to Northern Ireland: see s 35(3).
9 See eg the Gas Act 1986 s 9(3), Sch 3 para 4; the Electricity Act 1989 s 10(1), Sch 3 para 5; and FUEL AND ENERGY vols 19(1), (2) (Reissue) paras 636, 985.
10 See eg the New Towns Act 1981 s 10(1), Sch 4 Pt I (paras 1–6), where alternative but similar procedures are provided for.
11 See eg (1) the Airports Act 1986 s 59(1); and AVIATION vol 2 (Reissue) para 1117; (2) the Housing Act 1988 s 78(1), Sch 10 Pt I (paras 1–3); and HOUSING; (3) the Town and Country Planning Act 1990 s 226 (as prospectively amended), ss 228, 245; and TOWN AND COUNTRY PLANNING vol 46 (Reissue) para 760 et seq; (4) the Water Industry Act 1991 ss 155(4), 188, Sch 14; and WATER; (5) the Water Resources Act 1991 ss 154(4), 182, Sch 23; and WATER; and (5) the Leasehold Reform, Housing and Urban Development Act 1993 s 169(1), (2), Sch 20 Pt I (paras 1–3); and TRADE, INDUSTRY AND INDUSTRIAL RELATIONS vol 47 (Reissue) para 852.

(ii) Purchases by Authorities other than Ministers of the Crown

A. MAKING OF COMPULSORY PURCHASE ORDER

34. Making of compulsory purchase order. A compulsory purchase order[1] authorising a compulsory purchase by an authority other than a minister of the Crown must be made by that authority ('the acquiring authority')[2] and submitted to and confirmed by the authority having power under the empowering enactment to authorise the purchase (the 'confirming authority')[3] in accordance with the relevant statutory provisions[4]. Part II of the Acquisition of Land Act 1981[5] applies to any such compulsory acquisition made under Acts incorporating that Act[6].

1 Ie an order authorising a compulsory purchase: see the Acquisition of Land Act 1981 s 2(1). 'Compulsory purchase' means a compulsory purchase of land, being a compulsory purchase to which the Acquisition of Land Act 1981 applies by virtue of any enactment, whether or not passed or made before the 1981 Act was passed, or a compulsory purchase under a specified enactment (see para 33 note 8 ante): s 1(1). For the meaning of 'land' see para 28 note 3 ante.

2 'Acquiring authority', in relation to a compulsory purchase, means the minister, local authority or other person who may be authorised to purchase the land compulsorily: Acquisition of Land Act 1981 s 7(1). 'Local authority' means (1) a billing authority or a precepting authority as defined in the Local Government Finance Act 1992 s 69 (ie a county council in England, a police authority established under the Police Act 1964 s 3 (as substituted), a metropolitan county fire and civil defence authority, the London Fire and Civil Defence Authority, the Receiver for the Metropolitan Police District, the sub-treasurer of the Inner Temple and the under-treasurer of the Middle Temple, a parish or community council, the chairman of a parish meeting and charter trustees: see the Local Government Finance Act 1992 s 39(1), (2) (amended by the Police and Magistrates' Courts Act 1994 s 27(1); and by the Local Government (Wales) Act 1994 s 35(6); applied by the Local Government Finance Act 1992 s 69(1)); (2) a combined fire authority as defined in the Local Government Finance Act 1988 s 144; (3) a levying body within the meaning of s 74 (as amended) or a body as regards which s 75 (as amended) applies; (4) any joint board or joint committee if all the constituent authorities are such authorities as are described in heads (1)–(3) supra; and (5) the Honourable Society of the Inner Temple or the Honourable Society of the Middle Temple: Acquisition of Land Act 1981 s 7(1) (definition substituted by the Local Government Finance (Repeals, Savings and Consequential Amendments) Order 1990, SI 1990/776, art 8, Sch 3 para 23; amended by the Local Government Finance Act 1992 s 117(1), Sch 13 para 52; and by the Police and Magistrates' Courts Act 1994 s 93, Sch 9 Pt I).

3 'Confirming authority', in relation to a compulsory purchase, means, where the acquiring authority is not a minister, the minister having power to authorise the acquiring authority to purchase the land compulsorily: Acquisition of Land Act 1981 s 7(1).

4 Ibid s 2(2). See para 35 et seq post.

5 Ie ibid Pt II (ss 10–15) (as amended): see para 35 et seq post.

6 See ibid ss 1, 10(1); and para 33 ante. Part II (as amended) is also applied, subject to modifications, to compulsory rights orders in respect of opencast coal operations made under the Opencast Coal Act 1958 s 4 (as amended) by s 4(4A) (added by the Acquisition of Land Act 1981 s 34(1). Sch 4 para 11(1), (2)), subject to the provisions of s 29 (as amended): see para 83 post. Land occupied for opencast coal purposes is protected from compulsory acquisition by the Opencast Coal Act 1958 s 38 (as amended): see further MINES vol 31 para 307.

35. Form of compulsory purchase order.

The compulsory purchase order[1] must be made by the acquiring authority[2] in the prescribed form[3] and must describe the land[4] to which it applies by reference to a map[5]. A schedule attached to the order describes in detail the land to be acquired[6]. The purpose for which the order is made must be specified in it[7].

1 For the meaning of 'compulsory purchase' and 'compulsory purchase order' see para 34 note 1 ante.

2 For the meaning of 'acquiring authority' see para 34 note 2 ante.

3 Acquisition of Land Act 1981 s 10(2.) Guidance is issued by the Secretary of State as to the formalities to be complied with in sealing and identifying the documents required to be contained in an order: see Department of the Environment Circular 14/94. A compulsory purchase order will be valid notwithstanding that it is sealed on a date subsequent to the date on the order as long as there is no deliberate attempt to cause a landowner to act to his detriment: *Burke v Secretary of State for the Environment* (1992) 26 HLR 10, CA.

    Anything which, by the Acquisition of Land Act 1981 Pt II (ss 10–15) (as amended) (see the text and notes 4–6 infra; and para 36 et seq post); or Pt III (ss 16–22) (as amended) (see paras 41, 76 et seq post); or by s 2(3), Sch 1 (as amended) (see para 59 et seq post); or s 28, Sch 3 (as amended) (see para 79 et seq post), is required or authorised to be prescribed must be prescribed by regulations made by the Secretary of State by statutory instrument: s 7(2). The Secretary of State here concerned is the Secretary of State for the Environment. In exercise of the power so conferred, the Secretary of State has made the Compulsory Purchase of Land Regulations 1994, SI 1994/2145, which came into force on 1 October 1994: see reg 1. For the purposes of the Acquisition of Land Act 1981 s 10, the form of compulsory purchase order (other than a clearance compulsory purchase order) must be as set out in the Compulsory Purchase of Land Regulations 1994 reg 3(a)(i), Schedule, Form 1: reg 3(a)(i). If, however, (1) the order provides for the vesting of land given in exchange pursuant to the Acquisition of Land Act 1981 s 19 (as amended) or Sch 3 para 6 (as amended) (commons, open spaces etc: see paras 77, 82 post), the form of the order must be as set out in the Compulsory Purchase of Land Regulations 1994 Schedule, Form 2; or (2) if it does not so provide, but provides for discharging the land purchased from rights, trusts and incidents pursuant to the Acquisition of Land Act 1981 s 19 (as amended) or Sch 3 para 6 (as amended), the order must be as set out in the Compulsory Purchase of Land Regulations 1994 Schedule, Form 3: reg 3(a)(ii), (iii). The form of a clearance compulsory purchase order must be as set out in reg 3(b)(i), Schedule, Form 4 or, if it provides as mentioned in heads (1)–(2) supra, in the form set out in Schedule, Form 5 or Form 6 as the case may be: see reg 3(b)(i)–(iii). 'Clearance compulsory purchase order' means a compulsory purchase order made pursuant to the Housing Act 1985 s 290 (see HOUSING): Compulsory Purchase of Land Regulations 1994 reg 2. For the relevant form of compulsory rights order under the Opencast Coal Act 1958 s 4 (as amended) see the Opencast Coal (Compulsory Rights and Rights of Way) (Forms) Regulations 1987, SI 1987/1915, reg 4(a)(i), Schedule, Form 4. See further para 34 note 6 ante.

4 For the meaning of 'land' see para 28 note 3 ante. In relation to compulsory purchase under any enactment, 'land' includes anything falling within any definition of the expression in that enactment and within the definition set out in para 28 note 1 ante, but it does not include rights against the land (see *Grimley v Minister of Housing and Local Government* [1971] 2 QB 96, [1971] 2 All ER 431) unless special statutory provision is made (see para 30 ante). Whether or not incorporeal hereditaments fall within the definition of 'land' will be determined by construction of the empowering enactment.

5 Acquisition of Land Act 1981 s 10(2). The map should be of a sufficient scale to allow the extent of the acquisition to be clearly identified. For further guidance on making of compulsory purchase orders see Department of the Environment Circular 14/94; and for the content of the order see Appendix E thereto.

6 The schedule has five columns: (i) the number of the plot (if more than one) from the map; (ii) the extent, description and situation of the land in such detail as to allow the land to be identified; (iii) the names of the owners or reputed owners; (iv) the names of the lessees or reputed lessees; and (v) the names of the occupiers: see the Compulsory Purchase of Land Regulations 1994 Schedule, Forms 1–6 and the Schedules thereto.

7 See ibid Schedule, Forms 1–6. As to the purpose of the compulsory purchase order see para 24 ante.

36. Advertisement of compulsory purchase order.
Before submitting the order to the confirming authority[1], the acquiring authority[2] must place a copy of the order and of the accompanying map[3] at a place, such as the acquiring authority's offices, in the locality in which the land[4] comprised in the order is situated, so that interested persons may inspect them[5].

The acquiring authority must then, in two successive weeks, publish in one or more local newspapers circulating in the locality in which that land is situated a notice in the prescribed form[6] stating that the order has been made and is about to be submitted for confirmation, describing the land and stating the purpose for which it is required, naming the place where a copy of the order and map may be inspected, and specifying the time (not being less than 21 days from the first publication of the notice) within which, and the manner in which, objections to the order may be made[7].

1 For the meaning of 'confirming authority' see para 34 note 3 ante.
2 For the meaning of 'acquiring authority' see para 34 note 2 ante.
3 As to the map see para 35 note 5 ante.
4 For the meaning of 'land' see para 28 note 3 ante.
5 See the Acquisition of Land Act 1981 ss 10(3), 11(2)(c).
6 For the prescribed form of newspaper notice see the Compulsory Purchase of Land Regulations 1994, SI 1994/2145, reg 3(c), Schedule, Form 7. In the case of compulsory rights orders under the Opencast Coal Act 1958 s 4 (as amended) (see MINES), the relevant form of notice is contained in the Opencast

Coal (Compulsory Rights and Rights of Way) (Forms) Regulations 1987, SI 1987/1915, reg 4(a)(i), Schedule, Form 5. See further para 34 note 6 ante.

7 Acquisition of Land Act 1981 ss 10(3), 11(1), (2). As to objections see para 40 et seq post.

37. Notice of order to owners, lessees and occupiers. The acquiring authority[1] must serve[2] on every owner[3], lessee and occupier (except tenants for a month or any period less than a month)[4] of any land comprised in the order, a notice in the prescribed form[5] stating the effect of the order and that it is about to be submitted for confirmation and specifying the time (not being less than 21 days from the service of the notice) within which and the manner in which objections to the order may be made[6]. In the case of ecclesiastical property[7], notice must also be served on the Church Commissioners[8].

Acquiring authorities are also required to serve a copy of their statement of reasons for making the order on the persons mentioned above, and, in so far as practicable, such a statement should also be served on any short-term tenant and any applicant for planning permission in respect of the land[9].

1 For the meaning of 'acquiring authority' see para 34 note 2 ante.
2 As to the mode of service see para 38 post.
3 In relation to any land, 'owner' means a person, other than a mortgagee not in possession, who is for the time being entitled to dispose of the fee simple of the land, whether in possession or in reversion, and includes also (1) a person holding or entitled to the rents and profits of the land under a lease or agreement the unexpired term of which exceeds three years; and (2) a person who would have power to sell and convey or release the land to the acquiring authority if a compulsory purchase order were operative: Acquisition of Land Act 1981 s 7(1) (amended by the Planning and Compensation Act 1991 s 70, Sch 15 para 9). A person with an easement of support over land comprised in the order is not an owner of land entitled to service, even if the empowering enactment defines 'land' as easements and rights over land: *Grimley v Minister of Housing and Local Government* [1971] 2 QB 96, [1971] 2 All ER 341. See further paras 30-31 ante.
    To assist in identifying the persons entitled to service of notice, local authorities have a general power to require the occupier or other person having an interest in the land to state the name and address of the owner, mortgagee or lessee: see the Local Government (Miscellaneous Provisions) Act 1976 s 16 (as amended); and LOCAL GOVERNMENT vol 28 para 1243. Where title to the land is registered, office copies of the register can be obtained from the registrar: see the Land Registration Act 1988 s 1; and LAND REGISTRATION. A wife who acquired a house jointly with her husband was held not to be entitled to have a compulsory purchase order made in respect of the house quashed where a notice in the prescribed form had been served only on her husband but she had not been substantially prejudiced: *George v Secretary of State for the Environment* (1979) 38 P & CR 609, CA; sed quaere.
4 For these purposes, an occupier who is a statutory tenant within the meaning of the Rent Act 1977 or the Rent (Agriculture) Act 1976 or a licensee under an assured agricultural occupancy within the meaning of the Housing Act 1988 Pt I (ss 1-45) (as amended) is deemed to be a tenant for a period less than a month: Acquisition of Land Act 1981 s 12(2) (amended by the Housing Act 1988 s 140(1), Sch 17 para 32(1)). See further LANDLORD AND TENANT vols 27(1), (2) (Reissue) paras 677 et seq, 999 et seq, 1037 et seq. A tenancy which commences as a weekly tenancy has been held to continue as such however long it may last, and so not to entitle the owner to notice under these provisions: *EON Motors Ltd v Secretary of State for the Environment* [1981] 1 EGLR 19.
5 For the prescribed form see the Compulsory Purchase of Land Regulations 1994, SI 1994/2145, reg 3(d), Schedule, Form 8 or, if the order is made on behalf of a council, Schedule, Form 9. Where a compulsory purchase order is made under the Planning (Listed Buildings and Conservation Areas) Act 1990 s 47 (as prospectively amended) (compulsory acquisition of listed buildings in need of repair: see TOWN AND COUNTRY PLANNING vol 46 (Reissue) paras 945, 947), there must be included in the Compulsory Purchase of Land Regulations 1994 Schedule, Form 8, the following specified information: (1) in all such cases, an additional paragraph stating that any person having an interest in the listed building which it is proposed to acquire compulsorily may apply to the magistrates' court for an order staying further proceedings within 28 days after service of the notice, and an additional paragraph stating that the position with respect to the order is subject to any action taken under the Planning (Listed Buildings and Conservation Areas) Act 1990, which also provides for appeals against decisions of the court; (2) in any case where the notice is required by s 50(3) (minimum compensation in the case of

a building deliberately left derelict: see TOWN AND COUNTRY PLANNING vol 46 (Reissue) para 949) to include a statement that the authority has included a direction for minimum compensation, an additional paragraph stating that such a direction has been included, explaining the meaning of this and drawing attention to the right under s 50 to apply within 28 days after service of the notice to a magistrates' court that such a direction is not to be included: see the Compulsory Purchase of Land Regulations 1994 reg 4.

In the case of compulsory rights orders under the Opencast Coal Act 1958 s 4 (as amended) (see MINES): (1) the provisions of the Acquisition of Land Act 1981 s 12 (as amended) are substituted by s 29(4) (see para 83 post); and (2) the relevant form of notice is contained in the Opencast Coal (Compulsory Rights and Rights of Way) (Forms) Regulations 1987, SI 1987/1915, reg 4(a)(ii), Schedule, Form 6 (or, in the case of a limited rights order, Schedule, Form 7). See further para 34 note 6 ante.

6 Acquisition of Land Act 1981 ss 10(3), 12(1). As to objections see para 40 et seq post.
7 'Ecclesiastical property' means land (1) belonging to any ecclesiastical benefice; or (2) being or forming part of (a) a church subject to the jurisdiction of the bishop of any diocese or the site of such a church, or (b) a burial ground subject to such jurisdiction; or (3) being diocesan glebe land within the meaning of the Endowments and Glebe Measure 1976: Acquisition of Land Act 1981 s 12(3) (amended by the Planning and Compensation Act 1991 s 70, Sch 15 para 27).
8 Acquisition of Land Act 1981 s 12(3).
9 Department of the Environment Circular 14/94 para 17.

38. Service of notices. Any notice or other document required or authorised to be served in relation to the making and confirmation of the compulsory purchase order[1] may be served on any person either by delivering it to him or by leaving it at his proper address[2] or by post, but the document will not be duly served by post unless it is sent by registered letter or by the recorded delivery service[3]. Any such document required or authorised to be served upon an incorporated company or body will be duly served if it is served upon the secretary or clerk of the company or body[4].

Service of the notice on the occupier of the land may not be good service on the owner of the land even if the occupier of the land is the owner's agent[5].

If the authority with jurisdiction to make the order in connection with which the document is to be served is satisfied that reasonable inquiry has been made and that it is not practicable to ascertain the name or address of an owner[6], lessee or occupier of land[7] on whom any such document is to be served, the document may be served by addressing it to him by the description of 'owner', 'lessee' or 'occupier' of the land (describing it) to which it relates, and by delivering it to some person on the land or, if there is no person on the land to whom it may be delivered, by leaving it or a copy of it on or near the land[8].

1 Ie authorised or required to be served under the Acquisition of Land Act 1981.
2 For this purpose, and for the purposes of the Interpretation Act 1978 s 7 (service by post: see STATUTES vol 44(1) (Reissue) para 1388), the proper address of the secretary or clerk of any incorporated company or body is that of its registered or principal office, and the proper address of any other person is his last known address, except where the person to be served has furnished an address for service, in which case his proper address for these purposes is the address furnished: Acquisition of Land Act 1981 s 6(3). Service by post will be deemed to be effected by properly addressing, prepaying and posting a letter containing the document and, unless the contrary is proved, to have been effected at the time at which the letter would be delivered in the ordinary course of post: see the Interpretation Act 1978 s 7.
3 Acquisition of Land Act 1981 s 6(1).
4 Ibid s 6(2).
5 *Shepherd v Norwich Corpn* (1885) 30 ChD 553.
6 For the meaning of 'owner' see para 37 note 3 ante.
7 For the meaning of 'land' see para 28 note 3 ante.
8 Acquisition of Land Act 1981 s 6(4) (amended by the Planning and Compensation Act 1991 s 70, Sch 15 para 8). This provision does not, however, have effect in relation to an owner, lessee or occupier being a local authority, statutory undertakers or the National Trust: Acquisition of Land Act 1981 s 6(4)

proviso. Unless the context otherwise requires, 'statutory undertakers' means (1) any person authorised by any enactment to construct, work or carry on (a) any railway, light railway, tramway, road transport, water transport, canal or inland navigation undertaking; or (b) any dock, harbour, pier or lighthouse undertaking; or (c) any undertaking for the supply of hydraulic power; or (2) the Civil Aviation Authority; or (3) the Post Office; and for these purposes, 'enactment' means any Act or any order or scheme made under or confirmed by an Act: Acquisition of Land Act 1981 s 8(1) (amended by the Telecommunications Act 1984 s 109(6), Sch 7 Pt I; the Airports Act 1986 s 83(5), Sch 6 Pt I; the Gas Act 1986 s 67(3), (4), Sch 8 para 17, Sch 9 Pt I; the Electricity Act 1989 s 112(4), Sch 18; and the Water Act 1989 s 190(1), Sch 25 para 65). The following are deemed to be statutory undertakers, and their undertakings statutory undertakings, for this purpose: (i) a public gas supplier (see the Gas Act 1986 s 67(1), Sch 7 para 2(1)(xlii); (ii) a relevant airport operator within the meaning of the Airports Act 1986 (see s 58, Sch 2 para 1(1)); (iii) the National Rivers Authority, every water undertaker and every sewerage undertaker (see the Water Act 1989 Sch 25 para 1(1), (2)(xxvii)); (iv) the holder of a licence under the Electricity Act 1989 s 6 who is entitled to exercise any power of compulsory acquisition conferred by s 10, Sch 3 (as amended) (see s 112(1), Sch 16 para 2(2)(g), (9)). 'National Trust' means the National Trust for Places of Historic Interest or Natural Beauty incorporated by the National Trust Act 1907: Acquisition of Land Act 1981 s 7(1). For the meaning of 'local authority' see para 34 note 2 ante.

39. Submission of order for confirmation. When the making of a compulsory purchase order[1] has been advertised and the necessary notices have been served on the owners, lessees and occupiers[2], the order must be submitted to the confirming authority[3].

1 For the meaning of 'compulsory purchase order' see para 34 note 1 ante.
2 See paras 36–38 ante.
3 See the Acquisition of Land Act 1981 s 10(3). For the meaning of 'confirming authority' see para 34 note 3 ante. The empowering enactment may impose a time limit for the submission of the order for confirmation: see eg the Housing Act 1985 s 17(4).

40. Right of objection to compulsory purchase order. Objections to a compulsory purchase order[1] may be made in the manner and in the time provided in the notices[2] and must be made to the confirming authority[3]. They must be made in writing and the grounds of objection should be stated, for the confirming authority may require an objector to state the grounds in writing and may disregard the objection if it is satisfied that the objection relates exclusively to matters which can be dealt with by the tribunal by which the compensation is to be assessed[4].

1 For the meaning of 'compulsory purchase order' see para 34 note 1 ante.
2 See paras 37–38 ante. Objections to the inclusion of operational land of statutory undertakers may be made to the appropriate minister and the land may be excluded from the order: see para 41 post.
3 Objections may be made by owners, lessees and occupiers served with a notice of the order (see paras 37–38 ante) and other persons, but the objections of other persons may for certain purposes be disregarded (see para 42 post).
4 See the Acquisition of Land Act 1981 s 13(4); and para 43 post.

41. Representations by statutory undertakers as alternative to objections. Where the land[1] comprised in a compulsory purchase order[2] includes land which has been acquired by statutory undertakers[3] for the purposes of their undertaking, they may make representations, within the time within which objections to the order can be made[4], to the appropriate minister[5]. If that minister is satisfied that any of the land is used for the purposes of carrying on the undertaking, or that an interest in any of the land is held for those purposes[6], and provided that the representation made to him is not withdrawn[7], the order must not be confirmed, or made, so as to authorise the compulsory purchase of any land in respect of which that minister is so satisfied, except land in respect of which he certifies[8] that he is satisfied that its nature and situation are such that (1) it can be purchased and not replaced without serious detriment to the carrying on of the undertaking[9]; or (2) if purchased it can be replaced by other land belonging to, or available for acquisition by, the undertakers without such serious detriment[10].

In the case of acquisitions of land of statutory undertakers under the Town and Country Planning Act 1990[11], the Planning (Listed Buildings and Conservation Areas) Act 1990[12] or certain provisions of the Local Government, Planning and Land Act 1980[13], the order may be confirmed or made without the appropriate certificate[14] provided that it has been confirmed (or made) by the appropriate minister jointly with the minister or ministers who would normally make the order[15].

1 For the meaning of 'land' see para 28 note 3 ante. In relation to the compulsory purchase of a right under the Gas Act 1965 ss 12(1), 13(2) or (3) (as amended) (see FUEL AND ENERGY vol 19(1) (Reissue) paras 689–690), references to the land for these purposes include references to any land held with the stratum of land constituting the underground gas storage: see the Acquisition of Land Act 1981 s 30(2); and para 84 post.
2 For the meaning of 'compulsory purchase order' see para 34 note 1 ante.
3 For these purposes, 'statutory undertakers' include (1) a health service body, as defined in the National Health Service and Community Care Act 1990 s 60(7); and (2) a National Health Service trust established under Pt I (ss 1–26) (as amended): but in relation to a health service body as so defined, any reference in the Acquisition of Land Act 1981 s 16(1), (2) (as amended) (see the text and notes 4–10 infra) to land acquired or available for acquisition by the statutory undertakers is to be construed as a reference to land acquired or available for acquisition by the Secretary of State for use or occupation by that body: s 16(3) (added by the National Health Service and Community Care Act 1990 s 60, Sch 8 para 8(1)). For the meaning of 'statutory undertakers' generally see para 38 note 8 ante. The Secretary of State here concerned is the Secretary of State for Health or, as respects Wales, the Secretary of State for Wales.
4 As to the time within which objections may be made see the Acquisition of Land Act 1981 ss 11(2), (d), 12(1)(c); and paras 36–37 ante.
5 See ibid s 16(1) (as amended: see note 7 infra). 'Appropriate minister' means (1) in the Acquisition of Land Act 1981 in relation to any statutory undertakers, the Secretary of State (s 8(3)); or (2) the appropriate minister as prescribed in the empowering enactment (see eg the Gas Act 1986 s 67(1), Sch 7 para 2(10)(d); the Electricity Act 1989 s 112(1), Sch 16 para 3(2)(h); and the Water Act 1989 s 190(1), Sch 25 para 1(9), (10)(ix)). If a question arises as to which minister is the appropriate minister, the question is to be determined by the Treasury: Acquisition of Land Act 1981 s 8(4). As to the Treasury see CONSTITUTIONAL LAW.
6 Ibid s 16(1)(a), (b). This provision does not protect land acquired by statutory undertakers other than for the purposes of their undertaking.
7 Ibid s 16(1) (amended by the Planning and Compensation Act 1991 s 70, Sch 15 para 10(1)).
8 As soon as may be after the giving of a certificate under the Acquisition of Land Act 1981 Pt III (ss 16–22) (as amended), the acquiring authority must publish in one or more local newspapers circulating in the locality in which the land comprised in the order is situated a notice in the prescribed form stating that the certificate has been given: s 22. For the prescribed form see the Compulsory Purchase of Land Regulations 1994, SI 1994/2145, reg 3(f), Schedule, Form 11. In the case of compulsory rights orders under the Opencast Coal Act 1958 s 4 (as amended) (see MINES), the relevant form of notice is contained in the Opencast Coal (Compulsory Rights and Rights of Way) (Forms) Regulations 1987, SI 1987/1915, reg 4(a)(iii), Schedule, Form 9. See further para 34 note 6 ante. Subject to the Acquisition of Land Act 1981 s 24 (court's power to quash certificate: see para 87 post) the certificate becomes operative on the date on which the notice is first published: s 26(2).
9 Ibid s 16(2)(a).
10 Ibid s 16(2)(b).
11 See the Town and Country Planning Act 1990 s 226 (as prospectively amended), ss 228, 244, 245(1), (3); and TOWN AND COUNTRY PLANNING vol 46 (Reissue) para 760 et seq; and s 254; and HIGHWAYS vol 21 (Reissue) para 162.
12 See the Planning (Listed Buildings and Conservation Areas) Act 1990 s 47 (as prospectively amended); and TOWN AND COUNTRY PLANNING vol 46 (Reissue) para 945.

13 Ie under the Local Government, Planning and Land Act 1980 s 104 (as amended) (acquisition by the Land Authority for Wales); or s 142 (as amended) or s 143 (as amended) (acquisition by urban development corporation): see TOWN AND COUNTRY PLANNING vol 46 (Reissue) paras 806, 1297–1298.

14 Ie by virtue of the Acquisition of Land Act 1981 s 31(1), (2) (respectively amended and substituted by the Planning and Compensation Act 1991 ss 4, 70, Sch 2 para 53(2), Sch 15 para 10(2)), disapplying the Acquisition of Land Act 1981 s 16(2).

15 Ibid s 31(2) (as substituted: see note 14 supra). Where, in accordance with this provision, a compulsory acquisition is effected under a compulsory purchase order confirmed or made without the appropriate minister's certificate, the Town and Country Planning Act 1990 ss 280–282 (measure of compensation: see TOWN AND COUNTRY PLANNING vol 46 (Reissue) paras 843–845) apply in accordance with s 281(1)(c): Acquisition of Land Act 1981 s 31(4) (amended by the Planning and Compensation Act 1991 Sch 2 para 53(2)).

B. CONFIRMATION OF COMPULSORY PURCHASE ORDER

42. Confirmation where no objections are outstanding or objections are disregarded. If no objection is duly made by an owner, lessee or occupier[1], or if all objections so made are withdrawn[2], the confirming authority[3], upon being satisfied that the proper notices have been published and served[4], may[5], if it thinks fit and subject to any provisions protecting special categories of land[6], confirm the order with or without modifications[7], and without any hearing or inquiry[8]. An objection by a person other than an owner, lessee or occupier may therefore be disregarded and a hearing or inquiry will not be necessary if there is no objection by such a person. Moreover, even if there is an objection by an owner, lessee or occupier which has not been withdrawn, no hearing or inquiry will be required if it is the only objection and can be disregarded because it relates exclusively to matters which can be dealt with by the tribunal by which compensation is to be assessed[9].

1 Ie such an owner, lessee or occupier as is mentioned in the Acquisition of Land Act 1981 s 12(1): see para 37 ante. For the meaning of 'owner' see para 37 note 3 ante. In relation to compulsory rights orders under the Opencast Coal Act 1958 s 4 (as amended) (see MINES), references to persons directly concerned in relation to the order are substituted for references in the Acquisition of Land Act 1981 s 13 (as amended) (see the text and notes 2–9 infra) to owners, lessees or occupiers: see s 29(5); and para 83 post.

2 Objections must be validly withdrawn. In *Lord Howden v Simpson* (1839) 10 Ad & El 793 it was held that an agreement in consideration of the withdrawal of opposition to a private Bill was valid. An agreement by which the acquiring authority agreed to restrict its statutory powers to take land would generally be void. For the meaning of 'acquiring authority' see para 34 note 2 ante.

3 For the meaning of 'confirming authority' see para 34 note 3 ante.

4 As to the publication and service of notices see paras 36–38 ante.

5 If confirmation of the order would necessarily infringe some legal principle, the confirming authority must refuse to confirm it: see *London and Westcliff Properties Ltd v Minister of Housing and Local Government* [1961] 1 All ER 610, [1961] 1 WLR 519. The confirming authority is entitled to refuse to confirm an order where the acquiring authority has failed to convince it of the need for the order: see *R v Secretary of State for the Environment, ex p Melton Borough Council* (1986) 52 P & CR 318. As to the duties of the confirming authority see also para 57 post. For the meaning of 'acquiring authority' see para 34 note 2 ante.

6 Ie subject to the Acquisition of Land Act 1981 s 31 (as amended) (see para 41 ante): s 13(5). See also para 76 et seq post.

7 Ibid s 13(1). The order as confirmed by the confirming authority must not, unless all persons interested consent, authorise the acquiring authority to purchase compulsorily any land which the order would not have authorised that authority to purchase compulsorily if it had been confirmed without modification: s 14. For the meaning of 'land' see para 28 note 3 ante. It may be that the modifications could include a restriction on the period during which the powers granted by the order could be exercised. The power to modify orders is used sparingly: see Department of the Environment Circular 14/94 para 27. It will not be used to add or substitute for the purposes for which the order is made. As to

the 'purposes' of a compulsory purchase order see para 24 ante. In *Procter & Gamble v Secretary of State for the Environment* [1992] 1 EGLR 265, CA, it was confirmed that a compulsory purchase order made for one purpose cannot lawfully be confirmed for another or additional purpose. In *Glasgow City District Council v Secretary of State for Scotland* [1990] 2 EGLR 18, a decision by the confirming authority not to confirm an order with a modification excluding a parcel of land from the order, notwithstanding that the inspector had found that the development was possible with the modification, was upheld.

8 If there are objections by owners, lessees or occupiers, a hearing or inquiry must be held unless the objection is one which may be disregarded: see para 43 et seq post.

9 See the Acquisition of Land Act 1981 s 13(4). An objection may be disregarded in the case of a compulsory purchase order of land for development and other planning purposes under the Town and Country Planning Act 1990 s 226 (as prospectively amended) or s 228, if, in the opinion of the confirming authority or the Secretary of State, the objection amounts in substance to an objection to the provisions of the development plan defining the proposed use of that land and other land: see s 245(1); and TOWN AND COUNTRY PLANNING vol 46 (Reissue) para 767.

43. Local inquiry where objections are made and not withdrawn. If any objection is duly made by an owner, lessee or occupier[1], and is not withdrawn and may not be disregarded[2], the confirming authority must, before confirming the compulsory purchase order[3] either (1) cause a public local inquiry to be held[4]; or (2) afford to the objector an opportunity of appearing before and being heard by a person appointed by that authority for the purpose[5]. If the Secretary of State intends to cause an inquiry to be held, he must, within 14 days after the expiry of the time within which objections to the order may be made[6] or the submission of the order to him for confirmation (whichever is the later) give written notice[7]:

(a) to the acquiring authority[8] and to each statutory objector[9] of that intention[10]; and

(b) of the substance of each objection made by a statutory objector and, so far as practicable, of the substance of other objections[11].

1 Ie any objection as mentioned in the Acquisition of Land Act 1981 s 13(1): see para 42 ante. For the meaning of 'owner' see para 37 note 3 ante. See also para 42 note 1 ante.

2 Notwithstanding anything in ibid s 13(2), (3) (see the text and notes 3–5 infra; and paras 42 ante, 56 post), the confirming authority may require any person who has made an objection to state the grounds of the objection in writing, and may disregard the objection for these purposes if it is satisfied that the objection relates exclusively to matters which can be dealt with by the tribunal by whom the compensation is to be assessed: s 13(4). For the meaning of 'confirming authority' see para 34 note 3 ante. As to assessment of compensation see para 233 et seq post.

3 For the meaning of 'compulsory purchase order' see para 34 note 1 ante.

4 For the purposes of the execution of his duties under the Acquisition of Land Act 1981, a minister may cause such public local inquiries to be held as are directed by that Act and such other public local inquiries as he may think fit: s 5(1). As to the costs of an inquiry see para 54 post.

5 Ibid s 13(2). As to such hearings see para 55 post.

6 As to time limits for the making of objections see paras 36–37 ante.

7 Notices or documents required or authorised to be served or sent under any provision of the Compulsory Purchase by Non-ministerial Acquiring Authorities (Inquiries Procedure) Rules 1990, SI 1990/512, may be sent by post: r 20.

8 For these purposes, 'acquiring authority' means a local authority or any person other than a minister who may be authorised to purchase land compulsorily and who has made and submitted an order to the Secretary of State for confirmation in accordance with the Acquisition of Land Act 1981 Pt II (ss 10–15) (as amended) (see paras 34 et seq ante, 56 et seq post): Compulsory Purchase by Non-ministerial Acquiring Authorities (Inquiries Procedure) Rules 1990 r 2.

9 'Statutory objector' means any objector to whom the Secretary of State is obliged by virtue of the Acquisition of Land Act 1981 s 13(2) to afford an opportunity to be heard: Compulsory Purchase by Non-ministerial Acquiring Authorities (Inquiries Procedure) Rules 1990 r 2.

10 Ibid r 4(a).
11 Ibid r 4(b).

44. Representations by official bodies. Where an acquiring authority[1] proposes to rely, in its submissions at the inquiry[2], on an official representation[3], it must within seven days[4] of receipt either of that representation or of the relevant notice[5] (whichever is the later) send notification[6] to the official body concerned that an inquiry is to be held, and within 14 days of receipt of such notification, the official body must supply to the acquiring authority an official case[7], unless it has already done so[8].

1 For the meaning of 'acquiring authority' see para 43 note 8 ante.
2 For these purposes, 'inquiry' means an inquiry to which the Compulsory Purchase by Non-ministerial Acquiring Authorities (Inquiries Procedure) Rules 1990, SI 1990/512, apply: r 2. The Compulsory Purchase by Non-ministerial Acquiring Authorities (Inquiries Procedure) Rules 1990 were made by the Lord Chancellor under the Tribunals and Inquiries Act 1971 s 11 (repealed) and now have effect, by virtue of the Interpretation Act 1978 s 17(2)(a), under the Tribunals and Inquiries Act 1992 s 9. Those rules apply in relation to any inquiry which is caused by the Secretary of State to be held in England and Wales pursuant to the Acquisition of Land Act 1981 s 5 and which concerns an order made by an acquiring authority: Compulsory Purchase by Non-ministerial Acquiring Authorities (Inquiries Procedure) Rules 1990 r 3(1). For transitional provisions see r 3(2)–(4). Notwithstanding the provisions of r 3, the rules apply in relation to an inquiry concerning a clearance order only where that order is made on or after the coming into force of the Local Government and Housing Act 1989 s 165, Sch 9 paras 72, 73 (ie 1 April 1990: see the Local Government and Housing Act 1989 (Commencement No 5 and Transitional Provisions) Order 1990, SI 1990/431); Compulsory Purchase by Non-ministerial Acquiring Authorities (Inquiries Procedure) Rules 1990 r 22(1). 'Clearance order' means a compulsory purchase order made pursuant to the Housing Act 1985 s 290: Compulsory Purchase by Non-ministerial Acquiring Authorities (Inquiries Procedure) Rules 1990 r 2. See further HOUSING.
3 'Official representation' means a written representation made by an official body in support of an order; 'official body' means a minister of the Crown or a government department; and 'order' means a compulsory purchase order as defined in the Acquisition of Land Act 1981 s 7 (see para 34 note 1 ante) or a compulsory rights order made pursuant to the Opencast Coal Act 1958 s 4 (as amended) (see MINES): Compulsory Purchase by Non-ministerial Acquiring Authorities (Inquiries Procedure) Rules 1990 r 2.
4 The Secretary of State may at any time in any particular case allow further time for the taking of any step which is to be taken by virtue of the Compulsory Purchase by Non-ministerial Acquiring Authorities (Inquiries Procedure) Rules 1990, and references therein to a day by which, or a period within which, any step is to be taken are to be construed accordingly: r 19.
5 'Relevant notice' means the Secretary of State's notice to the acquiring authority under ibid r 4(a) (see para 43 ante): r 2.
6 As to the service of notices see para 43 note 7 ante.
7 'Official case' means a written statement by an official body setting out in detail its case in support of an order: Compulsory Purchase by Non-ministerial Acquiring Authorities (Inquiries Procedure) Rules 1990 r 2.
8 Ibid r 5.

45. Pre-inquiry meetings. The Secretary of State may cause a pre-inquiry meeting[1] to be held if it appears to him desirable, and where he does so he must serve with the relevant notice[2] a notification of his intention to cause a meeting to be held and a statement of matters[3]. Where an official representation[4] or an official case[5] has been made, its text must be included in the statement of matters and a copy of that statement must be served on the official body[6] concerned[7]. The acquiring authority[8] must cause a notice of the Secretary of State's intention to hold a meeting to be published in a newspaper circulating in the locality in which the land is situated and the notice must include the text of the statement of matters[9]. The acquiring authority must, not later than eight weeks[10] after the relevant date[11], serve on the Secretary of State and on each statutory objector[12] an outline statement[13] which must include the text of any official representation or official case[14]. A copy of the outline statement must be served on the official body concerned not later than eight weeks after the relevant date[15].

The Secretary of State may, by written notice, require any statutory objector, and any other person who has notified him of an intention or wish to appear at the inquiry, to serve an outline statement on him, on the acquiring authority and on any other person specified, within four weeks of the date of the notice[16].

The pre-inquiry meeting or, where there is more than one, the first meeting[17], must be held not later than 16 weeks after the relevant date[18], not less than 21 days' written notice having been given by the Secretary of State to the acquiring authority, to each statutory objector and to any other person whose presence at the meeting seems to the Secretary of State to be desirable[19].

The meeting is presided over by the inspector[20], who determines the matters to be discussed and the procedure to be followed[21].

If the Secretary of State has not caused a pre-inquiry meeting to be held, an inspector may hold one if he thinks it desirable[22]. In such a case he must arrange for not less than 14 days' written notice to be given to the acquiring authority, to each statutory objector, to any other person known at the date of the notice to be entitled to appear at the inquiry and to any other person whose presence at the meeting appears to the inspector to be desirable[23]. The inspector has the same powers over such a meeting as over one which the Secretary of State has caused to be held[24].

Where a pre-inquiry meeting is caused to be held by the Secretary of State the inspector must, and in any other case where there is a pre-inquiry meeting he may, arrange a timetable for the proceedings at the inquiry or at part of the inquiry; and he may vary the timetable at any time[25].

1　'Pre-inquiry meeting' means a meeting held before an inquiry to consider what may be done with a view to securing that the inquiry is conducted efficiently and expeditiously: Compulsory Purchase by Non-ministerial Acquiring Authorities (Inquiries Procedure) Rules 1990, SI 1990/512, r 2. For the meaning of 'inquiry' see para 44 note 2 ante.

2　For the meaning of 'relevant notice' see para 44 note 5 ante; and as to service of notices see para 43 note 7 ante.

3　Compulsory Purchase by Non-ministerial Acquiring Authorities (Inquiries Procedure) Rules 1990 r 6(1), (2). 'Statement of matters' means a statement by the Secretary of State of the matters which appear to him to be likely to be relevant to his consideration of the order in question: r 2. For the meaning of 'order' see para 44 note 3 ante.

4　For the meaning of 'official representation' see para 44 note 3 ante.

5　For the meaning of 'official case' see para 44 note 7 ante.

6　For the meaning of 'official body' see para 44 note 3 ante.

7　Compulsory Purchase by Non-ministerial Acquiring Authorities (Inquiries Procedure) Rules 1990 r 6(3).

8　For the meaning of 'acquiring authority' see para 43 note 8 ante.

9　Compulsory Purchase by Non-ministerial Acquiring Authorities (Inquiries Procedure) Rules 1990 r 6(4), (5).

10　As to the Secretary of State's power to allow further time see para 44 note 4 ante.

11　'Relevant date' means the date of the Secretary of State's notice to the acquiring authority under the Compulsory Purchase by Non-ministerial Acquiring Authorities (Inquiries Procedure) Rules 1990 r 4(a) (see para 44 ante): r 2.

12　For the meaning of 'statutory objector' see para 43 note 9 ante.

13　'Outline statement' means a written statement of the principal submissions which a person proposes to put forward at an inquiry: Compulsory Purchase by Non-ministerial Acquiring Authorities (Inquiries Procedure) Rules 1990 r 2.

14　Ibid r 6(6), (7).

15　Ibid r 6(7).

16　Ibid r 6(8).

17 Where a meeting has been held pursuant to ibid r 6(1), the inspector may hold a further meeting; and he must arrange for such notice to be given of a further meeting as appears to him to be necessary: r 6(12).

18 Ibid r 6(9).

19 Ibid r 6(10). The Secretary of State may require the acquiring authority (1) to post a notice of the meeting, not later than 14 days before the date fixed for the holding of the meeting, in a conspicuous place near to the land and also in one or more places where public notices are usually posted in the locality; (2) to publish, not later than 14 days before the date fixed for the holding of the meeting, a notice of the meeting in one or more of the newspapers circulating in the locality in which the land is situated: r 11(5), (6) (applied by r 6(10)). For these purposes, 'land' means the land to which the order relates or, where a right over land is proposed to be acquired, the land over which such a right would be exercised: r 2.

20 'Inspector' means a person appointed by the Secretary of State to hold an inquiry or a reopened inquiry: ibid r 2.

21 Ibid r 6(11). The inspector may require any person present at the meeting who, in his opinion, is behaving in a disruptive manner to leave and may refuse to permit that person to return or to attend any further meeting, or may permit him to return or attend only on such conditions as he may specify: r 6(11). Rule 6(11) applies to a further meeting as it applies to the first meeting: see r 6(12).

22 Ibid r 8(1).

23 Ibid r 8(2).

24 Ibid r 8(3), applying r 6(11).

25 Ibid r 9.

46. Appointment of assessor for public inquiry.
The Secretary of State may appoint an assessor, namely a person who will sit with the inspector[1] at an inquiry or a reopened inquiry[2] to advise the inspector on such matters arising as the Secretary of State may specify[3]. Where an assessor has been appointed, the Secretary of State must notify every person entitled to appear at the inquiry of the name of the assessor and of the matters on which he is to advise the inspector[4].

1 For the meaning of 'inspector' see para 45 note 20 ante.

2 For the meaning of 'inquiry' see para 44 note 2 ante.

3 See the Compulsory Purchase by Non-ministerial Acquiring Authorities (Inquiries Procedure) Rules 1990, SI 1990/512, r 2.

4 Ibid r 10. As to service of notices see para 43 note 7 ante.

47. Matters preliminary to inquiry.
The Secretary of State must fix a date[1], time and place for the holding of the inquiry[2] and must give not less than 42 days' written notice[3] of that date, time and place to any statutory objector[4], to the acquiring authority[5] and to any other person who has served an outline statement[6] or a statement of case[7]. The Secretary of State may vary the date, time and place fixed for the holding of the inquiry[8], but must give such notice of variation as appears to him to be reasonable[9].

Unless the Secretary of State otherwise directs, the acquiring authority must post notice of the inquiry in a conspicuous place near to the land[10] and also in one or more places where public notices are usually posted in the locality, not later than 14 days before the date of the inquiry[11], and must also, if directed by the Secretary of State, publish in one or more newspapers circulating in the locality in which the land is situated a notice of the inquiry[12]. Any notice of inquiry so posted or published must contain a clear statement of the date, time and place of the inquiry, and of the powers under which the order[13] has been made, together with a sufficient description of the land to identify approximately its location without reference to the map referred to in the order[14].

1 The date fixed for the inquiry must be (1) not later than 22 weeks after the relevant date; or (2) if the Secretary of State has caused a pre-inquiry meeting to be held pursuant to the Compulsory Purchase by

Non-ministerial Acquiring Authorities (Inquiries Procedure) Rules 1990, SI 1990/512, r 6 (see para 45 ante), not later than eight weeks after the conclusion of that meeting; or (3) where he is satisfied that in all the circumstances of the case it is impracticable to hold the inquiry within the applicable period mentioned in head (1) or head (2) supra, the earliest practicable date after the end of that period: r 11(1). Where two or more pre-inquiry meetings are held, references to the conclusion of a pre-inquiry meeting are references to the conclusion of the final meeting: r 2. For the meaning of 'inquiry' see para 44 note 2 ante.

2 Ibid r 11(1).
3 As to the Secretary of State's power to allow further time see para 44 note 4 ante. As to service of notices see para 43 note 7 ante.
4 For the meaning of 'statutory objector' see para 43 note 9 ante.
5 For the meaning of 'acquiring authority' see para 43 note 8 ante.
6 For the meaning of 'outline statement' see para 45 note 13 ante.
7 Compulsory Purchase by Non-ministerial Acquiring Authorities (Inquiries Procedure) Rules 1990 rr 11(2), 12(1). As to service of a statement of case see para 48 post.
8 Ibid r 11(3), (4). Rule 11(2) applies to a variation of a date as it applies to the date originally fixed: r 11(3).
9 Ibid r 11(4).
10 For the meaning of 'land' see para 45 note 19 ante.
11 Compulsory Purchase by Non-ministerial Acquiring Authorities (Inquiries Procedure) Rules 1990 r 11(5).
12 Ibid r 11(6).
13 For the meaning of 'order' see para 44 note 3 ante.
14 Compulsory Purchase by Non-ministerial Acquiring Authorities (Inquiries Procedure) Rules 1990 r 11(7).

48. Statements of case. At least 28 days[1] before the date fixed for the inquiry[2] and not later than (1) six weeks after the relevant date[3]; or (2) where a pre-inquiry meeting is held[4], four weeks after the conclusion of that meeting[5], the acquiring authority[6] must serve a statement of case[7] on the Secretary of State and on each statutory objector[8], and must supply a copy of the statement to the relevant official body[9] concerned within the relevant period for service[10]. There must be included in the statement[11] the text of any official case[12] or official representation[13]. The statement must be accompanied by copies of any documents, including any photographs, maps or plans, referred to in it, or the relevant extracts from them, together with a list of any documents to which the authority intends to refer, or which it intends to put in evidence, at the inquiry[14].

The Secretary of State may by notice in writing require any statutory objector or any other person who has notified him of an intention or a wish to appear at the inquiry, within four weeks of the date of the notice, to serve a statement of case on him, on the acquiring authority and on any other person specified in the notice[15]. He must supply any person who is not a statutory objector, but who has been so required to serve a statement of case, with a copy of the acquiring authority's statement of case[16].

Unless a statement of matters has already been served[17], the Secretary of State may serve such a statement on the acquiring authority within 12 weeks from the relevant date, and may also within that period serve such a statement on each statutory objector and on any person from whom he has required a statement of case[18].

The acquiring authority must afford to any person who so requests a reasonable opportunity to inspect and, where practicable, take copies of any statement or document[19] which, or a copy of which, has been served on or by it in accordance with any of the above provisions, and must specify in its statement of case the time and place at which the opportunity will be afforded[20].

1 As to the Secretary of State's power to allow further time see para 44 note 4 ante.
2 As to the date for the inquiry see para 47 ante; and for the meaning of 'inquiry' see para 44 note 2 ante.

3 For the meaning of 'relevant date' see para 45 note 11 ante.
4 Ie pursuant to the Compulsory Purchase by Non-ministerial Acquiring Authorities (Inquiries Procedure) Rules 1990, SI 1990/512, r 6: see para 45 ante. For the meaning of 'pre-inquiry meeting' see para 45 note 1 ante.
5 See para 47 note 1 ante.
6 For the meaning of 'acquiring authority' see para 43 note 8 ante.
7 'Statement of case' means a written statement containing full particulars of the case which a person proposes to put forward at the inquiry, including, where that person is the acquiring authority, the reasons for making the order: Compulsory Purchase by Non-ministerial Acquiring Authorities (Inquiries Procedure) Rules 1990 r 2. As to the service of notices see para 43 note 7 ante.
8 For the meaning of 'statutory objector' see para 43 note 9 ante.
9 For the meaning of 'official body' see para 44 note 3 ante.
10 Compulsory Purchase by Non-ministerial Acquiring Authorities (Inquiries Procedure) Rules 1990 r 7(1), (2).
11 Ie unless this has already been included in an outline statement under ibid r 6(6): see para 45 ante.
12 For the meaning of 'official case' see para 44 note 7 ante.
13 Compulsory Purchase by Non-ministerial Acquiring Authorities (Inquiries Procedure) Rules 1990 r 7(2). For the meaning of 'official representation' see para 44 note 3 ante.
14 Ibid r 2.
15 Ibid r 7(3).
16 Ibid r 7(4). The Secretary of State or an inspector may require any person who has served a statement of case in accordance with r 7 to provide such further information about the matters contained in the statement as he may specify: r 7(5). For the meaning of 'inspector' see para 45 note 20 ante.
17 Ie pursuant to ibid r 6(2): see para 45 ante. For the meaning of 'statement of matters' see para 45 note 3 ante.
18 Ibid r 7(6).
19 'Document' includes a photograph, map or plan: ibid r 2.
20 Ibid r 7(7).

49. Persons entitled to appear at the inquiry. The persons entitled to appear at an inquiry[1] are (1) any statutory objector[2]; (2) the acquiring authority[3]; and (3) any other person who has served an outline statement[4] or a statement of case[5]. This provision does not, however, prevent the inspector[6] from permitting any other person to appear at an inquiry and such permission must not be unreasonably withheld[7]. Any person entitled or permitted to appear may do so on his own behalf or be represented by counsel, solicitor or any other person[8]. An inspector may allow one or more persons to appear on behalf of some or all of any persons having a similar interest in the matter under inquiry[9].

An official body[10] must arrange for its representative to attend the inquiry if it has made an official case[11] and received, not later than 14 days[12] before the date fixed for the holding of an inquiry[13], a written request for such attendance from the acquiring authority, or from a statutory objector[14]. A person attending an inquiry as a representative in pursuance of this rule must state the reasons in support of the official case in question and must give evidence and be subject to cross-examination to the same extent as any other witness, but nothing in this provision requires him to answer any question which in the opinion of the inspector is directed to the merits of government policy[15].

1 For the meaning of 'inquiry' see para 44 note 3 ante.
2 For the meaning of 'statutory objector' see para 43 note 9 ante.
3 For the meaning of 'acquiring authority' see para 43 note 8 ante.
4 Ie under the Compulsory Purchase by Non-ministerial Acquiring Authorities (Inquiries Procedure) Rules 1990, SI 1990/512, r 6: see para 45 ante. For the meaning of 'outline statement' see para 45 note 13 ante.
5 Ibid r 12(1). The statement of case is served under r 7: see para 48 ante. For the meaning of 'statement of case' see para 48 note 7 ante; and as to the service of documents see para 43 note 7 ante.

6 For the meaning of 'inspector' see para 45 note 20 ante.
7 Compulsory Purchase by Non-ministerial Acquiring Authorities (Inquiries Procedure) Rules 1990 r 12(2).
8 Ibid r 12(3).
9 Ibid r 12(4).
10 For the meaning of 'official body' see para 44 note 3 ante.
11 Ie pursuant to the Compulsory Purchase by Non-ministerial Acquiring Authorities (Inquiries Procedure) Rules 1990 r 5: see para 44 ante. For the meaning of 'official case' see para 44 note 7 ante.
12 As to the Secretary of State's power to allow further time see para 44 note 4 ante.
13 As to the date fixed for the inquiry see para 47 ante.
14 Compulsory Purchase by Non-ministerial Acquiring Authorities (Inquiries Procedure) Rules 1990 r 13(1).
15 Ibid r 13(2), (3).

50. Inspection of land. The inspector[1] may make an unaccompanied inspection of the land[2], either before or during an inquiry[3], without giving notice of his intention to the persons entitled to appear[4] at the inquiry[5].

He may, and must if so requested by the acquiring authority[6] or any statutory objector[7] before or during the inquiry, inspect the land after the close of the inquiry in the company of a representative of the acquiring authority and any statutory objector[8], in which case he must, during the inquiry, announce the date and time at which he proposes to make the inspection[9]. He is not, however, bound to defer such an inspection where any person entitled to accompany him on his inspection is not present at the time appointed[10].

1 For the meaning of 'inspector' see para 45 note 20 ante.
2 For the meaning of 'land' see para 45 note 19 ante.
3 For the meaning of 'inquiry' see para 44 note 2 ante.
4 As to the persons entitled to appear see para 49 ante.
5 Compulsory Purchase by Non-ministerial Acquiring Authorities (Inquiries Procedure) Rules 1990, SI 1990/512, r 16(1).
6 For the meaning of 'acquiring authority' see para 43 note 8 ante.
7 For the meaning of 'statutory objector' see para 43 note 9 ante.
8 Compulsory Purchase by Non-ministerial Acquiring Authorities (Inquiries Procedure) Rules 1990 r 16(2).
9 Ibid r 16(3).
10 Ibid r 16(4).

51. Statements of evidence. The Secretary of State may by notice in writing require any person who is entitled to appear at the inquiry[1] and proposes to give, or call another person to give, evidence at it by reading a written statement, to serve a copy of that statement of evidence on the inspector[2] not later than three weeks[3] before the date on which he is due to give evidence in accordance with the arranged timetable[4] or, if there is no such timetable, three weeks before the date fixed for the holding of the inquiry[5]. An inspector may by written notice require any person who has served such a copy on him to supply to him, within a specified period, a written summary of the contents of that statement[6].

Where the acquiring authority[7] sends a copy of a statement of evidence or a summary to an inspector, it must at the same time send a copy to every person entitled to appear at the inquiry; and where any such person sends a copy statement or summary to the inspector he must at the same time send a copy to the acquiring authority[8]. Any person so required to send a copy of a statement of evidence to any other person must send with it a copy of the whole, or the relevant part, of any documents[9] referred to in it, unless copies of those documents or parts have already been made available[10] to that person[11].

Where the inspector has required a written summary of evidence, the person giving that evidence at the inquiry may do so only by reading the written summary, unless permitted by the inspector to do otherwise[12].

1 As to the persons entitled to appear at the inquiry see para 49 ante. For the meaning of 'inquiry' see para 44 note 2 ante.
2 For the meaning of 'inspector' see para 45 note 20 ante.
3 As to the Secretary of State's power to allow further time see para 44 note 4 ante.
4 Ie the timetable arranged pursuant to the Compulsory Purchase by Non-ministerial Acquiring Authorities (Inquiries Procedure) Rules 1990, SI 1990/512, r 9: see para 45 ante.
5 Ibid r 14(1). As to the service of documents see para 43 note 7 ante.
6 Ibid r 14(2).
7 For the meaning of 'acquiring authority' see para 43 note 8 ante.
8 Compulsory Purchase by Non-ministerial Acquiring Authorities (Inquiries Procedure) Rules 1990 r 14(3).
9 For the meaning of 'document' see para 48 note 19 ante.
10 Ie pursuant to the Compulsory Purchase by Non-ministerial Acquiring Authorities (Inquiries Procedure) Rules 1990 r 7: see para 48 ante.
11 Ibid r 14(5).
12 Ibid r 14(4).

52. Procedure at the inquiry. Subject to any express provision in the rules of procedure[1], the inspector[2] determines the procedure at an inquiry[3], save that unless in any particular case he determines otherwise with the consent of the acquiring authority[4], the acquiring authority must present its case first and must have the right of final reply[5]. The other persons entitled or permitted to appear[6] must be heard in such order as the inspector may determine[7].

The inspector may summons any person to attend to give evidence or produce documents in his custody or under his control relating to any matter in question at the inquiry[8], but he has no power to require the production of the title, or of any instrument relating to the title, of any land which is not the property of a local authority[9]. No person may be required to attend on a summons unless the necessary expenses are paid or tendered to him[10]. The inspector may direct that documents[11] tendered in evidence be inspected by any person entitled or permitted to appear[12] and that facilities be afforded to any such person to take or obtain copies of documentary evidence open to public inspection[13]. He may not require or permit evidence contrary to the public interest to be given[14], but otherwise he may admit any evidence at his discretion[15]. He may take evidence on oath, and for that purpose may administer oaths[16] or require a witness to make a solemn affirmation[17].

The inspector may proceed with an inquiry in the absence of any person entitled to appear at it[18] and may take into account any written representation or evidence or other document received by him from any person before an inquiry opens or during the inquiry, provided that he discloses it at the inquiry[19]. A person entitled to appear at an inquiry is entitled to call evidence, and the acquiring authority and the statutory objectors[20] are entitled to cross-examine persons giving evidence[21]. The calling of evidence and the cross-examination of persons giving it are otherwise[22] at the inspector's discretion[23]. Where the inspector refuses to permit the giving of oral evidence, the person wishing to give it may submit to him any evidence or other matter in writing before the close of the inquiry[24]. Where a person gives evidence by reading a summary[25] of his evidence, his statement of evidence[26] is treated as tendered in evidence unless the person giving the summary notifies the inspector that he now wishes to rely on that summary only, and that person is then subject to cross-examination on the statement of evidence to the same extent as if it were evidence he had given orally[27].

The inspector may allow any person to alter or add to a statement of case[28] so far as may be necessary for the purposes of the inquiry; but he must give every other person entitled to appear who is appearing at the inquiry an adequate opportunity of considering any fresh matter or document[29]. If necessary, he must adjourn the inquiry for this purpose; and he may in any case adjourn the inquiry from time to time[30].

The inspector may require any person appearing or present at an inquiry who, in his opinion, is behaving in a disruptive manner to leave and may refuse to permit that person to return, or may permit him to return only on such conditions as he may specify; but any such person may submit to him any evidence or other matter in writing before the close of the inquiry[31].

1 Ie any provision in the Compulsory Purchase by Non-Ministerial Acquiring Authorities (Inquiries Procedure) Rules 1990, SI 1990/512: see paras 43 et seq ante, 53 post.
2 For the meaning of 'inspector' see para 45 note 20 ante.
3 Compulsory Purchase by Non-ministerial Acquiring Authorities (Inquiries Procedure) Rules 1990 r 15(1). For the meaning of 'inquiry' see para 44 note 2 ante.
4 For the meaning of 'acquiring authority' see para 43 note 8 ante.
5 Compulsory Purchase by Non-ministerial Acquiring Authorities (Inquiries Procedure) Rules 1990 r 15(2).
6 As to the persons who are entitled, or may be permitted, to appear see para 49 ante.
7 Compulsory Purchase by Non-ministerial Acquiring Authorities (Inquiries Procedure) Rules 1990 r 15(2).
8 Local Government Act 1972 s 250(2) (applied by the Acquisition of Land Act 1981 s 5(2)). A person who refuses or deliberately fails to attend in obedience to the summons, or to give evidence, or who deliberately alters, suppresses, conceals, destroys or refuses to produce any document which he is so required or is liable to be required to produce is liable on summary conviction to a fine not exceeding level 3 on the standard scale, or to imprisonment for a term not exceeding six months, or to both: Local Government Act 1972 s 250(3) (as so applied; amended by virtue of the Criminal Justice Act 1982 ss 38, 46). As to the standard scale see para 14 note 6 ante.
9 Local Government Act 1972 s 250(2) proviso (b) (as applied: see note 8 supra).
10 Ibid s 250(2) proviso (a) (as applied: see note 8 supra).
11 For the meaning of 'document' see para 48 note 19 ante.
12 See the Compulsory Purchase by Non-Ministerial Acquiring Authorities (Inquiries Procedure) Rules 1990 rr 7(7), 14(5); and paras 48, 51 ante.
13 Ibid r 15(6).
14 See eg ibid r 13(3); and para 49 ante.
15 In particular, the inspector may refuse to permit the giving or production of evidence, the cross-examination of persons giving evidence, or the presentation of any matter, which he considers to be irrelevant or repetitious: ibid r 15(4). The inspector has a wide discretion as to what evidence is considered relevant and the court will only intervene in exceptional circumstances. For an example of when the court will intervene see *R v Secretary of State for the Environment, ex p Royal Borough of Kensington and Chelsea* [1987] JPL 567.
16 Local Government Act 1972 s 250(2) (as applied: see note 8 supra).
17 See the Oaths Act 1978 s 5; the Interpretation Act 1978 ss 5, 23(1), Sch 1; and STATUTES vol 44(1) (Reissue) para 1386.
18 Compulsory Purchase by Non-ministerial Acquiring Authorities (Inquiries Procedure) Rules 1990 r 15(9).
19 Ibid r 15(10).
20 For the meaning of 'statutory objector' see para 43 note 9 ante.
21 Compulsory Purchase by Non-ministerial Acquiring Authorities (Inquiries Procedure) Rules 1990 r 15(3).
22 Ie subject to ibid r 15(2), (4), (5), (7): r 15(3).
23 Ibid r 15(3).
24 Ibid r 15(4).
25 Ie in accordance with ibid r 14(4): see para 51 ante.

26 Ie the statement of evidence referred to in ibid r 14(1): see para 51 ante.
27 Ibid r 15(5).
28 Ie a statement of case served under ibid r 7: see para 48 ante. For the meaning of 'statement of case' see para 48 note 7 ante.
29 Ibid r 15(8).
30 Ibid r 15(8), (11). If the date, time and place of the adjourned inquiry are announced at the inquiry before the adjournment, no further notice is required: r 15(11). As to the circumstances in which the inspector would be obliged to adjourn the inquiry see *Orakpo v London Borough of Wandsworth and Secretary of State for the Environment* (1992) 24 HLR 370. For considerations to be taken into account when an objector seeks an adjournment see *Ostreicher v Secretary of State for the Environment* [1978] 3 All ER 82, [1978] 1 WLR 810, CA.
31 Compulsory Purchase by Non-ministerial Acquiring Authorities (Inquiries Procedure) Rules 1990 r 15(7).

53. Procedure after inquiry. After the close of an inquiry[1], the inspector[2] must make a report in writing to the Secretary of State which must include his conclusions and recommendations or his reasons for not making any recommendations[3]. Where an assessor has been appointed[4], he may make a report in writing after the close of the inquiry to the inspector in respect of the matters on which he was appointed to advise[5], in which case the inspector must append it to his own report and must state in his own report how far he agrees or disagrees with it, and, where he disagrees with the assessor, the reasons for that disagreement[6].

If, after the close of an inquiry, the Secretary of State:

(1) differs from the inspector on any matter of fact mentioned in, or appearing to him to be material to, a conclusion reached by the inspector; or

(2) takes into consideration any new evidence or new matter of fact which is not a matter of government policy,

and is for that reason disposed to disagree with a recommendation made by the inspector, he may not come to a decision which is at variance with that recommendation without first notifying the persons entitled to appear[7], and who did appear, at the inquiry of his disagreement and the reasons for it, and affording them an opportunity (a) of making written representations to him within 21 days[8] of the date of the notification; or (b) if he has taken into consideration any new evidence or matter in accordance with head (2) above, of asking within that period for the reopening of the inquiry[9]. He may cause an inquiry to be reopened to afford an opportunity for persons to be heard on such matters relating to the order[10] as he may specify, and must do so if asked by the acquiring authority[11] or a statutory objector[12] in the circumstances set out in heads (a) and (b) above[13].

The Secretary of State must notify his decision on the order and his reasons for it in writing to:

(i) the acquiring authority;

(ii) each statutory objector;

(iii) any person entitled to appear at the inquiry who did appear at it; and

(iv) any other person who appeared at the inquiry and has asked to be notified of the decision[14].

Where a copy of the inspector's report[15] is not sent with the notification of the decision, the notification must be accompanied by a copy of his conclusions and of any recommendations made by him; and if a person entitled to be notified of the decision has not received a copy of that report, he must be supplied with a copy of it on written application made to the Secretary of State within four weeks of the date of the decision[16].

1 For the meaning of 'inquiry' see para 44 note 2 ante.
2 For the meaning of 'inspector' see para 45 note 20 ante.
3 Compulsory Purchase by Non-ministerial Acquiring Authorities (Inquiries Procedure) Rules 1990, SI 1990/512, r 17(1). See also *Bushell v Secretary of State for the Environment* [1981] AC 75, [1980] 2 All ER 608, HL (a highways inquiry case), for comments on the purpose of the public inquiry procedure and the inspector's report. The report should contain a summary of the main evidence and arguments presented to the inspector along with findings of fact which led to his conclusions: see *Hope v Secretary of State for Environment* (1975) 31 P & CR 120. See also *Bolton Metropolitan Borough Council v Secretary of State for the Environment and Greater Manchester Waste Disposal Authority* (1990) 61 P & CR 343, CA.
4 As to the appointment of an assessor see para 46 ante.
5 Compulsory Purchase by Non-ministerial Acquiring Authorities (Inquiries Procedure) Rules 1990 r 17(2).
6 Ibid r 17(3).
7 As to the persons entitled to appear see para 49 ante.
8 As to the Secretary of State's power to allow more time see para 44 note 4 ante.
9 Compulsory Purchase by Non-ministerial Acquiring Authorities (Inquiries Procedure) Rules 1990 r 17(4). As to the service of notices see para 43 note 7 ante.
10 For the meaning of 'order' see para 44 note 3 ante.
11 For the meaning of 'acquiring authority' see para 43 note 8 ante.
12 For the meaning of 'statutory objector' see para 43 note 9 ante.
13 Compulsory Purchase by Non-ministerial Acquiring Authorities (Inquiries Procedure) Rules 1990 r 17(5). Where an inquiry is reopened, whether by the same or a different inspector, the Secretary of State must send to the persons entitled to appear, and who did appear, at the inquiry a written statement of the specified matters; and r 11(2)–(7) (preliminary matters: see para 47 ante) applies as if references to an inquiry were references to a reopened inquiry, but with the substitution in r 11(2) of '28 days' for '42 days': r 17(5).
14 Ibid r 18(1). Proper and adequate reasons must be given and must deal with the substantive issues that have been raised: see *Re Poyser and Mills' Arbitration* [1964] 2 QB 467, [1963] 1 All ER 612; *Westminster City Council v Great Portland Estates plc* [1985] AC 661, sub nom *Great Portland Estates v Westminster City Council* [1984] 3 All ER 744, HL; *Clarke Homes Ltd v Secretary of State for the Environment and East Staffordshire District Council* (1993) 66 P & CR 263 at 271–272, CA. An alleged deficiency of reasons is a ground of challenge if the interests of the applicant have been substantially prejudiced: see *George v Secretary of State for the Environment* (1979) 38 P & CR 609 at 617, 621, CA.
15 For these purposes, 'report' includes any assessor's report appended to the inspector's report but does not include any other documents so appended; but any person who has received a copy of the report may apply to the Secretary of State in writing, within six weeks of the publication of the notice of confirmation pursuant to the Acquisition of Land Act 1981 s 15 (see para 58 post), for an opportunity of inspecting such documents and the Secretary of State must afford him that opportunity: Compulsory Purchase by Non-ministerial Acquiring Authorities (Inquiries Procedure) Rules 1990 r 18(3). For the meaning of 'document' see para 48 note 19 ante.
16 Ibid r 18(2).

54. Costs of the inquiry. The Secretary of State may order the expenses of the inquiry to be paid by such local authority or party to the inquiry as he may direct, and may recover the amounts certified by him as payable, summarily as a civil debt[1]. He may also provide as between parties for the payment of their costs, and any party named in the order may have the order made a rule of the High Court and enforce payment accordingly[2]. It seems, however, to be the usual practice to refrain from making any order for costs as between the parties[3], save that an award of costs will normally be made to a successful objector whose land is excluded[4]. There is no rule of practice, such as commonly applies in courts of law, that the costs should follow the event.

1 Local Government Act 1972 s 250(4) (amended by the Housing and Planning Act 1986 s 49(2), Sch 12 Pt III; applied by the Acquisition of Land Act 1981 s 5(3)).
2 Local Government Act 1972 s 250(5) (as applied: see note 1 supra).
3 See, however, *Re Wood's Application* (1952) 3 P & CR 238, DC.
4 See Department of the Environment Circular 8/93 Annex 6 paras 1–7. Costs will not be awarded in favour of an unsuccessful objector. Costs may be awarded against a party who has acted unreasonably,

vexatiously or frivolously or who has necessitated a postponement or adjournment. As to the costs of planning inquiries cf the Town and Country Planning Act 1990 s 303A (added by the Town and Country Planning (Costs of Inquiries etc) Act 1995 s 1(1)); the Town and Country Planning (Costs of Inquiries etc) (Standard Daily Amount) Regulations 1996, SI 1996/24; and TOWN AND COUNTRY PLANNING.

55. Hearings before persons appointed to hear objections. Where no public local inquiry is to be held but objections are to be heard by a person appointed by the confirming authority[1] to hear objections[2], the provisions of the procedural rules applicable to public local inquiries[3] do not apply; but such a formal hearing must be distinguished from purely informal discussions which sometimes take place when objectors do not insist on an inquiry or hearing[4].

  1 For the meaning of 'confirming authority' see para 34 note 3 ante.
  2 See the Acquisition of Land Act 1981 s 13(2); and para 43 ante.
  3 Ie the Compulsory Purchase by Non-Ministerial Authorities (Inquiries Procedure) Rules 1990, SI 1990/512: see para 43 et seq ante.
  4 Cf *Ealing Borough Council v Minister of Housing and Local Government* [1952] Ch 856, [1952] 2 All ER 639, where a hearing was required under what is now the Town and Country Planning Act 1990 s 140(3), (4) (see TOWN AND COUNTRY PLANNING vol 46 (Reissue) para 722), and the discussions which in fact took place did not satisfy the statutory requirements.

56. Confirmation of order after hearing of objections. After considering the objections and the report of the person who held the public local inquiry[1] or of the person appointed to hear objections in lieu of holding an inquiry[2], and being satisfied that the proper notices have been published and served[3], the confirming authority[4] may[5] confirm the compulsory purchase order[6] with or without modifications[7]. Power may be given by the empowering enactment to confirm the order as to some of the land and postpone consideration as to the other land[8].

Unless all interested persons consent, the order as confirmed may not authorise the acquiring authority[9] to purchase compulsorily any land[10] which the order would not have authorised that authority so to purchase if it had been confirmed without modification[11].

  1 As to the public local inquiry see para 43 et seq ante.
  2 As to the hearing see para 55 ante.
  3 See paras 36–38 ante.
  4 For the meaning of 'confirming authority' see para 34 note 3 ante.
  5 As to the exercise of this discretion see paras 41 note 5 ante, 57 post.
  6 For the meaning of 'compulsory purchase order' see para 34 note 1 ante.
  7 Acquisition of Land Act 1981 s 13(2). If confirmation is refused there is no bar to the making of a fresh order with respect to the same land: see *Land Realisation Co Ltd v Postmaster-General* [1950] Ch 435, [1950] 1 All ER 1062. As to the confirmation of orders by special parliamentary procedure in the case of special land see para 78 post.
  8 See eg the Town and Country Planning Act 1990 s 245(2); and TOWN AND COUNTRY PLANNING vol 46 (Reissue) para 767.
  9 For the meaning of 'acquiring authority' see para 34 note 2 ante.
 10 For the meaning of 'land' see para 28 note 3 ante.
 11 Acquisition of Land Act 1981 s 14.

57. Confirming authority's duties as to confirmation. When the Secretary of State as the confirming authority[1] is considering representations made at a public inquiry and the inspector's report[2] he is acting in a quasi-judicial capacity[3] but when a confirming authority comes to make its substantive decision, its function is purely administrative, and the exercise of discretion vested in it to decide whether or not to confirm the order is an administrative act, the merits of which may not be challenged in the courts, but for which the confirming authority can be called upon to answer to Parliament[4]. In coming to its decision it may have regard to its own views as to general policy and to information acquired in its purely executive capacity[5]. So far as this information relates to general policy[6] or comes from extraneous sources[7], the confirming authority is under no obligation to disclose it, but if it relates to the answering of objections it must be disclosed to an objector to enable him to challenge it, even if the authority receives it after the end of the inquiry[8].

Accordingly, if the confirming authority properly considers objections and the report of the inquiry[9] before coming to its decision, and has acted in good faith and has fairly listened to both sides and followed the general principles of natural justice, its decision may not be questioned[10]. Its decision may be contrary to the recommendations of the person holding the inquiry or the person appointed to hear objections. However, where the confirming authority has not observed the procedural rules regarding the reopening of the inquiry[11], the order may be quashed[12].

1   For the meaning of 'confirming authority' see para 34 note 3 ante.
2   As to the contents of the inspector's report see para 53 ante.
3   See eg *B Johnson & Co (Builders) Ltd v Minister of Health* [1947] 2 All ER 395, CA; and *Bushell v Secretary of State for the Environment* [1981] AC 75, [1980] 2 All ER 608, HL. As the conduct of the inquiry see para 43 et seq ante.
4   See eg *Bushell v Secretary of State for the Environment* [1981] AC 75, [1980] 2 All ER 608, HL; *Franklin v Minister of Town and Country Planning* [1948] AC 87, [1947] 2 All ER 289, HL; *B Johnson & Co (Builders) Ltd v Minister of Health* [1947] 2 All ER 395 at 399, CA, per Lord Greene MR.
5   See *Price v Minister of Health* [1947] 1 All ER 47; *Summers v Minister of Health* [1947] 1 All ER 184; *B Johnson & Co (Builders) Ltd v Minister of Health* [1947] 2 All ER 395 at 401, CA.
6   *B Johnson & Co (Builders) Ltd v Minister of Health* [1947] 2 All ER 395, CA; *Re City of Plymouth (City Centre) Declaratory Order 1946, Robinson v Minister of Town and Country Planning* [1947] KB 702, CA; *Darlassis v Minister of Education* (1954) 118 JP 452. Cf *Franklin v Minister of Town and Country Planning* [1948] AC 87, [1947] 2 All ER 289, HL.
7   *Price v Minister of Health* [1947] 1 All ER 47 (letters received by minister before public inquiry not shown to objectors, nor in evidence at public inquiry); *Summers v Minister of Health* [1947] 1 All ER 184; *B Johnson & Co (Builders) Ltd v Minister of Health* [1947] 2 All ER 395 at 404, CA.
8   *Stafford v Minister of Health* [1946] KB 621; *Errington v Minister of Health* [1935] 1 KB 249, CA. See also *Hamilton v Roxburghshire County Council* 1970 SC 248.
9   Like other departmental documents, the inspector's report is privileged from disclosure: *Local Government Board v Arlidge* [1915] AC 120, HL; *William Denby & Sons Ltd v Minister of Health* [1936] 1 KB 337; *Darlassis v Minister of Education* (1954) 118 JP 452.
10   *Board of Education v Rice* [1911] AC 179 at 182, HL; *Local Government Board v Arlidge* [1915] AC 120, HL; *Stafford v Minister of Health* [1946] KB 621. If the decision letter of the Secretary of State is in agreement with the inspector's report and recommendation, there is no obligation on the Secretary of State to mention all the material considerations in the inspector's report: see *London Welsh Association Ltd v Secretary of State for the Environment* [1980] 2 EGLR 17, CA. As to the rules of natural justice see ADMINISTRATIVE LAW vol 1(1) (Reissue) para 84 et seq.
11   See the Compulsory Purchase by Non-ministerial Acquiring Authorities (Inquiries Procedure) Rules 1990, SI 1990/512, r 17(5); and para 53 ante.
12   *Meravale Builders Ltd v Secretary of State for the Environment* (1978) 36 P & CR 87.

58. Publication of confirmed order by acquiring authority. As soon as may be after the compulsory purchase order[1] has been confirmed, the acquiring authority[2] must publish in one or more local newspapers circulating in the locality in which the land[3] comprised in the order is situated a notice in the prescribed form[4], describing the land, stating that the order has been confirmed, and naming a place where a copy of the order as confirmed and the map referred to in it may be inspected at all reasonable hours, and must serve a similar notice and a copy of the order as confirmed on any person on whom notices were required to be served[5] before the submission of the order for confirmation[6].

1 For the meaning of 'compulsory purchase order' see para 34 note 1 ante.
2 For the meaning of 'acquiring authority' see para 34 note 2 ante.
3 For the meaning of 'land' see para 28 note 3 ante.
4 For the prescribed form see the Compulsory Purchase of Land Regulations 1994, SI 1994/2145, reg 3(e), Schedule, Form 10. In the case of compulsory rights orders under the Opencast Coal Act 1958 s 4 (as amended) (see MINES), the relevant form of notice is contained in the Opencast Coal (Compulsory Rights and Rights of Way) (Forms) Regulations 1987, SI 1987/1915, reg 4(a)(iii), Schedule, Form 8. See further para 34 note 6 ante.
5 Ie under the Acquisition of Land Act 1981 s 12 (as amended): see para 37 ante. As to the service of notices see para 38 ante.
6 Ibid s 15. As to orders made by ministers see para 59 et seq post.

(iii) Compulsory Purchase Orders made by Ministers

A. MAKING OF COMPULSORY PURCHASE ORDER IN DRAFT

59. Making of compulsory purchase orders by ministers. A compulsory purchase order[1] authorising a compulsory purchase by a minister under the Acquisition of Land Act 1981, so that the minister is both the acquiring[2] and the confirming authority[3], must be made in accordance with special statutory[4] procedures[5]. The order must be prepared in draft in such form as the minister may determine[6], but must describe the land[7] to which it applies by reference to a map[8].

1 For the meaning of 'compulsory purchase order' see para 34 note 1 ante.
2 For the meaning of 'acquiring authority' see para 34 note 2 ante.
3 For the meaning of 'confirming authority' see para 34 note 3 ante.
4 Ie in accordance with the Acquisition of Land Act 1981 s 2(3), Sch 1 (as amended): s 2(3), Sch 1 para 1(1).
5 Ibid Sch 1 para 1(1).
6 Ibid Sch 1 para 1(2), (3).
7 For the meaning of 'land' see para 28 note 3 ante.
8 Acquisition of Land Act 1981 Sch 1 para 1(2).

60. Advertisement of compulsory purchase order. As soon as may be after the draft of the order[1] has been prepared, and before making the order, the minister must publish a notice in the prescribed form[2], in two successive weeks, in one or more local newspapers circulating in the locality in which the land[3] comprised in the draft order is situated[4]. The notice must:

(1) state that the order has been prepared in draft and is about to be made;
(2) describe the land and state the purpose for which the land is required;
(3) name a place within the locality where a copy of the draft order and of the map referred to in it may be inspected; and
(4) specify the time, not being less than 21 days from the first publication of the notice, within which, and the manner in which, objections to the draft order can be made[5].

The minister must serve on every owner[6], lessee and occupier of any land comprised in the order, except tenants for a month or any period less than a month[7], a notice in the prescribed form[8] stating the effect of the draft order and that it is about to be made, and specifying the time, not being less than 21 days from service of the notice, within which, and the manner in which, objections to the draft order can be made[9]. Where any such notice is required to be served on an owner of land and the land is ecclesiastical property[10], a like notice must be served on the Church Commissioners[11].

  1 As to the draft order see para 59 ante.
  2 For the prescribed form see the Compulsory Purchase of Land Regulations 1994, SI 1994/2145, reg 3(c), Schedule, Form 7. The minister may make such modifications of the form of the notice as appear to him to be requisite: see the Acquisition of Land Act 1981 s 2(3), Sch 1 para 1(5).
  3 For the meaning of 'land' see para 28 note 3 ante.
  4 Acquisition of Land Act 1981 Sch 1 paras 1(4), 2(1).
  5 Ibid Sch 1 para 2(2).
  6 For the meaning of 'owner' see para 37 note 3 ante.
  7 For these purposes, an occupier who is a statutory tenant within the meaning of the Rent Act 1977 or the Rent (Agriculture) Act 1976 or a licensee under an assured agricultural occupancy within the meaning of the Housing Act 1988 Pt I (ss 1–45) (as amended) (see LANDLORD AND TENANT vols 27(1), (2) (Reissue) paras 677 et seq, 999 et seq, 1037 et seq respectively) is deemed to be a tenant for a period less than a month: Acquisition of Land Act 1981 Sch 1 para 3(2) (amended by the Housing Act 1988 s 140(1), Sch 17 para 32(2)).
  8 For the prescribed form see the Compulsory Purchase of Land Regulations 1994 reg 3(d), Schedule, Form 8. Where the order is made under the Planning (Listed Buildings and Conservation Areas) Act 1990 s 47 (as prospectively amended) (compulsory acquisition of listed buildings in need of repair: see TOWN AND COUNTRY PLANNING vol 46 (Reissue) para 945), additional information must be included in the notice: see the Compulsory Purchase of Land Regulations 1994 reg 4; and para 37 note 5 ante. The minister may make such modifications in the form of the notice as appear to him to be requisite: see the Acquisition of Land Act 1981 Sch 1 para 1(5).
  9 Ibid Sch 1 para 3(1). As to the service of notices see para 38 ante.
 10 For these purposes, 'ecclesiastical property' means land belonging to any ecclesiastical benefice, or being or forming part of a church or a burial ground subject to the jurisdiction of the bishop of any diocese, or the site of such a church, or being diocesan glebe land within the meaning of the Endowments and Glebe Measure 1976: Acquisition of Land Act 1981 Sch 1 para 3(3) (amended by the Planning and Compensation Act 1991 s 70, Sch 15 para 27).
 11 Acquisition of Land Act 1981 Sch 1 para 3(3).

61. Right of objection and representations by statutory undertakers. Objections to a compulsory purchase order[1] may be made in the manner and in the time provided in the notices[2] and must be made in the specified manner[3]. They must be made in writing and the grounds of objection should be stated, for the minister may require an objector to state the grounds in writing and may disregard the objection if he is satisfied that the objection relates exclusively to matters which can be dealt with by the tribunal by which the compensation is to be assessed[4].

Statutory undertakers[5] may make representations to the minister if their land[6] is included in the land comprised in a compulsory purchase order[7].

  1 For the meaning of 'compulsory purchase order' see para 34 note 1 ante.
  2 See para 60 ante.
  3 See the Acquisition of Land Act 1981 s 2(3), Sch 1 para 3(1)(c).
  4 See ibid Sch 1 para 4(5); and para 62 post.
  5 For the meaning of 'statutory undertakers' see para 38 note 8 ante.
  6 Ie land which has been acquired for the purposes of their undertaking: see the Acquisition of Land Act 1981 s 16(1) (as amended); and para 41 ante. For the extended meaning of 'statutory undertakers' for these purposes see para 41 note 3 ante.
  7 See para 41 ante.

B. MAKING OF FINAL ORDER

62. Making of order where no objections are outstanding or objections are disregarded. If no objection is duly made by an owner, lessee or occupier[1] or if all objections so made are withdrawn, and the minister is satisfied that the proper notices have been published and served[2], he may, if he thinks fit, make the compulsory purchase order[3] with or without modifications[4]. The minister, either alone or acting jointly with the planning minister[5] if the order is made in the exercise of highway land acquisition powers[6], may require any person who has made an objection to state the grounds of it in writing; and if he is or they are satisfied that the objection relates exclusively to matters which can be dealt with by the tribunal by whom the compensation is assessed[7], he or they may disregard the objection for the purposes of making the order[8].

The order as made by the minister must not authorise him to purchase compulsorily any land[9] which the draft order would not have authorised him to purchase compulsorily if it had been made without modification, unless all the persons interested consent[10].

1 Ie such an owner, lessee or occupier as is mentioned in the Acquisition of Land Act 1981 s 2(3), Sch 1 para 3 (as amended): see para 61 ante.
2 As to publication and service of notices see paras 38, 61 ante.
3 For the meaning of 'compulsory purchase order' see para 34 note 1 ante.
4 Acquisition of Land Act 1981 Sch 1 para 4(1).
5 For these purposes, 'the planning minister' means the Secretary of State for the time being have general responsibility in planning matters in relation to England and Wales, as the case may be: ibid Sch 1 para 4(6). The Secretary of State concerned is the Secretary of State for the Environment in relation to England and the Secretary of State for Wales in relation to Wales: see TOWN AND COUNTRY PLANNING vol 46 (Reissue) para 10.
6 For these purposes, 'highway land acquisition powers' has the meaning given by the Highways Act 1980 s 250(1) (ie powers in respect of the acquisition of land which are exercisable by a highway authority under any of ss 239–240, 242–246 and 250(2): see HIGHWAYS vol 21 (Reissue) paras 414 note 5, 800 et seq): Acquisition of Land Act 1981 Sch 1 para 4(6).
7 As to the assessment of compensation see para 233 et seq post.
8 Acquisition of Land Act 1981 Sch 1 para 4(5).
9 For the meaning of 'land' see para 28 note 3 ante.
10 Acquisition of Land Act 1981 Sch 1 para 5.

63. Local inquiry where objections are made and not withdrawn. If any objection is duly made[1] and not withdrawn, then before the minister makes the compulsory purchase order[2], either he or, in the case of an order proposed to be made in the exercise of highway land acquisition powers[3], he and the planning minister[4] acting jointly, must (1) cause a public local inquiry to be held; or (2) afford to any person by whom any objection has been duly made and not withdrawn an opportunity of appearing before and being heard by a person appointed by him or them for the purpose[5]. Where the minister[6] intends to cause an inquiry[7] to be held, he must give written notice of that intention, not later than four weeks[8] after the expiry of the time within which objections to the draft order may be made, to each statutory objector[9] at the address furnished to the minister[10]. Where he intends to cause a pre-inquiry meeting[11] to be held, he must serve with that notice a notification of his intention to do so[12] and must also cause notice of that intention to be published, not later than three weeks after the relevant date[13], in a newspaper circulating in the locality in which the land[14] is situated[15].

1 Ie as mentioned in the Acquisition of Land Act 1981 s 2(3), Sch 1 para 4(1): see para 62 ante.
2 For the meaning of 'compulsory purchase order' see para 34 note 1 ante.
3 For the meaning of 'highway land acquisition powers' see para 62 note 6 ante.
4 For the meaning of 'planning minister' see para 62 note 5 ante.
5 Acquisition of Land Act 1981 Sch 1 para 4(2).
6 For these purposes, 'minister' means the minister of the Crown who has, in accordance with the provisions of ibid Sch 1 (as amended), prepared in draft an order authorising the compulsory purchase of land by him: Compulsory Purchase by Ministers (Inquiries Procedure) Rules 1994, SI 1994/3264, r 2.
7 For these purposes, 'inquiry' means a local inquiry held under the provisions of the Acquisition of Land Act 1981 Sch 1 para 4(2): Compulsory Purchase by Ministers (Inquiries Procedure) Rules 1994 rr 2, 3.
8 At any time in any particular case, the minister may allow further time for the taking of any step which is to be taken by virtue of the Compulsory Purchase by Ministers (Inquiries Procedure) Rules 1994; and references therein to a day by which, or a period within which, any step is to be taken are to be construed accordingly: r 19.
9 'Statutory objector' means any objector on whom the minister is obliged by virtue of the Acquisition of Land Act 1981 Sch 1 para 3(1) (see para 60 ante) to serve a notice of the draft order and whose objection has not been withdrawn: Compulsory Purchase by Ministers (Inquiries Procedure) Rules 1994 r 2.
10 Ibid r 4. Notices or documents required or authorised to be served or sent under any of the provisions of the Compulsory Purchase by Ministers (Inquiries Procedure) Rules 1994 may be sent by post: r 20.
11 'Pre-inquiry meeting' means a meeting held before an inquiry to consider what may be done with a view to securing that the inquiry is conducted efficiently and expeditiously: ibid r 2.
12 Ibid r 5(2).
13 'Relevant date' means the date of the minister's notice under ibid r 4: r 2.
14 'Land' means the land to which the order relates or, where a right over land is proposed to be acquired, the land over which such a right would be exercised; and 'order' means a compulsory purchase order: ibid r 2. As to the acquisition of rights over land see para 79 et seq post.
15 Ibid r 5(3).

64. Pre-inquiry meeting. The minister[1] may cause a pre-inquiry meeting[2] to be held if it appears to him to be desirable[3]. The inspector[4] also has power to hold such a meeting[5].

Where the minister decides to hold a pre-inquiry meeting, he must serve his outline statement[6] on each statutory objector[7] not later than eight weeks after the relevant date[8] and may require any such objector and any other person who has notified him of any intention or wish to appear at the inquiry to serve an outline statement on him and on any other specified[9] person[10]. The meeting must be held not later than 16 weeks[11] after the relevant date[12] and the minister must give not less than three weeks' written notice of the date, time and location of the meeting to each statutory objector and any other person whose presence at the meeting seems to him to be desirable[13]. Where the inspector decides to hold the meeting, he must arrange for not less than three weeks' written notice to be given to the minister, each statutory objector, any other person known at the date of the notice to be entitled to appear at the inquiry[14] and any other person whose presence at the meeting appears to him to be desirable[15].

The inspector presides at the meeting and determines the matters to be discussed and the procedure to be followed[16]. He may hold a further meeting, in which case he must arrange for such notice of it to be given as appears to him to be necessary[17].

Where a pre-inquiry meeting is held following a decision of the minister to cause such a meeting to be held[18], an inspector must arrange a timetable for the proceedings at, or at part of, the inquiry[19]. In any other case he may[20] do so; and he may at any time vary any such timetable[21]. He may specify in any such timetable a date by which any proof of evidence or summary[22] may be sent to him[23].

1 For the meaning of 'minister' see para 63 note 6 ante.
2 For the meaning of 'pre-inquiry meeting' see para 63 note 11 ante.
3 Compulsory Purchase by Ministers (Inquiries Procedure) Rules 1994, SI 1994/3264, r 5(1).

4 'Inspector' means a person appointed by the minister to hold an inquiry or a reopened inquiry: ibid r 2. For the meaning of 'inquiry' see para 63 note 7 ante.
5 See ibid r 7(1).
6 In relation to a person, 'outline statement' means a written statement of the principal submissions which that person proposes to put forward at an inquiry: ibid r 2.
7 For the meaning of 'statutory objector' see para 63 note 9 ante.
8 For the meaning of 'relevant date' see para 63 note 13 ante. As to the service of notices see para 63 note 10 ante.
9 Ie any person specified in the notice: Compulsory Purchase by Ministers (Inquiries Procedure) Rules 1994 r 5(5).
10 Ibid r 5(5).
11 As to the Secretary of State's power to allow more time see para 63 note 8 ante.
12 Compulsory Purchase by Ministers (Inquiries Procedure) Rules 1994 r 5(6).
13 Ibid r 5(7).
14 As to the persons entitled to appear see para 68 post.
15 Compulsory Purchase by Ministers (Inquiries Procedure) Rules 1994 r 7(2).
16 Ibid rr 5(8), 7(3). He may require any person present at the meeting who, in his opinion, is behaving in a disruptive manner to leave and may refuse to permit that person to return or to attend any further meeting, or may permit him to return or attend only on such conditions as he may specify: rr 5(8), 7(3).
17 Ibid r 5(9). Rule 5(8) (see the text and note 16 supra) applies to such a meeting: r 5(9).
18 Ie a pre-inquiry meeting pursuant to ibid r 5: see the text and notes 1–17 supra.
19 Ibid r 8(1).
20 Ie subject to the provisions of ibid r 10(1): see para 66 post.
21 Ibid r 8(1).
22 Ie any proof of evidence or summary required by ibid r 14(1) to be sent to him: see para 70 post.
23 Ibid r 8(2).

65. Appointment of assessor for public inquiry. The minister[1] may appoint an assessor, namely a person who will sit with the inspector[2] at an inquiry or a reopened inquiry[3] to advise the inspector on such matters arising as the minister may specify[4]. Where an assessor has been appointed, the minister must notify every person entitled to appear at the inquiry[5] of the name of the assessor and of the matters on which he is to advise the inspector[6].

1 For the meaning of 'minister' see para 63 note 6 ante.
2 For the meaning of 'inspector' see para 64 note 4 ante.
3 For the meaning of 'inquiry' see para 63 note 7 ante.
4 See the Compulsory Purchase by Ministers (Inquiries Procedure) Rules 1994, SI 1994/3264, r 2.
5 As to the persons entitled to appear see para 68 post.
6 Compulsory Purchase by Ministers (Inquiries Procedure) Rules 1994 r 9.

66. Matters preliminary to inquiry. The minister must fix a date[1], time and place for the holding of the inquiry[2] and must give not less than six weeks' written notice[3] of that date, time and place to every statutory objector[4]. He may vary the date, time and place fixed for the holding of the inquiry[5], but must give the same notice of such variation as he gave of the date originally fixed[6].

Not later than two weeks before the date fixed for the holding of an inquiry, the minister must post notice of the inquiry in a conspicuous place near to the land[7] and also in one or more places where public notices are usually posted in the locality[8]. He must also publish in one or more newspapers circulating in the locality in which the land is situated a notice of the inquiry, not later than 14 days before the date fixed for the holding of the inquiry[9]. Any notice of inquiry so posted or published must contain a clear statement of the date, time and place of the inquiry, and of the powers under which the order[10] has been made, together with a sufficient description of the land to identify approximately its location without reference to the map referred to in the order[11].

1 The date fixed for the inquiry must be (1) not later than 22 weeks after the relevant date; or (2) if the minister has caused a pre-inquiry meeting to be held pursuant to the Compulsory Purchase by Ministers (Inquiries Procedure) Rules 1994, SI 1994/3264, r 5 (see para 64 ante), not later than eight weeks after the conclusion of that meeting; or (3) where he is satisfied that in all the circumstances of the case it is impracticable to hold the inquiry within the applicable period mentioned in head (1) or head (2) supra, the earliest practicable date after the end of that period: r 10(1). For the meaning of 'minister' see para 63 note 6 ante; and for the meaning of 'inquiry' see para 63 note 7 ante.
2 Ibid r 10(1). The place at which the inquiry is to be held must be determined by the minister and where he is satisfied, having regard to the nature of the draft order, that it is reasonable to do so, he may direct that it is to be held in more than one place: r 10(3).
3 As to the minister's power to allow further time see para 63 note 8 ante.
4 Compulsory Purchase by Ministers (Inquiries Procedure) Rules 1994 r 10(2). He may agree a lesser period with each statutory objector: r 10(2). For the meaning of 'statutory objector' see para 63 note 9 ante.
5 Ie whether or not the date as varied is within the applicable period mentioned in ibid r 10(1): r 10(4).
6 Ibid r 10(4).
7 Or, where the land extends for more than 5 km, at intervals of not more than 5 km: ibid r 10(5). For the meaning of 'land' see para 63 note 14 ante.
8 Ibid r 10(5).
9 Ibid r 10(6).
10 For the meaning of 'order' see para 63 note 14 ante.
11 Compulsory Purchase by Ministers (Inquiries Procedure) Rules 1994 r 10(7).

67. Statements of case. Not later than: (1) six weeks after the relevant date[1]; or (2) where a pre-inquiry meeting is held[2], four weeks after the conclusion of that meeting[3], the minister[4] must serve his statement of case[5] on each statutory objector[6]. The statement must be accompanied by a list of any documents[7] to which the minister intends to refer or which he intends to put in evidence at the inquiry[8]. He must also serve on each statutory objector a notice giving the names of all places, as close as reasonably possible to the land[9], where a copy of every such document or the relevant part of any such document may be inspected free of charge at all reasonable hours until the date of the commencement of the inquiry[10].

The minister may by notice in writing require any statutory objector or any other person who has notified him of an intention or a wish to appear at the inquiry, within six weeks of the date of the notice, to serve a statement of case on him and on any other person specified in the notice[11]. He must supply to any person who is not a statutory objector, but who has been so required to serve a statement of case, a copy of his own statement of case[12]. Either the minister or an inspector[13] may require any person who has so served a statement of case to provide such further information about the matters contained in the statement as he may specify[14].

The minister must afford to any person who so requests a reasonable opportunity to inspect and, where practicable, take copies of any statement or document which, or a copy of which, has been served on or by him in accordance with any of the above provisions, and must specify in his statement of case the time and place at which the opportunity will be afforded[15].

1 For the meaning of 'relevant date' see para 63 note 13 ante. As to the minister's power to allow further time see para 63 note 8 ante.
2 Ie pursuant to the Compulsory Purchase by Ministers (Inquiries Procedure) Rules 1994, SI 1994/3264, r 5: see para 64 ante. For the meaning of 'pre-inquiry meeting' see para 63 note 11 ante.

3 Where two or more such meetings are held, references to the conclusion of a pre-inquiry meeting are references to the conclusion of the final meeting: ibid r 2.
4 For the meaning of 'minister' see para 63 note 6 ante.
5 'Statement of case' means a written statement containing full particulars of the case which a person proposes to put forward at the inquiry, including, where that person is the minister, the reasons for making the order: Compulsory Purchase by Ministers (Inquiries Procedure) Rules 1994 r 2. For the meaning of 'order' see para 63 note 14 ante.
6 Ibid r 6(1). For the meaning of 'statutory objector' see para 63 note 9 ante. As to the service of documents see para 63 note 10 ante.
7 'Document' includes a photograph, map or plan: ibid r 2.
8 See ibid r 2.
9 For the meaning of 'land' see para 63 note 14 ante.
10 Compulsory Purchase by Ministers (Inquiries Procedure) Rules 1994 r 6(2). For the meaning of 'inquiry' see para 63 note 7 ante.
11 Ibid r 6(3). Every such person must also serve upon the minister a copy of every document or the relevant part of any document which that person intends to refer to or to put in evidence: r 6(4).
12 Ibid r 6(5).
13 For the meaning of 'inspector' see para 64 note 4 ante.
14 Compulsory Purchase by Ministers (Inquiries Procedure) Rules 1994 r 6(6).
15 Ibid r 6(7).

68. Representation and appearances at the inquiry. The minister[1] may be represented at the inquiry[2] by counsel or solicitor or by an officer of his department or other person authorised by him to represent him[3]. He must make a representative available at the inquiry to give evidence in elucidation of the statement of case[4] and that representative is subject to cross-examination to the same extent as any other witness[5] except that he is not required to answer any question which in the opinion of the inspector[6] is directed to the merits of government policy[7].

Every statutory objector[8] is entitled to appear at the inquiry[9]; but this provision does not prevent the inspector from permitting any other person to appear at the inquiry and such permission must not be unreasonably withheld[10]. Any person entitled or permitted to appear may do so on his own behalf or be represented by counsel, solicitor or any other person[11]. An inspector may allow one or more persons to appear on behalf of some or all of any persons having a similar interest in the matter under inquiry[12].

Where another government department has made a statement or representation in writing in support of the draft order and the minister has included that statement in his statement of case, a representative of the department concerned must be made available to attend the inquiry[13]. Any such representative must state at the inquiry the reasons for the view expressed by his department and must give evidence and be subject to cross-examination to the same extent as any other witness, but nothing in this provision requires him to answer any question which in the opinion of the inspector is directed to the merits of government policy[14].

1 For the meaning of 'minister' see para 63 note 6 ante.
2 For the meaning of 'inquiry' see para 63 note 7 ante.
3 Compulsory Purchase by Ministers (Inquiries Procedure) Rules 1994, SI 1994/3264, r 11(1).
4 For the meaning of 'statement of case' see para 67 note 5 ante.
5 Compulsory Purchase by Ministers (Inquiries Procedure) Rules 1994 r 11(2).
6 For the meaning of 'inspector' see para 64 note 4 ante.
7 Compulsory Purchase by Ministers (Inquiries Procedure) Rules 1994 r 11(3).
8 For the meaning of 'statutory objector' see para 63 note 9 ante.
9 Compulsory Purchase by Ministers (Inquiries Procedure) Rules 1994 r 13(1).
10 Ibid r 13(2).
11 Ibid r 13(3).
12 Ibid r 13(4).
13 Ibid r 12(1)
14 Ibid r 12(2), (3).

69. Inspection of land. The inspector[1] may make an unaccompanied inspection of the land[2], either before or during an inquiry[3], without giving notice of his intention to the persons entitled to appear[4] at the inquiry[5].

He may, and must if so requested by the minister[6] or any statutory objector[7] before or during the inquiry, inspect the land after the close of the inquiry in the company of a representative of the minister and any statutory objector[8], in which case he must, during the inquiry, announce the date and time at which he proposes to make the inspection[9]. He is not, however, bound to defer such an inspection where any person entitled to accompany him on his inspection is not present at the time appointed[10].

1 For the meaning of 'inspector' see para 64 note 4 ante.
2 For the meaning of 'land' see para 63 note 14 ante.
3 For the meaning of 'inquiry' see para 63 note 7 ante.
4 As to the persons entitled to appear see para 68 ante.
5 Compulsory Purchase by Ministers (Inquiries Procedure) Rules 1994, SI 1994/3264, r 16(1).
6 For the meaning of 'minister' see para 63 note 6 ante.
7 For the meaning of 'statutory objector' see para 63 note 9 ante.
8 Compulsory Purchase by Ministers (Inquiries Procedure) Rules 1994 r 16(2).
9 Ibid r 16(3).
10 Ibid r 16(4).

70. Statements of evidence. A person entitled to appear an inquiry[1] who proposes to give, or call another person to give, evidence at it by reading a proof of evidence must send to the inspector[2] and to the minister[3] a copy of the proof, and, where the proof contains in excess of 1,500 words, a written summary of it[4]. The proof and summary must be so sent not later than three weeks[5] before (1) the date fixed for the commencement of the inquiry; or (2) where a timetable has been arranged[6] which specifies a date by which the proof and summary must be sent to the inspector, that date[7]. Only the summary may be read at the inquiry unless the inspector permits or requires otherwise[8].

The minister must afford to any person who so requests a reasonable opportunity to inspect and, where practicable and on payment of a reasonable charge, take copies of any document[9] sent to or by him in accordance with these provisions[10].

1 As to the persons entitled to appear at the inquiry see para 68 ante. For the meaning of 'inquiry' see para 63 note 7 ante.
2 For the meaning of 'inspector' see para 64 note 4 ante.
3 For the meaning of 'minister' see para 63 note 6 ante.
4 Compulsory Purchase by Ministers (Inquiries Procedure) Rules 1994, SI 1994/3264, r 14(1), (2). As to the service of documents see para 63 note 10 ante.
5 As to the minister's power to allow further time see para 63 note 8 ante.
6 Ie pursuant to the Compulsory Purchase by Ministers (Inquiries Procedure) Rules 1994 r 8: see para 64 ante.
7 Ibid r 14(3).
8 Ibid r 14(4). This does not apply where the proof does not contain in excess of 1,500 words: see r 14(2), (4).
9 For the meaning of 'document' see para 67 note 7 ante.
10 Compulsory Purchase by Ministers (Inquiries Procedure) Rules 1994 r 14(5).

71. Procedure at the inquiry. Subject to any express provision in the rules of procedure[1], the inspector[2] determines the procedure at an inquiry[3], save that unless in any particular case he determines otherwise with the consent of the minister[4], the minister must present his case first and must have the right of final reply[5]. The other persons entitled or permitted to appear[6] must be heard in such order as the inspector may determine[7].

The inspector may summons any person to attend to give evidence or produce documents in his custody or under his control relating to any matter in question at the inquiry[8], but he has no power to require the production of the title, or of any instrument relating to the title, of any land which is not the property of a local authority[9]. No person may be required to attend on a summons unless the necessary expenses are paid or tendered to him[10]. The inspector may direct that the minister must afford to any person appearing at an inquiry a reasonable opportunity to inspect and, where practicable and on payment of a reasonable charge, take copies of any document[11] sent to or by him in accordance with these provisions[12]. He may not require or permit evidence contrary to the public interest to be given[13], but otherwise he may admit any evidence at his discretion[14]. He may take evidence on oath, and for that purpose may administer oaths[15] or require a witness to make a solemn affirmation[16].

The inspector may proceed with an inquiry in the absence of any person entitled to appear at it[17] and may take into account any written representation or evidence or other document received by him from any person before an inquiry opens or during the inquiry, provided that he discloses it at the inquiry[18]. A person entitled to appear at an inquiry is entitled to call evidence, and the minister and the statutory objectors[19] are entitled to cross-examine persons giving evidence[20]. The calling of evidence and the cross-examination of persons giving it are otherwise[21] at the inspector's discretion[22]. Where he refuses to permit the giving of oral evidence, the person wishing to give it may submit to him any evidence or other matter in writing before the close of the inquiry[23]. Where a person gives evidence by reading a summary[24] of his evidence, his proof of evidence[25] is treated as tendered in evidence unless the person giving the summary notifies the inspector that he now wishes to rely on that summary only, and that person is then subject to cross-examination on the proof of evidence to the same extent as if it were evidence he had given orally[26].

The inspector may allow any person to alter or add to a statement of case[27] so far as may be necessary for the purposes of the inquiry; but he must give every other person entitled to appear who is appearing at the inquiry an adequate opportunity of considering any fresh matter or document[28]. If necessary, he must adjourn the inquiry for this purpose; and he may in any case adjourn the inquiry from time to time[29].

The inspector may require any person appearing or present at an inquiry who, in his opinion, is behaving in a disruptive manner to leave and may refuse to permit that person to return, or may permit him to return only on such conditions as he may specify; but any such person may submit to him any evidence or other matter in writing before the close of the inquiry[30].

1 Ie any provision in the Compulsory Purchase by Ministers (Inquiries Procedure) Rules 1994, SI 1994/3264: see paras 63 et seq ante, 72 post.
2 For the meaning of 'inspector' see para 64 note 4 ante.
3 Compulsory Purchase by Ministers (Inquiries Procedure) Rules 1994 r 15(1). For the meaning of 'inquiry' see para 63 note 7 ante.
4 For the meaning of 'minister' see para 63 note 6 ante.
5 Compulsory Purchase by Ministers (Inquiries Procedure) Rules 1994 r 15(2).
6 As to the persons who are entitled, or may be permitted, to appear see para 68 ante.
7 Compulsory Purchase by Ministers (Inquiries Procedure) Rules 1994 r 15(2).
8 Local Government Act 1972 s 250(2) (applied by the Acquisition of Land Act 1981 s 5(2)). A person who refuses or deliberately fails to attend in obedience to the summons, or to give evidence, or who

deliberately alters, suppresses, conceals, destroys or refuses to produce any document which he is so required or is liable to be required to produce is liable on summary conviction to a fine not exceeding level 3 on the standard scale, or to imprisonment for a term not exceeding six months, or to both: Local Government Act 1972 s 250(3) (as so applied; amended by virtue of the Criminal Justice Act 1982 ss 38, 46). As to the standard scale see para 14 note 6 ante.

9 Local Government Act 1972 s 250(2) proviso (b) (as applied: see note 8 supra).

10 Ibid s 250(2) proviso (a) (as applied: see note 8 supra).

11 For the meaning of 'document' see para 67 note 7 ante.

12 Compulsory Purchase by Ministers (Inquiries Procedure) Rules 1994 r 15(6).

13 See eg ibid r 12(3); and para 68 ante.

14 Ibid r 15(4). In particular, the inspector may refuse to permit the giving or production of evidence, the cross-examination of persons giving evidence, or the presentation of any matter, which he considers to be irrelevant or repetitious: r 15(4). The inspector has a wide discretion as to what evidence is considered relevant and the court will only intervene in exceptional circumstances. For an example of when the court will intervene see *R v Secretary of State for the Environment, ex p Royal Borough of Kensington and Chelsea* [1987] JPL 567.

15 Local Government Act 1972 s 250(2) (as applied: see note 8 supra).

16 See the Oaths Act 1978 s 5; the Interpretation Act 1978 ss 5, 23(1); and STATUTES vol 44(1) (Reissue) para 1386.

17 Compulsory Purchase by Ministers (Inquiries Procedure) Rules 1994 r 15(9).

18 Ibid r 15(10).

19 For the meaning of 'statutory objector' see para 63 note 9 ante.

20 Compulsory Purchase by Ministers (Inquiries Procedure) Rules 1994 r 15(3).

21 Ie subject to ibid r 15(2), (4), (5), (7): r 15(3).

22 Ibid r 15(3).

23 Ibid r 15(4).

24 Ie in accordance with ibid r 14(4): see para 70 ante.

25 Ie the proof of evidence referred to in ibid r 14(1): see para 70 ante.

26 Compulsory Purchase by Ministers (Inquiries Procedure) Rules 1994 r 15(5).

27 Ie a statement of case served under ibid r 6: see para 67 ante. For the meaning of 'statement of case' see para 67 note 5 ante.

28 Ibid r 15(8).

29 Ibid r 15(8), (11). If the date, time and place of the adjourned inquiry are announced at the inquiry before the adjournment, no further notice is required: r 15(11). As for the circumstances in which the inspector would be obliged to adjourn the inquiry see *Orakpo v London Borough of Wandsworth and Secretary of State for the Environment* (1992) 24 HLR 370. For considerations to be taken into account when an objector seeks an adjournment see *Ostreicher v Secretary of State for the Environment* [1978] 3 All ER 82, [1978] 1 WLR 810, CA.

30 Compulsory Purchase by Ministers (Inquiries Procedure) Rules 1994 r 15(7).

72. Procedure after inquiry. After the close of an inquiry[1], the inspector[2] must make a report in writing to the minister[3] which must include his conclusions and recommendations or his reasons for not making any recommendations[4]. Where an assessor has been appointed[5], he may make a report in writing after the close of the inquiry to the inspector in respect of the matters on which he was appointed to advise[6], in which case the inspector must append it to his own report and must state in his own report how far he agrees or disagrees with it, and, where he disagrees with the assessor, the reasons for that disagreement[7].

If, after the close of an inquiry, the minister:

(1) differs from the inspector on any matter of fact mentioned in, or appearing to him to be material to, a conclusion reached by the inspector; or

(2) takes into consideration any new evidence or new matter of fact which is not a matter of government policy,

and is for that reason disposed to disagree with a recommendation made by the inspector, he may not come to a decision which is at variance with that recommendation without first notifying the persons entitled to appear[8], and who did appear, at the inquiry of his disagreement and the reasons for it, and affording them an opportunity (a) of making written representations to him within 21 days[9] of the date of the notification; or (b) if he has taken into consideration any new evidence or matter in accordance with head (2) above, of asking within that period for the reopening of the inquiry[10]. He may cause an inquiry to be reopened to afford an opportunity for persons to be heard on such matters relating to the order[11] as he may specify, and must do so if asked by a statutory objector[12] in the circumstances set out in heads (a) and (b) above[13].

The minister must notify his decision on the order and his reasons for it in writing to:

(i)   each statutory objector;

(ii) any person entitled to appear at the inquiry who did appear at it; and

(iii) any other person who appeared at the inquiry and has asked to be notified of the decision[14].

Where a copy of the inspector's report[15] is not sent with the notification of the decision, the notification must be accompanied by a copy of his conclusions and of any recommendations made by him; and if a person entitled to be notified of the decision has not received a copy of that report, he must be supplied with a copy of it on written application made to the minister within four weeks of the date of the decision[16].

1   For the meaning of 'inquiry' see para 63 note 7 ante.
2   For the meaning of 'inspector' see para 64 note 4 ante.
3   For the meaning of 'minister' see para 63 note 6 ante.
4   Compulsory Purchase by Ministers (Inquiries Procedure) Rules 1994, SI 1994/3264, r 17(1). See also *Bushell v Secretary of State for the Environment* [1981] AC 75, [1980] 2 All ER 608, HL (a highways inquiry case), for comments on the purpose of the public inquiry procedure and the inspector's report. The report should contain a summary of the main evidence and arguments presented to the inspector along with findings of fact which led to his conclusions: see *Hope v Secretary of State for Environment* (1975) 31 P & CR 120. See also *Bolton Metropolitan Borough Council v Secretary of State for the Environment and Greater Manchester Waste Disposal Authority* (1990) 61 P & CR 343, CA.
5   As to the appointment of an assessor see para 65 ante.
6   Compulsory Purchase by Ministers (Inquiries Procedure) Rules 1994 r 17(2).
7   Ibid r 17(3).
8   As to the persons entitled to appear see para 68 ante.
9   As to the minister's power to allow more time see para 63 note 8 ante.
10 Compulsory Purchase by Ministers (Inquiries Procedure) Rules 1994 r 17(4).
11 For the meaning of 'order' see para 63 note 14 ante.
12 For the meaning of 'statutory objector' see para 63 note 9 ante.
13 Compulsory Purchase by Ministers (Inquiries Procedure) Rules 1994 r 17(5). Where an inquiry is reopened, whether by the same or a different inspector, the minister must send to the persons entitled to appear, and who did appear, at the inquiry a written statement of the specified matters; and r 10(2)–(7) (preliminary matters: see para 66 ante) applies as if references to an inquiry were references to a reopened inquiry, but with the substitution in r 10(2) of 'four weeks' for 'six weeks': r 17(5).
14 Ibid r 18(1). Proper and adequate reasons must be given and must deal with the substantive issues that have been raised: see *Re Poyser and Mills' Arbitration* [1964] 2 QB 467, [1963] 1 All ER 612; *Westminster City Council v Great Portland Estates plc* [1985] AC 661, sub nom *Great Portland Estates v Westminster City Council* [1984] 3 All ER 744, HL; *Clarke Homes Ltd v Secretary of State for the Environment and East Staffordshire District Council* (1993) 66 P & CR 263 at 271–272, CA. An alleged deficiency of reasons is a ground of challenge if the interests of the applicant have been substantially prejudiced: see *George v Secretary of State for the Environment* (1979) 38 P & CR 609 at 617, 621, CA.
15 For these purposes, 'report' includes any assessor's report appended to the inspector's report but does not include any other documents so appended; but any person who has received a copy of the report may apply to the minister in writing, within six weeks of the publication of the notice of confirmation pursuant to the Acquisition of Land Act 1981 s 2(3), Sch 1 para 6 (see para 74 post), for an opportunity of inspecting such documents and the minister must afford him that opportunity: Compulsory Purchase by Ministers (Inquiries Procedure) Rules 1994 r 18(3). For the meaning of 'document' see para 67 note 7 ante.
16 Ibid r 18(2).

73. Hearings before persons appointed to hear objections. Where no public local inquiry is to be held but objections are to be heard by a person appointed by the minister to hear objections[1], the provisions of the procedural rules applicable to public local inquiries[2] do not apply; but such a formal hearing must be distinguished from purely informal discussions which sometimes take place when objectors do not insist on an inquiry or hearing[3].

If any person by whom an objection has been made avails himself of the opportunity of being heard, the minister and the planning minister[4] acting jointly or, as the case may be, the minister acting alone, must afford to any persons to whom it appears to them or to him expedient to afford it an opportunity of being heard on the same occasion[5].

1 See the Acquisition of Land Act 1981 s 2(3), Sch 1 para 4(2); and para 63 ante.
2 Ie the Compulsory Purchase by Ministers (Inquiries Procedure) Rules 1994, SI 1994/3264: see para 63 et seq ante.
3 Cf *Ealing Borough Council v Minister of Housing and Local Government* [1952] Ch 856, [1952] 2 All ER 639, where a hearing was required under what is now the Town and Country Planning Act 1990 s 140(3), (4) (see TOWN AND COUNTRY PLANNING vol 46 (Reissue) para 722), and the discussions which in fact took place did not satisfy the statutory requirements.
4 For the meaning of 'the planning minister' see para 62 note 5 ante.
5 Acquisition of Land Act 1981 Sch 1 para 4(4). As to the circumstances in which the minister must act jointly with the planning minister, and the circumstances in which he may act alone, see para 62 ante.

74. Making of order after hearing of objections. After the objections and the report of the person who held the public local inquiry[1] or of the person appointed to hear objections in lieu of holding an inquiry[2] have been considered by the minister or, in the case of an order proposed to be made in the exercise of highway land acquisition powers[3], by the minister and the planning minister[4] acting jointly, the minister may make the order either with or without modifications[5]. Unless all interested persons consent, the order as confirmed may not authorise the minister to purchase compulsorily any land[6] which the order would not have authorised him so to purchase if it had been confirmed without modification[7].

As soon as may be after the order has been made, the minister must publish, in one or more local newspapers circulating in the locality in which the land comprised in the order is situated, a notice in the prescribed form[8] describing the land, stating that the order has been made, and naming a place where a copy of the order as made and of the map referred to in it may be inspected at all reasonable hours[9].

1 As to the public local inquiry see para 63 et seq ante.
2 As to the hearing see para 73 ante.
3 For the meaning of 'highway land acquisition powers' see para 62 note 6 ante.
4 For the meaning of 'the planning minister' see para 62 note 5 ante.
5 Acquisition of Land Act 1981 s 2(3), Sch 1 para 4(3).
6 For the meaning of 'land' see para 28 note 3 ante.
7 Acquisition of Land Act 1981 Sch 1 para 5.
8 For the prescribed form of notice see the Compulsory Purchase of Land Regulations 1994, SI 1994/2145, reg 3(c), Schedule, Form 10.
9 Acquisition of Land Act 1981 Sch 1 para 6. The minister must serve a like notice, and a copy of the order as made, on any persons on whom notices with respect to the land were required to be served under Sch 1 para 3 (as amended) (see para 60 ante): Sch 1 para 6. As to the service of notices see para 38 ante.

(iv) Date of Operation of Compulsory Purchase Order

75. In general. Unless it is subject to special parliamentary procedure[1], a compulsory purchase order[2] becomes operative on the date on which the notice of confirmation, or, in the case of an order made by a minister, the making, of the order is first published[3] unless an application to the High Court has been made questioning the validity of the order and the order is suspended or quashed[4].

A compulsory rights order under the Opencast Coal Act 1958[5] becomes operative either on the date mentioned above or such later date, not being more than one year after confirmation of the order, as may be determined by the Secretary of State and specified in the order as confirmed[6].

1 As to special parliamentary procedure see para 78 post.
2 For the meaning of 'compulsory purchase order' see para 34 note 1 ante.
3 Acquisition of Land Act 1981 s 26(1). The publication must be in accordance with the statutory provisions (see paras 58, 74 ante): s 26(1).
4 See ibid s 24; and para 87 post.
5 Ie under the Opencast Coal Act 1958 s 4 (as amended): see MINES.
6 See the Acquisition of Land Act 1981 s 29(9); and para 83 post.

(v) Confirmation by Special Parliamentary Procedure

76. Compulsory purchase orders comprising land of local authorities, statutory undertakers and the National Trust. In so far as a compulsory purchase order[1] authorises the compulsory purchase of land[2] which:

(1) is the property of a local authority[3]; or

(2) has been acquired by statutory undertakers[4] (not being local authorities) for the purposes of their undertaking[5]; or

(3) belongs to, and is held inalienably[6] by, the National Trust[7],

the order will be subject to special parliamentary procedure[8] if an objection to the order has been made by the local authority, the statutory undertakers or the National Trust and that objection has not been withdrawn[9].

In order that the land may be protected by the requirement of special parliamentary procedure it must be land within the particular description at the time when objections may be duly made[10].

Except in relation to National Trust land these provisions do not, however, apply to the compulsory acquisition of an interest in land where the person acquiring the land is a specified local authority[11], an urban development corporation, the Land Authority for Wales, the Peak Park Joint Board or Lake District Special Planning Board, any specified statutory undertakers[12] or a minister[13].

1 For the meaning of 'compulsory purchase order' and 'compulsory purchase' see para 34 note 1 ante.
2 For the meaning of 'land' see para 28 note 3 ante. In relation to the compulsory purchase of a right under the Gas Act 1965 ss 12(1), 13(2) or (3) (as amended) (see FUEL AND ENERGY vol 19(1) (Reissue) paras 689–690), references to the land for these purposes include references to any land held with the stratum of land constituting the underground gas storage: see the Acquisition of Land Act 1981 s 30(2); and para 84 post.
3 Ibid s 17(1)(a). For the meaning of 'local authority' see para 34 note 2 ante.
4 Ibid s 16(3) (as added) (extended meaning of 'statutory undertakers': see para 41 note 3 ante) applies for these purposes as it applies in relation to s 16(1) (as amended), s 16(2) (see para 41 ante): s 17(2A) (added by the National Health Service and Community Care Act 1990 s 60, Sch 8 para 8(2)). For the meaning of 'statutory undertaker' generally see para 38 note 8 ante.
5 Acquisition of Land Act 1981 s 17(1)(b).

6 'Held inalienably' means that the land is inalienable under the National Trust Act 1907 s 21 or the National Trust Act 1939 s 8 (see OPEN SPACES vol 34 para 410): Acquisition of Land Act 1981 s 18(3).

7 Ibid s 18(1). For the meaning of 'National Trust' see para 38 note 8 ante.

8 As to special parliamentary procedure see para 78 post.

9 Acquisition of Land Act 1981 ss 17(2), 18(2).

10 An objection made by a local authority within the due time but before it acquired the ownership of the land is not an objection duly made for this purpose: *Middlesex County Council v Minister of Housing and Local Government* [1953] 1 QB 12, [1952] 2 All ER 709, CA.

11 The local authorities specified for these purposes are: (1) in relation to England, the council of a county or district, the Broads Authority, the council of a London borough, the Common Council of the City of London, a police authority established under the Police Act 1964 s 3 (as substituted) and a joint authority established by the Local Government Act 1985 Pt IV (ss 23–42) (as amended); and (2) in relation to Wales, the council of a county or district or a police authority established under the Police Act 1964 s 3 (as substituted); and this definition applies to the Isles of Scilly as if the Council of those Isles were the council of a county: Acquisition of Land Act 1981 s 17(4) (definition amended by the Local Government Act 1985 ss 84, 102(2), Sch 14 para 60, Sch 17; the Education Reform Act 1988 s 237(2), Sch 13 Pt I; the Norfolk and Suffolk Broads Act 1988 s 21, Sch 6 para 22; and the Police and Magistrates' Courts Act 1994 s 43, Sch 4 para 55; and prospectively amended by the Local Government (Wales) Act 1994 s 66(6), Sch 16 para 64(1), as from a day to be appointed under s 66(3), to substitute in head (2) supra for the word 'district' the words 'county borough').

12 For these purposes, 'statutory undertakers' includes (1) a National Health Service trust established under the National Health Service and Community Care Act 1990 Pt I (ss 1–26) (as amended); (2) the Funding Agency for Schools; (3) the Schools Funding Council for Wales; and (4) any authority, body or undertakers specified in an order made by the Secretary of State: Acquisition of Land Act 1981 s 17(4) (definition amended by the Coal Industry Act 1987 s 1(2), Sch 1 para 40; the National Health Service and Community Care Act 1990 s 66(1), Sch 9 para 23; the Education Act 1993 s 11; and by the Coal Industry Act 1994 s 67(1), (8), Sch 9 para 27(1), Sch 11 Pt II as from the restructuring date appointed under ss 7(1), 68(2)). For the purposes of the acquisition of land by the Urban Regeneration Agency by virtue of the Leasehold Reform, Housing and Urban Development Act 1993 s 162 (see TRADE, INDUSTRY AND INDUSTRIAL RELATIONS vol 47 (Reissue) para 852), this reference to 'statutory undertakers' also includes that agency: s 169(2), Sch 20 para 1, 3. An order under head (4) supra must be made by statutory instrument subject to annulment in pursuance of a resolution of either House of Parliament: Acquisition of Land Act 1981 s 17(5). At the date at which this volume states the law, no such order had been made.

13 Ibid s 17(3) (amended by the Planning and Compensation Act 1991 s 70, Sch 15 para 11; and prospectively amended by (1) the Local Government (Wales) Act 1994 s 20(4), Sch 6 para 17(1), as from a day to be appointed under s 66(3), so as to include a Welsh Planning Board; (2) the Environment Act 1995 ss 78, 120(3), Sch 10 para 21(1), Sch 24, as from a day to be appointed under s 125(3), so as to remove the words 'the Peak Park Joint or Lake District Special Planning Board' and include the words 'a National Park authority'). 'Welsh Planning Board' means a board constituted under (a) the Town and Country Planning Act 1990 s 2(1B) (as added); or (b) the Local Government Act 1972 s 184 (as amended), Sch 17 para 3A (as added): Acquisition of Land Act 1981 s 17(4) (definition prospectively added by the Local Government (Wales) Act 1994 Sch 6 para 17(1); prospectively amended so as to remove head (b) supra and the word 'or' immediately preceding it, by the Environment Act 1995 Sch 24). National Park authorities are established under ss 63, 64: see OPEN SPACES. The Acquisition of Land Act 1981 s 17 (as amended) does not apply in relation to compulsory rights orders under the Opencast Coal Act 1958 s 4 (as amended) (see MINES): see the Acquisition of Land Act 1981 s 29(6A) (as added): and para 83 post.

77. Compulsory purchase orders comprising commons, open spaces and allotments. In so far as a compulsory purchase order[1] authorises the purchase of any land[2] forming part of a common[3], open space[4] or fuel or field garden allotment[5], the order will be subject to special parliamentary procedure[6] except where excluded by a certificate of the Secretary of State[7]. Where it is proposed to give such a certificate, the Secretary of State must direct the acquiring authority[8] to give public notice of his intention to do so[9]. After affording opportunity to all persons interested to make representations and objections in relation thereto, and after causing a public local inquiry[10] to be held in any case where it appears to him to be expedient to do so, having regard to any representations or objections made, the Secretary of State may give the certificate after considering any such representations and objections and, if an inquiry has been held, the report of the person who held it[11].

Except where the Secretary of State has given a certificate that the land is being purchased to secure its preservation or improve its management[12], a compulsory purchase order may provide for vesting land given in exchange[13] in the persons in whom the land purchased was vested, and subject to the like rights, trusts and incidents as attach to the land purchased[14] and discharging the land purchased from all rights, trusts and incidents to which it was previously subject[15].

These provisions are modified in their application to compulsory rights orders under the Opencast Coal Act 1958[16] and do not apply in relation to the compulsory purchase of a right to store gas in an underground gas storage[17] or of any right[18] as respects wells, boreholes and shafts in a storage area or protective area[19].

1 For the meaning of 'compulsory purchase order' see para 34 note 1 ante.
2 For the meaning of 'land' see para 28 note 3 ante.
3 For the meaning of 'common' see para 29 note 3 ante.
4 For the meaning of 'open space' see para 29 note 4 ante.
5 For the meaning of 'fuel or field garden allotment' see para 29 note 5 ante.
6 As to special parliamentary procedure see para 78 post.
7 See the Acquisition of Land Act 1981 s 19(1) (as amended); and para 29 ante.
8 For the meaning of 'acquiring authority' see para 34 note 2 ante.
9 Acquisition of Land Act 1981 s 19(2) (amended by the Planning and Compensation Act 1991 s 70, Sch 15 para 12(1)(b)). Notice must be given in such form and manner as the Secretary of State may direct: Acquisition of Land Act 1981 s 19(2A) (added by the Planning and Compensation Act 1991 Sch 15 para 12(1)(c)).
10 As to the procedure applicable to a public local inquiry see the Acquisition of Land Act 1981 s 5; the Compulsory Purchase by Non-ministerial Acquiring Authorities (Inquiries Procedure) Rules 1990, SI 1990/512; and para 43 et seq ante.
11 Acquisition of Land Act 1981 s 19(2) (as amended: see note 9 supra). As to notice of the giving of the certificate see s 22; and para 41 note 8 ante; and for the prescribed form of notice see the Compulsory Purchase of Land Regulations 1994, SI 1994/2145, reg 3(f), Schedule, Form 11. Subject to the Acquisition of Land Act 1981 s 24 (court's power to quash certificate: see para 87 post), the certificate becomes operative on the date on which notice of the giving of it is first so published: s 26(2).
12 Ie a certificate in accordance with ibid s 19(1)(aa) (as aded): see para 29 head (2) ante.
13 Ie as mentioned in ibid s 19(1) (as amended): see para 29 ante.
14 Ie subject to the rights, trust and incidents mentioned in ibid s 19(1) (as amended): see para 29 head (1) ante.
15 Ibid s 19(3) (amended by the Planning and Compensation Act 1991 Sch 15 para 12(1)(d)). As to the acquisition of new rights over such land see para 82 post.
16 See the Acquisition of Land Act 1981 s 29(7); and para 80 post.
17 Ie under the Gas Act 1965 s 12(1) (as amended): see FUEL AND ENERGY vol 19(1) (Reissue) para 689.
18 Ie any right under ibid s 13(2) or (3) (as amended): see FUEL AND ENERGY vol 19(1) (Reissue) para 690.
19 See the Acquisition of Land Act 1981 s 30(2); and para 84 post.

78. Special parliamentary procedure. Where special parliamentary procedure applies to a compulsory purchase order[1], its effect is[2] that the order is of no effect until it has been laid before Parliament by the appropriate minister and has been brought into operation in accordance with the statutory provisions[3].

No order may be so laid before Parliament until the requirements of the empowering enactment preliminary to the making or confirmation of the order have been complied with, and a notice of the intention to lay the order before Parliament has been published in the London Gazette[4]. A short period is allowed for the presentation of petitions by way of general objection or for amendment to the order, and a further short period is allowed in which the order may be annulled by resolution of either House of Parliament, or referred to a joint committee of both Houses for the consideration of any petition[5]. If the joint committee's report is that the order should not be approved, or if amendments are made which are unacceptable to the minister concerned, authorisation of the acquisition requires the introduction and passing of a special type of confirming Bill[6]. In other cases an Act of Parliament is not needed[7], but amendments may have to be accepted. Thus, where this procedure is made applicable, a compulsory purchase order is subject to a measure of parliamentary control, in some ways resembling the procedure by provisional order but less cumbersome in practice[8]. Except in the few cases where a confirming Act is passed, a compulsory purchase order made under this procedure will be open to question in the court on the same limited grounds as would have been available if it had not been laid before Parliament[9].

1 See paras 76–77 ante. In the case of land falling within two or more of the categories specified in the Acquisition of Land Act 1981 ss 17–19 (as amended) (see paras 29, 76–77 ante) or s 28, Sch 3 paras 4–6 (as amended) (see paras 81–82 post), a compulsory purchase order will be subject to special parliamentary procedure if required to be subject to it by any of those provisions: s 21, Sch 3 para 8.

2 Special parliamentary procedure applies where, by any Act passed after 20 December 1945, power to make or confirm orders is conferred on any authority with the requirement that the order be subject to special parliamentary procedure: Statutory Orders (Special Procedure) Act 1945 s 1(1).

3 Ibid s 1(2). See further PARLIAMENT.

4 See ibid s 2(1).

5 See ibid ss 3–5 (as amended).

6 See ibid s 6(2) proviso, (3)–(5).

7 See ibid ss 4(3), 6(1), (2).

8 As to the provisional order procedure see para 9 ante.

9 See the Acquisition of Land Act 1981 s 23 (as amended), ss 26(1), 27; and paras 85–87 post.

(vi) Special Procedures relating to the Acquisition of Rights over Land

79. Acquisition of rights over land by the creation of new rights; in general. Specific statutory authority is generally required for the compulsory acquisition of rights over land by the creation of new rights. The Acquisition of Land Act 1981 provides a uniform code for such acquisitions as authorised by the Acts specified therein[1] and has effect with the modifications necessary to make it apply to the compulsory acquisition of a right[2] as it applies to the compulsory acquisition of land[3] so that, in appropriate contexts, references therein to land are read as referring to, or as including references to, the right acquired or to be acquired, or to land over which the right is, or is to be, exercisable, according to the requirements of the particular context[4]. Those provisions do not, however, apply to a compulsory purchase of a right to store gas in an underground gas storage[5] or of any right[6] as respects wells, boreholes and shafts in a storage area or protective area[7].

1 See the Acquisition of Land Act 1981 s 28, Sch 3 (as amended); and para 80 et seq post. Schedule 3 (as amended) applies to the compulsory acquisition under that Act of rights over land by the creation of new rights by virtue of (1) the Local Government (Miscellaneous Provisions) Act 1976 s 13(1) (see LOCAL GOVERNMENT vol 28 para 1219); (2) the Development of Rural Wales Act 1976 s 6(5) (as amended) (see TOWN AND COUNTRY PLANNING vol 46 (Reissue) para 1200); (3) the Local Government, Planning and Land Act 1980 s 142(4) (see TOWN AND COUNTRY PLANNING vol 46 (Reissue) para 1297); (4) the Highways Act 1980 s 250 (as amended) (see HIGHWAYS vol 21 (Reissue) para 808); (5) the Telecommunications Act 1984 s 34(3) (see TELECOMMUNICATIONS); (6) the Gas Act 1986 s 9(3), Sch 3 para 1 (see FUEL AND ENERGY vol 19(1) (Reissue) para 636); and (7) the Electricity Act 1989 s 10(1), Sch 3 para 1 (see FUEL AND ENERGY vol 19(2) (Reissue) para 984): Acquisition of Land Act 1981 s 28 (amended by the Telecommunications Act 1984 s 109(1), Sch 4 para 80(1); the Gas Act 1986 s 67(1), Sch 7 para 29; and the Electricity Act 1989 s 112(1), Sch 16 para 28).

2 For these purposes, 'right' means a right to which the Acquisition of Land Act 1981 s 28 (as amended) (see note 1 supra) applies, or any right to which Sch 3 (as amended) is applied by any Act passed after the Acquisition of Land Act 1981: Sch 3 para 1.

3 For the meaning of 'land' see para 28 note 3 ante.

4 Acquisition of Land Act 1981 Sch 3 para 2(1). Without prejudice to the generality of Sch 3 para 2(1), Sch 3 Pt II (paras 3–9) (as amended) (see para 80 et seq post) applies to the compulsory acquisition of a right in substitution for Pt III (ss 16–22) (as amended) (see paras 29, 41, 76–78 ante): Sch 3 para 2(2).

5 Ie under the Gas Act 1965 s 12(1) (as amended): see FUEL AND ENERGY vol 19(1) (Reissue) para 689.

6 Ie any right under ibid s 13(2) or (3) (as amended): see FUEL AND ENERGY vol 19(1) (Reissue) para 690.

7 See the Acquisition of Land Act 1981 s 30(3); and para 84 post.

80. Acquisition of new rights over statutory undertakers' land. The following provisions apply where (1) the land[1] over which a right[2] is to be acquired by virtue of a compulsory purchase order[3] includes land which has been acquired by statutory undertakers[4] for the purposes of their undertaking; and (2) on a representation made to the appropriate minister[5] before the expiration of the time within which objections can be made[6], he is satisfied that any of that land is used for the purposes of the carrying on of their undertaking, or that an interest in any of that land is held for those purposes[7]. If the representation is not withdrawn, the compulsory purchase order must not be confirmed or made so as to authorise the compulsory purchase of a right over any such land as to which that minister is so satisfied, except land as to which he is satisfied, and so certifies: (a) that its nature and situation are such that the right can be purchased without serious detriment to the carrying on of the undertaking; or (b) that any detriment to the carrying on of the undertaking, in consequence of the acquisition of the right, can be made good by the undertakers by the use of other land belonging to or available for acquisition by them[8]. As soon as may be after he has given such a certificate, the acquiring authority[9] must publish in one or more local newspapers circulating in the locality in which the land comprised in the order is situated a notice in the prescribed form[10] stating that the certificate has been given[11]. Subject to the court's power to quash the certificate[12], it becomes operative on the date on which such notice is first published[13].

In the case of acquisitions of land of statutory undertakers under the Town and Country Planning Act 1990[14], the Planning (Listed Buildings and Conservation Areas) Act 1990[15] or certain provisions of the Local Government, Planning and Land Act 1980[16], the order may be confirmed or made without the appropriate certificate[17] provided that it has been confirmed (or made) by the appropriate minister jointly with the minister or ministers who would normally make the order[18].

1 For the meaning of 'land' see para 28 note 3, 79 text to note 4 ante.

2 For the meaning of 'right' see para 79 note 2 ante.

3 For the meaning of 'compulsory purchase order' see para 34 note 1 ante.

4 For the meaning of 'statutory undertakers' see para 38 note 8 ante.

5 For the meaning of 'appropriate minister' see para 41 note 5 ante.

6 As to the making of objections see para 40 ante.

7 Acquisition of Land Act 1981 s 28 (as amended), Sch 3 para 3(1). As to the acquisitions to which Sch 3 (as amended) applies see para 79 ante.

8 Ibid Sch 3 para 3(1), (2) (Sch 3 para 3(1) amended by the Planning and Compensation Act 1991 s 70, Sch 15 para 10(1)).

9 For the meaning of 'acquiring authority' see para 34 note 2 ante.

10 For the prescribed form of notice stating that the certificate has been given see the Compulsory Purchase of Land Regulations 1994, SI 1994/2145, reg 3(f), Schedule, Form 11.

11 Acquisition of Land Act 1981 Sch 3 para 9.

12 Ie under ibid s 24: see para 87 post.

13 Ibid s 26(2).

14 See the Town and Country Planning Act 1990 s 226 (as prospectively amended), ss 228, 244, 245(1), (3); and TOWN AND COUNTRY PLANNING vol 46 (Reissue) para 760 et seq; and s 254; and HIGHWAYS vol 21 (Reissue) para 162.

15 See the Planning (Listed Buildings and Conservation Areas) Act 1990 s 47 (as prospectively amended); and TOWN AND COUNTRY PLANNING vol 46 (Reissue) para 945.
16 Ie under the Local Government, Planning and Land Act 1980 s 104 (as amended) (acquisition by the Land Authority for Wales); or s 142 (as amended) or s 143 (as amended) (acquisition by urban development corporation): see TOWN AND COUNTRY PLANNING vol 46 (Reissue) paras 806, 1297–1298.
17 Ie by virtue of the Acquisition of Land Act 1981 s 31(1), (2) (respectively amended and substituted by the Planning and Compensation Act 1991 ss 4, 70, Sch 2 para 53(2), Sch 15 para 10(2)), disapplying the Acquisition of Land Act 1981 s 16(2).
18 Ibid s 31(2) (as substituted: see note 14 supra). Where, in accordance with this provision, a compulsory acquisition is effected under a compulsory purchase order confirmed or made without the appropriate minister's certificate, the Town and Country Planning Act 1990 ss 280–282 (measure of compensation: see TOWN AND COUNTRY PLANNING vol 46 (Reissue) paras 843–845) apply in accordance with s 281(1)(c): Acquisition of Land Act 1981 s 31(4) (amended by the Planning and Compensation Act 1991 Sch 2 para 53(2)).

81. Acquisition of new rights where order subject to special parliamentary procedure.
In so far as a compulsory purchase order[1] authorises the compulsory purchase of rights[2] over land[3] which:

(1) is the property of a local authority[4]; or
(2) has been acquired by statutory undertakers[5] (not being local authorities) for the purposes of their undertaking[6]; or
(3) belongs to, and is held inalienably[7] by, the National Trust[8],

the order will be subject to special parliamentary procedure[9] if an objection to the order has been made by the local authority, the statutory undertakers or the National Trust and that objection has not been withdrawn[10].

Except in relation to National Trust land these provisions do not, however, apply to the compulsory acquisition of an interest in land where the person acquiring the land is a specified local authority[11], an urban development corporation, the Land Authority for Wales, the Peak Park Joint Board or Lake District Special Planning Board, any specified statutory undertakers[12] or a minister[13].

1 For the meaning of 'compulsory purchase order' see para 34 note 1 ante.
2 For the meaning of 'right' see para 79 note 2 ante.
3 For the meaning of 'land' see paras 28 note 3, 79 text to note 4 ante.
4 Acquisition of Land Act 1981 s 28 (as amended), Sch 3 para 4(1)(a). For the meaning of 'local authority' see para 34 note 2 ante.
5 For the meaning of 'statutory undertakers' see para 38 note 8 ante.
6 Acquisition of Land Act 1981 Sch 3 para 4(1)(b).
7 'Held inalienably' means that the land is inalienable under the National Trust Act 1907 s 21 or the National Trust Act 1939 s 8 (see OPEN SPACES vol 34 para 410): Acquisition of Land Act 1981 Sch 3 para 5(3).
8 Ibid Sch 3 para 5(1). For the meaning of 'National Trust' see para 38 note 8 ante.
9 As to special parliamentary procedure see para 78 ante.
10 Acquisition of Land Act 1981 Sch 3 paras 4(2), 5(2).
11 For these purposes, 'local authority' means (1) in relation to England, the council of a county or district, the council of a London borough and the Common Council of the City of London; and (2) in relation to Wales, the council of a county or district; and this definition applies to the Isles of Scilly as if the Council of those Isles were the council of a county: ibid Sch 3 para 4(4) (definition amended by virtue of the Local Government Act 1985 s 1; and prospectively amended to substitute, for the word 'district' in head (2) supra, the words 'county borough' by the Local Government (Wales) Act 1994 s 66(6), Sch 16 para 64(2), as from a day to be appointed under s 66(3)).
12 For these purposes, 'statutory undertakers' has the same meaning as in the Acquisition of Land Act 1981 s 17(3) (as amended) (see para 76 note 12 ante): Sch 3 para 4(3). That definition is in fact contained in s 17(4) (as amended) and may be amended by virtue of s 17(5): see para 76 note 12 ante.
13 Ibid Sch 3 para 4(3) (amended by the Planning and Compensation Act 1991 s 70, Sch 15 para 10(1)). The Acquisition of Land Act 1981 Sch 3 para 4(3) (as so amended) is further prospectively amended by

(1) the Local Government (Wales) Act 1994 s 20(4), Sch 6 para 17(2), as from a day to be appointed under s 66(3), to include a Welsh planning board; (2) the Environment Act 1995 ss 78, 120(3), Sch 10 para 21(2), Sch 24, as from a day to be appointed under s 125(3), so as to remove the words 'the Peak Park Joint or Lake District Special Planning Board' and include the words 'a National Park authority'. 'Welsh planning board' means a board constituted under (a) the Town and Country Planning Act 1990 s 2(1B) (as added); or (b) the Local Government Act 1972 s 184 (as amended), Sch 17 para 3A (as added): Acquisition of Land Act 1981 Sch 3 para 4(4) (definition prospectively added by the Local Government (Wales) Act 1994 Sch 6 para 17(2); prospectively amended, so as to remove head (b) supra and the word 'or' immediately preceding it, by the Environment Act 1995 Sch 24). National Park authorities are established under ss 63, 64: see further OPEN SPACES.

82. Acquisition of new rights over commons, open spaces and allotments.
In so far as a compulsory purchase order[1] authorises the acquisition of a right[2] over land[3] forming part of a common[4], open space[5] or fuel or field garden allotment[6], it is subject to special parliamentary procedure[7] unless the Secretary of State is satisfied:

(1) that the land, when burdened with that right, will be no less advantageous to those persons in whom it is vested and other persons, if any, entitled to rights of common and other rights, and to the public, than it was before[8];

(2) that the right is being acquired in order to secure the preservation or improve the management of the land[9];

(3) that there has been or will be given in exchange for the right additional land which will be adequate as respects the persons in whom there is vested the land over which the right is to be acquired, the persons, if any, entitled to rights of common or other rights over that land, and the public, to compensate them for the disadvantages which result from the acquisition of the right, and that the additional land has been or will be vested in the persons in whom there is vested the land over which the right is to be acquired, and subject to the like rights, trusts and incidents as attach to that land apart from the compulsory purchase order[10]; or

(4) that the land affected by the right to be acquired does not exceed 250 square yards in extent, and that the giving of other land in exchange for the right is unnecessary, whether in the interests of the persons, if any, entitled to rights of common or other rights or in the interests of the public[11], and certifies accordingly[12].

Where it is proposed to give a certificate under these provisions, the Secretary of State must direct the acquiring authority[13] to give public notice of his intention to do so[14]. After affording opportunity to all persons interested to make representations and objections in relation thereto, and after causing a public local inquiry[15] to be held in any case where it appears to him to be expedient to do so, having regard to any representations or objections so made, the Secretary of State may give the certificate after considering any representations and objections made and, if an inquiry has been held, the report of the person who held the inquiry[16].

A compulsory purchase order may provide for vesting land given in exchange as mentioned in head (3) above in the persons, and subject to the rights, there mentioned, and, except where the Secretary of State has given his certificate under head (2) above, for discharging the land over which any right is to be acquired from all rights, trusts and incidents to which it has previously been subject so far as their continuance would be inconsistent with the exercise of that right[17].

1 For the meaning of 'compulsory purchase order' see para 34 note 1 ante.
2 For the meaning of 'right' see para 79 note 2 ante.
3 For the meaning of 'land' see paras 28 note 3, 79 text to note 4 ante.

4 For these purposes, 'common' includes any land subject to be inclosed under the Inclosure Acts 1845 to 1882, and any town or village green: Acquisition of Land Act 1981 s 28 (as amended), Sch 3 para 6(5). As to the Inclosure Acts 1845 to 1882 see COMMONS vol 6 (Reissue) para 708 note 2.

5 For these purposes, 'open space' means any land laid out as a public garden, or used for the purpose of public recreation, or land being a disused burial ground: ibid Sch 3 para 6(5).

6 For these purposes, 'fuel or field garden allotment' means any allotment set out as fuel allotment, or a field garden allotment, under an Inclosure Act: Acquisition of Land Act 1981 Sch 3 para 6(5).

7 As to special parliamentary procedure see para 78 ante.

8 Acquisition of Land Act 1981 Sch 3 para 6(1)(a).

9 Ibid Sch 3 para 6(1)(aa) (added by the Planning and Compensation Act 1991 s 70, Sch 15 para 12(2)(a)).

10 Acquisition of Land Act 1981 Sch 3 para 6(1)(b).

11 Ibid Sch 3 para 6(1)(c). In the case of a compulsory purchase order under the Highways Act 1980, this provision has effect as if after the word 'extent' there were inserted the words 'or the right is required in connection with the widening or drainage of an existing highway or in connection partly with the widening and partly with the drainage of such a highway': Acquisition of Land Act 1981 Sch 3 para 6(2).

12 Ibid Sch 3 para 6(1). Schedule 3 para 9 (notice of giving of certificate: see para 80 ante) applies in relation to the giving of the certificate under these provisions: Sch 3 para 9. For the prescribed form of notice see the Compulsory Purchase of Land Regulations 1994, SI 1994/2145, reg 3(f), Schedule, Form 11.

13 For the meaning of 'acquiring authority' see para 34 note 2 ante.

14 Acquisition of Land Act 1981 Sch 3 para 6(3) (amended by the Planning and Compensation Act 1991 Sch 15 para 12(2)(b)). The notice must be given in such form and manner as the Secretary of State may direct: Acquisition of Land Act 1981 Sch 3 para 6(3A) (added by the Planning and Compensation Act 1991 Sch 15 para 12(2)(c)).

15 As to the procedure for the holding of the inquiry see the Acquisition of Land Act 1981 s 5; the Compulsory Purchase by Non-ministerial Acquiring Authorities (Inquiries Procedure) Rules 1990, SI 1990/512; and para 43 et seq ante.

16 Acquisition of Land Act 1981 Sch 3 para 6(3). Subject to s 24 (court's power to quash certificate: see para 87 post), the certificate becomes operative on the date on which notice of the giving of it is first published in accordance with the statutory provisions: s 26(2).

17 Ibid Sch 3 para 6(4) (amended by the Planning and Compensation Act 1991 Sch 15 para 12(2)(d)).

83. Compulsory rights orders under the Opencast Coal Act 1958. In its application to compulsory rights orders by the Opencast Coal Act 1958[1] the Acquisition of Land Act 1981 has effect subject to general[2] and specific[3] modifications[4].

1 Ie by the Opencast Coal Act 1958 s 4 (as amended): see MINES.

2 The general modifications are that the Acquisition of Land Act 1981 Pts II–IV (ss 10–27) (as amended) (see paras 34 et seq ante, 85 et seq post) apply as if in those provisions (1) any reference to a compulsory purchase order were a reference to a compulsory rights order; (2) any reference to the acquiring authority were a reference to the Coal Authority and any reference to the confirming authority were a reference to the Secretary of State; and (3) any reference to operating so as to confer on the Coal Authority temporary rights of occupation and use of land: s 29(1), (2) (s 29(2) amended by the Coal Industry Act 1987 s 1(2), Sch 1 para 40; and by the Coal Industry Act 1994 s 67(1), (8), Sch 9 para 27(2), Sch 11 Pt II, as from the restructuring date appointed under ss 7(1), 68(2)). For the meaning of 'compulsory purchase order' see para 34 note 1 ante; for the meaning of 'confirming authority' see para 34 note 3 ante; and for the meaning of 'land' see para 28 note 3 ante.

3 The specific modifications are as follows: (1) the Acquisition of Land Act 1981 Pt II (as amended) has effect as if for s 12 (as amended) (see para 37 ante) there were substituted the provisions set out in s 29(4) (see s 29(1), (4)); (2) s 13 (see paras 42–43 ante) applies as if for any reference to any owner, lessee or occupier there were substituted a reference to any person who, in relation to the order, is a person directly concerned (s 29(5)); (3) except where the Secretary of State is proceeding concurrently with respect to an application for opencast planning permission and a compulsory rights order, he may disregard an objection to such an order if he is satisfied that it relates to the question whether opencast planning permission should be granted or should have been granted and either (a) it relates exclusively to that question; or (b) in so far as it relates to other matters, they consist entirely of matters which can be dealt with in the assessment of compensation, but this is without prejudice to the operation of s 13 (s 29(6) (amended by the Housing and Planning Act 1986 s 39(3), Sch 8 para 18)); (4) the Acquisition of Land Act 1981 Pt III (as amended) is to apply as if s 17 (as amended) (see para 76 ante) were omitted (s 29(6A) (prospectively added by the Coal Industry Act 1994 s 67(1), (8), Sch 9 para 27(2) as from the

restructuring date); (5) in the Acquisition of Land Act 1981 s 19 (as amended) (see paras 29, 77 ante): (i) any reference to giving other land in exchange is to be construed as a reference to making other land available during the period for which the compulsory rights order is to have effect; (ii) the provisions of s 19 (as amended) as to the vesting of land, and as to its being subject to the like rights, trusts and incidents as the land purchased, apply with the necessary modifications; and (iii) s 19(3)(b) does not apply (s 29(7)); (6) s 23 (as amended) (see para 85 post) applies as if in s 23(1) for the first reference to the Acquisition of Land Act 1981 there were substituted a reference to the Opencast Coal Act 1958 and in the Acquisition of Land Act 1981 s 23(3)(a) the reference to the 1981 Act included a reference to the 1958 Act (Acquisition of Land Act 1981 s 29(8)); (7) the date on which the compulsory rights order becomes operative is to be that mentioned in s 26(1) (see para 75 ante) or such later date, not being more than one year after confirmation of the order, as may be determined by the Secretary of State and specified in the order as confirmed (s 29(9)); and (8) in the application of the 1981 Act to compulsory rights orders, 'prescribed' means prescribed by regulations under the Opencast Coal Act 1958 (Acquisition of Land Act 1981 s 29(10)). For these purposes, 'opencast planning permission' and 'persons directly concerned' have the same meanings as in the Opencast Coal Act 1958: Acquisition of Land Act 1981 s 29(11) (substituted by the Housing and Planning Act 1986 s 39(3), Sch 8 para 18). See further MINES.

4 Acquisition of Land Act 1981 s 29(1). Any modifications of particular provisions of the 1981 Act which are specified in s 29(4)–(11) (as amended: see note 3 supra) have effect, in relation to those provisions, in addition to the general modifications mentioned in s 29(2) (as amended: see note 2 supra): s 29(3).

84. Acquisition of rights in connection with the underground storage of gas.
In relation to the compulsory purchase of a right to store gas in an underground gas storage[1] or of any right as respects wells, boreholes and shafts in a storage area or protective area[2], the Acquisition of Land Act 1981, the enactments incorporated with it and the Compulsory Purchase Act 1965 have effect as if:

(1) references, whatever the terms used, to the land[3] comprised in the compulsory purchase order[4] were construed, where the context so requires, as references to the stratum of land constituting the underground gas storage or, as the case may be, the land comprising the well, borehole or shaft; and

(2) references to the obtaining or taking possession of the land so comprised were construed as references to the exercise of the right[5].

In relation to the compulsory purchase of a right to store gas in an underground gas storage the 1981 Act has effect subject to specified[6] modifications[7].

1 Ie under the Gas Act 1965 s 12(1) (as amended): see FUEL AND ENERGY vol 19(1) (Reissue) para 689.
2 Ie any right under ibid s 13(2) or (3) (as amended): see FUEL AND ENERGY vol 19(1) (Reissue) para 690.
3 For the meaning of 'land' see para 28 note 3 ante.
4 For the meaning of 'compulsory purchase order' see para 34 note 1 ante.
5 Acquisition of Land Act 1981 s 30(1).
6 In relation to the compulsory purchase of such a right, the Acquisition of Land Act 1981 has effect as if in ss 16–18 (as amended) (see paras 41, 76 ante) references to the land comprised in the compulsory purchase order included references to any land held with the stratum of land constituting the underground gas storage and as if s 19 (as amended) (see paras 29, 77 ante) were omitted: s 30(2).
7 Ibid s 30(2). Section 28, Sch 3 (as amended) (see para 80 et seq ante) does not apply to a compulsory purchase to which s 30 applies: s 30(3).

(vii) Validity of Orders and Certificates

85. Grounds for application to the High Court.
If any person aggrieved[1] by:

(1) a compulsory purchase order[2] desires to question its validity, or the validity of any provision contained in it, on the ground that the authorisation of a compulsory purchase granted by it is not empowered to be granted under the Acquisition of Land Act 1981 or the empowering enactment[3]; or

(2) a compulsory purchase order or a certificate[4] desires to question its validity on the ground that any relevant requirement[5] has not been complied with in relation to the order or certificate[6],

he may make an application to the High Court[7].

The application must be made within six weeks from the date on which notice of the confirmation or making of the order, or notice of the giving of the certificate, is first published[8] or, in the case of a compulsory purchase order subject to special parliamentary procedure[9] which is not excluded[10] from this provision, within six weeks from the date on which the order becomes operative[11].

Subject to this power to apply to the High Court, a compulsory purchase order or certificate may not be questioned in any legal proceedings whatsoever[12], either before or after it has been made, confirmed or given[13] and not even in a case of fraud or bad faith[14] or where the complainant has been given no opportunity of knowing of his right to apply to the High Court[15].

1 'Person aggrieved' means a person who has a particular grievance of his own beyond some inconvenience suffered by him in common with the rest of the public: see eg *R v Manchester Legal Aid Committee, ex p RA Brand & Co Ltd* [1952] 2 QB 413 at 431–432, [1952] 1 All ER 480 at 491, DC, citing *R v Nicholson* [1899] 2 QB 455 at 470, CA. It must be a legal grievance: see *Re Sidebotham, ex p Sidebotham* (1880) 14 ChD 458 at 465, CA. In *Martin v Bearsden and Milngavie District Council* 1987 SLT 300, Lord Clyde drew a distinction between those who might fairly be described as having a close interest in the outcome and those who have no such interest. Owners, lessees and occupiers of the land to be purchased who are entitled to be served with the notice of the making of the order would come within the definition, although in *George v Secretary of State for the Environment* (1979) 38 P & CR 609, CA, it was held that a wife who had acquired a house jointly with her husband was not entitled to challenge a compulsory purchase order made in respect of the house where only the husband had been served with notice of the making of the order, since she had not been substantially prejudiced by the failure to serve her; sed quaere.
   It may be that other persons not required to be served with notice of the making of the order would now be held to come within the definition of 'person aggrieved' despite the narrow view taken by earlier authorities: see eg *Buxton v Minister of Housing and Local Government* [1961] 1 QB 278, [1960] 3 All ER 408, in which it was held that a 'person aggrieved' was limited to a person whose legal rights had been infringed. Although there is no recent authority as to the meaning of 'persons aggrieved' under the Acquisition of Land Act 1981, the same phrase in relation to applications to quash planning permissions has been given a far wider meaning than simply those persons whose legal rights have been affected. In *Turner v Secretary of State for the Environment* (1973) 28 P & CR 123, a case under what is now the Town and Country Planning Act 1990 s 288, Ackner J declined to follow *Buxton v Minister of Housing and Local Government* supra and held that any person who, in the ordinary sense of the word, is aggrieved by the decision and certainly any person who has attended and made representations at the inquiry, should have rights to challenge the decision in the courts. It is submitted that in the absence of further authority as to the meaning of 'person aggrieved' under the Acquisition of Land Act 1981, the scope of the phrase will remain uncertain. See further ADMINISTRATIVE LAW vol 1(1) (Reissue) para 56; TOWN AND COUNTRY PLANNING vol 46 (Reissue) para 43 note 1.
2 For the meaning of 'compulsory purchase order' see para 34 note 1 ante.
3 Acquisition of Land Act 1981 s 23(1). The empowering enactment referred to is any such enactment as is mentioned in s 1(1) (see para 33 ante): s 23(1).
4 Ie a certificate under ibid Pt III (ss 16–22) (as amended) (see paras 29, 41, 76–77 ante) or s 28, Sch 3 (as amended) (see para 79 et seq ante): s 23(2)(b).
5 'Relevant requirement' means any requirement of (1) the Acquisition of Land Act 1981 or of any regulation under s 7(2) (see the Compulsory Purchase of Land Regulations 1994, SI 1994/2145; and para 35 et seq ante); or (2) the Tribunals and Inquiries Act 1992 (see eg s 10 (duty to give reasons) and ADMINISTRATIVE LAW) or of any rules made, or having effect as if made, under that Act (see eg the Compulsory Purchase by Non-ministerial Authorities (Inquiries Procedure) Rules 1990, SI 1990/512; the Compulsory Purchase by Ministers (Inquiries Procedure) Rules 1994, SI 1994/3264; and para 35 et seq ante): Acquisition of Land Act 1981 s 23(3) (amended by the Tribunals and Inquiries Act 1992 s 18(1), Sch 3 para 14).
6 Acquisition of Land Act 1981 s 23(2).
7 Ibid s 23(1), (2).

8 Ibid s 23(4)(b), (c). Publication must be in accordance with the Acquisition of Land Act 1981 (see paras 41, 58 ante): s 23(4)(b), (c).
9 Ie an order to which the Statutory Orders (Special Procedure) Act 1945 applies: see para 78 ante.
10 The Acquisition of Land Act 1981 Pt IV (ss 23–27) (as amended) does not apply to an order which is confirmed by Act of Parliament under the Statutory Orders (Special Procedure) Act 1945 s 6: see the Acquisition of Land Act 1981 s 27.
11 Ibid s 23(4)(a). The date referred to is the date on which the order becomes operative under the Statutory Orders (Special Procedure) Act 1945: Acquisition of Land Act 1981 s 23(4)(a). Section 23 (as amended) is modified in its application to compulsory rights orders under the Opencast Coal Act 1958: see s 29(8); and para 83 ante.
12 See *Smith v East Elloe RDC* [1956] AC 736, [1956] 1 All ER 855, HL, the principle being affirmed in *R v Secretary of State for the Environment, ex p Ostler* [1977] QB 122, [1976] 3 All ER 90, CA. See also *Tutin v Northallerton RDC* (1947) 91 Sol Jo 383, CA, where an application to the High Court for a declaration after the expiration of the six weeks' time limit was refused as being in effect an attempt to extend the time.
13 Acquisition of Land Act 1981 s 25.
14 See *Smith v East Elloe RDC* [1956] AC 736, [1956] 1 All ER 855, HL, in which a majority of the House of Lords expressed the view that these provisions give no opportunity to a person aggrieved to question the validity of an order on the ground that it was made or confirmed in bad faith; the only remedy is against the persons responsible for making the order. See also *R v Secretary of State for the Environment, ex p Ostler* [1977] QB 122, [1976] 3 All ER 90, CA.
15 See *Uttoxeter UDC v Clarke* [1952] 1 All ER 1318; *Woollett v Minister of Agriculture and Fisheries* [1955] 1 QB 103, [1954] 3 All ER 529, CA.

86. Mode of application. Application to the High Court to question the validity of a compulsory purchase order or minister's certificate is made to a single judge of the Queen's Bench Division[1] by originating motion[2], notice of which, stating the grounds of the application[3], must, within the time limited for making the application[4], be entered at the Crown Office and served on the confirming authority[5] and the acquiring authority[6] or, where a minister made the order or gave the certificate, on that minister[7].

Except in so far as the court at the hearing directs oral evidence to be given[8], the evidence on the hearing of the application is by affidavit[9]. Within 14 days after service of the notice of motion, the applicant must file his affidavit supporting the application, with a copy, in the Crown Office and serve a copy on the respondent[10], who must within a further 21 days file any opposing affidavit, with a copy, and serve a copy on the applicant and the Crown Office[11]. Unless the court otherwise orders, the application may not be heard earlier than 14 days after the time for filing the respondent's affidavit has expired[12].

1 RSC Ord 94 r 1(1). As to the right of appeal against a minister's certificate see para 85 ante.
2 For a form of originating notice of motion see 12(1) Court Forms (2nd Edn) (1996 issue) 109, Form 1.
3 RSC Ord 94 r 1(2). As to amendment of the notice see *Hanily v Minister of Local Government and Planning* [1951] 2 KB 917, [1951] 2 All ER 749, CA, in which it was held that amendment of the grounds upon which the application is based may be allowed after the six weeks' period has elapsed. The ground relied upon is important as the Acquisition of Land Act 1981 s 24(2)(b) (see para 87 post) provides that the court may only quash a compulsory purchase order or any provision contained therein, or any certificate, because of a failure to comply with any requirement of the legislation, if the interests of the applicant have been substantially prejudiced, whereas where the ground is that the order is outside the powers of the 1981 Act or the empowering enactment, no such substantial prejudice need be shown. As to 'substantial prejudice' see para 87 note 8 post. The courts have, at times, had difficulty in defining under which ground an order is challengeable (see *Gordondale Investments Ltd v Secretary of State for the Environment* (1971) 23 P & CR 334 at 342, CA, per Megaw LJ); but it would appear that a failure to comply with a procedural requirement (see the Acquisition of Land Act 1981 s 23(2); and para 85 ante) may also mean that the order thus made is not within the powers of the Act (see *Fairmount Investments Ltd v Secretary of State for the Environment* [1976] 2 All ER 865, [1976] 1 WLR 1255, HL, per Lord Russell).

4 In *Summers v Minister of Health* [1947] 1 All ER 184 it was held that the time for service of the notice of motion on the Secretary of State or other parties could be extended under what is now RSC Ord 3 r 5 as long as the originating notice of motion was served within the six week period prescribed by what is now the Acquisition of Land Act 1981 s 23.

5 For the meaning of 'confirming authority' see para 34 note 3 ante.

6 For the meaning of 'acquiring authority' see para 34 note 2 ante.

7 See RSC Ord 94 r 2(2), (3).

8 Ie under RSC Ord 38 r 2(3).

9 RSC Ord 94 r 3(1).

10 RSC Ord 94 r 3(2), (4). For a form of supporting affidavit see 12(1) Court Forms (2nd Edn) (1996 issue) 111, Form 3.

11 RSC Ord 94 r 3(3), (4).

12 RSC Ord 94 r 3(5). The procedure under Ord 94 rr 1–3 applies also to an application to suspend or quash a decision of the Secretary of State regarding a certificate of appropriate alternative development under the Land Compensation Act 1961 Pt III (ss 17–22) (as amended): see para 259 post.

87. Court's powers. Upon an application challenging the validity of a compulsory purchase order or certificate[1] the court may, by interim order[2], suspend the operation of the compulsory purchase order or any provision contained in it, or the operation of the certificate, either generally or in so far as it affects any property of the applicant, until the final determination of the proceedings[3].

In the case of an application on the ground that an order is not empowered to be granted[4], the court, if satisfied on that ground[5], may quash the order or any provision in it, or the certificate, either generally or in so far as it affects any property of the applicant[6]. In the case of an application on the grounds of failure to comply with any relevant requirement[7], the court may similarly quash the order or any provision in it, or the certificate, if satisfied that the applicant's interests have been substantially prejudiced[8].

In considering whether to quash an order, the court may take into consideration matters occurring between the making of the order and its confirmation[9] but must limit itself to matters available to the confirming authority[10].

1 Ie an application under the Acquisition of Land Act 1981 s 23 (as amended): see para 85 ante. For the meaning of 'compulsory purchase order' see para 34 note 1 ante.

2 For a form of interim order see 12(1) Court Forms (2nd Edn) (1996 issue) 113, Form 4.

3 Acquisition of Land Act 1981 s 24(1). Where the proper procedure for the order has not been followed, the court may prefer to quash the order rather than suspend it until the omission has been rectified: *Richardson v Minister of Housing and Local Government* (1956) 8 P & CR 29. As to the right of appeal against a minister's certificate see para 85 ante.

4 Ie under the Acquisition of Land Act 1981 or any such enactment as is mentioned in s 1(1) (see para 33 ante): s 24(2)(a).

5 Ie if satisfied that the order is, in purpose or object, ultra vires the statute under which the authority authorising it purports to act or is ultra vires the authorising authority. This will be so where any of the following are present: (1) there was no statutory basis for the order; (2) the confirming authority has made a decision which no reasonable confirming authority properly directed in the law could have made; (3) the confirming authority has taken into account an immaterial consideration or has failed to take into account a material consideration; and/or (4) confirmation of the order involved a breach of the rules of natural justice: see *Ashbridge Investments Ltd v Minister of Housing and Local Government* [1965] 3 All ER 371 at 374, [1965] 1 WLR 1320 at 1325, CA, per Lord Denning MR.

6 Acquisition of Land Act 1981 s 24(2)(a).

7 For the meaning of 'relevant requirement' see para 85 note 5 ante.

8 Acquisition of Land Act 1981 s 24(2)(b). 'Substantial prejudice' has been held to mean the loss of a chance of being better off in relation to the proposed order; and the applicant does not have to show that the decision would have been different if the requirement had been complied with: see *Hibernian Property Co Ltd v Secretary of State for the Environment* (1973) 27 P & CR 197. See also *Wilson v Secretary of State for the Environment* [1974] 1 All ER 428, [1973] 1 WLR 1083; *George v Secretary of State for the Environment* (1979) 38 P & CR 609, CA; *Martin v Bearsden and Milngavie District Council* 1987 SLT 300;

and *Greenwich London Borough v Secretary of State for the Environment and Spar Environments Ltd* [1981] JPL 809. See also *Save Britain's Heritage v Secretary of State for the Environment* [1991] 2 All ER 10, sub nom *Save Britain's Heritage v Number 1 Poultry Ltd* [1991] 1 WLR 153, HL ('substantial prejudice' caused where the reasons for the decision were so poorly expressed as to raise a real doubt as to whether the decision had been made within the powers of the relevant Act). Failure to serve notices on a person entitled to receive them, whereby, through lack of knowledge of the proposed order, he is deprived of the opportunity of objecting and of being heard at an inquiry, substantially prejudices his interests (*Brown v Ministry of Housing and Local Government* [1953] 2 All ER 1385 at 1387), unless he in fact knew of the proposed order (*Grimley v Minister of Housing and Local Government* [1971] 2 QB 96, [1971] 2 All ER 431). The onus of proof of substantial prejudice is on the applicant: see *Save Britain's Heritage v Secretary of State for the Environment* supra at 24–25 and 167–168 per Lord Bridge; *Gordondale Investments Ltd v Secretary of State for the Environment* (1971) 23 P & CR 334 at 340, CA, per Lord Denning MR. As to persons entitled to receive notices see para 37 ante; and as to prejudice of the applicant's interests see para 57 ante.

9   See *London and Westcliff Properties Ltd v Minister of Housing and Local Government* [1961] 1 All ER 610, [1961] 1 WLR 519.

10 See *Ashbridge Investments Ltd v Minister of Housing and Local Government* [1965] 3 All ER 371, [1965] 1 WLR 1320, CA.

2. RIGHTS OF OWNERS ETC TO REQUIRE PURCHASE OF INTERESTS

(1) INTERESTS AFFECTED BY PLANNING DECISIONS OR ORDERS

88. In general. Where, as a result of certain planning decisions[1], land is incapable of reasonably beneficial use[2], the owner of the land or a person entitled to an interest in the land may serve a purchase notice requiring the relevant council[3] of the area in which the land is situated to purchase his interest in that land[4]. The council on which the purchase notice was served must serve a response notice stating either:

(1) that it is willing to comply with the purchase notice, or that another local authority or specified statutory undertakers has or have agreed to comply with it in the council's place[5]; or

(2) that the council is not willing to comply and has not found any other local authority or statutory undertakers willing to comply, and that the council has sent a copy of the purchase notice and of the response notice to the Secretary of State[6].

Where a response notice has been served in accordance with head (1) above, the council or, as the case may be, the other local authority or statutory undertakers specified in it is or are deemed to be authorised to acquire the interest of the owner compulsorily[7] and to have served a notice to treat[8] in respect of it on the date of service of the response notice[9]. Where head (2) above applies, the Secretary of State must consider whether to confirm the purchase notice[10] or to take other action[11] in respect of it[12]. Where the land has a restricted use[13] he need not confirm the purchase notice[14]. Where he confirms the purchase notice, the council on which it was served, or another local authority or statutory undertakers substituted for that council by the Secretary of State[15], is or are deemed to be authorised to acquire the interest of the owner compulsorily and to have served a notice to treat in respect of it on such day as the Secretary of State may direct[16].

Special statutory provision is made with regard to agricultural units[17] and listed buildings[18].

All these provisions are considered in detail elsewhere in this work[19].

1 Ie the decisions mentioned in the Town and Country Planning Act 1990 s 137(1): see TOWN AND COUNTRY PLANNING vol 46 (Reissue) para 717.
2 As to the meaning of 'reasonably beneficial use' see TOWN AND COUNTRY PLANNING vol 46 (Reissue) para 720.
3 Ie the council of the district or London borough or, from a day to be appointed under the Local Government (Wales) Act 1994 s 66(3), the council of a Welsh county or county borough: Town and Country Planning Act 1990 s 137(2) (prospectively amended by the Local Government (Wales) Act 1994 s 20(4), Sch 6 para 24(3) as from a day to be so appointed). At the date at which this volume states the law, no such day had been appointed.
4 See the Town and Country Planning Act 1990 s 137(1), (2); and TOWN AND COUNTRY PLANNING vol 46 (Reissue) para 717.
5 See ibid s 139(1)(a), (b); and TOWN AND COUNTRY PLANNING vol 46 (Reissue) para 721 heads (1)–(2).
6 See ibid s 139(1)(c); and TOWN AND COUNTRY PLANNING vol 46 (Reissue) para 721 head (3).
7 Ie in accordance with ibid Pt IX (ss 226–246) (as amended) (see TOWN AND COUNTRY PLANNING vol 46 (Reissue) para 760 et seq) or, in the case of statutory undertakers, in accordance with any statutory provision, however expressed, under which they have power, or may be authorised, to purchase land compulsorily for the purposes of their undertaking: s 148(1). For the meaning of 'statutory undertakers' for these purposes see TOWN AND COUNTRY PLANNING vol 46 (Reissue) para 721 note 4.
8 As to the service of notices to treat see paras 100–104 post; and see TOWN AND COUNTRY PLANNING vol 46 (Reissue) para 707 note 5.
9 See the Town and Country Planning Act 1990 s 139(3); and TOWN AND COUNTRY PLANNING vol 46 (Reissue) para 721. A notice to treat which is deemed to have been so served may not be withdrawn under the Land Compensation Act 1961 s 31 (as amended) (see para 120 post): Town and Country Planning Act 1990 s 139(5).
10 As to confirmation of the purchase notice see TOWN AND COUNTRY PLANNING vol 46 (Reissue) paras 722–723, 725.
11 As to the action which he may take see TOWN AND COUNTRY PLANNING vol 46 (Reissue) para 723.
12 Town and Country Planning Act 1990 s 140(1).
13 For the meaning of 'restricted use' see TOWN AND COUNTRY PLANNING vol 46 (Reissue) para 724 note 3.
14 See the Town and Country Planning Act 1990 s 142(1), (3); and TOWN AND COUNTRY PLANNING vol 46 (Reissue) para 724.
15 Ie by virtue of a modification to the purchase notice made by virtue of ibid s 141(4): see TOWN AND COUNTRY PLANNING vol 46 (Reissue) para 723.
16 See TOWN AND COUNTRY PLANNING vol 46 (Reissue) para 725.
17 See TOWN AND COUNTRY PLANNING vol 46 (Reissue) paras 726–727.
18 See TOWN AND COUNTRY PLANNING vol 46 (Reissue) para 933 et seq.
19 See TOWN AND COUNTRY PLANNING vol 46 (Reissue) paras 717 et seq, 933 et seq.

89. Compensation. Where compensation is payable in respect of expenditure incurred in carrying out any works on land[1], any compensation payable in respect of the acquisition of an interest in the land in pursuance of a purchase notice[2] must be reduced by an amount equal to the value of those works[3].

Where the Secretary of State directs[4] that, if an application for it is made, planning permission[5] must be granted for the development[6] of any land, and it is shown that the permitted development value[7] of the interest in that land in respect of which the purchase notice was served is less than its value calculated on the assumption that planning permission would be granted for development consisting of (1) specified rebuilding operations or the maintenance, improvement or alteration of a building[8] subject to the statutory condition[9] relating thereto[10]; and (2) the use as two or more separate dwelling houses of any building which at a material date was used as a single dwelling house[11], the local planning authority[12], on a claim made to it, must pay the person entitled to that interest compensation of an amount equal to the difference[13].

1 Ie by virtue of the Town and Country Planning Act 1990 s 107 (as amended) (which provides for compensation for revocation or modification of planning permissions): see TOWN AND COUNTRY PLANNING vol 46 (Reissue) para 697.
2 As to purchase notices see para 88 ante; and TOWN AND COUNTRY PLANNING vol 46 (Reissue) para 717 et seq.
3 See the Town and Country Planning Act 1990 s 144(1); and TOWN AND COUNTRY PLANNING vol 46 (Reissue) para 728.
4 Ie under ibid s 141(3): see TOWN AND COUNTRY PLANNING vol 46 (Reissue) para 723.
5 'Planning permission' means permission under ibid Pt III (ss 55–106B) (as amended) (see TOWN AND COUNTRY PLANNING vol 46 (Reissue) para 144 et seq): s 336(1) (definition amended by the Planning and Compensation Act 1991 ss 32, 84(6), Sch 7 paras 8, 52(1), (2)(g), Sch 19 Pt I).
6 For the meaning of 'development' see TOWN AND COUNTRY PLANNING vol 46 (Reissue) para 144.
7 For these purposes, 'permitted development value', in relation to an interest in land in respect of which a direction is given under the Town and Country Planning Act 1990 s 141(3), means the value of that interest calculated with regard to that direction but on the assumption that no planning permission would be granted otherwise than in accordance with that direction: s 144(6).
8 Ie development of a class specified in ibid s 107(4) (as amended), Sch 3 para 1: see TOWN AND COUNTRY PLANNING vol 46 (Reissue) para 703. See also para 246 note 4 post.
9 Ie subject to the condition set out in ibid s 111(5) (as substituted), Sch 10: see TOWN AND COUNTRY PLANNING vol 46 (Reissue) para 704.
10 Ibid s 144(2)(b), (6) (amended by the Planning and Compensation Act 1991 s 31(4), Sch 6 paras 8, 19).
11 Ie development of a class specified in the Town and Country Planning Act 1990 Sch 3 para 2: see TOWN AND COUNTRY PLANNING vol 46 (Reissue) para 703. See also para 246 note 7 post.
12 As to local planning authorities see TOWN AND COUNTRY PLANNING vol 46 (Reissue) para 11 et seq.
13 Town and Country Planning Act 1990 s 144(2), (6) (as amended: see note 10 supra). See further TOWN AND COUNTRY PLANNING vol 46 (Reissue) para 728. For similar provisions with regard to listed buildings see TOWN AND COUNTRY PLANNING vol 46 (Reissue) para 938.

(2) INTERESTS AFFECTED BY PLANNING BLIGHT

90. In general. Land which is identified in ways to which the statutory provisions apply[1] as being affected by the planning proposals of public authorities is referred to as 'blighted land'[2]. A person with a qualifying interest[3] in blighted land who has made reasonable endeavours to sell that interest but has been unable to do so except at a price substantially lower than that for which it might reasonably have been expected to sell if no part of the relevant hereditament or agricultural unit[4] were, or were likely to be, comprised in blighted land, may serve a blight notice[5] on the appropriate authority[6] requiring it to purchase that interest to the extent specified in, and otherwise in accordance with, the relevant[7] statutory provisions[8].

The appropriate authority may serve a counter-notice objecting to the blight notice[9], in which case the claimant may require the objection to be referred to the Lands Tribunal[10].

Where a counter-notice has been served, and either (1) no counter-notice objecting to it is served; or (2) where such a counter-notice has been served, the objection is withdrawn or is not upheld on a reference to the tribunal, the appropriate authority is deemed to be authorised to acquire the claimant's interest compulsorily and to have served a notice to treat[11] in respect of it on the specified date[12]. Where the counter-notice specifies that the authority is willing to acquire part only of a hereditament or affected area[13], and the claimant accepts this proposal, or where on a reference to the Lands Tribunal the tribunal makes a declaration[14] in respect of that part of the hereditament or affected area, then the appropriate authority is deemed to be authorised to acquire compulsorily the claimant's interest in the specified part of the hereditament or affected area, but not in any other part, and to have served a notice to treat in respect of it on the specified date[15].

A blight notice may be withdrawn in certain circumstances[16].

Special statutory provision is made with regard to partially affected agricultural units[17] and the powers of personal representatives, mortgagees and partnerships[18].

All these provisions are considered in detail elsewhere in this work[19].

1 Ie land to which the Town and Country Planning Act 1990 s 149(1), Sch 13 paras 1–23 (as amended) apply: see TOWN AND COUNTRY PLANNING vol 46 (Reissue) para 734 et seq.

2 See ibid s 149(1).

3 For the meaning of 'qualifying interest' see ibid s 149(2); and TOWN AND COUNTRY PLANNING vol 46 (Reissue) para 729.

4 For the meaning of 'hereditament' and 'agricultural unit' see ibid s 171(1); and TOWN AND COUNTRY PLANNING vol 46 (Reissue) para 729 notes 6, 9.

5 As to blight notices see TOWN AND COUNTRY PLANNING vol 46 (Reissue) para 744 et seq.

6 For the meaning of 'the appropriate authority' see TOWN AND COUNTRY PLANNING vol 46 (Reissue) para 732.

7 Ie the Town and Country Planning Act 1990 Pt VI Ch II (ss 149–171) (as amended): see TOWN AND COUNTRY PLANNING vol 46 (Reissue) para 729 et seq.

8 See ibid s 150(1) (amended by the Planning and Compensation Act 1991 s 70, Sch 15 para 13); and TOWN AND COUNTRY PLANNING vol 46 (Reissue) para 744.

9 See TOWN AND COUNTRY PLANNING vol 46 (Reissue) para 745.

10 See TOWN AND COUNTRY PLANNING vol 46 (Reissue) para 748. As to the tribunal see para 202 et seq post.

11 As to the service of notices to treat see paras 100–104 post. See also TOWN AND COUNTRY PLANNING vol 46 (Reissue) para 707 note 5.

12 See the Town and Country Planning Act 1990 s 154(1), (2); and TOWN AND COUNTRY PLANNING vol 46 (Reissue) para 749. For the specified date see s 154(3); and TOWN AND COUNTRY PLANNING vol 46 (Reissue) para 749 note 11.

13 'The affected area', in relation to an agricultural unit, means so much of that unit as consists of blighted land on the date of service of a blight notice in respect of it: see ibid s 171(1), (5).

14 Ie in accordance with ibid s 153(6): see TOWN AND COUNTRY PLANNING vol 46 (Reissue) para 748.

15 See ibid s 154(4), (5); and TOWN AND COUNTRY PLANNING vol 46 (Reissue) para 749.

16 See ibid s 156; and TOWN AND COUNTRY PLANNING vol 46 (Reissue) para 751.

17 See TOWN AND COUNTRY PLANNING vol 46 (Reissue) paras 752–754.

18 See TOWN AND COUNTRY PLANNING vol 46 (Reissue) paras 755–758.

19 See TOWN AND COUNTRY PLANNING vol 46 (Reissue) para 729 et seq.

91. Compensation. If, where an interest in land is acquired in pursuance of a blight notice[1], there is a compulsory purchase order in force containing a direction for minimum compensation[2], the compensation payable must be assessed in accordance with that direction and as if the notice to treat deemed to have been served[3] had been served in pursuance of the compulsory purchase order[4]. If there is a compulsory purchase order in force under the statutory provisions relating to the acquisition of land for clearance[5], the compensation payable must be assessed in accordance with the Housing Act 1985 and as if the notice to treat deemed to have been served had been served in respect of that compulsory purchase order[6].

Compensation payable on the acquisition of an interest in the unaffected area of an agricultural unit[7], or so much of the affected area[8] as is not specified in a counter-notice, where one has been served[9], must be assessed on the normal[10] statutory assumptions[11].

1 See para 90 ante; and TOWN AND COUNTRY PLANNING vol 46 (Reissue) para 729 et seq.

2 Ie an order under the Acquisition of Land Act 1981 s 1 (see para 33 ante) as applied by the Planning (Listed Buildings and Conservation Areas) Act 1990 s 47 (as prospectively amended) and containing a direction under s 50: see TOWN AND COUNTRY PLANNING vol 46 (Reissue) paras 947, 949.

3 Ie under the Town and Country Planning Act 1990 s 154: see para 90 ante; and TOWN AND COUNTRY PLANNING vol 46 (Reissue) para 749. As to the service of notices to treat see paras 100–104 post; see also TOWN AND COUNTRY PLANNING vol 46 (Reissue) para 707 note 5.

4 See ibid s 157(1); and TOWN AND COUNTRY PLANNING vol 46 (Reissue) para 759.
5 Ie under the Housing Act 1985 s 290: see HOUSING.
6 See the Town and Country Planning Act 1990 s 157(2); and TOWN AND COUNTRY PLANNING vol 46 (Reissue) para 759.
7 For the meaning of 'agricultural unit' see ibid s 171(1); and TOWN AND COUNTRY PLANNING vol 46 (Reissue) para 729 note 9; and as to the unaffected area see TOWN AND COUNTRY PLANNING vol 46 (Reissue) para 752.
8 For the meaning of 'the affected area' see para 90 note 13 ante.
9 Ie served on the grounds specified in the Town and Country Planning Act 1990 s 151(4)(c): see TOWN AND COUNTRY PLANNING vol 46 (Reissue) para 745 head (3).
10 Ie the assumptions mentioned in the Land Compensation Act 1973 s 5(2)–(4) (as amended): see para 372 post.
11 Town and Country Planning Act 1990 s 157(3); and see TOWN AND COUNTRY PLANNING vol 46 (Reissue) para 759.

3. STEPS IN THE ACQUISITION OF LAND

(1) SURVEY BEFORE ACQUISITION

92. Power to enter land to survey. For the purpose merely of surveying and taking levels of any of the land[1] subject to compulsory purchase[2], of probing or boring to ascertain the nature of the soil and of setting out the line of the works[3], the undertakers[4] or the acquiring authority[5], after giving not less than three nor more than 14 days' notice[6] to the owners[7] or occupiers of that land, may enter[8] on that land; but the undertakers or the authority must make compensation for any damage thereby occasioned to the owners or occupiers of the land, and any question of disputed compensation[9] must be referred to the Lands Tribunal[10].

1 'Land' includes anything falling within any definition of that expression in the enactment under which the purchase is authorised: Compulsory Purchase Act 1965 s 1(3). See also para 13 text to note 7 ante.
2 'Subject to compulsory purchase', in relation to land, means land the compulsory purchase of which is authorised by the compulsory purchase order: ibid s 1(3).
3 'The works' means the works, of whatever nature, authorised to be executed by the special Act: ibid s 1(4). See also para 13 text to note 4 ante. For the meaning of 'special Act' see paras 11, 16 ante. Where, however, the Compulsory Purchase Act 1965 Pt I (ss 1–32) (as amended) applies by virtue of the Town and Country Planning Act 1990 Pt IX (ss 226–246) (as amended) (see TOWN AND COUNTRY PLANNING vol 46 (Reissue) para 760 et seq) or of the Planning (Listed Buildings and Conservation Areas) Act 1990 s 52 (as prospectively amended) (see TOWN AND COUNTRY PLANNING vol 46 (Reissue) para 951), references therein to the execution of works are to be construed in accordance with the Town and Country Planning Act 1990 s 245(4) or, as the case may be, the Planning (Listed Buildings and Conservation Areas) Act 1990 s 52(2) (see TOWN AND COUNTRY PLANNING vol 46 (Reissue) paras 767 note 4, 951 note 8 respectively): Compulsory Purchase Act 1965 s 1(4) (amended by the Planning (Consequential Provisions) Act 1990 s 4, Sch 2 para 13(1)).
4 For the meaning of 'the undertakers' see para 13 ante.
5 'Acquiring authority' means the person authorised by the compulsory purchase order to purchase the land: Compulsory Purchase Act 1965 s 1(3) (definition amended by the Acquisition of Land Act 1981 s 34(3), Sch 6 Pt I).
6 As to when an inspection will be granted if no notice is given see *Fooks v Wilts, Somerset and Weymouth Rly Co* (1846) 5 Hare 199.
7 Where any notice is to be given to the owner of any land, or where any act is authorised or required to be done with the consent of any such owner, the word 'owner', unless the context otherwise requires, means any person having power to sell and convey the land to the acquiring authority: Compulsory Purchase Act 1965 s 1(6); and see para 13 text to note 11 ante.
8 This does not, however, amount to entry in order to determine the date of valuation or the date from which to calculate interest on compensation: *Courage Ltd v Kingswood District Council* (1978) 35 P & CR 436, Lands Tribunal.

9 Compensation payable under the Compulsory Purchase Act 1965 s 11(3) carries interest at the rate for the time being prescribed under the Land Compensation Act 1961 s 32 (see para 125 post) for the withdrawal of the notice to treat: Planning and Compensation Act 1991 s 80(1), Sch 18 Pt I. Payments on account may be made of such compensation or interest (s 80(2)), recoverable where it is subsequently agreed or determined that there was no liability to pay the compensation or interest or that the payment on account was excessive (s 80(3)). The Compulsory Purchase Act 1965 s 11 has been modified in relation to the compulsory acquisition of rights by, inter alia, (1) a local authority, by the Local Government (Miscellaneous Provisions) Act 1976 s 13(3)(b) (as amended), Sch 1 para 9 (see LOCAL GOVERNMENT vol 28 para 1219); (2) the Development Board for Rural Wales, by the Development of Rural Wales Act 1976 s 6(7) (as amended), Sch 4 para 9 (see TOWN AND COUNTRY PLANNING vol 46 (Reissue) para 1200); (3) urban development corporations, by the Local Government, Planning and Land Act 1980 s 144, Sch 28 para 23(4) (see TOWN AND COUNTRY PLANNING vol 46 (Reissue) para 1297); (4) highway authorities, by the Highways Act 1980 s 250(5)(a) (as substituted), Sch 19 para 9 (see HIGHWAYS vol 21 (Reissue) para 808); (5) public gas suppliers, by the Gas Act 1986 s 9(3), Sch 3 para 10 (see FUEL AND ENERGY vol 19(1) (Reissue) para 636); (6) housing action trusts, by the Housing Act 1988 s 78(2), Sch 10 para 23(2) (see HOUSING); (7) licence holders under the Electricity Act 1989, by s 10(1), Sch 3 para 11 (see FUEL AND ENERGY vol 19(2) (Reissue) para 985); (8) the National Rivers Authority, by the Water Resources Act 1991 s 154(5), Sch 18 para 6 (see WATER); and (9) water and sewerage undertakers, by the Water Industry Act 1991 s 155(5), Sch 9 para 6 (see WATER).

10 Lands Clauses Consolidation Act 1845 s 84 proviso (where that Act applies: see para 11 ante); Compulsory Purchase Act 1965 s 11(3) (where that Act applies: see para 15 ante). Wider powers of entry for survey are given by some empowering enactments: see eg the Housing Act 1985 s 260; and HOUSING; the Local Government (Miscellaneous Provisions) Act 1976 s 15 (amended by the New Roads and Street Works Act 1991 s 168(1), Sch 8 para 106); and LOCAL GOVERNMENT vol 28 para 1242; and the Town and Country Planning Act 1990 ss 324(6), 325 (as amended); and TOWN AND COUNTRY PLANNING vol 46 (Reissue) paras 33–34.

(2) PURCHASE BY AGREEMENT

93. Purchase with or without service of notice to treat. Undertakers[1] or an acquiring authority[2] empowered to purchase land compulsorily need not exercise such compulsory powers of acquisition but may acquire it by agreement[3].

The undertakers or acquiring authority may agree with any of the owners[4] of the land subject to compulsory purchase[5], and with all parties having any estate or interest in any of the land or who are enabled[6] to sell and convey or release any of that land, for the absolute purchase, for a consideration in money or money's worth, of any of that land and of all estates and interests in it[7]. An agreement to purchase is not affected by the time limit imposed on the exercise of the power of compulsory purchase[8].

The agreement may be effected without the service of a notice to treat or after the service of a notice to treat and without using compulsory powers of reference following such notice[9]; but the land will nonetheless be acquired under the empowering enactment or special Act and the provisions of that Act, and any Act incorporated by it or applicable to it, will apply to the purchase except so far as they are inconsistent with a purchase by agreement[10].

Undertakers or an acquiring authority may, in the agreement, enter into restrictive covenants affecting the land purchased, but not so as to impose any fetter on the exercise of the statutory powers entrusted to them by Parliament[11], and any covenants which impose such a fetter are void[12]. Normally, the power to purchase compulsorily does not enable a compulsory acquisition of a stratum of land as a limited interest only in the land, or an easement over it, without acquiring it[13], but the undertakers or acquiring authority may acquire such a stratum or an interest or easement where the owner is willing to sell it, provided those rights are sufficient for the purposes contemplated by the special Act[14].

1 For the meaning of 'the undertakers' see para 13 ante.
2 For the meaning of 'acquiring authority' see para 92 note 5 ante.
3 Provision as to acquisition by agreement may be made in the special Act. The power to acquire by agreement is given by the Lands Clauses Consolidation Act 1845 s 6 (where that Act is incorporated: see para 11 ante); or by the Compulsory Purchase Act 1965 s 3 (as amended) (where that Act applies: see para 15 ante). See the text and notes 4–15 infra. For the meaning of 'special Act' see paras 11, 16 ante.
4 For the meaning of 'owner' see para 92 note 7 ante. See also para 13 text to note 11 ante.
5 For the meaning of 'land' and 'subject to compulsory purchase' see para 92 notes 1–2 ante. See also para 13 text to note 7 ante.
6 Ie by the special Act or by the Lands Clauses Consolidation Act 1845 s 6, or the Compulsory Purchase Act 1965 s 2, Sch 1 (as amended), as the case may be, or, where the 1965 Act applies, by any other enactment (see s 3 (as amended)): see para 96 post.
7 Lands Clauses Consolidation Act 1845 s 6 (referrring, however, only to consideration in money and not to consideration in money's worth); Compulsory Purchase Act 1965 s 3 (amended by the Planning and Compensation Act 1991 s 70, Sch 15 para 3).
8 As to the time limit imposed in the case of compulsory purchase see the Lands Clauses Consolidation Act 1845 s 123; and the Compulsory Purchase Act 1965 s 4 (amended by the Housing Act 1974 s 116; and by the Housing (Consequential Provisions) Act 1985 s 3, Sch 1 Pt I); and see *Webb v Direct London and Portsmouth Rly Co* (1851) 9 Hare 129 at 140; *Worsley v South Devon Rly Co* (1851) 16 QB 539 at 545; *Rangeley v Midland Rly Co* (1868) 3 Ch App 306; *Kemp v South Eastern Rly Co* (1872) 7 Ch App 364.
9 As to service of a notice to treat see para 102 post. Such service is not the exercise of compulsory powers, but a condition precedent to their exercise, and it may be followed by an agreement or by the enforcement of compulsory powers: *Re Uxbridge and Rickmansworth Rly Co* (1890) 43 ChD 536, CA; see also paras 100 note 2, 115–121 post.
10 *Hooper v Bourne* (1877) 3 QBD 258 at 273, CA; affd (1880) 5 App Cas 1, HL; *Kirby v Harrogate School Board* [1896] 1 Ch 437, CA. Where, however, an authority which has power to purchase land compulsorily on authorisation by a compulsory purchase order purchases land by agreement before being authorised to acquire it compulsorily, this will not be a purchase under a compulsory purchase power and only those provisions of the Compulsory Purchase Act 1965 relating to purchase by agreement will apply; thus, inter alia, s 10 (as amended), which gives a right to compensation for injurious works apart from compensation for land purchased (see paras 200, 354 post), will not apply: see eg the Small Holdings and Allotments Act 1908 s 38 (amended by the Compulsory Purchase Act 1965 s 38 (as amended), Sch 6); and ALLOTMENTS vol 2 (Reissue) para 16. There will accordingly be no power to do works to the injury of rights of way or to infringe restrictive covenants unless the statutory purpose would inevitably lead to that injury: see para 335 post. Where such power is required the authority should seek authorisation of the purchase by a compulsory purchase order.
    In many cases powers to cause such injury are not required and purchase by agreement without authorisation to purchase compulsorily takes place; but, with the right to have such authorisation, the purchase price is not likely to be other than the compulsory purchase price and accordingly various statutory provisions as to the assessment of the compulsory purchase price are applied also to the purchase price on such an agreement: see paras 277, 324 post. Other powers also are similarly applied: see para 253 post.
11 *Stourcliffe Estates Co Ltd v Bournemouth Corpn* [1910] 2 Ch 12, CA, where it was held that the undertakers could enter into a restrictive covenant which merely precluded them from exercising a subsidiary power, the exercise of which was not imperative for the purposes for which the land was acquired, but permissive only. The undertakers can grant an easement, provided it is not inconsistent with the purposes for which the land was acquired: *South Eastern Rly Co v Associated Portland Cement Manufacturers (1900) Ltd* [1910] 1 Ch 12, CA.
12 *Ayr Harbour Trustees v Oswald* (1883) 8 App Cas 623, HL; *Re Heywood's Conveyance, Cheshire Lines Committee v Liverpool Corpn* [1938] 2 All ER 230.
13 See para 30 ante.
14 *Great Western Rly Co v Swindon and Cheltenham Rly Co* (1884) 9 App Cas 787 at 801, HL: see para 30 ante.

94. Consideration for the sale. The consideration for the sale must be in money or money's worth[1]. Consideration may no longer comprise an annual rentcharge payable by the acquiring authority[2].

A person selling by agreement to an authority possessing compulsory purchase powers may apply for a certificate of appropriate alternative development[3].

1 See the Lands Clauses Consolidation Act 1845 s 6; the Compulsory Purchase Act 1965 s 3 (amended by the Planning and Compensation Act 1991 s 70, Sch 15 para 3); and para 93 text and note 7 ante.
2 See the Rentcharges Act 1977 ss 2, 17(2), Sch 2. The Lands Clauses Consolidation Act 1845 s 11 (amended by the Administration of Justice Act 1965 s 34, Sch 2; extended by the Lands Clauses Consolidation Acts Amendment Act 1860 s 2 (amended by the Rentcharges Act 1977 s 17(1), Sch 2) to all cases of sale and purchase or compensation under the 1845 Act where the parties interested in the sale, or entitled to the compensation, are under any disability or incapacity) which provides for the recovery of such rentcharges, is thus of little practical effect.
3 See the Land Compensation Act 1961 s 17 (as amended), s 22(2)(c); and para 253 post.

95. Application of general law to agreements. Agreements for the purchase of land by undertakers or an acquiring authority[1] are governed by the general law, as, for example, in regard to formalities[2], the time for completion[3], specific performance[4], and interest[5]. If the agreement provides that the price is to be fixed by reference to an arbitrator, the provisions of the Lands Clauses Acts[6] applicable to arbitrations, as, for example, those dealing with costs, will not apply to the reference[7] unless it is expressly so agreed.

1 See paras 93–94 ante.
2 See eg *Crampton v Varna Rly Co* (1872) 7 Ch App 562. As to the formalities required see the Law of Property (Miscellaneous Provisions) Act 1989 s 2; and LANDLORD AND TENANT vol 27(1) (Reissue) para 56; SPECIFIC PERFORMANCE vol 44(1) (Reissue) para 858. See also SALE OF LAND.
3 See *Baker v Metropolitan Rly Co* (1862) 31 Beav 504. As to the time for exercising an option to purchase see *Rangeley v Midland Rly Co* (1868) 3 Ch App 306; *Kemp v South Eastern Rly Co* (1872) 7 Ch App 364; and see *Tiverton and North Devon Rly Co v Loosemore* (1884) 9 App Cas 480, HL.
4 *Wilson v West Hartlepool Harbour and Rly Co* (1865) 34 LJ Ch 241; *Inge v Birmingham, Wolverhampton and Stour Valley Rly Co* (1853) 3 De GM & G 658; *Regent's Canal Co v Ware* (1857) 23 Beav 575; *Gunston v East Gloucestershire Rly Co* (1868) 18 LT 8; *Ingram v Midland Rly Co* (1860) 3 LT 533; *Tillett v Charing Cross Bridge Co* (1859) 28 LJ Ch 863.
5 *Catling v Great Northern Rly Co* (1869) 18 WR 121, CA; *Rhys v Dare Valley Rly Co* (1874) LR 19 Eq 93; *Re Pigott and Great Western Rly Co* (1881) 18 ChD 146; *Leggott v Metropolitan Rly Co* (1870) 5 Ch App 716; *Fletcher v Lancashire and Yorkshire Rly Co* [1902] 1 Ch 901; *Re Richard and Great Western Rly Co* [1905] 1 KB 68, CA; *Re Duke of Northumberland and Tynemouth Corpn* [1909] 2 KB 374.
6 As to the Lands Clauses Acts see para 11 ante.
7 *Catling v Great Northern Rly Co* (1869) 18 WR 121, CA; *Doulton v Metropolitan Board of Works* (1870) LR 5 QB 333; *Wombwell v Barnsley Corpn* (1877) 36 LT 708; *Bygrave v Metropolitan Board of Works* (1886) 32 ChD 147, CA; and see *Re Lindsay's Settlement* [1941] Ch 170, [1941] 1 All ER 104 (abandonment of arbitration under the Lands Clauses Acts by agreement).

96. Persons entitled to sell, including persons under disability. All persons who are seised, possessed of or entitled to any land[1], or any estate or interest in any of the land, which the undertakers[2] or acquiring authority[3] may agree to purchase, are authorised to sell and convey or release it to that authority, and to enter into all necessary agreements for that purpose[4]. This power applies, in particular, to corporations, tenants in tail or for life, trustees for charitable or other purposes[5] and persons for the time being entitled to the receipt of the rent and profits of any such land in possession or subject to any lease for years or for any less interest[6].

The powers so conferred on any person, other than a lessee for a term of years or for any less interest, may be exercised not only on behalf of himself and his successors, but also for and on behalf of every person entitled in reversion, remainder or expectancy after him, or in defeasance of his estate[7]. Trustees for a beneficiary under any disability may exercise those powers on behalf of that beneficiary to the same extent that the beneficiary could have exercised those powers if he had not been under any disability[8].

Any power of releasing land from any rent, charge or incumbrance, or of agreeing to the apportionment of any such rent, charge or incumbrance, may lawfully be exercised by any person enabled under the above provisions to sell and convey or release land to the undertakers or the acquiring authority[9].

In most cases in which persons under disability are beneficially interested, the legal estate in land should be able to be conveyed on acquisition of it by agreement either by trustees for sale[10] or under the Settled Land Act 1925[11], or by personal representatives[12]. In such cases there will be power to give a receipt for the purchase money without its being paid into court; but if it is payable to trustees for sale or Settled Land Act trustees it must be paid to two or more trustees or a trust corporation[13].

Nothing in the above provisions or in the special Act[14] enables a local authority to sell, without the prior consent of the Secretary of State, any land which it could not otherwise have sold without that consent, except where the undertakers are, or the acquiring authority is, authorised to purchase the land compulsorily[15]. In other cases the exercise of powers to sell is, by statute, subject to the obtaining of consent[16] and, if the necessary consent is not obtained, title in respect of persons under a disability will have to be made on payment into court[17].

If the sale purports to be carried out under the Lands Clauses Acts or the Compulsory Purchase Act 1965, its validity must be determined according to their provisions independently of other powers[18].

1 For the meaning of 'land' see para 92 note 1 ante. See also para 13 text to note 7 ante.
2 For the meaning of 'the undertakers' see para 13 ante.
3 For the meaning of 'acquiring authority' see para 92 note 5 ante.
4 Lands Clauses Consolidation Act 1845 s 7; Compulsory Purchase Act 1965 s 2, Sch 1 para 2(1). Lessees are thereby released from their covenants against assignment and for subsequent breaches of covenants which they are prevented from performing: *Slipper v Tottenham and Hampstead Junction Rly Co* (1867) LR 4 Eq 112; *Baily v De Crespigny* (1869) LR 4 QB 180; *Harding v Metropolitan Rly Co* (1872) 7 Ch App 154 at 159; and see *Mills v East London Union* (1872) LR 8 CP 79; *Wadham v Marlow* (1784) 8 East 315n.
5 Where notice to treat is served both on the trustees and on the beneficiary, but the purchase money is fixed as between the acquiring authority and the beneficiary by a reference to arbitration in which the trustees take no part, the authority cannot require the sale to be completed as a sale by the trustees, but it must be completed as a sale by the beneficiary: see *Re Pigott and Great Western Rly Co* (1881) 18 ChD 146. See also *Peters v Lewes and East Grinstead Rly Co* (1881) 18 ChD 429, CA; *Lippincott v Smyth* (1860) 29 LJ Ch 520; *Hall v London, Chatham and Dover Rly Co* (1866) 14 LT 351.
6 Lands Clauses Consolidation Act 1845 s 7 (amended by the Compulsory Purchase Act 1965 s 39(4), Sch 8 Pt II); Compulsory Purchase Act 1965 Sch 1 para 2(2). As to receivers appointed by the court see *Tink v Rundle* (1847) 10 Beav 318.
7 Lands Clauses Consolidation Act 1845 s 7 (as amended: see note 6 supra); Compulsory Purchase Act 1965 Sch 1 para 2(3). These provisions have effect subject to the Law of Property Act 1925 s 42(7), which provides that if, on a compulsory purchase, title could have been made without payment into court, title must be made in that way unless the purchaser otherwise elects: see the Compulsory Purchase Act 1965 Sch 1 paras 1(1), 2(3). As to payment into court see para 98 post. If the reversion is in the Crown, the Crown's consent is necessary: *Re Cuckfield Burial Board* (1854) 24 LJ Ch 585.
8 Lands Clauses Consolidation Act 1845 s 7 (as amended: see note 6 supra; further amended by the Mental Treatment Act 1930 ss 20(5), 22(3); and by virtue of the Mental Health Act 1983 s 148, Sch 5 para 29); Compulsory Purchase Act 1965 Sch 1 para 2(4). These provisions have effect as if references to disabilities did not include references to minors, married women or persons suffering from mental disorder: see the Law of Property (Amendment) Act 1924 s 9, Sch 9; the Compulsory Purchase Act 1965 Sch 1 para 1(2)(a). They are also excluded from effect in relation to patients and to persons as to whom powers are exercisable and have been exercised under the Mental Health Act 1983 s 98 (see MENTAL HEALTH vol 30 (Reissue) para 1443): Compulsory Purchase Act 1965 Sch 1 para 1(2)(b) (amended by the Mental Health Act 1983 s 148, Sch 4 para 20). Married women are in any case no longer subject to any legal disability in English law; and although the capacity of a married woman to contract is governed by the law of her domicile (see *Guepratte v Young* (1851) 4 De G & Sm 217), such incapacity, in relation to a contract where both parties are in England, may be invoked only if the other party was aware of it, or negligent in not being aware of it, at the time of the conclusion of the contract: see the Contracts (Applicable Law) Act 1990 ss 1, 2; the Rome Convention (ie the Convention on the

Law Applicable to Contractual Obligations (Rome, 19 June 1980) art 11; and CONFLICT OF LAWS para 853 post.

9 Lands Clauses Consolidation Act 1845 s 8 (amended by the Compulsory Purchase Act 1965 s 39(4), Sch 8 Pt II); Compulsory Purchase Act 1965 Sch 1 para 3(b). See further the Lands Clauses Consolidation Act 1845 ss 108–121 (as amended); the Compulsory Purchase Act 1965 ss 14–20 (as amended); and paras 180–196 post.

10 With regard to the overreaching powers upon conveyances of legal estates in land by trustees for sale see the Law of Property Act 1925 s 2 (as amended); and with regard to the creation of the statutory trusts for sale in land see REAL PROPERTY. Legal estates in land held for minors or persons suffering from mental disorder are subject to statutory provisions under which the estates should be disposable: see s 19, s 22 (substituted by the Mental Health Act 1959 s 149(1), Sch 7 Pt I; amended by the Mental Health Act 1983 s 148, Sch 4 para 5(a)); and cf note 11 infra.

11 See eg the Settled Land Act 1925 s 20 (as amended) (persons having powers of tenants for life, including tenants in tail and tenants for years determinable on life); s 23 (trustees of the settlement); s 29 (as amended) (land subject to charitable trusts); and see SETTLEMENTS. Powers of sale under the Settled Land Act 1925 are additional to powers under the Lands Clauses Acts: see the Settled Land Act 1925 s 108(1). See also the Mental Health Act 1983 ss 93(1), 94(1) (as amended), ss 94(2), 96(1), (5), 99, 112, replacing, in effect, the Settled Land Act 1925 s 28 (repealed) in relation to persons suffering from mental disorder; and see generally MENTAL HEALTH vol 30 (Reissue) para 1431 et seq. As to the Lands Clauses Acts see para 11 infra.

12 See the Administration of Estates Act 1925 ss 2, 39 (s 2 amended by the Law of Property (Miscellaneous Provisions) Act 1994 ss 16(1), 21(2), Sch 2); and EXECUTORS vol 17 para 1194.

13 Law of Property Act 1925 s 27(2) (substituted by the Law of Property (Amendment) Act 1926 s 7, Schedule); Settled Land Act 1925 s 94(1); Trustee Act 1925 s 14 (amended by the Law of Property (Amendment) Act 1926 Schedule). In these cases there will be no need for payment into court: see note 7 supra.

14 For the meaning of 'special Act' see paras 11, 16 ante.

15 Lands Clauses Consolidation Act 1845 s 15; Compulsory Purchase Act 1965 s 38(2); Secretary of State for the Environment Order 1970, SI 1970/1681, art 2(2). As to the application of the Compulsory Purchase Act 1965 Pt I (ss 1–32) (as amended) to sales by agreement under certain enactments see further s 38(3), (4). As to consent to sales see the Local Government Act 1972 ss 123(2), 128; and the Town and Country Planning Act 1959 s 26 (as amended), which, however, is excluded by the Local Government Act 1972 s 128(3); and see LOCAL GOVERNMENT.

16 See eg the Universities and College Estates Act 1925 s 2(2) (repealed except in relation to Winchester and Eton by the Universities and College Estates Act 1964 s 2, Sch 1 para 1).

17 See *Re Great Western Railway (New Railways) Act 1905, ex p Great Western Rly Co* (1909) 74 JP 21, CA.

18 *Peters v Lewes and East Grinstead Rly Co* (1881) 18 ChD 429, CA.

97. Assessment of consideration where persons under disability. When the land[1] is to be purchased or taken from any person under any disability[2] or incapacity, who has no power to sell or convey it except under the special Act[3], the Lands Clauses Acts[4], or the Compulsory Purchase Act 1965, the purchase money or compensation to be paid, and also the compensation for any permanent damage or injury to any land held by that person[5], must not be less than an amount determined by the valuation of two able practical surveyors[6], except where the amount has been determined[7] under compulsory powers[8].

1 For the meaning of 'land' see para 92 note 1 ante. See also para 13 text to note 7 ante.

2 For the meaning of 'disability' for these purposes see para 96 note 8 ante.

3 For the meaning of 'special Act' see paras 11, 16 ante.

4 As to the Lands Clauses Acts see para 11 ante.

5 *Stone v Yeovil Corpn* (1876) 2 CPD 99, CA.

6 Lands Clauses Consolidation Act 1845 s 9; Lands Clauses Consolidation Acts Amendment Act 1860 s 4; Compulsory Purchase Act 1965 s 2, Sch 1 paras 4(1), (5), 5(1). The valuation is to be by two able practical surveyors, one appointed by each party, and, in default of agreement between the surveyors, by a third surveyor nominated by two justices on the application of either party; and a certificate of the correctness of his valuation must be annexed by the surveyor to the valuation: Lands Clauses Consolidation Act 1845 s 9; Compulsory Purchase Act 1965 Sch 1 paras 4(1), (2), (3), (5), 5(1). A

certificate of value of the land being sold may be obtained by any person selling the land from the Lands Tribunal on written application to the registrar with such information as he may require: Land Compensation Act 1961 s 35; Lands Tribunal Rules 1975, SI 1975/299, r 46. This provision is unlikely to undergo substantial alteration in the Lands Tribunal Rules 1996, which are expected to come into force in April 1996. At the date at which this volume states the law, those new rules were still in draft and the final text had not been settled: see para 206 note 3 post.

This requirement as to valuation does not apply, it seems, where land is acquired, eg from statutory owners under powers conferred by the Settled Land Act 1925: see para 96 note 11 ante. As to the necessity for such a certificate in proceedings to enforce the sale see *Wycombe Rly Co v Donnington Hospital* (1866) 1 Ch App 268; *Bridgend Gas and Water Co v Dunraven* (1885) 31 ChD 219. A party cannot appoint himself as surveyor: *Peters v Lewes and East Grinstead Rly Co* (1881) 18 ChD 429 at 438, CA. Cf the statutory provisions respecting sales under the Settled Land Act 1925: see s 39 (as amended); and SETTLEMENTS vol 42 para 827 et seq.

A justice of the peace may act under the Compulsory Purchase Act 1965 in relation to land which is partly in one area, and partly in another, if he may act as respects land in either area, but no justice of the peace must so act if he is interested in the matter: s 1(5).

7 Ie where the amount has been determined by the Lands Tribunal, or by a member of the tribunal, or by the valuation of a surveyor selected by the tribunal in accordance with the Lands Tribunal Act 1949 s 3 (as amended) (see para 205 post), in the case of absent or untraced owners (see the Compulsory Purchase Act 1965 s 5(3), Sch 2 para 1(1)(b); and para 200 post): Sch 1 paras 4(1), (4), 5(1).

8 Lands Clauses Consolidation Act 1845 s 9; Lands Clauses Consolidation Acts Amendment Act 1860 s 4; Compulsory Purchase Act 1965 Sch 1 paras 4(1), (4), 5(1).

98. Payment into court where persons under disability. When the land[1] is purchased from persons under disability[2] who are enabled to sell and convey only under the special Act[3], the Lands Clauses Acts[4] or the Compulsory Purchase Act 1965[5], the purchase money or compensation must in general be paid into court for the benefit of the persons interested in the manner provided in those Acts[6].

1 For the meaning of 'land' see para 96 note 1 ante. See also para 13 text to note 7 ante.
2 For the meaning of 'disability' for these purposes see para 96 note 8 ante.
3 For the meaning of 'special Act' see paras 11, 16 ante.
4 As to the Lands Clauses Acts see para 11 ante.
5 See para 96 ante.
6 Lands Clauses Consolidation Act 1845 s 9; Compulsory Purchase Act 1965 s 2, Sch 1 para 6(1), (2). References to payment into court are references to payment into the Supreme Court: s 25(1). The Lands Clauses Consolidation Act 1845 s 9 refers to deposit in the Bank of England, but it is thought that this should now be construed as a reference to payment into the Supreme Court. As to acquisitions where there is power to acquire under a compulsory purchase order see paras 149–151 post. See further para 142 post. This requirement as to payment into court does not, it seems, apply where land is acquired eg from statutory owners under powers conferred by the Settled Land Act 1925: see para 96 note 11 ante. As to payment in and the application of the money see the Lands Clauses Consolidation Act 1845 ss 69–80 (as amended); the Compulsory Purchase Act 1965 Sch 1 para 6; and paras 149–151 post.

(3) CONDITIONS PRECEDENT TO EXERCISE OF COMPULSORY POWERS

(i) Subscription of Capital

99. Subscription of capital under binding contract to pay. Under the Lands Clauses Acts[1], where an undertaking is intended to be carried into effect by means of capital to be subscribed by the undertakers[2], the whole of the capital or estimated sum for defraying the expenses of the undertaking must be subscribed under a binding contract for payment before any of the powers in relation to the compulsory taking[3] can be put into force[4]. When the Lands Clauses Acts are not incorporated and the special Act[5] makes no provision in that behalf, the undertakers are not required to show a sufficiency of funds[6]; but if the undertaking cannot be completed, and the undertakers have made a mistake as to the sum necessary to complete it, an injunction may be granted to restrain further proceedings by them[7].

1 As to the Lands Clauses Acts see para 11 ante.
2 For the meaning of 'the undertakers' see para 13 ante.
3 For this purpose the service of notice to treat is not an exercise of compulsory powers: see *Guest v Poole and Bournemouth Rly Co* (1870) LR 5 CP 553; *Re Uxbridge and Rickmansworth Rly Co* (1890) 43 ChD 536, CA; and see *Goodwin Foster Brown Ltd v Derby Corpn* [1934] 2 KB 23. As to taking possession of an easement see *Great Western Rly Co v Swindon and Cheltenham Rly Co* (1884) 9 App Cas 787, HL.
4 Lands Clauses Consolidation Act 1845 s 16. As to evidence of subscription by a certificate of two justices see s 17; and see *Ystalyfera Iron Co v Neath and Brecon Rly Co* (1873) LR 17 Eq 142. The restriction does not apply to additional works by an existing company: see *R v Great Western Rly Co* (1852) 1 E & B 253; *Weld v South Western Rly Co* (1863) 32 Beav 340. Any exercise of powers contrary to this requirement is ultra vires: *R v Ambergate, Nottingham, and Boston, and Eastern Junction Rly Co* (1853) 1 E & B 372. See, however, the Companies Act 1985 ss 35–35B (as substituted and amended) (validity of company's acts; power of directors to bind company); and COMPANIES.
5 For the meaning of 'special Act' see paras 11, 16 ante.
6 *Salmon v Randall* (1838) 3 My & Cr 439.
7 *Agar v Regent's Canal Co* (1814) 1 Swan 250n; *King's Lynn Corpn v Pemberton* (1818) 1 Swan 244 at 250; *Blakemore v Glamorganshire Canal Navigation* (1832) 1 My & K 154 at 164; *Lee v Milner* (1837) 2 Y & C Ex 611 at 619; *Gray v Liverpool and Bury Rly Co* (1846) 9 Beav 391 at 394, 400; *Cohen v Wilkinson* (1849) 1 Mac & G 481. See also INJUNCTIONS.

(ii) Notice to Treat

100. Notice to treat to precede exercise of compulsory powers. If the undertakers[1] or the acquiring authority[2] need to use their compulsory powers[3] to purchase any of the land subject to compulsory purchase[4], they must give a notice (a 'notice to treat')[5] to all persons interested in[6], or having power to sell and convey or release[7], the land so far as known to them after making diligent inquiry[8]. A notice to treat ceases to have effect at the end of the period of three years beginning with the date on which it is served unless:

(1) the compensation has been agreed or awarded or has been either paid or paid into court[9];
(2) a general vesting declaration has been executed[10];
(3) the acquiring authority has entered on and taken possession of the land specified in the notice; or
(4) the question of compensation has been referred to the Lands Tribunal[11].

The time limit may be extended by agreement with the acquiring authority[12].

Where a notice to treat ceases to have effect[13], the acquiring authority must immediately give notice of that fact to the person on whom the notice to treat was served and any other person who, since it was served, could have made an agreement[14] to have the time limit extended[15]. The acquiring authority is liable to pay compensation to any person entitled to a notice to treat for any loss or expenses occasioned to him by the giving of the notice and its ceasing to have effect[16]. In default of agreement, the amount of any such compensation is to be determined by the Lands Tribunal[17].

A notice to treat may bear a date different from that on which it is served[18]. There is no specified form of notice[19] but every notice to treat must:

(a) give particulars of the land to which it relates;
(b) demand particulars of the recipient's estate and interest in the land, and of the claim he makes in respect of the land; and
(c) state that the undertakers or the acquiring authority are willing to treat for the purchase of the land and as to the compensation to be made for the damage which may be sustained by reason of the execution of the works[20].

If the appropriate person is prevented from treating because he is absent from the United Kingdom, or if he cannot be found after diligent inquiry has been made, the compensation or purchase money, including compensation for severance or other injurious affection, must be determined by the valuation of a surveyor and the money paid into court[21].

1 For the meaning of 'the undertakers' see para 13 ante.
2 For the meaning of 'acquiring authority' see para 92 note 5 ante.
3 As to the power to purchase by agreement without using such powers see para 93 ante.
4 For the meaning of 'land' and 'subject to compulsory purchase' see para 92 notes 1–2 ante. See also para 13 text to note 7 ante.
5 Although there is some authority for saying that, at least in some circumstances, the service of a notice to treat is not an exercise of compulsory powers, but is a condition precedent to their exercise (see *Guest v Poole and Bournemouth Rly Co* (1870) LR 5 CP 553; *Re Uxbridge and Rickmansworth Rly Co* (1890) 43 ChD 536, CA; *Goodwin Foster Brown Ltd v Derby Corpn* [1934] 2 KB 23), it is clear that the service of a notice within the prescribed time establishes the right to set in motion the machinery to complete a compulsory purchase (*Tiverton and North Devon Rly Co v Loosemore* (1884) 9 App Cas 480 at 484, HL; and see para 101 note 3 post). See also *Grice v Dudley Corpn* [1958] Ch 329 at 338, [1957] 2 All ER 673 at 678 per Upjohn J.
6 As to such persons see para 103 post.
7 As to such persons see para 96 ante.
8 Lands Clauses Consolidation Act 1845 s 18 (where that Act is incorporated: see para 11 ante); Compulsory Purchase Act 1965 s 5(1) (where that Act applies: see para 15 ante). There is, however, no requirement to serve a notice to treat where the authority seeks to acquire commonable rights and has followed the procedure for their acquisition laid down in s 21, Sch 4 (see COMMONS vol 6 (Reissue) paras 612–614): see *Mid Glamorgan County Council v Ogwr Borough Council* (1994) 68 P & CR 1, CA; on appeal sub nom *Lewis v Mid Glamorgan County Council* [1995] 1 All ER 760, [1995] 1 WLR 313, HL.
9 As to payment into court see paras 98 note 6 ante, 124 post.
10 Ie under the Compulsory Purchase (Vesting Declarations) Act 1981 s 4: see para 169 post.
11 Compulsory Purchase Act 1965 s 5(2A) (s 5(2A)–(2E) added by the Planning and Compensation Act 1991 s 67).
12 See the Compulsory Purchase Act 1965 s 5(2B) (as added: see note 11 supra). In the case of such agreement, the notice to treat ceases to have effect at the end of the period as extended unless (1) any of the events referred to in heads (1)–(4) in the text have then taken place; or (2) the parties have agreed to a further extension of the period, in which case this provision applies again at the end of the period as further extended, and so on: s 5(2B) (as so added).
13 Ie by virtue of ibid s 5(2A) or (2B) (as added): see the text and notes 10–12 supra.
14 Ie under ibid s 5(2B) (as added): see the text and note 12 supra.
15 Ibid s 5(2C)(a) (as added: see note 11 supra). Payments on account of such compensation may be made, which may be recoverable if it is later agreed or determined that the person making the payments is not liable to pay compensation, or that the amount paid was excessive: Planning and Compensation Act 1991 s 80(2), (3), Sch 18 Pt II.
16 Compulsory Purchase Act 1965 s 5(2C)(b) (as added: see note 11 supra).
17 Ibid s 5(2D) (as added: see note 11 supra). Compensation so payable to any person carries interest at the rate prescribed under the Land Compensation Act 1961 s 32 (see para 125 post) from the date on which he was entitled to be given notice under the Compulsory Purchase Act 1965 s 5(2C)(as added) until payment: s 5(2E) (as added: see note 11 supra). Payments on account of such interest may be made, which may be recoverable if it is later agreed or determined that the person making the payments is not liable to pay compensation, or that the amount paid was excessive: Planning and Compensation Act 1991 s 80(2), (3), Sch 18 Pt II.
18 *Cohen v Haringey London Borough Council* (1980) 42 P & CR 6, CA.
19 *Coats v Caledonian Railway Co* (1904) 6 F 1042; *Renton v North British Railway Co* (1845) 8 D 247.

20 Lands Clauses Consolidation Act 1845 s 18; Compulsory Purchase Act 1965 s 5(2)(a)–(c). See also *Lewis v Hackney London Borough Council* [1990] 2 EGLR 15, CA. For the meaning of 'the works' see para 92 note 3 ante. See also para 13 text to note 4 ante.

21 See para 200 text and notes 11–14 post. As to service of the notice to treat on the land in such a case see para 102 post. 'United Kingdom' means Great Britain and Northern Ireland: Interpretation Act 1978 s 5, Sch 1. 'Great Britain' means England, Scotland and Wales: Union with Scotland Act 1706, preamble art I; Interpretation Act 1978 s 22(1), Sch 2 para 5(a). Neither the Channel Islands nor the Isle of Man are within the United Kingdom.

101. Time for service of notice to treat. The time within which a notice to treat must be served may be prescribed by the empowering enactment or special Act[1]. If the Lands Clauses Acts are incorporated[2] the powers for the compulsory purchase or taking of land may not be exercised after (1) the expiration of the prescribed period; and (2) if no period is prescribed, the expiration of three years from the passing of the special Act[3].

If the special Act also limits the period of execution of the works and a notice to treat has been given within the prescribed time, but no further step has been taken by the acquiring authority or the owners, and the period for completion of the works has expired, neither of the parties can claim the benefit of the notice unless the delay can be explained[4].

The period for exercising compulsory powers may be extended by a subsequent Act which may validate notices previously given[5].

In the case of a compulsory purchase authorised by a compulsory purchase order to which the Compulsory Purchase Act 1965 applies[6], the enactment under which the purchase is empowered and the compulsory purchase order are deemed to be the special Act[7] and the time limit for service of the notice to treat is three years from the date when the order became operative[8].

1 For the meaning of 'special Act' see paras 11, 16 ante.
2 As to the Lands Clauses Acts and their incorporation see para 11 ante.
3 Lands Clauses Consolidation Act 1845 s 123. For the purpose of the right to exercise compulsory powers it is sufficient if a notice to treat is served within the prescribed time: see *Marquis of Salisbury v Great Northern Rly Co* (1852) 17 QB 840; *Tiverton and North Devon Rly Co v Loosemore* (1884) 9 App Cas 480 at 493, HL. In calculating the period, the day on which the special Act was passed is excluded: see *Goldsmiths' Co v West Metropolitan Rly Co* [1904] 1 KB 1, CA. Where periods are prescribed for taking land for specific purposes, but none for other purposes, the three years' limit will apply to those other purposes: *Seymour v London and South Western Rly Co* (1859) 5 Jur NS 753. If the Lands Clauses Consolidation Act 1845 s 123 is not incorporated and no time is limited by the special Act, a notice to treat may be served so long as power to do so is required for the purposes of the Act: see *Salmon v Randall* (1838) 3 My & Cr 439; *Thicknesse v Lancaster Canal Co* (1838) 4 M & W 472.
4 *Tiverton and North Devon Rly Co v Loosemore* (1884) 9 App Cas 480 at 493, HL; *R v Birmingham and Oxford Junction Rly Co* (1851) 15 QB 634, Ex Ch; *Sparrow v Oxford, Worcester and Wolverhampton Rly Co* (1851) 9 Hare 436; on appeal (1852) 2 De GM & G 94; and cf *Brocklebank v Whitehaven Junction Rly Co* (1847) 5 Ry & Can Cas 373; *Wood v North Staffordshire Rly Co* (1849) 3 De G & Sm 368. As to enforcing rights after the period fixed for the completion of the works see *Richmond v North London Rly Co* (1868) 3 Ch App 679. Works may be completed after that date if it is not necessary to rely upon statutory powers: see *Great Western Rly Co v Midland Rly Co* [1908] 2 Ch 644, CA; affd sub nom *Midland Rly Co v Great Western Rly Co* [1909] AC 445, HL.
5 *Ystalyfera Iron Co v Neath and Brecon Rly Co* (1873) LR 17 Eq 142; *Bentley v Rotherham and Kimberworth Local Board of Health* (1876) 4 ChD 588; and see *Williams v South Wales Rly Co* (1849) 3 De G & Sm 354; *Dun River Navigation Co v North Midland Rly Co* (1838) 1 Ry & Can Cas 135.
6 As to such orders see para 15 ante.
7 See para 16 ante.
8 Compulsory Purchase Act 1965 s 4. The date of operation of such an order is the date on which notice of the making or confirmation of the order is published, unless another date is stipulated in the order: see the Acquisition of Land Act 1981 s 26(1); and para 75 ante. No account is to be taken of any period

during which an authority is prevented from serving notice to treat by virtue of the Housing Act 1985 s 305 (as amended) (building subject to compulsory purchase order under s 290 becoming listed after the making of the order; no service of notice to treat without the Secretary of State's consent to demolition: see HOUSING): s 305(7).

102. Mode of service of notice to treat. In order that both parties may be bound, a notice to treat must be served in accordance with the statutory requirements[1].

If a notice to treat is not served on the proper person within the prescribed period, it may not be adopted by him by service of a counter-notice[2]; but if the counter-notice is acted upon the parties may be estopped from setting up the invalidity of the notice to treat[3]. Service on the occupier is not sufficient unless it can be shown that the owner could not be found, and if the notice relates to land in the occupation of more than one tenant, the notice for the owner must be served on each occupier, and must show that it is for the owner, service on an agent being insufficient[4].

1 *Shepherd v Norwich Corpn* (1885) 30 ChD 553 at 573; *R v Great Northern Rly Co* (1876) 2 QBD 151 at 154–155; *Fagan v Knowsley Metropolitan Borough* (1985) 50 P & CR 363, CA. The provisions of the Acquisition of Land Act 1981 s 6 (as amended) (see para 38 ante) apply to the service of notices to treat under the Compulsory Purchase Act 1965: s 30 (substituted by the Acquisition of Land Act 1981 s 34(1), Sch 4 para 14(4)). See also the Lands Clauses Consolidation Act 1845 ss 19, 20.
2 *Treadwell v London and South Western Rly Co* (1884) 54 LJ Ch 565, 51 LT 894. A counter-notice is one which, in relevant circumstances, may be served by the owner requiring all land to be taken where notice to take part only is given: see para 109 post. As to service on the undertakers under the Lands Clauses Consolidation Act 1845 see s 134. For the meaning of 'the undertakers' see para 13 ante.
3 *Pinchin v London and Blackwall Rly Co* (1854) 1 K & J 34; on appeal 5 De GM & G 851, 24 LJ Ch 417.
4 *Shepherd v Norwich Corpn* (1885) 30 ChD 553 at 570. See also *Fagan v Knowsley Metropolitan Borough* (1985) 50 P & CR 363, CA (notice served on brother as agent of owner living in Australia).

103. Persons entitled to be served with notice to treat. The persons entitled to be served with a notice to treat are all those who are interested in the land[1] or who have power to sell and convey or release it[2]. The freehold owner is entitled to be served, as is a person entitled under an enforceable contract of sale[3] or a person entitled to an option to purchase[4], but not a person entitled to a mere right of pre-emption[5].

Ecclesiastical property, the fee simple of which is in abeyance, is deemed to be vested in the Church Commissioners for the purpose of serving notice to treat[6].

Lessees must be served, including those who are holding under agreements equivalent to a lease in equity[7], but tenants with an interest from year to year or less are not entitled to a notice[8]. Mining lessees who have a right to sink pits in the surface of the land to be acquired are also entitled to a notice[9]. Mortgagees, including equitable mortgagees, must be served[10]. Licensees are not entitled to a notice to treat[11] unless there is special power to purchase such rights[12].

Where the owner of an interest in land creates an interest after the service on him of a notice to treat, that interest is not entitled to a notice to treat and compensation, and some interests, although entitled to a notice to treat, may be disregarded by the Lands Tribunal[13].

There is no power compulsorily to take less than the whole interest in the land and create and require a leasehold interest or to create and acquire an easement over the land unless there is a special power to acquire such a right[14]. If, however, there is such a power and the works cannot be executed before the easement is acquired, the owner of the land must be served with a notice to treat in respect of the easement[15]. So also, where there is a special power to acquire compulsorily a stratum only of the land, the owner of the land is entitled to a notice to treat[16].

Persons who have existing rights against the land to be acquired, such as rights of way or other easements or the benefit of restrictive covenants, are not entitled to a notice to treat because there is no power to acquire those rights unless special provision is made, but only a power injuriously to affect them[17]. If a power were given to acquire those rights, the right to a notice to treat would depend on the terms of the power[18].

1 See para 100 ante; and the text and notes 2–18 infra.
2 See para 96 ante.
3 *Hillingdon Estates Co v Stonefield Estates Ltd* [1952] Ch 627, [1952] 1 All ER 853.
4 *Oppenheimer v Minister of Transport* [1942] 1 KB 242, [1941] 3 All ER 485.
5 *Clout v Metropolitan and District Rlys Joint Committee* (1883) 48 LT 257. This includes a person who has acquired rights as a squatter: *Perry v Clissold* [1907] AC 73, PC. As to the effect of a notice to treat in respect of land subject to a lease see para 117 post.
6 Church of England (Miscellaneous Provisions) Measure 1978 s 8(1). For these purposes, 'ecclesiastical property' means land being or forming part of a church subject to the jurisdiction of a bishop of any diocese (other than the diocese of Sodor and Man) or the site of such a church, or being or forming part of a burial ground subject to such jurisdiction; and 'land' includes anything falling within any definition of that expression in the enactment under which the purchase is authorised: s 8(2).
7 *Re King's Leasehold Estates, ex p East of London Rly Co* (1873) LR 16 Eq 521; *Sweetman v Metropolitan Rly Co* (1864) 1 Hem & M 543; *Birmingham and District Land Co v London and North Western Rly Co* (1888) 40 ChD 268, CA.
8 See paras 180, 184 post. This includes a person who has acquired rights as a squatter: *Perry v Clissold* [1907] AC 73, PC.
9 *Re Masters and Great Western Rly Co* [1901] 2 KB 84, CA.
10 *Rogers v Kingston-upon-Hull Dock Co* (1864) 34 LJ Ch 165; *Martin v London, Chatham and Dover Rly Co* (1866) 1 Ch App 501 at 505; *Cooke v LCC* [1911] 1 Ch 604 at 609; *University Life Assurance Society v Metropolitan Rly Co* [1866] WN 167; *London and India Dock Co v North London Rly Co* (1903) Times, 6 February. As to special powers for acquisition of mortgagees' interests see further para 194 post.
11 See *Frank Warr & Co Ltd v LCC* [1904] 1 KB 713, CA (licence to use theatre premises for business of supplying refreshments), following *Municipal Freehold Land Co v Metropolitan and District Rlys Joint Committee* (1883) Cab & El 184 (licence to use boardroom and desk at certain times); *Bird v Great Eastern Rly Co* (1865) 19 CBNS 268 (licence to shoot over land); but the owner of the land may be liable for damages for breach of contract (see *Walton Harvey Ltd v Walker and Homfrays Ltd* [1931] 1 Ch 274, CA), and must claim for disturbance in respect of it: see para 295 post.
12 See note 18 infra.
13 See para 116 post.
14 See para 31 note 2 ante.
15 See *Ramsden v Manchester, South Junction and Altrincham Rly Co* (1848) 1 Exch 723; and para 31 note 2 ante. If the power to execute the works can be exercised without first acquiring a right or easement over the land, then the notice prescribed by the special Act will be sufficient and no notice to treat need be served, even if land is subsequently vested in the acquiring authority by virtue of the works executed: see *West Midlands Joint Electricity Authority v Pitt* [1932] 2 KB 1, CA; *Thornton v Nutter* (1867) 31 JP 419; *Roderick v Aston Local Board* (1877) 5 ChD 328, CA; *North London Rly Co v Metropolitan Board of Works* (1859) 28 LJ Ch 909; *Hughes v Metropolitan Board of Works* (1861) 4 LT 318. The execution of works such as the erection of posts is merely a power to affect the land injuriously: see *Escott v Newport Corpn* [1904] 2 KB 369. As to the special Act see paras 11, 16 ante.
16 See *Farmer v Waterloo and City Rly Co* [1895] 1 Ch 527; and para 32 note 1 ante.
17 See para 30 ante.
18 For a power to acquire rights over and against the land see eg the National Parks and Access to the Countryside Act 1949 s 103(6) (amended by the Acquisition of Land Act 1981 s 34(3), Sch 6 Pt I); the National Parks and Access to the Countryside Act 1949 s 114(1) (definition of 'interest'); and OPEN SPACES vol 34 para 465.

104. Service of further notice to treat. The acquiring authority may serve the same person with more than one notice to treat in respect of different areas of land. Thus, if the land specified in one notice is not sufficient for the purposes of its undertaking, it may serve another for the purchase of additional land[1], or, having purchased the surface under a power to purchase the surface and omit the minerals, it may serve a further notice in respect of the minerals[2]. If a notice to treat has been validly withdrawn, the authority may serve another in respect of the same or part of the same property, so long as the time for compulsory purchase remains unexpired[3]. Similarly, if the land required is mortgaged and only the mortgagor has been served with notice, the authority may subsequently serve a notice to treat on the mortgagee, although it may have entered into possession of the land as against the mortgagor[4].

1 *Simpson v Lancaster and Carlisle Rly Co* (1847) 15 Sim 580; *Stamps v Birmingham and Stour Valley Rly Co* (1848) 2 Ph 673; and see *Williams v South Wales Rly Co* (1849) 3 De G & Sm 354.
2 *Errington v Metropolitan District Rly Co* (1882) 19 ChD 559, CA. As to the omission of minerals see paras 17, 32 ante.
3 *Ashton Vale Iron Co v Bristol Corpn* [1901] 1 Ch 591, CA.
4 *Cooke v LCC* [1911] 1 Ch 604. As to such purchases see para 193 post.

(iii) Owner's Rights where Notice to Treat is for Part Only of Land

105. Restriction on taking part only of property. When the notice to treat relates to part only of any agricultural land, house or other building or manufactory, and the party served is able and willing to sell and convey the whole of his interest in it, then, in cases where the appropriate statutory provision applies, he may require the undertakers to purchase and take the whole, and he cannot be required at any time to sell and convey a part only[1].

If a notice to treat will sever land and leave less than half an acre in the owner's hands he may, in certain circumstances, require that to be purchased[2]; and if a notice to treat requires land to be taken so as to intersect the owner's land and he requires communications to be made, the undertakers may in certain circumstances require him to sell the two pieces[3].

It is a common provision in special Acts to authorise the undertakers expressly to take specified parts only of houses, buildings or manufactories[4].

1 See paras 106, 109, 112 post.
2 See para 113 post.
3 See para 114 post.
4 Eg to take the forecourts of houses in order to widen a street: see the clause construed by the court in *Genders v LCC* [1915] 1 Ch 1, CA. For the meaning of 'special Act' see paras 11, 16 ante.

106. Counter-notice where notice to treat is for part of agricultural land. Where an acquiring authority[1] serves notice to treat, or is deemed to have served a notice to treat[2], in respect of any agricultural land[3] on a person, whether in occupation or not, who has a greater interest in the land than as tenant for a year or from year to year[4], and that person has such an interest in other agricultural land[5] comprised in the same agricultural unit[6] as that to which the notice relates, the person on whom the notice is served ('the claimant') may, within the period of two months beginning with the date of the service or deemed service of the notice to treat, serve on the acquiring authority a counter-notice (1) claiming that the other land is not reasonably capable of being farmed[7], either by itself or in conjunction with other relevant land[8], as a separate agricultural unit[9]; and (2) requiring the acquiring authority to purchase his interest in the whole of the other land[10]. Where he serves a counter-notice, the claimant must also, within the same two months' period, serve a copy of it on any other person who has an interest in the land to which the requirement in the counter-notice relates, although failure to do so will not invalidate the counter-notice[11].

This power is without prejudice to the power of an owner of agricultural land who would otherwise be left with less than half an acre to insist[12] on the whole being taken, or the power of the acquiring authority to require the owner to sell to it land[13] of less than half an acre which the owner would otherwise be left with after severance[14].

These provisions[15] apply in relation to the acquisition of interests in land, whether compulsorily or by agreement, by government departments which are authorities possessing compulsory purchase powers[16] as they apply in relation to the acquisition of interests in land by such authorities which are not government departments[17].

1　In relation to an interest in land, 'acquiring authority' means the person or body of persons by whom the interest is, or is proposed to be, acquired: Land Compensation Act 1961 s 39(1) (definition applied by the Land Compensation Act 1973 s 87(1)).

2　Ie a notice to treat deemed to have been served by virtue of any of the provisions of the Compulsory Purchase (Vesting Declarations) Act 1981 Pt III (ss 7–9) (see paras 171, 175–176 post): see the Land Compensation Act 1973 s 53(5) (amended by the Land Compensation (Scotland) Act 1973 s 81(1), Sch 2 Pt I; the Compulsory Purchase (Vesting Declarations) Act 1981 s 16(1), Sch 3; and by the Planning (Consequential Provisions) Act 1990 s 4, Sch 1 Pt I).

3　'Agricultural land' means land used for agriculture which is so used for the purposes of a trade or business, or which is designated by the Minister of Agriculture, Fisheries and Food for the purposes of the Agriculture Act 1947 s 109(1), and includes any land so designated as land which in the minister's opinion ought to be brought into use for agriculture: s 109(1). Such designations must not extend to land used as pleasure grounds, private gardens or allotment gardens, or to land kept or preserved mainly or exclusively for the purposes of sport or recreation, except where the minister is satisfied that its use for agriculture would not be inconsistent with its use for those purposes and it is so stated in the designation: s 109(1) proviso. 'Agriculture' includes horticulture, fruit and seed growing, dairy farming, livestock keeping and breeding, the use of land as grazing, meadow or osier land, market gardens and nursery grounds, and the use of land for woodlands where that use is ancillary to the farming of land for other agricultural purposes; and 'agricultural' is to be construed accordingly: s 109(3). These definitions are applied by the Land Compensation Act 1973 s 87(1) (amended by the Land Compensation (Scotland) Act 1973 Sch 2 Pt I).

4　As to the right of a tenant for a year, or from year to year, to serve a counter-notice when served with a notice of entry on part of his holding see the Land Compensation Act 1973 s 55 (as amended), s 56(1); and paras 185–187 post.

5　Where an acquiring authority has served a notice to treat in respect of any of the other agricultural land, or such a notice is deemed to have been served by virtue of the Town and Country Planning Act 1990 ss 137–144 (as amended) (see TOWN AND COUNTRY PLANNING vol 46 (Reissue) para 717 et seq) then unless and until that notice to treat is withdrawn, the provisions of the Land Compensation Act 1973 s 53 (as amended) (see the text and notes 1–4 supra, 6–14 infra) and s 54 (as amended) (effect of counter-notice: see para 107 post) have effect as if that land did not form part of that other agricultural land: s 53(4) (amended by the Planning (Consequential Provisions) Act 1990 Sch 2 para 29(9)).

6　'Agricultural unit' has the meaning given in the Town and Country Planning Act 1990 s 171(1) (see TOWN AND COUNTRY PLANNING vol 46 (Reissue) para 729 note 9): Land Compensation Act 1973 s 87(1) (definition amended by the Planning (Consequential Provisions) Act 1990 s 4, Sch 2 para 29(1)).

7　For these purposes, references to the farming of land include references to the carrying on in relation to the land of any agricultural activities: Land Compensation Act 1973 s 87(1).

8　'Other relevant land' means (1) land comprised in the same agricultural unit as the land to which the notice to treat or deemed notice to treat relates, being land in which the claimant does not have an interest greater than as tenant for a year or from year to year (ibid s 53(3)(a), (5)); and (2) land comprised in any other agricultural unit occupied by him on the date of the service of the notice to treat or deemed notice to treat, being land in respect of which he is then entitled to a greater interest than as tenant for a year or from year to year (s 53(3)(b), (5)). Where the acquiring authority has served such a notice to treat in respect of the other relevant land, or such a notice is deemed to have been served by virtue of the Town and Country Planning Act 1990 ss 137–144 (as amended) (see TOWN AND COUNTRY PLAN-NING vol 46 (Reissue) para 717 et seq), then unless and until that notice is withdrawn, the provisions of the Land Compensation Act 1973 ss 53, 54 (as amended) have effect as if that land did not constitute other relevant land: s 53(4) (as amended: see note 5 supra).

9　Ibid s 53(1)(a).

10　Ibid s 53(1)(b).

11　Ibid s 53(2).

12 Ie under the Lands Clauses Consolidation Act 1845 s 93; or the Compulsory Purchase Act 1965 s 8(2): see para 113 post.
13 Ie under the Lands Clauses Consolidation Act 1845 s 94; or the Compulsory Purchase Act 1965 s 8(3): see para 114 post.
14 Land Compensation Act 1973 s 53(6) (amended by the Land Compensation (Scotland) Act 1977 Sch 2 Pt I).
15 Ie the Land Compensation Act 1973 Pt IV (ss 44–64) (as amended): see para 107 et seq post.
16 For the meaning of 'authority possessing compulsory purchase powers' see para 244 note 6 post (definition applied by ibid s 87(1)).
17 Ibid s 84(2).

107. Effect of counter-notice as to agricultural land compelling purchase of other land outside compulsory purchase powers. If the acquiring authority[1] does not, within the two months' period beginning with the date of service of a counter-notice[2], agree in writing to accept the counter-notice as valid, the claimant[3] or the authority may, within two months after the end of that period, refer it to the Lands Tribunal; and on that reference the tribunal must determine whether the claim in the counter-notice is justified and declare the counter-notice valid or invalid in accordance with that determination[4].

Where a counter-notice is accepted as, or declared to be, valid, the acquiring authority is deemed (1) to be authorised to acquire compulsorily, under the enactment by virtue of which it is empowered to acquire the land in respect of which the notice to treat was served or deemed to be served, the claimant's interest in the land to which the requirement in the counter-notice relates[5]; and (2) to have served a notice to treat in respect of that land on the date on which the first-mentioned notice to treat was served[6]. There is no power to withdraw that notice to treat deemed to have been served[7].

A claimant may withdraw a counter-notice at any time before the compensation payable in respect of a compulsory acquisition in pursuance of the counter-notice has been determined by the Lands Tribunal, or at any time before the end of six weeks beginning with the date on which the compensation is so determined; and where a counter-notice is so withdrawn any notice to treat deemed to have been served in consequence of it is to be deemed to have been withdrawn[8].

The compensation payable in respect of the acquisition of an interest in land in pursuance of a notice to treat deemed to have been served by virtue of these provisions must be assessed on the basis of certain statutory assumptions[9].

1 For the meaning of 'acquiring authority' for these purposes see para 106 note 1 ante.
2 Ie under the Land Compensation Act 1973 s 53(1): see para 106 ante.
3 For the meaning of 'the claimant' see para 106 ante.
4 Land Compensation Act 1973 s 54(1). As to the Lands Tribunal see para 202 et seq post.
5 Ibid s 54(2)(a).
6 Ibid s 54(2)(b).
7 See ibid s 54(4), which excludes the power conferred by the Land Compensation Act 1961 s 31 (see para 120 post) but which is expressed to be without prejudice to the Land Compensation Act 1973 s 54(3) (deemed withdrawal: see the text and note 8 infra).
8 Ibid s 54(3).
9 Ibid s 54(5). The assumptions referred to are those mentioned in s 5(2) (as substituted), s 5(3) (as amended), and s 5(4): see para 372 post.

108. Effect of counter-notice as to agricultural land where lessee's interest only in land outside compulsory purchase powers compelled to be taken. Where there is power to purchase land compulsorily, there is normally no power to require a leasehold interest only in the land to be acquired unless there is special provision to the contrary[1]. Where, however, an acquiring authority[2] is compelled to purchase an interest in other land by a counter-notice[3], the authority may find itself with the lessee's interest in the other land but without the lessor's interest. Where, therefore, the authority becomes, or will become, entitled[4] to a lease of any land, but not to the lessor's interest, the authority may offer to surrender the lease to the lessor on such terms as it considers reasonable[5].

The question of what terms are reasonable may be referred to the Lands Tribunal by the authority or the lessor and if, at the expiration of three months after the date of the offer to surrender the lease, the authority and the lessor have not agreed on that question, and that question has not been referred to the tribunal by the lessor, it must be so referred by the authority[6]. If the question is referred to the tribunal, the lessor is deemed to have accepted the surrender of the lease at the expiration of one month after the date of the tribunal's determination or on such other date as the tribunal may direct, and to have agreed with the authority on the terms of the surrender which the tribunal has held to be reasonable[7].

Where the lessor refuses to accept any sum payable to him by virtue of the tribunal's decision or refuses or fails to make out his title to the acquiring authority's satisfaction, that authority may pay into court any sum so payable to the lessor[8]. Where an acquiring authority which becomes so entitled to the lease of any land is a body incorporated by or under any enactment, the authority's corporate powers will, if they would not otherwise do so, include power to farm that land[9].

1 See para 31 ante.
2 For the meaning of 'acquiring authority' for these purposes see para 106 note 1 ante.
3 See para 106 ante.
4 Ie by virtue of the Land Compensation Act 1973 s 54 (as amended): see the text and notes 5–9 infra; and para 107 ante.
5 Ibid s 54(6)(a). For this purpose, any terms as to surrender contained in the lease must be disregarded: s 54(6).
6 Ibid s 54(6)(b). As to the Lands Tribunal see para 202 et seq post.
7 Ibid s 54(6)(c).
8 Ibid s 54(7). The provisions of the Compulsory Purchase Act 1965 s 9(2), (5) (deposit of compensation in cases of refusal to convey etc: see paras 142, 146 post) applies, with the necessary modifications, to the sum deposited: Land Compensation Act 1973 s 54(7). As to payment into court under the 1965 Act see para 98 note 6 ante.
9 Land Compensation Act 1973 s 54(8).

109. Counter-notice where notice to treat under the Lands Clauses Acts relates to part of premises. No party[1] may at any time be required to sell or convey to the undertakers[2] a part only of any house[3] or other building[4] or manufactory[5] if he is willing and able to sell and convey the whole of it[6]. It follows that if a notice to treat is served which relates to part only of a house or other building or manufactory, the party from whom the acquisition is to be made may, if he is willing and able to sell and convey the whole, by counter-notice require the undertakers to take the whole of the premises. No particular form of notice is required provided it is made clear what the undertakers are required to take[7].

The owner cannot require a different or larger part to be taken; what has to be offered is the whole[8]; but the insertion in the special Act[9], at the owner's instance, of provisions for the protection of his property will not prevent him from exercising his right to require the whole to be taken[10].

The owner may signify his desire that the undertakers should take the whole of the premises at any time before they have begun to put their compulsory powers into motion[11], provided he has not by his conduct estopped himself from doing so, as, for example, by agreeing to the price to be paid for the part[12]. The submission of a claim for a part, and uncompleted negotiations as to the compensation to be paid for the part, will not estop him from claiming that they should take the whole[13]. Where the special Act makes particular provisions relating to the acquisition of parts of premises, the owner may be required to serve notice in a particular form and within a particular time.

1 Ie no party able to sell and convey the whole of the property: see *Governors of St Thomas's Hospital v Charing Cross Rly Co* (1861) 1 John & H 400; *Lord Grosvenor v Hampstead Junction Rly Co* (1857) 26 LJ Ch 731. A lessee of a house may require the undertakers to purchase his interest in the whole house independently of the lessor's rights: *Pulling v London, Chatham and Dover Rly Co* (1864) 33 LJ Ch 505. Similarly, if a person has a leasehold interest in a house and part of a garden, and a freehold interest in the remaining part, the undertakers, if required to take the whole, cannot insist on taking either part: *Macgregor v Metropolitan Rly Co* (1866) 14 LT 354; *Richards v Swansea Improvement and Tramways Co* (1878) 9 ChD 425, CA; *Siegenberg v Metropolitan District Rly Co* (1883) 49 LT 554. If a lessor sells part and a lessee the whole of his land, the undertakers may remain liable on the covenants as to the parts not acquired from the lessor: *Piggott v Middlesex County Council* [1909] 1 Ch 134.
2 For the meaning of 'the undertakers' see para 13 ante.
3 For the meaning of 'house' see para 110 post.
4 Ie something in the nature of a house: see *Regent's Canal and Dock Co v LCC* [1912] 1 Ch 583; and para 110 post.
5 For the meaning of 'manufactory' see para 110 post.
6 Land Clauses Consolidation Act 1845 s 92 (where that Act is incorporated: see para 11 ante). As to the modified provision where the Compulsory Purchase Act 1965 applies see para 112 post.
7 *Gardner v Charing Cross Rly Co* (1861) 2 John & H 248; *Spackman v Great Western Rly Co* (1855) 1 Jur NS 790; *Pollard v Middlesex County Council* (1906) 95 LT 870; *Richards v Swansea Improvement and Tramways Co* (1878) 9 ChD 425, CA; *Binney v Hammersmith and City Rly Co* (1863) 8 LT 161.
8 *Pulling v London, Chatham and Dover Rly Co* (1864) 33 LJ Ch 505; *Thompson v Tottenham and Forest Gate Rly Co* (1892) 67 LT 416.
9 For the meaning of 'special Act' see para 11 ante.
10 See *Sparrow v Oxford, Worcester and Wolverhampton Rly Co* (1852) 2 De GM & G 94; *Governors of St Thomas's Hospital v Charing Cross Rly Co* (1861) 1 John & H 400. If the whole is taken the undertakers are released from the restrictive provision: *Governors of St Thomas's Hospital v Charing Cross Rly Co* supra at 401.
11 Service of the notice to treat is not by itself an exercise of compulsory powers: *Goodwin Foster Brown Ltd v Derby Corpn* [1934] 2 KB 23; and see para 100 note 5 ante.
12 *Gardner v Charing Cross Rly Co* (1861) 2 John & H 248; *Barker v North Staffordshire Rly Co* (1848) 5 Ry & Can Cas 401, 2 De G & Sm 55; *Pollard v Middlesex County Council* (1906) 95 LT 870.
13 *Lavers v LCC* (1905) 93 LT 233; *Pollard v Middlesex County Council* (1906) 95 LT 870.

110. Meaning of 'house', 'building' and 'manufactory'. By a 'house' or 'building' is meant more than the mere fabric. 'House' includes the house, garden and curtilage; in fact all that would pass on the conveyance of a house[1]. It also means more than a dwelling house or residence, and includes a shop, or an inn[2], or a building built for one purpose, such as a hospital[3]. 'Building' includes separate buildings in one ambit used for a common purpose[4]. Conversely, one building used as two dwelling houses, as in the case of semi-detached houses, is treated as two separate houses[5]. Unfinished houses are also considered to be houses[6].

In determining whether premises are a manufactory, regard must be had to the main use to which they are put[7]. If the main business is manufacturing, the undertakers may be required to take the whole of the premises, even though part may be used for other purposes[8], or may be temporarily let to another occupier[9]. If a manufactory is partly worked by water power, and undertakers desire to take the water and the arrangements for storing and conveying the power, they may be required to take the whole manufactory[10]. Where, however, the main business carried on upon premises is not manufacture, it is immaterial that some manufacture should be carried on incidentally to it and in such a case the undertakers may take the whole of the part used for manufacture without being required to take the other parts[11]. Similarly, they may take the part not used as the manufactory without taking the part so used[12].

The date of service of the notice to treat fixes the time when the premises are to be considered in order to determine whether the land proposed to be purchased or taken is part of a house, building, or manufactory[13]. Changes made after that date are immaterial[14]. If made in good faith, changes of use or occupation may be made at any time before the service of the notice[15].

1   *Grosvenor v Hampstead Junction Rly Co* (1857) 26 LJ Ch 731; *Cole v West London and Crystal Palace Rly Co* (1859) 28 LJ Ch 767; *Marson v London, Chatham and Dover Rly Co* (1868) LR 6 Eq 101 (further proceedings (1869) LR 7 Eq 546); *Governors of St Thomas's Hospital v Charing Cross Rly Co* (1861) 1 John & H 400; *Richards v Swansea Improvement and Tramways Co* (1878) 9 ChD 425, CA. Thus, it would include a shrubbery and the various orchards and gardens connected with a house (*Hewson v South Western Rly Co* (1860) 8 WR 467; *King v Wycombe Rly Co* (1860) 29 LJ Ch 462; *Salter v Metropolitan District Rly Co* (1870) LR 9 Eq 432), and might include a paddock behind a house and accessible only from the garden (*Barnes v Southsea Rly Co* (1884) 27 ChD 536; *Low v Staines Reservoir Joint Committee* (1900) 64 JP 212, CA); and also the courtyard to a house (*Caledonian Rly Co v Turcan* [1898] AC 256, HL). It does not, however, include all land which the owner of the house may possess and enjoy along with the house, such as fields used for grazing (*Pulling v London, Chatham and Dover Rly Co* (1864) 33 LJ Ch 505; *Steele v Midland Rly Co* (1866) 1 Ch App 275; *Fergusson v London, Brighton and South Coast Rly Co* (1863) 11 WR 1088), or gardens and stables on the opposite side of the road, purchased subsequently to the purchase of the house (*Kerford v Seacombe, Hoylake and Deeside Rly Co* (1888) 57 LJ Ch 270; and see *Chambers v London, Chatham and Dover Rly Co* (1863) 11 WR 479), or a private road leading to a mansion house (*Allhusen v Ealing and South Harrow Rly Co* (1898) 78 LT 285 at 286). Similarly, if a cottage stands in a nursery garden, the garden will not be deemed to be part of the house: *Falkner v Somerset and Dorset Rly Co* (1873) LR 16 Eq 458.

2   *Richards v Swansea Improvement and Tramways Co* (1878) 9 ChD 425 at 431, CA.

3   *Governors of St Thomas's Hospital v Charing Cross Rly Co* (1861) 1 John & H 400.

4   See eg *Richards v Swansea Improvement and Tramways Co* (1878) 9 ChD 425, CA; *Siegenberg v Metropolitan District Rly Co* (1883) 49 LT 554; *Greswolde-Williams v Newcastle-upon-Tyne Corpn* (1927) 92 JP 13 (building let out in offices). A church is a 'house or building' (and can be assumed to be a building) and includes adjacent halls and outbuildings: *London Transport Executive v Congregational Union of England and Wales (Inc)* (1978) 37 P & CR 155.

5   *Harvie v South Devon Rly Co* (1874) 32 LT 1, CA.

6   *Alexander v Crystal Palace Rly Co* (1862) 30 Beav 556.

7   *Richards v Swansea Improvement and Tramways Co* (1878) 9 ChD 425 at 434–436, CA.

8   Eg for a rubbish heap (*Sparrow v Oxford, Worcester and Wolverhampton Rly Co* (1852) 2 De GM & G 94), or warehouses (*Spackman v Great Western Rly Co* (1855) 1 Jur NS 790).

9   *Brook v Manchester, Sheffield and Lincolnshire Rly Co* [1895] 2 Ch 571.

10   *Furniss v Midland Rly Co* (1868) LR 6 Eq 473.

11   *Benington & Sons v Metropolitan Board of Works* (1886) 54 LT 837, where blending and packing tea was the principal business, and the making of packing cases an incidental part.

12   *Reddin v Metropolitan Board of Works* (1862) 4 De GF & J 532.

13   *Richards v Swansea Improvement and Tramways Co* (1878) 9 ChD 425, CA.

14   *Chambers v London, Chatham and Dover Rly Co* (1863) 11 WR 479; *Littler v Rhyl Improvement Comrs* [1878] WN 219.

15   *Richards v Swansea Improvement and Tramways Co* (1878) 9 ChD 425, CA.

111. Effect of counter-notice under the Lands Clauses Acts. The effect under the Lands Clauses Acts[1] of the counter-notice when validly given is to enable the undertakers either to purchase the whole or to withdraw their notice to treat[2]. If the notice to treat is withdrawn, the subsequent withdrawal of the counter-notice does not revive the original notice to treat[3]; the parties are relegated to the same position as they were in before the notice to treat was served, and if they so desire the undertakers can serve a fresh notice as to the same premises or as to a different part of them[4]. If, however, the owner withdraws his counter-notice before the undertakers have signified their desire either to take the whole or to withdraw the notice to treat, the original notice to treat stands[5]. No formal notice to take, or of their intention to take, the whole is required to be given by the undertakers on receiving a counter-notice, provided they signified their intention in such a way as to bind themselves[6]. The appointment of an arbitrator does not prevent them from withdrawing their notice to treat[7].

An owner who has served a valid counter-notice may obtain an injunction to restrain the undertakers from taking part only[8], or a declaration that they cannot purchase or take part[9], or, if they have entered, a declaration that they must take the whole[10]. In such a case, the deposit to be made on entry before the purchase is completed must be the value of the whole premises[11].

When the counter-notice is given in a case where it is not valid, the undertakers may disregard it and proceed with the notice to treat[12], and they will not be bound by the counter-notice, even though it may have been accepted by their solicitors[13]. A valid counter-notice given upon service of an invalid notice to treat, and acted upon, may estop the parties from setting up the invalidity[14].

1   As to the Lands Clauses Acts see para 11 ante.
2   *King v Wycombe Rly Co* (1860) 29 LJ Ch 462; *R v London and South Western Rly Co* (1848) 12 QB 775; *R v London and Greenwich Rly Co* (1842) 3 QB 166; *Wild v Woolwich Borough Council* [1910] 1 Ch 35, CA. As to withdrawal of notices to treat see generally para 120 post.
3   *Ex p Quicke* (1865) 12 LT 580.
4   *Ashton Vale Iron Co Ltd v Bristol Corpn* [1901] 1 Ch 591, CA.
5   *Pinchin v London and Blackwall Rly Co* (1854) 1 K & J 34; on appeal 5 De GM & G 851, 24 LJ Ch 417.
6   *Schwinge v London and Blackwall Rly Co* (1855) 24 LJ Ch 405.
7   *Grierson v Cheshire Lines Committee* (1874) LR 19 Eq 83; *Ashton Vale Iron Co v Bristol Corpn* [1901] 1 Ch 591 at 601, CA.
8   *Barnes v Southsea Rly Co* (1884) 27 ChD 536; *Lavers v LCC* (1905) 93 LT 233; *Marson v London, Chatham and Dover Rly Co* (1869) LR 7 Eq 546.
9   *Richards v Swansea Improvement and Tramways Co* (1878) 9 ChD 425, CA.
10   *King v Wycombe Rly Co* (1860) 29 LJ Ch 462; *Sparrow v Oxford, Worcester and Wolverhampton Rly Co* (1852) 2 De GM & G 94.
11   *Giles v London, Chatham and Dover Rly Co* (1861) 30 LJ Ch 603; *Underwood v Bedford and Cambridge Rly Co* (1861) 7 Jur NS 941; *Gardner v Charing Cross Rly Co* (1861) 2 John & H 248. As to entry see para 122 post.
12   *Harvie v South Devon Rly Co* (1874) 32 LT 1, CA; *Loosemore v Tiverton and North Devon Rly Co* (1882) 22 ChD 25 at 35, 50, CA; on appeal sub nom *Tiverton and North Devon Rly Co v Loosemore* (1884) 9 App Cas 480 at 484, HL.
13   *Treadwell v London and South Western Rly Co* (1884) 54 LJ Ch 565, 51 LT 894.
14   *Pinchin v London and Blackwall Rly Co* (1854) 5 De GM & G 851, 24 LJ Ch 417.

112. Counter-notice where notice to treat under the Compulsory Purchase Act 1965 relates to part of premises. Where the authorisation of the compulsory purchase is by a compulsory purchase order to which the Compulsory Purchase Act 1965 applies[1], no person is required to sell a part only of any house, building or manufactory[2], or of a park[3] or garden[4] belonging to a house, if he is willing and able to sell the whole of those premises, unless the Lands Tribunal determines that:

(1) in the case of a house, building or manufactory, the part proposed to be acquired can be taken without material detriment to the house, building or manufactory; or

(2) in the case of a park or garden, the part proposed to be acquired can be taken without seriously affecting the amenity[5] or convenience of the house[6].

If the tribunal so determines, it must award compensation in respect of any loss due to the severance of the part proposed to be acquired, in addition to its value; and thereupon the party interested is required to sell to the acquiring authority[7] that part of the premises[8].

In determining whether or not there is material detriment as mentioned in head (1) above, or whether or not amenity or convenience is seriously affected as mentioned in head (2) above, the tribunal may consider all the circumstances and the mode and manner in which the property is to be taken[9] and must take into account not only the effect of the severance but also the use to be made of the part proposed to be acquired and, in a case where the part is proposed to be acquired for works or other purposes extending to other land, the effect of the whole of the works and the use to be made of the other land[10].

1 As to such orders see para 15 ante.
2 For the meaning of 'house', 'building' and 'manufactory' see para 110 ante.
3 A 'park' need not be large and land may be a park although it is let for grazing: see *Re Ripon (Highfield) Housing Confirmation Order 1938, White and Collins v Minister of Health* [1939] 2 KB 838, [1939] 3 All ER 548, CA.
4 The 'root idea' of a garden is that it is 'a substantially homogenous area, substantially devoted to the growth of fruits, flowers and vegetables': see *Bomford v Osborne (Inspector of Taxes)* [1942] AC 14 at 40, [1941] 2 All ER 426 at 442, HL, per Lord Wright. Where there is a cultivated garden which is separated from an adjoining piece of rough pasture, the rough pasture cannot be regarded as part of the garden: *Methuen-Campbell v Walters* [1979] QB 525, [1979] 1 All ER 606, CA; and see *McAlpine v Secretary of State for the Environment* (1994) Times, 6 December.
5 As to the meaning of 'amenity' see TOWN AND COUNTRY PLANNING vol 46 (Reissue) para 42 note 4.
6 Compulsory Purchase Act 1965 s 8(1)(a), (b), (i), (ii). See *Ravenseft Properties Ltd v London Borough of Hillingdon* (1968) 20 P & CR 483, Lands Tribunal; *McMillan v Strathclyde Regional Council* [1983] 1 EGLR 188, Lands Tribunal for Scotland. Apart from the provision as to part of a park or garden and the Lands Tribunal's power to determine that the part can be taken without material detriment to the whole, the Compulsory Purchase Act 1965 s 8(1) is in the same terms as the Lands Clauses Consolidation Act 1845 s 92, and, subject to the above differences, the judicial decisions on the latter would appear to apply to the former: see paras 109–111 ante. As to the Lands Tribunal see para 202 et seq post.
7 For the meaning of 'acquiring authority' for these purposes see para 92 note 5 ante.
8 Compulsory Purchase Act 1965 s 8(1). Notice of an application for a determination by the Lands Tribunal must be served on an acquiring authority prior to the authority entering the property: *Glasshouse Properties Ltd v Secretary of State for Transport* (1993) 66 P & CR 285, Lands Tribunal. It seems that the compensation must be awarded on the same principles as compensation for severance etc where no counter-notice has been served: see para 291 et seq post. The Compulsory Purchase Act 1965 s 8(1) is substituted in relation to the compulsory acquisition of rights by, inter alia, (1) a local authority, by the Local Government (Miscellaneous Provisions) Act 1976 s 13(3)(b) (as amended), Sch 1 para 7 (see LOCAL GOVERNMENT vol 28 para 1219); (2) the Development Board for Rural Wales, by the Development of Rural Wales Act 1976 s 6(7) (as amended), Sch 4 para 7 (see TOWN AND COUNTRY PLANNING vol 46 (Reissue) para 1200); (3) urban development corporations, by the Local Government, Planning and Land Act 1980 s 144, Sch 28 para 23(2) (see TOWN AND COUNTRY PLANNING vol 46 (Reissue) para 1297); (4) highway authorities, by the Highways Act 1980 s 250(5)(a) (as substituted), Sch 19 para 7 (see HIGHWAYS vol 21 (Reissue) para 808); (5) public gas suppliers, by the Gas Act 1986 s 9(3), Sch 3 para 8 (see FUEL AND ENERGY vol 19(1) (Reissue) para 636); (6) housing action trusts, by the Housing Act 1988 s 78(2), Sch 10 para 22 (see HOUSING); (7) licence holders under the Electricity Act 1989, by s 10(1), Sch 3 para 9 (see FUEL AND ENERGY vol 19(2) (Reissue) para 985); (8) the National Rivers Authority, by the Water Resources Act 1991 s 154(5), Sch 18 para 4 (see WATER); and (9) water and sewerage undertakers, by the Water Industry Act 1991 s 155(5), Sch 9 para 4 (see WATER). In considering, for the purposes of heads (4)–(5), (7)–(9) supra, the extent of any material detriment to a house, building or manufactory or any extent to which the amenity or convenience of a house is affected, the Lands Tribunal must have regard not only to the right which is to be acquired over the land, but also to any adjoining or adjacent land belonging to the same owner and subject to compulsory purchase: Compulsory Purchase Act 1965 s 8(1A) (substituted as mentioned in those heads).

9 *Re Gouty and Manchester, Sheffield and Lincolnshire Rly Co* [1896] 2 QB 439, CA (decided on a similar decision in a local Act), where the taking of the land would have been materially detrimental by depriving the landowner of access to his remaining land but for the fact that the railway company had given an undertaking not to take his land in such a way as to deprive the landowner of access and to provide a permanent right of way equivalent to the original access; see also *Caledonian Rly Co v Turcan* [1898] AC 256, HL. A special Act may empower the tribunal, if the part proposed to be taken is not severable without material detriment to the whole, to determine whether or not any other part less than the whole is severable without material detriment, and may empower the undertakers to take that other part without being obliged to purchase the whole if it is so severable. For the meaning of 'special Act' see paras 11, 16 ante.

10 Land Compensation Act 1973 s 58(1) (amended by the Compulsory Purchase (Vesting Declarations) Act 1981 s 16(3), Sch 5; and by the Planning (Consequential Provisions) Act 1990 s 4, Sch 2 para 29(10)), which is applied with the necessary modifications (1) by the Land Compensation Act 1973 s 58(2)(a) (amended by the Highways Act 1980 s 343(2), Sch 24 para 23; the Gas Act 1986 s 67(1), Sch 7 para 14(2); the Water Act 1989 s 190(1), Sch 25 para 44(2); and by the Water Consolidation (Consequential Provisions) Act 1991 s 2(1), Sch 1 para 23) to any determination under the Compulsory Purchase Act 1965 s 8(1) substituted as mentioned in note 8 heads (4)–(5), (8)–(9) supra; and (2) by the Land Compensation Act 1973 s 58(2)(b) to any determination under any provision corresponding to or substituted for the Compulsory Purchase Act 1965 s 8(1), contained in, or in an instrument made under, any other enactment passed after the Land Compensation Act 1973: see s 58(2) (as so amended).

113. Intersected land not in a town or built upon. Where any land[1] which is not situated in a town or built upon[2] is cut through and divided by the authorised works so as to leave, either on both sides or on one side of the works[3], less than half an acre of land, the owner of that small piece of land may require the undertakers[4] or acquiring authority[5] to purchase it[6] along with the land subject to compulsory purchase[7], unless the owner has other adjoining land to which it can be joined, so as to be conveniently occupied with it, in which case, if so required by the owner, the undertakers or authority must at their own expense join the piece of land so left to the adjoining land by removing the fences and levelling the sites and by soiling it in a satisfactory and workmanlike manner[8].

1 For the meaning of 'land' see para 92 note 1 ante. See also para 13 text and note 7 ante.
2 'Town' is used in its popular sense, and 'built upon' means continuously built upon, as in a town: *Lord Carington v Wycombe Rly Co* (1868) 3 Ch App 377; *Directors etc of the London and South Western Rly Co v Blackmore* (1870) LR 4 HL 610; *R v Cottle* (1851) 16 QB 412 at 421–422; *Elliott v South Devon Rly Co* (1848) 2 Exch 725. A market garden with a cottage on it is not land built upon: *Falkner v Somerset and Dorset Rly Co* (1873) LR 16 Eq 458.
3 For the meaning of 'the works' see para 92 note 3 ante. See also para 13 text to note 4 ante.
4 For the meaning of 'the undertakers' see para 13 ante.
5 For the meaning of 'acquiring authority' for these purposes see para 92 note 5 ante.
6 As to including this land in a reference as to the purchase price see *Re North Staffordshire Rly Co and Wood* (1848) 2 Exch 244.
7 Lands Clauses Consolidation Act 1845 s 93; Compulsory Purchase Act 1965 s 8(2).
8 Lands Clauses Consolidation Act 1845 s 93 (which uses the phrase 'sufficient and workmanlike manner'); Compulsory Purchase Act 1965 s 8(2) proviso. Section 8 is completely substituted by the provisions mentioned in para 112 note 8 heads (2)–(3), (6) ante, so that the provisions set out in the text and notes 1–7 supra do not apply in relation to the acquisition of rights by the Development Board for Rural Wales, urban development corporations and housing action trusts.

114. Intersected land requiring expensive communications. Where any land[1], whether in a town or not, and whether built upon or not[2], is cut through and divided by the authorised works so as to leave, either on both sides or on one side of the works[3], a quantity of land which is less than half an acre, or of less value than the expense of making a bridge, culvert, or such other communication between the divided land as the undertakers[4] or acquiring authority[5] can be compelled to make under the provisions of the special and incorporated Acts[6], and the owner of the divided lands has no other land adjoining the small piece of land, and he requires the undertakers or the acquiring authority to make the communication, they may require the owner to sell to them the small piece of land[7]. Any dispute as to the value of the piece of land or as to what would be the expense of making the communication must be determined by the Lands Tribunal, and either party to proceedings for determining the compensation to be paid for the land may require the tribunal to make its determination in those proceedings[8].

1 For the meaning of 'land' see para 92 note 1 ante. See also para 13 text to note 7 ante.
2 See para 113 note 2 ante; and *Eastern Counties and London and Blackwall Rly Cos v Marriage* (1860) 9 HL Cas 32.
3 For the meaning of 'the works' see para 92 note 3 ante. See also para 13 text to note 4 ante.
4 For the meaning of 'the undertakers' see para 13 ante.
5 For the meaning of 'acquiring authority' see para 92 note 5 ante.
6 Eg under the Railways Clauses Consolidation Act 1845 s 68: see *Falls v Belfast and Ballymena Rly Co* (1849) 12 ILR 233, Ex Ch. The Compulsory Purchase Act 1965 s 8(3) simply uses the phrase '.... less value than the expense of making the communication between the divided land'. For the meaning of 'special Act' see paras 11, 16 ante.
7 Lands Clauses Consolidation Act 1845 s 94; Compulsory Purchase Act 1965 s 8(3).
8 Lands Clauses Consolidation Act 1845 s 94; Lands Tribunal Act 1949 s 1(3)(b) (amended by the Land Compensation Act 1961 s 40(3), Sch 5); Compulsory Purchase Act 1965 s 8(3). Section 8 is completely substituted by the provisions mentioned in para 112 note 8 heads (2)–(3), (6) ante, so that the provisions set out in the text and notes 1–7 supra do not apply in relation to the acquisition of rights by the Development Board for Rural Wales, urban development corporations and housing action trusts. As to costs in the proceedings see *Cobb v Mid Wales Rly Co* (1866) LR 1 QB 342; and para 227 post. As to the Lands Tribunal see para 202 et seq post.

(iv) Effect of Notice to Treat

115. Relation of parties as vendor and purchaser after notice to treat. The effect of serving a notice to treat is to establish a relation analogous in some respects to that of vendor and purchaser, a relation which binds the owner of the land to give up the land subject to compensation, and which binds the undertakers or acquiring authority to take the land; but there is no contract of sale until the price is ascertained and the land remains the property of the landowner[1]. Both parties have the right to have the price ascertained and the purchase completed in the manner provided by the Lands Clauses Acts[2] or the Compulsory Purchase Act 1965 or any Acts modifying those Acts[3]. The rights and obligations created by the service of the notice to treat are legal as distinct from equitable, and they bind all persons claiming under the owner, whether with notice of the service or not[4].

When the price has been ascertained, the relationship of vendor and purchaser exists between the parties as if there had been an ordinary agreement for sale, and, except so far as excluded by the special Act[5], the parties' rights and duties are the same as those arising out of an ordinary contract for the sale of land[6], including the right to have the contract enforced by specific performance[7], and the owner's interest then, but not before, becomes an interest in personalty[8]. When the price has been fixed, the agreement so constituted is registrable as an estate contract in the land charges register[9], and in the case of registered land may be protected by the registration of a notice[10].

1 *Fotherby v Metropolitan Rly Co* (1866) LR 2 CP 188 at 193; *Haynes v Haynes* (1861) 1 Drew & Sm 426 at 450; *Adams v London and Blackwall Rly Co* (1850) 2 Mac & G 118; *Tiverton and North Devon Rly Co v*

Loosemore (1884) 9 App Cas 480 at 493, 503, 511, HL; *Mercer v Liverpool, St Helen's and South Lancashire Rly Co* [1903] 1 KB 652 at 661, CA, per Stirling LJ; approved [1904] AC 461 at 463, 465, HL; *Cardiff Corpn v Cook* [1923] 2 Ch 115; and see *Edinburgh and District Water Trustees v Clippens Oil Co* (1902) 87 LT 275, HL; *Wild v Woolwich Borough Council* [1910] 1 Ch 35, CA. Quaere whether the Law of Property (Miscellaneous Provisions) Act 1989 s 2 (formalities required for a contract for the sale or other disposition of an interest in land: see LANDLORD AND TENANT vol 27(1) (Reissue) para 56; SPECIFIC PERFORMANCE vol 44(1) (Reissue) para 858; and SALE OF LAND) applies to the contract: see *Munton v GLC* [1976] 2 All ER 815, [1976] 1 WLR 649, CA (the provisions of the Law of Property Act 1925 s 40(1) (repealed) did not so apply).

2 As to the Lands Clauses Acts see para 11 ante.
3 *Fotherby v Metropolitan Rly Co* (1866) LR 2 CP 188; *Tiverton and North Devon Rly Co v Loosemore* (1884) 9 App Cas 480 at 493, HL; and see *R v Hungerford Market Co* (1832) 4 B & Ad 327; *Birch v St Marylebone Vestry* (1869) 20 LT 697. As to the assessment of compensation see paras 197, 233 et seq post.
4 *Mercer v Liverpool, St Helen's and South Lancashire Rly Co* [1903] 1 KB 652 at 662, CA, per Stirling LJ; approved [1904] AC 461 at 463, 465, HL. A claim for compensation by the purchaser of land in respect of which a notice to treat has already been served is not defeated by the submission that the purchaser has already received value for money: *Landlink Two Ltd and Barclays Bank plc v Sevenoaks District Council* (1985) 51 P & CR 100, Lands Tribunal.
5 For the meaning of 'special Act' see paras 11, 16 ante.
6 See the cases cited in note 1 supra. Where negotiations are still 'subject to contract', the agreement as to price will not be binding on the parties: *Munton v GLC* [1976] 2 All ER 815, [1976] 1 WLR 649, CA.
7 *Harding v Metropolitan Rly Co* (1872) 7 Ch App 154. This relationship, together with the right of enforcement, is subject to a right of withdrawal: see paras 120, 135 post. See also the cases cited in para 135 note 5 post.
8 *Haynes v Haynes* (1861) 1 Drew & Sm 426 at 451 et seq. As to the doctrine of conversion see EQUITY vol 16 (Reissue) para 819 et seq.
9 Land Charges Act 1972 s 2(4), Class C(iv). As to the effect of failure to register see LAND CHARGES.
10 Land Registration Act 1925 s 49(1)(c). See further LAND REGISTRATION.

116. Effect of notice to treat on owner's rights and duties.

The owner of an interest in land at the date of the notice to treat continues as owner until there is a contract of sale[1]. He may continue to deal with his interest as he likes and may sell, convey or otherwise deal with it[2], and it is for him, and not the undertakers or acquiring authority, to insure the premises[3].

The owner may not, however, increase the burden of compensation payable by the undertakers or acquiring authority either by the creation of a new interest in the land taken or the land held with it[4] or by effecting improvements to the land so as to alter the quality of the subject matter[5]. There would therefore be no obligation to serve a notice to treat in respect of any such new interest[6]. This restriction on the person served with a notice to treat relates to the creation of an interest and, as a person served with that notice can sell or convey it or otherwise deal with it, there is nothing to prevent the owner of a freehold interest determining or acquiring any leasehold interest or the owner of a leasehold interest acquiring the freehold[7].

Additional provision to similar effect is made by statute in certain cases. Where there is an acquisition under a compulsory purchase order to which the Acquisition of Land Act 1981 applies[8], the Lands Tribunal may not take into account any interest in land[9], or any enhancement of the value of any interest in land, by reason of any building erected, work done or improvement or alteration made, whether on the land purchased or on any other land with which the claimant is, or was at the time of the erection, doing or making of the building, works, improvement or alteration, directly or indirectly concerned, if the tribunal is satisfied that the creation of the interest[10], the erection of the building, the doing of the work, the making of the improvement or the alteration, as the case may be, was not reasonably necessary and was undertaken with a view to obtaining compensation or increased compensation[11].

1 See para 115 text and note 1 ante.
2 *Mercer v Liverpool, St Helen's and South Lancashire Rly Co* [1904] AC 461, HL; *Dawson v Great Northern and City Rly Co* [1905] 1 KB 260 at 268–269, CA; *Sewell v Harrow and Uxbridge Rly Co* (1902) 19 TLR 130; on appeal (1903) 20 TLR 21, CA; *Carnochan v Norwich and Spalding Rly Co* (1858) 26 Beav 169; *Cardiff Corpn v Cook* [1923] 2 Ch 115; and cf *Metropolitan Rly Co v Woodhouse* (1865) 34 LJ Ch 297.
3 See *Birmingham Corpn v West Midland Baptist (Trust) Association (Inc)* [1970] AC 874 at 899, 908, 911, [1969] 3 All ER 172 at 180, 187, 190, HL, overruling *Phoenix Assurance Co v Spooner* [1905] 2 KB 753. See also *Matthey v Curling* [1922] 2 AC 180, HL; *Re King, Robinson v Gray* [1963] Ch 459, [1963] 1 All ER 781, CA, as to the lessor's and lessee's rights as to insurance money payable after a fire.
4 As to such land and the right to compensation for severance or other injurious affection in respect of it see *Mercer v Liverpool, St Helen's and South Lancashire Rly Co* [1904] AC 461, HL; and para 291 post.
5 *Mercer v Liverpool, St Helen's and South Lancashire Rly Co* [1904] AC 461 at 465, HL, per Lord Lindley; *Cardiff Corpn v Cook* [1923] 2 Ch 115; *Re Marylebone (Stingo Lane) Improvement Act, ex p Edwards* (1871) LR 12 Eq 389; and see *Johnson v Edgware, Highgate and London Rly Co* (1866) 35 Beav 480, 14 LT 45; *Wilkins v Birmingham Corpn* (1883) 25 ChD 78. As to weekly tenants let in after the notice to treat having no right to compensation see *Re Marylebone (Stingo Lane) Improvement Act, ex p Edwards* supra. If such an interest is created, the compensation payable in respect of the interest out of which it is created is deemed to include the value of the new interest (see *Mercer v Liverpool, St Helen's and South Lancashire Rly Co* supra), and where the undertakers or acquiring authority as owners use their power of taking possession (see paras 123, 129 post) with respect to the new interest there would be eviction by title paramount (see *Cuthbertson v Irving* (1859) 4 H & N 742; affd (1860) 6 H & N 135) and the lessee would have no claim on his lessor (see *Manchester, Sheffield and Lincolnshire Rly Co v Anderson* [1898] 2 Ch 394, CA) unless the lessor had failed to disclose the existence of the compulsory purchase order and the notice to treat when creating the interest (see *Walton Harvey Ltd v Walker and Homfrays Ltd* [1931] 1 Ch 274, CA). The principle that the owner may not deal with his property so as to increase the undertakers' or acquiring authority's burden after service of a notice to treat applies equally to dealings with undertakings liable to compulsory acquisition in accordance with an Act of Parliament: see *Chocolate Express Omnibus Co v London Passenger Transport Board* (1934) 152 LT 63, CA.
6 Otherwise, if the owner so created an interest after the time for exercising the compulsory powers had expired, the undertakers or acquiring authority would be saddled with the interest with no power to acquire it compulsorily.
7 It was not unusual for undertakers or an acquiring authority to induce the landlord to terminate a tenancy (see para 180 post), or for a mortgagor to redeem the equity of redemption or to purchase the mortgagee's interest (see para 193 post). As to an ineffective surrender see *Zick v London United Tramways Ltd* [1908] 2 KB 126, CA; and as to the use of covenants by the lessor to obtain possession see para 117 post. As to the effect of the termination of a tenancy on the valuation of an interest see para 285 post.
8 As to such orders see the Acquisition of Land Act 1981 s 1 (as amended), s 2; and paras 33–34 ante.
9 For the meaning of 'land' see para 28 note 3 ante.
10 This would not be apt to effect an interest created after a notice to treat and excluded under the above provisions. There is no restriction on the termination of an interest or on its assignment.
11 Acquisition of Land Act 1981 s 4(1), (2). Section 4 is applied by, inter alia, the Water Industry Act 1991 s 167, Sch 11 para 6; and by the Water Resources Act 1991 s 168, Sch 19 para 6: see WATER. The increase in the acquiring authority's burden in respect of compensation which is so prohibited must arise from the alteration of the land or the creation of a new interest, and does not apply to the termination of an interest: see *Birmingham Corpn v West Midland Baptist (Trust) Association (Inc)* [1970] AC 874 at 893, 904, [1969] 3 All ER 172 at 175, 184, HL; *R v Kennedy* [1893] 1 QB 533; and the cases cited in note 5 supra. See, however, *Banham v London Borough of Hackney* (1970) 22 P & CR 922, Lands Tribunal, where the tribunal found it necessary to consider whether the termination of an interest increased the burden.

117. Effect of notice to treat on other interests. The service of a notice to treat on the owner of the interest in the land does not frustrate an enforceable contract of sale, and the purchaser is also entitled to a notice to treat[1]. A person entitled to an interest in land under a building agreement is not affected but is entitled to a notice to treat[2]. The liability of a lessee under covenants in the lease is not affected by the service of a notice to treat for his interest[3]. The lessor is entitled to the benefit of the covenants until the conveyance of his interest, and is entitled to recover damages for breaches of covenant by the lessee occurring before the conveyance of the lessor's interest, although he is not so entitled afterwards[4].

If a lease contains a proviso that if any part of the land leased is compulsorily acquired the lessor may re-enter and repossess it, the service of a notice to treat brings the proviso into operation[5], but where the lease contains a proviso enabling the lessor to re-enter for the purpose of building, the lessor cannot take advantage of the proviso to enhance the value of his interest[6].

1 *Hillingdon Estates Co v Stonefield Estates Ltd* [1952] Ch 627, [1952] 1 All ER 853.
2 *Birmingham and District Land Co v London and North Western Rly Co* (1888) 40 ChD 268, CA; *Re Furness and Willesden UDC* (1905) 70 JP 25.
3 *Mills v East London Union* (1872) LR 8 CP 79; *Harding v Metropolitan Rly Co* (1872) 7 Ch App 154; *Matthey v Curling* [1922] 2 AC 180, HL. The lessee remains liable after the assignment of his interest (but is entitled on that assignment to the usual covenants for indemnity) unless the tenancy is a new tenancy to which the Landlord and Tenant (Covenants) Act 1995 s 5 (tenant released from covenants on assignment of tenancy) applies, ie a new tenancy granted on or after 1 January 1996 otherwise than in pursuance of an agreement entered into, or a court order made, before that date: see ss 1(1), (3), 31(1); and the Landlord and Tenant (Covenants) Act 1995 (Commencement) Order 1995, SI 1995/2963.
4 *Re King, Robinson v Gray* [1963] Ch 459 at 488, 497, [1963] 1 All ER 781 at 792–793, 798, CA.
5 *Re Morgan and London and North Western Rly Co* [1896] 2 QB 469; *Re Athlone Rifle Range* [1902] 1 IR 433.
6 *Johnson v Edgware, Highgate and London Rly Co* (1866) 35 Beav 480, 14 LT 45.

118. Right to assessment of compensation. A person served with a notice to treat has the right to have the price ascertained and the purchase completed in accordance with statute[1].

The notice to treat confers the right to have the compensation ascertained in respect of all the land mentioned in it, and all the subsequent proceedings must have relation to the whole of the land to which the notice to treat refers[2]. Without the consent of the other, neither party can have the value of part only of the land assessed[3]. Each person on whom a notice to treat is served is entitled to have the compensation as regards his own particular interest assessed separately[4].

The right to the compensation to be assessed may be assigned and dealt with as property[5], but the sum which may be due is not a debt which can be attached by garnishee order until the conveyance has in fact been executed[6].

1 See para 115 text and notes 2–3 ante.
2 *Stone v Commercial Rly Co* (1839) 4 My & Cr 122; *Ecclesiastical Comrs v London Sewers Comrs* (1880) 14 ChD 305; *Ex p Bailey* (1852) Bail Ct Cas 66.
3 *Thompson v Tottenham and Forest Gate Rly Co* (1892) 67 LT 416.
4 See *Abrahams v London Corpn* (1868) LR 6 Eq 625.
5 *Dawson v Great Northern and City Rly Co* [1905] 1 KB 260 at 271, CA.
6 *Richardson v Elmit* (1876) 2 CPD 9; *Howell v Metropolitan District Rly Co* (1881) 19 ChD 508.

119. Time of valuation. The value of the land must be assessed at the prices current at the time of entry, agreement or assessment, whichever is the earliest; what is to be valued is the land and the interests in it at that time[1], subject to the rule that interests created or works beyond the necessities of continued enjoyment by the owner after service of the notice to treat, which add to the undertakers' or acquiring authority's burdens[2], must be disregarded; and interests created or works executed for the purpose of increasing compensation must be disregarded where the Acquisition of Land Act 1981 applies[3].

1   *Birmingham Corpn v West Midland Baptist (Trust) Association (Inc)* [1970] AC 874 at 899, 907, 911, [1969] 3 All ER 172 at 180, 187, 190, HL; applied in *Munton v GLC* [1976] 2 All ER 815, [1976] 1 WLR 649, CA. In a case where possession of land has been taken in separate parcels at different dates, the date for assessment of compensation is the date of the first taking of possession: *Chilton v Telford Development Corpn* [1987] 3 All ER 992, [1987] 1 WLR 872, CA. Where there is an appeal, compensation is assessed according to the market value at the date of the original hearing: *Hoveringham Gravels Ltd v Chiltern District Council* (1978) 39 P & CR 414, Lands Tribunal; *Washington Development Corpn v Bamlings (Washington) Ltd* (1984) 52 P & CR 267, [1985] 1 EGLR 16, CA (possession of land taken piecemeal).

2   *Birmingham Corpn v West Midland Baptist (Trust) Association (Inc)* [1970] AC 874 at 899, 904–905, 910, [1969] 3 All ER 172 at 180, 184–185, 189, HL.

3   See the authority cited in note 2 supra; and para 116 ante.

120. Withdrawal of notice to treat. Neither party can avoid the obligation imposed by a notice to treat without the consent of the other[1] unless the notice is withdrawn in accordance with a statutory power to do so. The right to withdraw, arising when the party served with the notice is entitled to require the undertakers to take more land than they desire and does so require[2], amounts to withdrawal by consent[3].

Where the person served with a notice to treat[4] has delivered to the acquiring authority[5] a notice in writing of the amount claimed by him containing the necessary particulars of the nature of his interest and the details of the amount claimed in time so as to enable the authority to make a proper offer[6], the authority may, at any time within six weeks after delivery of the notice of claim for compensation, withdraw any notice to treat served on the claimant or on any other person interested in the land authorised to be acquired[7]. The authority is, however, then liable to pay compensation to the claimant or other person for any loss[8] or expenses occasioned to him by the giving and withdrawal of the notice[9].

If the claimant fails to deliver a proper notice of claim[10], the acquiring authority may withdraw any notice to treat which has been served on him, or on any other person interested in the land authorised to be acquired, at any time after the decision of the Lands Tribunal on his claim but not later than six weeks after the final determination of the claim by the tribunal[11], unless the authority has entered into possession of the land by virtue of the notice to treat[12]. The person served with the notice to treat will be entitled to compensation for any loss or expense incurred before the time when, in the tribunal's opinion, a proper notice of claim should have been delivered[13]. So long as the authority is entitled to withdraw a notice to treat under this power, it cannot be compelled to take the land to which the notice relates or to pay any compensation awarded in respect of the taking[14].

Power to withdraw a notice to treat may also be given by the special Act[15].

The above powers to withdraw a notice to treat may be excluded[16].

1   *Haynes v Haynes* (1861) 1 Drew & Sm 426 at 456; *Tiverton and North Devon Rly Co v Loosemore* (1884) 9 App Cas 480 at 506, 516, HL; *Tawney v Lynn and Ely Rly Co* (1847) 16 LJ Ch 282. The consent may be implied from the conduct of the parties.

2   Eg to take a whole house, when part only is required: see para 109 ante.

3   *Wild v Woolwich Borough Council* [1910] 1 Ch 35, CA. See also para 121 post.

4   In relation to a compulsory acquisition in pursuance of a notice to treat, 'the notice to treat' means the notice to treat in pursuance of which the relevant interest is acquired: Land Compensation Act 1961 s 39(2). 'The relevant interest' means the interest acquired in pursuance of that notice: s 39(2). References in the 1961 Act to a notice to treat include references to a notice to treat which, under any enactment, is deemed to have been served, and references to the service of such a notice and to the date of service are to be construed accordingly: s 39(8). For the meaning of 'enactment' see para 1 note 3 ante. Any reference in s 39(2) to a notice to treat is to be construed, in relation to (1) the vesting of land in an urban development corporation, as a reference to a notice under the Local Government, Planning

and Land Act 1980 s 141 (as amended) (see TOWN AND COUNTRY PLANNING vol 46 (Reissue) para 1296) (s 141(5), Sch 27 paras 9, 13); (2) the vesting of land in a housing action trust, as a reference to an order under the Housing Act 1988 s 76 (see HOUSING) (s 76(6), Sch 9 paras 6, 10); (3) the vesting of land in the Urban Regeneration Agency, as a reference to an order under the Leasehold Reform, Housing and Urban Development Act 1993 s 161(1) (see TRADE, INDUSTRY AND INDUSTRIAL RELATIONS vol 47 (Reissue) para 851) (s 161(4), Sch 19 paras 1, 5); and references in the Land Compensation Act 1961 to the date of service of a notice to treat are to be treated for those purposes as references to the date on which the relevant order comes into force (see the Local Government, Planning and Land Act 1980 Sch 27 para 10; the Housing Act 1988 Sch 9 para 7; and the Leasehold Reform, Housing and Urban Development Act 1993 Sch 19 para 2).

 5 For these purposes, 'acquiring authority', in relation to an interest in land, means the person or body of persons by whom the interest is, or is proposed to be, acquired: Land Compensation Act 1961 s 39(1). For the meaning of 'land' see para 18 note 2 ante.
 6 Ie a notice under ibid s 4(1)(b), (2): see para 198 post.
 7 Ibid s 31(1). The notice may be withdrawn even after possession has been taken and an adequate payment made: *R v Northumbrian Water Ltd, ex p Able UK Ltd* [1995] TLR 683. In such an event the advance payment is returnable: *R v Northumbrian Water Ltd, ex p Able UK Ltd* supra.
 8 As to such loss see *Duke of Grafton v Secretary of State for Air* (1956) 6 P & CR 374, CA (surveyor's fees); *LCC v Montague Burton Ltd* [1934] 1 KB 360, DC (ground rent and interest on money borrowed).
 9 Land Compensation Act 1961 s 31(3). Compensation payable under s 31(3) carries interest at the rate for the time being prescribed under s 32 (see para 125 post) from the date of the withdrawal of the notice to treat: Planning and Compensation Act 1991 s 80(1), Sch 18 Pt I. Payments on account may be made of such compensation or interest (s 80(2)) and may be recoverable where it is subsequently agreed or determined that there was no liability to pay the compensation or interest or that the payment on account was excessive (s 80(3)). In default of agreement the amount of the compensation must be determined by the Lands Tribunal: Land Compensation Act 1961 s 31(4). The Lands Tribunal has jurisdiction to consider a disputed compensation claim even where the requirements of s 31 have not been met, if the parties have agreed that the acquiring authority can withdraw its notice to treat on condition that the landowner is to be compensated for proven losses: *Williams v Blaenau Gwent Borough Council* (1994) 67 P & CR 393, Lands Tribunal. As to the tribunal see para 202 et seq post.
10 See the text to note 6 supra.
11 The claim is not to be deemed to be finally determined so long as the time for requiring the Lands Tribunal to state a case with respect to it, or for appealing from any decision on the points raised by a case so stated, has not expired: Land Compensation Act 1961 s 31(6).
12 Ibid s 31(2).
13 Ibid s 31(3). As to the compensation see the text and note 9 supra; and see *Methodist Church Trustees v North Tyneside Metropolitan Borough Council* (1979) 38 P & CR 665.
14 Land Compensation Act 1961 s 31(5).
15 See eg the Small Holdings and Allotments Act 1908 s 39(8) (as amended); and ALLOTMENTS vol 2 (Reissue) para 26; and see *R v Woods and Forests Comrs* (1850) 15 QB 761 at 774. For the meaning of 'special Act' see paras 11, 16 ante.
16 Land Compensation Act 1961 s 40(2)(a). For provisions excluding the power, mostly in relation to notices deemed to have been served, see the Agriculture Act 1967 s 49(7)(ii); and AGRICULTURE vol 1(2) (Reissue) para 534 note 5; the Forestry Act 1967 s 22(5); and FORESTRY vol 19(1) (Reissue) para 70; the Town and Country Planning Act 1990 ss 139(5), 143(8), 146(6), 167; and TOWN AND COUNTRY PLANNING vol 46 (Reissue) paras 721, 725, 727, 749. See also the Land Compensation Act 1973 s 54(4); and para 107 ante; the Compulsory Purchase (Vesting Declarations) Act 1981 s 7(3); and para 171 post.

121. Effect of failure to take subsequent steps after notice to treat. A party who, by laches or misconduct, delays the completion of the quasi-contract to purchase may thereby deprive himself of the right to enforce the notice to treat[1]. Similarly, the conduct of the parties may amount to a waiver of their rights under the notice, as, for example, if after some delay the acquiring authority informs the owner of the land of its intention to abandon the undertaking[2]. The implied acceptance of an invalid notice as valid, by proceeding as if it were valid, may prevent the parties from contesting its validity at a later stage[3].

1 *Grice v Dudley Corpn* [1958] Ch 329, [1957] 2 All ER 673. A railway undertaker might do so by delaying to complete until the time for executing the authorised works had expired: *Tiverton and North Devon Rly Co v Loosemore* (1884) 9 App Cas 480 at 496, HL; *Richmond v North London Rly Co* (1868) LR 5 Eq 352; affd 3 Ch App 679 at 680 per Lord Cairns LC. A special power was given by the Town and Country Planning Act 1959 s 14 (repealed) to take steps to acquire land under long-standing notices to treat given before 6 August 1947 without affecting the question as to the validity of the notice to treat.

2 *Hedges v Metropolitan Rly Co* (1860) 28 Beav 109; *Stretton v Great Western and Brentford Rly Co* (1870) 5 Ch App 751. Thus, in an action by the undertakers to ascertain the validity of a notice to treat, the landowner is entitled to raise the defence that the undertakers have improperly depreciated the value of the property: *London Corpn v Horner* (1914) 111 LT 512, CA.

3 *Lynch v London Sewers Comrs* (1886) 32 ChD 72, CA; *R v South Holland Drainage Committee Men* (1838) 8 Ad & El 429; *Pinchin v London and Blackwall Rly Co* (1854) 5 De GM & G 851, 24 LJ Ch 417.

(4) ENTRY BEFORE COMPLETION

(i) Entry with Owner's Consent or after Payment of Compensation

122. Necessity for consent or payment. Except with the consent of the owners and occupiers[1], the undertakers[2] or acquiring authority[3] may not enter upon any of the land subject to compulsory purchase[4] until the compensation payable for the respective interests in the land has been agreed or awarded and has been paid to the persons having those interests or paid into court[5]. The undertakers or acquiring authority may, however, enter and use the land without having paid the compensation upon making certain payments into court by way of security and giving bonds[6]. Furthermore, some special Acts[7], and the Compulsory Purchase Act 1965 in its application to acquisitions authorised by a compulsory purchase order[8], provide for entry after service of a notice to treat without such payment into court[9].

If the undertakers are authorised by the special Act to enter upon land for the purpose of acquiring an interest in it, such as the appropriation and use of the subsoil in order to make a tunnel, they can only make the entry on such of the above conditions as apply to the particular authorisation[10]. Where the special Act enables the acquiring authority to compel the creation of an easement, an entry on land for the purpose of creating those easements is subject to the above limitations and conditions[11]. Some special Acts authorise the entry on land in order to acquire certain rights and to do certain work, as, for example, to lay pipes[12] without purchasing land or any easement over it, in which case the undertakers can enter without complying with the above conditions[13].

1 Once given, the consent cannot be withdrawn: see *Knapp v London, Chatham and Dover Rly Co* (1863) 2 H & C 212; and para 128 note 4 post. For a temporary purpose the occupier's consent may be sufficient: *Standish v Liverpool Corpn* (1852) 1 Drew 1.

2 For the meaning of 'the undertakers' see para 13 ante.

3 For the meaning of 'acquiring authority' for these purposes see para 92 note 5 ante.

4 Where the Lands Clauses Consolidation Act 1845 is incorporated (see para 11 ante), the land is that which the undertakers are empowered to take and which is required to be permanently used; and under certain Acts land may be required for temporary purposes: see eg the Railways Clauses Consolidation Act 1845 ss 30–44; and RAILWAYS. Where the Compulsory Purchase Act 1965 applies (see para 15 ante), the land is the land the compulsory purchase of which is authorised by the compulsory purchase order: see para 92 note 2 ante. For the meaning of 'land' see para 92 note 1 ante. See also para 13 text to note 7 ante.

5 Lands Clauses Consolidation Act 1845 s 84 (amended by the Administration of Justice Act 1965 s 17(1), Sch 1); Compulsory Purchase Act 1965 s 11(4). As to payment into court see paras 98 note 6 ante, 124 post. Section 11 (as amended) is modified in relation to the compulsory acquisition of rights by, inter alia, (1) a local authority, by the Local Government (Miscellaneous Provisions) Act 1976 s 13(3)(b) (as

amended), Sch 1 para 9 (see LOCAL GOVERNMENT vol 28 para 1219); (2) the Development Board for Rural Wales, by the Development of Rural Wales Act 1976 s 6(7) (as amended), Sch 4 para 9 (see TOWN AND COUNTRY PLANNING vol 46 (Reissue) para 1200); (3) urban development corporations, by the Local Government, Planning and Land Act 1980 s 144, Sch 28 para 23(4) (see TOWN AND COUNTRY PLANNING vol 46 (Reissue) para 1297); (4) highway authorities, by the Highways Act 1980 s 250(5)(a) (as substituted), Sch 19 para 9 (see HIGHWAYS vol 21 (Reissue) para 808); (5) public gas suppliers, by the Gas Act 1986 s 9(3), Sch 3 para 10 (see FUEL AND ENERGY vol 19(1) (Reissue) para 636); (6) housing action trusts, by the Housing Act 1988 s 78(2), Sch 10 para 23(2) (see HOUSING); (7) licence holders under the Electricity Act 1989, by s 10(1), Sch 3 para 11 (see FUEL AND ENERGY vol 19(2) (Reissue) para 985); (8) the National Rivers Authority, by the Water Resources Act 1991 s 154(5), Sch 18 para 6 (see WATER); and (9) water and sewerage undertakers, by the Water Industry Act 1991 s 155(5), Sch 9 para 6 (see WATER). See also para 123 et seq post.

6   See para 124 post.
7   For the meaning of 'special Act' see paras 11, 16 ante.
8   As to compulsory purchase orders see para 33 et seq ante.
9   See para 129 post. A notice to treat is not rendered invalid by reason of its being served after the authority has taken possession of the land: *Cohen v Haringey London Borough Council* (1980) 42 P & CR 6, CA.
10   *Farmer v Waterloo and City Rly Co* [1895] 1 Ch 527, applying *Metropolitan Rly Co v Fowler* [1893] AC 416 at 423, HL; and see *Spencer v Metropolitan Board of Works* (1882) 22 ChD 142, CA.
11   *Hill v Midland Rly Co* (1882) 21 ChD 143, as explained in *Great Western Rly Co v Swindon and Cheltenham Rly Co* (1884) 9 App Cas 787 at 802, 811, HL. See also *Midland Rly Co v Great Western Rly Co* [1909] AC 445, HL. The interference with an easement over the land taken is not an entry on land for the purposes of requiring the conditions for entry before completion to apply as respects the person entitled to the easement: *Clark v London School Board* (1874) 9 Ch App 120 at 124; *Bush v Trowbridge Waterworks Co* (1875) 10 Ch App 459; and see para 30 ante.
12   See eg the Water Industry Act 1991 s 158 (as amended), s 159; and WATER.
13   *Roderick v Aston Local Board* (1877) 5 ChD 328, CA; *North London Rly Co v Metropolitan Board of Works* (1859) 28 LJ Ch 909.

(ii) Entry without Consent or Payment, on Payment into Court or Bond

123. Entry on payment into court; bond securing purchase money. When the undertakers[1] or acquiring authority[2] desire[3] to enter upon and use, without consent, any of the land[4] which they require to purchase before an agreement has been come to or award made for the purchase money or compensation to be paid by them in respect of that land, they may do so, without having first paid or deposited the purchase money or compensation, on the terms of (1) paying into the Supreme Court by way of security either the amount of purchase money or compensation claimed by any party interested or entitled to sell and convey the land ('the owner')[5] who does not consent to that entry[6] or such a sum as is determined by an able practical surveyor[7] to be the value of that land, or of the interest in it which that party is entitled or able to sell and convey; and (2) delivering a bond with sureties[8] for a sum equal to the sum so deposited[9].

The value of the land to be so determined includes the damage by severance or other injurious affection so far as it can be estimated, as well as the value of the land itself[10]. The surveyor should properly examine the premises so as to form a fair judgment[11]; if he does so in good faith, the fact that the sum is inadequate, or that he valued without sufficient knowledge of the relevant facts, does not entitle the owner to an injunction restraining the undertakers or acquiring authority from taking possession of the land pending a proper valuation[12]. When the undertakers or authority are authorised to purchase a right in land the surveyor determines only the value of that right, and not of the whole land[13]. If there is a dispute as to the title, but both claimants are known, the amount must be settled by the appropriate procedure before the land can be vested in the undertakers[14].

1 For the meaning of 'the undertakers' see para 13 ante.
2 For the meaning of 'acquiring authority' for these purposes see para 92 note 5 ante.
3 The power of entry after deposit and bond does not appear to be confined to cases of urgent necessity: see *Loosemore v Tiverton and North Devon Rly Co* (1882) 22 ChD 25 at 39, 46, CA; on appeal sub nom *Tiverton and North Devon Rly Co v Loosemore* (1884) 9 App Cas 480, HL.
4 For the meaning of 'land' see para 92 note 1 ante. See also para 13 text to note 7 ante.
5 As to such persons see para 96 ante.
6 As to payment into court see paras 98 note 6 ante, 124 post.
7 Where the Lands Clauses Consolidation Act 1845 is incorporated (see para 11 ante), the surveyor must be appointed by two justices of the peace acting together: s 85 (the Lands Tribunal Act 1949 s 1(6) (as amended) (see para 200 post) does not in terms transfer the power of appointment). So also where the Compulsory Purchase Act 1965 applies (see para 15 ante), the surveyor must be appointed by two justices of the peace, acting together: s 11(2), Sch 3 para 2(2). Notice of an application to appoint a surveyor need not be given to the owner of the land: see *Bridges v Wilts, Somerset and Weymouth Rly Co* (1847) 16 LJ Ch 335; *Langham v Great Northern Rly Co* (1848) 1 De G & Sm 486 at 499.
8 As to bonds see para 125 post.
9 Lands Clauses Consolidation Act 1845 s 85 (amended by the Administration of Justice Act 1965 s 17(1), Sch 1); Compulsory Purchase Act 1965 s 25(1), Sch 3 paras 1, 2(1), 3(1). Where the undertakers or acquiring authority are required to take the whole of the premises after serving a notice to treat for part of them, the deposit must be the value of the whole: *Giles v London Chatham and Dover Rly Co* (1861) 30 LJ Ch 603; *Underwood v Bedford and Cambridge Rly Co* (1861) 7 Jur NS 941; *Gardner v Charing Cross Rly Co* (1861) 2 John & H 248. Where one notice to treat is served in respect of several parcels of land, the undertakers or authority must deposit the value of the whole before entering some only of the parcels: *Barker v North Staffordshire Rly Co* (1848) 5 Ry & Can Cas 401, 2 De G & Sm 55; *Ford v Plymouth, Devonport and South Western Junction Rly Co* (1848).
10 *Field v Carnarvon and Llanberis Rly Co* (1867) LR 5 Eq 190.
11 *Cotter v Metropolitan Rly Co* (1864) 4 New Rep 454, 12 WR 1021. See also *Barker v North Staffordshire Rly Co* (1848) 5 Ry & Can Cas 401, 2 De G & Sm 55; *Stamps v Birmingham, Wolverhampton and Stour Valley Rly Co* (1848) 7 Hare 251 at 256; on appeal on other grounds 2 Ph 673.
12 *River Roden Co Ltd v Barking Town UDC* (1902) 18 TLR 608, CA.
13 *Hill v Midland Rly Co* (1882) 21 ChD 143; and see *Lambert v Dublin, Wicklow and Wexford Rly Co* (1890) 25 LR Ir 163. See also *Loosemore v Tiverton and North Devon Rly Co* (1882) 22 ChD 25 at 42–43, CA; on appeal sub nom *Tiverton and North Devon Rly Co v Loosemore* (1884) 9 App Cas 480, HL; *Ex p Neath and Brecon Rly Co* (1876) 2 ChD 201 (minerals excluded).
14 *Ex p London and South Western Rly Co* (1869) 38 LJ Ch 527; *Re Lowestoft Manor and Great Eastern Rly Co, ex p Reeve* (1883) 24 ChD 253, CA.

124. Payment into court. The deposit is made by paying the money into the Supreme Court[1]. One or more accounts must be opened and kept in the Accountant General's name at such bank or banks as may be designated by the Lord Chancellor with Treasury concurrence[2]. Lodgments of money are made directly to the bank to the credit of the Accountant General's account[3]. Where the money lodged directly with the bank has been received and credited to the Accountant General's account, the bank must certify on the lodgment direction[4] that funds have been lodged and must send it to the Court Funds Office[5]. The deposit is for the benefit of the persons interested and is subject to the control and disposition of the High Court[6].

1 Lands Clauses Consolidation Act 1845 s 85 (amended by the Administration of Justice Act 1965 s 17(1), Sch 1) (where that Act is incorporated: see para 11 ante); Compulsory Purchase Act 1965 s 25(1).
2 Administration of Justice Act 1982 s 38(2). As to the Treasury see CONSTITUTIONAL LAW.
3 Court Funds Rules 1987 r 16(5).
4 Ie the lodgment direction issued under ibid r 14: see r 18.
5 Ibid r 18.
6 See para 126 post. As to the payment of costs see *Re London, Brighton and South Coast Rly Co, ex p Flower* (1866) 1 Ch App 599; *Ex p Morris* (1871) LR 12 Eq 418; *Charlton v Rolleston* (1884) 28 ChD 237, CA.

125. Bond. In addition to making the deposit[1], the undertakers[2] or acquiring authority[3] must give or tender to the owner a bond under their common or official seal if they are a corporation, or if not, then under the hands and seals of them or any two of them, with two sufficient sureties[4], in a penal sum equal to the sum to be deposited, conditioned for payment to the owner, or for payment into the Supreme Court, of all the purchase money or compensation which may be agreed or awarded, together with interest on it[5], from the time of entering on the land[6] until the purchase money or compensation is paid to that party or into court[7].

1　See para 124 ante.
2　For the meaning of 'the undertakers' see para 13 ante.
3　For the meaning of 'acquiring authority' see para 92 note 5 ante.
4　Where the parties do not agree as to the sureties they must be approved by two justices: Lands Clauses Consolidation Act 1845 s 85; Compulsory Purchase Act 1965 s 11(2), Sch 3 para 3(3). As to the procedure see *Bridges v Wilts, Somerset and Weymouth Rly Co* (1847) 16 LJ Ch 335; and as to the undertakers' solicitors acting as sureties see *Langham v Great Northern Rly Co* (1848) 1 De G & Sm 486. In special Acts it is often provided that the bond shall be sufficient without the addition of any sureties. For the meaning of 'special Act' see paras 11, 16 ante.
5　The rate of interest is that prescribed by regulations under the Land Compensation Act 1961 s 32. With effect from 31 December 1995, the Acquisition of Land (Rate of Interest after Entry) Regulations 1995, SI 1995/2262, prescribe a rate of 0.5% below the standard rate: reg 2(1). For these purposes, the standard rate is: (1) the base rate quoted by the reference banks and effective on the reference day most recently preceding the day on which entry onto the land has been made or, where that day is a reference day, such reference day; and (2) the base rate quoted by the reference banks and effective on each subsequent reference day preceding payment of compensation: regs 1, 2(2). If different base rates are quoted by different banks and effective on a reference day, the rate which, when the base rate quoted by each reference bank is ranked in a descending sequence of seven, is fourth in the sequence is to be used to obtain the standard rate: reg 2(3). If more than one base rate is quoted by a reference bank and effective on a reference day, the last quoted rate is to be treated as the base rate quoted by that reference bank and effective on that day: reg 2(4). The reference banks, in relation to any reference day, are the seven largest institutions authorised by the Bank of England under the Banking Act 1987 and incorporated in and carrying on a deposit-taking business in the United Kingdom which quote a base rate in sterling effective as mentioned in reg 2(2)–(4); and the size of an institution is to be determined by reference to its total consolidated gross assets (together with any subsidiary within the meaning of the Companies Act 1985 s 736 (as substituted: see COMPANIES)) denominated in sterling, as shown in its audited end-year accounts last published before the relevant day: Acquisition of Land (Rate of Interest after Entry) Regulations 1995 reg 2(5), (6). The reference days are 31 March, 30 June, 30 September and 31 December or, if any such day is not a business day, the next business day: reg 2(7). For the meaning of 'United Kingdom' see para 100 note 21 ante.
　　Payments on account may be made of any interest payable on any such bond, which are recoverable if the payments are subsequently agreed or determined not to be due, or shown to be excessive: see the Planning and Compensation Act 1991 s 80(2), (3).
6　For the meaning of 'land' see para 92 note 1 ante. See also para 13 text to note 7 ante.
7　Lands Clauses Consolidation Act 1845 s 85 (amended by the Administration of Justice Act 1965 s 17(1), Sch 1); Compulsory Purchase Act 1965 ss 11(2), 25(1), Sch 3 para 3(1)–(3). As to variations and additions in the form of the bond see *Hosking v Phillips* (1848) 3 Exch 168; *Poynder v Great Northern Rly Co* (1847) 2 Ph 330; *Langham v Great Northern Rly Co* (1848) 1 De G & Sm 486; *Cotter v Metropolitan Rly Co* (1864) 4 New Rep 454, 12 WR 1021; *Willey v South Eastern Rly Co* (1849) 1 Mac & G 58.

126. Application of money paid in until performance of bond. The money paid into court[1] must remain there by way of security to the parties whose land has been entered upon, for the performance of the condition of the bond given by the undertakers or the acquiring authority[2]. If dealt with under the Administration of Justice Act 1982[3], the money must be accumulated and, upon the condition of the bond being fully performed, the Chancery Division of the High Court may, on the application by summons[4] of the undertakers[5] or the acquiring authority[6], order the money or the proceeds of the securities in which it has been invested together with the accumulation of it to be paid to the undertakers or the authority[7]. If the condition has not been fully performed, the court may order the money to be applied in such manner as it thinks fit for the benefit of the parties for whose security it was paid[8].

In order that the money should be repaid, it is not necessary that all questions between the parties should be settled, as, for example, the payment of costs[9]. It is enough that the condition of the bond has been performed, either by payment to the person to whom the bond was given[10] or, in case of refusal by him, into court[11]. If the purchase is abandoned with the consent of the owner of the land, the undertakers or acquiring authority will be entitled to repayment of the money[12]. If the condition of the bond is not performed, the owner of the land will be entitled, on an application by him to the court, to have the money paid out to him[13]. If the price has been fixed by agreement or otherwise, he may also bring an action for specific performance[14], or he may enforce his lien on the land as an ordinary vendor, in which case the money in court will be paid in respect of the purchase price[15]. If the price fixed is larger than the sum in court, and there is delay in completion, the owner of the land is entitled to have the amount of the deposit increased until it is equal to the price[16].

1 See para 124 ante.
2 Lands Clauses Consolidation Act 1845 s 86 (substituted by the Administration of Justice Act 1965 s 17(1), Sch 1); Compulsory Purchase Act 1965 s 11(2), Sch 3 para 4(1).
3 Ie under the Administration of Justice Act 1982 s 38 (as amended): see COURTS.
4 See the Supreme Court Act 1981 s 61(1), (3), Sch 1 para 1 (as amended); and RSC Ord 7 r 2, Ord 92 r 5. See also *Re Neath and Brecon Rly Co* (1874) 9 Ch App 263; *Martin v London, Chatham and Dover Rly Co* (1866) 1 Ch App 501. For a form of summons for repayment of money deposited and a supporting affidavit see 12 Court Forms (2nd Edn) (1990 issue) 109, Forms 18, 19.
5 For the meaning of 'the undertakers' see para 13 ante.
6 For the meaning of 'acquiring authority' see para 92 note 5 ante.
7 Land Clauses Consolidation Act 1845 s 86 (as substituted: see note 2 supra; amended by the Administration of Justice Act 1982 s 46(2)(a)); Compulsory Purchase Act 1965 s 25(1), Sch 3 para 4(2), (3); Interpretation Act 1978 s 17(2)(a). As to costs see para 148 post.
8 Land Clauses Consolidation Act 1845 s 86 (as substituted: see note 2 supra); Compulsory Purchase Act 1965 Sch 3 para 4(4).
9 *Re London and South Western Railway Extension Act, ex p Stevens* (1848) 2 Ph 772; *Ex p Great Northern Rly Co* (1848) 16 Sim 169 (further proceedings 5 Ry & Can Cas 269); *Re Wimbledon and Dorking Railway Act 1857, ex p Wimbledon and Dorking Rly Co* (1863) 9 LT 703.
10 *Ex p Midland Rly Co* [1904] 1 Ch 61, CA.
11 *Ex p Midland Rly Co* [1904] 1 Ch 61, CA; *Re Fooks* (1849) 2 Mac & G 357. For an example where it had not been performed see *Ex p London and South Western Rly Co* (1869) 38 LJ Ch 527. As to the evidence necessary to show that the condition has been performed see *Re London and North Western Rly Co* (1872) 26 LT 687; *Ex p Midland Rly Co* (1894) 38 Sol Jo 289.
12 *Ex p Birmingham, Wolverhampton and Dudley Rly Co* (1863) 1 Hem & M 772; and cf *Royal Bank of Canada v R* [1913] AC 283, PC.
13 *Re Mutlow's Estate* (1878) 10 ChD 131.
14 *Earl of Jersey v Briton Ferry Floating Dock Co* (1869) LR 7 Eq 409 at 413.
15 *Walker v Ware, Hadham and Buntingford Rly Co* (1865) LR 1 Eq 195; *Betty v London, Chatham and Dover Rly Co* [1867] WN 169; *Wing v Tottenham and Hampstead Junction Rly Co* (1868) 3 Ch App 740.
16 *Ashford v London, Chatham and Dover Rly Co* (1866) 14 LT 787; *Ex p London, Tilbury and Southend Rly Co* (1853) 1 WR 533.

127. Time and mode of entry. Entry, upon making a deposit and giving a bond, is a right consequent upon the owner of the land and the undertakers or acquiring authority being placed by the notice to treat in a position analogous to that of vendor and purchaser[1]. If a notice to treat is served within the time limited for the exercise of the powers of compulsory purchase, entry may be made after the expiration of that period, at any rate up to the limit of the time, if any, prescribed for the construction of the works[2]. The undertakers or acquiring authority may exercise the power to enter before completion of the purchase, even though there is no urgent necessity for immediate entry[3]. The power to enter includes the power to use the land[4]. If the undertakers or acquiring authority purport to enter under this power, but are in fact acting ultra vires, the entry will not assist their title, and will render them liable in damages[5].

1   *Tiverton and North Devon Rly Co v Loosemore* (1884) 9 App Cas 480 at 488, 495, 503, HL; *Doe d Armitstead v North Staffordshire Rly Co* (1851) 16 QB 526 at 536; *Great Western Rly Co v Swindon and Cheltenham Rly Co* (1884) 9 App Cas 787 at 805, 810, HL. If an agreement for purchase has been made without a notice to treat, leaving the price to be ascertained as stipulated, the power of entry may be exercised: see *Ramsden v Manchester, South Junction and Altrincham Rly Co* (1848) 1 Exch 723; *Tiverton and North Devon Rly Co v Loosemore* supra at 502–503.
2   *Marquis of Salisbury v Great Northern Rly Co* (1852) 17 QB 840; *Tiverton and North Devon Rly Co v Loosemore* (1884) 9 App Cas 480 at 488, 495, 503, HL; *Doe d Armitstead v North Staffordshire Rly Co* (1851) 16 QB 526 at 536.
3   *Loosemore v Tiverton and North Devon Rly Co* (1882) 22 ChD 25 at 39, 46, CA; on appeal sub nom *Tiverton and North Devon Rly Co v Loosemore* (1884) 9 App Cas 480, HL, commenting on *Field v Carnarvon and Llanberis Rly Co* (1867) LR 5 Eq 190.
4   See the cases cited in note 2 supra.
5   *Batson v London School Board* (1903) 67 JP 457.

128. Unauthorised entry. If the undertakers or acquiring authority enter without complying with any of the conditions to be observed prior to entry, they may be sued in trespass for damages[1], or for possession[2], and an injunction may be granted to restrain them from remaining in possession or using the land until they have complied with the necessary conditions[3]. These proceedings will not lie, however, at the instance of a person who has consented to the entry but who subsequently desires to withdraw his consent[4], which may be presumed from that person's conduct[5]. They will lie at the instance of any person having a legal or equitable interest in the land[6], unless by a mistake, in good faith, there has been an omission to purchase his interest, in which case the undertakers or acquiring authority may remain in possession for a certain time to enable them to purchase the interest[7].

If the undertakers[8] or acquiring authority[9] or any of their contractors wilfully[10] enter on and take possession of any of the land subject to compulsory purchase[11] in contravention of the conditions to be observed before entry[12], the undertakers or authority are subject to a penalty payable to the person in possession of that land[13] with additional penalties for each day on which they so remain in possession after any such sum has been adjudged to be forfeited[14]. These penalties are recoverable in addition to the amount of any damage done to the land by reason of the entry and taking possession[15]. Distress may be levied for the recovery of the penalties[16].

1   *Ramsden v Manchester, South Junction and Altrincham Rly Co* (1848) 1 Exch 723. As to entry in order to secure the public safety see *Tower v Eastern Counties Rly Co* (1843) 3 Ry & Can Cas 374.
2   *Stretton v Great Western and Brentford Rly Co* (1870) 5 Ch App 751; *Marquis of Salisbury v Great Northern Rly Co* (1858) 5 CBNS 174.
3   *Ranken v East and West India Docks and Birmingham Junction Rly Co* (1849) 12 Beav 298; *Perks v Wycombe Rly Co* (1862) 10 WR 788; *Cardwell v Midland Rly Co* (1904) 21 TLR 22, CA; and see *Goodson v Richardson* (1874) 9 Ch App 221; *Marriott v East Grinstead Gas and Water Co* [1909] 1 Ch 70; *Deere v Guest* (1836) 1 My & Cr 516; *Poynder v Great Northern Rly Co* (1847) 2 Ph 330; *Willey v South Eastern Rly Co* (1849) 1 Mac & G 58; *Lind v Isle of Wight Ferry Co* (1862) 1 New Rep 13; *Wood v Charing Cross Rly Co* (1863) 33 Beav 290; *Armstrong v Waterford and Limerick Rly Co* (1846) 10 I Eq R 60.

4 *Doe d Hudson v Leeds and Bradford Rly Co* (1851) 16 QB 796; *Knapp v London, Chatham and Dover Rly Co* (1863) 2 H & C 212; and see *Langford v Brighton, Lewes and Hastings Rly Co* (1845) 4 Ry & Can Cas 69.

5 *Greenhalgh v Manchester and Birmingham Rly Co* (1838) 3 My & Cr 784; and see *Marquis of Salisbury v Great Northern Rly Co* (1858) 5 CBNS 174.

6 *Martin v London, Chatham and Dover Rly Co* (1866) 1 Ch App 501; *Rogers v Kingston-upon-Hull Dock Co* (1864) 34 LJ Ch 165; *Birmingham and District Land Co v London and North Western Rly Co* (1888) 40 ChD 268, CA; and cf *Cooke v LCC* [1911] 1 Ch 604, where it was held that the promoters could serve a notice to treat on mortgagees and proceed against them in the ordinary way, even though they had entered into possession of the land as against the mortgagor.

7 See para 132 post.

8 For the meaning of 'the undertakers' see para 13 ante.

9 For the meaning of 'acquiring authority' see para 92 note 5 ante.

10 Entry is not wilful if made under a mistaken idea that the conditions had been complied with (*Steele v Midland Rly Co* (1869) 21 LT 387; *Hutchinson v Manchester, Bury and Rossendale Rly Co* (1846) 15 M & W 314); and no penalty is incurred under these provisions if compensation has been paid in good faith and without collusion to any person whom the undertakers or acquiring authority reasonably believed to be entitled to it, or if it has been paid into court for the benefit of a person entitled to the land, or paid into court by way of security, even if that person was not in fact legally entitled to it (Lands Clauses Consolidation Act 1845 s 89 proviso; Compulsory Purchase Act 1965 s 12(6)).

11 For the meaning of 'land' and 'subject to compulsory purchase' see para 92 notes 1–2 ante. See also para 13 text to note 7 ante.

12 As to these conditions see para 123 ante, and as to the exclusion of those conditions and the substitution of alternative powers of entry see para 129 post.

13 Lands Clauses Consolidation Act 1845 s 89; Compulsory Purchase Act 1965 s 12(1). Penalties for wrongful entry are recoverable before a magistrates' court summarily as a civil debt: Lands Clauses Consolidation Act 1845 s 89; Compulsory Purchase Act 1965 s 12(2). Appeal lies from a magistrates' court to the Crown Court: Lands Clauses Consolidation Act 1845 s 146; Compulsory Purchase Act 1965 s 12(3) (both amended by the Courts Act 1971 s 56(2), Sch 9 Pt I).

14 Lands Clauses Consolidation Act 1845 s 89; Compulsory Purchase Act 1965 s 12(4). Penalties for wrongfully continuing in possession are recoverable in the High Court and in any such proceedings the magistrates' court's decision is not conclusive as to the undertakers' or acquiring authority's right of entry: Lands Clauses Consolidation Act 1845 s 89 (amended by the Administration of Justice Act 1965 s 34, Sch 2), Lands Clauses Consolidation Act 1845 ss 90, 136 (s 136 amended by the Summary Jurisdiction Act 1884 s 4, Schedule); Compulsory Purchase Act 1965 s 12(5). See also note 13 supra.

15 Lands Clauses Consolidation Act 1845 s 89; Compulsory Purchase Act 1965 s 12(1). Section 12 (as amended) is modified in order to correspond to the modifications made to s 11 (as amended) in relation to the compulsory acquisition of rights by, inter alia, (1) a local authority (see the Local Government (Miscellaneous Provisions) Act 1976 s 13(3)(b) (as amended), Sch 1 para 9; and LOCAL GOVERNMENT vol 28 para 1219); (2) the Development Board for Rural Wales (see the Development of Rural Wales Act 1976 s 6(7) (as amended), Sch 4 para 9; and TOWN AND COUNTRY PLANNING vol 46 (Reissue) para 1200); (3) urban development corporations (see the Local Government, Planning and Land Act 1980 s 144, Sch 28 para 23(4); and TOWN AND COUNTRY PLANNING vol 46 (Reissue) para 1297); (4) highway authorities (see the Highways Act 1980 s 250(5)(a) (as substituted), Sch 19 para 9; and HIGHWAYS vol 21 (Reissue) para 808); (5) public gas suppliers (see the Gas Act 1986 s 9(3), Sch 3 para 10; and FUEL AND ENERGY vol 19(1) (Reissue) para 636); (6) housing action trusts (see the Housing Act 1988 s 78(2), Sch 10 para 23(2); and HOUSING); (7) licence holders under the Electricity Act 1989 (see s 10(1), Sch 3 para 11; and FUEL AND ENERGY vol 19(2) (Reissue) para 985); (8) the National Rivers Authority (see the Water Resources Act 1991 s 154(5), Sch 18 para 6; and WATER); and (9) water and sewerage undertakers (see the Water Industry Act 1991 s 155(5), Sch 9 para 6; and WATER).

16 See the Compulsory Purchase Act 1965 s 29(1). The corresponding provisions of the Lands Clauses Consolidation Act 1845 (ie ss 138, 141) were, however, repealed by the Statute Law (Repeals) Act 1993 s 1, Sch 1 Pt XIV. No distress levied under the Compulsory Purchase Act 1965 is to be deemed unlawful, nor is the person making the distress to be deemed a trespasser on account of any defect or want of form in the warrant of distress or other proceedings relating to the distress; and the person making the distress is not to be deemed a trespasser ab initio on account of any irregularity afterwards committed by him so, however, that any person aggrieved by any defect or irregularity may recover full satisfaction for the special damage in civil proceedings: s 29(1).

(iii) Entry without Consent, Payment, Payment into Court or Bond

129. Entry on notice after notice to treat. If, where the power to acquire land is under a compulsory purchase order to which the Compulsory Purchase Act 1965 applies[1], the acquiring authority[2] has served notice to treat[3] in respect of any of the land[4] and has served on the owner[5], lessee and occupier of that land not less than 14 days' notice[6], the authority may enter[7] on and take possession of that land or such part of it as is specified in the notice[8]. Any compensation agreed or awarded for the land carries interest at the prescribed rate[9] from the time of entry until the compensation is paid or is paid into court[10]. Payments on account may be made of such compensation or interest so payable[11] which may be recoverable where it is subsequently agreed or determined that there was no liability to pay the compensation or interest or that the payment on account was excessive[12].

1   See para 15 ante.
2   For the meaning of 'acquiring authority' see para 92 note 5 ante.
3   As to the persons entitled to a notice to treat see para 102 ante. A tenant from year to year is not entitled to a notice to treat (see para 184 post), but may be given one, and his right to compensation will arise on entry: see *R v Stone* (1866) LR 1 QB 529, and para 183 note 2 post. However, his compensation will be derived from the Compulsory Purchase Act 1965 s 20 (as amended) (see paras 181–182, 184 post): see *R v Kennedy* [1893] 1 QB 533; *London Borough of Newham v Benjamin* [1968] 1 All ER 1195, [1968] 1 WLR 694, CA.
4   For the meaning of 'land' see para 92 note 1 ante.
5   For the meaning of 'owner' see para 92 note 7 ante.
6   Where the notice is required to be served on an owner of land which is ecclesiastical property as defined in the Acquisition of Land Act 1981 s 12(3) (as amended) (see para 37 note 7 ante), a similar notice must be served on the Church Commissioners: Compulsory Purchase Act 1965 s 11(1) (amended by the Acquisition of Land Act 1981 s 34(1), Sch 4 para 14(1), (3)).
7   As to unauthorised entry or entry on the wrong land see para 128 ante. As to the position where land is taken by stages following a single notice of entry see *Chilton v Telford Development Corpn* [1987] 3 All ER 992, [1987] 1 WLR 872, CA.
8   Compulsory Purchase Act 1965 s 11(1). As to the modification of s 11 (as amended: see note 6 supra) in relation to the compulsory acquisition of rights by, inter alia, local authorities, the Development Board for Rural Wales, urban development corporations, highway authorities, public gas suppliers, housing action trusts, licence holders under the Electricity Act 1989, the National Rivers Authority and water and sewerage undertakers, see para 122 note 5 ante.
9   Ie under the Land Compensation Act 1961 s 32: see para 125 note 5 ante.
10   Compulsory Purchase Act 1965 s 11(1). As to payment into court see para 124 ante.
11   Planning and Compensation Act 1991 s 80(2), Sch 18 Pt II.
12   Ibid s 80(3).

(iv) Enforcement of Right to Enter

130. Entry peaceably or on warrant for possession. If the undertakers[1] or acquiring authority[2] are authorised[3] to enter upon and take possession of land[4] required for the purposes of the undertaking, and the owner or occupier of any of that land or any other person refuses to give up possession, or hinders the undertakers or the authority from entering upon or taking possession of that land, the undertakers or the authority may enter peaceably[5] or issue their warrant to the sheriff[6] to deliver possession of the land to the person appointed in the warrant to receive it[7]. On receipt of the warrant, the sheriff must deliver possession of the land accordingly[8].

Nothing in the Protection from Eviction Act 1977 affects the operation of these provisions[9].

1 For the meaning of 'the undertakers' see para 13 ante.
2 For the meaning of 'acquiring authority' see para 92 note 5 ante.
3 Ie under the Lands Clauses Acts or the Compulsory Purchase Act 1965, or under the special Act or any Act incorporated therewith: see the Lands Clauses Consolidation Act 1845 s 91; and the Compulsory Purchase Act 1965 s 13(1). For the meaning of 'special Act' see paras 11, 16 ante; and as to the Lands Clauses Acts see para 11 note 1 ante.
4 For the meaning of 'land' see para 92 note 1 ante. See also para 13 text to note 7 ante.
5 The issue of a warrant is not necessary unless entry is actually resisted: *Loosemore v Tiverton and North Devon Rly Co* (1882) 22 ChD 25 at 41, CA; on appeal sub nom *Tiverton and North Devon Rly Co v Loosemore* (1884) 9 App Cas 480, HL.
6 'Sheriff' includes an under sheriff or legally competent deputy, and means the sheriff for the area where the land or any part of it is situated: Lands Clauses Consolidation Act 1845 s 3; Compulsory Purchase Act 1965 s 13(6).
7 Lands Clauses Consolidation Act 1845 s 91 (where that Act is incorporated: see para 11 ante); Compulsory Purchase Act 1965 s 13(1) (where that Act applies: see para 15 ante).
8 Lands Clauses Consolidation Act 1845 s 91; Compulsory Purchase Act 1965 s 13(2). Section 13(2) is modified in order to correspond to the modifications made to s 11 (as amended) in relation to the compulsory acquisition of rights by, inter alia, (1) a local authority (see the Local Government (Miscellaneous Provisions) Act 1976 s 13(3)(b) (as amended), Sch 1 para 9; and LOCAL GOVERNMENT vol 28 para 1219); (2) the Development Board for Rural Wales (see the Development of Rural Wales Act 1976 s 6(7) (as amended), Sch 4 para 9; and TOWN AND COUNTRY PLANNING vol 46 (Reissue) para 1200); (3) urban development corporations (see the Local Government, Planning and Land Act 1980 s 144, Sch 28 para 23(4); and TOWN AND COUNTRY PLANNING vol 46 (Reissue) para 1297); (4) highway authorities (see the Highways Act 1980 s 250(5)(a) (as substituted), Sch 19 para 9; and HIGHWAYS vol 21 (Reissue) para 808); (5) public gas suppliers (see the Gas Act 1986 s 9(3), Sch 3 para 10; and FUEL AND ENERGY vol 19(1) (Reissue) para 636); (6) housing action trusts (see the Housing Act 1988 s 78(2), Sch 10 para 23(2); and HOUSING); (7) licence holders under the Electricity Act 1989 (see s 10(1), Sch 3 para 11; and FUEL AND ENERGY vol 19(2) (Reissue) para 985); (8) the National Rivers Authority (see the Water Resources Act 1991 s 154(5), Sch 18 para 6; and WATER); and (9) water and sewerage undertakers (see the Water Industry Act 1991 s 155(5), Sch 9 para 6; and WATER).
9 Protection from Eviction Act 1977 s 9(4)(e). See further CRIMINAL LAW vol 11(1) (Reissue) paras 190–191; LANDLORD AND TENANT vol 27(1) (Reissue) paras 184–185, 547.

131. Costs of warrant for possession. The costs accruing by reason of the issue and execution of the warrant[1] must be settled by the sheriff[2] and paid by the person refusing to give possession, and the amount of those costs must be deducted from any compensation then payable to that person and retained by the undertakers[3] or the acquiring authority[4]. If no compensation is so payable, or if the compensation is less than the costs, then the costs or the excess beyond the compensation, if not paid on demand, must be levied by distress[5], and upon application to any justice of the peace for that purpose he must issue his warrant accordingly[6]. If the compensation has been paid into court, the costs may be ordered to be paid out of the fund in court[7].

1 Ie the warrant for delivery of possession: see para 130 ante.
2 For the meaning of 'sheriff' see para 130 note 6 ante.
3 For the meaning of 'the undertakers' see para 13 ante.
4 Lands Clauses Consolidation Act 1845 s 91; Compulsory Purchase Act 1965 s 13(3). For the meaning of 'acquiring authority' see para 92 note 5 ante.
5 As to distress see para 128 note 16 ante.
6 Lands Clauses Consolidation Act 1845 s 91; Compulsory Purchase Act 1965 s 13(4). Any surplus arising from the sale under the distress, after satisfying the amount due and the expenses of the distress and sale, must be returned on demand to the person whose goods and chattels have been distrained: Compulsory Purchase Act 1965 s 13(5). The corresponding provision of the Lands Clauses Consolidation Act 1845 (ie s 138) is now repealed: see para 128 note 16 ante.
7 *Re Schmarr* [1902] 1 Ch 326 at 331, CA; *Re Turner's Estate and Metropolitan Railway Act 1860* (1861) 5 LT 524. As to payment into court see paras 98 note 6, 124 ante.

(5) INTERESTS OMITTED BY MISTAKE FROM PURCHASE OR COMPENSATION

132. Acquiring authority's right to remain in possession. If, at any time after the undertakers[1] have entered upon any land which under the Lands Clauses Acts[2] or the special Act[3] or incorporated Acts they were authorised to purchase, which are permanently required for the purposes of the special Act, or after an acquiring authority[4] has entered upon any of the land subject to compulsory purchase[5], it appears that they have through mistake or inadvertence[6] failed or omitted duly to purchase or to pay compensation for any estate, right or interest in, or charge affecting, that land, then, whether the period allowed for the purchase of the land[7] has expired or not, the undertakers or the acquiring authority are entitled to remain in the undisturbed possession of the land, provided they purchase or pay compensation in the required time and manner[8]. Thus, if after the purchase and taking of land from an ostensible owner the undertakers or the acquiring authority become aware of the existence of a mortgage which they do not dispute, the mortgagee cannot eject them until the time has expired in which they may make compensation[9], nor can an owner do so if by reason of a mistake in the book of reference[10] they have taken more land than was shown by the measurements in that book[11].

If the undertakers or the authority dispute the existence of the right or interest, however, an action for possession may be brought against them by the claimant in order to establish his right, but in such a case execution will be postponed for the same period[12].

1 For the meaning of 'the undertakers' see para 13 ante.
2 As to the Lands Clauses Acts see para 11 ante.
3 For the meaning of 'special Act' see paras 11, 16 ante.
4 For the meaning of 'acquiring authority' see para 92 note 5 ante.
5 For the meaning of 'land' and 'subject to compulsory purchase' see para 92 notes 1–2 ante. See also para 13 text to note 7 ante.
6 The provision does not apply in the case of mere neglect, and, if the undertakers or the acquiring authority are aware of the existence of the right or interest, previous mistakes or ignorance will not bring them within the provision and they may be liable to actions for possession or in trespass and be restrained by injunction: see *Martin v London Chatham and Dover Rly Co* (1866) 1 Ch App 501; *Stretton v Great Western and Brentford Rly Co* (1870) 5 Ch App 751; *Thomas v Barry Dock and Rlys Co* (1889) 5 TLR 360; *Cardwell v Midland Rly Co* (1904) 21 TLR 22, CA; and see *Cooke v LCC* [1911] 1 Ch 604. As to the principles on which the courts act in granting injunctions in these cases see *Wood v Charing Cross Rly Co* (1863) 33 Beav 290; *Garrett v Banstead and Epsom Downs Rly Co* (1864) 13 WR 878; *Munro v Wivenhoe and Brightlingsea Rly Co* (1865) 13 WR 880; *Webster v South Eastern Rly Co* (1851) 1 Sim NS 272; *Lind v Isle of Wight Ferry Co* (1862) 1 New Rep 13.
7 Ie the period specified in the Compulsory Purchase Act 1965 s 4 (as amended): see para 101 ante.
8 Land Clauses Consolidation Act 1845 s 124 (where that Act is incorporated: see para 11 ante); Compulsory Purchase Act 1965 s 22(1), (2) (where that Act applies: see para 15 ante). The Compulsory Purchase Act 1965 s 22 is modified in relation to the compulsory acquisition of rights by, inter alia, (1) a local authority, by the Local Government (Miscellaneous Provisions) Act 1976 s 13(3)(b) (as amended), Sch 1 para 11 (see LOCAL GOVERNMENT vol 28 para 1219); (2) the Development Board for Rural Wales, by the Development of Rural Wales Act 1976 s 6(7) (as amended), Sch 4 para 11 (see TOWN AND COUNTRY PLANNING vol 46 (Reissue) para 1200); (3) urban development corporations, by the Local Government, Planning and Land Act 1980 s 144, Sch 28 para 23(6) (see TOWN AND COUNTRY PLANNING vol 46 (Reissue) para 1297); (4) highway authorities, by the Highways Act 1980 s 250(5)(a) (as substituted), Sch 19 para 11 (see HIGHWAYS vol 21 (Reissue) para 808); (5) public gas suppliers, by the Gas Act 1986 s 9(3), Sch 3 para 12 (see FUEL AND ENERGY vol 19(1) (Reissue) para 636); (6) housing action trusts, by the Housing Act 1988 s 78(2), Sch 10 para 23(4) (see HOUSING); (7) licence holders under the Electricity Act 1989, by s 10(1), Sch 3 para 13 (see FUEL AND ENERGY vol 19(2) (Reissue) para 985); (8) the National Rivers Authority, by the Water Resources Act 1991 s 154(5), Sch 18 para 8

(see WATER); and (9) water and sewerage undertakers, by the Water Industry Act 1991 s 155(5), Sch 9 para 8 (see WATER).

9 *Jolly v Wimbledon and Dorking Rly Co* (1861) 31 LJQB 95, Ex Ch.

10 The undertakers may have power under their special Act or an enactment incorporated with it to correct mistakes or omissions in deposited plans or books of reference: see para 23 note 2 ante.

11 *Hyde v Manchester Corpn* (1852) 5 De G & Sm 249; *Kemp v West End of London and Crystal Palace Rly Co* (1855) 1 K & J 681. Cf *Omagh Urban Council v Henderson* [1907] 2 IR 310.

12 *Marquis of Salisbury v Great Northern Rly Co* (1858) 5 CBNS 174; *Doe d Hyde v Manchester Corpn* (1852) 12 CB 474.

133. Possession on purchase or payment of compensation. The condition entitling the undertakers[1] or the acquiring authority[2] to remain in possession of the land[3] is that within six months after notice of the estate, right, interest or charge, in cases where they do not dispute the claim, or in cases of dispute then within six months after the claim has been finally established by law in favour of the claimant[4], they must purchase or pay compensation for the estate, right, interest in, or charge affecting the land[5] which they have failed or omitted to purchase or pay compensation for[6]. They must also, within that time, pay to any person who may establish a right to it full compensation for the mesne profits[7] or interest which would have accrued to those persons during the interval between the undertakers' or authority's entry on the land and the time of the payment of the purchase money or compensation, so far as the mesne profits or interest may be recoverable in any proceedings[8].

1 For the meaning of 'the undertakers' see para 13 ante.

2 For the meaning of 'acquiring authority' see para 92 note 5 ante.

3 Ie in the circumstances set out in para 132 ante.

4 Lands Clauses Consolidation Act 1845 s 124 (where that Act is incorporated: see para 11 ante); Compulsory Purchase Act 1965 s 22(3) (where that Act applies: see para 15 ante). Thus, if an action for possession is brought, and application is made for a new trial, the matter is not finally determined until the new trial is refused: *Hyde v Manchester Corpn* (1852) 5 De G & Sm 249. For a case on a dispute as to minerals decided after many years see *Caledonian Rly Co v Davidson* [1903] AC 22, HL.

5 For the meaning of 'land' see para 92 note 1 ante. See also para 13 text to note 7 ante.

6 Lands Clauses Consolidation Act 1845 s 124; Compulsory Purchase Act 1965 s 22(1)(a).

7 'Mesne profits' means the mesne profits or interest which would have accrued to the persons concerned during the interval between the entry of the acquiring authority and the time when the compensation is paid, so far as such mesne profits or interest may be recoverable in any proceedings: ibid s 22(5); and see the Lands Clauses Consolidation Act 1845 s 124.

8 Ibid s 124; Compulsory Purchase Act 1965 s 22(1)(b), (5). As to the modification of s 22 in relation to the compulsory acquisition of rights by, inter alia, a local authority, the Development Board for Rural Wales, urban development corporations, highway authorities, public gas suppliers, housing action trusts, licence holders under the Electricity Act 1989, the National Rivers Authority and water and sewerage undertakers see para 132 note 8 ante.

134. Ascertainment of compensation. The purchase money or compensation must be agreed on, or awarded and paid, whether to the claimants or into court, in the same manner as, according to the provisions of the Lands Clauses Acts[1] or the Compulsory Purchase Act 1965[2], it would have been agreed on or awarded and paid if the undertakers[3] or the acquiring authority[4] had purchased the estate, right, interest or charge before entering upon the land[5], or as near thereto as circumstances will admit[6]. In assessing the compensation the value of the land and of any estate or interest in it, or of any mesne profits[7] of the land, is to be taken to be the value when the undertakers or the acquiring authority entered on the land, and without regard to any improvements or works made in or upon the land by the undertakers or the acquiring authority, and as though the works had not been constructed[8].

1 As to the Lands Clauses Acts see para 11 ante.
2 As to the agreement, award and payment of compensation see paras 197, 233 et seq post.
3 For the meaning of 'the undertakers' see para 13 ante.
4 For the meaning of 'acquiring authority' see para 92 note 5 ante.
5 For the meaning of 'land' see para 92 note 1 ante. See also para 13 text to note 7 ante.
6 Lands Clauses Consolidation Act 1845 s 124 (where that Act is incorporated: see para 11 ante); Compulsory Purchase Act 1965 s 22(1) (where that Act applies: see para 15 ante). As to payment into court see paras 98 note 6, 124 ante.
7 For the meaning of 'mesne profits' see para 133 note 7 ante.
8 Lands Clauses Consolidation Act 1845 s 125; Compulsory Purchase Act 1965 s 22(4). As to the modification of s 22 in relation to the compulsory acquisition of rights by, inter alia, a local authority, the Development Board for Rural Wales, urban development corporations, highway authorities, public gas suppliers, housing action trusts, licence holders under the Electricity Act 1989, the National Rivers Authority and water and sewerage undertakers see para 132 note 8 ante. As to the measure of damages when the promoters have entered with notice of the interest see *Stretton v Great Western and Brentford Rly Co* (1870) 5 Ch App 751.

(6) COMPLETION OF PURCHASE

(i) Right to Completion and Specific Performance

135. Right to completion and specific performance after notice to treat or entry and ascertainment of price. When notice to treat has been served or land has been entered upon under an empowering enactment with which the Lands Clauses Acts are incorporated[1] or under a compulsory purchase order to which the Compulsory Purchase Act 1965[2] applies[3], and the price or compensation has been ascertained either by agreement or assessment, the relation of vendor and purchaser is established between the parties in the same way as under a formal agreement, subject to the purchaser's right to withdraw the notice to treat after determination of the amount of compensation where the vendor has failed to serve a proper notice of claim[4]. All the ordinary rules apply, unless the special Act contains provisions to the contrary[5].

Either the vendor[6] or the undertakers or acquiring authority[7] can accordingly enforce the contract by specific performance, but the owner must show that he has a good title to the land, and specific performance will therefore only be granted subject to his title being investigated and proved[8]. He must also be prepared to execute a conveyance, and it will be a defence to an action for the price that the conveyance has not been executed by him[9]. When there is no question as to title, he can compel the undertakers or authority to execute a conveyance[10] or accept an assignment of a lease with all proper covenants[11], even though they may have already paid the purchase money. After a good title is shown and possession is offered, they will be liable to pay interest on the purchase money[12], if there is nothing in the Act under which the land was acquired to indicate a contrary intention[13].

1 As to the Lands Clauses Acts and their incorporation see para 11 ante.
2 As to the application of the Compulsory Purchase Act 1965 in place of the Lands Clauses Acts see para 15 ante.
3 As to notices to treat see the Lands Clauses Consolidation Act 1845 s 18; the Compulsory Purchase Act 1965 s 5(1); and para 100 ante. As to the form of the notice see para 100 ante; and as to service of the notice see paras 101–102 ante.
   As to entry on land with or without consent see the Lands Clauses Consolidation Act 1845 ss 84, 85 (as amended); the Compulsory Purchase Act 1965 s 11 (as amended), Sch 3; and para 122 et seq ante.
4 See the Lands Compensation Act 1961 s 31; the Land Compensation Act 1973 s 54(4); and para 120 ante.
5 *Regent's Canal Co v Ware* (1857) 23 Beav 575; *Mason v Stokes Bay Rly and Pier Co* (1862) 32 LJ Ch 110; cf *London Corpn v Horner* (1914) 111 LT 512, CA; and see para 115 et seq ante, and generally SALE OF

LAND. Cf *John Hudson & Co Ltd v Kirkness (Inspector of Taxes)* [1954] 1 All ER 29, [1954] 1 WLR 40, CA, distinguishing between the compulsory vesting of property by a statute with fixed compensation provided and compulsory acquisition taking place under the authority of a statute. For the meaning of 'special Act' see paras 11, 16 ante.

6 *Adams v London and Blackwall Rly Co* (1850) 2 Mac & G 118.
7 See note 5 supra.
8 *Gunston v East Gloucestershire Rly Co* (1868) 18 LT 8. See further SPECIFIC PERFORMANCE vol 44(1) (Reissue) para 838.
9 *East London Union v Metropolitan Rly Co* (1869) LR 4 Exch 309, following the general principle in *Laird v Pim* (1841) 7 M & W 474.
10 *Re Cary-Elwes' Contract* [1906] 2 Ch 143.
11 *Harding v Metropolitan Rly Co* (1872) 7 Ch App 154.
12 *Re Pigott and Great Western Rly Co* (1881) 18 ChD 146.
13 *Inglewood Pulp and Paper Co v New Brunswick Electric Power Commission* [1928] AC 492, PC. Where entry has been made before completion interest is payable from the date of entry: see para 123 et seq ante. Where compensation is assessed by the Lands Tribunal before entry interest may be payable from the date of the award: see para 226 post. As to the right to interest where an advance payment has been made see para 138 post.

(ii) Advance Payment of Compensation

136. Making of advance payment of compensation. Where an acquiring authority[1] has taken possession of any land[2], the person entitled to the compensation ('the claimant') may request[3] the authority to make an advance payment on account of any compensation payable by it for the compulsory acquisition of any interest in that land[4], whereupon the authority must make an advance payment[5] equal to 90 per cent of (1) the agreed amount of the compensation[6]; or (2) if no agreement has been reached, an amount equal to the compensation as estimated by the authority[7]. No advance payment may, however, be made if the land is subject to a mortgage the principal of which exceeds 90 per cent of the above-mentioned amount; and where the land is subject to a mortgage with a lower principal, the advance must be reduced by such sum as the authority considers it will require for securing the release of the mortgagee's interest[8].

Any such advance payment must be made not later than three months after the date on which the request is made, or, if those three months end before the authority takes possession of the land[9], on the date on which it takes possession[10].

1 For the meaning of 'acquiring authority' for these purposes see para 106 note 1 ante.
2 Where, instead of taking possession of land, an acquiring authority serves a notice in respect of the land allowing tenants to continue in possession under the Housing Act 1985 s 583, this provision has effect as if it had taken possession of the land on the date on which that notice was served: Land Compensation Act 1973 s 52(11) (amended by the Housing (Consequential Provisions) Act 1985 s 4, Sch 2 para 24(6)). Where the authority has acquired a right over land, the reference in the text to taking possession of the land must be read as a reference to first entering the land for the purpose of exercising that right: Land Compensation Act 1973 s 52(12).
3 The request must be in writing, giving particulars of the claimant's interest in the land so far as not already given pursuant to a notice to treat, and must be accompanied or supplemented by such other particulars as the acquiring authority may reasonably require to enable it to estimate the amount of the compensation in respect of which the advance payment is to be made: ibid s 52(2). As to notice to treat see para 100 et seq ante.
4 This provision applies, with the necessary modifications, to compensation for the compulsory acquisition of a right over land as it does to compensation for the compulsory acquisition of an interest in land: ibid s 52(12). As to the right to accrued interest where an advance payment is made see para 138 post.
5 Ibid s 52(1), (2).
6 Ibid s 52(3)(a).

7 Ibid s 52(3)(b).
8 Ibid s 52(6).
9 See note 2 supra.
10 Land Compensation Act 1973 s 52(4). If the compensation is in respect of an interest which is settled land for the purposes of the Settled Land Act 1925, the advance must be made to the persons entitled to give a discharge for capital money and will be treated as capital money arising under that Act: Land Compensation Act 1973 s 52(7).

137. Effect of advance payment of compensation. Before an acquiring authority[1] makes an advance payment on account of compensation in respect of any interest in land[2], it must deposit with the council of the district or London borough in which the land is situated particulars of the payment to be made, the compensation and the interest in land to which it relates[3]. Any particulars so deposited are a local land charge and the council with whom any such particulars are deposited is treated[4] as the originating authority as respects the charge thereby constituted[5]. Where a local land charge is registered in the appropriate local land charges register[6] and the advance payment to which the charge relates is made to the claimant[7], then if he afterwards disposes of the interest in the land to, or creates an interest in the land in favour of, a person other than the acquiring authority, the amount of the advance payment, together with any accrued interest paid[8], must be set off against any sum payable by the authority to that other person in respect of the compulsory acquisition of the interest disposed of or the compulsory acquisition or release of the interest created[9].

Where, at any time after an advance payment has been made on the basis of the acquiring authority's estimate of the compensation, it appears to the acquiring authority that its estimate was too low, it must, if a request in that behalf is duly made[10], pay to the claimant the balance of the amount of the advance payment calculated as at that time[11]. Where the amount, or aggregate amount, of any payment made on the basis of the authority's estimate of the compensation exceeds the compensation as finally determined or agreed, the excess must be repaid; and if after any payment has been made to any person it is discovered that he was not entitled to it, the amount of the payment is recoverable by the acquiring authority[12].

Where an advance payment has been made under these provisions on account of any compensation, the statutory provisions relating to refusal to convey on tender of compensation[13] have effect as if references to the compensation were references to the unpaid balance of the compensation[14].

1 For the meaning of 'acquiring authority' for these purposes see para 106 note 1 ante.
2 Ie an advance payment under the Land Compensation Act 1973 s 52 (as amended): see para 136 ante.
3 Ibid s 52(8) (amended by the Local Land Charges Act 1975 s 19, Sch 1; further prospectively amended by the Local Government (Wales) Act 1994 s 66(6), Sch 16 para 40(3), as from a day to be appointed under s 66(3), to add, after the words 'London borough', the words 'or Welsh county or county borough').
4 Ie for the purposes of the Local Land Charges Act 1975: see LAND CHARGES.
5 Land Compensation Act 1973 s 52(8A) (added by the Local Land Charges Act 1975 s 17(2)).
6 Ie pursuant to the Land Compensation Act 1973 s 52(8A) (as added: see note 5 supra): s 52(9) (amended by the Local Land Charges Act 1975 s 17(2)).
7 For the meaning of 'the claimant' see para 136 ante.
8 Ie under the Land Compensation Act 1973 s 52A (as added): see para 138 post.
9 Ibid s 52(9) (amended by the Local Land Charges Act 1975 s 17(2); and by the Planning and Compensation Act 1991 s 70, Sch 15 para 24).
10 Ie in accordance with the Land Compensation Act 1973 s 52(2): see para 136 ante.
11 Ibid s 52(4A) (added by the Planning and Compensation Act 1991 s 63(1)).
12 Land Compensation Act 1973 s 52(5) (substituted by the Planning and Compensation Act 1991 s 63(1)).
13 Ie the Lands Clauses Consolidation Act 1845 s 76 (as amended); and the Compulsory Purchase Act 1965 s 9: see paras 142, 144, 146 post.

14 Land Compensation Act 1973 s 52(10) (amended by the Planning and Compensation Act 1991 s 84(6), Sch 19 Pt III).

138. Right to interest where advance payment made. Where the compensation to be paid by the acquiring authority[1] for the compulsory acquisition of any interest in land would otherwise carry interest[2], then, if the authority makes an advance payment[3] to any person on account of the compensation, it must at the same time make a payment to that person of accrued interest[4], for the period beginning with the date of entry, on the amount by reference to which the advance payment was calculated[5]. If the authority makes an increased payment[6] to any person on account of the compensation, it must at the same time make a payment to him of accrued interest, for the period beginning with the date of entry, on the amount by reference to which that payment was calculated, less the amount by reference to which the preceding payment[7] was calculated[8].

If, on an anniversary of the date on which the authority made an advance payment[9] to any person on account of the compensation, the amount of the accrued interest on the unpaid balance[10] or the aggregate amount of the accrued interest on any unpaid balances[11] exceeds £1,000[12], the authority must make a payment to the claimant[13] of the amount or aggregate amount[14]. On paying the outstanding compensation, the acquiring authority must pay the amount of the accrued interest on the unpaid balance or the aggregate amount of the accrued interest on any unpaid balances[15].

Where the amount, or aggregate amount, of any advance payment made on the basis of the acquiring authority's estimate of the compensation is greater than the compensation as finally determined or agreed and, accordingly, the interest paid is excessive, the excess must be repaid[16]. If, after any interest on any amount has been paid to any person under these provisions, it is discovered that he was not entitled to the amount, the interest is recoverable by the acquiring authority[17].

1 For the meaning of 'acquiring authority' for these purposes see para 106 note 1 ante.
2 Ie under the Compulsory Purchase Act 1965 s 11(1) (as amended) (see para 129 ante); or any bond under s 11(2) (as amended), Sch 3 or the Lands Clauses Consolidation Act 1845 s 85 (as amended) (see para 123 et seq ante): Land Compensation Act 1973 s 52A(1) (s 52A added by the Planning and Compensation Act 1991 s 63(2)). Where any payment has been made under the Land Compensation Act 1973 s 52(1) on account of any compensation (see para 136 ante), the acquiring authority is not required to pay interest under the Compulsory Purchase Act 1965 s 11(1) (as amended) or under any such bond: Land Compensation Act 1973 s 52A(9) (as so added).
3 Ie under ibid s 52(1): see para 136 ante.
4 For these purposes, interest accrues (1) at the rate prescribed under the Land Compensation Act 1961 s 32 (see para 125 note 5 ante); or (2) in the case of a bond under the Lands Clauses Consolidation Act 1845 s 85 (as amended), at the rate specified in that provision: Land Compensation Act 1973 s 52A(8) (as added: see note 2 supra). The Lands Clauses Consolidation Act 1845 s 85 (as amended) specifies a rate of interest of 5%; but the Land Compensation Act 1961 s 32 specifically states that the prescribed rate is to replace that rate of 5%; the effect of head (2) supra is therefore unclear, but it appears that for this purpose only the rate of interest of 5% is to be applied.
5 Land Compensation Act 1973 s 52A(1), (2)(a) (as added: see note 2 supra). For these purposes, the amount by reference to which a payment under s 52(1) or (4A) (as added) was calculated is the amount referred to in s 52(3)(a) or (b) for the purposes of that calculation (see para 136 ante): s 52A(8)(b) (as so added).
6 Ie a payment under ibid s 52(4A) (as added): see para 136 ante.
7 Ie under ibid s 52(1) or (4A) (as added): see para 136 ante.
8 Ibid s 52A(3) (as added: see note 2 supra). See also note 5 supra.
9 Ie under ibid s 52(1): see para 136 ante.
10 Ie under ibid s 52A(2) (as added: see note 2 supra): s 52A(5)(a) (as so added). The unpaid balance is the difference between the amount of the payment under s 52(1) and the amount by reference to which it was calculated (see note 5 supra): s 52A(2)(b) (as so added). For the purposes of s 52A(5), (6) (as so added)

(see the text and notes 9 supra, 11–15 infra), interest accrues on any unpaid balance for the period beginning with (1) the making of the payment under s 52(1) or, as the case may be, s 52(4A) (as added); or (2) if any payment has already been made in respect of that balance under s 52A(5) (as so added), the date of the preceding payment thereunder: s 52A(7) (as so added).

11 Where the authority makes a payment under ibid s 52(4A) (as added) on account of the compensation, the difference between (1) the amount of the payment; and (2) the amount by reference to which it was calculated (see note 5 supra) less the amount by reference to which the preceding payment under s 52(1) or (4A) (as added) was calculated, is an unpaid balance for these purposes: s 52A(4) (as added: see note 2 supra).

12 The Secretary of State may from time to time by order substitute another sum for the sum so specified; and the power to make such orders is exercisable by statutory instrument subject to annulment in pursuance of a resolution of either House of Parliament: ibid s 52A(12) (as added: see note 2 supra). At the date at which this volume states the law, no such order had been made. The Secretary of State here concerned is the Secretary of State for the Environment or, in relation to Wales, the Secretary of State for Wales.

13 For the meaning of 'the claimant' see para 136 ante.
14 Land Compensation Act 1973 s 52A(5) (as added: see note 2 supra).
15 Ibid s 52A(6) (as added: see note 2 supra).
16 Ibid s 52A(10) (as added: see note 2 supra).
17 Ibid s 52A(11) (as added: see note 2 supra).

(iii) Conveyance or Transfer

139. Form and execution of conveyance or transfer. Certain forms of conveyance are provided by the Lands Clauses Acts[1] and the Compulsory Purchase Act 1965 for acquisitions authorised by compulsory purchase order[2], but in practice these are seldom used and the conveyance is usually made in accordance with forms similar to those used on ordinary conveyances on sale[3]. In the case of registered land, the normal forms of transfer to a corporation may be adapted for use as appropriate[4].

If the compensation payable includes payment in respect of disturbance, the compensation for disturbance is part of the consideration for the sale, and the aggregate of that compensation and of all other compensation (including compensation for severance or other injurious affection payable) is the figure to be inserted in the conveyance or transfer on which stamp duty at the rate appropriate to the purchase money payable on a conveyance on sale is to be paid[5]. The instrument by which the transfer is effected must be produced to the Commissioners of Inland Revenue by the acquiring authority within 30 days of its execution[6], together with such other documents as are required[7]. Within three months of the completion of the purchase the authority must also produce to the commissioners that instrument duly stamped with the ad valorem duty payable on a conveyance on sale of the property[8].

Where the sale is by agreement[9], it seems that the same covenants for title should be given as in the case of an ordinary sale[10]; but where there is a compulsory purchase it seems that the undertakers or acquiring authority can only require a conveyance in the statutory form[11] or a form similar to it[12], and the statutory form includes no covenants for title, nor does its wording incorporate the covenants implied by statute[13]. If title is not made out to the undertakers' or authority's satisfaction, they can dispense with the conveyance and execute a deed poll vesting the land in themselves after making deposit[14].

1 As to the Lands Clauses Acts see para 11 ante.
2 See the Lands Clauses Consolidation Act 1845 s 81 (amended by the Compulsory Purchase Act 1965 s 39(4), Sch 8 Pt II); the Lands Clauses Consolidation Act 1845 Schs (A), (B) (where that Act is incorporated: see para 11 ante); and the Compulsory Purchase Act 1965 s 23(6), Sch 5 (where that Act applies: see para 15 ante). A conveyance made in the prescribed form, or as near to it as the

circumstances admit, is effectual to vest the land conveyed by it in the undertakers or the acquiring authority and operates to bar and destroy all estates, rights, titles, remainders, reversions, limitations, trusts and interests relating to the land which have been purchased or compensated for by the consideration mentioned in the conveyance: Lands Clauses Consolidation Act 1845 s 81 (as so amended); Compulsory Purchase Act 1965 s 23(6). As to purchase by vesting declaration for speedy acquisition see para 168 et seq post. For the meaning of 'acquiring authority' for these purposes see para 92 note 5 ante; for the meaning of 'the undertakers' see para 13 ante; and for the meaning of 'land' see para 92 note 1 ante. See also para 13 text to note 7 ante.

3 For forms of conveyance see 8 Forms & Precedents (5th Edn) (1994 Reissue) 353 et seq, Form 46 et seq.

4 See 8 Forms & Precedents (5th Edn) (1994 Reissue) 356–357, Form 49.

5 *IRC v Glasgow and South Western Rly Co* (1887) 12 App Cas 315, HL; *Horn v Sunderland Corpn* [1941] 2 KB 26 at 34, [1941] 1 All ER 480 at 485–486, CA.

6 Finance Act 1931 s 28(1).

7 Ibid s 28(1). The documents referred to are those required in order to comply with the provisions of s 28(1), Sch 2 (as amended), as set out in the Land Commission Act 1967 s 87(2), Sch 15. See STAMP DUTIES vol 44(1) (Reissue) para 1026.

8 Finance Act 1895 s 12. Both productions may be effected on the same occasion, whether by personal application or through the post, and may embrace an application for stamping with the appropriate duty, but the applicant should expressly indicate whether the instrument is presented by way of production under one or other of the statutory provisions or under both: see 51 LS Gaz 511 (December 1954).

9 See para 95 ante.

10 As to the implied covenants for title see the Law of Property (Miscellaneous Provisions) Act 1994 Pt I (ss 1–13); and REAL PROPERTY; SALE OF LAND.

11 See the Lands Clauses Consolidation Act 1845 Schs (A), (B); the Compulsory Purchase Act 1965 Sch 5.

12 See the Lands Clauses Consolidation Act 1845 s 81 (as amended: see note 2 supra); the Compulsory Purchase Act 1965 s 23(6).

13 The forms contained in the Lands Clauses Consolidation Act 1845 Schs (A), (B) and the Compulsory Purchase Act 1965 Sch 5 contain no wording which would have resulted in the implication of a covenant by virtue of the Law of Property Act 1925 s 76 (repealed); and the Law of Property (Miscellaneous Provisions) Act 1994 s 9 (modifications of statutory forms) is thus of no application.

14 See para 144 post.

140. Costs of conveyance. Under the Lands Clauses Acts[1] or, in the case of an acquisition authorised by a compulsory purchase order, under the Compulsory Purchase Act 1965[2], the costs of all conveyances of land purchased under the special Act[3] and the Acts incorporated in it, or of the land subject to compulsory purchase[4], must be borne by the undertakers[5] or by the acquiring authority[6], whether the sale is voluntary or compulsory[7]. These costs include all charges and expenses incurred on the vendor's as well as on the purchaser's part:

(1) of all conveyances and assurances of the land, and of any outstanding terms of interest in it;

(2) of deducing, evidencing and verifying the title to the land, terms or interests; and

(3) of making out and furnishing such abstracts and attested copies as the undertakers or authority may require,

and all other reasonable expenses incident to the investigation, deduction and verification of the title[8]. Where the sale takes place under an agreement, the provision as to costs may be varied by the agreement[9].

If, in order formally to complete a title otherwise good, the undertakers or authority require letters of administration to be taken out, or some act to be done which would not otherwise have been necessary, they must pay the costs occasioned by it[10]. The costs of any necessary application to the court to appoint a person to convey are also payable by the undertakers or authority[11], as are the costs of conveyancing counsel when required[12]. The costs of the conveyance do not include costs of preliminary negotiations, or the costs of apportioning ground rents when part of leasehold property is taken[13], or costs of collateral agreements[14].

The undertakers or acquiring authority are not entitled to refuse to take a conveyance merely to save expense[15].

1 As to the Lands Clauses Acts see para 11 ante.
2 As to the acquisitions to which the Compulsory Purchase Act 1965 applies see para 15 ante.
3 For the meaning of 'special Act' see paras 11, 16 ante.
4 For the meaning of 'land' and 'subject to compulsory purchase' see para 92 notes 1–2 ante. See also para 13 text to note 7 ante.
5 For the meaning of 'the undertakers' see para 13 ante.
6 For the meaning of 'acquiring authority' see para 92 note 5 ante.
7 Lands Clauses Consolidation Act 1845 s 82 (where that Act is incorporated: see para 11 ante); Compulsory Purchase Act 1965 s 23(1) (where that Act applies: see para 15 ante); *Re Burdekin* [1895] 2 Ch 136, CA. As to purchase by agreement see paras 93–98 ante.
8 Lands Clauses Consolidation Act 1845 s 82; Compulsory Purchase Act 1965 s 23(2). For examples under other Acts see *Re London and Greenwich Rly Co, ex p Addey's Charity Feoffees* (1843) 12 LJ Ch 513; *Re Strachan's Estate and Metropolitan Improvement Acts* (1851) 9 Hare 185. In certain circumstances, legal costs incurred before the notice to treat can be recovered: see *Prasad v Wolverhampton Borough Council* [1983] Ch 333, [1983] 2 All ER 140, CA.
9 See *Re London and South Western Railway Act 1855, ex p Phillips* (1862) 32 LJ Ch 102; *Re Middlesex County Light Railways Order 1903* [1908] WN 167.
10 *Re Liverpool Improvement Act* (1868) LR 5 Eq 282, overruling *Re South Wales Rly Co* (1851) 14 Beav 418; *Re Thames Tunnel (Rotherhithe and Ratcliff) Act 1900* [1908] 1 Ch 493, CA; and see *Re South City Market Co, ex p Keatley* (1890) 25 LR Ir 263; *Re Bear Island Defence Works and Doyle* [1903] 1 IR 164, CA. Costs of taking out probate to the estate of a deceased person who had agreed to sell a leasehold interest have been held not to be payable by the undertakers: *Re Elementary Education Acts 1870 and 1873* [1909] 1 Ch 55, CA. If the undertakers or acquiring authority pay the money into court by reason of the failure of an owner under a disability to make a good title, they will be required to pay similar costs on application to the court for payment out: see the Lands Clauses Consolidation Act 1845 s 80 (as amended); the Compulsory Purchase Act 1965 s 26(1)(c), (2), (3); and para 162 note 8 post. As to the costs of registering title see *Re Belfast and Northern Counties Rly Co, ex p Gilmore* [1895] 1 IR 297.
11 *Re Lowry's Will* (1872) LR 15 Eq 78; *Re Nash's Estate* (1855) 4 WR 111; *Re Eastern Counties and Tilbury Junction Rly Co, ex p Cave* (1855) 26 LTOS 176. However, they will not be obliged to pay costs incurred in respect of such part of the application as fails: see *Re Jacobs, Baldwin v Pescott* [1908] 2 Ch 691.
12 *Re Spooner's Estate* (1854) 1 K & J 220. As to solicitors' costs see generally SOLICITORS vol 44(1) (Reissue) para 158 et seq.
13 *Re Hampstead Junction Rly Co, ex p Buck* (1863) 1 Hem & M 519: see para 189 post.
14 Eg an agreement to carry the vendor's goods at a fixed price: *Re Lietch and Kewney (Solicitors)* (1867) 15 WR 1055.
15 *Re Cary-Elwes' Contract* [1906] 2 Ch 143.

141. Taxation and recovery of costs of conveyance. When the undertakers[1] or the acquiring authority[2] and the party entitled to costs cannot agree as to the amount, the costs must be taxed by one of the Supreme Court taxing masters on an order of the court obtained by either of the parties[3], although such an order cannot be obtained by the undertakers after the costs have been paid[4].

The expense of taxation is borne by the undertakers or the acquiring authority unless upon the taxation one-sixth of the amount of the costs is disallowed, in which case the costs of the taxation are borne by the party whose costs have been taxed, and the amount must be ascertained by the master and deducted by him accordingly in his certificate of taxation[5].

The undertakers or the acquiring authority must pay the sum certified by the master to be due in respect of the costs to the party entitled to them, and in default the sum may be recovered in the same way as any other costs payable under an order of the Supreme Court[6]. The master's taxation of these costs is open to review by the court[7].

1 For the meaning of 'the undertakers' see para 13 ante.
2 For the meaning of 'acquiring authority' see para 92 note 5 ante.
3 Lands Clauses Consolidation Act 1845 s 83 (amended by the Administration of Justice Act 1965 s 34, Sch 2) (where the 1845 Act is incorporated: see para 11 ante); Compulsory Purchase Act 1965 s 23(3) (where that Act applies: see para 15 ante). See further PRACTICE AND PROCEDURE; SOLICITORS. Where there is an agreement as to costs which includes matters not within the ambit of the above provisions, the order should not be made under the Land Clauses Consolidation Act 1845 s 83 (as amended): see *Middlesex County Light Railways Order 1903* [1908] WN 167; see also *Re North Eastern Railway Company Act 1901, Re Lands Clauses Consolidation Acts 1845, 1860, 1869, Holden v North Eastern Rly Co* (1904) 48 Sol Jo 526.
4 *Re South Eastern Rly Co, ex p Somerville* (1883) 23 ChD 167. Costs agreed to be paid on the abandonment of an inquisition are not taxable under this provision: *Marquis of Drogheda v Great Southern and Western Rly Co* (1847) 12 I Eq R 103.
5 Lands Clauses Consolidation Act 1845 s 83; Compulsory Purchase Act 1965 s 23(5).
6 Lands Clauses Consolidation Act 1845 s 83 (as amended: see note 3 supra); Compulsory Purchase Act 1965 s 23(4).
7 See *Re West Ferry Road, Poplar, London, Re Padwick's Estate* [1955] 2 All ER 638, [1955] 1 WLR 751, CA; see also *Owen v London and North Western Rly Co* (1867) LR 3 QB 54 at 60–61; *Sandback Charity Trustees v North Staffordshire Rly Co* (1877) 3 QBD 1 at 5, CA, per Brett LJ.

(iv) Deed Poll on Owner's Refusal to take Compensation etc or Absence

142. Payment into court; owner's refusal to take compensation, make title or convey. If the owner of any of the land[1] purchased by the undertakers[2] or the acquiring authority[3], or of any interest in the land so purchased, on tender of the purchase money or compensation either agreed or awarded to be paid in respect of the land or interest (1) refuses to accept it[4]; or (2) neglects or fails to make out a title to their satisfaction; or (3) refuses to convey or release the land as directed, the undertakers or authority may pay the purchase money or compensation[5] into court[6]. The compensation so paid into court must be placed to the credit of the parties interested in the land and the undertakers or acquiring authority must, so far as they can, give those parties' descriptions[7].

1 For the meaning of 'land' see para 92 note 1 ante. See also para 13 text to note 7 ante.
2 For the meaning of 'the undertakers' see para 13 ante.
3 For the meaning of 'acquiring authority' see para 92 note 5 ante.
4 If by reason of any disability the parties are unable to accept the purchase money this is not a refusal, even if other parties might complete for them: *Re Leeds Grammar School* [1901] 1 Ch 228. Other provision is made for such parties: see para 149 post.
5 If an advance payment of compensation has been made under the Land Compensation Act 1973 s 52(1) (see para 136 ante), the reference here to compensation must be read as if it were a reference to the balance of the compensation remaining unpaid: see s 52(10)(a); and para 137 ante.
6 Lands Clauses Consolidation Act 1845 s 76 (amended by the Administration of Justice Act 1965 s 17, Sch 1; and by the Compulsory Purchase Act 1965 s 39(4), Sch 8 Pt III) (where the 1845 Act is incorporated: see para 11 ante); Compulsory Purchase Act 1965 s 9(1) (where that Act applies: see para 15 ante). Similar provision is made for cases where an owner is abroad or cannot be found: see s 5(3), Sch 2 para 2(1); and para 143 post. As to payment into court see paras 98 note 6, 124 ante.
7 Ibid s 9(2).

143. Payment into court in owner's absence. Where the owner of the land[1] is absent from the United Kingdom[2], or cannot after diligent inquiry be found, and the undertakers[3] or the acquiring authority[4] have had the compensation assessed by a surveyor[5], they may pay into court the compensation so determined to the credit of the parties interested in the land, giving their descriptions so far as they are in a position to do so[6].

1 For the meaning of 'land' see para 92 note 1 ante. See also para 13 text to note 7 ante.
2 For the meaning of 'United Kingdom' see para 100 note 21 ante.
3 For the meaning of 'the undertakers' see para 13 ante.
4 For the meaning of 'acquiring authority' see para 92 note 5 ante.
5 See paras 100 ante, 200 post.
6 See the Lands Clauses Consolidation Act 1845 s 76 (amended by the Administration of Justice Act 1965 s 17, Sch 1; and by the Compulsory Purchase Act 1965 s 39(4), Sch 8 Pt III) (where the 1845 Act is incorporated: see para 11 ante); the Compulsory Purchase Act 1965 s 5(3), Sch 2 para 2(1) (where that Act applies: see para 15 ante). As to payment into court see paras 98 note 6, 124 ante. As to the execution of a deed poll see para 144 post; and as to payment out of court see para 146 post.

144. Execution of deed poll. After the payment of the purchase money or compensation into court[1], the undertakers[2] or the acquiring authority[3] may, if they think fit, execute a deed poll, under their common seal or by an officer duly appointed for that purpose[4] if they are a corporation, or if the undertakers are not a corporation under the hands of the undertakers or any two of them[5], containing a description of the land in respect of which the payment into court has been made[6] and declaring the circumstances under which and the names of the parties to whose credit the payment in has been made[7]. The deed poll must be stamped with the stamp duty which would have been payable upon a conveyance to the undertakers or acquiring authority of the land described in it[8]. Thereupon, all the estate and interest in the land of the parties for whose use, and in respect of which, the purchase money or compensation has been paid into court will vest absolutely in the undertakers or the authority, and as against those parties they will be entitled to immediate possession of the land[9]. The procedure confers no rights as against third parties, and is not applicable to cases where the person purporting to sell has no title at all to the land[10]. In order that an estate or interest may vest, the person who fails to make out a good title must have some title, and the failure to make out a title must arise from an independent estate or interest outstanding in a third party; the effect of this procedure is to vest in the undertakers or authority the estate and interest of the person so failing, and no more[11]. Thus, if the person whose interest has been agreed to be acquired proves to have only an inchoate possessory title, the undertakers or authority acquire this interest only, and the real owner will not afterwards be barred from asserting his rights[12].

The undertakers or acquiring authority, therefore, before adopting the above procedure of vesting the property by means of a deed poll, ought to give the owner an opportunity of making a good title[13]. If they have entered into an agreement with any person for the purchase of land, and that person fails to make out a good title, he cannot compel them to adopt this procedure; but if they do not, they cannot remain in possession under the agreement[14].

1 See paras 142–143 ante.
2 For the meaning of 'the undertakers' see para 13 ante.
3 For the meaning of 'acquiring authority' see para 92 note 5 ante.
4 Ie in accordance with the Law of Property Act 1925 s 74(4): see CORPORATIONS.
5 Any rule of law which required a seal for the valid execution of an instrument as a deed by an individual has, except in relation to a corporation sole, been abolished: Law of Property (Miscellaneous Provisions) Act 1989 s 1(1)(b), (10). By virtue of s 1(7), the provisions of s 1 (as amended) have effect as to signing, sealing or delivery of an instrument by an individual in place of any provision of the Lands Clauses Consolidation Act 1845 as to signing, sealing or delivery; and the requirement in s 77 (as amended) that, where the undertakers are not a corporation, the deed poll is to be executed under seal is accordingly of no effect in relation to deeds executed on or after 31 July 1990: see the Law of Property (Miscellaneous Provisions) Act 1989 (Commencement) Order 1990, SI 1990/1175. See further DEEDS.

6 See paras 142–143 ante.
7 Lands Clauses Consolidation Act 1845 s 77 (amended by the Administration of Justice Act 1965 s 17(1), Sch 1; and by the Compulsory Purchase Act 1965 s 39(4), Sch 8 Pt II) (where the 1845 Act is incorporated: see para 11 ante); Compulsory Purchase Act 1965 ss 9(3), 28(1) (where that Act applies: see para 15 ante). As to absent owners see s 5(3), Sch 2 para 2(2). The provisions of the 1965 Act as to the execution of deed polls have effect subject to the Law of Property Act 1925 s 7(4) (under which any such power of disposing of a legal estate exercisable by a person who is not the estate owner is, when practicable, to be exercised in the name and on behalf of the estate owner: see REAL PROPERTY vol 39 para 589): Compulsory Purchase Act 1965 s 28(3).
8 Lands Clauses Consolidation Act 1845 s 77 (as amended: see note 6 supra); Compulsory Purchase Act 1965 s 28(2). As to the requirements to be complied with as to the production of the instrument effecting the conveyance see para 139 ante.
9 Lands Clauses Consolidation Act 1845 s 77 (as amended: see note 6 supra); Compulsory Purchase Act 1965 s 9(4). As to absent owners see s 5(3), Sch 2 para 2(3). Section 9(4) and Sch 2 para 2(3) are modified in relation to the compulsory acquisition of rights by, inter alia, (1) a local authority, by the Local Government (Miscellaneous Provisions) Act 1976 s 13(3)(b) (as amended), Sch 1 para 8 (see LOCAL GOVERNMENT vol 28 para 1219); (2) the Development Board for Rural Wales, by the Development of Rural Wales Act 1976 s 6(7) (as amended), Sch 4 para 8 (see TOWN AND COUNTRY PLANNING vol 46 (Reissue) para 1200); (3) urban development corporations, by the Local Government, Planning and Land Act 1980 s 144, Sch 28 para 23(3) (see TOWN AND COUNTRY PLANNING vol 46 (Reissue) para 1297); (4) highway authorities, by the Highways Act 1980 s 250(5)(a) (as substituted), Sch 19 para 8 (see HIGHWAYS vol 21 (Reissue) para 808); (5) public gas suppliers, by the Gas Act 1986 s 9(3), Sch 3 para 9 (see FUEL AND ENERGY vol 19(1) (Reissue) para 636); (6) housing action trusts, by the Housing Act 1988 s 78(2), Sch 10 para 23(1) (see HOUSING); (7) licence holders under the Electricity Act 1989, by s 10(1), Sch 3 para 10 (see FUEL AND ENERGY vol 19(2) (Reissue) para 985); (8) the National Rivers Authority, by the Water Resources Act 1991 s 154(5), Sch 18 para 5 (see WATER); and (9) water and sewerage undertakers, by the Water Industry Act 1991 s 155(5), Sch 9 para 5 (see WATER).
10 *Wells v Chelmsford Local Board of Health* (1880) 15 ChD 108.
11 *Douglass v London and North Western Rly Co* (1857) 3 K & J 173.
12 *Ex p Winder* (1877) 6 ChD 696; *Gedye v Works and Public Buildings Comrs* [1891] 2 Ch 630, CA; *Wells v Chelmsford Local Board of Health* (1880) 15 ChD 108. See also *Re Harris, ex p LCC* [1901] 1 Ch 931; and *Ex p Burdett Coutts* [1927] 2 Ch 98.
13 *Doe d Hutchinson v Manchester, Bury and Rossendale Rly Co* (1845) 15 LJ Ex 208.
14 *Douglass v London and North Western Rly Co* (1857) 3 K & J 173.

145. Registered land. If, in the case of registered land, the proprietor refuses to execute a transfer, or his execution of a transfer cannot be obtained or can only be obtained after undue delay or expense, then, after due notice to the proprietor, on production of the land certificate unless the registrar makes an order to the contrary, and on such other evidence as he deems sufficient, the registrar at the Land Registry may make such entry in, or correction of, the register as he deems fit for vesting the land in the person in whom the legal estate would have been vested if the land had not been registered[1].

1 Land Registration Rules 1925, SR & O 1925/1093, r 131. As to dealings with registered land generally see LAND REGISTRATION.

146. Application for payment out. On the application of any person[1] claiming all or any part of the money paid into court[2], or claiming all or any part of the land[3] in respect of which it was paid into court, or any interest in it, the Chancery Division of the High Court may order its distribution according to the claimants' respective estates, titles or interests; and if, before the money is distributed, it is placed in an investment account or otherwise invested[4], the court may likewise order payment of the dividends of it, and may make such other order as it thinks fit[5]. The application to the court is by originating summons to be heard in chambers[6].

Thus, a legal or equitable mortgagee may apply for payment out to him of the amount due on his mortgage and of arrears of interest up to six years[7]. Persons may also apply who are entitled in respect of trade claims or loss of profits[8], or who have established their title by other proceedings[9]. If the undertakers pay off any of these interests, they may themselves apply for payment out[10].

1   As to such persons see the text and notes 7–10 infra; and para 147 post.
2   As to payment into court see paras 98 note 6, 124 ante.
3   For the meaning of 'land' see para 92 note 1 ante. See also para 13 text to note 7 ante.
4   Ie under the Administration of Justice Act 1982 s 38 (as amended): see COURTS; PRACTICE AND PROCEDURE.
5   Lands Clauses Consolidation Act 1845 s 78 (amended by the Administration of Justice Act 1965 ss 17(1), 34, Schs 1, 2; and by the Administration of Justice Act 1982 s 46(2)(a)(iii)) (where the 1845 Act is incorporated: see para 11 ante); Compulsory Purchase Act 1965 s 9(5) (where that Act applies: see para 15 ante); Interpretation Act 1978 s 17(2)(a); RSC Ord 92 r 5(1). As to absent owners see the Compulsory Purchase Act 1965 s 5(3), Sch 2 para 3(1).
6   RSC Ord 92 r 5(1)(d), (2). If the application is made in a pending cause or matter, or a similar application has previously been made by petition or originating summons, the application is by ordinary summons: Ord 29 r 5(2). Application for payment out of sums not exceeding £15,000 may be made ex parte on affidavit: see Ord 92 r 5(3).
7   *Re Marriage, ex p London, Tilbury and Southend Rly Co and Eastern Counties and London and Blackwall Rly Co* (1861) 9 WR 843; *Re Stead's Mortgaged Estates* (1876) 2 ChD 713; *Pile v Pile, ex p Lambton* (1876) 3 ChD 36, CA. See further LIMITATION OF ACTIONS.
8   *Cooper v Metropolitan Board of Works* (1883) 25 ChD 472, CA.
9   *Galliers v Metropolitan Rly Co* (1871) LR 11 Eq 410.
10 *Re Marriage, ex p London, Tilbury and Southend Rly Co and Eastern Counties and London and Blackwall Rly Co* (1861) 9 WR 843; *Cooper v Metropolitan Board of Works* (1883) 25 ChD 472 at 480, CA.

147. Court's powers as to distribution of money. The court uses its own machinery to determine the interest of the party applying, and also to apportion the amount due to him[1]. Thus, if the money paid in represents the value of more land or of a greater interest in land than that to which the claimant can make title, the court will order an inquiry as to the extent of his interest, and will order an amount equivalent to it to be paid to him, the balance being either retained in court or paid out to the undertakers[2].

If various persons having interests in the land apply, the court will also determine their respective rights[3]. When there are rival claims in respect of the money in court, the rival claimants may be brought before the court by permission being granted to the applicant to serve them, except in the case of the Crown, which cannot be so brought before the court[4]. The matter in dispute may, however, be settled by other proceedings[5], and the court may direct the application to stand over until it is so settled[6].

If any question arises respecting the title to the land in respect of which the money has been paid into court[7], the persons respectively in possession of the land as being the owners, or in receipt of the rents of the land as being entitled to them at the time the land was purchased or taken, are deemed to have been lawfully entitled to the land until the contrary is shown to the court's satisfaction; and, unless the contrary is so shown, the persons so in possession, and all persons claiming under them or consistently with their possession, are deemed to be entitled to the money so paid in, and to the interest or dividends of it or of the securities purchased with it, and the same must be paid and applied accordingly[8]. Thus, persons who have merely possessory titles[9], or titles which would have ripened into possessory titles but for the undertakers' action[10], are entitled to the deposited money or to the dividends. The court will not, however, order the corpus of the fund to be paid out until the possessory title would have ripened[11]. Similarly, where part of an owner's land is taken, the court, on being satisfied that he has a title which can be supported, will order the money or the dividends to be paid to him without further proof or argument because his title to the remainder of the land ought not to be jeopardised[12]. Persons in possession of closed burial grounds are similarly entitled to the fund in court[13].

A person who has gone into possession for a lesser interest than the fee simple, such as a lessee, and is in possession under that interest at the date of the payment in, cannot claim the whole of the money in court as the value of the land although the reversioner is unknown, as he is not in possession as owner, but is only entitled to so much as represents the value of the interest in respect of which he is in possession[14].

1 *Brandon v Brandon* (1864) 2 Drew & Sm 305.
2 *Re Alston's Estate* (1856) 5 WR 189, where it was admitted that a small part of the land originally claimed, and in respect of which the money was paid in, did not belong to the claimant; *Re Perks' Estate* (1853) 1 Sm & G 545; *Re North London Rly Co, ex p Cooper* (1865) 34 LJ Ch 373; *Re North London Rly Co, ex p Hayne* (1865) 12 LT 200.
3 *Re Marriage, ex p London, Tilbury and Southend Rly Co and Eastern Counties and London and Blackwall Rly Co* (1861) 9 WR 843; *Re Stead's Mortgaged Estates* (1876) 2 ChD 713; *Re County of London (Devons Road, Poplar) Housing Confirmation Order 1945* [1956] 1 All ER 818, [1956] 1 WLR 499.
4 *Re Lowestoft Manor and Great Eastern Rly Co, ex p Reeve* (1883) 24 ChD 253 at 256, CA.
5 *Bogg v Midland Rly Co* (1867) LR 4 Eq 310; *Cooper v Metropolitan Board of Works* (1883) 25 ChD 472, CA; *Pile v Pile, ex p Lambton* (1876) 3 ChD 36, CA; *Galliers v Metropolitan Rly Co* (1871) LR 11 Eq 410; *Birmingham and District Land Co v London and North Western Rly Co* (1888) 40 ChD 268, CA.
6 *Re Lowestoft Manor and Great Eastern Rly Co, ex p Reeve* (1883) 24 ChD 253, CA; and see *Re St Pancras Burial Ground* (1866) LR 3 Eq 173; *Ex p Freemen and Stallingers of Sunderland* (1852) 1 Drew 184.
7 See paras 142–143 ante.
8 Lands Clauses Consolidation Act 1845 s 79 (amended by the Administration of Justice Act 1965 s 17(1), Sch 1) (where the 1845 Act is incorporated: see para 11 ante); Compulsory Purchase Act 1965 s 25(3) (where that Act applies: see para 15 ante).
9 *Re Cook's Estate* (1863) 8 LT 759; *Re Alston's Estate* (1856) 5 WR 189; *Ex p Webster* [1866] WN 246. Cf *Perry v Clissold* [1907] AC 73, PC.
10 *Re Evans* (1873) 42 LJ Ch 357; *Ex p Winder* (1877) 6 ChD 696; *Re Metropolitan Street Improvement Act 1877, ex p Chamberlain* (1880) 14 ChD 323; *Re Harris, ex p LCC* [1901] 1 Ch 931; *Re Harris, Hansler v Harris* [1909] WN 181; and cf *Re Greenough, Re Hollinsworth* (1871) 19 WR 580. Where the payment into court was not made in pursuance of the provisions of the Lands Clauses Acts, the court, in *Ex p Burdett Coutts* [1927] 2 Ch 98, directed the money to be paid out to the person with whom the contract had been made, as his title had not been proved to be defective. As to the Lands Clauses Acts see para 11 ante.
11 *Re Harris, ex p LCC* [1901] 1 Ch 931.
12 *Re Sterry's Estate* (1855) 3 WR 561; *Re St Pancras Burial Ground* (1866) LR 3 Eq 173; and see *Ex p Freemen and Stallingers of Sunderland* (1852) 1 Drew 184 at 189.
13 *Re St Pancras Burial Ground* (1866) LR 3 Eq 173; and see *Campbell v Liverpool Corpn* (1870) LR 9 Eq 579.
14 *Gedye v Works and Public Buildings Comrs* [1891] 2 Ch 630, CA; *Re Harris, ex p LCC* [1901] 1 Ch 931; *Ex p Burdett Coutts* [1927] 2 Ch 98.

148. Court's power to award costs. Where the Lands Clauses Acts[1] are incorporated in the special Act[2] or the Compulsory Purchase Act 1965 applies[3], the court has power, in all cases of money paid into court as purchase money or compensation under those Acts[4], to order the undertakers[5] or acquiring authority[6] to pay the costs[7] of or incurred in consequence of the purchase of the land[8], and the cost of investing the money in court or of reinvesting it in other land[9], except where the money has been so paid or deposited by reason of the wilful refusal of any person entitled to it to accept or receive it or to convey or release the land in respect of which the money was payable, or by reason of the wilful neglect of any person to make out a good title to the land[10]. In these excepted cases, and in all cases of money paid into court under Acts not incorporating the Lands Clauses Acts, the costs of and incidental to all proceedings in the Supreme Court are in the discretion of the court or judge unless there are express statutory provisions or rules of court to the contrary[11].

By wilful refusal or wilful neglect is meant a refusal or neglect without any reason[12], or with only a frivolous reason, or by imposing an improper condition such as the prior payment of costs[13]. If the vendor has a substantial reason, whether invalid or not, the refusal or neglect is not considered wilful[14]. A refusal is not wilful because the service of the notice to treat is considered invalid on substantial, though wrong, grounds[15], or because the vendor is legally advised that the undertakers or acquiring authority have no power to take the land[16], or because he has not paid off incumbrances which exceed the price to be paid for the land or procured the holders to join in the conveyance[17]; but a refusal is wilful where, after the compulsory purchase order has been confirmed, the vendor is legally advised that the order may be bad[18].

 1 As to the Lands Clauses Acts see para 11 ante.
 2 This is subject to any variation in the special Act of the provisions in the Lands Clauses Acts, as to which see *Re St Katherine's Dock Co* (1866) 14 WR 978. For the meaning of 'special Act' see paras 11, 16 ante.
 3 As to the application of the Compulsory Purchase Act 1965 see para 15 ante.
 4 See paras 142–143 ante.
 5 For the meaning of 'the undertakers' see para 15 ante.
 6 For the meaning of 'acquiring authority' see para 92 note 5 ante.
 7 For these purposes, references to costs include references to all reasonable charges and expenses incidental to the matters mentioned in the Compulsory Purchase Act 1965 s 26 (see the text and notes 1–6 supra, 8–10 infra) and to the cost of (1) obtaining the proper orders for any of the purposes set out therein; (2) obtaining the orders for the payment of dividends out of the compensation; (3) obtaining the orders for the payment out of court of the principal amount of the compensation, or of any securities in which it is invested; and (4) all proceedings relating to such orders, except such as are occasioned by litigation between adverse claimants: s 26(3).
 8 For the meaning of 'land' see para 92 note 1 ante. See also para 13 text to note 7 ante.
 9 See the Lands Clauses Consolidation Act 1845 s 80 (amended by the Administration of Justice Act 1965 s 17(1), Sch 1) (where the 1845 Act is incorporated: see para 11 ante); and the Compulsory Purchase Act 1965 s 26(2) (where that Act applies: see para 15 ante). This also applies to money paid in respect of persons unknown, as they are not excepted cases. The costs of not more than one application for reinvestment may be allowed unless it appears to the High Court that it is for the benefit of the parties interested in the compensation that it should be invested in the purchase of land in different sums and at different times: s 26(4).
10 Lands Clauses Consolidation Act 1845 s 80 (amended by the Administration of Justice Act 1965 Sch 1); Compulsory Purchase Act 1965 s 26(1). This provision is not affected by RSC Ord 62 r 3(3), which gives the court a discretion as to costs: *Reeve v Gibson* [1891] 1 QB 652, CA; *Hasker v Wood* (1885) 54 LJQB 419, CA. An incumbrancer who has an honest claim and has to apply for payment out of court of his money will not be deprived of costs merely because his mortgagor had not conducted the proceedings in such a way as would entitle the mortgagor to costs: *Dublin Corpn v Carroll* (1915) 49 ILT 60, CA.
11 See the Supreme Court Act 1981 s 51(1) (substituted by the Courts and Legal Services Act 1990 s 4(1)); and *Re Schmarr* [1902] 1 Ch 326, CA; *Re Fisher* [1894] 1 Ch 450, CA; *Dublin Corpn v Carroll* (1915) 49 ILT 60, CA.
12 See *Re Dublin Corpn, ex p Dowling* (1881) 7 LR Ir 173.
13 *Re Turner's Estate and Metropolitan Railway Act 1860* (1861) 5 LT 524.
14 *Re Windsor, Staines and South Western Railway Act* (1850) 12 Beav 522; *Ex p Birkbeck Freehold Land Society* (1883) 24 ChD 119; *Re Leeds Grammar School* [1901] 1 Ch 228.
15 *Re East India Docks and Birmingham Junction Railway Act, ex p Bradshaw* (1848) 16 Sim 174; *Ex p Railstone* (1851) 15 Jur 1028; *Re Metropolitan District Rly Co, ex p Lawson* (1869) 17 WR 186.
16 *Re Ryde Comrs, ex p Dashwood* (1856) 26 LJ Ch 299; *Re St Luke's Vestry Middlesex and London School Board* [1889] WN 102.
17 *Re Crystal Palace Rly Co, Re Divers* (1855) 1 Jur NS 995; *Re Nash, Re London Tilbury and Southend Railway Act 1852* (1855) 25 LJ Ch 20, sub nom *Re Nash, Re Lands Clauses Consolidation Act 1945* 1 Jur NS 1082.
18 *Re Jones and Cardiganshire County Council* (1913) 57 Sol Jo 374.

(v) Deed Poll where Persons under Disability etc

149. Payment of purchase money into court or to trustees for persons under disability. Where any interest in land is purchased or taken from a person under disability who is not entitled to sell or convey except under the provisions of the special Act[1], the Lands Clauses Acts[2] or the Compulsory Purchase Act 1965, the purchase money or compensation, if it amounts to £200 or more, must be paid into the Supreme Court[3]. If it exceeds £20 but does not exceed £200, the purchase money or compensation may be paid into court or to two trustees[4], and if it does not exceed £20 it must be paid to the person entitled[5]. These provisions are limited in their application because the power to sell and convey land of a person under disability has been otherwise extended[6]. Where the undertakers have compulsory powers and title can be made under a subsisting contract, whether by virtue of a notice to treat or otherwise, without payment into court, title is to be made in that way unless, to avoid expense or delay or for any special reason, the undertakers consider it expedient that the money should be paid into court[7].

1 As to the Lands Clauses Acts see para 11 ante.
2 For the meaning of 'special Act' see paras 11, 16 ante.
3 See para 150 et seq post.
4 See para 166 post.
5 See para 167 post.
6 See para 96 ante.
7 Law of Property Act 1925 s 42(7). Apart from this provision, the undertakers could not insist on the sale being carried out under other statutory powers to save themselves expense: see *Re Pigott and Great Western Rly Co* (1881) 18 ChD 146; *Re Lady Bentinck and London and North Western Rly Co* (1895) 12 TLR 100; *Re Leeds Grammar School* [1901] 1 Ch 228.

150. Payment in respect of ecclesiastical, university or college land. Where the land[1] acquired under the authority of a compulsory purchase order to which the Compulsory Purchase Act 1965 applies[2] is ecclesiastical property[3], any sums agreed or awarded for the purchase of the land, or to be paid by way of compensation for damage sustained by reason of severance or injury affecting it, are not to be paid as otherwise directed by that Act[4] but must be paid (1) to the Church Commissioners, in the case of land which is not diocesan glebe land[5]; and (2) to the Diocesan Board of Finance[6] in which the land is vested, in the case of diocesan glebe land, and in either case must be applied for the purposes for which the proceeds of a sale by agreement of the land would be applicable under any enactment or Measure authorising such a sale or disposing of the proceeds of such a sale[7].

Where the land acquired belongs to the Universities of Oxford, Cambridge or Durham or any of their colleges[8], and the purchase money or compensation would otherwise be required to be paid, or has been paid, into court or to trustees, the money or compensation may instead be paid to the university or college[9].

1 For the meaning of 'land' see para 92 note 1 ante.
2 See para 15 ante.
3 Ie ecclesiastical property as defined in the Acquisition of Land Act 1981 s 12(3) (as amended): see para 37 note 7 ante.
4 As to the payment of purchase money and compensation see para 122 et seq ante.
5 For these purposes, 'diocesan glebe land' has the same meaning as in the Endowments and Glebe Measure 1976 (see ECCLESIASTICAL LAW): Compulsory Purchase Act 1965 s 31 (definition added by the Planning and Compensation Act 1991 s 70, Sch 15 para 19).

6　For these purposes, 'Diocesan Board of Finance' has the same meaning as in the Endowments and Glebe Measure 1976 (see ECCLESIASTICAL LAW): Compulsory Purchase Act 1965 s 31 (definition added by the Planning and Compensation Act 1991 Sch 15 para 19).

7　Compulsory Purchase Act 1965 s 31 (amended by the Acquisition of Land Act 1981 s 34(1), Sch 4 para 14(5); and by the Planning and Compensation Act 1991 Sch 15 para 19). The Compulsory Purchase Act 1965 s 31 (as so amended) does not apply in relation to a compulsory purchase order under the Pipe-lines Act 1962 s 11 (see RAILWAYS vol 38 para 1077): Compulsory Purchase Act 1965 s 37(2).

8　Ie a university or college to which the Universities and College Estates Act 1925 applies, other than Eton or Winchester: see s 1.

9　Ibid s 28(1), (2) (amended by virtue of the Universities and College Estates Act 1964 ss 2, 3, Sch 1 para 12(1)). In the case of Eton or Winchester, the money or compensation may be paid to the Minister of Agriculture, Fisheries and Food: Universities and College Estates Act 1925 ss 28(1), (2), 43; Transfer of Functions (Ministry of Food) Order 1955, SI 1955/554, art 3(1). Any such money held by the minister at 16 August 1964 in respect of the universities or colleges mentioned in the text was to be transferred to the college: Universities and College Estates Act 1964 ss 3(2), 5(4).

151. Payment into court of £200 or over. When any land[1] or any interest in it is purchased or taken from a person under disability who is not entitled to sell or convey it except under the provisions of the special Act[2], the Lands Clauses Acts[3] or the Compulsory Purchase Act 1965[4], the purchase price or compensation payable in respect of the land or interest, or in respect of any permanent damage to any such land, must be paid into the Supreme Court if it amounts to or exceeds £200[5].

Also all sums of money exceeding £200 payable by the undertakers[6] or the acquiring authority[7] in respect of the taking, using or interfering with any land under a contract or agreement with any person who is not entitled to dispose of the land absolutely for his own benefit must be paid into court[8] and any such contracting party may not retain for his own use (1) any part of any sums agreed or contracted to be paid for or in respect of the taking, using or interfering with any of the land; or (2) any part of any sums agreed or contracted to be paid in lieu of bridges, tunnels or other accommodation works[9]. All such money is deemed to be contracted to be paid for and on account of the several parties interested in the land, whether in possession or in remainder, reversion or expectancy[10].

Furthermore, if, in order to obtain possession, the undertakers or the acquiring authority have been compelled to pay the money to or on behalf of a person under disability, that person may be required to pay it into court[11].

If necessary, the undertakers or the authority will be compelled by mandamus to pay the money into court[12]; but as the requirement of the payment is for the safe custody of the money and is not necessary in order to perfect the title of the undertakers or the authority, the court may sanction the application of the money to some proper purpose without the payment in[13].

1　For the meaning of 'land' see para 92 note 1 ante. See also para 13 text to note 7 ante.

2　For the meaning of 'special Act' see paras 11, 16 ante.

3　Ie under the Lands Clauses Consolidation Act 1845 s 7 (as amended) (where that Act is incorporated: see para 11 ante): see para 96 ante. As to the classes of person referred to see *Kelland v Fulford* (1877) 6 ChD 491; *Newton v Metropolitan Rly Co* (1861) 8 Jur NS 738; *Re Chelsea Waterworks Co* (1887) 56 LJ Ch 640. As to the Lands Clauses Acts see para 11 ante.

4　Ie the Compulsory Purchase Act 1965 s 2, Sch 1 paras 1–3 (as amended) (where that Act applies: see para 15 ante): see paras 96–97 ante. See also note 5 infra.

5　See the Lands Clauses Consolidation Act 1845 s 69 (amended by the Administration of Justice Act 1965 s 17(1), Sch 1; and by the Compulsory Purchase Act 1965 Sch 8 Pt II); the Compulsory Purchase Act 1965 Sch 1 para 6(1), (2). This is subject to the provisions of Sch 1 (as amended): see paras 96–97 ante; the text and notes 6–10 infra; and para 152 et seq post. As to payment into court see paras 98 note 6, 124 ante. These provisions are limited in their application because the power to sell and convey land of a person under disability has been otherwise extended: see para 96 ante. As to when money paid in will pass under a conveyance of his property by the party entitled see *Ex p Ballinrobe and Claremorris Light Rly Co and Kenny* [1913] 1 IR 519.

6 For the meaning of 'the undertakers' see para 13 ante.

7 For the meaning of 'acquiring authority' see para 92 note 5 ante.

8 If the sum exceeds £20 but is less than £200, it may be paid to two trustees, instead of into court: see para 166 post.

9 Lands Clauses Consolidation Act 1845 s 73 (amended by the Administration of Justice Act 1965 Sch 1); Compulsory Purchase Act 1965 Sch 1 para 9(1), as read with the enactments cited in note 5 supra.

10 Lands Clauses Consolidation Act 1845 s 73 (as amended: see note 9 supra); Compulsory Purchase Act 1965 Sch 1 para 9(2). This provision does not otherwise affect contracts by persons under a disability under the Lands Clauses Consolidation Act 1845 s 7 (as amended) or the Compulsory Purchase Act 1965 Sch 1 paras 1–3 (as amended): see *Taylor v Directors etc of Chichester and Midhurst Rly Co* (1870) LR 4 HL 628. As to payment under contract to a tenant for life for not opposing a bill see *Pole v Pole* (1865) 2 Drew & Sm 420.

11 *London and North Western Rly Co v Lancaster Corpn* (1851) 15 Beav 22. Alternatively other provision for safety may be made by the court: see the text to note 13 infra.

12 *Barnett v Great Eastern Rly Co* (1868) 18 LT 408; *Williams v Llanelly Rly Co* (1868) 19 LT 310.

13 *Re London, Brighton and South Coast Rly Co, ex p Earl of Abergavenny* (1856) 4 WR 315; *Re Milnes (a Person of Unsound Mind)* (1875) 1 ChD 28, CA.

152. Execution of deed poll. When the compensation agreed or awarded in respect of the land purchased or taken has been paid into court[1], the owner of the land[2], when required so to do by the undertakers[3] or acquiring authority[4], must duly convey the land or interest to them or as they direct[5]. In default of doing so, or if he fails to make a good title to the land to their satisfaction, they may execute a deed poll containing a description of the land and reciting its acquisition by them, the names of the parties from whom it was purchased, the amount of the compensation paid into court, and the default[6].

On execution of the deed poll, all the estate and interest in the land belonging to, or capable of being sold and conveyed by, any person as between whom and the undertakers or authority the compensation was agreed or awarded and paid into court, will vest absolutely in the undertakers or authority; and as against all such persons, and all parties on behalf of whom they are enabled to sell and convey[7], the undertakers or authority will be entitled to immediate possession of the land[8].

1 See para 151 notes 2–3 ante.

2 In this context, 'owner' includes all parties who are enabled to sell or convey the land by the Lands Clauses Consolidation Act 1845 (see s 75 (as amended)) or by the Compulsory Purchase Act 1965 s 2, Sch 1 (as amended) (see Sch 1 para 10(1)). For the meaning of 'land' see para 92 note 1 ante. See also para 13 text to note 7 ante.

3 For the meaning of 'the undertakers' see para 13 ante.

4 For the meaning of 'acquiring authority' see para 92 note 5 ante.

5 Lands Clauses Consolidation Act 1845 s 75 (amended by the Administration of Justice Act 1965 s 17(1), Sch 1) (where the 1845 Act is incorporated: see para 11 ante); Compulsory Purchase Act 1965 Sch 1 para 10(1) (where that Act applies: see para 15 ante). These provisions are limited in their application because the power to sell and convey land of a person under disability has been otherwise extended: see para 96 ante. As to the sealing, stamping and execution of deeds poll see para 144 ante. The undertakers or authority may not execute a deed poll instead of a conveyance merely to save themselves expense: *Re Cary-Elwes' Contract* [1906] 2 Ch 143.

6 Lands Clauses Consolidation Act 1845 s 75 (as amended: see note 5 supra); Compulsory Purchase Act 1965 Sch 1 para 10(2).

7 See para 151 notes 2–3 ante.

8 Lands Clauses Consolidation Act 1845 s 75 (as amended: see note 5 supra); Compulsory Purchase Act 1965 Sch 1 para 10(3). Schedule 1 para 10(3) is modified in relation to the compulsory acquisition of rights by, inter alia, (1) a local authority, by the Local Government (Miscellaneous Provisions) Act 1976 s 13(3)(b) (as amended), Sch 1 para 8 (see LOCAL GOVERNMENT vol 28 para 1219); (2) the Development Board for Rural Wales, by the Development of Rural Wales Act 1976 s 6(7) (as amended), Sch 4

para 8 (see TOWN AND COUNTRY PLANNING vol 46 (Reissue) para 1200); (3) urban development corporations, by the Local Government, Planning and Land Act 1980 s 144, Sch 28 para 23(3) (see TOWN AND COUNTRY PLANNING vol 46 (Reissue) para 1297); (4) highway authorities, by the Highways Act 1980 s 250(5)(a) (as substituted), Sch 19 para 8 (see HIGHWAYS vol 21 (Reissue) para 808); (5) public gas suppliers, by the Gas Act 1986 s 9(3), Sch 3 para 9 (see FUEL AND ENERGY vol 19(1) (Reissue) para 636); (6) housing action trusts, by the Housing Act 1988 s 78(2), Sch 10 para 23(1) (see HOUSING); (7) licence holders under the Electricity Act 1989, by s 10(1), Sch 3 para 10 (see FUEL AND ENERGY vol 19(2) (Reissue) para 985); (8) the National Rivers Authority, by the Water Resources Act 1991 s 154(5), Sch 18 para 5 (see WATER); and (9) water and sewerage undertakers, by the Water Industry Act 1991 s 155(5), Sch 9 para 5 (see WATER).

153. Investment of money paid in and disposal of income. Until the money paid in is applied, it will be placed in an investment account or otherwise invested under the Administration of Justice Act 1982[1]. If the money paid in is so dealt with, the annual proceeds of it must be paid to the person who would for the time being have been entitled to the rents and profits of the land in respect of which the compensation was paid[2]. The interim investment and payment of the proceeds or income may be made on an order of the Chancery Division of the High Court made in chambers on the application by originating summons[3] of the party who would have been entitled to the rents and profits of the land in respect of which the money has been paid in[4]. If there is more than one sum of money in court in respect of two or more pieces of land to the rents and profits of which one person would have been entitled, the application of all the sums may be dealt with on one summons[5].

1   Lands Clauses Consolidation Act 1845 s 70 (amended by the Administration of Justice Act 1965 s 17(1), Sch 1; and by the Administration of Justice Act 1982 s 46(2)(a)(iii)); Compulsory Purchase Act 1965 s 25(1); Interpretation Act 1978 s 17(2)(a). The money is invested under the Administration of Justice Act 1982 s 38 (as amended): see COURTS; PRACTICE AND PROCEDURE. These provisions are limited in their application because the power to sell and convey land of a person under disability has been otherwise extended: see para 96 ante.
2   Lands Clauses Consolidation Act 1845 s 70 (as amended: see note 1 supra); Compulsory Purchase Act 1965 s 2, Sch 1 para 6(3). For the meaning of 'land' see para 92 note 1 ante. See also para 13 text to note 7 ante. The proceeds or income may be ordered to be paid to the person who was tenant for life of the land taken, even though the conveyance has not been executed, provided the undertakers or acquiring authority have taken possession (*Re Wrey* (1865) 13 WR 543; *Ex p Cofield* (1847) 11 Jur 1071; *Re Hungerford* (1855) 1 K & J 413). They may be ordered to be paid to trustees, whether private (see *Re Clinton* (1860) 6 Jur NS 601; *Re Coulson's Settlement* (1867) 17 LT 27; *Re Pryor's Settlement Trusts* (1876) 35 LT 202; *Re Foy's Trusts* (1875) 23 WR 744; *Re Metropolitan Rly Co and Maire* [1876] WN 245; *Re Goe's Estate* (1854) 3 WR 119), or charitable (see *Re Collins' Charity* (1851) 20 LJ Ch 168), and to persons entitled to the fees, if any, of disused burial grounds (*Ex p Rector of Liverpool* (1870) LR 11 Eq 15; *Ex p Rector of St Martin's, Birmingham* (1870) LR 11 Eq 23; *Re St Pancras Burial Ground* (1866) LR 3 Eq 173). Where there are successive interests the order may direct that the dividends be paid to the person entitled for the time being, as in the case of rectors and vicars (*Re Rector etc of St Benet's* (1865) 12 LT 762; *A-G v Brandreth* (1842) 1 Y & C Ch Cas 200; *Re East Lincolnshire Rly Co's Acts, ex p Archbishop of Canterbury* (1848) 5 Ry & Can Cas 699), or to a man for his life and then to his wife (*Re How's Trusts* (1850) 15 Jur 266; *Re Lowndes' Trust* (1851) 20 LJ Ch 422; *Re Brent's Trusts* (1860) 8 WR 270). If the order is not made in this form, a fresh order may be necessary: *Re Jolliffe's Estate* (1870) LR 9 Eq 668. The dividends unpaid at the date of the death of any person entitled to the rents and profits will be apportioned and paid to his personal representatives: Court Funds Rules 1987 r 43.
3   RSC Ord 92 r 5(1)(c), (2). An application in a pending cause or matter, or where an application for the same purpose has previously been made by petition or originating summons, is made by ordinary summons: Ord 92 r 5(2).
4   Lands Clauses Consolidation Act 1845 s 70 (as amended: see note 1 supra; further amended by the Administration of Justice Act 1965 s 34, Sch 2); Compulsory Purchase Act 1965 Sch 1 para 6(3), (4). As to costs see paras 154–155 post.
5   See para 157 text and note 8 post.

154. Costs of investment. Pending the permanent application of the money paid into court[1], the undertakers[2] or acquiring authority[3] may be ordered to pay the costs of investing the money[4], even if a contract for the purchase of land as a permanent investment has been entered into[5]. The order does not affect the liability of the undertakers or authority to pay the costs of a subsequent permanent investment[6]. The court also has power to order them to pay the costs of more than one interim investment, as, for example, of an investment on mortgage when under a previous order the money has been invested in consols[7]. Such an investment on mortgage may, however, be treated as a permanent investment[8]. When the money is ordered to be invested in stock, the official broker must be employed[9] and the whole sum ordered must be invested, as the undertakers or authority are required to pay the broker's charges[10].

1　See para 153 ante.
2　For the meaning of 'the undertakers' see para 13 ante.
3　For the meaning of 'acquiring authority' see para 92 note 5 ante.
4　See the Lands Clauses Consolidation Act 1845 s 80 (as amended); the Compulsory Purchase Act 1965 s 26(2)(b); and para 148 ante. These provisions are limited in their application because the power to sell and convey land of a person under disability has been otherwise extended: see para 96 ante.
5　*Re Liverpool etc Rly Co* (1853) 17 Beav 392.
6　*Re Dodd's Estate* (1871) 19 WR 741; *Re Wilkinson's Estate* (1868) 18 LT 17; *Re Gaselee* [1901] 1 Ch 923 at 928.
7　*Re Blyth's Trusts* (1873) LR 16 Eq 468 at 469 per Lord Selborne LC; *Re Hereford, Hay and Brecon Rly Co* (1864) 13 WR 134; *Re Nepton's Charity* (1906) 22 TLR 442; *Re Sewart's Estate* (1874) LR 18 Eq 278; *Re Smith's Estate* (1870) LR 9 Eq 178; *Reading v Hamilton* (1862) 5 LT 628. Before *Re Blyth's Trusts* (1873) LR 16 Eq 468, the practice was unsettled. See *Re Lomax* (1864) 34 Beav 294; *Re Flemon's Trusts* (1870) LR 10 Eq 612. For a case of reinvestment in stock see *Re Brown* (1890) 63 LT 131, CA.
8　*Re Gedling Rectory* (1885) 53 LT 244.
9　*Re West Riding and Lancashire Railways Bill* [1876] WN 48, 80; *Ex p Bolton Junction Rly Co* (1876) 24 WR 451.
10　*Ex p Trinity House Corpn* (1843) 3 Hare 95; *Re Kendal and Westmoreland Railway Act 1845 and Re Braithwaite's Trust* (1853) 1 Sm & G, App xv; *Re Gaselee* [1901] 1 Ch 923. In practice these are paid in the first instance by the applicant and recovered from the undertakers or authority as part of his reasonable costs and charges: *Re Gaselee* supra at 927; and see *Re Wilson* (1853) 1 WR 504; *Re Magdalen College, Oxford* [1901] 2 Ch 786.

155. Costs on payment of income. The undertakers[1] or acquiring authority[2] are liable to pay the costs of obtaining orders for the payment of dividends on the money paid into court[3]; however, if two applications are made when one would have sufficed, they will only be required to pay the costs of one[4].

1　For the meaning of 'the undertakers' see para 13 ante.
2　For the meaning of 'acquiring authority' see para 92 note 5 ante.
3　See the Lands Clauses Consolidation Act 1845 s 80 (as amended); the Compulsory Purchase Act 1965 s 26(3)(b); and para 148 ante. See also para 151 ante. As to payment into court see paras 98 note 6, 124 ante. These provisions are limited in their application because the power to sell and convey land of a person under disability has been otherwise extended: see para 96 ante.
4　Eg if a second order for payment of dividends is required because the first was not drawn so as to cover persons successively entitled, the court may exercise its discretion to order the undertakers or authority to pay the costs: *Re Pryor's Settlement Trusts* (1876) 35 LT 202; *Re Andenshaw School* (1863) 1 New Rep 255; *Re Goe's Estate* (1854) 3 WR 119; *Re Bazett's Trustees* (1850) 16 LTOS 279; *Ex p Ecclesiastical Comrs* (1870) 39 LJ Ch 623; *Re Grand Junction Railway Acts, ex p Hordern* (1848) 2 De G & Sm 263; *Re Metropolitan Rly Co and Maire* [1876] WN 245; *Re Ryder* (1887) 37 ChD 595. As to payment of dividends in case of resettlement see *Re Pick's Settlement* (1862) 31 LJ Ch 495; *Re Shakespeare Walk School* (1879) 12 ChD 178. Where there are several funds in court belonging to the same trust, and only one application is necessary, the costs of one only will be allowed: *Re Wilts, Somerset and Weymouth Rly Co, Re South Devon Rly Co, Re Cornwall Rly Co, ex p Lord Broke* (1863) 11 WR 505; *Re Pattison's Devised Estates, Re*

Pattison's Settled Estates (1876) 4 ChD 207; *Re Gore Langton's Estates* (1875) 10 Ch App 328; and cf *Re Midland Great Western Rly Co* (1881) 9 LR Ir 16. The various undertakers may be ordered to bear the costs in equal shares: *Ex p Sunbury-on-Thames UDC, ex p Staines Reservoirs Joint Committee* (1922) 86 JP Jo 153. For other examples see *Re Spooner's Estate* (1854) 1 K & J 220; *Re London and North Western Railway Co's Act 1846 and Rugby and Stamford Railway Act 1846, Re Baroness Braye's Settled Estates* (1863) 11 WR 333; *Re Long's Trust* (1864) 33 LJ Ch 620; *Re Nicholls's Trust Estates* (1866) 35 LJ Ch 516.

156. Application of purchase money or compensation.

The purchase money or compensation paid into court[1] must remain there until applied on an order of the High Court[2] to one or more of the following purposes:

(1) in the discharge of any debt or incumbrance affecting the land or affecting other land settled with it on the same or the like trusts or purposes[3]; or

(2) in the purchase of other land to be conveyed, limited and settled upon like trusts and purposes and in the same manner as the land stood settled in respect of which the purchase money or compensation was paid[4]; or

(3) if the money or compensation was paid in respect of any buildings taken or injured by the proximity of the works[5], in removing or replacing the buildings or substituting other buildings in such manner as the High Court may direct[6]; or

(4) in payment to any party becoming absolutely entitled to the purchase money or compensation[7].

1 See the Lands Clauses Consolidation Act 1845 s 69 (as amended); the Compulsory Purchase Act 1965 s 2, Sch 1 para 6(1), (2); and para 151 ante. These provisions are limited in their application because the power to sell and convey land of a person under disability has been otherwise extended: see para 96 ante.
2 As to applications for such orders see para 157 post.
3 Lands Clauses Consolidation Act 1845 s 69 (amended by the Administration of Justice Act 1965 s 17(1), Sch 1; and by the Compulsory Purchase Act 1965 s 39(4), Sch 8 Pt II) (where the 1845 Act is incorporated: see para 11 ante); Compulsory Purchase Act 1965 Sch 1 para 6(2)(a) (where that Act applies: see para 15 ante). For the meaning of 'land' see para 92 note 1 ante. See also para 13 text to note 7 ante.
   A corporation may be allowed to apply the money to pay off mortgages on other corporate land or tolls, or to pay off bonds the interest on which was payable out of the common fund, which was mainly made up of the rents and profits of land: *Re Derby Municipal Estates* (1876) 3 ChD 289; *Re Eastern Counties Rly Co, ex p Cambridge Corpn* (1848) 5 Ry & Can Cas 204; and see *Ex p Hythe Corpn* (1840) 4 Y & C Ex 55; *Re Dublin, Wicklow and Wexford Rly Co, ex p Tottenham* (1884) 13 LR Ir 479; *Re Dublin, Wicklow and Wexford Rly Co, ex p Richards* (1890) 25 LR Ir 175.
   The order may sanction the application of the money to purchasing the surrender of beneficial leaseholds (*Re Manchester, Sheffield and Lincolnshire Rly Co, ex p Sheffield Corpn* (1855) 21 Beav 162, 25 LJ Ch 587; *Ex p Bishop of London* (1860) 2 De GF & J 14; *Ex p London Corpn* (1868) LR 5 Eq 418; *Re Marquis of Townshend's Estates and Lynn and Fakenham Railway Act 1876* [1882] WN 7); or in paying off rent to prevent re-entry on leasehold premises (*Re London-Street, Greenwich and London, Chatham and Dover Railway (Further Powers) Act 1881* (1887) 57 LT 673); in redeeming quit rents and rentcharges (*Re Public Works Comrs, ex p Studdert* (1856) 6 I Ch R 53; *Re Comrs of Church Temporalities, Ireland, ex p Lord Leconfield* (1874) IR 8 Eq 559; *Re Dublin, Wicklow and Wexford Rly Co, ex p Tottenham* (1884) 13 LR Ir 479); in reinstating structures to prevent a sale under a building Act (*Re Davis' Estate and Crystal Palace and West Railway Act, ex p Davis* (1858) 3 De G & J 144); or in paying off expenses under Inclosure Acts (*Re Oxford, Worcester etc Rly Co, ex p Lockwood* (1851) 14 Beav 158; *Ex p Queen's College, Cambridge* (1849) 14 Beav 159n; *Vernon v Earl Manvers* (1862) 32 LJ Ch 244). It may not, however, be applied in paying off charges payable by the person in possession, and not charged on the inheritance: *Re Louth and East Coast Rly Co, ex p Rector of Grimoldby* (1876) 2 ChD 225; *Re Hull Railway and Dock Act, ex p Rector of Kirksmeaton* (1882) 20 ChD 203; *Re Public Works Comrs, ex p Studdert* (1856) 6 I Ch R 53; and cf *Ex p LCC, ex p Vicar of Christ Church, East Greenwich* [1896] 1 Ch 520. As to applications to the court see para 157 post; as to costs see para 159 post.
4 Lands Clauses Consolidation Act 1845 s 69; Compulsory Purchase Act 1965 Sch 1 para 6(2)(b). See *Kelland v Fulford* (1877) 6 ChD 491 at 494 per Jessel MR; and see *Ex p Vicar of Castle Bytham, ex p Midland Rly Co* [1895] 1 Ch 348; and cf *Re Eastern Counties Rly Co, ex p Vicar of Sawston* (1858) 27 LJ Ch 755; *Re Browne and Oxford and Bletchley Junction and Buckinghamshire Railway Acts* (1852) 6 Ry & Can Cas 733; *Re*

Cheshunt College (1855) 3 WR 638; *Dixon v Jackson* (1856) 25 LJ Ch 588; *Re Buckingham* (1876) 2 ChD 690, CA; *Re Taylor's Estate* (1871) 40 LJ Ch 454 (land in Isle of Man). In the absence of special circumstances, the purchase money for freehold land will not be allowed to be laid out in the purchase of leaseholds (*Re Lancashire and Yorkshire Rly Co, ex p Macaulay* (1854) 23 LJ Ch 815; *Ex p Master, Fellows and Scholars of Trinity College, Cambridge* (1868) 18 LT 849; *Re Rehoboth Chapel* (1874) 44 LJ Ch 375; *Re Cann's Estate, Re Norfolk Railway Co's Acts* (1850) 19 LJ Ch 376) or in equities of redemption (*Re Cheltenham and Great Western Rly Co, ex p Craven* (1848) 17 LJ Ch 215; *Ex p Portadown, Dungannon and Omagh Junction Rly Co* (1876) 10 IR Eq 368); but the purchase money for leaseholds may be laid out in buying freeholds (*Re Brasher's Trust* (1858) 6 WR 406; *Re Parker's Estate* (1872) LR 13 Eq 495; and cf *Re Coyte's Estate, Re Liverpool Docks Acts* (1851) 1 Sim NS 202). The erection of permanent buildings has been authorised where it was for the benefit of the estate or trust, on the ground that this was equivalent to a purchase: see *Re London and North Western Railway Act 1861, ex p Liverpool Corpn* (1866) 1 Ch App 596; *Re Leigh's Estate* (1871) 6 Ch App 887; *Drake v Trefusis* (1875) 10 Ch App 364. Money paid for part of a glebe has been allowed to be laid out in building a new rectory (*Re Incumbent of Whitfield* (1861) 1 John & H 610; *Ex p Rector of Bradfield St Claire* (1875) 32 LT 248; *Ex p Rector of Hartington* (1875) 23 WR 484; *Ex p Rector of Claypole* (1873) LR 16 Eq 574; *Ex p Vicar of St Botolph, Aldgate* [1894] 3 Ch 544); in drainage works on the glebe (*Re Vicar of Queen Camel, Re Great Western Railway Act and Wilts, Somerset and Weymouth Amendment Act 1846* (1863) 8 LT 233); and in repairing a church porch (*Ex p Parson etc of St Alphage* (1886) 55 LT 314). As to applications to the court see para 157 post; as to costs see para 159 post.

    When a small sum remains after such a purchase, the court may authorise it to be paid out to trustees to be applied on permanent improvements (*Re Kinsey* (1863) 1 New Rep 303; *Ex p Barrett* (1850) 19 LJ Ch 415); and if the balance remaining is less than £20 it may be paid out to the parties entitled to the rents and profits for their own use and benefit (see para 167 post). As to money paid in respect of leases and reversions see para 164 post. Additionally, where the money is liable to be laid out in the purchase of land to be made subject to a settlement, it may be invested or applied as capital money arising under the Settled Land Act 1925 on the like terms, if any, respecting costs and other things, as nearly as circumstances admit, and, notwithstanding anything in that Act according to the same procedure, as if the modes of investment or application authorised under that Act were authorised under the Lands Clauses Consolidation Act 1845 or the Compulsory Purchase Act 1965, as the case may be: see the Settled Land Act 1925 s 76; and SETTLEMENTS.

5 For the meaning of 'the works' see para 92 note 3 ante. See also para 13 text to note 4 ante.
6 Lands Clauses Consolidation Act 1845 s 69; Compulsory Purchase Act 1965 Sch 1 para 6(2)(c). Thus, money paid for land taken by a railway undertaking has been authorised to be laid out in removing and altering farm buildings rendered unsafe or unsuitable by reason of the construction of the railway (*Re Johnson's Settlements* (1869) LR 8 Eq 348), and in building new ones (*Re Oxford, Worcester and Wolverhampton Rly Co, ex p Milward* (1859) 29 LJ Ch 245; *Re Kent Coast Rly Co, ex p Dean and Chapter of Canterbury* (1862) 7 LT 240, 10 WR 505; *Re Buckinghamshire Rly Co, ex p Churchwardens and Overseers of Bicester* (1848) 5 Ry & Can Cas 205). Money paid for almshouses may be laid out in building others (*Re Southampton and Dorchester Railway Act, ex p Thorner's Charity* (1848) 12 LTOS 266; and see *Re St Thomas's Hospital* (1863) 11 WR 1018). As to applications to the court see para 157 post; as to costs see para 161 post.
7 Lands Clauses Consolidation Act 1845 s 69; Compulsory Purchase Act 1965 Sch 1 para 6(2)(d). Thus it may be paid to a person who comes of age if he is then entitled to it for his own use (*Kelland v Fulford* (1877) 6 ChD 491 at 495; *Re Hall's Estate* (1870) LR 9 Eq 179; *Re Cant's Estate* (1859) 4 De G & J 503), or to a tenant in tail but not as a person absolutely entitled until he has executed a disentailing deed (*Re Broadwood's Settled Estates* (1875) 1 ChD 438; *Re Reynolds* (1876) 3 ChD 61, CA), unless the sum is trifling (*Re Watson* (1864) 4 New Rep 528; *Stead v Harper* [1896] WN 46).
    Statutory bodies with or without powers of sale of land may be entitled to have the money paid out to them (*Re Chelsea Waterworks Co* (1887) 56 LJ Ch 640; *Re Brumby and Frodingham UDC* (1904) 69 JP 96; *Ex p King's College, Cambridge* [1891] 1 Ch 677; *Ex p Watford UDC* (1914) 78 JP Jo 160) if they have obtained any necessary consents (*Ex p Great Western Railway (New Railways) Act 1905, ex p Great Western Rly Co* (1909) 74 JP 21, CA). Trustees with power of sale may be authorised to receive payment out (*Re Gooch's Estate* (1876) 3 ChD 742; *Re Hobson's Trusts* (1878) 7 ChD 708, CA; *Re St Luke's, Middlesex, Vestry* [1880] WN 58; *Re Thomas's Settlement* (1882) 30 WR 244; *Re London, Brighton and South Coast Rly Co, ex p Bowman* [1888] WN 179; *Re Smith, ex p London and North Western Rly Co and Midland Rly Co* (1888) 40 ChD 386, CA; *Re Morgan, Smith v May* [1900] 2 Ch 474); and so may the trustees of a charity (*Re Faversham Charities* (1862) 5 LT 787; *Ex p Haberdashers' Co* (1886) 55 LT 758; *Re Clergy Orphan Corpn* [1894] 3 Ch 145, CA; *Re Sheffield Corpn and Trustees of St William's Roman Catholic Chapel and Schools, Sheffield* [1903] 1 Ch 208; *Re Islington Borough Council* (1907) 97 LT 78; *Re Wesleyan Methodist Chapel, South Street, Wandsworth* [1909] 1 Ch 454; but cf *Re Bristol Free Grammar School Estates*

(1878) 47 LJ Ch 317; *Re Bishop Monk's Horfield Trust* (1881) 29 WR 462; *Re Rector and Churchwardens of St Alban's, Wood Street* (1891) 66 LT 51). The transfer of a fund to another account is equivalent to payment out of court: *Melling v Bird* (1853) 22 LJ Ch 599. As to applications to the court see para 157 post; as to costs see para 162 post.

157. Application to court for disposal of money and payment out. The money paid into court may be applied or paid out on an order of the Chancery Division of the High Court, made at the instance of the party who would have been entitled to the rents and profits of the land in respect of which the money has been paid in[1]. Thus consecutive tenants for life may apply[2], but not a remainderman[3] or an annuitant[4]. In the case of disused burial grounds, the party entitled to the burial fees, if any, would be the proper person to apply[5].

The application is made by originating summons to be heard in chambers[6]. An affidavit must as a rule be made verifying the applicant's title[7]. If there is more than one sum of money in court in respect of two or more pieces of land to the rents and profits of which one person would have been entitled, the application of all the sums may be dealt with on one summons[8].

In cases of discharging incumbrances, or laying out the money in buildings and improvements, the remaindermen and the trustees of the settlement should generally be served, so that they may have an opportunity of objecting[9]. Incumbrancers should generally be served on applications for payment out, but the costs of their appearance, if not necessary, will not be payable by the undertakers or acquiring authority[10]. On applications by a trustee, it seems that the beneficiary need not be served[11], unless his presence is necessary for the purpose of distributing the fund[12]. A person having an ascertained share in the fund may apply for payment out without serving the other persons entitled to shares, but it would be otherwise if the shares had to be ascertained[13].

1 Lands Clauses Consolidation Act 1845 s 70 (amended by the Administration of Justice Act 1965 s 17(1), Sch 1) (where the 1845 Act is incorporated: see para 11 ante); Compulsory Purchase Act 1965 s 2, Sch 1 para 6(4) (where that Act applies: see para 15 ante). As to payment into court see paras 98 note 6, 124 ante. These provisions are limited in their application because the power to sell and convey land of a person under disability has been otherwise extended: see para 96 ante.
2 *Re Jolliffe's Estate* (1870) LR 9 Eq 668.
3 *Nash v Nash* (1868) 37 LJ Ch 927.
4 *Re St Katherine Dock Co* (1828) 2 Y & J 386; and see *Ex p Cofield* (1847) 11 Jur 1071; *Re London and Tilbury Rly Co, Re Pedley's Estate* (1855) 1 Jur NS 654.
5 Eg the rector (*Ex p Rector of Liverpool* (1870) LR 11 Eq 15; *Ex p Rector of St Martin's, Birmingham* (1870) LR 11 Eq 23), or the trustees of the ground (*Re St Pancras Burial Ground* (1866) LR 3 Eq 173; and cf *Champneys v Arrowsmith* (1867) LR 3 CP 107). The Charity Commissioners' consent to applications for investment in the case of charities is not required: see CHARITIES vol 5(2) (Reissue) paras 461 note 7, 463 note 8.
6 RSC Ord 92 r 5(1), (2). If the application is made in a pending cause or matter, or an application for the same purpose has previously been made by petition or originating summons, the application is by ordinary summons: Ord 92 r 5(2).
7 The affidavit should state that the applicant is unaware of any right in any other person, or of any claim by any other person, to the sum claimed or any part of it, or, if aware of any such right or claim, must state or refer to it: see the Supreme Court Practice 1995 note 92/5/14.
8 *Re Manchester, Sheffield and Lincolnshire Rly Co, ex p Sheffield Corpn* (1855) 21 Beav 162, 25 LJ Ch 587; *Re Lord Arden's Estates* (1875) 10 Ch App 445; *Re Browse's Trusts* (1866) 14 LT 37; *Re Southampton and Dorchester Rly Co, ex p King's College, Cambridge* (1852) 5 De G & Sm 621; *Re Gore Langton's Estates* (1875) 10 Ch App 328.
9 *Re Leigh's Estate* (1871) 6 Ch App 887; *Re Furness Rly Co, Re Romney* (1863) 3 New Rep 287; and see *Re Olive's Estate* (1890) 44 ChD 316; *Re Browne and Oxford and Bletchley Junction and Buckinghamshire Railway Acts* (1852) 6 Ry & Can Cas 733; *Re Cann's Estate, Re Norfolk Railway Co's Acts* (1850) 19 LJ Ch

376; *Re Piggin, ex p Mansfield Rly Co* [1913] 2 Ch 326. Patrons of a living should also be served: *Ex p Vicar of Castle Bytham, ex p Midland Rly Co* [1895] 1 Ch 348. The costs of an affidavit of service when required will be payable by the undertakers: *Re Halstead United Charities* (1875) LR 20 Eq 48; *Re Artisans' and Labourers' Dwellings Improvement Act 1875, ex p Jones* (1880) 14 ChD 624; *Re Ruck's Trusts* (1895) 13 R 637. As to the costs of persons served see para 158 post.

10 *Re Halstead United Charities* (1875) LR 20 Eq 48; *Re Artisans' and Labourers' Dwellings Improvement Act 1875, ex p Jones* (1880) 14 ChD 624; *Re Ruck's Trusts* (1895) 13 R 637; *Ex p Mercers' Co* (1879) 10 ChD 481. Cf *Re Hatfield's Estate (No 2)* (1863) 32 Beav 252; *Re Brooke* (1864) 12 WR 1128; *Re Baroness Braye's Settled Estates* (1863) 32 LJ Ch 432.

11 *Re East, ex p East* (1853) 2 WR 111; *Re Gooch's Estate* (1876) 3 ChD 742.

12 *Re Long's Trust* (1864) 10 Jur NS 417. As to the appearance of the trustees of a settlement on the application of a person becoming entitled absolutely see *Re Burnell's Estate* (1864) 12 WR 568; *Ex p Metropolitan Rly Co* (1868) 16 WR 996. As to the appearance of the tenant for life on the application of the trustees of the settlement see *Re Piggin, ex p Mansfield Rly Co* [1913] 2 Ch 326.

13 *Re Midland Rly Co* (1847) 11 Jur 1095; *Re Clarke's Devisees* (1858) 6 WR 812. As to separate applications by persons having the same interests and employing the same solicitor see *Re Nicholls' Trust Estates* (1866) 35 LJ Ch 516. As to the costs of payment out see para 162 post.

158. Costs of persons served. The undertakers or acquiring authority will only be ordered to pay the costs of service upon persons necessarily served; and if those persons, when served, appear unnecessarily, they will not be entitled to their costs[1].

If the application is simply for the reinvestment of money in land, and there are mortgagees or annuitants whose rights are not otherwise affected, the proper course is to serve them, giving them an intimation that if they appear at the hearing they will probably have to pay their own costs[2].

In the case of settled land, when the money is to be laid out in other land, the remainderman need not be served or appear, and the costs of service upon and of appearance by him will be disallowed[3].

When the money has been deposited in respect of land which is the subject of an action, the parties to the action should be served, and in a proper case will be allowed their costs of appearance[4].

Similar rules apply on an application for investment[5]. Thus, mortgagees and other incumbrancers should not be served[6] unless they are in occupation[7]. It is proper to serve the undertakers or acquiring authority[8]. The costs occasioned by improper service may be ordered to be paid by the applicant or out of the fund[9], and a similar order may be made where, by reason of default or delay, or the applicant's failure to serve, additional costs have been incurred[10].

1 As to the costs of service and appearance generally in connection with matters in the Chancery Division see RSC Ord 62; and PRACTICE AND PROCEDURE. Undertakers will not be ordered to pay costs of such parts of the summons as may have failed: *Re Jacobs, Baldwin v Pescott* [1908] 2 Ch 691.

2 *Re Gore Langton's Estates* (1875) 10 Ch App 328 at 333; *Re Duggan's Trusts* (1869) LR 8 Eq 697.

3 *Re Yorkshire, Doncaster and Goole Rly Co, Re Dylar's Estate* (1855) 1 Jur NS 975; *Re Browne and Oxford and Bletchley Junction and Buckinghamshire Railway Acts* (1852) 6 Ry & Can Cas 733; *Re Bowes's Estate* (1864) 10 Jur NS 817; *Re Gore Langton's Estates* (1875) 10 Ch App 328.

4 *Haynes v Barton* (1866) LR 1 Eq 422; *Picard v Mitchell* (1850) 12 Beav 486; *Re Brandon's Estate* (1862) 2 Drew & Sm 162.

5 *Re Dowling's Trusts* (1876) 45 LJ Ch 568; *Re Finch's Estate* (1866) 14 WR 472; *Re Leigh's Estate* (1871) 6 Ch App 887.

6 *Re Morris's Settled Estates* (1875) LR 20 Eq 470; *Re Webster's Settled Estates, South Eastern Railway Act and Lands Clauses Consolidation Act* (1854) 2 Sm & G, App vi; *Re Lancashire and Yorkshire Rly Co, ex p Smith* (1849) 6 Ry & Can Cas 150; *Ex p Bishop of London* (1860) 2 De GF & J 14; *Re Thomas's Estate, Re Ely Valley Railway Act 1857 and Lands Clauses Consolidation Act 1845, ex p Cozens* (1864) 12 WR 546; *Re Smith* (1865) 14 WR 218; *Ex p Cofield* (1847) 11 Jur 1071; *Re Ruck's Trusts* (1895) 13 R 637; *Re Osborne's Estate* [1878] WN 179.

7 *Re Hungerford's Trust* (1857) 3 K & J 455; *Re Nash, Re London, Tilbury and Southend Railway Act 1852* (1855) 25 LJ Ch 20, sub nom *Re Nash, Re Lands Clauses Consolidation Act 1845* 1 Jur NS 1082.
8 *Re Charity of King Edward VI's Almshouses at Saffron Walden* (1868) 37 LJ Ch 664.
9 *Re Lancashire and Yorkshire Rly Co, Wilson v Foster* (1859) 28 LJ Ch 410; *Re Incumbent of Whitfield* (1861) 1 John & H 610.
10 *Re Clarke's Estate* (1882) 21 ChD 776; *Re Leigh's Estate* (1871) 6 Ch App 887.

159. Costs of purchase and of discharging debts etc. The undertakers[1] or acquiring authority[2] may be ordered to pay the costs of, or incurred in consequence of, the purchase of the land, other than those otherwise provided for, including all reasonable charges and expenses incidental to the purchase, the costs of obtaining the proper orders, and the costs of all proceedings relating to such orders except such as are occasioned by litigation between adverse claimants[3]. They will also be liable to pay the costs for the discharge of any debt or incumbrance affecting the land or other land settled with it on the same or like trusts or purposes[4]. If the money is employed in discharging incumbrances or in the purchase of leaseholds by the reversioner, the practice is to order the undertakers or authority to pay only the costs of having the money paid out, but not of the reinvestment[5].

1 For the meaning of 'the undertakers' see para 13 ante.
2 For the meaning of 'acquiring authority' see para 92 note 5 ante.
3 Lands Clauses Consolidation Act 1845 s 80 (amended by the Administration of Justice Act 1965 s 17(1), Sch 1) (where the 1845 Act is incorporated; see para 11 ante); Compulsory Purchase Act 1965 s 26(2)(a), 3(a), (d) (where that Act applies: see para 15 ante); and see paras 148 ante, 160–163 post. As to such other costs see para 124 ante (costs on payment into court on entry without consent); para 140 ante (costs of conveyance), and paras 200 note 15, 227 post (costs of assessment). These provisions are limited in their application because the power to sell and convey land of a person under disability has been otherwise extended: see para 96 ante. For the meaning of 'land' see para 92 note 1 ante. See also para 13 text to note 7 ante.
4 See the Lands Clauses Consolidation Act 1845 s 69 (as amended); the Compulsory Purchase Act 1965 s 2, Sch 1 para 6(2)(a); and para 151 ante. As to the discharge of debts etc see para 156 ante.
5 *Re Manchester, Sheffield, and Lincolnshire Rly Co, ex p Sheffield Corpn* (1855) 21 Beav 162, 25 LJ Ch 587; *Re Sheffield Waterworks Co, ex p Sheffield Town Trustees* (1860) 8 WR 602; *Re Mark's Trusts* [1877] WN 63; *Ex p London Corpn* (1868) LR 5 Eq 418; and cf *Re Eastern Counties Rly Co, ex p Earl of Hardwicke* (1848) 17 LJ Ch 422; *Re Lancaster and Carlisle Rly Co, ex p Yeates* (1847) 12 Jur 279; *Re Lord Stanley of Alderley* (1872) LR 14 Eq 227; *Re Dublin, Wicklow and Wexford Rly Co, ex p Richards* (1890) 25 LR Ir 175.

160. Costs on purchase of other land. The undertakers[1] or acquiring authority[2] may be ordered to pay the costs of, or incurred in consequence of, the purchase of the land, other than those otherwise provided for[3]. They will be liable to pay the costs in respect of the purchase of other land to be conveyed, limited and settled upon like trusts and purposes, and in the same manner, as the land in respect of which the compensation was paid stood settled[4]; but the costs of not more than one application for reinvestment in land may be allowed unless it appears to the High Court that it is for the benefit of the parties interested in the compensation that it should be invested in the purchase of land in different sums and at different times[5], and not then if the undertakers or authority can show that the reinvestments are capricious, vexatious or unnecessary[6].

Where the money is invested with other money provided by the applicant, the undertakers or authority will be ordered to pay the whole costs of reinvestment, except so far as they are increased by reason of the purchase money exceeding the money paid in[7]. If there are two or more funds in court, and these are invested together, the undertakers or acquiring authorities are entitled to a contribution from others who are under a similar obligation to pay the costs[8]. The general costs of the application and of the purchase are borne equally, unless there are special circumstances, of which the inequality of the amounts is not necessarily one[9]; but the ad valorem stamp, the surveyor's fee, and, in some cases, the solicitor's charges, have been apportioned rateably[10]. If some of the parties who have paid money into court are not liable to pay costs, the other undertakers or authorities are only liable to pay the proportion they would have been liable to pay if all had been liable[11]. If some of those who have paid in have amalgamated, they will be treated as one for the purposes of costs[12]. If the deposited money belongs to persons who have become absolutely entitled, the undertakers or authority may be ordered to pay the costs of reinvestment[13]; and they may also be ordered to do so where, by reason of the owner's death, the land purchased will be held on trusts differing from those in existence when the land was taken[14].

If the court does not sanction the proposed investment, the undertakers or authority are not required to pay the costs of the abortive application, and may be allowed their costs out of the fund in court[15]; and if the applicant has acted in good faith for the benefit of the estate in making the application, his costs will also be allowed out of the money in court[16]. If the court approves the purchase, but it is not completed owing to the failure to make, or because of the great expense of making, a good title, the undertakers or authority are required to pay the costs[17], but not if the purchase is abandoned on insufficient grounds[18].

The costs which the undertakers or authority are ordinarily required to pay on the purchase of land as a reinvestment are such costs as, in the case of an open contract, would be purchaser's costs[19]. These include the costs of the reference to chambers for all investigation of title, and of the conveyancing counsel to the court when necessary[20]; and the costs of the petitioner's solicitor for investigation of the title and preparing and completing the conveyance[21]. They do not include costs of private counsel, except for consultation on difficult points[22], and they do not include costs ordinarily paid by the vendor even though the contract makes them payable by the purchaser[23]. If, by reason of the applicants being under disability, additional costs are incurred, as where the applicants are trustees of a charity[24] or hold ecclesiastical offices[25], or when the land or fund is subject to a suit[26], the undertakers or authority may be ordered to pay the costs reasonably incurred in consequence[27].

1 For the meaning of 'the undertakers' see para 13 ante.
2 For the meaning of 'acquiring authority' see para 92 note 5 ante.
3 See the Lands Clauses Consolidation Act 1845 s 80 (as amended); the Compulsory Purchase Act 1965 s 26(2)(a), (3)(a), (d); and para 159 text and note 3 ante. These provisions are limited in their application because the power to sell and convey land of a person under disability has been otherwise extended: see para 96 ante. The liability of the undertakers for costs of reinvestment appears to be the same whether the money is deposited as required by the Lands Clauses Acts or paid in an alternative manner in accordance with the provisions of other enactments, eg under the Universities and College Estates Act 1925 s 28 (as amended) (see para 150 ante): see the *Final Report of the Expert Committee on Compensation and Betterment* (Cmd 6386) (1942) para 179. For the meaning of 'land' see para 92 note 1 ante. See also para 13 text to note 7 ante.
4 See the Lands Clauses Consolidation Act 1845 s 69 (as amended); the Compulsory Purchase Act 1965 s 2, Sch 1 para 6(2)(b); and para 151 ante. As to the purchase of other land see para 156 ante.
5 Lands Clauses Consolidation Act 1845 s 80 proviso (amended by the Administration of Justice Act 1965 s 17(1), Sch 1) (where the 1845 Act is incorporated: see para 11 ante); Compulsory Purchase Act 1965 s 26(4) (where that Act applies: see para 15 ante).
6 *Re Brandon's Estate* (1862) 2 Drew & Sm 162 at 166; *Re Trustees of St Bartholomew's Hospital* (1859) 4 Drew 425 at 426; *Ex p Fishmongers' Co* (1862) 1 New Rep 85; *Re Woolley's Trust, Re East and West India Docks and Birmingham Junction Railway Act 1846* (1853) 17 Jur 850; and cf *Re London and Birmingham Rly Co, ex p Provost and Fellows of Eton College* (1842) 3 Ry & Can Cas 271; *Re London and Birmingham Rly Co, ex p Boxmoor Waste Lands Trustees* (1844) 3 Ry & Can Cas 513; *Re St Katherine's Dock Co* (1844) 3

Ry & Can Cas 514; *Re London and Birmingham Rly to Northampton, ex p Bouverie* (1846) 4 Ry & Can Cas 229; *Re Merchant Taylors' Co* (1847) 10 Beav 485; *Jones v Lewis* (1850) 2 Mac & G 163; *Ex p St Katharine's Hospital* (1881) 17 ChD 378, decided under similar provisions in special Acts. For the meaning of 'special Act' see paras 11, 16 ante.

7   *Re Clark* [1906] 1 Ch 615; *Re Metropolitan Rly Co and Gonville and Caius College, Cambridge* (1887) reported in [1906] 1 Ch 619n (stating the principle laid down in *Re Sheffield and Lincolnshire Railway Act, ex p Hodge* (1848) 16 Sim 159; *Re Southampton and Dorchester Rly Co, ex p King's College, Cambridge* (1852) 5 De G & Sm 621; *Re Branmer's Estate* (1849) 14 Jur 236; *Re Loveband's Settled Estates* (1860) 30 LJ Ch 94). The orders made in *Ex p Perpetual Curate of Bilston* (1889) 37 WR 460 and *Re Bagot's Settled Estates* (1866) 14 WR 471 are not now followed. The rule laid down in *Re Clark* supra applies to an application for payment out: see para 162 note 13 post.

8   *Ex p Bishop of London* (1860) 2 De GF & J 14; *A-G v Rochester Corpn* (1867) 16 LT 408, 15 WR 765; *Ex p Ecclesiastical Comrs for England* (1865) 11 Jur NS 461; *Re Metropolitan Rly Co and Gonville and Caius College, Cambridge* (1887) reported in [1906] 1 Ch 619n.

9   See the cases cited in note 8 supra, and *Ex p Governors of Christ's Hospital* (1864) 2 Hem & M 166; *Re Byron's Estate* (1863) 1 De GJ & Sm 358; *Re Merton College* (1864) 1 De GJ & Sm 361; *Ex p Master, Fellows and Scholars of Trinity College, Cambridge* (1868) 18 LT 849; and see *Re Leigh's Estate* (1871) 6 Ch App 887; *Re Manchester and Leeds Rly Co, ex p Gaskell* (1876) 2 ChD 360; *Ex p Governors of Christ's Hospital* (1879) 27 WR 458.

10 *Re Bishopsgate Foundation* [1894] 1 Ch 185; *Ex p Bishop of London* (1860) 2 De GF & J 14; *Ex p London Corpn* (1868) LR 5 Eq 418; and see *Ex p Christchurch* (1861) 9 WR 474; *Ex p Governors of St Bartholomew's Hospital* (1875) LR 20 Eq 369; *A-G v St John's Hospital, Bath* [1893] 3 Ch 151.

11 Thus, where there were 17 separate funds in court, and six of the defendants were not liable to pay costs, the remaining 11 were ordered each to pay one-seventeenth of the total costs: *Ex p Ecclesiastical Comrs for England* (1865) 11 Jur NS 461; *A-G v Rochester Corpn* (1867) 16 LT 408, 15 WR 765.

12 *Ex p Corpus Christi College, Oxford* (1871) LR 13 Eq 334; *Re Manchester and Leeds Rly Co, ex p Gaskell* (1876) 2 ChD 360; *Re Midland Great Western Rly Co* (1881) 9 LR Ir 16. If a line is leased, the lessors remain liable (*Re Carlisle and Silloth Rly Co* (1863) 33 Beav 253); if the undertaking is assigned, the assignors become liable (*Ex p Vicar of Sheffield* (1904) 68 JP 313).

13 *Re Jones's Trust Estate* (1870) as reported in 39 LJ Ch 190; *Re Dodd's Estate* (1871) 19 WR 741; and see *Re De Beauvoir* (1860) 29 LJ Ch 567 at 570, sub nom *Re Benyon's Trusts* 8 WR 425.

14 *Re De Beauvoir* (1860) 29 LJ Ch 567, sub nom *Re Benyon's Trusts* 8 WR 425; and cf *Re Parker's Estate* (1872) LR 13 Eq 495; *Re Eastern Counties Rly Co, Re Lands Clauses Consolidation Act 1845, ex p Peyton's Settlement* (1856) 4 WR 380.

15 *Re Hardy's Estate* (1854) 18 Jur 370; *Ex p Stevens* (1851) 15 Jur 243; *Re Macdonald's Trusts of the Will, Re London and Blackwall Rly Co* (1860) 2 LT 168. They must pay the costs of obtaining the particular order that is made, not of that part of the summons which failed: *Re Jacobs, Baldwin v Pescott* [1908] 2 Ch 691.

16 Cf *Re Leigh's Estate* (1871) 6 Ch App 887; and see the Lands Clauses Consolidation Act 1845 s 73 (as amended); the Compulsory Purchase Act 1965 Sch 1 para 9; and para 151 ante.

17 *Re Woolley's Trust, Re East and West India Docks and Birmingham Junction Railway Act 1846* (1853) 17 Jur 850; *Ex p Rector of Holywell* (1865) 2 Drew & Sm 463; *Re Carney's Trusts* (1872) 20 WR 407; *Re North Staffordshire Rly Co, ex p Vaudrey's Trusts* (1861) 3 Giff 224.

18 *Re Lands Clauses Consolidation Act 1845, ex p Copley* (1858) 4 Jur NS 297.

19 *Ex p Governors of Christ's Hospital* (1875) LR 20 Eq 605; *Re Temple Church Lands* (1877) 47 LJ Ch 160; *Re Eastern Counties Rly Co, ex p Vicar of Sawston* (1858) 27 LJ Ch 755; *Ex p Thavie's Charity Trustees* [1905] 1 Ch 403; *Re North Staffordshire Rly Co, ex p Incumbent of Alsager* (1854) 2 Eq Rep 327. See further SALE OF LAND.

20 These may be dispensed with if the amount is small: *Re Blomfield* (1876) 25 WR 37; *Re Lapworth Charity* [1879] WN 37. If the money is invested before the purchase is approved, the undertakers or authority are not required to pay the costs of purchase: *Ex p Bouverie* (1848) 5 Ry & Can Cas 431; *Re Bishop Monk's Horfield Trust* (1881) 29 WR 462.

21 *Re Merchant Taylors' Co* (1885) 30 ChD 28, CA; and see *Re Stewart* (1889) 41 ChD 494.

22 *Re Jones's Settled Estates* (1858) 6 WR 762.

23 See the cases cited in note 19 supra.

24 *Re Governors of Christ's Hospital* (1864) 12 WR 669 (costs of enrolment). Cf *Re St Paul's Schools, Finsbury* (1883) 52 LJ Ch 454 (costs connected with a new scheme required for other reasons than the taking of the land not included); and cf para 163 note 7 post.

25 *Ex p Vicar of Creech St Michael* (1852) 21 LJ Ch 677.

26 *Carpmael v Proffit* (1854) 17 Jur 875.

27 See also *Armitage v Askham* (1855) 1 Jur NS 227; *Re Brandon's Estate* (1862) 2 Drew & Sm 162.

161. Costs of payment in respect of removing or replacing buildings. The undertakers[1] or acquiring authority[2] may be ordered to pay the costs of, or in consequence of, the purchase of the land, other than those otherwise provided for[3], and will be liable, if the compensation was paid in respect of any buildings taken or injured by the proximity of the works, for costs in respect of removing or replacing the buildings or substituting other buildings[4]. If the money is applied in erecting buildings, whether in substitution for others or not, this is treated as a payment out, and the undertakers or authority pay only the costs of the application and of the payment out[5]. Thus, the costs of planning and superintending the buildings[6], or of the surveyor's certificate that the works have been completed[7], are not payable, but the costs of a certificate of the sum due will be payable by the undertakers or authority[8].

1 For the meaning of 'the undertakers' see para 13 ante.
2 For the meaning of 'acquiring authority' see para 92 note 5 ante.
3 See the Lands Clauses Consolidation Act 1845 s 80 (as amended); the Compulsory Purchase Act 1965 s 26(2)(a), (3)(a), (d); and para 159 text to note 3 ante. These provisions are limited in their application because the power to sell and convey land of a person under disability has been otherwise extended: see para 96 ante. For the meaning of 'land' see para 92 note 1 ante. See also para 13 text to note 7 ante.
4 See the Lands Clauses Consolidation Act 1845 s 69 (as amended); the Compulsory Purchase Act 1965 s 2, Sch 1 para 6(2)(c); and para 151 ante. As to the removal or replacement of buildings see para 156 ante. For the meaning of 'the works' see para 92 note 3 ante; and see also para 13 text to note 4 ante. As to the meaning of 'building' see para 110 ante.
5 *Re Incumbent of Whitfield* (1861) 1 John & H 610; *Re Lathropp's Charity* (1866) LR 1 Eq 467 (distinguishing *Re Buckinghamshire Rly Co* (1850) 14 Jur 1065); *Ex p Rector of Claypole* (1873) LR 16 Eq 574; *Ex p Rector of Shipton-under-Wychwood* (1871) 19 WR 549; *Ex p Rector of Gamston* (1876) 1 ChD 477. As to substituted buildings see *Re Southampton and Dorchester Railway Act, ex p Thorner's Charity* (1848) 12 LTOS 266; *Re Chelsea Waterworks Co, ex p Minister and Churchwardens of St John's, Fulham* (1856) 28 LTOS 173; *Re Kent Coast Rly Co, ex p Dean and Chapter of Canterbury* (1862) 7 LT 240, 10 WR 505; *Re St Thomas's Hospital* (1863) 11 WR 1018.
6 *Re Butcher's Co* (1885) 53 LT 491.
7 *Ex p Rector of Shipton-under-Wychwood* (1871) 19 WR 549.
8 *Re Arden* (1894) 70 LT 506, CA.

162. Costs of application for payment out. The undertakers[1] or the acquiring authority[2] are liable to pay costs of obtaining orders for the payment out of court of the principal amount of the purchase money or compensation or of any securities in which it is vested, except such as are occasioned by litigation between adverse claimants[3]. This will include the brokerage on the sale of the securities in which the money has been invested[4]. They will also be required to pay all costs incurred in investigating[5] and making good the claimant's title, such as the costs of a disentailing assurance[6], of a power of attorney[7] and of taking out letters of administration[8], in cases where the taking of the land has rendered these necessary when they would not otherwise have been required. They must also pay the extra costs incurred by the owner dealing in the ordinary way with the money after it has been paid into court[9]. For example, if the land taken was the subject of a settlement, and the tenant for life exercises a power of appointment under the settlement[10], or if a reversioner mortgages his reversionary interest[11], the undertakers or authority must pay the costs of the parties requiring to be served in consequence. If, by reason of the money having been deposited in respect of a lease, part of the corpus has to be sold periodically and paid out, they will also be liable for the costs of those sales[12].

Where the fund in court comprises not only the money paid into court on the compulsory acquisition of the land, but also other money, the undertakers or authority will be ordered to pay the whole costs of the application for payment out of the fund, except in so far as the costs have been increased by reason of the inclusion in the application of the other money[13].

When an application is made for the money to be transferred to another account in court, and the undertakers' or authority's name is omitted from the title to that other account, the transfer is deemed to be equivalent to a payment out, and the undertakers or authority will be ordered to pay the costs of the application and transfer[14], but thereafter their liability ceases[15]. If the transfer is to the credit of an action, all persons having the same interest in the money should be joined in the making of the application, unless there is good reason why they should not be joined, and, if they appear separately without good reason, the undertakers or authority ought not to be ordered to pay their costs[16]. All parties to the action should be served with the application and the undertakers or authority are liable to pay the costs of service and of the appearance of the parties[17] other than the cost of appearance of parties who, having no objection to the order sought, ought not to appear[18]. The appearance of the trustee of the settlement is usually necessary, and his costs will be allowed[19].

If several persons have interests in the fund, but their interests are not adverse, the undertakers or authority will be required to pay all the costs of determining the respective shares, including the costs of construing a will[20]. Thus, if the money has been deposited in respect of land the subject of a mortgage, they may be ordered to pay the costs of the inquiry as to the amount due to the mortgagee[21].

The undertakers or authority are not required to pay the costs of unsuccessful applications for payment out, and the unsuccessful applicant may be ordered to pay the undertakers' or authority's costs[22]. They are not required to pay the costs of litigation between adverse claimants to the money[23], but if they pay money into court because they know of such adverse claims they will be liable to pay the ordinary costs of investment and of payment out[24]. They will also be required to pay the costs of proving the rightful claimant's title, but not any additional costs caused by the adverse claim[25]. Similarly, if the right to the fund depends on the construction of a will or other document, they will be ordered to pay one set of costs in connection with it[26]. If two adverse claimants mutually agree to apply for payment out, the undertakers or authority will be required to pay the costs incurred in connection with the payment out[27].

1 For the meaning of 'the undertakers' see para 13 ante.
2 For the meaning of 'acquiring authority' see para 92 note 5 ante.
3 Land Clauses Consolidation Act 1845 s 80 (amended by the Administration of Justice Act 1965 s 17(1) Sch 1) (where the 1845 Act is incorporated: see para 11 ante); Compulsory Purchase Act 1965 s 26(2)(a), (3)(a), (c), (d) (where that Act applies: see para 15 ante); *Re Gooch's Estate* (1876) 3 ChD 742; *Re Ellison's Estate* (1856) 25 LJ Ch 379; *Re Wood Green Gospel Hall Charity, ex p Middlesex County Council* [1909] 1 Ch 263 (costs of application to Charity Commissioners for new scheme). These provisions are limited in their application because the power to sell and convey land of a person under disability has been otherwise extended: see para 96 ante. Under special Acts not incorporating the Lands Clauses Acts a different rule applied: see *Re Eastern Counties Rly Co, ex p Earl of Hardwicke* (1848) 17 LJ Ch 422; *Re Bristol and Exeter Rly Co, ex p Gore-Langton* (1847) 11 Jur 686. As to the allowance of fees for attendance before the Accountant General see *Re Butler's Will, ex p Metropolitan Board of Works* (1912) 106 LT 673. As to the Lands Clauses Acts see para 11 ante; and for the meaning of 'special Act' see paras 11, 16 ante.
4 *Re Magdalen College, Oxford* [1901] 2 Ch 786; see also *Ex p Emmanuel Hospital* (1908) 24 TLR 261.
5 *Re Spooner's Estate* (1854) 1 K & J 220; *Re Singleton's Estate, ex p Fleetwood Rly Co* (1863) 9 Jur NS 941.
6 *Brooking's Devisees v South Devon Rly Co* (1859) 2 Giff 31. Cf *Re Merchant Shipping Act 1854, ex p Allen* (1881) 7 LR Ir 124.
7 *Re Godley* (1847) 10 I Eq R 222; *Re Kearns, ex p Lurgan UDC* [1902] 1 IR 157. Cf *Re Belfast and Northern Counties Rly Co, ex p Gilmore* [1895] 1 IR 297.
8 *Re Lloyd and North London Railway (City Branch) Act 1861* [1896] 2 Ch 397, adopting decisions in *Re Dublin Junction Rlys, ex p Kelly* (1893) 31 LR Ir 137, and in *Re Midland Great Western (Ireland) Rly Co, ex p Rorke* [1894] 1 IR 146, and approved in *Re Griggs, ex p London School Board* [1914] 2 Ch 547, CA; and

see *Re Waterford and Limerick Rly Co, ex p Baron Harlech* [1896] 1 IR 507; *Re Kearns, ex p Lurgan UDC* [1902] 1 IR 157; *Re Bear Island Defence Works and Doyle* [1903] 1 IR 164, CA. See also para 140 ante.

9 *Eden v Thompson* (1864) 2 Hem & M 6 at 8 per Wood V-C; *Re Lye's Estate, Re Berks and Hants Extension Railway Act 1859* (1866) 13 LT 664. Cf *Re Gough's Trusts, ex p Great Western Rly Co* (1883) 24 ChD 569; *Re Jones's Trust Estate* (1870) 39 LJ Ch 190, 18 WR 312; *Re London-Street, Greenwich and London, Chatham and Dover Railway (Further Powers) Act 1881* (1887) 57 LT 673.

10 *Re Brooshooft's Settlement* (1889) 42 ChD 250; and cf *Re Byrom* (1859) 5 Jur NS 261.

11 *Re Olive's Estate* (1890) 44 ChD 316.

12 *Re Long's Estate* (1853) 1 WR 226; *Re Edmunds* (1866) 35 LJ Ch 538.

13 *Re Lynn and Fakenham Railway (Extension) Act 1880* (1909) 100 LT 432.

14 *Melling v Bird* (1853) 22 LJ Ch 599.

15 *Fisher v Fisher* (1874) LR 17 Eq 340 at 341; *Prescott v Wood* (1868) 37 LJ Ch 691; *Nock v Nock* [1879] WN 125. As to costs when the new account is still entitled to the undertakers' or authority's name see *Drake v Greaves* (1886) 33 ChD 609; *Brown v Fenwick* (1866) 35 LJ Ch 241.

16 *Melling v Bird* (1853) 22 LJ Ch 599; *Re Picton's Estate* (1855) 3 WR 327.

17 *Eden v Thompson* (1864) 2 Hem & M 6; *Dinning v Henderson* (1848) 2 De G & Sm 485; *Henniker v Chafy* (1860) 28 Beav 621; *Re English's Settlement* (1888) 39 ChD 556.

18 *Sidney v Wilmer (No 2)* (1862) 31 Beav 338; *Eden v Thompson* (1864) 2 Hem & M 6.

19 *Re English's Settlement* (1888) 39 ChD 556; *Re Burnell's Estate* (1864) 12 WR 568.
    On a transfer to the official custodian for charities, there is no need for service on corporations or persons interested and costs of service are not payable by the undertakers or authority: *Re Prebend of St Margaret, Leicester* (1864) 10 LT 221; *Re Rector and Churchwardens of St Alban's, Wood Street* (1891) 66 LT 51. Notwithstanding the changes to the court's power to vest property in the offical custodian which were made by the Charities Act 1992 s 29 (as amended), funds vested in the Accountant General on payment into court (see para 124 ante) may be transferred to the official custodian on application to him by the Charity Commissioners: see the Administration of Justice Act 1982 s 41(1); and CHARITIES vol 5(2) (Reissue) para 271.

20 *Askew v Woodhead* (1880) 14 ChD 27 at 36, CA; *Re Gregson's Trusts* (1864) 2 Hem & M 504; revsd on another point 2 De GJ & Sm 428; *Re Singleton's Estate, ex p Fleetwood Rly Co* (1863) 9 Jur NS 941; *Re Hinks's Estate* (1853) 2 WR 108; *Re Noake's Will* (1880) 28 WR 762; *Ex p Collins* (1850) 19 LJ Ch 244; and see *Re Williams, ex p Great Southern and Western Rly Co* (1877) 11 IR Eq 497.

21 *Re Bareham* (1881) 17 ChD 329, CA; *Re Olive's Estate* (1890) 44 ChD 316.

22 *Ex p Winder* (1877) 6 ChD 696 at 705; *Re Jacobs, Baldwin v Pescott* [1908] 2 Ch 691.

23 Lands Clauses Consolidation Act 1845 s 80; Compulsory Purchase Act 1965 s 26(3)(d).

24 *Ex p Palmer, Cox and Bellingham* (1849) 13 Jur 781; *Hore v Smith* (1849) 14 Jur 55; *Re North London Rly Co, ex p Cooper* (1865) 34 LJ Ch 373; *Re Duke of Norfolk's Settled Estates* (1874) 31 LT 79; *Re Courts of Justice Comrs* [1868] WN 124. If the money is paid in at the request of one of the claimants, and the other afterwards withdraws his claim, the undertakers or authority would appear not to be liable: *Re English* (1865) 13 WR 932. If they have treated both claimants as vendors and have paid two sums into court, they may have to pay the costs of both: *Re Butterfield* (1861) 9 WR 805.

25 *Re Spooner's Estate* (1854) 1 K & J 220; *Re Joliffe* (1857) 3 Jur NS 633; *Re North London Rly Co, ex p Cooper* (1865) 34 LJ Ch 373; *Re Catling's Estate* [1890] WN 75. For the form of order see *Re Cant's Estate* (1859) 1 De GF & J 153, and *Hood v West Ham Corpn, Re West Ham Corpn Act 1902* (1910) 74 JP 179. It is the taxing officer's duty to disallow such of the costs as are, in his opinion, occasioned by litigation between adverse claimants, whether the order follows the decision in *Re Cant's Estate* supra and excepts such costs, or is drawn up in accordance with the practice not to except such costs unless the question is raised at the hearing: *Hood v West Ham Corpn, Re West Ham Corpn Act 1902* supra. Costs of negotiations for the settlement of a dispute affecting the title of the land acquired are costs occasioned by adverse litigation: *Hood v West Ham Corpn, Re West Ham Corpn Act 1902* supra. Opposition by the Charity Commissioners to an application for payment out by a corporation claiming to be absolutely entitled on the ground that it had no power to sell without their consent does not constitute adverse litigation: *Re Clergy Orphan Corpn* [1894] 3 Ch 145 at 147, CA.

26 *Re Mid Kent Railway Act 1856, ex p Styan* (1859) John 387; *Re Tookey's Trust, Re Bucks Rly Co* (1852) 16 Jur 708; *Ex p Yates* (1869) 17 WR 872; *Re Longworth's Estate* (1853) 1 K & J 1.

27 *Re Spooner's Estate* (1854) 1 K & J 220.

163. Costs of purchasing and taking land. The undertakers[1] or acquiring authority[2] may be ordered to pay the costs of or incurred in consequence of the purchase of the land not otherwise provided for[3], including all reasonable charges and expenses incidental to the purchase, the costs of obtaining the proper orders and the costs of all proceedings relating to those orders except such as are occasioned by litigation between adverse clients[4]. Where, therefore, additional costs are incurred in applications to the court which are rendered necessary by reason of mental disorder[5] or because of the existence of an administration action[6], or, where the vendors are trustees of a charity, in applying to the Charity Commissioners and obtaining a new scheme[7], the undertakers or authority may be ordered to pay these additional costs.

When the money has been paid into court as security before entry by the undertakers or authority, they may be ordered to pay certain costs connected with the taking of the land, but not costs the payment of which is provided for under other provisions[8], even though these in fact remain unpaid[9]. When part of land subject to leases has been taken, the undertakers or authority have been ordered to pay the costs of apportioning the rents among the various parties and also the costs incurred with regard to settling accommodation works[10]. Similarly, when the undertaking was abandoned after entry subject to compensation to the landowner for disturbance, they have been ordered to pay the costs of ascertaining this compensation[11], but the court has power to make only a general order as to these costs, and cannot order them to be paid out of the money in court[12].

1 For the meaning of 'the undertakers' see para 13 ante.
2 For the meaning of 'acquiring authority' see para 92 note 5 ante.
3 See para 159 note 3 ante. For the meaning of 'land' see para 92 note 1 ante. See also para 13 text to note 7 ante.
4 See the Lands Clauses Consolidation Act 1845 s 80 (amended by the Administration of Justice Act 1965 s 17(1), Sch 1) (where the 1845 Act is incorporated: see para 11 ante); the Compulsory Purchase Act 1965 s 26(2)(a), (3)(a), (d) (where that Act applies: see para 15 ante); and para 159 text to note 3 ante. These provisions are limited in their application because the power to sell and convey land of a person under disability has been otherwise extended: see para 96 ante.
5 *Re Taylor and York and North Midland Rly Co* (1849) 1 Mac & G 210; *Re Walker, ex p Manchester and Leeds Rly Co* (1851) 7 Ry & Can Cas 129; *Re Briscoe* (1864) 2 De GJ & Sm 249.
6 *Haynes v Barton* (1861) 1 Drew & Sm 483; *Haynes v Barton* (1866) LR 1 Eq 422; *Picard v Mitchell* (1850) 12 Beav 486.
7 *Re Wood Green Gospel Hall Charity, ex p Middlesex County Council* [1909] 1 Ch 263. These costs will not be allowed where the formulation of a new scheme was not the direct result of the acquisition of the land: see para 160 note 24 ante.
8 See para 159 note 3 ante.
9 *Ex p Great Northern Rly Co* (1848) 5 Ry & Can Cas 269; and see *Ex p Morris* (1871) LR 12 Eq 418 (costs of summoning jury, which became unnecessary owing to agreement being reached); *Re Pardoe's Account and Epping Forest Act 1878* [1882] WN 33 (costs of assessing compensation when Lands Clauses Acts provisions as to costs not incorporated). See also *Metropolitan District Rly Co v Sharpe* (1880) 5 App Cas 425, HL (costs provisions of Lands Clauses Acts applied where procedure for assessment of compensation substituted by special Act). As to the Lands Clauses Acts see para 11 ante; and for the meaning of 'special Act' see paras 11, 16 ante.
10 *Re London, Brighton and South Coast Rly Co, ex p Flower* (1866) 1 Ch App 599; and see *Re Hampstead Junction Rly Co, ex p Buck* (1863) 1 Hem & M 519.
11 *Charlton v Rolleston* (1884) 28 ChD 237, CA.
12 *Re Neath and Brecon Rly Co* (1874) 9 Ch App 263.

164. Money paid into court in respect of leases or reversions. When the money or compensation paid into court has been paid in respect of any lease or agreement for a lease[1], or any estate in land[2] less than the whole fee simple, or of any reversion dependent on any such lease or estate, the High Court, on the application of any person interested in the money[3], may order it to be laid out, invested, accumulated and paid, in such manner as it may consider will give the persons interested in the money the same benefit as they might lawfully have had from the lease, estate or reversion, or as near to it as may be[4]. Such orders may also be made in respect of money paid for renewable leaseholds[5] or in respect of compensation for leaving minerals unworked so as to afford support when the minerals have been let on lease[6].

The method of distribution depends on the nature of the parties' interests. Thus, if leasehold had been settled in trust for a tenant for life with remainder over, he is entitled to be paid such yearly sum raised out of the income and corpus as will exhaust the fund in the number of years which the lease had to run[7]. Where it transpires that the lease would have terminated during the life of the tenant for life, he is entitled to the whole sum, so that if he has only been paid the income he becomes entitled, at the date when the lease would have terminated, to have the corpus paid to him[8]. If the lease was renewable from time to time so as to be practically perpetual, the tenant for life was only entitled to the income[9]. If a person is entitled to an annuity charged on the leasehold, and the income is not sufficient to pay it, a portion of the corpus will be sold from time to time to make up the deficiency[10].

When the money in court is in respect of reversions dependent on leases, a tenant for life is entitled to no more than the amount of the rent he received as lessor so long as the lease would have continued; so if the land was let at less than the rack rent, or if during the term the property had increased in value, he will only be paid the amount of the rent out of the income, and the balance will be accumulated until the end of the lease[11], after which he will be entitled to the income on the whole sum[12]. In the case of compensation paid for minerals required to be left unworked, which would have been worked out during the life of the tenant for life, and in respect of which he would have received royalties, the sum will be apportioned as rent accruing from day to day to the tenant for life during whose life tenancy the minerals would have been worked out[13]. In cases of property held by corporations not for their own beneficial interest, the court may authorise the whole of the income to be paid out, even where it is in excess of the rent received[14].

1 'Lease' includes an agreement for a lease: Lands Clauses Consolidation Act 1845 s 3; Compulsory Purchase Act 1965 s 1(3); and see *Re King's Leasehold Estates, ex p East of London Rly Co* (1873) LR 16 Eq 521.

2 For the meaning of 'land' see para 92 note 1 ante. See also para 13 text to note 7 ante.

3 The application is made by originating summons in the Chancery Division to be heard in chambers: see RSC Ord 92 r 5(1), (2). If the application is made in a pending cause or matter, or an application for the same purpose has previously been made by petition or originating summons, the application is by ordinary summons: Ord 92 r 5(2). As to service on the remainderman on applications by tenants for life see *Re Crane's Estate* (1869) LR 7 Eq 322. A tenant who has received notice to quit from the owner is not a party interested in the money: *Ex p Nadin* (1848) 17 LJ Ch 421.

4 Lands Clauses Consolidation Act 1845 s 74 (amended by the Administration of Justice Act 1965 ss 17(1), 34, Schs 1, 2; and by the Compulsory Purchase Act 1965 s 39(4), Sch 8 Pt II) (where the 1845 Act is incorporated: see para 11 ante); Compulsory Purchase Act 1965 s 25(2) (where that Act applies: see para 15 ante). These provisions are limited in their application because the power to sell and convey land of a person under disability has been otherwise extended: see para 96 ante. Cf the corresponding provision in the Settled Land Act 1925 s 79: see SETTLEMENTS. An order will not be made for payment out to the lessor of arrears of rent: *Re Dublin Corpn and Baker, ex p Thompson* [1912] 1 IR 498.

5 *Re Wood's Estate* (1870) LR 10 Eq 572.

6 *Re Barrington, Gamlen v Lyon* (1886) 33 ChD 523; *Cardigan v Curzon-Howe* (1898) 14 TLR 550. Cf *Re Robinson's Settlement Trusts* [1891] 3 Ch 129.

7 *Askew v Woodhead* (1880) 14 ChD 27, CA (approving *Re Phillips' Trusts* (1868) LR 6 Eq 250); *Re Sewell's Trusts* (1870) 23 LT 835; *Re Hunt's Estate* [1884] WN 181; *Re Walsh's Trust* (1881) 7 LR Ir 554; *Re South City Market Co, ex p Bergin* (1884) 13 LR Ir 245. See also *Re Duke of Leeds and Coal Acts 1938 to 1943, Duke of Leeds v Davenport* [1947] Ch 525, [1947] 2 All ER 200 (approved in *Williams v Sharpe* [1949] Ch 593, [1949] 2 All ER 102, CA); and *Re Scholfield's Will Trusts, Scholfield v Scholfield* [1949] Ch 341, [1949] 1 All ER 490 (war damage value payments derived from settled leaseholds invested in purchasing annuities for periods corresponding to the unexpired leasehold terms).

8 *Re Beaufoy's Estate* (1852) 1 Sm & G 20; cf *Phillips v Sarjent* (1848) 7 Hare 33 at 37.
9 *Re Wood's Estate* (1870) LR 10 Eq 572; and see *Re Barber's Settled Estates* (1881) 18 ChD 624. See also
    Ex p Precentor of St Paul's (1855) 1 K & J 538 (lease renewable as payment of fine). Perpetually renewable
    leases are converted into terms of 2,000 years by the Law of Property Act 1922 ss 145, 190, Sch 15, the
    fines payable on renewal being converted into additional rent: see LANDLORD AND TENANT vol 27(1)
    (Reissue) para 453.
10 *Re London, Brighton and South Coast Rly Co, ex p Wilkinson* (1849) 3 De G & Sm 633; *Re Treacher's
    Settlement* (1868) 18 LT 810.
11 *Re Wootton's Estate* (1866) LR 1 Eq 589; *Re Wilkes' Estate* (1880) 16 ChD 597; *Re Mette's Estate* (1868)
    LR 7 Eq 72; *Cottrell v Cottrell* (1885) 28 ChD 628; *Re Bowyer's Settled Estate* (1892) 36 Sol Jo 347; and cf
    Re Duke of Westminster's Settled Estates, Duke of Westminster v Earl of Shaftesbury [1921] 1 Ch 585. As
    regards ecclesiastical property to the like effect see *Re South Western Railway Co's Acts, ex p Rector of
    Lambeth* (1846) 4 Ry & Can Cas 231; *Ex p Bishop of Winchester* (1852) 10 Hare 137; *Ex p Dean and
    Chapter of Gloucester* (1850) 19 LJ Ch 400; *Ex p Dean and Chapter of Christchurch* (1853) 23 LJ Ch 149; *Re
    Wimbledon and Croydon Railway Act, ex p Archbishop of Canterbury* (1854) 23 LTOS 219.
12 *Re Wilkes' Estate* (1880) 16 ChD 597.
13 *Cardigan v Curzon-Howe* (1898) 14 TLR 550; *Re Barrington, Gamlen v Lyon* (1886) 33 ChD 523; and cf
    Re Robinson's Settlement Trusts [1891] 3 Ch 129.
14 *Re Dean of Westminster, Re Hampstead Junction Rly Co* (1858) 26 Beav 214; *Ex p Trustees of St Thomas's
    Church Lands and Temple Church Lands, Bristol* (1870) 23 LT 135; *Re South Western Railway Co's Acts, ex p
    Rector of Lambeth* (1846) 4 Ry & Can Cas 231.

165. Discretionary payments to tenants for life and limited owners. The
court, and trustees to whom sums of under £200 have been paid instead of payment
into court[1], may, if they think fit, allot to any tenant for life or for any other partial or
qualified estate, for his own use, a part of the sum paid into court or to the trustees, as
compensation for any injury, inconvenience or annoyance which he may have
sustained independently of the actual value of the land and of the damage occasioned to
the land held with it, by reason of the taking of the land and the execution of the
works[2]. A tenant for life is not allowed any capital sum for matters in respect of which
he is entitled to the income of the money in court, and the income may be deemed
sufficient compensation. Thus, he may not be entitled to any capital sum in respect of
minerals even though they might be worked out in his lifetime[3]. He may, however, be
allowed out of the money in court a sum to cover the costs he may properly have
incurred in connection with the purchase or taking of the land, such as the costs of
preliminary negotiation[4], of an arbitration as to the price of the land when the award
has been less than the amount offered[5], and other similar matters[6].

Costs incurred by a tenant for life in opposing the special Act[7] while passing as a Bill
through Parliament are not payable out of the fund in court under the Lands Clauses
Acts[8], but the court can authorise the payment of these costs out of the money in court
either under its general jurisdiction[9] or under the Settled Land Act 1925[10].

1 See the Lands Clauses Consolidation Act 1845 s 71 (as amended); the Compulsory Purchase Act 1965
    s 2, Sch 1 para 7(1); and para 166 post.
2 Land Clauses Consolidation Act 1845 s 73 (amended by the Administration of Justice Act 1965 s 17(1),
    Sch 1) (where the 1845 Act is incorporated: see para 11 ante); Compulsory Purchase Act 1965 Sch 1
    para 9(3) (where that Act applies: see para 15 ante); *Taylor v Directors etc of Chichester and Midhurst Rly Co*
    (1870) LR 4 HL 628 at 643. These provisions are limited in their application because the power to sell
    and convey land of a person under disability has been otherwise extended: see para 96 ante.
       Thus, a sum may be allowed to a rector for annoyance caused to him by the construction of a railway
    in what was part of his glebe (*Re East Lincolnshire Rly Co, ex p Rector of Little Steeping* (1848) 5 Ry & Can
    Cas 207; *Re Saunderton Glebe Lands, ex p Rector of Saunderton* [1903] 1 Ch 480; *Re Collis's Estate* (1866) 14
    LT 352); or to a tenant for life for money laid out on a road for which the promoters agreed to pay (*Re
    Duke of Marlborough's Estate Act, ex p Lord Churchill* (1849) 13 Jur 738; on appeal (1850) 15 LTOS 341).
    As to the present practice relating to the payment to the Church Commissioners or the Diocesan Board
    of Finance of compensation awarded to an owner of land which is ecclesiastical property see para 150

ante. For the meaning of 'land' and 'the works' see para 92 notes 1, 3 ante. See also para 13 text to notes 7, 4 respectively ante.

3 *Re Robinson's Settlement Trusts* [1891] 3 Ch 129; but see *Cardigan v Curzon-Howe* (1898) 14 TLR 550.
4 *Re Strathmore Estates* (1874) LR 18 Eq 338 at 339; *Re Oldham's Estate* [1871] WN 190.
5 *Re Earl of Berkeley's Will* (1874) 10 Ch App 56; *Re Aubrey's Estates and South Wales Railway Act* (1853) 17 Jur 874; *Ex p Perpetual Curate of Whitworth* (1871) 24 LT 126.
6 *Re Great Yeldham Glebe Lands* (1869) LR 9 Eq 68; *Blackford v Davis* (1869) 4 Ch App 304; *Rees v Metropolitan Board of Works* (1880) 14 ChD 372.
7 For the meaning of 'special Act' see paras 11, 16 ante.
8 *Re Earl of Berkeley's Will* (1874) 10 Ch App 56; *Re Nicoll's Estate* [1878] WN 154. As to the Lands Clauses Acts see para 11 ante.
9 *Re Ormrod's Settled Estate* [1892] 2 Ch 318; *Re LCC, ex p Pennington* (1901) 84 LT 808; and cf *A-G v Brecon Corpn* (1878) 10 ChD 204.
10 See the Settled Land Act 1925 s 92; and SETTLEMENTS.

(vi) Payment of Small Sums to Trustees or Persons Entitled instead of into Court

166. Payment to trustees of sums less than £200. If the purchase money or compensation exceeds £20 but does not exceed £200, it may, with the approval of the undertakers[1] or acquiring authority[2], be paid into court[3], or be paid to two trustees approved by the undertakers or authority and nominated in writing signed by the person entitled to the rents or profits of the land in respect of which it is paid[4]. Both the compensation paid to the trustees and the income arising from it must be applied by them in accordance with the statutory provisions applying to sums exceeding £200[5] save that it is unnecessary to obtain a High Court order, and until so applied the compensation may be invested in government or real securities[6].

1 For the meaning of 'the undertakers' see para 13 ante.
2 For the meaning of 'acquiring authority' see para 92 note 5 ante.
3 As to payment into court see the Compulsory Purchase Act 1965 s 25(1); and paras 98 note 6, 124 ante.
4 Lands Clauses Consolidation Act 1845 s 71 (amended by the Administration of Justice Act 1965 s 17(1), Sch 1; and by the Compulsory Purchase Act 1965 s 39(4), Sch 8 Pt II) (where the 1845 Act is incorporated: see para 11 ante); Compulsory Purchase Act 1965 s 2, Sch 1 para 7(1) (where that Act applies: see para 15 ante). These provisions are limited in their application because the power to sell and convey land of a person under disability has been otherwise extended: see para 96 ante. As to the application of sums paid into court see para 151 et seq ante. For the meaning of 'land' see para 92 note 1 ante. See also para 13 text to note 7 ante.
5 See para 151 et seq ante. As to the trustees' power to make discretionary payments to limited owners see para 165 ante.
6 Lands Clauses Consolidation Act 1845 s 71 (as amended: see note 4 supra) (applying s 70 (as amended): see para 153 ante); Compulsory Purchase Act 1965 Sch 1 para 7(2).

167. Payment to persons entitled of sums of £20 or less. If the purchase money or compensation does not exceed £20 it must be paid to the person entitled to the rents and profits of the land[1] in respect of which it is payable, for his own use and benefit[2].

1 For the meaning of 'land' see para 92 note 1 ante. See also para 13 text to note 7 ante.
2 Lands Clauses Consolidation Act 1845 s 72 (amended by the Compulsory Purchase Act 1965 s 39(4), Sch 8 Pt II) (where the 1845 Act is incorporated; see para 11 ante); Compulsory Purchase Act 1965 s 2, Sch 1 para 8 (where that Act applies: see para 15 ante); and see *Re Lord Egremont* (1848) 12 Jur 618; *Re London and Birmingham Railway Co's Act, ex p Rector of Loughton* (1849) 5 Ry & Can Cas 591; *Re Hichin's Estate* (1853) 1 WR 505; *Re Bateman's Estate* (1852) 21 LJ Ch 691; *Ex p Vicar of Sheffield* (1904) 68 JP 313. These provisions are limited in their application because the power to sell and convey land of a person under disability has been otherwise extended: see para 96 ante.

(7) VESTING DECLARATIONS AS ALTERNATIVE STEPS

(i) Making and Effect of Vesting Declarations

168. Condition precedent to power to make vesting declaration. Where any
minister or local or other public authority[1] authorised to acquire land[2] by means of a
compulsory purchase order[3] desires to make a general vesting declaration[4] with respect
to any land which is subject to the compulsory purchase order, that acquiring authority
must include in the statutory notice of making or confirmation of the order[5], or in a
notice[6] given subsequently and before the service of a notice to treat[7] in respect of that
land[8]:

(1) a prescribed statement[9] of the effect of the statutory provisions[10] relating to the
execution and effect of that declaration[11]; and

(2) a notification to the effect that every person who, if a general vesting declaration
were executed in respect of all the land comprised in the order, other than land
in respect of which notice to treat has been served, would be entitled to claim
compensation in respect of any of the land[12], is invited to give information to the
authority by making a declaration in the prescribed form[13] with respect to his
name and address and the land in question[14].

A notice complying with these provisions must be registered in the register of local
land charges by the proper officer of the local authority for the area in which that land,
or any part of that land, is situated[15].

1 Ie a minister or local or other public authority to whom or to which the provisions of the Compulsory
Purchase (Vesting Declarations) Act 1981 apply, and referred to therein as an 'acquiring authority': see
ss 1(2), 2(1). The 1981 Act enables any such authority to vest in himself or itself by a declaration land
which he or it is authorised by a compulsory purchase order to acquire: see s 1(1).
2 'Land', in relation to compulsory acquisition by an acquiring authority, has the same meaning as in the
relevant enactments; and 'relevant enactments', in relation to an acquiring authority, means the
enactments under which that authority may acquire or be authorised to acquire land compulsorily and
which prescribe a procedure for effecting the compulsory acquisition by that authority by means of a
compulsory purchase order: ibid s 2(1).
3 As to compulsory purchase orders see para 33 et seq ante.
4 'General vesting declaration' means a declaration executed under the Compulsory Purchase (Vesting
Declarations) Act 1981 s 4 (see para 169 post): s 2(1). The following orders have the same effect as
general vesting declarations, ie any order vesting land (1) in an urban development corporation under
the Local Government, Planning and Land Act 1980 s 141 (as amended) (see s 141(4) (as amended); and
TOWN AND COUNTRY PLANNING vol 46 (Reissue) para 1296); (2) in a housing action trust under the
Housing Act 1988 s 76 (see s 76(5); and HOUSING); (3) in the Urban Regeneration Agency under the
Leasehold Reform, Housing and Urban Development Act 1993 s 161(1) (see s 161(4); and TRADE,
INDUSTRY AND INDUSTRIAL RELATIONS vol 47 (Reissue) para 851). The Compulsory Purchase
(Vesting Declarations) Act 1981 is modified in relation to an order (a) under head (1) supra, by s 15,
Sch 2; (b) under head (2) supra, by the Housing Act 1988 s 76(5), Sch 9 para 12; (c) under head (3) supra,
by the Leasehold Reform, Housing and Urban Development Act 1993 s 161(5), Sch 19 paras 6, 7.
5 For these purposes, 'statutory notice of confirmation', in relation to a compulsory purchase order,
means the notice of the confirmation of the order which is required to be published or served by the
Acquisition of Land Act 1981 s 15 (see para 58 ante), or by any other provision of the relevant
enactments corresponding thereto; and where the acquiring authority is a minister, for references to the
statutory notice of confirmation of the order there are to be substituted references to the notice of the
making of the order which is required to be published or served by s 2(3), Sch 1 para 6 (see para 74 ante),
or any other provision of the relevant enactments corresponding thereto: Compulsory Purchase
(Vesting Declarations) Act 1981 s 3(5), (6).
6 Ie a notice to which the requirements of the relevant enactments with respect to the publication and
service of a notice of the making or confirmation of a compulsory purchase order apply: ibid s 3(1)(b), (6).
7 As to notices to treat see para 100 et seq ante.

8 Compulsory Purchase (Vesting Declarations) Act 1981 s 3(1), (2). These provisions apply except where a notice to treat has actually been served: see s 7(1), (2); and para 171 post.
9 'Prescribed' means prescribed by regulations made by the Secretary of State by statutory instrument subject to annulment in pursuance of a resolution of either House of Parliament: ibid s 2(1). The Secretary of State here concerned is the Secretary of State for the Environment. For the prescribed form of statement see the Compulsory Purchase of Land (Vesting Declarations) Regulations 1990, SI 1990/497, reg 3(b), Schedule, Form 2 Pt I.
10 Ie the effect of the Compulsory Purchase (Vesting Declarations) Act 1981 Pts II, III (ss 3–9) (as amended): see the text and notes 1–8 supra, 11–15 infra; and para 169 et seq post.
11 Ibid s 3(1), (3)(a). A notice under s 3 is not an exercise of powers of compulsory purchase under the Compulsory Purchase Act 1965 s 4 (as amended) (see para 101 ante): *Co-operative Insurance Society Ltd v Hastings Borough Council* [1993] 2 EGLR 19; not following *Westminster City Council v Quereshi* [1991] 1 EGLR 256.
12 As to the persons who would be entitled to compensation see paras 37, 103 ante, 197 post.
13 For the prescribed form see the Compulsory Purchase of Land (Vesting Declarations) Regulations 1990 Schedule, Form 2 Pt II.
14 Compulsory Purchase (Vesting Declarations) Act 1981 s 3(1), (3)(b). The Town and Country Planning Act 1990 s 330 (power to acquire information as to interests in land: see TOWN AND COUNTRY PLANNING vol 46 (Reissue) para 30) has effect as if the Compulsory Purchase (Vesting Declarations) Act 1981 were part of the 1990 Act: Compulsory Purchase (Vesting Declarations) Act 1981 s 2(3) (amended by the Planning (Consequential Provisions) Act 1990 s 4, Sch 2 para 52(1)).
15 Compulsory Purchase (Vesting Declarations) Act 1981 s 3(4). As to the registration of local land charges see the Local Land Charges Act 1975 s 3(2)(a); and LAND CHARGES.

169. Form, execution and vesting date of declaration. The acquiring authority[1] may execute a declaration in the prescribed form[2] in respect of any land[3] which it is authorised to acquire by the compulsory purchase order[4], vesting the land in itself from the end of a specified period which must not be less than 28 days from the date on which the service of the required notices[5] is completed[6]. The first day after the end of that period is the vesting date in relation to such a general vesting declaration[7].

The declaration may not be executed before the compulsory purchase order has come into operation[8]; and may not be executed before the end of the period of two months beginning with the date of the first publication of the notice of the making or confirmation of the compulsory purchase order or the subsequent notice containing the prescribed information[9] or such longer period, if any, as may be specified in that notice[10], except with the written consent of every occupier of any land specified in the declaration[11].

1 For the meaning of 'acquiring authority' see para 168 note 1 ante.
2 For the prescribed form see the Compulsory Purchase of Land (Vesting Declarations) Regulations 1990, SI 1990/497, reg 3(a), Schedule, Form 1.
3 For the meaning of 'land' see para 168 note 2 ante.
4 As to compulsory purchase orders see para 33 et seq ante.
5 Ie the notices required by the Compulsory Purchase (Vesting Declarations) Act 1981 s 6 (as amended): see para 170 post.
6 Ibid s 4(1). A certificate by the acquiring authority that the service of those notices was completed on a date specified in the certificate is conclusive evidence of the fact so stated: s 4(2).
7 Ibid s 4(3).
8 Ibid s 5(2). As to the date of coming into operation see para 75 ante. Section 5(2) applies in particular where the compulsory purchase order is subject to special parliamentary procedure (see paras 76–78 ante) and therefore does not come into operation in accordance with the Acquisition of Land Act 1981 s 26(1) (see para 75 ante) or any corresponding provision of the relevant enactments; Compulsory Purchase (Vesting Declarations) Act 1981 s 5(2). For the meaning of 'relevant enactments' see para 168 note 2 ante.
9 Ie the notice complying with ibid s 3: see para 168 ante.
10 Ibid s 5(1).
11 Ibid s 5(1) proviso.

170. Notice before vesting date to owners and occupiers of effect of declaration. As soon as may be after executing a general vesting declaration[1], the acquiring authority[2] must serve[3] (1) on every occupier of any of the land[4] specified in the declaration, other than land in which there subsists a minor tenancy[5] or a long tenancy which is about to expire[6]; and (2) on every other person who has given information to the authority with respect to any of that land in pursuance of the invitation published and served[7], a notice in the prescribed form[8] specifying the land and stating the effect of the declaration[9].

1   For the meaning of 'general vesting declaration' see para 168 note 4 ante.
2   For the meaning of 'acquiring authority' see para 168 note 1 ante.
3   The Town and Country Planning Act 1990 s 329 (as amended) (service of notices: see TOWN AND
    COUNTRY PLANNING vol 46 (Reissue) para 31) applies as if the Compulsory Purchase (Vesting
    Declarations) Act 1981 s 6 (as amended) formed part of the 1990 Act: Compulsory Purchase (Vesting
    Declarations) Act 1981 s 6(2) (amended by the Planning (Consequential Provisions) Act 1990 s 4, Sch 2
    para 52(2)).
4   For the meaning of 'land' see para 168 note 2 ante.
5   'Minor tenancy' means a tenancy for a year or from year to year or any lesser interest; and 'tenancy' has
    the same meaning as in the Landlord and Tenant Act 1954 (see s 69(1); and LANDLORD AND TENANT
    vol 27(1) (Reissue) para 369 note 1): Compulsory Purchase (Vesting Declarations) Act 1981 s 2(1).
6   Ibid s 6(1)(a). 'Long tenancy which is about to expire', in relation to a general vesting declaration,
    means a tenancy granted for an interest greater than a minor tenancy, but having on the vesting date a
    period still to run which is not more than the specified period (ie the period, longer than a year, specified
    for these purposes in the declaration in relation to the land in which the tenancy subsists): s 2(1), (2). In
    determining for these purposes what period a tenancy still has to run on the vesting date it must be
    assumed that (1) the tenant will exercise any option to renew and will not exercise any option to
    terminate the tenancy, then or thereafter available to him; and (2) the landlord will exercise any option
    to terminate the tenancy then or thereafter available to him: s 2(2). As to the vesting date see para 169
    ante.
7   Ibid s 6(1)(b). The invitation referred to is that published and served under s 3(1): see para 168 ante.
8   For the prescribed form of notice see the Compulsory Purchase of Land (Vesting Declarations)
    Regulations 1990, SI 1990/497, reg 3(c), Schedule, Form 3.
9   Compulsory Purchase (Vesting Declarations) Act 1981 s 6(1). As to evidence of the service of notices
    under s 6 (as amended) see para 169 note 6 ante.

171. Effect of vesting declaration. On the vesting date[1] the provisions of the Land Compensation Act 1961[2] and of the Compulsory Purchase Act 1965[3] will apply as if, on the date on which the general vesting declaration[4] was executed[5], a notice to treat[6] had been served on every person on whom the acquiring authority[7] could otherwise have served such a notice[8], other than any person entitled to an interest in the land in respect of which a notice to treat had actually been served before the vesting date[9] and other than any person entitled to a minor tenancy[10] or a long tenancy which is about to expire[11].

The power to withdraw a notice to treat[12] is not exercisable in respect of a notice to treat which is so deemed to be served[13].

1   As to the vesting date see para 169 ante.
2   Ie as modified by the Acquisition of Land Act 1981 s 4 (see para 116 ante): Compulsory Purchase
    (Vesting Declarations) Act 1981 s 7(1)(a). The Land Compensation Act 1961 relates to claims for
    compensation (see para 197 et seq post) and the measure and assessment of compensation (see paras 177,
    233 et seq post), and provides, inter alia, power to withdraw a notice to treat (see para 120 ante); but see
    the text and notes 12–13 infra.
3   The Compulsory Purchase Act 1965 provides for notices to treat (see para 100 ante), objections to
    taking only part of the land (see paras 112 ante, 172 post), the right of entry (see paras 100, 103, 122 et seq
    ante, 175, 197 post), the right to compensation or purchase money and apportionment of rent (see
    para 177 et seq post), interests omitted by mistake (but the provisions are excluded: see para 175 note 4
    post), and completion, inter alia, by deed poll (see para 142 et seq ante).

4 For the meaning of 'general vesting declaration' see para 168 note 4 ante.

5 As to the date on which a declaration may be made see para 169 ante.

6 As to notices to treat see para 100 et seq ante.

7 For the meaning of 'acquiring authority' see para 168 note 1 ante.

8 Ie on every person on whom the acquiring authority could have served a notice to treat under the Compulsory Purchase Act 1965 s 5 (as amended) (see para 103 ante), on the assumption that the authority required to take the whole of the land specified in the declaration and had knowledge of all those persons: Compulsory Purchase (Vesting Declarations) Act 1981 s 7(1), (2).

9 If notice to treat is actually served, the acquisition will continue on the ordinary procedure, which is available in the alternative.

10 For the meaning of 'minor tenancy' see para 170 note 5 ante. As to the effect of the declaration on such tenancies see para 176 post.

11 Compulsory Purchase (Vesting Declarations) Act 1981 s 7(1). For the meaning of 'long tenancy which is about to expire' see para 170 note 6 ante. As to the effect of the declaration on such tenancies see para 176 post.

12 Ie the power conferred by the Land Compensation Act 1961 s 31: see para 120 ante.

13 Compulsory Purchase (Vesting Declarations) Act 1981 s 7(3).

(ii) Counter-notice where Declaration comprises Part Only of Property

172. Counter-notice by person able and willing to sell the whole. If a general vesting declaration[1] comprises part only of a house, building or factory[2] or of a park[3] or garden[4] belonging to a house, any person who is able to sell the whole of it may, by a notice (a 'notice of objection to severance') served on the acquiring authority[5] within the time allowed[6], require it to purchase his interest in the whole[7]. Where notice of objection to severance is served within the time allowed, then, notwithstanding the provisions for vesting the land in the acquiring authority[8], the interest in respect of which the notice is served will not so vest[9]; and, if the person entitled to the interest is entitled to possession of the land[10], the authority will not be entitled to enter upon or take possession of it[11] until, in either case, the notice has been disposed of[12].

1 For the meaning of 'general vesting declaration' see para 168 note 4 ante.

2 As to the meaning of 'house, building or factory' cf para 110 ante.

3 As to the meaning of 'park' see para 112 note 3 ante.

4 As to the meaning of 'garden' see para 112 note 4 ante.

5 For the meaning of 'acquiring authority' see para 168 note 1 ante.

6 Except as provided by the Compulsory Purchase (Vesting Declarations) Act 1981 s 12, Sch 1 para 10 (see para 174 post), the notice will not have effect if it is served more than 28 days after the date on which notice under s 6 (as amended) (see para 170 ante) is served on the person given the notice of objection to severance: Sch 1 para 2(2).

7 Ibid Sch 1 paras 1, 2(1). No form of notice of objection to severance has been prescribed. The Compulsory Purchase Act 1965 s 8(1) (which makes other provision for objection to severance of buildings, gardens etc: see para 112 ante) does not apply to land in respect of which a general vesting declaration is made: Compulsory Purchase (Vesting Declarations) Act 1981 Sch 1 para 2(3).

8 Ie the provisions of ibid s 8: see para 175 post.

9 Ibid Sch 1 para 3(a).

10 For the meaning of 'land' see para 168 note 2 ante.

11 Compulsory Purchase (Vesting Declarations) Act 1981 Sch 1 para 3(b).

12 Ibid Sch 1 para 3. The notice must be disposed of in accordance with the provisions of Sch 1 paras 2–10: see para 173 et seq post.

173. Acquiring authority's response to counter-notice. Within three months after a person has served on an acquiring authority[1] a notice of objection to severance[2], the acquiring authority must either:

(1) serve notice on that person withdrawing the notice to treat deemed to have been served on him[3] in respect of his interest in the land proposed to be severed[4]; or

(2) serve notice on him that the general vesting declaration[5] is to have effect in relation to his interest in that land as if the whole of that land had been comprised in the declaration, and, if part only of that land was comprised in the compulsory purchase order, in that order[6]; or

(3) refer the notice of objection to severance to the Lands Tribunal and notify him that it has been so referred[7].

If the authority does not take any such action within the period allowed, then at the end of that period the authority will be deemed to have withdrawn the deemed notice to treat in accordance with head (1) above[8].

If a deemed notice to treat is so withdrawn in respect of a person's interest[9], or is so deemed to have been withdrawn[10], that interest will not vest in the acquiring authority by virtue of the general vesting declaration[11]; and if that person is entitled to possession of the land, the authority will not be entitled by virtue of the declaration to enter upon or take possession of it[12].

If the authority serves notice on the objector to severance that the general vesting declaration is to have effect as if the whole of the land had been comprised in the declaration[13], the declaration and, where applicable, the compulsory purchase order, will have effect as mentioned in head (2) above, whether or not the acquiring authority could otherwise[14] have been authorised to acquire the interest in question in the whole of the land proposed to be severed[15].

If the authority refers a notice of objection to severance to the Lands Tribunal[16] and on that reference the tribunal determines that the part of the land proposed to be severed which is comprised in the general vesting declaration can be taken, either, in the case of a house, building or factory[17], without material detriment, or, in the case of a park or garden[18], without seriously affecting the amenity[19] or convenience of the house[20], that notice will be disposed of and the suspension of vesting and right of entry will cease[21]. If, on such a reference, the tribunal does not make such a determination, it must determine the area of that land[22] which the acquiring authority ought to be required to take[23]. The general vesting declaration will then have effect in relation to the interest in that area of the person who served the notice of objection to severance as if the whole of that area had been comprised in the declaration, whether or not the authority could otherwise have been authorised to acquire that interest in the whole of that area; and where part of the area determined by the tribunal was not comprised in the compulsory purchase order, the declaration has effect as if the whole of that area had been comprised in the order as well as in the declaration[24].

1 For the meaning of 'acquiring authority' see para 168 note 1 ante.
2 See para 172 ante.
3 As to the deemed notice to treat see para 172 ante.
4 Compulsory Purchase (Vesting Declarations) Act 1981 s 12, Sch 1 para 4(1)(a). Deemed notice to treat cannot be withdrawn after the vesting date (see s 7(3); and para 171 ante); but Sch 1 para 4(1)(a) has effect notwithstanding s 7(3): Sch 1 para 4(2). 'Land proposed to be severed' means land in respect of which notice of objection to severance is served: Sch 1 para 1. For the meaning of 'land' see para 168 note 2 ante. As to the effect of a late notice see para 174 post.
5 For the meaning of 'general vesting declaration' see para 168 note 4 ante.
6 Compulsory Purchase (Vesting Declarations) Act 1981 Sch 1 para 4(1)(b). As to compulsory purchase orders see para 33 et seq ante.
7 Ibid Sch 1 para 4(1)(c).
8 Ibid Sch 1 para 5.
9 Ie in accordance with ibid Sch 1 para 4(1): see head (1) in the text.

10 Ie in accordance with ibid Sch 1 para 5: see the text to note 8 supra.
11 Ibid Sch 1 para 6(a).
12 Ibid Sch 1 para 6(b).
13 Ie the authority takes action in accordance with head (2) in the text: ibid Sch 1 para 7.
14 Ie apart from ibid Sch 1 Pt I (paras 1–10): see para 172 ante; the text and notes 1–13 supra, 15–24 infra; and para 174 post.
15 Ibid Sch 1 para 7.
16 Ie in accordance with head (3) in the text: ibid Sch 1 para 8(1). As to the Lands Tribunal see para 202 et seq post.
17 As to the meaning of 'house, building or factory' cf para 110 ante.
18 As to the meaning of 'park or garden' see para 112 notes 3–4 ante.
19 As to the meaning of 'amenity' see TOWN AND COUNTRY PLANNING vol 46 (Reissue) para 42 note 4.
20 In making a determination in any of the cases mentioned in the text to notes 16–19 supra, the Lands Tribunal must take into account not only the effect of the severance but also the use to be made of the part proposed to be acquired and, where the part is proposed to be acquired for works or other purposes extending to other land, the effect of the whole of the works and the use to be made of the other land: Compulsory Purchase (Vesting Declarations) Act 1981 Sch 1 para 8(2).
21 Ibid Sch 1 para 8(1). Schedule 1 para 3 (see para 172 ante) ceases to have effect in relation to the notice: Sch 1 para 8(1).
22 Ie the whole of the land, or a part which includes the part comprised in the general vesting declaration: ibid Sch 1 para 9(1).
23 Ibid Sch 1 para 9(1).
24 Ibid Sch 1 para 9(1), (2).

174. Effect of counter-notice served out of time. Where a person is entitled to serve a notice of objection to severance[1] and it is proved (1) that he never received the notice required to be served on him[2] or that he received that notice less than 28 days before, or on, or after, the date on which the period specified in the general vesting declaration[3] expired[4]; and (2) that a notice of objection to severance served by him was served not more than 28 days after the date on which he first had knowledge of the execution of the general vesting declaration[5], that notice has effect notwithstanding that it is served after the expiration of the time allowed[6].

1 Ie in accordance with the Compulsory Purchase (Vesting Declarations) Act 1981 s 12, Sch 1 para 2(1): see para 172 ante.
2 Ie required by ibid s 6 (as amended): see para 170 ante.
3 For the meaning of 'general vesting declaration' see para 168 note 4 ante.
4 Compulsory Purchase (Vesting Declarations) Act 1981 Sch 1 para 10(1)(a).
5 Ibid Sch 1 para 10(1)(b).
6 Ibid Sch 1 para 10(1). As to the time allowed see Sch 1 para 2(2); and para 172 note 3 ante. Where, in such circumstances, a person serves a notice of objection to severance after the end of the period specified in the general vesting declaration, then in relation to that notice: (1) Sch 1 paras 3, 6 (see paras 172–173 ante) do not have effect; (2) Sch 1 para 4 (see para 173 ante) has effect as if Sch 1 para 4(1)(a) (see para 173 head (1) ante) were omitted; (3) Sch 1 para 5 (see para 173 ante) has effect with the substitution, for the words 'sub-paragraph (1)(a)' of the words 'sub-paragraph (1)(b)'; and (4) Sch 1 para 8 (see para 173 ante) does not have effect, but without prejudice to the making by the Lands Tribunal of any such determination as is mentioned therein: Sch 1 para 10(2).

(iii) Entry onto and Vesting of Land

175. In general. On the vesting date[1], the land[2] specified in the general vesting declaration[3], together with the right to enter upon and take possession of it[4], vests in the acquiring authority[5] as if the circumstances in which an authority authorised to purchase land compulsorily has any power to execute a deed poll[6] had arisen in respect of all the land and all interests in it and the acquiring authority had duly exercised that power accordingly on the vesting date[7].

Where, after land has become vested in the acquiring authority, a person retains possession of any document relating to the title to the land, he is deemed to have given to the acquiring authority an acknowledgment in writing of the authority's right to production of that document and to delivery of copies of it, and, except where he retains possession of the document as mortgagee or trustee or otherwise in a fiduciary capacity, an undertaking for its safe custody[8].

1 As to the vesting date see para 169 ante.
2 For the meaning of 'land' see para 168 note 2 ante.
3 For the meaning of 'general vesting declaration' see para 168 note 4 ante.
4 The Compulsory Purchase Act 1965 s 11(1) (as amended) (power to enter upon land after service of notice to treat: see para 129 ante) does not apply to land specified in a general vesting declaration: Compulsory Purchase (Vesting Declarations) Act 1981 s 8(3). The power of entry is postponed in the case of land subject to a minor tenancy etc: see para 176 post.
5 This is subject to the special provisions with respect to land subject to a minor tenancy etc: see para 176 post. For the meaning of 'acquiring authority' see para 168 note 1 ante.
6 Ie any power to execute a deed poll under the Compulsory Purchase Act 1965 Pt I (ss 1–32) (as amended) (see para 142 et seq ante) and whether for vesting land or any interest in land in the acquiring authority or for extinguishing the whole or part of any rent-service, rentcharge, chief or other rent, or other payment or incumbrance: Compulsory Purchase (Vesting Declarations) Act 1981 s 8(1)(a), (2).
7 Ibid s 8(1).
8 Ibid s 14. The Law of Property Act 1925 s 64 (see REAL PROPERTY vol 39 para 586) has effect accordingly, and on the basis that the acknowledgment and undertaking did not contain any such expression of contrary intention as is mentioned in s 64: Compulsory Purchase (Vesting Declarations) Act 1981 s 14.

176. Minor tenancy or long tenancy which is about to expire. Where any land[1] specified in a general vesting declaration[2] is land in which there subsists a minor tenancy[3] or a long tenancy which is about to expire[4], the right of entry[5] is not exercisable with respect to that land unless, after serving a notice to treat in respect of that tenancy[6] (1) the acquiring authority[7] has served on every occupier of any of the land in which the tenancy subsists a notice stating that at the end of a specified period of not less than 14 days from the date on which the notice is served it intends to enter upon and take possession of the land specified in the notice; and (2) that period has expired[8]. The vesting of the land in the acquiring authority will be subject to the tenancy until that period expires or the tenancy comes to an end, whichever first occurs[9].

1 For the meaning of 'land' see para 168 note 2 ante.
2 For the meaning of 'general vesting declaration' see para 168 note 4 ante.
3 For the meaning of 'minor tenancy' see para 170 note 5 ante.
4 For the meaning of 'long tenancy which is about to expire' see para 170 note 6 ante.
5 Ie the right conferred by the Compulsory Purchase (Vesting Declarations) Act 1981 s 8(1): see para 175 ante.
6 Such a tenancy will not have been the subject of a deemed notice to treat under ibid s 7: see para 171 ante.
7 For the meaning of 'acquiring authority' see para 168 note 1 ante.
8 Compulsory Purchase (Vesting Declarations) Act 1981 s 9(1), (2).
9 Ibid s 9(3).

(iv) Compensation

177. Liability to pay compensation. Where any of the land[1] specified in a general vesting declaration[2] has become vested in an acquiring authority[3], the authority is liable to pay the same compensation and the same interest on the compensation agreed or awarded as it would have been liable to pay if it had taken possession of the land under the Compulsory Purchase Act 1965[4]; but the time within which a question of disputed compensation, arising out of an acquisition of an interest in land in respect of which a notice to treat is deemed[5] to have been served, may be referred to the Lands Tribunal is six years from the date at which the person claiming compensation, or a person under whom he derives title, first knew, or could reasonably be expected to have known, of the vesting of the interest[6].

Where after the execution of a general vesting declaration a person ('the claimant') claims compensation in respect of the acquisition by the acquiring authority of an interest in land by virtue of the declaration, and the authority pays compensation in respect of that interest, then if it is shown that (1) the land or the claimant's interest in it was subject to an incumbrance which was not disclosed in the particulars of his claim; and (2) by reason of that incumbrance, the compensation paid exceeded the compensation to which he was entitled in respect of that interest[7], the authority may recover the amount of the excess from the claimant[8]. Moreover, if after such payment it is subsequently shown that the claimant was not entitled to the interest, either in the whole or in part of the land to which the claim related, the authority may recover from him an amount equal to the compensation paid or to so much of that compensation as, on the proper apportionment of it[9], is attributable to that part of the land[10].

Any person who, in consequence of the vesting of the land in an acquiring authority[11], is relieved from any liability, whether in respect of a rentcharge, rent under a tenancy[12], mortgage interest or any other matter, and makes any payment as in satisfaction or in part satisfaction of that liability, is entitled to recover the sum paid as money had and received to his use by the person to whom it was paid, if he shows that when he made the payment he did not know of the facts which constituted the cause of his being so relieved or of one or more of those facts[13].

1 For the meaning of 'land' see para 168 note 2 ante.
2 For the meaning of 'general vesting declaration' see para 168 note 4 ante.
3 For the meaning of 'acquiring authority' see para 168 note 1 ante.
4 Ie under the Compulsory Purchase Act 1965 s 11(1) (as amended): see para 129 ante.
5 Ie by virtue of the Compulsory Purchase (Vesting Declarations) Act 1981 Pt III (ss 7–9): see para 171 et seq ante.
6 Ibid s 10(1), (3). Section 10(3) is to be construed as one with the Limitation Act 1980 Pt I (ss 1–27) (as amended): s 10(3). As to construction as one see STATUTES vol 44(1) (Reissue) para 1485. The Compulsory Purchase Act 1965 s 22 and Sch 2 (absent and untraced owners: see para 143 et seq ante) do not apply to the compensation to be paid for any interest in land in respect of which a notice to treat is deemed to have been served by virtue of the Compulsory Purchase (Vesting Declarations) Act 1981 Pt III: s 10(2).
7 Any question arising as to the amount of the compensation to which the claimant was entitled in respect of an interest in land is to be referred to and determined by the Lands Tribunal; and the Land Compensation Act 1961 s 2 (as amended) (public sittings, limitation on number of expert witnesses and other matters: see paras 218, 223–225 post) applies in relation to the determination of the question subject to any necessary modifications: Compulsory Purchase (Vesting Declarations) Act 1981 s 11(4).
8 Ibid s 11(1), (2). Subject to s 11(4) (see note 7 supra), any amount recoverable by the acquiring authority is recoverable in any court of competent jurisdiction: s 11(5). If the acquiring authority is a local authority as defined in the Town and Country Planning Act 1990 s 336(1) (as amended) (see TOWN AND COUNTRY PLANNING vol 46 (Reissue) para 5 note 1), any sum so recovered must be applied towards the repayment of any debt incurred in acquiring or redeveloping the land, or if no debt was so incurred must be paid into the account out of which sums incurred in the acquisition of that land were paid: Compulsory Purchase (Vesting Declarations) Act 1981 s 11(6) (amended by the Planning (Consequential Provisions) Act 1990 s 4, Sch 2 para 52(3)).
9 Any question arising as to the apportionment of any compensation paid must be referred to and determined by the Lands Tribunal: Compulsory Purchase (Vesting Declarations) Act 1981 s 11(4). See further note 7 supra.

10 Ibid s 11(3).
11 Ie under ibid Pt III: see para 171 et seq ante.
12 For the meaning of 'tenancy' see para 170 note 5 ante.
13 Compulsory Purchase (Vesting Declarations) Act 1981 s 13.

178. Rentcharges apportioned. Subject to any agreement[1], where land specified in a general vesting declaration[2], together with other land not so specified, is charged with a rentcharge, such proportion of the rentcharge as may be apportioned[3] to the land specified in the declaration must be treated as having been extinguished[4] on the vesting of that land in the acquiring authority[5]. Where in such a case a portion of a rentcharge is treated as having been extinguished, the provisions of the Compulsory Purchase Act 1965 as to rentcharges[6] have effect as if the extinguishment had taken place under them[7].

1 If the person entitled to the rentcharge and the owner of the land subject to it enter into an agreement to that effect, the Compulsory Purchase Act 1965 s 18 (see paras 191–192 post) has effect as if at the time the land vested in the acquiring authority under the Compulsory Purchase (Vesting Declarations) Act 1981 Pt III (ss 7–9) (see paras 171, 175–176 ante), the person entitled to the rentcharge had released the land from the rentcharge on the condition that the part of land remaining be exclusively subject to the whole of the rentcharge under the Compulsory Purchase Act 1965 s 18(2); and in that case no part of the rentcharge may be treated as having been extinguished as regards the remaining part of the land charged with it: Compulsory Purchase (Vesting Declarations) Act 1981 s 12, Sch 1 para 11(3). For these purposes, 'rentcharge' includes any other payment or incumbrance charged on the land not provided for in the Compulsory Purchase Act 1965 ss 1–17 (as amended): s 18(6) (applied by the Compulsory Purchase (Vesting Declarations) Act 1981 Sch 1 para 11(4)). For the meaning of 'acquiring authority' and 'land' see para 168 notes 1–2 ante.
2 For the meaning of 'general vesting declaration' see para 168 note 4 ante.
3 Ie under the Compulsory Purchase Act 1965 s 18: see paras 191–192 post.
4 Ie by virtue of the Compulsory Purchase (Vesting Declarations) Act 1981 Pt III: see paras 171, 175–176 ante.
5 Ibid Sch 1 para 11(1). As to the relief given where payments are made after such extinguishment see s 13; and para 177 ante.
6 Ie the Compulsory Purchase Act 1965 s 18: see paras 191–192 post.
7 Compulsory Purchase (Vesting Declarations) Act 1981 Sch 1 para 11(2).

179. Rent apportioned. Where land[1] specified in a general vesting declaration[2], together with other land not so specified, is comprised in a tenancy[3] for a term of years unexpired, the provisions of the Compulsory Purchase Act 1965 for the apportionment of rent[4] have effect as if for the references in them to the time of the apportionment of rent there were substituted references to the time of the vesting of the tenancy in the acquiring authority[5].

1 For the meaning of 'land' see para 168 note 2 ante.
2 For the meaning of 'general vesting declaration' see para 168 note 4 ante.
3 For the meaning of 'tenancy' see para 170 note 5 ante.
4 Ie the Compulsory Purchase Act 1965 s 19: see paras 189–190 post.
5 Compulsory Purchase (Vesting Declarations) Act 1981 s 12, Sch 1 para 12. As to the relief given where payments are made after the apportionment see s 13; and para 177 ante.

(8) STEPS WHERE LAND UNDER LEASE, SHORT TENANCY, RENTCHARGE OR MORTGAGE

(i) Leases and Short Tenancies

180. Leases allowed to expire or otherwise terminated. When undertakers[1] or an acquiring authority[2] require to purchase or take land in the possession of a person under a lease, they may purchase the lessor's interest and allow the lessee's interest to expire; and no compensation will be payable under the Lands Clauses Acts[3] or the Compulsory Purchase Act 1965[4], but the lessee may be entitled to compensation under some other enactment[5]. The same applies if the undertakers or acquiring authority determine the lease by notice and allow him to remain in possession[6] or if they induce the lessor to determine the lease before the acquisition of the lessee's interest[7].

Otherwise, if they require to enter on the lessee's interest, the undertakers or acquiring authority must serve on the lessee a notice to treat for the purchase of his interest[8]; but if he is allowed to remain in possession until his interest expires he will have no right to compensation under that notice[9]. In the case of tenants from year to year, however, the undertakers or authority need not serve a notice to treat but may avail themselves of special statutory provisions[10].

1 For the meaning of 'the undertakers' see para 13 ante.
2 For the meaning of 'acquiring authority' see para 92 note 5 ante.
3 As to the Lands Clauses Acts see para 11 ante.
4 *Holloway v Dover Corpn* [1960] 2 All ER 193, [1960] 1 WLR 604, CA; *Ex p Nadin* (1848) 17 LJ Ch 421; *Syers v Metropolitan Board of Works* (1877) 36 LT 277, CA; and see *Re Portsmouth Rly Co, ex p Merrett* (1860) 2 LT 471.
5 Compensation may become payable eg to a tenant whose tenancy is determined by notice to quit under the Landlord and Tenant Acts 1927 and 1954 (see LANDLORD AND TENANT vol 27(1) (Reissue) paras 607, 637 et seq); under the Agricultural Holdings Act 1986 (see AGRICULTURE vol 1(2) (Reissue) para 376 et seq) or the Agricultural Tenancies Act 1995 (see Pt III (ss 15–27); and AGRICULTURE); and under the Allotments Acts 1922 and 1950 (see ALLOTMENTS vol 2 (Reissue) para 46 et seq).
6 *Holloway v Dover Corpn* [1960] 2 All ER 193, [1960] 1 WLR 604, CA.
7 See the cases cited in note 4 supra.
8 See paras 100, 103 ante.
9 *Holloway v Dover Corpn* [1960] 2 All ER 193, [1960] 1 WLR 604, CA; *R v Kennedy* [1893] 1 QB 533.
10 See paras 181, 184 post.

181. Notice to tenants from year to year requiring possession. If any of the land subject to compulsory purchase[1] is in the possession of a person having no greater interest in it than as tenant for a year or from year to year[2] and that person is required to give up possession[3] of any land so occupied by him before the expiration of his term or interest in it, he is entitled to compensation for the value of his unexpired term or interest in the land, and for any just allowance which ought to be made to him by an incoming tenant, and for any loss or injury he may sustain[4]. If a part only of the land is required, he is also entitled to compensation for the damage done to him by severing the land held by him, or otherwise injuriously affecting it[5].

1 For the meaning of 'land' and 'subject to compulsory purchase' see para 92 notes 1–2 ante. See also para 13 text to note 7 ante.
2 As to tenancies within this provision see para 182 post.
3 As to possession being required see para 183 post.

4 Lands Clauses Consolidation Act 1845 s 121 (where that Act is incorporated: see para 11 ante); Compulsory Purchase Act 1965 s 20(1) (where that Act applies: see para 15 ante).

5 Lands Clauses Consolidation Act 1845 s 121; Compulsory Purchase Act 1965 s 20(2) (amended by the Planning and Compensation Act 1991 s 70, Sch 15 para 4). If the parties differ as to the amount of compensation payable under the Compulsory Purchase Act 1965 s 20(1), (2) (as so amended), the dispute must be referred to and determined by the Lands Tribunal: s 20(3). As to the tribunal see para 202 et seq post. The Compulsory Purchase Act 1965 s 20 (as so amended) has effect subject to the Landlord and Tenant Act 1954 s 39 (as amended) (see LANDLORD AND TENANT vol 27(1) (Reissue) para 558 note 8) (see the Compulsory Purchase Act 1965 s 20(6)); and is modified in relation to the compulsory acquisition of rights by, inter alia, (1) a local authority, by the Local Government (Miscellaneous Provisions) Act 1976 s 13(3)(b) (as amended), Sch 1 para 10 (see LOCAL GOVERNMENT vol 28 para 1219); (2) the Development Board for Rural Wales, by the Development of Rural Wales Act 1976 s 6(7) (as amended), Sch 4 para 10 (see TOWN AND COUNTRY PLANNING vol 46 (Reissue) para 1200); (3) urban development corporations, by the Local Government, Planning and Land Act 1980 s 144, Sch 28 para 23(5) (see TOWN AND COUNTRY PLANNING vol 46 (Reissue) para 1297); (4) highway authorities, by the Highways Act 1980 s 250(5)(a) (as substituted), Sch 19 para 10 (see HIGHWAYS vol 21 (Reissue) para 808); (5) public gas suppliers, by the Gas Act 1986 s 9(3), Sch 3 para 11 (see FUEL AND ENERGY vol 19(1) (Reissue) para 636); (6) housing action trusts, by the Housing Act 1988 s 78(2), Sch 10 para 23(3) (see HOUSING); (7) licence holders under the Electricity Act 1989, by s 10(1), Sch 3 para 12 (see FUEL AND ENERGY vol 19(2) (Reissue) para 985); (8) the National Rivers Authority, by the Water Resources Act 1991 s 154(5), Sch 18 para 7 (see WATER); and (9) water and sewerage undertakers, by the Water Industry Act 1991 s 155(5), Sch 9 para 7 (see WATER).

182. Interests entitled to compensation. The term or interest in respect of which notice requiring possession is given[1] must be a tenancy in law or in equity[2] and mere licensees[3], or persons holding under statutory controlled or regulated tenancies[4], are not included.

A person in possession as the owner of the residue of a long term, but of which less than a year remains, is a person falling within the provisions relating to compensation[5]. If a notice to treat is served in respect of an interest greater than a tenancy from year to year and nothing is done under that notice before the unexpired residue of the term is less than a year, a notice then served requiring possession in respect of the tenancy is effective for these purposes[6], but not if a notice to treat is so served and is not followed by a notice requiring possession[7].

If any person having a greater interest than as tenant at will claims compensation in respect of any unexpired term or interest under any lease[8] or grant of the land subject to compulsory purchase[9], the undertakers[10] or the acquiring authority[11] may require him to produce the lease or grant, or the best evidence of it in his power; and if, after written demand by the undertakers or authority, the lease, grant or best evidence is not produced within 21 days, that person will be considered as a tenant holding only from year to year, and will be entitled to compensation accordingly[12].

1 See para 181 ante.
2 *Municipal Freehold Land Co v Metropolitan and District Rlys Joint Committee* (1883) Cab & El 184. As to equitable interests see *Re King's Leasehold Estates, ex p East of London Rly Co* (1873) LR 16 Eq 521; *Sweetman v Metropolitan Rly Co* (1864) 1 Hem & M 543. A schoolmaster in possession of a house under the terms of his appointment which was terminable by three months' notice was held to be a tenant within the above provisions: *R v Manchester, Sheffield and Lincolnshire Rly Co* (1854) 4 E & B 88.
3 *Frank Warr & Co Ltd v LCC* [1904] 1 KB 713, CA (licence to use theatre for premises for supplying refreshments); *Bird v Great Eastern Rly Co* (1865) 19 CBNS 268.
4 *Re Dudley and District Benefit Building Society v Emerson* [1949] Ch 707 at 717, [1949] 2 All ER 252 at 257, CA.
5 *R v Great Northern Rly Co* (1876) 2 QBD 151.
6 *R v Kennedy* [1893] 1 QB 533, considered and explained in *Bexley Heath Rly Co v North* [1894] 2 QB 579, CA.
7 Cf *Tyson v London Corpn* (1871) LR 7 CP 18.

8   For the meaning of 'lease' see paras 13 note 7, 164 note 1 ante.
9   For the meaning of 'land' and 'subject to compulsory purchase' see para 92 notes 1–2 ante. See also para 13 text to note 7 ante.
10 For the meaning of 'the undertakers' see para 13 ante.
11 For the meaning of 'acquiring authority' see para 92 note 5 ante.
12 Lands Clauses Consolidation Act 1845 s 122 (where that Act is incorporated: see para 11 ante); Compulsory Purchase Act 1965 s 20(5) (where that Act applies: see para 15 ante). See *Sweetman v Metropolitan Rly Co* (1864) 1 Hem & M 543 (application to equitable interests).

183. Possession must be required.   In order for the provisions relating to compensation[1] to apply, there must be a notice requiring possession; the service of a notice to treat is not in itself such a requiring of possession[2], nor is it constituted by going out of possession on receipt of notice to treat[3], but a person who goes out of possession by agreement with the undertakers[4] or the acquiring authority[5] falls within those provisions[6].

1   See para 181 ante.
2   *R v Stone* (1866) LR 1 QB 529; *R v London and Southampton Rly Co* (1839) 10 Ad & El 3; cf *Tyson v London Corpn* (1871) LR 7 CP 18 at 22–23.
3   *Great Northern and City Rly Co v Tillett* [1902] 1 KB 874 at 876. If the lessee receives a notice to treat under the Compulsory Purchase Act 1965 s 11(1) (as amended) (see para 129 ante), to comply with that provision and he is then required to give up possession, his interest must be compensated under s 20 (as amended) as for a short tenancy: *London Borough of Newham v Benjamin* [1968] 1 All ER 1195, [1968] 1 WLR 694, CA.
4   For the meaning of 'the undertakers' see para 13 ante.
5   For the meaning of 'acquiring authority' see para 92 note 5 ante.
6   *Knapp v London, Chatham and Dover Rly Co* (1863) 32 LJ Ex 236; *R v Great Northern Rly Co* (1876) 2 QBD 151. A mere permission to continue in possession to a given date is not a requirement of possession: *Frisby v Chingford Corpn* (1957) 8 P & CR 423. However, tenants of unfit houses given permission to continue in possession under the Housing Act 1985 s 583 are deemed to have been required to give up possession for the purposes of the Compulsory Purchase Act 1965 s 20 (as amended): see the Housing Act 1985 s 583(3); and HOUSING.

184. Delivery of possession.   On payment or tender of the amount of the compensation[1], all persons who have been required to deliver up possession as having interests not greater than that of a tenant for a year or from year to year[2] must respectively deliver up to the undertakers[3] or the acquiring authority[4], or to the person appointed by them to take possession, any land subject to compulsory purchase[5] which is in their possession and is required by the undertakers or authority[6]. If this procedure is followed, no conveyance and no notice to treat is necessary in order to enable the undertakers or authority to acquire the tenant's interest[7].

1   As to the power to enter without tender or payment of compensation see para 123 et seq ante.
2   See para 181 ante.
3   For the meaning of 'the undertakers' see para 13 ante.
4   For the meaning of 'acquiring authority' see para 92 note 5 ante.
5   For the meaning of 'land' and 'subject to compulsory purchase' see para 92 notes 1–2 ante.
6   Lands Clauses Consolidation Act 1845 s 121 (amended by the Compulsory Purchase Act 1965 s 39(4), Sch 8 Pt III) (where the 1845 Act is incorporated: see para 11 ante); Compulsory Purchase Act 1965 s 20(4) (where that Act applies: see para 15 ante). As to the rights of a yearly tenant allowed to continue in possession after notice requiring possession see *Cranwell v London Corpn* (1870) LR 5 Exch 284 at 287, Ex Ch; *R v Rochdale Improvement Act Comrs* (1856) 2 Jur NS 861; *R v London and Southampton Rly Co* (1839) 10 Ad & El 3 (as explained in *Cranwell v London Corpn* supra).

7 *Syers v Metropolitan Board of Works* (1877) 36 LT 277 at 278, CA, per Jessel MR; *London Borough of Newham v Benjamin* [1968] 1 All ER 1195, [1968] 1 WLR 694, CA (see para 183 note 3 ante).

185. Counter-notice where possession required of part of agricultural holding by notice of entry after notice to treat. Where an acquiring authority[1] serves notice of entry[2] on the person in occupation of an agricultural holding[3], being a person having no greater interest in it than as tenant for a year or from year to year[4], and the notice relates to part only of that holding[5], the person on whom the notice is served ('the claimant'), may, within the period of two months beginning with the date of service of the notice of entry, serve on the acquiring authority a counter-notice (1) claiming that the remainder of the holding is not reasonably capable of being farmed, either by itself or in conjunction with other relevant land[6], as a separate agricultural unit[7]; and (2) electing to treat the notice of entry as a notice relating to the entire holding[8].

A claimant who serves a counter-notice must, within the same period, serve a copy of it on the landlord of the holding, although failure to do so will not invalidate the counter-notice[9].

These provisions have effect, subject to any necessary modifications, in relation to a notice of entry under certain provisions of the New Towns Act 1981[10] and of the Housing Act 1985[11]. They apply in relation to the acquisition of interests in land, whether compulsorily or by agreement, by government departments which are authorities possessing compulsory purchase powers[12] as they apply in relation to the acquisition of interests in land by such authorities which are not government departments[13].

1 For the meaning of 'acquiring authority' for these purposes see para 106 note 1 ante.
2 Ie under the Compulsory Purchase Act 1965 s 11(1): see para 129 ante.
3 'Agricultural holding' means the aggregate of the land (whether agricultural land or not) comprised in a contract of tenancy which is a contract for an agricultural tenancy, not being a contract under which that land is let to the tenant during his continuance in any office, appointment or employment held under the landlord: Agricultural Holdings Act 1986 s 1(1) (applied by the Land Compensation Act 1973 s 87(1) (amended for these purposes by the Land Compensation (Scotland) Act 1973 s 81(1), Sch 2 Pt I; and by the Agricultural Holdings Act 1986 s 100, Sch 14 para 56)). 'Tenant' means the holder of land under a contract of tenancy, and includes the executors, administrators, assigns or trustee in bankruptcy of a tenant, or other person deriving title from a tenant; and 'landlord' means any person for the time being entitled to receive the rents and profits of any land: s 96(1) (as so applied). These provisions do not apply to farm business tenancies under the Agricultural Tenancies Act 1995.
4 As to such an interest see para 182 ante.
5 Where, however, an acquiring authority has served a notice to treat in respect of land in the agricultural holding, other than that to which the notice of entry relates, then unless and until that notice to treat is withdrawn, the provisions of the Land Compensation Act 1973 s 55 (as amended) (service of a counter-notice: see the text and notes 1–4 supra, 6–9 infra), and of s 56 (as amended) (effect of service of that notice: see para 186 post), have effect as if that land did not form part of the holding: s 55(4).
6 'Other relevant land' means (1) land comprised in the same agricultural unit as the agricultural holding (ibid s 55(3)(a)); and (2) land comprised in any other agricultural unit occupied by the claimant on the date of service of the notice of entry, being land in respect of which he is then entitled to a greater interest than as tenant for a year or from year to year (s 55(3)(b)). Where, however, an acquiring authority has served a notice to treat in respect of other relevant land, then, unless and until that notice to treat is withdrawn, the provisions of ss 55, 56 (as amended) have effect as if that land did not constitute other relevant land: s 55(4). For the meaning of 'agricultural unit' see TOWN AND COUNTRY PLANNING vol 46 (Reissue) para 729 note 9; and as to the application of this definition see para 106 note 6 ante.
7 Ibid s 55(1)(a).
8 Ibid s 55(1)(b).

9 Ibid s 55(2).
10 Land Compensation Act 1973 s 57(2) (amended by the New Towns Act 1981 s 81, Sch 12). The notice of entry referred to is a notice under s 14(1), Sch 6 para 4 (provisions applicable to compulsory acquisition under that Act): see TOWN AND COUNTRY PLANNING vol 46 (Reissue) para 1121.
11 Land Compensation Act 1973 s 57(3) (amended by the Housing (Consequential Provisions) Act 1985 s 4, Sch 2 para 24(7)). The notice of entry referred to is a notice under the Housing Act 1985 s 584 (as amended) (power to enter and determine short tenancies of land acquired or appropriated for certain purposes of that Act): see further HOUSING.
12 For the meaning of 'authority possessing compulsory purchase powers' see para 244 note 6 post (definition applied by the Land Compensation Act 1973 s 87(1)).
13 See ibid s 84(2).

186. Effect of counter-notice where possession required of part of agricultural holding; in general.

If the acquiring authority[1] does not, within the period of two months beginning with the date of service of a counter-notice[2], agree in writing to accept it as valid, the claimant[3] or the authority may, within two months after the end of that period, refer it to the Lands Tribunal; and on any such reference the tribunal must determine whether the claim in the counter-notice is justified and declare the counter-notice valid or invalid in accordance with its determination of that question[4].

If, before the end of 12 months after a counter-notice has been accepted as, or declared to be, valid, the claimant has given up possession of every part of the agricultural holding[5] to the acquiring authority:

(1) the notice of entry is deemed to have extended to the part of the holding to which it did not relate; and

(2) the authority is deemed to have taken possession of that part in pursuance of that notice on the day before the expiration of the year of the tenancy which is current when the counter-notice is so accepted or declared[6].

These provisions have effect, subject to any necessary modifications, in relation to a notice of entry under certain provisions of the New Towns Act 1981[7] and of the Housing Act 1985[8].

1 For the meaning of 'acquiring authority' for these purposes see para 106 note 1 ante.
2 Ie under the Land Compensation Act 1973 s 55 (as amended): see para 185 ante. For exceptions see para 185 notes 5–6 ante.
3 Ie the person serving the counter-notice: see ibid s 55(1); and para 185 ante.
4 Ibid s 56(1). As to the tribunal see para 202 et seq post.
5 For the meaning of 'agricultural holding' see para 185 note 3 ante.
6 Land Compensation Act 1973 s 56(2). As to notice of entry see para 185 ante.
7 Ibid s 57(2) (amended by the New Towns Act 1981 s 81, Sch 12). The notice of entry referred to is a notice under s 14(1), Sch 6 para 4 (provisions applicable to compulsory acquisition under that Act): see TOWN AND COUNTRY PLANNING vol 46 (Reissue) para 1121.
8 Land Compensation Act 1973 s 57(3) (amended by the Housing (Consequential Provisions) Act 1985 s 4, Sch 2 para 24(7)). The notice of entry referred to is a notice under the Housing Act 1985 s 584 (as amended) (power to enter and determine short tenancies of land acquired or appropriated for certain purposes of that Act): see further HOUSING.

187. Effect of counter-notice where possession required of part of agricultural holding and entry on land not subject to compulsory purchase.

Where the claimant[1] gives up possession of an agricultural holding[2] to the acquiring authority[3] under a notice of entry[4], but the authority has not been authorised to acquire the landlord's[5] interest in, or in any of, the part of the holding to which the notice of entry did not relate ('the land not subject to compulsory purchase'), neither the claimant nor the authority is under any liability to the landlord by reason of the claimant giving up possession of the land not subject to compulsory purchase or the authority taking or being in possession of it[6], and immediately after the date on which the authority takes possession of that land it must give up to the landlord, and he must take, possession of that land[7].

Accordingly, the tenancy must be treated as terminated on the date on which the claimant gives up possession of the holding to the acquiring authority or, if he gives up possession of different parts at different times, gives up possession of the last part, but without prejudice to any rights or liabilities of the landlord or the claimant which have accrued before that date[8]. Thereafter, any rights of the claimant against, or liabilities of his to, the landlord which arise on or out of the termination of the tenancy by virtue of this provision, whether under the contract of tenancy, under the Agricultural Holdings Act 1986 or otherwise, will be rights and liabilities of the authority, and any question as to the payment to be made in respect of any such right or liability must be referred to and determined by the Lands Tribunal[9].

These provisions have effect, subject to any necessary modifications, in relation to a notice of entry under certain provisions of the New Towns Act 1981[10].

1 Ie the person serving the counter-notice after a notice of entry: see the Land Compensation Act 1973 s 55(1); and para 185 ante.
2 For the meaning of 'agricultural holding' see para 185 note 3 ante.
3 For the meaning of 'acquiring authority' for these purposes see para 106 note 1 ante.
4 See para 186 ante.
5 For the meaning of 'landlord' see para 185 note 3 ante.
6 Land Compensation Act 1973 s 56(3)(a).
7 Ibid s 56(3)(b). Any increase in the value of the land not subject to compulsory purchase which is attributable to the landlord's so taking possession must be deducted from the compensation payable in respect of the acquisition of his interest in the remainder of the holding: s 56(3)(c).
8 Ibid s 56(3)(c). Where a tenancy is so terminated, the Agricultural Holdings Act 1986 s 72 (landlord's right to compensation for deterioration of holding: see AGRICULTURE vol 1(2) (Reissue) paras 440–442) has effect as if s 72(4) required the landlord's notice of intention to claim compensation to be served on the acquiring authority and to be so served within three months after the termination of the tenancy: Land Compensation Act 1973 s 56(4) (amended by the Agricultural Holdings Act 1986 s 100, Sch 14 para 54).
9 Land Compensation Act 1973 s 56(3)(d) (amended by the Agricultural Holdings Act 1986 Sch 14 para 54). As to the tribunal see para 202 et seq post.
10 Land Compensation Act 1973 s 57(2) (amended by the New Towns Act 1981 s 81, Sch 12). The notice of entry referred to is a notice under s 14(1), Sch 6 para 4 (provisions applicable to compulsory acquisition under that Act): see TOWN AND COUNTRY PLANNING vol 46 (Reissue) para 1121. The Land Compensation Act 1973 s 56(3), (4) (as amended) does not, however, have effect in relation to a notice of entry under the Housing Act 1985 s 584 (as amended) (power to enter and determine short tenancies of land acquired or appropriated for certain purposes of that Act: see further HOUSING): see the Land Compensation Act 1973 s 57(3) (amended by the Housing (Consequential Provisions) Act 1985 s 4, Sch 2 para 24(7)).

188. Counter-notice where possession required of part of agricultural holding on deposit of compensation and giving of bond. Before taking possession of part only of an agricultural holding[1] under the power to enter after depositing in court the amount of the compensation and giving a bond[2], or under the statutory provisions relating to vesting declarations[3], the acquiring authority[4] must serve notice of its intention to do so on the person in occupation of the holding; and the provisions relating to the service and the effect of a counter-notice where possession is required by notice of entry after notice to treat[5] have effect, subject to any necessary modifications, as if possession were being obtained pursuant to a notice of entry under the Compulsory Purchase Act 1965[6].

1 For the meaning of 'agricultural holding' see para 185 note 3 ante.
2 Ie under the Lands Clauses Consolidation Act 1845 s 85 or the Compulsory Purchase Act 1965 s 11(2), Sch 3 (as amended): see para 123 ante.
3 Ie under the Compulsory Purchase (Vesting Declarations) Act 1981 Pt II (ss 7–9): see para 171 et seq ante.
4 For the meaning of 'acquiring authority' for these purposes see para 106 note 1 ante.
5 Ie the Land Compensation Act 1973 ss 55, 56 (as amended) (see paras 185–187 ante), which apply where notice of entry is given after notice to treat under the Compulsory Purchase Act 1965 s 11(1) (as amended) (see para 129 ante).
6 Land Compensation Act 1973 s 57(1) (amended by the Compulsory Purchase (Vesting Declarations) Act 1981 s 16(1), Sch 3 para 1).

189. Apportionment of rent under lease. If part only of the land[1] comprised in a lease[2] for an unexpired term of years is required by the undertakers[3] or the acquiring authority[4], the rent payable in respect of the land comprised in the lease must be apportioned between the land so required and the residue of the land[5]. The apportionment may be settled by agreement between the lessor and lessee, on the one part, and the undertakers or the authority, on the other part, and, if not so agreed, must be settled by the Lands Tribunal[6].

If the undertakers or authority agree with the lessee as to the apportionment, specific performance of an agreement to purchase the land agreed to be sold may be decreed even though the lessor's consent to the apportionment has not been obtained[7], and if he refuses consent the matter must be referred to the Lands Tribunal[8]. The costs of the apportionment are not payable as costs of the conveyance by the undertakers or authority[9], but it is within the court's discretion to order them to pay these costs where money has been paid into court[10]. Costs of proceedings before the Lands Tribunal are in general in the tribunal's discretion[11].

1 For the meaning of 'land' see para 92 note 1 ante. See also para 13 text to note 7 ante.
2 For the meaning of 'lease' see paras 13 note 7, 164 note 1 ante.
3 For the meaning of 'the undertakers' see para 13 ante.
4 For the meaning of 'acquiring authority' see para 92 note 5 ante.
5 Lands Clauses Consolidation Act 1845 s 119 (where that Act is incorporated: see para 11 ante); Compulsory Purchase Act 1965 s 19(1) (where that Act applies: see para 15 ante). The lessee may be entitled to compensation for the value of his lease (see paras 197, 280 post), and also for damage by severance or otherwise by the execution of the works (see para 291 post); and so also may a tenant from year to year (see para 294 post).
6 Lands Clauses Consolidation Act 1845 s 119; Land Compensation Act 1961 s 1; Compulsory Purchase Act 1965 s 19(2). As to the effect of the apportionment see para 190 post. As to the apportionment of rent where land is vested in the acquiring authority by a vesting declaration see para 179 ante; and as to the tribunal see para 202 et seq post.
7 *Slipper v Tottenham and Hampstead Junction Rly Co* (1867) LR 4 Eq 112; *Williams v East London Rly Co* (1869) 18 WR 159.
8 *Slipper v Tottenham and Hampstead Junction Rly Co* (1867) LR 4 Eq 112 at 115 per Romilly MR. It would seem to follow that the lessee and lessor together might take the undertakers or authority before the tribunal to have the rent apportioned.
9 *Re Hampstead Junction Rly Co, ex p Buck* (1863) 33 LJ Ch 79. As to the obligation to pay costs of the conveyance see para 139 ante.
10 See *Re London, Brighton and South Coast Rly Co, ex p Flower* (1866) 1 Ch App 599; and para 163 ante.
11 See para 227 post.

190. Effect of apportionment. After the apportionment[1], the lessee is liable to pay only so much of the future accruing rent[2] as is apportioned in respect of the land[3] not required by the undertakers[4] or acquiring authority[5]. The lessor has all the same rights and remedies against the lessee in respect of the land not so required for the recovery of the portion of rent as, before the apportionment, he had for the recovery of the whole rent reserved by the lease[6]; and all the covenants, conditions and terms of the lease, except as to the amount of rent to be paid, remain in force with regard to that part of the land not so required in the same manner as they would have done if that part only of the land had been included in the lease[7].

The lessee is entitled to receive from the undertakers or the acquiring authority compensation for the damage done to him in his tenancy by reason of the severance of the land required by them from that not required, or otherwise by reason of the execution of the works[8].

Where the land is acquired under an order providing for a vesting declaration, the time of apportionment is the time when the land is vested in the acquiring authority[9].

1 Ie under the Lands Clauses Consolidation Act 1845 s 119 or the Compulsory Purchase Act 1965 s 19(1), (2): see para 189 ante.
2 Rents accrue from day to day and are apportionable as to time accordingly in the absence of any express stipulation to the contrary: see the Apportionment Act 1870 ss 2, 7; and LANDLORD AND TENANT vol 27(1) (Reissue) para 245.
3 For the meaning of 'land' see para 92 note 1 ante. See also para 13 text to note 7 ante.
4 For the meaning of 'the undertakers' see para 13 ante.
5 Lands Clauses Consolidation Act 1845 s 119 (where that Act is incorporated: see para 11 ante); Compulsory Purchase Act 1965 s 19(3) (where that Act applies: see para 15 ante). For the meaning of 'acquiring authority' see para 92 note 5 ante.
6 For the meaning of 'lease' see paras 13 note 7, 164 note 3 ante.
7 Lands Clauses Consolidation Act 1845 s 119; Compulsory Purchase Act 1965 s 19(4). The apportioned rent becomes payable from the date of the apportionment or agreement: see *Ball v Graves* (1886) 18 LR Ir 224; *Re War Secretary and Hurley's Contract* [1904] 1 IR 354.
8 Lands Clauses Consolidation Act 1845 s 120; Compulsory Purchase Act 1965 s 19(5). For the meaning of 'the works' see paras 13 text to note 4, 92 note 3 ante.
9 See para 179 ante.

(ii) Rentcharges; Release on Payment or Tender

191. Proceedings preliminary to release from rentcharge. If any difference arises between the undertakers[1] or the acquiring authority[2] and a person entitled to a rentcharge[3] on any of the land subject to compulsory purchase[4] as to the compensation to be paid for the release of the land from the rentcharge or from the part of it affecting the land, it must be referred to and determined by the Lands Tribunal[5].

If part only of the land so charged is comprised in the land required by the undertakers or acquiring authority, the apportionment of the rentcharge may be settled by agreement between the party entitled to it and the owner of the land on the one part and the undertakers or the acquiring authority on the other[6]. If not so settled, the apportionment must be referred to and determined by the Lands Tribunal[7]. If however, the remaining part of the land so charged is a sufficient security for the rentcharge, the person entitled to the rentcharge may, with the consent of the owner of that part of the land, release the land required from it on condition or in consideration of that part of the land remaining exclusively subject to the whole of the rentcharge[8].

1 For the meaning of 'the undertakers' see para 13 ante.
2 For the meaning of 'acquiring authority' see para 92 note 5 ante.
3 For the meaning of 'rentcharge' see para 178 note 1 ante.
4 For the meaning of 'land' and 'subject to compulsory purchase' see para 92 notes 1–2 ante. See also para 13 text to note 7 ante.
5 Lands Clauses Consolidation Act 1845 s 115 (where that Act is incorporated: see para 11 ante); Land Compensation Act 1961 s 1; Compulsory Purchase Act 1965 s 18(1) (where that Act applies: see para 15

ante). In the case of a rentcharge belonging to a person suffering from mental disorder, the court has sanctioned the release of the rentcharge on the undertakers or authority purchasing, in lieu of it, a government annuity of the same amount: see *Re Brewer* (1875) 1 ChD 409, CA.

6 Lands Clauses Consolidation Act 1845 s 116; Compulsory Purchase Act 1965 s 18(2)(a).

7 Lands Clauses Consolidation Act 1845 s 116 (amended by the Compulsory Purchase Act 1965 s 39(4), Sch 8 Pt II); Land Compensation Act 1961 s 1; Compulsory Purchase Act 1965 s 18(2)(b).

8 Lands Clauses Consolidation Act 1845 s 116; Compulsory Purchase Act 1965 s 18(2). For an example of the remaining land being wholly charged by court order see *Powell v South Wales Rly Co* (1855) 1 Jur NS 773.

192. Release from rentcharge on payment of compensation. If, on payment or tender of the compensation agreed or awarded to the person entitled to the rentcharge[1], he fails to execute a release of the rentcharge in favour of the undertakers[2] or the acquiring authority[3], or if he fails to make out a good title to the rentcharge to their satisfaction, they may pay the amount of the compensation into court[4]. When they have paid the compensation into court, they may execute a deed poll[5], and thereupon the rentcharge, or the part of it in respect of which the compensation was paid ceases and is extinguished[6].

If, however, any of the land subject to compulsory purchase[7] is so released from a rentcharge, or part of a rentcharge, to which it was subject jointly with other land, that other land alone becomes charged with the whole of the rentcharge or with the remainder of it, as the case may be, and the person entitled to the rentcharge has all the same rights and remedies over that other land for the whole or the remainder of the rentcharge as he had previously over the whole of the land subject to the rentcharge[8]. Upon any such rentcharge or part of a rentcharge being so released, the deed or instrument creating or transferring it may be tendered to the undertakers or the acquiring authority, and they must affix their common or official seal to a memorandum of the release indorsed on the deed or instrument, declaring (1) what part of the land originally subject to the rentcharge has been purchased by virtue of the empowering enactment[9]; (2) if the land is released from part of the rentcharge, what part of it has been released, and how much continues payable[10]; and (3) if the land so required has been released from the whole of the rentcharge, then that the remaining land is thenceforward to remain exclusively charged with it[11]. The memorandum must be made and executed at the expense of the undertakers or acquiring authority and is evidence in all courts and elsewhere of the facts stated in it, but not so as to exclude any other evidence of the same facts[12].

Where land is acquired under an order providing for a vesting declaration, special provision is made as to land subject to a rentcharge[13].

1 See para 191 ante. For the meaning of 'rentcharge' see para 178 note 1 ante.

2 For the meaning of 'the undertakers' see para 13 ante.

3 For the meaning of 'acquiring authority' see para 92 note 5 ante.

4 Lands Clauses Consolidation Act 1845 s 117 (amended by the Administration of Justice Act 1965 s 17(1), Sch 1) (where the 1845 Act is incorporated: see para 11 ante); Compulsory Purchase Act 1965 s 18(3) (where that Act applies: see para 15 ante). As to payment into court see paras 98 note 6, 124, 142 ante.

5 As to the execution of deeds poll see the Lands Clauses Consolidation Act 1845 s 77 (as amended); the Compulsory Purchase Act 1965 ss 9(3), 28; and para 144 ante.

6 Lands Clauses Consolidation Act 1845 s 117 (amended by the Compulsory Purchase Act 1965 s 39(4), Sch 8 Pt II); Compulsory Purchase Act 1965 s 18(3).

7 For the meaning of 'land' and 'subject to compulsory purchase' see para 92 notes 1–2 ante. See also para 13 text to note 7 ante.

8 Lands Clauses Consolidation Act 1845 s 118; Compulsory Purchase Act 1965 s 18(4).

9 Lands Clauses Consolidation Act 1845 s 118; Compulsory Purchase Act 1965 s 18(5)(a).

10 Lands Clauses Consolidation Act 1845 s 118; Compulsory Purchase Act 1965 s 18(5)(b).
11 Lands Clauses Consolidation Act 1845 s 118; Compulsory Purchase Act 1965 s 18(5)(c).
12 Lands Clauses Consolidation Act 1845 s 118; Compulsory Purchase Act 1965 s 18(5).
13 See para 178 ante.

(iii) Mortgaged Land

193. Right to treat with mortgagor alone. The mortgagee as well as the mortgagor of land to be taken is entitled to a notice to treat[1]; but if a lump sum is paid into court in respect of both interests the court will apportion the amount between the mortgagee and mortgagor[2]. It is a common practice, however, when the mortgagee is not in possession, for the undertakers or the acquiring authority to treat with the mortgagor for the full value of the land, and to leave him to pay off or otherwise discharge the mortgage out of the purchase money. They are entitled so to proceed, but unless the mortgagee agrees to this procedure, they must take care that his interest is provided for, as otherwise they may be restrained from prosecuting their works on the mortgaged land until the mortgage has been redeemed or provision has been made in accordance with the statutory provisions for payment of compensation to the mortgagee[3].

If the undertakers or authority deal with the mortgagor only in respect both of his interest and of the mortgagee's interest, and the amount assessed is less than the sum due in respect of the mortgage, and if they have entered and destroyed the buildings on the land, they may be treated as being in the same position as the mortgagor, and be ordered to pay the total amount found due in respect of the principal, interest and costs[4]. Nevertheless, the fact that they take possession as against the mortgagor does not deprive them of their statutory right to serve a notice to treat on the mortgagee and to proceed in due course to assess the compensation under that notice[5].

1 *Martin v London, Chatham and Dover Rly Co* (1866) 1 Ch App 501; *R v Metropolitan Rly Co* (1865) 13 LT 444; *Cooke v LCC* [1911] 1 Ch 604; and see para 103 ante.
2 *Pile v Pile, ex p Lambton* (1876) 3 ChD 36, CA; *Cooper v Metropolitan Board of Works* (1883) 25 ChD 472, CA; and see *Re South City Market Co, ex p Bergin* (1884) 13 LR Ir 245.
3 *Ranken v East and West India Docks and Birmingham Junction Rly Co* (1849) 12 Beav 298; *Spencer-Bell to London and South Western Rly Co and Metropolitan District Rly Co* (1885) 33 WR 771; and see *Re Eastern Counties Rly Co, Re Lands Clauses Consolidation Act 1845, ex p Peyton's Settlement* (1856) 4 WR 380. For the position where the undertakers or authority enter into possession after treating only with the mortgagor and the assessed purchase money is less than the mortgage debt see the text and notes 4–5 infra.
4 *Martin v London, Chatham and Dover Rly Co* (1866) 1 Ch App 501. As to cases of entry where they have not known of the existence of a mortgage see para 132 ante.
5 *Cooke v LCC* [1911] 1 Ch 604.

194. Redemption of mortgagee's interest. Special statutory provision is made for the purchase or redemption of the mortgagee's interest by the undertakers[1] or acquiring authority[2], independently of the mortgagor[3]. The undertakers or authority may purchase or redeem the mortgagee's interest in any of the land subject to compulsory purchase[4], whether or not:

(1) they have previously purchased the equity of redemption[5];
(2) the mortgagee is a trustee[6];
(3) the mortgagee is in possession of the land[7];
(4) the mortgage includes other land in addition to the land subject to compulsory purchase[8].

The undertakers or authority may redeem the mortgage by paying or tendering to the mortgagee the principal and interest due on the mortgage, together with his costs and charges, if any, and also six months' additional interest[9]; and thereupon he must immediately convey or release his interest in the land comprised in the mortgage to them or as they may direct[10]. Alternatively, they may give written notice to the mortgagee that they will pay off the principal and interest due on the mortgage at the end of six months, computed from the day of giving the notice; and if they give this notice, or if the person entitled to the equity of redemption gives six months' notice of his intention to redeem the mortgage, then at the expiration of either of these notices, or at any intermediate period, on payment or tender by them to the mortgagee of the principal money due on the mortgage and the interest which would become due at the end of six months from the time of giving either of the notices, together with his costs and expenses, if any, the mortgagee must convey or release his interest in the land comprised in the mortgage to the undertakers or authority or as they direct[11].

If, in either of the above cases, on such payment or tender the mortgagee fails to convey or release his interest in the mortgage as directed by the undertakers or acquiring authority, or if he fails to make out a good title to that interest to their satisfaction, they may pay into court[12] the sums payable under the above provisions[13] and may then execute a deed poll[14] in the manner provided in the case of a purchase of land[15]. On the execution of the deed poll, as well as upon a conveyance by the mortgagee, all the estate and interest of the mortgagee, and of all persons in trust for him or for whom he may be a trustee, in the land vests in the undertakers or authority and, where he was entitled to possession of the land, they become similarly entitled[16].

1 For the meaning of 'the undertakers' see para 13 ante.
2 For the meaning of 'acquiring authority' see para 92 note 5 ante.
3 See the Lands Clauses Consolidation Act 1845 ss 108–114 (as amended) (where that Act is incorporated: see para 11 ante); and the Compulsory Purchase Act 1965 ss 14–17 (where that Act applies: see para 15 ante). These groups of sections do not form complete and exhaustive codes dealing with mortgagees' rights, but are supplementary to the general provisions of those Acts; and the Lands Clauses Consolidation Act 1845 ss 108, 110, and the Compulsory Purchase Act 1965 ss 14, 15, therefore, do not exclude mortgagees' rights, as owners, to recover compensation for injury by severance: *R v Clerk of the Peace for Middlesex* [1914] 3 KB 259. See also para 291 post.
4 Lands Clauses Consolidation Act 1845 s 108; Compulsory Purchase Act 1965 s 14(1). For the meaning of 'land' and 'subject to compulsory purchase' see para 92 notes 1–2 ante. See also para 13 text to note 7 ante.
5 Lands Clauses Consolidation Act 1845 s 108; Compulsory Purchase Act 1965 s 14(7)(a).
6 Lands Clauses Consolidation Act 1845 s 108; Compulsory Purchase Act 1965 s 14(7)(b).
7 Lands Clauses Consolidation Act 1845 s 108; Compulsory Purchase Act 1965 s 14(7)(c).
8 Lands Clauses Consolidation Act 1845 s 108; Compulsory Purchase Act 1965 s 14(7)(d).
9 If a time was limited in the mortgage deed for payment of the principal secured by it, and the mortgagee has been required under the Lands Clauses Consolidation Act 1845 ss 108–113 (as amended) or the Compulsory Purchase Act 1965 ss 14–16 to accept payment of the principal at a time earlier than the time so limited, the amounts payable to him will include all costs and expenses incurred by him in respect of, or as incidental to, the reinvestment of the sum so paid off: Lands Clauses Consolidation Act 1845 s 114; Compulsory Purchase Act 1965 s 17(1)(a). In case of difference these costs must be taxed, and their payment may be enforced in the manner provided by the Lands Clauses Consolidation Act 1845 s 83 (as amended); or the Compulsory Purchase Act 1965 s 23 (see para 141 ante), with respect to the costs of conveyances: Lands Clauses Consolidation Act 1845 s 114; Compulsory Purchase Act 1965 s 17(2). Further, if the rate of interest secured by the mortgage is higher than can reasonably be expected to be obtained on reinvestment at the time the mortgage is paid off, regard being had to the current rate of interest, the amount payable to the mortgagee will include compensation in respect of the loss thereby sustained: Lands Clauses Consolidation Act 1845 s 114; Compulsory Purchase Act 1965 s 17(1)(b). In case of difference the amount of the compensation must be referred to and determined by the Lands Tribunal: Lands Clauses Consolidation Act 1845 s 114; Land Compensation Act 1961 s 1; Compulsory Purchase Act 1965 s 17(2). As to references to the tribunal see para 208 et seq post. Entry

without payment of the amounts required will be an unauthorised entry: see the Lands Clauses Consolidation Act 1845 s 114. As to unauthorised entry see para 128 ante.

10 Lands Clauses Consolidation Act 1845 s 108; Compulsory Purchase Act 1965 s 14(2).
11 Lands Clauses Consolidation Act 1845 s 108; Compulsory Purchase Act 1965 s 14(3).
12 As to payment into court in such cases see para 142 ante.
13 Lands Clauses Consolidation Act 1845 s 109 (amended by the Administration of Justice Act 1965 s 17(1), Sch 1); Compulsory Purchase Act 1965 s 14(4). As to payment into court see paras 98 note 6, 124, 142 ante.
14 Ie in the manner provided by the Lands Clauses Consolidation Act 1845 s 77 (as amended); or the Compulsory Purchase Act 1965 ss 9(3), 28: see para 144 ante.
15 Lands Clauses Consolidation Act 1845 s 109; Compulsory Purchase Act 1965 s 14(5).
16 Lands Clauses Consolidation Act 1845 s 109; Compulsory Purchase Act 1965 s 14(6).

195. Mortgage debt exceeding value of land. If the value of any of the mortgaged land[1] is less than the principal, interest and costs secured on it, the value of the land, or the compensation to be paid by the undertakers[2] or acquiring authority[3] in respect of the land, must be settled by agreement between the mortgagee and the person entitled to the equity of redemption, on the one part, and the undertakers or authority, on the other part, or, if they fail to agree, must be determined by the Lands Tribunal[4]. The amount so agreed or awarded must be paid by the undertakers or authority to the mortgagee in satisfaction or part satisfaction of his mortgage debt[5]; and, on payment or tender of that amount[6], the mortgagee must convey or release all his interest in the mortgaged land to them or as they direct[7]. If he fails to do so, or fails to adduce a good title to that interest to their satisfaction, they may pay that amount into court[8].

When the undertakers or acquiring authority have paid the amount agreed or awarded into court, they may execute a deed poll[9] in the manner provided in the case of the purchase of land[10]; and thereupon the land, as to the estate and interest then vested in the mortgagee, or any person in trust for him, becomes absolutely vested in them and, where he was entitled to possession of the land, they become similarly entitled[11]. The payment to the mortgagee, or into court, of the amount agreed or awarded must be accepted by the mortgagee in satisfaction or part satisfaction of his mortgage debt, and is a full discharge of the mortgaged land from all money due on it[12]. Nevertheless all rights and remedies possessed by the mortgagee against the mortgagor by virtue of any bond, covenant or other obligation, other than the right to the land, remain in force in respect of so much of the mortgage debt as has not been satisfied by payment to the mortgagee or into court[13].

1 For the meaning of 'land' see para 92 note 1 ante. See also para 13 text to note 7 ante.
2 For the meaning of 'the undertakers' see para 13 ante.
3 For the meaning of 'acquiring authority' see para 92 note 5 ante.
4 Lands Clauses Consolidation Act 1845 s 110 (where that Act is incorporated: see para 11 ante); Land Compensation Act 1961 s 1; Compulsory Purchase Act 1965 s 15(1) (where that Act applies: see para 15 ante). As to the position where the undertakers or authority deal with the mortgagor alone and the mortgage debt exceeds the value of the land see para 193 ante. As to the Lands Tribunal see para 202 et seq post.
5 Lands Clauses Consolidation Act 1845 s 110; Compulsory Purchase Act 1965 s 15(2).
6 If the mortgage is paid off before the time stipulated in the mortgage, the costs and expenses of reinvestment and the loss arising from investment at a lower interest rate must also be paid: see para 194 note 9 ante.
7 Lands Clauses Consolidation Act 1845 s 110; Compulsory Purchase Act 1965 s 15(3).
8 Lands Clauses Consolidation Act 1845 s 111 (amended by the Administration of Justice Act 1965 s 17(1), Sch 1); Compulsory Purchase Act 1965 s 15(3). As to payment into court see paras 98 note 6, 124, 142 ante.

9 Ie in the manner provided by the Lands Clauses Consolidation Act 1845 s 77 (as amended); or the Compulsory Purchase Act 1965 ss 9(3), 28: see para 144 ante.
10 Lands Clauses Consolidation Act 1845 s 111; Compulsory Purchase Act 1965 s 15(4).
11 Lands Clauses Consolidation Act 1845 s 111; Compulsory Purchase Act 1965 s 15(5).
12 Lands Clauses Consolidation Act 1845 s 111; Compulsory Purchase Act 1965 s 15(6).
13 Lands Clauses Consolidation Act 1845 s 111 (as amended: see note 8 supra); Compulsory Purchase Act 1965 s 15(7).

196. Part only of mortgaged land taken. If a part only of any mortgaged land[1] is required by the undertakers[2] or the acquiring authority[3] and

(1) that part is of less value than the principal, interest and costs secured on the land; and

(2) the mortgagee does not consider the remaining part of the land a sufficient security for the money charged on it, or is not willing to release the part so required,

then the value of that part, and also the compensation, if any, to be paid in respect of the severance of it or otherwise, must be settled by agreement between the mortgagee and the person entitled to the equity of redemption, on the one part, and the undertakers or acquiring authority, on the other[4]. If they fail to agree as to the amount, it must be determined by the Lands Tribunal[5].

The amount so agreed or awarded[6] must be paid by the undertakers or authority to the mortgagee in satisfaction, or part satisfaction, of his mortgage debt[7], and on the payment or tender of the amount agreed or awarded the mortgagee must convey or release to them, or as they direct, all his interest in the mortgaged land to be taken[8]. A memorandum of what has been so paid must be indorsed on the deed creating the mortgage and signed by the mortgagee, and a copy of it must at the same time, if required, be furnished by the undertakers or authority at their expense to the person entitled to the equity of redemption of the land comprised in the mortgage[9].

If, upon payment or tender to any such mortgagee of the amount so agreed or determined, the mortgagee fails to convey or release to the undertakers or authority, or as they direct, his interest in the land in respect of which the compensation has been paid or tendered, or if he fails to adduce a good title to it to their satisfaction, they may pay the amount of the compensation into court[10]. When the undertakers or authority have paid the money into court, they may execute a deed poll[11] in the manner provided in the case of purchase of land[12]. Thereupon, all the estate and interest in the land then vested in the mortgagee or in any person in trust for him becomes absolutely vested in the undertakers or the authority; and if the mortgagee was entitled to possession of the land, they become similarly entitled[13].

The payment to the mortgagee, or into court, of the amount agreed or awarded must be accepted by the mortgagee in satisfaction or part satisfaction of his mortgage debt and is a full discharge of the mortgaged land from all money due on it[14]. The mortgagee has, however, the same powers and remedies for recovering and compelling payment of the mortgage money or the residue of it, as the case may be, and the interest on it respectively, as against the remaining land comprised in the mortgage, as he would have had for recovering or compelling payment of it as against the whole of the land originally comprised in the mortgage[15].

1 For the meaning of 'land' see para 92 note 1 ante. See also para 13 text to note 7 ante.
2 For the meaning of 'the undertakers' see para 13 ante.
3 For the meaning of 'acquiring authority' see para 113 note 5 ante.

4 Lands Clauses Consolidation Act 1845 s 112 (where that Act is incorporated: see para 11 ante); Land Compensation Act 1961 s 1; Compulsory Purchase Act 1965 s 16(1) (where that Act applies: see para 15 ante).

5 Lands Clauses Consolidation Act 1845 s 112; Land Compensation Act 1961 s 1; Compulsory Purchase Act 1965 s 16(1). As to the Lands Tribunal see para 202 et seq post; and as to the determination of disputed compensation see paras 233–234, 279 (value of the land) 291 (severance or other injurious affection) post.

6 If the mortgage is paid off before the time stipulated in the mortgage deed, the cost and expenses of reinvestment and the loss arising from reinvestment at a lower interest rate must also be paid: see para 194 note 9 ante.

7 Lands Clauses Consolidation Act 1845 s 112; Compulsory Purchase Act 1965 s 16(2).

8 Lands Clauses Consolidation Act 1845 s 112; Compulsory Purchase Act 1965 s 16(3).

9 Lands Clauses Consolidation Act 1845 s 112; Compulsory Purchase Act 1965 s 16(4).

10 Lands Clauses Consolidation Act 1845 s 113 (amended by the Administration of Justice Act 1965 s 17(1), Sch 1); Compulsory Purchase Act 1965 s 16(5). As to payment into court see paras 98 note 6, 124, 142 ante.

11 Ie in the manner provided by the Lands Clauses Consolidation Act 1845 s 77 or the Compulsory Purchase Act 1965 ss 9(3), 28: see para 144 ante.

12 Lands Clauses Consolidation Act 1845 s 113; Compulsory Purchase Act 1965 s 15(4) (applied by s 16(5)).

13 Lands Clauses Consolidation Act 1845 s 113; Compulsory Purchase Act 1965 s 15(5) (applied by s 16(5)).

14 Lands Clauses Consolidation Act 1845 s 113; Compulsory Purchase Act 1965 s 15(6) (applied by s 16(5)).

15 Lands Clauses Consolidation Act 1845 s 113; Compulsory Purchase Act 1965 s 16(6).

4. CLAIMS FOR PURCHASE MONEY OR COMPENSATION

(1) RIGHT TO AND CLAIMS FOR PURCHASE MONEY OR COMPENSATION

197. Persons interested in or having power to sell, convey or release land. When an acquiring authority[1] requires to purchase any land[2] authorised to be acquired compulsorily it must give a notice to treat[3] to all the persons interested in or having power to sell, convey or release the land, stating in it that it is willing to treat for the purchase of the land and as to the compensation for damage which may be sustained by reason of the execution of the works[4].

1 For the meaning of 'acquiring authority' see para 92 note 5 ante.

2 For the meaning of 'land' see para 92 note 1 ante. See also para 13 text to note 7 ante.

3 See para 100 et seq ante. For the time within which a notice to treat must be served see para 101 ante. As to withdrawal or abandonment of a notice to treat see paras 120–121 ante; and *Grice v Dudley Corpn* [1958] Ch 329, [1957] 2 All ER 673; *Simpsons Motor Sales (London) Ltd v Hendon Corpn* [1964] AC 1088, [1963] 2 All ER 484; *R v Carmarthen District Council, ex p Blewin Trust Ltd* (1989) 59 P & CR 379.

4 See the Lands Clauses Consolidation Act 1845 s 18 (where that Act is incorporated: see para 11 ante); the Compulsory Purchase Act 1965 s 5(1), (2)(c) (where that Act applies: see para 15 ante); and see para 198 post. As to the interests entitled to a notice to treat and claim compensation see para 103 et seq ante.

198. Making of claim, giving particulars of interest in land. A notice to treat must give particulars of the land to which the notice relates and demand from the party served with it particulars of his estate and interest in the land to be purchased or taken and of the claims made by him in respect of the land[1], but there is nothing in the Lands

Clauses Acts or the Compulsory Purchase Act 1965 to compel the owner of the land to supply the particulars demanded[2].

However, if the Lands Tribunal[3] is satisfied that a claimant has failed to deliver to the acquiring authority[4], in time to enable that authority to make a proper offer, a written notice of the amount claimed by him containing particulars of the exact nature of the interest in respect of which compensation is claimed, and giving details of the amounts claimed under separate heads and showing how the amount under each head is calculated[5], then, unless for special reasons the tribunal thinks it proper not to do so, it must order the claimant to bear his own costs and to pay the costs of the acquiring authority so far as they were incurred after the time when in the tribunal's opinion the notice should have been delivered[6].

Failure to deliver particulars also affects compensation payable where a notice to treat is withdrawn[7].

1　See the Lands Clauses Consolidation Act 1845 s 18; the Compulsory Purchase Act 1965 s 5(2)(a), (b); and paras 100, 197 ante.
2　*Birch v St Marylebone Vestry* (1869) 20 LT 697. As to the Lands Clauses Acts see para 11 ante.
3　As to the tribunal see para 202 et seq post.
4　For the meaning of 'acquiring authority' for these purposes see para 120 note 5 ante.
5　Land Compensation Act 1961 s 4(1)(b), (2).
6　Ibid s 4(1). Furthermore, where the particulars did not include a proper claim so that the acquiring authority would not know how much compensation it would have to pay, it was free to withdraw from the acquisition (provided that it had not entered into possession of the land): see *Trustees for Methodist Church Purposes v North Tyneside Metropolitan Borough Council* (1979) 38 P & CR 665. As to withdrawal of notices to treat see para 120 ante.
7　See para 120 ante.

199. Offers by claimant or acquiring authority. Where a claimant has delivered to the acquiring authority[1] written notice of his interest and claim[2] in time to enable that authority to make a proper offer and has made an unconditional offer in writing to accept any sum as compensation, then, if the sum awarded to him by the Lands Tribunal is equal to or exceeds that sum, the tribunal must, unless for special reasons it thinks it proper not to do so, order the authority to bear its own costs and pay the claimant's costs so far as they were incurred after his offer was made[3]. An owner, or the assignee of the original claimant's interest, may withdraw or amend a claim before acceptance[4].

The acquiring authority is not obliged to make an offer of a sum in compensation[5], but it may make such an offer, and if it is an unconditional offer in writing and the sum awarded to the claimant by the tribunal does not exceed the sum offered[6], the tribunal must, unless for special reasons it thinks it proper not to do so, order the claimant to bear his own costs and to pay the authority's costs so far as they were incurred after the offer was made[7].

An unconditional offer of any sum, or of readiness to accept any sum, as compensation must not be disclosed to the tribunal until it has decided on the amount of compensation to be awarded to the party to or by whom the offer was made, but a copy of the offer enclosed in a sealed cover may be sent to the registrar[8] or delivered to the tribunal at the hearing by the party who made the offer and must be opened by the tribunal after it has decided the amount of the compensation[9].

1　For the meaning of 'acquiring authority' see para 120 note 5 ante.
2　Ie a notice as required by the Land Compensation Act 1961 s 4(1)(b) containing the particulars set out in s 4(2): see para 198 ante.
3　Ibid s 4(3). As to the essentials of an offer see note 7 infra; and as to the tribunal see para 202 et seq post. With regard to pre-offer costs, the Lands Tribunal has a complete discretion and thus there is nothing to

prevent an award of such costs to a claimant who is awarded less than the authority's offer. However, it would be a wrong exercise of this discretion to award such costs to a claimant who eventually failed to establish any claim to compensation: *Pepys v London Transport Executive* [1975] 1 All ER 748, [1975] 1 WLR 234, CA.

4　*Cardiff Corpn v Cook* [1923] 2 Ch 115.

5　*Martin v Leicester Waterworks Co* (1858) 3 H & N 463. As to the withdrawal of an offer and the making of a new one see *Fitzhardinge v Gloucester and Berkeley Canal Co* (1872) LR 7 QB 776; *Gray v North Eastern Rly Co* (1876) 1 QBD 696; *Yates v Blackburn Corpn* (1860) 6 H & N 61; *Lascelles v Swansea School Board* (1899) 69 LJQB 24.

6　Land Compensation Act 1961 s 4(1)(a).

7　Ibid s 4(1). In order to affect the incidence of costs, the offer must be made in sufficient time to enable the claimant, before he has incurred any substantial expense, to make up his mind whether or not he will accept it: see *Fisher v Great Western Rly Co* [1911] 1 KB 551 at 555, CA. It must be a clear unconditional offer made in respect of the subject matter alone (see *Miles v Great Western Rly Co* [1896] 2 QB 432, CA; *Fisher v Great Western Rly Co* supra) and must not include costs (see *Balls v Metropolitan Board of Works* (1866) LR 1 QB 337) or the execution of works (see *Fisher v Great Western Rly Co* supra). If the claim is divided into parts, but there is really only one matter in dispute, the total of the sums awarded and offered determine the incidence of costs: see *Re Hayward and Metropolitan Rly Co* (1864) 4 B & S 787; and cf *R v Biram* (1852) 17 QB 969.

8　'The registrar' means the registrar of the Lands Tribunal or, as respects any powers or functions of the registrar, any officer of the Lands Tribunal authorised by the Lord Chancellor to exercise those powers or functions: Lands Tribunal Rules 1975, SI 1975/299, r 2(2).

9　Ibid r 50(1). This provision is unlikely to undergo substantial alteration in the Lands Tribunal Rules 1996, which are expected to come into force in April 1996. At the date at which this volume states the law, those new rules were still in draft and the final text had not been settled. See further para 206 note 3 post.

200. Reference of disputed claims to Lands Tribunal. If a person served with a notice to treat[1] does not within 21 days from the service of the notice state the particulars of his claim in respect of the land[2] to be purchased or taken or treat with the undertakers[3] or the acquiring authority[4] in respect of his claim, or if he and the authority do not agree as to the amount of the compensation[5] to be paid by the authority for the interest belonging to him, or which he has power to sell[6], or for any damage which may be sustained by him by reason of the execution of the works[7], the question of the disputed compensation must be referred to the Lands Tribunal[8].

Unless agreed between the parties, any question as to the apportionment of rent under a lease where part only of the land subject to the lease is taken must also be referred to the tribunal[9] and so also must questions as to the release and apportionment of rentcharges[10]. Where the parties entitled to the purchase money or compensation are absent from the United Kingdom[11] and are prevented from treating or cannot after diligent inquiry be found, the purchase money or compensation must be determined by an able practical surveyor selected from the members of the tribunal[12] and paid into court[13], but if such a party is later dissatisfied with that valuation he may, before applying for payment out or investment of the sum assessed and paid into court, require the submission to the tribunal of the question whether the compensation paid into court was sufficient or whether any and what further sum ought to be paid over or paid into court[14]. If the tribunal awards a further sum, the undertakers or the acquiring authority must pay it over, or pay it into court, as the case may require, within 14 days of the making of the award, and if they fail to do so, that further sum may be recovered in proceedings in the High Court[15].

If any person claims compensation in respect of any land, or any interest in land, which has been taken for, or injuriously affected by, the execution of the works, and for which the undertakers or the acquiring authority[16] have not made satisfaction[17], any dispute arising in relation to compensation must also be referred to and determined by the Lands Tribunal[18]. Any such compensation carries interest at the prescribed rate[19] from the date of the claim until payment[20].

1   As to service of the notice to treat see para 100 et seq ante.
2   For the meaning of 'land' see para 92 note 1 ante. See also para 13 text to note 7 ante.
3   For the meaning of 'the undertakers' see para 13 ante.
4   For the meaning of 'acquiring authority' see para 92 note 5 ante.
5   As to such compensation or purchase money see paras 233–234, 279 et seq post.
6   As to persons with power to sell see para 96 et seq ante.
7   Ie where compensation in respect of damage by severance or injurious affection arises as part of the purchase money for the land taken: see para 291 post. For the meaning of 'the works' see para 92 note 3 ante. See also para 13 text to note 4 ante.
8   Lands Clauses Consolidation Act 1845 s 21 (amended by the Compulsory Purchase Act 1965 s 39(4), Sch 8 Pt III) (where the 1845 Act is incorporated: see para 11 ante); Compulsory Purchase Act 1965 s 6 (where that Act applies: see para 15 ante). As to notice of reference to the tribunal see para 208 post.
9   See para 189 ante.
10 See para 191 ante.
11 For the meaning of 'United Kingdom' see para 100 note 21 ante.
12 Lands Clauses Consolidation Act 1845 s 58 (amended by the Compulsory Purchase Act 1965 Sch 8 Pt III); Lands Tribunal Act 1949 s 1(6) (amended by the Land Compensation Act 1961 s 40(2)(b), Sch 4 para 8; and by the Compulsory Purchase Act 1965 Sch 8 Pt III) (where the 1845 Act is incorporated); Compulsory Purchase Act 1965 s 5(3), Sch 2 para 1(1); and see para 100 ante. The selection is made in accordance with the Lands Tribunal Act 1949 s 3 (as amended): see para 205 post. The undertakers or the acquiring authority must preserve the valuation and produce it on demand to the owners of the land to which it relates and to all other interested parties: Lands Clauses Consolidation Act 1845 s 61; Compulsory Purchase Act 1965 Sch 2 para 1(3). All the expenses of and incident to the valuation must be borne by the undertakers or the acquiring authority: Lands Clauses Consolidation Act 1845 s 62; Compulsory Purchase Act 1965 Sch 2 para 1(4). The surveyor appointed may apply for a certificate of appropriate alternative development: see para 253 note 3 post. Payments on account may be made of such compensation, which may be recovered if later shown not to be payable or to be excessive: see the Planning and Compensation Act 1991 s 80(2), (3), Sch 18 Pt II.
13 See paras 142–143 ante.
14 Lands Clauses Consolidation Act 1845 ss 64, 65; Land Compensation Act 1961 s 1; Compulsory Purchase Act 1965 s 5(3), Sch 2 para 4(1).
15 Lands Clauses Consolidation Act 1845 s 66 (amended by the Administration of Justice Act 1965 s 34); Land Compensation Act 1961 s 1; Compulsory Purchase Act 1965 Sch 2 para 4(2). If the tribunal determines that the compensation paid into court was sufficient, the costs of and incident to the tribunal proceedings will be in the tribunal's discretion in accordance with the Lands Tribunal Act 1949 s 3(5) (see para 227 post), but if it determines that a further sum ought to be paid, all the costs of and incident to the proceedings must be paid by the undertakers or the acquiring authority: see the Lands Clauses Consolidation Act 1845 s 67; the Land Compensation Act 1961 s 1; the Compulsory Purchase Act 1965 Sch 2 para 4(3). As to references to the tribunal see para 208 et seq post.
16 Where ibid Pt I (ss 1–32) (as amended) applies by virtue of the Town and Country Planning Act 1990 Pt IX (ss 226–246) (as amended) (see TOWN AND COUNTRY PLANNING vol 46 (Reissue) para 760 et seq), this reference to the acquiring authority is to be construed in accordance with s 245(4)(b) (see TOWN AND COUNTRY PLANNING vol 46 (Reissue) para 767 note 4 head (2)): Compulsory Purchase Act 1965 s 10(3) (amended by the Planning (Consequential Provisions) Act 1990 s 4, Sch 2 para 13(2) (a), (b)).
17 Ie whether under the provisions of the Lands Clauses Consolidation Act 1845, of the Compulsory Purchase Act 1965, or of the special Act: Lands Clauses Consolidation Act 1845 s 68 (amended by the Compulsory Purchase Act 1965 Sch 8 Pt III); Compulsory Purchase Act 1965 s 10(1). For the meaning of 'special Act' see paras 11, 16 ante.
18 Lands Clauses Consolidation Act 1845 s 68 (as amended: see note 17 supra); Lands Tribunal Act 1949 s 1(3)(b) (amended by the Land Compensation Act 1961 s 40(3), Sch 5); Compulsory Purchase Act 1965 s 10(1). As to such rights to compensation and other similar rights see para 353 post. Section 10 (as amended: see note 16 supra) is to be construed as affording in all cases a right to compensation for injurious affection to land which is the same as the right which the Lands Clauses Consolidation Act 1845 s 68 (as so amended) has been construed as affording in cases where the amount claimed exceeds £50: Compulsory Purchase Act 1965 s 10(2). Despite the fact that the Lands Tribunal was the proper forum in respect of claims for injurious affection, the court refused to strike out a claim which involved

the construction of a private Act of Parliament and which claimed declarations in respect of such compensation: see *Argyle Motors (Birkenhead) Ltd v Birkenhead Corpn* (1971) 22 P & CR 829.

19 Ie at the rate for the time being prescribed under the Land Compensation Act 1961 s 32: see para 125 ante.

20 Land Compensation Act 1973 s 63(1). Payments on account may be made in respect of such interest, which are recoverable if it is subsequently found that the person making them is not liable to pay interest or that the amount of any payment is excessive: see the Planning and Compensation Act 1991 s 80(2), (3), Sch 18 Pt II.

201. Limitation of time for claim. The Lands Tribunal has no jurisdiction to decide questions of title[1]; it assesses the amount of the purchase money or compensation irrespective of the title. Whilst it is obvious that no action may be brought for any liquidated sum representing the purchase money prior to the date of the award[2], it does not follow that the provisions of the Limitation Act 1980[3] do not apply to the making of the reference to the Lands Tribunal for the purpose of assessing the appropriate purchase money or compensation.

Furthermore, in the case of an acquisition of land under the provisions for declaring the land to be vested in the acquiring authority, a question of disputed compensation or purchase money may not be referred to the tribunal after six years from the date of the vesting of the interest[4].

1 *Brierley Hill Local Board v Pearsall* (1884) 9 App Cas 595, HL; *Horrocks v Metropolitan Rly Co* (1863) 4 B & S 315; *Holt Bros and Whitford v Axbridge RDC* (1931) 95 JP 87; *Mountgarret (Rt Hon Viscount) v Claro Water Board* (1963) 15 P & CR 53, Lands Tribunal. As to the tribunal see para 202 et seq post.

2 *Turner v Midland Rly Co* [1911] 1 KB 832. Note that this was a case under the Lands Clauses Consolidation Act 1845 s 68 (as amended) (see para 200 ante; and cf the Compulsory Purchase Act 1965 s 10 (as amended)), ie a claim for injurious affection where no land was taken. The applicable limitation Act was the Statute of Limitations 1623 (21 Jac 1 c 16) which did not contain the equivalent of the Limitation Act 1980 s 9: see note 3 infra.

3 An action to recover any sum by virtue of any enactment may not be brought after the expiration of six years from the date on which the cause of action accrued: ibid s 9(1). This has been construed to mean that a claimant has six years, whether or not the compensation has been assessed: see *West Riding of Yorks County Council v Huddersfield Corpn* [1957] 1 QB 540, [1957] 1 All ER 669; *Central Electricity Board v Halifax Corpn* [1963] AC 785, sub nom *Central Electricity Generating Board v Halifax Corpn* [1962] 3 All ER 915, HL; and *Pegler v Rly Executive* [1948] AC 332, [1948] 1 All ER 559, HL. The six year period would thus appear to run from the date upon which the right to compensation (not the right to any particular amount of compensation) accrued. If the word 'action' in the Limitation Act 1980 s 9(1) is to embrace proceedings which are not actions in the true sense, it seems that for 'cause of action' must be read 'cause of proceeding': *China v Harrow UDC* [1954] 1 QB 178 at 185, [1953] 2 All ER 1296 at 1299, DC, per Lord Goddard.

4 See para 177 ante.

(2) SETTLEMENT OF CLAIMS BY LANDS TRIBUNAL

(i) Constitution and Jurisdiction

202. Constitution of Lands Tribunal. The Lands Tribunal[1] is appointed by the Lord Chancellor, and consists of a president and such number of other members as the Lord Chancellor may determine[2].

The president must be a person who has either (1) held judicial office under the Crown (whether in the United Kingdom[3] or not); or (2) has a seven year general qualification[4]; or (3) is a member of the Bar of Northern Ireland of at least seven years' standing[5]. Such number of the remaining members as the Lord Chancellor may determine must be persons falling within head (2) or head (3) above or solicitors of the Supreme Court of Northern Ireland of at least seven years' standing and the others must be persons having experience in the valuation of land appointed after consultation with the president of the Royal Institution of Chartered Surveyors⁶. The members may be paid such remuneration, travelling and subsistence allowances as the Lord Chancellor may with Treasury approval determine⁷. The appointments are for terms and on conditions determined by the Lord Chancellor with the prior approval of the Treasury, members being eligible for re-appointment⁸. If, however, a member of the tribunal becomes, in the Lord Chancellor's opinion, unfit to continue in office or incapable of performing his duties, the Lord Chancellor must immediately declare that member's office to be vacant and notify the fact in such manner as he thinks fit, and that office then becomes vacant⁹.

With the approval of the Treasury as to numbers and remuneration, the Lord Chancellor may appoint such officers and servants of the tribunal as he may determine¹⁰. The remuneration and allowances of members of the tribunal, the remuneration of the officers and servants appointed by the Lord Chancellor, and such other expenses as the Treasury may determine must be defrayed out of money provided by Parliament¹¹.

1 As to the establishment of the Lands Tribunal (with jurisdiction in England, Wales and Northern Ireland) see the Lands Tribunal Act 1949 s 1(1)(b). There is a separate tribunal for Scotland: see s 1(1)(a).
2 Ibid s 2(1). In case of the president's temporary absence or inability to act, the Lord Chancellor may appoint another member to act as deputy and the member so appointed has, when so acting, all the functions of the president: s 2(3).
3 For the meaning of 'United Kingdom' see para 100 note 21 ante.
4 Ie a general qualification within the meaning of the Courts and Legal Services Act 1990 s 71 (see SOLICITORS vol 44(1) (Reissue) para 91 head (3)): Lands Tribunal Act 1949 s 2(2)(b) (substituted by the Courts and Legal Services Act 1990 s 71(2), Sch 10 para 7).
5 Lands Tribunal Act 1949 s 2(2) (amended by the Courts and Legal Services Act 1990 Sch 10 para 7). All Lands Tribunal members are barred from legal practice: Courts and Legal Services Act 1990 s 75, Sch 11.
6 Lands Tribunal Act 1949 s 2(2) (as amended: see note 5 supra).
7 Lands Tribunal Act 1949 s 2(6) (amended by the Judicial Pensions Act 1981 s 36, Sch 4). The Judicial Pensions Act 1981 ss 10, 16 et seq (as amended) provide for the payment of pensions and lump sums on retirement or death of the chairman and members of the tribunal.
8 Lands Tribunal Act 1949 s 2(5). However, no person may be appointed a member of the tribunal for a term which extends beyond the day on which he attains the age of 70, except in accordance with the Judicial Pensions and Retirement Act 1993 s 26(4)–(6) (power to authorise continuance in office up to the age of 75): Lands Tribunal Act 1981 s 2(5A) (added by the Judicial Pensions and Retirement Act 1993 s 26(10), Sch 6 para 31). Similarly, the president and other members of the tribunal must vacate their offices on the day on which they attain the age of 70 or such lower age as may for the time being be specified for the purpose: see s 26(1), Sch 5. For transitional provisions see ss 26(11), 27, Sch 7.
9 Lands Tribunal Act 1949 s 2(4).
10 Ibid s 2(7).
11 Ibid s 2(8) (amended by the Judicial Pensions Act 1981 Sch 4).

203. Jurisdiction of Lands Tribunal. The jurisdiction conferred on the Lands Tribunal includes jurisdiction:
   (1) as to any question of disputed compensation where land¹ is authorised to be acquired compulsorily and, where any part of the land to be acquired is subject to a lease which comprises land not acquired, any question as to the apportionment of the rent payable under the lease²;
   (2) formerly exercised by members of certain panels³ but now transferred to the tribunal⁴;

(3) to discharge and modify[5] restrictive covenants[6];

(4) of statutory tribunals[7] to determine questions under any Act, including a local or private Act, or any instrument under any such Act[8];

(5) on the application of any person, to certify the value of any land being sold by him to a person possessing compulsory purchase powers[9], the sale of the land to that authority at the certified price being deemed to be a sale at the best price that can reasonably be obtained[10];

(6) to act as arbitrator under a reference by consent[11].

The jurisdiction of the Lands Tribunal is limited to questions of compensation and questions of title are outside its jurisdiction[12].

1 For the meaning of 'land' see para 18 note 2 ante.

2 Lands Tribunal Act 1949 s 1(3)(b), (c) (respectively amended by the Land Compensation Act 1961 s 40(3), Sch 5; and by the Compulsory Purchase Act 1965 s 39(4), Sch 8 Pt III); Land Compensation Act 1961 s 1; and see para 200 ante.

3 Ie the power (1) to determine any question which by any Act, including a local or private Act, is directed, in whatever terms, to be determined by a person or one or more persons selected from the panel of official arbitrators appointed under the Acquisition of Land (Assessment of Compensation) Act 1919 (repealed), or the panel of referees appointed under the Finance (1909–10) Act 1910 s 34 (repealed), or which is so directed to be determined in the absence of agreement to the contrary (Lands Tribunal Act 1949 s 1(3)(a)); (2) to exercise any other jurisdiction conferred by any Act, including a local or private Act, or instrument made under any such Act, on a person or one or more persons so selected (s 1(4)(b) (amended by the Land Compensation Act 1961 Sch 5)). The panel of official arbitrators formerly determined questions of disputed compensation or apportionment of rent where land was authorised to be acquired compulsorily: see the Acquisition of Land (Assessment of Compensation) Act 1919 s 1 (repealed). Subsequent enactments conferred other powers on the panel: see eg the Atomic Energy Act 1946 s 6(8), Sch 1 para 9 (amended by the Lands Tribunal Act 1949 s 10, Sch 2; and by virtue of the Land Compensation Act 1961 s 40(1)); and FUEL AND ENERGY vol 19(2) (Reissue) para 1193. All such jurisdiction is now exercisable by the Lands Tribunal. The principal jurisdiction formerly exercised by the panel of referees, and transferred to the tribunal, was over disputes concerning the valuation of land for estate duty (now abolished) and as to the valuation of land for mineral rights duty (now abolished) and other matters connected with that duty.

4 Lands Tribunal Act 1949 s 1(3)(a), (4)(b) (s 1(4)(b) as amended: see note 3 supra).

5 Ie under the Law of Property Act 1925 s 84 (as amended): see EQUITY vol 16 (Reissue) para 803 et seq.

6 Lands Tribunal Act 1949 s 1(4)(a). As to private and local Acts see STATUTES vol 41(1) (Reissue) paras 1211–1213. Except in so far as the context otherwise requires, any reference in the Lands Tribunal Act 1949 to an enactment is to be construed as referring to that enactment as amended, extended or applied by any other enactment: s 8(2).

7 'Statutory tribunal' means any government department, authority or person entrusted with the judicial determination as arbitrator or otherwise of questions arising under an Act, but does not include (1) any of the ordinary courts of law or a tribunal consisting of one or more judges of any of those courts; or (2) an arbitrator unless the person to act as arbitrator is designated, or is to be selected from a class or group of persons designated, by the Act or instrument requiring or authorising arbitration: ibid s 4(7).

8 See para 204 post.

9 For the meaning of 'authority possessing compulsory purchase powers' see para 244 note 6 post.

10 Land Compensation Act 1961 s 35. Application for the certificate of value must be made to the Lands Tribunal registrar in writing, and the applicant must provide the registrar on his request with such information as may be required to enable the certificate to be given: Lands Tribunal Rules 1975, SI 1975/299, r 46. This provision is unlikely to undergo substantial alteration in the Lands Tribunal Rules 1996, which are expected to come into force in April 1996. At the date at which this volume states the law, those new rules were still in draft and the final text had not been settled. See further para 206 post.

11 Lands Tribunal Act 1949 s 1(5). The Arbitration Act 1950 only applies in so far as the rules so provide: see the Lands Tribunal Act 1949 s 3(8); the Interpretation Act 1978 s 17(2)(a); and the Lands Tribunal Rules 1975 r 38. Further, any agreement entered into before 1 January 1950 (ie the commencement date of the Lands Tribunal Act 1949) which provides for referring any matter to arbitration by a person or one or more persons selected as mentioned in note 3 supra has effect, subject to any subsequent agreement, as if it provided for referring the matter to arbitration by the Lands Tribunal: s 1(5). Where the tribunal is acting as arbitrator under a reference by consent, the following sections of the Arbitration

Act 1950 apply (in addition to those referred to in para 208 note 10 post): ss 1, 2, 3, 4(1), 5, 18(3), (4), 24(2), (3) and 27: Lands Tribunal Rules 1975 r 38. The Lands Tribunal Rules 1996, which are expected to come into force in April 1996, are likely to apply, additionally, the Arbitration Act 1950 s 19A (as added) (power to award interest: see ARBITRATION vol 2 (Reissue) para 687). At the date at which this volume states the law, those new rules were still in draft and the final text had not been settled. See further para 206 note 3 post.

12 *Mountgarret (Rt Hon Viscount) v Claro Water Board* (1963) 15 P & CR 53, Lands Tribunal. This limitation might not apply where there is a reference by consent under the Lands Tribunal Act 1949 s 1(5). For other limitations see *Williams v Secretary of State for the Environment* (1976) 33 P & CR 131, Lands Tribunal (prior agreement between parties as to amount of compensation); cf *Cadwallader v Rochdale Metropolitan Borough Council* (1977) 19 RVR 302, Lands Tribunal. The tribunal will not investigate a solicitor's express instructions to reach agreement to settle: *Harford v Birmingham City Council* (1993) 66 P & CR 468, Lands Tribunal. Where land is owned by two or more persons jointly, any claim must be pursued by all the joint owners: *Williams v British Gas Corpn* (1980) 41 P & CR 106, Lands Tribunal. The tribunal has jurisdiction to determine a claim for compensation arising from the withdrawal of a notice to treat notwithstanding that the claimant had already recovered the expense of his professional fees in the county court: *Williams v Blaenau Gwent Borough Council* (1994) 67 P & CR 393, Lands Tribunal.

204. Power to add to jurisdiction of Lands Tribunal. Questions which are required or authorised by an Act (including a local or private Act)[1], or instrument made under any such Act, to be determined by any statutory tribunal[2] may be directed by Order in Council to be determined instead by the Lands Tribunal if it appears to Her Majesty: (1) that the questions are appropriate for the Lands Tribunal as involving valuation of land or for other reasons; and (2) that it is desirable to transfer the jurisdiction to determine those questions from the first-mentioned tribunal to the Lands Tribunal either (a) to promote uniformity of decision; or (b) to use economically the services of those having experience in the valuation of land or other special qualifications; or (c) to make possible the winding up of a statutory tribunal having little work to do[3]. Jurisdiction conferred on a tribunal by or under an Act passed after the Lands Tribunal Act 1949 may be so transferred unless the Act conferring the jurisdiction contains a direction to the contrary[4]; but where the jurisdiction is first conferred on a tribunal by or under an Act so passed, heads (a) and (b) above do not apply[5].

The Order in Council transferring jurisdiction may contain supplementary and consequential provisions which appear to Her Majesty to be expedient, and any such provisions may be revoked or varied by a subsequent order or, if the order so provides, by rules made under the Lands Tribunal Act 1949[6]. Without prejudice to this power, the supplementary and consequential provisions must include provisions for:

(i) the enforcement of the tribunal's decisions in the same way as those of the statutory tribunal from which the jurisdiction is transferred[7];

(ii) the selection of members to deal with a case and for their sitting with assessors[8];

(iii) applying with or without modifications to the exercise of that jurisdiction by the Lands Tribunal, or repealing, any procedural provisions governing its exercise by the statutory tribunal[9]; and

(iv) preserving the effect of things done in or for the purpose of the exercise of that jurisdiction by the statutory tribunal[10].

Where the Lands Tribunal is exercising a jurisdiction so transferred to it, the statutory provisions as to procedure, appeals, costs and fees[11] have effect subject to the provisions of any Order in Council with respect to that jurisdiction[12].

The transfer of any jurisdiction to the Lands Tribunal by or under the Lands Tribunal Act 1949 does not affect the principles on which any question is to be determined or the persons on whom the determination is binding, or any provision which requires particular matters to be expressly dealt with or embodied in the determination, or which relates to evidence[13]; nor is the transfer[14] of any jurisdiction conferred on some other tribunal or person by an instrument made under any Act to be taken as affecting any power by virtue of which that instrument was made[15].

The Treasury may by regulations provide for the payment of compensation to persons suffering loss of office or employment, or loss or diminution of emoluments, attributable to the transfer of any jurisdiction to the Lands Tribunal[16]. Such regulations may provide for the manner in which, and the persons to whom, compensation claims are to be made, and for the determination of questions arising[17].

  1 As to local and private Acts see STATUTES vol 44(1) (Reissue) paras 1211–1213.
  2 For the meaning of 'statutory tribunal' see para 203 note 7 ante.
  3 Lands Tribunal Act 1949 s 4(1). See the Lands Tribunal (War Damage Appeals Jurisdiction) Order 1950, SI 1950/513; the Lands Tribunal (Statutory Undertakers Compensation Jurisdiction) Order 1952, SI 1952/161 (partly revoked by SI 1956/1734). As to the constitution of the Lands Tribunal see para 203 ante.
  4 Lands Tribunal Act 1949 s 4(2). Such Orders in Council are subject to annulment by resolution of either House of Parliament: s 4(6).
  5 Ibid s 4(2) proviso. Many later Acts have conferred jurisdiction on the Lands Tribunal for the purposes of those Acts; this jurisdiction is referred to elsewhere in this work in the titles relevant to that jurisdiction.
  6 Ibid s 4(3). Any power to make rules under the Lands Tribunal Act 1949 is exercisable by statutory instrument: s 8(3).
  7 Ibid s 4(4)(a).
  8 Ibid s 4(4)(b).
  9 Ibid s 4(4)(c).
 10 Ibid s 4(4)(d).
 11 Ie the provisions contained in ibid s 3 (as amended): see paras 205–206, 221, 225, 227, 231 post.
 12 Ibid s 4(5). As to the application of s 4 to Northern Ireland see s 9(1)–(3). The Lands Tribunal Act 1949 does not otherwise affect the law in force in Northern Ireland: s 9(1).
 13 Ibid s 7(1) (amended by the Land Compensation Act 1961 s 40(3), Sch 5). Nothing in the Lands Tribunal Act 1949 affects the operation of any enactment applying or giving power to apply the Acquisition of Land (Assessment of Compensation) Act 1919 (repealed) or any of its provisions in relation to the exercise of a jurisdiction not transferred by or under the 1949 Act, except that any enactment applying or giving power to apply the Acquisition of Land (Assessment of Compensation) Act 1919 s 5(2) (repealed) has like operation in relation to the Lands Tribunal Act 1949 s 5 (repealed): ss 7(3), 8(1).
 14 Ie by ibid s 1(4) (as amended) (see para 203 ante) or by an Order in Council under s 4 (see the text and notes 1–12 supra): s 7(2).
 15 Ibid s 7(2). The provision conferring that power accordingly has effect as from the transfer as if it directed the jurisdiction to be exercised by the Lands Tribunal as provided by or under the Lands Tribunal Act 1949, except in so far as provision to the contrary is thereafter made in pursuance of that power: s 7(2).
 16 Ibid s 6(1). Any compensation must be paid out of money provided by Parliament: s 6(3).
 17 Ibid s 6(2). Such regulations are not made by statutory instrument, and are not recorded in this work.

205. Selection of members of tribunal and assessors to hear reference. The jurisdiction of the Lands Tribunal[1] may be exercised by any one or more of its members, except when there is statutory provision to the contrary[2].

If it appears to the president that any case coming before the tribunal calls for special knowledge and that it would be desirable for the tribunal to be assisted by assessors, he may direct that it is to hear or determine the case with the aid of an assessor or of assessors appointed by him after any consultations he may think fit[3].

  1 As to the jurisdiction of the tribunal see paras 203–204 ante.
  2 Lands Tribunal Act 1949 s 3(1). References in the Lands Tribunal Act 1949 to the tribunal are to be construed accordingly: s 3(1). The president may select a member or members of the Lands Tribunal to

deal with a particular case or class or group of cases (s 3(2)(a)); or he may select for a class or group of cases members from amongst whom a member or members to deal with any particular case are to be selected, in which case the selection from amongst those members of a member or members to deal with a particular case is to be made either by the president or, if he so directs, by one of those members appointed by him to be chairman (s 3(2)(b)). Section 3(2) applies to the selection of a member of the tribunal appointed as a surveyor for the purposes of s 1(6) (as amended) (see para 200 ante) as if the case were one to be dealt with by the tribunal: s 3(2). The president may, however, at any time substitute another member for any other previously selected to hear a case, or vary the members selected for any group or class: Lands Tribunal Rules 1975, SI 1975/299, r 31(1). Where he has appointed any member as chairman of the members selected for any group or class of cases, that chairman may exercise the same power of substituting one member for another previously selected as the tribunal, or as a member of the tribunal, to hear a case in that class or group of cases: r 31(2). This provision is unlikely to undergo substantial alteration in the Lands Tribunal Rules 1996, which are expected to come into force in April 1996. At the date at which this volume states the law, those new rules were still in draft and the final text had not been settled. See further para 206 note 3 post. As to the president see para 202 ante.

3 Lands Tribunal Rules 1975 r 35(1) (amended by SI 1977/1820). The remuneration of an assessor so appointed is such as the president may determine with the approval of the Treasury: r 35(2); Transfer of Functions (Minister for the Civil Service and Treasury) Order 1981, SI 1981/1670, art 2(2). As to the power to make rules of procedure see para 206 post.

206. Rules of procedure. Proceedings before the Lands Tribunal are regulated by rules[1] made by the Lord Chancellor[2], which supplement the statutory provisions[3]. In so far as the rules regulate the fees chargeable in respect of proceedings before the tribunal[4] they are subject to the approval of the Treasury[5]. Such rules may in particular:

(1) make provision as to the form in which any decision of the tribunal is to be given, and as to the amendment of any such decision in pursuance of any directions which may be given by the Court of Appeal[6];

(2) make provision as to the time within which any proceedings before the tribunal are to be instituted and as to the evidence which may be required or admitted in any such proceedings[7];

(3) provide for the tribunal to be assisted by assessors when dealing with cases calling for special knowledge and, subject to the Treasury's approval, provide for making payments to the assessor as part of the tribunal's expenses[8];

(4) apply any of the provisions of the Arbitration Act 1950 in relation to the tribunal[9];

(5) allow the tribunal to determine cases without an oral hearing[10].

The rules must:

(a) require that the determination without an oral hearing of any disputed claim for compensation which is payable in respect of a compulsory acquisition of land, or depends directly or indirectly on the value of any land, is to require the consent of the person making the claim[11];

(b) provide for preserving, so far as appears to the Lord Chancellor to be practicable, the effect of things done before 1 January 1950 in or for the purposes of the exercise of any jurisdiction transferred[12] to the tribunal[13].

In addition to general procedural provisions the rules which have been made make special provision for particular aspects of the tribunal's jurisdiction[14]. The Interpretation Act 1978 applies to the interpretation of the rules as it applies to the interpretation of an Act of Parliament[15].

Any failure of any person to comply with the rules does not render the proceedings or anything done in pursuance of them invalid unless the president or the tribunal so directs[16].

1 Ie rules made under the Lands Tribunal Act 1949 s 3 (as amended) by statutory instrument and subject to the provisions of the 1949 Act: ss 3(6), 8(3).

2 See ibid s 3(11)(b).

3 In exercise of the rule-making power conferred by ibid s 3(11)(b), the Lord Chancellor has made the Lands Tribunal Rules 1975, SI 1975/299 (amended by SI 1977/1820; SI 1981/105; SI 1981/600; SI 1989/440; SI 1990/1382; modified by SI 1991/2684), which came into operation on 1 April 1975: r 1. See paras 199, 203–205, 208 ante, 208 et seq post. At the date at which this volume states the law, however, new rules and new fees rules were in preparation, both of which are expected to come into force in April 1996 as the Lands Tribunal Rules 1996 and the Lands Tribunal (Fees) Rules 1996, which will replace the Lands Tribunal Rules 1975 (as amended). Those new rules were still in draft and the final text had not been settled. The principal changes which are anticipated in the new rules are:

 (1) the introduction of a new simplified procedure in relation to compensation cases, to be applied where the claimant consents to its use;

 (2) a simplification of the procedure for the determination of proceedings without a hearing (see para 219 post);

 (3) the introduction of a power to award interest on compensation in all cases (see paras 203 note 11 ante, 226 post);

 (4) a substantial increase in fees as a result of the new fees rules;

 (5) more flexibility in the use of forms, which will no longer be prescribed in the rules, with one possible exception in relation to rights of light;

 (6) the strengthening of sanctions in the event of failure to pursue proceedings diligently or to comply with the rules, including in particular a power to strike out proceedings or to debar any party from taking any further part in them;

 (7) a new provision for solicitors to be placed formally on the record when acting for a party to proceedings with responsibility to the tribunal for fees; and

 (8) new express procedural powers to legitimate that which is already standard practice, eg the embodiment of the tribunal's decision in an order.

4 At the date at which this volume states the law, new fees rules were in preparation: see note 3 supra. As to costs see paras 227–229 post.

5 Lands Tribunal Act 1949 s 3(6).

6 Ibid s 3(6)(a)(i), (11)(a). See further paras 225, 232 post.

7 Ibid s 3(6)(a)(ii), (iii). See further para 208 et seq post.

8 Ibid s 3(6)(b) (amended by the Local Government, Planning and Land Act 1980 s 193, Sch 33 para 3). See para 205 ante.

9 Lands Tribunal Act 1949 s 3(6)(c); Arbitration Act 1950 s 44(3). See the Lands Tribunal Rules 1975 r 38; and paras 203 note 11 ante, 208 post. Where the tribunal acts as arbitrator, the Arbitration Act 1950 applies only in so far as it is so applied by the rules: Lands Tribunal Act 1949 s 3(8); Arbitration Act 1950 s 44(3).

10 Lands Tribunal Act 1949 s 3(6A) (s 3(6A)–(6C) (added by the Local Government, Planning and Land Act 1980 Sch 33 para 3). Where the tribunal determines a case without an oral hearing, the Lands Tribunal Act 1949 s 3(3) (see paras 200, 205 ante) applies subject to such modifications as may be prescribed by the rules: s 3(6C) (as so added).

11 Ibid s 3(6C) (as added: see note 10 supra). As to determinations without an oral hearing see para 219 post.

12 Ie transferred by the Lands Tribunal Act 1949: see para 203 ante.

13 Ibid s 3(10). For other transitional provisions see s 3(9); and for transitional provisions made by the existing rules see the Lands Tribunal Rules 1975 r 62(1). As to the expected replacement of those rules see note 3 supra.

14 This title sets out the effect of the general provisions and the provisions relating to compulsory acquisition: see paras 205 ante, 208 et seq post. As to the provisions relating to, eg, applications under the Law of Property Act 1925 s 84 (as amended) (relief from restrictive covenants affecting land) see EQUITY vol 16 (Reissue) para 806 et seq. As to the expected replacement of the existing provisions see note 3 supra.

15 Lands Tribunal Rules 1975 r 2(1); Interpretation Act 1978 s 17(2)(a). As to the rules of statutory interpretation laid down by the 1978 Act see STATUTES vol 44(1) (Reissue) para 1380 et seq.

16 Ibid r 60. The tribunal has power to correct clerical mistakes or errors arising from an accidental slip or an omission in an award: see r 38, applying the Arbitration Act 1950 s 17; and ARBITRATION vol 2 (Reissue) para 683. As to failure to comply with the rules see also note 3 head (6) supra.

207. Legal aid. Legal aid may be given in proceedings in the Lands Tribunal[1]; and in general the ordinary provisions as to legal aid[2] apply to applications for legal aid for proceedings in the tribunal and to the conduct of all proceedings in it for which a civil legal aid certificate is granted as they apply to applications for legal aid for, and the conduct of, proceedings in any court[3]. Powers in respect of legal aid to do any act or exercise any jurisdiction or discretion conferred on a court are exercisable, in Lands Tribunal proceedings, by the tribunal and, unless exercisable only during the hearing, may be exercised by the registrar[4].

1   Legal Aid Act 1988 s 14(1), Sch 2 Pt I para 4.
2   See the Civil Legal Aid (General) Regulations 1989, SI 1989/339 (as amended); and LEGAL AID vol 27(2) (Reissue) para 1896.
3   Ibid reg 148(2).
4   Ibid reg 148(3). As to the taxation of costs see para 228 post.

(ii) Notice of Reference

208. Notice of reference instituting proceedings. Proceedings for the determination of a reference[1] may be instituted by a person entitled under any enactment to do so, or, if there is no such person, by any person who wishes the reference to be determined, sending to the registrar[2] a notice of reference[3] together with sufficient copies for service upon every other party to the proceedings[4]. Where the question is one of compensation payable on the compulsory acquisition of land, the notice of reference must be accompanied by a copy of the notice to treat (if such notice has been served)[5] and of any notice of claim and any amendment delivered[6] to the acquiring authority[7]. In any other case, the notice of reference must be accompanied by a copy of the order, direction, notice, decision, authorisation or other document in consequence of which proceedings for the determination of the reference are instituted[8].

A notice of reference relating to the assessment of compensation on the compulsory acquisition of land may not be given before the expiration of 28 days from the date of service or constructive service of the notice to treat or, where no notice to treat is served or is deemed to be served, of the notice of claim[9].

Certain provisions of the Arbitration Act 1950 apply to all proceedings before the tribunal[10].

1   A 'reference' means any question, dispute or case determinable by the Lands Tribunal other than one to which the Lands Tribunal Rules 1975, SI 1975/299, Pts I–III (rr 3–14) (as amended) or Pts V–VI (rr 18–30) apply: rr 2(2), 15.
2   Any application or communication to be made to the president or to any member of the Lands Tribunal in respect of any case must be addressed to the registrar at the tribunal's office: ibid rr 2(2), 57(2). The office is at present situated at 48–49 Chancery Lane, London WC2A 1JR. For the meaning of 'the registrar' see para 199 note 8 ante.
3   At the date at which this volume states the law, the notice must be in the form prescribed by ibid r 16(1) (amended by SI 1981/600), Sch 1, Form 4 or Form 4A as may be appropriate: see r 16(1) (as so amended), Sch 1 (amended by SI 1989/440). For the prescribed fee at the date at which this volume states the law see r 61(1), Sch 2 (substituted by SI 1990/1382). The Lands Tribunal Rules 1996, which are expected to come into force in April 1996, will no longer prescribe forms; and new fees rules are expected to be made which will come into force on the same date. At the date at which this volume states the law, those new rules were still in draft and the final text had not been settled. See further para 206 note 3 ante.
4   Lands Tribunal Rules 1975 r 16(1) (as amended: see note 3 supra).
5   As to service of the notice to treat see para 100 et seq ante.
6   Ie in pursuance of the Land Compensation Act 1961 s 4: see paras 198–199 ante.
7   Lands Tribunal Rules 1975 r 16(2)(i). For the meaning of 'acquiring authority' see para 120 note 5 ante.
8   Ibid r 16(2)(ii). A new simplified procedure in compensation cases is expected to be introduced in April 1996, to apply where the claimant consents to its use: see para 206 note 3 head (1) ante.

9 Ibid r 16(3).
10 See ibid r 38 which applies the following provisions of the Arbitration Act 1950: s 12 (as amended) (conduct of proceedings: see para 222 post), s 14 (interim awards: see para 225 post), s 17 (correction of slips: see para 225 post), s 18(5) (charge on property for solicitor's costs: see para 229 post), s 20 (subject to any enactment which prescribes a rate of interest) (interest on awards: see para 226 post) and s 26 (as substituted) (enforcement of award: see para 230 post). Additional provisions are applied where the tribunal is acting as an arbitrator under a reference by consent: see para 203 note 11 ante. See also para 206 note 3 head (3) ante.

209. Entry, withdrawal and dismissal of references. Upon receiving a notice of reference[1] the registrar[2] of the Lands Tribunal must (1) enter particulars of the reference in the register of references; and (2) send[3] a copy of the notice to every party to the proceedings (other than the party instituting the proceedings) and inform the parties of the number of the reference, which thereafter constitutes the title of the proceedings[4].

A reference[5] may be withdrawn by sending to the registrar a written notice of withdrawal signed by all the parties or by their solicitors or agents[6].

Where any party has failed to pursue any proceedings with due diligence or has failed to comply with any of the rules of procedure, the registrar may, after giving the parties an opportunity to be heard, make an order that the proceedings be heard by the tribunal or make such other order as may be appropriate for the purpose of expediting or disposing of the proceedings[7].

1 As to the notice of reference see para 208 ante; and for the meaning of 'reference' see para 208 note 1 ante.
2 For the meaning of 'the registrar' see para 199 note 8 ante.
3 Any notice or other document required or authorised to be served on any person for the purpose of the Lands Tribunal Rules 1975, SI 1975/299 (as amended), is deemed to have been duly served if sent by prepaid post to that person at his ordinary address or his address for service specified in any notice given under the rules; and any notice or other document required or authorised to be sent to the registrar must be sent to him at the tribunal's office: rr 2(2), 57(1). A party to any proceedings may change his address for service at any time by notice in writing to the registrar and to every other party to those proceedings: r 58.
    If any person to whom any notice or other document is required to be sent cannot be found, or has died and has no personal representative, or is out of the United Kingdom, or if for any other reason service upon him cannot readily be effected in accordance with the rules, the president or the tribunal may dispense with service upon him or may make an order for substituted service upon such other person or in such other form, whether by newspaper advertisement or otherwise, as the president or the tribunal may think fit: r 59. As to the president see para 202 ante; and for the meaning of 'United Kingdom' see para 100 note 21 ante. As to the expected replacement of the Lands Tribunal Rules 1975 (as amended) by new rules and new fees rules see para 206 note 3 ante. At the date at which this volume states the law, those new rules were still in draft and the final text had not been settled.
4 Ibid r 17.
5 This provision applies equally to an appeal or application: ibid r 51. An appellant or applicant may, at any time before the hearing of the proceedings, apply to the president for an order to dismiss the proceedings, and the president may make such order as may be just: ibid r 51(2). The provisions of r 45(2), (4), (5), (6) (see para 213 post) apply to an application for such an order to dismiss the proceedings with the substitution of references to the president for references to the registrar: r 51(3).
6 Ibid r 51(1). For these purposes, 'solicitor' includes a body corporate recognised by the Council of the Law Society under the Administration of Justice Act 1985 s 9 (as amended) (see SOLICITORS vol 44(1) (Reissue) para 383 et seq): see the Solicitors' Incorporated Practices Order 1991, SI 1991/2684, arts 2–5, Sch 1. Where a reference is conditionally withdrawn it is necessary for the tribunal to know the facts of the case, and so it may proceed to hear and determine the reference: *Perkins v Central Land Board* (1953) 4 P & CR 162, Lands Tribunal.
7 Lands Tribunal Rules 1975 r 51(4). Rule 45(8) (see para 213 post) applies to such an order of the registrar: r 51(5). These powers are expected to be strengthened in the Lands Tribunal Rules 1996, which are to come into force in April 1996: see para 206 note 3 head (6) ante. At the date at which this volume states the law, those new rules were still in draft and the final text had not been settled.

210. Consolidation of references etc. Where notices to treat have been served[1] for the acquisition of several interests in the land[2] to be acquired, then, if the acquiring authority[3] so desires, the disputed claims of the persons entitled to those interests must, so far as practicable, be heard and determined by the same member or members of the Lands Tribunal, but the value of the several interests must be separately assessed[4]. Where two or more notices of reference[5] have been given in respect of several interests in the same subject in dispute, an application may be made by any party to the proceedings that the references be heard together[6]. The president or the tribunal may also make an order that such references be consolidated or heard together without any application having been made in that behalf[7]. An order for consolidation may be made with respect to some only of the matters to which the notices of reference relate[8].

Where any question of disputed compensation under the Compulsory Purchase Act 1965 is referred to the tribunal, any related question concerning a disputed amount in respect of premises formerly used for the business of courts abolished by the Courts Act 1971[9] must, so far as practicable, be considered and disposed of by the tribunal on the same occasion[10].

1 As to the service of notices to treat see para 100 et seq ante.
2 For the meaning of 'land' see para 18 note 2 ante.
3 For the meaning of 'acquiring authority' see para 120 note 5 ante.
4 Land Compensation Act 1961 s 3. The Lord Chancellor may make rules under the Lands Tribunal Act 1949 providing that such claims are to be heard together: Land Compensation Act 1961 s 3. As to the general power to make procedural rules under the 1949 Act see para 206 ante; and as to the tribunal see paras 203–207 ante.
5 As to notices of reference see para 208 ante; and for the meaning of 'reference' see para 208 note 1 ante. This provision also applies where two or more notices of appeal have been given in respect of different lands or hereditaments raising the same issues: see the Lands Tribunal Rules 1975, SI 1975/299, r 36(2). Where more than one notice of appeal has been given in respect of the same land or hereditament, an application to the registrar in accordance with r 45 (see para 213 post) for an order that the appeals be consolidated may be made by any party to the appeals: r 36(1). For the meaning of 'the registrar' see para 199 note 8 ante. As to the expected replacement of the Lands Tribunal Rules 1975 (as amended) by new rules and new fees rules see para 206 note 3 ante. At the date at which this volume states the law, those new rules were still in draft and the final text had not been settled.
6 Ibid r 36(2).
7 Ibid r 36(3) (which also applies where any such notices of appeal as are referred to in r 36(1), (2) have been given: see r 36(3)).
8 Ibid r 36(4) (which also applies to notices of appeal: see r 36(4)).
9 Ie any dispute between a minister and a local authority as to whether any, and if so, what, amount is payable under the Courts Act 1971 s 28, Sch 3 (as amended): see COURTS.
10 Ibid Sch 3 para 10.
    Where two or more appeals against the decision of a valuation or community charge tribunal appear to the president to involve the same issues, he may, with the written consent of all parties, direct that one appeal, to be selected by him, will be heard in the first instance as a test case and that the parties to each appeal will, without prejudice to their right to require the Lands Tribunal to state a case for the decision of the Court of Appeal, be bound by the decision of the Lands Tribunal on the appeal so selected: Lands Tribunal Rules 1975 r 37 (amended by SI 1989/440). The community charge has now been abolished and replaced by council tax: see the Local Government Finance Act 1992 ss 1(1), 117(2), Sch 14. Valuation and community charge tribunals are now to be known as 'valuation tribunals': see s 15(1).

211. Disclosure of documents at registrar's request. The Lands Tribunal or, subject to any direction given by the tribunal, the registrar[1] may on the application of any party to the proceedings or of its or his own motion order any party:

(1) to deliver to the registrar any document or other information which the tribunal may require[2] and which it is in the power of the party to deliver[3];

(2) to afford to every other party to the proceedings an opportunity to inspect those documents or copies of them and to take copies[4];

(3) to deliver to the registrar an affidavit or make a list stating whether any document or class of document specified or described in the order or application is, or has at any time been, in his possession, custody or power, and stating when he parted with it[5];

(4) to deliver to the registrar a statement in the form of a pleading setting out further and better particulars of the grounds on which he intends to rely and any relevant facts or contentions[6];

(5) to answer interrogatories on affidavit relating to any matter at issue between the applicant and the other party[7]; or

(6) to deliver to the registrar a statement of agreed facts, facts in dispute and the issue or issues to be tried by the tribunal[8].

However, nothing in this provision must be deemed to require the furnishing of any information which it would be contrary to the public interest to disclose[9].

1 For the meaning of 'the registrar' see para 199 note 8 ante. As to the Lands Tribunal see paras 202–207 ante.

2 As to the tribunal's power to require documents not supplied see the Lands Tribunal Rules 1975, SI 1975/299, r 41; and para 220 post. Where an order is made in the case of proceedings other than those to which r 33A(5) (as added) (see para 219 post) applies, the tribunal or the registrar may give directions as to the time within which any document is to be sent to the registrar (being at least 14 days from the date of the direction) and the parties to whom copies of the document are to be sent: r 40(2) (r 40 substituted by SI 1981/105). The provisions of r 45 (see para 213 post) apply to r 40 (as so substituted) as appropriate to applications and in relation to cases where the registrar acts of his own motion: r 40(3) (as so substituted). As to the expected replacement of the Lands Tribunal Rules 1975 (as amended) by new rules and new fees rules see para 206 note 3 ante. At the date at which this volume states the law, those new rules were still in draft and the final text had not been settled.

3 Ibid r 40(1)(a) (as substituted: see note 2 supra).

4 Ibid r 40(1)(b) (as substituted: see note 2 supra).

5 Ibid r 40(1)(c) (as substituted: see note 2 supra).

6 Ibid r 40(1)(d) (as substituted: see note 2 supra).

7 Ibid r 40(1)(e) (as substituted: see note 2 supra).

8 Ibid r 40(1)(f) (as substituted: see note 2 supra).

9 Ibid r 40(1) proviso (as substituted: see note 2 supra). As to what documents are protected by the public interest from disclosure see DISCOVERY. The tribunal cannot require a person to produce any document or to answer any question which he would be entitled on the ground of privilege or confidentiality to refuse to produce or to answer if the proceedings were in a court of law: see *R v Lands Tribunal, ex p City of London Corpn* [1982] 1 All ER 892, [1982] 1 WLR 258, CA.

212. Consent orders. Where the parties to any proceedings have agreed upon the terms of any order to be made by the Lands Tribunal[1], particulars of the terms, signed by all the parties or their solicitors[2] or agents, must be sent to the registrar[3], and the order may be made by the tribunal in those terms in the absence of the parties[4].

1 As to the Lands Tribunal see paras 202–207 ante.

2 For these purposes, 'solicitor' includes a body corporate recognised by the Council of the Law Society under the Administration of Justice Act 1985 s 9 (as amended) (see SOLICITORS vol 44(1) (Reissue) para 383 et seq): see the Solicitors' Incorporated Practices Order 1991, SI 1991/2684, arts 2–5, Sch 1.

3 For the meaning of 'the registrar' see para 199 note 8 ante.

4 Lands Tribunal Rules 1975, SI 1975/299, r 55. For the prescribed fee at the date at which this volume states the law see r 61(1), Sch 2 (substituted by SI 1990/1382). As to the expected replacement of the Lands Tribunal Rules 1975 (as amended) by new rules and new fees rules see para 206 note 3 ante. At the date at which this volume states the law, those new rules were still in draft and the final text had not been settled.

(iii) Interlocutory Applications

213. Applications for directions. Unless otherwise ordered by the president, an application in Lands Tribunal proceedings for directions of an interlocutory nature for which the rules do not otherwise provide must be made to the registrar[1].

The application must be made in writing, stating the title of the proceedings and the grounds on which the application is made[2], and if made with the consent of all parties must be accompanied by consents signed by or on behalf of the parties[3]. If it is not made with the consent of every party, then before it is made a copy of the application must be served on every other party and the application must state that this has been done[4].

Any party who objects to the application may within seven days after service of a copy on him send a written notice of objection to the registrar and the applicant, and before making an order on the application the registrar must consider all the objections which he has received and, if any party wishes to appear before him, must give him and every other party an opportunity to do so[5].

The parties may appear on the application and be heard either in person or by counsel or solicitor or by any other person allowed by leave of the president or the registrar[6]. In dealing with any interlocutory application the registrar must have regard to the convenience of the parties and the desirability of limiting costs so far as practicable[7]. The registrar may, and must if the applicant or any party objecting to an application so requires[8], refer the application to the president for decision[9].

The registrar must communicate his decision on the application in writing to each party to it[10]. If any party is aggrieved by the registrar's decision he may appeal to the president by giving notice in writing to the registrar and to every other party within seven days after service on him of notice of the decision, or within such further time as the registrar may allow, but such an appeal does not act as a stay of proceedings unless the president so orders[11].

Where an application is made as respects a case included in a class or group of cases for special reference[12], or one for which a member or members of the tribunal has or have been selected, the president's powers and duties may be exercised and discharged in relation to the application by a member or members of the tribunal authorised in that behalf by the president[13].

1 Lands Tribunal Rules 1975, SI 1975/299, r 45(1). Application for an order for affidavit evidence is made to the president or the tribunal (see r 39(2); and para 217 post), and application for the disposal of a preliminary point of law is made to the president (see r 49(1); and para 216 post). Rule 45 applies to r 40 (as substituted) (see para 211 ante) as appropriate to applications and in relation to cases where the registrar acts of his own motion: see r 40(3) (as substituted); and para 211 note 2 ante. As to the expected replacement of the Lands Tribunal Rules 1975 (as amended) by new rules and new fees rules see para 206 note 3 ante. At the date at which this volume states the law, those new rules were still in draft and the final text had not been settled. As to the president see para 202 ante; and as to the tribunal see paras 202–207 ante. For the meaning of 'the registrar' see para 199 note 8 ante.
2 Ibid r 45(2). For a form of application see 24(2) Court Forms (2nd Edn) (1995 issue) 838, Form 17.
3 Lands Tribunal Rules 1975 r 45(3). For a form of consent see 24(2) Court Forms (2nd Edn) (1995 issue) 839, Form 18.
4 Lands Tribunal Rules 1975 r 45(4). As to service see para 209 note 3 ante.
5 Ibid r 45(5). For a form of objection see 24(2) Court Forms (2nd Edn) (1995 issue) 839, Form 19.
6 Lands Tribunal Rules 1975 r 44. 'Solicitor' in r 44 does not include a body corporate recognised by the Council of the Law Society under the Administration of Justice Act 1985 s 9 (as amended) (see SOLICITORS vol 44(1) (Reissue) para 383 et seq): see the Solicitors' Incorporated Practices Order 1991, SI 1991/2684, arts 2–5, Sch 1.
7 Ibid r 45(6). As to withdrawal of applications see r 51; and para 209 ante.
8 As to applications which must be made to the president see note 1 supra.
9 Lands Tribunal Rules 1975 r 45(7).

10 Ibid r 45(6).
11 Ibid r 45(8). For a form of notice of appeal to the president see 24(2) Court Forms (2nd Edn) (1995 issue) 840, Form 20.
12 Ie under the Lands Tribunal Act 1949 s 3(2): see para 205 ante.
13 Lands Tribunal Rules 1975 r 45(9).

214. Applications for extension of time. The time appointed[1] for doing any act or taking any steps in relation to any Lands Tribunal proceedings may be extended by the registrar[2] on application to him[3], upon such terms, if any, as the justice of the case may require; and an extension may be ordered even though the application is not made until after the expiration of the time appointed[4].

1 Ie by or under the Lands Tribunal Rules 1975, SI 1975/299 (as amended): see paras 199, 203 et seq ante, 215 et seq post. As to the expected replacement of the Lands Tribunal Rules 1975 (as amended) by new rules and new fees rules see para 206 note 3 ante. At the date at which this volume states the law, those new rules were still in draft and the final text had not been settled.
2 For the meaning of 'the registrar' see para 199 note 8 ante.
3 Ie under the Lands Tribunal Rules 1975, SI 1975/299, r 45: see para 213 ante.
4 Ibid r 48(1) (amended by SI 1981/105). The time appointed by r 11(1) for sending a statement of case and reply and the time appointed by r 42(4) (see para 223 post) for sending copies of documents to the registrar may, by consent of the parties and on written notification sent to the registrar and received by him before the expiration of the time appointed by the rules or fixed by a previous extension by consent, be extended for a period not exceeding two months on each notification and four months in aggregate: r 48(2).

215. Pre-trial review. The Lands Tribunal and, subject to any directions given by the tribunal, the registrar[1] may on the application of a party to the proceedings or of its or his own motion order a pre-trial review to be held on a day not less than 14 days after the making of the order unless the parties to the proceedings agree otherwise[2]. The registrar must send a notice to each party informing him of the place and date of the pre-trial review[3]. The provisions relating to interlocutory applications[4] have effect as if the pre-trial review were the hearing of an interlocutory application and accordingly the tribunal or the registrar may, of its or his own motion, exercise on the review any of the powers exercisable on an interlocutory application[5]. Where any party seeks a specific direction he must, so far as practicable, apply for it on the pre-trial review, giving notice of his intention to do so to the registrar and every other party[6]. On the pre-trial review the tribunal or the registrar must give all such directions as appear necessary or desirable for securing the just, expeditious and economical disposal of the proceedings[7]. In particular, the tribunal or registrar must endeavour on the pre-trial review to secure that the parties make all such admissions and agreements as ought reasonably to be made by them in relation to the proceedings and may record in the order made on the review any admission or agreement so made or any refusal to make one[8]. Where a party fails to appear on a pre-trial review, the tribunal or the registrar, after giving the parties an opportunity to be heard, may make such order as may be appropriate for the purpose of expediting or disposing of the proceedings[9].

1 For the meaning of 'the registrar' see para 199 note 8 ante.
2 Lands Tribunal Rules 1975, SI 1975/299, r 45A(1) (r 45A added by SI 1981/105). As to the tribunal see paras 202–207 ante. As to the expected replacement of the Lands Tribunal Rules 1975 (as amended) by new rules and new fees rules see para 206 note 3 ante. At the date at which this volume states the law, those new rules were still in draft and the final text had not been settled.
3 Ibid r 45A(1) (as added: see note 2 supra).
4 Ie the provisions in ibid r 45: see para 213 ante.

5 Ibid r 45A(5) (as added: see note 2 supra).
6 Ibid r 45A(4)(as added: see note 2 supra). If an application which might have been made on the review is made subsequently, the applicant must pay the costs of and occasioned by the application, unless the tribunal is of the opinion that there was sufficient reason for the application not having been made on the review: r 45A(4) (as so added).
7 Ibid r 45A(2) (as added: see note 2 supra). It is for the applicant to make his own case, therefore the tribunal will not order discovery from the district valuer to remedy a deficiency in the applicant's case. The test is whether it would be in the interests of securing a just, expeditious and economical disposal of the proceedings for the tribunal to require the records to be produced: see *Kingsley v IRC* [1987] 2 EGLR 217, Lands Tribunal.
8 Lands Tribunal Rules 1975 r 45A(3) (as added: see note 2 supra).
9 Ibid r 45A(6) (as added: see note 2 supra).

216. Applications for disposal of preliminary points of law. On the application of any party to proceedings before the Lands Tribunal, the president may order any point of law which appears to be in issue in the proceedings to be disposed of at a preliminary hearing before a member or members of the tribunal selected by the president for the purpose[1]. If in the opinion of such member or members the decision on the point of law substantially disposes of the proceedings, he or they may order that the argument is to be treated as the hearing of the case, or may make such other order as may seem just[2].

1 Lands Tribunal Rules 1975, SI 1975/229, r 49(1). The provisions of r 45(2)–(6) (see para 213 ante) apply to such an application with the substitution of references to the president for references to the registrar: r 49(2). For the meaning of 'reference' see para 208 note 1 ante. No application under r 49 should be made if there is a relevant and subsisting issue of fact between the parties, and one should only be made if the determination sought would dispense with a further hearing or at least with the determination of some substantial issue: *Lands Tribunal Practice Direction* (12 February 1987) (1987) 131 Sol Jo 254; see also *Western Steam Ship Co v Amaral Sutherland & Co Ltd* [1914] 3 KB 55, CA. As to the expected replacement of the Lands Tribunal Rules 1975 (as amended) by new rules and new fees rules see para 206 note 3 ante. At the date at which this volume states the law, those new rules were still in draft and the final text had not been settled. As to the tribunal see paras 202–207 ante; and as to the president see para 202 ante. For the meaning of 'the registrar' see para 199 note 8 ante.
  Occasionally, the preliminary determination of a question of fact or law might avoid or at least substantially reduce the potential costs of a reference; in such a case it is open to the parties jointly to apply for a split trial. Any such application should state the grounds upon which it is made and the precise question to be determined. However, no such application should be made in respect of matters which, by reason of the obscurity of the facts or the law, ought to be decided at the trial: *Lands Tribunal Practice Direction* supra; *Windsor Refrigerator Co Ltd v Branch Nominees Ltd* [1961] Ch 375, [1961] 1 All ER 277, CA.
2 Lands Tribunal Rules 1975 r 49(1). As to appeals on a point of law see the Lands Tribunal Act 1949 s 3(4) proviso; and para 231 post.

217. Applications as to evidence. Evidence before the Lands Tribunal may be given orally or, if the parties to the proceedings consent or the president or the tribunal so orders, by affidavit[1]. The tribunal may at any stage of the proceedings make an order requiring the personal attendance of any deponent for examination and cross-examination[2].

Application for leave to call more than one, or more than one additional, expert witness[3] may be made to the registrar as an interlocutory application[4] or may be made to the tribunal at the hearing[5].

1 Lands Tribunal Rules 1975, SI 1975/299, r 39(1). On an application to the president the provisions of r 45(2)–(6) (see para 213 ante) apply with the substitution of references to the president for references to the registrar: r 39(2). The registrar has the power to administer oaths and take affirmations for the

purpose of affidavits to be used in proceedings before the tribunal: r 47. As to the expected replacement of the Lands Tribunal Rules 1975 (as amended) by new rules and new fees rules see para 206 note 3 ante. At the date at which this volume states the law, those new rules were still in draft and the final text had not been settled. As to the tribunal see paras 202–207 ante; and as to the president see para 202 ante. For the meaning of 'the registrar' see para 199 note 8 ante.

2   Ibid r 39(1). Where an affidavit has been produced by consent in evidence or by order of the president, the tribunal may at any stage order the personal attendance of the deponent: *Mahboob Hussain v Oldham Metropolitan Borough Council* (1981) 42 P & CR 388, Lands Tribunal.

3   As to expert evidence generally see the Lands Tribunal Rules 1975 r 42 (as amended); and para 223 post.

4   Ie in accordance with the provisions of ibid r 45: see para 213 ante.

5   Ibid r 42(3). It is not necessary to obtain leave to call a witness who, although qualified as an expert, will give evidence only of comparable prices. If he is not to be asked to express his opinion his evidence is evidence of fact only, and he is not an expert for the purpose of r 42.

(iv) The Hearing

218. Place and notification of hearing. The Lands Tribunal[1] sits at such places in England and Wales as the president may from time to time determine[2]. The registrar[3] must send to each party to the proceedings before the tribunal a notice informing him of the place and date of the hearing[4], which, unless the parties otherwise agree, must be not earlier than 14 days after the date on which the notice is sent[5]. Upon receiving notice of intention to appear from a person who is not already a party to the proceedings, the registrar must send to that person a notice informing him of the place and date of the hearing[6]. Any person sent such a notice may apply to the registrar[7] for an alteration of the place or date of hearing[8].

The tribunal sits in public[9] unless it is determining an appeal, reference or application without a hearing[10] or it is acting as an arbitrator under a reference[11] by consent[12].

1   As to the selection of a tribunal to hear a reference see para 205 ante.

2   Lands Tribunal Rules 1975, SI 1975/299, r 32(1). As to the expected replacement of the Lands Tribunal Rules 1975 (as amended) by new rules and new fees rules see para 206 note 3 ante. At the date at which this volume states the law, those new rules were still in draft and the final text had not been settled. As to the tribunal see paras 202–207 ante; and as to the president see para 202 ante.

3   For the meaning of 'the registrar' see para 199 note 8 ante.

4   Unless the context otherwise requires, any reference to the hearing of any proceedings includes the determination of proceedings without an oral hearing: Lands Tribunal Rules 1975 r 2(2A) (added by SI 1977/1820).

5   Ibid r 32(2). As to the hearing fee at the date at which this volume states the law see r 61, Sch 2, Fee 6 (substituted by SI 1990/1382); but see para 206 note 3 head (4) ante. As to service see para 209 note 3 ante.

6   Ibid r 32(3).

7   Ie in accordance with the provisions of ibid r 45: see para 213 ante.

8   Ibid r 32(4).

9   Land Compensation Act 1961 s 2(1), (2). This does not, however, prevent the determination of cases without an oral hearing pursuant to rules under the Lands Tribunal Act 1949: s 2(2) proviso (added by the Community Land Act 1975 s 58(2), Sch 10 para 4(1); and by virtue of the Local Government, Planning and Land Act 1980 s 193, Sch 33 para 5). See also the Lands Tribunal Rules 1975 r 33 (substituted by SI 1977/1820).

10   Ie in accordance with the provisions of Lands Tribunal Rules 1975 r 33A (as added) (see para 219 post): r 33 (as substituted: see note 9 supra).

11   For the meaning of 'reference' see para 208 note 1 ante.

12   Lands Tribunal Rules 1975 r 33 (as substituted: see note 9 supra). As to the tribunal's power to act as an arbitrator under a reference by consent see the Lands Tribunal Act 1949 s 1(5); and para 203 ante.

219. Contested proceedings without a hearing. The Lands Tribunal has power to determine any appeal, reference[1] or application without an oral hearing[2] and any party to any proceedings[3] may apply[4] to the registrar[5] for a direction that the tribunal must exercise this power[6]. An order must not be made on such an application in respect of any proceedings relating to the amount of compensation which is payable in respect of the compulsory acquisition of land or which depends directly or indirectly on the value of any land, without the consent signed by or on behalf of the person who is claiming such compensation[7]. After an order has been made that the tribunal will determine certain proceedings without an oral hearing, the tribunal may, of its own motion or on the application of any party to those proceedings, require any such party to furnish such statements of case, reply or further or better particulars as the tribunal may specify[8]; and any party to the proceedings may submit to the tribunal, in writing, representations which he wishes to be taken into consideration[9]. This procedure is likely to be simplified with effect from April 1996[10].

The tribunal may, at any time and for any reason, order that proceedings which it was in the process of deciding without an oral hearing must be heard, and therefore give directions for the disposal[11] of those proceedings[12].

1 For the meaning of 'reference' see para 208 note 1 ante.
2 Ie notwithstanding the provisions of the Lands Tribunal Rules 1975, SI 1975/299, r 39 as to oral evidence (see para 217 ante) and of r 44 (right of audience: see para 213 ante); but subject to r 33A(2) (r 33A added by SI 1977/1820) (see the text and note 7 infra): r 33A(1) (as so added).
3 Ie any proceedings instituted under the Lands Tribunal Rules 1975 (as amended): r 33A(1) (as added: see note 2 supra).
4 Ie in accordance with the provisions of ibid r 45: see para 213 ante.
5 For the meaning of 'the registrar' see para 199 note 8 ante.
6 Lands Tribunal Rules 1975 r 33A(1) (as added: see note 2 supra). As to the expected replacement of the Lands Tribunal Rules 1975 (as amended) by new rules and new fees rules see para 206 note 3 ante. At the date at which this volume states the law, those new rules were still in draft and the final text had not been settled. As to the tribunal see paras 202–207 ante.
7 Ibid r 33A(2) (as added: see note 2 supra); and see the Lands Tribunal Act 1949 s 3(6B) (as added); and para 206 ante.
8 Ibid r 33A(3) (as added: see note 2 supra). Any such statements etc, any representations made by any party (see the text and note 9 infra), and any document or other information required to be delivered by any party to any proceedings to which r 33A (as so added) applies in accordance with r 40 (as substituted) (see para 211 ante), must be sent to the registrar together with sufficient copies for all the other parties to the proceedings within 28 days of the order or requirement: r 33A(5) (as so added). Within seven days of receiving them, the registrar must send copies of them to every other party to the proceedings: r 33A(6) (as so added). If, after having received a copy of such statements etc, any party to the proceedings wishes to make any representations to the tribunal he may submit them in writing to the registrar within 28 days of receiving them, and r 33A(5), (6) (as so added) applies to such representations; but no party may make representations on more than one occasion in those proceedings except by the leave of the tribunal or registrar: r 33A(7) (as so added).
9 Ibid r 33A(4) (as substituted: see note 4 supra). If any party to any proceedings to which r 33A (as so added) applies intends to rely upon the evidence of an expert witness, then the provisions of r 42 (as amended) (see para 223 post) apply as if references therein to the calling of witnesses and the hearing of evidence were references to representations: r 33A(8) (as so added).
10 See para 206 note 3 head (2) ante.
11 Ie disposal in accordance with the Lands Tribunal Rules 1975 (as amended): r 33A(9) (as added: see note 2 supra).
12 Ibid r 33A(9) (as added: see note 2 supra). Rules 52, 53 (see paras 220–221 post) do not apply to any proceedings to which r 33A (as so added) applies (r 33A(10)(b) (as so added); and rr 6, 10, 11, 13 (as amended) are subject to certain modifications: see r 33A(10)(a) (as so added).

220. Failure to appear at hearing or to supply documents. If any party to a reference[1] does not appear at the time and place appointed for the hearing, the Lands

Tribunal may hear and determine the reference in his absence and may make such order as to costs as it thinks fit[2]. However, on an application by that party within seven days of the determination, the tribunal may set it aside on such terms as to costs or otherwise as it thinks fit, if it is satisfied that that party had sufficient reason for his absence[3].

If it appears to the tribunal that any party to proceedings before it has failed to send a copy of any document required to be sent to any other party or to the registrar[4], the tribunal may direct that a copy of the document be sent as may be necessary and that the further hearing[5] of the proceedings be adjourned, and may require the party at fault to pay any additional costs occasioned by the adjournment[6].

1   Ie a reference under the Lands Tribunal Rules 1975, SI 1975/299, Pt IV (rr 15–17) (as amended): see paras 208–209 ante. For the meaning of 'reference' see para 208 note 1 ante.
2   Ibid r 53. If the appellant or applicant does not appear on an appeal under Pts I–III (rr 3–14) (as amended) or an application under Pt V (rr 18–26), the tribunal may dismiss the appeal or application, and if any other party to those proceedings does not appear, the tribunal may likewise proceed in that party's absence: r 53. As to the expected replacement of the Lands Tribunal Rules 1975 (as amended) by new rules and new fees rules see para 206 note 3 ante. At the date at which this volume states the law, those new rules were still in draft and the final text had not been settled. As to the Lands Tribunal see paras 202–207 ante.
3   Ibid r 53 proviso. A dismissal (see note 2 supra) may also be set aside in this manner: r 53. Rule 53 does not apply to any proceedings to which r 33A (as added) applies: see para 219 note 12 ante.
4   As to copies of documents required to be sent to the registrar see ibid r 16; and para 208 ante. For the meaning of 'the registrar' see para 199 note 8 ante.
5   For the meaning of 'hearing' see para 218 note 4 ante.
6   Ibid r 41.

221. Right of audience; control of procedure. In any proceedings before the Lands Tribunal, any party may appear and be heard either in person, or by counsel or solicitor, or by any other person allowed by leave of the tribunal to appear instead of any party[1].

The party claiming compensation or the party to whom any rent or rentcharge requiring apportionment is payable must begin on a reference[2], and in any other case the party by whom the proceedings were instituted begins[3]. Subject to the rules of procedure and to any directions given by the president, the procedure at the hearing of any proceedings is such as the tribunal may direct[4].

Where a case is dealt with by two or more members of the tribunal, of whom one is the president, the president will preside; if he does not sit, the person selecting the members to sit[5] must nominate one of them to preside[6].

1   See the Lands Tribunal Rules 1975, SI 1975/299, r 44; and para 213 ante. As to the expected replacement of the Lands Tribunal Rules 1975 (as amended) by new rules and new fees rules see para 206 note 3 ante. At the date at which this volume states the law, those new rules were still in draft and the final text had not been settled. As to counsel's costs see para 227 post. As to representation in interlocutory proceedings see para 213 ante; and as to the tribunal see paras 202–207 ante.
2   Ie on a reference under the Lands Tribunal Rules 1975 Pt IV (rr 15–17) (as amended): see r 52(1)(ii). For the meaning of 'reference' see para 208 note 1 ante.
3   Ibid r 52(1)(ii). On an appeal under Pts I–III (rr 3–12) (as amended) the appellant begins, and on an application under Pts V, VI (rr 27–30), the applicant begins: r 52(1)(i), (iii).
4   Ibid r 52(2). Rule 52 does not apply to any proceedings to which r 33A (as added) applies: see para 219 ante. As to the president see para 202 ante.
5   See para 205 ante.
6   Lands Tribunal Act 1949 s 3(3)(a). Where the tribunal determines a case without an oral hearing in accordance with the Lands Tribunal Rules 1975 r 33A (as added) (see para 219 ante) the Lands Tribunal Act 1949 s 3(3) applies subject to such modifications as may be prescribed by the rules: s 3(6C) (added by the Local Government, Planning and Land Act 1980 s 193, Sch 33 para 3).

222. Evidence generally. Evidence before the Lands Tribunal may be given orally or, if the parties consent or the president of the tribunal so orders, by affidavit; but the tribunal may at any stage of the proceedings make an order requiring the personal attendance of any deponent for examination and cross-examination[1]. Subject to legal objection, parties to the reference[2], all persons claiming through them, and any witnesses must submit to be examined on oath or affirmation in relation to the matters in dispute and must produce before the tribunal all documents within their possession or power which may be required or called for and do all other things during the proceedings which the tribunal may require[3].

Any party to a reference may sue out a writ of subpoena ad testificandum or subpoena duces tecum, but no person may be compelled under any such writ to produce any document which he could not be compelled to produce on the trial of an action; and the High Court or a judge thereof may order that a writ of subpoena ad testificandum or of subpoena duces tecum issue to compel the attendance before the tribunal of a witness wherever he may be within the United Kingdom[4] or that a writ of subpoena ad testificandum issue to bring up a prisoner for examination before the tribunal[5]. Further, for the purpose of, and in relation to, a reference, the High Court has the same powers of making a wide variety of interlocutory orders[6] as it has for the purpose of and in relation to an action or matter in the High Court[7], although the power does not prejudice any power already vested in the tribunal in respect of those matters[8].

1 Lands Tribunal Rules 1975, SI 1975/299, r 39(1). As to the expected replacement of the Lands Tribunal Rules 1975 (as amended) by new rules and new fees rules see para 206 note 3 ante. At the date at which this volume states the law, those new rules were still in draft and the final text had not been settled. As to interlocutory applications for affidavit evidence see para 217 ante; as to the tribunal see paras 202–207 ante; and as to the president see para 202 ante.
2 For the meaning of 'reference' see para 208 note 1 ante.
3 Arbitration Act 1950 s 12(1), (2), applied by the Lands Tribunal Rules 1975 r 38. The tribunal has power to administer oaths to or take the affirmations of the parties and witnesses: Arbitration Act 1950 s 12(3).
4 Ibid s 12(4).
5 Ibid s 12(5).
6 These include orders in respect of security for costs, affidavit evidence, examination of witnesses out of court, including examination out of the jurisdiction, securing the amount in dispute, entry on land, interim injunctions and the appointment of a receiver: see ibid s 12(6)(a)–(h) (amended by the Courts and Legal Services Act 1990 ss 103, 125(7), Sch 20).
7 Arbitration Act 1950 s 12(6).
8 Ibid s 12(6) proviso.

223. Expert evidence. Not more than one expert witness on either side may be heard unless the Lands Tribunal otherwise directs, except that where the reference[1] includes a claim in respect of minerals, or disturbance of business, as well as in respect of land[2], one additional expert witness on either side on the value of the minerals or on the damage caused by disturbance may be allowed[3].

Application for leave to call more than one or more than one additional expert witness may be made to the tribunal as well as to the registrar[4] on an interlocutory application[5]. Where more than one party intends to call an expert witness, every such party must, within 28 days after being so requested by the registrar, lodge copies of certain documents relating to the evidence of his expert witness[6], with sufficient copies for service upon the other parties[7]. Within seven days after receiving these documents the registrar must send to each party copies of the documents supplied by the other party[8].

If an application for leave to call more than one, or more than one additional, expert witness is made at the hearing and is granted by the tribunal, or if at the hearing any party seeks to rely upon any plans, valuations or particulars which appear to the tribunal not to have been sent to the registrar in accordance with his request on granting leave[9], then the tribunal may adjourn the hearing on such terms as to costs or otherwise as it thinks fit[10].

Nothing in the Civil Evidence Act 1972 or in rules of court made under it[11] prevents expert evidence from being adduced before the tribunal by any party, notwithstanding that no application has been made to the tribunal for a direction as to the disclosure of that evidence to any other party to the proceedings[12].

1   For the meaning of 'reference' see para 208 note 1 ante.
2   For the meaning of 'land' see para 18 note 2 ante.
3   Land Compensation Act 1961 s 2(3); Lands Tribunal Rules 1975, SI 1975/299, r 42(2). Rule 42 (as amended) applies to any proceedings except appeals from decisions of valuation or community charge tribunals (now known as 'valuation tribunals': see para 210 note 10 ante) under Pt II (rr 9–11) (as amended) and applications for certificates under Pt VI (rr 27–30): r 42(1) (amended by SI 1989/440). As to the expected replacement of the Lands Tribunal Rules 1975 (as amended) by new rules and new fees rules see para 206 note 3 ante. At the date at which this volume states the law, those new rules were still in draft and the final text had not been settled. As to the tribunal see paras 202–207 ante.
    Where any party to any proceedings to which r 33A (as added) (see para 219 ante) applies intends to rely on expert evidence then the provisions of r 42 (as amended) apply as if references to the calling of witnesses and the hearing of evidence were references to representations: r 33A(8) (added by SI 1977/1820).
4   Ie in accordance with the provisions of ibid r 45: see para 213 ante. For the meaning of 'the registrar' see para 199 note 8 ante.
5   Lands Tribunal Rules 1975 r 42(3).
6   The documents which must be so sent to the registrar are (1) every plan and valuation of the land or hereditament which is the subject of the proceedings, including particulars and computations in support of any valuation, which it is proposed to put in evidence (ibid r 42(4)(i)); and (2) either a statement of any prices, costs or other particulars and any plans relating to any other property which are proposed to be given in evidence in support of any such valuation, or a statement that no such prices, costs, particulars or plans will be relied on (r 42(4)(ii)).
    Although an expert may in evidence express his opinion on values he cannot give hearsay evidence as to the facts of transactions which lie outside his personal knowledge: *English Exporters (London) Ltd v Eldonwall Ltd* [1973] Ch 415, [1973] 1 All ER 726.
7   Lands Tribunal Rules 1975 r 42(4). This provision must be strictly complied with: *St Albans City Council v St Albans Waterworks Co and Clare (Valuation Officer)* (1954) 47 R & IT 191, Lands Tribunal.
8   Lands Tribunal Rules 1975 r 42(5). As to the service of documents see para 209 note 3 ante.
9   Ie in accordance with ibid r 42 (as amended): see the text and notes 1–8 supra.
10   Ibid r 42(6) (amended by SI 1981/105).
11   For the rules so made see RSC Ord 38 rr 7, 33, 35–44; CCR Ord 20 rr 25–28.
12   Lands Tribunal Rules 1975 r 39(3).

224. View of the land. A member of the Lands Tribunal dealing with the proceedings is entitled to enter on and inspect any land[1] which is the subject of them[2]. When the tribunal intends to enter on any premises it must give notice to the parties of its intention to do so and the parties are entitled to attend the inspection[3].

1   For the meaning of 'land' see para 18 note 2 ante.
2   Land Compensation Act 1961 s 2(4); Lands Tribunal Rules 1975, SI 1975/299, r 34. It is, however, wrong for the member of the tribunal himself to view the site and carry out his own experiments and thus give evidence to himself without such evidence being tested by the parties: *Hickmott v Dorset County Council* (1977) 35 P & CR 195, [1977] 2 EGLR 15, CA. As to the expected replacement of the Lands Tribunal Rules 1975 (as amended) by new rules and new fees rules see para 206 note 3 ante. At the date at which this volume states the law, those new rules were still in draft and the final text had not been settled.

3 Lands Tribunal Rules 1975 r 34(2). As to service of the notice see para 209 note 3 ante. The provisions of r 34 apply, so far as practicable, to any comparable land or hereditament to which the attention of the tribunal is directed as they apply to the land or hereditament which is the subject of the proceedings: r 34(3).

(v) Decision and Award

225. The tribunal's decision. The Lands Tribunal may, if it thinks fit, make an interim award[1]. In the event of a difference between the members dealing with the case, the decision is by a majority, and in the event of equality the person presiding[2] is entitled to a second or casting vote[3].

The tribunal's decision on a reference[4] is normally given in writing, together with a statement of the tribunal's reasons for its decision[5].

On the application of either party, the tribunal must specify the amount awarded in respect of any particular matter which is the subject of the award[6]. Where an amount awarded or value determined by the tribunal is dependent upon its decision on a question of law which is in dispute in the proceedings, the tribunal must ascertain, and state in its decision, the alternative amount or value, if any, which it would have awarded or determined if it had decided otherwise on the question of law[7].

The registrar[8] must send copies of the decision or, where the decision was given orally, a statement of its effect, to every party who has appeared before the tribunal[9]. A decision of the tribunal is final[10], subject to a right of appeal by way of case stated[11].

The tribunal has power to correct in an award any clerical mistake or error arising from any accidental slip or omission[12].

1 Arbitration Act 1950 s 14; applied by the Lands Tribunal Rules 1975, SI 1975/299, r 38. Any reference in the Arbitration Act 1950 Pt I (ss 1–34) (as amended) to an award includes a reference to an interim award: s 14. As to the expected replacement of the Lands Tribunal Rules 1975 (as amended) by new rules and new fees rules see para 206 note 3 ante. At the date at which this volume states the law, those new rules were still in draft and the final text had not been settled. As to the tribunal see paras 202–207 ante.

2 As to the person presiding see para 221 ante.

3 Lands Tribunal Act 1949 s 3(3)(b).

4 For the meaning of 'reference' see para 208 note 1 ante.

5 Tribunals and Inquiries Act 1992 s 10(1), Sch 1 para 27; Lands Tribunal Rules 1975 r 54(1) (which also applies to a decision on an appeal or application). The tribunal may only give its decision and reasons orally where it is satisfied that no injustice or inconvenience to the parties would be occasioned by its doing so (r 54(1) proviso). The tribunal may not make an award on a basis not relied on by either of the parties: *Aquilina v Havering London Borough Council* (1992) 66 P & CR 39, CA. The statement of reasons will be part of the 'speaking' record for the purposes of any case stated: *R v Northumberland Compensation Appeal Tribunal, ex p Shaw* [1952] 1 KB 338, [1952] 1 All ER 122, CA. To be adequate, reasons must not only be intelligible but must also deal with the substantial points which have been raised: *Re Poyser and Mills' Arbitration* [1964] 2 QB 467, [1963] 1 All ER 612. The Lands Tribunal should not regard itself as bound by its earlier decisions on points of law: *West Midland Baptist (Trust) Association (Inc) v Birmingham Corpn* [1968] 2 QB 188, [1968] 1 All ER 205, CA; affd sub nom *Birmingham Corpn v West Midland Baptist (Trust) Association (Inc)* [1970] AC 874, [1969] 3 All ER 172, HL.

On an appeal against a decision of a valuation or community charge tribunal (now known as a 'valuation tribunal': see para 210 note 10 ante), the Lands Tribunal must, if the appeal is a rating appeal, give such directions with respect to the manner in which the hereditament in question is to be treated in the valuation list as appear to the tribunal to be necessary to give effect to the contention of the appellant, if and so far as that contention appears to the tribunal to be well founded: Lands Tribunal Rules 1975 r 54(2)(i) (r 54(2) amended by SI 1989/440). If the appeal is a drainage rates appeal, the tribunal must quash the determination to which the appeal relates, alter the determination in such a manner as it thinks just or dismiss the appeal: r 54(2)(ii) (as so amended).

6 Land Compensation Act 1961 s 2(5).

7 Lands Tribunal Rules 1975 r 54(3).

8 For the meaning of 'the registrar' see para 199 note 8 ante.
9 Lands Tribunal Rules 1975 r 54(4). As to the power to embody the decision in an order, which is expected to be formalised in April 1996, see para 206 note 3 head (8) ante. As to the service of documents see para 209 note 3 ante. In the case of an appeal against the decision of a valuation tribunal, copies must be sent to the clerk of the local valuation panel from which that tribunal was constituted and, if the appeal is a rating appeal, to the valuation officer: r 54(4)(i) (which refers to a 'local valuation court'; this phrase in r 54(2) was amended to read 'valuation or community charge tribunal': see note 5 supra). In the case of an appeal under Pt III (rr 12–14) (as amended), copies must be sent to the court, authority or person from whose decision the appeal was brought: r 54(4)(ii).
   If any directions for amendment of the tribunal's decision are given by the Court of Appeal on any case stated, the amendment must be made by the tribunal accordingly and the registrar must send copies of the amended decision to all persons to whom copies of the original decision were sent: r 54(5).
10 Lands Tribunal Act 1949 s 3(4). Once a decision has been given the tribunal is *functus officio* and cannot subsequently give a direction as to interest payable on the compensation awarded: *Merediths Ltd v LCC (No 2)* (1957) 9 P & CR 258, Lands Tribunal.
11 See para 231 post.
12 Arbitration Act 1950 s 17; applied by the Lands Tribunal Rules 1975 r 38. An interim award may be corrected under the slip rule: *Craske v Norfolk County Council* [1991] 1 EGLR 221, Lands Tribunal.

226. Interest on awards. Where statute provides for interest to be payable on awards, the Lands Tribunal may, if it thinks fit, direct that any sum awarded by it should carry interest from the date of the award at such rate as may from time to time be prescribed[1] by regulations made by the Treasury[2]. If entry has been made before the date of the award, interest on the award will be payable from the date of entry[3]. There is no general jurisdiction[4] of the Lands Tribunal to award interest on compensation before the date of the award[5]; but the Secretary of State has power to make orders[6] providing that compensation payable under the statutory provisions named therein is to carry interest at the prescribed rate[7].

1 Ie prescribed by the Land Compensation Act 1961 s 32: see para 125 note 5 ante.
2 See the Acquisition of Land (Rate of Interest after Entry) Regulations 1995, SI 1995/2262; and para 125 ante. See also the Arbitration Act 1950 s 20 (applied, subject to any enactment which prescribes a rate of interest) by the Lands Tribunal Rules 1975 r 38); and the Judgment Debts (Rate of Interest) Order 1993, SI 1993/564. Application must be made at the time of the award, and the direction must be embodied in the decision: *Merediths Ltd v LCC (No 2)* (1957) 9 P & CR 258, Lands Tribunal. At the date at which this volume states the law, there was no inherent jurisdiction to award interest and, where the Lands Tribunal is acting as an arbitrator, there was no power to award interest because the Arbitration Act 1950 s 19A (as added) had not been applied to the Lands Tribunal by the Lands Tribunal Rules 1975, SI 1971/299, r 38 (see *St John's College, Oxford v Thames Water Authority* [1990] 1 EGLR 229, Lands Tribunal); but this position is expected to change in April 1996 (see para 206 note 3 head (3) ante). As to the expected replacement of the Lands Tribunal Rules 1975 (as amended) by new rules and new fees rules see para 206 note 3 ante. At the date at which this volume states the law, those new rules were still in draft and the final text had not been settled.
3 See the Lands Clauses Consolidation Act 1845 s 85 (as amended); the Compulsory Purchase Act 1965 s 11(1), (2) (as amended), Sch 3 para 3; and paras 123, 129 ante.
4 Ie under the Law Reform (Miscellaneous Provisions) Act 1934 s 3(1): see COUNTY COURTS vol 10 para 406.
5 *British Coal Corpn v Gwent County Council* (1995) Times, 18 July, CA. If, however, the Lands Tribunal has concurrent jurisdiction with some other tribunal and that other tribunal has the power to award interest, the Lands Tribunal has a similar power: *Knibb v National Coal Board* [1987] QB 906, [1986] 3 All ER 644, CA.
6 Any such order must be made by statutory instrument which is subject to annulment in pursuance of a resolution of either House of Parliament: Planning and Compensation Act 1991 s 80(5).
7 See ibid s 80(1), (4). At the date at which this volume states the law, no such order had been made.

227. Costs. The costs of and incidental to any proceedings before the Lands Tribunal are in the tribunal's discretion[1], except that (1) where an unconditional offer in writing to pay compensation has been made and the award does not exceed the offer, or a claimant has failed to make his claim in time to allow the acquiring authority[2] to make a proper offer, the tribunal must, unless for special reasons it thinks it proper not to do so, order the claimant to bear his own costs and pay the authority's costs incurred after the offer was made or, as the case may be, after the time when, in the tribunal's opinion, the claim should have been made[3]; and (2) where an unconditional offer to accept compensation has been made and the award exceeds the offer, the tribunal must, unless for special reasons it thinks it proper to do so, order the acquiring authority to bear its own costs and pay the claimant's costs incurred after the offer was made[4]. The registrar[5] may make a recommendation to the tribunal as to the award of costs in respect of any application or proceedings heard by him[6]. Any party dissatisfied with such a recommendation may, within ten days of it, appeal to the tribunal or, where no member has been selected[7] as respects the proceedings, to the president against the recommendation and the tribunal or, as the case may be, the president may make an order as it or he thinks just, including an order as to the payment of the costs of the appeal[8].

The tribunal may order that the costs incurred by any party be paid by any other party[9]. It may in any case before it disallow the costs of counsel[10]. Where the tribunal gives a final decision in writing, the decision must contain, in addition to any direction as to costs, a direction that the costs of any legally assisted person be taxed under the Legal Aid Act 1988[11].

1 Lands Tribunal Rules 1975, SI 1975/299, r 56(1). As to the expected replacement of the Lands Tribunal Rules 1975 (as amended) by new rules and new fees rules see para 206 note 3 ante. At the date at which this volume states the law, those new rules were still in draft and the final text had not been settled. The discretion to award costs must be exercised judicially: see *Gray v Lord Ashburton* [1917] AC 26, HL; *Bradshaw v Air Council* [1926] Ch 329 at 336; *Lloyd del Pacifico v Board of Trade* (1930) 46 TLR 476 at 477; *P Rosen & Co Ltd v Dowley and Selby* [1943] 2 All ER 172; *Wootton v Central Land Board* [1957] 1 All ER 441, [1957] 1 WLR 424, CA; *Church Cottage Investments Ltd v Hillingdon London Borough Council (No 2)* [1991] 2 EGLR 13, CA. Reasons should be given for any departure from the usual rule that costs follow the event: see *Pepys v London Transport Executive* [1975] 1 All ER 748, [1975] 1 WLR 234, CA. As to the tribunal see paras 202–207 ante.
2 For the meaning of 'acquiring authority' see para 120 note 5 ante.
3 See the Lands Tribunal Rules 1975 r 56(1), excepting cases to which the Land Compensation Act 1961 s 4(1), (2) (see paras 198–199 ante) applies.
4 See the Lands Tribunal Rules 1975 r 56(1), excepting cases to which the Land Compensation Act 1961 s 4(3) (see para 199 ante) applies. For a case where the award was above both parties' respective sealed offers see *Toye v Kensington and Chelsea Royal London Borough* [1994] 1 EGLR 204, Lands Tribunal.
5 For the meaning of 'the registrar' see para 199 note 8 ante.
6 Lands Tribunal Rules 1975 r 56(1A) (added by SI 1981/105).
7 As to the selection of members of the tribunal see para 205 ante.
8 Lands Tribunal Rules 1975 r 56(1B) (as added: see note 6 supra). As to the president see para 202 ante.
9 Lands Tribunal Act 1949 s 3(5). As to costs on a reference by a returned absent owner see para 200 note 15 ante. Legal and accountancy costs, like surveyors' and valuers' fees, are recoverable as part of the substantive compensation: see *LCC v Tobin* [1959] 1 All ER 649, [1959] 1 WLR 354, CA. For costs awarded against claimants see *Armstrong v Minister of Transport* (1951) 2 P & CR 36, Lands Tribunal; *Fooks v Minister of Supply* (1951) 2 P & CR 102, Lands Tribunal; *Ford v Hartley Wintney RDC* (1951) 2 P & CR 99, Lands Tribunal; and *Church Cottage Investments Ltd v Hillingdon London Borough Council (No 2)* [1991] 2 EGLR 13, CA. As to calculation of surveyors' fees see *Truman v Chatham Borough Council* (1974) 28 P & CR 326, Lands Tribunal.
    Where any costs of a litigant in person are ordered to be paid by any other party to the proceedings or in any other way, there may, subject to the Lands Tribunal Rules 1975 (as amended), be allowed on the taxation or other determination of those costs sums in respect of any work done, and any expenses and losses incurred, by the litigant in or in connection with the proceedings before the Lands Tribunal to which the order relates: see the Litigants in Person (Costs and Expenses) Act 1975 s 1(1)(b), (4)(a). As to the taxation of costs generally see para 228 post.
10 Land Compensation Act 1961 s 4(4).

11 See the Civil Legal Aid (General) Regulations 1989, SI 1989/339, reg 148(4); and LEGAL AID vol 27(2) (Reissue) para 1896.

228. Taxation of costs. The Lands Tribunal may order that the costs of any proceedings before it incurred by any party are to be paid by any other party and the tribunal may tax or settle the amount of any costs to be paid under any such order or direct in what manner they are to be taxed[1]. Thus it may settle the amount of the costs by fixing a lump sum or may direct that costs be taxed by the registrar[2] on a scale specified by the tribunal, being a scale prescribed by the Rules of the Supreme Court or by the County Court Rules[3].

If any party is dissatisfied with a taxation of costs directed by the tribunal, he may within seven days of the taxation serve on the registrar and any other interested party an objection in writing, specifying the items objected to and the grounds of the objection and applying for the taxation to be reviewed in respect of those items[4]. On such an application the registrar must review the taxation of the items objected to and state in writing the reasons for his decision[5].

Any party dissatisfied with the registrar's decision given on the review may, within ten days of the decision, apply to the president to review the taxation, and the president may thereupon make such order as he thinks just, including an order as to the payment of the costs of the review; but otherwise the taxation by the registrar is final in respect of all matters to which objection has not been taken[6].

1 Lands Tribunal Act 1949 s 3(5).
2 For the meaning of 'the registrar' see para 199 note 8 ante.
3 Lands Tribunal Rules 1975, SI 1975/299, r 56(2). As to the expected replacement of the Lands Tribunal Rules 1975 (as amended) by new rules and new fees rules see para 206 note 3 ante. At the date at which this volume states the law, those new rules were still in draft and the final text had not been settled. As to the taxation of costs of a legally assisted person (within the meaning of the Legal Aid Act 1988) see the Civil Legal Aid (General) Regulations 1989, SI 1989/339, reg 148(3), (4); and LEGAL AID vol 27(2) (Reissue) para 1896.
4 Lands Tribunal Rules 1975 r 56(3).
5 Ibid r 56(4).
6 Ibid r 56(5). As to the president see para 202 ante. It has been held that the president will only review the taxation by the registrar if it is shown that the registrar has erred on some question of principle; he will not review it on the ground of amount only: see *Tollemache v Richmond Borough Council* (1953) 4 P & CR 144, Lands Tribunal, applying the principles as to reviews of taxation in the High Court, as to which see *Coon v Diamond Tread Co (1938) Ltd* [1950] 2 All ER 385; read in the light of and qualified by the note on that case in [1956] 1 All ER 609n. However, whilst it is clear that the old limitations in respect of the review of costs by the High Court have been applied to the Lands Tribunal, it is not clear whether the Lands Tribunal has moved towards the current High Court practice which is that there is a discretion to reconsider the taxation afresh: see *Madurasinghe v Penguin Electronics* [1993] 3 All ER 20, [1993] 1 WLR 989, CA.

229. Recovery of costs. Where the Lands Tribunal orders the claimant to pay the costs, or any part of the costs, of the acquiring authority[1], the acquiring authority may deduct the amount so payable from the compensation payable to the claimant[2]; and, without prejudice to any other method of recovery, costs or any part of the costs not covered by the deduction may be recovered by the authority from him summarily as a civil debt[3]. The High Court has power to charge the land for the payment of solicitor's costs[4]. The right to costs is independent of the conveyance of the land, and a claimant in good faith may recover them, even though he is unable to make a good title[5].

1 For the meaning of 'acquiring authority' see para 120 note 5 ante.

2 Land Compensation Act 1961 s 4(5).

3 Ibid s 4(6).

4 See the Solicitors Act 1974 s 73(1) (as applied by the Arbitration Act 1950 s 18(5); and by virtue of the Lands Tribunal Rules 1975, SI 1975/299, r 38; and the Interpretation Act 1978 s 17(2)(a)); and SOLICITORS vol 44(1) (Reissue) para 243 et seq. As to the expected replacement of the Lands Tribunal Rules 1975 (as amended) by new rules and new fees rules see para 206 note 3 ante. At the date at which this volume states the law, those new rules were still in draft and the final text had not been settled.

5 *Capell v Great Western Rly Co* (1883) 11 QBD 345, CA. The vendor has no lien in respect of these costs: *Earl of Ferrers v Stafford and Uttoxeter Rly Co* (1872) LR 13 Eq 524.

230. Enforcement of decision. By leave of the High Court or a judge thereof an award of the Lands Tribunal may be enforced in the same manner as a judgment or order and, where leave is given, judgment may be entered in the terms of the award[1]. However, it is unlikely that leave would be given where a question of title was raised. In such circumstances the appropriate course would be to bring an action to enforce the award[2].

1 Arbitration Act 1950 s 26(1) (amended by the Administration of Justice Act 1977 s 17(2)); applied by the Lands Tribunal Rules 1975, SI 1975/299, r 38. As to the expected replacement of the Lands Tribunal Rules 1975 (as amended) by new rules and new fees rules see para 206 note 3 ante. At the date at which this volume states the law, those new rules were still in draft and the final text had not been settled. As to the tribunal see paras 202–207 ante.

2 As to the leave of the court in doubtful cases and as to actions to enforce awards see ARBITRATION vol 2 (Reissue) para 712.

(vi) Appeal to Court of Appeal

231. Appeal by case stated. Any person who is aggrieved[1] by a decision of the Lands Tribunal as being erroneous in point of law may, within such time as may be limited by rules of court[2] require the tribunal to state and sign a case for the decision of the Court of Appeal[3]. If an appellant properly identifies a point of law which was relevant to the tribunal's decision and is arguable, that point should be included as a question in the case stated; and the question whether there was any evidence to support a conclusion by the tribunal is a question of law[4]. The case stated must state the facts on which the decision was based and the decision must be signed by the member or members of the tribunal by whom it was given[5]. Where the decision in respect of which the case is stated states all the relevant facts found by the tribunal and indicates the questions of law to be decided by the Court of Appeal, a copy of the decision signed by the person who presided at the hearing must be annexed to the case, and the facts so found and the questions of law to be decided are sufficiently stated in the case by referring to the statement thereof in the decision[6].

The case must be stated as soon as may be after the application is made and must be sent by post to the applicant[7].

Within 21 days after receiving the case, the party at whose instance it was stated must serve on every other party to the proceedings a copy of the case together with a notice setting out his contentions on the question of law, and must serve a copy of the notice on the registrar[8]. Within two days after service of the notice the party serving the notice must lodge the case and two copies of the notice with the registrar of civil appeals[9], who must enter the case in the appropriate list; and the case may not be heard until after 21 days from the date of entry[10].

1 For the meaning of 'person aggrieved' see para 85 note 1 ante; and ADMINISTRATIVE LAW vol 1(1) (Reissue) para 56. Where the Lands Tribunal's decision is given on a review by way of appeal of the

previous decision of another person, that person, if dissatisfied with the decision, is treated for this purpose as a person aggrieved by it: Lands Tribunal Act 1949 s 3(4) proviso.

2 The time within which the person aggrieved may require the tribunal to state a case for the decision of the Court of Appeal is four weeks from the date of the decision: RSC Ord 61 r 1(1).

3 Lands Tribunal Act 1949 s 3(4) proviso, s 3(11)(a); RSC Ord 61 r 1(1). Where the Lands Tribunal inadequately states a case (as opposed to refusing to state a case) judicial review is an inappropriate remedy: *Hertfordshire County Council v Rothschild Trust Co (CI)* [1994] 2 EGLR 36, CA. It is not standard practice, but may on the facts of the case be appropriate, for the notes of evidence of the member who heard the reference to be annexed to the stated case: *Blue Circle Industries plc v West Midlands County Council* [1994] 1 EGLR 41, CA; cf *Festiniog Rly Co v Central Electricity Generating Board* (1962) 13 P & CR 248, 60 LGR 157, CA.

4 See *Hertfordshire County Council v Rothschild Trust Co (CI)* [1994] 2 EGLR 36, CA.

5 RSC Ord 61 r 1(2). See *RA Vine (Engineering) Ltd v Havant Borough Council* [1989] 2 EGLR 15.
    A proposed appellant who requires the tribunal to state a case for the decision of the Court of Appeal may set out the grounds of appeal in the application to the tribunal. If no grounds of appeal are specified in the application, the applicant will be invited to specify within 14 days the point or points of law which it is sought to raise in the Court of Appeal. It is the obligation of the proposed appellant to define concisely and with reasonable precision the question or questions of law which it is sought to raise. Unless the point at issue is already plainly identified in the tribunal's decision, a question of law stated in general or vague terms such as 'whether upon the findings of fact it came to a correct decision in law' will not be accepted. Such grounds of appeal as are specified in the application or subsequently, and which in the view of the tribunal raise a point of law for the decision of the Court of Appeal, will normally be reproduced in the case stated. The tribunal will decline to state a case if no grounds of appeal are specified, or if the grounds of appeal, when specified, in the view of the tribunal disclose no point of law: *Practice Note (No 1 of 1993)* [1993] 38 EG 159.

6 RSC Ord 61 r 1(4). See also *Practice Direction* [1956] 3 All ER 117, [1956] 1 WLR 1112. The word 'decision' in the Lands Tribunal Act 1949 s 3(4) means 'final decision' and there is no jurisdiction for a case to be stated in relation to an interlocutory ruling or order, eg an order refusing discovery of documents: *R v Lands Tribunal, ex p City of London Corpn* [1982] 1 All ER 892, [1982] 1 WLR 258, CA. The duty of the Lands Tribunal in stating a case is not fulfilled by appending a transcript of the whole or a large part of the evidence; it should select what was regarded as the relevant evidence and state factually to what it amounted: *Hertfordshire County Council v Rothschild Trust Co (CI)* [1994] 2 EGLR 36, CA, applying *Tersons Ltd v Stevenage Development Corpn* [1965] 1 QB 37, [1963] 3 All ER 863, CA. As to the person presiding see para 221 ante.

7 RSC Ord 61 r 1(3).

8 RSC Ord 61 r 3(1). Order 59 r 10 applies to a case stated by a tribunal to which Ord 61 applies: Ord 61 r 3(5). For the meaning of 'the registrar' see para 199 note 8 ante.

9 RSC Ord 61 r 3(2). Where a minister or government department has a statutory right to be heard in proceedings on the case, a copy of the case and the notice of motion served under Ord 61 r 3(1) must be served on him or it: Ord 61 r 3(3).

10 RSC Ord 61 r 3(2).

232. Powers of Court of Appeal. On the hearing of the case the Court of Appeal may amend the case or order it to be sent back to the Lands Tribunal for amendment[1]. The Court of Appeal has power to receive further evidence; it may draw inferences of fact, make any order which ought to have been made by the tribunal, and make such further or other order as the case may require[2].

The registrar of civil appeals must notify the registrar of the tribunal of the court's decision and of any directions given thereon[3]. If the Court of Appeal has given directions for the amendment of any decision on which a case has been stated, the amendment must be made by the tribunal accordingly, and the registrar must send copies of the amended decision to every person to whom copies of the original decision were sent[4].

1 RSC Ord 61 r 3(4). As to the tribunal see paras 202–207 ante.
2 See RSC Ord 59 r 10, applied by Ord 61 r 3(5).

3 RSC Ord 61 r 3(6).
4 Lands Tribunal Rules 1975, SI 1975/299, r 54(5). As to the expected replacement of the Lands Tribunal
   Rules 1975 (as amended) by new rules and new fees rules see para 206 note 3 ante. At the date at which
   this volume states the law, those new rules were still in draft and the final text had not been settled.

5. ASSESSMENT OF PURCHASE MONEY OR COMPENSATION

(1) THE RIGHT TO COMPENSATION

233. The right to compensation. The owner whose land is compulsorily acquired
is entitled to compensation no less than the loss imposed on him but on the other hand
no greater[1], since the purpose of compensation is to provide fair compensation for a
claimant whose land has been compulsorily taken from him. This is sometimes
described as the principle of equivalence[2]. Compensation or purchase money[3] is
assessed upon the basis of the value of the land to the owner[4] and in addition the owner
is entitled to compensation for disturbance[5], for severance of his retained land[6] or for
other injurious affection[7].

1 *Horn v Sunderland Corpn* [1941] 2 KB 26 at 42, [1941] 1 All ER 480 at 491, CA.
2 *Director of Buildings and Lands v Shun Fung Ironworks Ltd* [1995] 2 AC 111 at 125, [1995] 1 All ER 846 at
   852, PC, per Lord Nicholls.
3 Compensation or purchase money are the same thing under different names: see *IRC v Glasgow and
   South Western Rly Co* (1887) 12 App Cas 315, HL.
4 See para 244 et seq post. See also *Corrie v MacDermott* [1914] AC 1056, PC; *Cedar Rapids Manufacturing
   and Power Co v Lacoste* [1914] AC 569, PC; *Fraser v City of Fraserville* [1917] AC 187, PC; *Pastoral Finance
   Association Ltd v The Minister* [1914] AC 1083, PC; *IRC v Glasgow and South Western Rly Co* (1887) 12
   App Cas 315 at 320, HL.
5 See para 322 et seq post.
6 See para 291 et seq post.
7 See paras 292, 353 et seq post.

234. The alternative bases. The owner is entitled to the amount which the land[1] if
sold in the open market by a willing seller might be expected to realise[2], no allowance
being made on account of the acquisition being compulsory[3] and subject to specific
assumptions as to the valuation[4]. As an alternative, however, where the land is, and but
for the compulsory acquisition would continue to be, devoted to a purpose of such a
nature that there is no general demand or market for land for that purpose, the
compensation may, if the Lands Tribunal is satisfied that reinstatement in some other
place is bona fide intended, be assessed on the basis of the reasonable cost of equivalent
reinstatement[5]. Special provisions apply in relation to compensation for the acquisition
of unfit houses where, before 1 April 1990, an order was made declaring the house
unfit[6].

1 For the meaning of 'land' see para 18 note 2 ante.
2 Land Compensation Act 1961 s 5 r (2). This does not, however, affect the assessment of compensation
   for disturbance (see para 322 et seq post) or any other matter not directly based on the value of the land:
   s 5 r (6).
3 Ibid s 5 r (1).
4 See para 258 et seq post.
5 Land Compensation Act 1961 s 5 r (5): see para 281 post.
6 See para 241 post.

(2) DATE FOR ASSESSMENT OF COMPENSATION FOR LAND TAKEN

235. The date for assessment. The date at which compensation is to be assessed on the 'market value' basis is the date on which possession is taken or the date when the value is being agreed or assessed by the tribunal if earlier[1]. Where the land is acquired by means of a general vesting declaration[2], the valuation date will be the date of vesting[3]. Compensation on the 'equivalent reinstatement' basis must be assessed at the earliest date at which reinstatement could reasonably have been obtained[4] and the question whether the land would continue to be used for its existing use must be considered as at the date of the deemed notice to treat[5].

1 *Birmingham Corpn v West Midland Baptist (Trust) Association (Inc)* [1970] AC 874, [1969] 3 All ER 172, HL; *Miller & Partners Ltd v Edinburgh Corpn* 1978 SC 1; *Washington Development Corpn v Bamlings (Washington) Ltd* (1984) 52 P & CR 267, [1985] 1 EGLR 16, CA. The date of assessment by the tribunal is the last day of the hearing by the Lands Tribunal: *W & S (Long Eaton) Ltd v Derbyshire County Council* (1975) 31 P & CR 99, CA; see also *C & J Seymour (Investments) Ltd v Lewes District Council* [1992] 1 EGLR 237, Lands Tribunal; *Hoveringham Gravels Ltd v Chiltern District Council* (1978) 39 P & CR 414, Lands Tribunal.
2 See para 168 et seq ante.
3 *Renfrew's Trustees v Glasgow Corpn* 1972 SLT 2, Lands Tribunal for Scotland.
4 *Birmingham Corpn v West Midland Baptist (Trust) Association (Inc)* [1970] AC 874, [1969] 3 All ER 172, HL.
5 *Zoar Independent Church Trustees v Rochester Corpn* [1975] QB 246 at 255, [1974] 3 All ER 5 at 12, CA, per Buckley LJ.

236. Time for ascertaining the interest acquired. The usual principle is that the nature of the claimant's interest is to be ascertained at the time of (or immediately before or immediately after) the service of the notice to treat[1]. Regard has, however, been had in some circumstances to events occurring after service of the notice to treat which affect the nature of the claimant's interest; for instance, where a lease which subsists at the date of the notice to treat expires before possession is taken and the claim for compensation is made, regard will be had to the fact that the claimant tenant has had the beneficial use of the leasehold land and no land has in fact been compulsorily acquired[2].

1 *Rugby Joint Water Board v Foottit, Rugby Joint Water Board v Shaw-Fox* [1973] AC 202 at 216, [1972] 1 All ER 1057 at 1064, HL, per Lord Pearson; *Penny v Penny* (1867) LR 5 Eq 227; *Re Morgan and London and North Western Rly Co* [1896] 2 QB 469; *Re Rowton Houses Ltd's Leases, Square Grip Reinforcement Co (London) Ltd v Rowton Houses Ltd* [1967] Ch 877, [1966] 3 All ER 996. See also *Lyle v Bexley London Borough Council* [1972] RVR 318, Lands Tribunal; *Runcorn Association Football Club v Runcorn and Warrington Development Corpn* (1982) 45 P & CR 183, Lands Tribunal.
2 *Holloway v Dover Corpn* [1960] 2 All ER 193, [1960] 1 WLR 604, CA; see also *R v Kennedy* [1893] 1 QB 533; *Soper and Soper v Doncaster Corpn* (1964) 16 P & CR 53, Lands Tribunal; *Banham v London Borough of Hackney* (1970) 22 P & CR 922, Lands Tribunal; *Bradford Property Trust Ltd v Hertfordshire County Council* (1973) 27 P & CR 228, Lands Tribunal; *Midland Bank Trust Co Ltd (Executors) v London Borough of Lewisham* (1975) 30 P & CR 268, Lands Tribunal.

(3) THE LAND AND BUILDINGS TO BE VALUED

(i) Intrinsic Quality and Circumstances of Land and Buildings

237. Intrinsic quality and circumstances to be considered unless excluded. Every intrinsic quality of the land and buildings and every intrinsic circumstance must be taken into consideration[1], except so far as any statute requires the buildings or uses to be excluded[2].

The land may be fertile or infertile, cultivated or neglected and with or without adequate buildings in a proper state of repair or an adequate water supply. It may be crossed by a footpath or liable to flooding, but on the other hand it may be otherwise protected from the hazards of nature, and may have views sufficiently ensured[3].

1   *Robinson Bros (Brewers) Ltd v Houghton and Chester-le-Street Assessment Committee* [1937] 2 KB 445 at 469, [1937] 2 All ER 298 at 307, CA; affd sub nom *Robinson Bros (Brewers) Ltd v Durham County Assessment Committee (Area No 7)* [1938] AC 321, [1938] 2 All ER 79, HL. 'No one can suppose, in the case of land which is certain, or even likely, to be used in the immediate or reasonably near future for building purposes but which at the valuation date is waste land, or is being used for agricultural purposes, that the owner, however willing a vendor, will be content to sell the land for its value as waste or agricultural land, as the case may be. It is plain that in ascertaining its value the possibility of its being used for building purposes would have to be taken into account': *Vyricherla Narayana Gajapatiraju Bahadur Garu v Revenue Divisional Officer, Vizagapatam* [1939] AC 302 at 313, [1939] 2 All ER 317 at 322, PC, per Lord Romer.
2   See paras 239–241 post.
3   Where land has a potential or development value some of the advantages and disadvantages would be ignored and others would become important; however increases (or decreases) in value on account of the acquisition being compulsory must be ignored: see the Land Compensation Act 1961 s 5 r (1); and para 234 ante.

238. Circumstances affecting quality of the land. On a purchase of licensed premises the owner is entitled to a purchase price as of licensed premises[1]; nevertheless, the purchaser does not purchase the existing licence, although the right or chance of obtaining a similar licence would belong to him[2]. The value of the goodwill of licensed premises is included in the value of the land as licensed premises[3]. In valuing the interest of a lessor the probability of the continuance of the premises as licensed premises must be regarded[4] and, if the house is a tied house, the lessor will be entitled to a fine based on the benefit derived from the tying covenant[5].

The land may be fronting a highway maintainable at the public expense or fronting a private street and liable to street works charges[6] or be with or without services in respect of sewers, water, electricity and gas.

1   *Tadcaster Tower Brewery Co v Wilson* [1897] 1 Ch 705; *Belton v LCC* (1893) 68 LT 411.
2   *Earl Fitzwilliam v IRC* [1914] AC 753 at 757, HL.
3   *Re Kitchin, ex p Punnett* (1880) 16 ChD 226 at 233, CA (ie the goodwill so called arising from the establishment and existence of the business and its situation).
4   *Belton v LCC* (1893) 68 LT 411.
5   *Bourne v Liverpool Corpn* (1863) 33 LJQB 15; *Re Chandler's Wiltshire Brewery Co Ltd and LCC* [1903] 1 KB 569; *Re LCC and City of London Brewery Co* [1898] 1 QB 387. As to tied house covenants see LANDLORD AND TENANT vol 27(1) (Reissue) para 458; and see also the Supply of Beer (Tied Estate) Order 1989, SI 1989/2390; and TRADE, INDUSTRY AND INDUSTRIAL RELATIONS vol 47 (Reissue) para 125 note 11.
6   As to these liabilities see HIGHWAYS. As to market value as affected by development on adjoining land see para 268 et seq post.

(ii) Works on or Uses of Land to be Disregarded

239. Works executed with view to compensation. It has been held that works by the owner of the land altering the land after the notice to treat so as to increase the acquiring authority's burden with respect to the payment of purchase money or compensation must be disregarded[1]. The Lands Tribunal may not take into account any enhancement of the value of any interest in land by reason of any building erected, work done or improvement or alteration made, whether on the land purchased or on any other land[2] with which the claimant is, or was at the time of the erection, doing or making of the building, works, improvement or alteration, directly or indirectly concerned, if it is satisfied that the erection of the building, the doing of the work, the making of the improvement or the alteration, as the case may be, was not reasonably necessary and was undertaken with a view to obtaining compensation or increased compensation[3]. Works carried out after service of the notice to treat may, if they go beyond what is necessary for the owner's continued enjoyment of the land and add to the burden on the acquiring authority, be disregarded in the assessment of compensation[4].

1 See para 116 ante.
2 This provision will therefore affect compensation for severance or other injurious affection of land not taken: see para 291 post.
3 See the Acquisition of Land Act 1981 s 4(2) (where that Act applies: see para 33 ante); and para 116 ante.
4 *Cardiff Corpn v Cook* [1923] 2 Ch 115; cf *City of Glasgow Union Rly Co v James McEwen & Co* (1870) 8 M 747.

240. Uses or works contrary to law. Where the value of the land[1] is increased by reason of the use of the land or of any premises on it in a manner which could be restrained by any court or is contrary to law[2], or is detrimental to the health of the occupants of the premises or to the public health, the amount of that increase is not to be taken into account in assessing compensation in respect of compulsory acquisition[3]. However, there is no express statutory provision making buildings or works contrary to law liable to proceedings for their demolition or removal[4].

1 For the meaning of 'land' see para 18 note 2 ante.
2 Evidence of legal proceedings in respect of the use, or the possibility of legal proceedings, may be received: cf *Higham v Havant and Waterloo UDC* [1951] 2 KB 527, [1951] 2 All ER 178n, CA.
3 Land Compensation Act 1961 s 5 r (4). As to uses contrary to planning law see TOWN AND COUNTRY PLANNING. As to uses which are a nuisance see NUISANCE. There is no longer a distinction between a use which could not be enforced against (though it was unlawful) and a use which, though not permitted, was not unlawful: see the Town and Country Planning Act 1990 ss 191, 192 (substituted by the Planning and Compensation Act 1991 s 10(1)); and TOWN AND COUNTRY PLANNING vol 46 (Reissue) para 685 et seq. Accordingly the distinction relied on in *Hughes v Doncaster Metropolitan Borough Council* [1991] 1 AC 382, [1991] 1 All ER 295, HL, would no longer appear to be good law.
4 Any purchaser in the market would nevertheless take these matters into account. Buildings may, inter alia, be contrary to planning control (see TOWN AND COUNTRY PLANNING vol 46 (Reissue) para 654 et seq; and see in particular *Handoll v Warner Gooodman & Streat* [1995] 1 EGLR 173, CA) or contrary to building regulations (see PUBLIC HEALTH).

241. Transitional provisions relating to unfit houses whereby land purchased as cleared site. It was formerly provided under the housing legislation that where the land to be acquired comprised a house which was unfit for human habitation, the compensation or purchase money to be paid for the land was to be the value at the time the valuation was made of the land as a site cleared of buildings and available for development in accordance with the building regulations[1]. This provision was capable of working unfairly in practice, for example where an owner-occupier had paid more than site value because of the scarcity of housing, and, despite measures taken to ameliorate the harshness of the rule[2], the provision was much criticised and was repealed except in relation to orders declaring houses to be unfit made before 1 April 1990[3].

1 See the Housing Act 1985 s 585 et seq (repealed by the Local Government and Housing Act 1989 ss 165(1)(d), 194(4), Sch 9 para 76, Sch 12 Pt II).
2 Eg well-maintained payments under the Housing Act 1985 s 586, Sch 23 (repealed) and the owner-occupier supplement under s 587, Sch 24 (repealed).
3 Local Government and Housing Act 1989 (Commencement No 5 and Transitional Provisions) Order 1990, SI 1990/431, art 4, Sch 1 para 28.

(4) POTENTIAL USE OF LAND TO BE CONSIDERED

(i) In general

242. The general rule. The owner of land is entitled to its value to him; this comprises all the advantages, present and future, which the land possesses[1]. Nevertheless, it is only the present value of these advantages which fall to be considered, and not the advantages as realised in the hands of the acquiring authority, and there must be disregarded any increase in value due to the scheme underlying the acquisition[2]; although if the land is suitable for some purpose, that purpose is not excluded merely because the authority intends to apply the land to it[3].

If the owner holds the land subject to restrictions in his hands, they must be taken into account[4], but the possibility of the restrictions being discharged must also be kept in view[5]. Examples of restrictions are planning restrictions[6], restrictive covenants[7], and the restrictions which attach to an open space held for amenity[8] or which attach to ecclesiastical land[9].

The general right to the potential value is not limited to that value at the date of the notice to treat but applies at the date of entry or time of valuation[10]; nor is it restricted by assumed permission at the date of the notice to treat except to a limited extent by a certificate of appropriate alternative development[11].

1 *Cedar Rapids Manufacturing and Power Co v Lacoste* [1914] AC 569 at 576, PC; *Re Lucas and Chesterfield Gas and Water Board* [1909] 1 KB 16, CA; *Fraser v City of Fraserville* [1917] AC 187 at 194, PC; and see *R v Brown* (1867) LR 2 QB 630 (value of agricultural land as building land); *Ripley v Great Northern Rly Co* (1875) 10 Ch App 435 (land near a reservoir suitable for cotton mills); *Brown v Rlys Comr* (1890) 15 App Cas 240, PC (land suitable for mining); *Bailey v Isle of Thanet Light Rlys Co* [1900] 1 QB 722 (land bought and held by owner for intended school). In *Birmingham District Council v Morris and Jacombs Ltd* (1976) 33 P & CR 27, CA, a strip of land was compulsorily acquired that had been specifically conditioned as an access in a planning permission; compensation was assessed solely on access and not on residential value. These cases must, however, be read subject to restrictions on use but subject to the possibility of removal of those restrictions: see the text and notes 4–5 infra. They must also be read subject to the exclusion from market value of a purchaser for a purpose only attainable by statutory powers or for which there is no market apart from the special needs of a particular purchaser or the requirements of any authority possessing compulsory purchase powers as provided by the Land Compensation Act 1961 s 5 r (3) (as amended): see para 270 post. In summary, an owner whose land is acquired compulsorily is entitled to the higher of (1) its potential value (on the assumption that the present use is abandoned); or (2) its existing use value (together with any relevant compensation for disturbance), but not to both.
2 *Stebbing v Metropolitan Board of Works* (1870) LR 6 QB 37; *IRC v Glasgow and South Western Rly Co* (1887) 12 App Cas 315, HL; *Cedar Rapids Manufacturing and Power Co v Lacoste* [1914] AC 569 at 576, PC; *Penny v Penny* (1867) LR 5 Eq 227; *Re Lucas and Chesterfield Gas and Water Board* [1909] 1 KB 16,

CA; *Re Gough and Aspatria, Silloth and District Joint Water Board* [1904] 1 KB 417 at 423, CA. Since the assessment of compensation is on the same basis as at common law, it would be contrary to public policy to deduct from it the value of eg a regional development grant which was paid under a different statutory code and with different objectives: *Palatine Graphic Arts Co Ltd v Liverpool City Council* [1986] QB 335, [1986] 1 All ER 366, CA; cf *A & B Taxis Ltd v Secretary of State for Air* [1922] 2 KB 328, CA. See also the cases cited in para 268 note 1 post and the reservations set out in note 1 supra.

  3 *Re Riddell and Newcastle and Gateshead Water Co* (1878) Browne and Allan's Law of Compensation (2nd Edn) 672, 90 LT 44n, CA; *Re Countess Ossalinsky and Manchester Corpn* (1883) Browne and Allan's Law of Compensation (2nd Edn) 659, DC; *Re Gough and Aspatria, Silloth and District Joint Water Board* [1904] 1 KB 417, CA; *Cedar Rapids Manufacturing and Power Co v Lacoste* [1914] AC 569 at 579–580, PC; *Trent-Stoughton v Barbados Water Supply Co Ltd* [1893] AC 502, PC; *Re Lucas and Chesterfield Gas and Water Board* [1909] 1 KB 16 at 26, 31, CA. See also the reservations set out in note 1 supra.

  4 *Corrie v MacDermott* [1914] AC 1056 at 1062, PC.

  5 *Corrie v MacDermott* [1914] AC 1056 at 1063–1064, PC; and see *City and South London Rly Co v United Parishes of St Mary, Woolnoth and St Mary, Woolchurch Haw* [1905] AC 1, HL, where, in assessing the value of the subsoil of a church, the fact that the land might be made available for building purposes by an Order in Council under the Union of Benefices Act 1860 (repealed) was held to be rightly taken into account. As to the valuation of a church see also *Hilcoat v Archbishops of Canterbury and York* (1850) 19 LJCP 376; and as to the valuation of a burial ground see *Stebbing v Metropolitan Board of Works* (1870) LR 6 QB 37, considered in *Corrie v MacDermott* supra. However, such properties will be subject to reinstatement value if there is a genuine intention to reinstate. See also the reservation set out in note 1 supra.

  6 See para 243 post; and *Birmingham District Council v Morris and Jacombs Ltd* (1976) 33 P & CR 27, CA.

  7 As to the possibility of removal or discharge of a restrictive covenant see the Law of Property Act 1925 s 84 (as amended); and see EQUITY vol 16 (Reissue) para 903 et seq; and see *Re Abbey Homesteads (Developments) Ltd's Application, Abbey Homesteads (Developments) Ltd v Northamptonshire County Council* (1986) 53 P & CR 1, [1986] 1 EGLR 24, CA; *Abbey Homesteads (Developments) Ltd v Northamptonshire County Council* (1992) 64 P & CR 377, [1992] 2 EGLR 18, CA (effect on compensation).

  8 See *Re Edinburgh Corpn and North British Rly* (unreported arbitration), cited in *Corrie v MacDermott* [1914] AC 1056 at 1064, PC; but see now para 281 post (reinstatement value).

  9 See note 5 supra.

 10 See paras 119, 235–236 ante.

 11 See para 243 post.

243. Actual, possible and assumed planning permission. The enjoyment of the potentialities of land is restricted by the requirement of planning permission[1] for the carrying out of development[2]. The restriction may be removed by actual planning permission at the date of service of the notice to treat or by a permission assumed by statute[3]; and any planning permission which is to be assumed in accordance with the relevant statutory provisions is in addition to any planning permission which may be in force at the date of the service of the notice to treat[4].

The planning permissions which are to be assumed in relation to the relevant land[5] or any part of it in ascertaining the value of the interest in the land for the purpose of assessing compensation in respect of any compulsory acquisition are such one or more of the following as are applicable to that land[6]:

(1) an assumption of permission such as would permit development in accordance with the acquiring authority's proposals[7];

(2) an assumption of permission for development[8] included in the existing use of land[9];

(3) an assumption of permission for development defined or shown in a development plan[10]; and

(4) an assumption of permission for development certified by a planning authority as permission that would have been granted[11].

The provisions for the statutory assumption of planning permission must not, however, be construed as requiring it to be assumed that planning permission would necessarily be refused for any development which is not development for which the granting of planning permission is to be assumed[12]; but in determining whether planning permission for any development could in any particular circumstances reasonably have been expected to be granted in respect of any land, regard must be had to any contrary opinion expressed in relation to that land in any certificate[13] of appropriate alternative development[14].

1 'Planning permission' means permission under the Town and Country Planning Act 1990 Pt III (ss 55–106B) (as amended) (see TOWN AND COUNTRY PLANNING vol 46 (Reissue) para 144 et seq): Land Compensation Act 1961 s 39(1); Planning (Consequential Provisions) Act 1990 s 2(4). Whilst development potential must in some circumstances be assumed for the purpose of valuation, it does not follow that any relevant planning permission will automatically enhance the value of the land in the absence of demand: see *Bromilow v Greater Manchester Council* (1974) 29 P & CR 517, Lands Tribunal (affd (1975) 31 P & CR 398, CA); *Davy Ltd v London Borough of Hammersmith* (1975) 30 P & CR 469, Lands Tribunal.

2 'Development' has the meaning assigned to it by the Town and Country Planning Act 1990 s 55 (as amended) (see TOWN AND COUNTRY PLANNING vol 46 (Reissue) para 144 et seq): Land Compensation Act 1961 s 39(1); Planning (Consequential Provisions) Act 1990 s 2(4).

3 For the statutory assumptions see the Land Compensation Act 1961 s 15 (as amended), s 16; and para 246 et seq post.

4 Ibid s 14(2). This applies also where notice to treat is deemed to have been served: s 39(8). As to the time of the valuation see para 119 ante; and as to service of the notice to treat see paras 100–104 ante. For the meaning of 'the notice to treat' see para 120 note 4 ante. For these purposes, and for the purpose of any reference in s 15 (as amended) to planning permission which is in force on the date of service of the notice to treat, it is immaterial whether the planning permission was granted (1) unconditionally or subject to conditions; or (2) in respect of the land in question taken by itself or in respect of an area including that land; or (3) on an ordinary application or on an outline application or by virtue of a development order, or is planning permission which, in accordance with any direction or provision given or made by or under any enactment, is deemed to have been granted: s 14(4). 'Development order' means an order under the Town and Country Planning Act 1990 s 59(1) (see TOWN AND COUNTRY PLANNING vol 46 (Reissue) para 183): Land Compensation Act 1961 s 39(1); Planning (Consequential Provisions) Act 1990 s 2(4). See the Town and Country Planning (General Permitted Development) Order 1995, SI 1995/418; the Town and Country Planning (General Development Procedure) Order 1995, SI 1995/419 (both of which came into force on 3 June 1995); and TOWN AND COUNTRY PLANNING. 'Outline application' means an application for planning permission subject to subsequent approval on any matters: Land Compensation Act 1961 s 39(1). For the meaning of 'enactment' see para 1 note 3 ante.

5 For the meaning of 'land' see para 18 note 2 ante. 'The relevant land' means the land in which the relevant interest (ie the interest acquired in pursuance of the notice to treat) subsists: Land Compensation Act 1961 s 39(2).

6 Ibid s 14(1) (amended by the Planning and Compensation Act 1991 s 70, Sch 15 para 15(1)).

7 See the Land Compensation Act 1961 s 15(1), (2); and para 245 post.

8 Ie development of a class specified (1) in the Town and Country Planning Act 1990 s 107(4) (as amended), Sch 3 para 1 (subject to the condition set out in s 111(5) (as substituted)), Sch 10 (see TOWN AND COUNTRY PLANNING vol 46 (Reissue) paras 703–704); and (2) in Sch 3 para 2 (see TOWN AND COUNTRY PLANNING vol 46 (Reissue) para 703): Land Compensation Act 1961 s 15(3) (substituted by the Planning and Compensation Act 1991 s 31(4), Sch 6 para 1(1)(a)).

9 See the Land Compensation Act 1961 s 15(3) (as substituted: see note 8 supra), s 15(4) (as amended); and para 246 post.

10 See ibid s 16; and paras 247–251 post. As to development plans see TOWN AND COUNTRY PLANNING vol 46 (Reissue) para 36 et seq.

11 See ibid ss 15(5), 17–22 (as amended); and paras 252–259 post.

12 Ibid s 14(3) (amended by the Planning and Compensation Act 1991 Sch 15 para 15(2)).

13 Ie any certificate issued under the Land Compensation Act 1961 Pt III (ss 17–22) (as amended): see para 252 et seq post.

14 Ibid s 14(3A)(a) (added by the Planning and Compensation Act 1991 Sch 15 para 15(2)).

244. Statutory assumption where land required for highway use. If a determination mentioned in heads (a) and (b) below falls to be made in a case where (1) the relevant land[1] is to be acquired for use for or in connection with the construction of a highway[2]; or (2) the use of the relevant land for or in connection with such construction is being considered by a highway authority, that determination must be made on the assumption that, if the relevant land were not so used, no highway would be constructed to meet the same or substantially the same need as that highway would have been constructed to meet[3]. The determinations which must be made on this assumption are:

(a) a determination, for the purpose of assessing compensation in respect of any compulsory acquisition, whether planning permission[4] might reasonably be expected to be granted for any development[5] if no part of the relevant land were proposed to be acquired by an authority possessing compulsory purchase powers[6]; and

(b) a determination[7] as to the development for which, in the opinion of the local planning authority[8], planning permission would or would not have been granted if no part of the relevant land were proposed to be acquired by any authority possessing such powers[9].

1 For the meaning of 'the relevant land' see para 243 note 5 ante; and for the meaning of 'land' see para 18 note 2 ante.
2 For these purposes, references to the construction of a highway include references to its alteration or improvement: Land Compensation Act 1961 s 14(8) (s 14(5)–(8) added by the Planning and Compensation Act 1991 s 64).
3 Land Compensation Act 1961 s 14(5), (6) (as added: see note 2 supra).
4 For the meaning of 'planning permission' see para 243 note 1 ante.
5 For the meaning of 'development' see para 243 note 2 ante.
6 Land Compensation Act 1961 s 14(7)(a) (as added: see note 2 supra). 'Authority possessing compulsory purchase powers', where it occurs in the 1961 Act otherwise than in relation to a transaction, means any person or body of persons who could be or have been authorised to acquire an interest in land compulsorily, and, in relation to any transaction, means any person or body of persons who could be or have been so authorised for the purposes for which the transaction is or was effected, or a parish council, community council or parish meeting on whose behalf a district council or county council could be or have been so authorised: s 39(1) (definition amended by the Local Authorities etc (Miscellaneous Provisions) Order 1976, SI 1976/315, art 4(4); further prospectively amended by the Local Government (Wales) Act 1994 s 66(6), Sch 16 para 17, as from a day to be appointed under s 66(3), to substitute for the words 'or county council' the words 'county council or county borough council').
7 Ie under the Land Compensation Act 1961 s 17 (as amended): see para 253 post.
8 'Local planning authority' has the meaning assigned to it by the Town and Country Planning Act 1990 s 1 (as amended) (see TOWN AND COUNTRY PLANNING vol 46 (Reissue) para 11): Land Compensation Act 1961 s 39(1); Planning (Consequential Provisions) Act 1990 s 2(4). This definition is prospectively substituted by the Environment Act 1995 s 78, Sch 10 para 4(2), as from a day to be appointed under s 125(3), to read '"local planning authority" is to be construed in accordance with the Town and Country Planning Act 1990 Pt I (ss 1–9)' (as amended). At the date at which this volume states the law, no such day had been appointed.
9 Land Compensation Act 1961 s 14(7)(b) (as added: see note 2 supra).

(ii) Assumed Permission for Development in accordance with Acquiring Authority's Proposals

245. Where at the date of the notice to treat there is no permission already in force. In a case where the relevant interest to be acquired in pursuance of the notice to treat is to be acquired for purposes which involve the carrying out of the acquiring authority's[1] proposals for development[2] of the relevant land or any part of it[3], and on the date of service of the notice to treat there is not in force planning permission[4] for that development which will enure, while it is in force, for the benefit of the land and all persons interested in it[5], then it must be assumed that planning permission would be granted, in respect of that land or that part of it, such as would permit its development in accordance with the authority's proposals[6].

This assumed permission is in addition to any planning permission which may be in force at the date of the service of the notice to treat[7].

1 For the meaning of 'acquiring authority' see para 120 note 5 ante.
2 For the meaning of 'development' see para 243 note 2 ante.
3 Land Compensation Act 1961 s 15(1)(a). For the meaning of 'land' see para 18 note 2 ante; and for the meaning of 'the relevant land' and 'the relevant interest' see para 243 note 5 ante.
4 As to the meaning of 'planning permission' for this purpose see para 243 note 4 ante; and for the meaning of 'planning permission' generally see para 243 note 1 ante.
5 Land Compensation Act 1961 s 15(1)(b), (2). As to service of the notice to treat see paras 100–104 ante. See also para 120 note 4 ante.
6 Ibid s 15(1). Thus, as the assumed permission is only permission to develop in accordance with the proposals, it will be sufficient and proper to assume a permission in general terms and not for the actual scheme of the acquiring authority, which must in any case be disregarded: see *Myers v Milton Keynes Development Corpn* [1974] 2 All ER 1096, [1974] 1 WLR 696, CA. In valuing land acquired by the authority for residential and industrial purposes, with the assumed permission, the authority's actual scheme for development of the land must thus be ignored, in accordance with the principle in *Pointe Gourde Quarrying and Transport Co Ltd v Sub-Intendent of Crown Lands* [1947] AC 565, PC. The question is whether any other persons would be likely to want to purchase the land for development to the same or less extent, and if the development by those other persons would not be likely or would be deferred, the land must be valued accordingly: *Abbey Homesteads (Developments) Ltd v Northamptonshire County Council* (1992) 64 P & CR 377, [1992] 2 EGLR 18, CA. Planning permission alone does not raise the value of the land; it merely removes the restrictions on development so that demand for the development must be taken into account: *Viscount Camrose v Basingstoke Corpn* [1966] 3 All ER 161, [1966] 1 WLR 1100, CA.

An assumed permission for industrial purposes is satisfied by an assumed permission for a change of use to industrial purposes, and it must not be assumed that an industrial development certificate necessary for planning permission for building operations would be granted: *Viscount Camrose v Basingstoke Corpn* supra. Any increase in the value of the land by reason of development or the prospect of development of other land must also be excluded so far as it is development which would not be likely to be carried out if the authority did not propose to acquire any of that other land, or that other land had not been defined or designated for development as provided in the Land Compensation Act 1961 s 6, Sch 1 (as amended) (see para 269 et seq post): *Viscount Camrose v Basingstoke Corpn* supra.
7 Land Compensation Act 1961 s 14(2). It is not to be assumed that planning permission would necessarily be refused for development which is not development for which the granting of planning permission is assumed: see s 14(3) (as amended): and para 243 ante.

(iii) Assumed Permission included in Existing Use of Land

246. Assumed permission for development included in the existing use of land. For the purpose of assessing compensation in respect of any compulsory acquisition, it must be assumed that planning permission[1] would be granted, in respect of the relevant land[2] or any part of it, for development[3] consisting of (1) specified rebuilding operations or the maintenance, improvement or alteration of a building[4] subject to the statutory condition[5] relating thereto[6]; and (2) the use as two or more separate dwelling houses of any building which at a material date was used as a single dwelling house[7]. Where, however, at any time before the date of service of the notice to treat[8] an order was made[9] in respect of the relevant land or any part of it requiring the removal of any building[10] or the discontinuance of any use, and compensation became payable in respect of that order[11], it must not be assumed that planning permission would be granted in respect of the relevant land or part of it for the rebuilding of that building or the resumption of that use[12].

1 As to the meaning of 'planning permission' for these purposes see para 243 note 4 ante; and for the meaning of 'planning permission' generally see para 243 note 1 ante.
2 For the meaning of 'land' see para 18 note 2 ante; and for the meaning of 'the relevant land' see para 243 note 5 ante.
3 For the meaning of 'development' generally see para 243 note 2 ante.
4 Ie development of a class specified in the Town and Country Planning Act 1990 s 107(4) (as amended), Sch 3 para 1: see TOWN AND COUNTRY PLANNING vol 46 (Reissue) para 703. As to what amounts to rebuilding see *Re Walker's Settled Estate* [1894] 1 Ch 189; *Re Kensington Settled Estates* (1905) 21 TLR 351; *Re Windham's Settled Estate* [1912] 2 Ch 75; *Re Lord Gerard's Settled Estate* [1893] 3 Ch 252 at 267, CA; *Re Wright's Settled Estates* (1900) 83 LT 159; *Re De Teissier's Settled Estates* [1893] 1 Ch 153; and see SETTLEMENTS. The permission may be subject to any other control apart from the planning permission: cf *Trustees of the Walton-on-Thames Charities v Walton and Weybridge UDC* (1970) 21 P & CR 411, CA.
5 Ie subject to the condition set out in the Town and Country Planning Act 1990 s 111(5) (as substituted), Sch 10: see TOWN AND COUNTRY PLANNING vol 46 (Reissue) para 704.
6 Land Compensation Act 1961 s 15(3)(a) (substituted by the Planning and Compensation Act 1991 s 31(4), Sch 6 para 1(1)(a)).
7 Land Compensation Act 1961 s 15(3)(b) (as substituted: see note 6 supra). The development referred to is development of a class specified in the Town and Country Planning Act 1990 Sch 3 para 2: see TOWN AND COUNTRY PLANNING vol 46 (Reissue) para 703. As to what is a dwelling house see *Gravesham Borough Council v Secretary of State for the Environment* (1982) 47 P & CR 142; cf *Lewin v End* [1906] AC 299 at 302, 304, HL. It should not be assumed that assumed planning permissions under the Land Compensation Act 1961 s 15 (as amended) and the Town and Country Planning Act 1990 Sch 3 (as amended) automatically increase the value of the land: *Halliwell and Halliwell v Skelmersdale Development Corpn* (1965) 16 P & CR 305, Lands Tribunal.
8 As to service of the notice to treat see paras 100–104 ante; and for the meaning of 'the notice to treat' see para 120 note 4 ante.
9 Ie under the Town and Country Planning Act 1990: see s 102 (as amended); and TOWN AND COUNTRY PLANNING vol 46 (Reissue) para 474 et seq.
10 'Building' includes any structure or erection and any part of a building as so defined, but does not include plant or machinery comprised in a building: Land Compensation Act 1961 s 39(1).
11 As to compensation see the Town and Country Planning Act 1990 s 115; and TOWN AND COUNTRY PLANNING vol 46 (Reissue) para 709.
12 Land Compensation Act 1961 s 15(4)(c); Planning (Consequential Provisions) Act 1990 s 2(4).

(iv) Assumed Permission in respect of Certain Land in Development Plan

247. Land allocated for a particular purpose in the development plan. If the relevant land[1] or any part of it, not being land subject to comprehensive development[2], consists or forms part of a site defined in the current development plan as the site of proposed development[3] of a description specified in relation to it in the plan, it must be assumed that planning permission[4] would be granted for that development[5]. In determining whether this assumption is applicable to the relevant land or any part of it, regard must be had to any contrary opinion expressed in relation to that land in any certificate[6] of appropriate alternative development[7].

1 For the meaning of 'the relevant land' see para 243 note 5 ante; and for the meaning of 'land' see para 18 note 2 ante.
2 'Land subject to comprehensive development' means land which consists or forms part of an area defined in the current development plan as an area of comprehensive development: Land Compensation Act 1961 s 16(8). 'The current development plan', in relation to any land, means a development plan comprising that land, in the form in which, whether as originally approved or made or as for the time being amended, that plan is in force on the date of service of the notice to treat: s 39(1) (definition amended by Town and Country Planning Act 1968 s 108, Sch 11). Any reference in the Land Compensation Act 1961 to an area defined in the current development plan as an area of comprehensive development is to be construed as a reference to an action area for which a local plan is in force: Town and Country Planning Act 1990 s 54(5). An action area could be defined by a structure plan by virtue of the Town and Country Planning Act 1971 s 7(5) (repealed); and a local plan may designate any part of a

local planning authority's area as an action area, ie an area which the authority has selected for the commencement during a prescribed period of comprehensive treatment by development, redevelopment or improvement, or partly by one and partly by another method: see the Town and Country Planning Act 1990 s 36(7) (substituted by the Planning and Compensation Act 1991 s 27, Sch 4 para 17); and TOWN AND COUNTRY PLANNING vol 46 (Reissue) para 94. As to local plans see TOWN AND COUNTRY PLANNING vol 46 (Reissue) para 94 et seq. As to service of the notice to treat see paras 100–104 ante; and for the meaning of 'the notice to treat' see para 120 note 4 ante.

3 For the meaning of 'development' see para 243 note 2 ante.

4 For the meaning of 'planning permission' see para 243 note 1 ante. As to the nature and extent of the permission see para 251 post.

5 Land Compensation Act 1961 s 16(1).

6 Ie any certificate issued under ibid Pt III (ss 17–22) (as amended): see paras 252–259 post.

7 Ibid s 14(3A)(b) (added by the Planning and Compensation Act 1991 s 70, Sch 15 para 15(2)).

248. Land allocated for specified use in development plan. If the relevant land[1] or any part of it (not being land subject to comprehensive development[2]), consists or forms part of an area shown in the current development plan[3] as an area allocated primarily for a use specified in the plan in relation to that area, it must be assumed that planning permission[4] would be granted, in respect of that land or that part of it, as the case may be, for any development[5] which is development (1) for the purposes of that specified use of that land or part[6]; and (2) for which planning permission might reasonably have been expected to be granted in respect of that land or part[7] if no part of that land were proposed to be acquired by any authority possessing compulsory purchase powers[8].

In determining whether this assumption is applicable to the relevant land or any part of it, regard must be had to any contrary opinion expressed in relation to that land in any certificate[9] of appropriate alternative development[10].

1 For the meaning of 'the relevant land' see para 243 note 5 ante; and for the meaning of 'land' see para 18 note 2 ante.

2 For the meaning of 'land subject to comprehensive development' see para 247 note 2 ante.

3 For the meaning of 'current development plan' see para 247 note 2 ante.

4 For the meaning of 'planning permission' see para 243 note 1 ante. As to the nature and extent of the assumed permission see para 251 post.

5 For the meaning of 'development' see para 243 note 2 ante.

6 Land Compensation Act 1961 s 16(2)(a).

7 Ibid s 16(2)(b). The provisions of s 16(2)(a) and (b) must both be satisfied and applied together; it is not a matter of finding under s 16(2)(b) what kind of permission would be granted if s 16(2)(a) is satisfied and, accordingly, if no planning permission might reasonably have been expected, there can be no assumed permission: *Provincial Properties (London) Ltd v Caterham and Warlingham UDC* [1972] 1 QB 453, [1972] 1 All ER 60, CA. On the other hand, the likelihood of a planning permission actually being sought or granted is irrelevant to the making of the assumption: *Sutton v Secretary of State for the Environment* [1984] JPL 648. However if there is no demand for land with that permission, the value of the land may not be increased: *Bromilow v Greater Manchester Council* (1975) 31 P & CR 398, CA; *Davy Ltd v London Borough of Hammersmith* (1975) 30 P & CR 469, Lands Tribunal.

8 Land Compensation Act 1961 s 16(2), (7). For the meaning of 'authority possessing compulsory purchase powers' see para 244 note 6 ante. If, on considering whether planning permission might reasonably have been expected, there are traffic reasons against permission, but there is a proposal for a by-pass partly on the land to be acquired which has to be ignored under s 16(7), it is not to be assumed that there would be a by-pass elsewhere in relief of traffic, but evidence of the possibility of such a by-pass must be considered: see *Margate Corpn v Devotwill Investments Ltd* [1970] 3 All ER 864, HL. Any question as to whether planning permission might reasonably have been expected is within the exclusive jurisdiction of the Lands Tribunal: *Harrison v Croydon London Borough Council* [1968] Ch 479, [1967] 2 All ER 589. See also *Richardsons Developments Ltd v Stoke-on-Trent Corpn* (1971) 22 P & CR 958, Lands Tribunal; *Menzies Motors Ltd v Stirling District Council* 1977 SC 33, Lands Tribunal for Scotland. A local authority cannot specify a planning permission for a purpose which could only be achieved by an authority possessing compulsory purchase powers: *Scunthorpe Borough Council v Secretary of State for the Environment* [1977] JPL 653.

Special provisions apply where land is acquired for or in connection with the construction of a highway: see the Land Compensation Act 1961 s 14(5)–(8) (as added); and para 244 ante.
9 Ie any certificate issued under ibid Pt III (ss 17–22) (as amended): see paras 252–259 post.
10 Ibid s 14(3A)(b) (added by the Planning and Compensation Act 1991 s 70, Sch 15 para 15(2)).

249. Land allocated for range of specified uses in development plan. If the relevant land[1] or any part of it, not being land subject to comprehensive development[2], consists or forms part of an area shown in the current development plan[3] as an area allocated primarily for a range of two or more uses specified in the plan in relation to the whole of that area, it must be assumed that planning permission[4] would be granted in respect of that land or that part for any development[5] which (1) is development for the purposes of a use of that land or that part of it which is a use falling within that range of uses[6]; and (2) is development for which planning permission might reasonably have been expected to be granted in respect of that land or part if no part of that land were proposed to be acquired by any authority possessing compulsory purchase powers[7].

In determining whether this assumption is applicable to the relevant land or any part of it, regard must be had to any contrary opinion expressed in relation to that land in any certificate[8] of appropriate alternative development[9].

1 For the meaning of 'the relevant land' see para 243 note 5 ante; and for the meaning of 'land' see para 18 note 2 ante.
2 For the meaning of 'land subject to comprehensive development' see para 247 note 2 ante.
3 For the meaning of 'current development plan' see para 247 note 2 ante.
4 For the meaning of 'planning permission' see para 243 note 1 ante. As to the nature and extent of the assumed permission see para 251 post.
5 For the meaning of 'development' see para 243 note 2 ante.
6 Land Compensation Act 1961 s 16(3)(a).
7 Ibid s 16(3)(b), (7). Cf para 248 notes 7–8 ante. For the meaning of 'authority possessing compulsory purchase powers' see para 244 note 6 ante.
8 Ie any certificate issued under ibid Pt III (ss 17–22) (as amended): see paras 252–259 post.
9 Ibid s 14(3A)(b) (added by the Planning and Compensation Act 1991 s 70, Sch 15 para 15(2)).

250. Land allocated for comprehensive development in the development plan. If the relevant land[1] or any part of it is land subject to comprehensive development[2], it must be assumed that planning permission[3] would be granted in respect of that land or part for any development[4] for the purposes of a use of that land or part falling within the planned range of uses[5], being development for which planning permission might reasonably have been expected to be granted in respect of that land or part in the specified circumstances[6]. The specified circumstances are those which would have existed if:

(1) no part of that land were proposed to be acquired by any authority possessing compulsory purchase powers[7];

(2) the area in question had not been defined in the current development plan as an area of comprehensive development and no particulars or proposals relating to any land in that area had been comprised in the plan[8]; and

(3) in a case where, on the date of service of the notice to treat[9], land in that area has already been developed in the course of the development or redevelopment of the area in accordance with the plan, no land in that area had been so developed on or before that date[10].

In determining whether this assumption is applicable to the relevant land or any part of it, regard must be had to any contrary opinion expressed in relation to that land in any certificate[11] of appropriate alternative development[12].

1 For the meaning of 'the relevant land' see para 243 note 5 ante; and for the meaning of 'land' see para 18 note 2 ante.
2 For the meaning of 'land subject to comprehensive development' see para 247 note 2 ante.
3 For the meaning of 'planning permission' see para 243 note 1 ante. As to the nature and extent of the assumed permission see para 251 post.
4 For the meaning of 'development' see para 243 note 2 ante.
5 Ie whether it is the use which, in accordance with the particulars and proposals comprised in the current development plan in relation to the area in question, is indicated in the plan as the proposed use of the relevant land or that part of it, or is any other use falling within the planned range of uses: Land Compensation Act 1961 s 16(4). 'The planned range of uses' means the range of uses which, in accordance with the particulars and proposals comprised in the current development plan in relation to the area in question, are indicated in the plan as proposed uses of land in that area: s 16(5). For the meaning of 'current development plan' see para 247 note 2 ante.
6 Ibid s 16(4).
7 Ibid s 16(7). For the meaning of 'authority possessing compulsory purchase powers' see para 244 note 6 ante.
8 Ibid s 16(5)(a).
9 As to service of the notice to treat see paras 100–104 ante. For the meaning of 'the notice to treat' see para 120 note 4 ante.
10 Land Compensation Act 1961 s 16(5)(b).
11 Ie any certificate issued under ibid Pt III (ss 17–22) (as amended): see paras 252–259 post.
12 Ibid s 14(3A)(b) (added by the Planning and Compensation Act 1991 s 70, Sch 15 para 15(2)).

251. Nature and extent of assumed planning permission. Where in accordance with the statutory provisions[1] it is to be assumed that planning permission[2] would be granted, the assumption must be that permission would be granted subject to such conditions, if any, as, in the circumstances mentioned in relation to the assumed permission in question, might reasonably be expected to be imposed by the authority granting the permission[3]. Further, if, in accordance with any map or statement comprised in the current development plan[4], it is indicated that any such planning permission would be granted only at a future time, then, without prejudice to the above assumed conditions, the assumption must be that the planning permission in question would be granted at the time when, in accordance with the indications in the plan, that permission might reasonably be expected to be granted[5], if no part of that land were proposed to be acquired by any authority possessing compulsory purchase powers[6].

1 Ie in accordance with the Land Compensation Act 1961 s 16(1)–(5): see paras 247–250 ante.
2 For the meaning of 'planning permission' see para 243 note 1 ante.
3 Land Compensation Act 1961 s 16(6)(a).
4 For the meaning of 'current development plan' see para 247 note 2 ante.
5 Land Compensation Act 1961 s 16(6)(b).
6 Ibid s 16(7). For the meaning of 'authority possessing compulsory purchase powers' see para 244 note 6 ante.

(v) Assumed Permission in accordance with Certificate of Appropriate Alternative Development

252. Permission certified subject to conditions including condition as to time. Where a certificate of appropriate alternative development is issued[1], it must be assumed in the case of a compulsory acquisition[2] or purchase by agreement[3] that any planning permission[4] which, according to the certificate, would have been granted in respect of the relevant land[5] or part of it, if it were not proposed to be acquired by any authority possessing compulsory purchase powers[6], would be so granted[7]. Where, however, any conditions are specified[8] in the certificate, then it must be assumed that the permission would be granted only subject to those conditions and, if any future time is so specified, only at that time[9]. The general principle of the possibility of removal of restrictions is applied by such a certificate[10].

1   Ie under the provisions of the Land Compensation Act 1961 Pt III (ss 17–22) (as amended): see paras 253–259 post.
2   See ibid ss 17, 22(2)(a), (b); and para 253 post.
3   See ibid ss 17(2), 22(2)(c); and para 253 post.
4   For the meaning of 'planning permission' see para 243 note 1 ante.
5   For the meaning of 'the relevant land' see para 243 note 5 ante; and for the meaning of 'land' see para 18 note 2 ante.
6   For the meaning of 'authority possessing compulsory purchase powers' see para 244 note 6 ante.
7   Land Compensation Act 1961 s 15(5) (amended by the Community Land Act 1975 s 58(2), Sch 10 para 4(2), (5); and by virtue of the Local Government, Planning and Land Act 1980 s 193, Sch 33 para 5(1), (3)).
8   Ie in accordance with the provisions of the Land Compensation Act 1961 Pt III (as amended): see para 253 et seq post.
9   Ibid s 15(5). As to the specification of those matters in the certificate see s 17(5) (as amended); and para 255 post.
10   See paras 242–243 ante.

253. Right to apply for certificate of appropriate alternative development. Where an authority possessing compulsory purchase powers[1] proposes to acquire an interest in land[2], either of the parties directly concerned[3] may apply to the local planning authority[4] for a certificate of appropriate alternative development[5]. If, however, the authority proposing to acquire the interest has served a notice to treat[6] in respect of it, or if an agreement has been made[7] for the sale of that interest to the authority, and a reference has been made to the Lands Tribunal to determine the amount of the compensation payable in respect of that interest, then no such application for a certificate may be made by either of the parties after the date of that reference except either with the consent in writing of the other party or the leave of the Lands Tribunal[8].

1   For the meaning of 'authority possessing compulsory purchase powers' see para 244 note 6 ante.
2   For these purposes, an interest in land is to be taken to be an interest proposed to be acquired by an authority possessing compulsory purchase powers in the following, but no other, circumstances: (1) where, for the purpose of a compulsory acquisition by that authority of land consisting of or including land in which that interest subsists, a notice required to be published or served in connection with that acquisition, either by an Act or by any standing order of either House of Parliament relating to petitions for private Bills, has been published or served in accordance with that Act or order (Land Compensation Act 1961 s 22(2)(a)); or (2) where a notice requiring the purchase of that interest has been served under any enactment, and in accordance with that enactment that authority is deemed to have served a notice to treat in respect of that interest (see eg the Town and Country Planning Act 1990 s 139(3) (purchase notices), s 149(4) (blight notices); and TOWN AND COUNTRY PLANNING vol 46 (Reissue) paras 721, 729) (Land Compensation Act 1961 s 22(2)(b); and see *Jelson Ltd v Minister of Housing and Local Government* [1970] 1 QB 243, [1969] 3 All ER 147, CA); or (3) where a written offer has been made by or on behalf of that authority to negotiate for the purchase of that interest (Land Compensation Act 1961 s 22(2)(c)); or (4) where an order has been made under the Leasehold Reform, Housing and Urban Development Act 1993 s 161(1) vesting the land in which the interest subsists in the Urban Regeneration Agency (see TRADE, INDUSTRY AND INDUSTRIAL RELATIONS vol 47 (Reissue) para 851) (Land Compensation Act 1961 s 22(2)(ca) (added for the purposes of such orders by the Leasehold Reform, Housing and Urban Development Act 1993 s 161(4), Sch 19 paras 1, 4)); or (5) where an order has been made under the Local Government, Planning and Land Act 1980 s 141 (as amended) vesting the land in an urban development corporation (see TOWN AND COUNTRY PLANNING vol 46 (Reissue) para 1296) (Land Compensation Act 1961 s 22(2)(d) (added for the purposes of such orders by the Local Government, Planning and Land Act 1980 s 141(5), Sch 27 paras 9, 12)); or (6) where an order has been

made under the Housing Act 1988 s 76 vesting the land in a housing action trust (see HOUSING) (Land Compensation Act 1961 s 22(2)(cc) (added for the purposes of such orders by the Housing Act 1988 s 76(6), Sch 9 paras 6, 9). A certificate may be applied for where there is an express power to acquire any interest or right in or over the land without having to acquire the whole land: see paras 30–32 ante. For the meaning of 'land' see para 18 note 2 ante; and for the meaning of 'enactment' see para 1 note 3 ante.

3   'The parties directly concerned', in relation to an interest in land, means the person entitled to the interest and the authority by whom it is proposed to be acquired: Land Compensation Act 1961 s 22(1). See also para 255 post.
    A surveyor who has to determine the compensation or purchase money under the Lands Clauses Consolidation Act 1845 s 58 (as amended); or under the Compulsory Purchase Act 1965 s 5(3), Sch 2 (as amended) (see para 200 post), in respect of an interest in land (a) proposed to be acquired by an authority possessing compulsory purchase powers; and (b) to which a person who is absent from the United Kingdom or who cannot be found is entitled, may apply for a certificate under these provisions before carrying out his valuation: Land Compensation Act 1961 s 19(1) (amended by the Planning and Compensation Act 1991 s 70, Sch 15 para 17; applied by the Compulsory Purchase Act 1965 s 39(3), Sch 7). The provisions of the Land Compensation Act 1961 s 17 (as amended), s 18 (see paras 255–258 post) apply in relation to an application so made as they apply in relation to an application made by virtue of s 17(1) (as substituted): s 19(1). For the meaning of 'United Kingdom' see para 100 note 21 ante.

4   For the meaning of 'local planning authority' see para 244 note 8 ante. The Broads Authority is the sole district planning authority in respect of the Broads for these purposes and for the purposes of ibid ss 18, 19 (as amended); and 'the Broads' has the same meaning as in the Norfolk and Suffolk Broads Act 1988: Land Compensation Act 1961 s 17(10), (11) (added by the Norfolk and Suffolk Broads Act 1988 s 2(5), Sch 3 para 3). As to district planning authorities see TOWN AND COUNTRY PLANNING vol 46 (Reissue) para 11.
    The Lands Tribunal has indicated that wherever possible application under the Land Compensation Act 1961 s 17 (as amended) for a certificate (and if necessary appeal under s 18: see para 258 post) should be made instead of leaving the self-same question to be determined on a hypothetical basis by the tribunal: *Williamson and Stevens v Cambridgeshire County Council* [1977] 1 EGLR 165, Lands Tribunal.

5   Land Compensation Act 1961 s 17(1) (substituted by the Planning and Compensation Act 1991 s 65(1)). As to the contents of the certificate see para 257 post.

6   As to the service of notices to treat see paras 100–104 ante. For the meaning of 'the notice to treat' see para 120 note 4 ante.

7   The making of a contract means the execution of it or, if it was not in writing, the signing of the memorandum or note by which it was attested: Land Compensation Act 1961 s 39(4). It appears that this provision has not been affected by the Law of Property (Miscellaneous Provisions) Act 1989 s 2 (formalities required on a sale or other disposition of land: see LANDLORD AND TENANT vol 27(1) (Reissue) para 56; SPECIFIC PERFORMANCE vol 44(1) (Reissue) para 858); sed quaere.

8   Land Compensation Act 1961 s 17(2) (amended by the Planning and Compensation Act 1991 s 70, Sch 15 para 16(a)). The Land Compensation Act 1961 s 17(2) (as so amended) is modified in relation to an order vesting the land in (1) the Urban Regeneration Agency, by the Leasehold Reform, Housing and Urban Development Act 1993 Sch 19 paras 1, 3; (2) an urban development corporation, by the Local Government, Planning and Land Act 1980 Sch 27 paras 9, 11; and (3) a housing action trust, by the Housing Act 1988 Sch 9 paras 6, 8.

254. Power to prescribe relevant matters. The provisions which may be made by a development order[1] include provision for regulating the manner in which applications for certificates of appropriate alternative development[2] and appeals in relation to them[3] are to be made and dealt with respectively[4], and in particular:

(1)   for prescribing[5] the time within which a certificate is required[6] to be issued[7];

(2)   for prescribing the manner in which notices of appeals[8] are to be given, and the time for giving any such notice[9];

(3)   for requiring local planning authorities[10] to furnish the Secretary of State[11], and such other persons, if any, as may be prescribed by or under the order, with such information as may be so prescribed with respect to applications for such certificates, including information whether any such application has been made in respect of any particular land[12] and information as to the manner in which any

such application has been dealt with, together, in such cases as may be so prescribed, with copies of certificates issued[13];

(4) for requiring a local planning authority, on issuing a certificate specifying conditions by reference to general requirements[14], to supply a copy of those requirements, or so much of them as is relevant to the certificate, with each copy of the certificate, unless, before the certificate is issued, the requirements in question have been made available to the public in such manner as may be specified in the development order[15].

1 For the meaning of 'development order' see para 243 note 4 ante.
2 Ie under the Land Compensation Act 1961 ss 17, 19 (as amended): see paras 253 ante, 255 et seq post.
3 Ie under ibid s 18: see para 258 post.
4 Ibid s 20.
5 Ie subject to the provisions of ibid s 17(4) (as amended): see para 256 post.
6 Ie under ibid s 17 (as amended): see para 256 post.
7 Ibid s 20(a).
8 See note 3 supra.
9 Ibid s 20(b).
10 For the meaning of 'local planning authority' see para 244 note 8 ante.
11 The functions of the Minister of Housing and Local Government under the Land Compensation Act 1961 (see s 39(1)) were transferred to the Secretary of State for the Environment, in respect of England, by the Secretary of State for the Environment Order 1970, SI 1970/1681; and to the Secretary of State for Wales, in respect of Wales, by the Secretary of State for Wales and Minister of Land and Natural Resources Order 1965, SI 1965/319.
12 For the meaning of 'land' see para 18 note 2 ante.
13 Land Compensation Act 1961 s 20(c).
14 Ie in accordance with ibid s 17(6): see para 257 post.
15 Ibid s 20(d). In exercise of the powers conferred, inter alia, by s 20, the Secretary of State has made the Land Compensation Development Order 1974, SI 1974/539, which came into operation on 1 April 1974: art 1. See para 255 et seq post.

255. Application for certificate. An application for a certificate of appropriate alternative development[1] must be in writing[2] and must include a plan or map sufficient to identify the land[3] to which the application relates[4]. The application must state:

(1) whether or not there are, in the applicant's opinion, any classes of development[5] which would be appropriate for the land in question[6] if it were not proposed to be acquired by any authority possessing compulsory purchase powers[7] and, if so, must specify the classes of development and the times at which they would be so appropriate[8];

(2) the applicant's grounds for holding that opinion[9].

It must be accompanied by a statement specifying the date on which a copy of the application has been or will be served on the other party directly concerned[10].

On a written request to the local planning authority[11] by any person appearing to it to have an interest in the land which is the subject of an application for a certificate, that authority must furnish to that person the name and address of the applicant for the certificate and the date of the application and, after it is issued, a copy of the certificate[12]. The persons served with notice of an application may make written representations to the authority with respect to the application[13].

1 Ie a certificate under the Land Compensation Act 1961 s 17 (as amended): see para 253 ante; the text and notes 5–10 infra; and paras 256–257 post.
2 Land Compensation Development Order 1974, SI 1974/539, art 3(1).
3 For the meaning of 'land' see para 18 note 2 ante.
4 Land Compensation Development Order 1974 art 3(1).
5 For the meaning of 'development' see para 243 note 2 ante.

6 Ie either immediately or at a future time; Land Compensation Act 1961 s 17(3)(a) (s 17(3) substituted by the Community Land Act 1975 s 47(1), (2); and by virtue of the Local Government, Planning and Land Act 1980 s 121(2), Sch 24).

7 For the meaning of 'authority possessing compulsory purchase powers' see para 244 note 6 ante.

8 Land Compensation Act 1961 s 17(3)(a) (as substituted: see note 6 supra).

9 Ibid s 17(3)(b) (as substituted: see note 6 supra).

10 Ibid s 17(3)(c) (as substituted: see note 6 supra). In the case of an application for a certificate made by virtue of s 19(1) (as amended) in respect of the interest of a person absent or unknown (see para 253 ante), the statement must specify the date on which a copy of the application has been or will be served on each of the parties directly concerned: s 19(3) (amended by the Community Land Act 1975 s 58(2), Sch 10 para 4(3), (5); and by virtue of the Local Government, Planning and Land Act 1980 s 193, Sch 33 para 5). For the meaning of 'the parties directly concerned' see para 253 note 3 ante.

11 For the meaning of 'local planning authority' see para 244 note 8 ante.

12 Land Compensation Development Order 1974 art 5. Alternatively, the authority must pass the written request to the local planning authority whose function it is to issue the certificate, and that authority must then comply with the request: art 5. As to the power to prescribe other information see para 254 ante. As to service of a copy of the certificate see paras 256–257, 260 post.

13 See ibid art 3(3); and para 257 post.

256. Issue of certificate. Where an application is made to the local planning authority[1] for a certificate of appropriate alternative development in respect of an interest in land[2], the authority must issue a certificate to the applicant[3] not earlier than 21 days after the date specified in the statement accompanying the application[4] and not later than two months after receipt of the application[5]. On issuing a certificate in respect of an interest in land to one of the parties directly concerned[6], the local planning authority must serve a copy of the certificate on the other of those parties[7].

Where a certificate is issued by a county planning authority[8], that authority must send a copy to the district planning authority[9] for the area in which the land or any part of it is situated; and where a certificate is issued by a district planning authority and specifies a class or classes of development[10] relating to a county matter[11], the district authority must send a copy to the county authority[12]. The local planning authority must also, on written request, furnish a copy of the certificate to any person appearing to it to have an interest in the land[13].

1 For the meaning of 'local planning authority' see para 244 note 8 ante.

2 Ie a certificate under the Land Compensation Act 1961 s 17 (as amended): see paras 253–255 ante; the text and notes 3–7 infra; and para 257 post. For the meaning of 'land' see para 18 note 2 ante.

3 Ibid s 17(4). As to applications see para 255 ante.

4 Ie the date specified in the statement mentioned in ibid s 17(3)(c) (as substituted: see para 255 ante); or, in the case of a certificate applied for by virtue of s 19(1) (as amended) (ie an application by a surveyor in respect of the interest of a person absent or unknown: see para 253 ante), the date specified in the statement in accordance with s 19(3) (as amended) (see para 255 ante) or, where more than one date is so specified, the later of those dates: see s 17(4) (amended by the Community Land Act 1975 s 47(1), (3); and by virtue of the Local Government, Planning and Land Act 1980 s 121(2), Sch 24); and the Land Compensation Act 1961 s 19(3) (amended by the Community Land Act 1975 s 58(2), Sch 10 para 4(3), (5); and by virtue of the Local Government, Planning and Land Act 1980 s 193, Sch 33 para 5).

5 Land Compensation Act 1961 s 17(4) (as amended: see note 4 supra); Land Compensation Development Order 1974, SI 1974/539, art 3(2).

6 For the meaning of 'the parties directly concerned' see para 253 note 3 ante.

7 Land Compensation Act 1961 s 17(9). Where, in pursuance of an application made by virtue of s 19(1) (as amended), the local planning authority issues a certificate to the surveyor, it must serve copies of the certificate on both the parties directly concerned: s 19(2). The service on the person who is absent or unknown will, however, have to be postponed. As to service see further para 260 post.

8 As to county planning authorities see TOWN AND COUNTRY PLANNING vol 46 (Reissue) para 11.

9 As to district planning authorities see TOWN AND COUNTRY PLANNING vol 46 (Reissue) para 11.

10 For the meaning of 'development' see para 243 note 2 ante.

11 For the meaning of 'county matter' see TOWN AND COUNTRY PLANNING vol 46 (Reissue) para 20.

12 Land Compensation Development Order 1974 art 3(4) (substituted by SI 1986/435).
13 Ibid art 5.

257. Contents of certificate. The certificate of appropriate alternative development[1] issued to the applicant must state that it is the opinion of the local planning
authority[2] regarding the grant of planning permission[3] in respect of the land[4] in
question, that if it were not proposed to be acquired by an authority possessing
compulsory purchase powers[5], either:

(1) planning permission would have been granted for development[6] of one or more
    classes specified in the certificate, whether specified in the application or not,
    and for any development for which the land is to be acquired[7], but would not
    have been granted for any other development[8]; or

(2) planning permission would have been granted for any development for which
    the land is to be acquired, but would not have been granted for any other
    development[9].

In determining whether planning permission for any particular class of development
would have been granted in respect of any land, the local planning authority must not
treat development of that class as development for which planning permission would
have been refused by reason only that it would have involved development of the land
in question, or of that land together with other land, otherwise than in accordance with
the provisions of the development plan[10] relating to it[11].

Where, in the local planning authority's opinion, planning permission would have
been granted as mentioned in head (1) above, but would only have been granted
subject to conditions[12], or at a future time, or both subject to conditions and at a future
time, the certificate must specify those conditions or that future time, or both, as the
case may be, in addition to the other matters required to be contained in it[13].

If a local planning authority issues a certificate otherwise than for the class or classes
of development specified in the application made to it, or contrary to written
representations made to it by one of the parties directly concerned[14], it must include in
the certificate a written statement of its reasons for doing so and must give particulars of
the manner in which and the time within which an appeal may be made[15] to the
Secretary of State[16].

In assessing the compensation payable to any person in respect of any compulsory
acquisition[17], there must be taken into account any expenses reasonably incurred
by him[18] in connection with the issue of a certificate of appropriate alternative
development[19].

1 Ie the certificate under the Land Compensation Act 1961 s 17 (as amended): see paras 253–256 ante; and
   the text and notes 2–19 infra.
2 For the meaning of 'local planning authority' see para 244 note 8 ante.
3 For the meaning of 'planning permission' see para 243 note 1 ante.
4 For the meaning of 'land' see para 18 note 2 ante.
5 Land Compensation Act 1961 s 17(4) (amended by the Community Land Act 1975 s 47(1), (3); and by
   virtue of the Local Government, Planning and Land Act 1980 s 121(2), Sch 24). For the meaning of
   'authority possessing compulsory purchase powers' see para 244 note 6 ante.
6 For the meaning of 'development' see para 243 note 2 ante.
7 For these purposes, development is development for which the land is to be acquired if the land is to be
   acquired for purposes which involve the carrying out of proposals of the acquiring authority for that
   development: Land Compensation Act 1961 s 17(4) (amended by the Planning and Compensation Act
   1991 s 65(2)). For the meaning of 'acquiring authority' see para 120 note 5 ante.
8 Land Compensation Act 1961 s 17(4)(a) (substituted by the Planning and Compensation Act 1991
   s 65(2)). The local planning authority must determine what planning permission would be granted at
   the date of an actual notice to treat, or a deemed notice to treat or an offer to negotiate for the purchase

of the interest, as the case may be: *Jelson Ltd v Minister of Housing and Local Government* [1970] 1 QB 243, [1969] 3 All ER 147, CA; followed in *Fox v Secretary of State for the Environment and Surrey Heath Borough Council* (1991) 62 P & CR 459, [1991] 2 EGLR 13; cf *Robert Hitchins Builders Ltd v Secretary of State for the Environment* (1978) 37 P & CR 140. These cases were, however, decided before the Planning and Compensation Act 1991 s 65(2) came into force.

A potentiality may be taken into account under the general principle: see paras 242–243 ante; *Sutton v Secretary of State for the Environment* [1984] JPL 648; *ADP & E Farmers v Department of Transport* [1988] 1 EGLR 209, Lands Tribunal; *Corrin v Northampton Borough Council* [1980] 1 EGLR 148, Lands Tribunal. Where land otherwise available for urban development is taken for a public purpose, the certificate should reflect its urban development value: *Grampian Regional Council v Secretary of State for Scotland* [1983] 3 All ER 673, [1983] 1 WLR 1340, HL, distinguishing *Skelmersdale Development Corpn v Secretary of State for the Environment* [1980] JPL 322. Where a certificate of appropriate alternative development has been granted which enhances a particular site only part of which is subsequently acquired, the landowner may be entitled to additional compensation for severance of the land acquired from that retained: *Hoveringham Gravels Ltd v Chiltern District Council* (1978) 39 P & CR 414, Lands Tribunal; cf *Phipps v Wiltshire County Council* [1983] 1 EGLR 181, Lands Tribunal.

It is wrong for the authority to specify a use, such as public open space, which could be achieved only by an authority possessing compulsory purchase powers: *Scunthorpe Borough Council v Secretary of State for the Environment* [1977] JPL 653.

9   Land Compensation Act 1961 s 17(4)(b) (as substituted: see note 8 supra). Where an application is made for a certificate and at the expiry of the prescribed time for its issue (or, if an extended period is at any time agreed upon in writing by the parties and the local planning authority, at the end of that period), no certificate has been issued, s 18 (see para 258 post) applies as if the local planning authority had issued such a certificate containing such a statement as is mentioned in s 17(4)(b) (as so substituted): s 18(4).

10   As to development plans see TOWN AND COUNTRY PLANNING vol 46 (Reissue) para 36 et seq.

11   Land Compensation Act 1961 s 17(7) (amended by the Community Land Act 1975 s 47(1), (5); and by virtue of the Local Government, Planning and Land Act 1980 Sch 24).

12   For these purposes, a local planning authority may formulate general requirements applicable to such classes of case as may be described in them; and any conditions required to be specified in the certificate in accordance with these provisions may, if it appears to the local planning authority to be convenient to do so, be specified by reference to those requirements, subject to such special modifications of them, if any, as may be set out in the certificate: Land Compensation Act 1961 s 17(6). If a local planning authority, on issuing a certificate, specifies conditions by reference to general requirements so formulated, it must supply with the certificate and every copy of it a copy of those requirements, or so much of them as is relevant to the certificate, unless, before the certificate is issued, the requirements in question have been made available to the public by depositing them for public inspection at all reasonable hours at the authority's office and, where the issuing authority is a district planning authority, at the county planning authority's office, or, where, the issuing authority is a county planning authority, at the office of the district planning authority in whose area the land is situated: Land Compensation Development Order 1974, SI 1974/539, art 6 (amended by SI 1986/435). As to district planning authorities and county planning authorities see TOWN AND COUNTRY PLANNING vol 46 (Reissue) para 11.

13   Land Compensation Act 1961 s 17(5) (amended by the Community Land Act 1975 s 47(1), (5); and by virtue of the Local Government, Planning and Land Act 1980 Sch 24).

14   For the meaning of 'the parties directly concerned' see para 253 note 3 ante.

15   Ie under the Land Compensation Act 1961 s 18: see para 258 post.

16   Land Compensation Development Order 1974 art 3(3). A failure to include all the particulars so required invalidates the certificate: *London and Clydeside Estates Ltd v Aberdeen District Council* [1979] 3 All ER 876, [1980] 1 WLR 182, HL.

17   As to the assessment of compensation see paras 250 et seq ante, 261 et seq post.

18   Ie including expenses incurred in connection with an appeal under the Land Compensation Act 1961 s 18 where any of the issues on the appeal are determined in his favour: s 17(9A) (added by the Planning and Compensation Act 1991 s 65(3)).

19   Land Compensation Act 1961 s 17(9A) (as added: see note 18 supra).

258. Appeal to Secretary of State. Where the local planning authority[1] has issued a certificate of appropriate alternative development[2] in respect of an interest in land[3], the person for the time being entitled to that interest may appeal to the Secretary of State[4] against that certificate, as may any authority possessing compulsory purchase powers[5] by whom that interest is proposed to be acquired[6]. There is also a right of appeal where the authority has not issued a certificate within the prescribed period or any extended period which may have been agreed and the certificate is deemed to have been issued[7].

The appellant must give the Secretary of State written notice of appeal within one month of the receipt of the certificate or of the date when a certificate is deemed to have been issued, as the case may be[8], and must send a copy of the notice to the local planning authority and to the other of the parties directly concerned[9]. Within one month of giving notice of appeal, or such longer period as the Secretary of State may in any particular case allow[10], the appellant must furnish to him one copy of the application made to the local planning authority for the certificate, and one copy of the certificate, if any, issued by that authority together with a statement of the grounds of appeal[11]. If the appellant does not supply these copies within the time so limited, the appeal will be treated as withdrawn[12].

If any person or authority entitled to appeal so desires, the Secretary of State must, before determining the appeal, afford that person or authority and the local planning authority an opportunity of appearing before, and being heard by, a person appointed by the Secretary of State for the purpose[13].

On the appeal the Secretary of State must consider the matters to which the certificate relates as if the application for the certificate had been made to him in the first instance, and must either confirm the certificate, or vary it, or cancel it and issue a different certificate in its place, as he considers appropriate[14]. The Secretary of State may cause a local inquiry to be held for the purpose of the exercise of any of his functions under the Land Compensation Act 1961[15].

1 For the meaning of 'local planning authority' see para 244 note 8 ante.
2 Ie a certificate under the Land Compensation Act 1961 s 17 (as amended): see paras 253–257 ante.
3 For the meaning of 'land' see para 18 note 2 ante.
4 As to the Secretary of State see para 254 note 11 ante.
5 For the meaning of 'authority possessing compulsory purchase powers' see para 244 note 6 ante.
6 Land Compensation Act 1961 s 18(1). Section 18 also applies in relation to an application made by virtue of s 19(1) (as amended): see para 253 ante.
7 See ibid s 18(4); and para 257 ante.
8 Land Compensation Development Order 1974, SI 1974/539, art 4(1), (2).
9 Ibid art 4(2). For the meaning of 'the parties directly concerned' see para 253 note 3 ante.
10 Application for any extension of time must be made before expiry of the period: *R v Secretary of State for the Environment, ex p Ward, Ward v Secretary of State for the Environment and Secretary of State for Transport* [1995] JPL B39.
11 Land Compensation Development Order 1974 art 4(3).
12 Ibid art 4(4).
13 Land Compensation Act 1961 s 18(3).
14 Ibid s 18(2).
15 See ibid s 37. The provisions of the Local Government Act 1972 s 250 (as amended) which relate to the giving of evidence at, and defraying the cost of, local inquiries (see paras 52, 54 ante) have effect with respect to any such inquiry: Land Compensation Act 1961 s 37; Interpretation Act 1978 s 17(2)(a).

259. Appeal to High Court from Secretary of State. If the local planning authority[1] or any person aggrieved[2] by a decision of the Secretary of State[3] as to a certificate of appropriate alternative development[4] desires to question the validity of that decision on the ground that it is not within the statutory powers[5] or that any of the requirements of the relevant statutory provisions[6], or of a development order[7], or of the Tribunals and Inquiries Act 1992 or any enactment replaced thereby or rules made thereunder have not been complied with in relation to the decision, that person or authority may, within six weeks from the date of the decision, apply to the High Court[8], which may:

(1) by interim order suspend the operation of the decision until the determination of the proceedings[9];

(2) quash the decision if satisfied that it is not within the statutory powers or that the applicant's interests have been substantially prejudiced by a failure to comply with the relevant requirements[10].

Subject to such an application, the validity of the Secretary of State's decision may not be questioned in any legal proceedings whatsoever[11]; but this does not affect the exercise of the jurisdiction of any court in respect of any refusal or failure on the part of the Secretary of State to give a decision on an appeal[12] to him[13].

1 For the meaning of 'local planning authority' see para 244 note 8 ante.
2 For the meaning of 'person aggrieved' see ADMINISTRATIVE LAW vol 1(1) (Reissue) para 56.
3 As to the Secretary of State see para 254 note 11 ante.
4 Ie a decision on an appeal under the Land Compensation Act 1961 s 18: see para 258 ante.
5 Ie within the powers of the Land Compensation Act 1961: see Pt III (ss 17–22) (as amended); and paras 253–258 ante.
6 Ie the requirements of the Land Compensation Act 1961: see Pt III (as amended); and paras 253–258 ante.
7 For the meaning of 'development order' see para 243 note 4 ante.
8 Land Compensation Act 1961 s 21(1) (amended by the Tribunals and Inquiries Act 1992 s 18(1), Sch 3 para 1). As to the procedure on the application see RSC Ord 94 rr 1–3; and para 86 ante.
9 Land Compensation Act 1961 s 21(1)(a).
10 Ibid s 21(1)(b).
11 Ibid s 21(2). As to the effect of this provision see *Anisminic Ltd v Foreign Compensation Commission* [1969] 2 AC 147, [1969] 1 All ER 208, HL; and ADMINISTRATIVE LAW vol 1(1) (Reissue) para 21.
12 See note 4 supra.
13 Land Compensation Act 1961 s 21(3).

260. Service of notices and documents. Any notice or other document required or authorised to be served or given under the statutory provisions relating to certificates of appropriate alternative development[1] or compensation where permission for additional development is granted after acquisition[2] may be served or given either:

(1) by delivering it to the person on whom it is to be served or to whom it is to be delivered; or

(2) by leaving it at the usual or last known place of abode of that person or, in a case in which an address for service has been furnished by that person, at that address; or

(3) by sending it in a prepaid registered letter[3] addressed to that person at his usual or last known place of abode, or, in a case in which an address for service has been furnished by that person, at that address; or

(4) in the case of an incorporated company or body, by delivering it to the secretary or clerk of the company or body at its registered or principal office, or sending it in a prepaid registered letter addressed to the secretary or clerk of the company or body at that office[4].

Where the notice or document is required or authorised to be served on any person as having an interest in premises, and the name of that person cannot be ascertained after reasonable inquiry, the notice is deemed to be duly served if:

(a) being addressed to him either by name or by the description of 'the owner' of the premises (describing them) it is delivered or sent in the manner mentioned in heads (1), (2) or (3) above; or

(b) being so addressed, and marked in the prescribed manner[5], it is sent in a prepaid registered letter to the premises and is not returned to the authority sending it, or is delivered to some person on those premises or is affixed conspicuously to some object on those premises[6].

1 Ie under the Land Compensation Act 1961 Pt III (ss 17–22) (as amended): see para 252 et seq ante.
2 Ie under ibid Pt IV (ss 23–29) (as repealed, revived and amended): see para 262 et seq post.
3 It is thought that the recorded delivery service may be used as an alternative to registered post: see the Recorded Delivery Service Act 1962 s 1(1), (2), Schedule para 1.
4 Land Compensation Act 1961 s 38(1).
5 Ie marked in the manner for the time being prescribed by regulations under the Town and Country Planning Act 1990 for securing that notices thereunder are plainly identifiable as a communication of importance (see TOWN AND COUNTRY PLANNING vol 46 (Reissue) para 31): Land Compensation Act 1961 s 38(2); Planning (Consequential Provisions) Act 1990 s 2(4).
6 Land Compensation Act 1961 s 38(2).

(5) EFFECT OF PLANNING PERMISSIONS WHERE COMPENSATION FOR GRANT OR REFUSAL OF PERMISSION PAYABLE OR REPAYABLE

(i) Outstanding Right to Compensation for Refusal etc of Planning Permission

261. In general. The Town and Country Planning Act 1947 in effect attempted to nationalise the development value of land[1]. This scheme was abandoned in 1953[2] but there remained an extremely narrow and increasingly anachronistic class of cases where compensation had been paid for a refusal of planning permission in the period between 1947 and 1953 and where there was a possible liability on landowners in respect of certain land to pay a development charge on the enhancement of the value of their land as a result of the obtaining of planning permission. The relevant provisions were continued in effect by Part V of the Town and Country Planning Act 1990[3] but were repealed by the Planning and Compensation Act 1991 in relation to claims made after 25 September 1991[4] and are of historical relevance only.

Statutory provision is, however, still made for cases where there is an outstanding right to compensation for the refusal of planning permission[5]. Where, in the case of any compulsory acquisition, a planning decision[6] or order has been made before the service of the notice to treat[7], and in consequence of the decision or order any person is entitled[8] to compensation for the depreciation of the value of an interest in land[9] which consists of or includes the whole or part of the relevant land[10], then if (1) no notice stating that the compensation has become payable has been registered[11] before the date of service of the notice to treat, whether or not a claim for compensation has been made; but (2) such a notice is registered on or after that date, the compensation payable in respect of the compulsory acquisition must be assessed as if that notice had been registered before the date of service of the notice to treat and had remained on the register of local land charges on that date[12].

1 The Town and Country Planning Act 1947 imposed restrictions on the development of land by the requirement of planning permission and provided for the payment of compensation for those restrictions to the extent that they had depreciated the value of the land: see ss 58–68 (repealed). The compensation was to be paid out in full in 1953 (see s 65(2) (repealed)) and land was to be sold and acquired at existing use value, ie without the possibility of removal of permission (see s 51 (repealed)). On obtaining planning permission, owners of land were to pay a development charge and, in effect, to

buy back the development value for the loss of which they had been compensated: see ss 69–74 (repealed).

2   The development charge was abolished and the compensation was no longer payable: see the Town and Country Planning Act 1953 s 2 (repealed). It was later decided to attach it to the land on 1 January 1955 and to pay it on the refusal or conditional grant of planning permission so far as the value of the land was depreciated thereby (see the Town and Country Planning Act 1954 ss 19, 20 (repealed)), or when the land was acquired by compulsory purchase under the provisions as to sale at existing use, which continued until 30 October 1958 (see s 31 (repealed)): see the Town and Country Planning Act 1959 ss 1–13, 58, Sch 8 (repealed). Meanwhile, before 1 January 1955, the date on which the unexpended balance was to attach to the land, some claim holdings for such depreciation had been reduced or extinguished by pledges of the claim holding in respect of development charges, or payments in respect of war-damaged land, or by way of development charge, or in respect of land compulsorily acquired, or land disposed of by gift, or where claim holdings had been purchased: see the Town and Country Planning Act 1954 ss 1–14 (repealed). If these payments were less than the value of the claim holding before 1 January 1955, and that holding had not been extinguished by compensation payable in respect of refusals of permission or conditional grant or revocation or modification of it, then the claim holding became attached to the land as the unexpended balance of established development value: see s 17 (repealed). The attachment of the balance to the land required the land to be divided so that claim holdings coincided with respect to the same area of land and continued to require that division from time to time: see s 18(2), (5) (repealed). If a claim holding had not survived so as to found a balance, it could be restored to some extent by the repayment on development of compensation previously paid in respect of the claim holding: see s 46(2), (4) (repealed). The balance so attached then became subject to reduction or extinguishment in respect of subsequent acts and events: see the Town and Country Planning Act 1990 s 119 et seq, Sch 12 (repealed). On the other hand, the balance might have been restored or increased where compensation became payable in respect of the refusal or conditional grant of planning permission on or after 1 January 1955 and, on permission given later for new development, the compensation became recoverable; the balance then had to be restored to the extent of the amount recoverable for the purposes of reduction of the balance in respect of the new development: see eg the Town and Country Planning Act 1971 s 161 (repealed); the Town and Country Planning Act 1990 Sch 12 para 13 (repealed). There might also have been a restoration of the balance where compensation became payable in respect of the revocation or modification of permission on or after 1 January 1955 and, on permission given later for new development, the compensation became recoverable: see eg the Town and Country Planning Act 1971 ss 168, 292, Sch 24 para 1 (repealed); the Town and Country Planning Act 1990 Sch 12 para 14 (repealed).

A deemed balance may have arisen or an existing balance may have been increased where compensation for severance or other injurious affection of the land not taken was, in the case of acquisitions on or after 1 January 1955 and before 30 October 1958, limited to a basis of injury pending new development and not in perpetuity, and the land so severed or injured was subsequently acquired by an acquiring authority; without that deemed balance the owner would have been selling land in a state affected by severance or other injurious affection and he would have received compensation as for injury for a term of years pending new development: see the Town and Country Planning Act 1971 s 143(3), (6), (7) (repealed); the Town and Country Planning Act 1990 Sch 12 para 18 (repealed).

The Secretary of State was obliged, on application made to him, or might, of his own initiative, issue a certificate as to the original unexpended balance and state what had happened to it: see eg the Town and Country Planning Act 1971 s 145 (repealed); the Town and Country Planning Act 1990 Sch 12 para 20 (repealed).

3   See ibid Pt V (ss 119–136), Sch 12 (repealed).

4   See the Planning and Compensation Act 1991 s 31(1), (5); the Planning and Compensation Act 1991 (Commencement No 1 and Transitional Provisions) Order 1991, SI 1991/2067, art 3. Any amount recoverable under the Town and Country Planning Act 1990 s 133 (repealed) which had not been paid, including any interest on any such amount, ceased to be recoverable; and any mortgage, covenant or other obligation by which the payment of any such amount, or interest on it, was secured, was discharged: Planning and Compensation Act 1991 s 31(6).

5   See the Land Compensation Act 1961 s 11; and the text and notes 6–12 infra. Section 11 is expressed so as to refer to compensation under the Town and Country Planning Act 1990 Pt V (repealed) as well as to compensation under s 107(1) (compensation where planning permission is revoked or modified: see TOWN AND COUNTRY PLANNING vol 46 (Reissue) para 697) but in practice the former references are now obsolete.

6   For the meaning of 'planning decision' see para 262 note 4 post.

7   For the meaning of 'the notice to treat' see para 120 note 4 ante.

8 Ie subject to the making and determination of a claim in accordance with the relevant provisions, and to the effect of any direction by the Secretary of State under the Town and Country Planning Act 1990 ss 80, 81 (repealed) or any of their predecessors: Land Compensation Act 1961 s 12(1); Planning (Consequential Provisions) Act 1990 s 2(4). 'The relevant provisions' means the provisions of the Town and Country Planning Act 1990 Pt V (repealed) in relation to compensation formerly payable thereunder (see the text and notes 1–5 supra); and in relation to compensation under s 107(1), means the provisions of regulations made under the Town and Country Planning Act 1990 with respect to claims for compensation under s 107(1): Land Compensation Act 1961 s 12(2); Planning (Consequential Provisions) Act 1990 s 2(4). See further TOWN AND COUNTRY PLANNING vol 46 (Reissue) para 697 et seq.

9 For these purposes, any reference to compensation for depreciation of the value of an interest in land is a reference to compensation payable either (1) under the Town and Country Planning Act 1990 Pt V (repealed) in respect of depreciation of the value of that interest; or (2) under s 107(1) (see TOWN AND COUNTRY PLANNING vol 46 (Reissue) para 697) in respect of loss or damage consisting of depreciation of the value of that interest: Land Compensation Act 1961 s 12(2)(a), (b); Planning (Consequential Provisions) Act 1990 s 2(4). For the meaning of 'land' see para 18 note 2 ante.

10 For the meaning of 'the relevant land' see para 243 note 5 ante.

11 For these purposes, any reference to registration is a reference to registration in the register of local land charges under the Town and Country Planning Act 1990 s 110(4) (see TOWN AND COUNTRY PLANNING vol 46 (Reissue) para 700): Land Compensation Act 1961 s 12(2); Planning (Consequential Provisions) Act 1990 s 2(4).

12 Land Compensation Act 1961 s 12(1).

(ii) Compensation where Permission for Additional Development granted after Acquisition

A. IN GENERAL

262. Compensation where planning decision made after acquisition. Where:

(1) any interest in land[1] is compulsorily acquired or is sold to an authority possessing compulsory purchase powers[2] and, before the end of the period of ten years beginning with the date of completion[3], a planning decision[4] is made granting permission for the carrying out of additional development[5] of any of the land[6]; and

(2) the principal amount of the compensation[7] which was payable in respect of the compulsory acquisition or, in the case of a sale by agreement, the amount of the purchase price, was less than the specified amount[8],

then the person to whom the compensation or purchase price was payable is entitled[9], on a claim duly made[10] by him, to compensation from the acquiring authority of an amount equal to the difference[11].

The specified amount is the principal amount of the compensation which would have been payable in respect of a compulsory acquisition of the interest by the acquiring authority, in pursuance of a notice to treat[12] served on the relevant date[13], if the planning decision mentioned in head (1) above had been made before that date and the permission granted by it had been in force on that date[14].

No such compensation is, however, payable in respect of a planning decision in so far as it relates to land acquired by the acquiring authority, whether compulsorily or by agreement:

(a) under the statutory provisions[15] relating to acquisitions by urban development corporations and by highway authorities in connection with urban development areas[16];

(b) under the statutory provision[17] relating to acquisition by the Land Authority for Wales[18];

(c) under the New Towns Act 1981[19];

(d) where the compulsory purchase order[20] included a direction[21] for minimum compensation where a building had been deliberately allowed to fall into disrepair[22]; or

(e) under the statutory provisions[23] relating to acquisition by the Urban Regeneration Agency[24].

If the person who would have been entitled to such compensation has died before the planning decision in question, or any other act or event has occurred whereby the right to compensation, if vested in him immediately before that act or event, would thereupon have vested in some other person, the right to compensation is to be treated as having devolved as if that right had been vested in him immediately before his death or immediately before that act or event, and the compensation is payable to the person claiming under him accordingly[25].

Compensation so payable carries interest at the prescribed rate[26] from the date of the planning decision in question until payment[27]. If it appears to any person that he may become liable to pay to another any such compensation or interest, he may, on written request by that other person, make one or more payments on account of the compensation or interest[28]; and such payments on account, or any excess, are recoverable if it is subsequently agreed or determined either that he is not liable to pay the compensation or interest or that any such payment is excessive[29].

The statutory provisions relating to the determination of questions of disputed compensation[30] apply[31] in relation to the assessment of compensation under these provisions as they apply in relation to the assessment of compensation in respect of the compulsory acquisition of an interest in land[32].

1 For the meaning of 'land' see para 18 note 2 ante.

2 For the meaning of 'authority possessing compulsory purchase powers' see para 244 note 6 ante.

3 'Date of completion', in relation to an acquisition or sale of an interest in land, means the date on which the acquisition or sale is completed by the vesting of that interest in the acquiring authority: Land Compensation Act 1961 s 29(1) (s 29 repealed; revived by the Planning and Compensation Act 1991 s 66(1), Sch 14 para 1). For the meaning of 'acquiring authority' see para 120 note 5 ante.

4 'Planning decision' means a decision made on an application under the Town and Country Planning Act 1990 Pt III (ss 55–106B) (as amended) (see TOWN AND COUNTRY PLANNING vol 46 (Reissue) para 144 et seq): Land Compensation Act 1961 s 39(1); Planning (Consequential Provisions) Act 1990 s 2(4). As respects references for these purposes to planning decisions: (1) in relation to a decision altered on appeal by the reversal or variation of the whole or any part of it, such references are to be construed as references to the decision as so altered; (2) in relation to a decision upheld on appeal, such references are to be construed as references to the decision of the local planning authority and not to the decision of the Secretary of State on the appeal; (3) in relation to a decision given on an appeal made by virtue of the Town and Country Planning Act 1990 s 78(2) (as amended) (see TOWN AND COUNTRY PLANNING vol 46 (Reissue) para 846) in default of a decision by the local planning authority, such references are to be construed as references to the decision so given; and (4) the time of a planning decision, in a case where there is or was an appeal, is to be taken to be or to have been the time of the decision as made by the local planning authority, whether or not that decision is or was altered by the reversal or variation of the whole or any part of it on the appeal, or, in the case of such a decision as is mentioned in head (3) supra, the time when by virtue of s 78(5) the notification of a decision by the local planning authority is deemed to have been given: Land Compensation Act 1961 s 39(3); Planning (Consequential Provisions) Act 1990 s 2(4). The Secretary of State here concerned is the Secretary of State for the Environment in relation to England, and, in relation to Wales, the Secretary of State for Wales.

5 For the meaning of 'additional development' see para 263 post. For these purposes, any reference to the granting of permission for the carrying out of development of any land is a reference to the granting of permission (including where applicable outline permission) for that development either unconditionally or subject to conditions, and either in respect of that land by itself or in respect of an area including that land: Land Compensation Act 1961 s 29(2) (as revived: see note 3 supra). For the meaning of 'development' see para 243 note 2 ante. As to outline permission see TOWN AND COUNTRY PLANNING vol 46 (Reissue) paras 450–454.

6 Land Compensation Act 1961 s 23(1)(a) (s 23 repealed; revived by the Planning and Compensation Act 1991 Sch 14 para 1).

7 Any reference in ibid s 23 (as revived and amended: see notes 6 supra, 18–19, 22 infra) to the principal amount of the compensation is to be construed as including any sum attributable to disturbance, severance or injurious affection: Land Compensation Act 1961 s 27, Sch 3 para 1 (repealed; revived by the Planning and Compensation Act 1991 Sch 14 para 2). If, however, the person entitled to the compensation under the Land Compensation Act 1961 s 23 (as so revived and amended) (1) was, at the time of the compulsory acquisition or sale mentioned in head (2) in the text, entitled to an interest in other land contiguous or adjacent to the land acquired or purchased; but (2) is, at the time of the planning decision in question, no longer entitled to the interest, either in respect of the whole or in respect of part of that land, any reference in s 23 (as so revived) to the principal amount of any compensation or the amount of the purchase price is to be construed as excluding so much of the compensation or purchase price as was or would have been attributable to severance or injurious affection of that land or, as the case may be, of that part: Sch 3 para 2 (as so revived). For the purposes of the application of s 23 (as so revived and amended) and Sch 3 paras 1–4, 7–8 (as so revived) to a case falling within Sch 3 para 4 (as so revived) (provisions relating to mortgaged land: see note 9 infra), any reference to the principal amount of the compensation which was or would have been payable in respect of any compulsory acquisition is to be construed as a reference to the principal amount of the compensation which would have been payable if the interest in question had not been subject to a mortgage: Sch 3 para 5 (as so revived). References in Sch 3 (as so revived) to s 23 (as so revived and amended) include references to that section as applied by s 25 or s 26 (as so revived); and references to the time of any planning decision are to be construed accordingly: Sch 3 para 8 (as so revived).

'Contiguous' prima facie means 'touching': *Spillers Ltd v Cardiff Assessment Committee and Pritchard (Cardiff Revenue Officer)* [1931] 2 KB 21; *Haynes v King* [1893] 3 Ch 439 at 448; *Southwark Revenue Officer v R Hoe & Co Ltd* (1930) 143 LT 544. 'Adjacent' is less precise, particularly where, as here, used in contradistinction to 'contiguous': see *Wellington Corpn v Lower Hutt Corpn* [1904] AC 773, PC; cf *Re Ecclesiastical Comrs for England's Conveyance* [1936] Ch 430 ('adjoining or adjacent'); *English Clays Lovering Pochin & Co Ltd v Plymouth Corpn* [1974] 2 All ER 239, [1974] 1 WLR 742, CA; *James A Jobling & Co Ltd v Sunderland County Borough Assessment Committee* [1944] 1 All ER 207 (affd on other grounds [1944] 1 All ER 500, CA).

8 Land Compensation Act 1961 s 23(1)(b) (as revived: see note 6 supra). As to the specified amount see s 23(2) (as so revived) and the text and notes 12–14 infra.

9 Where, in a case falling within ibid s 23(1) (as revived: see note 6 supra), the interest in land which was acquired or sold was subject to a mortgage, any reference, however expressed, in s 23 (as revived and amended) or s 24 (as revived) (see para 265 post) to the person entitled to the compensation or purchase price is to be construed as a reference to the person who, subject to the mortgage, was entitled to that interest, and not as a reference to the mortgagee: Sch 3 para 4 (as revived: see note 7 supra). Where, however, the interest in land which was acquired or sold was subject to a settlement, and accordingly the compensation or purchase price was payable to the trustees of that settlement, any such reference, however expressed, is to be construed as a reference to the trustees for the time being of the settlement: Sch 3 para 7(1) (as so revived). 'Settlement' means a settlement within the meaning of the Settled Land Act 1925 or a trust for sale within the meaning of the Law of Property Act 1925: Land Compensation Act 1961 Sch 3 para 7(4) (as so revived).

10 As to making a claim see para 265 post.

11 Land Compensation Act 1961 s 23(1) (as revived: see note 6 supra). In determining that difference for these purposes, in a case where (1) the compensation or the purchase price was or would have been reduced (whether by virtue of s 7 (see para 316 post) or otherwise) by reason of an increase in the value of an interest in contiguous or adjacent land; and (2) at the time of the planning decision the person entitled to the compensation under s 23 (as revived and amended) is not entitled to the interest or is entitled to it only as respects part of the contiguous or adjacent land, the amount specified in s 23(2) (as so revived: see the text and notes 12–14 infra) and the principal amount or purchase price mentioned in s 23(1) (as so revived) are to be calculated as if the circumstances by reason of which the compensation or purchase price was or would have been so reduced had not existed or, as the case may be, as if the interest in the contiguous or adjacent land had subsisted only in that part of the land: Sch 3 para 3 (as revived: see note 7 supra).

12 As to the service of notices to treat see paras 100–104 ante.

13 'The relevant date', in relation to a compulsory acquisition of an interest in land, means the date of service of the notice to treat and, in relation to a sale of such an interest by agreement, means the date of the making of the contract in pursuance of which the sale was effected: Land Compensation Act 1961 s 29(1) (as revived: see note 3 supra). References in the 1961 Act to a contract are references to a contract in writing or a contract attested by a memorandum or note of it in writing, signed by the parties to it or

by some other person or persons authorised by them in that behalf and, in relation to an interest in land conveyed or assigned without a preliminary contract, are references to the conveyance or assignment: s 39(4). Cf, however, the Law of Property (Miscellaneous Provisions) Act 1989 s 2 (formalities required on a sale or other disposition of land); and LANDLORD AND TENANT vol 27(1) (Reissue) para 56; SPECIFIC PERFORMANCE vol 44(1) (Reissue) para 858; SALE OF LAND. As to the making of a contract see para 253 note 7 ante. For the meaning of 'the notice to treat' see para 120 note 4 ante.

14 Land Compensation Act 1961 s 23(2) (as revived: see note 6 supra).

15 Ie under the Local Government, Planning and Land Act 1980 s 142 or s 143 (as amended): see TOWN AND COUNTRY PLANNING vol 46 (Reissue) para 1297 et seq.

16 Land Compensation Act 1961 s 23(3)(a) (as revived: see note 6 supra). Nor is such compensation payable by virtue of an order under the Local Government, Planning and Land Act 1980 s 141 (as amended) vesting land in an urban development corporation: see s 141(5A) (as added); and TOWN AND COUNTRY PLANNING vol 46 (Reissue) para 1296.

17 Ie under the Local Government, Planning and Land Act 1980 s 104 (as amended): see TOWN AND COUNTRY PLANNING vol 46 (Reissue) para 806.

18 Land Compensation Act 1961 s 23(3)(aa) (added by the Leasehold Reform, Housing and Urban Development Act 1993 s 181(1), (2)).

19 Land Compensation Act 1961 s 23(3)(b) (as revived (see note 6 supra); amended by the Leasehold Reform, Housing and Urban Development Act 1993 s 187(2), Sch 22). As to acquisitions by development corporations and highway authorities in connection with new town areas see TOWN AND COUNTRY PLANNING vol 46 (Reissue) para 1104 et seq.

20 As to compulsory purchase orders see para 34 et seq ante.

21 Ie under the Planning (Listed Buildings and Conservation Areas) Act 1990 s 50: see TOWN AND COUNTRY PLANNING vol 46 (Reissue) para 949.

22 Land Compensation Act 1961 s 23(3)(c) (as revived (see note 6 supra); amended by the Leasehold Reform, Housing and Urban Development Act 1993 s 181(1), (3)).

23 Ie under the Leasehold Reform, Housing and Urban Development Act 1993 Pt III (ss 158–185): see TRADE, INDUSTRY AND INDUSTRIAL RELATIONS vol 47 (Reissue) para 844 et seq.

24 Land Compensation Act 1961 s 23(3)(d) (added by the Leasehold Reform, Housing and Urban Development Act 1993 s 181(1), (3)).

25 Land Compensation Act 1961 s 23(4) (as revived: see note 6 supra). Section 23(4) (as so revived) does not apply where Sch 3 para 7(1) (as revived: see note 7 supra) applies (see note 9 supra): Sch 3 para 7(2) (as so revived).

26 Ie the rate prescribed under ibid s 32: see para 125 note 5 ante.

27 Ibid s 23(5) (as revived: see note 6 supra).

28 Planning and Compensation Act 1991 s 80(2), Sch 18 Pt II.

29 Ibid s 80(3).

30 Ie the Land Compensation Act 1961 Pt I (ss 1–4) (as amended): see paras 18, 189, 198–199, 223–225, 227, 229 ante.

31 Ie so far as applicable and subject to ibid ss 24–29 (as revived: see note 6 supra): s 23(6) (as so revived).

32 Ibid s 23(6) (as revived: see note 6 supra).

263. Meaning of 'additional development'. For the purposes of the statutory provisions relating to compensation where a planning decision is made after acquisition[1], 'additional development', in relation to an acquisition or sale of an interest in land[2], means any development[3] which is not development:

(1) for the purposes of the functions for which a local authority[4] acquired the interest, when it is the acquiring authority[5] and acquired the interest for the purposes of any of its functions;

(2) for the purposes of the project for which the acquiring authority acquired the interest, when that authority is not a local authority;

(3) for which planning permission[6] was in force on the relevant date[7];

(4) for which it was assumed[8], for the purpose of assessing compensation in the case of compulsory acquisition, that planning permission would be granted; and

(5) for which it would have been so assumed, in the case of a sale by agreement, if the interest had been compulsorily acquired by the acquiring authority in

pursuance of a notice to treat[9] served on the relevant date, instead of being sold by agreement[10].

1 Ie the Land Compensation Act 1961 Pt IV (ss 23–29) (as repealed, revived and amended): see paras 262 ante, 265 et seq post.
2 For the meaning of 'land' see para 18 note 2 ante.
3 For the meaning of 'development' see para 243 note 2 ante.
4 For these purposes, 'local authority' means (1) a charging authority, a precepting authority, a combined police authority or a combined fire authority, as defined in the Local Government Finance Act 1988 s 144 (as amended); (2) a levying board within the meaning of s 74 (as amended); (3) a body as regards which s 75 (as amended) applies; (4) any joint board or joint committee if all the constituent authorities are such authorities as are described in heads (1)–(3) supra; and (5) the Honourable Society of the Inner Temple or the Honourable Society of the Middle Temple; and includes any internal drainage board under the Land Drainage Act 1991 s 1, Sch 1 (as amended): Land Compensation Act 1961 s 29(1) (repealed; revived by the Planning and Compensation Act 1991 s 66(1), Sch 14 para 1); Interpretation Act 1978 s 17(2)(a).
5 For the meaning of 'acquiring authority' see para 120 note 5 ante.
6 For the meaning of 'planning permission' see para 243 note 1 ante.
7 For the meaning of 'the relevant date' see para 262 note 13 ante.
8 Ie in accordance with the provisions of the Land Compensation Act 1961 ss 14–16 (as amended): see para 243 et seq ante.
9 As to the service of notices to treat see paras 100–104 ante.
10 Land Compensation Act 1961 s 29(1) (as revived: see note 4 supra).

264. Special provisions relating to mortgaged and settled land.

No compensation is payable where a planning decision is made after acquisition[1] in respect of a compulsory acquisition or sale by agreement where the interest acquired or sold was the interest of a mortgagee, as distinct from an interest subject to a mortgage[2].

Any compensation paid[3] to the trustees of a settlement[4] in respect of a compulsory acquisition or sale by agreement is applicable by the trustees as if it were proceeds of the sale of the interest acquired or sold[5].

1 Ie payable by virtue of the Land Compensation Act 1961 s 23 (as revived and amended) (see para 262 ante) or by virtue of that provision as applied by s 25 or s 26 (as revived) (see paras 265–266 post): s 27, Sch 3 paras 6, 8 (repealed; revived by the Planning and Compensation Act 1991 s 66(1), Sch 14 paras 1, 2).
2 Land Compensation Act 1961 Sch 3 para 6 (as revived: see note 1 supra).
3 Ie paid by virtue of ibid s 23 (as revived and amended) or by virtue of that provision as applied by s 25 or s 26 (as revived): Sch 3 paras 7(3), 8 (as revived: see note 1 supra).
4 For the meaning of 'settlement' see para 262 note 9 ante.
5 Land Compensation Act 1961 Sch 3 para 7(3) (as revived: see note 1 supra).

265. Claims for compensation where planning decision made after acquisition.

For the purpose of facilitating the making of claims for compensation where a planning decision is made after acquisition[1], the person entitled to receive the compensation or purchase price in respect of a relevant acquisition or sale[2] or any person claiming under him[3] may give to the acquiring authority[4] an address for service[5]. Where a planning decision is made[6] at any time after a person has so given an address for service and before the end of the specified period[7], the acquiring authority must give notice of the decision in the prescribed form[8] to that person at that address[9].

Where a person has given an address for service to an acquiring authority and that authority, before the end of the specified period, ceases to be entitled to an interest in the whole or part of the land[10] comprised in the acquisition or sale, without remaining or becoming entitled to a freehold interest in, or tenancy[11] of, that land or that part of it, that authority must notify the local planning authority[12]; and after that it is the duty of the local planning authority to give notice to the acquiring authority of any planning decision of which the acquiring authority is required to give notice under the above provisions[13].

A claim for compensation in respect of a planning decision[14] does not have effect if made more than six months after the date:

(1) of the decision[15], if the claim is made by a person who has not given the acquiring authority an address for service; or

(2) of the date on which notice of the decision is given to the person making the claim, if he has given the acquiring authority an address for service[16].

1 Ie claims under the Land Compensation Act 1961 s 23 (as repealed, revived and amended): see para 262 ante. For the meaning of 'planning decision' see para 262 note 4 ante.

2 Ie such an acquisition or sale as is mentioned in ibid s 23(1)(a) (as revived): see para 262 head (1) ante. As to the person entitled to receive the compensation see para 262 note 9 ante.

3 Ie any person claiming under him as being a person who, if compensation under ibid s 23 (as revived and amended) became payable, would be entitled to it by virtue of s 23(4) (as revived): see para 262 text and note 25 ante.

4 For the meaning of 'acquiring authority' see para 120 note 5 ante.

5 Land Compensation Act 1961 s 24(1) (s 24 repealed; revived by the Planning and Compensation Act 1991 s 66(1), Sch 14 para 1).

6 Ie such a planning decision as is mentioned in the Land Compensation Act 1961 s 23(1)(a) (as revived): see para 262 head (1) ante.

7 Ie the period mentioned in ibid s 23(1)(a) (as revived): see para 262 head (1) ante.

8 'Prescribed' means prescribed by regulations under ibid Pt IV (ss 23–29) (as repealed, revived and amended) (see paras 262 et seq ante, 266 et seq post): s 29(1). The Secretary of State may make regulations by statutory instrument, subject to annulment in pursuance of a resolution of either House of Parliament, prescribing the form of any notice required by Pt IV (as revived and amended) to be given in the prescribed form: s 28(1), (2) (repealed; revived by the Planning and Compensation Act 1991 Sch 14 para 1). The Secretary of State here concerned is the Secretary of State for the Environment in relation to England and, in relation to Wales, the Secretary of State for Wales. In exercise of the power so conferred, the Secretary of State has made the Land Compensation (Additional Development) (Forms) Regulations 1992, SI 1992/271, which came into force on 12 March 1992: reg 1. For the prescribed form of notice see reg 3(a), Schedule, Form 1.

9 Land Compensation Act 1961 s 24(2) (as revived: see note 5 supra). If, however, an address for service has been given by such a person as is mentioned in s 24(1)(b) (as so revived) (ie a person claiming under the person entitled as being a person who would be entitled to compensation by virtue of s 23(4) (as so revived): see note 3 supra; and para 262 ante), and the acquiring authority has reasonable grounds for believing that the person entitled is dead or that any other act or event has occurred as mentioned in s 23(4)(b) (as so revived) (see para 262 ante), the acquiring authority need not give a notice to the person entitled: s 24(3) (as so revived).

10 For the meaning of 'land' see para 18 note 2 ante.

11 For these purposes, 'tenancy' has the same meaning as in the Landlord and Tenant Act 1954 (see LANDLORD AND TENANT vol 27(1) (Reissue) para 369 note 1): Land Compensation Act 1961 s 39(1).

12 For the meaning of 'local planning authority' see para 244 note 8 ante; and see TOWN AND COUNTRY PLANNING vol 46 (Reissue) para 11 et seq.

13 Land Compensation Act 1961 s 24(6) (as revived: see note 5 supra). Notice of a planning decision must be given (1) in the case of a decision made by the local planning authority, within seven days after the making of the decision; and (2) in any other case, within seven days after the making of the decision has been notified to the local planning authority: s 24(7) (as so revived).

14 Ie a claim under ibid s 23 (as revived and amended): see para 262 ante.

15 Where there is an appeal against the planning decision, this reference to the date of the decision is to be read as a reference to the date of the decision on the appeal (ibid s 24(4) (as revived: see note 5 supra)); and references for these purposes to an appeal against a planning decision include an appeal made by virtue of the Town and Country Planning Act 1990 s 78(2) (as substituted) (appeals relating to advertisements: see TOWN AND COUNTRY PLANNING vol 46 (Reissue) para 850) (Land Compensation Act 1961 s 24(5) (as so revived)).

16 Ibid s 24(4) (as revived: see note 5 supra).

B. EXTENSION TO CASES WHERE NO PLANNING DECISION MADE

266. Extension to planning permission where no planning decision is made. The provisions relating to claims for compensation where a planning decision is made after acquisition[1] have effect:

   (1) in relation to planning permission[2] granted by a development order[3], as if a planning decision granting that permission had been made on the date when the development[4] is initiated[5];

   (2) in relation to planning permission granted by the adoption or approval of a simplified planning zone scheme[6], as if a planning decision granting that permission had been made on the date when the scheme is approved or adopted;

   (3) in relation to planning permission granted by an order designating an enterprise zone[7], as if a planning decision granting that permission had been made on the date when the designation takes effect;

   (4) in relation to planning permission deemed to be granted by a direction given by a government department or the Secretary of State[8], as if a planning decision granting that permission had been made on the date when the direction is given;

   (5) in relation to planning permission deemed to be granted by a local planning authority[9], as if a planning decision granting that permission had been made on the occurrence of the event in consequence of which the permission is deemed to be granted[10].

Where those provisions so have effect in relation to any planning permission falling within heads (1) to (5) above for any development, then if before the date shown in the relevant head a person who is entitled[11] to give an address for service has given such an address to the acquiring authority[12] and the development is proposed to be carried out by the acquiring authority or, if it is proposed to be carried out by a person other than that authority, notice of that proposal is given to the acquiring authority by the person proposing to carry it out, it is the duty of that authority to give notice of the proposal in the prescribed form[13] to the entitled person at the address given by him to the authority[14].

A claim for compensation[15] in respect of a planning permission falling with heads (1) to (5) above does not have effect if made more than six months after the date:

   (a) on which notice was given to the person who made the claim, if he is a person to whom notice has been given in accordance with the provisions[16]; or

   (b) shown in the relevant head, in any other case[17].

1 Ie the Land Compensation Act 1961 s 23 (as repealed, revived and amended) and s 24(1) (as repealed and revived): see para 262, 265 ante. For the meaning of 'planning decision' see para 262 note 4 ante.
2 For the meaning of 'planning permission' see para 243 note 1 ante.
3 For the meaning of 'development order' see para 243 note 4 ante.
4 For the meaning of 'development' see para 243 note 2 ante.
5 For these purposes, development of land is taken to be initiated (1) if the development consists of the carrying out of operations, at the time when those operations are begun; (2) if the development consists of a change of use, at the time when the new use is instituted; and (3) if the development consists both of the carrying out of operations and of a change in use, at the earlier of the times mentioned in heads (1)–(2) supra: Land Compensation Act 1961 s 39(7).
6 As to simplified planning zone schemes see TOWN AND COUNTRY PLANNING vol 46 (Reissue) para 361 et seq.
7 As to enterprise zones see TOWN AND COUNTRY PLANNING vol 46 (Reissue) paras 385, 1335 et seq.
8 Ie under the Town and Country Planning Act 1990 s 90 (as amended): see TOWN AND COUNTRY PLANNING vol 46 (Reissue) para 169.
9 For the meaning of 'local planning authority' see para 244 note 8 ante; and see TOWN AND COUNTRY PLANNING vol 46 (Reissue) para 11 et seq.

10 Land Compensation Act 1961 s 25(1) (s 25 repealed; revived by the Planning and Compensation Act 1991 s 66(1), Sch 14 para 1).
11 Ie under the Land Compensation Act 1961 s 24(1) (as revived: see para 265 ante) as applied by s 25(1) (as revived: see note 10 supra): see s 25(2)(a) (as so revived).
12 For the meaning of 'acquiring authority' see para 120 note 5 ante.
13 For the prescribed form see the Land Compensation (Additional Development) (Forms) Regulations 1992, SI 1992/271, reg 3(b), Schedule, Form 2.
14 Land Compensation Act 1961 s 25(2) (as revived: see note 10 supra). An acquiring authority is not, however, required to give such notice of proposed development to the entitled person if (1) an address for service has been given to the authority by such a person as is mentioned in s 24(1)(b) (as so revived) (ie any person claiming under the entitled person as being a person who, if compensation under s 23 (as revived and amended) became payable, would be entitled to it by virtue of s 23(4) (as so revived): see para 262 text and note 25 ante); and (2) the authority has reasonable grounds for believing that the entitled person is dead or that any other act or event has occurred as mentioned in s 23(4)(b) (as so revived): s 25(3) (as so revived).
15 Ie under ibid s 23 (as revived and amended): see para 262 ante.
16 Ie in accordance with ibid s 25(2) (as revived): see the text and notes 11–14 supra.
17 Ibid s 25(4) (as revived: see note 10 supra).

267. Extension to Crown development. Where:

(1) any interest in land[1] is compulsorily acquired or is sold to an authority possessing compulsory purchase powers[2], and before the end of the period of ten years beginning with the date of completion[3] there is initiated[4] any additional development[5] of any of the land which was comprised in the acquisition or sale[6]; and

(2) the development in question is development for which planning permission[7] is not required because it is initiated by or on behalf of the Crown[8] or there is a Crown or Duchy interest[9] in the land and the development is initiated in right of that interest[10],

the provisions relating to claims for compensation where a planning decision is made after acquisition[11] apply as if a planning decision granting permission for that development had been made at the time when the additional development is so initiated[12].

Where those provisions have effect as so applied in relation to the initiation of any development, and before the development is initiated a person who is entitled[13] to give an address for service has given such an address to the acquiring authority[14], it is the duty of that authority to give notice in the prescribed form[15] of the initiation of the development to the entitled person at the address given by him to the authority[16]. Where, however, this duty to give notice is the duty of a government department, and the minister in charge of the department certifies that for reasons of national security it is necessary that the nature of the development should not be disclosed, except to the extent specified in the certificate, the department must give notice of development but is not required to give any particulars of the nature of the development except to the extent so specified[17].

A claim for compensation[18] in respect of the initiation of any development does not have effect if made more than six months after:

(a) the date on which notice was given to the person making the claim, if he is a person to whom notice has been given[19]; or

(b) the time the development is initiated, in any other case[20].

1 For the meaning of 'land' see para 18 note 2 ante.
2 For the meaning of 'authority possessing compulsory purchase powers' see para 244 note 6 ante.
3 For the meaning of 'date of completion' see para 262 note 3 ante.
4 As to when development is initiated see para 266 note 5 ante; and for the meaning of 'development' see para 243 note 2 ante.

5 For the meaning of 'additional development' see para 263 ante.
6 Land Compensation Act 1961 s 26(1)(a) (s 26 repealed; revived by the Planning and Compensation Act 1991 s 66(1), Sch 14 para 1).
7 For the meaning of 'planning permission' see para 243 note 1 ante.
8 Land Compensation Act 1961 s 26(1)(b), (2)(a) (as revived: see note 6 supra).
9 For these purposes, 'Crown or Duchy interest' means an interest belong to Her Majesty in right of the Crown or of the Duchy of Lancaster, or belonging to the Duchy of Cornwall, or belonging to a government department or held in trust for Her Majesty for the purposes of a government department: ibid s 26(7) (as revived: see note 6 supra).
10 Ibid s 26(1)(b), (2)(b) (as revived: see note 6 supra).
11 Ie the provisions of ibid s 23 (as revived and amended) and s 24(1) (as revived): see paras 262, 265 ante. For the meaning of 'planning decision' see para 262 note 4 ante.
12 Ibid s 26(1) (as revived: see note 6 supra).
13 Ie under ibid s 24(1) (as revived) (see para 265 ante) as that provision is applied by s 26(1) (as revived: see note 6 supra): see s 26(3)(b) (as so revived).
14 For the meaning of 'acquiring authority' see para 120 note 5 ante.
15 For the prescribed form see the Land Compensation (Additional Development) (Forms) Regulations 1992, SI 1992/271, reg 3(c), Schedule, Form 3.
16 Land Compensation Act 1961 s 26(3) (as revived: see note 6 supra). An acquiring authority is not, however, required to give such notice of proposed development to the entitled person if (1) an address for service has been given to the authority by such a person as is mentioned in s 24(1)(b) (as so revived) (ie any person claiming under the entitled person as being a person who, if compensation under s 23 (as revived and amended) became payable, would be entitled to it by virtue of s 23(4) (as so revived): see para 262 text and note 25 ante); and (2) the authority has reasonable grounds for believing that the entitled person is dead or that any other act or event has occurred as mentioned in s 23(4)(b) (as so revived): s 26(5) (as so revived).
17 Ibid s 26(4) (as revived: see note 6 supra).
18 Ie under ibid s 23 (as revived and amended): see para 262 ante.
19 Ie under ibid s 26(3) (as revived: see note 6 supra): see the text and notes 13–16 supra.
20 Ibid s 26(6) (as revived: see note 6 supra).

(6) SCHEME FOR WHICH THE LAND IS TAKEN TO BE DISREGARDED

(i) In general

268. The general principle. In valuing the land taken there must be disregarded any increase in value which is due to the scheme for which the land is taken; it is well settled that compensation for the compulsory acquisition of land cannot include an increase in value which is entirely due to the scheme underlying the acquisition[1]. The purpose of this principle is to prevent the acquisition of the land being at a price which is inflated by the very project or scheme which gives rise to the acquisition[2]. Conversely, the compensation payable cannot include any decrease in value which is entirely due to this scheme[3]; no account is taken of any depreciation of the value of the relevant interest[4] which is attributable to the fact that (whether by way of allocation or other particulars contained in the current development plan[5] or by any other means[6]) an indication has been given that the relevant land[7] is, or is likely to be, acquired by an authority possessing compulsory purchase powers[8].

1 *Pointe Gourde Quarrying and Transport Co Ltd v Sub-Intendent of Crown Lands* [1947] AC 565, PC; approved in *Davy v Leeds Corpn* [1965] 1 All ER 753, [1965] 1 WLR 445, HL; *Penny v Penny* (1867) LR 5 Eq 227; *Re Lucas and Chesterfield Gas and Water Board* [1909] 1 KB 16, CA; *Cedar Rapids Manufacturing and Power Co v Lacoste* [1914] AC 569, PC; *Fraser v City of Fraserville* [1917] AC 187, PC; *Re Gough and Aspatria, Silloth and District Joint Water Board* [1904] 1 KB 417 at 423, CA; *Vyricherla Narayana Gajapatiraju v Revenue Divisional Officer, Vizagapatam* [1939] AC 302 at 313, [1939] 2 All ER 317 at 322, PC. The principle is commonly referred to as 'the Pointe Gourde principle' after *Pointe Gourde*

Quarrying and Transport Co Ltd v Sub-Intendent of Crown Lands supra. It applies to the value of the interest when ascertained and not to the ascertainment of what is the interest to be valued, and cannot affect the lessor's rights in relation to his lessee: see *Minister of Transport v Pettitt* (1968) 20 P & CR 344 at 355, CA; *Rugby Joint Water Board v Foottit, Rugby Joint Water Board v Shaw-Fox* [1973] AC 202, [1972] 1 All ER 1057, HL; *Abbey Homesteads (Developments) Ltd v Northamptonshire County Council* (1992) 64 P & CR 377, [1992] 2 EGLR 18, CA; but as to agricultural holdings see para 288 note 8 post. When valuing the land in relation to other land, the actual scheme of the acquiring authority on that other land must also be disregarded: see the cases cited supra; and para 271 post.

2   *Wilson v Liverpool City Council* [1971] 1 All ER 628 at 635, [1971] 1 WLR 302 at 310, CA, per Widgery LJ.
3   *Jelson Ltd v Blaby District Council* [1978] 1 All ER 548, [1977] 1 WLR 1020, CA.
4   For the meaning of 'relevant interest' see para 120 note 4 ante.
5   For the meaning of 'current development plan' see para 247 note 2 ante.
6   An indication given by 'other means' must provide information which is available not merely to the owner but also to a potential purchaser: *Abbey Homesteads (Developments) Ltd v Northamptonshire County Council* (1992) 64 P & CR 377 at 385, [1992] 2 EGLR 18 at 21, CA. See also *Thornton v Wakefield Metropolitan District Council* [1991] 2 EGLR 215, Lands Tribunal; *London Borough of Hackney v Macfarlane* (1970) 21 P & CR 342, CA; *Trocette Property Co Ltd v GLC* (1974) 28 P & CR 408, CA. As to the method of assessing the market value of the land acquired see paras 278–279 post.
7   For the meaning of 'the relevant land' see para 243 note 5 ante.
8   Land Compensation Act 1961 s 9 (amended by the Town and Country Planning Act 1968 s 108, Sch 11); and see *London Borough of Hackney v Macfarlane* (1970) 21 P & CR 342, CA; *Trocette Property Co Ltd v GLC* (1974) 28 P & CR 408, CA; *Tranter v Birmingham City District Council* (1975) 31 P & CR 327, Lands Tribunal; *London & Provincial Poster Group Ltd v Oldham Metropolitan Borough Council* [1991] 1 EGLR 214, Lands Tribunal; *Thornton v Wakefield Metropolitan District Council* [1991] 2 EGLR 215, Lands Tribunal. For the meaning of 'authority possessing compulsory purchase powers' see para 244 note 6 ante.

(ii) Statutory Disregard of Actual or Prospective Development in Certain Cases

A. IN GENERAL

269. Statutory disregard of the scheme for which land is acquired. No account is to be taken of any increase or diminution in the value of the relevant interest[1] which is attributable in certain circumstances[2] to the carrying out, or the prospect of, so much of the relevant development[3] as would not have been likely to be carried out if the statutory conditions[4] had been satisfied[5]. This statutory provision does not, however, affect the general principle[6]; both the statutory assumptions and the general principle operate concurrently[7]. Identification of the scheme which must be disregarded will turn on the facts of each case[8], but there is no provision for the disregard of any increase in value due to persons in the market who are prepared to develop the land to the same as, or to a lesser extent than, it would be developed under the acquiring authority's scheme[9].

1   For the meaning of 'relevant interest' see para 120 note 4 ante.
2   Ie the circumstances described in any of the Land Compensation Act 1961 s 6(1), Sch 1 paras 1–4B col 1 (as amended): see para 271 et seq post.
3   For these purposes, 'development' is to be construed as including the clearing of the land: ibid s 6(3). For the meaning of 'development' generally see para 243 note 2 ante. The relevant development referred to is the development mentioned, in relation to the circumstances described in any of Sch 1 paras 1–4B col 1 (as amended), in Sch 1 paras 1–4B col 2 (as amended): see para 271 et seq post.
4   Ie the conditions mentioned in ibid s 6(1)(a) (see para 271 post) or, where the circumstances are those described in any of Sch 1 paras 2–4B col 1 (as amended), the condition that the area or areas referred to therein had not been defined or designated as therein mentioned (see s 6(1)(b) (amended by the Housing Act 1988 s 78(4)); and para 272 et seq post.

5 Ibid s 6(1).
6 Ie 'the Pointe Gourde principle': see para 268 ante.
7 *Viscount Camrose v Basingstoke Corpn* [1966] 3 All ER 161, [1966] 1 WLR 1100, CA.
8 *Wilson v Liverpool City Council* [1971] 1 All ER 628 at 635, [1971] 1 WLR 302 at 310, CA, per Widgery LJ.
9 As to market value see further paras 278–279 post.

270. Disregard of special suitability or adaptability of land for certain purposes.

The special suitability or adaptability of the land for any purpose[1] must not be taken into account, in assessing compensation in respect of its compulsory acquisition, if that purpose is a purpose to which it could be applied only in pursuance of statutory powers[2], or for which there is no market apart from the requirements of any authority possessing compulsory purchase powers[3].

1 'Purpose' connotes an actual or potential use of the land itself; it cannot be regarded as meaning a purpose which is only concerned with the use of the products of that land elsewhere: see *Pointe Gourde Quarrying and Transport Co Ltd v Sub-Intendent of Crown Lands* [1947] AC 565, PC. The purchase of the freehold interest in land for the purposes of the merger with the leasehold interest is not a use of the land itself and a purchaser for such a purpose is not excluded: *Lambe v Secretary of State for War* [1955] 2 QB 612, [1955] 2 All ER 386, CA.
2 Statutory powers not related to the use of the land proposed to be acquired cannot justify the disregarding of the special suitability or adaptability of that land for the purposes of assessing compensation under this rule: see *Hertfordshire County Council v Ozanne* [1991] 1 All ER 769, 62 P & CR 1, HL.
3 Land Compensation Act 1961 s 5 r (3) (amended by the Planning and Compensation Act 1991 ss 70, 84(6), Sch 15 para 1, Sch 19 Pt III). For an example where the rule (as originally enacted) did not apply see *Batchelor v Kent County Council* [1990] 1 EGLR 32, CA (land comprised in the compulsory purchase order provided the most suitable, but not the only, access to a development site; held that 'most suitable' does not correspond with 'specially suitable'. See also *Blandrent Investment Developments Ltd v British Gas Corpn* [1979] 2 EGLR 18, HL. For the meaning of 'authority possessing compulsory purchase powers' see para 244 note 6 ante.

B. CIRCUMSTANCES INVOLVING INCREASE OR DECREASE IN VALUE OF RELEVANT INTEREST

271. Development on other land for purposes for which that land and the land to be valued is acquired.

An increase or diminution in the value of the relevant interest which must be disregarded[1] arises where the acquisition is for purposes involving development[2] of any of the land authorised to be acquired[3], if the increase or diminution is attributable to the carrying out, or the prospect, of development of any of the land authorised to be acquired (other than the relevant land[4]) which is development for any of the purposes for which any part of the land (including any part of the relevant land) is to be acquired, so far as that development would not have been likely to be carried out if the acquiring authority[5] had not acquired, and did not propose to acquire, any of the land so authorised[6].

1 Ie an increase or decrease which must be disregarded in accordance with the Land Compensation Act 1961 s 6(1) (as amended): see para 269 ante. For the meaning of 'relevant interest' see para 120 note 4 ante.
2 For the meaning of 'development' for these purposes see para 269 note 3 ante. See also para 243 note 2 ante.
3 'The land authorised to be acquired' means (1) in relation to an acquisition authorised by a compulsory purchase order or a special enactment, the aggregate of the land comprised in the authorisation (Land Compensation Act 1961 s 6(3)(a)); and (2) in relation to a compulsory acquisition not so authorised but effected under powers exercisable by virtue of any enactment for defence purposes, the aggregate of (a)

the land comprised in the notice to treat and (b) any land contiguous or adjacent to it which is comprised in any other notice to treat served under the like powers not more than one month before and not more than one month after the date of service of that notice (s 6(3)(b)). 'Special enactment' means a local enactment, or a provision contained in an Act other than a local or private Act, being a local enactment or provision authorising the compulsory acquisition of land specifically identified in it; and 'local enactment' means any local or private Act or an order confirmed by Parliament or brought into operation in accordance with special parliamentary procedure: s 39(1). 'Defence purposes' includes any purpose of any of Her Majesty's naval, military or air forces, the service of any visiting force within the Visiting Forces Act 1952 Pt I (ss 1–12) (as amended), and any purpose of the Secretary of State connected with the service of any of those forces: Land Powers (Defence) Act 1958 s 25(1) (applied by the Land Compensation Act 1961 s 6(3)). As to local and private Acts see STATUTES vol 44(1) (Reissue) paras 1211, 1213; and as to special parliamentary procedure see para 78 ante; and STATUTES vol 44(1) (Reissue) para 1514; PARLIAMENT.

4 For the meaning of 'the relevant land' see para 243 note 5 ante.
5 For the meaning of 'acquiring authority' see para 120 note 5 ante. Where the land acquired is included in and is part of a clearance area and is purchased for clearing the area, the clearance would not normally be likely to be carried out if the authority had not acquired or did not propose to acquire the land for the purpose, even though the acquiring authority could have proceeded to exercise its powers to make clearance orders instead of purchasing the land: *Davy v Leeds Corpn* [1965] 1 All ER 753, [1965] 1 WLR 445, HL. As to clearance areas see the Housing Act 1985 ss 289–298 (as amended); and HOUSING.
6 Land Compensation Act 1961 s 6(1)(a), Sch 1 Case 1.

272. Development in action area. An increase or diminution in the value of the relevant interest which must be disregarded[1] arises where any of the relevant land[2] forms part of an action area[3] for which a local plan is in force[4], if the increase is attributable to the carrying out, or the prospect, of development[5] of any land in that area (other than the relevant land) in the course of the development or redevelopment of the area in accordance with the plan, so far as that development would not have been likely to be carried out if the area had not been so defined[6].

1 Ie an increase or decrease which must be disregarded in accordance with the Land Compensation Act 1961 s 6(1) (as amended): see para 269 ante. For the meaning of 'relevant interest' see para 120 note 4 ante.
2 For the meaning of 'relevant land' see para 243 note 5 ante.
3 As to action areas see para 247 note 2 ante.
4 See the Town and Country Planning Act 1990 s 54(5), whereby the reference in the Land Compensation Act 1961 s 6(1), Sch 1 Case 2 to 'an area defined in the current development plan as an area of comprehensive development' is to be construed as a reference to an action area for which a local plan is in force; and para 247 note 2 ante. As to local plans see TOWN AND COUNTRY PLANNING vol 46 (Reissue) para 94 et seq.
5 For the meaning of 'development' for these purposes see para 269 note 3 ante; and see also para 243 note 2 ante.
6 Land Compensation Act 1961 s 6(1)(b) (amended by the Housing Act 1988 s 78(4)); Land Compensation Act 1961 Sch 1 Case 2.

273. Development in area designated as site, or extension of site, of new town. An increase or diminution in the value of the relevant interest which must be disregarded[1] arises where any of the relevant land[2], on the date of the service of the notice to treat[3], forms part of an area designated as the site of a new town[4] or as an extension of the site of a new town[5], if the increase is attributable to the carrying out, or the prospect, of:

(1) development[6] of any land in that area (other than the relevant land) in the course of development of that area as a new town, or as part of a new town[7]; or

(2) any public development[8] specified by direction of the Secretary of State[9] as development in connection with which, or in consequence of which, the

provision of housing or other facilities is required and for whose purposes an order designating any area as the site, or an extension of the site, of a new town is proposed to be made[10],
so far as that development would not have been likely to be carried out if the area had not been so designated[11].

1 Ie an increase or decrease which must be disregarded in accordance with the Land Compensation Act 1961 s 6(1) (as amended): see para 269 ante. For the meaning of 'relevant interest' see para 120 note 4 ante.
2 For the meaning of 'relevant land' see para 243 note 5 ante.
3 For the meaning of 'the notice to treat' see para 120 note 4 ante. As to the service of notices to treat see paras 100–104 ante.
4 Ie by an order under the New Towns Act 1946 (repealed) or the New Towns Act 1981: see TOWN AND COUNTRY PLANNING vol 46 (Reissue) para 1087 et seq. Land is not to be treated as forming part of such an area if the notice to treat is served on or after the transfer date, ie the date on which, by virtue of any enactment contained in any Act relating to new towns, whenever passed, the development corporation established for the purposes of that new town ceases to act, except for the purposes of or incidental to the winding up of its affairs: Land Compensation Act 1961 s 6(2), Sch 1 paras 5, 6 (Sch 1 para 6 amended by the New Towns Act 1966 s 2, Schedule Pt I). In determining whether the land to be acquired and valued forms part of an area designated as the site of a new town, in the case of an area designated by an order operative on or before 29 October 1958, regard must be had to the order as it was in force on that day, any variation becoming operative after that day being disregarded; and, in the case of an area so designated by an order becoming operative after that day, regard must be had to the order in its original form, any variation of the order being disregarded: Land Compensation Act 1961 Sch 1 para 7.
5 Ie by an order under the New Towns Act 1965 s 1 (repealed) or the New Towns Act 1981 s 1 (as amended): see TOWN AND COUNTRY PLANNING vol 46 (Reissue) para 1087 et seq.
6 For the meaning of 'development' for these purposes see para 269 note 3 ante; and see also para 243 note 2 ante.
7 For the purpose of determining whether any development of which there is a prospect on the date of service of the notice to treat would be such development, it is immaterial whether the time when that development will or may take place is a time before, on or after the date when the development corporation established for the purposes of the new town ceases to act except for the purposes of or incidental to the winding up of its affairs: Land Compensation Act 1961 s 6(2), Sch 1 paras 5, 8 (s 6(2), Sch 1 para 8 amended by the New Towns Act 1966 Schedule Pt I).
8 'Public development' means development, whether or not in the area designated under the New Towns Act 1981 s 1 (as amended), in the exercise of statutory powers by (1) a government department; (2) any statutory undertakers within the meaning of the Town and Country Planning Act 1990 (see TOWN AND COUNTRY PLANNING vol 46 (Reissue) para 822) or any body deemed by virtue of any enactment to be statutory undertakers for the purposes of, or of any provision of, that Act; or (3) without prejudice to head (2) supra, any body having power to borrow money with the consent of a minister, and it includes such development which has already been carried out when the direction in respect of it is given, as well as such development which is then proposed: Land Compensation Act 1973 s 51(6) (amended by the New Towns Act 1981 s 81, Sch 12 para 9; and by the Planning (Consequential Provisions) Act 1990 s 4, Sch 2 para 29(8)).
9 Ie a direction under the Land Compensation Act 1973 s 51 (as amended). Where the Secretary of State proposes to make an order under the New Towns Act 1981 s 1 (as amended) designating any area as the site of a new town, or an extension of the site of a new town, and the purpose or main purpose, or one of the main purposes, for which the order is proposed to be made is the provision of housing or other facilities required in connection with, or in consequence of the carrying out of, any public development, he may, before making the order, give a direction specifying that development for the purposes of the Land Compensation Act 1973 s 51 (as amended) in relation to that area: s 51(1) (amended by the New Towns Act 1981 Sch 12 para 9). No such direction may be given in relation to any area until the Secretary of State has prepared a draft of the order under the New Towns Act 1981 s 1 (as amended) in respect of that area and has published the notice required by s 1(4), Sch 1 para 2 (see TOWN AND COUNTRY PLANNING vol 46 (Reissue) para 1088): Land Compensation Act 1973 s 51(3) (amended by the New Towns Act 1981 Sch 12 para 9). Any direction must be given by order, and any order containing such a direction may be varied or revoked by a subsequent order: Land Compensation Act 1973 s 51(4). The power to make such orders is exercisable by statutory instrument, subject to annulment in pursuance of a resolution of either House of Parliament: s 51(5).

10 Ie an order under the New Towns Act 1981 s 1 (as amended): Land Compensation Act 1973 s 51(1) (amended by the New Towns Act 1981 Sch 12 para 9).
11 Land Compensation Act 1961 s 6(1)(b) (amended by the Housing Act 1988 s 78(4)); Land Compensation Act 1961 Sch 1 Cases 3, 3A (Sch 1 Case 3A added by the New Towns Act 1966 Schedule Pt I); Land Compensation Act 1973 s 51(2)(a). Where, before the date of service of the notice to treat for the purposes of a compulsory acquisition, the land has been disposed of by an authority or body in circumstances where the Land Compensation Act 1961 Sch 1 Case 3 or Case 3A (as added) would have applied if the authority or body had been compulsorily acquiring the land at the time of the disposal, then those Cases do not apply for the purposes of that acquisition: Sch 1 para 9 (added by the Local Government, Planning and Land Act 1980 s 133, Sch 25 para 8). The development excluded, as extended to public development (see the text and notes 8–10 supra), applies also so as to exclude any increase or diminution of value to be disregarded under any rule of law relating to the assessment of compensation: Land Compensation Act 1973 s 51(2)(a). As to those rules of law see paras 242–268 ante.

274. Development in area defined in development plan as area of town development. An increase or diminution in the value of the relevant interest which must be disregarded[1] arises where any of the relevant land[2] forms part of an area defined in the current development plan[3] as an area of town development[4], if the increase is attributable to the carrying out, or the prospect, of development[5] of any land in that area (other than the relevant land) in the course of town development so far as that development would not have been likely to be carried out if the area had not been so defined as an area of town development[6].

1 Ie an increase or decrease which must be disregarded in accordance with the Land Compensation Act 1961 s 6(1) (as amended): see para 269 ante. For the meaning of 'relevant interest' see para 120 note 4 ante.
2 For the meaning of 'relevant land' see para 243 note 5 ante.
3 For the meaning of 'current development plan' see para 247 note 2 ante.
4 Ie town development within the meaning of the Town Development Act 1952 (repealed): see s 1(1) (repealed, subject to a transitional provision, by the Local Government and Housing Act 1989 ss 175, 194(4), Sch 12 Pt II).
5 For the meaning of 'development' for these purposes see para 269 note 3 ante; and see also para 243 note 2 ante.
6 Land Compensation Act 1961 s 6(1)(b) (amended by the Housing Act 1988 s 78(4)); Land Compensation Act 1961 Sch 1 Case 4.

275. Development in area designated as urban development area. An increase or diminution in the value of the relevant interest which must be disregarded[1] arises where any of the relevant land[2] forms part of an area designated as an urban development area[3], if the increase is attributable to the carrying out, or the prospect, of development[4] of any land (other than the relevant land) in the course of the development or redevelopment of that area as an urban development area[5].

1 Ie an increase or decrease which must be disregarded in accordance with the Land Compensation Act 1961 s 6(1) (as amended): see para 269 ante. For the meaning of 'relevant interest' see para 120 note 4 ante.
2 For the meaning of 'relevant land' see para 243 note 5 ante.
3 Ie by an order under the Local Government, Planning and Land Act 1980 s 134 (as amended): see TOWN AND COUNTRY PLANNING vol 46 (Reissue) para 1270 et seq. In assessing the increase or diminution in value to be left out of account, no increase is to be excluded from being left out of account merely because it is attributable (1) to any development of land which was carried out before the area was designated as an urban development area; (2) to any development or prospect of development of land outside the urban development area; (3) to any development or prospect of development of land by an authority, other than the acquiring authority, possessing compulsory purchase powers: Land Compensation Act 1961 s 6(1)(b), (2) (respectively amended by the Housing Act 1988 s 78(4); and by the Local Government, Planning and Land Act 1980 s 145(3)); Land

Compensation Act 1961 Sch 1 para 10 (added by the Local Government, Planning and Land Act 1980 s 145(2)). The Land Compensation Act 1961 Sch 1 para 10 (as so added) has effect in relation to any increase or diminution in value to be left out of account by virtue of any rule of law relating to the assessment of compensation in respect of compulsory acquisition as it has effect in relation to any increase or diminution in value to be left out of account by virtue of s 6 (as so amended): Sch 1 para 11 (as so added). As to those rules of law see paras 242–268 ante. For the meaning of 'authority possessing compulsory purchase powers' see para 244 note 6 ante; and for the meaning of 'acquiring authority' see para 120 note 5 ante.

4 For the meaning of 'development' for these purposes see para 269 note 3 ante; and see also para 243 note 2 ante.
5 Land Compensation Act 1961 s 6(1)(b) (as amended: see note 3 supra), Sch 1 Case 4A (added by the Local Government, Planning and Land Act 1980 s 145(1)).

276. Development in housing action trust area. An increase or diminution in the value of the relevant interest which must be disregarded[1] arises where any of the relevant land[2] forms part of a housing action trust area[3], if the increase is attributable to the carrying out, or the prospect, of development[4] of any land (other than the relevant land) in the course of the development or redevelopment of that area as a housing action trust area[5].

1 Ie an increase or decrease which must be disregarded in accordance with the Land Compensation Act 1961 s 6(1) (as amended): see para 269 ante. For the meaning of 'relevant interest' see para 120 note 4 ante.
2 For the meaning of 'the relevant land' see para 243 note 5 ante.
3 Ie a housing action trust area established under the Housing Act 1988 Pt III (ss 60–92) (as amended): see HOUSING.
4 For the meaning of 'development' for these purposes see para 269 note 3 ante; and see also para 243 note 2 ante.
5 Land Compensation Act 1961 s 6(1)(b) (amended by the Housing Act 1988 s 78(4)); Land Compensation Act 1961 Sch 1 Case 4B (added by the Housing Act 1988 s 78(3)).

C. LAND SUBSEQUENTLY ACQUIRED; SEVERANCE OF LAND

277. Subsequent acquisition of adjacent land. Where, in connection with the compulsory acquisition of an interest in land[1], a diminution in the value of an interest in other land has been taken into account[2] in assessing compensation for injurious affection[3], then, in connection with any subsequent acquisition where either:

(1) the interest acquired thereby is the same as the interest previously taken into account[4] (whether the acquisition extends to the whole of the land in which that interest previously subsisted or only to part of that land)[5]; or

(2) the person entitled to the interest acquired is, or derives title[6] to that interest from, the person who at the time of the previous acquisition was entitled to the interest previously taken into account[7],

that diminution is not to be left out of account[8] in so far as it was taken into account in connection with the previous acquisition[9].

So also where, for the purpose of assessing compensation in respect of a compulsory acquisition of an interest in land[10], an increase in the value of an interest in other land has been taken into account[11], then that increase is not to be left out of account[12] in connection with any subsequent acquisition falling within head (1) or head (2) above, in so far as it was taken into account in connection with the previous acquisition[13].

Where, in connection with a sale of an interest in land by agreement, the circumstances are such that, if it had been a compulsory acquisition, an increase or diminution in value would have fallen to be taken into account as mentioned above, the above provisions apply, with the necessary modifications, as if that sale had been a compulsory acquisition and that increase or diminution in value had been taken into account accordingly[14].

1 For the meaning of 'land' see para 18 note 2 ante.
2 Ie in any of the circumstances mentioned in the Land Compensation Act 1961 s 6(1), Sch 1 Pt I col 1 (as amended) (see paras 271–276 ante): s 8(2).
3 As to compensation for injurious affection see para 292 post.
4 For these purposes, any reference to the interest previously taken into account is a reference to the interest whose increased or diminished value was taken into account as mentioned in the Land Compensation Act 1961 s 8(1) (see note 11 infra) or s 8(2) (see note 2 supra): s 8(3).
5 Ibid s 8(3)(a).
6 For these purposes, references (1) to a person from whom title is derived by another person include references to any predecessor in title of that other person; (2) to a person deriving title from another person include references to any successor in title of that other person; and (3) to deriving title are references to deriving title either directly or indirectly: ibid s 39(5).
7 Ibid s 8(3)(b).
8 Ie by virtue of ibid s 6 (as amended): see para 269 et seq ante.
9 Ibid s 8(2).
10 As to the interests entitled to compensation see paras 100, 103 ante.
11 Ie by virtue of the Land Compensation Act 1961 s 7 or any corresponding enactment and in any of the circumstances mentioned in Sch 1 Pt I col 1 (as amended) (see paras 271–276 ante): s 8(1). References for these purposes to a corresponding enactment are references to either the Light Railways Act 1896 s 13 (repealed, subject to transitional provisions: see para 323 post) or the Highways Act 1980 s 261(1) (or its predecessor, the Highways Act 1959 s 222(6) (repealed)): Land Compensation Act 1961 s 8(7) (amended by the Highways Act 1980 s 343(2), Sch 24 para 8; the Miscellaneous Financial Provisions Act 1983 s 8, Sch 3; and by the Housing (Consequential Provisions) Act 1985 s 3, Sch 1 Pt I). See further para 323 post.
12 Ie by virtue of the Land Compensation Act 1961 s 6 (as amended): s 8(1).
13 Ibid s 8(1).
14 Ibid s 8(4).

(7) MARKET OR REINSTATEMENT VALUE OF LAND TAKEN

(i) Market Value

278. In general. The market value is what will be paid by a willing purchaser to a willing seller in the market, and not the value which a valuer thinks ought to be the market value[1]. The invariable practice is, however, for the expert evidence of a valuer to be put before the Lands Tribunal[2].

1 *Fowler v Sheffield Corpn* (1960) 11 P & CR 440, Lands Tribunal. Valuers use a number of methods for valuing land; as to the common approaches see para 280 post.
2 As to the Lands Tribunal see para 202 et seq ante; and as to expert evidence see para 223 ante.

279. Value if sold in open market by willing seller to willing purchaser. The owner is entitled to the amount which the land[1] if sold in the open market by a willing seller might be expected to realise[2]. A value ascertained by reference to the amount obtainable in an open market shows an intention to include every possible purchaser; the amount to be assessed for the purpose of calculating compensation will be the amount the land might be expected to realise if offered under conditions enabling every person desirous of purchasing to come in and make an offer[3].

The owner is entitled to the value of the land at the time for valuation in its actual condition with its intrinsic qualities subject to certain exclusions[4] and to restrictions with respect to its potentialities[5], but subject also to the possibility of the removal of those restrictions[6]. Any enhanced value attaching to the land by reason of the fact that it has been compulsorily acquired for the purpose of the acquiring authority must be disregarded[7].

The compensation must therefore be ascertained by reference to that which a willing seller might expect to obtain from a willing seller in a hypothetical open market. The disinclination of the seller to part with his land and the urgent necessity of the purchaser to buy must alike be disregarded; neither must be considered to act under compulsion. This is implied in the common saying that the value of the land is not to be estimated at its value to the purchaser; but the fact that some particular purchaser might desire the land more than others is not necessarily to be disregarded. The wish of a particular purchaser, though not his compulsion, may always be taken into consideration for what it is worth[8]. 'Willing seller' does not mean a person willing to sell without reserve for any price that he can obtain, but one who is willing to sell, making the most in the circumstances of his property; and what is the most, in the circumstances, which he can make of his property cannot be determined without consideration of the circumstances and, in particular, cannot be ascertained while excluding the known requirements of a probable purchaser[9]. Some possible purchasers are willing to give a higher price than others because they know or think that they can make more profitable use of the land for any given purpose, and these possible purchasers create the market. As the basis of the value of the land is the value to the owner[10], he is a possible purchaser in the hypothetical market for what the land is worth to him, but he would not pay, nor is he entitled to, a value arrived at by the capitalisation of the profits made by him from the use of the land[11].

1 For the meaning of 'land' see para 18 note 2 ante.
2 See the Land Compensation Act 1961 s 5 r (2); and para 234 et seq ante.
3 *IRC v Clay* [1914] 3 KB 466 at 475, CA; *Glass v IRC* 1915 SC 449. Cf *Priestman Collieries Ltd v Northern District Valuation Board* [1950] 2 KB 398, [1950] 2 All ER 129, DC. The market value may be what a speculator proposing to dispose of the land would pay for it, if such a person would be the most likely purchaser: *Blue Jay Investments Ltd v Thames Water Authority* [1984] 1 EGLR 187, Lands Tribunal.
4 See para 288 et seq ante.
5 See para 258 et seq ante.
6 See para 262 et seq ante.
7 Land Compensation Act 1961 s 5 r (1). For the meaning of 'acquiring authority' see para 120 note 5 ante.
8 *Vyricherla Narayana Gajapatiraju v Revenue Divisional Officer, Vizagapatam* [1939] AC 302 at 312, [1939] 2 All ER 317 at 321, PC; *Lambe v Secretary of State for War* [1955] 2 QB 612 at 622–623, [1955] 2 All ER 386 at 390, CA. See also *FR Evans (Leeds) Ltd v English Electric Co Ltd* (1977) 36 P & CR 185 per Donaldson J (affd (1977) 245 Estates Gazette 657, CA); *Dennis & Robinson Ltd v Kiossos Establishment* (1987) 54 P & CR 282, [1987] 1 EGLR 133, CA (rent review cases concerning the 'open market'); and LANDLORD AND TENANT vol 27(1) (Reissue) para 274; and see *IRC v Gray* [1994] STC 360 at 372, CA.
9 *Glass v IRC* 1915 SC 449 at 465. 'A willing seller means one who is prepared to sell provided a fair price is obtained in all the circumstances of the case. I do not think it means only a seller who is prepared to sell at any price and on any terms, and who is actually at the time wishing to sell. In other words, I do not think it means an anxious seller': *IRC v Clay* [1914] 3 KB 466 at 478, CA, per Pickford LJ. It must not be assumed that the seller will act without due regard to his own interests: see *Robertson's Trustees v Glasgow Corpn* 1967 SC 124 (trustees were correct to insist, in respect of the valuation of a tenement block, on the separate valuation of each unit as opposed to a valuation of the property as a whole, since the former produced the higher figure).
10 See para 233 ante.
11 *Vyricherla Narayana Gajapatiraju v Revenue Divisional Officer, Vizagapatam* [1939] AC 302 at 314, [1939] 2 All ER 317 at 322, PC; *Pastoral Finance Association Ltd v The Minister* [1914] AC 1083 at 1088–1089, PC.

280. Valuation; common approaches. The prices paid for comparable property in the neighbourhood provide the usual evidence as to the market value[1]; but it should be noted that seemingly comparable transactions consisting of settlements by acquiring authorities are not themselves open market transactions and may be an unreliable guide to the true open market value[2].

In the case of freehold land in possession, if there are no comparable sales, the market value may be achieved by capitalising the best annual value or rent obtainable in the market[3].

If the land is let, the value of the reversion will be the capital value of the annual rent during the currency of the lease and then on the basis of the best rent available[4]. If land is let at a rent below its value, but with a proviso that in the event of any part being taken compulsorily the lessor could re-enter, he must be compensated on the basis of the full value and not on the rent actually paid[5]. Where a freehold interest is acquired subject to a leasehold interest, the 'marriage value' which the freehold interest would have to the lessee is to be taken into account in assessing the open market value of the freehold[6]. In the case of the value of the lease this will be the capital value of the profit rent, if any, paid by the lessee, namely, the difference between the rent under the lease and the market rent calculated by reference to the number of years unexpired[7]. If the land has potential for development and is let, the value for development will have to be divided between the lessor and lessee according to the lessor's right and power to obtain possession for development, or according to the unexpired term of the lease, because the value of the reversion to the lessee and the value of the lease to the reversioner is not to be disregarded[8]. The 'marriage value' which the lease would have to the freeholder (or subtenant) may be taken into account in assessing the open market value[9].

There is no statutory provision enabling the acquiring authority to acquire at its existing use value land highly valuable for development merely because it is let or subject to other rights such as rights of common; and there would appear to be no statutory restriction on the lessee or the commoners surrendering their interests to the lessor or lord of the manor, as the case may be, after the notice to treat[10]. Furthermore, if land is struck with sterility by Act of Parliament and is worth only a nominal sum in the owners' hands, it may be held for a purpose which will attract reinstatement value[11].

1   *Vyricherla Narayana Gajapatiraju v Revenue Divisional Officer, Vizagapatam* [1939] AC 302 at 313, [1939] 2 All ER 317 at 322, PC. Allowances for improvements on comparable properties may be required to be made: *Streatham and General Estates Co Ltd v Works and Public Buildings Comrs* (1888) 52 JP 615, DC; affd sub nom *Ex p Streatham and General Estates Co Ltd* (1888) 4 TLR 766, CA.

2   *Shaw v London Borough of Hackney* (1974) 28 P & CR 477, Lands Tribunal. Cf *Land Securities plc v Westminster City Council* [1993] 4 All ER 124, [1993] 1 WLR 286 (relative weight to be attached to open market transactions and settlements in rent review valuations).

3   This method has considerable disadvantages (see *Perkins v Middlesex County Council* (1951) 2 P & CR 42, Lands Tribunal) but will be accepted in the absence of good comparable evidence (see *Trocette Property Co Ltd v GLC* (1973) 27 P & CR 256, Lands Tribunal; affd (1974) 28 P & CR 408, CA). Cf *Re Morgan and London and North Western Rly Co* [1896] 2 QB 469.

4   See note 3 supra.

5   See note 3 supra. If the land is let at a special rent above comparable rents, the value of the land must be assessed on the special rent, subject to the possibility or probability of its continuance: *Earl of Eldon v North-Eastern Rly Co* (1899) 80 LT 723; *Re Athlone Rifle Range* [1902] 1 IR 433.

6   See *Hearts of Oak Benefit Society v Lewisham Borough Council* [1979] 1 EGLR 178, Lands Tribunal. Cf *Trocette Property Co Ltd v GLC* (1973) 27 P & CR 256, Lands Tribunal; affd (1974) 28 P & CR 408, CA.

7   *Penny v Penny* (1867) LR 5 Eq 227.

8   *Lambe v Secretary of State for War* [1955] 2 QB 612, [1955] 2 All ER 386, CA; *Mountview Estates Ltd v London Borough of Enfield* (1968) 20 P & CR 729, Lands Tribunal.

9 Cf *Trocette Property Co Ltd v GLC* (1973) 27 P & CR 256, Lands Tribunal; affd (1974) 28 P & CR 408, CA.
10 See paras 116 note 10 ante, 285 post.
11 See para 281 post.

(ii) Reinstatement Value

281. Equivalent reinstatement. As an alternative to compensation based upon the market value of the land acquired, the owner of the land will be entitled to damages assessed on the basis of the reasonable cost of equivalent reinstatement[1] where the owner can show:

(1) that the land acquired is devoted[2] to a purpose and but for the compulsory acquisition would continue to be so devoted[3];

(2) that the purpose is one for which there is no general demand or market for the land[4];

(3) the bona fide[5] intention to reinstate the use for that purpose on another site[6]; and

(4) these conditions being satisfied, that the Lands Tribunal's reasonable discretion should be exercised in his favour[7].

Compensation falls to be assessed by reference to the date when reinstatement of the premises first becomes reasonably practicable[8].

The word 'land' in the phrase 'no general demand or market for land' means land in general and not the subject land; accordingly the criterion that there be no general demand or market for land is not satisfied merely because there is no demand for the subject land[9]. Further, the word 'general' in this phrase qualifies only 'demand' and not 'market'; the underlying concept is that there cannot be a market unless both supply and demand exist, but there may be a general demand although there is no supply. In that case the demand will be unsatisfied[10].

The reasonable cost of equivalent reinstatement includes the cost of acquiring substituted premises and the cost of converting the substituted premises so that, in the case of a business, the former purpose may be carried on substantially unaltered and undiminished[11]. The claimant must, however, minimise his loss[12].

1 See the Land Compensation Act 1961 s 5 r (5) (embodying the recommendations of the *Second Report of the Committee Dealing with the Law and Practice relating to the Acquisition of Land for Public Purposes* (Cd 9229) (1918)); and para 234 ante. The special rules which formerly existed in relation to war-damaged land under the Land Compensation Act 1961 s 13(1) no longer apply, that section having been repealed by the Statute Law (Repeals) Act 1989.

2 'Devoted' connotes an intention to use the land for that particular purpose: *Aston Charities Trust Ltd v Stepney Borough Council* [1952] 2 QB 642, [1952] 2 All ER 228, CA (land continued to be devoted to purpose notwithstanding de facto use had been interrupted temporarily by bombing).

3 The date of the notice to treat is the date at which it must be shown that the premises are devoted to the purpose for which there is no general demand: *Zoar Independent Church Trustees v Rochester Corpn* [1975] QB 246, [1974] 3 All ER 5, CA. Although there is no requirement that the land must be committed to that purpose for any particular length of time, the probable duration of the continuance of the purpose is a matter which may affect how the Lands Tribunal exercises its discretion whether to apply the Land Compensation Act 1961 s 5 r (5): *Zoar Independent Church Trustees v Rochester Corpn* supra.

4 The question whether there is a general demand or market is to be determined at the time the compensation falls to be assessed: *Harrison & Hetherington Ltd v Cumbria County Council* (1985) 50 P & CR 396, HL.

5 *Zoar Independent Church Trustees v Rochester Corpn* [1975] QB 246, [1974] 3 All ER 5, CA (the fact that the realisation of the intention is dependent upon the receipt of compensation does not deprive the intention of any necessary quality).

6 It is the purpose that needs to be reinstated, not the precise use which had taken place on the acquired land: *Zoar Independent Church Trustees v Rochester Corpn* [1975] QB 246, [1974] 3 All ER 5, CA; *Trustee of*

the Nonentities Society v Kidderminster Borough Council (1970) 22 P & CR 224, Lands Tribunal; cf *Edge Hill Light Rly Co v Secretary of State for War* (1956) 6 P & CR 211, Lands Tribunal.

7 Before the tribunal exercises its discretion, it will require to know what constitutes equivalent reinstatement and its cost and the amount of compensation that would be payable under the Land Compensation Act 1961 s 5 rr (2), (6) (see para 234 ante) compared with s 5 r (5): *Harrison & Hetherington Ltd v Cumbria County Council* (1985) 50 P & CR 396 at 397, HL. In the case of a business, the relation between the cost of reinstatement and the value of the business may be paramount in considering the question of reasonableness (*Festiniog Rly Co v Central Electricity Generating Board* (1962) 13 P & CR 248, 60 LGR 157, CA); however, the relation between the cost of reinstatement and the value of the undertaking to be reinstated may be of less significance in considering the reinstatement of a social or charitable purpose (see *Sparks and Others (Trustees of East Hunslet Liberal Club) v Leeds City Council* [1977] 2 EGLR 163, Lands Tribunal).

8 See para 235 ante; *Birmingham Corpn v West Midland Baptist (Trust) Association (Inc)* [1970] AC 874, [1969] 3 All ER 172, HL.

9 *Harrison & Hetherington Ltd v Cumbria County Council* (1985) 50 P & CR 396 at 397, HL.

10 *Harrison & Hetherington Ltd v Cumbria County Council* (1985) 50 P & CR 396 at 397, HL; *Wilkinson v Middlesbrough Borough Council* (1981) 45 P & CR 142 at 148, CA.

11 See *A & B Taxis Ltd v Secretary of State for Air* [1922] 2 KB 328 at 344, CA. See also *Trustees of Zetland Lodge of Freemasons v Tamar Bridge Joint Committee* (1961) 12 P & CR 326, Lands Tribunal; *Trustees of Old Dagenham Methodist Church v Dagenham Borough Council* (1961) 179 Estates Gazette 295.

12 See *Service Welding Ltd v Tyne and Wear County Council* (1979) 38 P & CR 352, CA.

282. Examples of land devoted to a purpose for which there is no market.

Land with churches, schools or hospitals on it, or with buildings devoted to general religious and charitable purposes[1], or land with a club house[2], or carrying a light railway[3], or barracks[4], or houses of an exceptional character, or special business premises[5], provide examples of land which may be within the rule relating to reinstatement value[6].

Land held under a lease is not excluded[7]. Land is devoted to a purpose even though the use of that purpose is temporarily interrupted[8].

The land devoted to the purpose must be considered as a whole, and it seems that there is no right to take parts of the land separately and show that they could be used for some other purposes[9].

1 See *London School Board v South Eastern Rly Co* (1887) 3 TLR 710, CA; *Zoar Independent Church Trustees v Rochester Corpn* [1975] QB 246, [1974] 3 All ER 5, CA.

2 *St John's Wood Working Men's Club Trustees v LCC* (1947) 150 Estates Gazette 213; *Trustees of Zetland Lodge of Freemasons v Tamar Bridge Joint Committee* (1961) 12 P & CR 326, Lands Tribunal.

3 *Edge Hill Light Rly Co v Secretary of State for War* (1956) 6 P & CR 211, Lands Tribunal.

4 *Territorial Army Association of Devon v Plymouth Corpn* [1928] EGD 195.

5 *A & B Taxis Ltd v Secretary of State for Air* [1922] 2 KB 328 at 336–337, CA.

6 For the rule see the Land Compensation Act 1961 s 5 r (5); and paras 234, 281 ante.

7 *Territorial Army Association of Devon v Plymouth Corpn* [1928] EGD 195.

8 *Aston Charities Trust Ltd v Stepney Borough Council* [1952] 2 QB 642, [1952] 2 All ER 228, CA.

9 *London Diocesan Fund v Stepney Corpn* (1953) 4 P & CR 9, Lands Tribunal.

283. Application of equivalent reinstatement rule to dwelling specially adapted for disabled person where disabled person resident.

In the case of compulsory acquisition of an interest in a dwelling[1] which (1) has been constructed or substantially modified to meet the special needs of a disabled person[2]; and (2) is occupied by that person as his residence immediately before the date when the acquiring authority[3] takes possession of the dwelling or was last so occupied before that date[4], then, if the person whose interest is acquired so elects, the compensation is to be assessed as if the dwelling were land which is devoted to a purpose of such a nature that there is no general demand or market for that purpose[5]. The compensation will accordingly be on the basis of the reasonable cost of equivalent reinstatement, and the Lands Tribunal has no discretion in applying the measure of compensation; nor is it required to be satisfied of an intention to reinstate[6].

1   'Dwelling' means a building or part of a building occupied or, if not occupied, last occupied or intended to be occupied as a private dwelling, and includes any garden, yard, outhouses and appurtenances belonging to or usually enjoyed with that building or part: Land Compensation Act 1973 s 87(1) (definition amended by the Land Compensation (Scotland) Act 1973 s 81(1), Sch 2 Pt I).
2   Land Compensation Act 1973 s 45(1)(a). 'Disabled person' means a person who is substantially and permanently handicapped by illness, injury or congenital infirmity: s 87(1) (definition amended by the Land Compensation (Scotland) Act 1973 s 81(1), Sch 2 Pt I).
3   For the meaning of 'acquiring authority' see para 106 note 1 ante.
4   Land Compensation Act 1973 s 45(1)(b).
5   Ibid s 45(2).
6   As to land devoted to a purpose for which there is no market see generally paras 281–282 ante.

(8) COMPENSATION WHERE PERSON ENTITLED IS NOT IN OCCUPATION

284. Expenses of owners not in occupation. Where, in consequence of any compulsory acquisition of land[1], the acquiring authority[2] acquires an interest of a person who is not then in occupation of the land, and that person incurs incidental charges or expenses in acquiring, within the period of one year beginning with the date of entry, an interest in other land in the United Kingdom[3], the charges or expenses are to be taken into account in assessing his compensation as they would be taken into account if he were in occupation of the land[4].

1   For the meaning of 'land' see para 18 note 2 ante.
2   For the meaning of 'acquiring authority' see para 120 note 5 ante.
3   For the meaning of 'United Kingdom' see para 100 note 21 ante.
4   Land Compensation Act 1961 s 10A (added by the Planning and Compensation Act 1991 s 70, Sch 15 para 2).

285. Effect on value of interest of landlord or tenant. Where the owner of the interest in the land to be valued is not in occupation at the date of the notice to treat and the land is in the occupation of a tenant[1] or a subtenant, the value of the owner's interest will be affected by the owner's ability, at the time of valuation or date of entry, whichever is the earlier[2], to obtain possession and the time within which possession may be obtained by notice to quit or otherwise, and also by whether the person in occupation has gone out of occupation at the time of valuation or date of entry[3].

The length of the lease for a term of years affects the value of the landlord's interest, and if there is a right to renewal of the lease this must be taken into account[4], but not a mere expectation of renewal[5].

Where a lease contains a proviso for re-entry on any part of the land leased being compulsorily taken, the landlord is entitled to the value of the land free of the lease[6]. An invalid lease would not affect the landlord's compensation[7], and a lease granted after the date of the notice to treat cannot increase the burden on the acquiring authority[8], but in either case the tenant may have a remedy against the landlord.

The values of the interest of the landlord and the tenant are affected by statute; possession by the landlord arising out of the tenant's rehousing by an acquiring authority may fall to be disregarded[9], the right of renewal of a business tenancy is protected[10], and the landlord's right to serve notice to quit an agricultural holding is restricted[11]. These provisions do not, however, prevent a tenant from surrendering his interest after the notice to treat and before the time of valuation or date of entry[12].

1 As to the effect of rehousing tenants see para 286 post.
2 Land is to be valued as at the date of valuation or the date of entry, whichever is the earlier, and not as at the date of the notice to treat: see para 119 ante.
3 As to the statutory modification of rights to obtain possession and value where possession is obtained see paras 286–288 post.
4 *Bogg v Midland Rly Co* (1867) LR 4 Eq 310.
5 *Lynch v Glasgow Corpn* (1903) 5 F 1174. Other rights of a lessee must be taken into account (see *Re McIntosh and Pontypridd Improvements Co Ltd* (1892) 8 TLR 203, CA); and so must restrictions in the lease in favour of the landlord (cf *Priestman Collieries Ltd v Northern District Valuation Board* [1950] 2 KB 398, [1950] 2 All ER 129, DC).
6 *Re Morgan and London and North Western Rly Co* [1896] 2 QB 469. The proviso could operate as a surrender under the Landlord and Tenant Act 1954 s 24(2) ((as amended): see LANDLORD AND TENANT vol 27(1) (Reissue) para 567. A proviso in a lease giving the landlord power to resume possession for building does not, however, entitle him to resume possession where the acquiring authority acquires the land for some other purpose: *Johnson v Edgware, Highgate and London Rly Co* (1866) 35 Beav 480, 14 LT 45. Furthermore, an acquiring authority cannot, after acquisition, exercise a power of resuming possession reserved in the lease by the landlord for the purpose of reducing or taking away the tenant's right to compensation: see *Fleming v Newport Rly Co* (1883) 8 App Cas 265, HL, approving *Solway Junction Rly Co v Jackson* (1874) 1 R 831.
7 Cf *Re North London Rly Co, ex p Cooper* (1865) 34 LJ Ch 373.
8 See para 116 ante.
9 See para 286 post.
10 See para 287 post.
11 See para 288 post.
12 See para 280 ante.

286. Rehousing or prospect of rehousing tenants by acquiring authority not to enhance landlord's compensation. In assessing the compensation payable in respect of the compulsory acquisition of an interest in land which, on the date of service of the notice to treat[1] or deemed notice to treat[2], is subject to a tenancy[3], there must be left out of account any part of the value of that interest which is attributable to, or to the prospect of, the tenant giving up possession after that date in consequence of being provided with other accommodation by virtue of the duty[4] of an authority possessing compulsory purchase powers[5] to secure that a person displaced from residential accommodation on any land acquired by that authority will, if suitable alternative residential accommodation on reasonable terms is not otherwise available to that person, be provided with that other accommodation[6]. Accordingly, for the purpose of determining the date by reference to which that compensation is to be assessed, the acquiring authority[7] is to be deemed, where the tenant gives up possession, to have taken possession on the date on which it is given up by the tenant[8].

Thus, as compensation in respect of land acquired is to be assessed in respect of the interests and state of the land at the date of entry by the acquiring authority, or the date of assessment, whichever is the earlier[9], the removal of the tenant or the prospect of such removal will not enhance the amount of the purchase money to which the landlord would otherwise be entitled.

1 As to the service of a notice to treat and its effect see para 100 et seq ante.
2 Ie a notice to treat deemed to have been served by virtue of the Compulsory Purchase (Vesting Declarations) Act 1981 Pt III (ss 7–9) (general vesting declarations: see paras 171, 175–176 ante): Land Compensation Act 1973 s 50(4) (amended by the Land Compensation (Scotland) Act 1973 s 81(1), Sch 2 Pt I; and by the Compulsory Purchase (Vesting Declarations) Act 1981 s 16(1), Sch 3 para 1).

3 'Tenancy', otherwise than in relation to an agricultural holding, has the same meaning as in the Landlord and Tenant Act 1954 (see LANDLORD AND TENANT vol 27(1) (Reissue) para 369 note 1): Land Compensation Act 1973 s 87(1) (definition amended by the Land Compensation (Scotland) Act 1973 Sch 2 Pt I). For the meaning of 'agricultural holding' see para 185 note 3 ante.

4 Ie under the Land Compensation Act 1973 s 39(1)(a): see para 329 post; and HOUSING.

5 For the meaning of 'authority possessing compulsory purchase powers' see para 244 note 6 ante (definition applied by ibid s 87(1)).

6 Land Compensation Act 1973 s 50(2).

7 For the meaning of 'acquiring authority' see para 106 note 1 ante.

8 Land Compensation Act 1973 s 50(2).

9 See para 119 ante.

287. Compensation of landlord and tenant affected by right to apply for new business tenancy. Where, in pursuance of any enactment providing for the acquisition or taking of possession of land compulsorily, an acquiring authority[1] (1) acquires the landlord's interest in any land subject to a tenancy to which Part II of the Landlord and Tenant Act 1954[2] applies; or (2) acquires the tenant's interest in, or takes possession of, that land[3], then the tenant's right to apply under Part II of that Act for the grant of a new tenancy must be taken into account in assessing the compensation payable by the acquiring authority, whether to the landlord or the tenant, in connection with the acquisition of the interest or the taking of possession of the land, and, in assessing that compensation, it must be assumed that neither the acquiring authority nor any other authority possessing compulsory purchase powers[4] has acquired or proposes to acquire any interest in the land[5].

1 For the meaning of 'acquiring authority' see para 106 note 1 ante.

2 Ie the Landlord and Tenant Act 1954 Pt II (ss 23–46) (as amended) (security of tenure for business tenants): see LANDLORD AND TENANT vol 27(1) (Reissue) para 558 et seq. For the meaning of 'tenancy' see para 297 note 3 ante.

3 In the case of a tenancy greater than one for a year or from year to year, the interest would be acquired after a notice to treat (see para 100 et seq ante) and in the case of a tenancy for a year or from year to year or less, the interest would be dealt with by a notice requiring possession under the Lands Clauses Consolidation Act 1845 s 121 (as amended) or the Compulsory Purchase Act 1965 s 20 (as amended), or by notice of entry or entry after the deposit of security under s 11 (as amended) and compensation paid in respect of it accordingly (see paras 181 et seq ante, 300 et seq post). Further, if the amount of the compensation which would have been payable under the Landlord and Tenant Act 1954 s 37 (as amended) (see LANDLORD AND TENANT vol 27(1) (Reissue) para 607 et seq), if the tenancy had come to an end in circumstances giving rise to compensation under that provision and the date at which the acquiring authority obtained possession had been the termination of the current tenancy, exceeds the amount of the compensation payable under the Lands Clauses Consolidation Act 1845 s 121 (as amended) or the Compulsory Purchase Act 1965 s 20 (as amended), in the case of a tenancy to which the Landlord and Tenant Act 1954 Pt II (as amended) applies, that compensation will be increased by the amount of the excess: s 39(2) (amended by the Land Compensation Act 1973 s 47(3)); and see LANDLORD AND TENANT vol 27(1) (Reissue) para 558.

4 For the meaning of 'authority possessing compulsory purchase powers' see para 244 note 6 ante (definition applied by the Land Compensation Act 1973 s 87(1)).

5 Ibid s 47(1).

288. Compensation of landlord and tenant affected by restrictions on notices to quit agricultural holdings. Where, in pursuance of any enactment providing for the acquisition or taking of possession of land compulsorily, an acquiring authority[1] (1) acquires the landlord's[2] interest in an agricultural holding[3] or any part of it; or (2) acquires the interest of the tenant[4] in, or takes possession of[5], an agricultural holding or any part of it, then compensation is to be assessed as set out below[6].

In assessing the compensation payable by the acquiring authority to the landlord in connection with the acquisition of the landlord's interest in an agricultural holding or any part of it, there must be disregarded the landlord's right to serve a notice to quit, and any notice to quit already served by the landlord, which would not be or would not have been effective if:

(1) in the statutory provision for a case where notice to quit is given on the ground that the land is required for a use other than agriculture for which planning permission has been granted or is not required[7], the reference to the land being required did not include a reference to its being required by an acquiring authority[8]; and

(2) in the statutory provision[9] relating to the proposed termination of a tenancy for the purpose of the land's being used for a non-agricultural use not falling within head (1) above, the reference to the land's being used did not include a reference to its being used by an acquiring authority[10].

Furthermore, if the tenant has quitted the holding or any part of it by reason of a notice to quit which is to be so disregarded, it must be assumed that he has not done so[11].

In assessing the compensation payable by the acquiring authority to the tenant in connection with the acquisition of the tenant's interest in, or taking of possession of, an agricultural holding or any part of it ('the tenant's compensation'), there must be disregarded the landlord's right to serve a notice to quit and any notice to quit already served by him which would not be or would not have been effective[12] in the circumstances set out in heads (1) and (2) above[13]. The tenant's compensation is, however, to be reduced by an amount equal to any payment which the acquiring authority is liable to make to him in respect of the acquisition or taking of possession in question under the statutory provisions[14] relating to additional payments by an acquiring authority where it acquires the tenant's interest in, or takes possession of, an agricultural holding or any part of it[15].

If the tenant's compensation as determined in accordance with the above provisions[16] is less than it would have been if those provisions had not been enacted, it must be increased by the amount of the deficiency[17]; and in assessing his compensation no account is to be taken of any benefit which might accrue to him by virtue of the statutory provisions[18] relating to additional payments by the landlord for disturbance[19].

The above provisions do not, however, have effect where the tenancy of the agricultural holding is a tenancy to which the Agricultural Holdings Act 1986 does not apply[20] by virtue of the Agricultural Tenancies Act 1995[21].

1   For the meaning of 'acquiring authority' see para 106 note 1 ante.
2   For the meaning of 'landlord' see para 185 note 3 ante.
3   For the meaning of 'agricultural holding' see para 185 note 3 ante.
4   For the meaning of 'tenant' see para 185 note 3 ante.
5   In the case of a tenancy for a year or from year to year or less, the interest is taken possession of and, in the case of a greater interest, the lease is acquired, under a notice to treat: see para 287 note 3 ante.
6   Land Compensation Act 1973 s 48(1). Section 48(1) is subject to s 48(1A) (as added) (see the text and notes 20–21 infra): s 48(1) (amended by the Agricultural Tenancies Act 1995 s 40, Schedule para 24).
7   Ie in the Agricultural Holdings Act 1986 s 26(2), Sch 3 Pt I Case B (as substituted): see AGRICULTURE vol 1(2) (Reissue) para 345. For these purposes, 'notice to quit' has the same meaning as in the 1986 Act: Land Compensation Act 1973 s 87(1) (definition amended by the Land Compensation (Scotland) Act 1973 s 81(1), Sch 2 Pt I; and by virtue of the Agricultural Holdings Act 1986 s 100, Sch 14 para 56). As to such notices see AGRICULTURE vol 1(2) (Reissue) para 340 et seq.
8   Land Compensation Act 1973 s 48(2)(a)(i) (amended by the Agricultural Holdings Act 1986 Sch 14 para 53(1), (2)). The landlord is thus prevented from taking advantage of the acquiring authority's special needs as he could have done by virtue of the decision in *Rugby Joint Water Board v Foottit, Rugby Joint Water Board v Shaw-Fox* [1973] AC 202, [1972] 1 All ER 1057, HL, where land was acquired for a reservoir and it was held that the landlords were entitled to be compensated on the basis that they could have served an incontestable notice to quit on the tenants on the ground that the land was required for non-agricultural use for which planning permission had been obtained, although that permission had

been obtained by the acquiring authority. A landlord would, however, be entitled to have taken into account his right to serve a notice to quit, or a notice to quit served by him, based on his planning permission, or based on one obtained by the acquiring authority for a purpose not limited to that authority's special requirements, as eg the special requirements of any government department, local or public authority or statutory undertakers: cf the Land Compensation Act 1961 s 5 r (3) (as amended) (see para 270 ante); and see para 268 ante.

9 Ie the Agricultural Holdings Act 1986 s 27(3)(f): see AGRICULTURE vol 1(2) (Reissue) para 342.

10 Land Compensation Act 1973 s 48(2)(a)(ii) (amended by the Agricultural Holdings Act 1986 Sch 14 para 53(1), (2); also amended by the Agricultural Holdings (Notices to Quit) Act 1977 s 13(1), Sch 1 para 6 (repealed); and by virtue of the Agricultural Holdings Act 1986 s 101(1), Sch 14 para 53(2), Sch 15 Pt I).

11 Land Compensation Act 1973 s 48(2)(b).

12 Ie if the Agricultural Holdings Act 1986 Sch 3 Pt I Case B (as substituted) and s 27(3)(f) were construed in accordance with heads (1)–(2) in the text: Land Compensation Act 1973 s 48(3) (amended by the Agricultural Holdings Act 1986 Sch 14 para 53(1), (3)).

13 Land Compensation Act 1973 s 48(3) (as amended: see note 12 supra).

14 Ie under the Agriculture (Miscellaneous Provisions) Act 1968 s 12 (as amended): see AGRICULTURE vol 1(2) (Reissue) paras 396–397.

15 Land Compensation Act 1973 s 48(5).

16 Ie determined in accordance with ibid s 48(3) (as amended), s 48(5): see the text and notes 12–15 supra.

17 Ibid s 48(6).

18 Ie by virtue of the Agricultural Holdings Act 1986 s 60(2)(b) (see AGRICULTURE vol 1(2) (Reissue) para 427 et seq), but not by virtue of s 60(2)(b) as applied by the Agriculture (Miscellaneous Provisions) Act 1968 s 12 (as amended): Land Compensation Act 1973 s 48(6A) (added by the Agricultural Holdings Act 1986 Sch 14 para 53(1), (4)).

19 Land Compensation Act 1973 s 48(6A) (as added: see note 18 supra). As to the method of assessment of the compensation payable under s 48 (as amended) see *Wakerley v St Edmundsbury Borough Council* (1977) 33 P & CR 497, Lands Tribunal; *Dawson v Norwich City Council* (1978) 37 P & CR 516, Lands Tribunal.

20 Ie by virtue of the Agricultural Tenancies Act 1995 s 4: see AGRICULTURE.

21 Land Compensation Act 1973 s 48(1A) (added by the Agricultural Tenancies Act 1995 Schedule para 24).

(9) OTHER SPECIAL CASES

289. Measure of compensation to statutory undertakers etc. Special statutory provision is made with regard to the calculation of compensation to statutory undertakers[1] who are entitled to be compensated as a result of certain planning decisions and orders[2] or in consequence of a compulsory acquisition of land[3]. This special provision may, however, be excluded at the option of those undertakers when the right to compensation arises on a compulsory acquisition[4]; and in that case the normal rules[5] for the assessment of compensation apply[6].

Nothing in the Land Compensation Act 1961 applies to any purchase of the whole or any part of any statutory undertaking[7] under any enactment in that behalf prescribing the terms on which the purchase is to be effected[8].

1 For the meaning of 'statutory undertakers' see TOWN AND COUNTRY PLANNING vol 46 (Reissue) para 822. The special statutory provision also applies to the operator of a telecommunications code system: see TOWN AND COUNTRY PLANNING vol 46 (Reissue) para 843.

2 As to the right to compensation see the Town and Country Planning Act 1990 s 279; and TOWN AND COUNTRY PLANNING vol 46 (Reissue) para 842.

3 See ibid s 280; and TOWN AND COUNTRY PLANNING vol 46 (Reissue) para 843. As to the procedure for assessing compensation see s 282; and TOWN AND COUNTRY PLANNING vol 46 (Reissue) para 845. In relation to compulsory acquisitions of interests in land which has been acquired by statutory undertakers for the purposes of their undertaking, the provisions of the Land Compensation Act 1961 have effect subject to the Town and Country Planning Act 1990 s 280(1): Land Compensation Act 1961 s 11; Planning (Consequential Provisions) Act 1990 s 2(4). This provision does not, however, apply where

the Land Compensation Act 1961 s 36 excludes the provisions of the 1961 Act: see the text and notes 7–8 infra; and para 1 ante.

4 See the Town and Country Planning Act 1990 s 281; and TOWN AND COUNTRY PLANNING vol 46 (Reissue) para 844.

5 Ie with the exclusion of the Land Compensation Act 1961 s 5 r (5) (see paras 234, 281–282 ante): see the Town and Country Planning Act 1990 s 281(1); and TOWN AND COUNTRY PLANNING vol 46 (Reissue) para 844.

6 See ibid s 281(1); and TOWN AND COUNTRY PLANNING vol 46 (Reissue) para 844. As to the assessment of compensation under the normal rules see paras 233 et seq ante, 291 et seq post.

7 For the meaning of 'statutory undertaking' and 'enactment' see para 1 note 3 ante.

8 Land Compensation Act 1961 s 36(1).

290. Determination of compensation in cases of closing orders and demolition orders. Where a closing order[1] or a demolition order[2] is made in respect of any premises[3], the local housing authority[4] must pay to every owner[5] of the premises an amount equivalent to the diminution in the compulsory purchase value of the owner's interest in the premises[6] as a result of the making of the closing order or, as the case may be, the demolition order[7]. That amount must be determined, in default of agreement, as if it were compensation payable in respect of the compulsory purchase of the interest in question and must be dealt with accordingly[8]. In any case where a closing order which has been made in respect of any premises is revoked and a demolition order is made in its place[9], the amount so payable to the owner in connection with the demolition order must be reduced by the amount, if any, paid to the owner or a previous owner in connection with the closing order[10].

1 Ie under the Housing Act 1985 s 264 (as substituted): see HOUSING.

2 Ie under ibid s 265 (as substituted): see HOUSING.

3 'Premises', in relation to a demolition order or closing order, means the dwelling house, house in multiple occupation, building or part of a building in respect of which the order is made: see ibid s 322 (definition added by the Local Government and Housing Act 1989 s 165(1), Sch 9 para 42; applied by the Housing Act 1985 s 584A(4)) (s 584A added by the Local Government and Housing Act 1989 Sch 9 para 75).

4 'Local housing authority' means a district council, a London borough council, the Common Council of the City of London or the Council of the Isles of Scilly: Housing Act 1985 s 1 (prospectively amended by the Local Government (Wales) Act 1994 s 22(2), Sch 8 para 5(1), as from a day to be appointed under s 66(3), to include a Welsh county council or county borough council).

5 'Owner', in relation to premises or part of the premises, means a person, other than a mortgagee not in possession, who is for the time being entitled to dispose of the fee simple in the premises, whether in possession or in reversion, and includes also a person holding or entitled to the rents and profits of the premises under a lease of which the unexpired term exceeds three years: Housing Act 1985 s 602 (definition amended by the Local Government and Housing Act 1989 Sch 9 para 81).

6 'Compulsory purchase value', in relation to an owner's interest in premises, means the compensation which would be payable in respect of the compulsory purchase of that interest if it fell to be assessed in accordance with the Land Compensation Act 1961 (see para 233 et seq ante): Housing Act 1985 s 584A(4) (as added: see note 3 supra).

7 Ibid s 584A(1), (2) (as added: see note 3 supra).

8 Ibid s 584A(2)(b) (as added: see note 3 supra). The amount is determined as at the date of the making of the order in question: s 584(2)(a) (as so added).

9 Ie by virtue of ibid s 279 (as amended): see HOUSING.

10 Ibid s 584(3) (as added: see note 3 supra). As to repayment if the demolition or closing order is revoked see s 584B (as so added); and HOUSING.

6. COMPENSATION FOR SEVERANCE ETC AS PART OF PURCHASE MONEY

291. Right to compensation; severance. The Lands Clauses Acts[1] and the Compulsory Purchase Act 1965[2] provide that in assessing the purchase money or compensation to be paid by the undertakers[3] or the acquiring authority[4], regard must be had not only to the value of the land[5] to be purchased by them but also to the damage, if any, to be sustained by the owner of the land by reason of the severing of the land taken from his other land, or otherwise injuriously affecting that other land by the exercise of the statutory[6] powers[7]. The compensation is an additional head of compensation for the owner[8] of the land taken by reason of other retained land being severed from that land or otherwise injuriously affected by the compulsory purchase[9] and is part of the purchase money, purchase money and compensation being the same thing under different names[10].

The right to such compensation is not affected by the statutory provision[11] for the assessment of the value of the land taken[12].

The owner of the land is thus entitled to the market value of the land taken, and, if that land has been severed from other land of his, he is entitled to compensation for the depreciation in value of that other land by the severance or other injurious affection[13]. The owners entitled are those entitled to a notice to treat for the land to be purchased[14], but special though similar statutory provision is made with respect to the purchase of the interest of a lessee in land severed[15] and where a mortgage of the land severed exceeds the value of the land[16]. Where also the acquiring authority redeems the mortgage on the land taken, a mortgagee in possession with a power of sale is an owner entitled to compensation for severance or other injurious affection, notwithstanding the special statutory provision[17] as to mortgages[18].

Where different pieces of land are owned by the same person and are so near to each other and so situated that the possession and control of the parts of it gives an enhanced value to the whole, and one piece is compulsorily purchased, there will be a severance of the land purchased from the land held with it so as to give rise to a right to compensation for severance or other injurious affection within the above provisions[19]. The land taken must be so connected with or related to the part left that the owner of the latter is prejudiced in his ability to use or dispose of it to advantage by reason of the severance[20]. In order that there should be a severance, it is not necessary that the part taken and the part left should be in actual contiguity[21]; nor is it necessary that the owner should hold the land with respect to which damage is claimed by the same title as the land that is taken[22]. On the other hand, the bare fact that before the exercise of the compulsory power to take land the claimant was the common owner of both parts is insufficient[23].

Land held as described above[24] may be severed in effect by the owner himself, by his claim for a value of the land taken or part of it, as for a purpose different from the purpose for which the land was in fact so held, and to that extent there will be no right to compensation for severance[25].

There may be a lateral severance as well as a vertical one, as when the sub-soil is taken for a tunnel[26], and mines and minerals may be severed from the soil where there is special power to do so[27], but such severance may be subject to special statutory provisions[28].

1 As to the Lands Clauses Acts see para 11 note 1 ante.
2 Ie where acquisition is under a compulsory purchase order to which the Compulsory Purchase Act 1965 applies as being the special Act: see para 16 ante.
3 For the meaning of 'the undertakers' see para 13 ante.
4 For the meaning of 'acquiring authority' see para 92 note 5 ante.
5 For the meaning of 'land' see para 92 note 1 ante. See also para 13 text to note 7 ante.
6 Ie the powers of the Lands Clauses Consolidation Act 1845 or the special Act or any Act incorporated therewith (see the Lands Clauses Consolidation Act 1845 s 63), or the powers conferred by the Compulsory Purchase Act 1965 or the special Act (see the Compulsory Purchase Act 1965 s 7). For the meaning of 'the special Act' see paras 11, 16 ante.
7 Lands Clauses Consolidation Act 1845 s 63; Compulsory Purchase Act 1965 s 7. References in any enactment to the Lands Clauses Consolidation Act 1845 s 63 include references to the Compulsory Purchase Act 1965 s 7: s 39(3), Sch 7. There is no right to compensation etc in respect of interests created after the date of the notice to treat: see para 116 ante. The Compulsory Purchase Act 1965 s 7 is substituted in relation to the compulsory acquisition of rights by, inter alia, (1) a local authority, by the Local Government (Miscellaneous Provisions) Act 1976 s 13(3)(b) (as amended), Sch 1 para 6 (see LOCAL GOVERNMENT vol 28 para 1219); (2) the Development Board for Rural Wales, by the Development of Rural Wales Act 1976 s 6(7) (as amended), Sch 4 para 6 (see TOWN AND COUNTRY PLANNING vol 46 (Reissue) para 1200); (3) urban development corporations, by the Local Government, Planning and Land Act 1980 s 144, Sch 28 para 23(1) (see TOWN AND COUNTRY PLANNING vol 46 (Reissue) para 1297); (4) highway authorities, by the Highways Act 1980 s 250(5)(a) (as substituted), Sch 19 para 6 (see HIGHWAYS vol 21 (Reissue) para 808); (5) public gas suppliers, by the Gas Act 1986 s 9(3), Sch 3 para 7 (see FUEL AND ENERGY vol 19(1) (Reissue) para 636); (6) housing action trusts, by the Housing Act 1988 s 78(2), Sch 10 para 21 (see HOUSING); (7) licence holders under the Electricity Act 1989, by s 10(1), Sch 3 para 8 (see FUEL AND ENERGY vol 19(2) (Reissue) para 985); (8) the National Rivers Authority, by the Water Resources Act 1991 s 154(5), Sch 18 para 3 (see WATER); and (9) water and sewerage undertakers, by the Water Industry Act 1991 s 155(5), Sch 9 para 3 (see WATER).
8 It is sufficient if both parcels of land are held by one and the same owner and if the unity of ownership conduces to the advantage or protection of the property as one holding (*Cowper Essex v Acton Local Board* (1889) 14 App Cas 153 at 175, HL, per Lord Macnaghten); it is not necessary for the land taken and the other land not taken to be held under the same title (*Oppenheimer v Minister of Transport* [1942] 1 KB 242, [1941] 3 All ER 485).
9 See *Hoveringham Gravels Ltd v Chiltern District Council* (1977) 35 P & CR 295 at 305, CA. See also *Walker v Ware, Hadham and Buntingford Rly Co* (1865) LR 1 Eq 195 at 198; *Blundell v R* [1905] 1 KB 516 at 522–523 (approving *R v Abbott* [1897] 2 IR 362); *Watson v Secretary of State for Air* [1954] 3 All ER 582 at 584, [1954] 1 WLR 1477 at 1480, CA.
10 *IRC v Glasgow and South Western Rly Co* (1887) 12 App Cas 315, HL.
11 Ie the Land Compensation Act 1961 s 5 r (2): see paras 234, 279 ante. As to market value see generally para 278 et seq ante.
12 Ibid s 5 r (6); and cf *Horn v Sunderland Corpn* [1941] 2 KB 26 at 33–34, [1941] 1 All ER 480 at 485–486, CA.
13 See paras 278 et seq ante, 292 et seq post. He is also entitled to compensation for disturbance: see para 295 et seq post. The compensation thus given has been described as compensation on the basis of value to the owner, ie on the basis that the statutory provisions give to the owner the right to be put, so far as money can do it, in the same position as if his land had not been taken from him: *Corrie v MacDermott* [1914] AC 1056, PC; *Horn v Sunderland Corpn* [1941] 2 KB 26 at 42, [1941] 1 All ER 480 at 491, CA; *Hoveringham Gravels Ltd v Chiltern District Council* (1977) 35 P & CR 295, CA. It has also been described as reinstatement value and this has led to confusion with the reinstatement value which applies where no proper market value is ascertainable (see para 281 ante): see eg *R v Burrow* (1884) Times, 24 January, CA; affd sub nom *Metropolitan and District Rly Co v Burrow* (1884) Times, 22 November, HL. In assessing the value of the remaining land before severance, however, the effect of the scheme underlying the acquisition must be disregarded: see para 268 ante.
14 See para 103 ante; and in particular, *Oppenheimer v Minister of Transport* [1942] 1 KB 242, [1941] 3 All ER 485 (person with option to purchase has right to compensation for severance); *Clout v Metropolitan and District Rlys Joint Committee* (1883) 48 LT 257 (person with mere right of pre-emption has no such right). As to the right to compensation for severance given to tenants whose interests are not purchased see para 294 post.
15 See the Lands Clauses Consolidation Act 1845 s 120; the Compulsory Purchase Act 1965 s 19(5); and para 190 ante. The damage is that sustained during the period of the lease: see *Bexley Heath Rly Co v North* [1894] 2 QB 579, CA.

16 See the Lands Clauses Consolidation Act 1845 s 112; the Compulsory Purchase Act 1965 s 16; and para 196 ante.
17 See the text and note 16 supra.
18 See the Lands Clauses Consolidation Act 1845 s 108; the Compulsory Purchase Act 1965 s 14; *R v Clerk of the Peace for Middlesex* [1914] 3 KB 259; and para 194 ante.
19 See *Cowper Essex v Acton Local Board* (1889) 14 App Cas 153 at 167, HL; *Caledonian Rly Co v Lockhart* (1860) 3 Macq 808 at 815, HL.
20 *Holditch v Canadian Northern Ontario Rly Co* [1916] 1 AC 536, PC.
21 *Holt v Gas, Light and Coke Co* (1872) LR 7 QB 728; *Cowper Essex v Acton Local Board* (1889) 14 App Cas 153, HL; *Rockingham Sisters of Charity v R* [1922] 2 AC 315, PC.
22 *Holt v Gas, Light and Coke Co* (1872) LR 7 QB 728; and see note 8 supra.
23 *Holditch v Canadian Northern Ontario Rly Co* [1916] 1 AC 536, PC.
24 See the text and note 19 supra.
25 See *Horn v Sunderland Corpn* [1941] 2 KB 26, [1941] 1 All ER 480, CA, where the owner of the land claimed that the land which was being purchased from him should be treated as building land for the purpose of the valuation of that land but should also be treated as agricultural land from which he was being disturbed in respect of his farming business and entitled to compensation for disturbance in respect of it, but it was held that he could only realise the building value if he was willing to abandon the farming business in order to obtain the higher price. See also para 295 note 10 post.
26 *City and South London Rly Co v United Parishes of St Mary, Woolnoth and St Mary, Woolchurch Haw* [1905] AC 1, HL.
27 *Errington v Metropolitan District Rly Co* (1882) 19 ChD 559, CA.
28 See generally MINES.

292. Compensation for injurious affection as well as for severance. Compensation is payable not only in respect of injury to the land not taken which is caused by severance[1] but also for injury to that land caused by injurious affection, that is, by the acquiring authority's construction of works on the land taken, or partly on the land taken and partly elsewhere, or by the uses to which the land taken is to be put, whether the works require statutory authorisation to cause injury or not[2]. Compensation is not limited to works or uses for which there would be a right of action but for the statutory powers making lawful that which would otherwise be unlawful[3].

The works and uses are all those which the acquiring authority could carry out under its statutory authority, and it cannot reduce the amount of compensation payable by offering to enter into covenants not to use the land taken or part of it for the particular purpose for which its taking was authorised, as such an undertaking would be invalid; but an acquiring authority may undertake not to use the land for certain purposes where such an undertaking is compatible with the purposes for which the land is authorised to be acquired, and such an undertaking would be valid[4].

The injurious affection to the land not taken is no longer limited to injurious affection from the works on or use of the land taken from the same owner and 'held with' the land not taken and affected[5]. Where land[6] is acquired or taken from any person for the purpose of works which are to be situated partly on that land and partly elsewhere, compensation for injurious affection[7] of land retained by that person and given as part of the purchase money of land severed and taken[8] from that person is to be assessed by reference to the whole of the works[9] and not only the part situated on the land acquired or taken from him[10].

All damage that can be reasonably foreseen must be taken into account, and no subsequent claim may be made in respect of it[11]. The owner may, however, allow the question of compensation to stand over until after the execution of the works of the undertaking[12].

These provisions[13] apply in relation to the acquisition of interests in land, whether compulsorily or by agreement, by government departments which are authorities possessing compulsory purchase powers[14] as they apply in relation to the acquisition of interests in land by such authorities which are not government departments[15].

1 See para 291 ante.
2 *Re Stockport, Timperley and Altrincham Rly Co* (1864) 33 LJQB 251; *Duke of Buccleuch v Metropolitan Board of Works* (1872) LR 5 HL 418; *Cowper Essex v Acton Local Board* (1889) 14 App Cas 153 at 162, 178, HL; *Rockingham Sisters of Charity v R* [1922] 2 AC 315, PC. So where part of a person's land was taken for a railway and there was a resulting danger of fire to a mill on the land not taken, compensation for injurious affection was awarded: *Re Stockport, Timperley and Altrincham Rly Co* supra. So also where building land was rendered inaccessible (*R v Brown* (1867) LR 2 QB 630), where land was taken for the building of a highway (*Duke of Buccleuch v Metropolitan Board of Works* supra; *R v Mountford, ex p London United Tramways (1901) Ltd* [1906] 2 KB 814; *Re Great Eastern Rly Co and LCC* (1907) 98 LT 116, CA), or for a school, by reason of the noise from children (*R v Pearce, ex p London School Board* (1898) 67 LJ QB 842), or for military, naval or air force purposes (*Blundell v R* [1905] 1 KB 516, approving and following *R v Abbott* [1897] 2 IR 362; *Re Ned's Point Battery* [1903] 2 IR 192; *Master and Fellows of University College, Oxford v Secretary of State for Air* [1938] 1 KB 648, [1938] 1 All ER 69, DC; *Ainslie v Secretary of State for War* (1952) 2 P & CR 298; *Brooke-Hitching v The Admiralty* (1953) 4 P & CR 12); or where a reservoir was usable only on the land taken (*Ripley v Great Northern Rly Co* (1875) 10 Ch App 435).
3 See note 2 supra. Where the owner of land injuriously affected has had land taken but not held with the affected land, or has had no land taken, his only claim, subject to exceptions, is for compensation for injury by works or uses which would have given rise to an action but for the statute making lawful works otherwise unlawful (see para 353 post) and for compensation for injury by certain works, as provided by the Land Compensation Act 1973 ss 1 et seq (as amended) (see para 359 et seq post).
4 *Ayr Harbour Trustees v Oswald* (1883) 8 App Cas 623 at 634, HL, per Lord Blackburn, and at 640 per Lord Fitzgerald; *Re South Eastern Rly Co and Wiffin's Contract* [1907] 2 Ch 366; *Stourcliffe Estates Co Ltd v Bournemouth Corpn* [1910] 2 Ch 12, CA; *Re Heywood's Conveyance, Cheshire Lines Committee v Liverpool Corpn* [1938] 2 All ER 230.
5 As to the position before the coming into force of the Land Compensation Act 1973 s 44 (as amended) (ie 23 May 1973) see *Cowper Essex v Acton Local Board* (1889) 14 App Cas 153 at 166, HL; *Caledonian Rly Co v Ogilvy* (1855) 2 Macq 229, HL; *City of Glasgow Union Rly Co v Hunter* (1870) LR 2 Sc & Div 78 at 82, HL; *R v Mountford, ex p London United Tramways (1901) Ltd* [1906] 2 KB 814; *Re London and North Western Rly Co and Reddaway* (1907) 71 JP 150; *Horton v Colwyn Bay and Colwyn Urban Council* [1908] 1 KB 327, CA; *Rockingham Sisters of Charity v R* [1922] 2 AC 315, PC; *Edwards v Minister of Transport* [1964] 2 QB 134, [1964] 1 All ER 483, CA. If there was injurious affection to such land from works on or use of other land taken from that owner but not held with the land severed, or from works on or use of land taken from other owners, or from works on or use of land already owned by the acquiring authority, the compensation had to be sought under provisions other than the Lands Clauses Consolidation Act 1845 s 63 and the Compulsory Purchase Act 1965 s 7, as for compensation in lieu of a right of action: see para 353 post.
6 As to the meaning of 'land' see para 92 note 1 ante. See also para 13 text to note 7 ante.
7 For these purposes, 'compensation for injurious affection' means compensation for injurious affection under the Lands Clauses Consolidation Act 1845 s 63 or s 121 (as amended); or under the Compulsory Purchase Act 1965 s 7 or s 20 (as amended) (see paras 291 ante, 294 post): Land Compensation Act 1973 s 44(2).
8 This provision made by ibid s 44(1) also applies to compensation under the Compulsory Purchase Act 1965 s 7 as substituted by (1) the Highways Act 1980 s 250 (as amended), Sch 19 para 6; or (2) the Gas Act 1986 s 9(3), Sch 3 para 7; or (3) the Water Industry Act 1991 s 155(5), Sch 9 para 3; or (4) the Water Resources Act 1991 s 154(5), Sch 18 para 3, in relation to the acquisition of rights over land under those Acts, or by any corresponding enactment (see para 291 note 7 ante) including (except where otherwise provided) an enactment passed after 23 May 1973: Land Compensation Act 1973 s 44(2) (amended by the Highways Act 1980 s 343(2), Sch 24 para 23; the Gas Act 1986 s 67(1), Sch 7 para 14(1); the Water Act 1989 s 190(1), Sch 25 para 44(1); and by the Water Consolidation (Consequential Provisions) Act 1991 s 2(1), Sch 1 para 23). It also applies to compensation for severance or other injurious affection given to tenants for a year or from year to year whose interests in the land are not purchased but of which possession may be required under the Lands Clauses Consolidation Act 1845 s 121 (as amended) or the Compulsory Purchase Act 1965 s 20 (as amended) (see paras 181–184 ante, 294 post): see the Land Compensation Act 1973 s 44(2) (as so amended); and note 7 supra.
9 As to the meaning of 'the works' see para 92 note 3 ante; and see also para 13 text to note 4 ante.
10 Land Compensation Act 1973 s 44(1). The effect of this provision is that owners who have had land taken and suffer injurious affection to land held with that land and not taken from works on land taken from other owners or held by the acquiring authority are no longer, like other owners, limited, in

respect of that injury, to compensation under the Lands Clauses Consolidation Act 1845 s 68 (as amended) or the Compulsory Purchase Act 1965 s 10 (as amended): see para 200 ante. Under the extended rights to compensation for injurious affection by works conferred by the Land Compensation Act 1973 Pt I (ss 1–19 (as amended), where land is acquired for the purposes of any public works, and there is a right to claim compensation for injurious affection of retained land under the Lands Clauses Consolidation Act 1845 s 63 or the Compulsory Purchase Act 1965 s 7, no claim may be made for compensation under the Land Compensation Act 1973 Pt I (as amended): see s 8(2), (7); and para 364 text to note 13 post. If, however, an owner whose land is taken retains land held with it, or a person who claims under the Lands Clauses Consolidation Act 1845 s 121 (as amended) or the Compulsory Purchase Act 1965 s 20 (as amended) (tenants from year to year etc), as extended by the Land Compensation Act 1973 s 44 (as amended) (see para 294 note 3 post) has other land not held with the land taken from him which suffers injurious affection by the work, he may, in such a case, claim under the Lands Clauses Consolidation Act 1845 s 68 (as amended) or the Compulsory Purchase Act 1965 s 10 (as amended) (see paras 354–358 post), or under the Land Compensation Act 1973 Pt I (as amended): see s 8(5). But he cannot claim under both: s 8(7).

11 *Caledonian Rly Co v Lockhart* (1860) 3 Macq 808, HL; *Croft v London and North Western Rly Co* (1863) 32 LJQB 113; *Todd v Metropolitan District Rly Co* (1871) 24 LT 435; *Mercer v Liverpool, St Helen's and South Lancashire Rly Co* [1904] AC 461, HL.
12 *Caledonian Rly Co v Lockhart* (1860) 3 Macq 808, HL.
13 Ie the Land Compensation Act 1973 Pt IV (ss 44–64) (as amended): see para 293 et seq post.
14 For the meaning of 'authority possessing compulsory purchase powers' see para 244 note 6 ante (definition applied by ibid s 87(1)).
15 Ibid s 84(2).

293. Measure and assessment of compensation; mitigation of damage. The measure of compensation for damage to the land not taken by reason of severance or other injurious affection[1] is the extent to which it has depreciated in market value[2]. Damage by severance may be aggravated by injurious works on the land taken, or alternatively, it may be reduced by beneficial works on or uses of the land taken, and the land not taken may be so benefited that there is no depreciation in value, or the land not taken may even be enhanced in value[3]. However, except under special statutory provisions[4], any increased value may not be set off against the value of the land taken because in such a case the owner is entitled to sell the land taken without reference to the land held with it[5]. There would also appear to be a right to compensation for disturbance consequent on the severance or other injurious affection because the owner is entitled to compensation for all damage directly consequent on the taking of the land under the statutory powers[6].

In some public general Acts and in some local Acts[7] provisions are inserted enabling enhanced value to be taken into account in assessing the compensation[8]. These special statutory provisions for setting off the improved value of the land not taken against the value of the land taken apply not only where there would otherwise be a claim for severance or other injurious affection, but also where the land taken was not held with the land not taken and increased in value[9].

Where there is a proper claim for compensation for severance or other injurious affection to the land not taken and held with the land taken for the same purpose[10], which is the existing user of both parts of the land, or is for a purpose for which both parts have planning permission granted or assumed or which may reasonably be expected to be granted, the part taken and the part not taken must be valued as proportional parts of an unsevered whole[11], and the rules as to special suitability and adaptability[12] cannot therefore apply to that valuation. The part not taken must then be valued as affected by the severance or other injurious affection, and the rules as to special suitability and adaptability can then apply.

Injury by severance or other injurious affection may be avoided if there is power for an owner of part of agricultural land[13], or of part of a house, building or manufactory required to be purchased, to compel the acquiring authority to purchase the whole[14], or, in the case of the purchase leaving only a small area of land in the owner's hands, where power is given to the owner to require the purchase of the whole unless accommodation works for communication are carried out by the authority[15].

Some statutes compel the making of accommodation works to mitigate injury by severance[16], and otherwise the owner and authority may agree to construct such works which are not in restriction of their statutory powers and duties[17]. The compensation is, however, part of the purchase money[18], and the acquiring authority and the Lands Tribunal have no power, unless specifically provided[19], to compel the owner to accept accommodation works in mitigation of damage by severance[20], nor to award an additional sum in respect of such works[21].

1　See paras 291–292 ante.
2　Re Stockport, Timperley and Altrincham Rly Co (1864) 33 LJQB 251; Cowper Essex v Acton Local Board (1889) 14 App Cas 153, HL. See also Hoveringham Gravels Ltd v Chiltern District Council (1977) 35 P & CR 295, CA. As to market value see para 278 et seq ante.
3　See eg Wimpey & Co Ltd v Middlesex County Council [1938] 3 All ER 781, where land taken for an open space enhanced the value of the land not taken. As to betterment reducing compensation generally see para 316 et seq post.
4　See the text and notes 7–9 infra.
5　Re South Eastern Rly Co and LCC's Contract, South Eastern Rly Co v LCC [1915] 2 Ch 252 at 260, CA.
6　See eg Horn v Sunderland Corpn [1941] 2 KB 26 at 49, [1941] 1 All ER 480 at 491, CA; and para 295 note 20 post.
7　As to public general Acts and local Acts see STATUTES vol 44(1) (Reissue) paras 1210, 1213.
8　As an example of the application of such provisions see Harding v Board of Land and Works (1886) 11 App Cas 208, PC; Wimpey & Co Ltd v Middlesex County Council [1938] 3 All ER 781.
9　See para 316 post.
10　See para 291 ante.
11　If the parts are not so valued there will be no value before severance of the land not taken from which its diminution in value can be ascertained in relation to its value after severance.
12　See para 270 ante.
13　See the Land Compensation Act 1973 s 53 (as amended), s 54; and paras 106–107 ante.
14　See the Lands Clauses Consolidation Act 1845 s 92; and para 108 ante. Power to compel the acquiring authority to purchase the whole except where the part can be taken without material detriment to the part not taken lies in the case of acquisitions authorised by compulsory purchase orders under the Acquisition of Land Act 1981 to which the provisions of the Compulsory Purchase Act 1965 s 8(1) apply: see para 112 ante. As to the application of Pt I (ss 1–32) (as amended) to such compulsory purchase orders see para 15 ante.
15　See the Lands Clauses Consolidation Act 1845 ss 93, 94; the Compulsory Purchase Act 1965 s 8(2), (3); and paras 113–114 ante.
16　Eg the Railways Clauses Consolidation Act 1845 ss 68, 69; cf para 114 ante; and see RAILWAYS.
17　Ayr Harbour Trustees v Oswald (1883) 8 App Cas 623, HL; and see para 292 text and note 4 ante.
18　See para 291 ante.
19　Eg under the Railways Clauses Consolidation Act 1845: see note 16 supra.
20　Re Ware and Regent's Canal Co (1854) 9 Exch 395; and see R v South Holland Drainage Committee Men (1838) 8 Ad & El 429.
21　R v South Wales Rly Co (1849) 13 QB 988; cf Re Byles and Ipswich Dock Comrs (1855) 11 Exch 464. As to the Lands Tribunal see para 202 et seq ante.

294. Yearly tenancies and lesser interests. Yearly tenancies and lesser interests are not purchased but possession may be required[1]. However, the tenant is entitled, in addition to his other compensation, to compensation for the damage done to him in his tenancy by severing the land held by him, or otherwise injuriously affecting it[2], and it seems that the principles applicable to the severing of other interests[3] will apply[4], but the assessing tribunal has jurisdiction to assess such compensation only in respect of the period for which the land is held by the tenant[5].

Damage by severance may be mitigated by the power of a tenant of an agricultural holding, where part of the holding is proposed to be taken, to require the whole to be taken[6].

1 See para 181 et seq ante.
2 See the Lands Clauses Consolidation Act 1845 s 121 (as amended); the Compulsory Purchase Act 1965 s 20 (as amended); and para 181 et seq ante.
3 See para 291 et seq ante. As to the measure and assessment of compensation, and mitigation of damage by severance, see para 293 ante.
4 The provisions of the Land Compensation Act 1973 s 44(1) (see para 292 ante), extending the right to injurious affection from works on land not taken from the owner are, by s 44(2) (as amended), expressly applied to compensation for severance or other injurious affection under the Lands Clauses Consolidation Act 1845 s 121 (as amended) and the Compulsory Purchase Act 1965 s 20 (as amended): see para 292 note 10 ante.
5 *Bexley Heath Rly Co v North* [1894] 2 QB 579, CA.
6 See the Land Compensation Act 1973 ss 55–57 (as amended); and para 185 et seq ante.

7. COMPENSATION FOR DISTURBANCE FROM THE LAND ACQUIRED

(1) COMPENSATION TO OWNERS AS PART OF THE PURCHASE MONEY

295. Right to and assessment of compensation for disturbance. An owner[1] whose land is compulsorily acquired is entitled to compensation for disturbance[2] as part of the value to him of the land taken[3]. There is no express statutory provision which confers the right on owners to claim compensation for disturbance[4], but as a result of a long series of judicial decisions, it is established that the ascertainment of the value of land to the owner requires consideration of damage caused by the acquisition, for example by disturbance of the owner's business[5]. The owner is entitled to be compensated fully and fairly for his loss[6], and has the right to receive a money payment of an amount no more and no less than the amount of the loss imposed on him in the public interest[7]. In practice it is customary and convenient to assess the value of the land itself and the disturbance loss separately, but strictly in law these are no more than two elements in a single whole, together making up the value of the land to the owner[8].

The owner is entitled to recover any loss which flows from the compulsory acquisition provided that it is not too remote and that it is the natural and reasonable consequence of his dispossession[9]. If, however, the value of the land lies in its potential for development, which can only be realised by vacating the land, then payment for disturbance will only be made if the value of the land for its current use plus any compensation for disturbance exceeds the value of the land for development[10].

Until recently, only an owner-occupier could claim compensation for disturbance, but now an owner who is not in occupation can claim if he incurs incidental charges or expenses in acquiring, within the period of one year beginning with the date of entry, an interest in other land in the United Kingdom[11]. However, the question of occupation remains important in other circumstances. An owner of land who is not in occupation of it will not generally be entitled to compensation for disturbance suffered by the occupier, even if the occupier is a company of which he is the principal shareholder[12], although a parent company owning land on which a subsidiary company carries on business as agent for it is entitled to compensation for disturbance[13].

A claim for compensation for disturbance may include losses or expenses incurred before the service of a notice to treat or entry by the acquiring authority, provided that such losses or expenses were incurred in anticipation of the acquisition and because of the threat posed by the acquisition, and thus were causally connected with the acquisition[14].

As compensation for disturbance is to be assessed on the same basis as damages at common law, considerations of public policy may be relevant to the assessment, and it has been held to be contrary to public policy to lessen the inducement afforded by the payment of a regional development grant to assist in relocation in a development area by deducting the amount of the grant from the compensation for disturbance[15]. Compensation for disturbance is not payable if the use of land which is prevented by the acquisition is a use 'contrary to law'[16].

The normal date for the assessment of compensation for disturbance is the same as the date for the assessment of the value of the land itself, namely the date of entry or the date of the valuation itself, whichever is the earlier[17]; but it is possible, where appropriate, to deal with the assessment of compensation for disturbance after the assessment of the value of the land itself, in order to enable the actual losses to be considered[18].

The amount of compensation payable in respect of the compulsory acquisition of an interest in land must not be subject to any reduction on account of the fact that the acquiring authority[19] has provided, or undertaken to provide, or arranges for the provision of, residential accommodation under any enactment for the person entitled to the compensation, or that another authority will provide such accommodation[20].

1 Ie including a lessee for more than a year: see para 103 ante. For special provisions as to lessees see para 299 post.
2 Ie damage suffered consequent upon the acquisition.
3 See *Horn v Sunderland Corpn* [1941] 2 KB 26, [1941] 1 All ER 480, CA.
4 The Land Compensation Act 1961 s 5 r (6) merely states that s 5 r (2) (which requires open market value to be paid: see paras 234, 279 ante) does not affect the assessment of compensation for disturbance: see paras 234, 291 ante. Cf the express provision made for disturbance payments for non-owners without compensatable interests: see the Land Compensation Act 1973 ss 37, 38 (as amended); and paras 314–315 post.
5 *IRC v Glasgow and South Western Rly Co* (1887) 12 App Cas 315 at 320, HL; *Horn v Sunderland Corpn* [1941] 2 KB 26 at 32–33, 47, 49, [1941] 1 All ER 480 at 484, 495–496, CA.
6 See *Director of Buildings and Lands v Shun Fung Ironworks Ltd* [1995] 2 AC 111 at 125, [1995] 1 All ER 846 at 852, PC.
7 *Horn v Sunderland Corpn* [1941] 2 KB 26 at 42, [1941] 1 All ER 480 at 491, CA.
8 *Hughes v Doncaster Metropolitan Borough Council* [1991] 1 AC 382 at 392, [1991] 1 All ER 295 at 301, HL, per Lord Bridge.
9 See *Harvey v Crawley Development Corpn* [1957] 1 QB 485 at 494, [1957] 1 All ER 504 at 507, CA, per Romer LJ. See also *J Bibby & Sons Ltd v Merseyside County Council* (1979) 39 P & CR 53, CA; *Director of Buildings and Lands v Shun Fung Ironworks Ltd* [1995] 2 AC 111, [1995] 1 All ER 846, PC.
10 *Horn v Sunderland Corpn* [1941] 2 KB 26, [1941] 1 All ER 480, CA. Similarly, compensation will not be payable for disturbance if that disturbance has already been taken into account in assessing the compensation payable in respect of severance and injurious affection: see *Cooke v Secretary of State for the Environment* (1973) 27 P & CR 234, Lands Tribunal.
11 See the Land Compensation Act 1961 s 10A (added by the Planning and Compensation Act 1991 s 70, Sch 15 para 2); and para 284 ante. An owner who is not in occupation may also claim for other consequential loss: see *Wrexham Maelor Borough Council v MacDougall* [1993] 2 EGLR 23, CA (loss of a service contract). For the meaning of 'United Kingdom' see para 100 note 21 ante.
12 *Woolfson v Strathclyde Regional Council* (1978) 38 P & CR 521, HL. Cf *DHN Food Distributors Ltd v Tower Hamlets London Borough Council* [1976] 3 All ER 462, [1976] 1 WLR 852, CA.
13 *Smith, Stone and Knight Ltd v Birmingham Corpn* [1939] 4 All ER 116.

14 *Director of Buildings and Lands v Shun Fung Ironworks Ltd* [1995] 2 AC 111 at 137–138, [1995] 1 All ER 846 at 863–864, PC, approving and extending *Prasad v Wolverhampton Borough Council* [1983] Ch 333, [1983] 2 All ER 140, CA.

15 *Palatine Graphic Arts Co Ltd v Liverpool City Council* [1986] QB 335, [1986] 1 All ER 366, CA.

16 *Hughes v Doncaster Metropolitan Borough Council* [1991] 1 AC 382, [1991] 1 All ER 295, HL, applying the Land Compensation Act 1961 s 5 r (4). An unpermitted use which is immune from enforcement proceedings is not, however, contrary to law for these purposes: *Hughes v Doncaster Metropolitan Borough Council* supra.

17 See *Birmingham Corpn v West Midland Baptist (Trust) Association (Inc)* [1970] AC 874, [1969] 3 All ER 172, HL.

18 See *Munton v GLC* [1976] 2 All ER 815, [1976] 1 WLR 649, CA.

19 For the meaning of 'acquiring authority' see para 106 note 1 ante.

20 Land Compensation Act 1973 s 50(1). This provision applies also in relation to any payment to which a person is entitled under Pt III (ss 29–43) (as amended) (home loss payments, farm loss payments and payments to persons without compensatable interests) as it applies in relation to the compensation payable in respect of the compulsory acquisition of an interest in land, taking references to the acquiring authority as references to the authority responsible for making that payment: s 50(3). See also paras 310 text and note 25, 313 text and note 19, 315 text and note 14 post. As to the provision of housing for persons displaced by statutory works see para 329 et seq post.

296. Expense of finding new premises and removing goods. Costs incurred in preparing a claim for compensation should be included in the compensation payable, because such costs are incurred as a direct consequence of dispossession[1]. Such costs would not be excluded by any express statutory exclusion of compensation for disturbance, because compensation for such costs is properly described as compensation for 'any other matter not directly based on the value of land' as opposed to compensation for disturbance[2]. Costs reasonably incurred in connection with the issue of a certificate of appropriate alternative development should also be included[3].

The owner disturbed is also entitled to the legal costs and stamp duty on the purchase of a comparable property, to surveyors' fees in relation to it and to travelling expenses in finding such a property[4].

If the claimant has incurred increased operating costs (including an increased rent) after taking new premises, then he is entitled to compensation in respect of those costs if he had no alternative but to incur them and has obtained no benefit as a result of the extra costs which would make them worthwhile[5]. Costs of adaptation of new premises should be treated in a similar manner[6], but in relation to the acquisition or improvement of new premises there is a rebuttable presumption that value for money has been obtained by any extra cost[7].

The costs of removal of fixtures[8], furniture and goods[9] are payable as compensation. This includes depreciation in the value of furniture specially fitted[10] and in the case of a trader it includes the diminution in the value of his stock consequent on its removal or on a forced sale where such a sale is necessary[11]. The fact that a business is being carried on at a loss does not disentitle the claimant from claiming in respect of an increase in that loss caused by the acquisition, provided it is reasonable in the circumstances for the business to be continued[12].

If interest charges are incurred by the claimant in financing the development of new premises, then these will generally be treated as being part of the purchase price of the premises and thus, in view of the rebuttable presumption referred to above, the charges will not normally be payable as part of the compensation[13].

1 *LCC v Tobin* [1959] 1 All ER 649, [1959] 1 WLR 354, CA (legal and accountancy fees reasonably and properly incurred in preparing the claim for compensation). An interpreter's fees may be included: *Sadik v London Borough of Haringey* (1978) 37 P & CR 120.

2   See the Land Compensation Act 1961 s 5 r (6); *Judge Lee v Minister of Transport* [1966] 1 QB 111, [1965] 2 All ER 986, CA (surveyors' fees for negotiating the amount of the compensation).
3   See the Land Compensation Act 1961 s 17(9A) (added by the Planning and Compensation Act 1991 s 65(3)); and para 257 ante.
4   *Harvey v Crawley Development Corpn* [1957] 1 QB 485, [1957] 1 All ER 504, CA. The owner may also be entitled to the loss on an abortive purchase: *Harvey v Crawley Development Corpn* supra.
5   *J Bibby & Sons Ltd v Merseyside County Council* (1979) 39 P & CR 53, CA. See also *R v Burrow* (1884) Times, 24 January, CA; affd sub nom *Metropolitan and District Rly Co v Burrow* (1884) Times, 22 November, HL; *Harvey v Crawley Development Corpn* [1957] 1 QB 485, [1957] 1 All ER 504, CA; *Service Welding Ltd v Tyne and Wear County Council* (1979) 38 P & CR 352, CA.
6   See eg *Tamplins Brewery Ltd v County Borough of Brighton* (1971) 22 P & CR 746, Lands Tribunal.
7   See eg *Service Welding Ltd v Tyne and Wear County Council* (1979) 38 P & CR 352, CA.
8   *Gibson v Hammersmith and City Rly Co* (1863) 32 LJ Ch 337.
9   *Venables v Department of Agriculture for Scotland* 1932 SC 573.
10 See note 9 supra.
11 *Horn v Sunderland Corpn* [1941] 2 KB 26 at 49, [1941] 1 All ER 480 at 496, CA.
12 *R v Burrow* (1884) Times, 24 January, CA; affd sub nom *Metropolitan and District Rly Co v Burrow* (1884) Times, 22 November, HL. See also *Director of Buildings and Lands v Shung Fung Ironworks Ltd* [1995] 2 AC 111, [1995] 1 All ER 846, PC.
13 *Service Welding Ltd v Tyne and Wear County Council* (1979) 38 P & CR 352, CA.

297. Injury to goodwill and loss of profits until business re-established. Compensation is payable in respect of injury to goodwill by reason of the removal[1]. Goodwill is not purchased by the acquiring authority except where it is attached to the land, in which case it is part of the value of the land and is not strictly goodwill[2]. The injury may depend on the distance of the new premises from the old[3], and there may be a total loss of goodwill[4].

Compensation for injury to goodwill is often assessed on the average of the previous three years' profits[5], and the profit is multiplied by the appropriate number of years' purchase to find the value of the goodwill of which the depreciation is to be ascertained[6]. However, where the business has been running at a loss[7], or expenses are incurred for expansion but the business is not yet profitable, other methods must be applied. The objective is to assess the loss to the claimant, and even if the goodwill has no market value, because statute forbids the sale of the business, there is still a valid claim for the loss suffered by the sacrifice of potential business[8].

There may also be a claim for loss of profits during a period of re-establishment, whether or not there has been injury to goodwill[9]. In the case of a lessee's interest, this right will be affected by the length of his term and his right of renewal of his tenancy or its protection[10].

There is no right to the loss of profits which a building company could have made on the land acquired, because the profitability of the land is reflected in its market value[11].

There must be a causative link between the loss of profits and the dispossession of the claimant[12].

1   *Re Bidder and North Staffordshire Rly Co* (1878) 4 QBD 412 at 432, CA; *R v Scard* (1894) 10 TLR 545, DC; *R v Burrow* (1884) Times, 24 January, CA; affd sub nom *Metropolitan and District Rly Co v Burrow* (1884) Times, 22 November, HL.
2   As to so-called goodwill by reason of the situation of the premises see *Chissum v Dewes* (1828) 5 Russ 29; *King v Midland Rly Co* (1868) 17 WR 113; *Rutter v Daniel* (1882) 30 WR 724; on appeal (1882) 30 WR 801, CA; *Re Kitchin, ex p Punnett* (1880) 16 ChD 226 at 233, CA (goodwill of a public house passes with it).
3   See note 1 supra. Apart from the goodwill which is part of the value of the land (see note 2 supra), goodwill arising from the establishment of a business on premises and its maintenance is the goodwill which is entitled to compensation, and compensation for that goodwill will not pass to the mortgagee like that attached to the land: see *Cooper v Metropolitan Board of Works* (1883) 25 ChD 472, CA.

4 *White v Works and Public Buildings Comrs* (1870) 22 LT 591.
5 Ie according to the usual practice applied to a business of that nature or an ordinary sale where the goodwill is purchased; but there are no invariable rules; for an example see *Zarraga v Newcastle-upon-Tyne Corpn* (1968) 19 P & CR 609, Lands Tribunal.
6 *LCC v Tobin* [1959] 1 All ER 649, [1959] 1 WLR 354, CA.
7 See *R v Burrow* (1884) Times, 24 January, CA; affd sub nom *Metropolitan and District Rly Co v Burrow* (1884) Times, 22 November, HL.
8 *Roy v Westminster City Council* (1975) 31 P & CR 458, Lands Tribunal.
9 See *R v Burrow* (1884) Times, 24 January, CA; affd sub nom *Metropolitan and District Rly Co v Burrow* (1884) Times, 22 November, HL.
10 As to that right of renewal or protection see the Land Compensation Act 1973 s 47, s 48 (as amended); and paras 287–288 ante.
11 *Collins v Feltham UDC* [1937] 4 All ER 189; *George Wimpey & Co Ltd v Middlesex County Council* [1938] 3 All ER 781; but compensation may be allowed for abortive expenditure and increased overhead charges: *George Wimpey & Co Ltd v Middlesex County Council* supra. See also *D McEwing & Sons Ltd v Renfrew County Council* (1960) 11 P & CR 306; and cf *Pastoral Finance Association Ltd v The Minister* [1914] AC 1083 at 1088, PC.
12 *Emslie & Simpson Ltd v Aberdeen City District Council* [1994] 1 EGLR 33 (loss of profits caused by blight).

298. Compensation where not practicable to re-establish business. There may be cases where it is not reasonably practicable to re-establish a business after disturbance, in which case compensation will be payable for the total extinguishment of the business[1]. The extinguishment must, however, be caused by the acquisition and not, for example, by the claimant's ill-health[2].

Where a person is carrying on a trade or business, whether alone, in partnership[3] or through a company[4], on any land and, in consequence of the compulsory acquisition of the whole of that land, is required to give up possession of it to the acquiring authority[5], then if (1) on the date he gives up possession he has attained the age of 60[6]; and (2) the land then is or forms part of a hereditament[7] the annual value[8] of which does not exceed the prescribed amount[9]; and (3) that person has not disposed of the goodwill of the whole of the trade or business and gives to the acquiring authority certain statutory undertakings[10], the compensation payable to him in respect of the compulsory acquisition of his interest in the land[11], so far as attributable to disturbance, is to be assessed on the assumption that it is not reasonably practicable for him to carry on the trade or business or, as the case may be, the part of it the goodwill of which he has retained, elsewhere than on that land[12].

If an undertaking given by a person for these purposes is broken, the acquiring authority may recover from him an amount equal to the difference between the compensation paid and that which would have been payable had it been assessed without regard to these provisions[13].

It is sufficient for the purpose of these provisions that there should be a causal connection between the giving up of possession and the compulsory acquisition; the claimant does not have to await service of a notice of entry[14].

1 See eg *W Clibbett Ltd v Avon County Council* [1976] 1 EGLR 171, Lands Tribunal. There is no rule that a claimant can never be entitled to compensation for relocation if that exceeds the amount of compensation payable on an extinguishment basis; the question is whether a reasonable business person would relocate: *Director of Buildings and Lands v Shun Fung Ironworks Ltd* [1995] 2 AC 111, [1995] 1 All ER 846, PC.
2 *Bailey v Derby Corpn* [1965] 1 All ER 443, [1965] 1 WLR 213, CA. See, however, the text and notes 3–13 infra.
3 The Land Compensation Act 1973 s 46 (as amended) applies to a trade or business carried on by two or more persons in partnership as if references to the person by whom it is carried on were references to all the partners and as if the undertakings to be given (see note 10 infra) were required to be given by all the partners: s 46(5).

4 Ibid s 46 (as amended) applies to a trade or business carried on by a company (1) as if s 46(1)(a) (see head (1) in the text) required each shareholder, other than a minority shareholder, to be an individual who has attained the age of 60 on the date of giving up possession and each minority shareholder to be an individual who either has attained that age on that date, or is the spouse of a shareholder who has attained that age on that date; and (2) as if the undertakings to be given (see note 10 infra) were required to be given both by the company and by each shareholder: s 46(6). 'Shareholder' means a person who is beneficially entitled to a share or shares in the company carrying voting rights, and 'minority shareholder' means a person who is so entitled to less than 50% of those shares: s 46(6).

5 For the meaning of 'acquiring authority' see para 106 note 1 ante.

6 Land Compensation Act 1973 s 46(1)(a).

7 For these purposes, 'hereditament' has the meaning given in the Town and Country Planning Act 1990 s 171 (see TOWN AND COUNTRY PLANNING vol 46 (Reissue) para 729 note 6): Land Compensation Act 1973 s 46(2) (amended by the Planning (Consequential Provisions) Act 1990 s 4, Sch 2 para 29(7)).

8 For these purposes, 'annual value' has the meaning given in the Town and Country Planning Act 1990 s 171 (see TOWN AND COUNTRY PLANNING vol 46 (Reissue) para 729 note 12), taking references to the date of service of a notice under s 150 (as amended) (see TOWN AND COUNTRY PLANNING vol 46 (Reissue) para 744) as references to the date mentioned in the Land Compensation Act 1973 s 46(1) (see heads (1)–(3) in the text): s 46(2) (as amended: see note 7 supra).

9 Ibid s 46(1)(b). 'The prescribed amount' means the amount which, on the date on which he gives up possession, is the amount prescribed for the purposes of the Town and Country Planning Act 1990 s 149(3)(a) (interests qualifying for protection under planning blight provisions: see para 90 ante; and TOWN AND COUNTRY PLANNING vol 46 (Reissue) para 729), taking references to the date of service of a notice under s 150 (as amended) as references to the date on which the person gives up possession: Land Compensation Act 1973 s 46(2) (as amended: see note 7 supra).

10 Ibid s 46(1)(c). The undertakings to be given by the person claiming compensation are (1) an undertaking that he will not dispose of the goodwill of the trade or business, or, as the case may be, of the part of it the goodwill of which he has retained; and (2) an undertaking that he will not, within such area and for such time as the acquiring authority may require, directly or indirectly engage in or have any interest in any other trade or business of the same or substantially the same kind as that carried on by him on the land acquired: ibid s 46(3).

11 Ibid s 46 (as amended) applies also to compensation for disturbance to which a tenant for a year or from year to year is entitled under the Lands Clauses Consolidation Act 1845 s 121 (as amended), or the Compulsory Purchase Act 1965 s 20 (as amended) (see para 181 et seq ante): Land Compensation Act 1973 s 46(1). See further para 303 post. Those tenants are entitled to compensation for disturbance, although their interests are not purchased but are taken by requiring possession on payment of compensation: see para 300 post.

Section 46 (as amended) also applies to payments for disturbance under s 38(1)(b) (see para 315 post), payable to persons who have no interest in the land compulsorily acquired so as to entitle them to compensation for disturbance as part of the purchase money; it so applies subject to the necessary modifications and as if references to giving up of possession of the land to the acquiring authority, in consequence of its compulsory acquisition, were references to the displacement of a person from the land in consequence of the acquisition of the land by an authority possessing compulsory purchase powers as mentioned in s 37 (as amended) (see para 314 post): s 46(7).

12 Ibid s 46(1).

13 Ibid s 46(4).

14 *Sheffield Development Corpn v Glossop Sectional Buildings Ltd* [1994] 1 WLR 1676, [1994] 2 EGLR 29, CA.

(2) COMPENSATION TO TENANTS

299. In general. A tenant for more than a year has the rights of an owner on service of a notice to treat[1], but an acquiring authority which does not require early possession need not serve a notice to treat on a tenant[2], and may allow the interest to expire by effluxion of time or may give a notice to quit after acquiring the interest of the landlord[3], or it may induce the landlord to give that notice before the acquisition[4] or accept a surrender from the tenant[5], and, if the tenant is allowed to remain in possession until the tenancy expires, there will be no claim for disturbance[6].

If, however, a notice to treat has been given to a tenant having an interest greater than a tenancy from year to year, he will be entitled, in addition to the purchase money of his interest[7], to compensation for disturbance in relation to his unexpired term and in relation to any right of renewal which he may have[8], but not in relation to a mere expectation of renewal[9]. Unless special provision is made[10], a right of renewal under statute is not to be taken into account, and the length of the term is the earliest date on which the tenancy could have been terminated by notice to quit, or the date fixed for the expiration of the lease[11]. There are, however, special provisions[12] whereby the right of a business tenant to apply for the grant of a new tenancy is to be taken into account in assessing compensation[13], and whereby assumptions are to be made as to the security of tenure enjoyed by certain agricultural tenants[14].

1 See para 103 ante.
2 If the acquiring authority does not serve a notice to treat before the limit of time for exercise of its compulsory powers (see para 101 ante), a notice to quit will be its only way of acquiring possession. Delay may also lead to a claim that the freehold has been acquired in advance of requirements, unless there is that power to acquire.
3 As to the restriction of the rights of the acquiring authority to covenants for the benefit of the landlord see para 117 ante.
4 The value of the landlord's interest will be thereby increased at the time of valuation: see para 285 ante.
5 *R v Poulter* (1887) 20 QBD 132, CA.
6 *Ex p Nadin* (1848) 17 LJ Ch 421; *Re Portsmouth Rly Co, ex p Merrett* (1860) 2 LT 471; *Syers v Metropolitan Board of Works* (1877) 36 LT 277, CA.
7 See para 233 ante.
8 *Bogg v Midland Rly Co* (1867) LR 4 Eq 310.
9 *Lynch v Glasgow Corpn* (1903) 5 F 1174; *R v Liverpool and Manchester Rly Co* (1836) 4 Ad & El 650.
10 As to this special provision see the text and notes 12–14 infra.
11 *Watson v Secretary of State for Air* [1954] 3 All ER 582, [1954] 1 WLR 1477, CA; *Pearl v LCC* [1961] 1 QB 287 at 302, [1960] 3 All ER 588 at 592–593, CA.
12 See the Land Compensation Act 1973 s 47, s 48 (as amended); and paras 287–288 ante.
13 Ie under the Landlord and Tenant Act 1954 Pt II (ss 23–46) (as amended): see LANDLORD AND TENANT vol 27(1) (Reissue) para 558 et seq.
14 Ie tenants under the Agricultural Holdings Act 1986 (see AGRICULTURE vol 1(2) (Reissue) para 301 et seq); but not farm business tenants under the Agricultural Tenancies Act 1995 (see the Land Compensation Act 1973 s 48(1A) (as added); and para 288 ante). As to the method of assessment of the compensation payable to an agricultural tenant see the cases cited in para 288 note 19 ante.

(3) SHORT TENANCIES

300. Compensation payable on compulsory acquisition of short tenancies. There are special statutory provisions governing the position if any of the land subject to compulsory purchase is in the possession of a person having no greater interest in the land than as a tenant from year to year[1]. The acquiring authority[2] may acquire the landlord's interest and give a notice to quit to the tenant or accept a surrender from the tenant, or persuade the landlord to give a notice to quit before the acquisition[3]. Alternatively it may await the contractual expiry of the tenant's interest. In these cases, there is no compulsory acquisition of the tenant's interest and thus no compensation payable for it[4].

It may be, however, that the acquiring authority is not willing or able to await the termination of the tenant's interest in one of the ways mentioned above. If the tenant is required to give up possession of any of the land occupied by him before the expiration of his term or interest in the land, then he is entitled to compensation for the value of his unexpired term or interest in the land, and for any just allowance which ought to be made to him by an incoming tenant, and for any loss or injury he may sustain[5]. In this way, the tenant may obtain compensation for disturbance[6]. The compensation is assessed when the tenant is required to give up possession[7].

1 See the Compulsory Purchase Act 1965 s 20 (as amended); and para 181 et seq ante.
2 As to acquiring authorities generally see paras 3–5 ante.
3 See para 304 post. For provisions relating to agricultural tenancies (but not farm business tenancies) see paras 305–306 post.
4 Even though the tenant has no compensatable interest, he may nonetheless be entitled to a payment for disturbance: see paras 314–315 post.
5 See the Lands Clauses Consolidation Act 1845 s 121 (as amended); the Compulsory Purchase Act 1965 s 20 (as amended); and para 181 et seq ante.
6 See eg *Greenwoods Tyre Services Ltd v Manchester Corpn* (1972) 23 P & CR 246, Lands Tribunal.
7 *Newham London Borough Council v Benjamin* [1968] 1 All ER 1195, [1968] 1 WLR 694, CA. Thus, the service of a notice to treat is not a requirement for these purposes: see *Newham London Borough Council v Benjamin* supra. If the tenant gives up possession without a notice of entry he will lose his right to compensation: see *GW Roberts and Midland Bank Ltd v Bristol Corpn* (1960) 11 P & CR 205, Lands Tribunal.

301. Nature of compensation. Compensation for loss or injury[1] includes compensation for every kind of damage which the tenant may suffer[2]. The amount of any compensation payable in respect of the compulsory acquisition of an interest[3] in land must not be subject to any reduction on account of the fact that the acquiring authority[4] has provided, or undertakes to provide, or arranges for the provision of, or another authority will provide, residential accommodation under any enactment for the person entitled to the compensation[5].

1 See para 300 ante.
2 *R v Great Northern Rly Co* (1876) 2 QBD 151 at 156. The compensation therefore may include compensation for disturbance: see para 300 note 6 ante.
3 The interest of a tenant for a year, or from year to year, is not purchased under a notice to treat (see para 103 ante), but it is acquired by a notice requiring possession (see paras 181, 184 ante).
4 For the meaning of 'acquiring authority' see para 106 note 1 ante.
5 Land Compensation Act 1973 s 50(1). As to the provision of housing for persons displaced by statutory works see para 329 et seq post.

302. Loss of value of unexpired term. The tenant, when required to give up possession[1], is entitled to compensation for the value of his unexpired term[2]. There are statutory provisions[3] whereby the right of a business tenant to apply for a new tenancy[4] is to be taken into account, and the right of landlords of certain agricultural tenants to serve notice to quit[5] is to be disregarded[6].

1 *Newham London Borough Council v Benjamin* [1968] 1 All ER 1195, [1968] 1 WLR 694, CA.
2 See the Lands Clauses Consolidation Act 1845 s 121 (as amended); the Compulsory Purchase Act 1965 s 20 (as amended); and para 181 et seq ante.
3 Ie the Land Compensation Act 1973 s 47, s 48 (as amended): see paras 287–288 ante.
4 Ie under the Landlord and Tenant Act 1954 Pt II (ss 23–46) (as amended): see LANDLORD AND TENANT vol 27(1) (Reissue) para 558 et seq.
5 Ie under the Agricultural Holdings Act 1986 (see AGRICULTURE vol 1(2) (Reissue) para 301 et seq); but not under the Agricultural Tenancies Act 1995 (see the Land Compensation Act 1973 s 48(1A) (as added); and para 288 ante).
6 See note 3 supra.

303. Other grounds for compensation. A claim for compensation for the expenses of removal will depend on whether the tenant has given up possession. If he continues in possession, after a notice requiring possession, until the expiration of his fixed term[1], if any, or until the tenancy could have been determined by a notice to quit[2], he will have no claim under that head, except in so far as he has made preparations in good faith to give up possession on receiving the notice requiring possession[3].

Compensation for loss from injury to goodwill and loss of profits pending re-establishment of the business[4] will be restricted by the tenancy being one for a year or from year to year, subject to any right of renewal or other protection of the tenancy[5].

Where it is not reasonably practicable to re-establish the business, and compensation is payable for the extinguishment of the business[6], the amount will be affected by the shortness of the term and any right of renewal or protection[7]. If the statutory conditions are fulfilled it will be assumed that it will not be reasonably practicable to re-establish a business in the case of a person over 60 carrying on the business when possession is given up[8].

In addition to the compensation previously discussed[9], a tenant for a year or from year to year may be entitled to a home loss payment[10].

1 Ie where the unexpired residue of the term is less than a year: see *R v Great Northern Rly Co* (1876) 2 QBD 151.
2 *Watson v Secretary of State for Air* [1954] 3 All ER 582, [1954] 1 WLR 1477, CA; *Pearl v LCC* [1961] 1 QB 287 at 302, [1960] 3 All ER 588 at 592–593, CA.
3 *R v Rochdale Improvement Act Comrs* (1856) 2 Jur NS 861.
4 See para 297 ante.
5 See para 302 ante.
6 See para 298 ante.
7 See para 302 ante.
8 See the Land Compensation Act 1973 s 46 (as amended); and para 298 ante. This provision applies also to compensation under the Lands Clauses Consolidation Act 1845 s 121 (as amended); and the Compulsory Purchase Act 1965 s 20 (as amended): see para 298 note 11 ante.
9 See para 300 et seq ante.
10 The Land Compensation Act 1973 s 29 (as amended), s 29A (as added) and s 30 (as substituted), which give such a right (see para 308 et seq post), apply to any interest in the dwelling: s 39(4)(a).

304. When a notice to quit may be served instead of a notice requiring possession. Instead of giving a notice requiring possession[1], the acquiring authority[2] may acquire the landlord's interest and give a notice to quit[3], or accept a surrender from the tenant[4]; or, before the acquisition, the landlord may accept a surrender or give a notice to quit, or be persuaded by the acquiring authority to give a notice to quit[5].

Where, however, a notice to quit an agricultural holding, or part of it, is given, the tenant may have additional statutory rights[6]. Those rights do not, however, apply in relation to farm business tenancies under the Agricultural Tenancies Act 1995[7].

1 See paras 181, 300 ante.
2 As to acquiring authorities generally see paras 3–5 ante.
3 *Syers v Metropolitan Board of Works* (1877) 36 LT 277, CA.
4 Cf *R v Poulter* (1887) 20 QBD 132, CA.
5 *Ex p Nadin* (1848) 17 LJ Ch 421; *Re Portsmouth Rly Co, ex p Merrett* (1860) 2 LT 471.
6 See paras 305–306 post.
7 The Land Compensation Act 1973 ss 59, 61 (as amended) (see paras 305–306 post) apply to agricultural holdings as defined in the Agricultural Holdings Act 1986 s 1: see the Land Compensation Act 1973 s 87(1) (as amended); and para 185 note 3 ante. As to farm business tenancies see generally AGRICULTURE.

305. Notice to quit agricultural holding: right to opt for notice of entry compensation. A person in occupation of an agricultural holding[1], having no greater interest in it than as tenant[2] for a year or from year to year, may elect to take compensation for the acquisition of his interest[3] after service of a notice to quit the holding or part of it[4] as if the notice to quit had not been served[5]. These provisions apply where:

(1) the notice is served after an acquiring authority[6] has served notice to treat, or is deemed to have served such a notice[7], on the landlord of the holding, or, being an authority possessing compulsory purchase powers[8], has agreed to acquire his interest in the holding[9]; and

(2) either:

    (a) the statutory restriction on the operation of a notice to quit[10] does not apply because the land is required for non-agricultural use for which planning permission has been, or is deemed to have been, granted or is not required[11]; or

    (b) the Agricultural Land Tribunal has consented to the operation of the notice to quit and stated in the reasons for its decision that it is satisfied[12] that the land is required for non-agricultural use[13].

If the person served with the notice to quit elects that these provisions are to apply to the notice and gives up possession of the holding to the acquiring authority on or before the date on which his tenancy terminates in accordance with the notice, then the compensation provisions of the Compulsory Purchase Act 1965[14] and the Agriculture (Miscellaneous Provisions) Act 1968[15] are to have effect as if the notice to quit had not been served and the acquiring authority had taken possession of the holding in pursuance of a notice of entry[16] on the day before that on which the tenancy terminates in accordance with the notice to quit[17]. The provisions of the Agricultural Holdings Act 1986 relating to compensation to a tenant on the termination of his tenancy[18] do not, however, have effect in relation to the termination of the tenancy by reason of the notice to quit[19].

The election must be made by notice in writing served on the acquiring authority not later than the date on which possession of the holding is given up[20]. No such election may, however, be made or, if already made, continue to have effect in relation to any land[21] if, before the expiration of that notice, an acquiring authority takes possession of that land in pursuance of an enactment providing for the taking of possession of land compulsorily[22].

These provisions do not apply in relation to farm business tenancies under the Agricultural Tenancies Act 1995[23].

1 For the meaning of 'agricultural holding' see para 185 note 3 ante.
2 For the meaning of 'tenant' see para 185 note 3 ante.
3 A person served with a notice to quit part of an agricultural holding is not entitled, in relation to that notice, both to make an election under the Land Compensation Act 1973 s 59 (as amended) (see the text and notes 4–22 infra) and to give a counter-notice under the Agricultural Holdings Act 1986 s 32 (tenant's right to cause notice to quit part of holding to operate as notice to quit entire holding: see AGRICULTURE vol 1(2) (Reissue) para 363): Land Compensation Act 1973 s 59(6) (amended by the Agricultural Holdings Act 1986 s 100, Sch 14 para 55). For the meaning of 'notice to quit' see para 288 note 7 ante.
4 The Land Compensation Act 1973 s 59 (as amended) has effect in relation to a notice to quit part of an agricultural holding as it has effect in relation to a notice to quit an entire holding, and references to a holding and the termination of the tenancy are to be construed accordingly: s 59(5).
5 See ibid s 59(1), (2) (as amended); and the text and notes 6–19 infra.
6 For the meaning of 'acquiring authority' see para 106 note 1 ante.
7 This reference to a notice to treat served by an acquiring authority includes a reference to a notice to treat deemed to have been so served under any of the provisions of the Compulsory Purchase (Vesting

Declarations) Act 1981 Pt III (ss 7–9) (see paras 171, 175–176 ante): Land Compensation Act 1973 s 59(7) (applying s 53(5) (as amended) (see para 106 ante)).

8　This reference to an authority possessing compulsory purchase powers includes a person or body of persons who would be an authority possessing compulsory purchase powers if the landlord's interest were not an interest in Crown land as defined by the Town and Country Planning Act 1990 s 293 (see TOWN AND COUNTRY PLANNING vol 46 (Reissue) para 9 note 1): Land Compensation Act 1973 s 59(7) (amended by the Planning and Compensation Act 1991 s 70, Sch 15 para 7). See also the Land Compensation Act 1973 s 84(2) (cited in para 292 ante). For the meaning of 'authority possessing compulsory purchase powers' see para 244 note 6 ante (definition applied by s 87(1)). See also *Dawson v Norwich City Council* (1978) 37 P & CR 516, Lands Tribunal.

9　Land Compensation Act 1973 s 59(1)(a).

10　Ie the Agricultural Holdings Act 1986 s 26(1): see AGRICULTURE vol 1(2) (Reissue) para 341.

11　Ie by virtue of the Agricultural Holdings Act 1986 s 26(2), Sch 3 Pt I Case B (Case B as substituted): see AGRICULTURE vol 1(2) (Reissue) para 345.

12　Ie satisfied as to the matter mentioned in ibid s 27(3)(f): see AGRICULTURE vol 1(2) (Reissue) para 342.

13　Land Compensation Act 1973 s 59(1)(b) (amended by the Agricultural Holdings (Notices to Quit) Act 1977 s 13(1), Sch 1 para 6; and by the Agricultural Holdings Act 1986 Sch 14 para 55).

14　Ie the Compulsory Purchase Act 1965 s 20 (as amended) (compensation for tenants from year to year etc): see paras 181 et seq, 300 ante.

15　Ie the Agriculture (Miscellaneous Provisions) Act 1968 s 12 (as amended): see AGRICULTURE vol 1(2) (Reissue) para 433.

16　Ie under the Compulsory Purchase Act 1965 s 11(1) (as amended): see para 129 ante.

17　Land Compensation Act 1973 s 59(2)(a).

18　As to the statutory right to compensation under the Agricultural Holdings Act 1986 see AGRICULTURE vol 1(2) (Reissue) para 383 et seq.

19　Land Compensation Act 1973 s 59(2)(b) (amended by the Agricultural Holdings Act 1986 Sch 14 para 55).

20　Land Compensation Act 1973 s 59(4).

21　Ie whether the whole or part of the land to which the notice to quit relates: ibid s 59(3).

22　Ibid s 59(3). As to that power of taking possession see the Compulsory Purchase Act 1965 s 11(1) (as amended); and para 129 ante.

23　See para 304 text and note 7 ante.

306. Notice to quit part of agricultural holding by landlord after notice to treat; counter-notice to acquiring authority to take the whole.

Where a notice to quit part only of an agricultural holding[1] is served by the landlord on the tenant in circumstances where the tenant is entitled to make an election to take compensation as if a notice of entry has been served[2], and the tenant makes that election within the period of two months beginning with the date of the service of the notice to quit, or, if later, the decision of the Agricultural Land Tribunal[3], then the tenant may also within that period serve a notice on the acquiring authority[4] claiming that the remainder of the holding is not reasonably capable of being farmed, either by itself or in conjunction with other relevant land[5], as a separate agricultural unit[6]. If, within the period of two months beginning with the date of service of the notice by the claimant, the acquiring authority does not agree in writing to accept the notice as valid, the claimant or the authority may refer it to the Lands Tribunal within two months after the end of that period, and on that reference the tribunal must determine whether the claim in the claimant's notice is justified and declare the notice valid or invalid in accordance with its determination of that question[7].

Where the claimant's notice is accepted as, or is declared to be, valid, then, if before the end of 12 months after it has been so accepted or declared valid, the claimant has given up possession of part of the holding to which the notice relates to the acquiring authority, the provisions of the Compulsory Purchase Act 1965, relating to compensation to tenants for a year or from year to year[8], and the provisions of the Agriculture (Miscellaneous Provisions) Act 1968 giving compensation to tenants[9] have effect as if the acquiring authority had taken possession of that part in pursuance of a notice of entry[10] on the day before the expiration of the year of the tenancy which is current when the notice is so accepted or declared to be valid[11].

Under these provisions the acquiring authority may be compelled to take possession of part of an agricultural holding in land where it has not been authorised to acquire the landlord's interest in or in any part of that land[12], and, accordingly, where the claimant gives up possession of an agricultural holding to the acquiring authority, but the authority has not been authorised to acquire the landlord's interest in, or in any of, the part of the holding to which the notice to quit did not relate ('the land not subject to compulsory purchase'), neither the claimant nor the authority is to be under any liability to the landlord by reason of the claimant giving up possession of the land not subject to compulsory purchase or the authority taking or being in possession of it[13]. Furthermore, immediately after the date on which the authority takes possession of the land not subject to compulsory purchase, it must give up to the landlord, and he must take, possession of that land[14]; and any increase in the value of that land which is attributable to the landlord's taking possession of it must be deducted from the compensation payable in respect of the acquisition of his interest in the remainder of the holding[15].

The tenancy must also be treated as terminated on the date on which the claimant gives up possession of the holding to the acquiring authority, or, if he gives up possession of different parts at different times, gives up possession of the last part, but without prejudice to any rights or liabilities of the landlord or the claimant which have accrued before that date[16]; and any rights of the claimant against, or liabilities of the claimant to, the landlord, which arise on or out of the termination of the tenancy, whether under the contract of tenancy, under the Agricultural Holdings Act 1986[17] or otherwise, will be the rights and liabilities of the authority, and any question as to the payment to be made in respect of any such right or liability must be referred to and determined by the Lands Tribunal[18].

Where an election to take notice of entry compensation[19] ceases to have effect in relation to any land by virtue of the acquiring authority having taken possession of the land compulsorily[20], any counter-notice served by the claimant by virtue of the above provisions will also cease to have effect in relation to that land[21].

These provisions do not apply in relation to farm business tenancies under the Agricultural Tenancies Act 1995[22].

1 For the meaning of 'agricultural holding' see para 185 note 3 ante.
2 Ie under the Land Compensation Act 1973 s 59 (as amended): see para 305 ante.
3 Ie the decision to consent to the notice to quit under the Agricultural Holdings Act 1986 s 27: see para 305 ante.
4 For the meaning of 'acquiring authority' see para 106 note 1 ante.
5 For the meaning of 'other relevant land' see the Land Compensation Act 1973 s 55(3), (4) (applied, as is s 56(3) (as amended) by s 61(4) as if references to the notice of entry were references to the notice to quit); and para 185 ante.
6 Ibid s 61(1). For the meaning of 'agricultural unit' see para 106 note 6 ante. The claimant must also within the same period serve a copy of the notice on the landlord of the holding, but failure to do so will not invalidate the claimant's notice: see s 55(2) (applied by s 61(4)); and para 185 ante.
7 Ibid s 61(2). As to the Lands Tribunal see para 202 et seq ante.
8 Ie the provisions of the Compulsory Purchase Act 1965 s 20 (as amended): see paras 181 et seq, 300 ante.
9 Ie the provisions of the Agriculture (Miscellaneous Provisions) Act 1968 s 12 (as amended): see AGRICULTURE vol 1(2) (Reissue) para 433.
10 Ie under the Compulsory Purchase Act 1965 s 11(1) (as amended): see para 129 ante. On such entry the tenant is entitled to compensation under s 20 (as amended): see para 300 ante.
11 Land Compensation Act 1973 s 61(3).
12 The acquiring authority is not authorised to acquire that land because it does not need it.

13 Land Compensation Act 1973 s 56(3)(a) (applied by s 61(4)).
14 Ibid s 56(3)(b) (applied by s 61(4)).
15 Ibid s 56(3)(e) (applied by s 61(4)).
16 Ibid s 56(3)(c) (applied by s 61(4)).
17 As to these statutory rights see AGRICULTURE vol 1(2) (Reissue) para 383 et seq.
18 Land Compensation Act 1973 s 56(3)(d) (amended by the Agricultural Holdings Act 1986 s 100, Sch 14 para 54; applied by the Land Compensation Act 1973 s 61(4)).
19 Ie under ibid s 59 (as amended): see para 305 ante.
20 Ie under ibid s 59(3): see para 305 text to note 22 ante.
21 Ibid s 61(5).
22 See para 304 text and note 7 ante.

8. PAYMENTS FOR DISTURBANCE APART FROM COMPENSATION

(1) CLASSES OF PAYMENTS AND PERSONS ENTITLED

307. Payments additional to purchase money and compensation and payments where interests not acquirable. An owner of land who has an interest greater than a tenancy for a year or from year to year is entitled to compensation for disturbance as part of his purchase money[1] but, in addition and apart from it, he may be entitled to a home loss payment[2] and, in the case of an agricultural unit[3], he may be entitled to a farm loss payment if he intends to continue to farm[4].

A tenant for a year or from year to year or less is not entitled to a notice to treat and his interest is not purchased[5], but he is entitled to compensation for disturbance if he is required to give up possession and does so[6], and in addition to his compensation he may be entitled to a home loss payment[7].

Some occupiers of the land compulsorily acquired have no interest which gives a right to compensation under the above provisions, but certain of them may be entitled to payments for disturbance if they qualify by complying with certain statutory conditions[8], and in the case of others who do not so qualify the acquiring authority may make a voluntary payment[9]. Some occupiers in either class may be entitled to a home loss payment[10].

1 See para 295 et seq ante.
2 See para 308 post.
3 For the meaning of 'agricultural unit' see para 106 note 7 ante. Note that, unlike the definition of 'agricultural holding' (see para 185 note 3 ante), the definition of 'agricultural unit' does not exclude a farm business tenancy under the Agricultural Tenancies Act 1995. As to farm business tenancies see generally AGRICULTURE.
4 See para 311 post.
5 See para 181 ante.
6 See paras 184, 300 et seq ante.
7 See para 308 post.
8 See para 314 post.
9 See para 314 text to notes 16–19 post.
10 See para 315 post.

(2) HOME LOSS PAYMENTS

308. Right to home loss payment. Where a person is displaced[1] from a dwelling on any land in consequence of the compulsory acquisition of an interest in the dwelling or some other specified event[2] he will be entitled to receive a payment (a 'home loss payment') from the acquiring authority[3] or other specified authority or body[4] provided that the statutory conditions have been satisfied throughout the period of one year ending with the date of displacement[5]. Those conditions are that:

(1) he has been in occupation of the dwelling, or a substantial part of it, as his only or main residence[6]; and

(2) he has been in such occupation by virtue of any of the following interests or rights:

(a) any interest[7] in the dwelling[8];

(b) a right to occupy the dwelling as a statutory tenant[9] or under a restricted[10] contract[11];

(c) a right to occupy the dwelling under a contract of employment[12];

(d) a right to occupy the dwelling under a licence where either it is a right to occupy as a protected occupier[13], or the statutory provisions relating to secure tenancies[14] apply to the licence, or the licence is an assured[15] agricultural occupancy[16].

If these conditions have not been so satisfied throughout that period but are satisfied on the date of displacement, a discretionary payment may be made to that person of an amount not exceeding the amount to which he would have been entitled if he had satisfied those conditions throughout that period[17].

Where an authority possessing compulsory purchase powers acquires the interest of any person in a dwelling by agreement, then, in relation to any other person who is displaced from the dwelling in consequence of the acquisition, the above provisions have effect as if the acquisition were compulsory and the authority (if not authorised to acquire the interest compulsorily) had been so authorised on the date of the agreement[18].

Where by reason of the entitlement of one spouse ('A') to occupy a dwelling[19] by virtue of any such interest or right as is mentioned in heads (1) and (2) above, the other spouse ('B') acquires rights of occupation[20], then so long as:

(i) those rights of occupation continue;

(ii) B is in occupation of the dwelling and A is not; and

(iii) B is not otherwise treated as occupying the dwelling by virtue of such an interest or right,

then B is to be treated for the purposes of the above provisions as occupying the dwelling by virtue of such an interest[21].

A person residing in a caravan on a caravan site[22] who is displaced from that site may also be entitled to a home loss payment or discretionary payment[23], but no such payment may be made to any person by virtue of this provision except where no suitable alternative site for stationing a caravan is available to him on reasonable terms[24].

These provisions[25] apply in relation to the acquisition of interests in land, whether compulsorily or by agreement, by government departments which are authorities possessing compulsory purchase powers as they apply in relation to the acquisition of interests in land by such authorities which are not government departments[26].

1 For these purposes, a person is not to be treated as displaced from a dwelling in consequence of the compulsory acquisition of an interest in it if he gives up his occupation of it before the date on which the acquiring authority was authorised to acquire that interest, but, subject to that, it is not necessary for the authority to have required him to give up his occupation of the dwelling: Land Compensation Act 1973 s 29(3). Nor is a person to be treated as displaced from a dwelling in consequence of the acceptance of an undertaking or of the carrying out of any improvement to the dwelling unless he is permanently displaced from it in consequence of the carrying out of the works specified in the undertaking or notice or, as the case may be, of the improvement in question: s 29(3A) (added by the Housing Act 1974 s 130,

Sch 13 para 38(3); amended by the Planning and Compensation Act 1991 ss 70, 84(6), Sch 15 para 22(1), (3), Sch 19 Pt III). 'Improvement' includes alteration and enlargement: Land Compensation Act 1973 s 29(7A) (added by the Housing Act 1974 Sch 13 para 38(3)). For the meaning of 'dwelling' see para 283 note 1 ante; and for the meaning of 'acquiring authority' see para 106 note 1 ante.

2   Land Compensation Act 1973 s 29(1)(a). The other specified events are: (1) the making or acceptance of a housing order or undertaking in respect of the dwelling (s 29(1)(b) (amended by the Land Compensation (Scotland) Act 1973 s 81(1), Sch 2; and by the Local Government and Housing Act 1989 s 194(4), Sch 12 Pt II)); (2) where the land has been previously acquired by an authority possessing compulsory purchase powers or appropriated by a local authority and is for the time being held by the authority for the purposes for which it was acquired or appropriated, the carrying out of any improvement to the dwelling or of redevelopment on the land (Land Compensation Act 1973 s 29(1)(c) (amended by the Housing Act 1974 Sch 13 para 38(3))); (3) the carrying out of any improvement to the dwelling or of redevelopment on the land by a housing association which has previously acquired the land and at the date of the displacement is registered under the Housing Associations Act 1985 (see HOUSING) (Land Compensation Act 1973 s 29(1)(d) (substituted by the Housing (Consequential Provisions) Act 1985 s 4, Sch 2 para 24(2)(b))); and (4) the making of an order for possession on the grounds set out in the Housing Act 1985 s 84, Sch 2 Pt II Ground 10 or Ground 10A (as added) (see LANDLORD AND TENANT vol 27(2) (Reissue) paras 1182–1183): Land Compensation Act 1973 s 29(1)(e) (added by the Housing and Planning Act 1986 s 9(3)). For these purposes, 'a housing order or undertaking' means (a) a demolition or closing order, or an obstructive building order, under the Housing Act 1985 Pt IX (ss 264–323) (as amended) (slum clearance); (b) a closing order under s 368(4) (closing of multi-occupied house with inadequate means of escape from fire); (c) an undertaking accepted under s 368 (as amended): Land Compensation Act 1973 s 29(7) (substituted by the Housing (Consequential Provisions) Act 1985 Sch 2 para 24(2)(d); amended by the Local Government and Housing Act 1989 Sch 12 Pt II). See further HOUSING. 'Redevelopment' includes a change of use: Land Compensation Act 1973 s 29(7A) (as added: see note 1 supra). It has also been held to include demolition preceding the substitution of new buildings: see *R v Corby District Council, ex p McLean* [1975] 2 All ER 568, [1975] 1 WLR 735; *Follows v The Peabody Trust* (1983) 10 HLR 62, CA; *GLC v Holmes* [1986] QB 989, [1986] 1 All ER 739, CA. For the meaning of 'authority possessing compulsory purchase powers' see para 244 note 6 ante (definition applied by the Land Compensation Act 1973 s 87(1)).

3   Ie where ibid s 29(1)(a) (compulsory acquisition of an interest in the dwelling) applies: s 29(1)(i) (added by the Housing Act 1985 Sch 13 para 38(1)).

4   The specified authorities and bodies are as follows: (1) where the Land Compensation Act 1973 s 29(1)(b) (as amended) applies (see note 2 head (1) supra), the authority who made the order, accepted the undertaking or served the notice (s 29(1)(ii) (added by the Housing Act 1985 Sch 13 para 38(1); amended by the Planning and Compensation Act 1991 Sch 15 para 22(1), (2), Sch 19 Pt III)); (2) where the Land Compensation Act 1973 s 29(1)(c) (as amended) applies (see note 2 head (2) supra), the authority carrying out the improvement or redevelopment (s 29(1)(iii) (as so added and amended)); (3) where s 29(1)(d) (as substituted) applies (see note 2 head (3) supra), the housing association carrying out the improvement or redevelopment (s 29(1)(iv) (as so added; amended by the Planning and Compensation Act 1991 Sch 15 para 22(1), (2))); and (4) where the Land Compensation Act 1973 s 29(1)(e) (as added) applies (see note 2 head (4) supra), the landlord (s 29(1)(v) (added by the Housing and Planning Act 1986 s 9(3); amended by the Planning and Compensation Act 1991 Sch 15 para 22(1), (2))).

5   Land Compensation Act 1973 s 29(2) (substituted by the Planning and Compensation Act 1991 s 68(1)). Where the claimant has satisfied, throughout any period, the conditions mentioned in the Land Compensation Act 1973 s 29(2) (as so substituted), that period is treated for these purposes as including any immediately preceding period throughout which (1) he has resided in the dwelling as his only or main residence but without satisfying those conditions; and (2) another person or other persons have satisfied those conditions, and references to a dwelling include a reference to a substantial part of it: s 32(3) (substituted by the Planning and Compensation Act 1991 s 68(4)). Where he has satisfied those conditions throughout any period, that period (or that period as so extended) is treated for these purposes as including any immediately preceding period, or successive periods, throughout which he satisfied those conditions in relation to another dwelling or, as the case may be, other dwellings, applying heads (1)–(2) supra to determine the length of any period or periods: Land Compensation Act 1973 s 32(3A) (added by the Planning and Compensation Act 1991 s 68(4)). Where the claimant has successively been in occupation of or resided in different dwellings in the same building, being dwellings consisting of a room or rooms not structurally adapted for use as a separate dwelling, the Land Compensation Act 1973 s 29(2), (3), (3A) (as so substituted and added) has effect as if those dwellings were the same dwelling: s 32(5) (amended by the Planning and Compensation Act 1991 s 68(6)).

6   There is no statutory definition of 'only or main residence' for these purposes; but cf CAPITAL GAINS TAXATION vol 5(1) (Reissue) para 277.

7 Where an interest in a dwelling is vested in trustees (other than a sole tenant for life within the meaning of the Settled Land Act 1925) and a person beneficially entitled, whether directly or derivatively, under the trusts is entitled or permitted by reason of his interest to occupy the dwelling, he is to be treated for these purposes as occupying it by virtue of an interest in the dwelling: Land Compensation Act 1973 s 29(8) (amended by the Land Compensation (Scotland) Act 1973 Sch 2).

8 Land Compensation Act 1973 s 29(4)(a).

9 Ie within the meaning of the Rent (Agriculture) Act 1976 or the Rent Act 1977: see LANDLORD AND TENANT vol 27(1), (2) (Reissue) paras 999 et seq, 677 et seq respectively.

10 Ie under a contract to which ibid s 19 (repealed with savings by the Housing Act 1988 s 140(2), Sch 18 para 1) applies or would apply if the contract or dwelling were not excluded by s 19(3)–(5) (as so repealed) or s 144: see LANDLORD AND TENANT vol 27(1) (Reissue) para 848 et seq.

11 Land Compensation Act 1973 s 29(4)(b) (substituted by the Planning and Compensation Act 1991 Sch 15 para 22(1), (4)).

12 Land Compensation Act 1973 s 29(4)(d).

13 Ie within the meaning of the Rent (Agriculture) Act 1976; see LANDLORD AND TENANT vol 27(2) (Reissue) para 997.

14 Ie the Housing Act 1985 Pt IV (ss 79–117) (as amended): see LANDLORD AND TENANT vol 27(2) (Reissue) para 1125 et seq.

15 Ie within the meaning of the Housing Act 1988 Pt I (ss 1–45) (as amended): see LANDLORD AND TENANT vol 27(2) (Reissue) para 1037 et seq.

16 Land Compensation Act 1973 s 29(4)(e) (added by the Housing and Planning Act 1986 s 9(3); substituted by the Planning and Compensation Act 1991 Sch 15 para 22(1), (4)).

17 Land Compensation Act 1973 s 29(2) (as substituted: see note 5 supra).

18 Ibid s 29(6).

19 For these purposes, references to a dwelling include a reference to a substantial part of it: ibid s 29A(3) (s 29A added by the Planning and Compensation Act 1991 s 69).

20 Ie within the meaning of the Matrimonial Homes Act 1983: see HUSBAND AND WIFE.

21 Land Compensation Act 1973 s 29A(1), (2) (as added: see note 19 supra).

22 For these purposes, 'caravan site' means land on which a caravan is stationed for the purpose of human habitation and land which is used in conjunction with land on which a caravan is so stationed: ibid s 33(7). There is no statutory definition of 'caravan' for these purposes; but cf TOWN AND COUNTRY PLANNING vol 46 (Reissue) para 594.

23 See ibid s 33(1), applying ss 29–32 (as amended) (see the text and notes 1–21 supra; and para 309 et seq post) subject to certain modifications. For these purposes (1) s 29(1) (as amended) has effect as if for the words preceding s 29(1)(a) there were substituted the words 'Where a person residing in a caravan on a caravan site is displaced from that site in consequence of'; and s 29(2) (as substituted) has effect as if for s 29(2)(a), (b) there were substituted '(a) he has been in occupation of the caravan site by using a caravan stationed on it as his only or main residence; and (b) he has been in such occupation of the site by virtue of an interest or right to which this section applies' (s 33(3) (amended by the Planning and Compensation Act 1991 s 68(8)(b)); (2) the Land Compensation Act 1973 s 32 (as amended) has effect as if in s 32(3), (3A) (as substituted and added: see note 5 supra) the references to a dwelling were to a caravan site and as if for s 32(5) (as amended) (see note 5 supra) there were substituted 'Where any land comprises two or more caravan sites and the claimant has successively been in occupation of or resided in a caravan on different caravan sites on that land, s 29(2) and subsections (3) to (4) above have effect as if those sites were the same site' (s 33(5)(a), (c) (respectively substituted and amended by the Planning and Compensation Act 1991 s 68(8)(d))); and (3) the Land Compensation Act 1973 ss 29–32 (as amended) have effect as if in any provision not specifically modified, for any reference to a dwelling or land there were substituted a reference to a caravan site: s 33(6).

24 Ibid s 33(2) (amended by the Planning and Compensation Act 1991 s 68(8)(a)).

25 Ie the Land Compensation Act 1973 Pt III (ss 29–43) (as amended): see para 309 et seq post.

26 Ibid s 84(2).

309. Claim for home loss payment. No home loss payment[1] or discretionary payment[2] may be made except on a claim in writing made by the claimant within six years of the date of displacement[3]. The claim must give such particulars as the authority responsible for making the payment[4] may reasonably require for the purpose of determining whether the payment should be made and, if so, its amount[5].

Where a person ('the deceased') entitled to a home loss payment dies without having claimed it, a claim to the payment may be made by any person who is not a minor and who (1) throughout a period of not less than one year ending with the date of displacement of the deceased, has resided in the dwelling[6], or a substantial part of it, as his only or main residence[7]; and (2) is entitled to benefit by virtue of testamentary dispositions taking effect on the death of the deceased, or by virtue of the law of intestate succession or the right of survivorship between joint tenants as applied to that death[8].

A person residing in a caravan on a caravan site[9] who is displaced from that site may also make a claim for a home loss payment or discretionary payment[10], but no such payment may be made to any person by virtue of this provision except where no suitable alternative site for stationing a caravan is available to him on reasonable terms[11].

1 For the meaning of 'home loss payment' see para 308 ante.
2 For the meaning of 'discretionary payment' see para 308 ante.
3 Land Compensation Act 1973 s 32(1) (substituted by the Planning and Compensation Act 1991 s 68(4)); Land Compensation Act 1973 s 32(7A) (added by the Local Government, Planning and Land Act 1980 s 114; applying the Limitation Act 1980 by virtue of the Interpretation Act 1978 s 17(2)(a)). As to the date of displacement see para 308 ante.
4 As to the authorities responsible for making the payment see para 308 note 4 ante; and as to the application of these provisions to the Crown see para 308 text and notes 25–26 ante.
5 Land Compensation Act 1973 s 32(1). As to the amount of the payment see para 310 post.
6 For the meaning of 'dwelling' see para 283 note 1 ante. Where the claimant has successively been in occupation of or resided in different dwellings in the same building, being dwellings consisting of a room or rooms not constructed or structurally adapted for use as a separate dwelling, ibid s 32(4) (as amended) (see heads (1)–(2) in the text; and note 8 infra) has effect as if those dwellings were the same dwelling: s 32(5) (amended by the Planning and Compensation Act 1991 s 68(6)).
7 See para 308 note 6 ante.
8 Land Compensation Act 1973 s 32(4) (amended by the Local Government, Planning and Land Act 1980 s 114; and by the Planning and Compensation Act 1991 s 68(5)).
9 For the meaning of 'caravan site' see para 308 note 22 ante.
10 See the Land Compensation Act 1973 s 33(1), applying s 32 (as amended) with certain modifications.
11 Ibid s 33(2) (amended by the Planning and Compensation Act 1991 s 68(8)(a)). For these purposes, s 32 (as amended) has effect as if in s 32(4) (as amended) for the words 'resided in the dwelling, or a substantial part of it' there were substituted the words 'resided in a caravan on the caravan site': s 33(5)(b). See also s 33(6), cited in para 308 note 23 ante.

310. Payments for home loss. In the case of a person who on the date of displacement[1] is occupying, or is treated[2] as occupying, the dwelling[3] by virtue of an interest in it which is an owner's interest[4], the amount of the home loss payment[5] is 10 per cent of the market value of his interest in the dwelling[6] or, as the case may be, the interest in the dwelling vested in trustees, subject to a maximum of £15,000 and a minimum of £1,500[7]. In any other case, the amount of the home loss payment is £1,500[8].

Where a person is entitled to a home loss payment, the payment must be made on or before the latest of the following dates:

(1) the date of displacement[9];
(2) the last day of the period of three months beginning with the making of the claim[10]; and
(3) where the amount of the payment is to be determined on the basis that the interest in the dwelling is an owner's interest[11], the day on which the market value of the interest in question is agreed or finally determined[12].

Where the amount of the payment is to be determined as mentioned in head (3) above, the acquiring authority[13] may at any time make a payment in advance[14] and if, on the later of the dates referred to in heads (1) and (2) above, the market value of the interest in question has not been agreed or finally determined, the acquiring authority must make a payment in advance where it has not already done so[15]. Where the amount of a payment in advance differs from the amount of the home loss payment, the shortfall or excess must be paid by or, as the case may be, repaid to the acquiring authority when the market value of the interest in question is agreed or finally determined[16].

Where there are two or more persons entitled to make a claim to a home loss payment in respect of the same dwelling[17] the payment to be made on each claim is equal to the whole amount of the home loss payment divided by the number of such persons[18].

Where an interest in a dwelling is acquired by agreement by an authority possessing compulsory purchase powers[19], the authority may, in connection with the acquisition, make to the person from whom the interest is acquired a payment corresponding to any home loss payment or discretionary payment which it would be required or authorised to make to him if the acquisition were compulsory and the authority had been authorised to acquire that interest before he gave up occupation of the dwelling[20]. Where a landlord obtains possession by agreement of a dwelling subject to a secure tenancy[21] and either (a) notice of proceedings for possession of the dwelling has been, or might have been, served specifying certain grounds[22]; or (b) the landlord has applied, or could apply, to the Secretary of State, the Housing Corporation or Housing for Wales for approval[23] of a redevelopment scheme including the dwelling, or part of it, the landlord may make to any person giving up possession or occupation a payment corresponding to any home loss payment or discretionary payment which it would be required or authorised to make to him if an order for possession had been made on either of those grounds[24].

The amount of any home loss payment or discretionary payment must not be subject to any reduction on account of the fact that the authority responsible for making that payment has provided, or undertakes to provide, or arranges for the provision of, or another authority will provide, residential accommodation under any enactment for the person entitled to the payment[25].

Where a person residing in a caravan on a caravan site[26] who is displaced from that site is entitled to a home loss payment or discretionary payment[27], the statutory provisions relating to the amount of the payment[28] have effect as if the references to a person occupying a dwelling by virtue of an interest in it and to his interest in the dwelling were to a person occupying a caravan site by virtue of an interest in it and to that interest[29], and the statutory provisions relating to the date and method of payment[30] have effect with specified modifications[31].

1 As to the date of displacement see para 308 ante.
2 Ie for the purposes of the Land Compensation Act 1973 s 29 (as amended): see para 308 ante.
3 For the meaning of 'dwelling' see para 283 note 1 ante.
4 For these purposes, 'owner's interest' means the interest of a person who is an owner as defined in the Acquisition of Land Act 1981 s 7 (as amended) (see para 15 note 3 ante): Land Compensation Act 1973 s 30(7) (s 30 substituted by the Planning and Compensation Act 1991 s 68(3)). A spouse with a statutory right of occupation is not treated as occupying the dwelling by virtue of an owner's interest: see the Land Compensation Act 1973 s 29A(2) (added by the Planning and Compensation Act 1991 s 69); and para 308 ante.
5 For the meaning of 'home loss payment' see para 308 ante.
6 For these purposes, the market value of an interest in a dwelling is (1) in a case where the interest is compulsorily acquired, the amount assessed for the purposes of the acquisition as the value of the interest; and (2) in any other case, the amount which, if the interest were being compulsorily acquired in pursuance of a notice to treat served on the date of displacement, would be assessed for the purposes of the acquisition as the value of the interest, and any dispute as to the latter amount must be determined

by the Lands Tribunal: Land Compensation Act 1973 s 30(3) (as substituted: see note 4 supra). In determining the market value of an interest in a dwelling, the dwelling must be taken to include any garden, yard, outhouses and appurtenances belonging to or usually enjoyed with that dwelling: s 30(4) (as so substituted). As to the tribunal see para 202 et seq ante.

7   Ibid s 30(1) (as substituted: see note 4 supra). The Secretary of State may from time to time by regulations prescribe a different maximum or minimum for these purposes and a different amount for the purposes of s 30(2) (as so substituted) (see the text and note 8 infra); s 30(5) (as so substituted). The power to make such regulations is exercisable by statutory instrument subject to annulment in pursuance of a resolution of either House of Parliament: s 30(6) (as so substituted). At the date at which this volume states the law, no such regulations had been made.

8   Ibid s 30(2) (as substituted: see note 4 supra). See also note 7 supra.

9   Ibid s 32(2)(a) (s 32(2) substituted by the Planning and Compensation Act 1991 s 68(4)).

10 Land Compensation Act 1973 s 32(2)(b) (as substituted: see note 9 supra). As to making the claim see para 309 ante.

11 Ie determined in accordance with ibid s 30(1) (as substituted): see the text and notes 1–7 supra.

12 Ibid s 32(2)(c) (as substituted: see note 9 supra).

13 For the meaning of 'acquiring authority' see para 106 note 1 ante.

14 Land Compensation Act 1973 s 32(2A)(a) (s 32(2A)–(2C) added by the Planning and Compensation Act 1991 s 68(4)). The amount of the payment in advance must be the lesser of (1) the maximum amount for the purposes of the Land Compensation Act 1973 s 30(1) (as substituted: see note 4 supra); (2) 10% of the amount agreed to be the market value of the interest in question or, if there is no such agreement, 10% of the acquiring authority's estimate of that amount: s 32(2B) (as so added).

15 Ibid s 32(2A)(b) (as added; see note 14 supra).

16 Ibid s 32(2C) (as added: see note 14 supra).

17 Ie whether by virtue of joint occupation or by virtue of ibid s 32(4) (as amended) (see para 309 ante): s 32(6).

18 Ibid s 32(6).

19 For the meaning of 'authority possessing compulsory purchase powers' see para 244 note 6 ante (definition applied by ibid s 87(1)).

20 Ibid s 32(7) (amended by the Planning and Compensation Act 1991 s 68(7)). As to discretionary payments see further para 308 ante.

21 Ie within the meaning of the Housing Act 1985 Pt IV (ss 79–117) (as amended): see LANDLORD AND TENANT vol 27(2) (Reissue) para 1125 et seq.

22 Ie specifying ibid s 84, Sch 2 Pt II Ground 10 or Ground 10A (as added): see LANDLORD AND TENANT vol 27(2) (Reissue) paras 1182–1183.

23 Ie for the purposes of ibid Sch 2 Pt II Ground 10A (as added): see LANDLORD AND TENANT vol 27(2) (Reissue) para 1183.

24 Land Compensation Act 1973 s 32(7B) (added by the Housing and Planning Act 1986 s 9(4); amended by the Housing Act 1988 s 140(1), Sch 17 para 94; and by the Planning and Compensation Act 1991 s 68(7)).

25 See the Land Compensation Act 1973 s 50(1), (3); and para 295 ante.

26 For the meaning of 'caravan site' see para 308 note 22 ante.

27 No such payment may be made to any person except where no suitable alternative site for stationing a caravan is available to him on reasonable terms: see the Land Compensation Act 1973 s 33(2) (as amended); and para 308 ante.

28 Ie ibid s 30 (as substituted): see the text and notes 1–8 supra.

29 Ibid s 33(4) (substituted by the Planning and Compensation Act 1991 s 68(8)(c)).

30 Ie the Land Compensation Act 1973 s 32 (as amended): see the text and notes 9–24 supra.

31 See ibid s 33(5) (as amended); and paras 308 note 23, 309 note 11 ante. See also s 32(6); and para 308 note 23 ante.

(3) FARM LOSS PAYMENTS

311. Right to farm loss payment. The right to a farm loss payment may arise where a person has an owner's interest[1] and is in occupation of land constituting or included in an agricultural unit[2]. That person will be entitled to receive a farm loss payment from the acquiring authority[3] if:

(1) in consequence of the compulsory acquisition of his interest in the whole, or a sufficient part[4], of that land, he is displaced[5] from the land acquired; and

(2) not more than three years after the date of displacement[6] he begins to farm another agricultural unit ('the new unit') elsewhere in Great Britain[7].

No farm loss payment may, however, be made to any person unless on the date on which he begins to farm the new unit he is in occupation of the whole of that unit in right of a freehold interest in it or a tenancy of it, not having been entitled to any such interest or tenancy before the date on which the acquiring authority was authorised to acquire his interest in the land acquired[8]. Nor may such a payment be made by virtue of the displacement of a person from any land if he is entitled to a payment under the Agriculture (Miscellaneous Provisions) Act 1968[9] in consequence of the acquisition of an interest in, or the taking of possession of, that land[10].

Where the agricultural unit containing the land acquired is occupied for the purposes of a partnership firm, these provisions have effect in relation to the firm and not to the partners individually, any interest of a partner in the land acquired being treated as an interest of the firm, except that the requirements as to the new unit are treated as complied with in relation to the firm as soon as they are complied with by any one of the persons who were members of the firm[11].

These provisions[12] apply in relation to the acquisition of interests in land, whether compulsorily or by agreement, by government departments which are authorities possessing compulsory purchase powers as they apply in relation to the acquisition of interests in land by such authorities which are not government departments[13].

1 For these purposes, 'owner's interest' means a freehold interest or a tenancy where his interest is as tenant for a year or from year to year or a greater interest: Land Compensation Act 1973 s 34(2) (amended by the Planning and Compensation Act 1991 s 70, Sch 15 para 6(1), (3)).

2 See the Land Compensation Act 1973 s 34(1). For the meaning of 'agricultural unit' see para 106 note 6 ante. A farm business tenancy falls within this definition: see para 307 note 3 ante.

3 For the meaning of 'acquiring authority' see para 106 note 1 ante.

4 For these purposes, 'sufficient part' means not less than 0.5 hectares or such other area as the Secretary of State may by order specify: Land Compensation Act 1973 s 34(2) (as amended: see note 1 supra). The power to make such an order is exercisable by statutory instrument subject to annulment in pursuance of a resolution of either House of Parliament: s 34(2A) (added by the Planning and Compensation Act 1991 Sch 15 para 6(1), (4)).

5 For these purposes, a person is displaced from land in consequence of the compulsory acquisition of his interest in it if, and only if, he gives up possession of it (1) on being required to do so by the acquiring authority or on any date after the making or confirmation of the compulsory purchase order but before being required to do so by the acquiring authority; (2) on completion of the acquisition; or (3) where the acquiring authority permits him to remain in possession of the land under a tenancy or licence of a kind not making him a tenant as defined in the Agricultural Holdings Act 1986 (see AGRICULTURE vol 1(2) (Reissue) para 301 note 5), on the expiration of that tenancy or licence: Land Compensation Act 1973 s 34(3) (amended by the Agricultural Holdings Act 1986 s 100, Sch 14 para 52; and by the Planning and Compensation Act 1991 Sch 15 para 6(1), (5)).

6 For these purposes, and for the purposes of the Land Compensation Act 1973 s 35 (as amended) (see para 313 post), references to the date of displacement are references to the date on which the person concerned so gives up possession: s 34(3). As to the acquiring authority's power to require possession before completion see para 122 et seq ante; and as to completion of an acquisition see para 135 et seq ante.

7 Ibid s 34(1) (amended by the Planning and Compensation Act 1991 Sch 15 para 6(1), (2)). For the meaning of 'Great Britain' see para 100 note 21 ante.

8 Land Compensation Act 1973 s 34(4).

9 Ie under the Agriculture (Miscellaneous Provisions) Act 1968 s 12 (as amended): see AGRICULTURE vol 1(2) (Reissue) para 433.

10 Land Compensation Act 1973 s 34(5).

11 Ibid s 36(2).

12 Ie ibid Pt III (ss 29–43) (as amended): see paras 308–310 ante, 312 et seq post.

13 Ibid s 84(2).

312. Claim for farm loss payment. No farm loss payment[1] may be made except on a claim in that behalf made by the person entitled to it before the expiration of the period of one year beginning with the date on which the statutory requirement as to the farming of a new unit[2] is complied with[3]. The claim must be in writing and must be accompanied or supplemented by such particulars as the acquiring authority[4] may reasonably require to enable it to determine whether that person is entitled to a payment and, if so, its amount[5].

Where a person dies before the expiration of the period for making a claim to a farm loss payment, and would have been entitled to such a payment if he had made a claim within that period, a claim to that payment may be made, before the expiration of that period, by his personal representatives[6].

1 For the meaning of 'farm loss payment' see para 311 ante.
2 Ie the requirement in the Land Compensation Act 1973 s 34(1)(b): see para 311 ante. For transitional provisions, now effectively spent, see s 36(7).
3 Ibid s 36(1).
4 For the meaning of 'acquiring authority' see para 106 note 1 ante.
5 Ibid s 36(1). As to entitlement to a payment see para 311 ante; and as to the amount see para 313 post.
6 Ibid s 36(3).

313. Payments for farm loss. The amount of any farm loss payment[1] must be equal to the average annual profit derived from the use for agricultural purposes of the agricultural land[2] comprised in the land acquired, and that profit is to be computed[3] by reference to the profits for the three years ending with the date of displacement[4] or, if the person concerned has then been in occupation for a shorter period, that period[5]. In calculating the profits:

(1) there must be deducted a sum equal to the rent that might reasonably be expected to be payable in respect of the agricultural land comprised in the land acquired if it were let for agricultural purposes to a tenant responsible for rates, repairs and other outgoings, and that deduction must be made whether or not the land is in fact let and, if it is, must be made to the exclusion of any deduction for the rent actually payable[6];

(2) there must be left out of account profits from any activity if a sum in respect of loss of profits from that activity would fall to be included in the compensation, so far as attributable to disturbance, for the acquisition of the interest in the land acquired[7].

Where the value of the agricultural land[8] comprised in the land acquired exceeds the value of the agricultural land in the new unit, the amount of the farm loss payment must be proportionately reduced[9]. Moreover, the amount of a farm loss payment must not be greater than the amount, if any, by which that payment, calculated as above, together with the compensation for the acquisition of the interest in the land acquired, assessed on certain statutory assumptions[10], including any sum included as compensation for disturbance[11], exceeds the compensation actually payable for the acquisition of that interest[12]. Any dispute as to the amount of a farm loss payment must be referred to and determined by the Lands Tribunal[13].

Where a farm loss payment is made to any person, the authority making the payment must also pay any reasonable valuation or legal expenses incurred by that person for the purposes of the preparation and prosecution of his claim to the payment[14]. A farm loss payment carries interest at the prescribed rate[15] from the date when the statutory requirement as to the farming of a new unit[16] is complied with until payment[17]. Payments on account of the farm loss payment or interest may be made, on written request by the person entitled to the payment; and if it is subsequently agreed or determined that the person making the payment is not liable to pay the compensation or interest, or that any such payment is excessive, the payment or the excess is recoverable by him[18].

The amount of any payment in respect of farm loss must not be subject to any reduction on account of the fact that the authority responsible for making that payment has provided, or undertakes to provide, or arranges for the provision of, or another authority will provide, residential accommodation under any enactment for the person entitled to the payment[19].

Where an interest in land is acquired by agreement by an authority possessing compulsory purchase powers[20], the authority may, in connection with the acquisition, make to the person from whom the interest is acquired a payment corresponding to any farm loss payment which it would be required to make to him if the acquisition were compulsory and the authority, if not authorised to acquire the interest compulsorily, had been so authorised on the date of the agreement[21].

Where the agricultural unit containing the land acquired is occupied for the purposes of a partnership firm, the statutory provisions relating to payments for farm loss[22] have effect in relation to the firm and not the partners individually[23].

1 For the meaning of 'farm loss payment' see para 311 ante.
2 For the meaning of 'agricultural' and 'agricultural land' see para 106 note 3 ante.
3 Where the date of displacement is determined in accordance with the Land Compensation Act 1973 s 34(3)(c) (as amended) (see para 311 note 5 head (3) ante) and the person concerned has on that date been in occupation for more than three years, he may elect that, instead of being computed by reference to the profits for the three years ending with the date of displacement, the average annual profit shall be computed by reference to the profits: (1) for any three consecutive periods of 12 months for which accounts in respect of his profits have been made up, being periods for which he has been in occupation and the last of which ends on or after the date of completion of the acquisition; or (2) if there are no such periods, for any three consecutive years for which he has been in occupation and the last of which ends on or after the date of completion of the acquisition: s 35(3). For the meaning of 'date of displacement' see para 311 note 6 ante.
4 Where accounts have been made up in respect of the profits of the person concerned for a period or consecutive periods of 12 months and that period or the last of them ends not more than one year before the date of displacement, ibid s 35(1) has effect as if the date on which that period or the last of those periods ends were the date of displacement: s 35(2).
5 Ibid s 35(1).
6 Ibid s 35(4).
7 Ibid s 35(5).
8 The value of the agricultural land is to be assessed as follows: (1) on the basis of its value as land used solely for agriculture and as for a freehold interest in it with vacant possession; (2) by reference to the condition of the land and its surroundings and to prices current (a) in the case of the land comprised in the land acquired, on the date of displacement, or (b) in the case of land comprised in the new unit, on the date on which the person concerned begins to farm the new unit; (3) in accordance with the Land Compensation Act 1961 s 5 rr (2)–(4) (as amended) (see paras 234, 240, 270, 279 ante); (4) without regard to the principal dwelling, if any, comprised in the same agricultural unit as that land: Land Compensation Act 1973 s 35(7) (amended by the Land Compensation (Scotland) Act 1973 s 81(1), Sch 2 Pt I). As to the new unit see para 311 ante; and for the meaning of 'agricultural unit' see para 106 note 6 ante. See also para 307 note 3 ante.
9 Land Compensation Act 1973 s 35(6).
10 Ie the assumptions contained in ibid s 5(2)–(4) (as amended): see para 372 post.
11 As to compensation for disturbance see para 295 et seq ante.
12 Land Compensation Act 1973 s 35(8).

13 Ibid s 35(9) (amended by the Land Compensation (Scotland) Act 1973 Sch 2 Pt I). As to the Lands Tribunal see para 202 et seq ante.
14 Land Compensation Act 1973 s 36(5). This provision is without prejudice to the powers of the Lands Tribunal in respect of the costs of proceedings before the tribunal by virtue of s 35(9) (as amended: see note 13 supra)): s 36(5) (amended by the Land Compensation (Scotland) Act 1973 Sch 2 Pt I).
15 Ie the rate for the time being prescribed under the Land Compensation Act 1961 s 32: see para 125 ante.
16 Ie the date mentioned in the Land Compensation Act 1973 s 36(1): see para 312 ante.
17 Ibid s 36(6) (amended by the Land Compensation (Scotland) Act 1973 Sch 2 Pt I).
18 See the Planning and Compensation Act 1991 s 80(2), (3), Sch 18 Pt II.
19 See the Land Compensation Act 1973 s 50(1), (3); and para 295 ante.
20 For the meaning of 'authority possessing compulsory purchase powers' see para 244 note 6 ante (definition applied by ibid s 87(1)).
21 Ibid s 36(4).
22 Ie ibid s 35 (as amended): see the text and notes 1–13 supra.
23 Ibid s 36(2). Any interest of a partner in the land acquired is treated as an interest of the firm: s 36(2).

(4) PAYMENTS FOR DISTURBANCE TO PERSONS WITHOUT COMPENSATABLE INTERESTS

314. Right to disturbance payment. Where a person is displaced[1] from any land, other than land used for the purposes of agriculture[2], in consequence of the acquisition of the land by an authority possessing compulsory purchase powers[3] or some other specified event[4], he is entitled to receive a payment (a 'disturbance payment') from the acquiring authority[5] or other specified authority or body[6] if he fulfils the required conditions as to his displacement[7], possession and interest[8]. A disturbance payment is primarily intended to benefit those who do not otherwise qualify for compensation because they have no interest requiring to be purchased[9].

A person is not entitled to a disturbance payment unless he was in lawful possession of the land[10].

Where a person is displaced from land in such circumstances that he would otherwise be entitled to a disturbance payment from any authority and also to compensation from that authority where an order for a new tenancy of business premises is precluded on certain grounds[11], he will be entitled, at his option, to one or the other but not to both[12].

Where a person is displaced from any land in consequence of the acquisition of the land by an authority possessing compulsory purchase powers or some other specified event[13] but is not entitled as against the relevant authority to a disturbance payment, or to compensation for disturbance under any other enactment, the authority if it thinks fit may make a payment to him determined in accordance with the statutory provisions[14] determining the amount of a disturbance payment[15].

These provisions[16] apply in relation to the acquisition of interests in land, whether compulsorily or by agreement, by government departments which are authorities possessing compulsory purchase powers as they apply in relation to the acquisition of interests in land by such authorities which are not government departments[17].

1 As to when a person is treated as displaced for these purposes see note 7 infra. See also *Prasad v Wolverhampton Borough Council* [1983] Ch 333, [1983] 2 All ER 140, CA (a person is displaced in consequence of the acquisition if, under the threat of dispossession by virtue of a compulsory purchase order, he reasonably moves to other accommodation before the service of any notice to treat); approved in *Director of Buildings and Lands v Shun Fung Ironworks Ltd* [1995] 2 AC 111, [1995] 1 All ER 846, PC. If, however, a tenancy is surrendered to the authority, the interest created by it is extinguished and not acquired, so that nothing is payable by virtue of the Land Compensation Act 1973 s 37 (as amended): *R v Islington London Borough Council, ex p Knight* [1984] 1 All ER 154, [1984] 1 WLR 205.

2 Land Compensation Act 1973 s 37(7). For the meaning of 'agriculture' see para 106 note 3 ante.

3 Ibid s 37(1)(a). For the meaning of 'authority possessing compulsory purchase powers' see para 244 note 6 ante (definition applied by ibid s 87(1)).

4 The specified events are (1) the making or acceptance of a housing order or undertaking in respect of a house or building on the land (ibid s 37(1)(b) (amended by the Housing Act 1974 s 130, Sch 13 para 39; the Land Compensation (Scotland) Act 1973 s 81(1), Sch 3; and by the Local Government and Housing Act 1989 s 194(4), Sch 12 Pt II)); (2) where the land has been previously acquired by an authority possessing compulsory purchase powers or appropriated by a local authority and is for the time being held by the authority for the purposes for which it was acquired or appropriated, the carrying out of any improvement to a house or building on the land or of redevelopment on the land (Land Compensation Act 1973 s 37(1)(c) (amended by the Housing Act 1974 Sch 13 para 39)); (3) the carrying out of any improvement to a house or building on the land or of redevelopment on the land by a housing association which has previously acquired the land and at the date of the displacement is registered under the Housing Associations Act 1985 (see HOUSING) (Land Compensation Act 1973 s 37(1)(d) (added by the Housing Act 1974 Sch 13 para 39; substituted by the Housing (Consequential Provisions) Act 1985 s 4, Sch 2 para 24)). For these purposes, 'a housing order or undertaking', 'improvement' and 'redevelopment' have the same meanings as in the Land Compensation Act 1973 s 29 (as amended) (see para 308 notes 1–2 ante): s 37(9) (amended by the Land Compensation (Scotland) Act 1973 Sch 3 para 39(4)).

5 Land Compensation Act 1973 s 37(1)(i) (added by the Housing Act 1974 Sch 13 para 39).

6 Ie (1) where the Land Compensation Act 1973 s 37(1)(b) (as amended) applies (see note 4 head (1) supra), the authority who made the order, passed the resolution, accepted the undertaking or served the notice; (2) where s 37(1)(c) (as amended) applies (see note 4 head (2) supra), the authority carrying out the improvement or redevelopment; and (3) where s 37(1)(d) (as substituted) applies (see note 4 head (3) supra), the housing association carrying out the improvement or redevelopment: s 37(1)(ii)–(iv) (added by the Housing Act 1974 Sch 13 para 39).

7 A person is not to be treated as displaced in consequence of any such acquisition, improvement or redevelopment as is mentioned in the Land Compensation Act 1973 s 37(1)(a) (see the text and notes 1–3 supra), s 37(1)(c) (as amended) (see note 4 head (2) supra) or s 37(1)(d) (as substituted) (see note 4 head (3) supra) unless he was in lawful possession of the land (1) in the case of land acquired under a compulsory purchase order, at the time when notice was first published of the making of the compulsory purchase order prior to its submission for confirmation or, where the order did not require confirmation, of the preparation of the order in draft; (2) in the case of land acquired under an Act specifying the land as subject to compulsory acquisition, at the time when the provisions of the Bill for that Act specifying the land were first published; (3) in the case of land acquired by agreement, at the time when the agreement was made; and a person is not treated as displaced in consequence of any such order, undertaking or improvement notice as is mentioned in s 37(1)(b) (as amended) (see note 4 head (1) supra) unless he was in lawful possession of the land at the time when the order was made, the undertaking was accepted or the notice was served: s 37(3) (amended by the Land Compensation (Scotland) Act 1973 Sch 3; and by the Housing Act 1974 Sch 13 para 39). Nor is a person treated as displaced in consequence of the acceptance of an undertaking, the service of such an improvement notice as is mentioned in the Land Compensation Act 1973 s 37(1)(b) (as amended) or of the carrying out of any improvement to a house or building unless he is permanently displaced in consequence of the carrying out of the works specified in the undertaking or notice or, as the case may be, of the improvement in question: s 37(3A) (added by the Housing Act 1974 Sch 13 para 39).

8 Land Compensation Act 1973 s 37(1). A person is not entitled to a disturbance payment: (1) in a case within s 37(1)(a) (see the text and notes 1–3 supra) unless he has no interest in the land for the acquisition or extinguishment of which he is, or if the acquisition or extinguishment were compulsory would be, entitled to compensation under any other enactment; (2) in a case within s 37(1)(b) (as amended) (see note 4 head (1) supra), if he is entitled to a payment under the Housing Act 1985 s 584A(1) (as added) (compensation payable in cases of closing and demolition orders: see para 290 ante; and HOUSING); (3) in a case within the Land Compensation Act 1973 s 37(1)(d) (as substituted) (see note 4 head (3) supra) unless the displacement occurred on or after 31 July 1974: s 37(2)(b)–(d) (amended by the Housing Rents and Subsidies Act 1975 s 17(4), Sch 5; the Housing (Consequential Provisions) Act 1985 ss 3, 4, Sch 1 Pt I, Sch 2 para 24(3); and by the Local Government and Housing Act 1989 s 194, Sch 11 para 31, Sch 12 Pt II).

9 See *Prasad v Wolverhampton Borough Council* [1983] Ch 333 at 353, [1983] 2 All ER 140 at 152, CA, per Stephenson LJ.

10 Land Compensation Act 1973 s 37(2)(a). In this context, 'lawful possession' means physical occupation with the intention to exclude unauthorised intruders, with the permission of the person who has the

legal right to possession, so that a licensee who does not have exclusive possession may have a claim
under these provisions: *Wrexham Maelor Borough Council v MacDougall* [1993] 2 EGLR 23, CA.
11 Ie where he is entitled to compensation under the Landlord and Tenant Act 1954 s 37 (as amended): see
LANDLORD AND TENANT vol 27(1) (Reissue) paras 607–608.
12 Land Compensation Act 1973 s 37(4).
13 Ie where a person is displaced as mentioned in ibid s 37(1) (as amended): see the text and notes 1–8
supra.
14 Ie determined in accordance with ibid s 38(1)–(3): see para 315 post.
15 Ibid s 37(5). Any dispute as to the amount of such a discretionary payment, if the authority exercises its
discretion to make it, must be determined by the Lands Tribunal under s 38(4) (see para 315 post): *Gozra
v Hackney London Borough Council* (1988) 57 P & CR 211, CA. As to the tribunal see para 202 et seq ante.
16 Ie the Land Compensation Act 1973 Pt III (ss 29–43) (as amended): see paras 308 et seq ante, 315 et seq
post.
17 Ibid s 84(2).

315. Payments for disturbance. The amount of a disturbance payment[1] must be
equal to the reasonable expenses of the person entitled to the payment in removing
from the land from which he is displaced[2], and, if he was carrying on a trade or business
on that land, the loss he will sustain by reason of the disturbance of that trade or business
consequent upon his having to quit the land[3]. In estimating that loss, regard must be
had to the period for which the land occupied by him may reasonably have been
expected to be available for the purposes of his trade or business and to the availability
of other land suitable for that purpose[4]. In the case of a person over 60 who is displaced,
it must be assumed that it is not reasonably practicable to carry on the trade or business
elsewhere than on the land from which the person is displaced in the same circumstances and subject to the same conditions as must be assumed in cases of a person
owning an interest[5].

Where the displacement is from a dwelling[6] in respect of which structural modifications have been made for meeting the special needs of a disabled person[7], whether or
not he is the person entitled to the disturbance payment, then, if a local authority
having statutory welfare functions[8] provided assistance or would, had an application
been made, have provided assistance for making those modifications, the amount of
the disturbance payment must include an amount equal to any reasonable expenses
incurred by the person entitled to the payment in making, in respect of a dwelling to
which the disabled person removes, comparable modifications which are reasonably
required for meeting the disabled person's special needs[9].

Any dispute as to the amount of a disturbance payment must be referred to and
determined by the Lands Tribunal[10]. A disturbance payment carries interest at the
prescribed rate[11] from the date of displacement until payment[12]. Payments on account
of the disturbance payment or interest may be made, on written request by the person
entitled to the payment; and if it is subsequently agreed or determined that the person
who made the payment is not liable to pay the compensation or interest, or that any
such payment is excessive, the payment or the excess is recoverable by him[13].

The amount of any payment to persons without compensatable interests must not
be subject to any reduction on account of the fact that the authority responsible for
making that payment has provided, or undertakes to provide, or arranges for the
provision of, or another authority will provide, residential accommodation under any
enactment for the person entitled to the payment[14].

1 For the meaning of 'disturbance payment' see para 314 ante.
2 Land Compensation Act 1973 s 38(1)(a). The reasonable expenses of removal include all reasonable
expenses flowing from the need to move as a direct and natural consequence of it: see *Nolan v Sheffield*

Metropolitan District Council (1979) 38 P & CR 741, Lands Tribunal. They may include expenses reasonably incurred before the notice to treat: see para 314 note 1 ante.
3 Land Compensation Act 1973 s 38(1)(b). This may include compensation for the total extinguishment of a business: see *Wrexham Maelor Borough Council v MacDougall* [1993] 2 EGLR 23, CA; and see para 301 ante.
4 Land Compensation Act 1973 s 38(2).
5 See ibid ss 38(2), 46(7); and para 298 ante.
6 For the meaning of 'dwelling' see para 283 note 1 ante.
7 For the meaning of 'disabled person' see para 283 note 2 ante.
8 Ie under the National Assistance Act 1948 s 29 (as amended) (which relates to welfare arrangements for disabled persons): see PUBLIC HEALTH.
9 Land Compensation Act 1973 s 38(3) (amended by the Land Compensation (Scotland) Act 1973 s 81(1), Sch 2 Pt I).
10 Land Compensation Act 1973 s 38(4) (amended by the Land Compensation (Scotland) Act 1973 Sch 2 Pt I). As to the Lands Tribunal see para 202 et seq ante.
11 Ie the rate prescribed under the Land Compensation Act 1961 s 32: see para 125 note 5 ante.
12 Land Compensation Act 1973 s 37(6) (amended by the Land Compensation (Scotland) Act 1973 Sch 3).
13 See the Planning and Compensation Act 1991 s 80(2), (3), Sch 18 Pt II.
14 See the Land Compensation Act 1973 s 50(1), (3); and para 295 ante.

9. BETTERMENT REDUCING COMPENSATION

(1) GENERAL POWER OF DEDUCTION

316. Deduction under the Land Compensation Act 1961. Where, on the date of service of the notice to treat[1], the person entitled to the relevant interest[2] is also entitled in the same capacity[3] to an interest in other land[4] contiguous or adjacent[5] to the relevant land[6], there must be deducted from the amount of compensation which would otherwise be payable the amount, if any, of such an increase in the value of the interest in that other land as arises in certain circumstances[7] and is attributable to the carrying out, or the prospect, of so much of the relevant development[8] as would not have been likely to be carried out if the statutory conditions[9] had been satisfied[10]. This rule[11] does not apply to any compulsory acquisition in respect of which the compensation payable is subject to the provisions of any corresponding enactment[12], nor to any compulsory acquisition in respect of which the compensation payable is subject to the provisions of any local enactment[13] which provides, in whatever terms, that, in assessing compensation in respect of a compulsory acquisition thereunder account must be taken of any increase in the value of an interest in contiguous or adjacent land which is attributable to any of the works authorised by that enactment[14].

1 For the meaning of 'the notice to treat' see para 120 note 4 ante. As to service of notices to treat see paras 100–104 ante.
2 For the meaning of 'relevant interest' see para 120 note 4 ante.
3 A person entitled to two interests in land is to be taken to be entitled to them in the same capacity if, but only if, he is entitled (1) to both of them beneficially; or (2) to both of them as trustee of one particular trust; or (3) to both of them as personal representative of one particular person: Land Compensation Act 1961 s 39(6). A person will not be 'entitled' if his title is statute barred: *C & M Matthews Ltd v Marsden Building Society* [1951] Ch 758, sub nom *Re Martin's Mortgage Trusts* [1951] 1 All ER 1053, CA; cf *Re The Statutory Trusts Declared by Section 105 of the Law of Property Act 1925 Affecting the Proceeds of Sale of Moat House Farm, Thurlby* [1948] Ch 191, sub nom *Young v Clarey* [1948] 1 All ER 197.
4 For the meaning of 'land' see para 18 note 2 ante.
5 'Contiguous' prima facie means 'touching': *Spillers Ltd v Cardiff Assessment Committee and Pritchard (Cardiff Revenue Officer)* [1931] 2 KB 21; *Haynes v King* [1893] 3 Ch 439 at 448; *Southwark Revenue Officer v R Hoe & Co Ltd* (1930) 143 LT 544. 'Adjacent' is less precise, particularly where, as here, used in

contradistinction to 'contiguous': see *Wellington Corpn v Lower Hutt Corpn* [1904] AC 773, PC; cf *Re Ecclesiastical Comrs for England's Conveyance* [1936] Ch 430 ('adjoining or adjacent'); *English Clays Lovering Pochin & Co Ltd v Plymouth Corpn* [1974] 2 All ER 239, [1974] 1 WLR 742, CA; *James A Jobling & Co Ltd v Sunderland County Borough Assessment Committee* [1944] 1 All ER 207 (affd on other grounds [1944] 1 All ER 500, CA).

6   For the meaning of 'the relevant land' see para 243 note 5 ante.

7   Ie the circumstances described in any of the Land Compensation Act 1961 s 7(2), Sch 1 paras 1–4B col 1 (as amended): see para 317 et seq post.

8   For these purposes, 'the relevant development', in relation to the circumstances mentioned in note 7 supra, is that mentioned in relation thereto in ibid Sch 1 paras 1–4B col 2 (as amended), but modified, as respects the prospect of any development, by the omission of the words 'other than the relevant land' wherever they occur: s 7(2). For the meaning of 'development' see para 243 note 2 ante.

9   Ie the conditions mentioned in ibid s 6(1)(a), (b) (as amended): see para 269 et seq ante.

10 Ibid s 7(1). Apart from the statutory provisions discussed in this section of the title, and the Land Compensation Act 1973 s 6 (see para 373 post), there is no general power to set off against an owner's compensation any increased value to other land in his ownership: *Re South Eastern Rly Co and LCC's Contract, South Eastern Rly Co v LCC* [1915] 2 Ch 252 at 259–260, CA; and see para 293 ante; cf *Melwood Units Property Ltd v Comr of Main Roads* [1979] AC 426, [1979] 1 All ER 161, PC.

11 The rule may apply unfairly as between two owners who benefit from a scheme of public works, but only one of whom has any land taken. Furthermore, the enhancement in value of an owner's remaining land may be such that the compensation for the land taken is nil: *Cotswold Trailer Parks Ltd v Secretary of State for the Environment* (1972) 27 P & CR 219, Lands Tribunal. However, for the set-off provisions to apply it must be shown that the increase in value of the remaining land would not have occurred but for the scheme: *Laing Homes Ltd v Eastleigh Borough Council* (1978) 250 EG 350, 459, Lands Tribunal.

12 For the meaning of 'corresponding enactment' see para 277 note 11 ante. See further para 323 post.

13 For the meaning of 'local enactment' see para 271 note 3 ante. Where any such local enactment includes a provision restricting the assessment of the increase in value thereunder by reference to existing use (ie, by providing, in whatever terms, that the increase in value is to be assessed on the assumption that planning permission in respect of the contiguous or adjacent land in question would be granted for development of any class specified in the Town and Country Planning Act 1990 s 107(4), Sch 3 (as amended) (see TOWN AND COUNTRY PLANNING vol 46 (Reissue) paras 703–704) but would not be granted for any other development of that land), the enactment is to have effect as if it did not include that provision: Land Compensation Act 1961 s 8(6); Planning (Consequential Provisions) Act 1990 s 2(4). For the meaning of 'planning permission' see para 243 note 1 ante.

14 Land Compensation Act 1961 s 8(5).

(2) CIRCUMSTANCES INVOLVING INCREASE IN VALUE OF OTHER LAND

317. Development of land authorised to be acquired. An increase in the value of the interest in the other land to be deducted from compensation[1] arises where the acquisition is for purposes involving development[2] of any of the land authorised to be acquired[3], if the increase is attributable to the carrying out, or the prospect, of development of any of the land authorised to be acquired which is development for any of the purposes for which any part of the land (including any part of the relevant land[4]) is to be acquired, so far as that development would not have been likely to be carried out if the acquiring authority[5] had not acquired, and did not propose to acquire, any of the land so authorised[6].

1   Ie an increase which must be deducted from compensation under the Land Compensation Act 1961 s 7(1): see para 316 ante. For the meaning of 'land' see para 18 note 2 ante.

2   For these purposes, 'development' is to be construed as including the clearing of land: ibid ss 6(3), 7(2). For the meaning of 'development' generally see para 243 note 2 ante. See also *Cambridge City Council v Secretary of State for the Environment* (1992) 64 P & CR 257, CA.

3   For the meaning of 'land authorised to be acquired' see para 271 note 2 ante.

4   For the meaning of 'the relevant land' see para 243 note 5 ante.

5   For the meaning of 'acquiring authority' see para 120 note 5 ante.

6 Land Compensation Act 1961 ss 6(1)(a), 7(2), Sch 1 Case 1. It is the increase in value of the other land which is material; that increase in value must arise as the product of the development of the land for the purpose for which it is authorised to be acquired, and not from any alteration of the state of the other land or its profitability arising not as the product of the development but arising incidentally or by chance in the course of works for the development of the land for the purpose for which it is authorised to be acquired: see *Cooke v Secretary of State for the Environment* (1973) 27 P & CR 234, Lands Tribunal; cf *Marriage v East Norfolk Rivers Catchment Board* [1950] 1 KB 284 at 308–309, [1949] 2 All ER 1021 at 1035, CA. In valuing an increase from the prospects of development, only an increase in value from the product of the authorised development could be ascertained, and any incidental increase would be pure speculation. There may, however, be special statutory provision for accommodation works on the other land to reduce injury to it, and this may affect compensation.

318. Development in action area. An increase in the value of the interest in the other land to be deducted from compensation[1] arises where any of the relevant land[2] forms part of an action area[3] for which a local plan is in force[4], if the increase is attributable to the carrying out, or the prospect, of development[5] of any land in that area in the course of the development or redevelopment of the area in accordance with the plan, so far as that development would not have been likely to be carried out if the area had not been so defined[6].

1 Ie an increase which must be deducted from compensation under the Land Compensation Act 1961 s 7(1): see para 316 ante. For the meaning of 'land' see para 18 note 2 ante.
2 For the meaning of 'the relevant land' see para 243 note 5 ante.
3 As to action areas see para 247 note 2 ante.
4 See the Town and Country Planning Act 1990 s 54(5), whereby the reference in the Land Compensation Act 1961 s 7(2), Sch 1 Case 2 to 'an area defined in the current development plan as an area of comprehensive development' is to be construed as a reference to an action area for which a local plan is in force; and para 247 note 2 ante. As to local plans see TOWN AND COUNTRY PLANNING vol 46 (Reissue) para 94 et seq.
5 For the meaning of 'development' for these purposes see para 317 note 2 ante; and see also para 243 note 2 ante.
6 Land Compensation Act 1961 s 6(1)(b) (amended by the Housing Act 1988 s 78(4)); Land Compensation Act 1961 7(2), Sch 1 Case 2.

319. Development in area designated as site of or extension of site of new town. An increase in the value of the interest in the other land to be deducted from compensation[1] arises where any of the relevant land[2], on the date of the service of the notice to treat[3] for that interest, forms part of an area designated as the site of a new town[4] or as an extension of the site of a new town[5], if the increase is attributable to the carrying out, or the prospect, of:
(1) development[6] of any land in that area in the course of development of that area as a new town, or as part of a new town[7]; or
(2) any public development[8] specified by direction of the Secretary of State[9] as development in connection with which, or in consequence of which, the provision of housing or other facilities is required and for whose purposes an order designating any area as the site, or an extension of the site, of a new town is proposed to be made[10],
so far as that development would not have been likely to be carried out if the area had not been so designated[11].

1 Ie an increase which must be deducted from compensation under the Land Compensation Act 1961 s 7(1): see para 316 ante. For the meaning of 'land' see para 18 note 2 ante.
2 For the meaning of 'the relevant land' see para 243 note 5 ante.
3 For the meaning of 'the notice to treat' see para 120 note 4 ante. As to the service of notices to treat see paras 100–104 ante.

4 Ie by an order under the New Towns Act 1946 (repealed) or the New Towns Act 1981: see TOWN AND
   COUNTRY PLANNING vol 46 (Reissue) para 1087 et seq. As to determining whether the relevant land
   forms part of an area designated as the site of a new town see further the Land Compensation Act 1961
   s 6(2), Sch 1 paras 5–7 (as amended); and para 273 ante.
5 Ie by an order under the New Towns Act 1965 s 1 (repealed) or the New Towns Act 1981 s 1 (as
   amended): see TOWN AND COUNTRY PLANNING vol 46 (Reissue) para 1087 et seq.
6 For the meaning of 'development' for these purposes see para 317 note 2 ante; and see also para 243 note
   2 ante.
7 For the purpose of deciding whether any development of which there is a prospect on the date of
   service of the notice to treat would be such development, it is immaterial whether the time when that
   development will or may take place is a time before, on or after the date when the development
   corporation established for the purposes of the new town ceases to act except for the purposes of or
   incidental to the winding up of its affairs: Land Compensation Act 1961 s 6(1)(b) (amended by the
   Housing Act 1988 s 78(4)); Land Compensation Act 1961 ss 6(2), 7(2), Sch 1 paras 5, 8 (s 6(2), Sch 1 para
   8 amended by the New Towns Act 1966 s 2, Schedule Pt I).
8 For the meaning of 'public development' see para 273 note 7 ante.
9 Ie a direction under the Land Compensation Act 1973 s 51 (as amended): see para 273 ante.
10 Ie an order under the New Towns Act 1981 s 1 (as amended): Land Compensation Act 1973 s 51(1)
   (amended by the New Towns Act 1981 Sch 12 para 9).
11 Land Compensation Act 1961 s 6(1)(b) (as amended: see note 7 supra); Land Compensation Act 1961
   s 7(2), Sch 1 Cases 3, 3A (Sch 1 Case 3A added by the New Towns Act 1966 Schedule Pt I); Land
   Compensation Act 1973 s 51(2)(b). Where, before the date of service of the notice to treat for the
   purposes of a compulsory acquisition, the land has been disposed of by an authority or body in
   circumstances where the Land Compensation Act 1961 Sch 1 Case 3 or Case 3A (as added) would have
   applied if the authority or body had been compulsorily acquiring the land at the time of the disposal,
   then those Cases do not apply for the purposes of that acquisition: Sch 1 para 9 (added by the Local
   Government, Planning and Land Act 1980 s 133, Sch 25 para 8).

**320. Development in area defined in development plan as area of town
development.** An increase in the value of the interest in the other land to be
deducted from compensation[1] arises where any of the relevant land[2] forms part of an
area defined in the current development plan[3] as an area of town development[4], if the
increase is attributable to the carrying out, or the prospect, of development[5] of any land
in that area in the course of town development so far as that development would not
have been likely to be carried out if the area had not been so defined as an area of town
development[6].

1 Ie an increase which must be deducted from compensation under the Land Compensation Act 1961
   s 7(1): see para 316 ante. For the meaning of 'land' see para 18 note 2 ante.
2 For the meaning of 'the relevant land' see para 243 note 5 ante.
3 For the meaning of 'current development plan' see para 247 note 2 ante.
4 Ie town development within the meaning of the Town Development Act 1952 (repealed): see s 1(1)
   (repealed, subject to a transitional provision, by the Local Government and Housing Act 1989 ss 175,
   194(4), Sch 12 Pt II).
5 For the meaning of 'development' for these purposes see para 317 note 2 ante; and see also para 243 note
   2 ante.
6 Land Compensation Act 1961 s 6(1)(b) (amended by the Housing Act 1988 s 78(4)); Land Compensation Act 1961 s 7(2), Sch 1 Case 4.

321. Development in area designated as urban development area. An
increase in the value of the interest in the other land to be deducted from compensation[1] arises where any of the relevant land[2] forms part of an area designated as an
urban development area[3], if the increase is attributable to the carrying out, or the
prospect, of development[4] of any land in the course of the development or redevelopment of that area as an urban development area[5].

1 Ie an increase which must be deducted from compensation under the Land Compensation Act 1961
   s 7(1): see para 316 ante. For the meaning of 'land' see para 18 note 2 ante.

2 For the meaning of 'the relevant land' see para 243 note 5 ante.

3 Ie by an order under the Local Government, Planning and Land Act 1980 s 134 (as amended): see TOWN AND COUNTRY PLANNING vol 46 (Reissue) para 1270 et seq. In assessing the increase in value to be taken into account, no increase is to be excluded from being taken into account merely because it is attributable (1) to any development of land which was carried out before the area was designated as an urban development area; (2) to any development or prospect of development of land outside the urban development area; (3) to any development or prospect of development of land by an authority, other than the acquiring authority, possessing compulsory purchase powers: Land Compensation Act 1961 s 6(1)(b), (2) (respectively amended by the Housing Act 1988 s 78(4); and by the Local Government, Planning and Land Act 1980 s 145(3)); Land Compensation Act 1961 s 7(2), Sch 1 para 10 (added by the Local Government, Planning and Land Act 1980 s 145(2)).

4 For the meaning of 'development' for these purposes see para 317 note 2 ante; and see also para 243 note 2 ante.

5 Land Compensation Act 1961 s 6(1)(b) (as amended: see note 3 supra), s 7(2), Sch 1 Case 4A (added by the Local Government, Planning and Land Act 1980 s 145(1)).

322. Development in housing action trust area. An increase in the value of the interest in the other land to be deducted from compensation[1] arises where any of the relevant land[2] forms part of a housing action trust area[3], if the increase is attributable to the carrying out, or the prospect, of development[4] of any land in the course of the development or redevelopment of that area as a housing action trust area[5].

1 Ie an increase which must be deducted from compensation under the Land Compensation Act 1961 s 7(1): see para 316 ante. For the meaning of 'land' see para 18 note 2 ante.

2 For the meaning of 'the relevant land' see para 243 note 5 ante.

3 Ie a housing action trust area established under the Housing Act 1988 Pt III (ss 60–92) (as amended): see HOUSING.

4 For the meaning of 'development' for these purposes see para 317 note 2 ante; and see also para 243 note 2 ante.

5 Land Compensation Act 1961 s 6(1)(b) (amended by the Housing Act 1988 s 78(4)); Land Compensation Act 1961 s 7(2), Sch 1 Case 4B (added by the Housing Act 1988 s 78(3)).

(3) SPECIAL STATUTORY POWERS OF DEDUCTION; GENERAL POWER EXCLUDED

323. Purchases under corresponding enactments. There are two cases where specific provision is made by enactments corresponding to the deduction provisions of the Land Compensation Act 1961[1]; here the general power of deduction under that Act does not apply[2] but the provisions as to the protection of owners on any subsequent acquisition of the land benefited[3] do apply.

In determining the amount of compensation where land is acquired under the Light Railways Act 1896, the arbitrator must have regard to the extent to which the remaining and contiguous land and hereditaments belonging to the same proprietor may be benefited by the proposed light railway[4].

In assessing the compensation payable in respect of the compulsory acquisition of land by a highway authority[5] under certain provisions of the Highways Act 1980[6], the Lands Tribunal must have regard to the extent to which the remaining contiguous land belonging to the same person may be benefited by the purpose for which the land is authorised to be acquired[7]. Without prejudice to the generality of this duty, in the case of land authorised to be acquired for widening a highway, the tribunal must also set off against the value of the land to be acquired any increase in the value of other land belonging to the same person which will accrue to him by reason of the creation of a frontage to the highway as widened[8]. The tribunal must also take into account, and embody in its award, any undertaking given by the highway authority as to the use to which the land, or any part of it, will be put[9].

1 Ie the Land Compensation Act 1961 s 7: see para 316 et seq ante. For the meaning of 'corresponding enactment' see para 277 note 11 ante.
2 Ibid s 8(5). As to the general power of deduction see para 316 et seq ante.
3 See para 324 post.
4 Light Railways Act 1896 s 13 (repealed with transitional provisions; see the Transport and Works Act 1992 (Commencement No 3 and Transitional Provisions) Order 1992, SI 1992/2784).
5 As to highway authorities see HIGHWAYS vol 21 (Reissue) para 45 et seq.
6 Ie the Highways Act 1980 ss 239(1)–(5), 240, 246 (as amended), s 250(2): see HIGHWAYS vol 21 (Reissue) paras 800–801, 805, 808.
7 Ibid s 261(1)(a). For the way in which these provisions have been applied see *Cooke v Secretary of State for the Environment* (1973) 27 P & CR 234, Lands Tribunal; *Portsmouth Roman Catholic Diocesan Trustees v Hampshire County Council* (1979) 40 P & CR 579, Lands Tribunal; *Leicester City Council v Leicestershire County Council* (1995) 70 P & CR 435, Lands Tribunal. As to the tribunal see para 202 et seq ante.
8 Highways Act 1980 s 261(1)(b).
9 Ibid s 261(1)(c); and see HIGHWAYS vol 21 (Reissue) para 827.

(4) LAND SUBSEQUENTLY PURCHASED GIVING RISE TO DEDUCTION FOR BETTERMENT

324. No further deduction on subsequent purchase of other land. Where, for the purpose of assessing compensation in respect of a compulsory acquisition of an interest in land[1], an increase in the value of an interest in other land has been taken into account[2], then, in connection with any subsequent acquisition where either:

(1) the interest acquired thereby is the same as the interest previously taken into account[3] (whether the acquisition extends to the whole of the land in which that interest previously subsisted or only to part of that land)[4]; or

(2) the person entitled to the interest acquired is, or derives title[5] to that interest from, the person who at the time of the previous acquisition was entitled to the interest previously taken into account[6],

that increase is not to be taken into account[7] in so far as it was taken into account in connection with the previous acquisition[8].

Where, in connection with a sale of an interest in land by agreement, the circumstances are such that, if it had been a compulsory acquisition, an increase in value would have fallen to be taken into account as mentioned above, the same protection applies, with the necessary modifications, as if that sale had been a compulsory acquisition and that increase in value had been taken into account accordingly[9].

1 As to the interests entitled to compensation see paras 100, 103 ante. For the meaning of 'land' see para 18 note 2 ante.
2 Ie by virtue of the Land Compensation Act 1961 s 7 or any corresponding enactment and in any of the circumstances mentioned in s 7(2), Sch 1 Pt I col 1 (as amended) (see paras 316–322 ante): s 8(1). For the meaning of 'corresponding enactment' see para 277 note 11 ante; and see also para 323 ante.
3 For these purposes, any reference to the interest previously taken into account is a reference to the interest whose increased value was taken into account as mentioned in ibid s 8(1) (see note 2 supra): s 8(3).
4 Ibid s 8(3)(a).
5 For the meaning of 'derives title' see para 277 note 6 ante.
6 Land Compensation Act 1961 s 8(3)(b).
7 Ie by virtue of ibid s 7 or any corresponding enactment: s 8(1).

8 Ibid s 8(1).
9 Ibid s 8(4).

(5) OTHER STATUTORY POWERS OF DEDUCTION

325. Purchases under the Highways Act 1980 of land between street and improvement line. Any person whose property is injuriously affected by the prescribing of an improvement line[1] is entitled to recover from the authority which prescribed the line compensation for the injury sustained[2]. In assessing the compensation payable in respect of the compulsory acquisition by a highway authority of land[3] lying between an improvement line and the boundary of a street, the Lands Tribunal must take into account any benefit accruing to the vendor by reason of the improvement of the street except in so far as it may have been previously taken into account in the assessment of compensation[4] payable under the above provisions[5].

1 As to improvement lines see HIGHWAYS vol 21 (Reissue) para 351 et seq.
2 Highways Act 1980 s 73(9).
3 Ie under ibid s 241 (as amended): see HIGHWAYS vol 21 (Reissue) para 803.
4 Ie under ibid s 73(9): see the text and notes 1–2 supra.
5 Ibid s 261(5). As to the tribunal see para 202 et seq ante.

10. USE OF LAND ACQUIRED AND COMPENSATION FOR INJURY

(1) PERMISSIBLE WORKS ON AND USES OF LAND ACQUIRED

326. Authorised works and uses. The works which may be executed on the land acquired are works for the purposes for which the land was authorised to be acquired by the special Act or empowering enactment[1].

The works may be specified in the empowering enactment by plans, description and location and uses defined and limited, in which case there will be no power to construct works beyond those specified or beyond the limits, nor any power to use the works for purposes other than those defined[2], except for purposes fairly regarded as incidental to or consequential upon those purposes[3].

The works and uses for which land is acquired by local authorities are often specified in general terms. An object not expressly sanctioned but fairly derivable from the statutory powers is authorised by implication[4], and power is implied to do what is necessarily and properly required for carrying into effect the authorised purposes[5], or which may fairly be regarded as incidental to or consequential upon those things which the empowering enactment has authorised[6], but not works for collateral objects, however convenient they may be for carrying out the authorised purposes[7]. Where an authority had two purposes, one of which was within its powers and the other of which was not, its action is lawful only if the intra vires purpose is the dominant reason and the other purpose has not materially influenced its conduct[8].

An acquiring authority may not enter into a contract or undertaking not to use the land in accordance with its statutory powers[9] and, if it does so, the contract or undertaking will be void[10], but it may give an undertaking not inconsistent with the carrying out of the statutory powers[11], and may enter into restrictive covenants so long as it is not precluded by them from using the land for the purposes for which it was acquired[12].

If the acquiring authority executes works beyond its powers it may be restrained by action brought in the name of the Attorney General at the relation of a relator[13], or by judicial review[14], or an action may be brought by a person suffering special damage without involving the Attorney General, whether or not a private right of the individual is interfered with[15].

Where the carrying out of statutory purposes and the execution of works is permissive, no liability attaches for not exercising the power[16], and, where land has been acquired with a genuine intention to carry out works, the authority is not bound to complete the works if circumstances arise which make completion inadvisable[17]. Where, however, there is a duty to carry out the statutory purposes and execute the works in furtherance of them, an order of mandamus may issue to compel the acquiring authority to carry out the duties imposed upon it[18]; but the court will usually refuse such an order where there is an alternative remedy which is not less convenient, beneficial and effective[19]. If the duty is owed to any individual or class of individuals, the individual or one of the class may bring an action in respect of the failure to perform the duty[20].

1   *A-G v Manchester Corpn* [1906] 1 Ch 643 at 651; *Baroness Wenlock v River Dee Co* (1883) 36 ChD 675n at 685n, CA; on appeal (1885) 10 App Cas 354, HL; *Bayley v Great Western Rly Co* (1884) 26 ChD 434, CA. For the meaning of 'the special Act' see paras 11, 16 ante.

2   See *Colman v Eastern Counties Rly Co* (1846) 10 Beav 1.

3   See the cases cited in note 6 infra.

4   See *Cother v Midland Rly Co* (1848) 5 Ry & Can Cas 187; *Rangeley v Midland Rly Co* (1868) 3 Ch App 306; *Finck v London and South-Western Rly Co* (1890) 44 ChD 330 at 344, CA; *Lord Beauchamp v Great Western Rly Co* (1868) 3 Ch App 745; *Wilkinson v Hull etc Rly and Dock Co* (1882) 20 ChD 323, CA; *Sadd v Maldon, Witham and Braintree Rly Co* (1851) 6 Exch 143; *A-G v Sunderland Corpn* (1876) 2 ChD 634, CA; *London Association of Shipowners and Brokers v London and India Docks Joint Committee* [1892] 3 Ch 242 at 249–250, CA.

5   *Colman v Eastern Counties Rly Co* (1846) 10 Beav 1 at 14; *South Yorkshire Rly and River Dun Co v Great Northern Rly Co* (1853) 9 Exch 55 at 84; *S Pearson & Son Ltd v Dublin and South Eastern Rly Co* [1909] AC 217 at 220, HL; *Dundee Harbour Trustees v Nicol* [1915] AC 550, HL.

6   *A-G v Great Eastern Rly Co* (1880) 5 App Cas 473 at 478, HL; *Peel v London and North Western Rly Co* [1907] 1 Ch 5 at 13, CA.

7   Cf *Galloway v London Corpn* (1864) 2 De GJ & Sm 213 at 229; on appeal (1866) LR 1 HL 34; *A-G v West Hartlepool Improvement Comrs* (1870) LR 10 Eq 152; *Westminster Corpn v London and North Western Rly Co* [1905] AC 426 at 439, HL; *A-G v Fulham Corpn* [1921] 1 Ch 440; *Sydney Municipal Council v Campbell* [1925] AC 338, PC. Land acquired compulsorily for coastal protection cannot be used to provide a promenade for public amenity: *Webb v Minister of Housing and Local Government* [1965] 2 All ER 193, [1965] 1 WLR 755, CA. Powers under the Housing Act 1957 Pt V (ss 91–134) (repealed), including the power under s 107 (repealed) to lay out and construct roads on land acquired for the purposes of that Part, did not authorise the construction of a road to serve a function independent of the provision of housing accommodation: *Meravale Builders Ltd v Secretary of State for the Environment* (1978) 36 P & CR 87. See also *Procter & Gamble v Secretary of State for the Environment* [1992] 1 EGLR 265, CA.

8   *Hanks v Minister of Housing and Local Government* [1963] 1 QB 999, [1963] 1 All ER 47; *R v Inner London Education Authority, ex p Westminster City Council* [1986] 1 All ER 19, [1986] 1 WLR 28.

9   *Stourcliffe Estates Co Ltd v Bournemouth Corpn* [1910] 2 Ch 12, CA; *R v Hammersmith and Fulham London Borough Council, ex p Beddowes* [1987] QB 1050, [1987] 1 All ER 369, CA.

10 *Ayr Harbour Trustees v Oswald* (1883) 8 App Cas 623, HL; *Re Heywood's Conveyance, Cheshire Lines Committee v Liverpool Corpn* [1938] 2 All ER 230.

11 See the case cited in note 9 supra; and *Re Gonty and Manchester, Sheffield and Lincolnshire Rly Co* [1896] 2 QB 439, CA; *South Eastern Rly Co v Associated Portland Cement Manufacturers (1900) Ltd* [1910] 1 Ch 12, CA.

12 *Stourcliffe Estates Co Ltd v Bournemouth Corpn* [1910] 2 Ch 12, CA.

13 *A-G v Great Northern Rly Co* (1850) 15 Jur 387; *A-G v North Eastern Rly Co* [1915] 1 Ch 905, CA. As to the position generally of the relator and the Attorney General see CHARITIES vol 5(2) (Reissue) para 483.

14 *R v Carmarthen District Council, ex p Blewin Trust Ltd* (1989) 59 P & CR 379.

15 *Spencer v London and Birmingham Rly Co* (1836) 8 Sim 193; *Boyce v Paddington Borough Council* [1903] 1 Ch 109; and see PRACTICE AND PROCEDURE.

16 *Wilson v Halifax Corpn* (1868) LR 3 Exch 114; *Forbes v Lee Conservancy Board* (1879) 4 ExD 116; *Sheppard v Glossop Corpn* [1921] 3 KB 132, CA; *Gibraltar Sanitary Comrs v Orfila* (1890) 15 App Cas 400, PC.

17 *York and North Midland Rly Co v R* (1853) 22 LJQB 225; *Edinburgh, Perth and Dundee Rly Co v Philip* (1857) 28 LTOS 345, HL; *Scottish North-Eastern Rly Co v Stewart* (1859) 33 LTOS 307, HL; *R v Great Western Rly Co* (1893) 62 LJQB 572, CA; and see CORPORATIONS.

18 See *R v Marshland Smeeth and Fen District Comrs* [1920] 1 KB 155.

19 *Re Barlow, Rector of Ewhurst* (1861) 30 LJQB 271.

20 *Robinson v Beaconsfield Rural Council* [1911] 2 Ch 188, CA. Some other remedy may, however, be provided: see *Pasmore v Oswaldtwistle UDC* [1898] AC 387, HL; *Smeaton v Ilford Corpn* [1954] Ch 450, [1954] 1 All ER 923.

327. Temporary user for other purposes. The acquiring authority may continue to use the land acquired for the purposes for which it was being used at the time of the acquisition until such time as it can be used for the statutory purposes for which it was acquired[1]. The limit of time for that temporary use for other purposes would depend on what was reasonable in the circumstances, and if the time of user was not reasonable the use would be restrainable by injunction at the suit of the Attorney General[2]. Where the empowering enactment or special Act limits the time for the execution of works and incorporates the provisions of the Lands Clauses Consolidation Act 1845 as to the sale of superfluous lands, the time for temporary user will not be difficult to ascertain[3]. If, however, land is purchased in advance of requirements under a statutory power, the use of land until required for the statutory purpose for which it was acquired will depend on the terms of that power[4].

After being applied to the statutory purposes, the land acquired may become temporarily superfluous to requirements. In such a case there appears to be no objection to using the land for some other purpose within the capacity of the acquiring authority[5], or to letting the land under statutory powers[6].

1 *Bayley v Great Western Rly Co* (1884) 26 ChD 434 at 456, CA; *Foster v London, Chatham and Dover Rly Co* [1895] 1 QB 711, CA; *Onslow v Manchester, Sheffield and Lincolnshire Rly Co* (1895) 64 LJ Ch 355; *A-G v Teddington Urban Council* [1898] 1 Ch 66; and see *Leeds Corpn v Ryder* [1907] AC 420, HL (continuation of licensed premises).

2 *A-G v Hanwell Urban Council* [1900] 2 Ch 377, CA; *A-G v Pontypridd Urban Council* [1906] 2 Ch 257, CA.

3 For the limit of time for the execution of works see para 328 post; and as to the disposal of superfluous land see para 377 et seq post. For the meaning of 'special Act' see paras 11, 16 ante.

4 As to the power to purchase land in advance of requirements see para 24 note 1 ante.

5 See *Dundee Harbour Trustees v Nicol* [1915] AC 550 at 571, HL.

6 As to the powers of a local authority to let land see para 377 note 2 post.

328. Time for execution of works. Some special Acts or empowering enactments provide a limit of time for the execution of works, but if the land is properly entered on before the expiration of the time limited for execution, the acquiring authority may execute the works if it can do so as an ordinary owner of land, using its general powers, and without using some power which had been granted by the special Act but had expired by effluxion of time[1]. Some Acts which limit the time for completion of the works may incorporate a provision to do incidental works and alterations and improvements from time to time[2].

Public general Acts giving powers to local authorities and other public bodies to acquire land when required for the statutory purpose do not make provision for a time limit for the execution of the works on the land acquired.

1 *Tiverton and North Devon Rly Co v Loosemore* (1884) 9 App Cas 480 at 499, HL, per Lord Blackburn; *Great Western Rly Co v Midland Rly Co* [1908] 2 Ch 644, CA; affd sub nom *Midland Rly Co v Great Western Rly Co* [1909] AC 445, HL. For the meaning of 'special Act' see paras 11, 16 ante.
2 See eg the Railways Clauses Consolidation Act 1845 s 16; *Emsley v North Eastern Rly Co* [1896] 1 Ch 418, CA.

(2) REHOUSING AND RATING LIABILITIES OF ACQUIRING AUTHORITY

(i) Rehousing Liability

329. Local authority's duty to rehouse residential occupiers displaced by acquiring authority. Where a person is displaced from residential accommodation on any land in consequence of the acquisition of the land by an authority possessing compulsory purchase powers[1], and suitable alternative residential accommodation on reasonable terms is not otherwise available to that person, then, subject to the exemptions and qualifications mentioned below, it is the duty of the relevant authority[2] to secure that he is provided with such other accommodation[3].

Similarly, where a person residing in a caravan on a caravan site[4] is displaced from that site in consequence of the acquisition of the land by an authority possessing compulsory purchase powers, and neither suitable residential accommodation nor a suitable alternative site for stationing a caravan is available to that person on reasonable terms, then, subject to the exemptions and qualifications mentioned below, it is the duty of the relevant local authority to secure that he is provided with suitable residential accommodation[5].

The above provisions do not, however, apply to a person:
(1) if the acquisition is in pursuance of the service by him of a blight notice[6] under the Town and Country Planning Act 1990[7];
(2) if he is a trespasser on the land or, as the case may be, the caravan site, or has been permitted to reside in any house or building on it pending its demolition or improvement[8];
(3) if he is a person to whom money has been advanced for the purpose of enabling him to obtain accommodation in substitution for that from which he is displaced, either:
  (a) by the relevant authority to an owner-occupier displaced from a dwelling and wishing to construct or acquire another dwelling[9]; or
  (b) under certain provisions of the housing legislation[10]; or
  (c) by a development corporation or the Commission for the New Towns otherwise than under head (a) above[11]; or
  (d) by the Development Board for Rural Wales[12].

Nor must a person be treated as displaced in consequence of any such compulsory acquisition unless he was residing[13] in the accommodation in question or in a caravan on the caravan site in question, as the case may be:
  (i) in the case of land, or a caravan site, acquired under a compulsory purchase order[14], at the time when notice was first published of the making of the order

prior to its submission for confirmation[15], or, where the order did not require confirmation, of the preparation of the order in draft[16];

(ii)   in the case of land, or a caravan site, acquired under an Act specifying the land or site as subject to compulsory acquisition, at the time when the provisions of the Bill for the Act specifying the land were first published[17];

(iii) in the case of land, or a caravan site, acquired by agreement, at the time when the agreement was made[18].

Rehousing may affect the compensation payable; for example where a housing authority has rehoused tenants in advance of a compulsory purchase, the owner of the houses may be entitled to vacant possession value rather than sitting tenant value[19].

1   Land Compensation Act 1973 s 39(1)(a). For the meaning of 'authority possessing compulsory purchase powers' see para 244 note 6 ante (definition applied by s 87(1)). As to the application of these provisions to the Crown see paras 308, 311, 314 ante.

2   For these purposes, 'the relevant authority' is the local housing authority within the meaning of the Housing Act 1985 (see para 290 note 4 ante): Land Compensation Act 1973 s 39(7) (substituted by the Housing (Consequential Provisions) Act 1985 s 4(1), Sch 2 para 24(4)). Where, however, the land (or, in a case falling within the Land Compensation Act 1973 s 40 (see the text and notes 4–5 infra) the caravan site: see s 40(4)), is in an area designated as the site of a new town, then if the authority by which the land is acquired is (1) the development corporation, that corporation is the relevant authority (s 39(8)(b)); or (2) the Development Board for Rural Wales, that Board is the relevant authority (s 39(8)(d) (added by the Development of Rural Wales Act 1976 s 27, Sch 7 para 10). As to development corporations see TOWN AND COUNTRY PLANNING vol 46 (Reissue) para 1093 et seq; and as to the Development Board for Rural Wales see TOWN AND COUNTRY PLANNING vol 46 (Reissue) para 1185 et seq. The relevant authority's functions may be conferred on a housing action trust: see the Housing Act 1988 s 65(2)(c); and HOUSING.

3   Land Compensation Act 1973 s 39(1). Other specified events giving rise to a duty to rehouse are (1) the making or acceptance of a housing order or undertaking in respect of a house or building on the land (s 39(1)(b) (amended by the Land Compensation (Scotland) Act 1973 s 81(1), Sch 2 Pt I)); (2) where the land has been previously acquired by an authority possessing compulsory purchase powers or appropriated by a local authority and is for the time being held by the authority for the purposes for which it was acquired or appropriated, the carrying out of any improvement to a house or building on the land or of redevelopment on the land (s 39(1)(c) (amended by the Housing Act 1974 s 130(1), Sch 13 para 40)). For the meaning of 'housing order or undertaking' and 'redevelopment' see para 327 note 2 ante; and for the meaning of 'improvement' see para 327 note 1 ante (definitions applied by the Land Compensation Act 1973 s 39(9) (amended by the Land Compensation (Scotland) Act 1973 Sch 2 Pt I; and by the Housing Act 1974 Sch 13 para 40)).

    The local authority's duty is to act reasonably and to provide the displaced person with accommodation as soon as practicable; it is not required to give him priority over others on the housing list: *R v Bristol Corpn, ex p Hendy* [1974] 1 All ER 1047, [1974] 1 WLR 498, CA. As to whether the provision of temporary bed and breakfast accommodation amounts to a failure to comply with the duty under the Land Compensation Act 1973 s 39(1) (as amended) see *R v East Hertfordshire District Council, ex p Smith* (1991) 23 HLR 26, CA.

4   For the meaning of 'caravan site' see para 308 note 22 ante (definition applied by the Land Compensation Act 1973 s 40(5)).

5   Ibid s 40(1), (2).

6   Ie within the meaning of the Town and Country Planning Act 1990 s 149: see para 90 ante; and TOWN AND COUNTRY PLANNING vol 46 (Reissue) para 744 et seq.

7   Land Compensation Act 1973 s 39(2) (amended by Land Compensation (Scotland) Act 1973 Sch 2 Pt I; and by the Planning (Consequential Provisions) Act 1990 s 4, Sch 2 para 29(6)).

8   Land Compensation Act 1973 s 39(3) (amended by the Housing Act 1974 Sch 13 para 40); Land Compensation Act 1973 s 40(4).

9   Ie under the Land Compensation Act 1973 s 41 (as amended): see para 330 post. Local authorities may no longer make advances under s 41 (as amended): see the Local Government Act 1974 s 37(6) (repealed by the Housing (Consequential Provisions) Act 1985 s 3, Sch 1 without, however, reviving the repealed power: see the Interpretation Act 1978 s 16(1)(a); and STATUTES vol 44(1) (Reissue) para 1313). The powers of development corporations, the Commission for the New Towns, and the Development Board for Rural Wales to make such advances were not affected by the Local Govern-

ment Act 1974 s 37(6) (repealed). As to the Commission for the New Towns see TOWN AND
COUNTRY PLANNING vol 46 (Reissue) para 1159 et seq.
10 Ie under the Small Dwellings Acquisition Acts 1899 to 1923 (all repealed); the Housing (Financial
Provisions) Act 1958 s 43 (repealed); or the Housing Act 1985 s 435: see HOUSING.
11 Ie otherwise than under the Land Compensation Act 1973 s 41 (as amended): see the text and note 9
supra.
12 Land Compensation Act 1973 s 39(4)(a), (b), (d), (f) (s 39(4)(b) amended by the Housing (Consequential Provisions) Act 1985 Sch 2 para 24(4); the Land Compensation Act 1973 s 39(4)(f) added by the
Development of Rural Wales Act 1976 s 27, Sch 7 para 10).
13 Whether a person is resident in a particular place and whether that residence is permanent are questions
of fact and degree and it is possible to reside in accommodation such as a tent or a vehicle: see *Hipperson v
Newbury District Electoral Registration Officer* [1985] QB 1060, [1985] 2 All ER 456, CA. For observations
on the significance of intention to return and the element of permanence see *R v St Leonard' s,
Shoreditch, Inhabitants* (1865) LR 1 QB 21; *Levene v IRC* [1928] AC 217; and *Fox v Stirk* [1970] 2 QB 463,
[1970] 3 All ER 7, CA.
14 As to compulsory purchase orders see para 34 et seq ante.
15 As to the publication of these notices see paras 34–38 ante.
16 Land Compensation Act 1973 ss 39(6)(a), 40(3), (4). As to publication of the draft order see para 60 ante.
17 Ibid ss 39(6)(b), 40(3), (4).
18 Ibid ss 39(6)(c), 40(1), (3). For the purposes of other specified events (see note 3 supra), a person is not to
be treated as displaced in consequence of the acceptance of an undertaking, of the carrying out of any
improvement to a house or building or of the service of such an improvement notice as is mentioned in
s 39(1)(d) (repealed) unless he is permanently displaced from the residential accommodation in question
in consequence of the carrying out of the works specified in the undertaking, the carrying out of the
improvement or the carrying out of the work specified in the notice: s 39(6A) (added by the Housing
Act 1974 Sch 13 para 40).
19 *Bradford Property Trust Ltd v Hertfordshire County Council* (1973) 27 P & CR 228, Lands Tribunal.

330. Advances by relevant authorities to displaced residential owner-occupiers including certain lessees.

Where a person displaced from a dwelling[1] in consequence of the acquisition of land by an authority possessing compulsory purchase powers[2] (1) is an owner-occupier[3] of the dwelling; and (2) wishes to acquire or construct another dwelling in substitution for that from which he is displaced, the relevant authority[4] liable to rehouse the person displaced[5] may advance money to him for the purpose of enabling him to acquire or construct the other dwelling[6].

This power to advance money is without prejudice to any power to advance money exercisable by the authority under any other enactment[7]. It is only exercisable subject to such conditions as may be approved by the Secretary of State, and the following provisions also apply with respect to any advance made in the exercise of that power[8]. The advance may be made (a) on terms providing for the payment of the principal at the end of a fixed period, with or without a provision allowing the authority to extend that period, or upon notice given by the authority, subject, in either case, to a provision for earlier repayment on the happening of a specified event[9]; (b) on such other terms as the authority may think fit having regard to all the circumstances[10]. An advance for the construction of a dwelling may be made by instalments from time to time as the works of construction progress[11].

Before advancing money under the above provisions the authority must satisfy itself that the dwelling to be acquired is or will be made, or that the dwelling to be constructed will on completion be, in all respects fit for human habitation[12].

The principal of the advance, together with interest on it, must be secured by a mortgage of the borrower's interest in the dwelling, and the amount of the principal must not exceed the value which, in accordance with a valuation duly made on behalf of the relevant authority, it is estimated that the borrower's interest will bear, or, as the case may be, will bear when the dwelling has been constructed[13].

1 For the meaning of 'dwelling' see para 283 note 1 ante.
2 Ie under the Land Compensation Act 1973 s 39(1)(a): see para 329 ante. The text and notes 3–13 infra also apply where a person is displaced in consequence of any other event specified in s 39(1) (as amended): see para 329 note 3 ante. As to the application of s 39 (as amended) to persons displaced from caravan sites see s 40; and para 329 ante.
3 In relation to any dwelling, 'owner-occupier' for this purpose means a person who occupies it on the date of displacement either in right of a freehold interest in it or a tenancy of it granted or extended for a term of years certain of which not less than three years remain unexpired: ibid s 41(9)(a).
4 For the meaning of 'relevant authority' see para 329 note 2 ante. Local authorities may no longer make advances under ibid s 41 (as amended), but the powers of development corporations, the Commission for the New Towns, and the Development Board for Rural Wales are unaffected: see para 329 note 9 ante. As to local authorities' powers to advance money for certain housing purposes see the Housing Act 1985 Pt XIV (ss 435–459) (as amended); and HOUSING. As to the Commission for the New Towns see TOWN AND COUNTRY PLANNING vol 46 (Reissue) para 1159 et seq. As to development corporations see TOWN AND COUNTRY PLANNING vol 46 (Reissue) para 1093 et seq; and as to the Development Board for Rural Wales see TOWN AND COUNTRY PLANNING vol 46 (Reissue) para 1185 et seq. The relevant authority's functions may be conferred on a housing action trust: see the Housing Act 1988 s 65(2)(c); and HOUSING.
5 Ie under the Land Compensation Act 1973 s 39(1) (as amended): see para 329 ante.
6 Ibid s 41(1). References in s 41 (as amended) to the construction of a dwelling include references to the acquisition of a building and its conversion into a dwelling and to the conversion into a dwelling of a building previously acquired: s 41(10).
7 Ibid s 41(8).
8 Ibid s 41(2).
9 Ibid s 41(3)(a).
10 Ibid s 41(3)(b).
11 Ibid s 41(4).
12 Ibid s 41(6).
13 Ibid s 41(5).

331. Acquiring authority's duty to indemnify local authority in respect of losses on rehousing and advances to persons displaced. Where a relevant authority[1] provides or secures the provision of accommodation for any person displaced in consequence of a compulsory acquisition[2], then, if (1) the authority providing the accommodation ('the rehousing authority') is not the same as the authority by which the land in question is acquired ('the displacing authority')[3]; and (2) the displacing authority is not an authority having functions under Part II of the Housing Act 1985[4] or (if it is such an authority) the land is acquired or redeveloped by it otherwise than in the discharge of those functions[5], the displacing authority must make to the rehousing authority periodical payments, or, if the rehousing authority so requires, a lump sum payment, by way of indemnity against any net loss in respect of the rehousing authority's provision of that accommodation which may be incurred by that authority in any year during the period of ten years commencing with the year in which the accommodation is first provided[6].

For this purpose a local authority incurs a net loss in respect of its provision of accommodation for a person whom it is rehousing (a) if it rehouses him in a dwelling provided by it under Part II of the Housing Act 1985 for the purpose of rehousing him[7]; or (b) if it rehouses him in a housing revenue account dwelling[8] not so provided, and provides under Part II of the Housing Act 1985, in the financial year immediately preceding that in which he first occupies it, or in the period of three financial years commencing with the financial year in which he first occupies it, a dwelling of a similar type or size[9].

Losses by authorities making advances to persons displaced are also provided for, and where money has been advanced to a person displaced for the purpose of enabling him to obtain accommodation[10], then if (i) the authority making the advance ('the lending authority') is not the same as the displacing authority[11]; and (ii) the lending authority incurs a net loss in respect of the making of the advance[12], the displacing authority must make to the lending authority a lump sum payment by way of indemnity against that loss[13]. For this purpose a lending authority incurs a net loss in respect of the making of an advance to any person if he does not fully discharge his liability to the authority in respect of principal, interest and costs or expenses in accordance with the terms on which the advance is made[14] and the deficiency exceeds the net proceeds arising to the authority on a sale of the interest on which the principal and interest is secured[15].

1 For the meaning of 'relevant authority' see para 329 note 2 ante.
2 Ie in pursuance of the Land Compensation Act 1973 s 39(1)(a): see para 329 ante. As to the application of s 39 (as amended) to persons displaced from caravan sites see s 40; and para 329 ante. The text and notes 3–15 infra also apply where a person is displaced as a result of an event specified in s 39(1)(c) (as amended): see para 329 note 3 ante; and HOUSING.
3 Ibid s 42(1)(a).
4 Ie functions under the Housing Act 1985 Pt II (ss 8–57) (as amended) (provision of housing accommodation and related matters): see HOUSING.
5 Land Compensation Act 1973 s 42(1)(b) (amended by the Housing Act 1980 s 138; and by the Housing (Consequential Provisions) Act 1985 s 4, Sch 2).
6 Land Compensation Act 1973 s 42(1).
7 Ibid s 42(2)(a) (amended by the Land Compensation (Scotland) Act 1973 s 81(1), Sch 2 Pt I; and by the Housing (Consequential Provisions) Act 1985 s 4, Sch 2 para 24(5)).
8 'Housing revenue account dwelling' means a dwelling which is within the authority's housing revenue account within the meaning of the Local Government and Housing Act 1989 Pt VI (ss 74–88) (as amended) (see HOUSING): Land Compensation Act 1973 s 42(6) (substituted by the Housing (Consequential Provisions) Act 1985 s 4, Sch 2 para 24(5); amended by the Local Government and Housing Act 1989 s 194, Sch 11 para 32(1)).
9 Land Compensation Act 1973 s 42(2)(b), (6) (as respectively amended and substituted: see notes 7–8 supra). The Secretary of State may (1) for the purposes of s 42(1) (as amended: see note 5 supra), from time to time determine a method to be used generally in calculating net losses incurred by rehousing authorities (s 42(5)(a)); (2) for the purposes of s 42(1) (as so amended) or s 42(3), determine the net loss incurred by a rehousing authority, or by a lending authority (see head (i) in the text) in any particular case (s 42(5)(b)); and (3) give directions as to the manner in which any payment is to be made (s 42(5)(c)).
10 Ie as mentioned in ibid s 39(4) (as amended): see para 329 ante.
11 Ibid s 42(3)(a).
12 Ibid s 42(3)(b).
13 Ibid s 42(3). As to the determination of a net loss by the Secretary of State and payment under his direction see s 42(5); and note 9 supra.
14 Ibid s 42(4)(a).
15 Ibid s 42(4)(b).

332. Acquiring authority's power to pay expenses of displaced persons in acquiring another dwelling. Where a person displaced from a dwelling[1] in consequence of certain specified events[2] (1) has no interest in the dwelling, or no greater interest in it than as tenant for a year or from year to year; and (2) wishes to acquire another dwelling in substitution for that from which he is displaced, then, according to the nature of the event in consequence of which he was displaced, the acquiring authority[3] which made the order, passed the resolution, accepted the undertaking or served the notice or the authority carrying out the improvement or the redevelopment may pay any reasonable expenses incurred by him in connection with the acquisition, other than the purchase price[4].

This power does not apply to any person who is a trespasser on the land, or who has been permitted to reside in any house or building on the land pending its demolition or improvement[5]; and no payment may be made under this power in respect of expenses incurred by any person in connection with the acquisition of a dwelling unless the dwelling is acquired not later than one year after the displacement and is reasonably comparable with that from which he is displaced[6].

1 For the meaning of 'dwelling' see para 283 note 1 ante.
2 Ie in consequence of any of the events specified in the Land Compensation Act 1973 s 39(1)(a)-(c) (as amended): see para 329 ante. Section 43(1) (as amended: see note 4 supra) also refers to an event specified in s 39(1)(d) (repealed). As to when a person is to be treated as displaced see s 39(6) (as amended) (applied by s 43(4)); and para 329 ante.
3 For the meaning of 'acquiring authority' see para 106 note 1 ante.
4 Land Compensation Act 1973 s 43(1) (amended by the Housing Act 1974 s 130(1), Sch 13 para 41).
5 Ibid s 39(3) (amended by the Housing Act 1974 Sch 13 para 40; applied by the Land Compensation Act 1973 s 43(4)): see para 329 ante.
6 Ibid s 43(2). A dwelling acquired pursuant to a contract must be treated as acquired when the contract is made: s 43(3).

(ii) Liability to make good Deficiency in former General Rate

333. Acquiring authority's liability to make good rate deficiency during construction of works. If the undertakers[1] or the acquiring authority[2] became possessed, by virtue of the special Act[3], or of any incorporated Act, or of the Compulsory Purchase Act 1965, of any land[4] liable to be assessed to the general rate (now abolished)[5] then, in respect of any period up to the time the works were completed and assessed to the general rate, they were liable, under the Lands Clauses Consolidation Act 1845[6], if incorporated[7], or in respect of certain acquisitions under the Compulsory Purchase Act 1965[8], to make good the deficiency in the assessments for the general rate by reason of the taking or use of the land for the purpose of the works[9]. The repeal of the relevant statutory provisions does not affect any liability, whenever incurred, to make good a deficiency in respect of any period ending before 1 April 1990[10]. The statutory provisions regarding deficiency of general rates do not apply to non-domestic rates, community charge or council tax; but subject to the operation of the limitation period, arrears in respect of a deficiency of general rates remain recoverable[11].

1 For the meaning of 'the undertakers' see para 13 ante.
2 For the meaning of 'acquiring authority' see para 92 note 5 ante.
3 For the meaning of 'the special Act' see paras 11, 16 ante.
4 For the meaning of 'land' see para 92 note 1 ante. See also para 13 text to note 7 ante.
5 This was formerly the poor rate: see the Rating and Valuation Act 1925 s 2(1), (2) (repealed). The general rate was, in turn, abolished with effect from 1 April 1990: see the Local Government Finance Act 1988 ss 117(1), 149, Sch 13. For non-domestic property it was replaced by the non-domestic rate and for domestic property it was replaced initially by the community charge under the Local Government Finance Act 1988, and subsequently by the council tax under the Local Government Finance Act 1992: see RATING.
6 Ie under the Lands Clauses Consolidation Act 1845 s 133 (repealed with savings: see the text and note 10 infra).
7 As to incorporation of the Lands Clauses Acts see paras 11–12 ante.
8 See the Compulsory Purchase Act 1965 s 27(1) (repealed with savings: see the text and note 10 infra).
9 See the Lands Clauses Consolidation Act 1845 s 133; the Compulsory Purchase Act 1965 s 27 (both repealed with savings: see the text and note 10 infra).
10 Local Government Finance (Repeals, Savings and Consequential Amendments) Order 1990, SI 1990/776, art 3(1), (3), Sch 1.
11 As to the abolition and replacement of the general rate see note 5 supra. In *Stratton v Metropolitan Board of Works* (1874) LR 10 CP 76 it was held that a deficiency of assessment for 1865–71 was recoverable although not demanded until 1871–72. For the former general rate, recovery proceedings were to be commenced within six years of the first demand: *China v Harrow UDC* [1954] 1 QB 178, [1953] 2 All ER 1296, DC. Although the general rate was due and payable when made and published (*Thomson v*

Beckenham Borough Rating Authority [1947] KB 802) there was no statutory time limit on the issue of the demand; but enforcement sometimes failed due to lapse of time (*R v Lambeth London Borough Council, ex p Ahijah Sterling* [1986] RVR 27, CA).

(3) RIGHTS TO FACILITATE WORKS

334. Extinguishment of rights to facilitate works. Where a statute gives power to execute works and there is power to do the works even though they may injure the rights of others[1], those rights are not extinguished by the injurious works, but continue to exist as adversely affected[2].

However, provision is made for the stopping up or diversion of non-vehicular public rights of way where land is acquired compulsorily by a compulsory purchase order under the Acquisition of Land Act 1981 or by agreement[3], and several statutes make provision for extinguishing other public rights of way and also statutory rights on land acquired for the purpose of enabling the carrying into effect of the statutory purposes for which the land was acquired[4]. There is also statutory power to stop up and divert highways for the purpose of enabling the carrying out of development for which planning permission has been given under the Town and Country Planning Act 1990[5]. There are various other statutory powers to stop up and divert highways, to stop up means of access to highways, and to extinguish a right for vehicles to use a highway[6].

1 See para 335 post.
2 *Ellis v Rogers* (1885) 29 ChD 661 at 670, 672, CA: see paras 355, 382 post.
3 See the Acquisition of Land Act 1981 s 32 (as amended), s 33; and HIGHWAYS vol 21 (Reissue) para 171.
4 See eg the Housing Act 1985 ss 294–297 (as amended), s 611 (as amended); and HOUSING; the Town and Country Planning Act 1990 ss 236–237; and TOWN AND COUNTRY PLANNING vol 46 (Reissue) paras 777–778; Pt X (ss 247–261) (as prospectively amended); and HIGHWAYS vol 21 (Reissue) para 156 et seq; ss 271–274; and TOWN AND COUNTRY PLANNING vol 46 (Reissue) para 834.
5 See ibid s 247 (prospectively amended by the Local Government (Wales) Act 1994 s 20(4)(b), Sch 6 para 24(9) as from a day to be appointed under s 66(3)); and HIGHWAYS vol 21 (Reissue) paras 156–159.
6 See the Highways Act 1980 Pt VIII (ss 116–129) (as amended); and HIGHWAYS. See also the Town and Country Planning Act 1990 s 249; and HIGHWAYS vol 21 (Reissue) para 159. This may give rise to an entitlement to compensation if it can be proved that the extinguishment of the right caused loss: *Saleem v Bradford Metropolitan Borough Council* [1984] 2 EGLR 187, Lands Tribunal (where on the facts no compensation was payable).

(4) EXECUTION OF INJURIOUS WORKS

335. Power to execute injurious works. Where a public body is authorised by statute to exercise powers or execute works, whether for profit or not, it is subject to the same liabilities as an ordinary person[1] unless absolved by the terms of its statute or some other statute[2]. If the public body claims that its powers enable it to take away the common law rights of any person, it is bound to show that the statute clearly authorises it to do so, so as to make lawful that which would otherwise have been unlawful and to remove the remedy by action otherwise available[3].

A public body may be absolved from liability where Parliament has indicated that the works may be done notwithstanding injury to others, for example where there is a duty to do the works[4], or by the specification of the works in the statute by plans and sections[5], or where the works, although not prescribed by plans and sections, are of such a nature that in whatever form, as prescribed, they will inevitably cause injury[6], or by inference from special protective sections in the statute[7]. If the works do not fall clearly within this category, an implication of a power to do an act to the injury of the rights of others may be drawn from the provision of compensation for certain acts[8]. The implication is that Parliament contemplated that it was not feasible or practicable to do those acts for which compensation is provided without injury to the rights of others[9].

Where an Act authorises the acquisition of land for the construction of works, it may be a necessary implication that the Act authorised the operation of the completed works, with the result that there is no remedy so far as nuisance was the inevitable result of the authorised operation[10]. A nuisance clause providing that statutory powers may not be exercised so as to cause a nuisance may exclude an intention that an act may be done notwithstanding that it may cause injury to others[11]; but that clause cannot frustrate the discharge of a duty where the works will inevitably cause injury[12], or where the power to do works is prescribed as to place or manner[13], or, it seems, where the works are of such a nature with such a restricted area of execution that they will cause some injury whatever the case[14]. The body executing the works will only be liable in these cases if it is negligent in doing the works[15]. An injury will not be lawful unless it arises out of an authorised act and is one contemplated by the statute at the time when it was passed[16].

Where no provision is made for compensation, the question whether the person doing the works is acting strictly within his powers requires detailed consideration in order to establish liability for injury[17]; but where full compensation is provided for an injury it is questionable how far it is worthwhile going into matters of negligence[18]. However, in some cases an injunction may be proper even if provision is made for full compensation[19].

The standard of care is what is possible within practical feasibility and expense[20], but, to that extent, all statutory and common law powers must be used to avoid injury[21] unless the statute provides otherwise[22]; and, whether or not provision is made for compensation, the duty to take care applies both to the original construction and to subsequent maintenance, user and improvement, and if new practical means of preventing injury are discovered those means must be adopted[23].

Further powers and duties to mitigate injury by the effect of statutory works are now given whether compensation is provided or not[24].

There may also be negligence in the actual construction or use of the works, and if the undertakers carry out their authorised works without negligence in the choice of place or manner, but fail to take sufficient care to prevent damage in the course of the execution of the works, or their user, and cause injury which is not the product of the authorised works, they will be liable to an action in respect of that injury[25] and also to pay compensation for the damage caused by their authorised act[26].

If an act of God or of third parties makes injurious statutory works which would otherwise be innocuous, the undertakers are under the same liability as ordinary persons at common law and may be liable for continuing the nuisance on their land[27], but they will not be liable until they know or ought to have known of the nuisance[28] and have had a reasonable time to take steps to abate it[29]. However, the statutory works, in some cases, may not be the nuisance and the nuisance, in fact, may be the condition of the land arising from the failure of some person or body to perform a duty, in which case no liability will rest on the undertakers[30].

1   Ie an ordinary person with power to do no more than that authorised by the statute; the liability under a statutory power, eg to break open a street, cannot be compared with a common law power to do so with no liability if done in a reasonable manner and in a reasonable time. Without the statutory authorisation the public body would be liable for the act whatever the care.

2 See *Mersey Docks and Harbour Board Trustees v Gibbs* (1866) LR 1 HL 93 at 107, 110; *Gibraltar Sanitary Comrs v Orfila* (1890) 15 App Cas 400 at 412, PC; *Sharpness New Docks and Gloucester and Birmingham Navigation Co v A-G* [1915] AC 654 at 662, 665, HL.

3 *Clowes v Staffordshire Potteries Waterworks Co* (1872) 8 Ch App 125 at 139; *Metropolitan Asylum District Managers v Hill* (1881) 6 App Cas 193 at 203, 208, 212, HL; *Caledonian Rly Co v Walker's Trustees* (1882) 7 App Cas 259 at 293, HL; *T Tilling Ltd v Dick, Kerr & Co Ltd* [1905] 1 KB 562 at 568, 570; *Vernon v St James' Westminster Vestry* (1880) 16 ChD 449, CA.

4 *Metropolitan Asylum District Managers v Hill* (1881) 6 App Cas 193 at 203, 212, HL.

5 *Metropolitan Asylum District Managers v Hill* (1881) 6 App Cas 193, at 211–212, HL; *Manchester Corpn v Farnworth* [1930] AC 171 at 183, HL.

6 *Edgington v Swindon Corpn* [1939] 1 KB 86, [1938] 4 All ER 57; *WH Chaplin & Co Ltd v Westminster Corpn* [1901] 2 Ch 329; *Goldberg & Son Ltd v Liverpool Corpn* (1900) 82 LT 362, CA.

7 *Edgington v Swindon Corpn* [1939] 1 KB 86 at 90–91, [1938] 4 All ER 57 at 62–63.

8 'The legislature has very often interfered with the rights of private persons, but in modern times it has generally given compensation to those injured; and if no compensation is given it affords a reason, though not a conclusive one, for thinking that the intention of the legislature was, not that the thing should be done at all events, but only that it should be done, if it could be done, without injury to others. What was the intention of the legislature in any particular Act is a question of construction of the Act': see *Metropolitan Asylum District Managers v Hill* (1881) 6 App Cas 193 at 203, HL, per Lord Blackburn; *Price's Patent Candle Co Ltd v LCC* [1908] 2 Ch 526, CA; affd sub nom *LCC v Price's Candle Co Ltd* (1911) 75 JP 329, HL.

9 See note 8 supra.

10 *Allen v Gulf Oil Refining Ltd* [1981] AC 1001, [1981] 1 All ER 353, HL (the defence of statutory authority was available to an oil company seeking to resist a claim for nuisance from the operation of the company's oil refinery constructed on land compulsorily acquired under a private Act which expressly authorised the compulsory acquisition of land for that purpose. The Act contained no provision for compensation for nuisance arising from the operation of the refinery. The statutory powers must, however, be exercised without negligence, that word being used in a special sense so as to require the undertaker, as a condition of obtaining immunity from action, to carry out the work and conduct the operation with all reasonable regard and care for the interests of other persons).

11 *A-G v Gaslight and Coke Co* (1877) 7 ChD 217.

12 *Smeaton v Ilford Corpn* [1954] Ch 450 at 477, [1954] 1 All ER 923 at 936. A provision that nothing in a statute shall exonerate the undertakers from an action or suit does not render them liable, in the absence of negligence, for nuisance attributable to the performance of a statutory duty: *Department of Transport v North West Water Authority* [1984] AC 336, [1983] 3 All ER 273, HL.

13 *Jordeson v Sutton, Southcoates and Drypool Gas Co* [1899] 2 Ch 217 at 237, 257, CA.

14 Cf *Edgington v Swindon Corpn* [1939] 1 KB 86, [1938] 4 All ER 57.

15 See note 12 supra.

16 *Fisher v Ruislip-Northwood UDC and Middlesex County Council* [1945] KB 584 at 596, [1945] 2 All ER 458 at 463, CA; *R v Bradford Navigation Co* (1865) 34 LJQB 191 at 199–200.

17 *Southwark and Vauxhall Water Co v Wandsworth District Board of Works* [1898] 2 Ch 603, CA.

18 *Marriage v East Norfolk Rivers Catchment Board* [1950] 1 KB 284 at 299–300, [1949] 2 All ER 1021 at 1030, CA; *Colac v Summerfield* [1893] AC 187, PC.

19 *Jordeson v Sutton, Southcoates and Drypool Gas Co* [1899] 2 Ch 217, CA; *A-G v Metropolitan Board of Works* (1863) 1 Hem & M 298; *Holyoake v Shrewsbury and Birmingham Rly Co* (1848) 5 Ry & Can Cas 421; *Wintle v Bristol and South Wales Union Rly Co* (1862) 10 WR 210; *Ware v Regent's Canal Co* (1858) 3 De G & J 212 at 228; *Webster v Bakewell Rural Council (No 2)* (1916) 85 LJ Ch 89: and see note 21 supra.

20 The test of injury without negligence is not what is theoretically possible, but what is possible according to the state of scientific knowledge at the time, having also in view a certain common sense appreciation, which cannot be rigidly defined, of practical feasibility in view of the situation and expense: *Manchester Corpn v Farnworth* [1930] AC 171 at 183, HL, per Viscount Dunedin. If the choice of the place or manner of doing an act is made with skill, diligence and caution on proper advice, and is made reasonably and in good faith, the court will not hold that there is negligence: *Raleigh Corpn v Williams* [1893] AC 540 at 550, PC; *Marriage v East Norfolk Rivers Catchment Board* [1950] 1 KB 284 at 299, 309, [1949] 2 All ER 1021 at 1029, 1035, CA. The undertakers will not be liable in negligence for a genuine error of judgment or lack of foresight: *Marriage v East Norfolk Rivers Catchment Board* supra at 310 and 1036; *Sutton v Clarke* (1815) 6 Taunt 29. Cf *Tate & Lyle Industries Ltd v GLC* [1983] 2 AC 509, [1983] 1 All ER 1159, HL (held that damages were recoverable in respect of nuisance by the siltation of a river due to the construction of ferry terminals which restricted access to jetties and made dredging necessary; no immunity in respect of damage that was avoidable by taking all reasonable care for the interests of other persons).

21 *Geddis v Bann Reservoir Proprietors* (1878) 3 App Cas 430 at 456, HL; *Bond v Nottingham Corpn* [1940] Ch 429, [1940] 2 All ER 12, CA; but not where no right would otherwise be infringed: see *Southwark and Vauxhall Water Co v Wandsworth District Board of Works* [1898] 2 Ch 603 at 612, CA.

22 Eg by specifying the works by plans and sections or provision for compensation.

23 *Manchester Corpn v Farnworth* [1930] AC 171 at 202, HL; *Fisher v Ruislip-Northwood UDC and Middlesex County Council* [1945] KB 584 at 595–598, [1945] 2 All ER 458 at 462–464, CA; *Fremantle v London and North-Western Rly Co* (1860) 2 F & F 337 at 340; approved (1861) 10 CBNS 89; *Dimmock v North Staffordshire Rly Co* (1866) 4 F & F 1058; *Groom v Great Western Rly Co* (1892) 8 TLR 253.

24 See para 336 et seq post.

25 *Clothier v Webster* (1862) 12 CBNS 790; *Biscoe v Great Eastern Rly Co* (1873) LR 16 Eq 636; *Hall v Batley Corpn* (1877) 47 LJQB 148; *Fairbrother v Bury Rural Sanitary Authority* (1889) 37 WR 544; *Marriage v East Norfolk Rivers Catchment Board* [1950] 1 KB 284 at 309, [1949] 2 All ER 1021 at 1035, CA.

26 *Uttley v Todmorden Local Board of Health* (1874) 44 LJCP 19.

27 *A-G and Dommes v Basingstoke Corpn* (1876) 45 LJ Ch 726; *A-G v Tod Heatley* [1897] 1 Ch 560, CA; *Barker v Herbert* [1911] 2 KB 633, CA; *R v Bradford Navigation Co* (1865) 34 LJQB 191.

28 *Wringe v Cohen* [1940] 1 KB 229, [1939] 4 All ER 241, CA; *Mersey Docks and Harbour Board Trustees v Gibbs* (1866) LR 1 HL 93; *Lambert v Lowestoft Corpn* [1901] 1 KB 590.

29 *Barker v Herbert* [1911] 2 KB 633, CA; *Maitland v AT and J Raisbeck and Hewitt Ltd* [1944] KB 689 at 691–692, [1944] 2 All ER 272 at 272–273, CA; *Fisher v Ruislip-Northwood UDC and Middlesex County Council* [1945] KB 584 at 607–608, [1945] 2 All ER 458 at 468–469, CA; *Longhurst v Metropolitan Water Board* [1948] 2 All ER 834, HL.

30 *Thompson v Brighton Corpn* [1894] 1 QB 332, CA; *Moore v Lambeth Waterworks Co* (1886) 17 QBD 462, CA; *Railway Executive v West Riding of York County Council* [1949] Ch 423, [1949] 1 All ER 836, CA; *West Lancashire RDC v Lancashire and Yorkshire Rly Co* [1903] 2 KB 394.

(5) MITIGATION OF INJURIOUS EFFECT OF WORKS

336. In general. Where public bodies are authorised by statute to exercise powers or execute works, other than works prescribed by plans and sections, they must use all statutory and common law powers to avoid injury to the rights of others where it is possible to do so within practical feasibility and expense[1].

In addition to this duty and also where no such duty arises, regulations may impose on a highway authority and the person managing public works a duty to mitigate the injury caused by a highway or public works and may give them various powers to effect that purpose[2].

Highway authorities are given power to acquire land to mitigate the adverse effect of the use of a highway constructed or improved by them, or proposed to be constructed or improved, and to acquire land so adversely affected[3] and are also given power to execute works to effect that mitigation[4]. They may enter into agreements with respect to the use of land adjoining a highway so that the highway cannot now or in the future have an adverse effect on the use of that land[5]. Persons managing public works other than a highway may also acquire land to mitigate the adverse effect of the existence or use of their works and acquire land adversely affected[6], and are given power to execute works to effect that mitigation[7].

1 See para 335 ante.

2 See the Land Compensation Act 1973 s 20 (as amended); and para 337 et seq post.

3 See the Highways Act 1980 s 6(1) (as amended), ss 238(1), 246, 247 (as amended), ss 250(1), 261(1),(6); and HIGHWAYS vol 21 (Reissue) paras 805, 808, 826–827.

4 See ibid s 282; and HIGHWAYS vol 21 (Reissue) para 814.

5 See ibid s 253 (as amended); and HIGHWAYS vol 21 (Reissue) vol 21 paras 415, 815.

6 See the Land Compensation Act 1973 s 26 (as amended); and para 350 post.

7 See ibid s 27 (as amended); and para 351 post.

337. Regulations for sound-proofing buildings affected by public works. Where noise is caused or expected to be caused by the construction or use of public works[1], the Secretary of State may make regulations[2] imposing a duty or conferring a power on responsible authorities[3] to insulate buildings or to make grants in respect of the cost of such insulation[4]. Such regulations may:

(1) make provision as to the level of noise giving rise to a duty or power under the regulations and the area in which a building must be situated if a duty or power is to arise in respect of it[5];

(2) specify the classes of public works and of buildings in respect of which a duty or power is to arise, and the classes of persons entitled to make claims, under the regulations[6];

(3) specify the nature and extent of the work which is to be undertaken under the regulations and the expenditure in respect of which and the rate at which grants are to be made under them[7];

(4) make the carrying out of work or the making of grants under the regulations dependent upon compliance with conditions[8];

(5) make provision as to the funds out of which expenses incurred by responsible authorities under the regulations are to be defrayed[9];

(6) make provision for the settlement of disputes arising under the regulations[10].

If the regulations impose a duty or confer a power to carry out, or make a grant in respect of the cost of, work in respect of a building which is subject to a tenancy[11] on a claim in that behalf made by the landlord or the tenant, provision may also be made by the regulations for enabling the work to be carried out notwithstanding the withholding of consent by the other party to the tenancy[12]. Regulations may also:

(a) authorise or require local authorities to act as agents for responsible authorities in dealing with claims and in discharging or exercising the duties or powers of responsible authorities under them, and may provide for the making by responsible authorities of payments to local authorities in respect of anything done by them as such agents[13];

(b) authorise the council of a London borough to contribute towards expenses incurred under the regulations by a responsible authority in respect of the insulation of buildings against noise caused or expected to be caused by the use of any highway in that borough in relation to which a specified traffic order[14] has been made[15];

(c) contain such supplementary provisions as appear to the Secretary of State to be necessary or expedient and may make different provision with respect to different areas or different circumstances[16].

1 For these purposes, 'public works' means (1) any highway; and (2) any works or land (not being a highway or aerodrome) provided or used in the exercise of statutory powers: Land Compensation Act 1973 s 1(3)(a), (c) (applied by s 20(12)). 'Aerodrome' has the same meaning as in the Civil Aviation Act 1982 (see AVIATION vol 2 (Reissue) para 1102): Land Compensation Act 1973 s 87(1) (definition substituted by the Civil Aviation Act 1982 s 109, Sch 15 para 12(3)). References in the Land Compensation Act 1973 Pt II (ss 20–28) (as amended) to public works include references to any works which, apart from any Crown exemption, would be public works: s 84(1).

2 The power to make regulations under ibid s 20 (as amended) is exercisable by statutory instrument: s 20(8). A draft of any regulations so made must be laid before Parliament: s 20(9). The first regulations were subject to approval by a resolution of each House of Parliament: see s 20(9). The current regulations are the Noise Insulation Regulations 1975, SI 1975/1763 (amended by SI 1988/2000): see para 339 et seq post.

3 For these purposes, 'the responsible authority' in relation to a highway is the appropriate highway authority, including for this purpose any authority having power to make an order in respect of that highway under the Road Traffic Regulation Act 1984 s 1 (as amended) or s 6 (as amended): Land Compensation Act 1973 s 20(12) (amended by the Road Traffic Regulation Act 1984 s 146, Sch 13 para 29) (applying and extending the Land Compensation Act 1973 s 1(4)). In relation to other public works, the responsible authority is the person managing those works: ss 1(4), 20(12). References in the Land Compensation Act 1973 Pt II (ss 20–28) (as amended) to responsible authorities include references to any authority which, apart from any Crown exemption, would be a responsible authority: s 84(1). 'Appropriate highway authority' means (1) the highway authority which constructed the highway to which the claim relates or any other authority to which the functions of that authority in relation to that highway are transferred by virtue of the Local Government Act 1985; or (2) if and so far as the claim relates to depreciation that would not have been caused but for alterations to the carriageway of a highway, the highway authority which carried out the alterations or any other authority to which the functions of that authority in relation to that highway are transferred by virtue of that Act: Land Compensation Act 1973 s 19(1) (definition amended by the Local Government Act 1985 s 8, Sch 4 para 51). As from a day to be appointed the term 'appropriate highway authority' will also include any other authority to which functions have been transferred by the Local Government (Wales) Act 1994: Land Compensation Act 1973 s 19(1) (definition prospectively amended by the Local Government (Wales) Act 1994 s 66(6), Sch 16 para 40(2), as from a day to be appointed under s 66(3)). In the case of a highway which has not always since 17 October 1969 been a highway maintainable at the public expense, a reference to the highway authority for that highway must be substituted for the reference in head (1) supra to the highway authority which constructed it: Land Compensation Act 1973 s 19(3)(b). 'Highway' includes part of a highway and means a highway or part of a highway maintainable at the public expense as defined in the Highways Act 1980 s 329(1) (see HIGHWAYS vol 21 (Reissue) para 51 note 6): Land Compensation Act 1973 s 19(1) (definition amended by the Land Compensation (Scotland) Act 1973 s 81(1), Sch 2 Pt I; and by the Highways Act 1980 s 343(2), Sch 24 para 23).
4 Land Compensation Act 1973 s 20(1).
5 Ibid s 20(2)(a). Such regulations may provide for the relevant level of noise or the relevant area in a particular case to be determined by reference to a document published by or on behalf of the Secretary of State or by any other authority or body or in such other manner as may be provided in the regulations: s 20(3). This provision also applies in respect of any dwelling which is not a building, is occupied by a person as his only or main residence and is affected or likely to be affected by noise caused by the construction or use of public works: s 20A(4) (s 20A added by the Planning and Compensation Act 1991 s 70, Sch 15 para 5); see also para 338 post. For the meaning of 'dwelling' see para 283 note 1 ante. See also para 339 post.
6 Land Compensation Act 1973 s 20(2)(b). See also para 339 post.
7 Ibid s 20(2)(c). See also para 346 post.
8 Ibid s 20(2)(d). See also para 344 post.
9 Ibid s 20(2)(e).
10 Ibid s 20(2)(f). This power has not been exercised in the Noise Insulation Regulations 1975.
11 For the meaning of 'tenancy' see para 286 note 3 ante.
12 Land Compensation Act 1973 s 20(4). See also the Noise Insulation Regulations 1975 reg 12; and para 343 note 8 post.
13 Land Compensation Act 1973 s 20(5). See also the Noise Insulation Regulations 1975 reg 14; and para 342 post.
14 Ie an order under the Road Traffic Regulation Act 1967 s 6 (repealed) or the Road Traffic Regulation Act 1984 s 6 (as amended): see ROAD TRAFFIC.
15 Land Compensation Act 1973 s 20(6) (amended by the Road Traffic Regulation Act 1984 Sch 13 para 29).
16 Land Compensation Act 1973 s 20(7). This provision also applies in respect of any dwelling which is not a building, is occupied by a person as his only or main residence and is affected or likely to be affected by noise caused by the construction or use of public works: s 20A(4) (as added: see note 5 supra); see also para 338 post.

338. Power to make payments in respect of caravans and other structures affected by noise of public works. The Secretary of State may make regulations[1] empowering responsible authorities[2] to make a payment, not exceeding an amount specified in the regulations, in respect of any dwelling[3] which is not a building, is occupied by a person as his only or main residence and is affected or likely to be affected by noise caused by the construction or use of public works[4]. Such regulations may:

(1) make provision as to the level of noise giving rise to a power under the regulations and the area in which a dwelling must be situated if a power is to arise in respect of it[5];

(2) specify the classes of public works and of dwellings in respect of which a power is to arise, and the classes of persons entitled to make claims, under the regulations[6]; and

(3) make provision as to the funds out of which expenses incurred by responsible authorities under the regulations are to be defrayed[7].

1 The power to make regulations under the Land Compensation Act 1973 s 20A (added by the Planning and Compensation Act 1991 s 70, Sch 15 para 5) is exercisable by statutory instrument which is subject to annulment in pursuance of a resolution of either House of Parliament: Land Compensation Act 1973 s 20A(3) (as so added). At the date at which this volume states the law, no such regulations had been made.
2 For the meaning of 'responsible authority' see para 337 note 3 ante (definition applied by ibid s 20A(4)) (as added: see note 1 supra).
3 For the meaning of 'dwelling' see para 283 note 1 ante.
4 Land Compensation Act 1973 s 20A(1) (as added: see note 1 supra). For the meaning of 'public works' see para 337 note 1 ante (definition applied by s 20A(4)) (as so added).
5 Ibid s 20A(2)(a) (as added: see note 1 supra).
6 Ibid s 20A(2)(b) (as added: see note 1 supra).
7 Ibid s 20A(2)(c) (as added: see note 1 supra).

339. Sound-proofing buildings affected by public works. Where the use of certain highways[1] causes or is expected to cause noise at a level not less than the specified level[2], the appropriate highway authority[3] must carry out or make a grant in respect of the cost of carrying out insulation work[4] in or to an eligible building[5]. Where the use of certain other highways[6] causes or is expected to cause noise at a level not less than a specified level, that authority may carry out or make a grant in respect of such work[7].

Where a highway becomes a highway maintainable at public expense within three years after the relevant date, the highway authority for the highway may carry out or make a grant in respect of the cost of carrying out insulation work in or to an eligible building if a duty or power to do so would have arisen had the highway been a highway so maintainable at the relevant date and had the construction of the highway or an additional carriageway, or its alteration, been carried out by a highway authority[8].

Where construction works for the construction of a highway or additional carriageway or alteration of a highway cause, or are expected to cause, noise at a level which, in the opinion of the appropriate highway authority, seriously affects or will seriously affect for a substantial period of time the enjoyment of an eligible building adjacent to the site on which works are being or are to be carried out, but in respect of which building no duty or power to carry out insulation works or make grants has arisen[9], the appropriate authority may carry out or make a grant in respect of the cost of carrying out insulation works in or to the building[10].

The discharge or exercise by a highway authority of any duty or power imposed or conferred on the authority under these provisions may be the subject of advances by the Secretary of State[11].

1 'Highway' includes part of a highway and means a highway or part of a highway maintainable at the public expense as defined in the Highways Act 1980 s 329(1) (see HIGHWAYS vol 21 (Reissue) para 51 note 6): Noise Insulation Regulations 1975, SI 1975/1763, reg 2(1) (amended by SI 1988/2000). The

duty to carry out insulation work (see note 4 infra) or to make grants applies to a highway which has been or will be, and a highway for which an additional carriageway has been or will be, first open to public traffic after 16 October 1972: reg 3(3). 'Additional carriageway' means a carriageway constructed or proposed to be constructed for a highway beside, above or below an existing carriageway: reg 2(1).

2 As to the specified level see ibid reg 2(1). The use of a highway causes or is expected to cause noise at a level not less than the specified level if (1) the relevant noise level is greater by at least 1dB(A) than the prevailing noise level and is not less than the specified level; and (2) noise caused or expected to be caused by traffic using or expected to use that highway makes an effective contribution to the relevant noise level of at least 1dB(A): reg 3(2). As to the relevant noise level and the prevailing noise level see reg 2(1).

3 'Appropriate highway authority' in relation to a highway or the carriageway of a highway means the highway authority which constructed or propose to construct a highway or additional carriageway, or which altered or propose to alter a highway: ibid reg 2(1).

4 'Insulation work' means work carried out to insulate a building against noise and to provide for ventilation and solar control: ibid reg 2(1); see also reg 9, Sch 1.

5 Ibid reg 3(1). 'Eligible building' means a dwelling and other building used for residential purposes which will be not more than 300 metres from the nearest point on the carriageway of the highway after the construction of that highway or of an additional carriageway for it or the alteration of it as the case may be: regs 2(1), 7(1). The following are not eligible buildings:

(1) any building in respect of which a compulsory purchase order is in force, or in respect of which a compulsory purchase order has been submitted for confirmation to, or prepared in draft by, a minister and in respect of which a notice has been published under the Acquisition of Land Act 1981 s 11 (see para 36 ante), or under s 2(3), Sch 1 para 2 (see para 60 ante), or any corresponding enactment applicable, unless the order has been withdrawn or a decision has been taken not to confirm or make the order (Noise Insulation Regulations 1975 reg 7(2)(a) (amended by SI 1988/2000));

(2) any building liable to be acquired compulsorily under any local or private Act of Parliament or under an order, rule, regulation, byelaw or scheme made under an Act of Parliament (reg 7(2)(b));

(3) any building which is subject to (a) a demolition order under the Housing Act 1985 Pt IX (ss 264–323) (as amended); (b) a closing order under that Part; (c) a closing order under s 368(4); (d) an undertaking accepted under s 368(2) (Noise Insulation Regulations 1975 reg 7(2)(c) (substituted by SI 1988/2000));

(4) any building within an area declared to be a clearance area by a resolution under the Housing Act 1985 s 289 (as amended) (Noise Insulation Regulations 1975 reg 7(2)(d) (amended by SI 1988/2000));

(5) any building which was first occupied after the relevant date (reg 7(2)(e));

(6) any part of a building in respect of which part of a grant has been paid or is payable in respect of the carrying out of insulation work under any enactment other than the Land Compensation Act 1973 or any instrument made under any such enactment (Noise Insulation Regulations 1975 reg 7(2) (f)).

'Relevant date' means the date on which a highway or additional carriageway was first open to public traffic or, in the case of an altered highway, the date on which it was first open to public traffic after completion of the alteration: reg 2(1). Regulation 7(2)(c) (as substituted) (see head (3) supra) also refers to an undertaking accepted under the Housing Act 1985 s 264(4) (as originally enacted). Section 264 (as substituted) contains a power to make closing orders but no power to accept undertakings. See further HOUSING. See also the Land Compensation Act 1973 s 20(2)(b); and para 337 text and note 6 ante.

6 Ie (1) a highway and a highway for which an additional carriageway has been or is to be constructed if the highway or additional carriageway was first open to public traffic after 16 October 1969 and before 17 October 1972; or (2) an altered highway and a highway to which the Noise Insulation Regulations 1975 reg 3 applies before any duty under reg 8 has arisen: reg 4(2). 'Altered highway' means a highway of which the location, width or level of the carriageway has been or is to be altered, other than by resurfacing, after 16 October 1969: reg 2(1). See also the Land Compensation Act 1973 s 20(2)(b); and para 337 text and note 6 ante.

7 Noise Insulation Regulations 1975 reg 4(1). Where the authority is required by reg 3 or is empowered by reg 4(1) to carry out work or make a grant in respect of an eligible building it may also carry out work or make a grant in respect of the cost of carrying out insulation work in or to an eligible building in respect of which no duty under reg 3 or power under reg 4(1) or 4(3) has arisen if the facades of both buildings are contiguous or form part of a series of contiguous facades: reg 4(4). 'Facade' means a side of a building: reg 2(1).

8 Ibid reg 4(3).

9 Ie the duty under ibid reg 3(1) or the power under reg 4(1): see the text and notes 1–7 supra.

10 Ibid reg 5(1).
11 See the Highways Act 1980 s 272(1)(k); and HIGHWAYS vol 21 (Reissue) para 830.

340. Ascertainment of eligible buildings. The appropriate highway authority[1] for a highway[2] in respect of which it is under a duty to carry out insulation work[3] or make grants[4] must ascertain every eligible building[5] in respect of which that duty has arisen and must prepare a map or list, or both, identifying every such building[6]. Any such map or list must be deposited at the office of the appropriate highway authority or its agent[7] nearest to the building identified in it and made available for public inspection during the hours when the office is open, not later than six months after the relevant date[8] or, if the relevant date was before 7 November 1975, not later than six months after that date[9]. However, where the appropriate highway authority has merely the power and not the duty to carry out such insulation work and make such grants[10] there is no requirement for the preparation of any map or list or to require any map or list which is prepared to identify any building other than a building in respect of which an offer[11] is to be made; neither is there any requirement for such a map or list to be prepared before any date[12].

 1 For the meaning of 'appropriate highway authority' see para 339 note 3 ante.
 2 For the meaning of 'highway' see para 339 note 1 ante.
 3 For the meaning of 'insulation work' see para 339 note 4 ante.
 4 Ie the duty under the Noise Insulation Regulations 1975, SI 1975/1763, reg 3(1): see para 339 ante.
 5 For the meaning of 'eligible building' see para 339 note 5 ante.
 6 Noise Insulation Regulations 1975 reg 6(2).
 7 As to appropriate highway authorities and their agents see para 342 post.
 8 For the meaning of 'relevant date' see para 339 note 5 ante.
 9 Noise Insulation Regulations reg 6(3).
10 Ie under ibid reg 4(1): see para 339 ante.
11 Ie an offer made under ibid reg 8: see para 343 post.
12 See ibid reg 4(5).

341. Ascertainment of noise level. The ascertainment of the prevailing noise level, the relevant noise level and the effective contribution to the relevant noise level made by noise caused or expected to be caused by traffic using or expected to use a highway is to be made in accordance with the technical memoranda entitled 'Calculation of Road Traffic Noise' of 1975 or 1988, as applicable[1].

 1 Noise Insulation Regulations 1975, SI 1975/1763, regs 6(1), 15 (respectively amended and added by SI 1988/2000). In relation to any offer made on or after 1 December 1988 by the appropriate highway authority in pursuance of any duty or power under regs 3, 4 or 13 as provided in reg 8 (see para 343 post), the matter must be determined in accordance with the 1988 code: reg 15(3). 'The 1988 code' means the advice and instruction contained in the technical memorandum entitled 'Calculation of Road Traffic Noise' published by HMSO (1988).

342. Local authorities as agents of highway authorities. A local authority[1] may act as agent[2] for the appropriate highway authority[3] in the discharge and exercise of its duties and powers under the Noise Insulation Regulations 1975[4]. The appropriate highway authority alone, and not the agent local authority, unless that authority is also acting as agent of the appropriate highway authority in the construction or alteration of the highway[5] or carriageway in relation to which the functions are exercisable (1) must determine the buildings in respect of which insulation work[6] or a grant in respect of such work will be offered[7]; and (2) must consider and determine applications for reconsideration of buildings[8]. The appropriate highway authority must reimburse to each local authority the amounts paid by the local authority as agent[9] and such sums as may be reasonable in respect of the services rendered to the highway authority by that local authority[10].

1   'Local authority' in the Noise Insulation Regulations 1975, SI 1975/1763 (as amended), means (1) elsewhere than in Greater London, the council of a county or a district within the meaning of the Local Government Act 1972; (2) in Greater London, the council of a London borough and the Common Council of the City of London: Noise Insulation Regulations 1975 reg 14(5) (amended by SI 1988/2000).
2   As to agency generally see AGENCY.
3   For the meaning of 'appropriate highway authority' see para 339 note 3 ante.
4   Land Compensation Act 1973 s 20(5) (see para 337 text and note 14 ante); Noise Insulation Regulations 1975 reg 14(1).
5   For the meaning of 'highway' see para 339 note 1 ante.
6   For the meaning of 'insulation work' see para 339 note 4 ante.
7   Noise Insulation Regulations 1975 reg 14(2)(a).
8   Ie applications made under ibid reg 13(1) (see para 348 post): ibid reg 14(2)(b).
9   Ibid reg 14(3).
10 Ibid reg 14(4).

343. The appropriate highway authority's offer of insulation work or grant. The appropriate highway authority[1] must make a written offer in respect of every identified eligible building[2] to either (1) the person who is the occupier of the building or, if the building is unoccupied, the person who is entitled to occupy the building; or (2) the immediate landlord or licensor of that person, if any[3].

The offer must:

(a) identify the building to which it relates[4];
(b) offer to carry out or make a grant in respect of the cost of carrying out insulation work[5] in or to every eligible room[6] in the building[7];
(c) describe the work required to be carried out for this purpose[8];
(d) where the offer is made to the person who is the occupier of the building (or if the building is unoccupied, the person who is entitled to occupy the building) require that person, if he is not the owner of the building, to notify his immediate landlord or licensor of the terms of the offer[9];
(e) where the offer is made to the immediate landlord or licensor of the person named in head (d) above, require that person to notify the person who is the occupier of the building (or if the building is unoccupied the person who is entitled to occupy the building) of the terms of the offer[10];
(f) set out certain conditions[11] subject to which the offer is made[12];
(g) set out the restrictions[13] on acceptance of the offer[14].

1   For the meaning of 'appropriate highway authority' see para 339 note 3 ante.
2   For the meaning of 'eligible building' see para 339 note 5 ante.
3   Noise Insulation Regulations 1975, SI 1975/1763, reg 8(2). This duty arises once the authority has deposited the map or list pursuant to reg 6: see reg 8(1). As to the determination of noise levels for the purposes of the offer see para 341 note 1 ante.
4   Ibid reg 8(3)(a).
5   For the meaning of 'insulation work' see para 339 note 4 ante.
6   'Eligible room' means a living room or a bedroom having a qualifying door or window in an eligible building: Noise Insulation Regulations 1975 reg 2(1). As to qualifying doors and windows see reg 9, Sch 1.
7   Ibid reg 8(3)(b).
8   Ibid reg 8(3)(c).
9   Ibid reg 8(3)(d). Where an eligible building is subject to a tenancy and a claim to be entitled to the benefit of an offer is made by a landlord or tenant of the building, insulation may be carried out

notwithstanding that the consent of the other party to the tenancy is required and is withheld: reg 12. See also the Land Compensation Act 1973 s 20(4); and para 337 text and note 13 ante.
10 Noise Insulation Regulations 1975 reg 8(3)(e); and see note 9 supra.
11 See para 344 post.
12 Noise Insulation Regulations 1975 reg 8(3)(f).
13 See para 345 post.
14 Noise Insulation Regulations 1975 reg 8(3)(g).

344. Conditions for carrying out insulation work or making grants. The carrying out of insulation work[1] and the making of grants depend on compliance with the following conditions:

(1) the claimant[2] must have complied with certain regulations[3];
(2) a claimant who accepts an offer[4] to carry out insulation work must, if he is the occupier of or entitled to occupy the building, afford to the appropriate highway authority[5] or its agent[6] such access to the building as it may reasonably require for the purpose of carrying out and of inspecting the work to ascertain whether it complies with the relevant specifications[7]; or if he is not the occupier of, nor entitled to occupy, the building, procure the occupier or person entitled to occupy the building to afford them such access[8];
(3) a claimant who accepts an offer to make a grant in respect of the cost of insulation work must carry out the work in accordance with the relevant specifications and complete it before the expiration of 12 months from the date of acceptance and, if he is the occupier of, or entitled to occupy, the building, afford to the appropriate highway authority or its agent such access to the building as it may reasonably require for the purpose of inspecting the work to ascertain whether it complies with the relevant specifications, or if he is not the occupier of, nor entitled to occupy, the building, procure the occupier or person entitled to occupy the building to afford them such access[9].

1 For the meaning of 'insulation work' see para 339 note 4 ante.
2 'Claimant' means a person who accepts an offer made under the Noise Insulation Regulations 1975, SI 1975/1763, reg 8: reg 2(1).
3 Ie ibid regs 8(4)–(7) (see para 345 post): reg 10(1)(a).
4 As to the offer to carry out insulation work see para 343 ante.
5 For the meaning of 'appropriate highway authority' see para 339 note 3 ante.
6 As to local authorities as agents for highway authorities see para 342 ante.
7 As to the relevant specifications see reg 9, Sch 1; and the Land Compensation Act 1973 s 20(2)(c).
8 Noise Insulation Regulations 1975 reg 10(1)(b).
9 Ibid reg 10(1)(c); and see the Land Compensation Act 1973 s 20(2)(d); and para 337 text and note 8 ante.

345. Acceptance of the offer. The acceptance of the appropriate highway authority's[1] offer to carry out insulation work or to make grants[2] must be in writing[3]. It may be an acceptance of the offer to carry out insulation work in or to one or more or all of the rooms in respect of which the offer was made and may be an acceptance of the offer of a grant in respect of the cost of carrying out such work, but no offer of a grant must be accepted in respect of any room if an offer to carry out insulation work has been accepted in respect of it[4].

The acceptance of the offer must contain the following:

(1) the name and address of the claimant[5];
(2) particulars identifying the eligible building[6];
(3) a statement of the capacity (whether as occupier, person entitled to occupy, landlord or licensor) in which the claimant accepts the offer[7];

(4) if he is so required to notify any person[8] of the terms of the offer, a statement that he has so notified that person, and whether or not that person consents to the carrying out of insulation work[9];

(5) particulars of the rooms (if any) in respect of which he accepts the offered work[10];

(6) particulars of the rooms (if any) in respect of which he accepts the offered grant[11].

An offer may be accepted by the person to whom it was made or his successor and, if it has not been so accepted, it may after the expiration of three months after its date be accepted by any other person to whom it has or could have been notified and in that event it is not thereafter capable of being accepted by the person to whom it was made or his successor[12]. An offer may not be accepted except during one of the following periods (a) six months after its date; or (b) 12 months after the relevant date[13], provided that the appropriate highway authority may extend the time limit whether before or after its expiration[14].

Where the noise is created by works for the construction of a highway or additional carriageway or the alteration of a highway[15], an offer to carry out insulation work or make grants may not be accepted after the expiration of two months after the date of the offer or of such longer period as the appropriate highway authority may by extension at any time allow[16].

Where insulation work has been carried out in or to an eligible building and completed in accordance with the relevant specifications before the offer is made, an offer is deemed to be an offer of grant only, and may be accepted only by the person who incurred the cost of the work[17].

1 For the meaning of 'appropriate highway authority' see para 339 note 3 ante.
2 Ie an offer made under the Noise Insulation Regulations 1975, SI 1975/1763, reg 8. For the meaning of 'insulation work' see para 339 note 4 ante.
3 See ibid reg 8(5).
4 Ibid reg 8(5).
5 Ibid reg 8(6)(a). For the meaning of 'claimant' see para 344 note 2 ante.
6 Ibid reg 8(6)(b). For the meaning of 'eligible building' see para 339 note 5 ante.
7 Ibid reg 8(6)(c).
8 Ie pursuant to ibid reg 8(3)(d) or (e): see reg 8(6)(d).
9 Ibid reg 8(6)(d).
10 Ibid reg 8(6)(e).
11 Ibid reg 8(6)(f).
12 Ibid reg 8(4). This provision does not apply so as to limit the period within which any person may accept an offer where the noise is created by works for the construction of a highway or additional carriageway or the alteration of a highway: reg 5(2)(b). For the meaning of 'additional carriageway' see para 339 note 1 ante.
13 For the meaning of 'relevant date' see para 339 note 5 ante.
14 Noise Insulation Regulations 1973 reg 8(7).
15 Ie under ibid reg 5(1); see para 339 ante.
16 Ibid reg 5(2)(a).
17 Ibid reg 8(8).

346. Nature and extent of work to be undertaken. Insulation work[1] carried out must be in accordance with the relevant specifications[2]. Notwithstanding anything in the Noise Insulation Regulations 1975, no insulation work must be carried out and no grant in respect of the cost of carrying out insulation work must be made in or to any eligible room[3] in which there is installed any flueless combustion appliance other than a gas cooker, unless there will be in that room, after completion of the insulation work in or to that room in accordance with the relevant specifications, an uninsulated window capable of being opened[4]. Nothing in the regulations requires an authority to carry out work or to make a grant in respect of the carrying out of work required to remedy a defect in a building or to maintain or repair any equipment or apparatus installed in or on any building pursuant to the regulations[5].

1 For the meaning of 'insulation work' see para 339 note 4 ante.
2 Noise Insulation Regulations 1975, SI 1975/1763, reg 9(1). As to the relevant specifications see reg 9, Sch 1.
3 For the meaning of 'eligible room' see para 343 note 6 ante.
4 Noise Insulation Regulations 1975 reg 9(2).
5 Ibid reg 9(3).

347. Amount of grant. The amount of grant must be equal to the actual cost incurred by the claimant[1] in carrying out in accordance with the relevant specifications[2] the insulation work[3] in respect of which the claimant has accepted an offered grant, or to the reasonable cost of carrying out that work in accordance with those specifications, whichever is the less[4].

1 For the meaning of 'claimant' see para 344 note 2 ante.
2 As to the relevant specifications see the Noise Insulation Regulations 1975, SI 1975/1763, reg 9, Sch 1.
3 For the meaning of 'insulation work' see para 339 note 4 ante.
4 Noise Insulation Regulations 1975 reg 11.

348. Applications for reconsideration of building. Where there is a highway[1] to which the duty to carry out insulation work[2] or to make grants applies[3] and no offer[4] has been made in relation to an eligible building[5], any person[6] who claims that a duty has arisen with respect to the building may apply in writing to the appropriate highway authority[7], setting out the facts on which he relies, and may request the authority to make him an offer in accordance with the regulations[8]. Such an application must be made within six months after either (1) the date of depositing the map or list or both for public inspection[9]; or (2) the date six months after whichever is the later of the commencement date[10] and the relevant date[11]. On the commencement of each period within which applications may be made, the appropriate highway authority must publish once in a local newspaper circulating in the area of the highway a notice setting out particulars of the right to make an application, including particulars of the time within which, and the authority to which, such an application must be made[12].

On receiving an application the authority must review its noise level calculations[13] or make such calculations and, if it finds that a duty to carry out insulation work or to make grants[14] has arisen with respect to the building, it must comply with the request, but otherwise it must refuse it[15] and furnish the applicant with a written statement of its reasons for refusing[16].

1 For the meaning of 'highway' see para 339 note 1 ante.
2 For the meaning of 'insulation work' see para 339 note 4 ante.
3 Ie the duty under the Noise Insulation Regulations 1975, SI 1975/1763, reg 3.
4 Ie an offer under ibid reg 8(2).
5 For the meaning of 'eligible building' see para 339 note 5 ante.
6 Ie (1) the person who is the occupier of the building, or if the building is unoccupied, the person who is entitled to occupy the building; or (2) the immediate landlord or licensor of that person: Noise Insulation Regulations 1975 reg 13(2).
7 For the meaning of 'appropriate highway authority' see para 339 note 3 ante.
8 Noise Insulation Regulations 1975 reg 13(1).
9 See ibid reg 6; and para 340 ante.

10 The 'commencement date' means the date on which the Noise Insulation Regulations 1975 (as amended) came into force, ie 7 November 1975: see ibid reg 2(1).
11 Ibid reg 13(3). For the meaning of 'relevant date' see para 339 note 5 ante.
12 Ibid reg 13(6).
13 See ibid reg 6; and para 341 ante.
14 Ie under ibid reg 3; see para 339 ante.
15 Ibid reg 13(4). For transitional provisions see Sch 2.
16 Ibid reg 13(5).

349. Acquisition of land and execution of works to mitigate adverse effect of highways. A highway authority has the power to acquire land compulsorily or by agreement to mitigate any adverse effect on the surroundings caused by the existence or use of a highway constructed or improved by it[1]. The highway authority also has the power to carry out works on the land acquired and other nearby land to mitigate any such adverse effects, and may enter into an agreement with any person interested in adjoining land to restrict or regulate the use of the land in a particular way[2].

1 See the Highways Act 1980 ss 238, 246 (as amended); and HIGHWAYS vol 21 (Reissue) para 805.
2 See ibid ss 282, 253 (as amended); and HIGHWAYS vol 21 (Reissue) paras 415, 814–815.

350. Acquisition of land to mitigate effect of public works. A responsible authority[1] may acquire land by agreement[2] for the purpose of mitigating any adverse effect which the existence or use of any public works has or will have on the surroundings of the works[3]. A responsible authority may also acquire by agreement[4] (1) land the enjoyment of which is seriously affected by the carrying out of works by the authority for the construction or alteration of any public works[5]; or (2) land the enjoyment of which is seriously affected by the use of any public works[6], if the interest of the vendor is a qualifying interest[7].

Where the responsible authority proposes to carry out works on blighted land[8] for the construction or alteration of any public works, and is, in relation to that land, the appropriate authority[9], it may acquire by agreement land the enjoyment of which will in its opinion be seriously affected by the carrying out of the works or use of the public works if the interest of the vendor is a qualifying interest[10].

The question as to whether or not an agreement to acquire should be entered into by the highway authority requires to be considered in two stages, the first being whether in the opinion of the highway authority the enjoyment of the land would be seriously affected by the carrying out of the works or the use of the highway, and the second being whether (once the first criterion was met) the highway authority should exercise its discretion to acquire the land by agreement[11].

1 For these purposes, 'responsible authority' means the person managing the public works: Land Compensation Act 1973 s 1(4) (applied, with the necessary modification to exclude a highway authority, by s 26(6)). 'Public works' means (1) any aerodrome; and (2) any works or land (not being a highway or aerodrome) provided or used in the exercise of statutory powers: s 1(3)(b), (c) (as so applied). 'Public works' does not, however, include a highway or any works forming part of a statutory undertaking as defined in the Town and Country Planning Act 1990 s 336(1): Land Compensation Act 1973 s 26(6) (amended by the Land Compensation (Scotland) Act 1973 s 81(1), Sch 2 Pt I; and by the Planning (Consequential Provisions) Act 1990 s 4, Sch 2 para 29(3)). References to a responsible authority for these purposes do not include references to the National Rivers Authority, a water undertaker or a sewerage undertaker: see the Water Act 1989 s 190(1), Sch 25 para 1(6). References in the Land Compensation Act 1973 Pt II (ss 20–28) (as amended) to public works and responsible authorities include references to any works or authority which, apart from any Crown exemption, would be public works or a responsible authority: s 84(1). For the meaning of 'highway' see para 337 note 3 ante; and for the meaning of 'aerodrome' see para 337 note 1 ante.

2 The power applies only where the responsible authority has statutory powers to acquire land (whether compulsorily or by agreement) for the purposes of its functions but would not, apart from the Land Compensation Act 1973 s 26 (as amended) have power to acquire land as mentioned in s 26(1), (2) (as amended), s 26(2A) (as added): s 26(5) (amended by the Planning and Compensation Act 1991 s 70, Sch 15 para 21).

    Furthermore, the power is not exercisable unless the date on which the public works are first used falls on or after 17 October 1972, and (1) if that date fell not later than 23 May 1974, the power will not be exercisable unless the acquisition was begun before 23 May 1974, or one year after the date on which the public works were first used whichever ends later; and (2) if that date falls after 23 May 1974, the power will not be exercisable unless the acquisition was begun before the end of one year after that date: Land Compensation Act 1973 s 26(3)(a)(i), (b)(i). The acquisition of any land must be treated as begun when the agreement for its acquisition is made: s 26(4).

3 Ibid s 26(1). As to the execution of works on the land acquired and the development and disposal of the land see s 27 (as amended); and para 351 post.

4 As to the limitation of the power by the Land Compensation Act 1973 s 26(5) (as amended) see note 2 supra. As to the time for the exercise of the power see notes 5–6 infra.

5 Ibid s 26(2)(a). This power is not exercisable unless the date on which the public works, or the altered public works, are first used falls on or after 17 October 1972, and (1) if that date fell not later than 23 May 1974, the power will not be exercisable unless the acquisition was begun before 23 May 1974; and (2) if that date falls after 23 May 1974, the power will not be exercisable unless the acquisition was begun before that date: s 26(3)(a)(ii), (b)(ii). The acquisition of any land must be treated as begun when the agreement for its acquisition is made: s 26(4). For the considerations to be taken into account in deciding whether to exercise the similar power under the Highways Act 1980 s 246(2A) (as added) (see HIGHWAYS vol 21 (Reissue) para 805) see *R v Secretary of State for Transport, ex p Owen and Owen* [1995] RVR 117, CA.

6 Land Compensation Act 1973 s 26(2)(b). This power is not exercisable unless the date on which the public works are first used falls on or after 17 October 1971, and (1) if that date fell not later than 23 May 1974, the power will not be exercisable unless the acquisition was begun before 23 May 1974 or one year after the date on which the public works were first used, whichever ends later; and (2) if that date falls after 23 May 1974, the power will not be exercisable unless the acquisition was begun before the end of one year after that date: s 26(3)(a)(i), (b)(i). The acquisition of any land must be treated as begun when the agreement for its acquisition is made: s 26(4).

7 Ibid s 26(2) (amended by the Planning and Compensation Act 1991 Sch 15 para 21). 'Qualifying interest' has the meaning given in the Town and Country Planning Act 1990 s 149(2) (see para 90 ante; and TOWN AND COUNTRY PLANNING vol 46 (Reissue) para 729), taking references to the relevant date as references to the date on which the purchase agreement is made: Land Compensation Act 1973 s 26(2B) (added by the Planning and Compensation Act 1991 s 62(1)).

8 'Blighted land' has the meaning given in the Town and Country Planning Act 1990 s 149(1) (see para 90 ante; and TOWN AND COUNTRY PLANNING vol 46 (Reissue) para 729): Land Compensation Act 1973 s 26(2B) (as added: see note 7 supra).

9 'Appropriate authority' has the meaning given in the Town and Country Planning Act 1990 s 169(1) (see TOWN AND COUNTRY PLANNING vol 46 (Reissue) para 732): Land Compensation Act 1973 s 26(2B) (as added: see note 7 supra).

10 Ibid s 26(2A) (added by the Planning and Compensation Act 1991 s 62(1)).

11 See *R v Secretary of State for Transport, ex p Owen and Owen* [1995] RVR 117, CA (Secretary of State's refusal to purchase a dwelling quashed because he appeared to have accepted that the property was very considerably depreciated in value, but had failed to indicate how that was reconciled with his finding that the enjoyment of the land was not seriously affected; the question as to whether the land was seriously affected had not, therefore, been fully addressed by him). See also note 5 supra.

351. Execution of works etc. A responsible authority[1] may carry out works (1) if it has power to acquire land to mitigate the adverse effect of public works[2], on any land acquired by it under that power[3]; (2) on any other land belonging to it[4], for mitigating any adverse effect which the construction, alteration, existence or use of any public works has or will have on the surroundings of the works[5]. Without prejudice to the generality of this provision, the works that may be carried out include the planting of trees, shrubs or plants of any other description and the laying out of any area as grassland[6].

A responsible authority may also (a) develop or redevelop any land acquired by it[7], or any other land belonging to it, for the purpose of improving the surroundings of public works in any manner which it thinks desirable by reason of the construction, alteration, existence or use of the works[8]; and (b) dispose of any land acquired[9] by it[10].

1 For these purposes, 'responsible authority' means the person managing the public works: Land Compensation Act 1973 s 1(4) (applied, with the necessary modification to exclude a highway authority, by s 27(5)). 'Public works' means (1) any aerodrome; and (2) any works or land (not being a highway or aerodrome) provided or used in the exercise of statutory powers: s 1(3)(b), (c) (as so applied). 'Public works' does not, however, include a highway: s 27(5) (amended by the Land Compensation (Scotland) Act 1973 s 81(1), Sch 2 Pt I). The power applies only where the responsible authority is a body incorporated by or under any enactment and has effect only for extending the corporate powers of any such authority: Land Compensation Act 1973 s 27(4). For the meaning of 'highway' see para 337 note 3 ante; and for the meaning of 'aerodrome' see para 337 note 1 ante. As to application of these provisions to the Crown see para 350 note 1 ante.
2 Ie under ibid s 26 (as amended): see para 350 ante.
3 Ibid s 27(1)(a).
4 Ibid s 27(1)(b).
5 Ibid s 27(1).
6 Ibid s 27(2).
7 Ie under ibid s 26 (as amended): see para 350 ante.
8 Ibid s 27(3)(a).
9 Ie land acquired under ibid s 26 (as amended): see para 350 ante.
10 Ibid s 27(3)(b).

352. Expenses of persons moving temporarily during construction works etc. Where works are carried out by a highway authority[1] for the construction or improvement of a highway, or by a responsible authority[2] for the construction or alteration of any public works other than a highway, and the carrying out of those works affects the enjoyment of a dwelling[3] adjacent to the site on which they are being carried out to such an extent that continued occupation of the dwelling is not reasonably practicable[4], the highway authority or responsible authority, as the case may be, may pay any reasonable expenses incurred by the occupier of the dwelling in providing suitable alternative residential accommodation for himself and members of his household for the whole or any part of the period during which the works are being carried out[5].

No such payment may, however, be made to any person in respect of any expenses except in pursuance of an agreement made between that person and the authority concerned before the expenses are incurred, and no payment may be so made except in respect of the amount by which the expenses exceed those which that person would have incurred if the dwelling had continued to be occupied[6].

1 As to highway authorities see the Highways Act 1980 ss 1–3 (as amended); and HIGHWAYS vol 21 (Reissue) para 45 et seq.
2 In relation to a highway, 'responsible authority' means the appropriate highway authority (see para 337 note 3 ante) and, in relation to other public works, the person managing those works: Land Compensation Act 1973 ss 1(4), 28(4). 'Public works' means any highway, any aerodrome and any works or land, not being a highway or aerodrome, provided or used in the exercise of statutory powers: ss 1(3), 28(4). For the meaning of 'aerodrome' see para 337 note 1 ante; and for the meaning of 'highway' for the purposes of this definition see para 337 note 3 ante.
3 For the meaning of 'dwelling' see para 283 note 1 ante.
4 Land Compensation Act 1973 s 28(1).
5 Ibid s 28(2).
6 Ibid s 28(3).

(6) COMPENSATION FOR INJURY BY AUTHORISED WORKS

353. Compensation where statutory provision is made. Compensation for injury by the execution of statutory powers may be given by express provision in the special Act[1], or a public general Act[2], but if the special Act makes no such express provision, there will nevertheless be a right to compensation[3] if certain provisions of the Lands Clauses Consolidation Act 1845 are incorporated[4] or certain provisions of the Compulsory Purchase Act 1965 apply[5].

Where the special Act gives compensation for injury by works authorised by the statute, then injury by works on land already acquired or to be acquired by the acquiring authority, or on land which need not be acquired, may be the subject of compensation[6]; but if the provision of compensation is only by incorporation of the 1845 Act or application of the 1965 Act in, or to a compulsory purchase order as part of, the special Act for the purchase of specific land only, then the compensation provisions will apply only with respect to works on that land[7].

Activities authorised by another statute will not be the subject of compensation under the special Act[8]; but where the activity authorised by the other statute is in consequence of the injury or probability of it and a special power to do that which could be effected at common law, there would appear to be no reason to deprive the person suffering injury of his right to compensation[9].

The compensation is in lieu of a right of action which would lie but for the statutory authorisation of the works causing injury[10], but even when there would have been that right of action, compensation may be limited by the special Act to injury by construction and not by user[11]. However, other provision is made in these cases for compensation in respect of injury by noise, vibration, smell, fumes, smoke, artificial lighting and the discharge of any solid or liquid substances and also, in the case of highways, for that injury where there would not otherwise have been a right of action[12].

Where certain local councils[13] are authorised to acquire land by agreement[14], the provisions of Part I of the Compulsory Purchase Act 1965[15] apply[16]. Where an interest in land is held by a local authority[17] for a purpose for which the authority can by virtue of an enactment be authorised to acquire land compulsorily and (1) the interest was acquired by agreement by the authority or another body before 1 April 1974 and, where it was acquired by another body, has not since the acquisition been transferred otherwise than by an Act or an order made under an Act; and (2) provisions of the Lands Clauses Acts or the Compulsory Purchase Act 1965 apply to the acquisition but do not include certain specific provisions[18], the authority may by resolution provide that, on and after the date when the resolution comes into force, those specific provisions will be included among the statutory provisions which apply to the acquisition[19].

1 For the meaning of 'the special Act' see paras 11, 16 ante.
2 See eg the Public Health Act 1936 s 278 (as amended).
3 *R v St Luke's, Chelsea* (1871) LR 6 QB 572; affd (1871) LR 7 QB 148, Ex Ch; *Wright v President of the Air Council* (1929) 143 LT 43.
4 Ie the provisions of the Lands Clauses Consolidation Act 1845 s 68 (as amended): see para 354 post. As to the Lands Clauses Acts see para 11 ante. Whether s 68 (as amended) is incorporated depends on the construction of the Act incorporating the 1845 Act: see *Ferrar v London Sewers Comrs* (1869) LR 4 Exch 227, Ex Ch; *Dungey v London Corpn* (1869) 38 LJCP 298; *Broadbent v Imperial Gaslight Co* (1857) 26 LJ Ch

276, CA; on appeal sub nom *Imperial Gas Light and Coke Co v Broadbent* (1859) 7 HL Cas 600; *Kirby v Harrogate School Board* [1896] 1 Ch 437, CA. Some special Acts give an express right to compensation and apply the Lands Clauses Consolidation Act 1845 s 68 (as amended) (see eg the Land Drainage Act 1991 s 14(5), (6); and the Water Resources Act 1991 s 177, Sch 21 para 5(1), (2)), and some give no right to compensation and do not incorporate the Lands Clauses Consolidation Act 1845 s 68 (as amended) (see *Dungey v London Corpn* supra; *Baker v St Marylebone Vestry* (1876) 35 LT 129; *Burgess v Northwich Local Board* (1880) 6 QBD 264, DC).

5 Ie the provisions of the Compulsory Purchase Act 1965 s 10 (as amended): see para 354 post.

6 See *Lingké v Christchurch Corpn* [1912] 3 KB 595, CA.

7 *Joliffe v Exeter Corpn* [1967] 2 All ER 1099, [1967] 1 WLR 993, CA.

8 See note 7 supra.

9 See eg the Road Traffic Regulation Act 1984 ss 14, 15 (substituted by the Road Traffic (Temporary Restrictions) Act 1991 s 1(1), (2), Sch 1); and the Road Traffic Regulation Act 1984 ss 16A–16C (added by the Road Traffic Regulation (Special Events) Act 1994 s 1(1)).

10 See para 355 post.

11 See para 356 post.

12 See the Land Compensation Act 1973 Pt I (ss 1–19) (as amended); and para 359 et seq post.

13 Ie councils which are principal councils within the meaning of the Local Government Act 1972 s 270(1) (as amended) (ie a council elected for a non-metropolitan county, a district or a London borough and, by virtue of the Local Government (Wales) Act 1994 s 1(8), in relation to Wales, a county or county borough). See further LOCAL GOVERNMENT vol 28 para 1030 note 4.

14 Ie under the Local Government Act 1972 s 120: see LOCAL GOVERNMENT vol 28 para 1217.

15 Ie the provisions of the Compulsory Purchase Act 1965 Pt I (ss 1–32) (as amended) (see para 92 et seq ante) other than s 31 (as amended) (see para 150 ante): Local Government Act 1972 s 120(3).

16 Ibid s 120(3). This provision came into force on 1 April 1974: see s 273. In relation to acquisitions made before that date see note 18 infra. In the Compulsory Purchase Act 1965 Pt I (as amended) as so applied, 'land' has the meaning assigned to it by the Local Government Act 1972 and includes any interest in land and any easement or right in, to or over land (see s 270(1)): s 270(3).

17 For the meaning of 'local authority' see para 30 note 7 ante.

18 The provisions specifically excluded are the Lands Clauses Consolidation Act 1845 s 68 (as amended) (see para 354 post) under which there is among other things a right to compensation in respect of land injuriously affected by certain works, and the Compulsory Purchase Act 1965 s 10 (as amended) (see para 354 post) which re-enacts the Lands Clauses Consolidation Act 1845 s 68 (as amended): see the Local Government (Miscellaneous Provisions) Act 1976 s 14(1); and LOCAL GOVERNMENT vol 28 para 1217.

19 Ibid s 14(1). See LOCAL GOVERNMENT vol 28 para 1217. In relation to acquisitions before 1 April 1974 see note 18 supra.

354. Statutory provisions for compensation; parties entitled. Provision is made by the Lands Clauses Consolidation Act 1845, if incorporated[1], that if any party is entitled to compensation in respect of any land[2], or of any interest in it, which has been taken for or injuriously affected by the execution of the works, and for which the undertakers[3] have not made satisfaction under the provisions of that Act or the special Act[4], or any Act incorporated with it, that party may have the compensation settled[5].

An owner of land who has had land taken will have received compensation under the 1845 Act as part of his purchase money[6] for injury by works:

(1) on the land taken from him; and

(2) on the land taken from other persons,

to land not taken from him but held with land taken from him[7]; but not for injury by works to his land not held with land taken from him, either from works on the land taken from him or works on the land taken from other persons[8]. He is, therefore, entitled in respect of it to compensation under certain provisions of the 1845 Act[9]. Persons who have had no land taken are also entitled to compensation under those provisions because they are not entitled to compensation under the provisions relating to purchase money[10].

Provision is made by the Compulsory Purchase Act 1965, where it applies[11], that if any person claims compensation in respect of any land[12] or any interest in land which has been taken for, or injuriously affected by, the execution of the works and for which the acquiring authority[13] has not made satisfaction under the provisions of that Act or of the special Act, any dispute arising in relation to it must be referred to and determined by the Lands Tribunal[14]. This provision is to be construed as affording, in all cases, a right to compensation for injurious affection to land which is the same as the right which certain provisions of the Lands Clauses Consolidation Act 1845[15] have been construed as affording in cases where the amount claimed exceeds £50[16].

A person with a qualifying interest[17] may claim compensation in respect of injury by noise, vibration, smell, fumes, smoke, artificial lighting and the discharge of any solid or liquid substances and also, in the case of highways, for that injury where there would not otherwise have been a right of action[18].

1   See paras 11, 353 note 4 ante.
2   Compensation is limited to injury to land: see para 357 post. For the meaning of 'land' see para 13 text to note 7 ante.
3   For the meaning of 'the undertakers' see para 13 ante; and for the meaning of 'the works' see para 13 text to note 4 ante.
4   For the meaning of 'the special Act' see paras 11, 16 ante.
5   Lands Clauses Consolidation Act 1845 s 68 (amended by the Compulsory Purchase Act 1965 s 39(4), Sch 8 Pt III).This provision has long been construed as giving compensation for injury to the value of land by the execution of works in lieu of the right of action which would have lain but for the statutory authorisation of the works: see *Horn v Sunderland Corpn* [1941] 2 KB 26 at 42–43, [1941] 1 All ER 480 at 491–492, CA; and para 355 et seq post. As to the claim for and settlement of the compensation see para 358 post.
6   Ie under the Lands Clauses Consolidation Act 1845 s 63: see para 291 ante.
7   See ibid s 63; and the Compulsory Purchase Act 1965 s 7; and see para 292 ante.
8   Ie under the Lands Clauses Consolidation Act 1845 s 63: see para 291 ante.
9   Ie under the provisions of ibid s 68 (as amended). See also para 200 ante.
10 Ie under the provisions of ibid s 63: see para 291 ante.
11 As to the compulsory purchase orders to which the Compulsory Purchase Act 1965 applies see paras 15–16 ante.
12 For the meaning of 'land' see para 92 note 1 ante.
13 For the meaning of 'acquiring authority' see para 92 note 5 ante. See also para 200 note 16 ante.
14 Compulsory Purchase Act 1965 s 10(1): see further para 200 ante. As to claims for and the settlement of compensation see para 358 post. As to the tribunal see para 202 et seq ante.
15 Ie the provisions of the Lands Clauses Consolidation Act 1845 s 68 (as amended): see para 200 ante.
16 Compulsory Purchase Act 1965 s 10(2).
17 For the meaning of 'qualifying interest' see para 350 note 7 ante.
18 See the Land Compensation Act 1973 Pt I (ss 1–19) (as amended); and para 360 et seq post.

355. Damage from authorised works which would have been actionable.

The person whose rights have been injured can recover compensation for injury by authorised works[1] only in respect of losses sustained in consequence of what the undertakers or the acquiring authority have lawfully done under their statutory powers[2]. The damage must arise from something which would, if done without statutory authority, have given rise to a cause of action.[3] In other words, in order to have a right to compensation against the undertakers or the acquiring authority in respect of any act done under their statutory powers, the person claiming must have had a good cause of action in respect of that act, if it had been done by any person not so authorised[4]. The undertakers or the acquiring authority, having acquired land, may therefore use it in any way in which an ordinary owner might have lawfully used it without conferring any right to compensation, apart from any specific provision for compensation in a particular case, for example in respect of highways constructed by the highway authority[5].

Thus, the undertakers or the acquiring authority may:

(1) erect an embankment on the land acquired and destroy the amenity of adjoining property[6];

(2) block up access to light and air so long as no right of easement is interfered with[7];

(3) remove the support of buildings where no right of support has been acquired[8];

(4) draw off underground water[9];

(5) build a bridge and by doing so injure a ferry undertaking[10];

(6) cause loss of business to shops by pulling down neighbouring houses[11], or by demolishing and re-erecting party walls in accordance with requirements of building regulations[12];

(7) exercise the rights of ordinary riparian owners, if they are such owners[13]; and

(8) block up private roads on building estates unless the persons damaged can show they have a right to those roads[14].

Damage which would be too remote to be recovered in an action cannot be recovered as compensation[15].

The obstruction of a public way gives rise to no cause of action to a person unless he suffers special damage different from that suffered by the public generally[16].

However, interference with an adjoining owner's right of access from his premises to the highway, including a highway by water[17], is interference with a private right, which is distinct from the owner's right to use the highway which he enjoys as a member of the public[18]. If unauthorised, the interference will be actionable[19] and so, if authorised, it may be the subject of compensation for injurious affection, as for example where the interference makes access less convenient by the alteration of the level of the roadway[20], or by the blocking up of one of two means of access, whether by river or land[21].

The obstruction of easements, such as rights of way[22], of light[23], of obtaining a water supply[24], or of support[25] will also entitle the owner of the dominant tenement to compensation for any loss he may suffer as a result of it[26].

If land taken or used by the undertakers or the acquiring authority has been subject to restrictive covenants for the benefit of other land, the breach of such a covenant by the undertakers or the authority will confer upon the owner of that other land a right to compensation for injurious affection[27]. If acts done by the undertakers or the authority prevent covenants relating to land from being carried out, the undertakers or the authority will be liable in respect of those acts[28].

Rights over the land under licence may be the subject of compensation if coupled with an interest in land[29].

1 See paras 353–354 ante.

2 *Caledonian Rly Co v Colt* (1860) 3 Macq 833, HL; *Imperial Gas Light and Coke Co v Broadbent* (1859) 7 HL Cas 600. As to the authorised works see para 326 ante. This rule does not apply where the effects complained of are caused by activities on land taken from the claimant: *Re Stockport, Timperley and Altrincham Rly Co* (1864) 33 LJQB 251; *Cowper Essex v Acton Local Board* (1889) 14 App Cas 153, HL; and see the Compulsory Purchase Act 1965 s 7; and para 291 ante. If the powers are exceeded there will be a remedy by action: see para 326 ante.

3 *Glover v North Staffordshire Rly Co* (1851) 16 QB 912; *Ricket v Metropolitan Rly Co* (1867) LR 2 HL 175; *Metropolitan Board of Works v McCarthy* (1874) LR 7 HL 243; *Caledonian Rly Co v Walker's Trustees* (1882) 7 App Cas 259, HL; *Marriage v East Norfolk Rivers Catchment Board* [1949] 2 KB 456, [1949] 2 All ER 50; affd [1950] 1 KB 284, [1949] 2 All ER 1021, CA (applied eg in *Thameside Estates Ltd v GLC* [1979] 1 EGLR 167, Lands Tribunal). See also *R v Bristol Dock Co* (1810) 12 East 429 (interference with

right to water enjoyed in common with the rest of the public); *Day & Sons v Thames Water Authority* [1984] 1 EGLR 197, Lands Tribunal.

4 It is immaterial whether the right interfered with would be enforceable at law or in equity: *Furness Rly Co v Cumberland Co-operative Building Society* (1884) 52 LT 144, HL. See also para 335 note 1 ante.

5 See the Land Compensation Act 1973 Pt I (ss 1–19) (as amended); and para 360 et seq post.

6 *Re Penny* (1857) 7 E & B 660.

7 *Butt v Imperial Gas Co* (1866) 2 Ch App 158; *Eagle v Charing Cross Rly Co* (1867) LR 2 CP 638.

8 *Metropolitan Board of Works v Metropolitan Rly Co* (1868) LR 3 CP 612; affd (1869) LR 4 CP 192, Ex Ch.

9 *New River Co v Johnson* (1860) 29 LJMC 93; *R v Metropolitan Board of Works* (1863) 32 LJQB 105; and cf *Bradford Corpn v Pickles* [1895] AC 587, HL.

10 *Hopkins v Great Northern Rly Co* (1877) 2 QBD 224, CA; cf *R v Cambrian Rly Co* (1871) LR 6 QB 422; and see *Dibden v Skirrow* [1908] 1 Ch 41, CA.

11 *R v Vaughan* (1868) LR 4 QB 190; *R v London Dock Co* (1836) 5 Ad & El 163.

12 *R v Hungerford Market Co, ex p Yeates* (1834) 1 Ad & El 668; *R v Hungerford Market Co, ex p Eyre* (1834) 1 Ad & El 676.

13 *Rhodes v Airedale Drainage Comrs* (1876) 1 CPD 402, CA.

14 *Fleming v Newport Rly Co* (1883) 8 App Cas 265, HL; *Furness Rly Co v Cumberland Co-operative Building Society* (1884) 52 LT 144, HL.

15 *R v Poulter* (1887) 20 QBD 132, CA; *Re Clarke and Wandsworth District Board of Works* (1868) 17 LT 549; *Birkenhead Corpn v London and North Western Rly Co* (1885) 15 QBD 572, CA; and cf *Knock v Metropolitan Rly Co* (1868) LR 4 CP 131; *Sydney Municipal Council v Young* [1898] AC 457, PC. Thus, an occupier of a public house situated by the side of a public footway was held not to be entitled to recover compensation for loss of business caused by certain streets which led to this footway being temporarily obstructed, whereby the access to the house was rendered inconvenient: *Ricket v Metropolitan Rly Co* (1867) LR 2 HL 175; and see *Bigg v London Corpn* (1873) LR 15 Eq 376. As to remoteness of damage see generally DAMAGES.

16 See eg *Vanderpant v Mayfair Hotel Co Ltd* [1930] 1 Ch 138; *Harper v G N Haden & Sons Ltd* [1933] Ch 298, CA; *Ricket v Metropolitan Rly Co* (1867) LR 2 HL 175.

17 See *Lyon v Fishmongers' Co* (1876) 1 App Cas 662, HL; *North Shore Rly Co v Pion* (1889) 14 App Cas 612, PC (rivers); *R v Rynd* (1863) 16 ICLR 29; *A-G of Straits Settlement v Wemyss* (1888) 13 App Cas 192 at 195, PC (sea).

18 *A-G v Thames Conservators* (1862) 1 Hem & M 1 at 31–32; *Lyon v Fishmongers' Co* (1876) 1 App Cas 662, HL; *Marshall v Blackpool Corpn* [1935] AC 16 at 22, HL; *Rose v Groves* (1843) 5 Man & G 613. As to the right of access to the highway of an adjoining owner see further HIGHWAYS.

19 See para 326 ante.

20 *Moore v Great Southern and Western Rly Co* (1858) 10 ICLR 46, Ex Ch (lowering level of road alongside premises); *Tuohey v Great Southern and Western Rly Co* (1859) 10 ICLR 98 (raising level of road); *R v Eastern Counties Rly Co* (1841) 2 QB 347 (lowering level of road); *Caledonian Rly Co v Walker's Trustees* (1882) 7 App Cas 259, HL (access made steeper); *Beckett v Midland Rly Co* (1867) LR 3 CP 82; *Chamberlain v West End of London and Crystal Palace Rly Co* (1862) 2 B & S 605; affd (1863) 2 B & S 617, Ex Ch (access made narrower). See also *Wedmore v Bristol Corpn* (1862) 7 LT 459; *R v Wallasey Local Board of Health* (1869) LR 4 QB 351; *R v St Luke's, Chelsea* (1871) LR 7 QB 148, Ex Ch; *Pearsall v Brierley Hill Local Board* (1883) 11 QBD 735, CA; affd sub nom *Brierley Hill Local Board v Pearsall* (1884) 9 App Cas 595, HL; and see *R v Eastern Counties Rly Co* (1841) 2 QB 347; *Arnott v Whitby UDC* (1909) 101 LT 14; *Re McMullen and Ulster Rly Co* (1863) Ir Reserved Cas 35.

21 *Metropolitan Board of Works v McCarthy* (1874) LR 7 HL 243; *Macey v Metropolitan Board of Works* (1864) 33 LJ Ch 377; *Re Wadham and North Eastern Rly Co* (1884) 14 QBD 747; on appeal (1885) 16 QBD 227, CA; and cf *R v Metropolitan Board of Works* (1869) LR 4 QB 358; *Duke of Buccleuch v Metropolitan Board of Works* (1872) LR 5 HL 418; *Bell v Hull and Selby Rly Co* (1840) 6 M & W 699; *A-G of-Southern Nigeria v John Holt & Co (Liverpool) Ltd* [1915] AC 599, PC; *Hewett v Essex County Council* (1928) 138 LT 742; *Blundy, Clarke & Co v London and North Eastern Rly Co* [1931] 2 KB 334, CA; and see note 14 supra.

22 *Glover v North Staffordshire Rly Co* (1851) 16 QB 912; *Furness Rly Co v Cumberland Co-operative Building Society* (1884) 52 LT 144, HL; *Ford v Metropolitan and Metropolitan District Rly Companies* (1886) 17 QBD 12, CA; *Barnard v Great Western Rly Co* (1902) 86 LT 798; *London School Board v Smith* [1895] WN 37; and cf *Great Central Rly Co v Balby-with-Hexthorpe UDC, A-G v Great Central Rly Co* [1912] 2 Ch 110. As to blocking up access to a ferry see *R v Great Northern Rly Co* (1849) 14 QB 25. However, rights of way and statutory rights over land may be subject to special provisions for their extinguishment or special provision enabling them to be overridden: see eg the Town and Country Planning Act 1990 ss 236, 237, 251; and TOWN AND COUNTRY PLANNING vol 46 (Reissue) paras 778–779; HIGHWAYS vol 21 (Reissue) para 160.

23 *Eagle v Charing Cross Rly Co* (1867) LR 2 CP 638; *Clark v London School Board* (1874) 9 Ch App 120; *R v Poulter* (1887) 20 QBD 132, CA; *Wigram v Fryer* (1887) 36 ChD 87; *Re London, Tilbury and Southend Rly Co and Trustees of Gower's Walk Schools* (1889) 24 QBD 326, CA; *Courage & Co v South Eastern Rly Co* (1902) 19 TLR 61; *Emsley v North Eastern Rly Co* [1896] 1 Ch 418, CA.

24 See *Re Simeon and Isle of Wight RDC* [1937] Ch 525, [1937] 3 All ER 149.

25 See *Metropolitan Board of Works v Metropolitan Rly Co* (1868) LR 3 CP 612; affd (1869) LR 4 CP 192, Ex Ch; explained in *Roderick v Aston Local Board* (1877) 5 ChD 328, CA.

26 Riparian owners will be similarly entitled to compensation for interference with the natural flow of water (*R v Nottingham Old Waterworks Co* (1837) 6 Ad & El 355), as where part of the water is diverted, but where the whole of a stream was appropriated for waterworks under the Water Act 1945 s 24, Sch 3 (now repealed), it was deemed to be a taking and not merely an injurious affection, for the purposes of compensation (see *Ferrand v Bradford Corpn* (1856) 21 Beav 412; *Bush v Trowbridge Waterworks Co* (1875) 10 Ch App 459; *Stone v Yeovil Corpn* (1876) 2 CPD 99, CA; *Page v Kettering Waterworks Co* (1892) 8 TLR 228; and see *Stainton v Woolrych, Stainton v Metropolitan Board of Works and Lewisham District Board of Works* (1857) 26 LJ Ch 300); see also WATER. As to compensation for the occasional flooding of land even though the works were properly executed see *Ware v Regent's Canal Co* (1858) 3 De G & J 212 at 227; *Marriage v East Norfolk Rivers Catchment Board* [1950] 1 KB 284, [1949] 2 All ER 1021, CA.

27 *Kirby v Harrogate School Board* [1896] 1 Ch 437, CA; *Long Eaton Recreation Grounds Co v Midland Rly Co* [1902] 2 KB 574, CA; cf *Baily v De Crespigny* (1869) LR 4 QB 180 at 189. Thus, if land taken has been subject to a covenant restricting the class of buildings which may be erected, the erection by the undertakers or the acquiring authority of a different class will render them liable to pay compensation to the covenantee, and so will the breach by them of the covenant against carrying on a noisy and offensive trade (*Long Eaton Recreation Grounds Co v Midland Rly Co*, supra), or of a covenant for quiet enjoyment (*Manchester, Sheffield and Lincolnshire Rly Co v Anderson* [1898] 2 Ch 394 at 401, CA). Breach of a covenant not to interfere with the water supply from the land taken to the adjoining land may give rise to a claim for compensation: see *Re Simeon and Isle of Wight RDC* [1937] Ch 525, [1937] 3 All ER 149.

28 *Furness Rly Co v Cumberland Co-operative Building Society* (1884) 52 LT 144, HL (duty to lay out streets); and see *Re Masters and Great Western Rly Co* [1901] 2 KB 84, CA. As to the undertakers' duty to enter into a covenant to indemnify the lessee against breaches see *Harding v Metropolitan Rly Co* (1872) 7 Ch App 154. As to the effect of taking part of land let on a building agreement see *Re Furness and Willesden UDC* (1905) 70 JP 25.

29 As to sporting rights see *Bird v Great Eastern Rly Co* (1865) 34 LJCP 366; *Webber v Lee* (1882) 9 QBD 315, CA. However, these rights may be subject to acquisition as interests in land: see the National Parks and Access to the Countryside Act 1949 s 103(6) (amended by the Acquisition of Land Act 1980 s 34, Sch 6 Pt I).

356. Injury from construction or user of works. Where the special Act[1] provides for compensation for injury from construction of works, a claim for injury caused by the execution of works under the applicable provision of the Lands Clauses Consolidation Act 1845[2] or of the Compulsory Purchase Act 1965[3] is limited to injury from construction of works[4] and no claim will lie for injury by user[5], for example by noise, vibration and smoke[6], except under other statutory provisions for compensation[7].

In Acts authorising underground railways in London a clause providing for compensation for injurious affection by reason of vibration caused by the working of the railway has been inserted, and clauses with a similar object are commonly inserted in special Acts for the protection of individual owners[8].

Where an Act authorises the acquisition of land for the construction of works, it may be a necessary implication that the Act authorised the operation of the completed works, with the result that there is no remedy so far as nuisance was the inevitable result of the authorised operation[9].

1 For the meaning of 'the special Act' see paras 11, 16 ante.

2 Ie under the Lands Clauses Consolidation Act 1845 s 68 (as amended): see paras 200, 354 ante.

3 Ie under the Compulsory Purchase Act 1965 s 10 (as amended): see paras 200, 354 ante.

4 Injury to the trade of a ferry by the opening and use of a bridge constructed under statutory powers is not an injury by construction: see *Hopkins v Great Northern Rly Co* (1877) 2 QBD 224, CA; overruling *R v Cambrian Rly Co* (1871) LR 6 QB 422.

5 *Hammersmith and City Rly Co v Brand* (1869) LR 4 HL 171, decided with respect to the Railways Clauses Consolidation Act 1845 s 6 (as amended), which incorporates the Lands Clauses Acts and requires compensation to be paid in respect of injurious affection by the 'construction' of the railway. As to the Lands Clauses Acts see para 11 ante.

6 See *A-G v Metropolitan Rly Co* [1894] 1 QB 384, CA; *Caledonian Rly Co v Ogilvy* (1855) 2 Macq 229, HL; *Holditch v Canadian Northern Ontario Rly Co* [1916] 1 AC 536, PC.

7 See the Land Compensation Act 1973 Pt I (ss 1–19) (as amended); and para 359 et seq post. Where, however, the special Act provides for compensation in respect of construction and maintenance there is a right to compensation for construction and user: *Fletcher v Birkenhead Corpn* [1907] 1 KB 205, CA (distinguishing *Hammersmith and City Rly Co v Brand* (1869) LR 4 HL 171); applied in *Re Simeon and Isle of Wight RDC* [1937] Ch 525 at 539, [1937] 3 All ER 149 at 155–156 per Luxmoore J.

8 See eg *Re London and North Western Rly Co and Reddaway* (1907) 71 JP 150. In Acts authorising railway works the undertakers may be required to underpin or strengthen nearby houses or buildings at the request of owners and lessees to avoid injury in the execution and maintenance of the works, and are liable to compensate for loss or damage resulting from this power to underpin and strengthen: see the British Transport Commission Act 1949 s 17 (repealed). The British Transport Commission was dissolved on 1 January 1964. The functions of the Commission were transferred to other bodies, and in this case to the British Railways Board: see the Transport Act 1962 s 32.

9 *Allen v Gulf Oil Refining Ltd* [1981] AC 1001, [1981] 1 All ER 353, HL; and see para 335 text and note 10 ante.

357. Injury to the value of land. Where the right to compensation is derived only from the Lands Clauses Acts or the Compulsory Purchase Act 1965, compensation may be claimed only in respect of injury to the value of the land or an interest in land[1]. If there is a physical interference with some right, public or private, which the owners or occupiers of property are by law entitled to make use of in connection with that property, and which right gives an additional market value to that property apart from the uses to which any particular owner or occupier might put it, and by reason of that interference the property is lessened in value, there will be a right to compensation[2].

Where the interference is only temporary but is such that, if perpetual, it would give a ground for compensation, it will attract compensation[3].

1 As to the terms of that compensation see paras 353–354 ante; and *Caledonian Rly Co v Walker's Trustees* (1882) 7 App Cas 259 at 276, HL, per Lord Selborne LC. Under other Acts, such as the Public Health Act 1936 s 278 (as amended), compensation may be claimed for losses of a personal nature. See eg *Re Bater and Birkenhead Corpn* [1893] 1 QB 679; affd [1893] 2 QB 77, CA; *Lingké v Christchurch Corpn* [1912] 3 KB 595, CA. However, the only compensation which can be awarded under the Lands Clauses Consolidation Act 1845 s 68 (as amended), is compensation in respect of some loss of value of the land; compensation cannot be awarded for loss which is personal to the owner of the land or which is related to some particular user of the land: *Argyle Motors (Birkenhead) Ltd v Birkenhead Corpn* [1975] AC 99, [1974] 1 All ER 201, HL. As to the Lands Clauses Acts see para 11 ante.

2 *Metropolitan Board of Works v McCarthy* (1874) LR 7 HL 243 at 253, 256. Personal inconvenience caused by a level crossing near a house will not furnish a ground for compensation if the property itself is not depreciated in value (*Caledonian Rly Co v Ogilvy* (1855) 2 Macq 229, HL; *Wood v Stourbridge Rly Co* (1864) 16 CBNS 222), nor will loss of trade or custom occasioned by a work not otherwise directly affecting the house or land in or upon which the trade has been carried on, or any right properly incident to that house or land (*Caledonian Rly Co v Walker's Trustees* (1882) 7 App Cas 259 at 276, HL, per Lord Selborne LC), unless the interference depreciates the value of the land (see *Metropolitan Board of Works v Howard* (1889) 5 TLR 732, HL (diversion of traffic by erection of new bridge)). See also *Hewett v Essex County Council* (1928) 138 LT 742 (interference with access to a wharf where all loss, apart from depreciation of the value of the wharf was excluded). Further, loss of trade or diminution in the value of goodwill is excluded unless it affects the market value of the premises: see *Re Harvey and LCC* [1909] 1 Ch 528; *Eagle v Charing Cross Rly Co* (1867) LR 2 CP 638; *Hammersmith and City Rly Co v Brand* (1869) LR 4 HL 171 at 198; *Argyle Motors (Birkenhead) Ltd v Birkenhead Corpn* [1975] AC 99 at 114, [1973] 1 All ER 866 at 877, CA; affd [1975] AC 99, [1974] 1 All ER 201, HL.

3 *Ford v Metropolitan and Metropolitan District Rly Companies* (1886) 17 QBD 12, CA; *Lingké v Christchurch Corpn* [1912] 3 KB 595 at 607, CA.

358. Claim for compensation. A claim for compensation may be made when the injury by the works has occurred[1], but no claim lies for an injury which is merely prospective[2]. The claim must then be made for all damage which is capable of being foreseen, and the compensation must be assessed once and for all; no further claim may be made in respect of that injury[3], but new acts which would otherwise give rise to a further cause of action will be ground for a new claim[4].

The period of limitation is six years from the time when the cause of claim for compensation arose[5]. Any question of disputed compensation is within the jurisdiction of the Lands Tribunal[6].

If the right to compensation is established, the amount of compensation under the Lands Clauses Acts is commonly determined by the ordinary rules applicable to damages in actions in tort[7]. The compensation is for injury to the market value of the land as it is, and also in respect of any use to which the land may be put in its existing state[8]; it is the difference between the market value before injury and the market value after injury[9], and in assessing the value after injury there is no right to take into account a general increase in the value of property by reason of the works or their imminence[10]. When, under a statute, a person is entitled to full compensation for all damage, once the right to it is established, the amount of compensation may properly include a sum for damage caused by acts in themselves legal, but which could not have been committed had there been no interference with the claimant's legal rights[11].

Compensation[12] carries interest at the rate for the time being prescribed[13] from the date of the claim until payment[14]. There is provision for advance payments on account of compensation and accrued interest[15].

1   *Macey v Metropolitan Board of Works* (1864) 33 LJ Ch 377; *Stone v Yeovil Corpn* (1876) 2 CPD 99, CA; *Chamberlain v West End of London and Crystal Palace Rly Co* (1863) 2 B & S 617 at 638, Ex Ch.
2   *R v Poulter* (1887) 20 QBD 132, CA.
3   See the cases cited in note 1 supra.
4   *Stone v Yeovil Corpn* (1876) 2 CPD 99, CA; and cf *Darley Main Colliery Co v Mitchell* (1886) 11 App Cas 127, HL.
5   *Pegler v Rly Executive* [1948] AC 332, [1948] 1 All ER 559, HL; applied *in Vincent v Thames Conservancy* (1953) 4 P & CR 66, Lands Tribunal. See now the Limitation Act 1980 ss 9, 34.
6   Lands Tribunal Act 1949 s 1(3)(b) (amended by the Land Compensation Act 1961 s 40(3), Sch 5): see para 200 ante.
7   *Re London, Tilbury and Southend Rly Co and Trustees of Gower's Walk Schools* (1889) 24 QBD 326 at 329, CA, per Lord Fisher; *Re Clarke and Wandsworth District Board of Works* (1868) 17 LT 549; cf *R v Thames and Isis Navigation Comrs* (1836) 5 Ad & El 804; and see DAMAGES. As to the Lands Clauses Acts see para 11 ante.
8   *Beckett v Midland Rly Co* (1867) LR 3 CP 82 at 95; *Re Wadham and North Eastern Rly Co* (1884) 14 QBD 747; on appeal (1885) 16 QBD 227, CA; and see *Metropolitan Board of Works v Howard* (1889) 5 TLR 732, HL; *Hewett v Essex County Council* (1928) 138 LT 742.
9   *Re Wadham and North Eastern Rly Co* (1884) 14 QBD 747; on appeal (1885) 16 QBD 227, CA.
10 See *Eagle v Charing Cross Rly Co* (1867) LR 2 CP 638; *Senior v Metropolitan Rly Co* (1863) 32 LJ Ex 225.
11 *Re London, Tilbury and Southend Rly Co and Trustees of Gower's Walk Schools* (1889) 24 QBD 326, CA, where a railway company had erected a warehouse which obstructed some ancient lights of the claimants and also some other lights in respect of which no right existed, which latter could not have been interfered with but for the interference with the former; the company was held liable to pay for all the damage occasioned to the property. However, see *Horton v Colwyn Bay and Colwyn UDC* [1907] 1 KB 14 at 22–23 per Bigham J; on appeal [1908] 1 KB 327, CA, where at 339, 343, it was held that the owner who received compensation in respect of land taken and land held with it injuriously affected was not entitled to compensation for injury to other land of his by works on the land taken from him because he would not have had a right of action for that injury but for the statutory powers. The measure of compensation may be given by express enactment as in the Railway Fires Act 1905 s 2(3). As to the meaning of 'full compensation' in relation to costs see *Barnett v Eccles Corpn* [1900] 2 QB 423, CA.
12 Ie under the Lands Clauses Consolidation Act 1845 s 68 (as amended); or the Compulsory Purchase Act 1965 s 10 (as amended): see paras 200, 354 ante.

13 Ie under the Land Compensation Act 1961 s 32: see para 125 ante.
14 See the Land Compensation Act 1973 s 63(1); and para 200 ante.
15 See ibid s 52 (as amended), s 52A (as added); and paras 136–138 ante. Payments on account may be recoverable where it is subsequently agreed or determined that there was no liability to pay the compensation or interest or that the payment on account was excessive: see the Planning and Compensation Act s 80(2), (3), Sch 18 Pt II; and para 200 ante.

(7) COMPENSATION FOR INJURY BY NOISE, VIBRATION ETC

(i) Right to Compensation

359. Extension of rights to compensation. Some special Acts[1] and some public general Acts which give powers and authorise works contain a compensation clause of the widest kind, not limited to injury to the value of the land[2]. In most modern statutes compensation for injury to land by the execution of statutory powers is provided for by the incorporation in the special Act of certain provisions of the Lands Clauses Consolidation Act 1845[3] or by the application to the empowering enactment of certain provisions of the Compulsory Purchase Act 1965[4], and the compensation may by virtue of the empowering enactment be applicable to injury by the construction and maintenance of works, so that there will be a right to compensation for such things as noise and vibration in use and construction[5]. In some cases, however, the right to compensation is limited to injury by construction, and then there can be no compensation for injury by such things as noise and vibration except during the period of construction[6].

However, the Land Compensation Act 1973, where it applies,[7] gives a right to compensation for injury to the value of land by noise, vibration, smell etc by the use of public works for which there would otherwise be a right of action arising after the first use of the works after completion, or alteration, or change of use after construction[8], and there may be a claim under that Act and under the statutes mentioned above, but compensation is not payable twice in respect of the same depreciation[9]. Moreover, that first use must have occurred after 17 October 1969[10].

In the case of highways, anyone may dedicate a highway and if the public accepts it by user there is no right of action for injury to the value of land by the user by the public, except in the case of special damage by excessive or negligent user by a member of the public using the highway[11]. The construction and dedication of a highway under statute by the highway authority opening it to the public is not, therefore, a statutory authorisation of that which would otherwise be unlawful, and no compensation for injury by user of the highway is payable, even where the provisions of the Lands Clauses Consolidation Act 1845[12] or of the Compulsory Purchase Act 1965[13] are applicable; but a right to compensation for injury to the value of land by the use of a highway is given by certain provisions of the Land Compensation Act 1973[14] in the case of a highway maintainable at the public expense when constructed or where the carriageway of the highway is altered[15] if the highway is first open to public traffic after 17 October 1969[16]; and such a claim is not subject to the limitation that compensation is only payable where there would otherwise be a right of action[17].

1 For the meaning of 'the special Act' see paras 11, 16 ante.
2 See eg the Public Health Act 1936 s 278 (as amended). In *George Whitehouse Ltd (t/a Clarke Bros (Services)) v Anglian Water Authority* [1978] 2 EGLR 168, Lands Tribunal, claimants were held entitled

under the Public Health Act 1936 s 278 (as amended) for losses caused by the laying in the highway of a public sewer, including damage caused by the breaking open of the street, the cost of removing mud and dust from cars displayed for sale, and for loss of profits due to obstruction of the road during the works. See also the Public Health (Control of Disease) Act 1984 s 57; and PUBLIC HEALTH.

3   Ie the Lands Clauses Consolidation Act 1845 s 68 (as amended): see paras 200, 354 ante.
4   Ie by the Compulsory Purchase Act 1965 s 10 (as amended): see paras 200, 354 ante.
5   See para 354 ante.
6   See para 356 ante.
7   Ie the Land Compensation Act 1973 Pt I (ss 1–19) (as amended): see para 360 et seq post.
8   See ibid s 1 (as amended), s 9; and paras 360–361 post.
9   See ibid s 8(7); and para 364 post.
10 See ibid s 1(8); and para 367 post.
11 See HIGHWAYS.
12 Ie the provisions of the Lands Clauses Consolidation Act 1845 s 68 (as amended): see para 354 ante.
13 Ie the provisions of the Compulsory Purchase Act 1965 s 10 (as amended): see para 354 ante.
14 Ie the Land Compensation Act 1973 Pt I (as amended): see para 360 et seq post.
15 See ibid ss 1 (as amended), 9; and paras 360–361 post.
16 See ibid s 1(8); and para 367 post.
17 See ibid s 1(6) (as amended); and para 360 post.

360. Compensation after construction and use of public works. Where the value of an interest in land[1] is depreciated by physical factors[2] (other than those which are caused by accidents involving vehicles on a highway[3] or accidents involving aircraft[4]), caused by the use of public works[5], then, if (1) the interest qualifies for compensation[6]; and (2) the person entitled to the interest makes a claim after the time provided by, and otherwise in accordance with, the appropriate provisions[7], compensation for that depreciation may be payable by the responsible authority[8] to the person making the claim ('the claimant')[9].

No compensation is payable on any claim unless the relevant date[10] in relation to the claim falls on or after 17 October 1969[11].

Compensation is not payable in respect of physical factors caused by the use of any public works other than a highway unless immunity from actions for nuisance in respect of that use is conferred, whether expressly or by implication, by an enactment relating to those works[12], or, in the case of an aerodrome and physical factors caused by aircraft, the aerodrome is one in respect of which the Civil Aviation Act 1982[13] gives immunity from actions for nuisance in respect of noise and vibration caused by aircraft on an aerodrome[14].

There is no right to compensation under these provisions in respect of any aerodrome in the occupation of a government department[15].

1   'Land' includes, among other things, houses and buildings: see the Interpretation Act 1978 ss 5, 22, Sch 1 para 4(1)(a), Sch 2 para 5(b).
2   'Physical factors' means noise, vibration, smell, fumes, smoke, artificial lighting or the discharge on to the land in respect of which the claim is made of any solid or liquid substance: Land Compensation Act 1973 s 1(2). Physical factors caused by all aircraft arriving at or departing from an aerodrome must be treated as caused by the use of the aerodrome, but, otherwise, the source of the physical factors must be situated on or in the public works the use of which is alleged to be their cause: s 1(5). 'Claim' means a claim under Pt I (ss 1–19) (as amended): s 19(1). For the meaning of 'public works' see note 5 infra; and for the meaning of 'aerodrome' see para 337 note 1 ante. Danger and appreciation of danger are not physical factors; nor are they expressly covered in s 1(2): *Hickmott v Dorset County Council* (1975) 233 EG 1009, Lands Tribunal; affd (1977) 35 P & CR 195, [1977] 2 EGLR 15, CA; *Stuart and Stuart v British Airports Authority* [1983] RVR 161, Lands Tribunal for Scotland. In *Barb v Secretary of State for Transport, Rigby v Secretary of State for Transport* [1978] 2 EGLR 171, Lands Tribunal, depreciation to the value of two residential properties by traffic noise from a nearby motorway was held to be 7.5% of value, the properties being 620 metres and 730 metres from the motorway. £1,000 compensation was awarded

for motorway traffic noise in *Marchant v Secretary of State for Transport* [1979] 1 EGLR 194, Lands Tribunal; and £2000 in *Maile and Brock v West Sussex County Council* [1984] 1 EGLR 194, Lands Tribunal; but nil eg in *Hallows v Welsh Office* [1995] 1 EGLR 191, Lands Tribunal. As to the effect of physical factors generally see *Arkell v Department of Transport* [1983] 2 EGLR 181, Lands Tribunal; *Fallows v Gateshead Metropolitan Borough Council* (1993) 66 P & CR 460, Lands Tribunal. The upgrading of an existing road was the cause of the physical factors in *Broom and Broom v Department of Transport* [1993] RVR 218, Lands Tribunal. Compensation for the effect of aircraft noise was assessed at 10% for a house situated near a new runway constructed at Turnhouse Airport, Edinburgh: see *Inglis v British Airports Authority (No 2)* [1979] RVR 266, Lands Tribunal. Work carried out in three phases to Cardiff (South Wales) Airport was held a single project and compensation of £1,600 was payable to the owner of a nearby house: *Davies v Mid-Glamorgan County Council* [1979] 2 EGLR 158, Lands Tribunal. Compensation for loss in value of a house caused by noise and fumes from traffic on a length of highway which had undergone minor alterations as part of a larger scheme, including a new river bridge, could take into account the increase in traffic on the altered highway due to the bridge: *Williamson v Cumbria County Council* [1995] RVR 102, Lands Tribunal. No compensation is payable in respect of the psychological effect of a rubbish tip: *Shepherd v Lancashire County Council* (1976) 33 P & CR 296, Lands Tribunal. Artificial lighting refers to illumination caused by street lighting, even if that illumination is of low intensity, and not to the lighting structures themselves: *Blower v Suffolk County Council* (1994) 67 P & CR 228, Lands Tribunal.

 3 For the meaning of 'highway' see para 337 note 3 ante.
 4 Land Compensation Act 1973 s 1(7).
 5 'Public works' for this purpose means any highway, any aerodrome, and any works or land (not being a highway or aerodrome) provided or used in the exercise of statutory powers: ibid s 1(3). See also note 15 infra.
 6 Ibid s 1(1)(a). As to interests which qualify see para 362 post.
 7 Ibid s 1(1)(b) (amended by the Local Government, Planning and Land Act 1980 s 112(1), (3)). As to the appropriate procedures see paras 366–367 post.
 8 In relation to a highway, 'responsible authority' means the appropriate highway authority and in relation to other public works it means the person managing those works: Land Compensation Act 1973 s 1(4). See also note 15 infra. For the meaning of 'appropriate highway authority' see para 337 note 3 ante.
 9 Ibid s 1(1). As to claims see s 3 (as amended); and paras 366–367 post. As to the assessment of compensation see ss 4, 5 (as amended); and para 368 et seq post. As to betterment reducing compensation see s 6 (as amended); and para 373 post.
10 'Relevant date' means (1) in relation to a claim in respect of a highway, the date on which it was first open to public traffic (ibid s 1(9)(a)); or, in the case of a highway which has not always since 17 October 1969 been a highway maintainable at the public expense, the date on which it was first so open whether or not as a highway so maintainable (s 19(3)(a)), and no claim may be made if the relevant date falls at a time when the highway was not so maintainable and the highway does not become so maintainable within three years of that date (s 19(3) (amended by the Local Government, Planning and Land Act 1980 s 112(1), (8), Sch 34 Pt XII); and (2) in relation to a claim in respect of other public works, the date on which they were first used after completion (Land Compensation Act 1973 s 1(9)(b)).
    The responsible authority must keep a record and, on demand, furnish a statement in writing of the date on which the highway was first open to public traffic and of the date when public works were first used after completion: see s 15(1)(a), (b); and para 361 post.
11 Ibid s 1(8).
12 As to immunity from actions for nuisance by implication, ie by a statute making lawful that which would otherwise be unlawful, see paras 353–358 ante. In *Vickers v Dover District Council* [1993] 1 EGLR 193, Lands Tribunal, a claim under the Land Compensation Act 1973 s 1 (as amended) for depreciation in the value of land by physical factors caused by the use of public works was dismissed; the tribunal held that the Road Traffic Regulation Act 1984 s 32 (as amended) was entirely permissive and therefore did not, either expressly or by implication, confer on the council immunity from actions for nuisance within the meaning of the Land Compensation Act 1973 s 1(6) (as amended: see note 14 infra).
13 Ie the Civil Aviation Act 1982 s 77(2): see AVIATION vol 2 (Reissue) paras 1185, 1687.
14 Land Compensation Act 1973 s 1(6) (amended by the Civil Aviation Act 1982 s 109(2), Sch 15 para 12(1)).
15 Land Compensation Act 1973 s 84(1). Subject to that, references in Pt I (ss 1–19) (as amended) to public works and responsible authorities include any works or authority which, apart from any Crown exemption, would be public works or a responsible authority: s 84(1).

361. Alterations to and changes of use of public works. Where, whether before, on or after 23 June 1973[1]:

    (1) the carriageway of a highway[2] has been altered[3] after the highway has been open to public traffic[4];

    (2) any public works[5] other than a highway have been reconstructed, extended or otherwise altered after they have been first used[6]; or

    (3) there has been a change of use[7] in respect of any public works, other than a highway or aerodrome[8],

then if and so far as a claim[9] in respect of the highway or other public works relates to depreciation that would not have been caused but for the alterations[10] or change of use, the relevant date for the purposes of a claim will be:

    (a) the date on which the highway was first open to public traffic after completion of the alterations to the carriageway[11];

    (b) the date on which the other public works were first used after completion of the alterations[12]; or

    (c) the date of the change of use[13],

as the case may be[14].

  1 Ie the commencement date of the Land Compensation Act 1973 Pt I (ss 1–19) (as amended): ss 19(1), 89(2).

  2 For the meaning of 'highway' see para 337 note 3 ante.

  3 For these purposes, the carriageway of a highway is altered if, and only if, (1) the location, width or level of the carriageway is altered otherwise than by resurfacing; or (2) an additional carriageway is provided for the highway beside, above or below an existing one: Land Compensation Act 1973 s 9(5)(a), (b).

  4 Ibid s 9(1)(a). As to compensation for injury after the first opening for public traffic by use after construction of a highway see s 1 (as amended); and para 360 ante.

  5 For the meaning of 'public works' see para 360 note 4 ante.

  6 Land Compensation Act 1973 s 9(1)(b). As to compensation for injury after the date of the first use after completion of the works see s 1 (as amended); and para 360 ante.

  7 References to a change of use do not include references to the intensification of an existing use: ibid s 9(7).

  8 Ibid s 9(1)(c). For the meaning of 'aerodrome' see para 337 note 1 ante.

  9 For the meaning of 'claim' see para 360 note 2 ante. As to claims see ibid s 3 (as amended); and paras 366–367 post. As to the assessment of compensation see ss 4, 5 (as amended); and para 368 et seq post. As to betterment reducing compensation see s 6 (as amended); and para 373 post.

     The responsible authority in relation to a highway or other public works must keep a record and, on demand, furnish a written statement of: (1) the date on which the highway was first open to public traffic after completion of any particular alterations to the carriageway of the highway; (2) the date on which the public works were first used after completion of any particular alterations to those works; (3) in the case of public works other than a highway or aerodrome, the date on which there was a change of use in respect of the public works: s 15(1). However, the above duty will apply only in respect of the dates mentioned in heads (1)–(3) supra which fall on or after 23 June 1973: see s 15(3). References to alterations to the carriageway of a highway, to runway or apron alterations and to a change of use must be construed in the sane way as in s 9: s 15(3); and see notes 7 supra, 10 infra. A certificate by the Secretary of State stating that runway or apron alterations (see note 10 infra) have or have not been carried out at an aerodrome and the date on which an aerodrome at which any such alterations have been carried out was first used after completion of the alterations is conclusive evidence of the facts stated: s 15(2). As to the responsible authority see para 360 note 8 ante.

  10 Ibid s 9(2) (see the text and notes 11–14 infra) does not, by virtue of any alterations to an aerodrome, apply to a claim in respect of physical factors caused by aircraft, unless the alterations are runway or apron alterations: ibid s 9(3). 'Runway or apron alterations' means (1) the construction of a new runway, the major realignment of an existing runway or the extension or strengthening of an existing runway; or (2) a substantial addition to, or alteration of, a taxiway or apron, being an addition or alteration whose purpose or main purpose is the provision of facilities for a greater number of aircraft: s 9(6). As to the meaning of 'physical factors' see para 360 note 2 ante.

  11 Ibid s 9(2)(a). The reference to depreciation that would not have been caused but for alterations to the carriageway of a highway is a reference to such depreciation by physical factors which are caused by the use of, and the source of which is situated on, the length of carriageway which has been altered as

mentioned in s 9(5)(a) (see note 3 head (1) supra) or, as the case may be, the additional carriageway and the corresponding length of the existing one mentioned in s 9(5)(b) (see note 3 head (2) supra): s 9(5).
12 Ibid s 9(2)(b).
13 Ibid s 9(2)(c).
14 Ibid s 9(2). As to the time for claims in relation to the relevant date see s 1(8), (9); and para 360 text and notes 9–10 ante.

362. Interests qualifying for compensation; in general.

An interest which is an owner's interest[1] or an owner-occupier's interest[2] qualifies for compensation if it was acquired[3] by the claimant before the relevant date[4]. However, this does not apply to any interest acquired by the claimant by inheritance[5] from a person who acquired that interest, or a greater interest out of which it is derived, before the relevant date[6].

On the date on which notice of claim for compensation in respect of an interest is served, the claimant, if and so far as the interest is in land which is a dwelling[7], must have an owner's interest[8]; and where the interest carries the right to occupy the land, the land must be occupied by the claimant in right of that interest as his residence[9]. If and so far as the interest is not in land which is a dwelling, the claimant must have an interest which is that of an owner-occupier[10] and the land must be or form part of either a hereditament, the annual value[11] of which does not exceed the prescribed amount[12], or an agricultural unit[13].

1   In relation to any land 'owner's interest' means the legal fee simple in the land, or a tenancy of it granted or extended for a term of years certain of which, on the date of service of the notice of claim in respect of it, not less than three years remain unexpired: Land Compensation Act 1973 s 2(4). As to tenancies treated as owner's interests for these purposes see para 363 post. As to the situation where a potential claimant has disposed of a qualifying interest see para 365 post.
2   In relation to land in a hereditament, 'owner-occupier' means a person who occupies the whole or a substantial part of the land in right of an owner's interest in it and, in relation to land in an agricultural unit, means a person who occupies the whole of that unit and is entitled, while so occupying it, to an owner's interest in the whole or any part of that land: ibid s 2(5). 'Hereditament' has the meaning given in the Town and Country Planning Act 1990 s 171 (see TOWN AND COUNTRY PLANNING vol 46 (Reissue) para 729 note 6): Land Compensation Act 1973 s 2(6) (amended by the Planning (Consequential Provisions) Act 1990 s 4, Sch 2 para 29(1)). For the meaning of 'agricultural unit' see para 106 note 6 ante; and TOWN AND COUNTRY PLANNING vol 46 (Reissue) para 729 note 9.
3   An interest acquired pursuant to a contract must be treated as acquired when the contract was made: see the Land Compensation Act 1973 s 19(2).
4   See ibid s 2(1). For the meaning of 'relevant date' see para 360 note 9 ante.
5   An interest is acquired by a person by inheritance if it devolves on him by virtue only of testamentary dispositions taking effect on, or the law of intestate succession or the right of survivorship between joint tenants as applied to, the death of another person or the successive deaths of two or more other persons: ibid ss 2(7), 11(2). A person who acquires an interest by appropriation of it in or towards satisfaction of any legacy, share in residue or other share in the estate of a deceased person must be treated as a person on whom the interest devolves by direct bequest: ss 2(7), 11(3).
    Where an interest is settled land for the purposes of the Settled Land Act 1925 and on the death of a tenant for life within the meaning of that Act a person becomes entitled to the interest in accordance with the settlement, or by any appropriation by the personal representatives in respect of the settled land, the Land Compensation Act 1973 s 11(2) applies as if the interest had belonged to the tenant for life absolutely and the trusts of the settlement taking effect after his death had been the trusts of his will: ss 2(7), 11(4). This provision as to settled land applies, with any necessary modifications, where a person becomes entitled to an interest on the termination of a settlement as it would apply if he had become entitled in accordance with the terms of the settlement: ss 2(7), 11(5).
6   Ibid ss 2(7), 11(1).
7   For the meaning of 'dwelling' see para 283 note 1 ante.
8   Land Compensation Act 1973 s 2(1), (2)(a).
9   Ibid s 2(1), (2)(b). Where an interest in land is vested in trustees other than a sole tenant for life within the meaning of the Settled Land Act 1925 and a person beneficially entitled, whether directly or derivatively, under the trusts is entitled or permitted by reason of his interest to occupy the land, these provisions have effect as if occupation by that person were occupation by the trustees in right of the interest vested in them: Land Compensation Act 1973 ss 2(7), 10(4).

10 Ibid s 2(1), (3)(a).
11 'Annual value' has the meaning given in the Town and Country Planning Act 1990 s 171 (see TOWN
    AND COUNTRY PLANNING vol 46 (Reissue) para 729 note 12), taking references to the date of service
    of a notice under s 150 (as amended) as references to the date on which notice of the claim is served:
    Land Compensation Act 1973 s 2(6) (as amended: see note 2 supra).
12 'The prescribed amount' means the amount prescribed for the purposes of the Town and Country
    Planning Act 1990 s 149(3)(a) (see TOWN AND COUNTRY PLANNING vol 46 (Reissue) para 729 note
    13): Land Compensation Act 1973 s 2(6) (as amended: see note 2 supra). The prescribed amount is
    currently £18,000: see the Town and Country Planning (Blight Provisions) Order 1990, SI 1990/465,
    art 4 (having effect by virtue of the Planning (Consequential Provisions) Act 1990 s 2).
13 Land Compensation Act 1973 s 2(1), (3)(b).

363. Interests qualifying for compensation; qualifying tenancies. Certain
qualifying tenancies are treated as owner's interests for the purposes of the statutory
provisions relating to compensation for injury by noise or other physical factors[1]
whether or not the unexpired term on the date of service of the notice of claim[2] is of
the specified[3] length[4]. Such qualifying tenancies are:

(1) any tenancy by virtue of which a person is entitled under Part I of the Leasehold
     Reform Act 1967[5] to acquire the freehold or an extended lease of a house,
     where that person has on or before the relevant date[6] given the landlord notice
     under that Act of his desire to have the freehold or an extended lease, and has not
     acquired the freehold or an extended lease before that date[7];

(2) a tenancy where on the relevant date the tenant:
     (a) is a qualifying tenant in respect of the tenancy for the purposes of the
          provisions of the Leasehold Reform, Housing and Urban Development Act
          1993 relating to collective enfranchisement[8];
     (b) is by virtue of the tenancy either a participating tenant[9] in relation to a claim
          to exercise the right to collective enfranchisement under those provisions or
          one of the participating tenants on whose behalf the acquisition by the
          nominee purchaser[10] has been made in pursuance of such a claim[11];

(3) a tenancy where, on the relevant date and in respect of the tenancy, the tenant is
     a qualifying tenant for the purposes of the provisions of the 1993 Act conferring
     the individual right to acquire a new lease[12] who has given notice of a claim to
     exercise that right on or before the relevant date and who has not acquired a new
     lease before that date[13].

1 Ie owner's interests as defined in the Land Compensation Act 1973 s 2(4): see para 362 ante.
2 As to the notice of claim see para 366 post; and for the meaning of 'claim' see para 360 note 2 ante.
3 Ie the length specified in the Land Compensation Act 1973 s 2(4): see para 362 ante.
4 Ibid ss 12(2), 12A(1) (s 12A added by the Leasehold Reform, Housing and Urban Development Act
   1993 s 187(1), Sch 21 para 5).
5 Ie under the Leasehold Reform Act 1967 Pt I (ss 1–37) (as amended): see LANDLORD AND TENANT vol
   27(2) (Reissue) para 1253 et seq.
6 For the meaning of 'the relevant date' see para 360 note 9 ante.
7 Land Compensation Act 1973 s 12(1), (2). If no claim is made in respect of the qualifying tenancy before
   the claimant has ceased to be entitled to it by reason of his acquisition of the freehold or an extended
   lease, he may claim in respect of the qualifying tenancy as if he were still entitled to it: s 12(3). As to the
   time for that claim see s 12(4), (5) (as amended); and para 365 post. As to notice of claim see s 12(6); and
   para 366 post. As to assessment of the claim see ss 4(4), 12(7); and para 371 post.
8 Ie the Leasehold Reform, Housing and Urban Development Act 1993 Pt I Ch I (ss 1–38): see
   LANDLORD AND TENANT vol 27(2) (Reissue) para 1406 et seq.
9 For these purposes, 'participating tenant' is to be construed in accordance with ibid s 14 (see
   LANDLORD AND TENANT vol 27(2) (Reissue) paras 1441–1445): Land Compensation Act 1973
   s 12A(9) (as added: see note 4 supra).
10 For these purposes, 'nominee purchaser' is to be construed in accordance with the Leasehold Reform,
    Housing and Urban Development Act 1993 s 15; and 'the acquisition by the nominee purchaser' is to

be construed in accordance with s 38(2) (see LANDLORD AND TENANT vol 27(2) (Reissue) paras 1446–1450, 1451 note 8 respectively): Land Compensation Act 1973 s 12A(9) (as added: see note 4 supra).
11 Land Compensation Act 1973 s 12A(1), (2), (9)(a) (as added: see note 4 supra).
12 Ie the Leasehold Reform, Housing and Urban Development Act 1993 Pt I Ch II (ss 39–62): see LANDLORD AND TENANT vol 27(2) (Reissue) para 1523 et seq.
13 Land Compensation Act 1973 s 12A(1), (3), (9)(a) (as added: see note 4 supra). Section 12A (as so added) only applies where the relevant date occurs after 1 November 1993: Leasehold Reform, Housing and Urban Development Act 1993 (Commencement and Transitional Provisions No 1) Order 1993, SI 1993/2134, Sch 1 para 9. If no claim is made in respect of the qualifying tenancy before the claimant has ceased to be entitled to it in consequence of a lease being granted to him by the nominee purchaser or, as the case may be, under the Leasehold Reform, Housing and Urban Development Act 1993 Pt I Ch II, he may make a claim in respect of the qualifying tenancy as if he were still entitled to it: Land Compensation Act 1973 s 12A(4) (as so added). As to the time for that claim see s 12A(5), (6) (as so added); and para 365 post. As to notice of claim see s 12A(7) (as so added); and para 366 post. As to assessment of the claim see ss 4(4), 12A(8) (as so added); and para 371 post.

364. Limitation on right to compensation. Compensation is not payable in respect of the same depreciation both under the provisions relating to compensation for noise and other physical factors[1] and under any other enactment, except to the extent provided below[2].

Where a claim has been made in respect of depreciation of the value of an interest in land caused by the use of any public works[3] and compensation has been paid or is payable on that claim, compensation is not payable on any subsequent claim in relation to the same works and the same land or any part of it, whether in respect of the same or a different interest, except that, in the case of land which is a dwelling[4], this provision does not preclude the payment of compensation both on a claim in respect of the fee simple and on a claim in respect of a tenancy[5]. Furthermore, in the case of a claim for compensation for depreciation in the value of land after alterations of a highway or other public works or the change of use of public works other than a highway or aerodrome[6], these provisions do not preclude the payment of compensation unless the previous claim was in respect of depreciation that would not have been caused but for the same alterations or change of use[7]. Where a person is entitled to compensation in respect of the acquisition of an interest in land by an authority possessing compulsory purchase powers[8], or would be so entitled if the acquisition were compulsory, and

(1) the land is acquired for the purposes of any public works; and
(2) that person retains land which, in relation to the land acquired, constitutes other land within the meaning of the Lands Clauses Consolidation Act 1845[9] or the Compulsory Purchase Act 1965[10], so that the compensation for the acquisition will include compensation for injurious affection of that other land retained,

then, whether or not any sum is paid or payable in respect of injurious affection of the land retained, compensation is not payable under the provisions relating to noise or other physical factors[11] on any claim in relation to those works made after the date of service of the notice to treat[12], or, if the acquisition is by agreement, the date of the agreement, in respect of any interest in the land retained[13]. The above provisions do not, however, preclude the payment of compensation in the case of a claim for compensation for depreciation in the value of land after alterations of a highway or other public works or the change of use of public works other than a highway or aerodrome[14], unless the works for which the land was acquired were works resulting from the alterations, or works used for the purpose, to which the claim relates[15].

Where on or after 23 June 1973[16] an authority possessing compulsory purchase powers acquires land for the purposes of any public works and the person from whom the land is acquired retains land which, in relation to the land acquired, constitutes other land or lands within the meaning of the statutory provisions relating to injurious affection[17], the authority must deposit particulars of the land retained and the nature and extent of those works with the council of the district or London borough in which the land retained is situated[18]. Any particulars so deposited are a local land charge and for the purposes of the Local Land Charges Act 1975 the council with which any such particulars are deposited is treated as the originating authority as respects the charge thereby constituted[19]. Where the acquisition is on or after 23 June 1973, the public works for the purposes of which the land is acquired must be taken to be those specified in the relevant particulars registered as set out above[20].

1　Ie the Land Compensation Act 1973 Pt I (ss 1–19) (as amended): see paras 359 et seq ante, 365 et seq post.
2　Ibid s 8(7).
3　As to that claim see ibid s 1 (as amended), s 9; and paras 360–361 ante; and as to particulars of claim and service see s 3 (as amended); and para 366 post. For the meaning of 'public works' see para 360 note 4 ante.
4　For the meaning of 'dwelling' see para 283 note 1 ante.
5　Land Compensation Act 1973 s 8(1); and see *Bannocks v Secretary of State for Transport* [1995] RVR 57, Lands Tribunal.
6　See Land Compensation Act 1973 s 9(1)-(3); and para 361 ante. For the meaning of 'aerodrome' see para 337 note 1 ante.
7　Ibid s 9(4)(b).
8　For the meaning of 'authority possessing compulsory purchase powers' see para 244 note 6 ante (definition applied by ibid s 87(1)).
9　Ie within the meaning of the Lands Clauses Consolidation Act 1845 s 63: see para 291 ante.
10　Ie within the meaning of the Compulsory Purchase Act 1965 s 7: see para 291 ante.
11　See note 1 supra.
12　As to notice to treat see para 100 et seq ante.
13　Land Compensation Act 1973 s 8(2). Section 8(2) applies whether the acquisition is before, on or after 23 June 1973: s 8(3). The right to compensation under the Lands Clauses Consolidation Act 1845 s 63 or the Compulsory Purchase Act 1965 s 7 for injurious affection to the land retained is in respect of any works on the land taken from the owner and held with the land retained and also in respect of the statutory works partly on the land taken from the owner and partly elsewhere: see para 292 ante. Furthermore, the owner of the land taken may have other land not held with the land taken but injuriously affected by statutory works on land taken from him and on the land of others and for the injurious affection he may have a claim under the Lands Clauses Consolidation Act 1845 s 68 (as amended), or the Compulsory Purchase Act of 1965 s 10 (as amended) (see paras 200, 354 ante), and he is not precluded from the payment of compensation under the Land Compensation Act 1973 Pt I (as amended) in respect of depreciation by public works so far as situated elsewhere than on the land acquired (s 8(5)); nor would it seem that s 8(2) can operate to preclude a claim under Pt I (as amended) in respect of injury by works on the land acquired where the claim is not in respect of land severed and retained. However, compensation is not payable in respect of the same depreciation both under Pt I (as amended) and under any other enactment: see s 8(7); and the text and notes 1–2 supra.
14　See ibid s 9(1), (3); and para 361 ante.
15　Ibid s 9(4)(b).
16　As to this date see para 361 note 1 ante.
17　Ie the Lands Clauses Consolidation Act 1845 s 63 or the Compulsory Purchase Act 1965 s 7: see para 291 ante.
18　Land Compensation Act 1973 s 8(2)(b), (4) (s 8(4) amended by the Local Land Charges Act 1975 ss 17(2), 19(2)–(4), Sch 1; further prospectively amended by the Local Government (Wales) Act 1994 s 66(6), Sch 16 para 40(1), as from a day to be appointed under s 66(3), so as to include the words 'or Welsh county or county borough').
19　Land Compensation Act 1973 s 8(4A) (added by the Local Land Charges Act 1975 ss 17(2), 19(2)–(4), Sch 1).
20　Land Compensation Act 1973 s 8(3).

(ii) Claims for Compensation

365. Persons entitled to claim. The persons who may claim compensation are those who have a qualifying interest[1].

Where an interest is subject to a mortgage, a claim may be made by any mortgagee of the interest as if he were the person entitled to that interest but without prejudice to the making of a claim by that person[2] and no compensation is payable in respect of the interest of the mortgagee, as distinct from the interest which is subject to the mortgage[3].

In the case of a person who is entitled by virtue of a qualifying tenancy to claim as having an owner's interest[4], but who has not made a claim in respect of the qualifying tenancy before he has ceased to be entitled to it by reason of his acquisition of the freehold or an extended lease[5], a lease granted by the nominee purchaser[6] or a new lease[7], he may make a claim in respect of the qualifying tenancy as if he were still entitled to it[8]. He may not, however, make that claim after he has ceased to be entitled to the freehold, extended lease, lease granted by the nominee purchaser or new lease, as the case may be, but he may make the claim before the first claim day[9] if it is made before the claimant has disposed of the freehold or of the lease in question and after he has made a contract for disposing of it[10]. No compensation is payable before the first claim day on any claim made by virtue of these provisions[11].

1 See the Land Compensation Act 1973 ss 1, 2 (as amended); and paras 360, 362 ante.
2 Ibid s 10(1)(a). As to mortgage generally see MORTGAGE.
3 Ibid s 10(1)(b). As to the payment of the compensation to the mortgagee and the application by him see s 10(1)(c); and para 374 post.
4 As to that entitlement see ibid s 12(1), (2), s 12A(1)-(3) (as added); and para 363 ante.
5 Ie under the Leasehold Reform Act 1967 Pt I (ss 1–37) (as amended): see LANDLORD AND TENANT vol 27(1) (Reissue) para 1253 et seq.
6 As to the nominee purchaser see para 363 note 10 ante; and LANDLORD AND TENANT vol 27(2) (Reissue) paras 1446–1450.
7 Ie under the Leasehold Reform, Housing and Urban Development Act 1993 Pt I Ch II (ss 39–62): see LANDLORD AND TENANT vol 27(2) (Reissue) para 1523 et seq.
8 Land Compensation Act 1973 ss 12(3), 12A(4) (s 12A added by the Leasehold Reform, Housing and Urban Development Act 1993 s 187(1), Sch 21 para 5).
9 As to the first claim day see para 367 post.
10 Land Compensation Act 1973 s 12(4) (amended by the Local Government, Planning and Land Act 1980 s 112); Land Compensation Act 12A(5) (as added: see note 7 supra). As to notice of the claim see s 3 (as amended), s 12(6), s 12A(7) (as added); and para 366 post. As to the assessment see ss 4(4)(a), 12(7), s 12A(8) (as added); and para 371 post.
11 Ibid s 12(5) (amended by the Local Government, Planning and Land Act 1980 s 112(1), (4)); Land Compensation Act 1973 12A(6) (as added: see note 7 supra).

366. Notice of claim and service. A claim for compensation in respect of noise and other physical factors[1] is made by serving on the responsible authority[2] a notice containing particulars of:

(1) the land in respect of which the claim is made[3];
(2) the claimant's interest and the date on which, and the manner in which, it was acquired[4];
(3) the claimant's occupation of the land, except where the interest qualifies for compensation without occupation[5];
(4) any other interests in the land so far as known to the claimant[6];
(5) the public works[7] to which the claim relates[8];
(6) the amount of compensation claimed[9];

(7) any land contiguous or adjacent to the land in respect of which the claim is made, being land to which the claimant was entitled in the same capacity[10] on the relevant date[11];

(8) in the case of a claim relating to the depreciation in the value of land after the alteration of a highway or other public works or the change of use of public works other than a highway or aerodrome[12], the alterations or change of use alleged to give rise to the depreciation[13].

In the case of a person who is entitled by virtue of a qualifying tenancy to claim as having an owner's interest[14], the notice of claim must state that he makes his claim in respect of that qualifying tenancy[15]; and if he claims after he has ceased to be entitled to the qualifying tenancy[16], or if, having disposed of the freehold or extended lease acquired by him[17] or of the lease granted to him[18], he has made a claim before that disposal[19], he must include sufficient particulars in the notice of claim to show that he has the right to make that claim[20].

1 Ie a claim under the Land Compensation Act 1973 Pt I (ss 1–19) (as amended): see paras 360 et seq ante, 367 et seq post.
2 For the meaning of 'responsible authority' see para 360 note 8 ante.
3 Land Compensation Act 1973 s 3(1)(a).
4 Ibid s 3(1)(b); and see s 2 (as amended), s 10(4), s 11 (as amended); and para 362 ante.
5 Ibid s 3(1)(c); and see s 2 (as amended), s 10(4), s 11 (as amended); and para 362 ante.
6 Ibid s 3(1)(d).
7 For the meaning of 'public works' see para 360 note 4 ante.
8 Land Compensation Act 1973 s 3(1)(e).
9 Ibid s 3(1)(f).
10 Ie within the meaning of ibid s 6(5): see para 373 post.
11 Ibid s 3(1)(g). For the meaning of 'relevant date', which must fall on or after 17 October 1969 (s 1(8)), see para 360 note 9 ante.
12 See ibid s 9(1)-(3); and para 361 ante. As to public works other than a highway see para 361 ante. For the meaning of 'aerodrome' and 'highway' see para 337 notes 1, 3 respectively ante.
13 Ibid s 9(4).
14 See para 363 ante.
15 Land Compensation Act 1973 ss 12(6), 12A(7) (s 12A added by the Leasehold Reform, Housing and Urban Development Act 1993 s 187(1), Sch 21 para 5).
16 Ie if he claims under the Land Compensation Act 1973 s 12(3) or s 12A(4) (as added: see note 15 supra): see para 363 ante.
17 Ie acquired by him under the Leasehold Reform Act 1967 Pt I (ss 1–37) (as amended): see LANDLORD AND TENANT vol 27(2) (Reissue) para 1253 et seq.
18 Ie granted to him under the Leasehold Reform, Housing and Urban Development Act 1993 Pt I Ch I (ss 1–38) (collective enfranchisement) or under Pt I Ch II (ss 39–62) (individual right to new lease): see LANDLORD AND TENANT vol 27(2) (Reissue) paras 1406 et seq, 1523 et seq.
19 Ie if he claims under the Land Compensation Act 1973 s 12(4) (as amended) or s 12A(5) (as added): see para 365 ante.
20 Ibid s 12(6), s 12A(7) (as added: see note 15 supra).

367. Time for claim. No claim may be made before the expiration of 12 months from the relevant date[1] and the day next following the expiration of the 12 months is referred to as the first claim day[2].

However, this will not preclude the making of a claim in respect of an interest in land before the first claim day if (1) the claimant has during the 12 months after the relevant date made a contract for disposing of that interest, or, in so far as the interest is in land which is not a dwelling[3], for the grant of a tenancy[4] of that land; and (2) the claim is made before the interest is disposed of or the tenancy is granted; but compensation is not payable before the first claim day on any claim so made[5].

Claims before the first claim day may also be made by persons having a qualifying tenancy under the Leasehold Reform Act 1967 or the Leasehold Reform, Housing and Urban Development Act 1993[6].

Provision was made by the Local Government, Planning and Land Act 1980 to extend the claim period for certain claims which were out of time on 13 November 1980[7]. A person's right of action to recover compensation on a claim made by virtue of that special provision is, however, deemed to have accrued on that date for the purposes of the limitation period[8].

1   As to the relevant date, which in any case must fall on or after 17 October 1969 (s 1(8)), see ss 1(9), 9(2); and paras 360 note 9, 361 ante.
2   Land Compensation Act 1973 s 3(2) (amended by the Local Government, Planning and Land Act 1980 s 112(1), (2)). This provision is subject to the Land Compensation Act 1973 s 12 (as amended): s 3(2); and see the text and note 6 infra. For the purposes of the Limitation Act 1980 a person's right of action to recover compensation under the Land Compensation Act 1973 Pt I (ss 1–19) (as amended) is deemed to have accrued on the first claim day: s 19(2A) (added by the Local Government, Planning and Land Act 1980 s 112(1), (6)); Interpretation Act 1978 s 17(2)(a). The limitation period is six years: see the Limitation Act 1980 s 9(1).
3   For the meaning of 'dwelling' see para 283 note 1 ante.
4   For the meaning of 'tenancy' see para 286 note 3 ante.
5   Land Compensation Act 1973 s 3(3) (amended by the Local Government, Planning and Land Act 1980 s 112(1), (4)).
6   See the Land Compensation Act 1973 s 12(4) (as amended), s 12A(5) (as added); and para 365 ante. As to the treatment of qualifying tenancies as owner's interests see para 363 ante.
7   See the Local Government, Planning and Land Act 1980 s 113.
8   Ibid s 113(10); Interpretation Act 1978 s 17(2)(a). See also note 2 supra.

(iii) Assessment of Compensation

368. Entry to survey and value. Where notice of a claim[1] has been served on a responsible authority[2], any person authorised by that authority, on giving reasonable notice, may enter the land to which the claim relates for the purpose of surveying it and ascertaining its value in connection with the claim, and any person who wilfully obstructs[3] a person in the exercise of the powers so conferred is guilty of an offence and liable on summary conviction to a fine not exceeding level 1 on the standard scale[4].

1   As to notices of claim see para 366 ante; and for the meaning of 'claim' see para 360 note 2 ante.
2   For the meaning of 'responsible authority' see para 360 note 8 ante.
3   In order to be wilful, obstruction must be deliberate and intentional (*R v Senior* [1899] 1 QB 283 at 290–291); it is therefore necessary for the prosecution to prove that the act was done with the intention of obstructing (*Willmott v Atack* [1977] QB 498, [1976] 3 All ER 794, DC). It is immaterial that the person prosecuted did not appreciate that what he did amounted in law to obstruction or that his actions were not aimed primarily at the person obstructed: see eg *Hills v Ellis* [1983] QB 680, [1983] 1 All ER 667; *Lewis v Cox* [1985] QB 509, [1984] 3 All ER 672. See also *Department of Transport v Williams* (1993) 138 Sol Jo LB 5, CA.
4   Land Compensation Act 1973 s 3(4) (amended by virtue of the Criminal Justice Act 1982 ss 38, 46). As to the standard scale see para 14 note 6 ante.

369. Lands Tribunal's jurisdiction. Any question of disputed compensation must be referred to and determined by the Lands Tribunal[1], but no such question arising out of a claim[2] made before the first claim day[3] may be referred to the tribunal before the beginning of that day[4].

1   Land Compensation Act 1973 s 16(1) (amended by the Land Compensation (Scotland) Act 1973 s 81(1), Sch 2).

2 For the meaning of 'claim' see para 360 note 2 ante.

3 As to the first claim day see para 367 ante.

4 Land Compensation Act 1973 s 16(2) (amended by the Land Compensation (Scotland) Act 1973 Sch 2; and by the Local Government, Planning and Land Act 1980 s 112(1), (4)). As to the Lands Tribunal see para 200 et seq ante.

370. Action for nuisance where responsible authority has disclaimed statutory immunity. Where, in resisting a claim[1], a responsible authority[2] contends that no enactment relating to the works in question confers immunity from actions for nuisance[3] in respect of the use to which the claim relates so as to give a ground for compensation[4], then if (1) compensation is not paid on the claim; and (2) an action for nuisance in respect of the matters which were the subject of the claim is subsequently brought by the claimant against the authority, no enactment relating to those works, being an enactment in force when the contention was made, is to afford a defence to that action in so far as it relates to those matters[5].

1 For the meaning of 'claim' see para 360 note 2 ante.

2 For the meaning of 'responsible authority' see para 360 note 8 ante.

3 As to nuisance generally see NUISANCE.

4 See the Land Compensation Act 1973 s 1(6) (as amended); and para 360 ante.

5 Ibid s 17.

371. Relevant matters in assessing compensation. The compensation payable on any claim[1] must be assessed by reference to prices current on the first claim day[2].

In assessing depreciation due to the physical factors[3] caused by the use of any public works[4], account must be taken of the use of those works as it exists on the first claim day, and of any intensification that may then be reasonably expected of the use of those works in the state in which they are on that date[5]. In assessing the extent of the depreciation, there must be taken into account the benefit of any relevant works (1) which have been carried out, or in respect of which a grant has been paid, under the statutory powers for sound-proofing of buildings affected by public works[6] or by aerodromes[7], or any corresponding local enactment or under any provision of a scheme operated by a person managing an aerodrome which provides for the payment of sound-proofing grants[8] in respect of buildings near the aerodrome[9]; and (2) which have been carried out[10] to mitigate any adverse effect of the construction, improvement, existence or use of a highway or other public works on the land surrounding the highway or public works[11].

The value of the interest in respect of which the claim is made must be assessed:

(a) by reference to the nature of the interest and the condition of the land as it subsisted on the date of service of notice of the claim[12], subject to certain exceptions[13];

(b) in accordance with certain rules set out in the Land Compensation Act 1961[14], subject to certain exceptions[15];

(c) if the interest is subject to a mortgage, to a contract of sale or to a contract made after the relevant date for the grant of a tenancy[16], as if it were not subject to the mortgage or contract[17].

However, in assessing the value of the interest in respect of which the claim is made there must be left out of account any part of that value which is attributable to any building, or improvement or extension of a building, on the land if the building or, as the case may be, the building as improved or extended, was first occupied after the relevant date[18], and any change in the use of the land made after that date[19].

1 For the meaning of 'claim' see para 360 note 2 ante.
2 Land Compensation Act 1973 s 4(1) (amended by the Local Government, Planning and Land Act 1980 s 112(1), (4)). As to the first claim day see para 367 ante.
3 As to the meaning of 'physical factors' see para 360 note 2 ante.
4 As to the meaning of 'public works' see para 360 note 4 ante.
5 Land Compensation Act 1973 s 4(2) (amended by the Local Government, Planning and Land Act 1980 s 112(1), (4)).
6 Ie under the Land Compensation Act 1973 s 20 (as amended): see para 337 ante.
7 Ie under the Airports Authority Act 1965 s 15 (repealed), the Civil Aviation Act 1971 s 29A (repealed) and the Civil Aviation Act 1982 s 79 (as prospectively amended): see AVIATION vol 2 (Reissue) para 1188. For the meaning of 'aerodrome' see para 337 note 1 ante.
8 'Sound-proofing grants' in relation to any buildings, means grants towards the cost of insulating those buildings or parts of those buildings against noise: Land Compensation Act 1973 s 4(3) (definition added by the Civil Aviation Act 1980 s 20(1)).
9 Land Compensation Act 1973 s 4(3)(a) (amended by the Airports Authority Act 1975 s 25(2), Sch 5 Pt II; the Civil Aviation Act 1980 s 20(1); and by the Civil Aviation Act 1982 s 109(2), Sch 15 para 12(2)). It must be assumed that any relevant works which could be or could have been carried out, or in respect of which a grant could be or could have been paid, have been carried out, but, in a case where the authority having functions has a discretion whether or not to carry out the works or pay the grant, only if it has undertaken to do so: s 4(3).
10 Ie under the Highways Act 1980 s 282; or the Land Compensation Act 1973 s 27 (as amended): see HIGHWAYS vol 21 (Reissue) para 814; and para 351 ante respectively.
11 Ibid s 4(3)(b).
12 As to the notice of claim see ibid s 3 (as amended); and para 366 ante. In the case of a person claiming in respect of a qualifying tenancy (see para 363 ante), the reference to the date of service of the notice of claim is to have effect as if it were a reference to the relevant date: s 12(7), s 12A(8) (added by the Leasehold Reform, Housing and Urban Development Act 1993 s 187(1), Sch 21 para 5). For the meaning of 'the relevant date' see para 360 note 9 ante.
13 Ie excluding value attributable to certain buildings and uses under the Land Compensation Act 1973 s 4(5) (see the text and notes 18–19 infra): s 4(4)(a).
14 Ie under the rules set out in the Land Compensation Act 1961 s 5 rr (2)–(4) (as amended): see paras 234, 279, 270, 240 respectively ante.
15 Ie excluding value attributable to certain buildings and uses under the Land Compensation Act 1973 s 4(5) (see the text and notes 18–19 infra): s 4(4)(b).
16 For the meaning of 'tenancy' see para 286 note 3 ante.
17 Land Compensation Act 1973 s 4(4)(c).
18 Ibid s 4(5)(a).
19 Ibid s 4(5)(b).

372. Assumptions as to planning permission in assessing value. The following assumptions must be made in assessing the value of the interest in respect of which the claim is made[1].

It must be assumed that planning permission[2] would be granted in respect of the land in which the interest subsists ('the relevant land') or any part of it, for any development[3] consisting of (1) specified rebuilding operations or the maintenance, improvement or alteration of a building[4] subject to the statutory condition[5] relating thereto[6]; and (2) the use as two or more separate dwelling houses of any building which at a material date was used as a single dwelling house[7]. Where, however, an order has been made[8] in respect of the relevant land or any part of it requiring the removal of any building or the discontinuance of any use[9], and compensation has become payable in respect of that order[10], it must not be assumed that planning permission would be granted in respect of the relevant land or any part of it for the rebuilding of that building or the resumption of that use[11].

It must be assumed that planning permission would not be granted in respect of the relevant land or any part of it for any development other than the development mentioned above, and, if planning permission has been granted in respect of the relevant land or any part of it for that other development, it must be assumed that the planning permission has not been granted in so far as it relates to development that has not been carried out[12].

1 Land Compensation Act 1973 s 5(1). For the meaning of 'claim' see para 360 note 2 ante.
2 For these purposes, 'planning permission' has the same meaning as in the Town and Country Planning Act 1990 (see TOWN AND COUNTRY PLANNING vol 46 (Reissue) para 21 note 9): Land Compensation Act 1973 s 5(5) (amended by the Planning (Consequential Provisions) Act 1990 s 4, Sch 2 para 29(2)(c)).
3 For the meaning of 'development' see TOWN AND COUNTRY PLANNING vol 46 (Reissue) para 144 et seq (definition applied by the Land Compensation Act 1973 s 5(5)) (as amended: see note 2 supra).
4 Ie development of a class specified in the Town and Country Planning Act 1990 s 107(4) (as amended), Sch 3 para 1: see TOWN AND COUNTRY PLANNING vol 46 (Reissue) para 703. See also para 246 note 4 ante.
5 Ie subject to the condition set out in ibid s 111(5) (as substituted), Sch 10: see TOWN AND COUNTRY PLANNING vol 46 (Reissue) para 704.
6 Land Compensation Act 1973 s 5(2)(a) (substituted by the Planning and Compensation Act 1991 s 31(4), Sch 6 para 5).
7 Land Compensation Act 1973 s 5(2)(b) (as substituted: see note 6 supra). The development referred to is development of a class specified in the Town and Country Planning Act 1990 Sch 3 para 2: see TOWN AND COUNTRY PLANNING vol 46 (Reissue) para 703. See also para 246 note 7 ante.
8 Ie an order under ibid s 102 (as amended) or Sch 9 para 1: see TOWN AND COUNTRY PLANNING vol 46 para 474 et seq.
9 For the meaning of 'use' see TOWN AND COUNTRY PLANNING vol 46 (Reissue) para 9 note 11 (definition applied by the Land Compensation Act 1973 s 5(5) (as amended: see note 2 supra).
10 Ie under the Town and Country Planning Act 1990 s 115: see TOWN AND COUNTRY PLANNING vol 46 (Reissue) para 709.
11 Land Compensation Act 1973 s 5(3)(c) (amended by the Planning (Consequential Provisions) Act 1990 Sch 2 para 29(2)(b)(iii)). Any expression which is also used in the Town and Country Planning Act 1990 has the same meaning for these purposes as in that Act and references to any provision of that Act include references to any corresponding provision previously in force: Land Compensation Act 1973 s 5(5) (as amended: see note 2 supra).
12 Ibid s 5(4).

373. Compensation reduced by betterment of claimant's land. The compensation payable on a claim[1] must be reduced by an amount equal to any increase in the value of (1) the claimant's interest in the land in respect of which the claim is made[2]; and (2) any interest in other land contiguous or adjacent[3] to that land to which the claimant was entitled in the same capacity[4] on the relevant date[5], if, in either case, that increase is attributable to the existence of, or the use or prospective use of, the public works[6] to which the claim relates[7]. In the case of a claim for compensation for depreciation in the value of land after alterations of a highway or other public works or the change of use of public works other than a highway or aerodrome[8], the increase in value to be taken into account is any increase that would not have been caused but for the alteration or change of use in question[9].

Where, however, an increase in the value of an interest in other land has been taken into account under the above provisions, then, in connection with any subsequent acquisition of that other land[10], that increase must not be left out of account by virtue of the provisions of the Land Compensation Act 1961[11] which require increases in value of the land compulsorily acquired arising from development or prospective development of certain areas to be disregarded on assessing the value of that land, or taken into account by virtue of the provisions of that Act[12] which require the deduction from the value of land compulsorily acquired of any increase in the value of other adjacent or contiguous land owned by the same owner arising from development or prospective development of certain areas, or any corresponding enactment[13], in so far as it was taken into account in connection with that claim[14].

1 For the meaning of 'claim' see para 360 note 2 ante.
2 Land Compensation Act 1973 s 6(1)(a). The provisions previously mentioned in ss 4, 5 (as amended) (see paras 371–372 ante), which apply to the assessment of the depreciation in the value of the land to which the claim relates, do not apply to the assessment for these purposes of the value of the interest mentioned in head (1) in the text: s 6(2). As to the consideration by the Lands Tribunal of the deductions for benefits due to the scheme in highways cases see para 323 note 7 ante. See also *Hallows v Welsh Office* [1995] 1 EGLR 191, Lands Tribunal.
3 The expression 'adjacent' has in ordinary language no precise and uniform meaning, but is not confined to places adjoining and includes places close to or near: *Wellington Corpn v Lower Hutt Corpn* [1904] AC 773, PC. The proper meaning of 'contiguous' is 'touching': *Haynes v King* [1893] 3 Ch 439 at 448.
4 A person entitled to two interests in land must be taken to be entitled to them in the same capacity if, but only if, he is entitled (1) to both of them beneficially; or (2) to both of them as trustee of one particular trust; or (3) to both of them as personal representative of one particular person: Land Compensation Act 1973 s 6(5).
5 Ibid s 6(1)(b). For the meaning of 'relevant date' see para 360 note 9 ante.
6 For the meaning of 'public works' see para 360 note 4 ante.
7 Land Compensation Act 1973 s 6(1).
8 See ibid s 9(1)–(3); and para 360 ante. For the meaning of 'aerodrome' and 'highway' see para 337 notes 1, 3 ante. Compensation for loss in value of a house caused by noise and fumes from traffic on a length of highway which had undergone minor alterations as part of a larger scheme including a new river bridge, could take into account the increase in traffic on the altered highway due to the bridge: *Williamson v Cumbria County Council* [1995] RVR 102, Lands Tribunal.
9 Land Compensation Act 1973 s 9(4)(a).
10 Ie where either (1) the interest acquired by the subsequent acquisition is the same as the interest the increased value of which was previously taken into account as mentioned in ibid s 6(3), whether the acquisition extends to the whole of the land in which that interest previously subsisted or only to part of that land; or (2) the person entitled to the interest acquired is, or directly or indirectly derives title to that interest from, the person who at the time of the claim mentioned was entitled to the interest increased value of which was previously so taken into account: s 6(4). A reference to a person deriving title from another person includes a reference to any successor in title of that other person: s 6(5).
11 Ie the provisions of the Land Compensation Act 1961 s 6 (as amended): see para 269 et seq ante. Cf s 8(1); and paras 277, 324 ante.
12 Ie the provisions of ibid s 7: see para 316 et seq ante. Cf s 8(1); and paras 277, 324 ante.
13 'Corresponding enactment' has the same meaning as in the Land Compensation Act 1961 s 8 (see para 277 note 11 ante): Land Compensation Act 1973 s 6(6).
14 Ibid s 6(3).

(iv) Payment of Compensation

374. Persons to whom compensation is payable, and limits and extent of compensation. Where an interest is subject to a mortgage, any compensation which is payable in respect of the interest which is subject to the mortgage must be paid to the mortgagee or, if there is more than one mortgagee, to the first mortgagee, and must in either case be applied by him as if it were proceeds of sale[1].

Where the interest is held on trust for sale, the compensation must be dealt with as if it were proceeds of sale arising under the trust[2]; and where it is settled land for the purposes of the Settled Land Act 1925, the compensation must be treated as capital money arising under that Act[3].

Any compensation payable in respect of land which is ecclesiastical property[4] must be paid (1) in the case of land which is not diocesan glebe land, to the Church Commissioners; and (2) in the case of diocesan glebe land, to the Diocesan Board of Finance[5] in which the land is vested, and in either case the compensation must be applied for the purposes for which the proceeds of a sale by agreement of the land would be applicable under any enactment or Measure authorising, or disposing of the proceeds of, such a sale[6].

Compensation is not payable on any claim unless the amount of the compensation exceeds £50[7]. Where compensation is payable by a responsible authority[8] on a claim[9], the authority must pay, in addition to the compensation, any reasonable valuation or legal expenses incurred by the claimant for the purposes of the preparation and prosecution of the claim, but without prejudice to the Lands Tribunal's powers in respect of the costs of proceedings[10] before the tribunal[11].

1 Land Compensation Act 1973 s 10(1)(c). As to mortgage generally see MORTGAGE.
2 Ibid s 10(2). As to trusts for sale see SETTLEMENTS vol 42 para 896.
3 Ibid s 10(3): see SETTLEMENTS.
4 'Ecclesiastical property' means land belonging to an ecclesiastical benefice of the Church of England, or being or forming part of a church subject to the jurisdiction of a bishop of any diocese of the Church of England or the site of such a church, or being or forming part of a burial ground subject to that jurisdiction or being diocesan glebe land: ibid s 13(2) (s 13 amended by the Planning and Compensation Act 1991 s 70, Sch 15 para 20). 'Diocesan glebe land' has the same meaning as in the Endowments and Glebe Measure 1976: Land Compensation Act 1973 s 13(2) (as so amended).
5 'Diocesan Board of Finance' has the same meaning as in the Endowments and Glebe Measure 1976: Land Compensation Act 1973 s 13(2) (as amended: see note 4 supra). See ECCLESIASTICAL LAW.
6 Ibid s 13(1) (as amended: see note 4 supra).
7 Ibid s 7. As to the limits on the right to compensation see para 364 ante.
8 For the meaning of 'responsible authority' see para 360 note 8 ante.
9 For the meaning of 'claim' see para 360 note 2 ante.
10 Ie by virtue of the Land Compensation Act 1973 s 16 (as amended): see para 369 ante.
11 Ibid s 3(5) (amended by the Land Compensation (Scotland) Act 1973 s 81(2), Sch 2 Pt I). As to the tribunal see para 202 et seq ante.

375. Effect of payment when land is compulsorily acquired after claim. Where, after a claim[1] has been made in respect of any interest in land, the whole or part of the land in which that interest subsists is compulsorily acquired, then, if the value of that land has been diminished by the public works[2] to which the claim relates, but the compensation in respect of the compulsory acquisition falls to be assessed without regard to the diminution[3], the compensation in respect of the acquisition must be reduced by an amount equal to the compensation paid or payable on the claim, or, if the acquisition extends only to part of the land, to so much of that compensation as is attributable to that part[4].

1 For the meaning of 'claim' see para 360 note 2 ante.
2 For the meaning of 'public works' see para 360 note 4 ante.
3 As to these cases see the Land Compensation Act 1973 s 6(3); and para 373 ante. See also the Land Compensation Act 1961 s 8(1); and paras 277, 324 ante.
4 Land Compensation Act 1973 s 8(6).

376. Interest on compensation. Compensation[1] carries interest at the rate for the time being prescribed under the Land Compensation Act 1961[2] from (1) the date of service of the notice of claim[3]; or (2) if that date is before the first claim day[4], from the beginning of the claim period, until payment[5]. If it appears to any person that he may become liable to pay to another compensation or interest thereon under this provision he may, if the other person requests him in writing to do so, make one or more payments on account of such compensation or interest[6]. If after payment has been made by such person it is agreed or determined that he is not liable to pay the compensation or interest or, by reason of any agreement or determination, any such payment is shown to have been excessive, the payment or excess is recoverable by that person[7].

1 Ie compensation under the Land Compensation Act 1973 Pt I (ss 1–19) (as amended): see para 359 et seq ante.
2 Ie at the rate prescribed under the Land Compensation Act 1961 s 32: see para 125 note 5 ante.
3 As to service of the notice of claim see para 366 ante.
4 As to the first claim day see para 367 ante.
5 Land Compensation Act 1973 s 18(1) (amended by the Local Government, Planning and Land Act 1980 s 112(1), (4)).
6 Planning and Compensation Act 1991 s 80(2), Sch 18 Pt II.
7 Ibid s 80(3), Sch 18 Pt II.

(8) DISPOSAL OF SUPERFLUOUS LAND

377. Various powers of disposal. Where land is compulsorily acquired under an empowering enactment by an authority to which the Compulsory Purchase Act 1965 applies[1], there is no provision for the disposal of superfluous land unless it is made by the empowering enactment or special Act[2] or the authority has power to appropriate superfluous land to other statutory purposes[3]. Where, however, there is a compulsory purchase of land by an authority under a special Act incorporating certain provisions of the Lands Clauses Consolidation Act 1845[4], or those provisions are specially applied[5], the disposal of superfluous land is controlled by those provisions[6].

1 As to these authorities see para 15 ante.
2 Ie special provisions for sale or exchange or letting (see eg the Local Government Act 1972 ss 123, 127 (as amended)) or by specific incorporation or application of the Lands Clauses Consolidation Act 1845 ss 127–132 (see eg the incorporation of those sections in the Pipe-lines Act 1962 by the Compulsory Purchase Act 1965 s 37(3): see para 11 ante). For the meaning of 'the special Act' see paras 11, 16 ante.
3 See eg the Town and Country Planning Act 1990 s 232; and TOWN AND COUNTRY PLANNING vol 46 (Reissue) para 770; the Local Government Act 1972 ss 122, 123, 126, 127 (all as amended); and LOCAL GOVERNMENT.
4 Ie the Lands Clauses Consolidation Act 1845 ss 127–132: see para 378 et seq post.
5 See note 2 supra.
6 See para 378 et seq post.

378. Superfluous land under the Lands Clauses Acts. The Lands Clauses Consolidation Act 1845 makes provision with respect to superfluous land[1]. This is land acquired under the provisions of the special Act, either compulsorily or by negotiations undertaken by virtue of the compulsory powers, but subsequently found not to be required for the purposes of the undertaking[2]. These provisions[3] are deemed to be incorporated unless expressly or impliedly excluded[4].

The object of the relevant provisions is to secure to the landowners from whom land is taken by compulsion a reversion, as nearly as the legislature can accomplish it, of all land which is not required for the undertaking[5]. When incorporated, those provisions apply to all land acquired directly or indirectly under compulsory powers, but they do not apply to land bought under mere powers of purchase by agreement[6], among which is included land bought for extraordinary purposes[7], nor do they apply to cases where the land ceases to be required because of the partial or total abandonment of the undertaking[8].

1 See the Lands Clauses Consolidation Act 1845 ss 127–132. As to the incorporation of these sections see paras 11–12 ante, and as to their exclusion in the case of acquisitions to which the Acquisition of Land Act 1981 applies by the re-enactment of the Lands Clauses Acts in the Compulsory Purchase Act 1965 in substitution for those Acts and omitting provisions as to superfluous land see the Compulsory Purchase Act 1965 s 1(1) (substituted by the Acquisition of Land Act 1981 s 34, Sch 4 para 14(2)); and para 15 ante.

2 See the introductory words to the Lands Clauses Consolidation Act 1845 ss 127–132; and see *Great Western Rly Co v May* (1874) LR 7 HL 283 at 292 per Lord Cairns LC; *Hooper v Bourne* (1877) 3 QBD 258 at 272, CA, per Bramwell LJ; affd (1880) 5 App Cas 1, HL. For the meaning of 'the undertaking' see para 13 ante; and for the meaning of 'the special Act' see paras 11, 16 ante.

3 Ie the Lands Clauses Consolidation Act 1845 ss 127–132.

4 See note 1 supra.

5 *Great Western Rly Co v May* (1874) LR 7 HL 283 at 295 per Lord Cairns LC. For the causes of land becoming superfluous see *Great Western Rly Co v May* supra at 292–293.

6 *Horne v Lymington Rly Co* (1874) 31 LT 167.

7 *City of Glasgow Union Rly Co v Caledonian Rly Co* (1871) LR 2 Sc & Div 160, HL; *Hooper v Bourne* (1877) 3 QBD 258, CA; affd (1880) 5 App Cas 1, HL.

8 *Astley v Manchester, Sheffield and Lincolnshire Rly Co* (1858) 27 LJ Ch 478; *Smith v Smith* (1868) LR 3 Exch 282; *Re Duffy's Estate* [1897] 1 IR 307 at 315, CA. In case of abandonment the Act authorising the abandonment usually makes provision as to the disposal of the land: see eg the Transport Act 1962 s 14(1)(e).

379. Evidence that land is superfluous. It would be cogent evidence that land had become superfluous if it had been permanently devoted to some object which was not a purpose of the undertaking, such as the making of a highway[1], or if the undertakers had sold it[2] or advertised it for sale and described it as surplus land[3], but even these facts are not conclusive, as the acts of the undertakers may have been ultra vires[4]. The compulsory purchase by another company is not evidence that the land was superfluous[5]. On the other hand, land above a tunnel[6] or underneath an archway[7] is not superfluous land, because the term 'land' in that case is not considered to include a horizontal stratum, and that land might also be required for repairs. It is immaterial that the land is let to tenants or used for other purposes, because undertakers may use their land in any way not inconsistent with their statutory powers or contrary to the rights of others[8].

1 *Lord Beauchamp v Great Western Rly Co* (1868) 3 Ch App 745.

2 *Lord Carington v Wycombe Rly Co* (1868) 3 Ch App 377 at 384.

3 *London and South Western Rly Co v Blackmore* (1870) LR 4 HL 610.

4 *Macfie v Callander and Oban Rly Co* [1898] AC 270 at 284, HL; *Hobbs v Midland Rly Co* (1882) 20 ChD 418.

5 *Dunhill v North Eastern Rly Co* [1896] 1 Ch 121, CA. Land acquired for spoilbanks and no longer required for that or any fresh purpose is superfluous: *Great Western Rly Co v May* (1874) LR 7 HL 283; and see, for another example, *Moody v Corbett* (1865) 5 B & S 859; affd in part, and revsd in part (1866) LR 1 QB 509, Ex Ch. Land between a decayed fence and ditch alongside a railway, which had been cultivated by the adjoining owner, has been held to be superfluous: *Norton v London and North Western Rly Co* (1879) 13 ChD 268, CA; and see *Ware v London, Brighton and South Coast Rly Co* (1882) 52 LJ Ch 198.

6 *Re Metropolitan District Rly Co and Cosh* (1880) 13 ChD 607, CA; *Rosenberg v Cook* (1881) 8 QBD 162, CA; and see *Hooper v Bourne* (1877) 3 QBD 258, CA; *Re Lancashire and Yorkshire Rly Co and Earl of Derby's Contract* (1908) 100 LT 44. A good possessory title to such land may be acquired by adverse possession: *Midland Rly Co v Wright* [1901] 1 Ch 738; and see further LIMITATION OF ACTIONS.

7 *Mulliner v Midland Rly Co* (1879) 11 ChD 611.

8 *Bostock v North Staffordshire Rly Co* (1855) 4 E & B 798; *Grand Junction Canal Co v Petty* (1888) 21 QBD 273, CA; *Teebay v Manchester, Sheffield and Lincolnshire Rly Co* (1883) 24 ChD 572; *Foster v London, Chatham and Dover Rly Co* [1895] 1 QB 711, CA; *Onslow v Manchester, Sheffield and Lincolnshire Rly Co* (1895) 64 LJ Ch 355; *Great Western Rly Co v Solihull RDC* (1902) 86 LT 852, CA; *Lancashire and Yorkshire Rly Co v Davenport* (1906) 70 JP 129, CA.

380. Obligation to sell superfluous land. The undertakers[1] are required under the provisions of the Lands Clauses Acts to sell and dispose absolutely[2] of all superfluous land[3] within the period prescribed in the special Act[4] or, if no period is so prescribed, within ten years after the expiration of the time limited in the special Act for the completion of works[5], and apply the purchase money arising from the sale to the purposes of the special Act[6].

1 For the meaning of 'the undertakers' see para 13 ante.
2 A conditional sale providing for repurchase by the undertakers was void (see *London and South Western Rly Co v Gomm* (1882) 20 ChD 562, CA; *Ray v Walker* [1892] 2 QB 88); and a sale providing a lien on the land for unpaid purchase money might also be void (see *Re Thackwray and Young* (1888) 40 ChD 34). However, the undertakers could impose restrictive covenants on the land: see *Re Higgins and Hitchman's Contract* (1882) 21 ChD 95. As to the Lands Clauses Acts see para 11 ante.
3 As to superfluous land see para 378 ante.
4 For the meaning of 'the special Act' see paras 11, 16 ante.
5 For the meaning of 'works' see para 13 text to note 4 ante. As to when a time for completion of works is prescribed see para 328 ante.
6 Lands Clauses Consolidation Act 1845 s 127.

381. Right of pre-emption. Before the undertakers[1] dispose of any superfluous land[2], either by sale or by applying it to some purpose not a purpose of the undertaking[3], then unless the land is situated within a town or built upon[4] or used for building purposes[5], they must first offer to sell it to the person then entitled to the land, if any, from which it was originally severed[6]. This right of pre-emption arises whenever the undertakers decide that the land is superfluous and proceed to dispose of it, and it is not necessary that the prescribed period should have elapsed[7]. If the person entitled refuses to purchase the land, or cannot after diligent inquiry be found, then a similar offer must be made to the person or to the several persons[8] whose land immediately adjoins the land so proposed to be sold[9], provided those persons are capable of entering into a contract for the purchase of the land[10].

This right of pre-emption must be claimed within six weeks after the offer, and ceases if not accepted within that time[11]. The right of pre-emption may be released, and if not released remains in force as an equitable interest only[12]. In the absence of agreement the price of the land must be ascertained by arbitration and the costs of the arbitration are in the discretion of the arbitrators[13].

1 For the meaning of 'the undertakers' see para 13 ante.
2 An agreement for sale is not in itself a disposal of the land: *London and Greenwich Rly Co v Goodchild* (1844) 3 Ry & Can Cas 507 at 511. As to superfluous land see para 378 ante.
3 *London and South Western Rly Co v Blackmore* (1870) LR 4 HL 610; *Lord Carington v Wycombe Rly Co* (1868) 3 Ch App 377; *Lord Beauchamp v Great Western Rly Co* (1868) 3 Ch App 745. Applying the land to an extension of the undertaking sanctioned by another Act is not a disposal (*Astley v Manchester, Sheffield and Lincolnshire Rly Co* (1858) 27 LJ Ch 478); nor is a compulsory purchase by other promoters (*Dunhill v North Eastern Rly Co* [1896] 1 Ch 121, CA).
4 'Town' is used in its popular sense, and 'land built upon' means continuously built upon, as in a town: *Lord Carington v Wycombe Rly Co* (1868) 3 Ch App 377; *London and South Western Rly Co v Blackmore* (1870) LR 4 HL 610; *R v Cottle* (1851) 16 QB 412 at 421–422; *Elliott v South Devon Rly Co* (1848) 2 Exch 725; and see para 113 note 2 ante.
5 'Used for building purposes' means actually used, or at least laid out and sold or leased as building land: see the cases cited in note 3 supra; and *Coventry v London, Brighton and South Coast Rly Co* (1867) LR 5 Eq 104.
6 Lands Clauses Consolidation Act 1845 s 128. For the meaning of 'severed' see *Hobbs v Midland Rly Co* (1882) 20 ChD 418 at 429; and see para 291 ante.
7 *Great Western Rly Co v May* (1874) LR 7 HL 283 at 295 per Lord Cairns LC; *Lord Carington v Wycombe Rly Co* (1868) 3 Ch App 377; *London and South Western Rly Co v Gomm* (1882) 20 ChD 562 at 584, CA, per Jessel MR. As to the prescribed period see para 380 ante.
8 Where more than one person is entitled the offer has to be made to each in succession in such order as the undertakers think fit: Lands Clauses Consolidation Act 1845 s 128.

9   For the meaning of 'adjoining' see *Coventry v London, Brighton and South Coast Rly Co* (1867) LR 5 Eq
    104 (in which lessees were held entitled to a right of pre-emption); *London and South Western Rly Co v
    Blackmore* (1870) LR 4 HL 610; *Re Baroness Bateman and Parker's Contract* [1899] 1 Ch 599.
10 Lands Clauses Consolidation Act 1845 s 128. As to enforcing this right and for the form of order see
    London and South Western Rly Co v Blackmore (1870) LR 4 HL 610 at 627.
11 Lands Clauses Consolidation Act 1845 s 129. A declaration in writing made before a justice by some
    person not interested in the matter in question, stating that (1) such an offer was made and was refused or
    not accepted within six weeks from the time of making the offer; or (2) that the person or all the persons
    entitled to the right of pre-emption were out of the country, or could not after diligent inquiry be
    found, or were not capable of entering into a contract for the purchase of such lands, is sufficient
    evidence in all courts of the facts stated: Lands Clauses Consolidation Act 1845 s 129.
12 Law of Property Act 1925 s 186. Contracts by estate owners conferring by statutory implication a right
    of pre-emption are registrable as estate contracts under the Land Charges Act 1972 s 2(1), (4) (as
    amended), Class C(iv). In the case of registered land the right of pre-emption may be protected by
    registration of a notice under the Land Registration Act 1925 Pt IV (ss 48–62) (as amended): see s 3(ix)
    (as substituted), ss 49(1)(c), 59(2). See further LAND CHARGES; LAND REGISTRATION.
13 Lands Clauses Consolidation Act 1845 s 130. The arbitration provisions of that Act are not applicable to
    the arbitration, but those of the Arbitration Act 1950 will apply: see *Jones v South Staffordshire Rly Co*
    (1869) 19 LT 603; *Re Eyre's Trusts* [1869] WN 76. For the provisions of the Arbitration Act 1950
    applicable to statutory arbitrations see ARBITRATION.

382. Conveyance of land. Upon payment or tender to the undertakers[1] of the
purchase money agreed or determined for the sale of superfluous land[2], the undertakers
must convey the land to the purchaser by deed under the common seal of the
undertakers if they are a corporation, or if they are not a corporation under the hands
and seals of the undertakers or any two of the directors or managers acting by the
authority of the body; and a deed so executed is effectual to vest the lands in the
purchaser and a receipt under such a common seal or under the hands of two of the
directors or managers of the undertaking is a sufficient discharge to the purchaser for
the purchase money[3]. The purchaser will acquire no greater right than that of the
undertakers[4], and restrictions existing before the land was taken compulsorily are
revived[5].

In the absence of express limitations in the conveyances the use of the word 'grant'
in conveyances by the undertakers operates as the following express covenants: (1) a
covenant that, notwithstanding any act or default done by the undertakers, they were
at the time of the execution of the conveyance seised or possessed of the lands or
premises thereby granted for an indefeasible estate of inheritance in fee simple, free
from all incumbrances done or occasioned by them, or otherwise for such estate or
interest as therein expressed to be thereby granted, free from incumbrances done or
occasioned by them; (2) a covenant that the grantee of such lands and all his heirs,
successors, executors, administrators and assigns (as the case may be) will quietly enjoy
the lands against the undertakers and their successors and all other persons claiming
under them, and be indemnified by the undertakers and their successors from all
incumbrances created by the undertakers; and (3) a covenant for further assurance of
such lands, at the expense of such grantee, his heirs, successors, executors, administrators or assigns (as the case may be) by the undertakers, or their successors and all
other persons claiming under them[6].

All such grantees and their successors, heirs, executors, administrators and assigns,
according to their respective quality or nature and the estate or interest in the
conveyance, may in all actions brought by them assign breaches of covenants as they
might do if such covenants were expressly inserted in the conveyance[7].

1   For the meaning of 'the undertakers' see para 13 ante.
2   As to superfluous land see para 378 ante.

3 Lands Clauses Consolidation Act 1845 s 131. Any rule of law which required a seal for the valid execution of an instrument as a deed by an individual has, however, been abolished, except in relation to a corporation sole: see the Law of Property (Miscellaneous Provisions) Act 1989 s 1(1)(b), (10); and DEEDS.

4 *Pountney v Clayton* (1883) 11 QBD 820, CA; *Myers v Catterson* (1889) 43 ChD 470, CA.

5 *Ellis v Rogers* (1885) 29 ChD 661; *Pountney v Clayton* (1883) 11 QBD 820, CA; *Bird v Eggleton* (1885) 29 ChD 1012.

6 Lands Clauses Consolidation Act 1845 s 132. The use of the word 'grant' is no longer necessary in conveyances, and apart from a provision such as that in this section does not imply any covenant in law: see the Law of Property Act 1925 ss 51(2), 59(2). As to the covenants for title implied by statute on the disposition of a property see the Law of Property (Miscellaneous Provisions) Act 1994 Pt I (ss 1–13); and REAL PROPERTY; SALE OF LAND.

7 Lands Clauses Consolidation Act 1845 s 132.

383. Default in disposal of superfluous land. If the undertakers[1] make default in disposing of superfluous land, the land remaining unsold at the expiration of the prescribed period vests in and becomes the property of the adjoining owners in proportion to the extent of their lands respectively adjoining the land[2]. The land has to be superfluous at the expiry of the statutory period[3]. If it becomes superfluous afterwards these clauses do not apply[4].

The question whether at the expiration of the ten years or other specified period land was superfluous or not is a mixed question of law and fact[5]. The issue to be determined is whether at the expiration of the period the land had become either requisite for the undertaking or would in all probability become requisite within a reasonable time after that date; if it may be so requisite, it is not superfluous[6].

1 For the meaning of 'the undertakers' see para 13 ante.

2 Lands Clauses Consolidation Act 1845 s 127. Where several properties are in contact with the superfluous land, that land will be divided in proportion to the frontage of each: *Moody v Corbett* (1866) LR 1 QB 510, Ex Ch; and see *Smith v Smith* (1868) LR 3 Exch 282 at 287; *Great Western Rly Co v May* (1874) LR 7 HL 283 at 303. If the undertakers continue to occupy the land and let it to a tenant, he cannot raise the question as to its being superfluous land: *London and North Western Rly Co v West* (1867) LR 2 CP 553. As to superfluous land see para 378 ante.

3 *Great Western Rly Co v May* (1874) LR 7 HL 283 at 294 per Lord Cairns LC; *Macfie v Callander and Oban Rly Co* [1898] AC 270 at 276, 278, HL; *Hooper v Bourne* (1880) 5 App Cas 1 at 9, 11, HL; *Re Metropolitan District Rly Co and Cosh* (1880) 13 ChD 607 at 615, CA. A subsequent extension by an Act, passed at the time of vesting, of the time for disposing of superfluous land does not affect the vesting: *Great Western Rly Co v May* supra; *London and South Western Rly Co v Gomm* (1882) 20 ChD 562 at 584, CA, per Jessel MR; *Moody v Corbett* (1865) 5 B & S 859; affd on this point (1866) LR 1 QB 510, Ex Ch. As to the statutory period see para 380 ante.

4 *Macfie v Callander and Oban Rly Co* [1898] AC 270, HL.

5 *Smith v North Staffordshire Rly Co* (1880) 44 LT 85.

6 *Macfie v Callander and Oban Rly Co* [1898] AC 270 at 284, HL, per Lord Watson: *Hooper v Bourne* (1877) 3 QBD 258 at 274–275, CA, per Bramwell, LJ; affd (1880) 5 App Cas 1, HL.

384–400. Letting superfluous land. Land held by undertakers[1] until the time arrives for deciding whether or not it is superfluous[2] may also be let or used for purposes other than those directly connected with the undertaking[3].

1 For the meaning of 'undertakers' see para 13 ante.

2 As to superfluous land see para 378 ante.

3 *Bayley v Great Western Rly Co* (1884) 26 ChD 434, CA; and see the cases cited in para 379 notes 7–8 ante.

CONFIDENCE AND
DATA PROTECTION

For access to medical records.. *see* MEDICINE	
agents, duties of..	AGENCY
barristers, generally	BARRISTERS
bribery...	CRIMINAL LAW, EVIDENCE
	AND PROCEDURE
children, confidentiality in proceedings relating to	CHILDREN AND YOUNG
	PERSONS; CRIMINAL LAW,
	EVIDENCE AND PROCEDURE
computers, misuse of..	CRIMINAL LAW, EVIDENCE
	AND PROCEDURE
constructive trusts..	TRUSTS
contractual obligations..	CONTRACT
conversion of chattels...	TORT
copyright..	COPYRIGHT
defamation..	LIBEL AND SLANDER
directors, duties of...	COMPANIES
discovery..	DISCOVERY
employees, duties of	EMPLOYMENT
evidence...	EVIDENCE
fiduciary relationships...	EQUITY
Human Fertilisation and Embryology Authority,	CHILDREN AND YOUNG
information held by..	PERSONS; MEDICINE
insider dealing	COMPANIES
interception of communications	CRIMINAL LAW, EVIDENCE
	AND PROCEDURE
Legal Aid Board, information held by...........................	LEGAL AID
misrepresentation	MISREPRESENTATION AND
	FRAUD
official secrets	CRIMINAL LAW, EVIDENCE
	AND PROCEDURE
partners, duties of..	PARTNERSHIP
patent law...	PATENTS AND REGISTERED
	DESIGNS
public interest immunity..	DISCOVERY; EVIDENCE
rehabilitation of offenders, confidentiality relating to	CRIMINAL LAW, EVIDENCE
	AND PROCEDURE
solicitors, generally	SOLICITORS
trade secrets	TRADE, INDUSTRY AND
	INDUSTRIAL RELATIONS
trespass to goods..	TORT
trover	TORT
trustees, duties of...	TRUSTS

1. CONFIDENCE

(1) OBLIGATIONS OF CONFIDENCE

401. Introduction. Although early isolated instances of protection for confidences can be found[1], the modern law dates essentially from the mid-nineteenth century, when the court restrained the unauthorised copying and advertising of etchings which the Prince Consort had arranged to have reproduced for private circulation[2]. Obligations of confidence may now be of significance in governmental, commercial and personal contexts. In public law they may restrain undue publicity for the internal working of central and local government[3].

These obligations have supplemented copyright[4] and patent law[5] by protecting related matters not falling within their limits. Whilst copyright protects the form of expression, confidence protects the substance, as when the plot of a play is not to be disclosed until the opening night[6] or an idea for a dramatic work is communicated orally[7]. Confidence may protect an invention prior to the grant of a patent[8] or provide alternative protection if it is not desired to make the public disclosures required for patenting. Obligations of confidence also enable employers to prevent the abuse of their trade secrets and goodwill by present and former employees[9]. In personal matters the protection of matrimonial and family confidences goes some way to making good the lack of general protection for privacy[10] and the association of confidence with professional and fiduciary relationships furthers the proper attainment of their purposes[11].

1 *Duke of Queensberry v Shebbeare* (1758) 2 Eden 329 (printer restrained from publishing confidential material); *Thompson v Stanhope* (1774) Amb 737 (family letters); *Wyatt v Wilson* (1820, unreported) (doctor); *Evitt v Price* (1827) 1 Sim 483 (accountant). The lines attributed to Sir Thomas More 'three things are to be help in Conscience, Fraud, Accident and Things of Confidence' *(Coco v A N Clark (Engineers) Ltd* [1969] RPC 41 at 46) indicate a long history in equity.

  There appears to be no distinction consistently drawn by the authorities or by statute between 'confidence' and 'confidentiality'. In this title the usage of the authority or statute relied on in any particular instance has been followed.

2 *Prince Albert v Strange* (1849) 2 De G & Sm 652; on appeal 1 Mac & G 25.

3 *A-G v Jonathan Cape Ltd, A-G v Times Newspapers Ltd* [1976] QB 752, [1975] 3 All ER 484 (diary of cabinet minister). Detriment is necessary for governmental confidences to give effect to a special element of public interest, but the question was specifically not decided in relation to private law confidences: see *A-G v Observer Ltd, A-G v Times Newspapers Ltd* [1990] 1 AC 109 at 256–258, sub nom *A-G v Guardian Newspapers Ltd (No 2)* [1988] 3 All ER 545 at 642–643, HL, per Lord Keith of Kinkel and at 281–282, 659 per Lord Goff of Chieveley.

4 As to copyright see generally COPYRIGHT.

5 As to patent law see generally PATENTS AND REGISTERED DESIGNS.

6 *Gilbert v Star Newspaper Co Ltd* (1894) 11 TLR 4. Cf *Times Newspapers Ltd v MGN Ltd* [1993] EMLR 443, CA.

7 *Fraser v Thames Television Ltd* [1984] QB 44, [1983] 2 All ER 101.

8 See the Patents Act 1977 s 2(4)(a),(b); *Prout v British Gas plc* [1992] FSR 478, Patents County Court (employer on notice that employee would apply for patent based on idea in confidential suggestion scheme); *Triplex Safety Glass Co Ltd v Scorah* [1938] Ch 211, [1937] 4 All ER 693.

9 See *Herbert Morris Ltd v Saxelby* [1916] 1 AC 688, HL; *Robb v Green* [1895] 2 QB 315, CA; *Amber Size and Chemical Co Ltd v Menzel* [1913] 2 Ch 239; *Wessex Dairies Ltd v Smith* [1935] 2 KB 80, CA; *Hivac Ltd v Park Royal Scientific Instruments Ltd* [1946] Ch 169, [1946] 1 All ER 350, CA; *Stevenson Jordan & Harrison Ltd v MacDonald & Evans* [1952] 1 TLR 101, 69 RPC 10, CA;

10 *Duchess of Argyll v Duke of Argyll* [1967] Ch 302, [1965] 1 All ER 611 (recently divorced defendant restrained from publishing matrimonial confidences); *Thompson v Stanhope* (1774) Amb 737 (letters of father to son). But contrast *Lennon v News Group Newspapers Ltd and Twist* [1978] FSR 573, CA.

11 *Tournier v National Provincial and Union Bank of England* [1924] 1 KB 461, CA (banker); *Carter v Palmer* (1839) 1 Dr & W 722; affd (1842) 8 Cl & Fin 657 (barrister); *Davies v Clough* (1837) 8 Sim 262 (solicitor);

Hunter v Mann [1974] QB 767, [1974] 2 All ER 414, DC (referring to doctor and priest); *W v Egdell* [1990] Ch 359, [1990] 1 All ER 835, CA (doctor).

402. Prerequisites of liability for breach of confidence. If a party is to be held liable for breach of confidence it must be shown that: (1) the material communicated to him had the necessary quality of confidence; (2) it was communicated or became known to him in circumstances entailing an obligation of confidence; and (3) there was an unauthorised use of that material[1].

   1 See *Coco v A N Clark (Engineers) Ltd* [1969] RPC 41 at 47–48 per Megarry J, who noted that some authorities require that the unauthorised use be to the detriment of the plaintiff, but left open the question whether detriment was necessary in every case; *Dunford & Elliott Ltd v Johnson & Firth Brown Ltd* [1978] FSR 143 at 148, CA; and *Jarman & Platt Ltd v I Barget Ltd* [1977] FSR 260 at 276–277, CA (an obligation of confidence which is or becomes unreasonable may not be enforced even if detriment to the plaintiff is shown). See further paras 482–483 post.

(2) DERIVATION OF JURISDICTION

403. Derivation and heads of jurisdiction. Obligations of confidence may be derived from contract[1], tort[2], equity[3], property[4] or bailment[5] or may be imposed by statute[6].

The courts have been flexible in handling these heads of jurisdiction so as to extend the scope and range of remedies. For example, two heads of liability have been relied on to eliminate consequences which might have resulted from their origins in common law and equity[7]. In contract, express terms have been supplemented by implied[8] terms, and a case involving both contract and equity has been decided in equity alone to avoid problems of construing contractual terms[9].

   1 See para 404 post.
   2 See para 405 post.
   3 See para 406 post.
   4 See para 407 post.
   5 See para 408 post.
   6 See para 409 post.
   7 *Morison v Moat* (1851) 9 Hare 241 at 255; *Robb v Green* [1895] 2 QB 315 at 317–318, 319–320, CA; *Nichrotherm Electrical Co Ltd v Percy* [1957] RPC 207 at 213–214, CA; *Ackroyds (London) Ltd v Islington Plastics Ltd* [1962] RPC 97; contra *British Celanese Ltd v Moncrieff* [1948] Ch 564 at 578, [1948] 2 All ER 44 at 47, CA.
   8 *Wessex Dairies Ltd v Smith* [1935] 2 KB 80, CA; *Triplex Safety Glass Co Ltd v Scorah* [1938] Ch 211, [1937] 4 All ER 693; *Thomas Marshall (Exports) Ltd v Guinle* [1979] Ch 227, [1978] 3 All ER 193; but see *Potters-Ballotini Ltd v Weston-Baker* [1977] RPC 202, CA; *Roger Bullivant Ltd v Ellis* [1987] ICR 464, [1987] FSR 172, CA.
   9 *Peter Pan Manufacturing Corpn v Corsets Silhouette Ltd* [1963] 3 All ER 402, [1964] 1 WLR 96.

404. Contract. Contractual terms imposing obligations of confidence may be oral[1] or written, express or implied[2], but will be subject to the requirements of consideration[3] and privity[4] and hence may be narrower in scope than obligations arising under other heads of jurisdiction such as equity[5]. Compensatory damages will be available where such terms are breached whilst it is still doubtful whether such damages are generally available for breach of obligations in equity[6].

When contractual obligations of confidence take the form of terms in restraint of trade in contracts of employment they are subject to the rules of public policy governing such terms[7]. The employer can secure fuller protection whilst the employment subsists than after it terminates[8], when the terms must be no wider than is reasonably necessary to protect the employer's goodwill and trade secrets[9]. The terms must not purport to prevent the former employee using his acquired skills and knowledge when to do so would not prejudice the goodwill or trade secrets[10]. Matters covered by a term in restraint of trade may also be covered by implied obligations in the contract of employment[11]. If an express term is narrower than these implied obligations this will not of itself prevent effect being given to the wider implied obligation[12]. The same facts and the same criteria which give rise to an implied contractual obligation of confidence may also found an equitable obligation of confidence[13].

1 *Fraser v Thames Television Ltd* [1984] QB 44, [1983] 2 All ER 101 (idea for television series).
2 *Lamb v Evans* [1893] 1 Ch 218 at 229, CA, per Bowen LJ (term implied to give 'that effect which the parties must have intended it to have and without which it would be futile'); *Amber Size and Chemical Co Ltd v Menzel* [1913] 2 Ch 239 at 244.
3 *New Zealand Needle Manufacturers Ltd v Taylor* [1975] 2 NZLR 33 at 40–41 (implied obligation of confidence found to evade failure of express term for lack of consideration).
4 Privity has also been evaded by finding an implied contract: *Mechanical and General Invention Co Ltd and Lehwess v Austin and the Austin Motor Co Ltd* [1935] AC 346, HL; *Nichrotherm Electrical Co Ltd v Percy* [1957] RPC 207 at 214–215, CA.
5 Thus where confidence involving a trade secret for a carpet grip arose in pre-contractual negotiations the court had recourse to equity: *Seager v Copydex Ltd* [1967] 2 All ER 415, [1967] 1 WLR 923.
6 See the ambiguous dicta in *Nichrotherm Electrical Co Ltd v Percy* [1956] RPC 272 at 279; on appeal [1957] RPC 207 at 214, CA; *Seager v Copydex Ltd* [1967] 2 All ER 415 at 419, [1967] 1 WLR 923 at 932; *Seager v Copydex Ltd (No 2)* [1969] 2 All ER 718 at 719, 721, [1969] 1 WLR 809 at 812, 814–815; *Dowson & Mason Ltd v Potter* [1986] 2 All ER 418 at 421, [1986] 1 WLR 1419 at 1422.
7 See para 464 post; and CONTRACT vol 9 para 415; EMPLOYMENT vol 16 (Reissue) para 17.
8 In current employment mere competition may be barred: *Thomas Marshall (Exports) Ltd v Guinle* [1979] Ch 227, [1978] 3 All ER 193; *Printers and Finishers Ltd v Holloway* [1964] 3 All ER 731 at 737, [1965] 1 WLR 1 at 7; *Faccenda Chicken Ltd v Fowler, Fowler v Faccenda Chicken Ltd* [1987] Ch 117 at 135–136, [1986] 1 All ER 617 at 625, CA.
9 *Herbert Morris Ltd v Saxelby* [1916] 1 AC 688, HL.
10 *Faccenda Chicken Ltd v Fowler, Fowler v Faccenda Chicken Ltd* [1987] Ch 117, [1986] 1 All ER 617, CA.
11 *Lamb v Evans* [1893] 1 Ch 218, CA. This will cover trade secrets and goodwill. For a summary of the tests to determine whether a matter falls within the implied term, ie the nature of the employment and the nature of the information which, if not a trade secret, must be so confidential as to require the same protection, see *Faccenda Chicken Ltd v Fowler, Fowler v Faccenda Chicken Ltd* [1987] Ch 117 at 137, [1986] 1 All ER 617 at 625, CA.
12 *Wessex Dairies Ltd v Smith* [1935] 2 KB 80, CA; *Triplex Safety Glass Co Ltd v Scorah* [1938] Ch 211, [1937] 4 All ER 693 (unreasonably wide express term does not preclude enforcement of reasonable narrower implied term). See also *Initial Services Ltd v Putterill* [1968] 1 QB 396, [1967] 3 All ER 145; *Thomas Marshall (Exports) Ltd v Guinle* [1979] Ch 227, [1978] 3 All ER 193; but see *Potters-Ballotini Ltd v Weston-Baker* [1977] RPC 202, CA; *Roger Bullivant Ltd v Ellis* [1987] ICR 464, [1987] FSR 172, CA.
13 *Robb v Green* [1895] 2 QB 315, CA; *Nichrotherm Electrical Co Ltd v Percy* [1957] RPC 207, CA; *Ackroyds (London) Ltd v Islington Plastics Ltd* [1962] RPC 97.

405. Tort. Many torts, such as inducing breach of contract[1], conspiracy[2], intimidation[3], interference with business[4] and conversion of chattels[5], may involve the misuse or infringement of confidence. Some authorities, however, have treated a party imparting confidential information as having a right of property in that information, and infringement of this right may be an independent tort[6]. This duty of confidence has been discussed in terms similar to the duty of care[7], the measure of damages in terms similar to that in tort[8] and the defence of public interest for breach of confidence as similar to privilege in defamation[9]. On the other hand, however, it has been said that claims for breach of confidence do not arise in tort at all, but only within the equitable jurisdiction of the court[10].

1 See TORT vol 45 paras 1518–1524; and see *Hivac Ltd v Park Royal Scientific Instruments Ltd* [1946] Ch 169, [1946] 1 All ER 350, CA; *Bents Brewery Co Ltd v Hogan* [1945] 2 All ER 570; *Exchange Telegraph Co Ltd v Gregory & Co* [1896] 1 QB 147, CA; *Hamlyn v John Houston & Co* [1903] 1 KB 81, CA; *Summers & Co Ltd v Boyce* (1907) 23 TLR 724; *Lowenadler v Lee* (1924) 158 LT 372; *Scophony Ltd v Traub* [1937] 4 All ER 279, CA; *British Industrial Plastics Ltd v Ferguson* [1940] 1 All ER 479, HL; *B O Morris Ltd v F Gilman (BST) Ltd* (1943) 60 RPC 20; *Under Water Welders and Repairers Ltd v Street and Longthorne* [1968] RPC 498. See further para 481 post.

2 See TORT vol 45 paras 1526–1530. See *Spermolin Ltd v John Winter* [1962] CLY 2441; *Westminster Chemical NZ Ltd v McKinley* [1973] 1 NZLR 659; *British Industrial Plastics Ltd v Ferguson* [1940] 1 All ER 479, HL; *B O Morris Ltd v F Gilman (BST) Ltd* (1943) 60 RPC 20; *Greenwood & Batley Ltd v West* (1951) 68 RPC 268; *Jarman & Platt Ltd v I Barget Ltd* [1977] FSR 260 at 267–268, CA.

3 See TORT vol 45 para 1524.

4 See TORT vol 45 para 1525. When a confidence has been committed to writing or print, trespass to goods or conversion may be invoked if the material is dealt with tortiously: see para 407 post.

5 See TORT vol 45 para 1422 et seq.

6 For authorities on the question whether there is a proprietary right in information see para 407 notes 7–8 post. An independent tort would supplement jurisdiction available in equity and property to restrain or remedy abuse of confidence by parties not privy to a contractual obligation of confidence. The Law Commission proposed the creation of a new tort of breach of confidence but effect has not been given to this: see *Breach of Confidence* (Law Com no 110) (Cmnd 8388, 1981) para 2.10; and North 'Breach of Confidence: is there a new Tort?' (1971) 12 JS PTL 149; Jones 'Restitution of Benefits Obtained in Breach of Another's Confidence' (1970) 86 LQR 463.

7 *Coco v A N Clark (Engineers) Ltd* [1969] RPC 41 at 48; *Yates Circuit Foil Co v Electrofoils Ltd* [1976] FSR 345 at 380 ('reasonable man' test used to determine whether defendant ought to have known of confidentiality).

8 *Seager v Copydex Ltd (No 2)* [1969] 2 All ER 718, [1969] 1 WLR 809, CA (analogy with conversion); distinguished in *Dowson & Mason Ltd v Potter* [1986] 2 All ER 418, [1986] 1 WLR 1419.

9 *Initial Services Ltd v Putterill* [1968] 1 QB 396, [1967] 3 All ER 145, CA; *Fraser v Evans* [1969] 1 QB 349, [1969] 1 All ER 8, CA; cf *Khashoggi v Smith* (1980) 124 Sol Jo 149, CA; *Schering Chemicals Ltd v Falkman Ltd* [1982] QB 1, [1981] 2 All ER 321, CA.

10 *Kitechnology BV v Unicor GmbH Plastmaschinen* [1995] FSR 765 at 777–778, CA, per Evans LJ.

406. Equity. It is well established that there is jurisdiction in equity to protect confidence[1]. This may be involved when (1) a party receives information known to be confidential under an agreement not having contractual force[2]; or (2) when a third party receives information which is the subject of an agreement or contract creating an obligation of confidence, having induced a party to the contract or agreement to act in breach of the obligation[3]; or (3) when information is received without inducement but when the recipient knows or ought to know that it is being imparted in breach of confidence[4]; or (4) when the information is initially received innocently but the recipient later becomes aware that it was imparted in breach of confidence[5].

The equitable jurisdiction is broader than that in contract in that it does not require a binding contractual agreement or consideration[6] and is not subject to the requirements of privity[7]. It is wider than the tort of inducing breach of contract since it does not require the intentional inducement of a breach of contract[8].

Remedies may be more restricted in that common law damages may not be available[9]. The appropriate remedies for a claim in equity will be any or all of the following: (a) an injunction[10]; (b) an account of profits[11]; (c) an order for the delivery up or destruction of offending material[12]. Where the Court of Appeal or High Court has jurisdiction to entertain an application for an injunction or specific performance[13], it may award damages in addition to, or in substitution for, an injunction[14]. It is not settled whether equitable compensation is available for breach of an equitable obligation of confidence[15].

1 *A-G v Observer Ltd, A-G v Times Newspapers Ltd* [1990] 1 AC 109 at 255, 268, 281–282, sub nom *A-G v Guardian Newspapers Ltd (No 2)* [1988] 3 All ER 545 at 639–640, 648–649, 658–659, HL; *A-G v Guardian*

Newspapers Ltd [1987] 3 All ER 316 at 352–353, 359–360; [1987] 1 WLR 1248 at 1293, 1302, HL; *Saltman Engineering Co Ltd v Campbell Engineering Co Ltd* (1948) [1963] 3 All ER 413n, 65 RPC 203, CA; *Peter Pan Manufacturing Corpn v Corsets Silhouette Ltd* [1963] 3 All ER 402, [1964] 1 WLR 96; *Auto Securities Ltd v Standard Telephones and Cable Co* [1965] RPC 92 at 93; *Cranleigh Precision Engineering Ltd v Bryant* [1964] 3 All ER 289, [1965] 1 WLR 1293; *Seager v Copydex Ltd* [1967] 2 All ER 415, [1967] 1 WLR 923; *Duchess of Argyll v Duke of Argyll* [1967] Ch 302, [1965] 1 All ER 611; *Coco v A N Clark (Engineers) Ltd* [1969] RPC 41; *Fraser v Evans* [1969] 1 QB 349, [1969] 1 All ER 8, CA; *Hubbard v Vosper* [1972] 2 QB 84, [1972] 1 All ER 1023; *Baker v Gibbons* [1972] 2 All ER 759, [1972] 1 WLR 693; *New Zealand Netherlands Society 'Oranje' Inc v Kuys* [1973] 2 All ER 1222, [1973] 1 WLR 1126, PC; *Potters-Ballotini Ltd v Weston-Baker* [1977] RPC 202, CA; *Schering Chemicals Ltd v Falkman Ltd* [1982] QB 1, [1981] 2 All ER 321, CA; *Francome v Mirror Group Newspapers Ltd* [1984] 2 All ER 408, [1984] 1 WLR 892, CA; *Stephens v Avery* [1988] Ch 449, [1988] 2 All ER 477; *Kitechnology BV v Unicor GmbH Plastmaschinen* [1995] FSR 765, CA.

 2 *Seager v Copydex Ltd* [1967] 2 All ER 415, [1967] 1 WLR 923 (pre-contractual negotiations).
 3 *Under Water Welders and Repairers Ltd v Street and Longthorne* [1968] RPC 498 at 503–504 (injunction granted against procuring any person to act 'in breach of any contractual or other obligation of confidence'); and see cases cited in para 405 note 1 ante.
 4 *Prince Albert v Strange* (1849) 2 De G & Sm 652 at 714; *London and Provincial Sporting News Agency Ltd v Levy* (1928) [1923–1928] MacG Cop Cas 340.
 5 See para 420 text and note 7–8 post.
 6 *Seager v Copydex Ltd* [1967] 2 All ER 415, [1967] 1 WLR 923.
 7 See the cases cited in para 420 text and notes 7–8 post.
 8 See the cases cited in para 405 note 1 ante.
 9 *Nichrotherm Electrical Co Ltd v Percy* [1957] RPC 207 at 213–214, CA.
10 See paras 491–492 post; and INJUNCTIONS vol 24 (Reissue) para 801 et seq.
11 See para 495 post; and EQUITY vol 16 (Reissue) para 744.
12 See para 493 post; and EQUITY vol 16 (Reissue) paras 726–727.
13 See generally SPECIFIC PERFORMANCE.
14 Supreme Court Act 1981 s 50 (which is derived from the Chancery Amendment Act 1858 (Lord Cairns' Act) s 2). Damages in lieu are an alternative to an account and because of difficulties attendant on that remedy are often preferred in commercial cases; see *A-G v Observer Ltd, A-G v Times Newspapers Ltd* [1990] 1 AC 109 at 286, sub nom *A-G v Guardian Newspapers Ltd (No 2)* [1988] 3 All ER 545 at 662, HL, per Lord Goff of Chieveley. See further para 494 post.
15 The following New Zealand cases support the remedy: *Coleman v Myers* [1977] 2 NZLR 225 at 359–363, 379, NZ CA; *A B Consolidated Ltd v Europe Strength Food Co Pty Ltd* [1978] 2 NZLR 515 at 525, NZ CA; *Van Camp Chocolates Ltd v Aulsebrooks Ltd* [1984] 1 NZLR 354 at 361, NZ CA; *Day v Mead* [1987] 2 NZLR 443 at 450–451, 460–462, 467, 469, NZ CA; *A-G for the United Kingdom v Wellington Newspapers Ltd* [1988] 1 NZLR 129 at 172, NZ CA; *Aquaculture Corpn v New Zealand Green Mussel Co Ltd* [1990] 3 NZLR 299, NZ CA.

407. Property. If a confidence is embodied in printed or written material, the torts of trespass to goods[1] or conversion (trover)[2] may be available if the material is improperly acquired or exploited[3]. Damages may reflect the value of the information in question[4]. Conversion would permit an action against a party who improperly acquired or interfered with the embodying material in good faith; trespass would give an action against one who merely interfered with possession of the material[5]. These options facilitate actions against parties who are not privy to the original confidential relationship and, unlike the equitable jurisdiction, do not depend on the defendant's knowledge of an infringement of confidence. The torts of conversion and trespass to goods do depend on an interference with tangible chattels but, whether or not the confidence has been put in written form, it may be possible to rely on a restricted proprietary right in the information itself. This might be confined to trade secrets and literary, dramatic and artistic works, differing from copyright in protecting substance as well as form, and from patents in not giving a monopoly, the information remaining available for discovery by research or analysis of products[6]. There is conflicting authority as to whether there may be property in confidential material[7] or whether, more accurately, in the process of protecting it, the courts have allowed it certain proprietary characteristics[8]. Proprietary protection would supplement equitable protection of confidence by providing an action against a person who improperly acquired confidential information without having notice of or being party to a confidential relationship with the person entitled to the information. There is little, if any, indication that the courts would take the analogy with other forms of property so far as to apply the nemo dat rule[9] and its exceptions to information. On the other hand there is some support for the view that the court will favour an analogy between an entrustment of confidential information and a bailment[10]. This analogy would at least have the advantage of permitting the imposition of liability for negligent misuse or disclosure[11].

1   As to trespass to goods see generally TORT vol 45 para 1491 et seq.
2   As to conversion of goods see generally TORT vol 45 para 1422 et seq.
3   *Borden Chemical Co (Canada) Ltd v J G Beukers Ltd* (1972) 29 DLR (3d) 337; *Thurston v Charles* (1905) 21 TLR 659.
4   *Borden Chemical Co (Canada) Ltd v J G Beukers Ltd* (1972) 29 DLR (3d) 337; *Bavins & Sims v London and South Western Bank Ltd* [1900] 1 QB 270, CA (non-negotiable instrument); *Building and Civil Engineering Holiday Scheme Management Ltd v Post Office* [1966] 1 QB 247, [1965] 1 All ER 163, CA. As to the entrustment of confidential information as a bailment see paras 408, 467 post.
5   As to wrongful interference with goods see TORT vol 45 para 1416 et seq.
6   *Fraser v Thames Television Ltd* [1984] QB 44, [1983] 2 All ER 101 (substance of orally imparted idea); *James v James* (1872) LR 13 Eq 421 at 424 (independent discovery); *Estcourt v Estcourt Hop Essence Co* (1875) 10 Ch App 276; *Saltman Engineering Co Ltd v Campbell Engineering Co Ltd* (1948) [1963] 3 All ER 413n at 414, 65 RPC 203 at 215, CA (analysis or dismantling of products publicly available). Subconscious copying will amount to breach: *Seager v Copydex Ltd* [1967] 2 All ER 415, [1967] 1 WLR 923, CA.
7   The following dicta recognise property in information: *Prince Albert v Strange* (1849) 1 Mac & G 25 at 42–43; *Exchange Telegraph Co Ltd v Gregory & Co* [1896] 1 QB 147, CA; *Exchange Telegraph Co Ltd v Howard* (1906) 22 TLR 375; *Dean v Macdowell* (1878) 8 ChD 345 at 354; *Aas v Benham* [1891] 2 Ch 244 at 255, CA; *Scott v Scott* [1913] AC 417 at 443, 450, 483; *Herbert Morris Ltd v Saxelby* [1916] 1 AC 688 at 714, HL; *Re Keene* [1922] 2 Ch 475; *Evans Medical Supplies Ltd v Moriarty (Inspector of Taxes)* [1957] 1 All ER 336, [1957] 1 WLR 288; *Rolls-Royce Ltd v Jeffrey* [1962] 1 All ER at 805, [1962] 1 WLR 425 at 430, HL; *Musker v English Electric Co Ltd* (1964) 41 TC 556; *Boardman v Phipps* [1967] 2 AC 46 at 89–91, 107–111, 115–116, [1966] 3 All ER 721 at 734–735, 745–748, 751, HL; *Technograph Printed Circuits Ltd v Chalwyn Ltd* [1967] RPC 339 at 344; *Duchess of Argyll v Duke of Argyll* [1967] Ch 302 at 320, [1965] 1 All ER 611; *Butler v Board of Trade* [1971] Ch 680 at 691, [1970] 3 All ER 593 at 600; *Diamond Stylus Co Ltd v Bauden Precision Diamonds Ltd* [1973] RPC 675 at 676; *Yates Circuit Foil Co Ltd v Electrofoils Ltd* [1976] FSR 345 at 384–385; *Searle & Co Ltd v Celltech Ltd* [1982] FSR 92, CA; *A-G v Guardian Newspapers Ltd* [1987] 3 All ER 316 at 327–328, [1987] 1 WLR 1248 at 1263 per Browne-Wilkinson V-C; *Smith Kline & French Laboratories (Australia) Ltd v Secretary, Department of Community Services* (1990) 99 ALR 679, Aust Fed Ct. A trade secret has been held to be trust property (*Green v Folgham* (1823) 1 Sim & St 398), sold with a business (*Bryson v Whitehead* (1822) 1 Sim & St 74), passed to a trustee in bankruptcy (*Re Keene* [1922] 2 Ch 475), left by will (*Canham v Jones* (1813) 2 Ves & B 218), treated as partnership property (*Dean v MacDowell* (1878) 8 ChD 345) and passed to a successor in title (*IBCOS Computers v Barclays Mercantile Highland Finance* [1994] FSR 275).
8   Dicta denying or doubting property in information are to be found in the following: *Butterworth (Inspector of Taxes) v Page* (1935) 153 LT 34 at 43, HL; *Nichrotherm Electrical Co Ltd v Percy* [1957] RPC 207 at 209, CA; *Fraser v Evans* [1969] 1 QB 349 at 361, [1969] 1 All ER 8 at 11; *Boardman v Phipps* [1967] 2 AC 46 at 127-128, [1966] 3 All ER 721 at 759, HL, per Lord Upjohn ('In general, information is not property at all . . . information is not property in any normal sense'); *North and South Trust v Berkeley* [1971] 1 All ER 980 at 993, [1971] 1 WLR 470 at 485; *Oxford v Moss* (1978) 68 Cr App Rep 183 (information not property for the purposes of theft).
9   Ie *nemo dat quod non habet* (no one can give what he does not have).
10 See *Hospital Products Ltd v United States Surgical Corpn* (1984) 156 CLR 41 at 101; *Watson v Dolmark Industries Ltd* [1992] 3 NZLR 311, NZ CA; *Gartside v Outram* (1856) 26 LJCh 113; *Foster v Mountford*

[1978] FSR 582; *Federal Comr of Taxation v United Aircraft Corpn* (1943–1944) 68 CLR 525 at 534; and paras 408, 467 post.
11 Such liability may be indicated by liability for subconscious copying: see *Seager v Copydex Ltd* [1967] 2 All ER 415, [1967] 1 WLR 923.

408. Bailment. Bailment is traditionally confined to the entrustment of tangible chattels[1]. Obligations of confidentiality can arise where the bailment of a chattel is accompanied by an entrustment of confidential information relating to that chattel or its market, or where the recipient can derive confidential information from the chattel itself. This can occur where a temporary delivery of goods (such as industrial prototypes, patterns, drawings or specifications) is made in order to facilitate industrial or commercial processes[2], or where goods which are the subject of litigation are bailed for analysis or report[3]. In such a case, where a bailment co-exists with some other relationship imposing a duty of confidentiality, an action to restrain or repair the misuse of the information can be founded on the bailment as well as on the contract or other general ground of confidence[4].

An entrustment of confidential and intangible material may, however, be treated as a bailment of information, creating rights and duties akin to those which arise under a true bailment[5]; this is on the basis that confidential information can be property[6]. There is no direct authority that information may be the subject of a bailment, but there are decisions which appear to favour an analogy between bailment and the entrustment of information, or which use the language of bailment in describing such entrustment[7]. If the analogy is accepted, a person to whom confidential information is entrusted can be restrained, by means of remedies akin to those arising on a bailment, from dealing with the information contrary to the terms of the entrustment[8], and monetary remedies can be awarded in similar fashion to those which issue in respect of interference with chattels[9].

However, there are judicial observations denying an equation between bailments and entrustments of information[10]; there is no modern English decision on the question[11].

1 As to bailment generally see BAILMENT. As to bailees' obligations of confidence see para 467 post.
2 See *Suhner & Co AG v Transradio Ltd* [1967] RPC 329 at 336 (plaintiffs' drawings wrongfully used by defendants to prepare their own manufacturing drawings); *Watson v Dolmark Industries Ltd* [1992] 3 NZLR 311, NZ CA (use of dyes in return for royalties); *McAlpine & Sons Ltd v Minimax Ltd* [1970] 1 Lloyd's Rep 397 at 422 per Thesiger J (bailee under duty to deliver report on defective fire extinguisher to the bailors as a benefit derived from their use of the subject of the bailment); *Borden Chemical Co (Canada) Ltd v J G Beukers Ltd* (1972) 29 DLR (3d) 337, BC SC. The agreement must be examined closely to determine whether there is an original bailment: cf *Federal Comr of Taxation v United Aircraft Corpn* (1943) 68 CLR 525 at 534–535, Aust HC, per Latham CJ (money payable under agreement not derived from property of licensors where agreement required return of aircraft specifications and drawings but lacked provision stating that the material remained the licensor's property).
3 Cf *McAlpine & Sons Ltd v Minimax Ltd* [1970] 1 Lloyd's Rep 397 at 422 per Thesiger J.
4 See further paras 403–407 ante.
5 See Palmer and Kohler, Information as Property, in Palmer & McKendrick *Interests in Goods* (1993) 199–201; Palmer on Bailment (2nd edn, 1991) 13–15.
6 See para 407 ante. 'It is by no means clear that information is property in this context': *North and South Trust Co v Berkeley* [1971] 1 All ER 980 at 993, [1971] 1 WLR 470 at 485 per Donaldson J.
7 *Gartside v Outram* (1856) 26 LJCh 113 at 116 per Wood V-C (employer's communication of business secrets to employee constitutes 'a solemn and sacred deposit'); *North and South Trust Co v Berkeley* [1971] 1 All ER 980 at 993, [1971] 1 WLR 470 at 485 per Donaldson J (if information entrusted to Lloyd's brokers were property, such property was not acquired by the brokers so as to enable acquisition by their principals, but was 'merely in their custody'); *Reading v The King* [1949] 2 KB 232 at 236, CA, per Asquith LJ; affd sub nom *Reading v A-G* [1951] AC 507 at 516, HL, per Lord Porter (fiduciary relationship can arise giving rise to fiduciary obligations in the recipient, where one party entrusts to

another property 'including intangible property as, for instance, confidential information' on terms restricting its use); *Hospital Products Ltd v United States Surgical Corpn* (1984) 156 CLR 41 at 70, HC Aust, per Gibb CJ; *Watson v Dolmark Industries Ltd* [1992] 3 NZLR 311 at 315, NZ CA, per Cooke P. See further *Federal Comr of Taxation v United Aircraft Corpn* (1943) 68 CLR 525 at 547–548 per Williams J; but cf at 534–536 per Latham CJ.

The analogy derives support from judicial observations in Commonwealth cases that duties akin to those owed by a bailee can arise from an entrustment of other forms of intangible property, such as goodwill: see eg *Hospital Products Ltd v United States Surgical Corpn* supra at 101, 105–106 per Mason J; *Watson v Dolmark Industries Ltd* supra at 315 per Cooke P.

8 *Reading v The King* [1949] 2 KB 232 at 236, CA, per Asquith LJ; affd sub nom *Reading v A-G* [1951] AC 507 at 516, HL, per Lord Porter; *Watson v Dolmark Industries Ltd* [1992] 3 NZLR 311 at 315, NZ CA, per Cooke P, and at 318 per Gault J.

9 *Seager v Copydex Ltd (No 2)* [1969] 2 All ER 718, [1969] 1 WLR 809, CA (damages awarded for misuse of confidential information on similar basis to damages for conversion); cf *Watson v Dolmark Industries Ltd* [1992] 3 NZLR 311 at 315, NZ CA. See also generally paras 494–495 post.

10 *Federal Comr of Taxation v United Aircraft Corpn* (1943) 68 CLR 525 at 534–535, Aust HC, per Latham CJ; cf at 546–548 per Williams J.

11 See note 6 supra.

409. Legislation. Statute or subordinate legislation may impose obligations of confidence or negate obligations which might otherwise have arisen, this varying with the subject matter and the provisions of the relevant legislation. Legislation prohibiting publication includes such disparate topics as national security[1] and aspects of medical confidentiality[2] and such specialised topics as interception of communications[3], insider dealing[4] and data protection[5]. Examples of negation include the requirements of the Companies Act 1985 in respect of publication of balance sheets, profit and loss accounts and directors' and auditors' reports[6] and in civil procedure the disclosures required for discovery[7] and under Anton Piller orders[8]. Disclosure in a particular case may, by statute or subordinate legislation, be a criminal offence, but since criminal law can be enforced by injunction this provides a link with civil obligations of confidence[9] and on occasion statute may provide for a direct private action for damages[10].

1 See the Official Secrets Act 1911; and CRIMINAL LAW vol 11(1) (Reissue) para 243 et seq.
2 See para 448 et seq post.
3 See CRIMINAL LAW vol 11(1) (Reissue) para 270 et seq.
4 See COMPANIES.
5 See para 501 et seq post.
6 See the Companies Act 1985 Pt VII Ch I (ss 221–245C) (as amended); and generally COMPANIES.
7 See DISCOVERY vol 13 para 1 et seq.
8 See INJUNCTIONS vol 24 (Reissue) para 872 et seq.
9 See *Francome v Mirror Group Newspapers Ltd* [1984] 2 All ER 408, [1984] 1 WLR 892, CA; and INJUNCTIONS vol 24 (Reissue) para 943.
10 See *Francome v Mirror Group Newspapers Ltd* [1984] 2 All ER 408 at 412, 416, [1984] 1 WLR 892 at 896, 901, CA. As to when the plaintiff has a special interest over and above that of the general public and the statute does not contemplate exclusive enforcement by criminal law see *Gouriet v Union of Post Office Workers* [1978] AC 435, [1977] 3 All ER 70, HL. In imposing a duty statute may contemplate reasonable disclosure, thus providing a defence: *Hoechst UK Ltd v Chemiculture Ltd* [1993] FSR 270.

(3) GENERAL REQUIREMENTS OF PROTECTED CONFIDENCE

410. Essential features of confidentiality. The material for which protection is claimed must be (1) of limited public availability[1]; and (2) of a specific character[2], capable of clear definition. It need not be original or novel[3], complex[4], commercially valuable[5], personally damaging or discreditable to the confider[6] nor, in general, need it take any specific form[7]; but if it does not possess the two basic characteristics of limited availability and specific character it will not be protected even though it is expressly described as confidential[8]. In a marginal case such a description could be crucial[9].

1 See *A-G v Observer Ltd, AG v Times Newspapers Ltd* [1990] 1 AC 109 at 215, sub nom *A-G v Guardian Newspapers Ltd (No 2)* [1988] 3 All ER 545 at 624, CA, per Bingham LJ, where the term 'inaccessibility' was adopted; affd [1990] 1 AC 109, [1988] 3 All ER 545, HL. See also para 411 post.
2 See para 412 post.
3 See para 414 post.
4 See para 414 post.
5 See para 413 ante.
6 See para 415 post.
7 See para 417 post.
8 *Re Dalrymple's Application* [1957] RPC 449; *Mainmet Holdings plc v Austin* [1991] FSR 538.
9 *Sun Printers Ltd v Westminster Press Ltd* (1982) 126 Sol Jo 260, CA, per Donaldson LJ.

411. Limited availability. For material to be protected as confidential its availability to the public must be restricted[1], but the question is one of degree and the restrictions need not be narrow[2]. If information is assembled and communicated to recipients subject to an agreement or understanding that it is for their use alone, even if all the component items are available to the public the fact that others would have to expend time, work or money marshalling them in the form in which they were communicated may establish the necessary restriction on availability[3]. If information is not widely available in this country but is available elsewhere and it is common practice for those interested in the topic to consult the foreign sources then it may not be protected here, although much will depend on the degree of availability[4]. If information is published only in part, confidence may still protect the part which is undisclosed[5]. The offering for sale of a product embodying confidential information will not of itself destroy the confidence even though the relevant information could be discovered by analysing the product; if the effort and expense of analysis can be avoided or reduced by revealing the information it will retain protection, but in time it may become so generally known that protection will be lost[6]. If material was once public but its significance was not generally appreciated, or it was ignored, or forgotten, it may become confidential[7]. Where persons are required to disclose documents on discovery, they are entitled to the protection of the court against any use of the documents for any purpose other than in the action for which they were disclosed[8]. A duty to preserve confidentiality may well not be eroded or terminated by adventitious publicity[9].

1 *Robb v Green* [1895] 2 QB 1 at 18–19; *Louis v Smellie* (1895) 73 LT 226; *Exchange Telegraph Co Ltd v Central News Ltd* [1897] 2 Ch 48 at 53; *Brian D Collins (Engineers) Ltd v Charles Roberts & Co Ltd* [1965] RPC 429 at 431–432; *Terrapin Ltd v Builders' Supply Co (Hayes) Ltd* (1959) [1967] RPC 375 (on appeal, but the appeal reported first, [1960] RPC 128, CA); *Under Water Welders and Repairers Ltd v Street and Longthorne* [1968] RPC 498; *Littlewoods Organisation Ltd v Harris* [1978] 1 All ER 1026 at 1034, [1977] 1 WLR 1472 at 1480, CA; *A-G v Observer Ltd, A-G v Times Newspapers Ltd* [1990] 1 AC 109, sub nom *A-G v Guardian Newspapers Ltd (No 2)* [1988] 3 All ER 545, HL; *O Mustad & Son v S Allcock & Co Ltd and Dosen* (1928) [1963] 3 All ER 416, [1964] 1 WLR 109n, HL.
2 *Prince Albert v Strange* (1849) 1 Mac & G 25 (printers); *Gilbert v Star Newspaper Ltd* (1894) 11 TLR 4 (theatrical cast); *B O Morris v F Gilman (BST) Ltd* (1943) 60 RPC 20 (workers on machine); *Franchi v Franchi* [1967] RPC 149 at 153 (foreign patent too widely known); *A-G v Observer Ltd, A-G v Times Newspapers Ltd* [1990] 1 AC 109, sub nom *A-G v Guardian Newspapers Ltd (No 2)* [1988] 3 All ER 545, HL (wide knowledge defeats even government confidentiality in security matters). In employment contexts the fact that the employer has not sought to restrict knowledge or to give instructions as to restraint will go to defeat confidentiality: *United Indigo Chemical Co Ltd v Robinson* (1932) 49 RPC 178; *G D Searle & Co Ltd v Celltech Ltd* [1982] FSR 92, CA; *E Worsley & Co Ltd v Cooper* [1939] 1 All ER 290 at 309; *Sun Printers Ltd v Westminster Press Ltd* (1982) 126 Sol Jo 260, CA.

3 *Exchange Telegraph Co Ltd v Central News Ltd* [1897] 2 Ch 48 (racing results); *Ackroyds (London) Ltd v Islington Plastics Ltd* [1962] RPC 97 at 104 (making and selling plastic swizzle sticks did not amount to a publication defeating confidentiality 'if work would have to be done' to make information available).

4 *Franchi v Franchi* [1967] RPC 149 (foreign patent too well known in this country).

5 *O Mustad & Son v S Allcock & Co Ltd and Dosen* (1928) [1963] 3 All ER 416, [1964] 1 WLR 109n, HL.

6 *Ackroyds (London) Ltd v Islington Plastics Ltd* [1962] RPC 97 at 104; *Cranleigh Precision Engineering Ltd v Bryant* [1964] 3 All ER 289, [1965] 1 WLR 1293; and see *Yates Circuit Foil Co Ltd v Electrofoils Ltd* [1976] FSR 345. If others are prepared to pay for the information this may show that it is not generally available: *Potters-Ballotini v Weston-Baker* [1977] RPC 202 at 206, CA.

7 *Coco v A N Clark (Engineers) Ltd* [1969] RPC 41 at 47.

8 *Distillers Co (Biochemicals) Ltd v Times Newspapers Ltd, Distillers Co (Biochemicals) Ltd v Phillips* [1975] QB 613, [1975] 1 All ER 41. As to discovery see generally DISCOVERY.

9 *Schering Chemicals Ltd v Falkman Ltd* [1982] QB 1 at 28, [1981] 2 All ER 321 at 339, CA.

412. Specific character. For material to be protected as confidential it must be possible to point to a definite body of material or source of information[1]. The material must not be so intermingled with material publicly available that it is impossible to indicate its limits[2]. This has been stressed by the courts in relation to injunctions which must be so drafted as to leave the party enjoined in no doubt as to what is forbidden[3].

Clear definition as to the scope of the confidential information is important in employment contracts where it is essential to distinguish knowledge of an employer's goodwill and trade secrets, which can be protected as confidential by the employer, from the employee's personal skills, experience and knowledge, which cannot be subject to restraint[4]. 'Know-how' in the sense of the employee's personal attributes cannot be protected as confidential to the employer, but 'know-how' which amounts to knowledge of scientific and industrial processes may be protected if it meets the general requirements of restricted availability and definite character which will enable it to be treated as a trade secret[5]. Knowledge of the reasonable mode of general organisation and management of a business may well not be a trade secret[6].

1 *Terrapin Ltd v Builders Supply Co (Hayes) Ltd* (1959) [1967] RPC 375 at 391; on appeal (but the appeal reported first) [1960] RPC 128, CA; *Lawrence David Ltd v Ashton* [1991] 1 All ER 385, [1989] ICR 123; *Maudsley v Palumbo* [1995] TLR 690.

2 *Amway Corpn v Eurway International Ltd* [1974] RPC 82.

3 *Amway Corpn v Eurway International Ltd* [1974] RPC 82 at 85–86; *G D Searle & Co Ltd v Celltech Ltd* [1982] FSR 92 at 104, 109, CA; *Woodward v Hutchins* [1977] 2 All ER 751 at 754, [1977] 1 WLR 760 at 764, CA; *Bjorlow (Great Britain) Ltd v Minter* (1954) 71 RPC 321 at 322–323; *P A Thomas & Co v Mould* [1968] 2 QB 913 at 922–923; *Suhner & Co AG v Transradio Ltd* [1967] RPC 329 at 334.

4 *Herbert Morris Ltd v Saxelby* [1916] 1 AC 688, HL; *E Worsley & Co Ltd v Cooper* [1939] 1 All ER 290; *Stevenson Jordan & Harrison Ltd v Macdonald & Evans* [1952] 1 TLR 101, 69 RPC 10, CA; *Printers and Finishers Ltd v Holloway* [1964] 3 All ER 731, [1965] 1 WLR 1; *Coral Index Ltd v Regent Index Ltd* [1970] RPC 147; *Faccenda Chicken Ltd v Fowler, Fowler v Faccenda Chicken Ltd* [1987] Ch 117, [1986] 1 All ER 617, CA (separability not regarded as conclusive but the fact that the alleged confidential material was part of a package containing non-confidential material could throw light on its status. Not everything carried in the memory from former employment can be used in a new employment); *Johnson & Bloy (Holdings) v Wolstenholme Rink plc* [1989] FSR 135, CA; see also *Poly Lina Ltd v Finch* [1995] FSR 751.

5 As to matters to be considered when deciding what is a trade secret see *Faccenda Chicken Ltd v Fowler, Fowler v Faccenda Chicken Ltd* [1987] Ch 117 at 137–138, [1986] 1 All ER 617 at 626–627, CA. Special methods of design and construction may be trade secrets: *Reid & Sigrist Ltd v Moss and Mechanism Ltd* (1932) 49 RPC 461 (manufacture of aircraft turn indicators).

6 *Herbert Morris Ltd v Saxelby* [1916] 1 AC 688 at 705, HL, (approving *Sir W C Leng & Co Ltd v Andrews* [1909] 1 Ch 763 at 774). Prices charged or to be charged may or may not be trade secrets: see *Faccenda Chicken Ltd v Fowler, Fowler v Faccenda Chicken Ltd* [1987] Ch 117 at 140, [1986] 1 All ER 617 at 627–628, CA; *Thomas Marshall (Exports) Ltd v Guinle* [1979] Ch 227 at 248, [1978] 3 All ER 193 at 209; cf *Berkeley Administration Inc v McClelland* [1990] FSR 505.

413. Value. No protection will be given to material which is 'perfectly useless'[1], 'pernicious nonsense'[2] or 'trivial tittle-tattle'[3]. While the absence of current commercial value will not of itself debar protection it will affect the quantum of damages or the exercise of discretion in granting an injunction[4]. These factors may also apply to the protection of personal, domestic and matrimonial confidences[5]. An idea communicated in confidence but not in writing must have potential commercial merit to be protected[6].

1   *McNicol v Sportsman's Book Stores* (1930) [1928–1935] MacG Cop Cas 116; cited in *A-G v Observer Ltd, A-G v Times Newspapers Ltd* [1990] 1 AC 109 at 149, sub nom *A-G v Guardian Newspapers Ltd (No 2)* [1988] 3 All ER 545 at 574 per Scott J; affd [1990] 1 AC 109, [1988] 3 All ER 545, CA and HL.
2   *Church of Scientology of California v Kaufman* [1973] RPC 635.
3   *Coco v A N Clark (Engineers) Ltd* [1969] RPC 41 at 48.
4   *Nichrotherm Electrical Co Ltd v Percy* [1956] RPC 272 at 273; affd [1957] RPC 207, CA.
5   *Stephens v Avery* [1988] Ch 449 at 454, [1988] 2 All ER 477 at 481 (information as to sexual conduct not necessarily 'trivial' tittle-tattle and can be protected unless relating to conduct which is grossly immoral). See also *M and N v MacKenzie and News Group Newspapers Ltd* (18 Jan 1988, unreported) (cited in *Stephens v Avery* [1988] Ch 449 at 456, [1988] 2 All ER 477 at 482–483); *Khashoggi v Smith* (1980) 124 Sol Jo 149.
6   *Fraser v Thames Television Ltd* [1984] QB 44, [1983] 2 All ER 101.

414. Simplicity, originality and novelty. The fact that confidential material is simple will not restrict its claim to protection; in fact it may enhance it[1].

In general, protected material need not be novel or original[2], but these characteristics may be evidence going to show that it is not publicly available[3]. Originality may be essential if an idea not reduced to writing is to be protected[4].

1   *Coco v A N Clark (Engineers) Ltd* [1969] RPC 41 at 47; *Cranleigh Precision Engineering Ltd v Bryant* [1964] 3 All ER 289 at 295, [1965] 1 WLR 1293 at 1310; *Under Water Welders & Repairers Ltd v Street and Longthorne* [1968] RPC 498 at 506.
2   *Saltman Engineering Co Ltd v Campbell Engineering Co Ltd* (1948) [1963] 3 All ER 413n at 414, 65 RPC 203 at 215–216, CA; and see *House of Spring Gardens Ltd v Point Blank Ltd* [1983] FSR 213 (Ireland); on appeal [1985] FSR 327.
3   As to availability see para 411 ante.
4   *Fraser v Thames Television Ltd* [1984] QB 44, [1983] 2 All ER 101.

(4) LIMITS OF CONFIDENCE

415. Protective scope of an obligation of confidence. The obligation of confidence will bind the confidant whether or not the information covered by it would be to the credit of the creator[1], and whether or not it is of current economic value in commercial matters[2]; but it will not protect illegality, gross immorality or conduct contrary to public policy[3].

1   *Prince Albert v Strange* (1849) 2 De G & Sm 652 at 697 (recreational art); *Pollard v Photographic Co* (1888) 40 ChD 345 (public display of portrait photograph a 'gross breach of faith'). 'The anonymous donor of a very large sum to a very worthy cause has his own reasons for wishing to remain anonymous, which are unlikely to be discreditable. He should surely be in a position to restrain disclosure': *A-G v Observer Ltd, A-G v Times Newspapers Ltd* [1990] 1 AC 109 at 256, sub nom *A-G v Guardian Newspapers Ltd (No 2)* [1988] 3 All ER 545 at 640, HL, per Lord Keith of Kinkel.
2   *Nichrotherm Electrical Co Ltd v Percy* [1956] RPC 272 at 273; affd [1957] RPC 207, CA.
3   See para 416 post.

416. Illegality, immorality and public policy. The confidentiality of information concerning misconduct or iniquity which in the public interest ought to be disclosed will not be protected[1]. This applies to matters relating to past and contemplated crime[2], health risks to the public[3], the reliability of equipment used by the police for evidential purposes[4], matters within the purview of the Inland Revenue or of regulatory bodies[5] or public inquiries set up to investigate the efficiency of public bodies or institutions[6]. The interests of justice may require disclosure in these circumstances[7].

There is authority that past, as distinct from contemplated, civil wrongs can be protected by confidence, since disclosure of past torts may revive old disputes and so not be for the public good[8]. The court may prohibit, or decline to prohibit, contemplated prima facie defamatory breaches of confidence even though the defendant intends to justify the alleged defamation[9]. There may be disclosure to correct words or conduct amounting to misrepresentations misleading the public[10]. The disclosure of misconduct or conduct detrimental to the public will be justified[11], but possible benefit to the public from the disclosure of a scientific discovery or invention covered by confidence will not[12]. Negligence or incompetence (as distinct from misconduct) will not justify disclosure[13]. Well-founded suspicion of misconduct as well as knowledge of wrongdoing will justify disclosure[14]. Doctors, bankers and other professional practitioners are subject to requirements of disclosure peculiar to their professions[15].

1 *Gartside v Outram* (1856) 26 LJCh 113; *Initial Services Ltd v Putterill* [1968] 1 QB 396, [1967] 3 All ER 145; *Khashoggi v Smith* (1980) 124 Sol Jo 149, CA; *British Steel Corpn v Granada Television Ltd* [1981] AC 1096, [1981] 1 All ER 417, HL; *Francome v Mirror Group Newspapers Ltd* [1984] 2 All ER 408, [1984] 1 WLR 892, CA; *Lion Laboratories Ltd v Evans* [1985] QB 526, [1984] 2 All ER 417, CA; *Stephens v Avery* [1988] Ch 449, [1988] 2 All ER 477; *A-G v Observer Ltd, A-G v Times Newspapers Ltd* [1990] 1 AC 109, sub nom *A-G v Guardian Newspapers Ltd (No 2)* [1988] 3 All ER 545, HL. See also *Fraser v Evans* [1969] 1 QB 349 at 362, [1969] 1 All ER 8 at 11–12, CA, per Lord Denning MR (no injunction against newspaper which failed to make out ground of iniquity but nevertheless intended to plead justification of alleged prospective breach of copyright; see also text and note 9 infra).

2 *Initial Services Ltd v Putterill* [1968] 1 QB 396 at 405, [1967] 3 All ER 145 at 148, CA (approved in *British Steel Corpn v Granada Television Ltd* [1981] AC 1096 at 1169, 1201, [1981] 1 All ER 417 at 455, 479, HL); *Weld-Blundell v Stephens* [1919] 1 KB 520 at 527, 533, CA; *Tournier v National Provincial Bank Ltd* [1924] 1 KB 461 at 468, 473, 481, CA; *Beloff v Pressdram Ltd* [1973] 1 All ER 241 at 260; *Malone v Metropolitan Police Comr* [1979] Ch 344, [1979] 2 All ER 620; *Francome v Mirror Group Newspapers Ltd* [1984] 2 All ER 408, [1984] 1 WLR 892, CA; *A-G v Observer Ltd, A-G v Times Newspapers Ltd* [1990] 1 AC 109 at 282, sub nom *A-G v Guardian Newspapers Ltd (No 2)* [1988] 3 All ER 545 at 659, HL, per Lord Goff of Chieveley (only limited disclosure may be allowed as being in the public interest in a case of alleged iniquity in the security services).

3 *Hubbard v Vosper* [1972] 2 QB 84, [1972] 1 All ER 1023, CA; *Church of Scientology of California v Kaufman* [1973] RPC 635; *Beloff v Pressdram Ltd* [1973] 1 All ER 241 at 260. The defence will not apply if the damage has ceased: *Schering Chemicals Ltd v Falkman Ltd* [1982] QB 1, [1981] 2 All ER 321, CA; *Distillers Co (Biochemicals) Ltd v Times Newspapers Ltd, Distillers Co (Biochemicals) Ltd v Phillips* [1975] QB 613, [1975] 1 All ER 41.

4 *Lion Laboratories Ltd v Evans* [1985] QB 526, [1984] 2 All ER 417, CA.

5 *Re a company's application* [1989] Ch 477, [1989] 2 All ER 248.

6 *Price Waterhouse v BCCI Holdings (Luxembourg) SA* [1991] TLR 478.

7 *Lion Laboratories Ltd v Evans* [1985] QB 526, [1984] 2 All ER 417, CA.

8 See *Weld-Blundell v Stephens* [1919] 1 KB 520 at 527–529, 533–535, CA; not fully considered on appeal [1920] AC 956 at 993, 1000, HL; disapproved in *Initial Services Ltd v Putterill* [1968] 1 QB 396 at 405, [1967] 3 All ER 145 at 148, CA, per Lord Denning MR. Dictum approved in *British Steel Corpn v Granada Television Ltd* [1981] AC 1096 at 1169, 1201, [1981] 1 All ER 417 at 455, 480, HL. See also *Beloff v Pressdram Ltd* [1973] 1 All ER 241 at 260; *Malone v Metropolitan Police Comr* [1979] Ch 344 at 361, [1979] 2 All ER 620 at 634–635.

9 *Fraser v Evans* [1969] 1 QB 349 at 361–362, [1969] 1 All ER 8 at 11–12, CA. See also LIBEL AND SLANDER vol 28 para 8; but see text and note 1 supra. As to justification as a defence to defamation see LIBEL AND SLANDER vol 28 para 81 et seq.

10　*Church of Scientology of California v Kaufman* [1973] RPC 635; *Initial Services Ltd v Putterill* [1968] 1 QB 396 at 407, 410–411, [1967] 3 All ER 145 at 149, 151–152, CA; *Woodward v Hutchins* [1977] 2 All ER 751, [1977] 1 WLR 760, CA.

11　Whilst material of a grossly immoral tendency may not be protected, in the absence of a generally accepted moral code it is difficult to identify such material: *Stephens v Avery* [1988] Ch 449 at 453, [1988] 2 All ER 477 at 480. But see *M and N v MacKenzie and News Group Newspapers Ltd* (18 January 1988, unreported; cited in *Stephens v Avery* supra at 456 and at 482–483.

12　*Church of Scientology of California v Kaufman* [1973] RPC 635 at 649; *Beloff v Pressdram Ltd* [1973] 1 All ER 241 at 260. However, prevention of impending disaster may excuse disclosure: *Malone v Metropolitan Police Comr* [1979] Ch 344 at 362, [1979] 2 All ER 620 at 635.

13　See *British Steel Corpn v Granada Television Ltd* [1981] AC 1096, [1981] 1 All ER 417, HL; and *Distillers Co (Biochemicals) Ltd v Times Newspapers Ltd, Distillers Co (Biochemicals) Ltd v Phillips* [1975] QB 613 at 622, [1975] 1 All ER 41 at 49–50.

14　*Gartside v Outram* (1856) 26 LJCh 113 at 114; *Butler v Board of Trade* [1971] Ch 680 at 689, [1970] 3 All ER 593; *Malone v Metropolitan Police Comr* [1979] Ch 344 at 377, [1979] 2 All ER 620 at 646.

15　See para 436 et seq post.

417. Form. In general neither the obligation of confidentiality nor the subject matter need be in any special form.

The obligation may be written[1] or oral[2]. It may be specifically agreed[3], expressly or impliedly[4], or may arise as a necessary or traditional incident of a relationship such as marriage[5] or professional employment[6]. An express contractual term will not necessarily exclude or restrict a wider implied term; nor, conversely, will an unreasonably wide express term prevent the enforcement of a similar, but less restrictive, implied term[7].

The subject matter may be oral[8], written[9] or graphic as when confidence attaches to etchings prepared for private circulation amongst friends[10] or to a portrait photograph[11]. It may take the form of tables[12], diagrams[13], formulae[14], maps and plans[15], personal correspondence[16] or plots and ideas for dramatic works[17]. It may be embodied in machinery or its products[18].

The subject matter of the confidence may be carried in the memory[19]. An ex-employee is not necessarily free to use in his new employment all the material he carried in his memory from his former employment[20]. An idea not reduced into writing but communicated in confidence will be protected provided that it is original, clearly identifiable, has potential commercial merit and is capable of reaching fruition[21].

The fact that material claimed to be confidential is not easily separable from other material does not preclude the enforcement of confidentiality, but if the allegedly confidential material is part of a package which also contains non-confidential material this may go to show that the material in dispute is not confidential[22].

1　*Litholite Ltd v Travis and Insulators Ltd* (1913) 30 RPC 266; *Potters-Ballotini Ltd v Weston-Baker* [1977] RPC 202, CA.

2　*Portal v Hine* (1887) 4 TLR 330; *Fraser v Thames Television Ltd* [1984] QB 44, [1983] 2 All ER 101.

3　*Portal v Hine* (1887) 4 TLR 330; *Stephens v Avery* [1988] Ch 449, [1988] 2 All ER 477 (non-contractual understanding without any prior relationship is enough).

4　*Seager v Copydex Ltd* [1967] 2 All ER 415, [1967] 1 WLR 923, CA (contractual negotiations).

5　*Duchess of Argyll v Duke of Argyll* [1967] Ch 302, [1965] 1 All ER 611 (marriage).

6　*Tournier v National Provincial Bank* [1924] 1 KB 461, CA (banker and customer); *Hunter v Mann* [1974] QB 767, [1974] 2 All ER 414, DC (doctor and patient).

7　*Wessex Dairies Ltd v Smith* [1935] 2 KB 80, CA; *Fraser v Evans* [1969] 1 QB 349, [1969] 1 All ER 8; and see para 416 text and notes 1, 9 ante.

8　*Fraser v Thames Television Ltd* [1984] QB 44, [1983] 2 All ER 101.

9　*Thompson v Stanhope* (1774) Amb 737 (family letters).

10　*Prince Albert v Strange* (1849) 1 Mac & G 25.

11 *Pollard v Photographic Co* (1888) 40 ChD 345. See also *Tuck & Sons v Priester* (1887) 19 QBD 629 (copies of a drawing).
12 *Merryweather v Moore* [1892] 2 Ch 518 (table of engineering specifications).
13 *Nichrotherm Electrical Co Ltd v Percy* [1957] RPC 207, CA (diagrams of pig-feeding machine).
14 *Johnson & Bloy (Holdings) Ltd v Wolstenholme Rink plc* [1989] FSR 135, CA (formulae for ink manufacture); *Alperton Rubber Co Ltd v Manning* (1917) 86 LJCh 377.
15 *Brian D Collins (Engineers) Ltd v Charles Roberts & Co Ltd* [1965] RPC 429 (drawings of tank trucks); *Floydd v Cheney* [1970] Ch 602, [1970] 1 All ER 446.
16 *Thompson v Stanhope* (1774) Amb 737.
17 *Gilbert v Star Newspaper Ltd* (1894) 11 TLR 4 (plot of a comic opera); *Fraser v Thames Television Ltd* [1984] QB 44, [1983] 2 All ER 101; *Talbot v General Television Pty Ltd* [1981] RPC 1 (Vict) (idea for television programme).
18 *Ackroyds (London) Ltd v Islington Plastics Ltd* [1962] RPC 97 (machine for making plastic swizzle sticks); *IBCOS Computers Ltd v Barclays Mercantile Highland Finance Ltd* [1994] FSR 275 (computer software).
19 *Amber Size and Chemical Co v Menzel* [1913] 2 Ch 239.
20 *Johnson & Bloy (Holdings) Ltd v Wolstenholme Rink plc* [1989] FSR 135, CA.
21 *Fraser v Thames Television Ltd* [1984] QB 44, [1983] 2 All ER 101.
22 *Faccenda Chicken Ltd v Fowler, Fowler v Faccenda Chicken Ltd* [1987] Ch 117 at 138, 140, [1986] 1 All ER 617 at 627, CA.

(5) CREATION OF CONFIDENCE

418. Creation of confidence by statute or subordinate legislation. The commencement, content and limits of an obligation of confidentiality created by or under statute will depend on the terms of the relevant legislation[1].

1 See para 409 ante.

419. Creation of confidence otherwise than by legislation. In order to be protected, the information or other material must not only possess the attributes of limited availability[1] and specific character[2], but must also have been communicated to, obtained by or become known to the recipient in circumstances imposing an obligation of confidence[3]. Express terms must be such as to maintain the restricted availability and specific character essential to protected confidence. If the material is so widely published or disseminated as to negate these attributes[4], or if no instructions or administrative procedures are employed to safeguard them[5], no obligation will exist.

In both equity and contract an obligation of confidence will be impliedly constituted when material is imparted in circumstances which make it clear that it is being communicated subject to restrictions of confidentiality[6], as in the professional employment of a doctor[7] or banker[8]. However, an obligation of confidence may be specifically constituted without any such special relationship[9], as for instance where the recipient is placed in a position where confidential information can be acquired by observation[10]. It is uncertain how far the unsolicited communication of material with an indication that it is to be treated as confidential can impose an obligation on the recipient. It is settled that if the information is already independently available to the recipient no obligation arises[11]. Pre-contractual negotiations may give rise to an obligation if the requirements of protected confidence are present[12].

Similar criteria have been used in both contract and equity for establishing implied obligations of confidence[13] (although in contract reference has been made to the 'business efficacy test'[14]). The test, which is objective, is whether the recipient ought to have known that the material was confidential since there will be liability not only for deliberate but also subconscious misuse[15], and the test of the reasonable man has been invoked to determine what ought to have been appreciated by the recipient[16]. An obligation may also be created when one party agrees to acquire information for another subject to confidence[17].

1 See para 411 ante.
2 See para 412 ante.
3 'Information must have been imparted in circumstances importing an obligation of confidence': *Coco v A N Clark (Engineers) Ltd* [1969] RPC 41 at 47 per Megarry J.
4 *G D Searle & Co Ltd v Celltech Ltd* [1982] FSR 92, CA; *United Indigo Chemical Co Ltd v Robinson* (1932) 49 RPC 495; *E Worsley & Co Ltd v Cooper* [1939] 1 All ER 290; *Amway Corpn v Eurway International Ltd* [1974] RPC 82; *Aveley/Cybervox Ltd v Boman and Sign Erections Ltd* [1975] FSR 139; *Sun Printers Ltd v Westminster Press Ltd* (1982) 126 Sol Jo 260, CA; and see *Faccenda Chicken Ltd v Fowler, Fowler v Faccenda Chicken Ltd* [1987] Ch 117 at 138, 140, [1986] 1 All ER 617 at 627, 629, CA.
5 *G D Searle & Co Ltd v Celltech Ltd* [1982] FSR 92, CA; *Yates Circuit Foil Co v Electrofoils Ltd* [1976] FSR 345; *Aveley/Cybervox Ltd v Boman and Sign Erections Ltd* [1975] FSR 139; *Faccenda Chicken Ltd v Fowler, Fowler v Faccenda Chicken Ltd* [1987] Ch 117 at 138, 140, [1986] 1 All ER 617 at 627, 629, CA. If precautions are taken this will support confidentiality: *Standex International Ltd v C B Blades Ltd* [1976] FSR 114 at 121, CA.
6 The restrictions will often indicate the special purpose for which the material is being communicated: *Morison v Moat* (1851) 9 Hare 241; *Pollard v Photographic Co* (1888) 40 ChD 345; *Lamb v Evans* [1893] 1 Ch 218, CA; *Mechanical and General Inventions Co Ltd v Austin and Austin Motor Co* [1935] AC 346, HL; *Saltman Engineering Co Ltd v Campbell Engineering Co Ltd* (1948) [1963] 3 All ER 413n, 65 RPC 203, CA; *Nichrotherm Electrical Co Ltd v Percy* [1957] RPC 207, CA; *Ackroyds (London) Ltd v Islington Plastics Ltd* [1962] RPC 97; *Bostitch Inc v McGarry & Cole Ltd* [1964] RPC 173; *Brian D Collins (Engineers) Ltd v Charles Roberts & Co Ltd* [1965] RPC 429; *Torrington Manufacturing Co v Smith & Sons (England) Ltd* [1966] RPC 285; *Terrapin Ltd v Builders' Supply Co (Hayes) Ltd* (1959) [1967] RPC 375; on appeal (but the appeal reported first) [1960] RPC 128, CA; *Suhner & Co AG v Transradio Ltd* [1967] RPC 329; *Schering Chemicals Ltd v Falkman Ltd* [1982] QB 1, [1981] 2 All ER 321, CA.
7 See para 436 post.
8 See para 456 post.
9 *Seager v Copydex Ltd* [1967] 2 All ER 415, [1967] 1 WLR 923, CA (implied); *Stephens v Avery* [1988] Ch 449 at 455–456, [1988] 2 All ER 477 at 482 (express).
10 *Amber Size and Chemical Co Ltd v Menzel* [1913] 2 Ch 239.
11 The recipient may be wise to return the embodying material to the confider with a statement that he does not accept it on terms of confidentiality: *Johnson v Heat and Air Systems Ltd* (1941) 58 RPC 229.
12 *Gunston v Winox Ltd* (1920) 37 TLR 74 (injunction granted as information not independently available); *Mechanical and General Inventions Co Ltd v Austin and Austin Motor Co* [1935] AC 346, HL; *Seager v Copydex Ltd* [1967] 2 All ER 415, [1967] 1 WLR 923, CA; *Harrison v Project and Design Co (Redcar) Ltd* [1978] FSR 81. But see *Auto Securities Ltd v Standard Telephones and Cables* [1965] RPC 92 (injunction refused on balance of convenience); *Coco v A N Clark (Engineers) Ltd* [1967] RPC 41 (all requirements not shown).
13 *Saltman Engineering Co Ltd v Campbell Engineering Co Ltd* (1948) [1963] 3 All ER 413n, 65 RPC 203, CA; *Brian D Collins (Engineers) Ltd v Charles Roberts & Co Ltd* [1965] RPC 429. See also *Lamb v Evans* [1893] 1 Ch 218, CA; *Alperton Rubber Co v Manning* (1917) 86 LJCh 377; *National Broach and Machine Co v Churchill Gear Machines Ltd* [1965] RPC 61 (on appeal on the question of damages only [1965] 2 All ER 961, [1965] 1 WLR 1199, CA; affd [1966] 3 All ER 923n, [1967] 1 WLR 384, HL).
14 See *The Moorcock* (1889) 14 PD 64, CA; *Lamb v Evans* [1893] 1 Ch 218, CA; *Ackroyds (London) Ltd v Islington Plastics Ltd* [1962] RPC 97; and see CONTRACT vol 9 para 355.
15 *Seager v Copydex Ltd* [1967] 2 All ER 415, [1967] 1 WLR 923, CA.
16 *Coco v A N Clark (Engineers) Ltd* [1969] RPC 41 at 48 (cited in *Yates Circuit Foil Co v Electrofoils Ltd* [1976] FSR 345 at 380; *G D Searle & Co Ltd v Celltech Ltd* [1982] FSR 92 at 108, CA.) The test may be assisted by surrounding circumstances as when the recipient occupies an appointment of obvious trust (*Reid & Sigrist Ltd v Moss and Mechanism Ltd* (1932) 49 RPC 461 at 480) or by relevant custom and practice (*Gilbert v Star Newspaper Co Ltd* (1894) 11 TLR 4). Professional codes of conduct and circulars may provide evidence of such custom and practice. As to eg medicine see the General Medical Council guidelines approved in *W v Egdell* [1989] 1 All ER 1089 at 1101–1102; affd [1990] Ch 359 at 420, [1990] 1 All ER 835 at 849, CA; and as to those guidelines generally see para 436 et seq post.
17 *A-G v Guardian Newspapers Ltd* [1987] 3 All ER 316, [1987] 1 WLR 1248; *A-G v Observer Ltd, A-G v Times Newspapers Ltd* [1990] 1 AC 109 at 144, 214, sub nom *A-G v Guardian Newspapers (No 2)* [1988]

3 All ER 545 at 571, 624 (Scott J and CA) (newspapers publishing memoirs of intelligence officer which had been published in book form in breach of confidence); *Industrial Furnaces Ltd v Reaves* [1970] RPC 605.

420. Third party recipients of confidential material. A third party who acquires or receives confidential material which he knew or ought to have known was subject to confidence may be restrained by injunction from any further dealing[1] or may be liable to an account of profits[2]. If the third party knowingly induces a party under a contractual obligation of confidence to break that contract, the third party may be liable for the tort of inducing breach of contract[3] and if the third party improperly handles some document or other tangible embodiment of the confidential material he may be liable for trespass to goods[4] or conversion[5].

Constructive notice will be found if a third party can be shown to have deliberately refrained from inquiring whether material was being communicated in breach of confidence[6]. If the third party initially receives the confidential material innocently, without knowledge or notice that it has been communicated in breach of confidence, no liability will be incurred. Liability will be incurred only when the innocent party knows or ought to know of the impropriety affecting the communication[7]. It is doubtful whether bona fide purchase for value is a defence[8].

1 *Prince Albert v Strange* (1849) 2 De G & Sm 652 (on appeal (1849) 1 Mac & G 25); *Morison v Moat* (1851) 9 Hare 241; *Liquid Veneer Co Ltd v Scott* (1912) 29 RPC 639; *A-G v Guardian Newspapers Ltd* [1987] 3 All ER 316, [1987] 1 WLR 1248; *A-G v Observer Ltd, A-G v Times Newspapers Ltd* [1990] 1 AC 109, sub nom *A-G v Guardian Newspapers (No 2)* [1988] 3 All ER 545, HL (injunction not granted since wide publicity for the confidential material had rendered it futile).

2 'The fact that a primary confidant, having communicated the confidential information to a third party in breach of obligation, is about to reveal it similarly to someone else, does not entitle that third party to do the same': *A-G v Observer Ltd, A-G v Times Newspapers Ltd* [1990] 1 AC 109 at 261, sub nom *A-G v Guardian Newspapers Ltd (No 2)* [1988] 3 All ER 545 at 644, HL, per Lord Keith of Kinkel.

3 See para 405 ante.

4 See para 405 ante; and TORT vol 45 para 1491 et seq.

5 See para 405 ante; and TORT vol 45 para 1422 et seq.

6 *London and Provincial Sporting News Agency Ltd v Levy* (1928) [1923–1928] MacG Cop Cas 340. Companies formed to use information obtained in breach of confidence will be regarded as affected by notice: *Liquid Veneer Co Ltd v Scott* (1912) 29 RPC 639; *Litholite Ltd v Travis* (1913) 30 RPC 266; *Reid & Sigrist Ltd v Moss and Mechanism Ltd* (1932) 49 RPC 461; *Cranleigh Precision Engineering v Bryant* [1964] 3 All ER 289, [1965] 1 WLR 1293; *Industrial Furnaces Ltd v Reaves* [1970] RPC 605; *Standex International Ltd v Blades* [1976] FSR 114; and see *A-G v Guardian Newspapers Ltd* [1987] 3 All ER 316, [1987] 1 WLR 1248, HL; *A-G v Observer Ltd, A-G v Times Newspapers Ltd* [1990] 1 AC 109 at 144, 214, sub nom *A-G v Guardian Newspapers Ltd (No 2)* [1988] 3 All ER 545 at 658–659, HL, per Lord Goff of Chieveley.

7 *Prince Albert v Strange* (1849) 2 De G & Sm 652 (on appeal 1 Mac & G 25); *Rex Company and Rex Research Corpn v C H Muirhead and HM Comptroller of Patents* (1926) 44 RPC 38; *Stevenson Jordan & Harrison Ltd v Macdonald & Evans* (1951) 68 RPC 190; revsd on other grounds [1952] 1 TLR 101, 69 RPC 10, CA; *Printers and Finishers Ltd v Holloway* [1964] 3 All ER 731, [1965] RPC 239; *Fraser v Evans* [1969] 1 QB 349, [1969] 1 All ER 8, CA; *Butler v Board of Trade* [1971] Ch 680, [1970] 3 All ER 593; *Malone v Metropolitan Police Comr* [1979] Ch 344, [1979] 2 All ER 620; *Dowson & Mason Ltd v Potter* [1986] 2 All ER 418, [1986] 1 WLR 1419, CA; *Hoechst UK Ltd v Chemiculture Ltd* [1993] FSR 270. See also *A-G v Observer Ltd, A-G v Times Newspapers Ltd* [1990] 1 AC 109 at 255, 268, 281–282, sub nom *A-G v Guardian Newspapers Ltd (No 2)* [1988] 3 All ER 545, 639–640, 648–649, 658–659, HL, per Lord Goff of Chieveley.

8 *Duke of Queensberry v Shebbeare* (1758) 2 Eden 329; *Richards v Dobell* (1912) [1911–1916] MacG Cop Cas 51; *Stevenson, Jordan & Harrison Ltd v Macdonald & Evans* (1951) 68 RPC 190 at 195; on appeal [1952] 1 TLR 101, 69 RPC 10, CA, suggest not; contra *Morison v Moat* (1851) 9 Hare 241 at 263. See also Nourse LJ in *A-G v Observer Ltd* [1986] CA Transcript 696; cited in *A-G v Guardian Newspapers Ltd* [1987] 3 All ER 316 at 327–328, [1987] 1 WLR 1248 at 1265 per Browne-Wilkinson V-C; *A-G v Observer Ltd, A-G v Times Newspapers Ltd* [1990] 1 AC 109 at 144, 214, sub nom *A-G v Guardian Newspapers Ltd (No 2)* [1988] 3 All ER 545 at 596, CA. See Jones 'Restitution of Benefits Obtained in Breach of Another's Confidence' (1970) 86 LQR 463 at 479–481. Some Canadian authorities have

accepted the defence of bona fide purchase for value: see *International Tools v Kollar* (1968) 67 DLR (2d) 386 at 391; *Tenatronics Ltd v Hauf* (1972) 23 DLR (3d) 60. Bona fide purchasers may be protected by change of position: *Lipkin Gorman (a firm) v Karpnale Ltd* [1991] 2 AC 548; [1992] 4 All ER 512, HL.

(6) CONTINUANCE OF OBLIGATIONS OF CONFIDENCE

421. Duration of an obligation. The duration of an obligation arising from an agreement, contractual or otherwise, will depend primarily on the terms, express or implied, of the agreement. In contracts of employment such terms will be subject to the requirements of reasonableness resulting from public policy[1] and if these requirements are not observed then, subject to the possibility of severance[2], the terms will not be binding. An employee may continue to be bound by a contractual obligation of confidence even if the public could obtain the relevant information by buying and dismantling or analysing products in which it is embodied[3]. This may apply only when others have to expend work or money to obtain the information[4]. If the information is freely available without the need for significant investigation then the obligation of confidence may cease to bind[5].

Terms in restraint of trade[6] may continue to bind ex-employees who have had access to trade secrets or opportunities to influence goodwill, but the longer the term and the wider the scope of the covenant, the heavier will be the onus of proving that it is reasonable[7]. In appropriate circumstances lifelong and worldwide covenants may be upheld[8]. If an express term of an agreement makes it clear that all obligations of confidence are to lapse with the expiry of a specified period, then that will happen, but if the agreement states merely that an obligation of confidence will continue for a specified period, that obligation will not necessarily lapse when that period expires, since an implied term or equitable obligation which has not been excluded by the express term may continue to apply[9].

With governmental confidences, public interest in freedom of information may allow a relaxation[10] or security considerations may require perpetual non-disclosure[11]. A member of the intelligence services owes a lifelong obligation of confidence to the Crown in relation to governmental secrets[12], but a former cabinet minister may, after a sufficient interval, publish diaries recording proceedings at cabinet meetings where there is no indefinitely continuing public interest in maintaining the confidentiality of cabinet meetings and the disclosures are unlikely to raise an issue of national security[13].

Publication of confidential material in an application for a patent may involve sufficiently full disclosure to terminate the obligation in whole or in part[14]. If information is disclosed in confidence to a party for a special purpose and in a fiduciary capacity, that party may be restrained from using the information for his own purposes even if much of it is available to the public[15]. It may be that the duty to preserve confidentiality will not be eroded or terminated by adventitious publicity[16]. If a confidant improperly destroys confidentiality by publication of the entrusted material he may continue to be under a duty of confidence[17].

The discloser may be liable in damages or to an account of profits and may come under a specific duty, akin to the 'springboard' doctrine[18], not to use the formerly confidential material to his own advantage. An injunction granted by the court to restrict a defendant's freedom so as to prevent him from gaining an unfair advantage from confidential information obtained in former employment should be restricted to a period during which any advantage might last[19].

 1 *A-G v Barker* [1990] 3 All ER 257, CA (lifelong and worldwide restriction held to be valid since it did not restrict future employment).
 2 *Nordenfelt v Maxim-Nordenfelt Guns and Ammunition Co* [1894] Ch 535, HL; *Attwood v Lamont* [1920] 3 KB 571, CA; *Mason v Provident Clothing Supply Co* [1913] AC 724 at 745, HL; *Putsman v Taylor* [1927] 1 KB 637; *Scorer v Seymour-Johns* [1966] 3 All ER 347, [1966] 1 WLR 1419.
 3 *Merryweather v Moore* [1892] 2 Ch 518; *Reid & Sigrist Ltd v Moss and Mechanism Ltd* (1932) 49 RPC 461.
 4 *Ackroyds (London) Ltd v Islington Plastics Ltd* [1962] RPC 97 at 104. See also para 422 post.
 5 See *A-G v Observer Ltd, A-G v Times Newspapers Ltd* [1990] 1 AC 109, sub nom *A-G v Guardian Newspapers Ltd (No 2)* [1988] 3 All ER 545, HL (improper disclosure did not terminate an obligation to account); and see note 17 infra.
 6 *A-G v Barker* [1990] 3 All ER 257, CA (an express lifelong and worldwide covenant not to reveal personal confidential information during and after the employment was upheld since it was not in restraint of trade). As to restraint of trade see TRADE, INDUSTRY AND INDUSTRIAL RELATIONS vol 47 (Reissue) para 13 et seq.
 7 *Attwood v Lamont* [1920] 3 KB 571 at 589.
 8 *Nordenfelt v Maxim Nordenfelt Guns and Ammunition Co* [1894] AC 535, HL; *Fitch v Dewes* [1921] 2 AC 158, HL.
 9 *Wessex Dairies Ltd v Smith* [1935] 2 KB 80, CA; *Triplex Safety Glass Co Ltd v Scorah* [1938] Ch 211, [1937] 4 All ER 693; *Thomas Marshall (Exports) Ltd v Guinle* [1979] Ch 227, [1978] 3 All ER 193; contra *Potters-Ballotini Ltd v Weston-Baker* [1977] RPC 202, CA. See also *Roger Bullivant Ltd v Ellis* [1987] ICR 464, [1987] FSR 172, CA.
10 *A-G v Jonathan Cape Ltd, A-G v Times Newspapers Ltd* [1976] QB 752, [1975] 3 All ER 484.
11 *A-G v Observer Ltd, A-G v Times Newspapers Ltd* [1990] 1 AC 109, sub nom *A-G v Guardian Newspapers Ltd (No 2)* [1988] 3 All ER 545, HL.
12 *A-G v Observer Ltd, A-G v Times Newspapers Ltd* [1990] 1 AC 109 at 226, sub nom *A-G v Guardian Newspapers Ltd (No 2)* [1988] 3 All ER 545 at 633, CA, per Bingham LJ, at 268 and 647, HL, per Lord Brightman, and at 284 and 660 per Lord Goff of Chieveley.
13 *A-G v Jonathan Cape Ltd, A-G v Times Newspapers Ltd* [1976] QB 752, [1975] 3 All ER 484.
14 *O Mustad & Son v S Allcock & Co Ltd and Dosen* (1928) [1963] 3 All ER 416, [1964] 1 WLR 109n, HL; *Franchi v Franchi* [1967] RPC 149. However, local disclosure of information may not destroy confidentiality elsewhere: *Exchange Telegraph Co Ltd v Central News Ltd* [1897] 2 Ch 48; *Exchange Telegraph Ltd v Gregory & Co* [1896] 1 QBD 147; *Exchange Telegraph Ltd v Howard* (1906) 22 TLR 375.
15 *Schering Chemicals Ltd v Falkman Ltd* [1982] QB 1, [1981] 2 All ER 321, CA (journalist who obtains confidential information during employment as a professional adviser is under a fiduciary obligation not to use it for his own purposes); explained as an application of the 'springboard' doctrine (see para 422 post) in *A-G v Observer Ltd, A-G v Times Newspapers Ltd* [1990] 1 AC 109 at 149, sub nom *A-G v Guardian Newspapers Ltd (No 2)* [1988] 3 All ER 545 at 575 per Scott J, and at 177 and 595–596, CA, per Donaldson MR; affd [1990] 1 AC 109, [1988] 3 All ER 545, HL; and *A-G v Guardian Newspapers Ltd* [1987] 3 All ER 316 at 328, [1987] 1 WLR 1248 at 1263 per Browne-Wilkinson V-C.
16 *Schering Chemicals Ltd v Falkman Ltd* [1982] QB 1 at 28, [1981] 2 All ER 321 at 339, CA, per Shaw LJ.
17 *Speed Seal Products Ltd v Paddington* [1986] 1 All ER 91, [1985] 1 WLR 1327, CA. But this has been doubted on the grounds of absurdity, including the possible consequence that third parties dealing with the confidant would come under a duty of confidence even although the information was common knowledge: see *A-G v Observer Ltd, A-G v Times Newspapers Ltd* [1990] 1 AC 109 at 285 et seq, sub nom *A-G v Guardian Newspapers Ltd (No 2)* [1988] 3 All ER 545 at 661 et seq, HL.
18 See para 422 post.
19 *Roger Bullivant Ltd v Ellis* [1987] ICR 464, [1987] FSR 172, CA.

422. The 'springboard' doctrine. This doctrine expresses the principle that a party in possession of confidential information which is the subject-matter of an equitable obligation of confidence will not be allowed to use that information as a 'springboard' to enable him to enter the market more cheaply and speedily than others who would have to work or spend money to obtain it. Thus a party may be restrained from acting in breach of such an obligation even if others, not so bound, could acquire the information by buying, dismantling, analysing or examining products embodying it[1]. The doctrine will apply only if the relevant information retains partial confidentiality, and it is a question of fact and degree in each case whether the information has become so generally available that the person bound would have no advantage over members of the public[2]. The doctrine therefore operates for a limited period only[3].

1 For the doctrine's original formulation see *Terrapin Ltd v Builders' Supply Co (Hayes) Ltd* (1959) [1967] RPC 375 at 391 per Roxburgh J ('As I understand it, the essence of this branch of the law . . . is that a person who has obtained information in confidence is not allowed to use it as a springboard for activities detrimental to the person who made the confidential communication, and springboard it remains even when all the features have been published or can be ascertained by actual inspection by any member of the public'); on appeal (but the appeal reported first) [1960] RPC 128, CA. See also *Ackroyds (London) Ltd v Islington Plastics Ltd* [1962] RPC 97 at 103; *Cranleigh Precision Engineering Ltd v Bryant* [1964] 3 All ER 289, [1965] 1 WLR 1293; *Seager v Copydex Ltd* [1967] 2 All ER 415, [1967] 1 WLR 923, CA; *Peter Pan Manufacturing Corpn v Corsets Silhouette Ltd* [1963] 3 All ER 402, [1964] 1 WLR 96; and see *Yates Circuit Foil Co v Electrofoils Ltd* [1976] FSR 345 at 387; *Potters-Ballotini Ltd v Weston-Baker* [1977] RPC 202 at 206, CA; *Harrison v Project and Design Co (Redcar) Ltd* [1978] FSR 81 at 88; *Schering Chemicals Ltd v Falkman Ltd* [1982] QB 1, [1981] 2 All ER 321, CA; and see *A-G v Guardian Newspapers Ltd* [1987] 3 All ER 316, [1987] 1 WLR 1248 at 327, HL; *A-G v Observer Ltd, A-G v Times Newspapers Ltd* [1990] 1 AC 109 at 285, 288, sub nom *A-G v Guardian Newspapers Ltd (No 2)* [1988] 3 All ER 545 at 661, 664, HL.
2 *Yates Circuit Foil Co v Electrofoils Ltd* [1976] FSR 345 at 387; *Harrison v Project and Design Co (Redcar) Ltd* [1978] FSR 81 at 88; and see *Ackroyds (London) Ltd v Islington Plastics* [1962] RPC 97 at 104; *Franchi v Franchi* [1967] RPC 149 at 153.
3 *Potters-Ballotini Ltd v Weston-Baker* [1977] RPC 202 at 206–207, CA; *Peter Pan Manufacturing Corpn v Corsets Silhouette Ltd* [1963] 3 All ER 402 at 407, [1964] 1 WLR 96; *Harrison v Project and Design Co (Redcar) Ltd* [1978] FSR 81 at 87; *Prout v British Gas plc* [1992] FSR 478, Patents County Court (doctrine ended on filing patent application); *Roger Bullivant Ltd v Ellis* [1987] ICR 464, [1987] FSR 172, CA; *Fisher-Karpark Industries Ltd v Nichols* [1982] FSR 351.

(7) TERMINATION OF OBLIGATIONS OF CONFIDENCE

423. Release from obligation of confidence. Release may be express or implied, total or partial[1], as when restricted to a specific transaction or to part of the information covered[2]. Release must be effected by the person to whom the obligation of confidence is owed[3]. If that person makes the information publicly available, as in a patent application, this may amount to an implied release[4]. It is unclear whether a party under an obligation of confidence who improperly makes the information publicly available will continue to be bound[5]; some authority suggests that he will not continue to be bound but may nevertheless be liable in damages or to an account of profits[6]. A party who owes an obligation of confidence will not be impliedly released from it merely by showing that the person to whom it is owed knows that he has already endangered the confidence or is likely to act in breach of it[7]. If the obligation is owed to a trustee or fiduciary, the agreement of the beneficiaries or principals to a release is essential[8].

1 *Tournier v National Provincial and Union Bank of England* [1924] 1 KB 461 at 473, 485–486, CA; *Sunderland v Barclays Bank Ltd* (1938) 5 Legal Decisions Affecting Bankers 163 at 164; *Ackroyds (London) Ltd v Islington Plastics Ltd* [1962] RPC 97; *Hunter v Mann* [1974] QB 767 at 772, [1974] 2 All ER 414, DC; *O Mustad & Son v S Allcock & Co Ltd and Dosen* (1928) [1963] 3 All ER 416, [1964] 1 WLR 109n, HL; explained in *A-G v Observer Ltd, A-G v Times Newspapers Ltd* [1990] 1 AC 109 at 285, sub nom *A-G v Guardian Newspapers Ltd (No 2)* [1988] 3 All ER 545 at 662, HL, per Lord Goff of Chieveley. In the release of a contractual obligation problems of accord and satisfaction and equitable estoppel may arise: see *Ackroyds (London) Ltd v Islington Plastics Ltd* supra at 104; and CONTRACT vol 9 para 594 et seq.
2 *Tournier v National Provincial and Union Bank of England* [1924] 1 KB 461 at 486, CA; *O Mustad & Son v S Allcock & Co Ltd and Dosen* (1928) [1963] 3 All ER 416 at 418, [1964] 1 WLR 109n at 111–112.
3 *A-G v Jonathan Cape Ltd, A-G v Times Newspapers Ltd* [1976] QB 752 at 770, [1975] 3 All ER 485 at 495 (cabinet minister owes obligation to Queen and cannot be released from it by colleagues); but see *Harman v Secretary of State for the Home Department* [1983] 1 AC 280 at 326, sub nom *Home Office v Harman* [1982] 1 All ER 532 at 554–555, HL (party obtaining discovery owes duty to court but can be released

from it by the other party). A patient may release a doctor from medical confidentiality: *C v C* [1946] 1 All ER 562. A client may waive legal professional privilege: *Wilson v Rastall* (1792) 4 Term Rep 753.

4 *O Mustad & Son v S Allcock & Co Ltd and Dosen* (1928) [1963] 3 All ER 416, [1964] 1 WLR 109n, HL as explained in *A-G v Observer Ltd, A-G v Times Newspapers Ltd* [1990] 1 AC 109 at 285, sub nom *A-G v Guardian Newspapers Ltd (No 2)* [1988] 3 All ER 545 at 662, HL, per Lord Goff of Chieveley.

5 *Speed Seal Products Ltd v Paddington* [1986] 1 All ER 91, [1985] 1 WLR 1327, CA; *A-G v Observer Ltd, A-G v Times Newspapers Ltd* [1990] 1 AC 109, sub nom *A-G v Guardian Newspapers Ltd (No 2)* [1988] 3 All ER 545, Scott J and CA.

6 *A-G v Observer Ltd, A-G v Times Newspapers Ltd* [1990] 1 AC 109 at 286–288, sub nom *A-G v Guardian Newspapers Ltd (No 2)* [1988] 3 All ER 545 at 662–664, HL, per Lord Goff of Chieveley.

7 *A-G v Jonathan Cape Ltd, A-G v Times Newspapers Ltd* [1976] QB 752 at 768, [1975] 3 All ER 484 at 493; *Taylor v Blacklow* (1836) 3 Bing (NC) 235 (solicitor acting for both parties not released); *A-G v Observer Ltd, A-G v Times Newspapers Ltd* [1990] 1 AC 109 at 261, 292, sub nom *A-G v Guardian Newspapers Ltd (No 2)* [1988] 3 All ER 545 at 644, 667, HL.

8 *Boardman v Phipps* [1967] 2 AC 46 at 105, [1966] 3 All ER 721 at 743–744, HL; *Carter v Palmer* (1842) 8 Cl & Fin 657.

424. Frustration. An obligation of confidence created by contract may be frustrated[1] by supervening illegality if statute prohibits the continued preservation of confidence[2] or if a change of circumstance renders its continuance contrary to public policy[3]. If a business where trade secrets or goodwill are protected by confidence ceases to exist without those assets being transferred to a successor, the obligations also cease to exist[4]. If the relevant information becomes so widely known that it can be regarded as fully in the public domain this, too, may determine obligations of confidence[5].

The death of a party to whom the obligation is owed will not necessarily frustrate the obligation of confidence[6].

1 As to frustration see CONTRACT vol 6 para 450 et seq.

2 As to statutory duties of disclosure see the Criminal Justice Act 1988 s 93B (added by the Criminal Justice Act 1993 s 30); the Northern Ireland (Emergency Provisions) Act 1991 s 54A (added by the Criminal Justice Act 1993 s 48); and the Prevention of Terrorism (Temporary Provisions) Act 1989 s 18A (added by the Criminal Justice Act 1993 s 51).

3 See *W v Egdell* [1990] Ch 359, [1990] 1 All ER 835, CA, where the confidentiality of a medical opinion that a mental patient was dangerous was defeated by the obligation to disclose when the patient was applying for release from hospital; and para 441 post.

4 Cf *Rhodes v Forwood* (1876) 1 App Cas 256 at 274, HL (closure of business ends agency); *Measures Bros Ltd v Measures* [1910] 2 Ch 248; *General Billposting Co Ltd v Atkinson* [1909] AC 118, HL (wrongful dismissal repudiates contract; employee no longer bound); *Northey v Trevillion* (1902) 18 TLR 648. It would seem that obligations of confidence arising from equity, contract and tort would similarly cease.

5 *O Mustad & Son v S Allcock & Co Ltd and Dosen* (1928) [1963] 3 All ER 416, [1964] 1 WLR 109n, HL; *Speed Seal Products Ltd v Paddington* [1986] 1 All ER 91, [1985] 1 WLR 1327, CA. As to the view that it is absurd for the bound party to remain bound once his wrongful act has caused it to become public see *A-G v Observer Ltd, A-G v Times Newspapers Ltd* [1990] 1 AC 109 at 286–288, sub nom *A-G v Guardian Newspapers Ltd (No 2)* [1988] 3 All ER 545 at 662–664, HL, per Lord Goff of Chieveley.

6 See para 426 post.

425. Repudiation. Repudiatory breach on the part of the party entitled to confidence will release the party bound by the obligation[1].

1 *General Billposting Co Ltd v Atkinson* [1909] AC 118, HL; *Measures Bros Ltd v Measures* [1910] 2 Ch 248; cf *Yasouda Fire and Marine Insurance Co of Europe Ltd v Orion Marine Insurance Underwriting Agency Ltd* [1995] QB 174, [1995] 3 All ER 211.

426. Death. A doctor's obligation of confidence is not necessarily ended by the death of his patient but will depend on all the circumstances, including the nature of the information, the extent to which it is already available and the length of time since death[1]. Where an application for access to the health records of a deceased patient is made by the patient's personal representatives or any person who may have a claim arising out of the patient's death, access must not be given if the record includes a note, made at the patient's request, that he did not wish access to be given on such an application[2]. Where such an application is made, access must not be given to any part of the record which, in the opinion of the holder of the record, would disclose information which is not relevant to any claim which may arise out of the patient's death[3]. Similarly, a banker or solicitor may continue to be bound by an appropriate obligation of confidence after the death of a customer or client[4].

In so far as confidential information possesses the character of property, it devolves on death on personal representatives[5]. With commercial, literary and dramatic confidences this is assisted by the close links with patents, designs and copyright law[6].

1 See Confidentiality: Guidance from the General Medical Council (1995), Principle 13; and para 440 post.
2 Access to Health Records Act 1990 ss 3(1)(f), 4(3).
3 Ibid s 5(4).
4 For bankers this is in accordance with principle, and there appears to be no authority to the contrary. For solicitors see the Guide to the Professional Conduct of Solicitors (6th Edn, 1993) Principle 16.03.
5 *Canham v Jones* (1813) 2 V & B 218; and see para 407 note 7 ante.
6 See para 401 notes 4–8 ante.

427. Divorce. Divorce does not terminate the obligations of matrimonial confidence[1].

1 *Duchess of Argyll v Duke of Argyll* [1967] Ch 302, [1965] 1 All ER 611; but see *Lennon v News Group Newspapers Ltd and Twist* [1978] FSR 573, CA (no protection where parties had previously made disclosures to the press).

428. Purchase by third party. It may be that a bona fide purchaser for value without notice of confidential information will take the information free of the restrictions of confidence, but this is not free from doubt[1].

1 See para 420 text and note 8 ante.

(8) CLASSIFICATION OF CONFIDENCES

(i) Personal Confidences

429. General. There is in general no protection of privacy at common law, but the right to privacy in certain personal matters, particularly marital confidences, has been held to be one which the law should seek to protect[1]. If it is in the public interest that confidences should be respected, the encouragement of such respect may in itself constitute a sufficient ground for recognising and enforcing the obligation of confidence even where the confider can point to no specific detriment to himself[2]. A high-profile media personality who actively seeks publicity for what might otherwise have remained private will not be protected[3], and nor will protection be given to conduct that is grossly immoral[4] or otherwise inimical to public policy[5]. Protection has been extended not merely to family and domestic matters[6], but also to recreational activities[7] and in order to counter unsought publicity[8]. Protection extends not only to the confider but also to others who were to be shielded by the confidence[9].

1　*Duchess of Argyll v Duke of Argyll* [1967] Ch 302, [1965] 1 All ER 611; *A-G v Observer Ltd, A-G v Times Newspapers Ltd* [1990] 1 AC 109 at 255, sub nom *A-G v Guardian Newspapers Ltd (No 2)* [1988] 3 All ER 545 at 639, HL, per Lord Keith of Kinkel.
2　*A-G v Observer Ltd, A-G v Times Newspapers Ltd* [1990] 1 AC 109 at 255, sub nom *A-G v Guardian Newspapers Ltd (No 2)* [1988] 3 All ER 545 at 640, HL, per Lord Keith of Kinkel.
3　*Woodward v Hutchins* [1977] 2 All ER 751, [1977] 1 WLR 760, CA; *Lennon v News Group Newspapers Ltd and Twist* [1978] FSR 573, CA.
4　*Stephens v Avery* [1988] Ch 449 at 453, [1988] 2 All ER 477 at 481; and see *M and N v MacKenzie and News Group Newspapers Ltd and Twist* (18 January 1988, unreported) cited in *Stephens v Avery* supra at 456 and 482.
5　See paras 416 ante, 485 post.
6　*Duchess of Argyll v Duke of Argyll* [1967] Ch 302, [1965] 1 All ER 611 (matrimonial); *Thompson v Stanhope* (1774) Amb 737.
7　*Prince Albert v Strange* (1849) 2 De G & Sm 652; affd (1849) 1 Mac & G 25 (etchings for private circulation).
8　*Pollard v Photographic Co* (1888) 40 ChD 345 (public display of portrait photograph for advertising purposes). But see *Corelli v Wall* (1906) [1905–1910] MacG Cop Cas 41; *A-G v Observer Ltd, A-G v Times Newspapers Ltd* [1990] 1 AC 109 at 256, sub nom *A-G v Guardian Newspapers Ltd (No 2)* [1988] 3 All ER 545 at 640, HL, per Lord Keith of Kinkel (protection of anonymity of donor to charity).
9　*Coco v A N Clark (Engineers) Ltd* [1969] RPC 41 at 48 (a breach may show the entruster in a favourable light but gravely injure some friend or relation of his whom he wishes to protect).

430. Obligations of confidence between parent and child. Letters from a father to his son have been held to be protected by an obligation of confidence[1].

1　*Thompson v Stanhope* (1774) Amb 737. It is probable that the principle would extend to confidences arising out of other, analogous, family relationships.

431. Obligations of confidence between husband and wife. Matrimonial confidences will be protected even after divorce[1] unless both parties have assented to making their private lives public[2]. The implied obligation of confidence is a concomitant of marriage and remains enforceable even where the party seeking to restrain publication has published limited details and does not come with 'clean hands', provided that the 'balance of perfidy' is in that party's favour in that the plaintiff's publication was less pernicious than that proposed or published by the defendant[3]. A spouse's infidelity does not negate entitlement to protection for past confidences[4]. In view of the number of persons likely to be interested in disclosures the extent of an injunction may differ from that used to protect other forms of confidence[5].

1　*Duchess of Argyll v Duke of Argyll* [1967] Ch 302, [1965] 1 All ER 611.
2　*Lennon v News Group Newspapers Ltd and Twist* [1978] FSR 573, CA.
3　*Duchess of Argyll v Duke of Argyll* [1967] Ch 302 at 330, [1965] 1 All ER 611 at 625 per Ungoed-Thomas J.
4　*Duchess of Argyll v Duke of Argyll* [1967] Ch 302 at 331 [1965] 1 All ER 611 at 626.
5　*A-G v Observer Ltd, A-G v Times Newspapers Ltd* [1990] 1 AC 109 at 255–256, sub nom *A-G v Guardian Newspapers Ltd (No 2)* [1988] 3 All ER 545 at 643, HL.

432. Personal conduct. It has been held that there is nothing to support the view that information relating to sexual conduct cannot be the subject matter of a duty of confidentiality[1]. An express agreement to maintain confidentiality in regard to a lesbian relationship is enforceable[2]. Although the court will not give effect to an agreement relating to 'grossly immoral' conduct, the absence of a generally accepted moral code makes it difficult to identify such conduct and, indeed, 'there is no common view that sexual conduct of any kind between consenting adults is grossly immoral'[3]. If parties encourage publicity for what otherwise would be their private lives, protection will not be extended to them[4].

1 *Stephens v Avery* [1988] Ch 449 at 455, [1988] 2 All ER 477 at 482 per Browne-Wilkinson V-C.
2 *Stephens v Avery* [1988] Ch 449, [1988] 2 All ER 477.
3 *Stephens v Avery* [1988] Ch 449 at 453, [1988] 2 All ER 477 at 480. See also *Khashoggi v Smith* (1980) 124 Sol Jo 149, CA. It has been suggested that the mere existence of a homosexual relationship does not raise a duty of confidence between the parties or as against third parties: see *M and N v MacKenzie and News Group Newspapers Ltd* (18 January 1988, unreported); but this point was expressly left open in *Stephens v Avery* supra at 456 and 482.
4 *Woodward v Hutchins* [1977] 2 All ER 751, [1977] 1 WLR 760, CA; *Lennon v News Group Newspapers Ltd and Twist* [1978] FSR 573, CA.

433. Miscellaneous aspects of personal privacy. Almost every aspect of private life may be covered by obligations of confidence, provided that the basic requirements for protection[1] are present and no rules of law or public policy are infringed[2]. If a photographer takes a picture of a person without that person's consent, use of the picture for advertising cannot be restrained, whereas if the picture is taken in accordance with an agreement whose terms are subsequently breached, protection is available[3].

1 As to the basic requirements for protection see para 410 ante.
2 *A-G v Barker* [1990] 3 All ER 257, CA (lifelong and worldwide ban on revealing details of employers' private lives upheld since it did not restrict future employment). See *Francome v Mirror Group Newspapers Ltd* [1984] 2 All ER 408, [1984] 1 WLR 892, CA; and see also the authorities cited in para 429 notes 7–9 ante.
3 *Pollard v Photographic Co* (1888) 40 ChD 345.

(ii) Governmental Confidences

434. National and local government. The courts recognise the need to balance the public interest requiring many governmental activities to be protected by full or partial confidence with the countervailing public interest in making available information about public affairs[1]. The law of confidence provides the only civil ground for restraining publication of information relating to national security which is, of its nature, prima facie confidential[2], but, because of the need to consider the countervailing interest which favours disclosure, the party seeking to restrain publication must show not only that the material is confidential but also that it is in the public interest for it to remain undisclosed[3]. In view of the wide variety of matters covered, these countervailing interests will be balanced to different effect according to the circumstances[4].

Whilst current cabinet discussions are fully confidential, the passage of time may render them of merely historical interest so that publication will not be restrained if they have no security implications[5]. Members of the security services are under a lifelong obligation of confidence and both they and third parties, such as newspapers who receive information from them which they know or ought to know is confidential, may be restrained by injunction from disclosing the information unless the information has been so widely disseminated as to render an injunction futile[6]. A party intending to publish material already in the public domain will not be penalised by an injunction but may nevertheless be liable to an account of profits[7]. It is doubtful whether a party who, by improper disclosure, has made public information that was once confidential can continue to be restrained, but he may be liable for damages or to an account of profits[8]. In the security service the duty of confidence applies to all information except 'trivia of the most humdrum kind'[9]. The defence of iniquity[10] will, at best, justify complaint through internal channels or very restricted publication[11].

Comprehensive and indefinitely prolonged confidentiality for security matters does not infringe the duty, bestowed by the Convention for the Protection of Human Rights and Fundamental Freedoms, to protect freedom of speech, as the Convention permits restrictions which are prescribed by law and necessary in a democratic society 'in the interests of national security' and 'preventing the disclosure of information received in confidence'[12].

Matters which have attracted governmental confidentiality include the functioning of aspects of government such as cabinet collective responsibility (until lapse of time may have made protection no longer necessary)[13], the security services[14] and matters tending to prejudice foreign relations[15]. The fact that a third party knows that a party bound by an obligation of confidence intends to act in breach of that obligation and destroy confidentiality by publication will not of itself release the third party from his obligations[16]. If it is conceded in a particular case that publication of material in breach of confidence will not prejudice national security, a third party who obtains the material innocently will not be restrained from further publishing it merely in order to assert the lifelong obligation of confidence of the security officer who was its original author[17].

A newspaper that publishes material which is known to have been disclosed in breach of confidence, and which other newspapers have been restrained from publishing by injunction, may be in criminal contempt of court. The mens rea required to establish contempt is a specific intention to impede or prejudice the administration of justice and not mere recklessness as to whether that obstruction or prejudice would occur[18].

A local authority, although under a statutory duty to provide an efficient and comprehensive library service[19], is in contempt of court if it makes available a book containing material published in breach of confidence when the further dissemination of that material by newspapers is the subject of an interim injunction, but the authority need not examine all newspapers, books and periodicals taken in its libraries to see if they contain material infringing the injunction[20].

It is probable that a duty of confidence may, in principle, be owed by a government department[21] and by a local authority[22].

1 *A-G v Observer Ltd, A-G v Times Newspapers Ltd* [1990] 1 AC 109 at 256, 265, 282, sub nom *A-G v Guardian Newspapers Ltd (No 2)* [1988] 3 All ER 545 at 640, 646–647 and 659–660, HL; *A-G v Jonathan Cape Ltd, A-G v Times Newspapers Ltd* [1976] QB 752, [1975] 3 All ER 485; *Commonwealth of Australia v John Fairfax & Sons Ltd* (1980) 32 ALR 485, Aust HC.

2 *A-G v Observer Ltd, A-G v Times Newspapers Ltd* [1990] 1 AC 109 at 291, sub nom *A-G v Guardian Newspapers Ltd (No 2)* [1988] 3 All ER 545 at 666, HL, per Lord Goff of Chieveley. As to the protection of official secrets in criminal law see CRIMINAL LAW vol 11(1) (Reissue) para 243 et seq.

3 *A-G v Observer Ltd, A-G v Times Newspapers Ltd* [1990] 1 AC 109 at 256–258, sub nom *A-G v Guardian Newspapers Ltd (No 2)* [1988] 3 All ER 545 at 640–642, HL, per Lord Keith of Kinkel, and at 282 and 659 per Lord Goff of Chieveley; *A-G v Jonathan Cape Ltd, A-G v Times Newspapers Ltd* [1976] QB 752 at 770–771, [1975] 3 All ER 484 at 495 per Lord Widgery CJ; *Commonwealth of Australia v John Fairfax & Sons Ltd* (1980) 32 ALR 485 at 492–493, Aust HC, per Mason J.

4 *A-G v Jonathan Cape Ltd, A-G v Times Newspapers Ltd* [1976] QB 752 at 767, [1975] 3 All ER 484 at 492 per Lord Widgery CJ. Secrets relating to national security may require to be preserved indefinitely: *A-G v Jonathan Cape Ltd, A-G v Times Newspapers Ltd* supra at 770 and at 495 per Lord Widgery CJ.

5   *A-G v Jonathan Cape Ltd, A-G v Times Newspapers Ltd* [1976] QB 752, [1975] 3 All ER 484.

6   *A-G v Observer Ltd, A-G v Times Newspapers Ltd* [1990] 1 AC 109 at 260, 267, 288–289, sub nom *A-G v Guardian Newspapers Ltd (No 2)* [1988] 3 All ER 545 at 643, 648, 664–665, HL.

7   *A-G v Observer Ltd, A-G v Times Newspapers Ltd* [1990] 1 AC 109 at 260, 267, 288–289, sub nom *A-G v Guardian Newspapers Ltd (No 2)* [1988] 3 All ER 545 at 643, 647–648, 663–664, HL.

8   It has been suggested that the person who breaches his obligation may also continue to be bound by 'some limited obligation analogous to the springboard doctrine' to prevent him exploiting his knowledge, but the point was not argued before the court and the question was expressly reserved: see *A-G v Observer Ltd, A-G v Times Newspapers Ltd* [1990] 1 AC 109 at 288, sub nom *A-G v Guardian Newspapers Ltd (No 2)* [1988] 3 All ER 545 at 664, HL, per Lord Goff of Chieveley. As to the 'springboard' doctrine see para 422 ante.

9   *A-G v Observer Ltd, A-G v Times Newspapers Ltd* [1990] 1 AC 109 at 284, sub nom *A-G v Guardian Newspapers Ltd (No 2)* [1988] 3 All ER 545 at 660, HL, per Lord Goff of Chieveley; contra at 269 and 650 per Lord Griffiths.

10   As to the defence of iniquity see paras 416 ante, 485 post.

11   *A-G v Observer Ltd, A-G v Times Newspapers Ltd* [1990] 1 AC 109 at 259, sub nom *A-G v Guardian Newspapers Ltd (No 2)* [1988] 3 All ER 545 at 642, HL, per Lord Keith of Kinkel, and at 282–283 and 659–660 per Lord Goff of Chieveley.

12   See the Convention for the Protection of Human Rights and Fundamental Freedoms (Rome, 4 November 1950; TS 71 (1953); Cmd 8969) Art 10; and FOREIGN RELATIONS LAW vol 18 para 1694. 'Necessary' implies 'the existence of a pressing social need' and the interference with freedom of expression should be no more than is proportionate to the legitimate aim pursued: see *A-G v Observer Ltd, A-G v Times Newspapers Ltd* [1990] 1 AC 109 at 256, sub nom *A-G v Guardian Newspapers Ltd (No 2)* [1988] 3 All ER 545 at 640, HL, per Lord Keith of Kinkel, and at 288 and 660 per Lord Goff of Chieveley. See also *Lingens v Austria* (1986) 8 EHRR 407, ECtHR (discussed in *A-G v Observer Ltd, A-G v Times Newspapers Ltd* supra at 156–159, 580–582 per Scott J). An interlocutory injunction might infringe the Convention for the Protection of Human Rights and Fundamental Freedoms art 10 if the material to which it relates has been so widely published as to undermine the case for restraint: *A-G v Guardian Newspapers Ltd* [1987] 3 All ER 316, [1987] 1 WLR 1248, HL (injunction granted); *Observer and Guardian v UK* (1991) 14 EHRR 153, ECtHR; *Sunday Times v UK* (1991) 14 EHRR 229, ECtHR (injunction held to infringe the Convention for the Protection of Human Rights and Fundamental Freedoms art 10).

13   *A-G v Jonathan Cape Ltd, A-G v Times Newspapers Ltd* [1976] QB 752, [1975] 3 All ER 484.

14   *A-G v Observer Ltd, A-G v Times Newspapers Ltd* [1990] 1 AC 109, sub nom *A-G v Guardian Newspapers Ltd (No 2)* [1988] 3 All ER 345; *A-G v Guardian Newspapers Ltd* [1987] 3 All ER 316, [1987] 1 WLR 1248, HL.

15   *Commonwealth of Australia v John Fairfax & Co Ltd* (1980) 32 ALR 485, Aust HC.

16   *A-G v Observer Ltd, A-G v Times Newspapers Ltd* [1990] 1 AC 109 at 261, sub nom *A-G v Guardian Newspapers Ltd (No 2)* [1988] 3 All ER 545 at 644, HL, per Lord Keith of Kinkel, and at 292 and 667 per Lord Goff of Chieveley.

17   *Lord Advocate v The Scotsman Publications Ltd* [1990] 1 AC 812, [1989] 2 All ER 852, HL.

18   *A-G v Newspaper Publishing plc* [1988] Ch 333, [1987] 3 All ER 276, CA. As to mens rea generally see CRIMINAL LAW vol 11(1) (Reissue) para 10 et seq.

19   See the Public Libraries and Museums Act 1964 s 7 (as amended); and LIBRARIES AND SCIENTIFIC AND CULTURAL INSTITUTIONS vol 28 para 319.

20   *A-G v Observer Ltd, Re an application by Derbyshire County Council* [1988] 1 All ER 385.

21   *Norwich Pharmacal Co v Comrs of Customs and Excise* [1974] AC 133 at 181–182, [1973] 2 All ER 943 at 954, HL, per Lord Morris of Borth-y-Gest, and at 189–190 and 961 per Viscount Dilhorne; *Butler v Board of Trade* [1971] Ch 680, [1970] 3 All ER 593. However, because injunctions may not generally be granted against the Crown or any officer of the Crown (see the Crown Proceedings Act 1947 s 21(1), (2)), the only preventative remedy will be a declaration.

22   To the extent that a local authority is less concerned than a national government with issues of national security the public interest in preserving confidentiality is likely to be reduced, while the defence of iniquity might be allowed greater scope: see generally *A-G v Jonathan Cape Ltd, A-G v Times Newspapers Ltd* [1976] QB 752 at 767, [1975] 3 All ER 484 at 592 per Lord Widgery CJ; *Commonwealth of Australia v John Fairfax & Sons Ltd* (1980) 32 ALR 485 at 492–493, Aust HC, per Mason J. See also the text and notes 19–20 supra.

435. Public corporations and utilities. Public corporations and utilities are to be treated on the same basis as private companies, and their confidences are therefore not assessed according to the competing public interests in confidentiality and disclosure which apply to governmental organisations[1].

  1 See *British Steel Corpn v Granada Television Ltd* [1981] AC 1096 at 1202, [1981] 1 All ER 417 at 480, HL, per Lord Fraser of Tullybelton. As to trade secrets see TRADE, INDUSTRY AND INDUSTRIAL RELATIONS vol 47 (Reissue) para 44 et seq. As to the matters which directors of a company must disclose see COMPANIES.

(iii) Medical and other Professional Confidences

A. CONFIDENCES RELATING TO HEALTH

436. In general. The relationship of doctor and patient is one to which confidence attaches as a necessary or traditional incident[1] in order to ensure that patients make frank disclosure when seeking diagnosis and treatment[2].

The General Medical Council[3] has issued rules which, whilst not carrying statutory authority[4], indicate matters which might lead to disciplinary proceedings under the General Medical Council's statutory powers. Statute and subordinate legislation have also in part delimited the obligation of confidence[5]. To reinforce the general obligation of confidence the General Medical Council sets out certain general principles to apply in all circumstances[6].

  1 *Wyatt v Wilson* (unreported, 1820) (cited in *Prince Albert v Strange* (1849) 1 Mac & G 25 at 46 per Lord Cottenham); *Kitson v Playfair* (1896) Times, 28 March; *Hunter v Mann* [1974] QB 767 at 772, [1974] 2 All ER 414 at 417–418, DC; *Goddard v Nationwide Building Society* [1987] QB 670 at 685, [1986] 3 All ER 264 at 271; *X v Y* [1988] 2 All ER 648 at 656; *W v Egdell* [1990] Ch 359, [1990] 1 All ER 835, CA; *A-G v Observer Ltd, A-G v Times Newspapers Ltd* [1990] 1 AC 109 at 177, sub nom *A-G v Guardian Newspapers Ltd (No 2)* [1988] 3 All ER 545 at 595, CA, per Donaldson MR, and at 255 and 639, HL, per Lord Keith of Kinkel. Confidence may be waived by the patient and disclosure is not then a breach: *C v C* [1946] 1 All ER 562.
  2 *X v Y* [1988] 2 All ER 648; *W v Egdell* [1990] Ch 359 at 423, [1990] 1 All ER 835 at 851, CA.
  3 As to the General Medical Council see MEDICINE vol 30 (Reissue) para 111 et seq.
  4 *W v Egdell* [1990] Ch 359 at 412, [1990] 1 All ER 835 at 843, CA, per Sir Stephen Brown P. Since the Medical Act 1969 introduced a further range of penalties, conduct once not regarded as infringing professional standards may now be so treated: *McCandless v General Medical Council* [1995] TLR 668, PC.
  5 See para 447 post.
  6 See 'Confidentiality: Guidance from the General Medical Council' (1995) (contained in Duties of a Doctor), Principle 1.
     Information contained in, and extracts from, Duties of a Doctor – Guidance from the General Medical Council, are used in this title with grateful acknowledgment to the General Medical Council.

437. Doctors' obligation of confidence to patient. A patient has a right to expect that his doctor will not pass on any personal information which he learns in the course of his professional duties, unless the patient gives permission[1]. A doctor who is responsible for confidential information must ensure that it is effectively protected against improper disclosure when disposed of, stored, transmitted or received[2]. When a patient consents to disclosure of information the doctor must make sure that the patient understands the extent of, the reasons for and the likely consequences of disclosure[3]. The doctor must make sure that patients are informed whenever information about them is likely to be disclosed to others involved in their health care, and that they have the opportunity to withhold permission[4]. Only in exceptional circumstances where the health or safety of others would otherwise be at serious risk should a request by a patient for disclosure not to be made to third parties be overridden[5]. When disclosure is justified only so much information as is necessary for the purpose should be released, and the doctor must make sure that health workers to whom disclosure is made understand that it is in confidence[6]. If the doctor decides to disclose confidential information, he must be prepared to explain and justify his decision[7].

1 See Good Medical Practice: Guidance from the General Medical Council (1995), Principles 11, 16; Confidentiality: Guidance from the General Medical Council (1995), Principle 1. Confidence may be waived by the patient and disclosure is not then a breach: *C v C* [1946] 1 All ER 562. As to the authority of, and weight to be accorded to, guidance from the General Medical Council see para 436 ante.
2 See Confidentiality: Guidance from the General Medical Council (1995), Principle 1.
3 See ibid Principle 1.
4 See ibid Principle 1.
5 See ibid Principle 1.
6 See ibid Principle 1.
7 See ibid Principle 1.

438. Sharing of information among medical team. A doctor may release confidential information only in strict accordance with the patient's consent or with the consent of a person properly authorised on the patient's behalf[1]. When treatment is provided by a medical team, the doctor must explain to the patient the need to share information between team members, and any circumstances in which team members providing non-medical care may be required to disclose information to third parties, but it is not necessary to obtain explicit permission for the disclosures necessary for such matters as the obtaining of X-ray photographs or the preparation of correspondence relating to treatment to which the patient has agreed[2]. Disclosure without specific consent is also permissible in a medical emergency where the patient's consent cannot be obtained[3], or if the patient has given a discretion to the doctor to disclose information to other team members as required, but if a patient explicitly refuses to allow disclosure to all or any other members of the team this must be respected[4]. Doctors must ensure that other members of a medical team understand and observe confidentiality[5]. When a doctor assesses a patient for a third party (such as an employer or insurance company) the doctor must ensure that the patient (1) understands the purpose of the assessment; (2) is aware of the obligations of the doctor to the third party and that this may necessitate the disclosure of personal information; and (3) gives written consent[6].

1 See Confidentiality: Guidance from the General Medical Council (1995), Principle 2. Note that, in Canada, in suing a doctor the patient waives confidentiality: *Hay v University of Alberta* (1991) 2 Med LR 204. As to the authority of, and weight to be accorded to, guidance from the General Medical Council see para 436 ante.
2 See Confidentiality: Guidance from the General Medical Council (1995), Principles 3, 4, 5.
3 See ibid Principle 6.
4 See ibid Principle 7.
5 See ibid Principle 8.
6 See ibid Principle 9. As to the patient's ability to give consent see para 439 post.

439. Patient's ability to consent to disclosure of information. If, because of illness, immaturity or mental incapacity the patient is considered incapable of giving consent and has not allowed an appropriate third party to be involved in the consultation, then disclosure may be made to an appropriate person or authority if the doctor considers this essential in the medical interests of the patient (who must be informed)[1].

The judgment of whether a patient is capable of giving or withholding consent to treatment or disclosure must be based on the patient's ability to understand what the treatment may involve, and not solely on the patient's age[2]. If a patient appears to the doctor to be neglected or abused and unable to give consent, the doctor may inform an appropriate responsible person or statutory agency to prevent further harm to the patient[3]. Exceptionally, a doctor may consider it damaging to the patient to obtain his consent to disclosure but that disclosure should nevertheless be made in the patient's medical interests[4]; in such a case disclosure may be made to a close relative without the patient's consent[5].

1 See Confidentiality: Guidance from the General Medical Council (1995), Principle 10. As to the authority of, and weight to be accorded to, guidance from the General Medical Council see para 436 ante.
2 See ibid Principle 10.
3 See ibid Principle 11.
4 For example where a relative should know about the patient's terminal condition but the patient himself might be seriously harmed by the information; see ibid Principle 12.
5 See ibid Principle 12; and *Furniss v Fitchett* [1958] NZLR 396.

440. Death of the patient. The death of a patient may modify, but does not terminate, the doctor's duty of confidence; the extent of modification will depend on the circumstances, including the nature of the information, whether it is already public knowledge and the length of time since the patient's death[1]. When there is a conflict of interests between the parties affected by the patient's death, the doctor must not disclose information without the consent of the deceased patient's personal representatives or a close relative, who has been fully informed of the consequences of disclosure[2]. Third parties have rights of access to medical records of a deceased patient in certain circumstances[3].

1 See Confidentiality: Guidance from the General Medical Council (1995), Principle 13. See also para 426 ante. As to the authority of, and weight to be accorded to, guidance from the General Medical Council see para 436 ante.
2 See ibid Principle 13.
3 See ibid Principle 14; the Access to Health Records Act 1990 s 4(3); and para 426 ante.

441. Circumstances where patient's consent is not a prerequisite to disclosure. Disclosure of confidential information without the patient's consent is justified where the public interest overrides the duty of confidentiality[1].

Where, for the purposes of medical research, there is a need to disclose information whose subjects cannot effectively be rendered anonymous, every reasonable effort must be made to inform the patients concerned, or those who may properly give permission on their behalf, that they may, at any stage, withhold their consent to disclosure[2]. Where consent cannot be obtained, this fact must be drawn to the attention of the research ethics committee which must decide whether the public interest in research outweighs the patient's right to confidentiality[3].

The patient's consent to disclosure of information for teaching and audit must be obtained unless the data have been effectively rendered incapable of identifying patients[4].

Disclosure may be necessary in the public interest when failure to disclose may expose the patient or others to the risk of death or serious harm[5]. In such circumstances the doctor must disclose information promptly to an appropriate person or authority[6]. Disclosure is justified for the detection and prevention of serious crime[7].

Disclosure may be made to satisfy a statutory requirement[8] or on the direction of a judge, presiding officer of the court, coroner or other similar officer for the purpose of proceedings, but only so much of the patient's notes and records as is relevant must be disclosed[9]. The doctor must object to any attempt to compel further disclosure, such as references to persons not party to the proceedings[10]. If there is no court order, a request for disclosure by a third party such as a solicitor, police officer or officer of the court does not justify disclosure without the consent of the patient[11].

When a committee of the General Medical Council is investigating a doctor's fitness to practise[12] and has determined that the interests of justice require disclosure of confidential information, this may be made provided every reasonable effort has been made to obtain the consent of the patient concerned[13]. If consent is refused, disclosure must not be made[14]. In the case of a doctor in private practice, disclosure may be made at the request of an inspector of taxes provided that every effort has been made to separate financial from clinical information[15].

1 See *C (A Minor) (Evidence: Confidential Information)* [1991] 2 FLR 478, CA (in adoption proceedings, public interest and the best interests of the child prevailed over confidentiality of mother's medical records). See also *Re L (Minors) Police Investigation: Privilege* [1995] TLR 239.
2 See Confidentiality: Guidance from the General Medical Council (1995), Principle 15. As to the authority of, and weight to be accorded to, guidance from the General Medical Council see para 436 ante.
3 See ibid Principle 16.
4 See ibid Principle 17.
5 See ibid Principle 18.
6 See ibid Principle 18; *W v Egdell* [1990] Ch 359, [1990] 1 All ER 835, CA; *R v Crozier* [1991] Crim LR 138, CA; and the text and note 7 infra. Where a patient continues to drive when unfit to do so, having been warned by the doctor of the consequences of his actions, the doctor must make disclosure to the Driver and Vehicle Licensing Authority in accordance with the guidelines laid down in Confidentiality: Guidance from the General Medical Council (1995), Appendix 1: see Principle 19. Disclosure may also be made by a doctor where a colleague who is also a patient continues to practise when doing so may endanger others: Principle 19.
7 Ibid Principle 19. See *W v Egdell* [1990] Ch 359, [1990] 1 All ER 835, CA (public interest in safety overrode public interest in confidentiality where mental patient was considered too dangerous by a psychiatrist for early release from prison); and *R v Crozier* [1991] Crim LR 138, CA.
8 Such as those relating to controlled drugs or communicable diseases: see Confidentiality: Guidance from the General Medical Council (1995), Principle 20.
9 See ibid Principle 20.
10 See ibid Principle 20.
11 See ibid Principle 21.
12 See MEDICINE vol 30 (Reissue) para 126 et seq.
13 See Confidentiality: Guidance from the General Medical Council (1995), Principle 22.
14 See ibid Principle 22.
15 See ibid Principle 23.

442. Confidentiality relating to patients with sexually transmitted diseases.
There is a specific duty of confidence in relation to patients with sexually transmitted diseases[1]. Every regional and district health authority and every special health authority[2] must take all necessary steps to secure that any information obtained by the officers of the authority, with respect to persons examined or treated for any sexually transmitted disease, capable of identifying an individual, must not be disclosed except (1) for the purpose of communicating that information to a medical practitioner, or to a person employed under the direction of a medical practitioner in connection with the treatment of persons suffering from such disease or the prevention of its spread; and (2) for the purpose of such treatment or prevention[3].

1 See the National Health Service (Venereal Diseases) Regulations 1974, SI 1974/29 (as amended). As to AIDS and HIV see para 443 post.
2 As to health authorities see NATIONAL HEALTH vol 33 para 153 et seq.
3 National Health Service (Venereal Diseases) Regulations 1974 reg 2 (amended by SI 1982/288; modified by SI 1990/1525).

443. Confidentiality relating to patients with HIV or AIDS. Specific guidance applies to AIDS (acquired immune deficiency syndrome) and HIV (human immuno-deficiency virus) infection[1]. If a doctor knows that a health care worker is infected with HIV and has not sought or followed advice to modify his professional practice, the doctor has a duty to inform the appropriate regulatory body and an appropriate person, normally the senior doctor, in the infected person's employing authority[2].

A doctor infected with HIV is entitled to the same confidentiality as other patients[3] and only in the most exceptional circumstances, where the release of the doctor's name is essential for the protection of patients, may the HIV status of the doctor be revealed without his consent[4]. If an infected patient declines to allow a specialist to inform a general practitioner of his condition, this refusal should only be overridden if the doctor considers that failure to disclose would put the health of other members of the health care team at serious risk[5]. This also applies to disclosure to dentists[6], nurses[7] and laboratory technicians and these must be under the same general obligation of confidentiality as the doctor primarily responsible[8].

In the case of spouses and other sexual partners, where there is a serious and identifiable risk to a specific individual who, if not informed, would be exposed to infection, the doctor may be under a duty to inform that person in order to safeguard the person at risk despite refusal of consent by the patient[9].

1 See HIV and AIDS: the ethical considerations: Guidance from the General Medical Council (1995). As to the authority of, and weight to be accorded, guidance from the General Medical Council see para 436 ante.
2 See ibid Principle 9.
3 See *X v Y* [1988] 2 All ER 648 (newspaper attempting to induce health authority to disclose confidential medical records showing that doctors were suffering from AIDS).
4 See HIV and AIDS: the ethical considerations: Guidance from the General Medical Council (1995), Principle 10.
5 See ibid Principle 17.
6 As to dentists' obligations of confidentiality generally see para 450 post.
7 As to nurses' obligations of confidentiality generally see para 451 post.
8 See HIV and AIDS: the ethical considerations: Guidance from the General Medical Council (1995), Principle 18.
9 See ibid Principle 19.

444. Filming of patients for television. Specific guidance applies to television programmes which contain pictures of consultations[1]. A doctor must never take part in, or assist the recording of, a patient who does not wish to be filmed[2]. The interests of the patient must always take precedence over the public interest in the programme[3]. Doctors must be especially vigilant where the mentally ill, the disabled, the seriously ill, children or other vulnerable people are involved[4]. The doctor must personally obtain the consent of the patient, in writing if possible[5], and when doing so must ensure that the patient fully understands the purpose and context of the recording[6], and if the patient wishes to place restrictions on its use these should be agreed in writing before filming begins[7]. Consent forms (with translations where necessary) should be in a form which can be readily understood by the patient[8]. The patient must also understand that he can withhold or withdraw his consent at any time during filming without affecting his treatment or the relationship with his doctor[9] but that after filming has been completed programme makers may not be prepared to accept withdrawal of consent to screening of the material[10]. Where a patient suffers mental disability or is otherwise unable to give consent, agreement to filming should be sought from a close relative or carer[11]. For children who lack understanding to consent on their own behalf, the consent of a parent or guardian must be obtained[12]. The doctor should ensure that the person giving consent also understands the rights of the patient[13]. It is the responsibility of doctors to ensure that programme makers understand, agree to and observe the requirements of medical confidentiality[14]. Such an agreement should, when possible, be confirmed in writing between the doctors and the programme makers[15].

1 See the guidance set out by the Standards Committee in the General Medical Council News Review October 1995 Issue No 7 p 2. As to the authority of, and weight to be accorded to, guidance from the General Medical Council see para 436 ante.
2 See ibid para 1.
3 See ibid para 2.
4 See ibid para 2.
5 See ibid para 1.
6 See ibid para 3(a).
7 See ibid para 3(b).
8 See ibid para 3(c).
9 See ibid para 3(d).
10 See ibid para 3(e).
11 See ibid para 3(f).
12 See ibid para 3(f).
13 See ibid para 3(f).
14 See ibid para 4.
15 See ibid para 4.

445. Evidential privilege of doctors. A doctor does not enjoy any evidential privilege similar to legal professional privilege[1] and can therefore be compelled to disclose in court information covered by medical confidentiality. However, he may seek the protection of the court which may, at its discretion, allow him to decline to answer[2].

1 As to legal professional privilege see BARRISTERS vol 3(1) (Reissue) para 524–527; CRIMINAL LAW vol 11(2) (Reissue) para 1163; DISCOVERY vol 13 para 79; EVIDENCE vol 17 para 237; SOLICITORS vol 44(1) (Reissue) paras 90, 150.
2 *Hunter v Mann* [1974] QB 767 at 775, [1974] 2 All ER 414 at 419, DC, per Lord Widgery CJ. See also *Duchess of Kingston's Case* (1776) 20 State Tr 355; *R v Gibbons* (1823) 1 C & P 97; *Wheeler v Le Marchant* (1881) 17 ChD 675 at 681; *Garner v Garner* (1920) 36 TLR 196.

446. Patients below the age of 16. A person over the age of 16 is entitled to full confidentiality, but in the case of patients below that age, if the doctor is not satisfied that the patient has sufficient maturity and understanding to appreciate what is involved in a medical treatment or procedure, the doctor may inform the patient's parents or guardian, provided that the doctor informs the patient that this is being done[1]. If the doctor is satisfied that the patient has sufficient maturity and understanding then full confidentiality applies[2].

1 See *Gillick v West Norfolk and Wisbech Area Health Authority and DHSS* [1986] AC 112, [1985] 3 All ER 402, HL.
2 *Gillick v West Norfolk and Wisbech Area Health Authority and DHSS* [1986] AC 112 at 174, 189–190, 195, [1985] 3 All ER 402 at 413, 424, 427–428, HL.

447. Duty of disclosure imposed by statute. Certain statutes and statutory instruments impose obligations of disclosure in relation to medical information[1].

1 See the Abortion Act 1967 s 2 (as amended), and the Abortion Regulations 1991, SI 1991/499; and MEDICINE vol 30 (Reissue) para 46; the National Health Service Act 1977 s 124 (as amended), and the National Health Service (Notification of Births and Deaths) Regulations 1982, SI 1982/286; and REGISTRATION CONCERNING THE INDIVIDUAL vol 39 para 1081; the Police and Criminal Evidence Act 1984 ss 9–12; and CRIMINAL LAW vol 11(1) (Reissue) para 674; the Road Traffic Act 1988 s 172 (as substituted); and ROAD TRAFFIC; the Prevention of Terrorism (Temporary Provisions) Act 1989 ss 18, 18A (as added); and CRIMINAL LAW vol 11(1) (Reissue) para 113; and the Public Health (Control of Disease) Act 1984 s 11 (as amended), and the Public Health (Infectious Diseases) Regulations 1988, SI 1988/1546; and PUBLIC HEALTH.

448. Access to medical records. Legislation concerning data protection and access to medical reports and records contains provisions designed to safeguard confidentiality[1].

Access to medical records can be obtained by discovery[2] but the order to disclose such documents may direct that disclosure be limited to legal or medical advisers[3].

1 See the Data Protection Act 1984 and subordinate legislation made thereunder; and para 501 et seq post; the Access to Medical Reports Act 1988; the Access to Health Records Act 1990; the Access to Health Records (Control of Access) Regulations 1993, SI 1993/746; and MEDICINE vol 30 (Reissue) paras 19–20.
2 As to discovery generally see DISCOVERY.
3 See the Supreme Court Act 1981 s 34(1), (2). See also *McIvor v Southern Health and Social Services Board, Northern Ireland* [1978] 2 All ER 625, [1978] 1 WLR 757, HL; and DISCOVERY vol 13 para 13.

449. Information relating to human fertilisation and embryology. The Human Fertilisation and Embryology Authority ('the authority')[1] is under a duty to maintain a register[2] of relevant information, and the authority may not disclose any information contained within that register or any other information acquired by the authority in circumstances requiring it to be held in confidence[3].

The authority may make disclosure in certain circumstances in accordance with the statutory provisions[4].

1 As to the Human Fertilisation and Embryology Authority see CHILDREN vol 5(2) (Reissue) para 703; MEDICINE vol 30 (Reissue) para 59 et seq.
2 As to the register see the Human Fertilisation and Embryology Act 1990 s 31; and CHILDREN vol 5(2) (Reissue) para 703.
3 See ibid s 33 (as amended); and CHILDREN vol 5(2) (Reissue) para 705.
4 See ibid ss 31, 32, 34, 35; and CHILDREN vol 5(2) (Reissue) paras 704, 706.

450. Dentists. Dentists, as professional persons, appear to be under obligations of confidence similar to those of doctors[1]. Dentists who disclose to third parties, without the patient's permission, information about a patient acquired in a professional capacity may be considered to have been guilty of an improper breach of confidence, although there may be circumstances in which the public interest outweighs the dentist's duty with regard to confidentiality and in which disclosure would be justified[2]. Dentists' obligations of confidence extend to their staff[3]. For the purposes of legislation relating to access to health records a dentist, together with doctors, nurses and others professionally associated with medicine, is a 'health professional'[4].

1 'In common with other professional men, for instance a priest and there are of course others, the doctor is under a duty not to disclose without the consent of his patient, information which the doctor has

gained in his professional capacity': *Hunter v Mann* [1974] QB 767 at 772, [1974] 2 All ER 414 at 417, DC, per Boreham J.
2 See the General Dental Council – Professional Conduct and Fitness to Practise (1993), Clause 34(i).
3 See ibid Clause 34(i).
4 Ie within the meaning of the Data Protection (Subject Access Modification) (Health) Order 1987, SI 1987/1903, art 2, Schedule (as prospectively amended) (see para 531 note 6 post); and the Access to Health Records Act 1990 s 2(1) (see MEDICINE vol 39 (Reissue) para 20).

451. Nurses, midwives and health visitors. Nurses, midwives and health visitors, as professional persons, appear to be bound by obligations of confidence similar to those which bind doctors and dentists[1]. Those covered by the United Kingdom Central Council for Nursing, Midwifery and Health Visiting Code of Professional Conduct must protect all confidential information concerning patients and clients obtained in the course of professional practice and make disclosure only with consent, where required to do so by the order of a court or where disclosure can be justified in the wider public interest[2]. For the purposes of legislation giving access to medical records, nurses, midwives and health visitors are 'health professionals'[3]. The legislation gives the right of access but the health professional most directly concerned is permitted to withhold information which he or she believes might cause serious harm to the physical or mental health of the patient or client or which would identify a third party[4].

1 See *Hunter v Mann* [1974] QB 767 at 772, [1974] 2 All ER 414 at 417, DC.
2 The United Kingdom Central Council for Nursing, Midwifery and Health Visiting Code of Professional Conduct, Clause 10.
3 See the Data Protection (Subject Access Modification) (Health) Order 1987, SI 1987/1903, art 2, Schedule (as prospectively amended) (see para 531 note 6 post); and the Access to Health Records Act 1990 s 2(1) (as prospectively amended) (see MEDICINE vol 39 (Reissue) para 20).
4 See the United Kingdom Central Council for Nursing, Midwifery and Health Visiting Code of Professional Conduct, Clause 34.

452. Other health professionals. Other members of the health professions appear to be bound by obligations similar to those for doctors, dentists and nurses[1].
For the purposes of legislation giving access to health records[2], in addition to doctors[3], dentists[4] and registered nurses, midwives and health visitors[5], the following are 'health professionals': (1) registered optician[6]; (2) registered pharmaceutical chemist[7]; (3) registered chiropodist, dietician, occupational therapist, orthoptist or physiotherapist[8]; (4) clinical psychologist, child psychotherapist or speech therapist[9]; (5) art or music therapist employed by a health service body[10]; and (6) scientist employed by such a body as a head of department[11]. As from a day or days to be appointed, 'health professional' will also include an osteopath and a chiropractor[12].

1 See *Hunter v Mann* [1974] QB 767 at 772, [1974] 2 All ER 414 at 417, DC.
2 See the Data Protection (Subject Access Modification) (Health) Order 1987, SI 1987/1903, art 2, Schedule (as prospectively amended) (see para 531 note 6 post); and the Access to Health Records Act 1990 s 2(1) (as prospectively amended) (see MEDICINE vol 39 (Reissue) para 20).
3 See para 436 et seq ante.
4 See para 450 ante.
5 See para 451 ante.
6 Access to Health Records Act 1990 s 2(1)(c).
7 Ibid s 2(1)(d).
8 Ibid s 2(1)(f).
9 Ibid s 2(1)(g).
10 Ibid s 2(1)(h).

11 Ibid s 2(1)(i).
12 Ibid s 2(1)(fa)(ff) (prospectively added by the Chiropractors Act 1994 s 38(1) and the Osteopaths Act 1993 s 38(1) respectively).

B. OTHER PROFESSIONAL CONFIDENCES

453. Clergy. The relationship between priest and penitent has been held to be one of professional confidence[1]. The obligation of confidence may extend to all pastoral work of the clergy, for example conciliation[2], but the authorities appear inconsistent as to the circumstances in which the obligation of confidence may be overruled and, therefore, how far it extends to the pastoral work of the clergy generally[3].

1   *Goddard v Nationwide Building Society* [1987] QB 670 at 685, [1986] 3 All ER 264 at 271; *A-G v Observer Ltd, A-G v Times Newspapers Ltd* [1990] 1 AC 109 at 177, sub nom *A-G v Guardian Newspapers Ltd (No 2)* [1988] 3 All ER 545 at 595, CA, per Donaldson MR, and at 255 and 639, HL, per Lord Keith of Kinkel.
      See also *Hunter v Mann* [1974] QB 767 at 772, [1974] 2 All ER 414 at 417, DC; *Stephens v Avery* [1988] Ch 449 at 455, [1988] 2 All ER 477 at 482; *W v Egdell* [1990] Ch 359 at 419, [1990] 1 All ER 835 at 848, CA.
2   See *Henley v Henley* [1955] P 202, [1955] 1 All ER 590n (vicar's conversation in his character as 'conciliator' with party to subsequent divorce is privileged).
3   *R v Hay* (1860) 2 F & F 4 (priest who received watch in confessional required to say from whom he received it, but not what was said between him and the giver); *Broad v Pitt* (1828) 3 C & P 518; but see *Wheeler v Le Marchant* (1881) 17 ChD 675 at 681, per Jessel MR ('the principle protecting confidential communications is of a very limited character . . . communications made to a priest in the confessional on matters perhaps considered by the penitent to be more important even than his life or his fortune, are not protected'); *Normanshaw v Normanshaw* (1893) 69 LT 468 (clergyman called as witness on behalf of petitioner objected to disclose content of conversation; objection disallowed); *Francome v Mirror Group Newspapers Ltd* [1984] 2 All ER 408 at 413, [1984] 1 WLR 892 at 897, CA.

454. Barristers. The relationship of barrister and client is one to which confidence attaches as a necessary or traditional incident[1]. This obligation of confidence is codified in the Code of Conduct of the Bar of England and Wales[2].

1   *A-G v Observer Ltd, A-G v Times Newspapers Ltd* [1990] 1 AC 109 at 177, sub nom *A-G v Guardian Newspapers Ltd (No 2)* [1988] 3 All ER 545 at 595, CA, per Donaldson MR, and at 255 and 639, HL, per Lord Keith of Kinkel; *Carter v Palmer* (1839) 1 Dr & W 722; affd (1842) 8 Cl & Fin 657. As to legal professional privilege see BARRISTERS vol 3(1) (Reissue) para 524–527; CRIMINAL LAW vol 11(2) (Reissue) para 1163; DISCOVERY vol 13 para 79; EVIDENCE vol 17 para 237.
2   See the Code of Conduct of the Bar of England and Wales; and BARRISTERS vol 3(1) para 468.

455. Solicitors. As with barristers[1], the relationship of solicitor and client is one to which confidence attaches as a necessary or traditional incident[2]. Since solicitors are officers of the court a higher standard may be required of them than of other confidants[3]. Communications between solicitor and client are also covered by legal professional privilege which protects the solicitor from being compelled to reveal professional communications[4], provided they are legitimate and not made to promote fraud or crime[5].

The Law Society has formulated detailed guidance on the professional conduct of solicitors including the practical applications of the duty of confidentiality[6]. However, in certain circumstances the Solicitors Accounts Rules[7] may override a duty of confidence[8], as may the requirements for legal aid applications[9].

If privileged documents from counsel acting for the other side are mistakenly sent to a solicitor he should not read them but return them[10]. Before this, he may consult his client, advising that the court may grant an injunction to prevent the overt use of the material contained in the documents[11].

1 See para 454 ante.
2 See SOLICITORS vol 44(1) (Reissue) paras 90, 150.
3 *Rakusen v Ellis, Munday & Clarke* [1912] 1 Ch 831 at 840, CA, per Fletcher Moulton LJ; and see SOLICITORS vol 44(1) (Reissue) para 150. The protection of confidential information is a basis for restraining a former partner in the firm which is acting for one party in litigation from acting for another party to the litigation; but where the evidence did not show that the former partner had ever been in possession of confidential information relating to the litigation, the mere perception of impropriety was insufficient basis for intervention: *Re a Firm of Solicitors* [1995] FSR 783. A solicitor acting for both parties to a transaction may owe duties to each party: *Halifax Mortgage Services (formerly BNP Mortages Ltd) v Stepsky* [1996] Ch 1, [1995] 4 All ER 656; see also *Mortgage Express Ltd v Bowerman & Partners (a firm)* [1995] TLR 450, CA.
4 As to legal professional privilege see SOLICITORS vol 44(1) (Reissue) paras 90, 150; DISCOVERY vol 13 para 79; EVIDENCE vol 17 para 237; CRIMINAL LAW vol 11(2) (Reissue) para 1163. It has been held that legal professional privilege does not extend to information which the client could lawfully be required to reveal: see *Re Murjani (a bankrupt)* [1996] 1 All ER 65. As to whether the client's identity is confidential see *Conoco (UK) Ltd v The Commercial Law Practice* (1996) Times, 13 February.
5 See *R v Cox and Railton* (1884) 14 QBD 153, CCR; *Finers (a firm) v Miro* [1991] 1 All ER 182, [1991] 1 WLR 35, CA. The privilege prevails over any public interest in securing relevant and admissible evidence: *R v Derby Magistrates' Court, ex p B* [1995] 4 All ER 526, HL. A client suing a solicitor waives privilege: *Kershaw v Whelan* [1995] TLR 695; and see SOLICITORS vol 44(1) (Reissue) para 90.
6 See the Guide to the Professional Conduct of Solicitors (6th Edn, 1993); and SOLICITORS vol 44(1) (Reissue) paras 90, 150. The solicitor's duty of confidentiality is not determined by the end of the retainer, nor by the conclusion of the particular matter on which the solicitor or the firm was engaged nor by the death of the client: Guide to the Professional Conduct of Solicitors (6th Edn, 1993), Principle 16.03.
7 As to the Solicitors Accounts Rules 1991 see SOLICITORS vol 44(1) (Reissue) para 465 et seq.
8 See *Parry-Jones v Law Society* [1969] 1 Ch 1, [1968] 1 All ER 177, CA.
9 See LEGAL AID vol 27(2) (Reissue) para 1873.
10 See *English and American Insurance Co Ltd v Herbert Smith* [1988] FSR 232.
11 See the Guide to the Professional Conduct of Solicitors (6th Edn, 1993) para 16.07; but cf *Ablitt v Mills & Reeve (a firm)* [1995] TLR 535 (when such documents were read in full by the solicitor on the instructions of his client, the guidance as to taking instructions was judicially described as 'surprising' and the solicitor was restrained by injunction from taking any further part in the proceedings).

456. Bankers. A banker owes an obligation of confidence to his customer but this is subject to qualification both at common law and by statute[1]. The duty covers information derived not only from the customer's account but also from other sources, so far as they are related to banking, as when advice is given to a customer on business matters, or decisions are taken by the bank as to the treatment of customers[2]; the duty may continue after the relationship ends[3].

Disclosure is, however, allowed where required by (1) compulsion of law; (2) public interest; (3) the interests of the bank; or (4) the express or implied consent of the customer[4]. A bank is not under a duty to withhold from a customer the fact that it has been required to produce his account in court, nor is it under an absolute duty to inform him of the fact, but it should use its best endeavours to inform him. There is no head of legal privilege for bank accounts and it is uncertain whether there may be an implied term or duty to object on the customer's behalf or to inform the court that disclosure is being made without the consent of the customer and whether the bank, if in breach of such a term, can claim the immunity of a witness[5]. In civil proceedings, confidential reports disclosed voluntarily by a bank to regulatory authorities relating to its private client operations are not, as a class, entitled to public interest immunity since a heavy onus lies on the person asserting a new claim to such immunity[6]. In a criminal investigation a banker is not obliged to inform a customer of an order allowing police to inspect an account in a criminal investigation, nor is he obliged to resist such an order, although he is free to disregard a request by the police not to inform his client of the application for such an order[7]. A banker may be required by letters rogatory from a foreign court to submit to oral examination even if he is thereby required to disclose confidential advice given to a customer[8]. When, however, English law is the proper law of a banking contract[9] and the balance of convenience is appropriate, an injunction will be granted to prevent a bank breaching confidentiality to comply with an order of a foreign court claiming excessive jurisdiction[10].

1 See *Tournier v National Provincial and Union Bank of England* [1924] 1 KB 461, CA; and BANKING vol 3(1) (Reissue) paras 240–250.
2 *Tournier v National Provincial and Union Bank of England* [1924] 1 KB 461 at 473, CA, per Bankes LJ, and at 485 per Atkin LJ; contra at 481 per Scrutton LJ who excluded knowledge from other sources.
3 *Tournier v National Provincial and Union Bank of England* [1924] 1 KB 461 at 485, CA, per Atkin LJ; contra at 481 per Scrutton LJ.
4 *Tournier v National Provincial and Union Bank of England* [1924] 1 KB 461 at 473, CA, per Bankes LJ. Illustrations of head (1) in the text are revenue legislation and the Bankers' Books Evidence Act 1879; and of head (4) in the text, *Sunderland v Barclays Bank Ltd* (1938) 5 Legal Decisions Affecting Bankers 163 (where a husband took over a telephone conversation between his wife and a bank manager).
5 *Robertson v Canadian Imperial Bank of Commerce* [1995] 1 All ER 824, [1994] 1 WLR 1493, PC.
6 *Kaufmann v Credit Lyonnais Bank* (1995) Times, 1 February.
7 *Barclays Bank plc v Taylor, Trustee Savings Bank of Wales and Border Counties v Taylor* [1989] 3 All ER 563, [1989] 1 WLR 1066, CA.
8 *Re State of Norway's Application, Re State of Norway's Application (No 2)* [1990] 1 AC 723, sub nom *Re State of Norway's Applications (Nos 1 and 2)* [1989] 1 All ER 745, HL.
9 As to proper law of the contract see CONFLICT OF LAWS para 859 et seq post.
10 *X AG v A bank* [1983] 2 All ER 464, [1983] 2 Lloyd's Rep 535.

457. Fiduciaries' obligations of confidence. Fiduciary relationships[1], which by their nature are relationships of good faith, involve obligations of confidence[2]. The principle that a person who has obtained confidential information from another must not use that information to the prejudice of the person who gave it applies with particular force as between a director[3] and his company by reason of the fiduciary character of the duty owed by the one to the other[4]. The existence of a fiduciary relationship, however, does not operate to extend obligations of confidentiality to what would not otherwise be confidential[5].

1 As to fiduciary relationships see generally EQUITY vol 16 (Reissue) para 902 et seq.
2 See *Baker v Gibbons* [1972] 2 All ER 759 at 764–765, [1972] 1 WLR 693 at 700; *Schering Chemicals Ltd v Falkman Ltd* [1982] QB 1, [1981] 2 All ER 321, CA.
3 As to directors' obligations of confidence see para 460 post.
4 *Baker v Gibbons* [1972] 2 All ER 759 at 764–765, [1972] 1 WLR 693 at 700.
5 See *Yates Circuit Foil Co v Electrofoils Ltd* [1976] FSR 345 at 394. As to the characteristics of confidentiality see para 410 et seq ante.

458. Other professional advisers. A professional adviser (such as an accountant[1], an architect or engineer[2], a factor, a stockbroker or a surveyor[3]) is in a fiduciary relationship[4] to his client[5] and may therefore be under an obligation of confidence[6].

1 See *Chantrey Martin (a firm) v Martin* [1953] 2 QB 286, [1953] 2 All ER 691.
2 See *Brian D Collins (Engineers) Ltd v Charles Roberts & Co Ltd* [1965] RPC 429. See also *Abernethy v Hutchinson* (1825) 3 LJCh 209; *Floydd v Cheney, Cheney v Floydd* [1970] Ch 602, [1970] 1 All ER 446; *Terrapin Ltd v Builders' Supply Co (Hayes) Ltd* (1959) [1967] RPC 375; on appeal (but the appeal reported first) [1960] RPC 128, CA. See also, for cases involving engineers or engineering processes: *Reid & Sigrist Ltd v Moss and Mechanism Ltd* (1932) 49 RPC 461; *Mechanical and General Invention Co Ltd and*

Lehwess v Austin and the Austin Motor Co Ltd [1935] AC 346, HL; *B O Morris Ltd v F Gilman (BST) Ltd* (1943) 60 RPC 20; *Johnson v Heat and Air Systems Ltd* (1941) 58 RPC 229; *Hivac Ltd v Park Royal Scientific Instruments Ltd* [1946] Ch 169, [1946] 1 All ER 350, CA; *Nichrotherm Electrical Co Ltd v Percy* [1957] RPC 207, CA; *O Mustad & Son v S Allcock & Co Ltd and Dosen* (1928) [1963] 3 All ER 416, [1964] 1 WLR 109n, HL; *Saltman Engineering Co Ltd v Campbell Engineering Co Ltd* (1948) [1963] 3 All ER 413n, 65 RPC 203, CA; *K S Paul (Printing Machinery) Ltd v Southern Instruments (Communications) Ltd and E P Ellis (t/a Ellis & Sons)* [1964] RPC 118; *Bostitch Inc v McGarry & Cole Ltd* [1964] RPC 173; *Cranleigh Precision Engineering Ltd v Bryant* [1964] 3 All ER 289, [1965] 1 WLR 1293; *Torrington Manufacturing Co v Smith & Sons (England) Ltd* [1966] RPC 285; *National Broach and Machine Co v Churchill Gear Machines Ltd* [1965] RPC 61; on appeal on the question of damages only [1965] 2 All ER 961, [1965] 1 WLR 1199, CA; affd [1966] 3 All ER 923n, [1967] 1 WLR 384, HL; *Seager v Copydex Ltd* [1967] 2 All ER 415, [1967] 1 WLR 923; *Franchi v Franchi* [1967] RPC 149; *Suhner & Co AG v Transradio Ltd* [1967] RPC 329; *Technography Printed Circuits Ltd v Chalwyn Ltd* [1967] RPC 339; *Under Water Welders and Repairers Ltd v Street and Longthorne* [1968] RPC 498; *Coco v A N Clark (Engineers) Ltd* [1969] RPC 41; *Industrial Furnaces Ltd v Reaves* [1970] RPC 605; *Regina Glass Fibre Ltd v Werner Schuller* [1972] RPC 229; *Diamond Stylus Co Ltd v Bauden Precision Diamonds Ltd* [1973] RPC 675; *Standtex International Ltd v Blades and C B Blades Ltd* [1976] FSR 114; *Yates Circuit Foil Co Ltd v Electrofoils Ltd* [1976] FSR 345; *Potters-Ballotini v Weston-Baker* [1977] RPC 202, CA; *Harrison v Project and Design Co (Redcar) Ltd* [1978] FSR 81.

3 See *Brown v IRC* [1965] AC 244 at 265, [1964] 3 All ER 119 at 127, HL.

4 As to fiduciaries' obligations of confidence see para 457 ante. As to fiduciary relationships generally see EQUITY vol 16 (Reissue) para 902 et seq.

5 *Brown v IRC* [1965] AC 244 at 265, [1964] 3 All ER 119 at 127, HL.

6 See *Baker v Gibbons* [1972] 2 All ER 759 at 764–765, [1972] 1 WLR 693 at 700; *Hunter v Mann* [1974] QB 767 at 772, [1974] 2 All ER 414 at 417–418, DC; *W v Egdell* [1990] Ch 359 at 419, [1990] 1 All ER 835 at 848, CA; *Chantrey Martin (a firm) v Martin* [1953] 2 QB 286, [1953] 2 All ER 691.

459. Agents. An agent owes a fiduciary duty to his principal[1] which includes the duty to use information obtained by virtue of the agency solely for the purposes of the agency[2] and not to divulge it to third parties[3].

An agent may be under distinct and separate obligations when acting for two or more principals and therefore an estate agent is not under an implied obligation to reveal to one principal confidential information relating to a rival principal[4].

1 See eg *Parker v McKenna* (1874) 10 Ch App 96 at 119; and AGENCY vol 1(2) (Reissue) para 87. As to fiduciaries' obligations of confidence see para 457 ante. As to fiduciary relationships generally see EQUITY vol 16 (Reissue) para 902 et seq.

2 See AGENCY vol 1(2) (Reissue) para 90.

3 See AGENCY vol 1(2) (Reissue) para 90.

4 *Kelly v Cooper* [1993] AC 205, [1992] 3 WLR 936, PC.

460. Directors. Directors owe a fiduciary duty to the company[1] and have been described as agents of the company[2]. A director may coincidentally, but not by virtue of his position, be a trustee[3]. The principle that where a person has obtained confidential information from another he must not use that information to the prejudice of the person who gave it applies with particular force as between a director and his company by reason of the fiduciary character of the duty owed by the one to the other[4]. However, the fact that an individual is a director does not extend his obligations of confidentiality to what would not otherwise be confidential[5]. A non-executive director may engage in a competing business (unless debarred by express terms in his contract of employment) but he must not use or put at risk confidential information of the company and must not solicit customers of the company on behalf of the competing business[6].

1 *Regal (Hastings) Ltd v Gulliver* (1942) [1967] 2 AC 134n at 159n, [1942] 1 All ER 378 at 395, HL, per Lord Porter. As to directors and their duties see COMPANIES. As to fiduciary relationships generally see EQUITY vol 16 (Reissue) para 902 et seq. As to fiduciaries' obligations of confidence see para 457 ante.

2 See *Great Eastern Rly Co v Turner* (1872) 8 Ch App 149 at 152. As to agents see para 459 ante; and AGENCY.

3 See *Smith v Anderson* (1880) 15 ChD 247 at 275, CA, per James LJ, criticising the description of a director as trustee as a 'fallacy'.

4 *Baker v Gibbons* [1972] 2 All ER 759 at 764–765, [1972] 1 WLR 693 at 700. See also *Aubanel and Alabaster Ltd v Aubanel* (1949) 66 RPC 343; *Cranleigh Precision Engineering Ltd v Bryant* [1964] 3 All ER 289, [1965] 1 WLR 1293; *Industrial Furnaces Ltd v Reaves* [1970] RPC 605; *Industrial Development Consultants Ltd v Cooley* [1972] 2 All ER 162, [1972] 1 WLR 443; *Thomas Marshall (Exports) Ltd v Guinle* [1979] Ch 227, [1978] 3 All ER 193.

5 See *Yates Circuit Foil Co Ltd v Electrofoils Ltd* [1976] FSR 345 at 394.

6 *Aubanel and Alabaster Ltd v Aubanel* (1949) 66 RPC 343. See also para 464 post.

461. Partners and those involved in joint ventures. Partners owe each other a duty of good faith[1], which has been held to include mutual obligations of confidence[2]. They may, therefore, be held to be in breach of confidence[3]. If partners and parties to licensing agreements and joint ventures also owe each other a fiduciary duty[4], it is likely that the same principles applicable to other fiduciaries and agents would apply, so that the relationship between them will not of itself render confidential what would otherwise not be so, but will lead to obligations of confidence being applied with particular force[5].

1 See eg *Floydd v Cheney, Cheney v Floydd* [1970] Ch 602, [1970] 1 All ER 446. The principle is embodied in the Partnership Act 1890 ss 28, 29, 30; see PARTNERSHIP vol 35 (Reissue) paras 93–95.

2 See note 1 supra.

3 *Glassington v Thwaites* (1823) 1 Sim & St 124 (partnership); *Floydd v Cheney, Cheney v Floydd* [1970] Ch 602, [1970] 1 All ER 446 (partnership); *Re Gallay Ltd's Application* [1959] RPC 141 (partnership); *Torrington Manufacturing Co v Smith & Sons (England) Ltd* [1966] RPC 285 (licensing agreement); *National Broach and Machine Co v Churchill Gear Machines Ltd* [1965] RPC 61; on appeal on the question of damages only [1965] 2 All ER 961, [1965] 1 WLR 1199, CA; affd [1966] 3 All ER 923n, [1967] 1 WLR 384, HL (licensing agreement); *International Scientific Communications Inc v Pattison* [1979] FSR 429 (joint venture); *Coco v A N Clark (Engineers) Ltd* [1969] RPC 41 at 48 (joint venture); *LAC Minerals Ltd v International Corona Resources Ltd* (1989) 61 DLR (4th) 14, [1990] FSR 441, Can SC (mutual obligations of confidence existed in relation to information revealed by one party to the other for the purposes of possible joint business venture); see also *Worthington Pumping Engine v Moore* (1902) 20 RPC 41 at 46.

4 This issue is not conclusively decided, but is supported by some authority; see PARTNERSHIP vol 35 (Reissue) para 93. As to fiduciary relationships generally see EQUITY vol 16 (Reissue) para 902 et seq.

5 See *Baker v Gibbons* [1972] 2 All ER 759 at 764–765, [1972] 1 WLR 693 at 700.

462. Consultants. Obligations of confidence may be incidental to consultancies[1].

1 *Schering Chemicals Ltd v Falkman Ltd* [1982] QB 1, [1981] 2 All ER 321, CA; cf *Dunford & Elliott Ltd v Johnson & Firth Brown Ltd* [1977] 1 Lloyd's Rep 505, [1978] FSR 143, CA (confidence negated by wide circulation of report).

463. Independent contractors and sub–contractors. Whilst relationships with independent contractors and sub-contractors may not ordinarily be relationships of confidence, they may involve confidence[1]. The application of basic rules of European Community competition law to these relations may be modified by block exemptions[2].

1 *Brian D Collins (Engineers) Ltd v Charles Roberts & Co Ltd* [1965] RPC 429; *Ackroyds (London) Ltd v Islington Plastics Ltd* [1962] RPC 97; *Terrapin Ltd v Builders' Supply Co (Hayes) Ltd* (1959) [1967] RPC 375; on appeal (but the appeal reported first) [1960] RPC 128, CA.

2 See EUROPEAN COMMUNITIES vol 52 paras 19.356–19.364 and 19.196; and para 477 post.

464. Employees. Employees owe an implied duty of good faith to their employers which may include an obligation of confidence[1]. This duty may continue after the employment has terminated[2], and in order to protect trade secrets or goodwill[3] the employer can rely on an express term of a contract to restrain trade, provided that the term is no more widely drafted than is necessary or reasonable[4].

1 See EMPLOYMENT vol 16 (Reissue) para 49.
2 See EMPLOYMENT vol 16 (Reissue) para 51. A lifelong and worldwide ban on disclosing confidential information about the private lives of employers will be upheld if it does not restrict future employment and competition by the former employee: *A-G v Barker* [1990] 3 All ER 257 (ex-employee of the royal household seeking to publish book disclosing confidential information about the royal family was held to be in breach of contract of employment). See further paras 404, 421 ante. Note that many of the cases from which the principles relating to the law of confidence and confidentiality are drawn are cases involving an employer/employee relationship.
3 The employer must have trade secrets or goodwill, otherwise the court will not intervene: see *Mainmet Holdings plc v Austin* [1991] FSR 538; *Berkeley Administration Inc v McClelland* [1990] FSR 505.
4 See TRADE, INDUSTRY AND INDUSTRIAL RELATIONS vol 47 (Reissue) para 44 et seq.

465. Patent agents and registered trade mark agents. As professional advisers, patent agents[1] and registered trade mark agents[2] owe an obligation of confidentiality to their clients[3]. Statute makes special provision for professional privilege when such agents are consulted for particular purposes[4].

1 As to patent agents generally see PATENTS AND REGISTERED DESIGNS vol 35 (Reissue) para 692 et seq.
2 As to registered trade mark agents generally see TRADE MARKS vol 48 (Reissue) para 17 et seq.
3 See *Hunter v Mann* [1974] QB 767 at 772, [1974] 2 All ER 414 at 417–418, DC; *Brown v IRC* [1965] AC 244 at 265, [1964] 3 All ER 119 at 127, HL; and para 458 ante.
    The test of business efficacy for implying an obligation of confidentiality in a contract would appear to apply particularly to the engagement of a patent agent since premature publicity for the subject matter of a patent would destroy its patentability. As to the business efficacy test see para 419 text and note 14 ante.
4 See the Patents Act 1977 s 104 (repealed with savings); the Copyright, Designs and Patents Act 1988 s 280; and PATENTS AND REGISTERED DESIGNS vol 35 (Reissue) paras 306, 617; the Trade Marks Act 1994 s 87; and TRADE MARKS vol 48 (Reissue) para 20.

466. Publishers and broadcasters. If an idea for a book or theatre or television production is outlined to a publisher or broadcaster (for example a theatre or television producer) in circumstances importing an obligation of confidence the publisher or broadcaster comes under a corresponding obligation[1], and he will also be bound if he acquires work when he knows or ought to know that the person tendering it acquired it in breach of confidence[2]. The obligation applies not only to the principal work but also to any advertising or publicity for that work[3]. Work intended for publication may not have the quality of confidentiality even if there is a commercial interest in suppressing it for a specific time[4].

1 *Fraser v Thames Television Ltd* [1984] QB 44, [1983] 2 All ER 101; and see *Tuck & Sons v Priester* (1887) 19 QBD 48; revsd in part 19 QBD 629, CA; *Gilbert v Star Newspaper Co Ltd* (1894) 11 TLR 4; *Talbot v General Television Pty Ltd* [1981] RPC 1, Vict SC.
2 *Prince Albert v Strange* (1849) 2 De G & Sm 652; on appeal (1849) 1 Mac & G 25.
3 *Prince Albert v Strange* (1849) 2 De G & Sm 652; on appeal (1849) 1 Mac & G 25 (copies of catalogue to be destroyed).
4 *Times Newspapers Ltd v MGN Ltd* [1993] EMLR 443, CA.

467. Bailees. A bailee[1] who derives information from the possession of another's goods may deal with that information only in a manner expressly or impliedly stipulated by the terms of the bailment[2]. The unauthorised disclosure or use of confidential information gained by reason of a bailment can accordingly attract redress equivalent to that which applies to bailments in general[3].

An action to enforce the bailee's obligation of confidentiality may be founded purely on the bailment, although the obligation itself will often coincide with obligations derived from other sources, such as a contract[4]. Even where the bailment is founded on contract, the action for breach of bailment is distinct and independent both of contract and of tort[5]. Liability for breach of bailment may also follow irrespective of whether the bailment stems from a contract or other agreement between the parties[6]. A borrower or an unrewarded depositary of goods may therefore be liable to the lender or depositor for an unauthorised disclosure or misuse of information derived from the bailment[7]. A sub-bailee may, by virtue of his status as a bailee of the head bailor, be answerable to the head bailor as well as to the intermediate bailee for unauthorised disclosure[8]. It is also possible that a finder of goods, by virtue of being treated generally as a bailee, owes a duty of confidentiality to the owner in certain cases[9].

Where the bailment belongs to that class which imposes fiduciary responsibilities[10] on the bailee, the bailment may support equitable obligations of confidentiality[11]. However, not all bailments give rise to fiduciary obligations[12]. In general, the fiduciary class is restricted to those bailments under which the bailor entrusts to the bailee goods to be held or dealt with by the bailee for the benefit of the bailor, or for limited purposes stipulated by the bailor[13]. Whereas the bailee to whom goods are entrusted for safekeeping, or for skill and labour, or for carriage, may well owe fiduciary obligations to the bailor, a bailee who undertakes no service for the bailor (such as a buyer of goods subject to a title retention clause, or a hirer) is, in general, unlikely to owe such obligations[14].

Where the information derived from the bailment is in tangible form, such as a written document or computer disc, the court may order delivery up of that tangible record as a benefit derived by the bailee from the bailment[15]. Where information is recorded in tangible form, misuse of the tangible record may give rise to liability in tort, enabling the owner of the tangible record to sue, according to circumstances, in trespass to[16], or conversion of, goods[17]. In special cases, the owner of the tangible record who sues in trespass or conversion may recover a reasonable charge for the use of the information contained in, and abstracted from, the record[18]. In other cases, the owner of the tangible record may elect to recover the benefit which the converter or other wrongdoer derives from its misuse rather than compensatory damages[19]. It may be that, by analogy with the law regarding tangible chattels, information can be bailed, or can be treated as bailed for the purposes of determining the rights of entruster and recipient; if so, the confider can restrain the recipient from dealing with the information contrary to the terms of the entrustment, or can claim monetary remedies, in a manner akin to that which arises on a bailment[20].

1　As to bailment see para 408 ante; and BAILMENT.
2　*Reading v The King* [1949] 2 KB 232 at 236, CA, per Asquith LJ; affd sub nom *Reading v A-G* [1951] AC 507 at 516, HL, per Lord Porter; *Hospital Products Ltd v United States Surgical Corpn* (1984) 156 CLR 41 at 70, HC Aust, per Gibb CJ; *Watson v Dolmark Industries Ltd* [1992] 3 NZLR 311 at 315, NZ CA, per Cooke P, and at 318 per Gault J. See further *Federal Comr of Taxation v United Aircraft Corpn* (1943) 68 CLR 525 at 547–548 per Williams J; but cf at 534–536 per Latham CJ.
3　See generally BAILMENT vol 2 (Reissue) paras 1885–1887; TORT vol 45 paras 1451–1474.
4　As to contract see para 404 ante; and generally CONTRACT.
5　*Sutcliffe v Chief Constable of West Yorkshire* (1995) 159 JP 770, CA, per Otton LJ.
6　See BAILMENT vol 2 (Reissue) para 1801 et seq.
7　See BAILMENT vol 2 (Reissue) paras 1816, 1830.
8　See BAILMENT vol 2 (Reissue) para 1841.

9 See BAILMENT vol 2 (Reissue) para 1811. Bailment arises whenever one person is voluntarily in possession of another's goods: *The Pioneer Container* [1994] 2 AC 324 at 342, [1994] 2 All ER 250 at 262, HL, per Lord Goff of Chieveley.

10 As to fiduciary relationships generally see EQUITY vol 16 (Reissue) para 902 et seq.

11 *Reading v The King* [1949] 2 KB 232 at 236, CA, per Asquith LJ; affd sub nom *Reading v A-G* [1951] AC 507 at 516, HL, per Lord Porter (upholding the discovery of a fiduciary relationship, giving rise to fiduciary obligations in the recipient, wherever one person entrusts to another property, including intangible property such as confidential information, on terms which delimit its use); *Hospital Products Ltd v United States Surgical Corpn* (1984) 156 CLR 41 at 70, Aust HC, per Gibb CJ; *Watson v Dolmark Industries Ltd* [1992] 3 NZLR 311 at 315, NZ CA, per Cooke P, and at 318 per Gault J; see also *Federal Comr of Taxation v United Aircraft Corpn* (1943) 68 CLR 525 at 547–548 per Williams J; but cf at 534–536 per Latham CJ.

12 *Hendy Lennox (Industrial Engines) Ltd v Grahame Puttick Ltd* [1984] 2 All ER 152 at 162–163 per Staughton J (presumption that bailee a fiduciary); *Re Andrabell Ltd* [1984] 3 All ER 407 at 414 (no presumption that bailee a fiduciary); *Re E Dibbens & Sons Ltd (in liquidation)* [1990] BCLC 577; and see *Re Goldcorp Exchange Ltd* (in receivership) [1995] 1 AC 74 at 98, [1994] 2 All ER 806 at 821–822, PC.

13 *Re Hallett's Estate* (1880) 13 ChD 696 at 708–709, CA, per Jessel MR; *Hospital Products Ltd v United States Surgical Corpn* (1984) 156 CLR 41 at 101, Aust HC, per Mason J; and see Palmer on Bailment (2nd edn, 1991) pp 189–192.

14 *Hendy Lennox (Industrial Engines) Ltd v Grahame Puttick Ltd* [1984] 2 All ER 152 at 162–163 per Staughton J; *Re Andrabell Ltd* [1984] 3 All ER 407 at 414. In commercial bailments, express provision is often made for the bailee's observance of confidentiality: *Re Andrabell Ltd* supra.

15 *McAlpine & Sons Ltd v Minimax Ltd* [1970] 1 Lloyd's Rep 397 at 422 per Thesiger J; following *Strand Electric and Engineering Co Ltd v Brisford Entertainments Ltd* [1952] 2 QB 246 at 254–255, [1952] 1 All ER 796 at 800–801, CA, per Denning LJ; and see para 408 ante.

16 *Thurston v Charles* (1905) 21 TLR 659 per Walton J. As to trespass to goods see para 405 ante; and TORT vol 45 para 1491 et seq.

17 *Thurston v Charles* (1905) 21 TLR 659 (unauthorised disclosure of letter); *Borden Chemical Co (Canada) Ltd v J G Beukers Ltd* (1972) 29 DLR (3d) 337, BC SC (unauthorised exploitation of customer list). As to conversion of goods see para 405 ante; and TORT vol 45 para 1422 et seq.

18 Semble, following *Strand Electric and Engineering Co Ltd v Brisford Entertainments Ltd* [1952] 2 QB 246, [1952] 1 All ER 796; and see *McAlpine & Sons Ltd v Minimax Ltd* [1970] 1 Lloyd's Rep 397 at 422 per Thesiger J; and para 408 ante.

19 *Strand Electric and Engineering Co Ltd v Brisford Entertainments Ltd* [1952] 2 QB 246 at 254–255, [1952] 1 All ER 796 at 800–801, CA, per Denning LJ (followed in *McAlpine & Sons Ltd v Minimax Ltd* [1970] 1 Lloyd's Rep 397 at 422 per Thesiger J); and see TORT vol 45 paras 1452, 1473 (waiver of tort); *Borden Chemical Co (Canada) Ltd v J G Beukers Ltd* (1972) 29 DLR (3d) 337, BC SC (action in tort for conversion of customer list bailed by way of security resulted in bailor recovering as damages the value of the list to the bailee). See further para 408 ante.

20 See para 408 ante.

468. Teachers and lecturers. In respect of educational and pastoral duties, teachers and lecturers may be bound by the general obligations of the professions[1], coupled with special obligations in respect of personal information to which they may have access relating to pupils, students and their families[2]. Pupils and students may come under an obligation not to make improper use of instructional information and materials communicated to them in the course of teaching[3].

1 As to professional obligations generally see *Brown v IRC* [1965] AC 244 at 265, [1964] 3 All ER 119 at 127, HL; *Hunter v Mann* [1974] QB 767 at 772, [1974] 2 All ER 414 at 417–418, DC. Production of confidential records relating to the behavioural problems of a pupil may be required in the interests of justice: *M v British Railways Board* (1995) The Scotsman, 13 September.

2 As to the general obligation of confidence in relation to personal information see *Duchess of Argyll v Duke of Argyll* [1967] Ch 302, [1965] 1 All ER 611; *Stephens v Avery* [1988] Ch 449, [1988] 2 All ER 477; *Prince Albert v Strange* (1849) 2 De G & Sm 652; on appeal (1849) 1 Mac & G 25; *Thompson v Stanhope and Dodsley* (1774) Amb 737.

3 *Caird v Sime* (1887) 12 App Cas 326, HL; *Abernethy v Hutchinson* (1825) 3 LJCh 209; *Nichols v Pitman* (1884) 26 ChD 374 (all cases concerned with the wrongful publication of lectures).

469. Liquidators and receivers. Liquidators and receivers are covered by the obligations of their professions (usually accountancy[1]) and the general obligations of members of advisory professions[2]. Confidential information obtained by liquidators should not voluntarily be disclosed by them to defendants in collateral criminal proceedings in the absence of compelling reasons such as an order of the Crown Court[3].

1 As to accountants' duty of confidence see para 458 ante; and *Evitt v Price* (1827) 1 Sim 483; cf *Parry-Jones v Law Society* [1969] 1 Ch 1 at 9, [1968] 1 All ER 177 at 180, CA.
2 As to professional obligations generally see *Brown v IRC* [1965] AC 244 at 265, [1964] 3 All ER 119 at 127, HL; *Hunter v Mann* [1974] QB 767 at 772, [1974] 2 All ER 414 at 417–418, DC. As to professional advisers' obligations of confidence see para 458 ante.
3 *Re Barlow Clowes Gilt Managers Ltd* [1992] Ch 208, [1991] 4 All ER 385.

470. Arbitrators. Arbitrators may give restricted reasons for an award which are to be used only for the purposes of the award[1]. Although these have also been termed 'confidential reasons'[2], such characterisation may be inappropriate. Whereas, as a matter of practice, the courts usually do not consider these reasons in order to preserve the finality of the award, the parties cannot by their agreement exclude such consideration since any attempt to do so would be void as purporting to oust the jurisdiction of the court[3]. Documents voluntarily disclosed in arbitration are not privileged in later public litigation since, as they were not disclosed under compulsion, there was no risk that parties would be discouraged from frank disclosure[4].

1 As to arbitration generally see ARBITRATION.
2 See *Mutual Shipping Corpn of New York v Bayshore Shipping Corpn of Monrovia, The Montan* [1985] 1 All ER 520, sub nom *Mutual Shipping Corpn v Bayshore Shipping Co Ltd* [1985] 1 WLR 625, CA.
3 See *Czarnikow v Roth Schmidt & Co* [1922] 2 KB 478; but see the Arbitration Act 1979 s 3.
4 *Shearson Lehman Hutton Inc v Maclaine Watson & Co Ltd* [1989] 1 All ER 1056, [1988] 1 WLR 946; and see DISCOVERY.

471. Insurance brokers. When an insurance broker acts on behalf of both the policyholder and the underwriter, he is not obliged to disclose to the policyholder a report prepared whilst he was specifically acting on behalf of the underwriter[1]. This is a qualification to the general rule that a person employed is under a duty not only to preserve confidential information from disclosure to third parties but also to disclose to his employer relevant information which becomes available to him in the course of his employment[2]. The fact that an insurance broker is under a duty of utmost good faith to reveal material facts when effecting a policy may operate as an implied release in respect of otherwise confidential information[3].

Any information acquired by an insurance broker from his client must not be used or disclosed except in the normal course of negotiating, maintaining or renewing a contract of insurance, or in handling a claim for that client, unless the consent of the client has been obtained or the information is required by a court of competent jurisdiction[4].

1 *North and South Trust Co v Berkeley* [1971] 1 All ER 980, [1971] 1 WLR 470. As to insurance generally see INSURANCE.
2 *Cranleigh Precision Engineering Ltd v Bryant* [1964] 3 All ER 289, [1965] 1 WLR 1293; *Saunders v Parry* [1967] 2 All ER 803, [1967] 1 WLR 753; *Industrial Furnaces Ltd v Reaves* [1970] RPC 605; *Industrial Development Consultants Ltd v Cooley* [1972] 2 All ER 162, [1972] 1 WLR 443. See also para 464 ante.
3 *Pryke v Gibbs Hartley Cooper Ltd* [1991] 1 Lloyd's Rep 602. The obligation (breach of which is neither a breach of contract nor a tort) is owed by the broker to the insurer personally and not as agent of the

insured. It can be enforced only by avoidance of the policy: *Banque Keiser Ullman SA v Skandia (UK) Insurance Co Ltd* [1990] 1 QB 665, [1989] 2 All ER 952, CA. The appeal did not involve this issue but approval was given at [1991] 2 AC 249 at 280, [1990] 2 All ER 947 at 959, HL, per Lord Templeman.

4 Insurance Brokers Registration Council (Code of Conduct) Approval Order 1994, SI 1994/2569, reg 2, Schedule para 2(19). As to the insurance brokers' code of conduct see INSURANCE vol 25 (Reissue) vol 882 et seq.

472. Journalists. A journalist may incur obligations of confidence, similar to those binding members of other professions[1], in particular to his sources. At common law a journalist who refused to identify his sources when called upon to do so by the court might be held in contempt[2]. However, it is now provided by statute that no court may require a person to disclose, nor is any person guilty of contempt for refusing to disclose, the source of information contained in a publication for which he is responsible, unless it is established to the satisfaction of the court that the disclosure is necessary in the interests of justice or national security or for the prevention of disorder or crime[3].

The court retains a discretion to decline to order sources to be identified even in the excepted cases, but this is rarely exercised unless, for instance, a crime is very minor or disclosure would put the journalist at risk[4]. In cases other than those excepted, the court will not make orders which would indirectly identify a source, as by ordering the delivery up of a document from whose format the source could be traced[5]. The courts have taken different approaches to the interpretation of the exceptions, those for crime and national security being interpreted broadly to extend the exceptions, while the interests of justice have been treated more restrictively. In regard to the phrase 'necessary for the prevention of crime' it has been held that 'necessary', although stronger than 'useful or expedient', was less strong than 'indispensable'[6], while 'prevention of crime' is not restricted to a specific future crime but means the deterrence and control of crime generally, so that crimes allegedly already committed might come within the exception[7]. 'Necessary in the interests of justice' means more than merely relevant[8]. Further, while prevention of crime and national security are good reasons for limiting the public interest in the confidentiality of sources, the interests of justice allow more detailed evaluation, including the importance of the case for the plaintiff, the public interest in the information from the source and the method by which the source obtained the material; 'necessary' has been further interpreted to mean 'really needed'[9]. It is not sufficient for a party seeking disclosure of a protected source to show merely that he will otherwise be unable to exercise a legal right or avert a threatened legal wrong[10].

There is also protection against police search and seizure of journalistic material[11] if it comes within the definition of excluded material[12] or special procedure material[13].

When confidential material becomes available to a journalist the defence of public interest, iniquity or impropriety[14] or a serious health hazard[15] may, but will not always, justify full media publication[16] but sometimes it may merely justify notifying those with corrective or regulatory powers[17]. With national security it is hard to envisage circumstances which would give rise to a public interest defence for external publicity since there are established internal means of complaint and investigation[18]. Public interest will not justify the commission of a crime to obtain evidence of iniquity or impropriety[19]. A party who, by widespread publicity, destroys the confidentiality of material may be restrained by injunction from using or disseminating it even though all others are free to use it, although this has been doubted[20]. For personal information different terms of restraint may be imposed from those applicable to other types of information[21] and although gross immorality will not be protected by confidence it is difficult to define[22]. A newspaper which publishes confidential material without justification may be liable to an account of profits[23].

1   See *W v Egdell* [1990] Ch 359 at 419, [1990] 1 All ER 835 at 848, CA, per Bingham LJ.
2   *A-G v Mulholland, A-G v Foster* [1963] 2 QB 477, [1963] 1 All ER 767, CA; *British Steel Corpn v Granada Television Ltd* [1981] AC 1096, [1981] 1 All ER 417. There was an exception in libel actions: see *Broadcasting Corpn of New Zealand v Alex Harvey Industries Ltd* [1980] 1 NZLR 163, NZ CA; *British Steel Corpn v Granada Television Ltd* supra.
3   Contempt of Court Act 1981 s 10.
4   *Re an Inquiry under the Company Securities (Insider Dealing) Act 1985* [1988] AC 660 at 703, [1988] 1 All ER 203 at 208, HL.
5   *Secretary of State for Defence v Guardian Newspapers Ltd* [1985] AC 339 at 349–350, [1984] 3 All ER 601 at 606–607 (a civil servant remaining in post after disclosing a departmental memorandum was a threat to national security and therefore the handing over of the memorandum, from which that civil servant could be identified, was ordered).
6   *Re an Inquiry under the Company Securities (Insider Dealing) Act 1985* [1988] AC 660 at 704–705, [1988] 1 All ER 203 at 208–209, HL (the prosecution did not therefore have to show that it was only by the journalist's disclosure that a source could be identified).
7   *Re an Inquiry under the Company Securities (Insider Dealing) Act 1985* [1988] AC 660 at 704–705, [1988] 1 All ER 203 at 208–209, HL.
8   *Maxwell v Pressdram Ltd* [1987] 1 All ER 656, [1987] 1 WLR 298, CA (the fact that a plaintiff had added claims for exemplary and aggravated damages, which required identification of sources, to a claim in defamation did not bring the exception into operation).
9   *X Ltd v Morgan-Grampian (Publishers) Ltd* [1991] 1 AC 1 at 53, [1990] 2 All ER 1 at 16, HL, per Lord Oliver of Aylmerton.
10 *X Ltd v Morgan-Grampian (Publishers) Ltd* [1991] 1 AC 1 at 43, [1990] 2 All ER 1 at 9, HL, per Lord Bridge of Harwich. Hence the discovery of material from which a source who had disclosed the business plan of a company could be identified was ordered: see *X Ltd v Morgan-Grampian (Publishers) Ltd* supra.
11 For the meaning of 'journalistic material' see the Police and Criminal Evidence Act 1984 s 13; and CRIMINAL LAW vol 11(1) (Reissue) para 674.
12 For the meaning of 'excluded material' see ibid s 11; and CRIMINAL LAW vol 11(1) (Reissue) paras 673–674.
13 For the meaning of 'special procedure material' see ibid s 14; and CRIMINAL LAW vol 11(1) (Reissue) para 675.
14 See *Woodward v Hutchins* [1977] 2 All ER 751, [1977] 1 WLR 760, CA (conduct misleading public).
15 *Church of Scientology of California v Kaufman* [1973] RPC 627 (book justified).
16 *Lion Laboratories Ltd v Evans* [1985] QB 526, [1984] 2 All ER 417, CA (defective breathalyser).
17 *Francome v Mirror Group Newspapers Ltd* [1984] 2 All ER 408, [1984] 1 WLR 892, CA (alleged racing irregularities should be revealed to police or Jockey Club); and see *Initial Services Ltd v Putterill* [1968] 1 QB 396, [1967] 3 All ER 145, CA.
18 *A-G v Observer Ltd, A-G v Times Newspapers Ltd* [1990] 1 AC 109 at 269, sub nom *A-G v Guardian Newspapers Ltd (No 2)* [1988] 3 All ER 545 at 650, HL, per Lord Griffiths, and at 282–283 and 659–660 per Lord Goff of Chieveley.
19 *Francome v Mirror Group Newspapers Ltd* [1984] 2 All ER 408, [1984] 1 WLR 892, CA (telephone tapping). Nor will it justify breach of medical confidentiality: *X v Y* [1988] 2 All ER 648.
20 *Speed Seal Products Ltd v Paddington* [1986] 1 All ER 91, [1985] 1 WLR 1327, CA; *A-G v Observer Ltd, A-G v Times Newspapers Ltd* [1990] 1 AC 109, sub nom *A-G v Guardian Newspapers Ltd (No 2)* [1988] 3 All ER 545, HL (but see at 286–289 and 662–664 per Lord Goff of Chieveley, dissenting on this point, (discloser should be liable and perhaps under a restraint akin to the 'springboard' doctrine, but perpetually enjoining the discloser will have absurd consequences)).
21 *A-G v Observer Ltd, A-G v Times Newspapers Ltd* [1990] 1 AC 109 at 260, sub nom *A-G v Guardian Newspapers Ltd (No 2)* [1988] 3 All ER 545 at 643, HL, per Lord Keith of Kinkel.
22 See *Stephens v Avery* [1988] Ch 449 at 453, [1988] 2 All ER 477 at 480 per Browne-Wilkinson V-C.
23 *A-G v Observer Ltd, A-G v Times Newspapers Ltd* [1990] 1 AC 109, sub nom *A-G v Guardian Newspapers Ltd (No 2)* [1988] 3 All ER 545, HL. As to account of profits see para 495 post.

473. Police. Police documents may be covered by public interest immunity and so be exempt from production on discovery[1]. A class claim to public interest immunity for evidence relating to an investigation under Part IX of the Police and Criminal Evidence Act 1984[2] has been rejected and earlier authorities overruled, but a contents claim might apply to documents that came into existence in consequence of an investigation into a complaint of police misconduct[3]. The determination of the claim is for the court not the litigant and it is to be resolved by weighing the public interests in disclosure and confidentiality in the actual litigation, without taking account of any collateral proceedings[4]. If the police seize documents in the course of a criminal investigation they are bound to produce them on a subpoena in civil proceedings unless there is a ground of challenge such as legal professional privilege or self-incrimination[5]; and neither the fact that the documents are held for the public purpose of combating crime nor confidentiality between the police and the owner of the documents will bar their production[6].

It is within the official duties of the police to give information, including information relating to offences which are spent under the Rehabilitation of Offenders Act 1974[7], to Interpol, and therefore it is not an offence on the part of the police to provide this information[8].

It is a disciplinary offence for a member of a police force improperly to disclose information which he has in his possession as a member of the force[9].

1 *Conway v Rimmer* [1968] AC 910, [1968] 1 All ER 874, HL (report on probationary constable; disclosure ordered on the facts). As to discovery generally see DISCOVERY.
2 Ie the Police and Criminal Evidence Act 1984 Pt IX (ss 83–112): see POLICE.
3 *R v Chief Constable of the West Midlands Police, ex p Wiley* [1995] 1 AC 274, [1994] 3 All ER 420, HL.
4 *R v Chief Constable of the West Midlands Police, ex p Wiley* [1995] 1 AC 274, [1994] 3 All ER 420, HL.
5 As to legal professional privilege see BARRISTERS vol 3(1) (Reissue) para 524–527; CRIMINAL LAW vol 11(2) (Reissue) para 1163; DISCOVERY vol 13 para 79; EVIDENCE vol 17 para 237; SOLICITORS vol 44(1) (Reissue) paras 90, 150. As to self-incrimination see EVIDENCE vol 17 para 240; CRIMINAL LAW vol 11(2) (Reissue) para 1160 et seq.
6 *Marcel v Metropolitan Police Comr* [1992] Ch 225, [1992] 1 All ER 72, CA.
7 As to the rehabilitation of offenders see para 478 post; and CRIMINAL LAW vol 11(2) (Reissue) para 1078–1085, 1566 et seq.
8 *X v Metropolitan Police Comr* [1985] 1 All ER 890, [1985] 1 WLR 420. See the Rehabilitation of Offenders Act 1974 s 9(2); and CRIMINAL LAW vol 11(1) (Reissue) para 294.
9 Police (Discipline) Regulations 1985, SI 1985/518, regs 4(1), 5, Sch 1 para 6; see POLICE vol 36 para 272. As to the use of information retrieved from the police national computer see *R v Brown* [1994] QB 547, 99 Cr App Rep 69, CA; affd [1996] 1 All ER 545, HL; and para 513 post.

(9) SPECIAL SITUATIONS OF CONFIDENCE

474. Children. In adoption proceedings[1] the public interest and the child's best interests will prevail over the confidentiality of the mother's medical records[2]. Proceedings under the Children Act 1989 are confidential[3]. However, information which has been voluntarily filed with the court may be disclosed to other parties[4]. Proceedings under the Children Act 1989 are not adversarial and it is for the court to achieve a result having regard to the welfare of the child in question[5]. To this end the court has power to override legal professional privilege[6] and to order the disclosure of reports which would be privileged in other proceedings[7].

The court has a discretion to disclose confidential material relating to adoption[8], wardship[9] and care proceedings[10]. Factors to be taken into account in assessing whether disclosure should be made include the interests of justice[11] and the welfare of the child[12]. The Attorney General may be required to determine to what extent disclosure should be made[13] and he is now to be represented by counsel in cases where, for example, disclosure may be relevant to criminal proceedings[14].

1 As to adoption see CHILDREN vol 5(2) (Reissue) para 1021 et seq.
2 *Re C (A Minor) (Evidence: Confidential Information)* [1991] 2 FLR 478, CA. As to legal proceedings relating to children see generally CHILDREN; CRIMINAL LAW vol 11(2) para 1263 et seq. As to access to medical records see para 448 ante.
3 An admission by a mother to a guardian ad litem that she was responsible for her children's injuries should not have been disclosed by the guardian to a social worker and should not have been further disclosed to the police, who should have obtained a court order before interviewing the guardian: *Oxfordshire County Council v P* [1995] Fam 163, [1995] 2 All ER 225. A guardian should not make a promise to children that whatever they tell her will not be disclosed to other parties, as it is a promise the guardian may not be able to keep if the court orders disclosure: *Re D (Minors) (Adoption Reports: Confidentiality)* [1995] 1 WLR 356, CA; on appeal [1995] 4 All ER 385 at 393, 399, HL, per Lord Mustill (there is a presumption in favour of disclosure). A social worker, however, does not need the leave of the court in order to disclose to the police oral statements made by parents in relation to unexplained injuries sustained by their child: *Re G (Minor) (Social worker: Disclosure)* [1995] TLR 588, CA.
4 Where, in care proceedings, a mother voluntarily obtained a medical expert's report which she was ordered to file with the court and which then became available to all parties, the police authority could obtain disclosure of the report in order to consider whether to prosecute: *Re L (Police Investigation: Privilege)* [1995] 1 FLR 999, CA.
5 As to the welfare principle see CHILDREN vol 5(2) (Reissue) para 809 et seq.
6 As to legal professional privilege see BARRISTERS vol 3(1) (Reissue) para 524–527; CRIMINAL LAW vol 11(2) (Reissue) para 1163; DISCOVERY vol 13 para 79; EVIDENCE vol 17 para 237; SOLICITORS vol 44(1) (Reissue) paras 90, 150; and para 455 ante.
7 *Oxfordshire County Council v M* [1994] Fam 151, [1994] 2 All ER 269, CA.
8 *Re G (TJ) (an infant)* [1963] 2 QB 73, [1963] 1 All ER 20, CA; *Re JS (an infant)* [1959] 3 All ER 856, [1959] 1 WLR 1218; *Re PA (an infant)* [1971] 3 All ER 522, [1971] 1 WLR 1530, CA; *Re D (Adoption reports: Confidentiality)* [1995] 1 WLR 356, CA.
9 *B v W (Wardship Appeal)* [1979] 3 All ER 83, [1979] 1 WLR 1041, HL; *Re H (A Minor)* [1985] 3 All ER 1, [1985] 1 WLR 1164, CA; *Re S (Minors) (Wardship: Police Investigation)* [1987] Fam 199, [1987] 3 All ER 1076; *Re F (Minors) (Wardship: Police Investigation)* [1989] Fam 18; *Re Manda* [1993] Fam 183, [1993] 1 All ER 733, CA. As to wardship see CHILDREN vol 5(2) (Reissue) para 760 et seq.
10 *Re K (Minors) (Disclosure of Privileged Material)* [1994] 3 All ER 230. As to care orders see CHILDREN vol 5(2) (Reissue) para 788 et seq. See also *Cleveland County Council v F* [1995] 2 All ER 236 for factors in exercising discretion.
11 *Re S (Minors: Wardship: Police Investigation)* [1987] Fam 199, [1987] 3 All ER 1076 (prevention of crime prevailed over confidentiality); *Re K (Minors) (Disclosure of Privileged Material)* [1994] 3 All ER 230 (need for fair trial prevailed over confidentiality).
12 *B v W (Wardship Appeal)* [1979] 3 All ER 83, [1979] 1 WLR 1041, HL (disclosure not harmful); *Re K (Minors) (Disclosure of Privileged Material)* [1994] 3 All ER 230 (disclosure no detriment to children); *Re Manda* [1993] Fam 183, [1993] 1 All ER 733, CA (disclosure might be for benefit of ward).
13 *Re an ex parte originating summons in an adoption application* [1990] 1 All ER 639n, sub nom *Re an Adoption Application* [1990] 1 WLR 520 (disclosure sought for the defence of a parent accused of an offence against a child in care).
14 *Practice Note* [1990] 1 All ER 640.

475. Credit reference agencies. An individual has the right to find out whether a credit reference agency[1] has been consulted about him in any credit transaction in which he is involved, and to discover (and amend if necessary) the information any credit reference agency has compiled about him[2]. However, subject to certain exceptions, information obtained under or by virtue of the Consumer Credit Act 1974 about any individual or business must not be disclosed without the consent of the individual or business concerned[3].

1 As to credit reference agencies see HIRE PURCHASE AND CONSUMER CREDIT.

2 See the Consumer Credit Act 1974 ss 157–160 (s 158 as amended); and HIRE PURCHASE AND CONSUMER CREDIT. There is an exemption under the Data Protection Act 1984 s 34(3) where an individual has the right described in the text: see para 536 text and notes 8–10 post.

3 See Consumer Credit Act 1974 s 174 (as amended); and HIRE PURCHASE AND CONSUMER CREDIT.

476. Interception of communications. It is an offence intentionally to intercept communications by post or public telecommunications systems except where the interception is undertaken by an authority in accordance with the prescribed statutory requirements[1]. If and when it is undertaken without authority it may be both an infringement of confidence and a criminal offence[2].

Legislation further provides criminal sanctions for unauthorised access to or modification of materials held on computers, with additional sanctions if this is done with a view to the commission of a crime[3].

1 See the Interception of Communications Act 1985; and CRIMINAL LAW vol 11(1) (Reissue) para 270 et seq.

2 See eg *Francome v Mirror Group Newspapers Ltd* [1984] 2 All ER 408, [1984] 1 WLR 892, CA.

3 See the Computer Misuse Act 1990 ss 1, 2, 3; and CRIMINAL LAW vol 11(1) (Reissue) (Supp) para 604A et seq.

477. European Community. Information which the European Commission[1] acquires from its inquiries or investigations must be used only for the purposes of the relevant request or investigation and it must not disclose any information so acquired which is covered by an obligation of professional secrecy, but this is qualified in respect of the publication of decisions and observance of the right to be heard[2]. There is now access to Commission files but this is subject to exceptions for business secrets, internal Commission documents and matters communicated by informants who wish to remain anonymous[3].

The Commission may be liable in damages if it releases documents in a form which enables an informant to be identified, although the damages may be reduced if the informant has not taken reasonable steps to protect his own interests[4]. National legislation may provide for exceptions to a directive imposing a duty of professional confidence and when such exceptions are general in character the national court must balance the interest in establishing the truth against the interest in secrecy before deciding whether a witness should answer[5]. If a company against which complaints of anti-competitive practices have been made is not allowed to object to the production to the complainant of documents containing trade secrets, the decision of the Commission will be annulled without deciding whether or not there were trade secrets[6]. Provision is made for professional privilege and in competition law there is provision for the regulation of confidentiality in relation to 'know-how', sub-contracting agreements, research and development agreements and the assignment of 'know-how'[7]. 'Block exemptions' may qualify the application of general rules in relation to some of these topics[8].

The public has access to EC Council and Commission documents[9] except where disclosure could undermine the protection of the public interest, privacy, business secrets, the Community's financial interests or the confidentiality of any person who supplied information contained in the relevant document[10]. It has been held that the Council may refuse a request for access to documents in order to protect the confidentiality of its proceedings[11], but in exercising this discretion the Council must genuinely balance the interest of citizens in gaining access to its documents against any interest of its own in maintaining confidentiality of its deliberations[12].

1 As to the European Commission see EUROPEAN COMMUNITIES vol 51 para 1.84 et seq.
2 See EEC Council Regulation 17 of 6 February 1962; and EUROPEAN COMMUNITIES vol 52 paras 19.163–19.168.
3 See EUROPEAN COMMUNITIES vol 52 para 19.172.
4 Cases 145/83, 53/84 *Adams v EC Commission* [1986] QB 138, [1986] 1 CMLR 506, ECJ.
5 Case 110/84 *Municipality of Hillegom v Hillenius* [1985] ECR 3947, [1986] 3 CMLR 422, ECJ.
6 Case 53/85 *Akzo Chemie BV and Akzo Chemie UK Ltd v EC Commission, Engineering and Chemical Supplies, Epsom and Gloucester intervening* [1986] ECR 1965, [1987] 1 CMLR 231, ECJ.
7 See EUROPEAN COMMUNITIES vol 52 para 19.356 et seq. A professional person exercising the right of establishment in another Member State may be required to comply with that State's professional ethics: Case C-55/94 *Gebhard v Consiglio dell 'Ordine degli Avvocati e Procuratori di Milano* [1995] TLR 672, ECJ.
8 See EUROPEAN COMMUNITIES vol 52 para 19.196.
9 EC Council Decision 93/731 (OJ L 340, 20.12.93, p 43) art 1; EC Commission Decision 94/90 (OJ L 46, 18.2.94, p 58). As to the EC Council and EC Commission see EUROPEAN COMMUNITIES vol 51 paras 1.78 et seq, 1.84 et seq.
10 EC Council Decision 93/731 art 4(1); EC Commission Decision 94/90 annex.
11 EC Council Decision 93/731 art 4(2); EC Commission Decision 94/90 annex.
12 Case T-194/94 *Carvel v EU Council (Denmark intervening)* [1996] All ER (EC) 53 at 63–64.

478. Rehabilitation of offenders. Legislation provides that many criminal offences, other than the most serious, are, after the lapse of prescribed periods of time, to be treated as spent and the person convicted is thereafter to be treated for all purposes in law as not having committed, been charged with, prosecuted for or convicted and sentenced for the spent offences[1]. There is a general prohibition on the admissibility in evidence of such offences but this is restricted by wide qualifications in respect of criminal and family law and where the interests of justice require disclosure[2]. However, it is an offence to make unauthorised disclosure of spent convictions[3].

1 See the Rehabilitation of Offenders Act 1974 s 4; and CRIMINAL LAW vol 11(2) (Reissue) paras 1081–1084, 1571–1573.
2 See ibid s 7 (as amended); and CRIMINAL LAW vol 11(2) (Reissue) paras 1083–1084. 'Needs of justice' are to be assessed by the trial judge: *Reynolds v Phoenix Assurance Co Ltd* [1978] 2 Lloyds Rep 22, CA.
3 See the Rehabilitation of Offenders Act 1974 s 9 (as amended); and CRIMINAL LAW vol 11(2) (Reissue) paras 287, 294. See also *X v Metropolitan Police Comr* [1985] 1 All ER 890, [1985] 1 WLR 420; and para 473 ante.

479. Compromises and settlements. If a client authorises a solicitor to negotiate a settlement prior to the issue of a writ, this instruction will not be covered by legal professional privilege[1] because the solicitor is authorised to communicate the client's offer to the other side and any rule to the contrary would undermine settlements negotiated at this stage before a solicitor has implied authority to settle the case[2]. When an action is compromised, an implied obligation not to use the documents produced in the course of that action for further proceedings abroad applies to witness statements but not to expert reports[3].

1 As to legal professional privilege see BARRISTERS vol 3(1) (Reissue) para 524–527; CRIMINAL LAW vol 11(2) (Reissue) para 1163; DISCOVERY vol 13 para 79; EVIDENCE vol 17 para 237; SOLICITORS vol 44(1) (Reissue) paras 90, 150.
2 *Conlon v Conlons Ltd* [1952] 2 All ER 462, [1952] WN 403, CA.
3 *Prudential Assurance Co Ltd v Fountain Page Ltd* [1991] 3 All ER 878, [1991] 1 WLR 756.

(10) BREACH OF OBLIGATIONS OF CONFIDENCE

480. Breach of confidence. Breach of confidence may be constituted by the unjustified disclosure or use[1], or by the unjustified putting at risk of such disclosure or use[2], of the information imparted or, in the case of third parties, by the improper obtaining of confidential material[3] or, if the material was initially obtained innocently, by the improper retention or use of the confidential material when the recipient knew or ought to have known that it was confidential[4]. The disclosure or use may be partial provided that it is significant and substantial[5].

Breach of confidence may result not only from the disclosure of the primary material but also from ancillary or subsidiary public references to it, as when a catalogue containing details of protected etchings was held to be a breach of the confidence protecting the etchings[6]. Overhearing information by accident[7] or obtaining information as a bona fide purchaser for value without notice may not involve liability[8]. There is no irrebuttable presumption that an employee who has stolen confidential material from the employer and used it to contact customers has thereby obtained business from customers; it is a question of fact whether business has resulted from the misuse or from the employee's own skills[9].

1 *Terrapin Ltd v Builders' Supply Co (Hayes) Ltd* [1960] RPC 128, CA; *National Broach and Machine Co v Churchill Gear Machines Ltd* [1965] RPC 61; on appeal on the question of damages only [1965] 2 All ER 961, [1965] 1 WLR 1199, CA; affd [1966] 3 All ER 923n, [1967] 1 WLR 384, HL; *Seager v Copydex Ltd* [1967] 2 All ER 415, [1967] 1 WLR 923, CA. A statutory duty of confidence will not be broken by a reasonable disclosure envisaged by the statute: *Hoechst UK Ltd v Chemiculture Ltd* [1993] FSR 270.
2 *Hivac Ltd v Park Royal Scientific Instruments Ltd* [1946] Ch 169, [1946] 1 All ER 350, CA.
3 See *Under Water Welders and Repairers Ltd v Street and Longthorne* [1968] RPC 498 at 503–504.
4 *Prince Albert v Strange* (1849) 2 De G & Sm 652; on appeal (1849) 1 Mac & G 25; *Richards v Dobell* (1912) [1911–1916] MacG Cop Cas 51; *Rex Company and Rex Research Corpn v C H Muirhead and HM Comptroller of Patents* (1927) 44 RPC 38; *London and Provincial Sporting News Agency Ltd v Levy* (1928) [1923–1928] MacG Cop Cas 340; *Stevenson Jordan & Harrison Ltd v Macdonald & Evans* (1951) 68 RPC 190; revsd on other grounds [1952] 1 TLR 101, 69 RPC 10, CA; *Printers and Finishers Ltd v Holloway* [1964] 3 All ER 731, [1965] RPC 239 at 253; *Fraser v Evans* [1969] 1 QB 349 at 361, [1969] 1 All ER 8 at 11, CA; *Butler v Board of Trade* [1971] Ch 680, [1970] 3 All ER 593; *Malone v Metropolitan Police Comr* [1979] Ch 344, [1979] 2 All ER 620; *A-G v Observer Ltd, A-G v Times Newspapers Ltd* [1990] 1 AC 109 at 281, sub nom *A-G v Guardian Newspapers Ltd (No 2)* [1988] 3 All ER 545 at 658–659, HL; *A-G v Guardian Newspapers Ltd* [1987] 3 All ER 316, [1987] 1 WLR 1248, HL.
5 *Amber Size and Chemical Co Ltd v Menzel* [1913] 2 Ch 239 at 246–248.
6 *Prince Albert v Strange* (1849) 2 De G & Sm 652; on appeal (1849) 1 Mac & G 25.
7 *Malone v Metropolitan Police Comr* [1979] Ch 344, [1979] 2 All ER 620.
8 *A-G v Guardian Newspapers Ltd* [1987] 3 All ER 316 at 328, [1987] 1 WLR 1248 at 1265 per Browne-Wilkinson V-C; *A-G v Observer Ltd, A-G v Times Newspapers Ltd* [1990] 1 AC 109 at 177, sub nom *A-G v Guardian Newspapers Ltd (No 2)* [1988] 3 All ER 545 at 596, CA; *Morison v Moat* (1851) 9 Hare 241 at 263. See para 420 note 8 ante for authorities which suggest the contrary.
9 *Universal Thermosensors Ltd v Hibben* [1992] 3 All ER 257, [1992] 1 WLR 840.

481. Intention or negligence. In relation to claims for damages for breach of confidence it is, in general, immaterial why the defendant failed to fulfil his obligation, and it is no defence to plead that he has done his best[1]. If liability is to be based on conspiracy[2], or conversion[3] of, or trespass[4] to, material embodying the confidence, the state of mind and degree of unjustified interference required by those torts must be shown[5].

To establish the tort of inducing breach of contract it must be shown that the defendant knowingly and intentionally induced the breach[6] and a similar rule may apply to the knowing and intentional inducing of the breach of an equitable obligation[7]. If the obligation is equitable, intention or negligence will found liability both in immediate parties to the confidence and in third party recipients, since it has been held that even subconscious plagiarism is sufficient for liability[8]. An innocent third party who voluntarily receives material may also be liable after he has discovered the confidential character of the material, but it may be that a bona fide purchaser for value without notice will not be liable[9]. Intent or negligence may be taken into account when discretion is exercised to grant an injunction[10]. Many of the sources of liability mentioned may co-exist and be actionable in the same case[11].

1 See *Raineri v Miles* [1981] AC 1050 at 1086, [1980] 2 All ER 145 at 158, HL, per Lord Edmund-Davis. Contracts for professional services, such as those provided by accountants, architects, doctors and solicitors, merely impose duties of care in respect of primary professional duties since success cannot be guaranteed, but this qualification may not extend to subsidiary obligations to preserve confidences. As to the general professional obligation of confidence see paras 436–473 ante.

2 As to conspiracy see para 405 ante; and TORT vol 45 paras 1526–1530.

3 As to conversion see paras 405, 407 ante; and TORT vol 45 para 1422 et seq.

4 As to trespass to goods see paras 405, 407 ante; and TORT vol 45 para 1491 et seq.

5 See the text and notes infra; and generally TORT.

6 As to inducing breach of contract see para 405 ante; and TORT vol 45 paras 1518–1524.

7 See *Prudential Assurance Co Ltd v Lorenz* (1971) 11 KIR 78 (breach of equitable duty); *Bents Brewery Co Ltd v Hogan* [1945] 2 All ER 570; *Thomas Marshall (Exports) Ltd v Guinle* [1979] Ch 227, [1978] 3 All ER 193.

8 *Seager v Copydex Ltd* [1967] 2 All ER 415, [1967] 1 WLR 923, CA; and see *Terrapin Ltd v Builders' Supply Co (Hayes) Ltd* (1959) [1967] RPC 375; on appeal (but the appeal reported first) [1960] RPC 128, CA.

9 It has been held that no action will lie against an innocent person who uses information originally obtained in breach of confidence without knowing of the improper origin: *Cooksley v Johnson & Sons* (1905) 25 NZLR 834. See further para 420 text and notes 7–8 ante.

10 See *Coco v A N Clark (Engineers) Ltd* [1969] RPC 41 at 50 per Megarry J. As to injunctions see paras 491–492 post.

11 As to the interrelation of the heads of jurisdiction see para 403 ante.

482. Detriment. It has been suggested that detriment is a necessary element of actionable breach of confidence[1]. However, this has been doubted on good authority, at least in relation to personal confidences where, if detriment must be shown at all, it may be merely to the extent that the information given by the confider has been disclosed to persons whom he would prefer not to know of it, even though the disclosure would not be harmful to him in any positive way[2]. In the case of governmental secrets and confidences it has been said that the element of public interest in preserving confidence which the Crown must show to enforce its rights carries with it a requirement to show that publication would be harmful to the public interest[3] and this was accepted even when reservation was expressed on whether detriment was an essential requirement for actionable breach in private law[4]. Intention or negligence[5] may be taken into account when exercising discretion in granting an injunction[6].

1 See eg *Lamb v Evans* [1893] 1 Ch 218 at 236, CA; *Amber Size and Chemical Co Ltd v Menzel* [1913] 2 Ch 239 at 245; *Reid & Sigrist Ltd v Moss and Mechanism Ltd* (1932) 49 RPC 461 at 480; *Seager v Copydex Ltd* [1967] 2 All ER 415 at 417, [1967] 1 WLR 923 at 931, CA, per Lord Denning MR (information obtained in confidence not to be used 'to the prejudice of him who gave it without obtaining his consent').

2 *A-G v Observer Ltd, A-G v Times Newspapers Ltd* [1990] 1 AC 109 at 256, sub nom *A-G v Guardian Newspapers Ltd (No 2)* [1988] 3 All ER 545 at 640, HL, per Lord Keith of Kinkel. See also *Prince Albert v Strange* (1849) 2 De G & Sm 652 at 697 ('produce of private hours' to be protected); *Pollard v Photographic Co* (1888) 40 ChD 345 (unwanted publicity for portrait restrained).

3 *A-G v Observer Ltd, A-G v Times Newspapers Ltd* [1990] 1 AC 109 at 256–258, sub nom *A-G v Guardian Newspapers Ltd (No 2)* [1988] 3 All ER 545 at 640–642, HL, per Lord Keith of Kinkel, citing *A-G v Jonathan Cape Ltd, A-G v Times Newspapers Ltd* [1976] QB 752, [1975] 3 All ER 484 (where the decision depended on the fact that the publication would do no harm) and *Commonwealth of Australia v John Fairfax & Sons Ltd* (1980) 32 ALR 485 at 492–493, Aust HC, per Mason J. See also *A-G v Observer Ltd, A-G v Times Newspapers Ltd* supra at 270–271 and 650–651 per Lord Griffiths, accepting the same authorities.

4 *A-G v Observer Ltd, A-G v Times Newspapers Ltd* [1990] 1 AC 109 at 281–282, sub nom *A-G v Guardian Newspapers Ltd (No 2)* [1988] 3 All ER 545 at 659, HL, per Lord Goff of Chieveley; citing *Coco v A N Clark (Engineers) Ltd* [1969] RPC 41 at 48 per Megarry J. See also *A-G v Observer, A-G v Times Newspapers Ltd* supra at 265 and 646 per Lord Brightman (expressing agreement with the majority); at 293 and 668 per Lord Jauncey of Tullichettle (agreeing with Lord Keith of Kinkel); and at 270 and 650 per Lord Griffiths (regarding detriment or potential detriment as essential in private litigation since the remedy is to protect the confider not punish the confidant).

5 As to intention and negligence see para 481 ante.

6 See *Coco v A N Clark (Engineers) Ltd* [1969] RPC 41 at 50 per Megarry J. As to injunctions as a remedy see paras 491–492 post.

(11) PARTIES TO AN ACTION

483. Plaintiff. Only the person to whom the duty of confidence is owed may bring an action for breach of confidence and this person may not necessarily be the creator of the information[1]. Although privity of contract may apply to the creation of a confidence, the fact that contractual and equitable obligations may co-exist in the same case and the same criteria be used for their implication[2], together with the fact that the equitable obligation is not subject to the contractual requirement of privity, may enable a plaintiff to sue a party who is not privy to the contractual obligation[3].

The plaintiff must establish that: (1) the information had the quality of confidentiality; (2) it was imparted in confidence; and (3) unauthorised use, possibly to the plaintiff's detriment, was made of it[4]. If the original creator was acting as an agent or in some other fiduciary or subsidiary capacity, such as a servant or independent contractor, then the person entitled to the confidence and thereby able to sue will be the principal, the beneficiary or the employer[5]. In so far as confidential information possesses the character of property then those to whom the information has been transferred by way of sale, licence or operation of law[6], together with personal representatives and successors in title of a deceased person entitled to protection may, it seems, sue[7].

1 *Fraser v Evans* [1969] 1 QB 349, [1969] 1 All ER 8, CA (where a consultant was engaged to prepare a confidential report and wished to sue a third party who had obtained it and proposed to publish a copy, only the employer, and not the consultant, could sue).

2 *Saltman Engineering Co Ltd v Campbell Engineering Co* (1948) [1963] 3 All ER 413n, 65 RPC 203, CA; *Brian D Collins (Engineers) Ltd v Charles Roberts & Co Ltd* [1965] RPC 429 at 431; *Lamb v Evans* [1893] 1 Ch 218, 229; *Robb v Green* [1895] 2 QB 315, CA; *Nichrotherm Electrical Co Ltd v Percy* [1957] RPC 207, CA; *Ackroyds (London) Ltd v Islington Plastics Ltd* [1962] RPC 97. See also para 403 ante.

3 *Prince Albert v Strange* (1849) 2 De G & Sm 652; on appeal (1849) 1 Mac & G 25; *A-G v Observer Ltd, A-G v Times Newspapers Ltd* [1990] 1 AC 109, sub nom *A-G v Guardian Newspapers Ltd (No 2)* [1988] 3 All ER 545.

4 *Coco v A N Clark (Engineers) Ltd* [1969] RPC 41 (where only head (2) in the text was established); *Johnson v Heat and Air Systems Ltd* (1941) 58 RPC 229 (head (2) in the text established but there was no misuse since defendants already possessed the information). As to detriment see para 482 ante.

5 *Fraser v Evans* [1969] 1 QB 349, [1969] 1 All ER 8, CA.

6 If the opinion of Lord Upjohn in *Boardman v Phipps* [1967] 2 AC 46 at 128, [1966] 3 All ER 721 at 759, HL, that information is not 'property in any normal sense but equity will restrain its transmission to another if in breach of some confidential relationship' were to prevail, then a transferee or assignee would merely have a right to compel the transferor to sue an infringer but a majority in that case favoured the view that information is property, as do the majority of dicta in other cases (see para 407 note 7 ante). A trade secret has been held to be trust property: (*Green v Folgham* (1823) 1 Sim & Stu 398); and sold with a business (*Bryson v Whitehead* (1822) 1 Sim & St 74).

7 A trade secret has (1) passed to a trustee in bankruptcy (*Re Keene* [1922] 2 Ch 475); (2) been left by will (*Canham v Jones* (1813) 2 Ves & B 218); and (3) been treated as partnership property (*Dean v McDowell*

(1878) 8 ChD 345). The professional codes issued by the General Medical Council and the Law Society contemplate obligations of confidence of doctors (see para 440 ante) and solicitors (see paras 426, 455 ante) surviving their patients or clients.

484. Defendant. The initial recipient of protected confidential information will be liable in the event of his making unauthorised disclosure or use of the material or putting the material at risk of unauthorised disclosure or use[1]. Third parties who acquire by underhand, dishonest or improper means information which they know or ought to know is subject to protected confidence may also be sued, as may third parties who initially acquire such information innocently but subsequently learn of its confidential character[2]. Such third parties incur liability from the time of knowledge or notice[3]. It may be that a bona fide purchaser for value without notice does not incur liability[4]. A party acting in breach of confidence will not be allowed to use a company to evade liability, as knowledge or notice will be imputed to the company[5].

Under the 'springboard' doctrine a party who has had authorised access to confidential material not fully available to the public will be restrained from taking advantage of his position until the relevant information has been made fully public[6]. An employer or principal may be entrusted with confidential information which is to be further disclosed to employees or agents; and, in the event of breach, the liability of the employer or principal will primarily depend on the express or implied terms of the contract or equitable obligation under which the material was first imparted[7]. If the subordinate or agent improperly discloses or misuses the information knowing of its confidential character, the employer or principal may be directly liable to the creator of the confidence, as may the employee[8]. Otherwise, such employees or agents may be treated as third parties, thereby becoming immediately liable if they disclose or misuse the material knowing it to be confidential but otherwise incurring liability only when they receive notice or knowledge of its character[9].

1 See *Coco v A N Clark (Engineers) Ltd* [1969] RPC 41; *Dunford & Elliott Ltd v Johnson & Firth Brown Ltd* [1978] FSR 143, CA; and *Jarman & Platt Ltd v I Barget Ltd* [1977] FSR 260, CA; and para 402 ante.
2 *A-G v Observer Ltd, A-G v Times Newspapers Ltd* [1990] 1 AC 109, sub nom *A-G v Guardian Newspapers Ltd (No 2)* [1988] 3 All ER 545, HL.
3 *A-G v Observer Ltd, A-G v Times Newspapers Ltd* [1990] 1 AC 109 at 281, sub nom *A-G v Guardian Newspapers Ltd (No 2)* [1988] 3 All ER 545 at 658–659, HL, per Lord Goff of Chieveley. See further para 420 text and note 7 ante.
4 See para 420 text and note 8 ante.
5 See para 420 text and note 6 ante.
6 As to the 'springboard' doctrine see para 422 ante.
7 See paras 404, 464 ante.
8 Obligations of this type, both for the employer or principal and for the employee or agent, may continue after the employment has ceased if that is necessary to give business efficacy to the obligation of confidence: see *Schering Chemicals Ltd v Falkman Ltd* [1982] QB 1 at 27, [1981] 2 All ER 321 at 338, CA. Cf *Easton v Hitchcock* [1912] 1 KB 535, DC. See also *Faccenda Chicken Ltd v Fowler, Fowler v Faccenda Chicken Ltd* [1987] Ch 117, [1986] 1 All ER 617, CA.
9 *A-G v Observer Ltd, A-G v Times Newspapers Ltd* [1990] 1 AC 109 at 281, sub nom *A-G v Guardian Newspapers Ltd (No 2)* [1988] 3 All ER 545 at 658–659, HL, per Lord Goff of Chieveley. See further para 420 text and note 7 ante.

(12) DEFENCES

485. Just cause or excuse and public interest. It has long been established that there is no confidence as to the disclosure of iniquity, and therefore obligations of confidence will not require the concealment of wrongdoing[1]. This defence to disclosure has been progressively expanded and older references to iniquity must be taken to be illustrative rather than definitive of the degree of wrongdoing which will suffice for the operation of this defence[2]. It has been said to extend to crimes, frauds and misdeeds, both those actually committed as well as those contemplated, provided always that disclosure is justified in the public interest[3].

The defence covers both past and contemplated crimes[4]. In relation to civil wrongs, there seems to be no doubt that contemplated wrongdoing can be revealed and older authority suggesting that past torts should not be revealed[5] has been disapproved, provided that the disclosure of the tort is in the public interest[6]. Current or future medical hazards will also be covered[7], but not those which have ceased to be operative[8]. If a doctor believes that his mental patient, who is seeking release, is likely to be more dangerous than other doctors believe, he will be justified in revealing this to the appropriate authorities[9]. Disclosure of unreliability in equipment used to provide evidence for use at criminal trials has also been held to be justified, and it has been said that what is disclosed in the public interest need not be wrongdoing to be covered by the defence[10]. Conduct and misrepresentations which mislead the public[11] may also be disclosed, as may gross immorality, but in the absence of a generally accepted moral code it is difficult to define the scope of the latter[12].

Whether the intended disclosure is in the public interest must be judged at the time when disclosure is sought[13]. It is difficult to envisage circumstances when a defence of iniquity or public interest would justify media disclosure of the work of the security services, since there are established internal channels for representations[14]. It is not permissible to commit a criminal offence in order to obtain confidential material which the acquirer proposes to reveal in the public interest[15].

Negligence and incompetence may not be enough to bring the defence into operation[16]. Four factors are to be considered in applying the defence: (1) the difference between that in which the public is interested and that which it is in the public interest to disclose; (2) the special interest of the media in publicity; (3) the fact that limited publicity may be appropriate in a given case; and (4) the fact that what is to be regarded as iniquity changes over the years[17]. A statutory duty of confidence will not be broken by a reasonable disclosure of a type envisaged by the statute, such as to the Health and Safety Executive in regard to the packaging of chemicals[18].

1 *Gartside v Outram* (1856) 26 LJCh 113 at 114. See also *Annesley v Earl of Anglesea* (1743) 17 State Tr 1139 at 1223–1246 cited in *Initial Services Ltd v Putterill* [1968] 1 QB 396 at 405, [1967] 3 All ER 145 at 148, CA.

2 See *Fraser v Evans* [1969] 1 QB 349 at 362, [1969] 1 All ER 8 at 11, CA; *Lion Laboratories Ltd v Evans* [1985] QB 526 at 537–538, 548, [1984] 2 All ER 417 at 423, 431, CA, and at 538, 550 and 423–424, 432–433, suggesting that the defence does not require any wrongdoing. In *Francome v Mirror Group Newspapers Ltd* [1984] 2 All ER 408 at 411, [1984] 1 WLR 892 at 895–896, CA, Donaldson MR suggested the justifying conduct could be termed 'anti-social'.

3 *Initial Services Ltd v Putterill* [1968] 1 QB 396 at 405, [1967] 3 All ER 145 at 148, CA, per Lord Denning MR; approved in *British Steel Corpn v Granada Television Ltd* [1981] AC 1096 at 1169, 1201, [1981] 1 All ER 417 at 455, 480, HL; *Lion Laboratories Ltd v Evans* [1985] QB 526 at 537–538, [1984] 2 All ER 417 at 423, CA.

4 *Tournier v National Provincial and Union Bank of England* [1924] 1 KB 461 at 481, 486, CA (banker); *Kitson v Playfair* (1896) Times, 28 March (doctor); *Weld-Blundell v Stephens* [1919] 1 KB 520 at 527, 533, CA; *Malone v Metropolitan Police Comr* [1979] Ch 344 at 377, [1979] 2 All ER 620 at 646; *Khashoggi v Smith* (1980) 124 Sol Jo 149, CA.

5 See *Weld-Blundell v Stephens* [1919] 1 KB 520 at 527, CA; on appeal [1920] AC 956, HL.

6 *Initial Services Ltd v Putterill* [1968] 1 QB 396 at 405, [1967] 3 All ER 145 at 148, CA; *Beloff v Pressdram Ltd* [1973] 1 All ER 241 at 260–261; *Malone v Metropolitan Police Comr* [1979] Ch 344 at 361–362, [1979] 2 All ER 620 at 634–635.

7 *Hubbard v Vosper* [1972] 2 QB 84, [1972] 1 All ER 1023, CA; *Church of Scientology of California v Kaufman* [1973] RPC 627; affd (1972) 117 So Jo 72, CA (interlocutory proceedings); *Church of Scientology of California v Kaufman* [1973] RPC 635 (trial of action).
8 *Schering Chemicals Ltd v Falkman Ltd* [1982] QB 1 at 27, [1981] 2 All ER 321 at 337–338, CA.
9 *W v Egdell* [1990] Ch 359, [1990] 1 All ER 835, CA. See also *Tarasoff v Regents of the University of California* (1976) 17 Cal (3d) 425.
10 *Lion Laboratories Ltd v Evans* [1985] QB 526 at 538, 550, [1984] 2 All ER 417 at 423, 432–433, CA.
11 *Woodward v Hutchins* [1977] 2 All ER 751, [1977] 1 WLR 760, CA.
12 *Stephens v Avery* [1988] Ch 449 at 453–454, [1988] 2 All ER 477 at 480–481 (specific agreement to conceal relationship); but see per Garland J in *M and N v MacKenzie and News Group Newspapers* (18 January 1988, unreported), holding that a homosexual relationship does not per se create an obligation of confidence; cited, without expressing an opinion on the case, in *Stephens v Avery* supra at 456 and at 482–483.
13 *Dunford & Elliott Ltd v Johnson & Firth Brown Ltd* [1977] 1 Lloyd's Rep 505 at 509, CA.
14 *A-G v Observer Ltd, A-G v Times Newspapers Ltd* [1990] 1 AC 109 at 269, sub nom *A-G v Guardian Newspapers Ltd (No 2)* [1988] 3 All ER 545 at 650, HL, per Lord Griffiths, and at 282–283 and 659–660 per Lord Goff of Chieveley.
15 *Francome v Mirror Group Newspapers Ltd* [1984] 2 All ER 408 at 412, 415, [1984] 1 WLR 892 at 897, 901, CA (illegal private phone tapping).
16 *Distillers Co (Biochemicals) Ltd v Times Newspapers Ltd, Distillers Co (Biochemicals) Ltd v Phillips* [1975] QB 613 at 622, [1975] 1 All ER 41 at 49–50.
17 *Lion Laboratories Ltd v Evans* [1985] QB 526 at 537, [1984] 2 All ER 417 at 423, CA.
18 *Hoechst UK Ltd v Chemiculture Ltd* [1993] FSR 270.

486. Evidential basis for the defence. Full knowledge of the conduct believed to justify disclosure of confidential information is not required in order for the defence of just cause or excuse or public interest[1] to operate[2]. In a rare situation where the defence might apply to media publicity for the work of the security services it has been said that a mere allegation is not sufficient but would have to be followed by investigations reasonably open to the recipient, which then (in the particular circumstances) rendered it a credible allegation from an apparently reliable source[3]. Otherwise, well-founded suspicion, not a mere roving suggestion or even a general suggestion[4], will be required[5].

1 See para 485 ante.
2 See notes 3–5 infra.
3 *A-G v Observer Ltd, A-G v Times Newspapers Ltd* [1990] 1 AC 109 at 283, sub nom *A-G v Guardian Newspapers Ltd (No 2)* [1988] 3 All ER 545 at 660, HL, per Lord Goff of Chieveley.
4 *Gartside v Outram* (1856) 26 LJCh 113 at 114.
5 *Malone v Metropolitan Police Comr* [1979] Ch 344 at 377, [1979] 2 All ER 620 at 646.

487. Extent of relaxation of the defence. Even if the defence of just cause or excuse or public interest[1] operates to relax or negate an obligation of confidence, it may not justify full publicity; it will depend on the circumstances[2]. For the security services, knowledge or suspicion of wrongdoing would, except in the rarest cases, justify complaints only within internal channels[3]. In other cases, complaints to those with authority to prevent or correct the wrongdoing or other unsatisfactory situation may be justified[4], but where the public is being prejudiced or misled, full publicity in the media may be justified[5].

1 See para 485 ante.
2 See notes 3–5 infra.
3 *A-G v Observer Ltd, A-G v Times Newspapers Ltd* [1990] 1 AC 109 at 282–283, sub nom *A-G v Guardian Newspapers Ltd (No 2)* [1988] 3 All ER 545 at 659–660, HL, per Lord Goff of Chieveley.
4 *Francome v Mirror Group Newspapers Ltd* [1984] 2 All ER 408 at 414, 416, [1984] 1 WLR 892 at 899, 902, CA (suspected racing irregularities might be revealed to police or Jockey Club). Crime should be

revealed to the police or the Director of Public Prosecutions and breach of statutory duty should be revealed to the regulatory authority: *Initial Services Ltd v Putterill* [1968] 1 QB 396 at 405–406, [1967] 3 All ER 145 at 148, CA. However, some wrongdoing may justify going to the press, such as a misleading business practice or misleading conduct: *Woodward v Hutchins* [1977] 2 All ER 751, [1977] 1 WLR 760, CA. See also *Church of Scientology v Kaufman* [1973] RPC 627; affd (1972) 117 Sol Jo 72, CA (interlocutory proceedings); *Church of Scientology of California v Kaufman* [1973] RPC 635 (trial of action) (medical hazard justified a book); *Lion Laboratories Ltd v Evans* [1985] QB 526, [1984] 2 All ER 417, CA (defective breathalyser justified going to the press). An intended tort may be revealed to the prospective victim: see *Gartside v Outram* (1856) 26 LJCh 113.
5 *Woodward v Hutchins* [1977] 2 All ER 751, [1977] 1 WLR 760, CA; *Lion Laboratories Ltd v Evans* [1985] QB 526, [1984] 2 All ER 417, CA (media); *Church of Scientology v Kaufman* [1973] RPC 627; affd (1972) 117 Sol Jo 72, CA (interlocutory proceedings); *Church of Scientology of California v Kaufman* [1973] RPC 635 (trial of action).

488. Unclean hands. The maxim that 'he who comes to equity must come with clean hands' applies whenever a plaintiff seeks an equitable remedy for breach of confidence[1]. For conduct to amount to having unclean hands it must be improper but not necessarily illegal and it must be more than an error of judgment[2]. Whilst the defence is not dissimilar to the defence of just cause[3] and the two defences may coincide in an individual case[4], the just cause defence is primarily directed to the public interest and the unclean hands defence is directed to personal conduct; the attempted preservation of confidence by deplorable means by a plaintiff has been held to fall within this defence, the improper conduct being required to relate to the cause of action[5]. The defence is discretionary and when each party has been guilty of impropriety the court may, in the exercise of its discretion and on the balance of perfidy, grant remedies to a plaintiff who has been less guilty than the defendant[6]. Whilst impropriety may exclude present and future confidence it will not retroactively destroy past confidence[7].

1 As to the 'clean hands' maxim see EQUITY vol 16 (Reissue) para 751.
2 *Stevenson Jordan & Harrison Ltd v Macdonald & Evans* (1951) 68 RPC 190 at 196; revsd on other grounds [1952] 1 TLR 101, 69 RPC 10, CA.
3 See para 485 ante.
4 *Church of Scientology of California v Kaufman* [1973] RPC 635 at 654–656.
5 *Hubbard v Vosper* [1972] 2 QB 84 at 101, [1972] 1 All ER 1023 at 1033, CA; cited in *Church of Scientology of California v Kaufman* [1973] RPC 635 at 656.
6 *Duchess of Argyll v Duke of Argyll* [1967] Ch 302, [1965] 1 All ER 611.
7 *Duchess of Argyll v Duke of Argyll* [1967] Ch 302, [1965] 1 All ER 611.

489. Delay and laches. The maxim that 'equity aids the vigilant' applies to equitable remedies for breach of confidence[1]. The operation of the defence may depend on the lapse of time being so long that it has led the defendant to believe that the plaintiff has acquiesced in the breach and in consequence has changed his position, or so long that it has led to the loss of evidence[2]. However, delay will not be fatal to a plaintiff if, having objected to disclosure, he reserves his position until he has an opportunity to evaluate a disclosure he has been told will be made in the future[3]. Ignorance and incapacity will also explain delay[4].

1 As to delay see INJUNCTIONS vol 24 (Reissue) paras 844, 862, 919. As to acquiescence and laches see EQUITY vol 16 (Reissue) para 924 et seq.
2 *International Scientific Communications Inc v Pattison* [1979] FSR 429 (equitable remedy of account lost by delay but plaintiff recovered damages); *Prout v British Gas plc* [1992] FSR 478, Patents County Court (concession that delay defeated application for an injunction); *Faccenda Chicken Ltd v Fowler, Fowler v Faccenda Chicken Ltd* [1987] Ch 117 at 130–131, [1986] 1 All ER 617 at 621, CA (claim for injunction not pursued owing to lapse of time).

3 *Schering Chemicals Ltd v Falkman Ltd* [1982] QB 1 at 38, [1981] 2 All ER 321 at 346, CA (waiting to see film which would contain disclosures).

4 See *Rees v De Bernardy* [1896] 2 Ch 437; *Allcard v Skinner* (1887) 36 ChD 145.

(13) REMEDIES

490. Anton Piller orders. Anton Piller orders will be granted, subject to the usual conditions[1], at any stage in the proceedings, to enable the inspection of premises where there is strong evidence that infringing documents or articles may be found[2]. The plaintiff may be allowed to inspect and photograph articles and documents relating to the right allegedly infringed and to remove articles and documents which belong to him[3].

The order may be accompanied by an injunction restraining the defendant from altering or removing documents or articles covered by the order. The injunction must not be so wide in its terms as to restrain mere competition by former employees even if it would otherwise be difficult to quantify damages[4]. The plaintiff must normally give an undertaking in damages and if, because of the grant of an injunction too wide in its terms, the defendant is prevented from fulfilling existing orders, the plaintiff may be liable on the undertaking[5].

Safeguards to avoid oppression in the execution of an order have been formulated by the court[6]. The plaintiff must make full disclosure of material facts[7] but failure to advert to a legal conclusion which might have led to the exclusion of some of the evidence will not have an invalidating effect[8].

1 As to Anton Piller orders generally see INJUNCTIONS vol 24 (Reissue) para 872 et seq.

2 *Anton Piller KG v Manufacturing Processes Ltd* [1976] Ch 55, [1976] 1 All ER 779, CA; *EMI Ltd v Pandit* [1975] 1 All ER 418, [1975] 1 WLR 302; *Columbia Picture Industries Inc v Robinson* [1987] Ch 38 at 69–76, [1986] 3 All ER 338 at 365–372; *Lock International plc v Beswick* [1989] 3 All ER 373, [1989] 1 WLR 1268.

3 *EMI Ltd v Pandit* [1975] 1 All ER 418, [1975] 1 WLR 302; *Roberts v Northwest Fixings* [1993] FSR 281, CA (list of customers removed). Where a plaintiff recovers property allegedly stolen from him by the defendant, the rule that documents obtained on the execution of an Anton Piller order should not be used for purposes other than the litigation in which the order was made does not apply, and the plaintiff may disclose to the police the information that such property has been recovered from the defendant, but not the supervising solicitor's report: *Process Development Ltd v Hogg* [1996] FSR 45, CA.

4 *Roberts v Northwest Fixings* [1993] FSR 281, CA.

5 *Universal Thermosensors Ltd v Hibben* [1992] 3 All ER 257, [1992] 1 WLR, 840.

6 *Universal Thermosensors Ltd v Hibben* [1992] 3 All ER 257 at 275–276, [1992] 1 WLR 840 at 860–861.

7 *Lock International plc v Beswick* [1989] 3 All ER 373, [1989] 1 WLR 1268.

8 *Hoechst UK Ltd v Chemiculture Ltd* [1993] FSR 270.

491. Interlocutory injunctions. In view of the need for swift action to check disclosure, interlocutory injunctions[1] are of special importance in cases of disclosure of confidential information. The general principles that there should be a serious question to be tried, and that the balance of convenience should be satisfied, apply[2]. A wide variety of factors have been taken into account in the exercise of the court's discretion in granting such relief, including whether the plaintiff would be adequately compensated in damages if the injunction were refused[3], or conversely whether the defendant would be adequately compensated on the undertaking in damages required of the plaintiff if the injunction were inappropriately granted[4]. The court will consider not only the nature of the case but also the financial ability of the parties to make compensation[5].

The balance of harm may also be relevant. If the harm done to a defendant by closing his business would outweigh any harm done to the plaintiff by allowing continuance this will tell against the grant of an interlocutory injunction[6]. The court may be readier to protect an existing product than a mere idea in which the creator had made no investment[7]. The market share or market position of the plaintiff may be such that to refuse any injunction would do him grave harm[8]. The preservation of the status quo may tell in favour of granting an injunction, but not if it would destroy the defendant's case[9].

Where the public interest in the defence of the realm prevailed over the right of the public to be informed by the press, an injunction was extended to cover reports of court proceedings abroad[10]. Where the public interest in the unreliability of a breathalyser which might lead to the conviction of the innocent prevailed over the public interest in preserving confidentiality, the injunction was discharged[11].

The court will be readier to grant an injunction where the plaintiff cannot be adequately compensated in damages[12]. In cases involving defamation[13] an injunction will not normally be granted when the defendant intends to justify or plead fair comment[14]. The material to be protected must not be trivial tittle-tattle or otherwise worthless[15], but if the importance of the material warrants it, a worldwide interlocutory injunction may be granted[16]. If material is to be published in any event in the near future this will be a factor against granting the injunction, as commercial interest in delaying publication will not be enough to confer confidentiality[17].

No injunction will be granted when there is inadequate particularity as to what material is confidential, even if the balance of convenience would otherwise favour an injunction[18]. An injunction may be varied or granted on appeal to define more clearly the trade secrets covered by it and may prevent a defendant from fulfilling orders, although the court should be cautious in interfering with the rights of innocent third parties[19]. The injunction must be clear and definite in its terms so that the party to whom it is directed may know how it is to be observed[20]. No injunction will be granted to enforce an employee's covenant which is so widely drawn as to be unreasonable in covering matters in which the employee was not engaged or purporting to restrict his personal skill and knowledge[21].

1 As to interlocutory injunctions see INJUNCTIONS vol 24 (Reissue) para 853 et seq.
2 *American Cyanamid Co v Ethicon Ltd* [1975] AC 396, [1975] 1 All ER 504, HL.
3 *American Cyanamid Co v Ethicon Ltd* [1975] AC 396 at 408, [1975] 1 All ER 504 at 510, HL; *Brian D Collins (Engineers) Ltd v Charles Roberts & Co Ltd* [1965] RPC 429 at 433; *United Sterling Corpn Ltd v Felton* [1974] RPC 162 at 167–168; *Coco v A N Clark (Engineers) Ltd* [1969] RPC 41 (royalty on motorcycle engines to be paid into account to await outcome of trial); *Schering Chemicals Ltd v Falkman Ltd* [1982] QB 1, [1981] 2 All ER 321, CA (bad publicity).
4 *Bostitch Inc v McGarry & Cole Ltd* [1964] RPC 173; *Lock International plc v Beswick* [1989] 3 All ER 373, [1989] 1 WLR 1268.
5 *American Cyanamid Co v Ethicon Ltd* [1975] AC 396 at 408, [1975] 1 All ER 504 at 510, HL.
6 *Bostitch Inc v McGarry & Cole Ltd* [1964] RPC 173.
7 *Coco v A N Clark (Engineers) Ltd* [1969] RPC 41 at 54.
8 *Brian D Collins (Engineers) Ltd v Charles Roberts & Co Ltd* [1965] RPC 429; and see *United Sterling Corpn Ltd v Felton* [1974] RPC 162.
9 *Dunford & Elliott Ltd v Johnson & Firth Brown Ltd* [1977] 1 Lloyd's Rep 505, CA (defendant unable to reinstate a take-over bid). Where there was no letter before action and there was delay after the issue of the writ before service, it was the time of service that fixed the status quo: *Graham v Delderfield* [1992] FSR 313, CA.
10 *A-G v Guardian Newspapers Ltd* [1987] 3 All ER 316, [1987] 1 WLR 1248, HL (further publicity involving the publishing of a security officer's memoirs would destroy all confidentiality in the material and deprive the Attorney General of any possibility of success at the trial).
11 *Lion Laboratories Ltd v Evans* [1985] QB 526, [1984] 2 All ER 417, CA.
12 *Francome v Mirror Group Newspapers Ltd* [1984] 2 All ER 408 at 415, [1984] 1 WLR 892 at 900, CA.
13 As to defamation see generally LIBEL AND SLANDER.

14 *Bonnard v Perryman* [1891] 2 Ch 269, CA; *Fraser v Evans* [1969] 1 QB 349, [1969] 1 All ER 8, CA; and see *Woodward v Hutchins* [1977] 2 All ER 751, [1977] 1 WLR 760, CA (case in substance involved defamation).

15 *Coco v A N Clark (Engineers) Ltd* [1969] RPC 41 at 48.

16 See *A-G v Barker* [1990] 3 All ER 257, CA (although the case was held to be one of breach of contract rather than confidentiality).

17 *Times Newspapers Ltd v MGN Ltd* [1993] EMLR 443, CA.

18 *Mainmet Holdings plc v Austin* [1991] FSR 538.

19 *Lawrence David Ltd v Ashton* [1989] ICR 123, [1991] 1 All ER 385, CA; and see *PSM International v Whitehouse and Willenhall Automation* [1993] IRLR 279, CA.

20 See *Amway Corpn v Eurway International Ltd* [1974] RPC 82 at 86–87; *P A Thomas & Co v Mould* [1968] 2 QB 913, [1968] 1 All ER 963; *Lawrence David Ltd v Ashton* [1989] ICR 123, [1991] 1 All ER 385, CA; *Times Newspapers Ltd v MGN Ltd* [1995] EMLR 443, CA.

21 *Commercial Plastics Ltd v Vincent* [1965] 1 QB 623, [1964] 3 All ER 546, CA; *Technograph Printed Circuits Ltd v Chalwyn Ltd* [1967] RPC 339; *Austin Knight (UK) v Hinds* [1994] FSR 52.

492. Final injunctions. Final injunctions[1] may be granted subject to the ordinary principles of equitable relief in respect of both threatened[2] and actual[3] breaches of confidence arising from any of the sources of jurisdiction on which an obligation of confidence may be founded[4].

An injunction may be more readily granted in respect of personal information than in the case of trade secrets, the harm in the latter case being more readily assessed in monetary terms for an award of damages[5]. The terms of an injunction in respect of geographical area may also differ for these types of obligation[6]. The importance of the material will also be taken into account since the court will not protect trivial tittle-tattle[7].

If the information has been so widely published or so extensively used that restraint would be of no practical benefit this will tell against the grant of an injunction, but if some element of restriction and confidence remains this may be protected[8].

Another consideration is the extent to which possession of the confidential material would spare the defendant effort and expense in obtaining it by other means[9].

The court will also consider the extent to which use was made of the confidential material by the defendant, since the greater the use the more ready the court will be to grant the injunction[10]. If the defendant himself was responsible for disclosures which deprive the information of confidentiality, he may remain bound by the injunction even though all others are not bound[11]. The court will be reluctant to grant broad general injunctions against a class of persons and a class of acts, even in aid of national security, since injunctions are normally aimed at the prevention of some specific wrong, not at the prevention of wrongdoing in general[12]. It would not be appropriate to subject a person to an injunction on the ground that he is the sort of person who is likely to commit some kind of wrong or that he has an interest in doing so[13].

It is doubtful if, and to what extent, a plaintiff must prove detriment[14]. For personal confidences, it is enough if persons whom the plaintiff did not wish to know the information have obtained it, whether or not it is to his detriment[15], and for medical professional confidences it is sufficient that those requiring treatment may be deterred from seeking it[16]. If information is disclosed in inconclusive negotiations, the recipient may not be obliged to avoid the topic or carry out parallel research, but instead to use the information on payment[17]. Account may be taken of good or bad faith on the part of the defendant but these factors will not necessarily be conclusive[18]. The injunction may be drawn to achieve a balance of justice, for example by including a time limit[19], but it must be sufficiently certain in its terms to allow the defendant to know how it is to be observed[20].

1   As to injunctions generally see INJUNCTIONS.

2   *Duchess of Argyll v Duke of Argyll* [1967] Ch 302, [1965] 1 All ER 611; but cf *Lennon v News Group Newspapers Ltd and Twist* [1978] FSR 573, CA.

3   *Ackroyds (London) Ltd v Islington Plastics Ltd* [1962] RPC 97; cf *National Broach and Machine Co v Churchill Gear Machines Ltd* [1965] RPC 61; on appeal on the question of damages only [1965] 2 All ER 961, [1965] 1 WLR 1199, CA; affd [1966] 3 All ER 923n, [1967] 1 WLR 384, HL; *Peter Pan Manufacturing Corpn v Corsets Silhouette Ltd* [1963] 3 All ER 402, [1964]1 WLR 96; *Industrial Furnaces Ltd v Reaves* [1970] RPC 605.

4   *Prince Albert v Strange* (1849) 2 De G & Sm 652; on appeal (1849) 1 Mac & G 25; *Robb v Green* [1895] 2 QB 315, CA; *Nichrotherm Electrical Co Ltd v Percy* [1957] RPC 207, CA; *Ackroyds (London) Ltd v Islington Plastics Ltd* [1962] RPC 97; *Peter Pan Manufacturing Corpn v Corsets Silhouette Ltd* [1963] 3 All ER 402, [1964] 1 WLR 96; *Cranleigh Precision Engineering Ltd v Bryant* [1964] 3 All ER 289, [1965] 1 WLR 1293. See also para 403 ante.

5   *Coco v A N Clark (Engineers) Ltd* [1969] RPC 41 at 50. See also *Francome v Mirror Group Newspapers Ltd* [1984] 2 All ER 408 at 415, [1984] 1 WLR 892 at 900, CA.

6   See *A-G v Observer Ltd, A-G v Times Newspapers Ltd* [1990] 1 AC 109 at 260, sub nom *A-G v Guardian Newspapers Ltd (No 2)* [1988] 3 All ER 545 at 643, HL, per Lord Keith of Kinkel.

7   See *Coco v A N Clark (Engineers) Ltd* [1969] RPC 41 at 48. See also *McNicol v Sportsman's Book Stores* (1930) [1928–1935] MacG Cop Cas 116; cited in *A-G v Observer Ltd, A-G v Times Newspapers Ltd* [1990] 1 AC 109 at 149, sub nom *A-G v Guardian Newspapers Ltd (No 2)* [1988] 3 All ER 545 at 574 per Scott J; and see at 282–284, and 659–660, HL, per Lord Goff of Chieveley; *Church of Scientology of California v Kaufman* [1973] RPC 635 at 658.

8   *A-G v Observer Ltd, A-G v Times Newspapers Ltd* [1990] 1 AC 109, sub nom *A-G v Guardian Newspapers Ltd (No 2)* [1988] 3 All ER 545, HL; *O Mustad & Son v S Allcock & Co Ltd and Dosen* (1928) [1963] 3 All ER 416, [1964] 1 WLR 109n, HL; *Gilbert v Star Newspaper Co Ltd* (1894) 11 TLR 4.

9   As to the 'springboard' doctrine see para 422 ante.

10   *Reid & Sigrist Ltd v Moss and Mechanism Ltd* (1932) 49 RPC 461; *Peter Pan Manufacturing Corpn v Corsets Silhouette* [1963] 3 All ER 402. Conversely, if the contribution of the misused information is small it may be an award of damages only: *Bostitch Inc v McGarry & Cole Ltd* [1964] RPC 173; *Seager v Copydex Ltd* [1967] 2 All ER 415, [1967] 1 WLR 923, CA; *Seager v Copydex Ltd (No 2)* [1969] 2 All ER 718, [1969] 1 WLR 809; *Printers and Finishers Ltd v Holloway* [1964] 3 All ER 731, [1965] 1 WLR 1; *Cranleigh Precision Engineering Ltd v Bryant* [1964] 3 All ER 289, [1965] 1 WLR 1293.

11   *Speed Seal Products Ltd v Paddington* [1986] 1 All ER 91, [1985] 1 WLR 1327, CA; *A-G v Observer Ltd, A-G v Times Newspapers Ltd* [1990] 1 AC 109 at 260, sub nom *A-G v Guardian Newspapers Ltd (No 2)* [1988] 3 All ER 545, HL. This has been criticised as absurd, although it is recognised that damages and some restriction on use analogous to the 'springboard' doctrine may be appropriate: *A-G v Observer Ltd, A-G v Times Newspapers Ltd* supra per Lord Goff of Chieveley.

12   *A-G v Observer Ltd, A-G v Times Newspapers Ltd* [1990] 1 AC 109 at 264, sub nom *A-G v Guardian Newspapers Ltd (No 2)* [1988] 3 All ER 545 at 646, HL, per Lord Keith of Kinkel.

13   *A-G v Observer Ltd, A-G v Times Newspapers Ltd* [1990] 1 AC 109 at 264, sub nom *A-G v Guardian Newspapers Ltd (No 2)* [1988] 3 All ER 545 at 645–646, HL, per Lord Keith of Kinkel, with whom the majority agreed, though Lord Brightman was doubtful (see at 267 and 648). Once confidentiality had been lost, the collateral purposes of sustaining morale in the colleagues of the breaker of confidence and dissuading him from further publication were not enough to justify the grant of a final injunction: *A-G v Observer Ltd, A-G v Times Newspapers Ltd* supra at 275–276 and 545 at 654 per Lord Keith of Kinkel.

14   *Coco v A N Clark (Engineers) Ltd* [1969] RPC 41 at 48; *A-G v Observer Ltd, A-G v Times Newspapers Ltd* [1990] 1 AC 109 at 281–282, sub nom *A-G v Guardian Newspapers Ltd (No 2)* [1988] 3 All ER 545 at 659, HL, per Lord Goff of Chieveley, pointing out that in the case of governmental secrets the Crown has to establish not only breach of confidence but also that the breach is to its detriment in that there is a public interest in maintaining confidence. Detriment may be necessary in private law confidences: see *Jarman & Platt Ltd v I Barget Ltd* [1977] FSR 260, CA; and *Dunford & Elliott Ltd v Johnson & Firth Brown Ltd* [1977] 1 Lloyd's Rep 505 at 509, CA. As to detriment see para 482 ante.

15   *A-G v Observer Ltd, A-G v Times Newspapers Ltd* [1990] 1 AC 109 at 255–256, sub nom *A-G v Guardian Newspapers Ltd (No 2)* [1988] 3 All ER 545 at 639–640, HL, per Lord Keith of Kinkel, but contra at 270 and 650 per Lord Griffiths.

16   *X v Y* [1988] 2 All ER 648.

17   *Coco v A N Clark (Engineers) Ltd* [1969] RPC 41 at 49 (damages in lieu of an injunction).

18   *Seager v Copydex Ltd* [1967] 2 All ER 415, [1967] 1 WLR 923, CA (subconscious plagiarism resulting in damages but no injunction); but see *National Broach and Machine Co v Churchill Gear Machines Ltd* [1965] RPC 61 (on appeal on the question of damages only [1965] 2 All ER 961, [1965] 1 WLR 1199, CA; affd [1966] 3 All ER 923n, [1967] 1 WLR 384, HL) (injunction granted against continued use of plans even

though this was a mistake); *Printers and Finishers Ltd v Holloway* [1964] 3 All ER 731, [1965] 1 WLR 1; *Cranleigh Precision Engineering Ltd v Bryant* [1964] 3 All ER 289, [1965] 1 WLR 1293 (injunction for conscious wrongful use unless it is trifling).

19 See *Roger Bullivant Ltd v Ellis* [1987] ICR 464, [1987] FSR 172, CA (injunction not to extend beyond 'springboard' period).

20 *P A Thomas & Co v Mould* [1968] 2 QB 913, [1968] 1 All ER 963; *Amway Corpn v Eurway International Ltd* [1974] RPC 82 at 87; *Potters-Ballotini Ltd v Weston-Baker* [1977] RPC 202 at 206, CA; *Thomas Marshall (Exports) Ltd v Guinle* [1979] Ch 227, [1978] 3 All ER 193; *G D Searle & Co Ltd v Celltech Ltd* [1982] FSR 92, CA; *Mainmet Holdings plc v Austin* [1991] FSR 538; *Times Newspapers Ltd v MGN Ltd* [1993] EMLR 443, CA. An injunction may be varied on appeal to define more clearly trade secrets covered by it: *PSM International v Whitehouse and Willenhall* [1993] IRLR 279, CA. A number of the authorities involve interlocutory injunctions but the same principle applies: *Lock International plc v Beswick* [1989] 3 All ER 373, [1989] 1 WLR 1268; *Lawrence David Ltd v Ashton* [1991] 1 All ER 385, [1989] ICR 123, CA; *Maudsley v Palumbo* [1995] TLR 690.

493. Delivery up and destruction.

Orders for delivery up or destruction of documents, articles or machinery obtained or made in breach of confidence will be made to give full effect to prohibitory injunctions[1]. An order is discretionary and is made under the inherent jurisdiction of the court; and the processes directed must be carried out on oath[2]. Delivery up will be ordered when the plaintiff is the owner of the infringing articles or documents[3]; and destruction will be ordered when the documents or articles, such as copies, are the property of the defendant[4]. Where the defendants fully appreciate their obligations, the protected information makes an important contribution to what they are producing and an award of damages will not suffice, the court may order the destruction of machinery used to produce infringing articles or such articles[5]. In a less serious case damages may be awarded[6].

1 As to injunctions see paras 491–492 ante.

2 *Prince Albert v Strange* (1849) 2 De G & Sm 652; on appeal (1849) 1 Mac & G 25; cf *Industrial Furnaces Ltd v Reaves* [1970] RPC 605 at 627–628 per Graham J (order for delivery up of documents, rather than for their destruction on oath, as the court took the view that the defendant was not to be relied on); see EQUITY vol 16 (Reissue) paras 726–727.

3 *Evitt v Price* (1827) 1 Sim 483; *Alperton Rubber Co v Manning* (1917) 86 LJCh 377 (books removed by employees). Delivery up may be ordered even if the defendant has added confidential material of his own: *Industrial Furnaces Ltd v Reaves* [1970] RPC 605 at 628; and see note 1 supra. For a case where both delivery up and destruction were ordered see *Prince Albert v Strange* (1849) 2 De G & Sm 652; on appeal (1849) 1 Mac & G 25.

4 See *Peter Pan Corpn v Corsets Silhouette Ltd* [1963] 3 All ER 402, [1964] 1 WLR 96.

5 *Reid & Sigrist Ltd v Moss and Mechanism Ltd* (1932) 49 RPC 461.

6 *Saltman Engineering Co Ltd v Campbell Engineering Co Ltd* (1948) [1963] 3 All ER 413n at 415, 65 RPC 203 at 219, CA. See also the Supreme Court Act 1981 s 50.

494. Damages.

Damages may be awarded on ordinary common law principles for breaches of confidence arising from obligations in contract, tort and property[1] and under the jurisdiction originally conferred by Lord Cairns' Act in addition to, or in substitution for, an injunction[2]. Damages have been awarded for the breach of an equitable obligation of confidence in order to avoid wasteful destruction of otherwise useful property[3]. On the wording of the current legislation it is enough to ground an award in substitution if the court has power to entertain an application for an injunction[4]. It would not seem necessary that the court be satisfied that all the conditions for the grant of an injunction should be fulfilled[5].

When an injunction is granted to enforce a purely equitable obligation of confidence, damages may be awarded in addition to the injunction[6]. As damages may be awarded in substitution for a *quia timet* injunction, such damages may be awarded in respect of prospective breaches of confidence[7]. Where there is an established breach of confidence, damages can be awarded in lieu for both past and future losses[8]. It is doubtful if there is an inherent jurisdiction to award damages in equity[9]. Many authorities are not explicit as to the basis of an award and almost all of those dealing with breach of confidence can be explained under the statutory jurisdiction to award damages in addition to, or substitution for, an injunction or a claim for specific performance created by Lord Cairns' Act[10]. However, the court has refused to strike out a claim for damages even though there appeared to be no common law ground such as contract and no injunction was claimed[11]. It is also doubtful whether equitable compensation can be claimed for breach of confidence[12].

On assessment of damages in a case involving licensing of confidential information it has been said that if there is 'nothing very special' about the information, it being such as could be obtained from a competent consultant, damages should be the amount of his fee; but if it is 'something special' as, for instance, where it involves an inventive step, then the amount of damages should be the price which would be paid by a willing buyer to a willing seller; and if it is 'very special' then damages should be the capitalised value of a royalty[13]. In arriving at the willing seller's price the special circumstances of the plaintiff are to be taken into account[14]. On analogy with conversion[15] it was further said that when damages were satisfied the information would become the property of the defendant to exploit as he wished and he could patent it[16], in which case it remains doubtful whether the successful plaintiff could still utilise the information; if it were patented by the defendant it would seem that he could not. This approach has been criticised for laying undue stress on the benefit to the defendant and the reversal of unjust enrichment rather than on the compensation for loss suffered by the plaintiff. Where, however, the plaintiff is a manufacturer who would not have licensed the information, it has been held, following the rule for economic torts[17], that the proper measure of damages is the plaintiff's loss of profits on sales[18]. The authorities cover commercial and industrial confidences and there is little guidance on damages for breach of personal confidence[19]. Where an injunction and damages are awarded and an inquiry as to damages is ordered, this need not be limited to breaches proved or admitted at the trial but may extend to the same field as the injunction[20]. Damages will normally be assessed from the day of the breach unless this would work injustice, in which case the date of the hearing may be taken[21].

1 See DAMAGES vol 12 para 1101 et seq.
2 Chancery Amendment Act 1853 s 2 (Lord Cairns' Act) (repealed). See now the Supreme Court Act 1981 s 50.
3 *Saltman Engineering Co Ltd v Campbell Engineering Co Ltd* (1948) [1963] 3 All ER 413n at 415, 65 RPC 203 at 219, CA.
4 See the Supreme Court Act 1981 s 50.
5 As to the conditions for the grant of an injunction see generally INJUNCTIONS.
6 *London and Provincial Sporting News Agency Ltd v Levy* (1928) [1923–1928] MacG Cop Cas 340; *Nichrotherm Electrical Co Ltd v Percy* [1956] RPC 272; on appeal [1957] RPC 207, CA (decided in contract), where plaintiffs were required to elect, for the purposes of an inquiry as to damages, to pursue damages either for breach of copyright or for breach of confidence, but not both; *Ackroyds (London) Ltd v Islington Plastics Ltd* [1962] RPC 97; *Cranleigh Precision Engineering Ltd v Bryant* [1964] 3 All ER 289, [1965] 1 WLR 1293; *Peter Pan Manufacturing Corpn Ltd v Corsets Silhouette Ltd* [1963] 3 All ER 402, [1964] 1 WLR 96 (order for account of profits rather than damages).
7 See INJUNCTIONS vol 24 (Reissue) para 834 et seq. See also *Johnson v Agnew* [1980] AC 367 at 400, [1979] 1 All ER 883 at 895, HL; *Surrey County Council v Bredero Homes Ltd* [1992] 3 All ER 302 at 309, 310.
8 *Saltman Engineering Co Ltd v Campbell Engineering Co Ltd* (1948) [1963] 3 All ER 413n at 415, 65 RPC 203 at 219, CA.
9 See *Todd v Gee* (1810) 17 Ves 273; *Grant v Dawkins* [1973] 3 All ER 897, [1973] 1 WLR 1406.

10 See generally SPECIFIC PERFORMANCE.

11 *Stephens v Avery* [1988] Ch 449, [1988] 2 All ER 477 (but amendment of pleadings might cover this).

12 See para 406 note 15 ante.

13 *Seager v Copydex Ltd (No 2)* [1969] 2 All ER 718, [1969] 1 WLR 809, CA.

14 *Seager v Copydex Ltd (No 2)* [1969] 2 All ER 718 at 720, [1969] 1 WLR 809 at 813, CA, per Lord Denning MR. No clear indication was given of the time over which the royalty was to be capitalised. As Lord Denning MR later referred to the possibility of the defendant patenting the information, the court may have had the patent period in mind.

15 As to conversion see para 405 ante; and TORT vol 45 para 1422 et seq.

16 *Seager v Copydex Ltd (No 2)* [1969] 2 All ER 718 at 720–721, [1969] 1 WLR 809 at 813, CA, per Lord Denning MR. As to patents generally see PATENTS AND REGISTERED DESIGNS.

17 See *General Tire and Rubber Co v Firestone Tyre and Rubber Co Ltd* [1975] 2 All ER 173 at 177, [1975] 1 WLR 819 at 824, HL, per Lord Wilberforce.

18 *Dowson & Mason Ltd v Potter* [1986] 2 All ER 418 [1986] 1 WLR 1419, CA; distinguishing *Seager v Copydex Ltd (No 2)* [1969] 2 All ER 718, [1969] 1 WLR 809, CA.

19 See *Beloff v Pressdram Ltd* [1973] 1 All ER 241 (which, however, was pleaded in copyright).

20 *National Broach and Machine Co v Churchill Gear Machines Ltd* [1965] 2 All ER 961, [1965] 1 WLR 1199, CA; affd without considering this point [1966] 3 All ER 923n, [1967] 1 WLR 384, HL.

21 See *Johnson v Agnew* [1980] AC 367, [1979] 1 All ER 883, HL (a case concerning damages for breach of a contract to sell land).

495. Account of profits. Account of profits is a discretionary equitable remedy which assumes that the defendant has profited from the misuse of confidential information and that he should be deprived of those profits for the benefit of the plaintiff[1]. Whilst damages or an order for account of profits can be awarded with either an injunction or an order for delivery, damages and account of profits cannot both be awarded in the same action[2]. Account of profits can be used as a remedy not only for breach of an equitable obligation but also for breach of contract[3] or bailment[4].

The ascertainment of the amount of accountable profits may be prolonged and, in practice, damages are normally preferred[5]. Damages may also be appropriate where the information made only a restricted contribution to what the defendant did, whereas when he acted with full knowledge and the information made a major contribution, the plaintiff has been allowed to make an election between an account of profits and damages[6]. When the information is essential to the defendant he will be required to account for the total profits accrued[7]. If, however, the defendant could have obtained the information by independent research and the breach merely saved work and expense, then it may be that an apportionment should be made by comparing what the defendant would have spent acting independently and what he in fact spent because of the breach; the accounting would then be confined to the difference[8].

1 See EQUITY vol 16 (Reissue) para 691 et seq.

2 *Peter Pan Manufacturing Corpn v Corsets Silhouette Ltd* [1963] 3 All ER 402, [1964] 1 WLR 96 (injunction, destruction and account); *Industrial Furnaces Ltd v Reaves* [1970] RPC 605 (injunction, delivery up and damages).

3 Cases on agency support this: see *Beaumont v Boultbee* (1802) 7 Ves 599; *Mackenzie v Johnston and Meaburn* (1819) 4 Madd 373; and *Parker v McKenna* (1874) 10 Ch App 96 (directors acting as agents of bank).

4 As to bailment see paras 408, 467 ante; and BAILMENT.

5 *Siddell v Vickers* (1892) 9 RPC 152 at 162; *A-G v Observer Ltd, A-G v Times Newspapers Ltd* [1990] 1 AC 109 at 286, sub nom *A-G v Guardian Newspapers Ltd (No 2)* [1988] 3 All ER 545 at 662, HL, per Lord Goff of Chieveley (account ordered against newspaper publishing in breach of confidence). Where a defendant has acted innocently the court may either award damages (see *Seager v Copydex Ltd (No 2)* [1969] 2 All ER 718, [1969] 1 WLR 809, CA (subconscious plagiarism not making very substantial contribution, not a case for injunction or account but damages)), or, presumably, limit accounting to the period after the defendant had notice that he was infringing confidence.

6 *Peter Pan Manufacturing Corpn v Corsets Silhouette Ltd* [1963] 3 All ER 402, [1964] 1 WLR 96 (election allowed); *A-G v Observer Ltd, A-G v Times Newspapers Ltd* [1990] 1 AC 109, sub nom *A-G v Guardian*

Newspapers Ltd (No 2) [1988] 3 All ER 545, HL (account ordered against newspaper publishing with full knowledge).
7 *Peter Pan Manufacturing Corpn v Corsets Silhouette Ltd* [1963] 3 All ER 402, [1964] 1 WLR 96.
8 *Siddell v Vickers* (1892) 9 RPC 152 (patent); distinguished in *Peter Pan Manufacturing Corpn v Corsets Silhouette Ltd* [1963] 3 All ER 402, [1964] 1 WLR 96.

496. Recovery of bribe. If an agent[1], employee[2] or other fiduciary[3] abuses a position of confidence by accepting a bribe[4], the employer or principal may summarily dismiss that person[5], refuse payment of remuneration and indemnity[6] and recover the amount of the bribe if it has been paid to the agent or employee, whether or not any loss has been suffered[7]. If the bribe has not been paid, the employee or agent cannot recover it from the promisor[8], but if it has been paid the employer or principal can recover it[9]. If the employee or agent has been instrumental in entering into some associated transaction with the promisor on behalf of the employer or principal, that transaction can be avoided by the employer or principal[10]. The employer or principal may sue the agent and third party as jointly and severally liable for the bribe and for any additional loss that he may have suffered, but he must elect between recovery of the bribe and recovery of damages[11]. Older authority indicates that the third party would be fully liable without any deduction for recovery from the agent[12] but this has now been disapproved[13]. The employee or agent holds the amount of the bribe (and any property representing the bribe or in which the bribe has been invested) in trust for the employer or principal[14]. The principal's entitlement to recover the property which represents an original bribe is not limited to the amount of the bribe but extends to the whole of that property[15]. Interest is payable from the date when the bribe was received[16].

1 See *Swale v Ipswich Tannery Ltd* (1906) 11 Com Cas 88; and see *Boston Deep Sea Fishing and Ice Co v Ansell* (1888) 39 ChD 339, CA; *Temperley v Blackrod Manufacturing Co Ltd* (1907) 71 JP Jo 341. As to agents see para 459 ante; and AGENCY vol 1(2) (Reissue) para 108.
2 See *Boston Deep Sea Fishing and Ice Co v Ansell* (1888) 39 ChD 339, CA.
3 A wide meaning has been given to 'fiduciary' in this context: see *Reading v A-G* [1951] AC 507 at 516, [1951] 1 All ER 617 at 620, HL. For the meaning of 'bribe' see *Industries and General Mortgage Co Ltd v Lewis* [1949] 2 All ER 573; *Taylor v Walker* [1958] 1 Lloyd's Rep 490. As to fiduciaries' obligations of confidence see para 457 ante. As to fiduciary relationships generally see EQUITY vol 16 (Reissue) para 902 et seq.
4 As to bribery see CRIMINAL LAW vol 11(1) (Reissue) para 281 et seq; and AGENCY vol 1(2) Reissue) para 108.
5 A servant or agent who accepts a bribe need not have been influenced or departed from duty; acceptance suffices: *Harrington v Victoria Graving Dock Co* (1878) 3 QBD 549; and see *Shipway v Broadwood* [1899] 1 QB 369; *Re a Debtor* [1927] 2 Ch 367. As to summary dismissal see EMPLOYMENT vol 16 (Reissue) para 298 et seq.
6 *Andrews v Ramsay & Co* [1903] 2 KB 635; *Nicholson v J Mansfield & Co* (1901) 17 TLR 259. Other untainted transactions are unaffected: *Boston Deep Sea Fishing and Ice Co v Ansell* (1888) 39 ChD 339, CA.
7 *Reading v A-G* [1951] AC 507, [1951] 1 All ER 617, HL.
8 See *Harrington v Victoria Graving Dock Co* (1878) 3 QBD 549.
9 See *Industries and General Mortgage Co Ltd v Lewis* [1949] 2 All ER 573.
10 *Panama and South Pacific Telegraph Co v India Rubber, Gutta Percha and Telegraph Works Co* (1875) 10 Ch App 515; *Taylor v Walker* [1958] 1 Lloyd's Rep 490.
11 *Mahesan v Malaysian Government Officers' Cooperative Housing Society Ltd* [1979] AC 374, [1978] 2 All ER 405, PC.
12 *Salford Corpn v Lever* [1891] 1 QB 168, CA; *Hovenden & Sons v Millhoff* (1900) 83 LT 41, CA; *Morgan v Elford* (1876) 4 ChD 352; *Phosphate Sewage Co v Hartmont* (1877) 5 ChD 394, CA; *Grant v Gold Exploration and Development Syndicate Ltd* [1900] 1 QB 233, CA.
13 *Mahesan v Malaysian Government Officers' Cooperative Housing Society Ltd* [1979] AC 374, [1978] 2 All ER 405, PC.

14 *A-G for Hong Kong v Reid* [1994] 1 AC 324, [1994] 1 All ER 1, PC; doubting *Lister & Co v Stubbs* (1890) 45 ChD 1.
15 *A-G for Hong Kong v Reid* [1994] 1 AC 324, [1994] 1 All ER 1, PC.
16 *Nant-y-glo and Blaina Iron Works Co v Grave* (1878) 12 ChD 738.

497. Constructive trust. It has been held that, where parties proposing a joint venture or partnership[1] undertook exploratory drilling for minerals but then parted and the defendant, using the plaintiff's confidential information, successfully bid against the plaintiff for adjacent land, the defendant held the land on constructive trust for the plaintiff[2].

1 As to joint ventures and partnership see para 461 ante.
2 *LAC Minerals Ltd v International Corona Resources Ltd* (1989) 61 DLR (4th) 14, [1990] FSR 441, Can SC; cf *Agip (Africa) Ltd v Jackson* [1990] Ch 265 at 289–292, [1992] 4 All ER 385 at 402–404 per Millett J; affd [1991] Ch 547, [1992] 4 All ER 451, CA. As to constructive trusts generally see TRUSTS vol 48 (Reissue) para 585 et seq.

(14) EVIDENCE AND PROCEDURE

498. Defamation and confidentiality. A claim that communications are 'confidential' will not of itself confer any immunity in defamation[1], but the proven existence of a confidential relationship may assist to demonstrate a reciprocity of duty and interest[2] or mutual interest[3] to sustain a defence of qualified privilege.

1 *Brooks v Blanshard* (1833) 1 Cr & M 779 at 783 (letter for which privilege was claimed but denied); and see *Picton v Jackman* (1830) 4 C & P 257 (conversation 'confidential'). As to defamation generally see LIBEL AND SLANDER.
2 *Watt v Longsdon* [1930] 1 KB 130, CA; *Todd v Hawkins* (1837) 8 C & P 88 (relative warns about fiancé); *Stuart v Bell* [1891] 2 QB 341, CA (host warns guest); *Kelly v Partington* (1833) 4 B & Ad 700 (former employer giving reference). As to character references see generally EMPLOYMENT vol 16 (Reissue) para 278.
3 *Longdon-Griffiths v Smith* [1951] 1 KB 295, [1950] 2 All ER 662 (trustee at friendly society meeting); *Hunt v Great Northern Rly Co* [1891] 2 QB 189, CA.

499. Evidential privilege. Confidentiality does not of itself confer any evidential privilege[1] and hence, in general, confidential communications may be subject to disclosure on discovery[2]. This is true of personal, commercial, industrial and the majority of professional confidences[3], but confidential information or material covered by legal professional privilege and public interest immunity are wholly or partly exempt from disclosure[4]. Whilst confidentiality is not a separate head of privilege it may be a material consideration when privilege is claimed on the ground of public interest[5] and may be significant even when there is no privilege[6]. It has been held that general discovery of confidential documents should not be made on the ground of relevance alone unless it is necessary for disposing fairly of the case[7]. The court should inspect the documents and consider covering up or, in rare cases, hearing in camera[8].

Legal professional privilege exists between a client and his solicitor, barrister or foreign legal adviser[9] in respect of communications seeking legal advice[10], provided they are not directed to the commission of crime or fraud[11]. There need not be a retainer[12], nor need litigation be contemplated[13]. Documents and communications made for pending or contemplated litigation are also privileged; this is not confined to communications between a solicitor and a barrister but extends to those between a solicitor and a witness[14], between a party and a person instructed to report on the cause of an accident[15] and between a party and a patent agent or registered trade mark agent[16]. Privilege is confined to communications and does not extend to facts arising in the context of the relationship between the client and the adviser or another relationship[17]. The privilege is that of the party, and the party alone can waive it[18], but if an opponent can produce secondary evidence of the privileged material this will be admitted[19].

Public interest immunity covers not only official secrets and cabinet minutes, where the court would accept without query a ministerial certificate[20], but a wider class of material where the courts will endeavour to balance the interest in confidence and the ministerial claim to immunity against the interest that justice should not be restricted by the withholding of evidence[21]. A party seeking disclosure must show that the material sought is likely to support him on an issue and that without it the party would be deprived of proper representation[22]. Disclosure of material probably already publicly available may be refused since it would not assist the claimant[23]. Public interest immunity is not confined to the Crown, government departments and the police[24] but may sometimes be claimed between parties[25]. Thus it was held to apply when the protection of the anonymity of informants would help to maintain the supply of relevant information on cruelty to children to an organisation authorised by Parliament to take proceedings on their behalf[26], but confidential reports by a bank to regulatory authorities relating to its private client operations would not, as a class, be entitled to public interest immunity, since a heavy onus lies on a person seeking to assert a new class claim to such immunity[27].

There is no specific privilege for bank accounts[28] or for documents previously disclosed voluntarily in arbitration proceedings[29].

 1 *Alfred Crompton Amusement Machines Ltd v Customs and Excise Comrs (No 2)* [1974] AC 405 at 433, [1973] 2 All ER 1169 at 1184, HL, per Lord Cross of Chelsea. See also *D v NSPCC* [1978] AC 171 at 218, 230, 238–239, 245, [1977] 1 All ER 589 at 594, 604–605, 612, 615, 618, HL; *Science Research Council v Nassé, Leyland Cars (BL Cars Ltd) v Vyas* [1980] AC 1028 at 1065, 1070–1072, 1074–1078, 1080–1081, 1087, [1979] 3 All ER 673 at 679, 684–685, 686, 691–693, 697, HL.
 2 As to discovery generally see DISCOVERY.
 3 *W v Egdell* [1990] Ch 359 at 419, [1990] 1 All ER 835 at 848–849, CA, per Bingham LJ; citing *A-G v Mulholland* [1963] 2 QB 477, 489–490, [1963] 1 All ER 767 at 771, CA; *Chantrey Martin & Co v Martin* [1953] 2 QB 286, [1953] 2 All ER 691, CA; *Parry-Jones v Law Society* [1969] 1 Ch 1, [1968] 1 All ER 177, CA; *Hunter v Mann* [1974] QB 767, [1974] 2 All ER 414, DC; *Tournier v National Provincial and Union Bank of England* [1924] 1 KB 461 at 473, 486, CA.
 4 As to legal professional privilege see BARRISTERS vol 3(1) (Reissue) para 524–527; CRIMINAL LAW vol 11(2) (Reissue) para 1163; DISCOVERY vol 13 para 79; EVIDENCE vol 17 para 237; SOLICITORS vol 44(1) (Reissue) paras 90, 150. As to public interest immunity see EVIDENCE vol 17 paras 237, 238; DISCOVERY vol 13 para 86 et seq. A client suing a solicitor impliedly waives privilege in respect of all relevant matters, including files of other solicitors formerly retained by him that are now held by his present solicitors: *Kershaw v Whelan* [1995] TLR 695.
 5 *Alfred Crompton Amusement Machines Ltd v Customs and Excise Comrs (No 2)* [1974] AC 405 at 433, [1973] 2 All ER 1169 at 1184, HL, per Lord Cross of Chelsea.
 6 *Science Research Council v Nassé, Leyland Cars (BL Cars Ltd) v Vyas* [1980] AC 1028, [1979] 3 All ER 673, HL.
 7 *Science Research Council v Nassé, Leyland Cars (BL Cars Ltd) v Vyas* [1980] AC 1028 at 1066, [1979] 3 All ER 673 at 680, HL.
 8 *Science Research Council v Nassé, Leyland Cars (BL Cars Ltd) v Vyas* [1980] AC 1028 at 1073, 1085, [1979] 3 All ER 673 at 685, 695, HL.
 9 *Re Duncan, Garfield v Fay* [1968] P 306, [1968] 2 All ER 395.
10 See note 4 supra.
11 *R v Cox and Railton* (1884) 14 QBD 153, CCR; *Williams v Quebrada Rly, Land and Copper Co* [1895] 2 Ch 751.
12 See *Calcraft v Guest* [1898] 1 QB 759 at 761, CA; *Minter v Priest* [1930] AC 558, HL.

13 *Wheeler v Le Marchant* (1881) 17 ChD 675, CA (but a communication by a third party to the solicitor will not be privileged).

14 *Friend v London, Chatham and Dover Rly Co* (1877) 2 ExD 437, CA; *Southwark Water Co v Quick* (1878) 3 QBD 315, CA.

15 But only if the dominant purpose of the report was to obtain legal advice: *Waugh v British Railways Board* [1980] AC 521, [1979] 2 All ER 1169, HL.

16 See the Copyright, Designs and Patents Act 1988 s 280 (as amended); the Trade Marks Act 1994 s 87; PATENTS AND REGISTERED DESIGNS vol 35 (Reissue) para 617; and TRADE MARKS vol 48 (Reissue) para 20.

17 *Brown v Foster* (1857) 1 H & N 736; *Dwyer v Collins* (1852) 7 Exch 639 (possession of books and documents); *Conlon v Conlons Ltd* [1952] 2 All ER 462, [1952] WN 403, CA (whether solicitor had been authorised to negotiate a settlement before issue of the writ).

18 *Wilson v Rastall* (1792) 4 Term Rep 753; *R v Derby Magistrates' Court, ex p B* [1995] 4 All ER 526, HL. If a client sues the solicitor the privilege is waived: *Kershaw v Whelan* [1995] TLR 695.

19 *Calcraft v Guest* [1898] 1 QB 759, CA. Secondary evidence will not, however, be admitted if it was obtained by a trick: *ITC Film Distributors Ltd v Video Exchange Ltd* [1982] Ch 431, [1982] 2 All ER 241. Secondary evidence obtained by accident or mistake may be used for a prosecution since the need to enforce criminal law overrides a private claim to confidence: *Butler v Board of Trade* [1971] Ch 680 at 691, [1970] 3 All ER 593 at 600 per Goff J (solicitor handing over copy of privileged letter). This does not apply in civil cases where the court will use its equitable powers to prevent a party taking advantage of a clear mistake in disclosing privileged documents: *Derby & Co Ltd v Weldon (No 8)* [1990] 3 All ER 762, [1991] 1 WLR 73, CA; *English and American Insurance Co Ltd v Herbert Smith* [1988] FSR 232; *Ablitt v Mills & Reeve (a firm)* [1995] TLR 535. But see *Kenning v Eve Construction Ltd* [1989] 1 WLR 1189 (copy of a report by an expert witness sent to plaintiffs, and a confidential letter from the expert to the defendants accidentally included; the letter could be used).

20 See *Conway v Rimmer* [1968] AC 910, [1968] 1 All ER 874, HL; and note 4 supra.

21 See *Conway v Rimmer* [1968] AC 910, [1968] 1 All ER 874, HL; *Burmah Oil Co Ltd v Bank of England (A-G intervening)* [1980] AC 1090, [1979] 3 All ER 700, HL.

22 *Air Canada v Secretary of State for Trade* [1983] 2 AC 394, [1983] 1 All ER 910, HL.

23 *Air Canada v Secretary of State for Trade* [1983] 2 AC 394, [1983] 1 All ER 910, HL.

24 *Conway v Rimmer* [1968] AC 910, [1968] 1 All ER 874, HL. A class claim to public interest immunity for evidence relating to an investigation under the Police and Criminal Evidence Act 1984 Pt IX (ss 83–112) (as amended) has been rejected, but a contents claim can be made for specific documents: *R v Chief Constable of West Midlands Police, ex p Wiley* [1995] 1 AC 274, [1994] 3 All ER 420, HL. Confidentiality between the police and the owners of seized documents is not, of itself, enough to prevent their production on a subpoena to the police; there must be a recognised head of privilege, such as legal professional privilege: *Marcel v Metropolitan Police Comr* [1992] Ch 225, [1992] 1 All ER 72, CA.

25 *Alfred Crompton Amusement Machines Ltd v Customs and Excise Comrs (No 2)* [1974] AC 405, [1973] 2 All ER 1169, HL.

26 See *D v NSPCC* [1978] AC 171, [1977] 1 All ER 589, HL.

27 *Kaufmann v Credit Lyonnais Bank* (1995) Times, 1 February; and see *R v Chief Constable of West Midlands Police, ex p Wiley* [1995] 1 AC 274, [1994] 3 All ER 420, HL.

28 *Robertson v Canadian Imperial Bank of Commerce* [1995] 1 All ER 824, [1994] 1 WLR 1493, PC. As to bankers' obligations of confidentiality see para 456 ante.

29 *Shearson Lehman Hutton Inc v Maclaine Watson & Co Ltd* [1989] 1 All ER 1056, [1988] 1 WLR 946 per Webster J. As to arbitrators' obligations of confidentiality see para 470 ante.

500. Restriction of disclosure in litigation. In enforcing obligations of confidence by litigation, particularly in relation to trade secrets, the degree of disclosure required may defeat the purpose of the process. In some authorities the courts were prepared to accept restricted disclosure[1] but this appears inconsistent with the requirements of discovery, with the principles for the framing of injunctions and with other authorities[2]. The court has discretion in relation to discovery and may direct either that information be disclosed only to the legal advisers of the parties and their experts, or that documents be partially covered to conceal confidential material[3]. In order to prevent the confidences allegedly infringed from being made publicly available in court and thereby destroying the subject matter of the proceedings, the court can direct that the trial be held in camera[4]. If the court has no jurisdiction at the trial of the action or at the effective hearing of an interlocutory application to refuse to allow a party to proceedings to see evidence on which the other party relies, so also a party against whom an ex parte injunction is granted must be entitled to see the evidence on which the injunction was granted, so that he can consider whether he can and should apply to discharge it[5].

When material is disclosed by way of discovery the court will restrain not only the party who obtains it but also any third party who further obtains it from making use of it for any purpose other than the action for which it was disclosed[6]. When an action was compromised, an implied undertaking not to use documents produced under compulsion was held to cover witness statements but not experts' reports[7].

1 *Amber Size and Chemical Co Ltd v Menzel* [1913] 2 Ch 239; *Under Water Welders and Repairers Ltd v Street and Longthorne* [1968] RPC 498.
2 *Suhner & Co AG v Transradio Ltd* [1967] RPC 329; *Diamond Stylus Co Ltd v Bauden Precision Diamonds Ltd* [1973] RPC 675; *John Zink Co Ltd v Lloyds Bank Ltd and Airoil Burner Co (GB) Ltd* [1975] RPC 385; *G D Searle & Co Ltd v Celltech Ltd* [1982] FSR 92, CA. See also *P A Thomas & Co v Mould* [1968] 2 QB 913, [1968] 1 All ER 963. As to injunctions generally see INJUNCTIONS; and paras 491–492 ante. As to discovery generally see DISCOVERY.
3 *Science Research Council v Nassé, Leyland Cars (BL Cars Ltd) v Vyas* [1980] AC 1028, [1979] 3 All ER 673, HL; *Church of Scientology of California v Department of Health and Social Security* [1979] 3 All ER 97, [1979] 1 WLR 723, CA; *Sorbo Rubber Sponge Products Ltd v Defries* (1930) 47 RPC 454.
4 *Yates Circuit Foil Co v Electrofoils Ltd* [1976] FSR 345 at 346; *Industrial Furnaces Ltd v Reaves* [1970] RPC 605. The court will not mention secret processes in the judgment: see *Yates Circuit Foil Co v Electrofoils Ltd* supra. The publication of information relating to proceedings before any court sitting in private is not of itself contempt of court except where the information relates to a secret process, discovery or invention which is in issue in the proceedings: Administration of Justice Act 1960 s 12(1)(d). As to the exclusion of the public see also *Scott v Scott* [1913] AC 417 at 437–443, HL, per Viscount Haldane LC.
5 *VNU Publications Ltd v Ziff Davis (UK) Ltd* [1992] RPC 269 at 275 per Vinelott J (disclosure merely to the defendant's legal advisers was insufficient; the defendant was entitled to see all the evidence and comment on or challenge it; the case was not analogous to discovery where the courts restrict inspection of documents to counsel, solicitors and expert advisers); and see *WEA Records Ltd v Visions Channel 4 Ltd* [1983] 2 All ER 589, [1983] 1 WLR 721, CA (on an application for an ex parte order a judge should not hear confidential information which will not be made available to the defendant at a later stage).
6 *Riddick v Thames Board Mills Ltd* [1977] QB 881, [1977] 3 All ER 677, CA; *Distillers Co (Biochemicals) Ltd v Times Newspapers Ltd, Distillers Co (Biochemicals) Ltd v Phillips* [1975] QB 613, [1975] 1 All ER 41; *Harman v Secretary of State for the Home Department* [1983] 1 AC 280, sub nom *Home Office v Harman* [1982] 1 All ER 532, HL; *Sybron Corpn v Barclays Bank plc* [1985] Ch 299 (documents produced on discovery not to be used in other proceedings without leave of the court although information from the court record could be used).
7 *Prudential Assurance Co Ltd v Fountain Page Ltd* [1991] 3 All ER 878, [1991] 1 WLR 756.

2. DATA PROTECTION

(1) INTRODUCTION AND SCOPE OF LEGISLATION

501. The legislation. The Data Protection Act 1984 implements the White Paper on Data Protection[1] and enables the United Kingdom to ratify the Council of Europe Convention for the Protection of Individuals with regard to Automatic Processing of Personal Data[2]. The 1984 Act establishes a system of registration for, and supervision of, data users and computer bureaux[3] to ensure that personal data is used in accordance with the data protection principles[4]. With certain exceptions[5], the 1984 Act (1) applies to government departments and the police[6]; but (2) does not apply to a data user in respect of data held[7], or to a person carrying on a computer bureau in respect of services provided[8], outside the United Kingdom[9]. Nor does the 1984 Act apply to data processed wholly outside the United Kingdom unless the data are used or intended to be used in the United Kingdom[10].

Separate statutory provision is made with regard to medical reports and health records[11], records kept by credit reference agencies[12] and the provision of access to personal files held by certain local authorities[13].

Unauthorised access to, and modification of, computer material is punishable under the Computer Misuse Act 1990[14].

1 Ie *Data Protection: The Government's Proposals for Legislation* (Cmnd 8539) (1982). See also the Report of the Committee on Privacy (Cmnd 5012) (1972); the Report of the Committee on Data Protection (Cmnd 7341) (1978).

2 For the text of the Council of Europe Convention for the Protection of Individuals with regard to Automatic Processing of Personal Data, which was opened for signature on 28 January 1981 (referred to below as 'the European Convention': see the Data Protection Act 1984 s 41) see *Data Protection: The Government's Proposals for Legislation* (Cmnd 8539) (1982) Annex A. The designated authority for the purposes of the European Convention art 13 (rendering of mutual assistance) is the Data Protection Registrar (see further para 506 post): Data Protection Act 1984 s 37. The Secretary of State may by order make provision as to the functions to be discharged by the registrar in that capacity: s 37. Any power conferred by the Data Protection Act 1984 to make regulations, rules or orders is exercisable by statutory instrument; such regulations, rules or orders may make different provision for different cases or circumstances: s 40(1), (2). A statutory instrument containing an order under s 37 is subject to annulment in pursuance of a resolution of either House of Parliament: s 40(5). Before making any order under ss 1–39 (as amended) the Secretary of State must consult the registrar: s 40(3). In exercise of the power conferred by s 37, the Secretary of State has made the Data Protection (Functions of Designated Authority) Order 1987, SI 1987/2028, which came into force on 1 January 1988: art 1. The Secretary of State here concerned is the Home Secretary.

  Amendment to the data protection legislation will be required in order to comply with EC Council Directive 95/46 (OJ L281, 23.11.95, p 31) on the protection of individuals with regard to the processing of personal data (including data held in manual filing systems) and on the free movement of such data, which must be implemented within three years of its adoption. See further EUROPEAN COMMUNITIES.

3 See para 508 et seq post. For the meaning of 'data user' see para 502 post; and as to a 'computer bureau' see para 502 post.

4 As to the data protection principles see paras 503–505 post.

5 Ie the exceptions set out in the Data Protection Act 1984 ss 38(2), 39(3). A government department is not liable to prosecution under the 1984 Act; but ss 5(3), 15(2) (see paras 513–514 post) and, so far as relating to those provisions, s 5(5) (as amended) and s 15(3) (see para 524 post) apply to any person who by virtue of s 38 falls to be treated as a servant of the government department in question: s 38(2)(a). Section 6(6), and s 16, Sch 4 para 12 (see para 524 post) apply to a person in the public service of the Crown as they apply to any other person: s 38(2)(b).

6 See ibid s 38(1). Except as provided in s 38(2) (see note 5 supra), a government department is subject to the same obligations and liabilities under the 1984 Act as a private person; and for these purposes, each government department is treated as a person separate from any other government department and a person in the public service of the Crown is treated as a servant of the government department to which his responsibilities or duties relate: s 38(1). The constables under the direction and control of a chief officer of police are treated as his servants for these purposes; and the members of any body of constables maintained otherwise than by a police authority are treated as the servants (1) of the authority or person by whom that body is maintained; and (2) in the case of any members of such a body who are under the direction and control of a chief officer, of that officer: s 38(3). As to the application of s 38(3) to Scotland and Northern Ireland see s 38(4), (5).

7 For these purposes, data are treated as held where the data user exercises the control referred to in ibid s 1(5)(b) (see para 502 head (2) post) in relation to the data: s 39(2)(a).

8 For these purposes, services are treated as provided where the person carrying on the computer bureau does any of the things referred to in ibid s 1(6)(a) or (b) (see para 502 text to notes 10–11 post): s 39(2)(b).

9 Ibid s 39(1). Where a person who is not resident in the United Kingdom (1) exercises the control mentioned in note 7 supra; or (2) does any of the things mentioned in note 8 supra, through a servant or agent in the United Kingdom, the Data Protection Act 1984 applies as if that control were exercised or, as the case may be, those things were done in the United Kingdom by the servant or agent acting on his

own account and not on behalf of the person whose servant or agent he is: s 39(3). Where by virtue of this provision a servant or agent is treated as a data user or as a person carrying on a computer bureau, he may be described for the purposes of registration by the position or office which he holds; and any such description in an entry in the register is to be treated as applying to the person for the time being holding the position or office in question: s 39(4). As to control by the registrar of data to be transferred abroad see s 12; and para 517 post; and as to registration see para 508 et seq post. 'United Kingdom' means Great Britain and Northern Ireland: Interpretation Act 1978 s 5, Sch 1. 'Great Britain' means England, Scotland and Wales: Union with Scotland Act 1706, preamble art I; Interpretation Act 1978 s 22(1), Sch 2 para 5(a). Neither the Channel Islands nor the Isle of Man is within the United Kingdom.

10 Data Protection Act 1984 s 39(5). Section 4(3)(e) (see para 508 note 7 head (5) post), s 5(2)(e) (see para 513 head (5) post) and s 12(1) (see para 517 post) do not apply to the transfer of data which are already outside the United Kingdom; but references in s 12 to a contravention of the data protection principles include references to anything that would constitute such a contravention if it occurred in relation to the data when held in the United Kingdom: s 39(6).

11 See the Access to Medical Reports Act 1988; the Access to Health Records Act 1990; the Access to Health Records (Control of Access) Regulations 1993, SI 1993/746; and MEDICINE vol 30 (Reissue) paras 19–20.

12 See the Consumer Credit Act 1974 ss 157–160 (as amended); and para 475 ante. See also HIRE PURCHASE AND CONSUMER CREDIT.

13 See the Access to Personal Files Act 1987; and para 538 et seq post.

14 See CRIMINAL LAW vol 11(1) (Supp) para 604A.

502. Meaning of 'data' and related expressions. For the purposes of the Data Protection Act 1984, 'data' means information recorded in a form in which it can be processed[1] by equipment operating automatically in response to instructions given for that purpose[2]; and 'personal data' means data consisting of information which relates to a living individual who can be identified from that information, or from that and other information in the possession of the data user, including any expression of opinion about the individual, but not any indication of the intentions of the data user in respect of that individual[3]. An individual who is the subject of personal data is referred to as a 'data subject'[4].

'Data user' means a person who holds data[5]; and a person holds data if

(1) the data form part of a collection of data processed or intended to be processed[6] by or on behalf of that person[7]; and

(2) that person, either alone or jointly or in common with other persons, controls the contents and use of the data comprised in the collection[8]; and

(3) the data are in the form in which they have been or are intended to be processed either as mentioned in head (1) above or, though not for the time being in that form, in a form into which they have been converted after being so processed and with a view to being further so processed on a subsequent occasion[9].

A person carries on a 'computer bureau' if that person provides others with services in respect of data, either by causing data held by other persons for whom he acts as agent to be processed[10] or by allowing other persons the use of equipment in his possession for the processing of data held by them[11].

1 'Processing', in relation to data, means amending, augmenting, deleting or rearranging the data or extracting the information constituting the data and, in the case of personal data, means performing any of those operations by reference to the data subject: Data Protection Act 1984 s 1(7). This is not, however, to be construed as applying to any operation performed only for the purpose of preparing the text of documents: s 1(8).

2 Ibid s 1(1), (2).

3 Ibid s 1(1), (3). The use of the word 'individual' in this context excludes bodies of persons corporate or unincorporate: cf the Interpretation Act 1978 s 5, Sch 1; STATUTES vol 44(1) (Reissue) para 1382; and *Whitney v IRC* [1926] AC 37 at 43, HL, per Viscount Cave LC.

   References to personal data in any provision of the Data Protection Act 1984 Pt II (ss 4–20) (as amended) (see para 508 et seq post) or Pt III (ss 21–25) (see para 525 et seq post) do not include references to data which by virtue of Pt IV (ss 26–35A) (as amended) (see para 529 et seq post) are exempt from that provision: s 26(1).

4   Ibid s 1(1), (4).
5   Ibid s 1(1), (5).
6   Ie processed as mentioned in ibid s 1(2): see the text to notes 1–2 supra.
7   Ibid s 1(1), (5)(a).
8   Ibid s 1(1), (5)(b). As to where data are treated as held see para 501 note 7 ante.
9   Ibid s 1(1), (5)(c).
10   See note 6 supra.
11   Data Protection Act 1984 s 1(1), (6).

(2) THE DATA PROTECTION PRINCIPLES

503. In general. The data protection principles[1] are set out in Schedule 1 to the Data Protection Act 1984 and must be interpreted accordingly[2]. The Secretary of State may by order modify or supplement those principles for the purpose of providing additional safeguards in relation to personal data[3] consisting of information as to:

(1)   the racial origin of the data subject[4];
(2)   his political opinions or religious or other beliefs;
(3)   his physical or mental health or his sexual life; or
(4)   his criminal convictions[5].

Any such order may:

(a)   modify a principle either by modifying the principle itself or by modifying its interpretation[6];
(b)   make different provision in relation to data or information of different descriptions[7];

but no such order may be made unless a draft of it has been laid before and approved by a resolution of each House of Parliament[8].

1   As to the data protection principles see paras 504–505 post.
2   Data Protection Act 1984 s 2(1).
3   For the meaning of 'personal data' and 'data' see para 502 ante.
4   For the meaning of 'data subject' see para 502 ante.
5   Data Protection Act 1984 s 2(3)(a)–(d). References to the data protection principles include, except where the context otherwise requires, references to any modified or additional principle having effect by virtue of an order under s 2: s 2(3).
6   Ibid s 2(4). Where an order modifies a principle or provides for an additional principle it may contain provisions for the interpretation of the modified or additional principle: s 2(4). An order modifying the third data protection principle (see para 504 head (3) post) may, to such extent as the Secretary of State thinks appropriate, exclude or modify in relation to that principle any exemption from the non-disclosure provisions which is contained in Pt IV (ss 26–35A) (as amended) (see para 529 et seq post); and the exemptions from those provisions contained in Pt IV (as amended) accordingly have effect subject to any order so made: s 2(5). For the meaning of 'the non-disclosure provisions' see para 529 note 7 post. As to the Secretary of State see para 501 note 2 ante.
7   Ibid s 2(6).
8   Ibid s 40(4). As to the making of orders generally see para 501 note 2 ante. At the date at which this volume states the law, no such order had been made.

504. The seven principles applying to personal data held by data users. The following seven principles apply to personal data held[1] by data users[2]:

(1)   the information to be contained in personal data must be obtained, and personal data must be processed[3], fairly[4] and lawfully[5];
(2)   personal data must be held only for one or more specified[6] and lawful purpose or purposes[7];

(3) personal data held for any purpose or purposes must not be used or disclosed[8] in any manner incompatible with that purpose or those purposes[9];

(4) personal data held for any purpose or purposes must be adequate, relevant and not excessive in relation to that purpose or those purposes[10];

(5) personal data must be accurate[11] and, where necessary, kept up to date[12];

(6) personal data held for any purpose or purposes must not be kept for longer than is necessary therefor[13];

(7) an individual is entitled:

    (a) at reasonable intervals[14] and without undue delay or expense (i) to be informed by any data user whether that person holds personal data of which that individual is the subject and (ii) to access to any such data held by a data user[15]; and

    (b) where appropriate[16], to have such data corrected or erased[17].

1   For the meaning of 'personal data', 'data' and 'held' see para 502 ante.

2   Data Protection Act 1984 s 2(2). For the meaning of 'data user' see para 502 ante.

3   As to the meaning of 'processed' see para 502 note 1 ante.

4   In determining whether information was obtained fairly, regard must be had to the method by which it was obtained, including in particular whether any person from whom it was obtained was deceived or misled as to the purpose or purposes for which it is to be held, used or disclosed: Data Protection Act 1984 s 2(1), Sch 1 Pt II para 1(1). Information is in any event treated as obtained fairly if it is obtained from a person who is authorised by or under any enactment to supply it, or who is required to supply it by or under any enactment or by any convention or other instrument imposing an international obligation on the United Kingdom: Sch 1 Pt II para 1(2). In determining whether information was obtained fairly there must be disregarded any disclosure of the information which is authorised or required by or under any enactment or required by any such convention or other such instrument: Sch 1 Pt II para 1(2). Where personal data are held for historical, statistical or research purposes and not used in such a way that damage or distress is, or is likely to be, caused to any data subject, the information contained in the data is not regarded as obtained unfairly by reason only that its use for any such purpose was not disclosed when it was obtained: Sch 1 Pt II para 7(a). For the meaning of 'data subject' see para 502 ante; for the meaning of 'United Kingdom' see para 501 note 9 ante; as to the meaning of 'processed' see para 502 note 1 ante; and as to the meaning of 'disclosed' see note 8 infra.

5   Ibid Sch 1 Pt I principle 1.

6   Personal data are not treated as held for a specified purpose unless that purpose is described in particulars registered under the Data Protection Act 1984 in relation to the data: Sch 1 Pt II para 2. As to registration see para 508 et seq post.

7   Ibid Sch 1 Pt I principle 2.

8   'Disclosing', in relation to data, includes disclosing information extracted from the data; and where the identification of the individual who is the subject of personal data depends partly on the information constituting the data and partly on other information in the possession of the data user, the data are not to be regarded as disclosed or transferred unless the other information is also disclosed or transferred: ibid s 1(9).

9   Ibid Sch 1 Pt I principle 3. Personal data are not treated as used or disclosed in contravention of this principle unless (1) used otherwise than for a purpose of a description registered under the Data Protection Act 1984 in relation to the data; or (2) disclosed otherwise than to a person of a description so registered: Sch 1 Pt II para 3.

10   Ibid Sch 1 Pt I principle 4.

11   Any question whether or not personal data are accurate is to be determined as for the purposes of ibid s 22 (see para 526 post) but, in the case of such data as are mentioned in s 22(2), this principle is not to be regarded as having been contravened by reason of any inaccuracy in the information there mentioned if the requirements specified in s 22(2) have been complied with: Sch 1 Pt II para 4.

12   Ibid Sch 1 Pt I principle 5.

13   Ibid Sch 1 Pt I principle 6. However, data held for historical, statistical or research purposes and not used in such a way that damage or distress is, or is likely to be, caused to any data subject may be kept indefinitely: Sch 1 Pt II para 7(b).

14   In determining whether access to personal data is sought at reasonable intervals, regard must be had to the nature of the data, the purpose for which the data are held and the frequency with which they are altered: ibid Sch 1 Pt II para 5(2).

15 Ibid Sch 1 Pt I principle 7(a). Principle 7(a) must not be construed as conferring any rights inconsistent
with s 21 (see para 525 post): Sch 1 Pt II para 5(1).
16 The correction or erasure of personal data is appropriate only where necessary for ensuring compliance
with the other data protection principles: ibid Sch 1 Pt II para 5(3).
17 Ibid Sch 1 Pt I principle 7(b).

505. The eighth principle. The eighth data protection principle[1], which applies
both to personal data held by data users[2] and to personal data in respect of which
services are provided by persons carrying on computer bureaux[3], is that appropriate
security measures must be taken against unauthorised access to, or alteration, disclosure[4] or destruction of, personal data and against accidental loss or destruction of such
data[5]. Regard must be had for these purposes:

(1) to the nature of the personal data and the harm that would result from such
access, alteration, disclosure, loss or destruction; and

(2) to the place where the personal data are stored, to security measures pro-
grammed into the relevant equipment and to measures taken for ensuring the
reliability of staff having access to the data[6].

1 As to the data protection principles in general see para 503 ante; and as to the seven principles applying
only to personal data held by data users see para 504 ante.
2 For the meaning of 'personal data', 'data user', 'data' and 'held' see para 502 ante.
3 Data Protection Act 1984 s 1(2). As to persons carrying on computer bureaux see para 502 ante.
4 As to the meaning of 'disclosure' see para 504 note 8 ante.
5 Data Protection Act 1984 s 2(1), Sch 1 Pt I principle 8.
6 Ibid Sch 1 Pt II para 6.

(3) THE REGISTRAR AND THE TRIBUNAL

506. The Data Protection Registrar. The Data Protection Registrar ('the registrar') is an officer appointed by Her Majesty by Letters Patent[1]. He holds office for five
years but may be relieved of his office at his own request or removed from it in
pursuance of an address from both Houses of Parliament, and must in any case retire
when he attains the age of 65 years[2]. He must appoint a deputy registrar[3] and may
appoint such number of other officers and servants as he may determine[4]. It is his duty
to keep proper accounts and other records in relation to them[5] and to prepare a
statement of account in respect of each financial year[6].

It is the registrar's duty:

(1) to perform his statutory functions so as to promote the observance of the data
protection principles[7] by data users[8] and persons carrying on computer
bureaux[9];

(2) where he considers it appropriate to do so, to encourage trade associations or
other bodies representing data users to prepare, and to disseminate to their
members, codes of practice for guidance in complying with the data protection
principles[10].

He must also arrange for the dissemination, in such form and manner as he considers
appropriate, of such information as it may appear to him expedient to give to the public
about the operation of the Data Protection Act 1984 and any other matters within the
scope of his functions thereunder and he may give advice to any person as to any of
those matters[11]. He must annually lay before each House of Parliament a general report
on the performance of his statutory functions and may from time to time lay before
each House of Parliament such other reports with respect to those functions as he
thinks fit[12].

The registrar may consider any complaint that any of the data protection principles or any provision of the 1984 Act has been or is being contravened and must do so if the complaint appears to him to raise a matter of substance and to have been made without undue delay by a person directly affected; and where he considers any such complaint, he must notify the complainant of the result of his consideration and of any action which he proposes to take[13].

The registrar must also discharge his functions as the designated authority for the purposes of the European Convention[14].

No enactment, whenever passed, and no rule of law prohibiting or restricting the disclosure of information may preclude a person from furnishing the registrar with any information necessary for the discharge of his statutory functions[15].

1 Data Protection Act 1984 s 3(1)(a), (2). The registrar is a corporation sole; and his officers and servants are not to be regarded as servants or agents of the Crown: s 3(6), Sch 2 para 1(1), (2) (amended by the Official Secrets Act 1989 s 16(4), Sch 2).
2 Data Protection Act 1984 Sch 2 para 2(1)–(4). Subject to the retirement age, a person who ceases to be registrar on the expiration of his term of office is eligible for re-appointment: Sch 2 para 2(5). As to the registrar's salary and pension see Sch 2 para 3.
3 The deputy registrar must perform the functions conferred on the registrar by the Data Protection Act 1984 during any vacancy in that office or at any time when the registrar is for any reason unable to act: Sch 2 para 5(1).
4 Ibid Sch 2 para 4(1). Any functions of the registrar under the Data Protection Act 1984 may, to the extent authorised by him, be performed by any of his officers: Sch 2 para 5(2). As to remuneration and other conditions of service of persons appointed by the registrar see Sch 2 para 4(2)–(5); and as to the registrar's expenses see Sch 2 para 6(2).
5 Ibid Sch 2 para 7(1)(a).
6 See ibid Sch 2 para 7(1)(b), (c), (2)–(3).
7 As to the data protection principles see paras 503–505 ante.
8 For the meaning of 'data user' and 'data' see para 502 ante.
9 Data Protection Act 1984 s 36(1). As to persons carrying on computer bureaux see para 502 ante.
10 Ibid s 36(4).
11 Ibid s 36(3). The registrar has published guidelines explaining the requirements of the Data Protection Act 1984 which are available from the Office of the Data Protection Registrar, Wycliffe House, Water Land, Wilmslow, Cheshire, SK9 5AX.
12 Ibid s 36(5).
13 Ibid s 36(2).
14 See the Data Protection (Functions of Designated Authority) Order 1987, SI 1987/2028, art 2, Schedule. As to the European Convention see para 501 note 2 ante.
15 Data Protection Act 1984 ss 17(1), 41.

507. The Data Protection Tribunal. The Data Protection Tribunal ('the tribunal') is an appeal tribunal against certain decisions of the registrar and against certain notices issued by him[1]. The tribunal consists of a chairman appointed by the Lord Chancellor after consultation with the Lord Advocate[2], a number of deputy chairmen appointed in the same manner[3], and a number of other members (to represent the interests of data users[4] and data subjects[5]) appointed by the Secretary of State[6]. A member of the tribunal holds and vacates his office in accordance with the terms of his appointment except that a chairman or deputy chairman must vacate his office on the day on which he attains the age of 70 years[7]. He may resign at any time[8].

The Secretary of State must pay to the members of the tribunal such remuneration and allowances as he may with the approval of the Treasury determine[9] and may provide the tribunal with such officers and servants as he thinks necessary for the proper discharge of its functions[10].

No enactment, whenever passed, and no rule of law prohibiting or restricting the disclosure of information may preclude a person from furnishing the tribunal with any information necessary for the discharge of its statutory functions[11].

1 See the Data Protection Act 1984 s 3(1)(b). As to appeals to the tribunal and the practice and procedure of the tribunal see para 518 et seq post.
2 Ibid s 3(3)(a). The chairman must be either (1) a person who has a seven year general qualification within the meaning of the Courts and Legal Services Act 1990 s 71 (see SOLICITORS vol 44(1) (Reissue) para 91 head (3)); (2) an advocate or solicitor in Scotland of at least seven years' standing; or (3) a member of the Bar of Northern Ireland or a solicitor of the Supreme Court of Northern Ireland of at least seven years' standing: Data Protection Act 1984 s 3(4) (amended by the Courts and Legal Services Act 1990 s 7(2), Sch 10 para 58).
3 Data Protection Act 1984 s 3(3)(b). The number of deputy chairmen to be appointed is determined by the Lord Chancellor: s 3(3)(b). They must be qualified as mentioned in note 2 heads (1)–(3) supra: see s 3(4) (as amended: see note 2 supra).
4 For the meaning of 'data user' and 'data' see para 502 ante.
5 Data Protection Act 1984 s 3(5). For the meaning of 'data subject' see para 502 ante.
6 Ibid s 3(3)(c). The number of such other members to be appointed is determined by the Secretary of State: s 3(3)(c). As to the Secretary of State see para 501 note 2 ante.
7 Ibid s 3(6), Sch 2 para 8(1), (3) (respectively amended and added by the Judicial Pensions and Retirement Act 1993 s 26(10), Sch 6 para 51). This provision is subject to s 26(4)–(6) (power to authorise continuance in office up to the age of 75 years): Data Protection Act 1984 Sch 2 para 8(3) (as so added).
8 See ibid Sch 2 para 8(2).
9 Ibid Sch 2 para 9. The money is provided by Parliament: see Sch 2 para 9.
10 Ibid Sch 2 para 10. As to the tribunal's expenses see Sch 2 para 11.
11 Ibid ss 17(1), 41.

(4) REGISTRATION AND SUPERVISION OF DATA USERS AND COMPUTER BUREAUX

(i) Registration

508. Registration. The Data Protection Registrar must maintain a register of data users who hold[1], and of computer bureaux which provide services[2] in respect of, personal data[3] and must make an entry in the register in pursuance of each application for registration[4] accepted by him[5]. Each entry must state whether it is in respect of a data user, of a person carrying on a computer bureau or of a data user who also carries on such a bureau[6]. An entry in respect of:

(1) a data user must consist of the specified particulars[7];
(2) a person carrying on a computer bureau must consist of that person's name and address[8];
(3) a data user who also carries on a computer bureau must consist of that person's name and address and certain other specified particulars[9] as respects the personal data to be held by him[10].

The Secretary of State may by order vary the particulars to be included in entries made in the register[11].

1 For the meaning of 'data user', 'data' and 'hold' see para 502 ante.
2 As to computer bureaux providing services see para 502 ante.
3 For the meaning of 'personal data' see para 502 ante.
4 Ie under the Data Protection Act 1984 Pt II (ss 4–20) (as amended): see para 509 et seq post.
5 Ibid s 4(1). As to the registrar see para 506 ante.
6 Ibid s 4(2).
7 Ibid s 4(3). The specified particulars are: (1) the name and address of the data user; (2) a description of the personal data to be held by him and of the purpose or purposes for which the data are to be held or used;

(3) a description of the source or sources from which he intends or may wish to obtain the data or the information to be contained in the data; (4) a description of any person or persons to whom he intends or may wish to disclose the data; (5) the names or a description of any countries or territories outside the United Kingdom to which he intends or may wish directly or indirectly to transfer the data; and (6) one or more addresses for the receipt of requests from data subjects for access to the data: s 4(3)(a)–(f). In the case of a registered company (ie a company registered under the Companies Act 1985: see the Data Protection Act 1984 s 41), the address referred to is that of its registered office, and the particulars to be included in the entry include the company's number in the register of companies (s 4(6)); and in the case of a person other than such a company carrying on a business, the address is that of his principal place of business (s 4(7)). Head (5) supra does not apply to the transfer of data which are already outside the United Kingdom: see s 39(6); and para 501 note 10 ante. For the meaning of 'United Kingdom' see para 501 note 9 ante. As to the data subject's right of access see para 525 post. For the meaning of 'data subject' see para 502 ante; and as to the meaning of 'disclose' and 'transfer' see para 504 note 8 ante.

8 Ibid s 4(4). Section 4(6), (7) applies in respect of the address: see note 7 supra.
9 Ie the particulars specified in ibid s 4(3)(b)–(f): see note 7 heads (2)–(6) supra.
10 Ibid s 4(5). Section 4(6), (7) applies in respect of the address: see note 7 supra.
11 Ibid s 4(8). No such order may be made unless a draft of the order has been laid before and approved by a resolution of each House of Parliament: s 40(4). As to the making of orders generally, and as to the Secretary of State, see para 501 note 2 ante. At the date at which this volume states the law, no such order had been made.

509. Applications for registration and for amendment of registered particulars. A person applying for registration[1] must state whether he wishes to be registered as a data user[2], as a person carrying on a computer bureau[3] or as a data user who also carries on such a bureau, and must furnish the Data Protection Registrar, in such form as he may require, with the particulars required to be included in the entry to be made in pursuance of the application[4]. Where a person intends to hold personal data[5] for two or more purposes he may make separate applications for registration in respect of any of those purposes[6].

A registered person may at any time apply to the registrar for the alteration of any particulars included in the entry or entries relating to that person[7] or, where the alteration would consist of the addition of a purpose for which personal data are held, may instead of making an application for alteration make a fresh application for registration in respect of the additional purpose[8].

Every application for registration or for alteration to the register must be accompanied by the prescribed fee[9]. Any such application may be withdrawn by notice in writing to the registrar at any time before the applicant receives a notification from the registrar[10] that the application has been accepted or refused[11].

1 Ie under the Data Protection Act 1984 Pt I (ss 4–20) (as amended): see paras 508 ante, 510 et seq post.
2 For the meaning of 'data user' and 'data' see para 502 ante.
3 As to carrying on a computer bureau see para 502 ante.
4 Data Protection Act 1984 s 6(1). As to the required particulars see para 508 ante; and as to the offence of furnishing misleading etc particulars see s 6(6); and para 524 post. As to the registrar see para 506 ante.
5 For the meaning of 'personal data' see para 502 ante.
6 Data Protection Act 1984 s 6(2).
7 Ibid s 6(3). A registered person must make an application under s 6(3) whenever necessary for ensuring that the entry or entries relating to that person contain his current address (see para 508 note 7 ante) and any person who fails to comply with this provision is guilty of an offence: s 6(5). As to the penalties for such an offence see para 524 post.
8 Ibid s 6(4).
9 Ibid s 6(7). Regulations prescribing fees for the purposes of any provision of the Data Protection Act 1984 must be made by the Secretary of State and laid before Parliament after being made: ss 40(6), 41. Where the regulations prescribe fees payable to the registrar they must be made after consultation with him and with the approval of the Treasury; and in making any such regulations, the Secretary of State must have regard to the desirability of securing that those fees are sufficient to offset the expenses

incurred by the registrar and the Data Protection Tribunal in discharging their statutory functions and any expenses of the Secretary of State in respect of the tribunal: s 40(7). In exercise of the power so conferred, the Secretary of State has made the Data Protection (Fees) Regulations 1991, SI 1991/1160, which came into force on 1 June 1991: reg 1. For the prescribed fee see reg 2. As to the Secretary of State see para 501 note 2 ante; and as to the tribunal see para 507 ante.

In relation to the functions of the registrar, the tribunal and the Secretary of State which fall to be taken into account in exercising this power to fix fees, any deficit incurred before the exercise of the power may also be taken into account in determining the costs of those functions: see the Data Protection Registration Fee Order 1991, SI 1991/1142, art 2.

10 Ie under the Data Protection Act 1984 s 7(1): see para 510 post.
11 Ibid s 6(8).

510. Acceptance and refusal of applications. As soon as practicable, and in any case within the period of six months after receiving an application for registration or for the alteration of registered particulars[1], the Data Protection Registrar must notify the applicant in writing whether the application has been accepted or refused[2]. If, however, it appears to the registrar in any case that an application needs more consideration than can be given to it in that period, he must notify[3] the applicant in writing to that effect, in which event no notification need be given until after the end of that period[4].

Where the registrar notifies an applicant that his application has been accepted, the notification must contain a statement of (1) the particulars entered in the register, or the alteration made, in pursuance of the application; and (2) the date on which the particulars were entered or the alteration was made[5]. Where the registrar refuses an application he must give his reasons and inform the applicant of the statutory rights[6] of appeal[7]. He may not refuse an application duly made unless:

(a) he considers that the particulars proposed for registration or, as the case may be, the particulars that would result from the proposed alteration, will not give sufficient information as to the matters to which they relate[8]; or

(b) he is satisfied that the applicant is likely to contravene any of the data protection principles[9]; or

(c) he considers that the information available to him is insufficient to satisfy him that the applicant is unlikely to contravene any of those principles[10].

Subject to certain exceptions[11], a person who has made an application[12] is treated for the purposes of the statutory prohibition of unregistered holding of data[13] as if his application had been accepted and the particulars contained in it had been entered, or the alteration requested in it had been made, in the register on the date on which the application was made, until either he receives a notification of acceptance or refusal or the application is withdrawn[14]. Furthermore, if he receives a notification of refusal, he is so treated until the end of the period within which an appeal may be brought against the refusal and, if an appeal is brought, until its determination or withdrawal[15], unless by reason of special circumstances the registrar considers that a refusal notified by him to an applicant should take effect as a matter of urgency[16].

1 As to applications for registration etc see para 509 ante.
2 Data Protection Act 1984 s 7(1). Any notice or notification authorised or required to be served on or given to any person by the registrar may be served (1) on that person, if he is an individual, by delivering it to him, by sending it to him by post addressed to him at his usual or last-known place of residence or business, or by leaving it for him at that place; (2) on that body, if that person is a body corporate or unincorporate, by sending it by post to the proper officer of the body at its principal office, or by addressing it to the proper officer of the body and leaving it at that office: s 18(1). 'Principal office', in relation to a company registered under the Companies Act 1985, means its registered office; and 'proper officer', in relation to any body, means the secretary or other executive officer charged with the

conduct of its general affairs: Data Protection Act 1984 ss 18(2), 41. These provisions are without prejudice to any other lawful method of serving or giving a notice or notification: s 18(3). As to the registrar see para 506 ante.

3 Ie as soon as practicable and in any case before the end of the six month period mentioned in ibid s 7(1): s 7(5).

4 Ibid s 7(5).

5 Ibid s 7(1)(a), (b).

6 Ie the rights conferred by ibid s 13: see para 518 post.

7 Ibid s 7(4).

8 Ibid s 7(2)(a). Section 7(2)(a) is not, however, to be construed as precluding the acceptance by the registrar of particulars expressed in general terms in cases where that is appropriate, and he must accept particulars expressed in such terms in any case in which he is satisfied that more specific particulars would be likely to prejudice the purpose or purposes for which the data are to be held: s 7(3). For the meaning of 'data' and 'held' see para 502 ante.

9 Ibid s 7(2)(b). As to the data protection principles see paras 503–505 ante.

10 Ibid s 7(2)(c).

11 Ibid s 7(6) (see the text and notes 12–14 infra) does not apply to an application made by any person if in the previous two years (1) an application by that person has been refused; or (2) all or any of the particulars constituting an entry contained in the register in respect of that person have been removed in pursuance of a deregistration notice: s 7(8)(a), (b). In the case of any such application s 7(1) applies as if for the reference to six months there were substituted a reference to two months and, where the registrar gives a notification under s 7(5) in respect of any such application, s 7(6) applies to it as if for the reference to the date on which the application was made there were substituted a reference to the date on which that notification is received: s 7(8). For the purposes of head (1) supra, an application is not to be treated as having been refused so long as an appeal against the refusal can be brought, while such an appeal is pending or if such an appeal has been allowed: s 7(9). As to deregistration notices see para 516 post.

12 Ie in accordance with ibid s 6: see para 509 ante.

13 For the meaning of 'personal data' see para 502 ante.

14 Data Protection Act 1984 s 7(6)(a). For the purposes of s 7(6), an application is treated as made or withdrawn (1) if the application or notice of withdrawal is sent by registered post or the recorded delivery service, on the date on which it is received for dispatch by the Post Office; (2) in any other case, on the date on which it is received by the registrar: s 7(9)(a), (b).

15 Ibid s 7(6)(b).

16 Ibid s 7(7). In such a case the registrar may include a statement to that effect in the notification of the refusal; and in that event s 7(6)(b) has effect as if for the words from 'the period' onwards there were substituted the words 'the period of seven days beginning with the date on which that notification is received': s 7(7).

511. Duration and renewal of registration. No entry may be retained in the register[1] after the expiration of the initial period of registration except in pursuance of a renewal application made to the Data Protection Registrar[2]. The initial period of registration and the period for which an entry is to be retained in pursuance of a renewal application ('the renewal period') are to be a prescribed period[3] of not less than three years beginning with the date on which the entry in question was made or the date on which that entry would fall to be removed if the renewal application had not been made[4]. The person making an application for registration or a renewal application may specify in his application a period shorter than that prescribed as the initial period or renewal period, but the specified period must consist of one or more complete years[5].

Where the registrar notifies an applicant for registration that his application has been accepted[6], the notification must include a statement of the date when the initial period of registration will expire[7].

Every renewal application must be accompanied by the prescribed fee[8] and no such application may be made except in the period of six months ending with the expiration of the initial period of registration or, if there have been one or more previous renewal applications, the current renewal period[9]. Any renewal application may be sent by post, and the registrar must acknowledge its receipt and notify the applicant in writing of the date until which the entry in question will be retained in the register in pursuance of the application[10].

Without prejudice to these provisions, the registrar may at any time remove an entry from the register at the request of the person to whom it relates[11].

1 As to registration see para 508 ante.
2 Data Protection Act 1984 s 8(1). As to the registrar see para 506 ante.
3 Ie the period prescribed by regulations made by the Secretary of State: see ibid s 41. Regulations prescribing such a period must be made after consultation with the registrar and with the approval of the Treasury (s 40(7)) and must be laid before Parliament after being made (s 40(6)). As to the power to make regulations generally see para 501 note 2 ante. In exercise of the power so conferred, the Secretary of State has made the Data Protection Regulations 1985, SI 1985/1465 (amended by SI 1987/1304), prescribing a period of three years: see reg 3. As to the Secretary of State see para 501 note 2 ante.
4 Data Protection Act 1984 s 8(2).
5 Ibid s 8(3).
6 Ie under ibid s 7: see para 510 ante.
7 Ibid s 8(4).
8 As to the power to prescribe fees see para 509 note 9 ante; and for the prescribed fee see the Data Protection (Fees) Regulations 1991, SI 1991/1160, reg 2.
9 Data Protection Act 1984 s 8(5).
10 Ibid s 8(6). As to service of notices see para 510 note 2 ante.
11 Ibid s 8(7).

512. Inspection etc of registered particulars. The Data Protection Registrar must provide facilities for making the information contained in the entries in the register[1] available for inspection, in visible and legible form, by members of the public at all reasonable hours and free of charge[2]. On payment of such fee, if any, as may be prescribed[3], he must supply any member of the public with a duly certified copy in writing of the particulars contained in the entry made in the register in pursuance of any application for registration[4].

1 As to registration see para 508 ante; and as to the registrar see para 506 ante.
2 Data Protection Act 1984 s 9(1).
3 As to the power to prescribe fees see para 509 note 9 ante; and for the prescribed fee see the Data Protection (Fees) Regulations 1986, SI 1986/1899, reg 2.
4 Data Protection Act 1984 s 9(2).

(ii) Prohibition on Unregistered Holding or Unauthorised Disclosure of Data

513. Prohibition on unregistered holding etc of personal data. A person must not hold personal data[1] unless an entry in respect of that person as a data user[2], or as a data user who also carries on a computer bureau[3], is for the time being contained in the register[4].

A person in respect of whom such an entry is contained in the register must not:
(1) hold personal data of any description other than that specified in the entry;
(2) hold any such data, or use[5] any such data held by him, for any purpose other than the purpose or purposes described in the entry;
(3) obtain such data, or information to be contained in such data, to be held by him from any source which is not described in the entry;
(4) disclose[6] such data held by him to any person who is not described in the entry; or

(5) directly or indirectly transfer[7] such data held by him to any country or territory outside the United Kingdom[8] other than one named or described in the entry[9].

A person must not, in carrying on a computer bureau, provide services in respect of personal data unless an entry in respect of that person as a person carrying on such a bureau, or as a data user who also carries on such a bureau, is for the time being contained in the register[10].

A servant or agent of a person to whom heads (1) to (5) above apply is subject, as respects personal data held by that person, to the same restrictions on the use, disclosure or transfer of the data as those to which that person is subject under heads (2), (4) and (5) above and, as respects personal data to be held by that person, to the same restrictions as those to which he is subject under head (3) above[11].

Contravention of these provisions is a criminal offence[12].

1 For the meaning of 'personal data', 'data' and 'hold' see para 502 ante.
2 For the meaning of 'data user' see para 502 ante.
3 As to carrying on a computer bureau see para 502 ante.
4 Data Protection Act 1984 s 5(1). As to registration see para 508 et seq ante; and as to exemptions see para 529 et seq post.
5 'Using' data for these purposes involves more than merely accessing a computer and viewing the data on the screen: see *R v Brown* [1994] QB 547, 99 Cr App Rep 69, CA; affd [1996] 1 All ER 945, HL.
6 For the meaning of 'disclose' see para 504 note 8 ante. As to unauthorised disclosure see also para 514 post.
7 As to when data are transferred see para 504 note 8 ante.
8 For the meaning of 'United Kingdom' see para 501 note 9 ante.
9 Data Protection Act 1984 s 5(2). Head (5) in the text does not apply to the transfer of data which are already outside the United Kingdom: see s 39(6); and para 501 note 10 ante.
10 Ibid s 5(4).
11 Ibid s 5(3). Section 5(3) applies to any person who by virtue of s 38 (see para 501 ante) falls to be treated as a servant of a government department: see s 38(2)(a); and para 501 note 5 ante.
12 See ibid s 5(5) (as amended); and para 524 post. Section 5(5) (as so amended), so far as applying to s 5(3), applies to any person who by virtue of s 38 (see para 501 ante) falls to be treated as a servant of a government department: see s 38(2)(a); and para 501 note 5 ante.

514. Unauthorised disclosure etc and sale of personal data. A person is guilty of an offence[1] if he:

(1) procures the disclosure[2] to him of personal data[3] in contravention of the statutory prohibition[4] and knowing or believing that the disclosure constitutes such a contravention[5];

(2) sells personal data, or information extracted from the data, if he has procured the disclosure of the data to him in the circumstances set out in head (1) above[6];

(3) offers to sell[7] personal data, or information extracted from the data, if he has procured the disclosure of the data to him in such circumstances[8].

Personal data in respect of which services are provided by a person carrying on a computer bureau must not be disclosed by him without the prior authority of the person for whom those services are provided[9].

1 As to the penalties for such an offence see para 524 post.
2 For the meaning of 'disclose' see para 504 note 8 ante.
3 For the meaning of 'personal data' and 'data' see para 502 ante.
4 Ie in contravention of the Data Protection Act 1984 s 5(2) or (3): see para 513 ante. In determining for these purposes, and for the purposes of heads (2)–(3) in the text, whether a disclosure is in contravention of s 5(2) or (3), s 34(6)(d) (see para 536 post) must be disregarded: s 5(10) (s 5(6)–(11) added by the Criminal Justice and Public Order Act 1994 s 161(1)).
5 Data Protection Act 1984 s 5(6) (as added: see note 4 supra).
6 Ibid s 5(7), (10) (as added: see note 4 supra).

7 For these purposes, an advertisement indicating that personal data are or may be for sale is an offer to sell the data: ibid s 5(9) (as added: see note 4 supra).

8 Ibid s 5(8) (as added: see note 4 supra).

9 Ibid s 15(1). This restriction applies also to any servant or agent of a person carrying on a computer bureau: s 15(2). Contravention of the restriction is a criminal offence: see s 15(3); and para 524 post. Section 15(2) and, so far as applying thereto, s 15(3) apply to any person who by virtue of s 38 (see para 501 ante) falls to be treated as a servant of a government department: see s 38(2)(a); and para 501 note 5 ante.

(iii) Supervision

515. Enforcement notices. If the Data Protection Registrar is satisfied that a registered person[1] has contravened or is contravening any of the data protection principles[2], he may serve him with a notice ('an enforcement notice') requiring him to take, within the time specified in the notice[3], specified steps for complying with the principle or principles in question[4]. In deciding whether to serve such a notice the registrar must consider whether the contravention has caused or is likely to cause damage or distress to any person[5]. If by reason of special circumstances the registrar considers that the steps required by an enforcement notice should be taken as a matter of urgency, he may include a statement to that effect in the notice[6].

An enforcement notice must contain a statement of the principle or principles which the registrar is satisfied has or have been, or is or are being, contravened and his reasons for reaching that conclusion[7]. It must also contain particulars of the statutory rights[8] of appeal[9]. A notice in respect of a contravention of the fifth data protection principle[10] may require the data user[11] to rectify or erase the data and any other data held by him and containing an expression of opinion which appears to the registrar to be based on the inaccurate data[12]. Alternatively, in the case of data which accurately record information received or obtained from the data subject[13] or a third party[14], the notice may require the data user to take specified steps for securing compliance with the statutory provisions relating to inaccuracy[15] and, if the registrar thinks fit, for supplementing the data with such statement of the true facts relating to the matters dealt with by the data as the registrar may approve[16].

The registrar may not serve an enforcement notice requiring the person served with it to take steps for complying with the information and access requirements of the seventh principle[17] in respect of any data subject unless he is satisfied that the person served has contravened that subject's statutory rights[18] by failing to supply information to which the data subject is entitled and which has been duly[19] requested[20].

The registrar may cancel an enforcement notice by written notification to the person on whom it was served[21].

Any person who fails to comply with an enforcement notice is guilty of an offence[22].

1 As to registration see para 508 et seq ante; and as to the registrar see para 506 ante.

2 As to the data protection principles see paras 503–505 ante.

3 Subject to the Data Protection Act 1984 s 10(7) (see the text to note 6 infra) the time specified in an enforcement notice for taking the steps which it requires must not expire before the end of the period within which an appeal can be brought against the notice and, if such an appeal is brought, those steps need not be taken pending the determination or withdrawal of the appeal: s 10(6).

4 Ibid s 10(1). As to service of notices see para 510 note 2 ante.

5 Ibid s 10(2).

6 Ibid s 10(7). In that event, s 10(6) (see note 3 supra) does not apply but the notice may not require the steps to be taken before the end of the period of seven days beginning with the date on which the notice is served: s 10(7).

7 Ibid s 10(5)(a).

8 Ie the rights conferred by ibid s 13: see para 518 post.
9 Ibid s 10(5)(b).
10 See para 504 head (5) ante.
11 For the meaning of 'data user' and 'data' see para 502 ante.
12 Data Protection Act 1984 s 10(3)(a).
13 For the meaning of 'data subject' see para 502 ante.
14 Ie such data as are mentioned in the Data Protection Act 1984 s 22(2): see para 526 post.
15 Ie the requirements specified in ibid s 22(2): see para 526 post.
16 Ibid s 10(3)(b).
17 See para 504 head (7)(a) ante.
18 Ie has contravened the Data Protection Act 1984 s 21: see para 525 post.
19 Ie in accordance with ibid s 21: see para 525 post.
20 Ibid s 10(4).
21 Ibid s 10(8).
22 See ibid s 10(9); and para 524 post.

516. Deregistration notices. If the Data Protection Registrar is satisfied that a registered person[1] has contravened or is contravening any of the data protection principles[2], he may:

(1) serve him with a notice ('a deregistration notice') stating that he proposes, at the expiration of a specified period[3], to remove from the register all or any of the particulars constituting the entry or any of the entries contained in the register in respect of that person[4]; and

(2) remove those particulars from the register at the expiration of that period[5].

In deciding whether to serve a deregistration notice, the registrar must consider whether the contravention has caused or is likely to cause any person damage or distress, and he must not serve such a notice unless he is satisfied that compliance with the principle or principles in question cannot be adequately secured by the service of an enforcement notice[6]. If by reason of special circumstances he considers that any particulars should be removed from the register as a matter of urgency, he may include a statement to that effect in the deregistration notice[7].

A deregistration notice must contain a statement of the principle or principles which the registrar is satisfied has or have been, or is or are being, contravened and his reasons for reaching that conclusion and for deciding that compliance cannot be adequately secured by the service of an enforcement notice[8]. It must also contain particulars of the statutory rights[9] of appeal[10].

The registrar may cancel a deregistration notice by written notification to the person on whom it was served[11].

1 As to registration see para 508 et seq ante; and as to the registrar see para 506 ante.
2 As to the data protection principles see paras 503–505 ante.
3 Subject to the Data Protection Act 1984 s 11(5) (see the text to note 7 infra), the period specified in a deregistration notice may not expire before the end of the period within which an appeal can be brought against the notice and, if such an appeal is brought, the particulars must not be removed pending the determination or withdrawal of the appeal: s 11(4). For these purposes, references to removing any particulars include references to restricting any description which forms part of any particulars: s 11(7).
4 Ibid s 11(1)(a). As to service of notices see para 510 note 2 ante.
5 Ibid s 11(1)(b).
6 Ibid s 11(2). As to enforcement notices see para 515 ante.
7 Ibid s 11(5). In that event s 11(4) (see note 3 supra) does not apply but the particulars may not be removed before the end of the period of seven days beginning with the date on which the notice is served: s 11(5).
8 Ibid s 11(3)(a).

9 Ie the rights conferred by ibid s 13: see para 518 post.
10 Ibid s 11(3)(b).
11 Ibid s 11(6).

517. Transfer prohibition notices. If it appears to the Data Protection Registrar that a person registered[1] as a data user[2] or as a data user who also carries on a computer bureau[3], or a person treated[4] as so registered, proposes to transfer[5] personal data held[6] by him to a place outside the United Kingdom[7], and the registrar is satisfied as to the specified matters[8], he may serve that person with a notice ('a transfer prohibition notice') prohibiting him from transferring the data either absolutely or until he has taken specified steps for protecting the interests of the data subjects[9] in question[10]. In deciding whether to serve a transfer prohibition notice, the registrar must consider whether the notice is required for preventing damage or distress to any person and he must have regard to the general desirability of facilitating the free transfer of data between the United Kingdom and other states or territories[11].

A transfer prohibition notice must specify the time[12] when it is to take effect and contain a statement of the principle or principles which the registrar is satisfied is or are likely to be contravened and his reasons for reaching that conclusion[13]. It must also contain particulars of the statutory rights[14] of appeal[15]. If by reason of special circumstances the registrar considers that the prohibition should take effect as a matter of urgency, he may include a statement to that effect in the transfer prohibition notice[16].

No transfer prohibition notice may prohibit the transfer of any data where the transfer of the information constituting the data is required or authorised by or under any enactment, whenever passed, or required by any convention or other instrument imposing an international obligation on the United Kingdom[17].

The registrar may cancel a transfer prohibition notice by written notification to the person on whom it was served[18].

Any person who contravenes a transfer prohibition notice is guilty of an offence[19].

1 As to registration see para 508 et seq ante; and as to the registrar see para 506 ante.
2 For the meaning of 'data user' and 'data' see para 502 ante.
3 As to carrying on a computer bureau see para 502 ante.
4 Ie by virtue of the Data Protection Act 1984 s 7(6): see para 510 ante.
5 As to when data are transferred see para 504 note 8 ante.
6 For the meaning of 'personal data' and 'held' see para 502 ante.
7 For the meaning of 'United Kingdom' see para 501 note 9 ante.
8 Ie the matters mentioned in the Data Protection Act 1984 s 12(2), (3): s 12(1). Where the place to which the data are to be transferred is not in a state bound by the European Convention, the registrar must be satisfied that the transfer is likely to contravene, or lead to a contravention of, any of the data protection principles: Data Protection Act 1984 s 12(2). For these purposes, a place is treated as in a state bound by the European Convention if it is in any territory in respect of which the state is bound: Data Protection Act 1984 s 12(11). As to the European Convention see para 501 note 2 ante; and as to the data protection principles see paras 503–505 ante. References in the Data Protection Act 1984 s 12 to a contravention of the data protection principles include references to anything that would constitute such a contravention if it occurred in relation to the data when held in the United Kingdom: see s 39(6); and para 501 note 10 ante.

   Where the place to which the data are to be transferred is in a state bound by that convention, the registrar must be satisfied either that (1) the person in question intends to give instructions for their further transfer to a place which is not in such a state and that the further transfer is likely to contravene, or lead to a contravention of, any of the data protection principles; or (2) in the case of data to which an order under the Data Protection Act 1984 s 2(3) (see para 503 ante) applies, that the transfer is likely to contravene, or lead to a contravention of, any of the data protection principles as they have effect in relation to such data: s 12(3).
9 For the meaning of 'data subject' see para 502 ante.

10 Data Protection Act 1984 s 12(1). Section 12(1) does not apply to the transfer of data which are already outside the United Kingdom: see s 39(6); and para 501 note 10 ante. As to service of notices see para 510 note 2 ante.
11 Ibid s 12(4).
12 Subject to ibid s 12(7) (see the text and note 16 infra), the time so specified must not be before the end of the period within which an appeal can be brought against the notice and, if such an appeal is brought, the notice does not take effect pending the determination or withdrawal of the appeal: s 12(6).
13 Ibid s 12(5)(a).
14 Ie the rights conferred by ibid s 13: see para 518 post.
15 Ibid s 12(5)(b).
16 Ibid s 12(7). In that event s 12(6) (see note 12 supra) does not apply but the notice does not take effect before the end of the period of seven days beginning with the date on which it is served: s 12(7).
17 Ibid ss 12(9), 41.
18 Ibid s 12(8).
19 See ibid s 12(10); and para 524 post.

(iv) Appeals

518. Rights of appeal and preliminary matters. A person may appeal to the Data Protection Tribunal against:

(1) any refusal by the Data Protection Registrar of an application by that person for registration or for the alteration of registered particulars[1];

(2) any enforcement notice[2], deregistration notice[3] or transfer prohibition notice[4] with which that person has been served[5].

There is also a right of appeal against the registrar's decision to include:

(a) a statement that a refusal of an application should take effect as a matter of urgency[6] in a notification that an application has been refused[7];

(b) a statement that the notice should take effect as a matter of urgency[8] in an enforcement notice, deregistration notice or transfer prohibition notice[9],

and in each case that right is exercisable whether or not the applicant or the person served with the notice appeals against the refusal of the application or against the notice in question[10].

An appeal is brought by notice of appeal served on the tribunal within 28 days[11] of the date on which the notice or notification relating to the disputed decision was served on or given to the appellant[12]. A proper officer[13] must send an acknowledgment of service to the appellant and a copy of the notice of appeal to the registrar[14]. Where the appeal is under head (1) or head (2) above, the registrar must send to the tribunal a copy of the notification or notice relating to the disputed decision within such time after receiving the notice of appeal as the tribunal may allow[15]; and where the appeal is under head (a) or head (b) above he must, if required by the tribunal, send it a copy of the notification or notice relating to the disputed decision and a statement of his reasons for making that decision, within such time as the tribunal may allow[16].

The tribunal has power to order either party to furnish particulars[17], power to order discovery[18] and power to require entry on premises for the testing of data equipment and material[19].

The Secretary of State may make rules for regulating the exercise of these rights of appeal and the practice and procedure of the tribunal[20].

The appellant may withdraw his appeal at any time by sending to the tribunal a notice of withdrawal signed by him or on his behalf[21] but where an appeal is so withdrawn, a fresh appeal may not be brought in relation to the same disputed decision except with the leave of the tribunal[22].

1 Data Protection Act 1984 s 13(1)(a). As to applications for registration or for the alteration of registered particulars see para 509 ante; and as to the registrar and the tribunal see paras 506–507 ante.
2 As to enforcement notices see para 515 ante.
3 As to deregistration notices see para 516 ante.
4 As to transfer prohibition notices see para 517 ante.
5 Data Protection Act 1984 s 13(1)(b).
6 Ie a statement in accordance with ibid s 7(7): see para 510 ante.
7 Ibid s 13(2).
8 Ie a statement in accordance with ibid s 10(7) (see para 515 ante), s 11(5) (see para 516 ante) or s 12(7) (see para 517 ante): s 13(3).
9 Ibid s 13(3).
10 See ibid s 13(2), (3). Such an appeal may be determined without a hearing (see the Data Protection Tribunal Rules 1985, SI 1985/1568, r 10(1)(b)) and may be expedited (see r 21). The tribunal's jurisdiction in respect of such an appeal may be exercised ex parte by the chairman or a deputy chairman sitting alone: Data Protection Act 1984 s 13(4), Sch 3 para 3. See further the Data Protection Tribunal Rules 1985 r 21.
11 The tribunal may accept later service if it is of the opinion that, by reason of special circumstances, it is just and right to do so: ibid r 4(2). If sent by post in a registered letter or by the recorded delivery service and addressed in accordance with r 28, a notice of appeal is treated as having been served on the date on which it is received for dispatch by the Post Office: r 4(3).
12 Ibid rr 3(1), 4(1). As to the contents of the notice see r 3(2).
13 'Proper officer' means an officer or servant of the tribunal appointed by the chairman to perform the duties of a proper officer: ibid r 2.
14 Ibid r 5.
15 Ibid r 6(1).
16 Ibid r 6(2).
17 See ibid r 7.
18 See ibid r 8.
19 See ibid r 9. The chairman may act for the tribunal as regards such preliminary or incidental matters; see r 26. 'Data equipment' means equipment for the automatic processing of data or for recording information so that it can be automatically processed; and 'data material' means any document or other material used in connection with data equipment: Data Protection Act 1984 s 41.
20 Ibid s 13(4), Sch 3 para 4(1). As to the matters for which the rules may make provision see Sch 3 para 4(2). A statutory instrument containing such rules is subject to annulment in pursuance of a resolution of either House of Parliament: s 40(5). As to the power to make rules generally see para 501 note 2 ante. In exercise of the power so conferred, the Secretary of State has made the Data Protection Tribunal Rules 1985 which came into operation on 11 December 1985: r 1. As to the Secretary of State see para 501 note 2 ante.
21 Ibid r 25(1). If sent by post in accordance with r 28, the notice of withdrawal has effect on the date on which it is received for dispatch by the Post Office: r 25(2).
22 Ibid r 25(3).

519. Hearing and determination of the appeal. As soon as practicable after notice of appeal has been given[1], the Data Protection Tribunal must appoint a time and place for a hearing[2], having regard, so far as practicable, to the convenience of the appellant in travelling to it[3]. A proper officer[4] must send each party a notice of the time and place of any hearing[5] and a notice to the effect that if he fails, without sufficient reason, to appear at the hearing, the tribunal may either dismiss the appeal if he is the appellant or, in any case, hear and determine the appeal in his absence and make such order as to costs as the tribunal thinks fit[6].

For the purpose of hearing and determining appeals or any matter preliminary or incidental to an appeal, the tribunal must sit at such times and in such places as the chairman or a deputy chairman may direct, and may sit in two or more divisions[7]. It is duly constituted for an appeal[8] if it consists of the chairman or a deputy chairman, presiding, and an equal number of persons appointed to represent the interests of data users[9] and persons appointed to represent the interests of data subjects[10]. The determination of any question before the tribunal is according to the opinion of the majority of the members hearing the appeal[11].

The hearing must be in public unless, having regard to the desirability of safeguarding the privacy of data subjects, the tribunal directs that the hearing or any part of the hearing should take place in private[12].

A party may conduct his case himself or may appear and be represented by any person whom he may appoint for the purpose[13]. The tribunal has power to summon witnesses[14] and expert evidence may be given[15]. Each party must be given an opportunity to address the tribunal, amplify previously furnished written statements, give evidence, call witnesses, put questions to any person giving evidence and make representations on the evidence and on the subject matter of the appeal[16]. Oral evidence may be given on oath or affirmation and the tribunal may receive in evidence any document or information notwithstanding that it would be inadmissible in a court of law[17].

In any proceedings before the tribunal it is for the Data Protection Registrar to satisfy the tribunal that the disputed decision should be upheld[18].

If on an appeal against the refusal of an application or against a notice[19] the tribunal considers that the refusal or notice is not in accordance with the law, or that, to the extent that the refusal or notice involved an exercise of discretion by the registrar, he ought to have exercised his discretion differently, the tribunal must allow the appeal or substitute such other decision or notice as could have been made or served by the registrar, and in any other case it must dismiss the appeal[20]. On an appeal against the registrar's decision to include a statement that a refusal of an application should take effect as a matter of urgency in a notification that an application has been refused[21], the tribunal may direct that the notification of the refusal is to be treated as if it did not contain any such statement[22]. On an appeal against his decision to include a statement that the notice should take effect as a matter of urgency in an enforcement notice, deregistration notice or transfer prohibition notice[23], the tribunal may direct that the notice in question should have effect as if it did not contain any such statement or that the inclusion of the statement should not have effect in relation to any part of the notice and may make such modifications in the notice as may be required for giving effect to the direction[24].

Any irregularity resulting from failure to comply with the rules of procedure[25] before the tribunal has reached its decision does not by itself render the proceedings void, but the tribunal may, and must if it considers that any person may have been prejudiced, take such steps as it thinks fit before reaching its decision to cure the irregularity, whether by amendment of any document, the giving of any notice or otherwise[26].

At the conclusion of a hearing the decision of the tribunal may be announced by the chairman, but must in any event be recorded in a document, signed by him and dated when so signed, which must contain all findings of fact by the tribunal and the reasons for the decision[27]. The tribunal has power to make an order awarding costs against either party[28].

The tribunal may make arrangements for the publication of its decisions but in doing so it must have regard to the desirability of safeguarding the privacy of data subjects, and for that purpose the tribunal may make any necessary amendments to the text of a decision to conceal the identity of a data subject[29].

If any person is guilty of any act or omission in relation to proceedings before the tribunal which, if those proceedings were proceedings before a court having power to commit for contempt, would constitute contempt of court, the tribunal may certify the offence to the High Court[30]. The court may inquire into the matter and, after hearing any witness who may be produced against or on behalf of the person charged with the offence, and after hearing any statement that may be offered in defence, deal with him in any manner in which it could deal with him if he had committed the like offence in relation to the court[31].

1　As to notice of appeal see para 518 ante.
2　Data Protection Tribunal Rules 1985, SI 1985/1568, r 10(1). An appeal may be determined without a hearing where (1) neither party wishes one to be held; (2) the appeal is under the Data Protection Act 1984 s 13(2) or (3) (see para 518 ante); or (3) it appears to the tribunal that the issues raised on the appeal have been determined on a previous appeal brought by the appellant on the basis of facts which did not materially differ from those to which the appeal relates and the tribunal has given the parties an opportunity of making representations to the effect that the appeal ought not to be determined without a hearing: Data Protection Tribunal Rules 1985 r 10(1) proviso. As to the tribunal see para 507 ante.
3　Ibid r 10(2). The hearings of two or more appeals may be combined where some common question of law or fact arises in both or all of them, or it appears desirable so to proceed for some other reason: see r 22. The time may be postponed, the place altered, or the hearing adjourned: see r 23.
4　For the meaning of 'proper officer' see para 518 note 13 ante.
5　The time must not be earlier than 14 days after the date on which the notice is sent, unless the parties otherwise agree: Data Protection Tribunal Rules 1985 r 11(a).
6　See ibid rr 11, 14.
7　Data Protection Act 1984 s 13(4), Sch 3 para 1. As to the chairman and deputy chairmen see para 507 ante.
8　Ie an appeal under ibid s 13(1): see para 518 ante.
9　Ie persons appointed under ibid s 3(5)(a): see para 507 ante. For the meaning of 'data user' and 'data' see para 502 ante.
10　Ibid Sch 3 para 2(1). The members who are to constitute the tribunal must be nominated by the chairman or, if he is for any reason unable to act, by a deputy chairman: Sch 3 para 2(2). Persons to represent the interests of data subjects are appointed under s 3(5)(b): see para 507 ante. For the meaning of 'data subject' see para 502 ante.
11　Ibid Sch 2 para 2(3).
12　Data Protection Tribunal Rules 1985 r 12(1). Notwithstanding that a hearing is in private, the chairman, any deputy chairman or any member of the tribunal may attend it in his capacity as such, as may any member of the Council on Tribunals or the Scottish Committee of the Council on Tribunals in his capacity as such, and any other person with the leave of the tribunal or the consent of the parties present: r 12(2). As to the Council on Tribunals see ADMINISTRATIVE LAW vol 1(1) (Reissue) para 50.
13　Ibid r 13.
14　See ibid r 15.
15　See ibid r 16. Not more than one expert witness on either side may be heard unless otherwise ordered by the tribunal: r 16(1).
16　See ibid r 17. Subject to this, the tribunal must conduct the proceedings in such manner as it considers appropriate in the circumstances for ascertaining the matters in dispute and determining the appeal and it must, so far as appropriate, seek to avoid formality in its proceedings: r 17.
17　See ibid r 18(1), (3). No person may be compelled to give any evidence or produce any document which he could not be compelled to give or produce on the trial of an action in that part of the United Kingdom where the hearing takes place: r 18(2). For the meaning of 'United Kingdom' see para 501 note 9 ante.
18　Ibid r 19.
19　Ie an appeal under the Data Protection Act 1984 s 13(1): see para 518 ante.
20　Ibid s 14(1). The tribunal may review any determination of fact on which the refusal or notice in question was based: s 14(2).
21　Ie an appeal under ibid s 13(2): see para 518 ante.
22　Ibid s 14(3).
23　Ie an appeal under ibid s 13(3): see para 518 ante.
24　Ibid s 14(4).
25　Ie the Data Protection Tribunal Rules 1985: see para 518 ante; the text and notes 1–18 supra; and para 520 post.
26　Ibid r 27(1).
27　Ibid r 20(1). Clerical mistakes in the document or errors arising in it from an accidental slip or omission may at any time be corrected by the chairman by certificate under his hand: r 27(2). A proper officer

must send a copy of the document to each party and, except where a decision has been announced at the conclusion of the hearing, the decision is treated as having been made on the date on which the copy is sent to the appellant: r 20(2), (3).

28 See ibid r 24.
29 Ibid r 30.
30 Data Protection Act 1984 Sch 3 para 5(1).
31 Ibid Sch 3 para 5(2).

520. Application for review of tribunal's decision. The Data Protection Tribunal has power to review and to revoke or vary its decision, by certificate under the chairman's hand, on the grounds that new evidence has become available since the making of the decision, provided that its existence could not have been reasonably known of or foreseen, or that the interests of justice require such a review[1]. An application for such a review must be made to the chairman at any time within 14 days from when the decision was made and must be in writing stating the grounds in full[2]. The chairman may refuse the application if in his opinion it has no reasonable prospect of success[3]. If he does not so refuse it, it must be determined by the tribunal constituted as far as practicable as for the appeal, and if the application is granted the tribunal must proceed to a review of the decision[4]. After having reviewed the decision, the tribunal may confirm, vary or revoke it, and if the tribunal revokes the decision, it must proceed to determine the appeal again[5].

1 Data Protection Tribunal Rules 1985, SI 1985/1568, r 29(1). As to the tribunal see para 507 ante.
2 Ibid r 29(2).
3 Ibid r 29(3).
4 Ibid r 29(4). As to the constitution of the tribunal for the appeal see para 519 ante.
5 Ibid r 29(4). As to the procedure on the appeal see para 519 ante.

521. Right of appeal to the High Court. Any party to an appeal to the Data Protection Tribunal[1] may appeal from the decision of the tribunal on a point of law to the High Court if the address[2] of the person who was the appellant before the tribunal is in England and Wales[3].

1 As to the right of appeal see para 518 ante; as to the hearing and determination of the appeal see para 519 ante; and as to the tribunal see para 507 ante.
2 This reference to the address of the appellant before the tribunal is a reference to his address as included or proposed for inclusion in the register: Data Protection Act 1984 s 14(6). As to registration see para 508 et seq ante.
3 Ibid s 14(5)(a). As to the procedure on appeals to the High Court see generally PRACTICE AND PROCEDURE. As to the appropriate court where the appellant's address is in Scotland or Northern Ireland see s 14(5)(b), (c).

(v) Powers of Entry and Inspection

522. Issue and execution of warrants. If a circuit judge is satisfied by information on oath supplied by the Data Protection Registrar[1] that there are reasonable grounds for suspecting that an offence[2] in relation to data protection has been or is being committed, or that any of the data protection principles[3] have been or are being contravened by a registered person[4] and that evidence of the commission of the offence or of the contravention is to be found on any premises[5] specified in the information, he may grant a warrant authorising the registrar or any of his officers or servants at any time within seven days of the date of the warrant to enter those premises, to search them, to inspect, examine, operate and test any data equipment[6] found there and to inspect and seize any documents or other material found there which may be such evidence[7]. Unless the case is one of urgency or the judge is satisfied that compliance with the following provisions would defeat the object of the entry, he may not, however, issue such a warrant unless he is satisfied that:

(1) the registrar has given seven days' notice in writing to the occupier of the premises in question demanding access to them;

(2) access was demanded at a reasonable hour and was unreasonably refused; and

(3) the occupier has, after the refusal, been notified by the registrar of the application for the warrant and has had an opportunity of being heard by the judge on the question whether or not it should be issued[8].

A warrant so issued must be executed at a reasonable hour unless it appears to the person executing it that there are grounds for suspecting that the evidence in question would not be found if it were so executed[9]. The person executing it may use such reasonable force as may be necessary[10]. If the person who occupies the premises is present when the warrant is executed, he must be shown the warrant and supplied with a copy of it; and if he is not present a copy must be left in a prominent place on the premises[11].

A person seizing anything in pursuance of such a warrant must give a receipt if asked to do so[12]. Anything so seized may be retained for so long as is necessary in all the circumstances, but the person in occupation of the premises in question must be given a copy of anything that is seized if he so requests and the person executing the warrant considers that it can be done without undue delay[13].

A warrant so issued must be returned to the court from which it was issued either after being executed or if it is not executed within the time authorised for its execution; and the person by whom it is executed must make an indorsement on it stating what powers have been exercised by him under the warrant[14].

It is an offence intentionally to obstruct a person executing such a warrant or to refuse him reasonable assistance[15].

1 As to the registrar see para 506 ante.
2 Ie an offence under the Data Protection Act 1984: see para 524 post.
3 As to the data protection principles see paras 503–505 ante.
4 As to registration see para 508 et seq ante.
5 For these purposes, 'premises' includes any vessel, vehicle, aircraft or hovercraft, and references to the occupier of any premises include references to the person in charge of any vessel, vehicle, aircraft or hovercraft: Data Protection Act 1984 s 16, Sch 4 para 13.
6 For the meaning of 'data equipment' see para 518 note 19 ante.
7 Data Protection Act 1984 Sch 4 para 1. As to the application of these provisions to Scotland and Northern Ireland see Sch 4 paras 14, 15.
8 Ibid Sch 4 para 2. As to service of notices see para 510 note 2 ante.
9 Ibid Sch 4 para 5.
10 Ibid Sch 4 para 4.
11 Ibid Sch 4 para 6. A judge who issues such a warrant must also issue two copies of it and certify them clearly as copies: Sch 4 para 3.
12 Ibid Sch 4 para 7(1). As to matters exempt from seizure see para 523 post.
13 Ibid Sch 4 para 7(2).
14 Ibid Sch 4 para 11.
15 See ibid Sch 4 para 12; and para 524 post.

523. Matters exempt from inspection and seizure. The powers of inspection and seizure conferred by a warrant[1] are not exercisable in respect of:

(1) personal data[2] which are exempt from Part II[3] of the Data Protection Act 1984[4];
(2) any communication between a professional legal adviser and his client[5] in connection with the giving of legal advice to the client with respect to his obligations, liabilities and rights under that Act, any copy or other record of any such communication or any document or article enclosed with or referred to in any such communication if made in connection with the giving of any such advice[6];
(3) any communication between a professional legal adviser and his client, or between such an adviser or his client and any other person, made in connection with or in contemplation of proceedings under or arising out of the Data Protection Act 1984[7] and for the purposes of such proceedings, any copy or other record of any such communication or any document or article enclosed with or referred to in any such communication if made in connection with or in contemplation of and for the purposes of such proceedings[8].

Heads (2) and (3) above do not, however, apply to anything in the possession of any person other than the professional legal adviser or his client or to anything held with the intention of furthering a criminal purpose[9].

If the person in occupation of any premises in respect of which a warrant is issued[10] objects to the inspection or seizure under the warrant of any material on the grounds that it consists partly of matters in respect of which those powers are not exercisable, he must, if the person executing the warrant so requests, furnish that person with a copy of so much of the material as is not exempt from those powers[11].

1 Ie a warrant issued under the Data Protection Act 1984 s 16, Sch 4: see para 522 ante.
2 For the meaning of 'personal data' and 'data' see para 502 ante.
3 Ie exempt from the Data Protection Act 1984 Pt II (ss 4–20) (as amended): see paras 508 et seq ante, 524 post. As to exempt personal data see para 529 et seq post.
4 Ibid Sch 4 para 8.
5 For these purposes, references to the client of a professional legal adviser include references to any person representing such a client: ibid Sch 4 para 9(4).
6 Ibid Sch 4 para 9(1)(a), (2).
7 Ie including proceedings before the Data Protection Tribunal: ibid Sch 4 para 9(1)(b). As to proceedings before the tribunal see paras 518–520 ante; and as to the tribunal see para 507 ante.
8 Ibid Sch 4 para 9(1)(b), (2).
9 Ibid Sch 4 para 9(3).
10 Ie under ibid Sch 4: see para 522 ante.
11 Ibid Sch 4 para 10.

(vi) Offences

524. Offences, prosecutions and penalties. Under the Data Protection Act 1984, it is an offence for a person:
(1) to contravene the statutory prohibition[1] on the unregistered holding of personal data[2];
(2) knowingly or recklessly to contravene the prohibitions[3] on the holding, use, obtaining or disclosure of certain personal data by a registered person or a servant or agent of such a person[4];
(3) knowingly or recklessly to provide services in respect of personal data while carrying on a computer bureau[5] unless an entry in respect of the person carrying on the bureau[6] is for the time being contained in the register[7];

(4) to procure the disclosure of personal data while knowing or having reason to believe that the disclosure constitutes a contravention of the prohibition mentioned in head (2) above[8];

(5) to sell personal data whose disclosure has been procured as mentioned in head (4) above[9];

(6) to offer to sell personal data whose disclosure has been or is subsequently procured as mentioned in head (4) above[10];

(7) knowingly or recklessly to contravene the prohibition[11] on the unauthorised disclosure of personal data by computer bureaux or by any servant or agent of person carrying on a computer bureau[12];

(8) to fail to comply with the statutory requirement[13] to make an application for the alteration of particulars in the register[14] whenever necessary for ensuring that the entry or entries relating to the person in question contain his current address[15];

(9) knowingly or recklessly to furnish the Data Protection Registrar, in connection with an application for registration or for the alteration of registered particulars, with information which is false or misleading in a material respect[16];

(10) to fail to comply with an enforcement notice[17] (but it is a defence for a person charged with this offence to prove that he exercised all due diligence to comply with the notice in question[18]);

(11) to contravene a transfer prohibition notice[19] (but it is a defence for a person charged with this offence to prove that he exercised all due diligence to avoid contravention of the notice in question[20]);

(12) intentionally to obstruct a person in the execution of a warrant issued under the statutory powers of entry and inspection[21] or fail without reasonable excuse to give any person executing such a warrant such assistance as he may reasonably require for the execution of the warrant[22].

No proceedings for such an offence may be instituted in England and Wales except by the registrar or by or with the consent of the Director of Public Prosecutions[23].

A person guilty of an offence under head (8), head (9) or head (12) above is liable on summary conviction to a fine not exceeding level 5 on the standard scale[24]. A person guilty of any other offence under the Data Protection Act 1984 is liable on conviction on indictment to a fine or on summary conviction to a fine not exceeding the statutory maximum[25]. Where any such offence has been committed by a body corporate and is proved to have been committed with the consent or connivance of, or to be attributable to any neglect on the part of, any director, manager, secretary or similar officer of the body corporate or any person who was purporting to act in any such capacity, he as well as the body corporate is guilty of that offence and is liable to be proceeded against and punished accordingly[26].

The court by which a person is convicted of an offence under any of heads (1) to (7) or head (10) or head (11) above may order any data material[27] appearing to the court to be connected with the commission of the offence to be forfeited, destroyed or erased[28].

Information disclosed by any person in compliance with certain notices, requests or orders is not admissible against him in proceedings for an offence under the 1984 Act[29]

1 Ie the Data Protection Act 1984 s 5(1): see para 513 ante.
2 Ibid s 5(5) (amended by the Criminal Justice and Public Order Act 1994 s 162(2)(a)). For the meaning of 'personal data' see para 502 ante.
3 Ie the Data Protection Act 1984 s 5(2), (3): see para 513 ante.

4 Ibid s 5(5) (as amended: see note 2 supra). Section 5(5) (as so amended), so far as applying to s 5(3), applies to any person who by virtue of s 38 (see para 501 ante) falls to be treated as a servant of a government department: see s 38(2)(a); and para 501 note 5 ante. For the purposes of s 5(5) (as so amended), 'recklessness' requires consideration of whether there was foresight of the consequences identified in s 5 (as amended): see *Data Protection Registrar v Amnesty International (British Section)* (1994) Times, 23 November.

5 As to carrying on a computer bureau see para 502 ante.

6 Ie whether as a person carrying on such a bureau or as a data user who also carries on such a bureau: Data Protection Act 1984 s 5(4). For the meaning of 'data user' see para 502 ante.

7 Ibid s 5(4), (5) (as amended: see note 2 supra). As to registration see para 508 et seq ante.

8 See ibid s 5(6) (as added); and para 514 ante.

9 See ibid s 5(7) (as added); and para 514 ante.

10 See ibid s 5(8) (as added); and para 514 ante.

11 Ie ibid s 15(1), (2): see para 514 ante.

12 Ibid s 15(3). Section 15(3), so far as applying to s 15(2), applies to any person who by virtue of s 38 (see para 501 ante) falls to be treated as a servant of a government department: see s 38(2)(a); and para 501 note 5 ante.

13 Ie ibid s 6(5): see para 509 ante.

14 Ie under ibid s 6(3): see para 509 ante.

15 Ibid s 6(5).

16 Ibid s 6(6). Section 6(6) applies to a person in the public service of the Crown as it applies to any other person: see s 38(2)(b); and para 501 note 5 ante. As to the registrar see para 506 ante.

17 As to enforcement notices see para 515 ante.

18 Data Protection Act 1984 s 10(9).

19 As to transfer prohibition notices see para 517 ante.

20 Data Protection Act 1984 s 12(10).

21 Ie under ibid s 16, Sch 4: see paras 522–523 ante.

22 Ibid Sch 4 para 12. Schedule 4 para 12 applies to a person in the public service of the Crown as it applies to any other person: see s 38(2)(b); and para 501 note 5 ante.

23 Ibid s 19(1)(a). As to prosecutions in Northern Ireland see s 19(1)(b).

24 Ibid s 19(3). The 'standard scale' means the standard scale of maximum fines for summary offences as set out in the Criminal Justice Act 1982 s 37(2) (as substituted): Interpretation Act 1978 s 5, Sch 1 (amended by the Criminal Justice Act 1988 s 170(1), Sch 15 para 58(a)). See CRIMINAL LAW vol 11(2) (Reissue) para 808; and MAGISTRATES. At the date at which this volume states the law, the standard scale is as follows: level 1, £200; level 2, £500; level 3, £1,000; level 4, £2,500; level 5, £5,000: Criminal Justice Act 1982 s 37(2) (substituted by the Criminal Justice Act 1991 s 17(1)). As to the determination of the amount of the fine actually imposed, as distinct from the level on the standard scale which it may not exceed, see the Criminal Justice Act 1991 s 18 (substituted by the Criminal Justice Act 1993 s 65); and MAGISTRATES.

25 Data Protection Act 1984 s 19(2). The 'statutory maximum' is the prescribed sum within the meaning of the Magistrates' Courts Act 1980 s 32 (as amended) and, as from 1 October 1992, is £5,000: s 32(9) (amended by the Criminal Justice Act 1991 s 17(2)).

26 Data Protection Act 1984 s 20(1). Where the affairs of a body corporate are managed by its members, s 20(1) applies in relation to the acts and defaults of a member in connection with his functions of management as if he were a director of the body corporate: s 20(2).

27 For the meaning of 'data material' see para 518 note 19 ante.

28 Data Protection Act 1984 s 19(4). The court may not, however, make such an order in relation to any material where a person, other than the offender, claiming to be the owner or otherwise interested in it applies to be heard by the court unless an opportunity is given to him to show cause why the order should not be made: s 19(5).

29 See ibid s 34(9); and para 536 post.

(5) RIGHTS OF DATA SUBJECTS

525. Rights of access to personal data. An individual is entitled (1) to be informed by any data user[1] whether the data held by him include personal data[2] of which that individual is the data subject[3]; and (2) to be supplied by any data user with a copy of the information constituting any such personal data held by him[4]. Where any of that

information is expressed in terms which are not intelligible without explanation, the
information must be accompanied by an explanation of those terms[5]. A data user is not
obliged to supply any such information except in response to a request in writing and
on payment of such fee, not exceeding the prescribed maximum[6], as he may require[7].
In the case of a data user having separate entries in the register in respect of data held for
different purposes, a separate request must be made and a separate fee paid in respect of
the data to which each entry relates[8].

A data user is not obliged to comply with such a request:

(a) unless he is supplied with such information as he may reasonably require in
order to satisfy himself as to the identity of the person making the request and to
locate the information which he seeks[9]; and

(b) if he cannot comply with the request without disclosing[10] information relating
to another individual[11] who can be identified from that information, unless he is
satisfied that the other individual has consented to the disclosure of the information to the person making the request[12].

A data user must comply with a request under these provisions within 40 days of
receiving the request or, if later, receiving the information referred to in head (a) above
and, where it is required, the consent referred to in head (b) above[13]. The information
to be supplied pursuant to such a request must be supplied by reference to the data in
question at the time the request is received except that it may take account of any
amendment or deletion made between that time and the time when the information is
supplied, if that amendment or deletion would have been made regardless of the
receipt of the request[14]. If the High Court or a county court is satisfied on the
application of any person who has made such a request that the data user in question has
failed to comply with the request in contravention of these provisions, the court may
order him to comply with the request[15].

Where an individual is, or would but for any exemption[16] be, entitled under these
provisions to be supplied with information constituting personal data of which he is the
subject, no obligation arises under the Access to Personal Files Act 1987 to give him
access to that information[17].

1 For the meaning of 'data user' and 'data' see para 502 ante.
2 For the meaning of 'personal data' and 'held' see para 502 ante.
3 Data Protection Act 1984 s 21(1)(a). For the meaning of 'data subject' see para 502 ante.
4 Ibid s 21(1)(b).
5 Ibid s 21(1). As to exemptions from s 21 see para 529 et seq post.
    In the case of personal data consisting of marks or other information held by a data user for the
    purpose of determining the results of an academic, professional or other examination or of enabling the
    results of any such examination to be determined, or in consequence of the determination of any such
    results, s 21 has effect subject to certain modifications: s 35(1). See further note 13 infra. For these
    purposes, 'examination' includes any process for determining the knowledge, intelligence, skill or
    ability of a candidate by reference to his performance in any test, work or other activity: s 35(5).
6 For the prescribed maximum fee see the Data Protection (Subject Access) (Fees) Regulations 1987,
    SI 1987/1507, reg 2; and as to the power to prescribe fees see para 509 note 9 ante.
7 Data Protection Act 1984 s 21(2). A request for information under both heads (1) and (2) in the text
    must be treated as a single request and a request under head (1) is to be treated as extending also to
    information under head (2) in the absence of any indication to the contrary: s 21(2). The Secretary of
    State may by order provide for enabling a request under s 21 to be made on behalf of any individual who
    is incapable by reason of mental disorder of managing his own affairs: s 21(9). A statutory instrument
    containing such an order is subject to annulment in pursuance of a resolution of either House of
    Parliament: s 40(5). At the date at which this volume states the law, no such order had been made. As to
    the making of orders generally, and as to the Secretary of State, see para 501 note 2 ante.
8 Ibid s 21(3).
9 Ibid s 21(4)(a).

10   For the meaning of 'disclosing' see para 504 note 8 ante.

11   This reference to information relating to another individual includes a reference to information identifying that individual as the source of the information sought by the request; and head (b) in the text is not to be construed as excusing a data user from supplying so much of the information sought by the request as can be supplied without disclosing the identity of the other individual concerned, whether by the omission of names or other identifying particulars or otherwise: Data Protection Act 1984 s 21(5).

12   Ibid s 21(4)(b).

13   Ibid s 21(6). Where s 35 applies (see note 5 supra) and the period mentioned in s 21(6) begins before the results of an examination are announced, that period is to be extended until (1) the end of five months from the beginning of that period; or (2) the end of 40 days after the date of the announcement, whichever is the earlier: s 35(2). Where by virtue of s 35(2) a request is complied with more than 40 days after the beginning of the period mentioned in s 21(6), the information to be supplied pursuant to the request must be supplied both by reference to the data in question at the time when the request is received and, if different, by reference to the data as from time to time held in the period beginning when the request is received and ending when it is complied with: s 35(3). For these purposes, the results of an examination are treated as announced when they are first published or, if not published, when they are first made available or communicated to the candidate in question: s 35(4).

14   Ibid s 21(7).

15   Ibid ss 21(8), 25(1). The court may not, however, make such an order if it considers that it would in all the circumstances be unreasonable to do so, whether because of the frequency with which the applicant has made requests for access to the data user or for any other reason: s 21(8). For the purpose of determining any question whether an applicant is entitled to the information which he seeks, including any question whether any relevant data are exempt from s 21 by virtue of Pt IV (ss 26–35A) (as amended) (see para 529 et seq post), a court may require the relevant information constituting any data held by the data user to be made available for its own inspection but may not, pending the determination of that question in the applicant's favour, require the information sought by the applicant to be disclosed to him or his representatives whether by discovery or otherwise: s 25(2).

16   As to exemptions see para 529 et seq post.

17   Access to Personal Files Act 1987 s 1(2). As to the rights of access under the 1987 Act see para 538 et seq post.

526. Compensation for inaccuracy. An individual who is the subject of personal data held[1] by a data user[2] and who suffers damage by reason of the inaccuracy[3] of the data is entitled to compensation from the data user for that damage and for any distress which the individual has suffered by reason of the inaccuracy[4]. In the case of data which accurately record information received or obtained by the data user from the data subject[5] or a third party, this provision does not, however, apply if the following requirements have been complied with[6]:

(1)   the data indicate that the information was received or obtained by the data user from the data subject or a third party or the information has not been extracted from the data except in a form which includes an indication to that effect[7];

(2)   if the data subject has notified the data user that he regards the information as incorrect or misleading, an indication to that effect has been included in the data or the information has not been extracted from the data except in a form which includes an indication to that effect[8].

In proceedings brought against any person by virtue of these provisions it is a defence to prove that he had taken such care as in all the circumstances was reasonably required to ensure the accuracy of the data at the material time[9].

1   For the meaning of 'personal data', 'data' and 'held' see para 502 ante.

2   For the meaning of 'data user' see para 502 ante.

3   Data are inaccurate for these purposes if incorrect or misleading as to any matter of fact: Data Protection Act 1984 s 22(4).

4   Ibid s 22(1).

5   For the meaning of 'data subject' see para 502 ante.

6 Data Protection Act 1984 s 22(2).
7 Ibid s 22(2)(a).
8 Ibid s 22(2)(b).
9 Ibid s 22(3).

527. Compensation for loss or unauthorised disclosure. An individual who is the subject of personal data held[1] by a data user[2] or in respect of which services are provided by a person carrying on a computer bureau[3] and who suffers damage by reason of the loss, unauthorised destruction[4] or unauthorised disclosure[5] of the data, or from access having been obtained to the data without authority[6], is entitled to compensation from the data user or the person carrying on the bureau for that damage and for any distress which the individual has suffered by reason of the loss, destruction, disclosure or access[7]. In proceedings brought against any person by virtue of these provisions it is a defence to prove that he had taken such care as in all the circumstances was reasonably required to prevent the loss, destruction, disclosure or access in question[8].

1 For the meaning of 'personal data' , 'data' and 'held' see para 502 ante.
2 For the meaning of 'data user' see para 502 ante.
3 As to carrying on a computer bureau see para 502 ante.
4 Ie destruction without the authority of the data user or the person carrying on the bureau: Data Protection Act 1984 s 23(1)(b).
5 Ie disclosure without the authority of the data user or the person carrying on the bureau: ibid s 23(1)(c). In the case of a registered data user, s 23(1)(c) does not apply to disclosure to any person falling within a description specified pursuant to s 4(3)(d) (see para 508 note 7 head (4) ante) in an entry in the register relating to that data user: s 23(2). As to the meaning of 'disclosure' see para 504 note 8 ante; and as to registration see para 508 et seq ante.
6 Ie access having been obtained without the authority of the data user or the person carrying on the bureau: ibid s 23(1)(c). In the case of a registered data user, s 23(1)(c) does not apply to access by any person falling within a description specified pursuant to s 4(3)(d) (see para 508 note 7 head (4) ante) in an entry in the register relating to that data user: s 23(2).
7 Ibid s 23(1).
8 Ibid s 23(3).

528. Rectification and erasure. If the High Court or a county court[1] is satisfied, on the application of a data subject[2], that personal data held[3] by a data user[4] are inaccurate[5], it may order the rectification or erasure of the data and of any data held by the data user and containing an expression of opinion which appears to the court to be based on the inaccurate data[6]. This provision applies whether or not the data accurately record information received or obtained by the data user from the data subject or a third party[7] but where the data accurately record such information, then:

(1) if the requirements mentioned in the provisions relating to compensation for inaccuracy[8] have been complied with, the court may, instead of making such an order, make an order requiring the data to be supplemented by such statement of the true facts relating to the matters dealt with by the data as the court may approve[9]; and

(2) if all or any of those requirements have not been complied with, the court may, instead of making such an order, make such order as it thinks fit for securing compliance with those requirements with or without a further order requiring the data to be supplemented by such a statement as is mentioned in head (1) above[10].

If the court is satisfied, on the application of a data subject, that he has suffered damage by reason of the disclosure[11] of personal data, or of access having been obtained to personal data, in circumstances entitling him to compensation[12], and that there is a substantial risk of further unauthorised disclosure of, or access to, the data, the court may order erasure of the data[13].

1 See the Data Protection Act 1984 s 25(1).
2 For the meaning of 'data subject' and 'data' see para 502 ante.
3 For the meaning of 'personal data' and 'held' see para 502 ante.
4 For the meaning of 'data user' see para 502 ante.
5 Data are inaccurate for these purposes if incorrect or misleading as to any matter of fact: Data Protection Act 1984 s 22(4) (applied by s 24(1)).
6 Ibid s 24(1).
7 Ibid s 24(2).
8 Ie ibid s 22(2): see para 526 ante.
9 Ibid s 24(2)(a).
10 Ibid s 24(2)(b).
11 As to the meaning of 'disclosure' see para 504 note 8 ante.
12 Ie under the Data Protection Act 1984 s 23: see para 527 ante.
13 Ibid s 24(3). In the case of data in respect of which services were being provided by a person carrying on a computer bureau, the court may not make such an order unless such steps as are reasonably practicable have been taken for notifying the person for whom those services were provided and giving him an opportunity to be heard: s 24(3). As to carrying on a computer bureau see para 502 ante.

(6) EXEMPTIONS

529. Exemption for the purpose of safeguarding national security. Personal data[1] are exempt from Part II of the Data Protection Act 1984[2] and from the provisions relating to the rights of data subjects[3] if the exemption is required for the purpose of safeguarding national security[4]. Any question whether this exemption is or at any time was required for that purpose in respect of any personal data must be determined by a minister of the Crown[5] and a certificate signed by such a minister certifying that the exemption is or at any time was so required is conclusive evidence of that fact[6].

Personal data which are not so exempt are exempt from the non-disclosure provisions[7] in any case in which the disclosure of the data is for the purpose of safeguarding national security[8].

1 For the meaning of 'personal data' and 'data' see para 502 ante.
2 Ie the Data Protection Act 1984 Pt II (ss 4–20) (as amended): see para 508 et seq ante.
3 Ie ibid ss 21–24 (as amended): see paras 525–528 ante.
4 Ibid s 27(1).
5 The powers so conferred on a minister of the Crown are not exercisable except by a minister who is a member of the cabinet or by the Attorney General or the Lord Advocate: ibid s 27(6).
6 Ibid s 27(2). A document purporting to be such a certificate is to be received in evidence and deemed to be such a certificate unless the contrary is proved: s 27(5).
7 'The non-disclosure provisions' means (1) ibid ss 5(2)(d), 15 (see paras 513–514 ante); and (2) any provision of the Data Protection Act 1984 Pt II (as amended) conferring a power on the Data Protection Registrar to the extent to which it is exercisable by reference to any data protection principle inconsistent with the disclosure in question: s 26(3). As to the meaning of 'disclosure' see para 504 note 8 ante; as to the data protection principles see paras 503–505 ante; and as to the registrar see para 506 ante. As to the Secretary of State's power to exclude or modify exemptions from the non-disclosure provisions see s 2(5); and para 503 note 6 ante.
8 Ibid s 27(3). For these purposes, a certificate signed by a minister of the Crown (see note 5 supra) certifying that personal data are or have been disclosed for the purpose of safeguarding national security is conclusive evidence of that fact: s 27(4). See also s 27(5) cited in note 6 supra.

530. Exemptions relating to crime and taxation. Personal data[1] held for any of the following purposes:

(1) the prevention or detection of crime;

(2) the apprehension or prosecution of offenders; or

(3) the assessment or collection of any tax or duty,

are exempt from the subject access provisions[2] in any case in which the application of those provisions to the data would be likely to prejudice any of the matters mentioned above[3]. Personal data which are held for the purpose of discharging statutory functions and which consist of information obtained for such a purpose from a person who had it in his possession for any of the purposes mentioned above are exempt from the subject access provisions to the same extent as personal data held for any of the purposes mentioned in heads (1) to (3) above[4].

Personal data are exempt from the non-disclosure provisions[5] in any case in which the disclosure is for any of the purposes mentioned in heads (1) to (3) above and the application of those provisions in relation to the disclosure would be likely to prejudice any of the matters mentioned in those heads[6]. Personal data are also exempt from the provisions of Part II of the Data Protection Act 1984 conferring powers on the Data Protection Registrar, to the extent to which they are exercisable by reference to the first data protection principle[7], in any case in which the application of those provisions to the data would be likely to prejudice any of the matters so mentioned[8].

1 For the meaning of 'personal data' and 'data' see para 502 ante.

2 'The subject access provisions' means (1) the Data Protection Act 1984 s 21 (see para 525 ante); and (2) any provision of Pt II (ss 4–20) (as amended) (see para 508 et seq ante) conferring a power on the Data Protection Registrar to the extent to which it is exercisable by reference to s 2(1), Sch 1 Pt I principle 7(a) (see para 504 head (7)(a) ante): s 26(2). Except as provided by Pt III (ss 26–35A) (as amended) (see paras 529 ante, 531 et seq post and the text and notes 3–8 infra), the subject access provisions apply notwithstanding any enactment, whenever passed, or any rule of law prohibiting or restricting the disclosure, or authorising the withholding, of information: ss 26(4), 41. As to the meaning of 'disclosure' see para 504 note 8 ante. As to the registrar see para 506 ante.

3 Ibid s 28(1).

4 Ibid s 28(2).

5 For the meaning of 'the non-disclosure provisions' see para 529 note 7 ante.

6 Data Protection Act 1984 s 28(3)(a), (b). In proceedings against any person for contravening s 5(2)(d) (see para 513 ante) or s 15 (see para 514 ante) or for an offence under s 5(6) (as added) (see para 514 ante), it is a defence to prove that he had reasonable grounds for believing that failure to make (or in the case of s 5(6) (as added) to procure) the disclosure in question would have been likely to prejudice any of the matters mentioned in s 28(1) (see heads (1)–(3) in the text): s 28(3) (amended by the Criminal Justice and Public Order Act 1994 s 162(2)(b)).

7 As to the first data protection principle see para 504 head (1) ante.

8 Data Protection Act 1984 s 28(4).

531. Exemptions relating to health and social work. The Secretary of State may by order exempt from the subject access provisions[1], or modify those provisions in relation to:

(1) personal data[2] consisting of information as to the physical or mental health of the data subject[3];

(2) personal data of such other descriptions as may be specified in the order, being information held by government departments or local authorities or by voluntary organisations or other bodies designated by or under the order and appearing to him to be held for, or acquired in the course of, carrying out social work in relation to the data subject or other individuals[4].

An order so made may make different provision in relation to data consisting of information of different descriptions[5].

These powers have been exercised in relation to data consisting of information as to the physical or mental health of the data subject and either (a) held by a health professional[6]; or (b) held by another person but where the information constituting the data was first recorded by or on behalf of a health professional[7]. They have also been exercised in relation to personal data held by local authorities and other persons and bodies in relation to social work and welfare functions[8].

1 For the meaning of 'the subject access provisions' see para 530 note 2 ante.
2 For the meaning of 'personal data' and 'data' see para 502 ante.
3 Data Protection Act 1984 s 29(1). No order may be made under s 29 unless a draft of the order has been laid before and approved by a resolution of each House of Parliament: s 40(4). As to the making of orders generally, and as to the Secretary of State, see para 501 note 2 ante. For the meaning of 'data subject' see para 502 ante. As to the exercise of this power see the text and notes 6–7 infra.
4 Ibid s 29(2)(a), (b). The Secretary of State may not, however, confer any exemption or make any modification under s 29(2) except so far as he considers that the application to the data of those provisions, or of those provisions without modification, would be likely to prejudice the carrying out of social work: s 29(2). As to the exercise of this power see the text and note 8 infra.
5 Ibid s 29(3).
6 For the meaning of 'health professional' for these purposes see the Data Protection (Subject Access Modification) (Health) Order 1987, SI 1987/1903, art 2, Schedule (prospectively amended by the Osteopaths Act 1993 s 38(2)(a), (3), as from a day to be appointed under s 42(2); and by the Chiropractors Act 1994 s 38(3)(a), (4), as from a day to be appointed under s 44(3)).
7 See the Data Protection (Subject Access Modification) (Health) Order 1987 arts 2–4.
8 See the Data Protection (Subject Access Modification) (Social Work) Order 1987, SI 1987/1904, arts 2–4.

532. Exemptions relating to the regulation of financial services etc. Personal data[1] held for the purpose of discharging designated statutory functions are exempt from the subject access provisions[2] in any case in which the application of those provisions to the data would be likely to prejudice the proper discharge of those functions[3]. The functions which may be so designated, by order of the Secretary of State, are functions conferred by or under any enactment, whenever passed[4], appearing to him to be designed for protecting members of the public against financial loss due to dishonesty, incompetence or malpractice by persons concerned in the provision of banking, insurance, investment or other financial services or in the management of companies or due to the conduct of discharged or undischarged bankrupts[5]. Such an order may also designate for these purposes any functions of the Charity Commissioners appearing to the Secretary of State to be connected with the protection of charities against misconduct or mismanagement in their administration, whether by trustees or other persons, or connected with the protection of the property of charities from loss or misapplication or with the recovery of such property[6].

These powers have been exercised in relation to a number of relevant statutory functions[7].

1 For the meaning of 'personal data' and 'data' see para 502 ante.
2 For the meaning of 'the subject access provisions' see para 530 note 2 ante.
3 Data Protection Act 1984 s 30(1). Section 30 has effect as if the reference to prejudicing the proper discharge of statutory functions includes a reference to (1) contravening EC Council Directive 77/780 (OJ L322, 17.12.77, p 30) art 12 (see the Banking Co-ordination (Second Council Directive) Regulations 1992, SI 1992/3218, reg 82(1), Sch 10 para 15(a)); (2) contravening EC Council Directive 92/49 (OJ L228, 11.8.92, p 1) art 16 or EC Council Directive 92/96 (OJ L360, 3.2.92, p 1) art 16 (see the Insurance Companies (Third Insurance Directives) Regulations 1994, SI 1994/1696, reg 68(1), Sch 8 para 8); (3) contravening the Investment Services Regulations 1995, SI 1995/3275, reg 48 (see reg 57(1), Sch 10 para 3(a)).
4 The Data Protection Act 1984 s 30 has effect as if this reference to any enactment included a reference to (1) the Banking Co-ordination (Second Council Directive) Regulations 1992 (as amended) (see Sch 10 para 15(b)); (2) the Investment Services Regulations 1995 (see Sch 10 para 3(b)).

5 Data Protection Act 1984 ss 30(2), 41. No such order may be made unless a draft of the order has been laid before and approved by a resolution of each House of Parliament: s 40(4). As to the making of orders generally, and as to the Secretary of State, see para 501 note 2 ante. As to the exercise of this power see the text and note 7 infra.

6 Charities Act 1993 s 12.

7 See the Data Protection (Regulation of Financial Services etc) (Subject Access Exemption) Order 1987, SI 1987/1905 (amended by SI 1990/310; SI 1992/1855; modified by SI 1992/3218). See also the Financial Services Act 1986 s 190; and MONEY.

533. Exemptions in relation to judicial appointments and legal professional privilege. Personal data[1] held by a government department are exempt from the subject access provisions[2] if the data consist of information which has been received from a third party and is held as information relevant to the making of judicial appointments[3].

Personal data are exempt from the subject access provisions if the data consist of information in respect of which a claim to legal professional privilege[4] could be maintained in legal proceedings[5].

1 For the meaning of 'personal data' and 'data' see para 502 ante.
2 For the meaning of 'the subject access provisions' see para 530 note 2 ante.
3 Data Protection Act 1984 s 31(1).
4 As to legal professional privilege see BARRISTERS vol 3(1) (Reissue) para 524–527; CRIMINAL LAW vol 11(2) (Reissue) para 1163; DISCOVERY vol 13 para 79; EVIDENCE vol 17 para 237; SOLICITORS vol 44(1) (Reissue) paras 90, 150; and paras 454–455 ante.
5 Data Protection Act 1984 s 31(2).

534. Exemptions relating to payrolls and accounts. Personal data[1] are exempt from Part II of the Data Protection Act 1984[2] and from the provisions relating to the rights of data subjects[3] if they are held by a data user[4] only for one or more of the following purposes[5]:

(1) calculating amounts payable by way of remuneration[6] or pensions[7] in respect of service in any employment or office or making payments of, or of sums deducted from, such remuneration or pensions[8]; or

(2) keeping accounts relating to any business, trade or profession or other activity carried on by the data user or keeping records of purchases, sales or other transactions for the purpose of ensuring that the requisite payments are made by or to him in respect of those transactions or for the purpose of making financial or management forecasts to assist him in the conduct of any such business, trade, profession or activity[9].

It is a condition of the exemption of any data under these provisions that the data are not used for any purpose other than the purpose or purposes for which they are held and are not disclosed[10] except as permitted[11]; but the exemption is not lost by any disclosure in breach of that condition if the data user shows that he had taken such care to prevent it as in all the circumstances was reasonably required[12].

1 For the meaning of 'data' and 'personal data' see para 502 ante.
2 Ie the Data Protection Act 1984 Pt II (ss 4–20) (as amended): see para 508 et seq ante.
3 Ie ibid ss 21–24: see paras 525–528 ante. For the meaning of 'data subject' see para 502 ante.
4 For the meaning of 'data user' and 'held' see para 502 ante.
5 Data Protection Act 1984 s 32(1).
6 'Remuneration' includes remuneration in kind: ibid s 32(5).
7 'Pensions' includes gratuities and similar benefits: ibid s 32(5).
8 Ibid s 32(1)(a).

9 Ibid ss 32(1)(b), 41.
10 As to the meaning of 'disclosed' see para 504 note 8 ante.
11 Data held only for one or more of the purposes mentioned in the Data Protection Act 1984 s 32(1)(a) (see head (1) in the text) may be disclosed: (1) to any person, other than the data user, by whom the remuneration or pensions in question are payable; (2) for the purpose of obtaining actuarial advice; (3) for the purpose of giving information as to the persons in any employment or office for use in medical research into the health of, or injuries suffered by, persons engaged in particular occupations or working in particular places or areas; (4) if the data subject, or a person acting on his behalf, has requested or consented to the disclosure of the data either generally or in the circumstances in which the disclosure in question is made; or (5) if the person making the disclosure has reasonable grounds for believing that the disclosure falls within head (4) supra: s 32(3). Data held for any of the purposes mentioned in s 32(1) (see heads (1)–(2) in the text) may be disclosed (a) for the purpose of audit or where the disclosure is for the purpose only of giving information about the data user's financial affairs; or (b) in any case in which disclosure would be permitted by any other provision of Pt IV (ss 26–35A) (as amended) (see paras 529 et seq ante, 535 et seq post) if s 32(2) were included among the non-disclosure provisions: s 32(4). For the meaning of 'the non-disclosure provisions' see para 529 note 7 ante.
12 Ibid s 32(2).

535. Exemptions for domestic or other limited purposes. Personal data held[1]:
(1) by an individual and concerned only with the management of his personal, family or household affairs or held by him only for recreational purposes[2];
(2) by an unincorporated members' club and relating only to members of the club[3];
(3) by a data user[4] only for the purpose of distributing, or recording the distribution of, articles or information to the data subjects[5] and consisting only of their names, addresses or other particulars necessary for effecting the distribution[6],
are exempt from the provisions of Part II of the Data Protection Act 1984[7] and of the provisions[8] relating to the rights of data subjects[9]. Neither head (2) nor head (3) above, however, applies to personal data relating to any data subject unless he has been asked by the club or data user whether he objects to the data relating to him being held as mentioned therein and he has not objected[10]; and it is a condition of the exemption of any data under head (3) above that the data are not used for any purpose other than that for which they are held and of the exemption of any data under either head (2) or head (3) above that the data are not disclosed[11] except as permitted[12]. The first exemption is not lost by any use, and neither exemption is lost by any disclosure, in breach of this condition if the data user shows that he had taken such care to prevent it as in all the circumstances was reasonably required[13].

Personal data held only for preparing statistics or carrying out research are exempt from the subject access provisions[14] but it is a condition of this exemption that the data are not used or disclosed for any other purpose and that the resulting statistics or the results of the research are not made available in a form which identifies the data subjects or any of them[15].

1 For the meaning of 'personal data', 'data' and 'held' see para 502 ante.
2 Data Protection Act 1984 s 33(1).
3 Ibid s 33(2)(a).
4 For the meaning of 'data user' see para 502 ante.
5 For the meaning of 'data subject' see para 502 ante.
6 Data Protection Act 1984 s 33(2)(b).
7 Ie ibid Pt II (ss 4–20) (as amended): see para 508 et seq ante.
8 Ie ibid ss 21–24: see paras 525–528 ante.
9 Ibid s 33(1), (2).
10 Ibid s 33(3).
11 As to the meaning of 'disclosed' see para 504 note 8 ante.
12 Data Protection Act 1984 s 33(4). Such data may be disclosed: (1) if the data subject, or a person acting on his behalf, has requested or consented to the disclosure of the data either generally or in the

circumstances in which the disclosure in question is made; (2) if the person making the disclosure has reasonable grounds for believing that the disclosure falls within head (1) supra; or (3) in any other case in which disclosure would be permitted by any other provision of Pt IV (ss 26–35A) (as amended) (see paras 529 et seq ante, 536–537 post) if s 33(4) were included among the non-disclosure provisions: s 33(5). For the meaning of 'the non-disclosure provisions' see para 529 note 7 ante.

13 Ibid s 33(4).
14 For the meaning of 'the subject access provisions' see para 530 note 2 ante.
15 Data Protection Act 1984 s 33(6). Section 4(3)(d) (see para 508 note 7 head (4) ante) applies to this restriction on disclosure as it applies to the non-disclosure provisions: s 34(7).

536. Miscellaneous exemptions. Personal data held[1] by any person are exempt from the provisions of Part II of the Data Protection Act 1984[2] and of the provisions relating to the rights of data subjects[3] if the data consist of information which that person is required by or under any enactment, whenever passed, to make available to the public, whether by publishing it, making it available for inspection or otherwise and whether gratuitously or on payment of a fee[4]. The Secretary of State may by order exempt from the subject access provisions[5] personal data consisting of information the disclosure[6] of which is prohibited or restricted by or under any enactment, whenever passed, if he considers that the prohibition or restriction ought to prevail over those provisions in the interests of the data subject or of any other individual[7].

Where all the personal data relating to a data subject held by a data user[8], or all such data in respect of which a data user has a separate entry in the register, consist of information in respect of which the data subject is entitled to make a request under the statutory provisions relating to the files of credit reference agencies[9], the data are exempt from the subject access provisions[10]. Personal data are also exempt from the subject access provisions if the data are kept only for the purpose of replacing other data in the event of the latter being lost, destroyed or impaired[11].

Personal data are exempt from the non-disclosure provisions[12] in any case in which:

(1) the disclosure is required by or under any enactment, whenever passed, by any rule of law or by the order of a court[13] or made for the purpose of obtaining legal advice or for the purposes of, or in the course of, legal proceedings in which the person making the disclosure is a party or a witness[14]; or

(2) the disclosure is to the data subject or a person acting on his behalf[15]; or

(3) the data subject or any such person has requested or consented to the particular disclosure in question[16]; or

(4) the disclosure is by a data user or a person carrying on a computer bureau[17] to his servant or agent for the purpose of enabling the servant or agent to perform his functions as such[18]; or

(5) the person making the disclosure has reasonable grounds for believing that the disclosure falls within any of heads (2) to (4) above[19]; or

(6) the disclosure is urgently required for preventing injury or other damage to the health of any person or persons[20].

A person need not comply with a notice, request or order under the subject access provisions if compliance would expose him to proceedings for any offence other than an offence under the Data Protection Act 1984[21]. Information disclosed by any person in compliance with such a notice, request or order is not admissible against him in proceedings for an offence under the 1984 Act[22].

1 For the meaning of 'personal data', 'data' and 'held' see para 502 ante.
2 Ie the Data Protection Act 1984 Pt II (ss 4–20) (as amended): see para 508 et seq ante.
3 Ie ibid ss 21–24: see paras 525–528 ante. For the meaning of 'data subject' see para 502 ante.
4 Ibid ss 34(1), 41.

5 For the meaning of 'the subject access provisions' see para 530 note 2 ante.

6 As to the meaning of 'disclosure' see para 504 note 8 ante.

7 Data Protection Act 1984 ss 34(2), 41. No such order may be made unless a draft of the order has been laid before and approved by a resolution of each House of Parliament: s 40(4). As to the making of orders generally see para 501 note 2 ante. In exercise of the power so conferred, the Home Secretary (see para 501 note 2 ante) has made the Data Protection (Miscellaneous Subject Access Exemptions) Order 1987, SI 1987/1906, which came into force on 11 November 1987: art 1. There are exempted from the subject access provisions any personal data consisting of information the disclosure of which is prohibited or restricted by the enactments or instruments listed in art 2, Schedule, being enactments or instruments which impose prohibitions or restrictions on disclosure which ought to prevail over those provisions in the interests of data subjects or other individuals: art 2. The enactments and instruments so listed relate to adoption and to special educational needs: see Schedule Pt I.

8 For the meaning of 'data user' see para 502 ante.

9 Ie under the Consumer Credit Act 1974 s 158 (as amended): see para 475 ante; and HIRE PURCHASE AND CONSUMER CREDIT.

10 Data Protection Act 1984 s 34(3). Any request in respect of the data under s 21 (see para 525 ante) is to be treated for all purposes as if it were a request under the Consumer Credit Act 1974 s 158 (as amended): Data Protection Act 1984 s 34(3)(b).

11 Ibid s 34(4).

12 For the meaning of 'the non-disclosure provisions' see para 529 note 7 ante.

13 Data Protection Act 1984 ss 34(5)(a), 41.

14 Ibid s 34(5)(b).

15 Ibid s 34(6)(a). Section 4(3)(d) (see para 508 note 7 head (4) ante) does not apply to any such disclosure: s 34(7).

16 Ibid s 34(6)(b). Section 4(3)(d) (see para 508 note 7 head (4) ante) does not apply to any such disclosure: s 34(7).

17 As to carrying on a computer bureau see para 502 ante.

18 Data Protection Act 1984 s 34(6)(c). Section 4(3)(d) (see para 508 note 7 head (4) ante) does not apply to any such disclosure: s 34(7).

19 Ibid s 34(6)(d).

20 Ibid s 34(8). In proceedings against any person for contravening s 5(2)(d) (see para 513 ante) or s 15 (see para 514 ante), it is a defence to prove that he had reasonable grounds for believing that the disclosure in question was urgently required for that purpose: s 34(8) (applying s 26(3)(a)).

21 Ibid s 34(9).

22 Ibid s 34(9). As to offences under the Data Protection Act 1984 see para 524 ante.

537. Exemption for information about human embryos etc. Personal data[1] consisting of information showing that an identifiable individual was, or may have been, born in consequence of treatment services within the meaning of the Human Fertilisation and Embryology Act 1990[2] are exempt from the subject access provisions[3] except so far as their disclosure[4] under those provisions is made in accordance with the statutory provisions[5] relating to the register of information kept by the Human Fertilisation and Embryology Authority[6].

1 For the meaning of 'personal data' and 'data' see para 502 ante.

2 Ie within the meaning of the Human Fertilisation and Embryology Act 1990 s 2(1) (ie medical, surgical or obstetric services provided to the public or a section of the public for the purpose of assisting women to carry children): see CHILDREN vol 5(2) (Reissue) para 699 note 10.

3 For the meaning of 'the subject access provisions' see para 530 note 2 ante.

4 As to the meaning of 'disclosure' see para 504 note 8 ante.

5 Ie in accordance with the Human Fertilisation and Embryology Act 1990 s 31: see CHILDREN vol 5(2) (Reissue) para 703.

6 Data Protection Act 1984 s 35A (added by the Human Fertilisation and Embryology Act 1990 s 33(8)). As to the Human Fertilisation and Embryology Authority see MEDICINE vol 30 (Reissue) para 60; and as to the general restrictions on disclosure of information held in the register or other confidential information relating to treatment services etc see CHILDREN vol 5(2) (Reissue) para 705.

(7) ACCESS TO PERSONAL FILES HELD BY LOCAL AUTHORITIES ETC

(i) In general

538. Statutory obligation to give access to personal files. Any authority keeping records containing personal information[1] which is accessible personal information[2] has such obligations as regards access to, and the accuracy of, that information as are imposed by access regulations[3] made by the Secretary of State[4]. The statutory obligation to give access to information applies, subject to any exemptions or restrictions prescribed in the regulations, notwithstanding any enactment or rule of law prohibiting or restricting the disclosure, or authorising the withholding, of information[5].

1 'Personal information' means information which relates to a living individual who can be identified from that information, or from that and other information in the possession of the authority keeping the record, including any expression of opinion about the individual but not any indication of the intentions of the authority with respect to that individual: Access to Personal Files Act 1987 s 2(1), (2).
2 For the meaning of 'accessible personal information' see para 539 post.
3 Ie regulations under the Access to Personal Files Act 1987 s 3: s 1(1). The Secretary of State may by regulations make such provision as he considers appropriate for securing access by individuals to accessible personal information of which they are, or are treated as, the subjects and the rectification and erasure of inaccurate records containing such information: s 3(1). The regulations may make different provision for different descriptions of information, different authorities or other different circumstances: s 3(3). As to the particular matters for which they may provide see s 3(2), (6). Before making such regulations the Secretary of State must consult such authorities or bodies representing authorities as he thinks appropriate: s 3(4). The power to make such regulations is exercisable by statutory instrument but no such regulations may be made unless a draft of them has been laid before and approved by a resolution of each House of Parliament: s 3(5). In exercise of the power so conferred, the Secretary of State for Health has made the Access to Personal Files (Social Services) Regulations 1989, SI 1989/206; and the Access to Personal Files (Social Services) (Amendment) Regulations 1991, SI 1991/1587; and the Secretary of State for the Environment has made the Access to Personal Files (Housing) Regulations 1989, SI 1989/503. See para 540 et seq post.
4 Access to Personal Files Act 1987 s 3(1). Where an individual is, or would but for any exemption be, entitled under the Data Protection Act 1984 s 21 (see para 525 ante) to be supplied with information constituting personal data of which he is the subject, no obligation arises under the Access to Personal Files Act 1987 to give him access to that information: s 1(2).
5 Ibid s 1(5). The Housing Act 1985 s 106(5) (duty of landlord authority to give access to certain information: see HOUSING) does not apply in respect of any information recorded by a landlord authority in respect of which the authority is under an obligation to give access under the Access to Personal Files Act 1987: s 1(3).

539. Meaning of 'accessible personal information'. Information is 'accessible personal information' if it is held in a record kept by a specified authority[1] and is information of a description specified in relation to that authority[2]. Any obligation to give access to information is an obligation to give access to the individual who is the subject of it or is to be treated[3] as such[4]. As respects any access regulations[5], however, information is not accessible personal information if recorded before the commencement date of the regulations or the first commencement date of regulations imposing a corresponding obligation except to the extent that access to it is required to make intelligible information recorded on or after that date[6].

The authorities and information so specified are (1) a Housing Act local authority[7] and personal information held by it for any purpose of the authority's tenancies[8]; and (2) a local social services authority[9] and personal information held by it for any purpose of the authority's social services functions[10].

1   Ie an authority specified in the Access to Personal Files Act 1987 s 2(3), Sch 1 para 1, Table: see heads (1)–(2) in the text. For the meaning of 'personal information' see para 538 note 1 ante.
2   Ibid s 2(1), (3).
3   Ie under ibid Sch 1 (as amended): see note 8 infra.
4   Ibid s 2(3).
5   Ie any regulations made under ibid s 3: see paras 538 ante, 540 et seq post.
6   Ibid s 2(1), (4).
7   Any authority which by virtue of the Housing Act 1985 s 4(e) (as amended) is a local authority for the purpose of any provision of that Act is a Housing Act local authority for these purposes and so is any residuary body established under the Local Government Act 1985 s 57 and any housing action trust established under the Housing Act 1988 Pt III (ss 60–92) (as amended): Access to Personal Files Act 1987 Sch 1 para 2(1), (2) (amended by the Housing Act 1988 s 140(1), Sch 17 para 80). See further HOUSING. The Access to Personal Files Act 1987 Sch 1 para 1 has effect as if the reference to a Housing Act local authority included a reference to the Residuary Body for Wales or Corff Gweddilliol Cymru: see the Local Government (Wales) Act 1994 s 39(2), Sch 13 para 30.
8   See the Access to Personal Files Act 1987 Sch 1 para 1, Table. Personal information contained in records kept by a Housing Act local authority is 'held for any purpose of the authority's tenancies' if it is held for any purpose of the relationship of landlord and tenant of a dwelling which subsists, or has subsisted or may subsist, between the authority and any individual who is, has been or has applied to be a tenant of the authority: Access to Personal Files Act 1987 Sch 1 para 2(1), (3). For these purposes, information about any member of the individual's family held for any purpose of that relationship or potential relationship is to be treated as information of which he is the subject and accessible by him accordingly: Sch 1 para 2(3). For the meaning of 'tenancy' and 'tenant' see the Housing Act 1985 s 621 (applied by the Access to Personal Files Act 1987 Sch 1 para 2(1), (5)); and HOUSING.
9   Any authority which, by virtue of the Local Authority Social Services Act 1970 s 1 (as amended) or s 12, is or is treated as a local authority for the purposes of that Act is a 'local social services authority' for these purposes: Access to Personal Files Act 1987 Sch 1 para 2(1), (4). See further LOCAL GOVERNMENT vol 28 paras 1145, 1362.
10 See ibid Sch 1 para 1, Table. Personal information contained in records kept by such an authority as is mentioned in note 9 supra is 'held for any purpose of the authority's social services functions' if it is held for the purpose of any past, current or proposed exercise of such a function in any case: Sch 1 para 2(4). For the meaning of 'social services functions' see the Local Authority Social Services Act 1970 s 15(2) (as amended) (applied by the Access to Personal Files Act 1987 Sch 1 para 2(5)).

(ii) Rights of Access to Housing and Social Services Information

540. Right of access to personal information held by local social services authority. A local social services authority[1] is obliged (1) to inform any individual whether the accessible personal information[2] which the authority holds includes personal information[3] of which that individual is the subject; and (2) to give him access to any personal information of which he is the subject[4]. The obligation does not arise except in response to a request in writing and on payment of a fee[5] and the authority is not obliged to comply with such a request unless it is supplied with such information as it may reasonably require in order to satisfy itself as to the identity of the person making the request and to locate the information which he seeks[6].

If the accessible personal information in respect of which the authority has received such a request contains information relating to another individual who can be identified from it[7], the authority must within 14 days of receiving the request or, if later, of receiving the further information required[8], inform that other individual in writing of the request and that the accessible personal information contains information relating to him and ask that other individual whether he consents to the information relating to him being disclosed to the person making the request[9]. The authority must comply with a request under these provisions within 40 days of receiving it or, if later, receiving the further information required and, if necessary, the consent asked for[10]. The information to which access is to be given pursuant to such a request is the information held at the time when the request is received, except that it may take into account any amendment or deletion made between that time and the time when access is given, if it is an amendment or deletion that would have been made regardless of the receipt of the request[11].

1　For the meaning of 'local social services authority' see para 539 note 9 ante.
2　For the meaning of 'accessible personal information' see para 539 ante.
3　For the meaning of 'personal information' see para 538 note 1 ante.
4　Access to Personal Files (Social Services) Regulations 1989, SI 1989/206, reg 2(1). As to exemptions from this obligation see reg 8 (as amended), reg 9; and paras 542–543 post. A local social services authority complies with its obligation under head (2) in the text if it supplies the individual with a copy of any personal information of which he is the subject, but if it gives him access to that information by any other means it is in addition obliged to supply him with a copy of so much of the information as he may require: reg 2(2). If a copy is so supplied and the information is expressed in terms which are not intelligible without explanation, the information must be accompanied by an explanation of those terms: reg 2(3).
5　Ibid reg 3. The fee must not exceed £10: reg 3. A request under heads (1) and (2) in the text is treated as a single request and a request to be informed under head (1) is, in the absence of any indication to the contrary, treated as extending also to being given access to any personal information under head (2): reg 3.
6　Ibid reg 4.
7　Ie other than an individual to whom ibid reg 8(5)(b) (health professionals) or reg 9(3)(a) (social workers etc) applies: see paras 542–543 post.
8　Ie the information referred to in ibid reg 4: see the text and note 6 supra.
9　Ibid reg 5.
10　Ibid reg 6.
11　Ibid reg 7. As to review of the authority's decision to allow access to information see para 545 post.

541. Right of access to personal information held by Housing Act local authority. Where a tenant[1] requires a Housing Act local authority[2] in writing to inform him whether that authority holds relevant information[3] of which he is or is treated[4] as the subject, the authority must within 40 days of receiving that requirement, or of the giving of any necessary consent[5], (1) inform the tenant in writing whether it holds such information; and, if so, (2) either supply a copy of the relevant information free of any charge for the copy, or notify the tenant that its duty to do so does not arise, for a specified reason[6], unless the authority otherwise gives the tenant access to the information within that period and the tenant informs the authority that he does not want a copy[7]. These duties arise only where the tenant has paid any fee charged by the authority to a tenant making such a requirement[8] and has supplied information reasonably required to establish his identity, or the identity of any relevant member of his family, and to locate the information sought[9]; and where these conditions are not satisfied at the time of the written requirement, the time limit runs from the date on which they are satisfied[10].

These duties of the authority apply to any relevant information held by the authority at the time of the written requirement, but the authority may supply information taking account of any correction or erasure made between that time and the time when the information is supplied, if that correction or erasure would have been made regardless of the receipt of the requirement[11].

1　'Tenant' means (1) the tenant of a dwelling whose immediate landlord is a Housing Act local authority; (2) the former tenant of a dwelling where at any time the immediate landlord was such an authority; (3) an individual who is in the process of applying for, or who has applied for, a tenancy of a dwelling from such an authority: Access to Personal Files (Housing) Regulations 1989, SI 1989/503, reg 2. For the meaning of 'Housing Act local authority' see para 539 note 7 ante (definition applied by reg 2).
2　Ie within the meaning of the Access to Personal Files Act 1987: see para 539 note 7 ante.

3 'Relevant information' means, in relation to any tenant, accessible personal information held by the
   authority to which the tenant has addressed a requirement under the Access to Personal Files (Housing)
   Regulations 1989: reg 2. For the meaning of 'accessible personal information' see para 539 ante.
4 Ie under the Access to Personal Files Act 1987: see para 539 note 8 ante.
5 Ie the consent referred to in the Access to Personal Files (Housing) Regulations 1989 reg 4(1)(a): see
   para 542 post.
6 Ie a reason specified in one or more of ibid reg 4(1)(a)–(d): see para 542 post.
7 Ibid regs 3(1), 5(1), (2)(a), (b). Where the authority is obliged to give a copy of part only of the
   information and the remainder is exempt from access, the authority must comply with its duties as
   appropriate in relation to each part: see reg 5(2). Where a copy of information is supplied to the tenant
   in terms which cannot easily be understood without explanation, the information must be
   accompanied by a written explanation of those terms: reg 5(3).
8 Ibid reg 3(2)(a). The authority may charge a fee not exceeding £10 to a tenant making a requirement
   and no separate fee may be charged for giving access to that information under head (2) in the text:
   reg 3(4).
9 Ibid reg 3(2)(b).
10 Ibid reg 3(2).
11 Ibid reg 3(3).

**542. Exemptions from access to personal information relating to
health.** The duty of a Housing Act local authority[1] to give access to relevant
information[2] does not arise where the information sought would be likely if supplied to
cause serious harm to the physical or mental health of the tenant or any other person[3]:

(1) in the opinion of an appropriate health professional[4], where the information
     relates to the physical or mental health of an individual and the authority
     believes it was provided by or on behalf of such a professional[5]; or
(2) in the authority's opinion, in any other case[6].

Where part only of the information falls within this exemption, the authority's duty
arises in relation to the part that does not[7]; and in respect of information falling within
the exemption the authority must supply so much of it as can, in the opinion of the
appropriate health professional or of the authority, be supplied without causing serious
harm[8].

A local social services authority[9] is exempted from the obligation to give access to
personal information[10] in so far as it relates to information as to the physical or mental
health of an individual which originated from, or was supplied to the authority by or
on behalf of, a health professional[11] or which the authority believes to have so
originated or to have been so supplied[12], if the health authority, National Health
Service Trust or appropriate health professional informs[13] the local social services
authority that the information must not be disclosed because its disclosure:

(a) would be likely to cause serious harm to the physical or mental health of the
     individual who is the subject of the information or any other person[14]; or
(b) would be likely to disclose to the individual who is the subject of the
     information the identity of another individual who has not consented to its
     disclosure, either as a person to whom the information or part of it relates or as
     the source of the information, or enable that identity to be deduced by the
     individual who is the subject of the information, either from the information
     itself or from a combination of that information and other information which
     the individual who is the subject of the information has or is likely to have[15].

In such a case the obligation to give access to personal information nonetheless
applies to so much of the information sought as can be supplied without causing such
serious harm, or enabling the identity of another individual to be disclosed or deduced,
whether by the omission of names or other particulars or otherwise[16]. The obligation
also applies if the only individual whose identity is likely to be disclosed or deduced is a

health professional who has been involved in the care of the individual the subject of the information and the information relates to him or he supplied the information in his capacity as a health professional[17].

1 Ie the duty under the Access to Personal Files (Housing) Regulations 1989, SI 1989/503, reg 3(1)(b): see para 541 ante. For the meaning of 'Housing Act local authority' see para 539 note 7 ante (definition applied by reg 2).
2 For the meaning of 'relevant information' see para 541 note 3 ante.
3 Access to Personal Files (Housing) Regulations 1989 reg 4(1)(b).
4 'Appropriate health professional' means (1) the medical practitioner (ie person registered under the Medical Act 1983) or dental practitioner (ie person registered under the Dentists Act 1984) who is currently or was most recently responsible for the clinical care (including examination, investigation and diagnosis) of the tenant or the member of his family who is the subject of the relevant information in connection with the matters on which information is sought; or (2) where there is more than one such practitioner, the one who is the most suitable to advise on those matters; or (3) where there is no practitioner available falling within head (1) or head (2) supra, a health professional who has the necessary experience and qualifications to advise on those matters: Access to Personal Files (Housing) Regulations 1989 reg 2. For the meaning of 'health professional' see reg 2, Schedule (prospectively amended by the Osteopaths Act 1993 s 38(2)(d), (3) as from a day to be appointed under s 42(2); and by the Chiropractors Act 1994 s 38(3)(d), (4), as from a day to be appointed under s 44(3)). For the meaning of 'tenant' see para 541 note 1 ante.
5 Access to Personal Files (Housing) Regulations 1989 reg 4(1)(b)(i). The authority must seek the health professional's opinion within 14 days of receiving the request for access, and that opinion must be notified to the authority within the 40-day period referred to in reg 3(1) (see para 541 ante): see reg 6.
6 Ibid reg 4(1)(b)(ii).
7 Ibid reg 4(1).
8 Ibid reg 4(4).
9 For the meaning of 'local social services authority' see para 539 note 9 ante.
10 Ie the obligation imposed by the Access to Personal Files (Social Services) Regulations 1989, SI 1989/206, reg 2(1)(b): see para 540 ante.
11 For the meaning of 'health professional' see ibid reg 1(2), Schedule (amended by SI 1991/1587; prospectively amended by the Osteopaths Act 1993 s 38(2)(b), (3) as from a day to be appointed under s 42(2); and by the Chiropractors Act 1994 s 38(3)(b), (4), as from a day to be appointed under s 44(3)).
12 Access to Personal Files (Social Services) Regulations 1989 reg 8(1), (4) (reg 8(4) amended by SI 1991/1587). The exemption applies if the authority has, within 14 days of receiving a request under reg 3, informed the health authority or National Health Service Trust concerned or the appropriate health professional: see reg 8(3) (amended by SI 1991/1587). For the meaning of 'appropriate health professional' see reg 8(2) (which is expressed in almost identical terms to the definition set out in note 4 supra).
13 Ie before the end of the 40-day period provided for by ibid reg 6: see para 540 ante.
14 Ibid reg 8(4)(a).
15 Ibid reg 8(4)(b).
16 Ibid reg 8(5)(a).
17 Ibid reg 8(5)(b).

543. Other exemptions. The duty of a Housing Act local authority[1] to give access to relevant information[2] does not arise where the information sought:
  (1) would itself or with other available information identify another individual, other than a member of the tenant's[3] family, who has not consented to the disclosure, including an individual who has provided that information[4];
  (2) is information held by the authority for the purposes of prevention or detection of crime, or apprehension or prosecution of offenders, and disclosure of it would prejudice those matters[5];
  (3) is information in respect of which a claim to legal professional privilege could be maintained in legal proceedings[6],
and where part only of the information falls within one or more of these exemptions, the authority's duty arises in relation to the part that does not[7].

As regards accessible personal information[8] which is not personal health information from a health professional[9], a local social services authority[10] is exempted from the obligation to give access to personal information[11] if any of the following conditions are satisfied[12]:

(a) the carrying out of the social services functions[13] of the authority would be likely to be prejudiced by reason of the fact that serious harm to the physical or mental health or emotional condition of the individual who is the subject of the information or any other person would be likely to be caused[14];

(b) the identity of another individual, who has not consented to the disclosure of the information, either as a person to whom the information or part of it relates or as the source of the information, would be likely to be disclosed to, or deduced by, the individual the subject of the information or any other person who is likely to obtain access to it, either from the information itself or from a combination of that information and other information which the individual the subject of the information or such other person has, or is likely to have[15];

(c) the information is held by the authority for the purposes of the prevention or detection of crime or the apprehension or prosecution of offenders and to give an individual access to it[16] would be likely to prejudice either of those matters[17];

(d) the information consists of a report given or to be given to a court by the local social services authority in the course of any proceedings[18] where the information may be withheld by the court[19] in whole or in part from the individual who is the subject of the information[20];

(e) the information consists of information the disclosure of which is restricted or prohibited by certain enactments, rules and regulations relating to adoption and special educational needs[21];

(f) the information consists of information in respect of which a claim to legal professional privilege could be maintained in legal proceedings[22].

1 Ie the duty under the Access to Personal Files (Housing) Regulations 1989, SI 1989/503, reg 3(1)(b): see para 541 ante. For the meaning of 'Housing Act local authority' see para 539 note 7 ante (definition applied by reg 2).
2 For the meaning of 'relevant information' see para 541 note 3 ante.
3 For the meaning of 'tenant' see para 541 note 1 ante.
4 Access to Personal Files (Housing) Regulations 1989 reg 4(1)(a). Such information is not exempt from disclosure on the ground that it identifies an individual where the individual identified is one who (1) is or was a health professional and who provided the information in his capacity as such having been involved with the care of the person the subject of the information; or (2) acted in the course of his employment by the authority in connection with its functions as a landlord and who for reward provided services on behalf of the authority in performance of its duties as a landlord: reg 4(3). For the meaning of 'health professional' and 'care' see para 542 note 4 ante. Where such information is not as described in heads (1)–(2) supra, the authority must (a) within the period referred to in reg 3(1) (see para 541 ante) supply so much of the information sought as can be supplied without disclosing the identity of the other individual; (b) within 14 days of its duties arising under reg 3(1), inform that other individual in writing that the relevant information contains information which would identify him and ask whether he consents to that information being disclosed to the tenant: reg 4(2).
5 Ibid reg 4(1)(c).
6 Ibid reg 4(1)(d).
7 Ibid reg 4(1).
8 For the meaning of 'accessible personal information' see para 539 ante.
9 Ie information to which the Access to Personal Files (Social Services) Regulations 1989, SI 1989/206, reg 8 (see para 542 ante) does not apply: reg 9(1).
10 For the meaning of 'local social services authority' see para 539 note 9 ante.
11 Ie the obligation imposed by the Access to Personal Files (Social Services) Regulations 1989 reg 2(1)(b): see para 540 ante.
12 Ibid reg 9(1).

13 As to the meaning of 'social services functions' see para 539 note 10 ante.
14 Access to Personal Files (Social Services) Regulations 1989 reg 9(2). This condition does not apply to so much of the information sought by the request as can be supplied without causing serious harm, whether by the omission of names or other particulars or otherwise: reg 9(2). There is no requirement that evidence as to the risk of serious harm should be given by a medically qualified witness: *R v Derbyshire County Council, ex p K* [1994] 2 FLR 653 (permissible for social workers to give such evidence).
15 Access to Personal Files (Social Services) Regulations 1989 reg 9(3). This condition does not apply (1) if the only individual whose identity would be likely to be disclosed or deduced is or has been employed by the local social services authority in connection with that authority's social services functions or has provided for reward a service similar to a service provided by that authority in the exercise of those functions and the information relates to him or he supplied it in his official capacity or in connection with the provision of that service; or (2) to so much of the information sought by the request as can be supplied without enabling the identity of another individual to be disclosed or deduced, whether by the omission of names or other particulars or otherwise: reg 9(3)(a), (b).
16 Ie to apply ibid reg 2(1)(b) to the information: reg 9(4).
17 Ibid reg 9(4).
18 Ie proceedings to which the Magistrates' Courts (Children and Young Persons) Rules 1992, SI 1992/2071, apply: see CHILDREN vol 5(2) (Reissue) paras 1329–1331.
19 Ie in accordance with the provisions of the rules mentioned in note 18 supra: Access to Personal Files (Social Services) Regulations 1989 reg 9(5).
20 Ibid reg 9(5); Interpretation Act 1978 s 17(2)(a).
21 See the Access to Personal Files (Social Services) Regulations 1989 reg 9(6).
22 Ibid reg 9(7).

544. Correction and erasure of inaccurate information. A tenant[1] wishing a Housing Act local authority[2] (1) to correct or erase relevant information[3] which is inaccurate and of which he is or is treated[4] as the subject[5]; or (2) to correct relevant information which consists of an expression of opinion about the tenant or a member of his family which is based on such inaccurate information or which implies the existence of facts which are incorrect or misleading[6], may by notice in writing require the authority to do so[7]. Unless the authority forms the view that the relevant information is not inaccurate information or is not an opinion based on, or does not imply the existence of, incorrect or misleading facts in the manner described by the tenant[8], it must on receipt of such a requirement as is mentioned in head (1) above correct or erase the information as required by the tenant's notice and as soon as is reasonably practicable send a copy of the revised information to the tenant free of charge[9]; and on receipt of such a requirement as is mentioned in head (2) above it must clearly mark on any document on which that expression of opinion appears that the authority accepts that the opinion was based on inaccurate information or implies the existence of facts which are incorrect or misleading, and as soon as is reasonably practicable send to the tenant a copy of the document so marked free of charge[10]. Where, however, the authority forms the view described above, it must place a written note recording the tenant's view with the information which it has decided not to correct or erase[11] and send a copy of the note to the tenant together with a copy of the information to which it relates[12]. The authority must also, if it forms such a view, send a notice accompanying those copies to the tenant stating that the information is not inaccurate information or is not an opinion based on, or does not imply the existence of, incorrect or misleading facts in the manner described by the tenant and giving its reasons[13]. The authority must make no charge for supplying those copies or that notice[14].

Where the authority forms the view that part only of the relevant information is inaccurate, or is an opinion based on, or implies the existence of, incorrect or misleading facts in the manner described in the tenant's notice, it must comply with the procedure for correction, erasure or marking of documents[15] as appropriate in relation to that part, and with the procedure for sending copies and notices to the tenant[16] as to the remainder[17].

If an individual who is the subject of accessible personal information[18] regards that information, or part of it, as inaccurate, he may by notice in writing require the local social services authority[19] holding the information to rectify or erase the information which he regards as inaccurate[20]. If, following such a notice, the authority is satisfied that the information specified in it is inaccurate, the authority must rectify or erase the inaccurate information and any information held by the authority containing an expression of opinion which appears to the authority to be based on the inaccurate information[21]. If the authority is not so satisfied, it must place with the information regarded as inaccurate by the individual who served the notice a written note that that individual regards that information as inaccurate[22]. If a local social services authority so rectifies any information or so places a written note with any information, it must give the individual who is the subject of the information access to the rectified information or the written note without the payment of any fee[23].

1 For the meaning of 'tenant' see para 541 note 1 ante.
2 For the meaning of 'Housing Act local authority' see para 539 note 7 ante (definition applied by the Access to Personal Files (Housing) Regulations 1989, SI 1989/503, reg 2).
3 For the meaning of 'relevant information' see para 541 note 3 ante.
4 Ie under the Access to Personal Files Act 1987: see para 539 note 8 ante.
5 Access to Personal Files (Housing) Regulations 1989 regs 2, 7(1)(a).
6 Ibid reg 7(1)(b).
7 Ibid reg 7(1). That requirement must be accompanied by (1) sufficient information to enable the authority to identify the information and the record in which it is held; (2) a statement of the correct information; and (3) any written evidence on which the tenant relies as supporting his view that the information is, or is based on or implies the existence of facts which are, incorrect or misleading: reg 7(1)(i)–(iii).
8 Ie the view described in ibid reg 7(4): see the text and notes 11–14 infra.
9 Ibid reg 7(2).
10 Ibid reg 7(3).
11 Ibid reg 7(4)(a).
12 Ibid reg 7(4)(b).
13 Ibid reg 7(4)(c).
14 Ibid reg 7(4).
15 Ie the procedure set out in ibid reg 7(2): see the text to notes 8–9 supra.
16 Ie the procedure set out in ibid reg 7(3): see the text to note 10 supra.
17 Ibid reg 7(5). As to review of the authority's decision see para 545 post.
18 For the meaning of 'accessible personal information' see para 539 ante.
19 For the meaning of 'local social services authority' see para 539 note 9 ante.
20 Access to Personal Files (Social Services) Regulations 1989, SI 1989/206, reg 10(1). He is entitled to submit with the notice such written evidence of the inaccuracy of the information as he considers appropriate: reg 10(3). An authority is not obliged to take any action in response to such a notice unless the notice (1) supplies sufficient information for the authority to locate the information regarded as inaccurate; (2) specifies in what respect the individual regards that information as inaccurate; and (3) specifies how he considers the authority should rectify the information or what part of it he considers the authority should erase: reg 10(2).
21 Ibid reg 10(4).
22 Ibid reg 10(5).
23 Ibid reg 10(6). An authority has complied with its obligation under reg 10(6) if it supplies the individual with a copy of the rectified information or the note, but if the authority gives the individual access to that rectified information or note by other means, it is in addition obliged to supply him with a copy of so much of that rectified information or written note as he may require: reg 10(7).

545–600. Review of authority's decisions.

Where the tenant[1] is or is treated[2] as the subject of relevant information[3] held by a Housing Act local authority[4] and where he or a member of his family is aggrieved by any decision of that authority concerning his access to, or correction or erasure of, that information, the tenant may, within 28 days of his being notified of the decision, require that decision to be reviewed or reconsidered by the authority[5]. The authority must make such arrangements for the review of the decision as it thinks appropriate to ensure that the decision is either reviewed by members of that authority who took no part in making the decision to be reviewed or reconsidered by a meeting of the full authority[6]. The tenant may make oral or written representations[7].

An individual who is the subject of information held by a local social services authority[8] and who is aggrieved by any decision of that authority concerning his access to, or correction or erasure of, that information, may within 28 days of his being notified of the decision require that decision to be reviewed by a committee of three members of that authority appointed for that purpose[9]. The individual may make representations in writing to the members of the authority appointed for the purposes of the review and, if he so wishes, may make representations orally before them[10].

1 For the meaning of 'tenant' see para 541 note 1 ante.
2 Ie under the Access to Personal Files Act 1987: see para 539 note 8 ante.
3 For the meaning of 'relevant information' see para 541 note 3 ante.
4 For the meaning of 'Housing Act local authority' see para 539 note 7 ante (definition applied by the Access to Personal Files (Housing) Regulations 1989, SI 1989/503, reg 2).
5 Ibid reg 8(1).
6 Ibid reg 8(2)(a), (b).
7 Ibid reg 8(2).
8 For the meaning of 'local social services authority' see para 539 note 9 ante.
9 Access to Personal Files (Social Services) Regulations 1989, SI 1989/206, reg 11(1). Not more than one of the members of the committee may be a member of the committee established under the Local Authority Social Services Act 1970 s 2(1) (see LOCAL GOVERNMENT vol 28 paras 1145, 1362): Access to Personal Files (Social Services) Regulations 1989 reg 11(1).
10 Ibid reg 11(2).

CONFLICT OF LAWS

11. PROCEDURE

1. INTRODUCTION

(1) WHAT IS MEANT BY THE CONFLICT OF LAWS

601. Nature of the subject. The branch of English law[1] known as the conflict of laws, or private international law[2], in contradistinction to the ordinary local or domestic law of England[3], is concerned with cases having a foreign element. By a 'foreign element' is meant a contact with some system of law other than English law. Such a contact may exist, for example, because a contract was made or to be performed in a foreign country[4], or because a tort was committed there, or because property was situated there, or because the parties are not English[5]. In the conflict of laws, 'foreign element' and 'foreign country' mean a non-English element and a country other than England. From the point of view of the conflict of laws, Scotland or Northern Ireland is for many purposes as much a foreign country as France or Germany.

  1 As to the meaning of 'English law' see para 604 post.
  2 For a discussion of the various names given to the subject see Dicey and Morris *The Conflict of Laws* (12th Edn, 1993) 33.
  3 For the meaning of 'England' see para 604 post.
  4 For the meaning of 'country' see para 603 post.
  5 Ie English by domicile (see para 680 et seq post) or by residence (see paras 703–705 post). Traditionally, nationality is not a factor to which weight is attached in the English rules of the conflict of laws, because of the difficulty of determining the national law of a British subject (see para 609 note 5 post). However, as it is a relevant factor in the conflict of laws rules of many continental European countries, there is an increasing tendency for English statutes implementing international conventions on the conflict of laws to refer to a person's national law: see eg the Wills Act 1963; and para 964 post; the Family Law Act 1986; and para 744 post.

602. Public and private international law. The conflict of laws[1] has little in common with public international law[2]. The conflict of laws is a necessary part of the law of every country because different countries have different legal systems containing different legal rules, and some adjustment between them is necessary when events or transactions are not confined within the borders of a single country.

On the other hand, public international law seeks primarily to regulate the relations between different sovereign states; and, based as it is on the usage of nations and on judgments of the International Court of Justice[3], it is, at any rate in theory, the same everywhere. However, the rules of the conflict of laws are different from country to country. Even between England and Scotland there are some significant differences, while between England and other common law countries such as Australia, New Zealand and the United States on the one hand, and the continental European countries on the other, the differences are much more deep-rooted.

  1 For the meaning of this term see para 601 ante.
  2 For the principles of public international law see FOREIGN RELATIONS LAW.
  3 As to the International Court of Justice see FOREIGN RELATIONS LAW vol 18 para 1816 et seq.

603. Meaning of 'country'. A state in the sense of public international law may or may not coincide with a 'country' in the sense of the conflict of laws. Unitary states like France, Italy and New Zealand are countries in this sense, because the law is the same throughout the state. On the other hand, England, Scotland and Northern Ireland, each of the Australian and American states, and each Canadian province is a country in the sense of the conflict of laws, because each has a separate legal system, although none of them is a state known to public international law. However, for some purposes larger units than these may constitute countries. Thus, the United Kingdom is one country for purposes of the law of bills of exchange[1]; Great Britain is one country for most purposes of the law of companies[2]; Australia is one country for purposes of the law of matrimonial causes[3]; and Canada is one country for purposes of the law of divorce[4]. On the other hand, Wales is not a country, because its system of law is the same as that of England[5].

1 See the Bills of Exchange Act 1882; and BILLS OF EXCHANGE. For the meaning of 'United Kingdom' see para 604 post.
2 See the Companies Act 1985; and COMPANIES. For the meaning of 'Great Britain' see para 604 post.
3 Family Law Act 1975 (Aust), ss 39(3), (4), 103.
4 Divorce Act (RS Can 1970 c D-8), ss 5(1) (a), 14.
5 See para 604 post.

604. Geographical definitions. In this title the following terms are used:
'the United Kingdom' means Great Britain and Northern Ireland[1];
'Great Britain' means England, Scotland and Wales[2];
'the British Isles' or 'the British Islands' means the United Kingdom, the Channel Islands and the Isle of Man[3].
In older statutes 'England' included the principality of Wales, Monmouthshire and the town of Berwick on Tweed[1]; modern statutes refer separately to England and Wales, and those terms are defined by reference to local government boundaries[5].
Throughout this title the terms 'English law' and 'law of England' refer, in line with convention, to the law of England and Wales, since Wales does not have a separate jurisdiction, and 'English' and 'England', in relation to courts and jurisdiction, should be construed accordingly. Where a statute refers expressly to England and Wales (or may be taken so to refer), the terminology of that statute has been followed.

1 See the Interpretation Act 1978 s 5, Sch 1. Cf the definition of 'part of the United Kingdom' contained in the Civil Jurisdiction and Judgments Act 1982 s 50: see para 619 note 4 post.
2 See the Union with Scotland Act 1706 preamble, art 1.
3 See the Interpretation Act 1978 Sch 1.
4 See the Wales and Berwick Act 1746 s 3.
5 See the Interpretation Act 1978 Sch 1, where 'England' means, subject to any alteration of boundaries under the Local Government Act 1972 Pt IV (ss 46–78) (as amended), the areas consisting of the counties established by s 1, Greater London and the Isles of Scilly; and 'Wales' means the combined areas of the counties created by s 20 of that Act as originally enacted, but subject to any alteration made under s 73 (as amended); and CONSTITUTIONAL LAW; LOCAL GOVERNMENT. The Welsh Language Act 1967 s 4 (repealed) provided that references to England in future Acts of Parliament were no longer to include Wales. As to Greater London see LONDON GOVERNMENT vol 29 para 19. For an example of a statute defining 'England' as including Wales see the Maintenance Orders Act 1950 s 28(1).

605. Jurisdiction and choice of law. The questions that arise in conflict of laws cases are: (1) has the English court[1] jurisdiction to entertain the case; and (2) if so, what system of law, English or foreign, should it apply? There may sometimes be a third question, namely, will the English court recognise or enforce a foreign judgment purporting to determine the issue between the parties?
There are many situations in which, if the English court has jurisdiction, it will apply English domestic law[2]. Conversely, there are many situations in which, if a foreign court has jurisdiction according to English rules of the conflict of laws, its judgment

will be recognised or enforced in England, regardless of the grounds on which it was based or the choice of law rules which the foreign court applied[3]. Thus, in the English conflict of laws, questions of jurisdiction frequently tend to overshadow questions of choice of law[4].

1 As to the meaning of 'English' in relation to courts see para 604 ante.
2 See eg para 743 post (divorce and judicial separation).
3 See eg para 744 et seq post (divorce, judicial separation and annulment of marriage).
4 As to jurisdiction generally see para 615 et seq post.

(2) APPLICATION OF FOREIGN LAW

606. Renvoi. Where a foreign law governs a case by virtue of the English[1] rules as to choice of law, the English court must decide whether to apply the domestic law of the foreign country, that is, the law applicable in that country to a case having no material connection with any other country[2], or whether to apply the whole of the law of the foreign country, including its rules as to the conflict of laws[3]. If the latter course is adopted, it may be that the foreign country's rules as to the conflict of laws may make a reference back, or 'renvoi', as it is called, to the law of England[4], and in that event the English court must decide whether to accept the renvoi and apply its own internal law[5] or how otherwise to deal with the case.

1 As to the meaning of 'English' see para 604 ante.
2 This was recommended in *Re Annesley, Davidson v Annesley* [1926] Ch 692 at 709; *Re Askew, Marjoribanks v Askew* [1930] 2 Ch 259 at 278. It is the course usually adopted by the English court: see para 609 post.
3 This was preferred in *Re Ross, Ross v Waterfield* [1930] 1 Ch 377, especially at 389–390, after a full review of the authorities. See para 607 post.
4 The reference may be to the law of a third country, in which case the English court may apply that law, as in *Re Trufort, Trafford v Blanc* (1887) 36 ChD 600; and *Re Johnson, Roberts v A-G* [1903] 1 Ch 821.
5 This is the doctrine of 'partial renvoi'. See Dicey and Morris *The Conflict of Laws* (12th Edn, 1993) 72, where it is suggested that this is not the approach favoured by the courts, who prefer the doctrine of 'total renvoi': see para 607 post.

607. Total renvoi. In those cases in which the English court[1] applies the whole law of a foreign country, including its rules as to the conflict of laws, it will decide the case in the same manner as would the court of that foreign country having regard to all the actual facts of the case which it would consider relevant[2]. This method of dealing with the matter is in accordance with what is known as the 'doctrine of total renvoi' or 'foreign court doctrine'[3].

1 As to the meaning of 'English' in relation to courts see para 604 ante.
2 See *Re Ross, Ross v Waterfield* [1930] 1 Ch 377, especially at 389–390; and see the cases cited in para 609 notes 2–6 post. English law will, however, apply to matters of procedure.
3 See Dicey and Morris *The Conflict of Laws* (12th Edn, 1993) 72.

608. Difficulties of total renvoi doctrine. Certain difficulties may arise in the application of the total renvoi doctrine. First, it involves the English court[1] in the ascertainment of the rules of the conflict of laws of a foreign country, including its rules as to renvoi, and that ascertainment may in certain cases present much difficulty[2]. Secondly, the doctrine cannot be applied if the law of the foreign country also adopts the same doctrine, as otherwise a vicious circle or endless oscillation backwards and forwards from one law to the other would result[3]. If such a case were to come before an English court[4], it is thought that the domestic law of the foreign country would be applied by the English court[5].

1 As to the meaning of 'English' in relation to courts see para 604 ante.
2 See eg *Re Annesley, Davidson v Annesley* [1926] Ch 692 at 706–708; *Re Askew, Marjoribanks v Askew* [1930] 2 Ch 259 at 277–278; *Re Duke of Wellington, Glentanar v Wellington* [1947] Ch 506 at 515, [1947] 2 All ER 854 at 858–859; on appeal without referring to this point [1948] Ch 118, [1947] 2 All ER 854, 864, CA.
3 *Re Annesley, Davidson v Annesley* [1926] Ch 692 at 709; *Re Ross, Ross v Waterfield* [1930] 1 Ch 377 at 389; contra at 389–390; *Re Askew, Marjoribanks v Askew* [1930] 2 Ch 259 at 267; and see the First Report of the Private International Law Committee (Cmnd 9068), para 23; and Dicey and Morris *The Conflict of Laws* (12th Edn, 1993) 84–85.
4 At the date at which this volume states the law, no such case is known to have arisen.
5 *Casdagli v Casdagli* [1918] P 89 at 111, CA; on appeal [1919] AC 145, HL.

609. Scope of the renvoi doctrine. Where a foreign law governs a case by virtue of English[1] rules of the conflict of laws, the English court usually applies the domestic law of the foreign country[2]. The doctrine of renvoi has been applied primarily to cases of succession to movables[3] and immovables[4], as where a British national dies domiciled in a country by whose law succession is governed by the *lex patriae*, the law of the nationality[5]. Apart from such cases, the doctrine seems only to have been applied in a case of legitimation by subsequent marriage[6]. It also seems to be applicable as an alternative method of upholding the formal validity of a marriage, so that it will be formally valid if it complies either with the domestic rules or with the conflict rules of the *lex loci celebrationis*[7]. There is a strong case for the application of the doctrine to cases concerning the title to movables[8] or immovables[9] situated abroad.

1 As to the meaning of 'English' see para 604 ante.
2 See Dicey and Morris *The Conflict of Laws* (12th Edn, 1993) Rule 1 (p 70); and at 78. The doctrine does not apply in cases of contract: Rome Convention art 15 (set out in the Contracts (Applicable Law) Act 1990 s 2(1), Sch 1: see para 844 et seq post); *Re United Railways of Havana and Regla Warehouses Ltd* [1960] Ch 52 at 96–97, 115, [1959] 1 All ER 214 at 236, 246, CA. It does not apply to the formal validity of wills in cases governed by the Wills Act 1963: see ss 1, 2, 6(1); and para 964 post.
3 *Collier v Rivaz* (1841) 2 Curt 855; *Frere v Frere* (1847) 5 Notes of Cases 593; *Re Trufort, Trafford v Blanc* (1887) 36 ChD 600; *Re Brown-Séquard* (1894) 70 LT 811; *Re Johnson, Roberts v A-G* [1903] 1 Ch 821 (disapproved on another point in *Casdagli v Casdagli* [1918] P 89, CA; on appeal [1919] AC 145, HL; *Re Annesley, Davidson v Annesley* [1926] Ch 692; *Re Ross, Ross v Waterfield* [1930] 1 Ch 377; *Re Askew, Marjoribanks v Askew* [1930] 2 Ch 259); *Re Annesley, Davidson v Annesley* supra; *Re Ross, Ross v Waterfield* supra; *Re O'Keefe, Poingdestre v Sherman* [1940] Ch 124, [1940] 1 All ER 216; *Re Fuld's Estate (No 3), Hartley v Fuld* [1968] P 675, [1965] 3 All ER 776. Cf *Enohin v Wylie* (1862) 10 HL Cas 1; *Abd-ul-Messih v Farra* (1888) 13 App Cas 431 at 444–445, PC. See para 957 post.
4 *Re Ross, Ross v Waterfield* [1930] 1 Ch 377; *Re Duke of Wellington, Glentanar v Wellington* [1947] Ch 506, [1947] 2 All ER 854; on appeal without referring to this point [1948] Ch 118, [1947] 2 All ER 854, 864, CA, following *Kotia v Nahas* [1941] AC 403, [1941] 3 All ER 20, PC. See para 957 post.
5 The ascertainment of the national law of a British subject may give rise to questions of great difficulty. In *Re Johnson, Roberts v A-G* [1903] 1 Ch 821 at 826, and in *Re O'Keefe, Poingdestre v Sherman* [1940] Ch 124 at 129, [1940] 1 All ER 216 at 218, it was assumed, without evidence of foreign law, that this is the domicile of origin, but this is questionable: the question ought to be decided as the foreign court would decide it.
6 *Re Askew, Marjoribanks v Askew* [1930] 2 Ch 259: see para 786 post.
7 *Taczanowska (otherwise Roth) v Taczanowski* [1957] P 301 at 305, [1956] 3 All ER 457 at 460; on appeal [1957] P 301 at 318, [1957] 2 All ER 563 at 566, CA. See further para 706 note 3 post.
8 See para 930 post.
9 See the cases cited in note 3 supra; *Bank of Africa Ltd v Cohen* [1909] 2 Ch 129 at 146–147, CA. See further para 924 post.

(3) EXCLUSION OF FOREIGN LAW

610. Foreign law generally applied. Where by English[1] choice of law rules a foreign law is applicable to a case, the English court will generally apply that law even though the result may be contrary to a policy of English law which the court would apply in a purely domestic case[2]. Thus, the English court will generally enforce a contract which is valid by its governing law[3], even if it is made without consideration[4], or is champertous[5], or ousts the jurisdiction of a foreign court[6], or is for a loan which is irrecoverable under English domestic law[7]. Similarly, in cases involving personal status, the English court has recognised polygamy[8], marriage by proxy[9], marriage within the English prohibited degrees[10], and marriage below the age of consent[11].

1 As to the meaning of 'English' see para 604 ante.
2 See the cases cited in notes 4–11 infra.
3 As to the law applicable to a contract see para 844 et seq post.
4 *Re Bonacina, Le Brasseur v Bonacina* [1912] 2 Ch 394, CA.
5 *Re Trepca Mines Ltd (No 2)* [1963] Ch 199 at 218, [1962] 3 All ER 351 at 354, CA (litigation in foreign country); contrast *Grell v Levy* (1864) 16 CBNS 73; *Trendtex Trading Corpn v Crédit Suisse* [1982] AC 679, [1981] 3 All ER 520, HL (litigation in England).
6 *Addison v Brown* [1954] 2 All ER 213 at 217, [1954] 1 WLR 779 at 784.
7 *Saxby v Fulton* [1909] 2 KB 208, CA (betting loan); *Shrichand & Co v Lacon* (1906) 22 TLR 245 (loan at rate of interest in excess of that permitted by English Moneylenders Acts); see generally para 849 post.
8 *Baindail (otherwise Lawson) v Baindail* [1946] P 122, [1946] 1 All ER 342, CA: see para 737 post.
9 *Apt v Apt* [1948] P 83, [1947] 2 All ER 677, CA: see para 707 post.
10 *Re Bozzelli's Settlement, Husey-Hunt v Bozzelli* [1902] 1 Ch 751; *Cheni (otherwise Rodriguez) v Cheni* [1965] P 85, [1962] 3 All ER 873; and see para 726 post.
11 *Alhaji Mohamed v Knott* [1969] 1 QB 1, [1968] 2 All ER 563, DC: see para 727 post.

611. Public policy. Exceptionally, the English court[1] will not enforce or recognise a right conferred or a duty imposed by a foreign law where, on the facts of the particular case, enforcement or, as the case may be, recognition, would be contrary to a fundamental policy of English law[2]. The court has, therefore, refused in certain cases to apply foreign law where to do so would in the particular circumstances be contrary to the interests of the United Kingdom[3] or contrary to justice or morality[4]. So, in cases involving personal status, the English court will refuse to recognise a penal[5] status existing under a foreign law[6] or a penal incapacity or disability imposed by that law[7]. Foreign decrees affecting status may in certain cases be refused recognition on grounds of public policy[8]; and the court retains a residual discretion to refuse to recognise a foreign status where, on the facts of the particular case, recognition would be unjust or unconscionable[9]. However, this discretion is one to be most sparingly exercised[10].

The application of a rule of law which forms part of the law applicable to a contract may be refused if to apply it would be manifestly incompatible with English public policy[11]. In cases decided before the statutory provision to this effect was enacted, the English court refused to enforce a contract entered into under duress[12] and a contract to trade with the enemy[13], although in each case the contract was valid by its proper law; and it has also refused to enforce a champertous contract[14], a contract in restraint of trade[15], and a contract to procure a divorce[16].

1 As to the meaning of 'English' in relation to courts see para 604 ante.
2 See *Robinson v Bland* (1760) 2 Burr 1077; *Hope v Hope* (1857) 8 De GM & G 731; *Grell v Levy* (1864) 12

CBNS 73; *Sottomayor v De Barros* (1877) 3 PD 1 at 7, CA; *Rousillon v Rousillon* (1880) 14 ChD 351 at 369; *Kaufman v Gerson* [1904] 1 KB 591, CA; *Dynamit AG v Rio Tinto Co Ltd* [1918] AC 292, HL; *Baindail (otherwise Lawson) v Baindail* [1946] P 122 at 128–129, [1946] 1 All ER 342 at 346–347, CA; *Re Langley's Settlement Trusts, Lloyds Bank Ltd v Langley* [1962] Ch 541, [1961] 3 All ER 803, CA; *Cheni (otherwise Rodriguez) v Cheni* [1965] P 85 at 98–99, [1962] 3 All ER 873 at 882–883; and see the text and notes infra.

3   *De Wütz v Hendricks* (1824) 2 Bing 314; *Rousillon v Rousillon* (1880) 14 ChD 351; *Dynamit AG v Rio Tinto Co Ltd* [1918] AC 292, HL.

4   *Sottomayor v De Barros* (1877) 3 PD 1 at 7, CA; *Sottomayer v De Barros* (1879) 5 PD 94; *Kaufman v Gerson* [1904] 1 KB 591, CA; *Chetti v Chetti* [1909] P 67; *Re Langley's Settlement Trusts, Lloyds Bank Ltd v Langley* [1962] Ch 541, [1961] 3 All ER 803, CA; *Gray (otherwise Formosa) v Formosa* [1963] P 259, [1962] 3 All ER 419, CA; *Lepre v Lepre* [1965] P 52, [1963] 2 All ER 49. Cf *Cheni (otherwise Rodriguez) v Cheni* [1965] P 85 at 98–99, [1962] 3 All ER 873 at 882–883; *Re Fuld's Estate (No 3), Hartley v Fuld* [1968] P 675 at 698, [1965] 3 All ER 776 at 781. See also *Empresa Exportadora De Azucar v Industria Azucarera Nacional SA, The Playa Larga and The Marble Islands* [1983] 2 Lloyd's Rep 171 at 190, CA.

5   Ie discriminatory, as distinct from 'penal' in the sense in which the word is used in para 612 post.

6   *Re Metcalfe's Trusts* (1864) 2 De GJ & Sm 122 ('civil death' on entering a religious order); *Baindail (otherwise Lawson) v Baindail* [1946] P 122 at 128, [1946] 1 All ER 342 at 346, CA; *Regazzoni v KC Sethia (1944) Ltd* [1956] 2 QB 490 at 524, [1956] 2 All ER 487 at 496, CA, per Parker LJ; on appeal [1958] AC 301, [1957] 3 All ER 286, HL (slavery); but see *Santos v Illidge* (1860) 8 CBNS 861.

7   See *Worms v De Valdor* (1880) 49 LJCh 261; and *Re Selot's Trust* [1902] 1 Ch 488 (refusal to recognise incapacity imposed by French law upon French prodigal), applied in *Re Langley's Settlement Trusts, Lloyds Bank Ltd v Langley* [1962] Ch 541, [1961] 3 All ER 803, CA (Californian 'incompetent'). As to capacity to contract see para 853 post; as to incapacity to marry see para 729 post; and as to governmental seizure of property see para 937 post.

8   See para 747 post.

9   *Re Langley's Settlement Trusts, Lloyds Bank Ltd v Langley* [1962] Ch 541 at 555, 557–558, [1961] 3 All ER 803 at 807, 809, CA; *Russ (otherwise Geffers) v Russ (Russ otherwise De Waele intervening)* [1964] P 315 at 327–328, 334–335, [1962] 3 All ER 193 at 199, 203, CA; *Cheni (otherwise Rodriguez) v Cheni* [1965] P 85 at 98, [1962] 3 All ER 873 at 882–883; *Qureshi v Qureshi* [1972] Fam 173 at 201, [1971] 1 All ER 325 at 346.

10   *Cheni (otherwise Rodriguez) v Cheni* [1965] P 85 at 98–99, [1962] 3 All ER 873 at 882–883; *R v Brentwood Superintendent Registrar of Marriages, ex p Arias* [1968] 2 QB 956 at 968–969, 971, [1968] 3 All ER 279 at 282–283, 285, DC; *Qureshi v Qureshi* [1972] Fam 173 at 201, [1971] 1 All ER 325 at 346; and see *Vervaeke (formerly Messina) v Smith* [1983] 1 AC 145, 164.

11   Rome Convention art 16 (set out in the Contracts (Applicable Law) Act 1990 s 2(1), Sch 1: see para 844 et seq post).

12   *Kaufman v Gerson* [1904] 1 KB 591, CA. Cf *Re Meyer* [1971] P 298, [1971] 1 All ER 378 (divorce decree obtained under duress).

13   *Dynamit AG v Rio Tinto Co Ltd* [1918] AC 292, HL. For other cases concerned with trading with an enemy see CONTRACT.

14   *Grell v Levy* (1864) 16 CBNS 73. In this case the litigation was in England; it would be different if the litigation were in a foreign country by whose law champerty was lawful: *Re Trepca Mines Ltd (No 2)* [1963] Ch 199 at 218, [1962] 3 All ER 351 at 354, CA; see para 610 ante.

15   *Rousillon v Rousillon* (1880) 14 ChD 351 (restraint of trade in England). Cf *Apple Corpn Ltd v Apple Computer Inc* [1992] FSR 431.

16   *Hope v Hope* (1857) 8 De GM & G 731 (divorce in England; note that collusion is no longer a bar to the granting of a divorce decree: see DIVORCE).

612. Foreign penal law. The English court[1] will not enforce a foreign penal law, either directly or indirectly[2]. A penal law is one which imposes punishment for some breach of duty to the state, as opposed to a remedial law directed to securing compensation for a private person who has suffered damage as a result of a breach of duty owed to him[3]. The question whether a foreign law is penal is determined by the English court and is not affected by the view taken by the courts of the foreign country[4]. A sum of money claimed to be due to a plaintiff in an English court under the provisions of a foreign law is not considered as a penalty unless it is recoverable only at the instance of the foreign state concerned or by one of its officials as such or by a common informer[5]. Where a particular foreign law is partly penal and partly remedial, the English court will only enforce rights arising out of the part which is remedial[6]. Although the English court will not enforce a foreign penal law, it may recognise it for other purposes[7].

1   As to the meaning of 'English' in relation to courts see para 604 ante.
2   *Huntington v Attrill* [1893] AC 150, PC; *Folliott v Ogden* (1789) 1 Hy Bl 124; affd sub nom *Ogden v Folliott* (1790) 3 Term Rep 726; on appeal (1792) 4 Bro Parl Cas 111, HL; *Wolff v Oxholm* (1817) 6 M & S 92; *Le Louis* (1817) 2 Dods 210; *Banco de Vizcaya v Don Alfonso de Borbon y Austria* [1935] 1 KB 140; *Williams & Humbert Ltd v W & H Trade Marks (Jersey) Ltd* [1986] AC 368, [1986] 1 All ER 129; *United States of America v Inkley* [1989] QB 255, [1988] 3 All ER 144, CA. As to governmental seizure of property see para 937 post.
3   *Huntington v Attrill* [1893] AC 150 at 156, PC.
4   *Huntington v Attrill* [1893] AC 150 at 155, PC; *A-G for New Zealand v Ortiz* [1984] AC 1, [1983] 2 All ER 93, HL; *Larkins v National Union of Mineworkers* [1985] IR 671. However, see *United States of America v Inkley* [1989] QB 255 at 265, [1988] 3 All ER 144 at 150, CA, where it was stated that serious attention will be paid to the views of the foreign court, which may on occasions be decisive.
5   *Huntington v Attrill* [1893] AC 150 at 157–158, PC.
6   *Raulin v Fischer* [1911] 2 KB 93; and see para 1014 post.
7   *Regazzoni v KC Sethia (1944) Ltd* [1958] AC 301 at 322, [1957] 3 All ER 286 at 292, HL. Cf para 613 post. See also *Oppenheimer v Cattermole (Inspector of Taxes)* [1973] Ch 264, [1972] 3 All ER 1106, CA; affd on other grounds [1976] AC 249, [1975] 1 All ER 538, HL (deprivation of Jew's German nationality).

613. Foreign revenue law. The English court[1] will not enforce a foreign revenue law, either directly or indirectly[2]. An action to collect the taxes of a foreign country will not be entertained in England[3], irrespective of the identity of the plaintiff[4] or the form in which it is brought[5]. Although the English court will not enforce a foreign revenue law, it may recognise it for other purposes[6].

1   As to the meaning of 'English' in relation to courts see para 604 ante.
2   *Government of India, Ministry of Finance (Revenue Division) v Taylor* [1955] AC 491, [1955] 1 All ER 292, HL (capital gains tax); *Holman v Johnson* (1775) 1 Cowp 341 at 343 (customs duty); *Planché v Fletcher* (1779) 1 Doug KB 251 at 253 (customs duty); *James v Catherwood* (1823) 3 Dow Ry KB 190 at 191 (stamp duty); *Sydney Municipal Council v Bull* [1909] 1 KB 7 (rates); *Cotton v R* [1914] AC 176 at 195, PC (succession duty); *Indian and General Investment Trust Ltd v Borax Consolidated Ltd* [1920] 1 KB 539 at 550 (income tax); *Re Visser, Queen of Holland v Drukker* [1928] Ch 877 (succession duty); *Re Cohen (a bankrupt), ex p The Bankrupt v IRC* [1950] 2 All ER 36 at 39, CA (income tax); *Rossano v Manufacturers' Life Insurance Co* [1963] 2 QB 352 at 376–378, [1962] 2 All ER 214 at 228–229; *Brokaw v Seatrain UK Ltd* [1971] 2 QB 476, [1971] 2 All ER 98, CA; *A-G for Canada v Schulze & Co* (1901) 9 SLT 4 (customs duty); *Peter Buchanan Ltd and Macharg v McVey* [1955] AC 516n, [1954] IR 89 (profits tax); *Metal Industries (Salvage) Ltd v Harle (Owners)* 1962 SLT 114 (national insurance contributions); *Re Lord Cable (decd), Garratt v Waters* [1976] 3 All ER 417, [1977] 1 WLR 7. Cf *Re State of Norway's Application, Re State of Norway's Application (No 2)* [1990] 1 AC 723, sub nom *Re State of Norway's Applications (Nos 1 and 2)* [1989] 1 All ER 745 (assisting foreign court to obtain evidence for proceedings to enforce a revenue law in the foreign country did not constitute enforcement, direct or indirect).
3   As to the meaning of 'England' see para 604 ante.
4   *Peter Buchanan Ltd and Macharg v McVey* [1955] AC 516n, [1954] IR 89 (claim by liquidator in winding up of company); approved in *Government of India, Ministry of Finance (Revenue Division) v Taylor* [1955] AC 491 at 510–511, [1955] 1 All ER 292 at 298–299, HL.
5   *Rossano v Manufacturers' Life Insurance Co* [1963] 2 QB 352, [1962] 2 All ER 214 (garnishee order in respect of tax due by plaintiff in foreign country raised as defence to action for debt); *Brokaw v Seatrain UK Ltd* [1971] 2 QB 476, [1971] 2 All ER 98, CA (claim to possessory interest in goods by virtue of notice of levy in respect of unpaid tax).

6 *Regazzoni v KC Sethia (1944) Ltd* [1958] AC 301 at 319–322, [1957] 3 All ER 286 at 290–292, HL; *Re Emery's Investment Trusts, Emery v Emery* [1959] Ch 410, [1959] 1 All ER 577; and see paras 879, 881–882 post.

614. Foreign public law. Although the scope of the principle remains unclear, the English court will not enforce the public law of a foreign country[1].

1 See *United States of America v Inkley* [1989] QB 255, [1988] 3 All ER 144, CA; *A-G (UK) v Heinemann Publishers Australia Pty Ltd* (1988) 165 CLR 30, Aust HC. Cf *A-G for New Zealand v Ortiz* [1984] AC 1, [1983] 2 All ER 93, HL; *Williams & Humbert Ltd v W & H Trade Marks (Jersey) Ltd* [1986] AC 368, [1986] 1 All ER 129, HL. See also Dicey and Morris *The Conflict of Laws* (12th Edn, 1993) 103–108.

2. JURISDICTION

(1) IN GENERAL

615. Jurisdiction in actions in personam and in actions in rem. The jurisdiction of an English court[1] in an action in personam broadly depends upon the service of the writ of summons, or other originating process, upon the defendant[2]. If the writ may be served (and any challenge to the legality or regularity of such service overcome[3]) the court will have jurisdiction. As a matter of common law it was necessary to draw a distinction between service upon a defendant within the jurisdiction, and service upon a defendant outside the jurisdiction. In the former case, service was permissible as of right, for the defendant was under the authority of the sovereign, and was therefore liable to be summoned, when present within the jurisdiction[4]. By contrast, the intended defendant who is outside the jurisdiction is not so liable; and in the case of such a defendant, service upon him was permissible only with the leave of the court granted pursuant to the Rules of the Supreme Court[5] or pursuant to the County Court Rules[6].

The principles of jurisdiction in admiralty actions in rem are covered elsewhere[7], but where these impinge upon the provisions of the Brussels Convention[8] or the Lugano Convention[9], attention is drawn in this title to the particular problem.

1 As to the meaning of 'English' in relation to courts see para 604 ante.
2 See RSC Ord 5, Ord 10 r 5, Ord 11 r 9. For convenience, reference in this title to service of the writ is taken to include service of other forms of process. This paragraph and paras 616–679 post deal with jurisdiction in civil or commercial disputes. Jurisdiction in matrimonial matters is discussed elsewhere: as to divorce and judicial separation see para 741 post; as to nullity see para 742 post; as to presumptions of death and dissolution of marriage see para 751 post; as to declarations of status see para 754 post; as to financial relief see para 755 post; as to children see para 774 et seq post; and as to declarations of status and legitimacy see para 783 post.
3 The challenge will be made pursuant to RSC Ord 12 r 8; see para 617 post. Irregularity in service may be cured by the court: RSC Ord 2 r 1.
4 For the proposition that the power of the sovereign to summon a defendant is also the basis of the recognition of foreign judgments under the common law see *Adams v Cape Industries plc* [1990] Ch 433, [1991] 1 All ER 929, CA.
5 See RSC Ord 11.
6 See CCR Ord 8.
7 See ADMIRALTY vol 1 (1) (Reissue) para 307 et seq.
8 As to the Brussels Convention see para 618 text and note 1 post.
9 As to the Lugano Convention see para 618 text and note 2 post.

616. Immunity from the jurisdiction of the court. Certain individuals and bodies have immunity from the jurisdiction of the courts of the United Kingdom. Predominant among these are states, and others entitled to plead sovereign or diplomatic immunity, although the nature and extent of the immunity varies according to the identity of the claimant and the nature of the claim brought[1]. Similar immunities may be conferred upon an international organisation[2].

1 See FOREIGN RELATIONS LAW vol 18 paras 1548–1612.
2 Ie by Order made under the International Organisations Act 1968: see FOREIGN RELATIONS LAW vol 18 para 1597 et seq.

617. Contesting the jurisdiction of the court. A defendant who has been served with a writ within or out of the jurisdiction[1] is permitted, after acknowledging service and giving notice of intention to defend, and within the time fixed for the service of the defence[2], to challenge the jurisdiction of the court over him[3]. He may claim, inter alia, that service of the writ was irregular or ineffective, and should be set aside, or in the case of service on him out of the jurisdiction, that the court should not have granted leave to the plaintiff to serve the writ out of the jurisdiction, and that the writ, the order granting leave to serve it, and service of the writ, should be set aside[4]. If the court makes no order on the application, or dismisses it, the defendant is permitted a further period in which to re-acknowledge service and to give notice of intention to defend[5].

An application to challenge the jurisdiction of the court must be made at the outset of the proceedings, for if the defendant takes any step in the proceedings other than a step to challenge the jurisdiction, he will be taken to have waived any opportunity for challenge which he might otherwise have had, and to have submitted to the jurisdiction of the court[6].

1 Ie the jurisdiction of the English courts: see para 615 ante. As to the meaning of 'English' in relation to courts see para 604 ante.
2 See RSC Ord 12 r 8(1), (3).
3 See RSC Ord 12 r 8(1). The procedure by which a challenge to the jurisdiction is made, and the nature of the relief sought by such proceedings, is to be distinguished sharply from an application by a defendant, who does not dispute the existence of jurisdiction, for a stay of proceedings (a procedural stay). An application to the court that it should stay the exercise of its jurisdiction must, ex hypothesi, involve the admission that the court has such jurisdiction in the first place. It follows that an application for a stay should not be made within the procedure for making a challenge to the jurisdiction, for it is antithetical to it; and the mere making of it may itself compel the conclusion that the defendant has already submitted to the jurisdiction of the court: see *The Messiniaki Tolmi* [1984] 1 Lloyd's Rep 266, CA; *Bankers Trust Co v Galadari* [1986] 2 Lloyd's Rep 446, CA. But cf *Finnish Marine Insurance Co Ltd v Protective National Insurance Co* [1990] 1 QB 1078, [1989] 2 All ER 929; *Kuwait Airways Corpn v Iraq Airways Co* [1995] 1 Lloyd's Rep 25 at 32, 34, 38, CA; revsd, but not on this point, [1995] 3 All ER 694, [1995] 1 WLR 1147, HL. If the application for a stay is clearly shown to be alternative and subordinate to the application under RSC Ord 12 r 8, it may not be damaging to the applicant-defendant.
   It also follows that the obtaining of a such a stay is a matter of procedural law; and is discussed in this title in the context of procedural relief available to the parties during preparation for trial: see paras 1084–1091 post.
4 See RSC Ord 12 rr 7, 8(1).
5 See RSC Ord 12 r 8(6). If the defendant has made an application under Ord 12 r 8(1), the original notice of intention to defend does not constitute the submission of the defendant to the jurisdiction: Ord 12 r 8(6). Fresh acknowledgment will constitute submission to the jurisdiction: Ord 12 r 8(7); *E D & F Man (Sugar) Ltd v Haryanto (No 2)* [1991] 1 Lloyd's Rep 429, CA.
6 See *Williams & Glyn's Bank plc v Astro Dinamico Naviera SA* [1984] 1 All ER 760, [1984] 1 WLR 438, HL; *Kurz v Stella Musical Veranstaltungs GmbH* [1992] Ch 196, [1992] 1 All ER 630. See also *Ngcobo v Thor Chemicals Holdings Ltd* [1995] TLR 579, CA, where notice of appeal against a refusal of a stay was struck out because the appellant had, after being given leave to appeal, served a defence to the action, and was therefore to be seen as having withdrawn his objection to the trial being held in England.

(2) JURISDICTIONAL PROVISIONS OF THE BRUSSELS AND LUGANO CONVENTIONS

(i) In general

A. INTRODUCTORY

618. Jurisdiction according to the Conventions. The United Kingdom is party to two European conventions providing for the recognition and enforcement of judgments in civil and commercial matters, namely the Brussels Convention[1] and the Lugano Convention[2]. In consequence, the jurisdiction of a court in the United Kingdom in a civil or commercial matter is largely a matter of regulation by one of the two Conventions. In effect, the Conventions may provide:

(1) that the courts of the United Kingdom have jurisdiction in a particular case;
(2) that the courts of the United Kingdom and those of another contracting state[3] have jurisdiction in a particular case; or
(3) that the courts of the United Kingdom have no jurisdiction in a particular case.

If the rules of the Conventions (a) are inapplicable[4], or (b) provide that the jurisdiction of a national court in the particular case is to be determined by the national law of that court[5], the indigenous jurisdictional rules of English law are applicable[6].

In order to determine whether an English court has, or does not have, jurisdiction, the jurisdictional rules as set out in the Conventions must first be applied. The principal basis for jurisdiction is the domicile of the defendant[7], but a number of provisions of the Conventions are applicable without regard to the domicile of the defendant[8].

Where the Conventions give jurisdiction to the courts of the United Kingdom, an internal jurisdictional scheme operates to identify the particular part of the United Kingdom which has jurisdiction in the particular case[9].

The Conventions supersede previous treaties and conventions between contracting states (except where the conventions do not apply)[10]. The Civil Jurisdiction and Judgments Act 1982 may be amended by Order in Council in consequence of any revision of the Conventions[11].

1 The Convention on Jurisdiction and the Enforcement of Judgments in Civil and Commercial Matters (including the Protocol annexed to that Convention) was signed at Brussels on 27 September 1968. It was entered into by the six original members of the European Community, namely: Belgium, France, Germany (the former Federal Republic), Italy, Luxembourg and the Netherlands. This Convention is referred to in the Civil Jurisdiction and Judgments Act 1982 as 'the 1968 Convention': s 1(1). A Protocol on the interpretation of the Convention was signed at Luxembourg on 3 June 1971. This Protocol is referred to in the Civil Jurisdiction and Judgments Act 1982 (and throughout this title) as 'the 1971 Protocol': s 1(1). For convenience of reference the 1971 Protocol (as amended: see infra) is set out in the Civil Jurisdiction and Judgments Act 1982 Sch 2: s 2(2)(b) (s 2(2) and Sch 2 both substituted by the Civil Jurisdiction and Judgments Act 1982 (Amendment) Order 1990, SI 1990/2591). The obligation upon states entering into membership of the European Community to accede to the Convention was contained in the Treaty of Rome (ie the EC Treaty) art 220.
   The 1968 Convention and the 1971 Protocol have been amended, consequent upon the accession of further states to the European Community, as follows:
   (1) by the Convention on the accession to the 1968 Convention and the 1971 Protocol of Denmark, the Republic of Ireland and the United Kingdom, signed at Luxembourg on 9 October 1978 ('the Accession Convention': Civil Jurisdiction and Judgments Act 1982 s 1(1));
   (2) by the Convention on the accession of the Hellenic Republic to the 1968 Convention and the 1971 Protocol, with the adjustments made to them by the Accession Convention, signed at Luxembourg on 25 October 1982 ('the 1982 Accession Convention': Civil Jurisdiction and Judgments Act 1982 s 1(1) (definition added by the Civil Jurisdiction and Judgments Act 1982 (Amendment) Order 1989, SI 1989/1346));

(3) by the Convention on the accession of the Kingdom of Spain and the Portuguese Republic to the 1968 Convention and the 1971 Protocol, with the adjustments made to them by the Accession Convention and the 1982 Accession Convention, signed at Donostia–San Sebastián on 26 May 1989 ('the 1989 Accession Convention': Civil Jurisdiction and Judgments Act 1982 s 1(1) (definition added by the Civil Jurisdiction and Judgments Act 1982 (Amendment) Order 1990)).

The Civil Jurisdiction and Judgments Act 1982 provides that the Brussels Conventions are to have force of law in the United Kingdom, and that judicial notice is to be taken of them: s 2(1) (amended by the Civil Jurisdiction and Judgments Act 1991 s 3, Sch 2 para 1). 'The Brussels Conventions' means the 1968 Convention, the 1971 Protocol, the Accession Convention, the 1982 Accession Convention and the 1989 Accession Convention: Civil Jurisdiction and Judgments Act 1982 s 1(1) (definition added by the Civil Jurisdiction and Judgments Act 1982 (Amendment) Order 1990, and amended by the Civil Jurisdiction and Judgments Act 1991 s 2(1), (2)).

For convenience, this title uses the singular form 'the Brussels Convention' to denote the 1968 Convention as amended and adhered to by the United Kingdom. This is the form in which it is set out, for convenience of reference, in the Civil Jurisdiction and Judgments Act 1982 Sch 1: s 2(2)(a) (both substituted by the Civil Jurisdiction and Judgments Act 1982 (Amendment) Order 1990). The parties to the Brussels Convention (see supra) are referred to in the Civil Jurisdiction and Judgments Act 1982 as 'Brussels contracting states': s 1(3) (substituted by the Civil Jurisdiction and Judgments Act 1982 (Amendment) Order 1990; definition amended by the Civil Jurisdiction and Judgments Act 1991 s 2(5)).

2 Ie the Convention on jurisdiction and the enforcement of judgments in civil and commercial matters (including the Protocols annexed to that Convention) opened for signature at Lugano on 16 September 1988 and signed by the United Kingdom on 18 September 1989: see the Civil Jurisdiction and Judgments Act 1982 s 1(1) (definition added by the Civil Jurisdiction and Judgments Act 1991 s 2(3)). The Lugano Convention has force of law in the United Kingdom, and judicial notice must be taken of it: Civil Jurisdiction and Judgments Act 1982 s 3A(1) (s 3A added by the Civil Jurisdiction and Judgments Act 1991 s 1(1)). For convenience of reference the Lugano Convention is set out in the Civil Jurisdiction and Judgments Act 1982 Sch 3C: s 3A(2) (s 3A as so added; Sch 3C added by the Civil Jurisdiction and Judgments Act 1991 s 1(3), Sch 1). The relevant amendments to the Civil Jurisdiction and Judgments Act 1982 took effect, and consequently the Convention came into force in the United Kingdom, on 1 May 1992: Civil Jurisdiction and Judgments Act 1991 (Commencement) Order 1992, SI 1992/745.

The contracting states to the Lugano Convention, referred to as 'Lugano contracting states', are the 12 states party to the Brussels Convention (see note 1 supra) plus the member states of the European Free Trade Association, namely: Austria, Finland, Iceland, Norway, Sweden and Switzerland: see the Civil Jurisdiction and Judgments Act 1982 s 1(3) (as substituted: see note 1 supra; definition added by the Civil Jurisdiction and Judgments Act 1991 s 2(6)). At the date at which this volume states the law, all the Lugano contracting states except Austria had brought that Convention into effect.

3 In the Civil Jurisdiction and Judgments Act 1982, 'contracting state', without more, means, as applicable, a Brussels contracting state (see note 1 supra) and a Lugano contracting state (see note 2 supra): s 1(3) (as substituted, and the definition as amended: see note 1 supra).

4 See para 625 et seq post.

5 Ie pursuant to art 4 of the Conventions: see para 639 post. In the Civil Jurisdiction and Judgments Act 1982, any reference to a numbered article, without more, is a reference to the article so numbered in the Brussels Convention and the Lugano Convention, as appropriate: Civil Jurisdiction and Judgments Act 1982 s 1(2)(b) (substituted by the Civil Jurisdiction and Judgments Act 1991 s 2(4)). In line with this, a reference in this title to a numbered article 'of the Conventions' is a reference to the article so numbered in both the Brussels Convention and the Lugano Convention: see eg notes 7–8 infra. However, the citation of each such article separately is generally preferred where it is noted as authority: see eg para 627 note 3 post.

6 See para 648 et seq post.

7 See arts 2, 3 of the Conventions; the Civil Jurisdiction and Judgments Act 1982 s 41 (as amended); and para 634 post.

8 See paras 627–633 post. It is notable, however, that those provisions of the Conventions which permit proceedings to be brought against a defendant in courts other than those of his domicile are often accorded a restrictive or narrow interpretation: see the cases cited in relation to arts 16 (see paras 627–628 post), 13–15 (see para 632 post), 5, 6 (see paras 640–644 post) of the Conventions.

9 See para 619 post.

10 Brussels Convention arts 55, 56; Lugano Convention arts 55, 56. See the Civil Jurisdiction and Judgments Act 1982 s 9(1) (amended by the Civil Jurisdiction and Judgments Act 1991 Sch 2 para 4),

which states that those provisions have the same effect in relation to any statutory provision or rule of law of the United Kingdom which implements a superseded convention, as they have in relation to the superseded conventions themselves.

11 See the Civil Jurisdiction and Judgments Act 1982 s 14 (amended by the Civil Jurisdiction and Judgments Act 1991 Sch 2 para 9). The Orders in Council made under this power are the Civil Jurisdiction and Judgments Act 1982 (Amendment) Order 1989, SI 1989/346; the Civil Jurisdiction and Judgments Act 1982 (Amendment) Order 1990; and the Civil Jurisdiction and Judgments Act 1982 (Amendment) Order 1993, SI 1993/603.

619. Jurisdiction between different parts of the United Kingdom. Where the Brussels Convention[1] or the Lugano Convention[2] confers jurisdiction on the courts of the United Kingdom[3], jurisdiction as between different parts of the United Kingdom[4] is determined under the Civil Jurisdiction and Judgments Act 1982, which applies a modified version of the jurisdictional provisions of the Conventions[5].

However, the relevant provisions of that Act do not apply to certain specified proceedings[6].

1 As to the Brussels Convention see para 618 text and note 1 ante.
2 As to the Lugano Convention see para 618 text and note 2 ante.
3 For the meaning of 'United Kingdom' see para 604 ante.
4 'Part of the United Kingdom' means England and Wales, Scotland or Northern Ireland: Civil Jurisdiction and Judgments Act 1982 s 50.
5 Ibid s 16(1), (2), Sch 4 (s 16(1) amended by the Civil Jurisdiction and Judgments Act 1991 Sch 2 para 11; Sch 4 amended by the Civil Jurisdiction and Judgments Act 1982 (Amendment) Order 1993, SI 1993/603). Reference is made to that Schedule where necessary; see also para 625 post.
6 See the Civil Jurisdiction and Judgments Act 1982 s 17(1). For the proceedings so excluded see Sch 5 (as amended). The list of proceedings there contained may be amended by Order in Council: s 17(2). Such an Order in Council may make different provision for different descriptions of proceedings, for the same description of proceedings in different courts or for different parts of the United Kingdom, and may contain such transitional or incidental provisions as appear appropriate: s 17(3). An Order in Council may not be made unless a draft of it has been laid before and approved by each House of Parliament: s 17(4). At the date at which this volume states the law, no such Order in Council had been made in relation to England.

B. INTERPRETATION

620. Interpretation of the Brussels Convention. The Brussels Convention[1] is the common jurisdictional statute of the member states of the European Community. Accordingly, the Court of Justice of the European Community has been given the jurisdiction to give rulings upon the interpretation of the Convention[2], on references made by certain national courts[3]. Where such a question is raised in a case pending before such a court, the court must, or in certain circumstances may, request a ruling from the European Court[4] if it considers that a decision on the question is necessary to enable it to give judgment[5].

The competent authority[6] of a contracting state may request the European Court to give a ruling on a question of interpretation if judgments of the courts of that state conflict with either a previous interpretation given by the European Court or a judgment in another contracting state[7]. The registrar of the European Court must notify the contracting states and the institutions of the European Community, who have two months in which to submit statements or observations to the European Court[8]. No fees may be levied, or costs or expenses awarded, in respect of proceedings upon such a request[9].

In the United Kingdom, any question as to the meaning or effect of any provision of the Brussels Conventions[10] must, if not referred to the European Court as described above, be decided in accordance with the principles laid down by, and any relevant decision of, the European Court[11]. Without prejudice to this, certain specified reports may be considered in ascertaining the meaning or effect of any provision of the Brussels Conventions, and must be given such weight as is appropriate in the circumstances[12]. Judicial notice must be taken of any decision of, or expression of opinion by, the European Court on any such question[13].

It has been declared that in interpreting provisions of the Brussels Convention, it is appropriate for the European Court to pay due account to the decisions of national courts on the Lugano Convention[14].

1 As to the Brussels Convention see para 618 text and note 1 ante.
2 See the 1971 Protocol art 1. As to the 1971 Protocol see para 618 note 1 ante. The Court of Justice of the European Community also has jurisdiction in relation to the interpretation of the Protocol itself, of the Accession Convention, of the 1982 Accession Convention and of the 1989 Accession Convention: art 1. As to the Accession Convention, the 1982 Accession Convention and the 1989 Accession Convention see para 618 note 1 heads (1)–(3) ante. The provisions of the EEC Treaty, and of the Protocol on the Statute of the Court of Justice, which apply on requests to that court for preliminary rulings, apply to questions of interpretation as described in this paragraph: see 1971 Protocol art 5.
3 1971 Protocol art 1. The courts which may request the European Court to give a preliminary ruling on a question of interpretation are as follows:
  (1) specifically named courts of the contracting states, which in the case of the United Kingdom are the House of Lords and courts to which application has been made under the Brussels Convention art 37 para 2 (see para 1051 post) or art 41 (see para 1054 post) (1971 Protocol art 2 para 1);
  (2) the courts of the contracting states when they are sitting in an appellate capacity (art 2 para 2);
  (3) in cases provided under the Brussels Convention art 37 (see paras 1050–1051 post), the courts referred to therein (1971 Protocol art 2 para 3).
  For the meaning of 'contracting state' see para 618 note 3 ante.
4 In the 1971 Protocol the Court of Justice of the European Community is referred to as the Court of Justice; however, in English statutes, it is known as the 'European Court': see the European Communities Act 1972 s 1, Sch 1 Pt II, applied by the Interpretation Act 1978 s 5, Sch 1. To avoid confusion, the latter usage is preferred in this title, even where the usage in a particular authority may differ.
5 1971 Protocol art 3. The circumstances in which a reference is mandatory are where the court is one of those referred to in note 3 head (1) supra: see art 3 para 1. Where the court is one referred to in note 3 head (2) or (3) supra, the reference is discretionary: see art 3 para 2. For the procedure in English law see RSC Ord 114. However, the European Court has no jurisdiction to accept a reference from a national court seeking assistance in the interpretation of comparable (but not identical) domestic legislation: see Case C-346/93 *Kleinwort Benson Ltd v Glasgow City Council* [1995] ECR I-615, [1995] All ER (EC) 514, ECJ.
6 See the 1971 Protocol art 4 para 3. In the United Kingdom the competent authority is the appropriate law officer: see Dicey and Morris *The Conflict of Laws* (12th Edn, 1993) 286.
7 1971 Protocol art 4 para 1. The interpretation given by the European Court in response to a request does not affect the judgments which gave rise to the request: art 4 para 2.
8 Ibid art 4 para 4.
9 Ibid art 4 para 5.
10 For the meaning of 'the Brussels Conventions', distinct here from 'the Brussels Convention', see para 618 note 1 ante.
11 Civil Jurisdiction and Judgments Act 1982 s 3(1) (amended by the Civil Jurisdiction and Judgments Act 1991 s 3, Sch 2 para 1).
12 Civil Jurisdiction and Judgments Act 1982 s 3(3) (amended by the Civil Jurisdiction and Judgments Act 1991 Sch 2 para 1; the Civil Jurisdiction and Judgments Act 1982 (Amendment) Order 1989, SI 1989/1346; and the Civil Jurisdiction and Judgments Act 1982 (Amendment) Order 1990, SI 1990/2591). The reports to which reference may be made are: (1) the reports by Mr P Jenard on the 1968 Convention and the 1971 Protocol: (OJ C59, 5.3.79, p 1, 66); (2) the report by Professor Peter Schlosser on the Accession Convention (OJ C59, 5.3.79, p 71); (3) the report by Professor Demetrios I Evrigenis and Professor K D Kerameus on the 1982 Accession Convention (OJ C298, 24.11.86, p 1); and (4) the report by Mr Martinho de Almeida Cruz, Mr Manuel Desantes Real and Mr P Jenard on the 1989 Accession Convention (OJ C189, 28.7.90, p 35): Civil Jurisdiction and Judgments Act 1982

   s 3(3)(a)–(d) (as so amended). For the meaning of 'the 1968 Convention', 'the Accession Convention', 'the 1982 Accession Convention' and 'the 1989 Accession Convention' see para 618 note 1 ante.
13 Civil Jurisdiction and Judgments Act 1982 s 3(2).
14 See para 621 text and notes 3–6 post.

621. Interpretation of the Lugano Convention. The courts of each contracting state to the Lugano Convention[1], when applying and interpreting the provisions of that Convention, must pay due account to the principles laid down by the courts of other contracting states in decisions concerning the Convention[2]. This has been declared to mean that it is appropriate for the European Court[3], in ruling upon the Brussels Convention[4], to pay due account to the case-law of national courts concerning the Lugano Convention, and appropriate for the national courts of states interpreting the Lugano Convention[5] to pay due account to case-law of national courts, and of the European Court, upon the Brussels Convention[6].

   In the United Kingdom, in accordance with the provisions described above, a court must take account of any principles laid down in any relevant decision delivered by a court of any other Lugano contracting state concerning provisions of the Convention[7]. Without prejudice to this, a specified report on the Convention may be considered in ascertaining the meaning or effect of any provision of the Convention, and must be given such weight as is appropriate in the circumstances[8].

  1 As to the Lugano Convention see para 618 text and note 2 ante. For the meaning of 'contracting state' see para 618 note 3 ante.
  2 Lugano Convention Protocol No 2 art 1. As to the Protocols to the Lugano Convention see para 618 note 2 ante.
  3 As to the meaning of 'European Court' see para 620 note 4 ante.
  4 As to the Brussels Convention see para 618 text and note 1 ante.
  5 Ie states which are Lugano contracting states but not Brussels contracting states: see para 618 notes 1–2 ante.
  6 See the Report on the Lugano Convention by Mr P Jenard and Mr G Möller (OJ C 189, 28.7.90, p 57 at 90–91).
  7 Civil Jurisdiction and Judgments Act 1982 s 3B(1) (s 3B added by the Civil Jurisdiction and Judgments Act 1991 s 1(1)).
  8 Civil Jurisdiction and Judgments Act 1982 s 3B(2) (as added: see note 7 supra). The report referred to is that mentioned in note 6 supra.

622. Interpretation provisions common to both Conventions. The Brussels[1] and Lugano[2] Conventions have each been drafted in a number of different languages. It is expressly provided that each language version is equally authentic[3]; and it follows that it is permissible to refer to the texts of the Conventions in the other authentic languages, whether or not the English-language text appears to be ambiguous[4].

   Furthermore, it is apparent that many of the terms used in the Conventions bear a meaning distinct from that which would be accorded to them under national law[5].

  1 As to the Brussels Convention see para 618 text and note 1 ante.
  2 As to the Lugano Convention see para 618 text and note 2 ante.
  3 Brussels Convention art 68; Lugano Convention art 68; 1971 Protocol art 14. As to the 1971 Protocol see para 618 note 1 ante.
  4 See Dicey and Morris *The Conflict of Laws* (12th Edn, 1993) 284–285.
  5 See paras 626–645 post.

623. Interpretation of provisions regarding jurisdiction as between parts of the United Kingdom. In determining any question as to the meaning or effect of any provision for the determination of jurisdiction as between different parts of the United Kingdom[1], regard must be had to any relevant principles laid down by the European Court[2] in connection with the equivalent provisions of the Brussels Convention[3] and to any relevant decision of the European Court as to the meaning or effect of those provisions[4]. Without prejudice to this, the reports which may be considered with regard to the Brussels Convention[5] may also be considered with regard to the determination of jurisdiction as between parts of the United Kingdom and must, so far as relevant, be given such weight as is appropriate in the circumstances[6].

The European Court has no jurisdiction to give a preliminary ruling upon a provision of the Brussels Convention merely to enable the English court to give judgment on the basis of like provisions contained in the internal rules[7].

1 Ie any provision of the Civil Jurisdiction and Judgments Act 1982 Sch 4 (as amended) (as to which see para 619 ante): s 16(3). For the meaning of 'part of the United Kingdom' see para 619 note 4 ante.
2 As to the meaning of 'European Court' see para 620 note 4 ante.
3 Ie the Brussels Convention Title II (arts 2–24). As to the Brussels Convention see para 618 text and note 1 ante.
4 Civil Jurisdiction and Judgments Act 1982 s 16(3)(a). Where the text of Sch 4 is identical to the text of the Brussels Convention, this means that the interpretation of the United Kingdom provision must be the same as that of the Convention: *Kleinwort Benson Ltd v Glasgow City Council* (1996) Times, 1 February, CA.
5 See para 620 note 12 ante.
6 Civil Jurisdiction and Judgments Act 1982 16(3)(b).
7 See Case C-346/93 *Kleinwort Benson Ltd v Glasgow City Council* [1995] ECR I-615, [1995] All ER (EC) 514, ECJ, declining jurisdiction on a reference from *Barclays Bank plc v Glasgow City Council, Kleinwort Benson Ltd v Glasgow City Council* [1994] QB 404, [1994] 4 All ER 865, CA.

C. SERVICE OF PROCEEDINGS

624. Service of proceedings in cases covered by the Conventions. In any case in which the court has jurisdiction to hear a claim by reason of the Brussels Convention[1] or the Lugano Convention[2], but the person on whom the writ is to be served is out of the jurisdiction, the writ may be served as of right without the necessity for obtaining the leave of the court[3]. But any such writ must be indorsed with a statement that the court has power to hear and determine the claim[4].

1 As to the Brussels Convention see para 618 text and note 1 ante.
2 As to the Lugano Convention see para 618 text and note 2 ante.
3 See RSC Ord 11 r 1(2); and para 673 post. 'Person' includes a body of persons corporate or unincorporate: Interpretation Act 1978 s 5, Sch 1, applied by RSC Ord 1 r 3.
4 See RSC Ord 6 r 7(1).

D. SCOPE OF THE CONVENTIONS

625. Time of proceedings; application of a Convention by reference to states. For the purposes of jurisdiction, the Brussels Convention[1] or the Lugano Convention[2] is applicable only to proceedings commenced, or documents formally drawn up or registered as authentic instruments, on or after the day upon which it came into force[3].

Any question as to whether a case falls under the provisions of the Brussels Convention or the Lugano Convention is determined by the relevant provisions of the latter[4]. Accordingly, for proceedings to which both Conventions are in theory applicable, an English court dealing with a question of jurisdiction must apply the Brussels Convention[5] unless: (1) the defendant is domiciled in a Lugano contracting state which is not also a Brussels contracting state or the Lugano Convention confers jurisdiction[6] on the courts of such a state[7]; (2) in relation to lis pendens or to related actions[8], when proceedings are instituted in (a) a Lugano contracting state which is not a Brussels contracting state and (b) a Lugano contracting state which is a Brussels contracting state[9]; or (3) in matters of recognition and enforcement[10], where either the state of origin or the state addressed is not a member of the European Community[11].

Where the Brussels Convention or the Lugano Convention allocates jurisdiction to the courts of a contracting state[12], and that state is the United Kingdom, a separate jurisdictional scheme, internal to the United Kingdom and not subject to the jurisdiction of the European Court[13], will determine which part of the United Kingdom is to have jurisdiction[14].

1　As to the Brussels Convention see para 618 text and note 1 ante.
2　As to the Lugano Convention see para 618 text and note 2 ante.
3　Brussels Convention art 54 1st para; Lugano Convention art 54 1st para. As far as proceedings in the English courts are concerned, any proceedings commenced on or after 1 December 1991 are subject to the jurisdictional rules as contained in the 1968 Convention as modified by the 1989 Accession Convention (see para 618 note 1 ante). The Lugano Convention is potentially applicable to proceedings commenced in the English courts on or after 1 May 1992: see para 618 note 2 ante. See also *Trade Indemnity plc v Försäkringsaktiebolaget Njord (in liquidation)* [1995] 1 All ER 796.
4　Civil Jurisdiction and Judgments Act 1982 s 9(1A) (added by the Civil Jurisdiction and Judgments Act 1991 s 1(2)). The relevant provisions of the Lugano Convention are those contained in art 54B: see text and notes 5–11 infra.
5　See ibid art 54B para 1, which provides that the Lugano Convention does not prejudice the operation of the Brussels Convention.
6　Ie under the Lugano Convention art 16 or art 17: see paras 627–628, 633 post.
7　Ibid art 54B para 2(a). For the meaning of 'Brussels contracting state' and 'Lugano contracting state' see para 618 notes 1, 2 respectively ante.
8　Ie as provided for by ibid arts 21, 22: see para 645 post.
9　Ibid art 54B para 2(b).
10　See para 1040 et seq post.
11　Lugano Convention art 54B para 2(c).
12　Ie as distinct from allocating jurisdiction to the courts for a place, and in such a case there is no need for a separate provision of internal United Kingdom law.
13　Regard must be had, however, to principles laid down by the court in relation to the Brussels Convention: see para 623 ante. As to the meaning of 'European Court' see para 620 note 4 ante.
14　See generally the Civil Jurisdiction and Judgments Act 1982 Sch 4 (as amended); and para 619 ante. Reference to this is made where appropriate in this title.

626. Subject matter of the dispute. The Brussels Convention[1] and the Lugano Convention[2] apply to civil and commercial matters[3], but do not apply, in particular, to revenue, customs or administrative matters[4]. Further, the Conventions do not apply to: (1) the status or legal capacity of natural persons, rights in property arising out of a matrimonial relationship, wills and succession[5]; (2) bankruptcy, proceedings relating to the winding-up of insolvent companies or other legal persons, judicial arrangements, compositions and analogous proceedings[6]; (3) social security[7]; and (4) arbitration[8]. If the Conventions are inapplicable on this ground the jurisdiction of the court is determined solely by the indigenous rules of national law[9].

The Conventions have no application to matters relating to those rules of procedure which can be applied without jeopardising the jurisdictional rules of the Conventions[10]. The Conventions may also be inapplicable in a purely internal case in which there is no connection with any other contracting state[11]. Nor do they apply to proceedings for the recognition or enforcement of the judgment of a non-contracting state, even if the proceedings by which it is decided whether the judgment is entitled to recognition will involve a trial of what would otherwise appear to be a civil or commercial dispute[12].

If a plaintiff seeks to rely upon the jurisdictional provisions of another convention against a defendant who would otherwise be entitled to object to the jurisdiction of the English court[13], then at least in principle the plaintiff is entitled to invoke the provisions of the other convention[14], but he may be prevented from doing so if the same cause of action is pending between the same parties in the courts of another contracting state[15].

1 As to the Brussels Convention see para 618 text and note 1 ante.
2 As to the Lugano Convention see para 618 text and note 2 ante.
3 The meaning of 'civil and commercial matters' has been illustrated by decisions of the European Court: see Case 29/76 *LTU Lufttransportunternehmen GmbH & Co KG v Eurocontrol* [1976] ECR 1541, ECJ; Case 814/79 *Netherlands State v Rüffer* [1980] ECR 3807, ECJ; Case C-172/91 *Sonntag v Waidmann* [1993] ECR I-1963, ECJ. In effect it describes claims which are to be seen as matters of private law, rather than public law. It is not decisive that a body which is created under public law, or which is vested with public law powers, is a party to the litigation, for such a body can enter into a private law engagement with another party; but if the body is being proceeded against in relation to the exercise (or non-exercise) of powers which it has, and private individuals do not, or if it is alleged that it is liable for a legal reason which binds it as a public law body, but which would be inapplicable to a private individual, then the subject matter of the claim is excluded: Case C-172/91 *Sonntag v Waidmann* supra. Thus revenue, customs or administrative matters would be unlikely to have fallen within the scope of the Conventions, even without the use of the express words used to exclude them. As to the meaning of 'European Court' see para 620 note 4 ante.
4 Brussels Convention art 1; Lugano Convention art 1. See also note 3 supra.
5 Brussels Convention art 1 para 1; Lugano Convention art 1 para 1.
6 Brussels Convention art 1 para 2; Lugano Convention art 1 para 2. This exclusion is only for claims and matters which fall strictly within the rubric of bankruptcy and insolvent winding-up: Case 133/78 *Gourdain v Nadler* [1979] ECR 733, ECJ. A claim, therefore, made by the liquidator of an insolvent company against a defendant debtor to the company is not a claim peculiar to the context of bankruptcy; and is therefore not excluded: Case C-214/89 *Powell Duffryn plc v Petereit* [1992] ECR I-1745, ECJ. By contrast, a claim against the director of an insolvent company under the Insolvency Act 1986, requiring him to contribute to the assets of the insolvent company, would be excluded from the Convention: see the Insolvency Act 1986 ss 212–214; and Case 133/78 *Gourdain v Nadler* supra.
7 Brussels Convention art 1 para 3; Lugano Convention art 1 para 3.
8 Brussels Convention art 1 para 4; Lugano Convention art 1 para 4. This exclusion also extends to, and the Conventions are therefore inapplicable to, procedural and supervisory judicial proceedings brought prior to or during, and as part of, the arbitration process. Accordingly an application for the appointment of an arbitrator would not be subject to the provisions of the Conventions: Case C-190/89 *Marc Rich & Co AG v Società Italiana Impianti PA* [1991] ECR I-3855, ECJ. The further effect of the Conventions is unclear. As a matter of English law, a court is required to deny recognition to a foreign judgment rendered in breach of an arbitration agreement: Civil Jurisdiction and Judgments Act 1982 s 32(1), (3). But if the defendant submitted to the proceedings, he loses the protection of s 32: s 32(1)(b). It is unclear whether a court would be at liberty to apply this provision to deny recognition of a judgment otherwise entitled to recognition under the Conventions, on the ground that the national court's law of arbitration requires this result, and is entitled to be applied without interference from the Conventions; *Marc Rich & Co AG v Società Italiana Impianti PA (No 2)* [1992] 1 Lloyd's Rep 624, CA, suggests that a court may not do so, but the expression of opinion is obiter dicta, as the defendant had submitted to the jurisdiction of the court which had rendered judgment. See also *Qingdao Ocean Shipping Co v Grace Shipping Establishment, Transatlantic Schiffahrtskontor GmbH, Ode and Heath Chartering (UK) Ltd, The Xing Su Hai* [1995] 2 Lloyd's Rep 15 at 21.
9 See para 648 et seq post.
10 Case C-365/88 *Kongress Agentur Hagen GmbH v Zeehaghe BV* [1990] ECR I-1845, ECJ. As to the account which must be paid in the interpretation of either Convention to decisions of courts in relation to the other Convention, see paras 620–621 ante.
11 See the Preambles to the Conventions.
12 Case C-129/92 *Owens Bank Ltd v Bracco* [1994] ECR I-117, [1994] QB 509, [1994] 1 All ER 336, ECJ.
13 Ie by virtue of the Brussels Convention or the Lugano Convention.

14 See the Brussels Convention art 57; the Lugano Convention art 57: see para 677 et seq post.
15 Ie on the footing that the conventions are to be interpreted harmoniously, and if the other Convention has no provision dealing with lis alibi pendens, the provisions of the Brussels or Lugano Convention would apply: see Case C–406/92 *The Tatry (cargo owners) v The Maciej Rataj (owners)* [1994] ECR I-5439, [1995] All ER (EC) 229, ECJ.

(ii) Exclusive Jurisdiction regardless of Domicile

627. Immovable property. Proceedings which have as their object rights in rem in immovable property or tenancies of immovable property fall within the exclusive jurisdiction of the courts of the contracting state[1] or of the particular part of the United Kingdom[2], as the case may be, in which the property is situated[3]. The fraction of the claim falling within this definition must represent the dominant or principal part of the claim made[4]. In relation to tenancies, the rule covers claims which are brought to enforce the rent and other common covenants in a lease, but not covenants which, although contained in a lease, are substantively distinct from the obligations of lease[5]. The jurisdiction of the court cannot be denied by the bare allegation that there existed no legally enforceable lease[6]. A claim has as its object rights in rem in immovable property if it is brought to vindicate legal ownership of the land in question, but it is otherwise where the claim is brought to enforce personal obligations owed by the legal owner of the land, even if the ultimate ambition of the plaintiff in commencing the proceedings is to obtain a transfer of legal title to the land[7]. Accordingly an action to enforce a contract for the conveyance of land does not constitute such proceedings, and if the claim does not involve the application of rules of land law, and is governed instead by rules applicable to all property, it is unlikely that it will constitute such proceedings[8].

However, in relation to proceedings which have as their object tenancies of immovable property concluded for temporary private use for a maximum period of six consecutive months, the courts of the contracting state in which the defendant is domiciled also have jurisdiction provided that: (1) as regards the Brussels Convention and the determination of jurisdiction within the United Kingdom, the landlord and tenant are natural persons and domiciled in the same contracting state (or, as the case may be, part of the United Kingdom); or (2) as regards the Lugano Convention, the tenant is a natural person and neither party is domiciled in the contracting state in which the property is situated[9].

1 For the meaning of 'contracting state' see para 618 note 3 ante.
2 For the meaning of 'part of the United Kingdom' see para 619 note 4 ante.
3 Brussels Convention art 16 para 1(a); Lugano Convention art 16 para 1(a); Civil Jurisdiction and Judgments Act 1982 s 16(1) (as amended), (2), Sch 4 art 16(1)(a) (art 16(1) substituted by the Civil Jurisdiction and Judgments Act 1982 (Amendment) Order 1993, SI 1993/603). For a case involving land straddling an international frontier see Case 158/87 *Scherrens v Maenhout* [1988] ECR 3791, ECJ. For a qualification of this rule in its application to short private lettings see text and note 9 infra. As to the Brussels Convention see para 618 text and note 1 ante. As to the Lugano Convention see para 618 text and note 2 ante. As to the adaptation of the provisions of the Conventions by the Civil Jurisdiction and Judgments Act 1982 Sch 4, to a scheme applying as between parts of the United Kingdom, see para 619 ante. As to the interpretation of the scheme by reference to decisions under the Conventions see para 623 ante.
4 Case C–280/90 *Hacker v Euro-Relais* [1992] ECR I-1111, ECJ.
5 Contrast Case 73/77 *Sanders v van der Putte* [1977] ECR 2383, ECJ, with Case 241/83 *Rösler v Rottwinkel* [1985] ECR 99, [1985] 1 CMLR 806, ECJ. See also *Barratt International Resorts Ltd v Martin* 1994 SLT 434, Ct of Sess, where a contract of management of a time-share development was not a tenancy within this provision.

6 See Case 73/77 *Sanders v van der Putte* [1977] ECR 2383, ECJ; Case 158/87 *Scherrens v Maenhout* [1988] ECR 3791, ECJ.
7 Case C–294/92 *Webb v Webb* [1994] ECR I-1717, [1994] QB 696, [1994] 3 All ER 911, ECJ; *Barratt International Resorts Ltd v Martin* 1994 SLT 434, Ct of Sess. See also Case C–292/93 *Lieber v Göbel* [1994] ECR I-2535, ECJ.
8 See Case C–294/92 *Webb v Webb* [1994] ECR I-1717, [1994] QB 696, [1994] 3 All ER 911, ECJ; and Case 115/88 *Reichert v Dresdner Bank AG* [1990] ECR I-27, ECJ.
9 Brussels Convention art 16 para 1(b); Lugano Convention art 16 para 1(b); Civil Jurisdiction and Judgments Act 1982 Sch 4 art 16(1)(b) (as substituted: see note 3 supra). This provision was made as an amendment to the Brussels Convention (see the Civil Jurisdiction and Judgments Act 1982 (Amendment) Order 1990, SI 1990/2591, and to the Civil Jurisdiction and Judgments Act 1982 Sch 4 (see note 3 supra), and incorporated in the Lugano Convention prior to its enactment in the United Kingdom. It was designed to reverse the effect of the decision in Case 241/83 *Rösler v Rottwinkel* [1985] ECR 99, [1985] 1 CMLR 806, ECJ. It is intended to ensure that disputes as to tenancies arising out of holiday lettings are not confined to the exclusive jurisdiction of the contracting state in which the land is situated: see Dicey and Morris *The Conflict of Laws* (12th Edn, 1993) 948–950. As to which of the Brussels Convention and the Lugano Convention applies to a dispute see para 625 ante.

628. Other grounds. Apart from proceedings concerning immovable property[1], the other cases in which exclusive jurisdiction, regardless of domicile, is conferred on the courts of a particular contracting state[2], are as follows:

(1) in proceedings which have as their object the validity of the constitution, the nullity or the dissolution of companies or other legal persons or associations of natural or legal persons, or the decisions of their organs, exclusive jurisdiction is conferred upon the courts of the contracting state in which the company, legal person or association has its seat[3];

(2) in proceedings which have as their object the validity of entries in public registers, exclusive jurisdiction is conferred upon the courts of the contracting state in which the register is kept[4];

(3) in proceedings concerned with the registration or validity of patents, trade marks, designs or other similar rights required to be deposited or registered, exclusive jurisdiction is conferred upon the courts of the contracting state in which the deposit or registration has been applied for, has taken place, or is under the terms of an international convention deemed to have taken place[5];

(4) in proceedings concerned with the enforcement of judgments[6], exclusive jurisdiction is conferred upon the courts of the contracting state in which the judgment has been or is to be enforced[7].

The Conventions make no specific provision for a case in which the land, corporate seat, public register, or place of deposit or registration, is in a non–contracting state[8].

The provisions described above apply, with certain modifications[9], so as to confer exclusive jurisdiction on the courts of one particular part of the United Kingdom rather than another[10].

1 See para 627 ante.
2 For the meaning of 'contracting state' see para 618 note 3 ante.
3 Brussels Convention art 16 para 2; Lugano Convention art 16 para 2. As to the Brussels Convention see para 618 text and note 1 ante. As to the Lugano Convention see para 618 text and note 2 ante. It must be the validity of the decisions of organs, as distinct from the decisions themselves, which is the object of the proceedings: *Newtherapeutics Ltd v Katz* [1991] Ch 226, [1991] 2 All ER 151. Claims alleging want or excess of authority may fall within the article, but those alleging abuse of authority will not, as the latter are not concerned with the acts of the organs of a company, but wrongful acts of individuals: *Grupo Torras SA v Sheikh Fahad Mohammed al Sabeh* [1996] 1 Lloyd's Rep 7, CA.
4 Brussels Convention art 16 para 3; Lugano Convention art 16 para 3. See *Re Fagin's Bookshop plc* [1992] BCLC 118 (company's register of members).

5 Brussels Convention art 16 para 4; Lugano Convention art 16 para 4. This will apply to a case where the essential validity of a patent is in issue, but not (for example) to an action for the infringement of a patent: Case 288/82 *Duijnstee v Goderbauer* [1983] ECR 3663, [1985] 1 CMLR 220, ECJ (obligation of employee to transfer patent rights to employer).

6 'Judgment' means any judgment given by a court or tribunal of a contracting state, whatever the judgment may be called, including a decree, order, decision or writ of execution, as well as the determination of costs or expenses by an officer of the court: Brussels Convention art 25; Lugano Convention art 25.

7 Brussels Convention art 16 para 5; Lugano Convention art 16 para 5. The manner and form of enforcement proceedings, such as means of execution, fall within the article: see the report by Mr P Jenard on the 1968 Convention (OJ C59, 5.3.79, p 1 at 36); and Case C–129/92 *Owens Bank Ltd v Bracco* [1994] ECR I–117, [1994] QB 509, [1994] 1 All ER 336, ECJ. Measures pre-emptively taken to make the future enforcement of a contracting state judgment more successful are not within this provision: Case C–261/90 *Reichert v Dresdner Bank AG (No 2)* [1992] ECR I–2149, ECJ. The provision does not apply, and the Conventions as a whole have no application, to proceedings concerned with the recognition or enforcement of judgments from non-contracting states: Case C–129/92 *Owens Bank Ltd v Bracco* [1994] ECR I–117, [1994] QB 509, [1994] 1 All ER 336, ECJ. For the meaning of 'the 1968 Convention' see para 618 note 1 ante.

8 In such a case it appears that the jurisdiction of the court may be asserted under one of the other provisions of the Conventions; the question whether an English court could, in such a case, order a discretionary stay of proceedings is unclear: see para 646 post.

9 The modifications are that (1) head (3) in the text is omitted; (2) in each case, a reference to 'part of the United Kingdom' is substituted for the reference to 'contracting state'; and (3) in head (1) in the text, the reference to the decisions of the organs of persons, companies etc, is omitted. For the meaning of 'part of the United Kingdom' see para 619 note 4 ante. As to the adaptation of the provisions of the Conventions by the Civil Jurisdiction and Judgments Act 1982 Sch 4, to a scheme applying as between parts of the United Kingdom, see para 619 ante. As to the interpretation of the scheme by reference to decisions under the Conventions see para 623 ante.

10 See ibid s 16(1) (as amended), (2), Sch 4 art 16(2)–(5).

629. Consequences of exclusive jurisdiction. If a court of a contracting state[1] to the Brussels or Lugano Convention[2], or of a particular part of the United Kingdom[3], is seised of a claim which is principally concerned with a matter over which the courts of another contracting state (or, as the case may be, another part of the United Kingdom) have exclusive jurisdiction[4] the court must declare of its own motion that it has no jurisdiction[5]. Agreements or provisions of trust instruments conferring jurisdiction have no legal force if the court whose jurisdiction they purport to exclude has exclusive jurisdiction[6]; and it is not open to the defendant to submit to the jurisdiction of any other court[7].

Where actions come within the exclusive jurisdiction of several courts, any court other than the court first seised must decline jurisdiction in favour of that court[8].

Under the Conventions[9], a judgment from another court in circumstances which conflict with the exclusive jurisdiction must not be recognised[10].

1 For the meaning of 'contracting state' see para 618 note 3 ante.

2 As to the Brussels Convention see para 618 text and note 1 ante. As to the Lugano Convention see para 618 text and note 2 ante.

3 For the meaning of 'part of the United Kingdom' see para 619 note 4 ante. As to the adaptation of the provisions of the Conventions by the Civil Jurisdiction and Judgments Act 1982 s 16 (as amended), Sch 4, to a scheme applying as between parts of the United Kingdom, see para 619 ante. As to the interpretation of the scheme by reference to decisions under the Conventions see para 623 ante.

4 Ie under the Brussels Convention art 16; the Lugano Convention art 16; or the Civil Jurisdiction and Judgments Act 1982 Sch 4 art 16: see paras 627–628 ante.

5 Brussels Convention art 19; Lugano Convention art 19; Civil Jurisdiction and Judgments Act 1982 Sch 4 art 19.

6 Brussels Convention art 17, 4th para; Lugano Convention art 17 para 3; Civil Jurisdiction and Judgments Act 1982 Sch 4 art 17, 3rd para. As to the meaning of 'exclusive' in art 17 of the Conventions see

para 633 note 3 post. As to references to numbered articles 'of the Conventions' see para 618 note 5 ante.

7 Brussels Convention art 18; Lugano Convention art 18; Civil Jurisdiction and Judgments Act 1982 Sch 4 art 18.

8 Brussels Convention art 23; Lugano Convention art 23. As to which court is first seised of proceedings see para 645 post.

9 This does not apply to the application of provisions to the United Kingdom.

10 See the Brussels Convention art 28, 1st para; Lugano Convention art 28, 1st para. As to refusal of recognition generally under art 28 of the Conventions see para 1045 post.

(iii) Jurisdiction by Submission

630. Jurisdiction by submission. Apart from other provisions under which jurisdiction may be specifically conferred[1], a court before which a defendant enters an appearance has jurisdiction[2]. However, this does not apply where exclusive jurisdiction is conferred[3] on the courts of a particular contracting state[4] or, as the case may be, of a particular part of the United Kingdom[5].

Jurisdiction is not conferred if appearance was entered solely to contest the jurisdiction[6]. Thus if the defendant takes the steps prescribed by national procedural law for a challenge to the jurisdiction of the court, on the first available opportunity, he will not be treated as having conferred jurisdiction on the court by the entering of an appearance[7]. If national procedural law also requires that he lodge a defence on the merits, a court is still entitled to find that the defendant has not conferred jurisdiction by entering his appearance[8].

1 See paras 631–644 post; and note 2 infra.

2 Brussels Convention art 18; Lugano Convention art 18; Civil Jurisdiction and Judgments Act 1982 s 16(1) (as amended), (2), Sch 4 art 18. As to the Brussels Convention see para 618 text and note 1 ante. As to the Lugano Convention see para 618 text and note 2 ante. As to the adaptation of the provisions of the Conventions by the Civil Jurisdiction and Judgments Act 1982 Sch 4, to a scheme applying as between parts of the United Kingdom, see para 619 ante. As to the interpretation of the scheme by reference to decisions under the Conventions see para 623 ante. In English law the entry of an appearance is constituted by the acknowledgment of service: see RSC Ord 12 r 10. As to contesting the jurisdiction see para 617 ante.

 Note that the provisions cited supra are expressed in each case to be subject only to 'art 16' (see text and notes 3–5 infra). It follows that the other provisions of the Conventions (and the 1982 Act Sch 4) which confer jurisdiction, referred to in the text and note 1 supra, may be defeated by submission to jurisdiction.

3 Ie by the Brussels Convention art 16; the Lugano Convention art 16; or the Civil Jurisdiction and Judgments Act 1982 Sch 4 art 16 (as amended): see paras 627–628 ante.

4 Brussels Convention art 18; Lugano Convention art 18. For the meaning of 'contracting state' see para 618 note 3 ante.

5 Civil Jurisdiction and Judgments Act 1982 Sch 4 art 18. For the meaning of 'part of the United Kingdom' see para 619 note 4 ante.

6 Brussels Convention art 18; Lugano Convention art 18; Civil Jurisdiction and Judgments Act 1982 Sch 4 art 18.

7 Case 150/80 *Elefanten Schuh GmbH v Jacqmain* [1981] ECR 1671, [1982] 3 CMLR 1, ECJ; Case 27/81 *Etablissements Rohr SA v Ossberger* [1981] ECR 2431, [1982] 3 CMLR 29, ECJ. See also *Kurz v Stella Musical Veranstaltungs GmbH* [1992] Ch 196, [1992] 1 All ER 630. It is the purpose for which he enters an appearance, not the form of the appearance itself, which is determinative.

8 See Case 150/80 *Elefanten Schuh GmbH v Jacqmain* [1981] ECR 1671, [1982] 3 CMLR 1, ECJ; Case 27/81 *Etablissements Rohr SA v Ossberger* [1981] ECR 2431, [1982] 3 CMLR 29, ECJ.

(iv) Jurisdiction in cases of certain Contracts

631. Insurance contracts. Jurisdiction under the Brussels and Lugano Conventions in matters relating to insurance is determined according to a separate scheme contained in the Brussels and Lugano Conventions, as described below[1]. A judgment must not be recognised if it conflicts with the provisions of the scheme[2].

Actions against an insurer domiciled in a contracting state[3] may be brought where the insurer is domiciled[4], or in the contracting state in which the policyholder is domiciled[5], or (if the insurer is a co-insurer) where proceedings are being brought against the leading insurer[6]. Additionally, the insurer may be sued in the courts for the place where the harmful event occurred in the case of liability insurance or insurance of immovable property, or if movable and immovable property are covered by the same policy and both are adversely affected by the same contingency[7].

In respect of liability insurance, if the law of the court permits it, the insurer may be joined in proceedings which the injured party has brought against the insured[8].

An insurer not domiciled in a contracting state is nevertheless deemed to be so domiciled if the dispute arises out of the operations of a branch or agency in a contracting state[9].

An action may be brought by an insurer only in the courts of the contracting state in which the defendant is domiciled, whether he is the policyholder, the insured or the beneficiary[10].

The provisions of the scheme described above may be departed from by agreement[11] only if the agreement:

(1) is entered into after the dispute has arisen[12];

(2) allows the policyholder, the insured or the beneficiary to bring proceedings to be brought in courts other than those indicated above[13];

(3) is concluded between a policyholder and an insurer both of whom are at that time domiciled or habitually resident in the same contracting state, and it confers jurisdiction on the courts of that state even if the harmful event were to occur abroad, provided that the agreement is not contrary to the law of the state[14];

(4) is concluded with a policyholder who is not domiciled in a contracting state, except in so far as the insurance is compulsory or relates to immovable property in a contracting state[15]; or

(5) relates to a contract of insurance covering one or more of the following risks[16]:

    (a) any loss of or damage to (i) sea-going ships, installations situated offshore or on the high seas, or aircraft, arising from perils relating to their use for commercial purposes; or (ii) goods in transit, other than passengers' baggage where the transit consists of or includes carriage by such ships or aircraft[17];

    (b) any liability, other than for bodily injury to passengers or loss of or damage to their baggage, (i) arising out of the use or operation of such ships, installations or aircraft in so far as the law of the contracting state in which such aircraft are registered does not prohibit agreements on jurisdiction regarding insurance of such risks, (ii) for loss or damage as described in head (a) above[18];

    (c) any financial loss connected with the use or operation of ships, installations or aircraft, in particular loss of freight or charter hire[19];

    (d) any risk or interest connected with any of those referred to in heads (a) to (c) above[20].

1	Brussels Convention art 7; Lugano Convention art 7. The scheme is comprised in Section 3 (arts 7–12A) of each of the Conventions. The restrictions which they impose will not be applicable if the defendant enters an appearance in the courts of the contracting state in which he is sued: see para 630 ante. Neither do they apply if art 4 or art 5 para 5 of the Conventions (see paras 639, 643 post, and note 9 infra) applies to give the court jurisdiction: Brussels Convention art 7; Lugano Convention art 7; but see also the text to note 11 infra. As to the Brussels Convention see para 618 text and note 1 ante. As to the Lugano Convention see para 618 text and note 2 ante. As to references to numbered articles 'of the Conventions' see para 618 note 5 ante.

It is unclear whether the jurisdictional scheme provided by the Conventions applies to reinsurance: see the report by Professor Peter Schlosser on the Accession Convention (OJ C59, 5.3.79, p 71 at 117). The European Court declined to give its opinion on the point in C-351/89 *Overseas Union Insurance Ltd v New Hampshire Insurance Co* [1991] ECR I-3317; cf *New Hampshire Insurance Co v Strabag Bau AG* [1992] 1 Lloyd's Rep 361, CA; *Trade Indemnity plc v Forsäkringsaktiebolaget Njord (in liquidation)* [1995] 1 All ER 796 at 804. As to the meaning of 'European Court' see para 620 note 4 ante.

2	Brussels Convention art 28, 1st para; Lugano Convention art 28, 1st para. As to refusal of recognition generally under art 28 of the Conventions see para 1045 post.

3	For the meaning of 'contracting state' see para 618 note 3 ante.

4	Brussels Convention art 8 para 1; Lugano Convention art 8 para 1. As to domicile see para 634 et seq post.

5	Brussels Convention art 8 para 2; Lugano Convention art 8 para 2.

6	Brussels Convention art 8 para 3; Lugano Convention art 8 para 3.

7	Brussels Convention art 9; Lugano Convention art 9.

8	Brussels Convention art 10, 1st para; Lugano Convention art 10, 1st para. In such a case, the provisions of arts 7–9 of the Conventions (see text and notes 4–7 supra, 9 infra) apply to such actions: see Brussels Convention art 10, 2nd para; Lugano Convention art 10, 2nd para. If the law governing direct actions provides that the policyholder or the insured may be joined, the same court has jurisdiction over them: Brussels Convention art 10, 3rd para; Lugano Convention art 10, 3rd para. As to the importance of the distinction between the terms 'insured', 'policyholder' and 'beneficiary' as used in the Conventions see Dicey and Morris *The Conflict of Laws* (12th Edn, 1993) 375–376.

9	Brussels Convention art 8; Lugano Convention art 8. Note that any party domiciled in a contracting state may be sued in another contracting state if it has a branch, agency or other establishment there, out of the operations of which the dispute has arisen: Brussels Convention art 5 para 5; Lugano Convention art 5 para 5. Further, a counterclaim may always be brought in the court in which the main proceedings are pending: see art 6 para 3 of the Conventions; and para 644 post. For the purpose of such proceedings, a person is treated as domiciled in the part of the United Kingdom in which the branch, agency or establishment, out of whose operations the proceedings arose, is situated: Civil Jurisdiction and Judgments Act 1982 s 44(1)(a), (2) (amended by the Civil Jurisdiction and Judgments Act 1991 s 3, Sch 2 para 19).

10	See the Brussels Convention art 11, 1st para; and the Lugano Convention art 11, 1st para, which in each case is expressed to be without prejudice to art 10, 3rd para (see note 8 supra). This does not, however, affect the right to bring a counterclaim in the court in which the original claim is pending: Brussels Convention art 11, 2nd para; Lugano Convention art 11, 2nd para. As to the right to bring counterclaims see note 9 supra; and para 644 post. See also *New Hampshire Insurance Co v Strabag Bau AG* [1992] 1 Lloyd's Rep 361, CA.

11	Brussels Convention art 12; Lugano Convention art 12. As to the effect of agreements of this nature generally, known as 'choice of court agreements', see further para 633 post.

12	Brussels Convention art 12 para 1; Lugano Convention art 12 para 1.

13	Brussels Convention art 12 para 2; Lugano Convention art 12 para 2.

14	Brussels Convention art 12 para 3; Lugano Convention art 12 para 3.

15	Brussels Convention art 12 para 4; Lugano Convention art 12 para 4.

16	Brussels Convention art 12 para 5; Lugano Convention art 12 para 5.

17	Brussels Convention art 12A para 1; Lugano Convention art 12A para 1.

18	Brussels Convention art 12A para 2; Lugano Convention art 12A para 2.

19	Brussels Convention art 12A para 3; Lugano Convention art 12A para 3.

20	Brussels Convention art 12A para 4; Lugano Convention art 12A para 4.

632. Certain consumer contracts. Jurisdiction under the Brussels and Lugano Conventions in matters relating to consumer contracts is determined according to a separate scheme contained in the Brussels and Lugano Conventions, as described below[1]. A judgment must not be recognised if it conflicts with the provisions of the scheme[2]. Jurisdiction as between different parts of the United Kingdom in matters relating to consumer contracts is determined according to a similar scheme[3].

In proceedings concerning a contract made by a consumer[4] jurisdiction is determined by the scheme if the contract is:

    (1) a contract for the sale of goods on instalment credit terms[5]; or

    (2) a contract for a loan repayable by instalments, or for any other form of credit, to finance the sale of goods[6]; or

    (3) any other contract for the supply of goods, or for the supply of services, and

        (a) in relation to the Conventions, in the state of the consumer's domicile the conclusion of the contract was preceded by a specific invitation addressed to the consumer, or by advertising, and the consumer took in that state the steps necessary to conclude the contract[7]; or

        (b) within the United Kingdom, the consumer took in the part of the United Kingdom in which he is domiciled the steps necessary for the conclusion of the contract[8].

A consumer may bring proceedings in the contracting state or, as the case may be, the part of the United Kingdom, in which he is domiciled or in the contracting state in which the other party to the contract is domiciled[9]; but that other party may bring proceedings only in the contracting state in which the consumer is domiciled[10].

The provisions described above may be departed from only by an agreement[11] which (i) is entered into after the dispute has arisen; or (ii) allows the consumer to bring proceedings in courts other than those indicated above; or (iii) is entered into by the consumer and the other party, both of whom are at the time domiciled or habitually resident in the same contracting state or, as the case may be, the same part of the United Kingdom, and confers jurisdiction on the courts of that state or part, provided that such an agreement is not contrary to the law of that state or part[12].

1 See the Brussels Convention art 13; Lugano Convention art 13. The scheme is comprised in Section 4 (arts 13–15) of each of the Conventions. The restrictions which they impose will not be applicable if the defendant enters an appearance in the courts of the contracting state in which he is sued: see para 630 ante. Neither do they apply if art 4 or art 5 para 5 of the Conventions (see paras 639, 643 post, and note 9 infra) applies to give the court jurisdiction: Brussels Convention art 13; Lugano Convention art 13; but see also art 15 of the Conventions; and text to note 11 infra. As to the Brussels Convention see para 618 text and note 1 ante. As to the Lugano Convention see para 618 text and note 2 ante. As to references to numbered articles 'of the Conventions' see para 618 note 5 ante. For the meaning of 'contracting state' see para 618 note 3 ante.
    The code is inapplicable to contracts of transport: Brussels Convention art 13; Lugano Convention art 13.

2 Brussels Convention art 28, 1st para; Lugano Convention art 28, 1st para. As to refusal of recognition generally under art 28 of the Conventions see para 1045 post.

3 See the Civil Jurisdiction and Judgments Act 1982 s 16(1) (as amended), (2), Sch 4 art 13. The scheme, which is comprised in Section 4 (arts 13–15) of the Schedule, does not apply to contracts of transport or insurance: Sch 4 art 13. The scheme does not apply if the defendant enters an appearance: (see para 630 ante), and applies subject to art 5(5), (8)(b) (see para 643 post): art 13.

4 'Consumer' means someone who concludes a contract for a purpose which can be regarded as being outside his trade or profession: Brussels Convention art 13; Lugano Convention art 13; Civil Jurisdiction and Judgments Act 1982 Sch 4 art 13; and see Case 150/77 *Société Bertrand v Paul Ott KG* [1978] ECR 1431, ECJ. It is not clear whether it is a requirement that the other party to the contract makes the contract in the course of his business, but it is established that a non-consumer assignee of the consumer's contractual rights is not entitled to the privileges of these rules: Case C-89/91 *Shearson Lehmann Hutton Inc v TVB Treuhandgesellschaft für Vermögensverwaltung und Beteiligungen mbH* [1993] ECR I-139, ECJ.

5 Brussels Convention art 13 para 1; Lugano Convention art 13 para 1; Civil Jurisdiction and Judgments Act 1982 Sch 4 art 13(1).

6 Brussels Convention art 13 para 2; Lugano Convention art 13 para 2; Civil Jurisdiction and Judgments Act 1982 Sch 4 art 13(2).
7 Brussels Convention art 13 para 3; Lugano Convention art 13 para 3.
8 Civil Jurisdiction and Judgments Act 1982 Sch 4 art 13(3).
9 Brussels Convention art 14, 1st para; Lugano Convention art 14, 1st para; Civil Jurisdiction and Judgments Act 1982 Sch 4 art 14, 1st para. Under the Conventions, when a consumer enters into a contract with a party who is not domiciled in a contracting state but has a branch, agency or other establishment in a contracting state, then if the dispute arises out of the operations of that branch, agency or establishment, that party is deemed to be domiciled in that state: Brussels Convention art 13; Lugano Convention art 13. For the purpose of such proceedings, a person is treated as domiciled in the part of the United Kingdom in which the branch, agency or establishment, out of whose operations the proceedings arose, is situated: Civil Jurisdiction and Judgments Act 1982 s 44(1)(b), (2) (amended by the Civil Jurisdiction and Judgments Act 1991 s 3, Sch 2 para 19). Any proceedings brought in the United Kingdom by a consumer on the ground that he is domiciled there must be brought in the part of the United Kingdom in which he is domiciled: Civil Jurisdiction and Judgments Act 1982 s 10(3).
   A consumer does not have the right to bring proceedings in the courts of the contracting state in which he is domiciled unless the other party is also domiciled, or deemed to be so, in a contracting state: Case C-318/93 *Brenner v Dean Witter Reynolds Inc* [1994] ECR I-4725, [1995] All ER (EC) 278, ECJ.
   Note that any party domiciled in a contracting state (or part of the United Kingdom) may be sued in another contracting state (or part) if it has a branch, agency or other establishment there, out of the operations of which the dispute has arisen: Brussels Convention art 5 para 5; Lugano Convention art 5 para 5; Civil Jurisdiction and Judgments Act 1982 Sch 4 art 5(5). Further, a counterclaim may always be brought in the court in which the main proceedings are pending: see art 6 para 3, and art 14, 3rd para of the Conventions; and the Civil Jurisdiction and Judgments Act 1982 Sch 4 arts 6(3), 14, 3rd para; and para 644 post.
10 Brussels Convention art 14, 2nd para; Lugano Convention art 14, 2nd para; Civil Jurisdiction and Judgments Act 1982 Sch 4 art 14, 2nd para.
11 As to the effect of agreements of this nature generally, known as 'choice of court agreements', see further para 633 post.
12 Brussels Convention art 15; Lugano Convention art 15; Civil Jurisdiction and Judgments Act 1982 Sch 4 art 15. See further para 633 post.

(v) Jurisdiction derived from Choice of Court Agreement

633. Jurisdiction derived from a choice of court agreement. If the parties, one or more of whom is domiciled in a contracting state[1], have agreed that a court or the courts of a contracting state[2] are to have jurisdiction to settle any disputes which have arisen or which may arise in connection with a particular legal relationship, that court or those courts have exclusive[3] jurisdiction[4]. Similarly, the court or courts of a contracting state on which a trust instrument has conferred jurisdiction have exclusive jurisdiction in any proceedings brought against a settlor, trustee or beneficiary, if relations between those persons or their rights or obligations under the trust are involved[5].

   However, if a defendant enters an appearance in another court, he is taken to have waived a breach of this exclusive jurisdiction[6]. Agreements or provisions of a trust instrument conferring jurisdiction have no legal force if they are contrary to the provisions of the schemes regarding jurisdiction over insurance contracts[7] or consumer contracts[8], or if the courts whose jurisdiction they purport to exclude have exclusive jurisdiction[9] under the Conventions[10]. A judgment given by a court accepting jurisdiction in violation of the above provisions may not, on that account, be denied recognition[11].

   For a choice of court agreement to confer exclusive jurisdiction, one of the parties must be domiciled in a contracting state[12]: if this is not so, the courts of other contracting states have no jurisdiction unless the court chosen has declined jurisdiction[13]. The form in which the agreement is recorded must be either: (1) in writing or evidenced in writing; or (2) in a form which accords with the practices which the parties have established between themselves; or (3) in international trade or commerce, in a form which accords with a usage of which the parties are or ought to have been aware, and which in such trade or commerce is widely known to, and regularly observed by, parties to contracts of the type involved in the particular trade or commerce concerned[14].

The parties must have agreed to the clause; and a national court must assure itself both that they did agree, and that the agreement covers the proceedings which the plaintiff now brings[15], but it is not open to a court to deny the legal effect of the clause by reason of its failure also to comply with formal requirements of national law[16], nor on the ground of its incompatibility with other mandatory laws of the forum which would have rendered the agreement void of legal effect[17]. However, if the agreement is shown to have been entered into for the benefit of only one of the parties to it, that party retains the right to waive the agreement and sue in another court which would otherwise have jurisdiction over the defendant[18].

In the context of an individual contract of employment, the Brussels Convention provides that an agreement conferring jurisdiction has legal force only if it is entered into after the dispute has arisen or if the employee invokes it to seise courts other than those for the defendant's domicile or those specified by the Conventions[19]. Under the Lugano Convention an agreement in relation to such matters has effect only if it is entered into after the dispute has arisen[20].

Under the scheme for determining jurisdiction within the United Kingdom[21], if the parties have agreed that a court or courts of a part of the United Kingdom[22] are to have jurisdiction to settle any disputes which have arisen or may arise in connection with a particular legal relationship and the agreement would be effective[23] to confer jurisdiction under the law of that part, that court or those courts have jurisdiction[24]. The court or courts of a part of the United Kingdom on which a trust instrument has conferred jurisdiction has jurisdiction in any proceedings brought against a settlor, trustee or beneficiary, if relations between those persons or their rights or obligations under the trust are involved[25]. Agreements or provisions of a trust instrument conferring jurisdiction have no legal force if they are contrary to the provisions of the scheme regarding jurisdiction over consumer contracts[26], or if the courts whose jurisdiction they purport to exclude have exclusive jurisdiction[27] under the scheme[28]. In matters relating to individual contracts of employment, an agreement conferring jurisdiction has legal force only if it is entered into after the dispute has arisen or if the employee invokes it to seise courts other than those for the defendant's domicile or those specified by the scheme[29].

1 For the meaning of 'contracting state' see para 618 note 3 ante.
2 It is clear that art 17 of the Conventions applies only to choice of court agreements for the courts of a contracting state, and has no application in the case of an agreement upon the courts of a non-contracting state. As to the position where proceedings are sought to be stayed, by virtue of a choice of court agreement, in favour of a court of a non-contracting state, see para 646 post. As to references to numbered articles 'of the Conventions' see para 618 note 5 ante.
3 It appears that 'exclusive' does not here mean 'unique', and accordingly art 17 of the Conventions does not require the parties to agree upon a single jurisdiction; rather it means that the jurisdiction they agree upon excludes jurisdiction which would otherwise be conferred by the Conventions: see *Kurz v Stella Musical Veranstaltungs GmbH* [1992] Ch 196, [1992] 1 All ER 630. Thus if a single court is expressed to be competent for actions against A, and another for actions against B, there is no doubt that the clause will be effective: see Case 23/78 *Meeth v Glacetal Sarl* [1978] ECR 2133, [1979] 1 CMLR 520, ECJ. It seems that the courts of two contracting states may be chosen; and a clause purporting to confer non-exclusive jurisdiction on the courts of a contracting state may be held to be valid and effective: cf

Kurz v Stella Musical Veranstaltungs GmbH supra. Cf the position as regards jurisdiction within the United Kingdom: see text and note 24 infra.

4   Brussels Convention art 17, 1st para; Lugano Convention art 17 para 1. As to the Brussels Convention see para 618 text and note 1 ante. As to the Lugano Convention see para 618 text and note 2 ante. Note that the Brussels Convention art 17 has been considerably amended on each occasion upon which a new member state (except in the case of the accession of Greece) has acceded to the Convention (see para 618 note 1 ante). Early decisions of the European Court must be read with this in mind. As to the meaning of 'European Court' see para 620 note 4 ante.

5   Brussels Convention art 17, 3rd para; Lugano Convention art 17 para 2.

6   Case 150/80 *Elefanten Schuh GmbH v Jacqmain* [1981] ECR 1671, [1982] 3 CMLR 1, ECJ (variation of a contract by consent).

7   Ie art 12 of the Conventions: see para 631 text and notes 10–20 ante.

8   Ie art 15 of the Conventions: see para 632 text and notes 11–12 ante.

9   Ie conferred by art 16 of the Conventions: see paras 627–628 ante. As to references to numbered articles 'of the Conventions' see para 618 note 5 ante.

10   Brussels Convention art 17, 4th para; Lugano Convention art 17 para 3.

11   See the Brussels Convention art 28, 3rd para; the Lugano Convention art 28, 4th para. See also the Civil Jurisdiction and Judgments Act 1982 s 32(4) (as amended), which provides that s 32(1) (refusal of recognition or enforcement where proceedings in breach of agreement) does not apply to judgments required to be recognised under the Conventions: see para 1004 post. It has been held that a court seised second, which believes that it has jurisdiction under the Brussels Convention art 17 or the Lugano Convention art 17, is entitled to proceed to hear the case: *Kloeckner & Co AG v Gatoil Overseas Inc* [1990] 2 Lloyd's Rep 177; *Continental Bank NA v Aeakos Compania Naviera SA* [1994] 2 All ER 540, [1994] 1 WLR 588, CA; and see para 645 post.

12   Brussels Convention art 17, 1st para; Lugano Convention art 17 para 1.

13   Brussels Convention art 17, 2nd para; Lugano Convention art 17 para 1.

14   Brussels Convention art 17, 1st para (a)–(c); Lugano Convention art 17 para 1 (a)–(c). Early decisions of the European Court tended to give a very strict construction to these requirements, demanding clear writing to demonstrate that the defendant had seen the clause and had assented to it: Case 24/76 *Estasis Salotti di Colzani Aimo e Gianmario Colzani v RUWA Polstereimaschinen GmbH* [1976] ECR 1831, ECJ; Case 25/76 *Galeries Segoura SPRL v Bonakdarian* [1976] ECR 1851, [1977] 1 CMLR 361, ECJ. But in recent decisions there has been a relaxation of this standard. It is now possible to dispense with the need to comply with the formalities in a proper case: if the insistence by one party on compliance with the formalities would constitute bad faith on his part, such compliance may be dispensed with: cf Case 71/83 *Partenereederei ms Tilly Russ v Haven und Vervoerbedriff Nova NV & Goeminne Hout NV* [1984] ECR 2417, [1984] 3 CMLR 499, ECJ; Case 221/84 *Berghoefer GmbH & Co v ASA SA* [1985] ECR 2699, [1986] 1 CMLR 3, ECJ; Case 313/85 *Iveco Fiat SpA v NV Van Hool* [1986] ECR 3337, [1988] 1 CMLR 57, ECJ. If one party says he had no knowledge of the written clause, but did have the means of knowledge thereof, he may be deemed to have known of it, and hence to be bound: Case C-214/89 *Powell Duffryn plc v Petereit* [1992] ECR I-1745, ECJ (jurisdiction agreement in the constitution of a company in which the defendant was a shareholder; the wider application of the decision is uncertain). Best practice is to require the clause, and the assent of the parties to it, to be in written form. In the case of a Luxembourg domiciliary see the Brussels Convention, Annexed protocol art I (Civil Jurisdiction and Judgments Act 1982 s 2, Sch 1, Annexed Protocol); and Case 784/79 *Porta-Leasing GmbH v Prestige International SA* [1980] ECR 1517, [1981] 1 CMLR 135, ECJ.

15   Case C-214/89 *Powell Duffryn plc v Petereit* [1992] ECR I-1745, ECJ; *I P Metal Ltd v Ruote OZ SpA (No 2)* [1994] 2 Lloyd's Rep 560, CA. Cf *Harbour Assurance Co (UK) Ltd v Kansa General International Insurance Co Ltd* [1993] QB 701, [1993] 3 All ER 897, CA; *Pacific Resources Corpn v Credit Lyonnais Rouse* (7 October 1994, unreported), CA.

16   Case 150/80 *Elefanten Schuh GmbH v Jacqmain* [1981] ECR 1671, [1982] 3 CMLR 1, ECJ.

17   Case 25/79 *Sanicentral GmbH v Collin* [1979] ECR 3423, [1980] 2 CMLR 164, ECJ.

18   Brussels Convention art 17, 5th para; Lugano Convention art 17 para 4. If the clause expressly states that it was for the benefit of one party only, that will suffice: see Case 22/85 *Anterist v Crédit Lyonnais* [1986] ECR 1951, [1987] 1 CMLR 333, ECJ.

19   Brussels Convention art 17, 6th para. The reference in the text to specified courts is to courts specified in art 5 para 1: see para 641 post.

20   Lugano Convention art 17 para 5.

21   For the meaning of 'United Kingdom' see para 604 ante. As to the adaptation of the provisions of the Conventions by the Civil Jurisdiction and Judgments Act 1982 Sch 4, to a scheme applying as between parts of the United Kingdom, see para 619 ante. As to the interpretation of the scheme by reference to decisions under the Conventions see para 623 ante.

22   For the meaning of 'part of the United Kingdom' see para 619 note 4 ante.

23   Ie under the Civil Jurisdiction and Judgments Act 1982 s 16(1) (as amended), (2), Sch 4 (as amended).

24   Ibid Sch 4 art 17, 1st para. Note that, unlike its counterpart in the Brussels and Lugano Conventions, this provision does not refer to 'exclusive' jurisdiction.

25   Civil Jurisdiction and Judgments Act 1982 Sch 4 art 17, 2nd para.

26   Ie ibid Sch 4 art 15: see para 632 text and notes 11–12 ante.

27   Ie conferred by ibid Sch 4 art 16: see paras 627–628 ante.

28   Ibid Sch 4 art 17, 3rd para.

29   Ibid Sch 4 art 17, 4th para (added by the Civil Jurisdiction and Judgments Act 1982 (Amendment) Order 1993, SI 1993/603). The reference in the text to specified courts is to courts specified in the Civil Jurisdiction and Judgments Act 1982 Sch 4 art 5(1): see para 641 post.

(vi) Jurisdiction otherwise based on Domicile

A. DOMICILE IN A CONTRACTING STATE

634. Defendant domiciled in contracting state. Subject to the provisions discussed in other paragraphs[1], persons domiciled in a contracting state[2] must, whatever their nationality, be sued in the courts of that state[3], and persons who are not nationals of the state in which they are domiciled are governed by rules of jurisdiction applicable to nationals of that state[4]. As regards the determination of jurisdiction within the United Kingdom[5], persons domiciled in a part of the United Kingdom[6] must be sued in the courts of that part[7].

In order to determine whether a person is domiciled in the contracting state whose courts are seised of a matter, the court must apply its internal law; if a party is not domiciled in the state whose courts are so seised, then in order to determine whether he is domiciled in another contracting state, the court must apply the law of that state[8].

The seat of a company or other legal person or association of natural or legal persons, is treated as its domicile and is ascertained by applying the private international law of the court seised[9]. In order to determine whether a trust is domiciled in the contracting state whose courts are seised, the court must apply its rules of private international law[10].

Persons domiciled in a contracting state may be sued in the courts of another contracting state only by virtue of the rules of the Conventions[11]. Similarly, persons domiciled in a part of the United Kingdom may be sued in the courts of another part of the United Kingdom only by virtue of the scheme for determining jurisdiction between parts of the United Kingdom[12].

1   See paras 627–633 ante, 639–645 post.

2   For the meaning of 'contracting state' see para 618 note 3 ante.

3   Brussels Convention art 2, 1st para; Lugano Convention art 2, 1st para. As to the Brussels Convention see para 618 text and note 1 ante. As to the Lugano Convention see para 618 text and note 2 ante.

4   Brussels Convention art 2, 2nd para; Lugano Convention art 2, 2nd para. This represents the basic principle of the Conventions, namely that a defendant is entitled to defend himself in his home courts; exceptions to it are, for that reason at least, accorded a restricted or narrow interpretation. See in particular Case 220/88 *Dumez France SA v Hessische Landesbank* [1990] ECR I-49, ECJ; Case C-89/91 *Shearson Lehmann Hutton Inc v TVB Treuhandgesellschaft für Vermögensverwaltung und Beteiligungen mbH* [1993] ECR I-139, ECJ. A construction of a provision in the Conventions which would allow the plaintiff to sue in his home courts will be particularly carefully scrutinised: Case C-68/93 *Shevill v Presse Alliance SA* [1995] ECR I-415, [1995] 2 AC 18, [1995] All ER (EC) 289, ECJ; Case C-364/93 *Marinari v Lloyd's Bank plc (Zubaidi Trading Co intervening)* [1996] All ER (EC) 84, [1996] 2 WLR 159, ECJ. On the question of who is the defendant being sued see *The Deichland* [1990] 1 QB 361, CA; *The Anna H* [1995] 1 Lloyd's Rep 11, CA.

5   For the meaning of 'United Kingdom' see para 604 ante.

6 For the meaning of 'part of the United Kingdom' see para 619 note 4 ante.
7 Civil Jurisdiction and Judgments Act 1982 s 16(1) (as amended), (2), Sch 4 art 2. As to the adaptation of the provisions of the Conventions by the Civil Jurisdiction and Judgments Act 1982 Sch 4, to a scheme applying as between parts of the United Kingdom, see para 619 ante. As to the interpretation of the scheme by reference to decisions under the Conventions see para 623 ante.
8 Brussels Convention art 52; Lugano Convention art 52. As to the law to be applied in the United Kingdom see para 635 post.
9 Ie as distinct from the law of the contracting state in which it is supposed that the company or other legal person has its domicile: Brussels Convention art 53, 1st para; Lugano Convention art 53, 1st para. As to the law to be applied in the United Kingdom see para 636 post. As to the domicile of the Crown see para 638 post.
10 Brussels Convention art 53, 2nd para; Lugano Convention art 53, 2nd para. As to the law to be applied in the United Kingdom see para 637 post.
11 Brussels Convention art 3; Lugano Convention art 3.
The rules enabling jurisdiction in the United Kingdom over a defendant domiciled in another contracting state to be founded on:
(1) service of a writ on the defendant during temporary presence in the United Kingdom (the Brussels Convention refers to the document instituting the proceedings having been served on the defendant); or
(2) the presence within the United Kingdom of property belonging to the defendant; or
(3) the seizure by the plaintiff of property situated in the United Kingdom,
are inapplicable: see the Brussels Convention art 3; and the Lugano Convention art 3.
12 Civil Jurisdiction and Judgments Act 1982 Sch 4 art 3.

B. DOMICILE IN THE UNITED KINGDOM

635. Individuals. Subject to the provisions of the Brussels and Lugano Conventions[1], an individual is domiciled in the United Kingdom[2] if he is resident in the United Kingdom, and the nature and circumstances of his residence indicate that he has a substantial connection with the United Kingdom[3]. Similarly, an individual is resident in a particular part of the United Kingdom[4] if he is resident there, and the nature and circumstances of his residence indicate that he has a substantial connection with that part[5]. An individual is domiciled in a particular place in the United Kingdom if, and only if, he is domiciled in the part of the United Kingdom in which that place is situated, and he is resident in that place[6].

1 Ie subject to art 52 of the Conventions: see para 634 ante. As to the Brussels Convention see para 618 text and note 1 ante. As to the Lugano Convention see para 618 text and note 2 ante. As to references to numbered articles 'of the Conventions' see para 618 note 5 ante.
2 For the meaning of 'United Kingdom' see para 604 ante.
3 Civil Jurisdiction and Judgments Act 1982 s 41(1), (2) (s 41(1) amended by the Civil Jurisdiction and Judgments Act 1991 s 3, Sch 2 para 16). The requirement as to substantial connection is presumed to be fulfilled, unless the contrary is proved, if the individual has been resident in the United Kingdom for at least three months: Civil Jurisdiction and Judgments Act 1982 s 41(6).
4 For the meaning of 'part of the United Kingdom' see para 619 note 4 ante.
5 Civil Jurisdiction and Judgments Act 1982 s 41(3). If the requirements as to a substantial connection with a particular part of the United Kingdom are not satisfied, he is treated as domiciled in the part of the United Kingdom in which he is resident: s 41(5). Section 41(6) (see note 3 supra) also applies to s 41(3).
6 Ibid s 41(4)

636. Corporations and associations. For the purposes of the Brussels and Lugano Conventions[1] and the Civil Jurisdiction and Judgments Act 1982, the seat of a corporation or association is to be treated as its domicile[2].
A corporation or association has its seat in the United Kingdom[3] if, and only if, it was incorporated or formed under the law of a part of the United Kingdom[4] and has its

registered office or some other official address[5] in the United Kingdom, or its central management and control are exercised in that part[6]. It has its seat in a particular part of the United Kingdom if and only if it has its seat in the United Kingdom and (1) it has its registered office or some other official address in that part; (2) its central management and control are exercised in that part; or (3) it has a place of business[7] in that part[8]. It has its seat in a particular place in the United Kingdom if, and only if, it has its seat in the part of the United Kingdom in which that place is situated, and (a) it has its registered office or some other official address in that place; (b) its central management and control are exercised in that place; or (c) it has a place of business in that place[9].

A corporation or association has its seat in a state other than the United Kingdom if, and only if, it was incorporated or formed under the law of that state and has its registered office or some other official address there, or its central management and control are exercised in that state[10]. However, it is not regarded as having its seat in a contracting state other than the United Kingdom if it is shown that the courts of that state would not regard it as having its seat there[11].

For the purposes of the provisions conferring exclusive jurisdiction over proceedings relating to the formation or dissolution of corporations and associations, or decisions of their organs[12], a corporation or association has its seat in the United Kingdom if, and only if, it was incorporated or formed under the law of a part of the United Kingdom and its central management and control are exercised in the United Kingdom[13]. It has its seat in a particular part of the United Kingdom if and only if it has its seat in the United Kingdom and it was incorporated or formed under the law of that part[14], or, being incorporated or formed under the law of a state other than the United Kingdom, its central management and control are exercised in that part[15]. For the purposes of the same provisions, a corporation or association has its seat in a contracting state other than the United Kingdom if, and only if, it was formed or incorporated under the law of that state, or its central management and control are exercised in that state[16].

1 Ie for the purposes of art 53 of the Conventions: see para 634 ante. As to the Brussels Convention see para 618 text and note 1 ante. As to the Lugano Convention see para 618 text and note 2 ante. As to references to numbered articles 'of the Conventions' see para 618 note 5 ante. Certain other provisions apply in relation to art 16 para 2 of the Conventions: see text and notes 12–16 infra.

2 Civil Jurisdiction and Judgments Act 1982 42(1), (2) (amended by the Civil Jurisdiction and Judgments Act 1991 s 3, Sch 2 para 17). Certain other provisions apply in relation to the Civil Jurisdiction and Judgments Act 1982 Sch 4 arts 5A, 16(2): see text and notes 12–16 infra.

3 For the meaning of 'United Kingdom' see para 604 ante.

4 For the meaning of 'part of the United Kingdom' see para 619 note 4 ante.

5 'Official address', in relation to a corporation or association, means an address which it is required by law to register, notify or maintain for the purpose of receiving notices or other communications: Civil Jurisdiction and Judgments Act 1982 s 42(8).

6 Ibid s 42(3).

7 'Business' includes any activity carried on by a corporation or association, and 'place of business' must be construed accordingly: ibid s 42(8).

8 Ibid s 42(4).

9 Ibid s 42(5).

10 Ibid s 42(6).

11 Ibid s 42(7).

12 See the Brussels Convention art 16 para 2; Lugano Convention art 16 para 2; the Civil Jurisdiction and Judgments Act 1982 s 16 (as amended), Sch 4 arts 5A, 16(2); and para 628 text and note 3 ante.

13 Ibid s 43(1), (2) (s 43(1) amended by the Civil Jurisdiction and Judgments Act 1991 Sch 2 para 18).

14 A corporation or association formed under an enactment forming part of the law of more than one part of the United Kingdom, or an instrument having effect in the domestic law of more than one part of the United Kingdom must, if it has a registered office, be taken to have its seat in the part of the United

Kingdom in which that office is situated, and not in any other part of the United Kingdom: Civil Jurisdiction and Judgments Act 1982 s 43(5).

15 Ibid s 43(3), which is expressed to be subject to s 43(5) (see note 14 supra). For particular provision relating to Scotland see s 43(4).

16 Ibid s 43(6). However, a corporation or association must not be regarded as having its seat in a contracting state other than the United Kingdom if it has its seat in the United Kingdom by virtue of s 43(2)(a) (see text and note 13 supra), or if it is shown that the courts of that state would not regard it for the relevant purposes as having its seat there: s 43(7).

637. Trusts. For the purposes of the Brussels and Lugano Conventions[1] and the Civil Jurisdiction and Judgments Act 1982, a trust is domiciled in the United Kingdom[2] if, and only if, it is domiciled in a part of the United Kingdom[3]; it is domiciled in a part of the United Kingdom if, and only if, the system of law of that part is the system of law with which the trust has its closest and most real connection[4].

1 As to the Brussels Convention see para 618 text and note 1 ante. As to the Lugano Convention see para 618 text and note 2 ante.
2 For the meaning of 'United Kingdom' see para 604 ante.
3 Civil Jurisdiction and Judgments Act 1982 s 45(1), (2) (s 45(1) amended by the Civil Jurisdiction and Judgments Act 1991 s 3, Sch 2 para 20). For the meaning of 'part of the United Kingdom' see para 619 note 4 ante.
4 Civil Jurisdiction and Judgments Act 1982 s 45(3).

638. The Crown. For the purposes of the Civil Jurisdiction and Judgments Act 1982, the seat of the Crown is treated as its domicile[1]. For the purposes of the Brussels and Lugano Conventions[2] and the Civil Jurisdiction and Judgments Act 1982, the Crown in right of Her Majesty's government in the United Kingdom[3] has its seat in every part of, and in every place in, the United Kingdom[4]. However, Her Majesty may by Order in Council provide that in the case of proceedings of any specified description against the Crown in right of Her Majesty's government in the United Kingdom, the Crown is to be treated for the purposes of the Conventions as having its seat in, and in every place in, a specified part of the United Kingdom and not in any other part of the United Kingdom[5].

1 Civil Jurisdiction and Judgments Act 1982 s 46(1).
2 As to the Brussels Convention see para 618 text and note 1 ante. As to the Lugano Convention see para 618 text and note 2 ante. Article 53 of the Conventions equates the domicile of a legal person with its seat: see para 634 ante.
3 For the meaning of 'United Kingdom' see para 604 ante. Equivalent provision is made in relation to Her Majesty's government in Northern Ireland: see Civil Jurisdiction and Judgments Act 1982 s 46(3)(b). Nothing in these provisions applies to the Crown otherwise than in right of Her Majesty's government in the United Kingdom or Her Majesty's government in Northern Ireland: s 46(7).
4 Ibid s 46(2), (3)(a) (s 46(2) amended by the Civil Jurisdiction and Judgments Act 1991 s 3, Sch 2 para 21). For the meaning of 'part of the United Kingdom' see para 619 note 4 ante.
5 Civil Jurisdiction and Judgments Act 1982 s 46(4) (amended by the Civil Jurisdiction and Judgments Act 1991 Sch 2 para 21). Such an Order in Council may frame a description of proceedings in any way, and in particular may do so by reference to the government department or officer of the Crown against which or whom they fall to be instituted: Civil Jurisdiction and Judgments Act 1982 s 46(5). Any such Order in Council is subject to annulment in pursuance of a resolution of either House of Parliament: s 46(6). At the date at which this volume states the law, no such Order in Council had been made.

C. DEFENDANT NOT DOMICILED IN CONTRACTING STATE

639. Defendant not domiciled in any contracting state. If the defendant is not domiciled in a contracting state[1], nor is deemed to have such a domicile under the deeming provisions applicable to insurance and consumer contracts[2], and if jurisdiction is not otherwise conferred on a court by the Brussels and Lugano Conventions[3], the jurisdiction of the courts of each contracting state is to be determined by the law of that state[4]. As against such a defendant, any person domiciled in a contracting state may, whatever his nationality, avail himself in that state of the rules of jurisdiction there in force, in the same way as nationals of that state[5].

This means that the indigenous rules of the common law, as supplemented by statute, may be resorted to[6]. But it does not follow from this provision that the Conventions are in some sense inapplicable; for a court which proposes to assert jurisdiction by reason of this provision may not do so if the same cause of action, between the same parties, was first brought before the courts of another contracting state; and a court which proposes to assert jurisdiction under one of the provisions of the Conventions may not do so if in the courts of another contracting state the same cause of action, between the same parties, was commenced first[7].

1 For the meaning of 'contracting state' see para 618 note 3 ante. Under English law an individual is domiciled in a state other than a contracting state only if he is resident in that state, and the nature and circumstances of his residence indicate that he has a substantial connection with that state: Civil Jurisdiction and Judgments Act 1982 s 41(7).

2 See paras 631 note 9, 632 note 9 ante.

3 See paras 627–633 ante. As to the Brussels Convention see para 618 text and note 1 ante. As to the Lugano Convention see para 618 text and note 2 ante.

4 Brussels Convention art 4, 1st para; Lugano Convention art 4, 1st para. These are expressly subject to the provisions of art 16 of the Conventions: see paras 627–628 ante. As to references to numbered articles 'of the Conventions' see para 618 note 5 ante.

5 Brussels Convention art 4, 2nd para; Lugano Convention art 4, 2nd para. In particular, these provisions refer to those excluded as against a defendant domiciled in a contracting state by art 3 of the conventions: see para 634 note 11 ante.

6 See para 648 et seq post.

7 Case 351/89 *Overseas Union Insurance Ltd v New Hampshire Insurance Co* [1991] ECR I-3317, ECJ. In other words the jurisdiction of a court over a non-contracting state domiciliary, invoked by reason of art 4 of the Conventions, is itself derived from, and subject to the other restrictions contained in, the Conventions.

D. DEFENDANT DOMICILED IN ANOTHER CONTRACTING STATE

640. Special jurisdiction. A defendant who is domiciled in a contracting state[1] may nevertheless be sued in another contracting state if the matter is subject to the special jurisdiction of the courts of that other contracting state[2]. Because these provisions, which apply exclusively to those domiciled in another contracting state, derogate from a defendant's presumptive right to be sued in his home courts, they are construed restrictively[3]. Although they are in principle intended to get the litigation into a court with which it is closely connected, it is not open to the defendant to argue in a particular case that, because the special jurisdictional rule would lead to litigation in a court which in fact had little connection with the dispute, the court should on that account alone, determine that it has no special jurisdiction[4]. In all cases falling within the special jurisdiction provisions, there will be at least one other contracting state which has jurisdiction, and the provisions which regulate a situation of lis alibi pendens may well have to be used to resolve the problem of parallel proceedings[5].

Similarly, a defendant who is domiciled in a particular part of the United Kingdom⁶ may nevertheless be sued in another part of the United Kingdom if the matter is subject to the special jurisdiction of the courts of that other part of the United Kingdom⁷.

1 For the meaning of 'contracting state' see para 618 note 3 ante.
2 See the Brussels Convention art 5; the Lugano Convention art 5; and paras 641–643 post. As to the Brussels Convention see para 618 text and note 1 ante. As to the Lugano Convention see para 618 text and note 2 ante.
   The term 'special jurisdiction' is not defined, being taken from the heading of Section 2 (arts 5–6A) of the Conventions and of the United Kingdom scheme. As to references to numbered articles 'of the Conventions' see para 618 note 5 ante.
3 See in particular Case C-220/88 *Dumez France SA v Hessische Landesbank* [1990] ECR I-49, ECJ. The court is likely to be especially hostile to a construction which will routinely permit a plaintiff to bring proceedings in his home court: Case C-364/93 *Marinari v Lloyd's Bank plc (Zubaidi Trading Co intervening)* [1996] All ER (EC), 84, [1996] 2 WLR 159, ECJ.
4 Case C-288/92 *Custom Made Commercial Ltd v Stawa Metallbau GmbH* [1994] ECR I-2913, ECJ.
5 See para 645 post.
6 For the meaning of 'part of the United Kingdom' see para 619 note 4 ante.
7 See the Civil Jurisdiction and Judgments Act 1982 s 16(1) (as amended), (2), Sch 4 art 5; and paras 641–643 post. As to the adaptation of the provisions of the Conventions by the Civil Jurisdiction and Judgments Act 1982 Sch 4, to a scheme applying as between parts of the United Kingdom, see para 619 ante. As to the interpretation of the scheme by reference to decisions under the Conventions see para 623 ante.
   The term 'special jurisdiction' is not defined, being taken from the heading of Section 2 (arts 5–6A) of the scheme.

641. Matters relating to contract. A defendant domiciled in a contracting state¹ may be sued in another contracting state, in matters relating to a contract, in the courts for the place of performance of the obligation in question². Similarly, a person domiciled in a part of the United Kingdom³ may be sued in another part of the United Kingdom, in matters relating to a contract, in the courts for the place of performance of the obligation in question⁴.

A court may exercise this jurisdiction even if the defendant contends that there was no contract between the parties⁵. The court may accept jurisdiction if there is a good arguable case that there was such a contract as would confer jurisdiction upon it⁶.

'Matter relating to a contract' bears an autonomous meaning, not to be interpreted by reference to national law⁷. Its defining characteristic is that there is an obligation, freely entered into with regard to another⁸. The 'obligation in question' means the obligation in respect of which the plaintiff brings his claim, or upon the non-performance of which he founds his action⁹. Where there is more than one such obligation, the court may conclude that one of them is the principal to which the others are merely accessory; the principal one will determine the jurisdiction¹⁰. Where there is a single obligation calling for performance in more contracting states than one it will be the contracting state in which it was principally to be performed which will have jurisdiction¹¹. Under the United Kingdom scheme, a matter may apparently be a 'matter relating to a contract' even if the contract is void¹².

The place where the obligation was to be performed is determined by the court applying its rules of national law, including its conflicts rules¹³.

In relation to an individual contract of employment, the Brussels Convention and the scheme applicable within the United Kingdom provide that the place in question is that where the employee habitually carries out his work, or if the employee does not habitually carry out his work in any one country, the employer may also be sued in the courts for the place where the business which engaged the employee was or is now situated¹⁴. Under the Lugano Convention in matters relating to individual contracts of employment, the place of performance of the obligation is the place where the employee habitually carries on his work, or if he does not carry out his work in any one country, the place of business through which he was engaged[15].

1 For the meaning of 'contracting state' see para 618 note 3 ante.
2 Brussels Convention art 5 para 1; Lugano Convention art 5 para 1. As to the Brussels Convention see para 618 text and note 1 ante. As to the Lugano Convention see para 618 text and note 2 ante.
3 For the meaning of 'part of the United Kingdom' see para 619 note 4 ante.
4 Civil Jurisdiction and Judgments Act 1982 s 16(1) (as amended), (2), Sch 4 art 5(1). As to the adaptation of the provisions of the Conventions by the Civil Jurisdiction and Judgments Act 1982 Sch 4, to a scheme applying as between parts of the United Kingdom, see para 619 ante. As to the interpretation of the scheme by reference to decisions under the Conventions see para 623 ante.
5 Case 38/81 *Effer SpA v Kantner* [1982] ECR 825, [1984] 2 CMLR 667, ECJ.
6 *Tesam Distribution Ltd v Schuh Mode Team GmbH* [1990] ILPr 149, CA; *Mölnlycke AB v Procter & Gamble Ltd* [1992] 4 All ER 47, [1992] 1 WLR 1112, CA.
7 Case 34/82 *Peters v ZNAV* [1983] ECR 987, ECJ; Case C-26/91 *Jakob Handte GmbH v Traitements Mécano-chimiques des Surfaces* [1992] ECR I-3967, ECJ; and see Case C-214/89 *Powell Duffryn plc v Petereit* [1992] ECR I-1745, ECJ. This definition would probably encompass all actions seen as contractual in English law. See, however, *Kleinwort Benson Ltd v Glasgow City Council* (1996) Times, 1 February, CA; and text and notes 8, 12 infra.
8 Case C-26/91 *Jakob Handte GmbH v Traitements Mécano-chimiques des Surfaces* [1992] ECR I-3967, ECJ. See also *Atlas Shipping Agency (UK) Ltd v Suisse Atlantique Société d'Armament Maritime SA* [1995] ILPr 600 (commission payment to shipbroker provided for in contract between buyer and seller was a 'matter relating to a contract' when claimed by the shipbroker). But cf *Trade Indemnity plc v Försäkrings-saktiebølaget Njord (in liquidation)* [1995] 1 All ER 796. It therefore excludes an action by a sub-buyer against the manufacturer, who does not freely enter into an engagement with the sub-buyer: see Case C-26/91 *Jakob Handte GmbH v Traitements Mécano-chimiques des Surfaces* supra, where according to the national law of court seised the claim would have been contractual. Certain quasi-contractual or restitutionary claims, especially where these are closely linked to the existence of an actual or supposed contract, may fall within this provision, but it is unclear whether a claim by a plaintiff that a supposed contract is a nullity, or is unenforceable, illegal or void, can be brought within it: see *Barclays Bank plc v Glasgow City Council, Kleinwort Benson Ltd v Glasgow City Council* [1994] QB 404, [1994] 4 All ER 865, CA, where the question was referred to the European Court, which, however, sub nom Case C-346/93 *Kleinwort Benson Ltd v Glasgow City Council* [1995] ECR I-615, [1995] All ER (EC) 514, ECJ, declined jurisdiction because the question arose in the context of the internal jurisdictional provisions of the United Kingdom rather than the Brussels Convention: see para 623 text and note 7 ante. On resumption of the proceedings in the Court of Appeal, it was held by a majority that such a restitutionary claim could be a 'matter relating to a contract' within the United Kingdom jurisdictional scheme: *Kleinwort Benson Ltd v Glasgow City Council* (1996) Times, 1 February, CA; but it remains open for the European Court to reach a different conclusion when such a question falls to be decided under the Brussels or Lugano Convention.
9 Case 14/76 *De Bloos Sprl v Société en commandite par actions Bouyer* [1976] ECR 1497, [1977] 1 CMLR 60, ECJ; Case 266/85 *Shenavai v Kreischer* [1987] ECR 239, ECJ; *Union Transport plc v Continental Lines SA* [1992] 1 All ER 161, [1992] 1 WLR 15, HL; *Medway Packaging Ltd v Meurer Maschinen GmbH & Co KG* [1990] 2 Lloyd's Rep 112, CA. The obligation to pay damages for breach will not usually be seen as the obligation in question, unless it can be see as a primary, rather than compensatory or remedial, obligation: Case 14/76 *De Bloos Sprl v Société en commandite par actions Bouyer* supra.
10 Case 266/85 *Shenavai v Kreischer* [1987] ECR 239, ECJ; *Union Transport plc v Continental Lines SA* [1992] 1 All ER 161, [1992] 1 WLR 15, HL.
11 Case C-125/92 *Mulox IBC Ltd v Geels* [1993] ECR I-4075, ECJ.
12 See *Kleinwort Benson Ltd v Glasgow City Council* (1996) Times, 1 February, CA; that case, however, is decided under the Civil Jurisdiction and Judgments Act 1982 Sch 4, and cannot be taken to be a decision on the Brussels or Lugano Convention.
13 Case 12/76 *Industrie Tessili v Dunlop AG* [1976] ECR 1473, [1977] 1 CMLR 26, ECJ; Case C-288/92 *Custom Made Commercial Ltd v Stawa Metallbau GmbH* [1994] ECR I-2913, ECJ. Accordingly, in England, the court must ascertain the law which governs the contract, and construe the contract according to that law to determine where the obligation in question was to be performed: see para 844 et seq post. In general English law supposes that money payable under a contract is due to be paid at the place where the creditor resides, and that, as a result, an unpaid English seller under a contract governed

by English law may sue the recalcitrant purchaser in England: *The Eider* [1893] P 119, CA; *Bank of Scotland v Seitz* 1990 SLT 584, Ct of Sess.

14 Brussels Convention art 5 para 1; Civil Jurisdiction and Judgments Act 1982 Sch 4 art 5(1) (amended by the Civil Jurisdiction and Judgments Act 1982 (Amendment) Order 1993, SI 1993/603). It is unclear whether, in a case where the employee works in more than one contracting state, the place is where the main bulk of the work is done, or whether instead the second half of the provision alone applies in such a case: cf Case C-125/92 *Mulox IBC Ltd v Geels* [1993] ECR I-4075, ECJ, decided under the Brussels Convention prior to its amendment by the 1989 Accession Convention (as to which see para 618 note 1 ante).

15 Lugano Convention art 5 para 1.

642. Matters relating to tort. A defendant domiciled in a contracting state[1] may be sued in another contracting state, in matters relating to tort, delict or quasi-delict, in the courts for the place where the harmful event occurred[2]. A person domiciled in a part of the United Kingdom[3] may be sued in another part of the United Kingdom, in matters relating to tort, delict or quasi-delict, in the courts for the place where the harmful event occurred or in the case of a threatened wrong is likely to occur[4].

The definition of a matter 'relating to tort' is an autonomous one, and has been held to cover any action which seeks to establish the liability of a defendant, but which is not a matter relating to a contract[5].

The courts given jurisdiction are those for the place where the damage occurred, and those for the place of the event giving rise to the damage[6]. The damage which defines jurisdiction is that done to the immediate victim of the wrongful act, and not loss caused to indirect victims. It may be economic or non-economic, but the place where it is suffered is not a competent jurisdiction if the place where it occurred is elsewhere[7]. If damage occurs in a number of contracting states, each state may exercise special jurisdiction over so much of the damage as occurred within its territorial jurisdiction[8].

1 For the meaning of 'contracting state' see para 618 note 3 ante.
2 Brussels Convention art 5 para 3; Lugano Convention art 5 para 3. As to the Brussels Convention see para 618 text and note 1 ante. As to the Lugano Convention see para 618 text and note 2 ante.
3 For the meaning of 'part of the United Kingdom' see para 619 note 4 ante.
4 Civil Jurisdiction and Judgments Act 1982 s 16(1) (as amended), (2), Sch 4 art 5(3). As to the adaptation of the provisions of the Conventions by the Civil Jurisdiction and Judgments Act 1982 Sch 4, to a scheme applying as between parts of the United Kingdom, see para 619 ante. As to the interpretation of the scheme by reference to decisions under the Conventions see para 623 ante.
   Note that the jurisdiction conferred on the courts of a part of the United Kingdom on the basis of a threatened harmful event has no equivalent in the Conventions, and there is no decision of the European Court on this point.
5 Case 189/87 *Kalfelis v Schröder* [1988] ECR 5565, ECJ; Case C-364/93 *Marinari v Lloyd's Bank plc (Zubaidi Trading Co intervening)* [1996] All ER (EC) 84, [1996] 2 WLR 159, ECJ; *Kitechnology BV v Unicor GmbH Plastmaschinen* [1994] ILPr 568, CA (breach of confidence). As to matters relating to a contract see para 641 ante. Cf *Barclays Bank plc v Glasgow City Council, Kleinwort Benson Ltd v Glasgow City Council* [1994] QB 404, [1994] 4 All ER 865, CA, where the question whether special jurisdiction was conferred as a matter relating to a contract or tort was referred to the European Court, which, however, sub nom Case C 346/93 *Kleinwort Benson Ltd v Glasgow City Council* [1995] ECR I-615, [1995] All ER (EC) 514, ECJ, declined jurisdiction because the question arose in the context of the internal jurisdictional provisions of the United Kingdom rather than the Brussels Convention: see para 623 text and note 7 ante.
   It appears that the definition has been subject to qualification, for the special jurisdiction has also been held to be inapplicable to an action for a declaration that a transfer of property to a transferee was ineffective as against a creditor of the transferor, on the ground that the action did not seek to establish the 'liability' of the defendant: Case C-261/90 *Reichert v Dresdner Bank AG (No 2)* [1992] ECR I-2149, ECJ. It is unclear whether 'liability' in that context means 'liability for wrongdoing' or 'liability to perform an obligation owed to the plaintiff'.

6 Case 21/76 *Handelskwekerij GJ Bier BV und Stichting Reinwater v Mines de Potasse d'Alsace SA* [1976] ECR 1735, [1978] QB 708, ECJ, where effluent pumped into the river Rhine in France caused damage to the market-garden of the plaintiff in Holland; the Dutch and the French courts had special jurisdiction, and the plaintiff was entitled to elect between them. See also Case C-68/93 *Shevill v Presse Alliance SA* [1995] ECR I-415, [1995] 2 AC 18, [1995] All ER (EC) 289, ECJ (action for defamation may be brought where newspaper is distributed only in respect of distribution within that contracting state).

7 Case C-220/88 *Dumez France v Hessische Landesbank* [1990] ECR I-49, ECJ; Case C-364/93 *Marinari v Lloyd's Bank plc (Zubaidi Trading Co intervening)* [1996] All ER (EC) 84, [1996] 2 WLR 159, ECJ.

8 *Shevill v Presse Alliance SA* [1992] 1 All ER 409, [1992] 2 WLR 1, CA; and the proceedings in the European Court: Case C-68/93 *Shevill v Presse Alliance SA* [1995] ECR I-415, [1995] 2 AC 18, [1995] All ER (EC) 289, ECJ.

643. Other matters giving rise to special jurisdiction. A defendant domiciled in a contracting state[1], or a particular part of the United Kingdom[2], may be sued in another contracting state (or as the case may be, another part of the United Kingdom), in matters relating to maintenance, in the courts for the place where the maintenance creditor is domiciled or habitually resident[3].

As regards a claim for damages or restitution based on an act giving rise to criminal proceedings, jurisdiction is given to the court seised of the criminal proceedings to the extent that the court has jurisdiction under its own law to entertain civil proceedings[4].

As regards a dispute arising out of the operation of a branch, agency or other establishment, jurisdiction is given to the courts for the place in which the establishment is situated[5].

A defendant sued as trustee, settlor or beneficiary of a trust created by the operation of a statute, or by a written instrument, or created orally and evidenced in writing, may be sued in the courts for the contracting state (or, as the case may be, for the part of the United Kingdom), in which the trust is domiciled[6].

As regards a dispute concerning the payment of remuneration claimed in respect of the salvage of a cargo or freight, a defendant may be sued in the court under the authority of which the cargo or freight has been arrested to secure payment, or could have been arrested but bail or other security has been given, provided that this applies only if the defendant is claimed to have an interest in the cargo or freight or to have had such an interest at the time of salvage[7].

In relation to the determination of jurisdiction as between parts of the United Kingdom, in proceedings concerning a debt secured on immovable property, or brought to assert or declare proprietary or possessory rights, or rights of security, in or over movable property, or to obtain authority to dispose of movable property, jurisdiction is given to the courts of the part of the United Kingdom in which the property is situated[8]. Also within the United Kingdom, proceedings which have as their object a decision of an organ of a company or other legal person may be brought in the courts of the part of the United Kingdom in which that company, legal person or association has its seat[9].

1 For the meaning of 'contracting state' see para 618 note 3 ante.

2 For the meaning of 'part of the United Kingdom' see para 619 note 4 ante.

3 Brussels Convention art 5 para 2; Lugano Convention art 5 para 2; Civil Jurisdiction and Judgments Act 1982 s 16(1) (as amended), (2), Sch 4 art 5(2); and see Case 120/79 *De Cavel v De Cavel (No 2)* [1980] ECR 731. If the matter is ancillary to proceedings concerning the status of a person, the defendant may be sued in the court which, according to its own law, has jurisdiction to entertain those proceedings, unless that jurisdiction is based solely on the nationality of one of the parties: Brussels Convention art 5 para 2; Lugano Convention art 5 para 2; Civil Jurisdiction and Judgments Act 1982 Sch 4 art 5(2). As to the Brussels Convention see para 618 text and note 1 ante. As to the Lugano Convention see para 618 text and note 2 ante.

As to the adaptation of the provisions of the Conventions by the Civil Jurisdiction and Judgments Act 1982 Sch 4, to a scheme applying as between parts of the United Kingdom, see para 619 ante. As to the interpretation of the scheme by reference to decisions under the Conventions see para 623 ante.

4 Brussels Convention art 5 para 4; Lugano Convention art 5 para 4; Civil Jurisdiction and Judgments Act 1982 Sch 4 art 5(4); and see Case C-172/91 *Sonntag v Waidmann* [1993] ECR I-1963, ECJ.

5 Brussels Convention art 5 para 5; Lugano Convention art 5 para 5; Civil Jurisdiction and Judgments Act 1982 Sch 4 art 5(5). As to what is a branch, agency or establishment see Case 14/76 *De Bloos Sprl v Société en commandite par actions Bouyer* [1976] ECR 1497, [1977] 1 CMLR 60, ECJ (exclusive distributor); Case 33/78 *Etablissements Somafer SA v Saar-Ferngas AG* [1978] ECR 2183, [1979] 1 CMLR 490, ECJ (appearance of permanency); Case 139/80 *Blankaert and Willems PVBA v Trost* [1981] ECR 819, [1982] 2 CMLR 1, ECJ (independent commercial agent); Case 218/86 *SAR Schotte GmbH v Parfums Rothschild Sarl* [1987] ECR 4905, ECJ (appearance created by letterhead). It is not necessary for the purpose of art 5 para 5 of the Conventions that the undertakings entered into by the branch are to be performed in the contracting state in which that branch is situated: Case C-439/93 *Lloyd's Register of Shipping v Société Campenon Bernard* [1995] ECR I-961, [1995] All ER (EC) 531, ECJ. See also the opinion of the Advocate General in Case C-89/91 *Shearson Lehmann Hutton Inc v TVB Treuhandgesellschaft für Vermögensverwaltung und Beteiligungen mbH* [1993] ECR I-139, ECJ, suggesting that in order to be seen as an establishment to which this provision may apply, there must be sufficient control for the body by an agent, but enough independence for it to be able to make contracts which bind the parent body.

6 Brussels Convention art 5 para 6; Lugano Convention art 5 para 6; Civil Jurisdiction and Judgments Act 1982 Sch 4 art 5(6). Any proceedings brought by virtue of these provisions in the United Kingdom must be brought in the courts of the part of the United Kingdom in which the trust is domiciled: s 10(2). As to the determination of domicile of a trust see paras 634 text and note 10, 637 ante.

7 Brussels Convention art 5 para 7; Lugano Convention art 5 para 7; Civil Jurisdiction and Judgments Act 1982 Sch 4 art 5(7). Where a court of a contracting state (or, as the case may be, of a part of the United Kingdom), has jurisdiction in actions relating to liability arising from the use of a ship, that court, or any other court substituted for the purpose by the internal law of the state (or part) also has jurisdiction over claims for the limitation of such liability: Brussels Convention art 6A; Lugano Convention art 6A; Civil Jurisdiction and Judgments Act 1982 Sch 4 art 6A.

8 Ibid Sch 4 art 5(8).

9 Ibid Sch 4 art 5A. As to where a corporation or other legal person has its seat under English law see para 636 ante.

644. Additional parties and related claims.

A defendant domiciled in a contracting state[1], or a particular part of the United Kingdom[2], may also be sued in other specified courts, as follows[3]:

(1) where he is one of a number of defendants, in the courts for the place where any one of them is domiciled[4]; or

(2) as a third party in an action on a warranty or guarantee, or in any other third party proceedings, in the court seised of the original proceedings unless these were instituted solely with the object of removing him from the jurisdiction of the court which would otherwise have been competent[5]; or

(3) on a counterclaim arising from the same contract or facts on which the original claim is based, in the court in which the original claim is pending[6]; or

(4) in matters relating to a contract, if this may be combined with an action against the same defendant in matters relating to rights in rem in immovable property, in the courts for the contracting state (or, as the case may be, the part of the United Kingdom), in which the property is situated[7].

It appears that the court probably has a discretion permitting it to decline jurisdiction on procedural grounds which relate to the efficient disposal of the proceedings; the applicant is not entitled to invoke this jurisdiction without regard to the usual procedural conditions of national law. But these procedural rules must not be applied so as to produce a direct conflict with the Conventions[8].

1 For the meaning of 'contracting state' see para 618 note 3 ante.

2 For the meaning of 'part of the United Kingdom' see para 619 note 4 ante.

3 Brussels Convention art 6; Lugano Convention art 6; Civil Jurisdiction and Judgments Act 1982 s 16(1 (as amended), (2), Sch 4 art 6. These provisions seek to ensure that separate claims which ought to be heard together are efficiently dealt with. As to the Brussels Convention see para 618 text and note ante. As to the Lugano Convention see para 618 text and note 2 ante. As to the adaptation of the provisions of the Conventions by the Civil Jurisdiction and Judgments Act 1982 Sch 4, to a scheme applying as between parts of the United Kingdom, see para 619 ante. As to the interpretation of the scheme by reference to decisions under the Conventions see para 623 ante.

4 Brussels Convention art 6 para 1; Lugano Convention art 6 para 1; Civil Jurisdiction and Judgments Ac 1982 Sch 4 art 6(1). It is not necessary that the 'one' defendant be the principal defendant, but it i required that the claim against the second defendant be one which needs to be heard with the claim against the first defendant in order to prevent irreconcilable judgments: Case 189/87 *Kalfelis v Schröde* [1988] ECR 5565, ECJ; *Mölnlycke AB v Procter & Gamble Ltd* [1992] 4 All ER 47, [1992] 1 WLR 1112 CA; *The Eras Eil Actions* [1995] 1 Lloyd's Rep 64 at 74–79; *Qingdao Ocean Shipping Co v Grace Shipping Establishment, Transatlantic Schiffahrtskontor GmbH, Ode and Health Chartering (UK) Ltd, The Xing Su Ha* [1995] 2 Lloyd's Rep 15.

5 Brussels Convention art 6 para 2; Lugano Convention art 6 para 2; Civil Jurisdiction and Judgments Ac 1982 Sch 4 art 6(2); and see Case 365/88 *Kongress Agentur Hagen GmbH v Zeehaghe BV* [1990] ECR I-1845, ECJ; *Kinnear v Falconfilms NV* [1994] 3 All ER 42.

6 Brussels Convention art 6 para 3; Lugano Convention art 6 para 3; Civil Jurisdiction and Judgments Ac 1982 Sch 4 art 6(3); and see Case 220/84 *A-S Autoteile Service GmbH v Malhé* [1985] ECR 2267, [1986] 3 CMLR 321, ECJ. A defence of set-off is not a counterclaim, and need not comply with the article: Case C-341/93 *Danvaern Production A/S v Schuhfabriken Otterbeck GmbH & Co* [1995] ILPr 649, ECJ.

7 Brussels Convention art 6 para 4; Lugano Convention art 6 para 4; Civil Jurisdiction and Judgments Ac 1982 Sch 4 art 6(4) (added by the Civil Jurisdiction and Judgments Act 1982 (Amendment) Order 1993 SI 1993/603). As regards actions in rem within the United Kingdom see also para 643 text and note 8 ante.

8 Case 365/88 *Kongress Agentur Hagen GmbH v Zeehaghe BV* [1990] ECR I-1845, ECJ.

(vii) Removal of Convention Jurisdiction

645. Examination of jurisdiction and lis alibi pendens. Where a defendant domiciled in one contracting state[1] is sued in the courts of another contracting state and does not enter an appearance, the court must declare of its own motion that it has no jurisdiction unless its jurisdiction is derived from the Conventions[2]. Similarly, where a defendant domiciled in one part of the United Kingdom[3] is sued in the courts of another part of the United Kingdom and does not enter an appearance, the court must declare of its own motion that it has no jurisdiction unless it is derived from the scheme for determining jurisdiction between parts of the United Kingdom[4]. In either case, the court must stay the proceedings so long as it is not shown that the defendant has been able to receive the document instituting the proceedings or an equivalent document in sufficient time to enable him to arrange for his defence, or that all necessary steps have been taken to this end[5].

Where proceedings involving the same cause of action and between the same parties are brought in the courts of different contracting states[6], any court other than the court first seised must of its own motion stay its proceedings until such time as the jurisdiction of the court first seised is established[7]. Where the jurisdiction of the court first seised is established, any other court must decline jurisdiction in favour of that court[8]. A court seised second is not permitted to continue to hear the case on the ground that it considers that the court first seised does not have, or should not be exercising, jurisdiction[9].

In order to prevent irreconcilable judgments within the scope of the Conventions, this provision is to be given a broad and flexible interpretation[10]. Proceedings involve the same cause of action where they advance claims which might give rise to irreconcilable judgments, even if they appear to involve separate aspects of a single transaction; the two claims do not have to be identical; thus an action for damages for breach of contract may involve the same cause of action as one for rescission of the same contract[11]. Proceedings are between the same parties if there is a common plaintiff and a common defendant, even if there are other parties additionally involved, but the obligation to decline jurisdiction extends only to the parties which are common to both sets of proceedings[12]. Proceedings do not cease to be between the same parties or arise from the same cause of action merely because the proceedings in one contracting state are in the form of an admiralty action in rem and those in the other take the form of an action in personam[13].

The date at which a court is seised must be determined, by the national law of the court seised, by ascertaining when proceedings became definitively pending between the parties[14]. As far as English law is concerned, this date is, for the purpose of the Conventions, the date of service (as distinct from the issue) of the writ[15]. This remains so even if the court has already made orders in the litigation prior to the service of the writ in the substantive proceedings[16].

A court may stay proceedings where related actions are brought in the courts of other contracting states, or may decline jurisdiction to enable the consolidation of related actions[17].

1 For the meaning of 'contracting state' see para 618 note 3 ante.
2 Brussels Convention art 20, 1st para; Lugano Convention art 20, 1st para. As to the Brussels Convention see para 618 text and note 1 ante. As to the Lugano Convention see para 618 text and note 2 ante.
3 For the meaning of 'part of the United Kingdom' see para 619 note 4 ante. As to the adaptation of the provisions of the Conventions by the Civil Jurisdiction and Judgments Act 1982 s 16 (as amended), Sch 4, to a scheme applying as between parts of the United Kingdom, see para 619 ante. As to the interpretation of the scheme by reference to decisions under the Conventions see para 623 ante.
4 Civil Jurisdiction and Judgments Act 1982 Sch 4 art 20, 1st para.
5 Brussels Convention art 20, 2nd para; Lugano Convention art 20, 2nd para; Civil Jurisdiction and Judgments Act 1982 Sch 4 art 20, 2nd para. As to the position where a contracting state is bound to serve judicial and extra-judicial documents in accordance with its international obligations, see the Brussels Convention art 20, 3rd para, Annexed Protocol art IV; Lugano Convention art 20, 3rd para, Protocol No I art IV.
6 It has been held that art 21 of the Conventions applies also as between the courts of England and Scotland; and that the common law principle of forum non conveniens does not: *Foxen v Scotsman Publications Ltd* (1994) Times, 17 February; not followed in *Cumming v Scottish Daily Record and Sunday Mail Ltd* (1995) Times, 8 June. However, the Civil Jurisdiction and Judgments Act 1982 Sch 4 (as amended), as to which see para 619 ante, does not contain provisions analogous to those of the Conventions, and therefore the latter decision is to be preferred. As to references to numbered articles 'of the Conventions' see para 618 note 5 ante.
7 Brussels Convention art 21, 1st para; Lugano Convention art 21, 1st para. These provisions provide a mechanism to ensure that parallel litigation does not occur where the effect of the rules previously discussed (see paras 627–644 ante) would be to confer jurisdiction upon the courts of two or more contracting states; see eg para 633 note 3 ante.
8 Brussels Convention art 21, 2nd para; Lugano Convention art 21, 2nd para.
9 Case C-351/89 *Overseas Union Insurance Ltd v New Hampshire Insurance Co* [1991] ECR I-3317, ECJ. The European Court in that case did not decide the question whether a court seised second may proceed to hear the case if it has exclusive jurisdiction under the Conventions; contrast, however, *Continental Bank NA v Aeakos Compania Naviera SA* [1994] 2 All ER 540, [1994] 1 WLR 588, CA, where a choice of court agreement validly gave exclusive jurisdiction to the English courts under art 17 of the Conventions; it was held that art 17 took precedence over arts 21, 22, so that the English court had jurisdiction notwithstanding that proceedings had already been begun in the Greek courts. As to references to numbered articles 'of the Conventions' see para 618 note 5 ante.
10 See Case 144/86 *Gubisch Maschinenfabrik KG v Palumbo* [1987] ECR 4861, ECJ; Case C-351/89 *Overseas Union Insurance Ltd v New Hampshire Insurance Co* [1991] ECR I-3317, ECJ.
11 Case 144/86 *Gubisch Maschinenfabrik KG v Palumbo* [1987] ECR 4861, ECJ. Similarly proceedings for a declaration of non-liability involve the same cause of action as proceedings to enforce the liability

which is denied: Case C-406/92 *The Tatry (cargo owners) v The Maciej Rataj (owners)* [1994] ECR I-543 [1995] All ER (EC) 229, ECJ.

12 Case C-406/92 *The Tatry (cargo owners) v The Maciej Rataj (owners)* [1994] ECR I-5439, [1995] All El (EC) 229, ECJ. See also *Grupo Torras SA v Sheikh Fahad Mohammed al Sabah* [1996] 1 Lloyd's Rep 7, C/ It was pointed out by the European Court in Case C-406/92 *The Tatry (cargo owners) v The Maciej Rat (owners)* supra that under art 22 of the Conventions (see para 1090 post), it is open to the court in i discretion to stay proceedings or decline jurisdiction in order to avoid fragmenting the proceeding

13 See Case C-406/92 *The Tatry (cargo owners) v The Maciej Rataj (owners)* [1994] ECR I-5439, [1995] All El (EC) 229, ECJ; *The Anna H* [1995] 1 Lloyd's Rep 11, CA. It would in any event presumably be open t the court in its discretion to stay the proceedings or decline jurisdiction under art 22 of the Conventio on the ground that the proceedings were related: see para 1090 post.

14 Case 129/83 *Zelger v Salinitri (No 2)* [1984] ECR 2397, [1985] 3 CMLR 366, ECJ.

15 *Dresser (UK) Ltd v Falcongate Freight Management Ltd* [1992] QB 502, [1992] 2 All ER 450, CA.

16 *Neste Chemicals SA v DK Line SA, The Sargasso* [1994] 3 All ER 180, [1994] 2 Lloyd's Rep 6, C/ disapproving dicta to the contrary in *Dresser (UK) Ltd v Falcongate Freight Management Ltd* [1992] Q 502, [1992] 2 All ER 450, CA.

17 See the Brussels Convention art 22; the Lugano Convention art 22; and para 1090 post. For th meaning of 'related actions' see Case C-406/92 *the Tatry (cargo owners) v The Maciej Rataj (owners)* [199 ECR I-5439, [1995] All ER (EC) 229, ECJ.

(viii) Discretion

646. Discretion in the exercise of Convention jurisdiction. It is generall supposed that the Brussels and Lugano Conventions[1] do not authorise a court t decline jurisdiction in favour of the courts of another contracting state, on discretion ary grounds otherwise permitted by national procedural law; but where the court i favour of which a stay is sought is in a non-contracting state, it has been held that th Conventions do not prevent a court exercising its discretion to stay proceedings[2].

1 As to the Brussels Convention see para 618 text and note 1 ante. As to the Lugano Convention se para 618 text and note 2 ante.

2 *Re Harrods (Buenos Aires) Ltd* [1992] Ch 72, [1991] 4 All ER 334, CA. See further para 1090 post. It i believed that a court may stay proceedings, on the basis of a choice of court agreement, in favour of th courts of a non-contracting state; it is possible proceedings may be stayed on the ground that there is, i favour of a non-contracting state, a connection which would, within the contracting states, hav conferred exclusive jurisdiction under art 16 of the Conventions (see paras 627–628 ante).

(ix) Provisional Measures

647. Provisional and protective measures. Application may be made to th courts of a contracting state[1] for such provisional, including protective, measures a may be available under the law of that state, even if under the Brussels or Lugan Convention[2], or the scheme applicable within the United Kingdom[3], the courts o another contracting state or, as the case may be, of another part of the Unite Kingdom, have jurisdiction as to the substance of the matter[4].

1 For the meaning of 'contracting state' see para 618 note 3 ante.

2 As to the Brussels and Lugano Conventions see para 618 text and notes 1–2 ante.

3 As to the adaptation of the provisions of the Conventions by the Civil Jurisdiction and Judgments Ac 1982 s 16 (as amended), Sch 4, to a scheme applying as between parts of the United Kingdom, se

para 619 ante. As to the interpretation of the scheme by reference to decisions under the Conventions see para 623 ante. For the meaning of 'part of the United Kingdom' see para 619 note 4 ante.
4 Brussels Convention art 24; Lugano Convention art 24; Civil Jurisdiction and Judgments Act 1982 Sch 4 art 24. See further para 1076 post.

(3) JURISDICTION UNDER THE COMMON LAW RULES AND UNDER STATUTORY RULES OTHER THAN THE CONVENTIONS

648. In general. The fundamental principle of jurisdiction as it is exercised under the rules of the common law is that a defendant who is liable to be served with the writ, whether within[1] or out of[2] the jurisdiction, is subject to the jurisdiction of the court[3].

1 See para 649 post.
2 See para 650 et seq post.
3 See Dicey and Morris *The Conflict of Laws* (12th Edn, 1993) 298, 300–303. As to whether a court which has jurisdiction over the defendant may be entitled to decline to exercise it see para 1085 post. In this sense the rules of the Brussels and Lugano Conventions, and subordinate legislation relating to them, may be seen as a partial definition or redefinition of whether it is lawful to serve process upon a defendant. As to the Brussels Convention see para 618 text and note 1 ante. As to the Lugano Convention see para 618 text and note 2 ante. For the subordinate legislation see RSC Ord 11 r 1(2)(a), Ord 6 r 7.

649. Defendant present within the jurisdiction. If the defendant is present within the jurisdiction of the court, he is liable to be served with the writ in an action in personam. In relation to the existence of jurisdiction, it is irrelevant that his presence is fleeting, or that the dispute in question has no real or substantial connection with England[1]. The principal question which arises in such a case, therefore, is as to the manner in which service must be made in order for it to be effective service within the jurisdiction; this is considered fully elsewhere in this work[2].

1 *Maharanee of Baroda v Wildenstein* [1972] 2 QB 283, [1972] 2 All ER 689, CA; cf *Adams v Cape Industries plc* [1990] Ch 433, [1991] 1 All ER 929, CA. In such a case, however, it may be open to a court, upon the defendant's application, to stay its proceedings in favour of a court with a closer connection with the dispute or with the parties: see para 1085 post.
2 See PRACTICE AND PROCEDURE vol 37 paras 145–170.

650. Service on a defendant out of the jurisdiction. The circumstances in which the process of the court may be served out of the jurisdiction[1], and the practice and procedure to be followed, are largely governed by Rules of the Supreme Court[2]. Service out of the jurisdiction is treated as the exercise by the English court of judicial power over a foreigner who owes no allegiance to the United Kingdom or over a person who is resident or domiciled out of the jurisdiction, but is nevertheless called upon to answer claims made against him in England and Wales[3]. However, since the exercise of judicial power over such persons in other countries is prima facie a trespass upon the sovereignty of the other country[4], a plaintiff is not entitled as of right, save for certain specified and extremely significant exceptions[5], to issue and serve judicial process out of the jurisdiction: he must first obtain the leave of the court to do so[6]. Where application for such leave is made, the court must decide (1) whether it has jurisdiction to grant such leave[7]; and (2) even if the court has such jurisdiction, whether the case is a proper one for service out of the jurisdiction[8].

1   'Jurisdiction' refers to the territorial jurisdiction of the High Court: *Re Smith* (1876) 1 PD 300; *Th Fagernes* [1927] P 311, CA. This jurisdiction extends over the whole of England and Wales: se PRACTICE AND PROCEDURE vol 37 para 149 note 9. As to the meaning of 'England and Wales' se para 604 ante.

2   See RSC Ord 11; and see also Ord 16 r 3(4), which applies Ord 11 to third party proceedings, as if th third party notice were a writ and the proceedings were therefore an action, and the defendant issuin the notice were the plaintiff in such an action and the third party were a defendant of summons. As t the service out of the jurisdiction of a writ in certain Admiralty actions in personam see Ord 75 r 4; an ADMIRALTY vol 1(1) (Reissue) para 403. However, there can be no service out of the jurisdiction of writ in an Admiralty action in rem: RSC Ord 75 r 4(3). For the corresponding provisions in the count court see CCR Ord 8. Where the text of CCR Ord 8 is at variance with RSC Ord 11 r 1(1), the forme will, if at all possible, be construed to conform to the latter: *Agrafax Public Relations Ltd v United Scottis Society Inc* [1995] ILPr 753, CA.

3   *Société Générale de Paris v Dreyfus Bros* (1885) 29 ChD 239 at 242; *The Hagen* [1908] P 189, CA; *Wyler Lyons* [1963] P 274, [1963] 1 All ER 821.

4   See RSC Ord 11 r 5(2), which provides that nothing in Ord 11 r 5(1) (which applies Ord 10 r 1(1) (4)–(6) and Ord 65 r 4 to writs to be served out of the jurisdiction), or in any court order or directio made by virtue of it is to authorise or require the doing of anything in a country in which service is to b effected which is contrary to the law of that country.

5   For cases of jurisdiction in which leave is not required see para 673 post. Most such cases are founded o the jurisdictional provisions of an international convention to which the United Kingdom is party: se para 673 post. If the court has jurisdiction pursuant to the Brussels and Lugano Conventions (se para 618 notes 1–2 ante), service of the writ is permitted without the leave of the court: RSC Ord 1 r 1(2).

6   See RSC Ord 6 r 7(1) (writ), applied to originating summonses by Ord 7 r 5(3).

7   See RSC Ord 11 r 1(1); and para 651 et seq post.

8   See RSC Ord 11 r 4(2); and see *Seaconsar Far East Ltd v Bank Markazi Jomhouri Islami Iran* [1994] 1 AC 438, [1993] 4 All ER 456, HL; and para 671 post.

651. Service of writ out of the jurisdiction with leave. Service of a writ o summons[1] out of the jurisdiction is permissible with the leave of the court[2] in a numbe of specified cases[3], but always provided (1) that the writ does not contain a claim ove which the court has jurisdiction by reason of the Brussels Convention or the Lugano Convention[4], or by virtue of any other enactment[5]; and (2) the writ does not contain a claim suitable for an Admiralty action[6]. The several cases specified must be read disjunctively, so that the plaintiff may choose to rely on whichever one suits him best[7]. Nevertheless, they are each separate, self-contained and independent of the others. If the writ contains more than one claim, each individual claim must fall within one or more of the provisions of the applicable rule[8].

If it is unclear whether, or it is disputed that, a claim made by the plaintiff falls within the definition of the particular sub-rule upon which reliance is placed, the doubt is to be resolved as follows: (a) a question whether the admitted facts fall within the legal definition of the head of the sub-rule, is a question as to the legal construction of statutory words, and the court must determine for itself the correct interpretation[9]; (b) if it is disputed that the facts of the case, which if admitted would bring the case within the sub-rule, have been sufficiently shown, the plaintiff must demonstrate a good arguable case that the relevant facts are as he alleges them to be[10].

1   As to the service of other process with leave see paras 668–669 post.

2   As to applications for leave see para 670 post.

3   For these cases see RSC Ord 11 r 1(1)(a)–(u); and para 652 et seq post. The provisions of RSC Ord 11 r 1(1)(a)–(u) are commonly known as, and may for convenience be referred to in this title as, the 'heads' or 'sub-rules' of RSC Ord 11 r 1(1).

4   As to the Brussels Convention see para 618 text and note 1 ante. As to the Lugano Convention see para 618 text and note 2 ante.

5   RSC Ord 11 r 1(1), (2). Where the court does have jurisdiction pursuant to the Brussels or Lugano Convention service of the writ out of the jurisdiction is permissible as of right; as to this and other

jurisdiction founded on other enactments in respect of which service out of the jurisdiction is available as of right see para 673 post.

6 Ie such a claim as is mentioned in RSC Ord 75 r 2(1)(a): RSC Ord 11 r 1(1). In these cases, service out of the jurisdiction is permissible with leave in the circumstances mentioned in Ord 75 r 4: see ADMIRALTY vol 1(1) (Reissue) para 403.

7 *Matthews v Kuwait Bechtel Corpn* [1959] 2 QB 57, [1959] 2 All ER 345, CA.

8 *Saipem SpA v Dredging VO2 BV, The Volvox Hollandia* [1988] 2 Lloyd's Rep 361, CA; *Metall und Rohstoff AG v Donaldson Lufkin & Jenrette Inc* [1990] 1 QB 391, [1989] 3 All ER 14, CA.

9 *E F Hutton & Co (London) Ltd v Moffarij* [1989] 2 All ER 633 at 639, [1989] 1 WLR 488 at 495, CA.

10 *Seaconsar Far East Ltd v Bank Markazi Jomhouri Islami Iran* [1994] 1 AC 438, [1993] 4 All ER 456, HL; *Agrafax Public Relations Ltd v United Scottish Society Inc* [1995] ILPr 753, CA. This is wholly distinct from the requirement, imposed in relation to RSC Ord 11 r 4(2) as to whether the case is a proper one for service out of the jurisdiction, that the plaintiff merely demonstrate in relation to the merits of the claim that there is a serious issue to be tried: *Seaconsar Far East Ltd v Bank Markazi Jomhouri Islami Iran* supra; and see further para 671 post. That case has superseded previous confused authorities, such as *Vitkovice Horni a Hutni Tezirstvo v Korner* [1951] AC 869, [1951] 2 All ER 334, HL, which are no longer reliable.

652. Defendant domiciled within the jurisdiction. Leave may be given[1] to serve out of the jurisdiction if relief[2] is sought in the action against a person[3] domiciled[4] within the jurisdiction[5].

1 As to applications for leave see para 670 post.

2 This provision is very wide and includes any relief in respect of any legal claim, whether it sounds in contract or tort or quasi-contract or declaration or other remedy such as rectification or rescission. It does not matter for this purpose where the contract was made or where the cause of action arose, whether within or out of the jurisdiction: *Lenders v Anderson* (1883) 12 QBD 50; *Hadad v Bruce* (1892) 8 TLR 409. The basis of this jurisdiction is the domicile of the person against whom the relief is sought: see *Re Liddell's Settlement Trusts* [1936] Ch 365, [1936] 1 All ER 239, CA.

3 As to the meaning of 'person' see para 624 note 3 ante.

4 'Domicile' in this provision means domicile as defined by the Civil Jurisdiction and Judgments Act 1982 ss 41–46 (as amended): RSC Ord 11 r 1(4). See paras 631 note 9, 632 note 9, 635–638 ante.

5 RSC Ord 11 r 1(1)(a). This rule will be applicable only rarely, for in a civil or commercial matter, a defendant domiciled in the United Kingdom falls within the jurisdictional régime of the Brussels and Lugano Conventions (as to which see para 618 notes 1–2 ante), and service upon him will, in principle, be as of right, and will not require the leave of the court: RSC Ord 11 r 1(1), (2). See paras 624 ante, 673 post.

653. Injunctions. Leave may be given[1] to serve a writ out of the jurisdiction if in the action begun by the writ an injunction[2] is sought ordering the defendant to do or to refrain from doing anything within the jurisdiction[3], whether or not damages are also claimed in respect of a failure to do, or the doing of, that thing[4].

1 As to applications for leave see para 670 post.

2 This does not include an interlocutory injunction: *Siskina (Cargo Owners) v Distos Compania Naviera SA* [1979] AC 210, [1977] 3 All ER 803, HL. As the claim for an interlocutory injunction is not by itself a cause of action, service of the writ on the defendant out of the jurisdiction will not be possible if this is the only claim which is advanced against him. If it is sought to obtain an interlocutory injunction against a defendant out of the jurisdiction, it must be shown that there is another head of RSC Ord 11 which applies to the claim made against him: *Siskina (Cargo Owners) v Distos Compania Naviera SA* supra; *Channel Tunnel Group Ltd v Balfour Beatty Construction Ltd* [1993] AC 334, [1993] 1 All ER 664, HL. If no such claim is advanced (the applicant seeking only a Mareva injunction to preserve assets against which a foreign judgment will later be enforced), the claim does not fall within RSC Ord 11 r 1(1)(b): *Mercedes-Benz AG v Leiduck* [1995] 3 All ER 929, [1995] 3 WLR 718, PC. See also *Qingdao Ocean Shipping Co v Grace Shipping Establishment, Transatlantic Schiffahrtskontor GmbH, Ode and Heath Chartering (UK) Ltd, The Xing Su Hai* [1995] 2 Lloyd's Rep 15. The Civil Jurisdiction and Judgments Act 1982 s 25 (as amended) authorises interim relief to be granted in a case in which the dispute between the parties will be heard in the courts of another contracting state to the Brussels Convention or to the

Lugano Convention (as to which see para 618 notes 1–2 ante): see further para 1076 post. In such a case it is unclear whether the writ by which such relief is sought may be served out of the jurisdiction under RSC Ord 11 r 1(1)(b); it was held that it could be in *X v Y* [1990] 1 QB 220, [1989] 3 All ER 689, but this decision was doubted in *Mercedes-Benz AG v Leiduck* supra.

3 The act to be restrained or ordered must be one within the jurisdiction: *Kinahan v Kinahan* (1890) 45 ChD 78; *Re De Penny, De Penny v Christie* [1891] 2 Ch 63 at 68–69. A claim that the defendant be required to account within the jurisdiction, or that he be ordered to pay money within the jurisdiction, does not fall within RSC Ord 11 r 1(1)(b): *ISC Technologies Ltd v Guerin* [1992] 2 Lloyd's Rep 430.

4 RSC Ord 11 r 1(1)(b). See further INJUNCTIONS vol 24 (Reissue) para 959. Whilst it is not necessary that an injunction should be the only relief claimed (*Lisbon-Berlyn (Transvaal) Gold Fields Ltd v Heddle* (1884) 52 LT 796), or that it should be ancillary to some other claim in respect of which leave may be granted under RSC Ord 11 r 1(1)(b) (*Tozier v Hawkins* (1885) 15 QBD 650 at 680, CA), the claim for the injunction must not be one added to a substantive claim for pecuniary relief not otherwise within RSC Ord 11 r 1(1) (*Rosler v Hilbery* [1925] Ch 250, CA); it must itself be part of the substantive relief to which the plaintiff's cause of action entitles him (*Siskina (Cargo Owners) v Distos Compania Naviera SA* [1979] AC 210, [1977] 3 All ER 803, HL); and see *James North & Sons Ltd v North Cape Textiles Ltd* [1984] 1 WLR 1428, CA. RSC Ord 11 r 1(1)(b) does not extend to the service on a foreigner out of the jurisdiction of a writ or other process claiming only Mareva relief: *Mercedes-Benz AG v Leiduck* [1995] 3 All ER 929, [1995] 3 WLR 718, PC.

654. Necessary or proper parties. Leave may be given[1] to serve a writ out of the jurisdiction if the claim[2] has been brought[3] against a person[4] duly served[5] within or out of the jurisdiction, and a person out of the jurisdiction is a necessary or proper party[6] to the claim[7].

1 As to applications for leave see para 670 post.

2 This applies equally to a counterclaim: *Derby & Co Ltd v Larsson* [1976] 1 All ER 401, [1976] 1 WLR 202, HL.

3 The plaintiff must depose that to his belief there is between him and the person duly served a real issue which he may reasonably ask the court to try: see RSC Ord 11 r 4(1)(d); and *Witted v Galbraith* [1893] 1 QB 577, CA; *Deutsche National Bank v Paul* [1898] 1 Ch 283; *The Brabo* [1949] AC 326, [1949] 1 All ER 294, HL, where it was apparent that the action against the defendants within the jurisdiction was bound to fail. The action against the defendant duly served must not be merely subsidiary to the cause of action against the person outside the jurisdiction: *Re Schintz, Schintz v Warr* [1926] Ch 710, CA. The action against the person within the jurisdiction must have been brought in good faith and not merely for the purpose of bringing before the court the person out of the jurisdiction: *Witted v Galbraith* supra; *The Brabo* supra. Moreover, the plaintiff must show a reasonable cause of action against the defendant duly served and not one to which he would have an absolute defence: *The Brabo* supra. It is not necessary to show that the plaintiff is bound to succeed against the defendant within the jurisdiction, but there must be a real issue to be tried between them: *Ellinger v Guinness, Mahon & Co, Frankfurter Bank AG and Metall Gesellschaft AG* [1939] 4 All ER 16.

4 As to the meaning of 'person' see para 624 note 3 ante.

5 The defendant must have been actually served before leave can be given: *Collins v North British and Mercantile Insurance Co* [1894] 3 Ch 228; *The Duc d'Aumale* [1903] P 18, CA; *Yorkshire Tannery Ltd v Eglington Co* (1884) 54 LJCh 81; *Camera Care Ltd v Victor Hasselblad AB* [1986] 1 FTLR 348, CA; *Qingdao Ocean Shipping Co v Grace Shipping Establishment, Transatlantic Schiffahrtskontor GmbH, Ode and Heath Chartering (UK) Ltd, The Xing Su Hai* [1995] 2 Lloyd's Rep 15 at 26. But if the plaintiff has not served the other party by the time he makes the application, this may nevertheless be a curable irregularity: see RSC Ord 2; and *Camera Care Ltd v Victor Hasselblad AB* supra. As to due service in England and Wales see PRACTICE AND PROCEDURE vol 37 paras 145–170.

6 A necessary or proper party is one who, if he were subject to the jurisdiction, could properly be joined as a defendant: *Massey v Heynes & Co and Schenker & Co* (1888) 21 QBD 330, CA, where the action was in contract against a principal, with an alternative claim for breach of warranty against an agent. He need not be both a necessary and a proper party, for RSC Ord 11 r 1(1)(b) is disjunctive: *Massey v Heynes* supra; *Witted v Galbraith* [1893] 1 QB 577, CA. The provision applies to an action on a tort alleged to have been committed by defendants jointly or severally: *Re Beck, Attia v Seed* (1918) 87 LJCh 335, CA. See also *Qatar Petroleum v Shell International Petroleum Maatschappij BV* [1983] 2 Lloyd's Rep 35, CA; *Golden Ocean Assurance Ltd v Martin, The Goldean Mariner* [1990] 2 Lloyd's Rep 215, CA. As to the application of RSC Ord 11 r 1(1)(b) to a third party notice see Ord 16 r 3(4); *The Eras Eil Appeals* [1992]

1 Lloyd's Rep 570 at 591–593, CA; *International Commercial Bank v Insurance Corporation of Ireland plc* [1989] IR 453.
7 RSC Ord 11 r 1(1)(c). This provision is wide and independent of the other heads of Ord 11 r 1(1), and may apply even though the subject matter of the action is outside those other heads. This provision reflects the view that all necessary persons should be before the court at once: see *Derby & Co Ltd v Larsson* [1976] 1 All ER 401, [1976] 1 WLR 202, HL; *Electric Furnace Corpn v Selas Corpn of America* [1987] RPC 23, CA. But the width of the provision is such that the court should be careful to see that it is not abused: *Multinational Gas and Petrochemical Co v Multinational Gas and Petrochemical Services Ltd* [1983] Ch 258, [1983] 2 All ER 563, CA; *Golden Ocean Assurance Ltd v Martin, The Goldean Mariner* [1990] 2 Lloyd's Rep 215, CA. Nevertheless, if the conditions prescribed are complied with, leave may be given in a case in which leave could not be given under any other head: see eg *Thanemore SS Ltd v Thompson* (1885) 52 LT 522; *Jenney v Mackintosh* (1886) 33 ChD 595; *Croft v King* [1893] 1 QB 419, DC; *Williams v Cartwright* [1895] 1 QB 142, CA; *Duder v Amsterdamsch Trustees Kantoor* [1902] 2 Ch 132; *The Duc d'Aumale* [1903] P 18, CA; *Oesterreichische Export AG v British Indemnity Insurance Co Ltd* [1914] 2 KB 747, CA.

655. Contracts. The court has jurisdiction to grant leave[1] to serve a writ out of the jurisdiction where the action begun by the writ is brought to enforce, rescind, dissolve, annul or otherwise affect[2] a contract, or to recover damages or obtain other relief in respect of the breach of a contract[3], being, in either case, a contract which (1) was made within the jurisdiction[4]; or (2) was made by or through an agent trading or residing within the jurisdiction, on behalf of a principal trading or residing out of the jurisdiction[5]; or (3) is by its terms, or by implication, governed by English law[6]; or (4) contains a term to the effect that the High Court is to have jurisdiction to hear and determine any action in respect of the contract[7].

The court also has jurisdiction to grant leave to serve a writ out of the jurisdiction when the claim is brought in respect of a breach committed within the jurisdiction of a contract made within or out of the jurisdiction[8], and irrespective of the fact, if such be the case, that the breach was preceded or accompanied by a breach committed out of the jurisdiction[9] that rendered impossible the performance of so much of the contract as ought to have been performed within the jurisdiction[10].

1 As to applications for leave see para 670 post.
2 See *BP Exploration Co (Libya) Ltd v Hunt* [1976] 3 All ER 879, [1976] 1 WLR 788; *E F Hutton & Co (London) Ltd v Mofsarij* [1989] 2 All ER 633, [1989] 1 WLR 488, CA. If the plaintiff seeks a declaration that there was no concluded contract, it has been held that the case is not within the sub-rule: *Finnish Maritime Insurance Co Ltd v Protective National Insurance Co* [1990] 1 QB 1078, [1989] 2 All ER 929; not followed in *D R Insurance v Central National Insurance Co* [1996] 1 Lloyd's Rep 74.
3 RSC Ord 11 r 1(1)(d). It is sufficient if the plaintiff can bring his case within one of heads (1)–(4) in the text: *Wansborough Paper Co Ltd v Laughland* [1920] WN 344, CA. There must be a good arguable case that there was a concluded contract (see *Seaconsar Far East Ltd v Bank Markazi Jomhouri Islami Iran* [1994] 1 AC 438, [1993] 4 All ER 456, HL; *Agrafax Public Relations Ltd v United Scottish Society Inc* [1995] ILPr 753, CA; and see para 651 ante), even if it is an implied contract (*Bowling v Cox* [1926] AC 751, PC), such as a quasi-contractual promise to repay; see also *Re Jogia (a bankrupt)* [1988] 2 All ER 328, [1988] 1 WLR 484. The holding of office as director is not as such (that is, in the absence of a contract of employment) a contract: *Newtherapeutics Ltd v Katz* [1991] Ch 226, [1991] 2 All ER 151. As to contracts in English law see generally CONTRACT.
4 RSC Ord 11 r 1(1)(d)(i). This includes a contract 'arising' in England and Wales: *Re An Intended Action, Trustee of Rousou (a bankrupt) v Rousou* [1955] 2 All ER 169, [1955] 1 WLR 545; and further proceedings sub nom *Trustee of Rousou (a bankrupt) v Rousou* [1955] 3 All ER 486; *Re Jogia (a bankrupt)* [1988] 2 All ER 328, [1988] 1 WLR 484. In accordance with principle, a contract is made where the offer is accepted: see *Cowan v O'Connor* (1888) 20 QBD 640, DC. But in the case of telex communications, the contract is made at the place where the offeror receives the acceptance: *Entores Ltd v Miles Far East Corpn* [1955] 2 QB 327, [1955] 2 All ER 493, CA; *Brinkibon Ltd v Stahag Stahl und Stahlwarenhandelgesellschaft mbH* [1983] 2 AC 34, [1982] 1 All ER 293, HL. If a contract made within the jurisdiction is amended outside the jurisdiction, it is still treated as having been made within the jurisdiction unless a new agreement is made by the amendment: *BP Exploration Co (Libya) Ltd v Hunt* [1976] 3 All ER 879, [1976] 1 WLR 788.

5 RSC Ord 11 r 1(i)(d)(ii). This includes a contract whose terms have been arranged through an agent who had no authority to bind his principal, the contract having been made with the principal himself: *National Mortgage and Agency Co of New Zealand Ltd v Gosselin and Stordeur* (1922) 38 TLR 832, CA. See also *Mauroux v Sociedade Comercial Abel Pereira da Fonseca SARL* [1972] 2 All ER 1085, [1972] 1 WLR 962. The rule is inapplicable where the principal of the agent is the plaintiff as opposed to the defendant: *Union International Insurance Co Ltd v Jubilee Insurance Co Ltd* [1991] 1 All ER 740, [1991] 1 WLR 415. For an alternative method of service in such cases see RSC Ord 10 r 2.

6 RSC Ord 11 r 1(1)(d)(iii). For the provisions of law which determine whether a contract is governed by English law see para 844 et seq post. The law as set out in the Rome Convention (set out in the Contracts (Applicable Law) Act 1990 s 2, Sch 1: see para 844 et seq post) is applicable for these purposes: *Bank of Baroda v Vysya Bank Ltd* [1994] 2 Lloyd's Rep 87. Note the particular transitional provision in art 54 of the Brussels and Lugano Conventions, under which an English court may exercise jurisdiction over a defendant domiciled in a contracting state on the basis of a written provision in a contract that it is to be governed by English law: see para 625 ante; and see *New Hampshire Insurance Co v Strabag Bau AG* [1992] 1 Lloyd's Rep 361, CA.

7 RSC Ord 11 r 1(1)(d)(iv). Note that in a case falling within this head the court will usually have jurisdiction under Ord 11 r 1(2), and no leave will be required (see para 673 post). See the cases cited in para 633 note 15 ante on the construction of choice of court clauses.

8 The breach of contract must occur within the jurisdiction: *Cordova Land Co Ltd v Victor Bros Inc* [1966] 1 WLR 793. See also *Cuban Atlantic Sugar Sales Corpn v Compania de Vapores San Elefterio Ltda* [1960] 1 QB 187, [1960] 1 All ER 141, CA, where there was no contractual obligation to be performed in England, and therefore no breach within the jurisdiction. The breach being assumed, the court has to be satisfied on the affidavits that there is a good arguable case that it was committed within the jurisdiction: see *Seaconsar Far East Ltd v Bank Markazi Jomhouri Islami Iran* [1994] 1 AC 438, [1993] 4 All ER 456, HL; *Agrafax Public Relations Ltd v United Scottish Society Inc* [1995] ILPr 753, CA. Failure to pay a debt due to a plaintiff in England is a breach within the jurisdiction: *Robey v Snaefell Mining Co* (1887) 20 QBD 152, DC; *The Eider* [1893] P 119, CA; *Thompson v Palmer* [1893] 2 QB 80, CA. So is the dismissal of an employee by a letter posted in England: *Oppenheimer v Louis Rosenthal & Co* [1937] 1 All ER 23, CA.

9 This provision negatives *Johnson v Taylor Bros & Co Ltd* [1920] AC 144, HL.

10 RSC Ord 11 r 1(1)(e).

656. Torts. Leave may be given[1] to serve a writ out of the jurisdiction if the action begun by the writ is founded on a tort and the damage was sustained, or resulted from an act committed, within the jurisdiction[2].

1 As to applications for leave see para 670 post.

2 RSC Ord 11 r 1(1)(f). This sub-rule is drafted to reflect the provisions of the Brussels Convention art 5 para 3; the Lugano Convention art 5 para 3; and the Civil Jurisdiction and Judgments Act 1982 s 16(1) (as amended), (2), Sch 4 art 5(3): see para 642 ante. As to the Brussels Convention see para 618 text and note 1 ante. As to the Lugano Convention see para 618 text and note 2 ante. The concept of a tort referred to a tort according to English law, as distinct from other forms of civil liability under English or under a foreign law: *Metall und Rohstoff AG v Donaldson Lufkin & Jenrette Inc* [1990] 1 QB 391, [1989] 3 All ER 14, CA. However, on the coming into force of the Private International Law (Miscellaneous Provisions) Act 1995 Pt III (ss 9–15) (see paras 897–901 post), it may be sufficient for the claim to be characterised as a tort for the purposes of the conflict of laws, although not amounting to a tort in English law. *Metall und Rohstoff AG v Donaldson Lufkin & Jenrette Inc* supra also established that damage is sustained within the jurisdiction if there is some significant damage within the jurisdiction, and that an act was committed within the jurisdiction if the damage resulted from substantial and efficacious acts committed within the jurisdiction, whether or not it was accompanied by other substantial and efficacious acts committed elsewhere: see *Metall und Rohstoff AG v Donaldson Lufkin & Jenrette Inc* supra at 437, 25. It is possible that a distinction exists between where damage occurred and where it was sustained: see para 642 note 6 ante. If RSC Ord 11 r 1(1)(f) is to be interpreted to conform to the provisions of the Conventions, it may be necessary to read 'sustained' as 'occurred'.

The question of where the tort occurred, which was of decisive importance under the former version of RSC Ord 11 r 1(1)(f) and which continues to be relevant in relation to the new version in the sense that it must be shown that there was a tort committed, and whether there was such a tort, is determined by choice of law rules which are predicated upon the location of a tort; the test is where in substance the cause of action arose: see further para 893 post.

As to tort generally see NEGLIGENCE; NUISANCE; TORT.

657. Land within the jurisdiction. Leave may be given[1] to serve a writ out of the jurisdiction if the whole subject matter of the action begun by the writ is land situated within the jurisdiction[2], with or without rents or profits[3], or the perpetuation of testimony[4] relating to land so situated[5].

1   As to applications for leave see para 670 post.
2   The land must be the subject matter of the claim, which may be an action for possession and may relate to title: *Agnew v Usher* (1884) 51 LT 752, CA.
3   It follows that a claim for rents or profits must be ancillary to the claim to the land, and not the subject matter of the action.
4   See *Slingsby v Slingsby* [1912] 2 Ch 21, CA, the decision in which led to the addition of these words in RSC Ord 11 r 1(1)(g).
5   RSC Ord 11 r 1(1)(g).

658. Documents affecting land within the jurisdiction. Leave may be given[1] to serve a writ out of the jurisdiction if the claim is made to construe, rectify, set aside or enforce an act, deed, will, contract obligation or liability affecting land situated within the jurisdiction[2].

1   As to applications for leave see para 670 post.
2   RSC Ord 11 r 1(1)(h). This provision includes an action for possession and for breach of covenant to repair: *Tassell v Hallen* [1892] 1 QB 321. It may also include an action for rent, which may be an obligation affecting land being enforced in the action (see *Iveagh v Harris* [1929] 2 Ch 142; but see *Agnew v Usher* (1884) 14 QBD 78, DC; affd 51 LT 752, CA). See also *Kaye v Sutherland* (1887) 20 QBD 147; *A-G v Draper's Co* [1894] 1 IR 185, Ir CA (claim for breach of trust); *Mority v Stephan* (1888) 58 LT 850; *Kolchmann v Meurice* [1903] 1 KB 534, CA. A claim for slander of title to land is not within this provision: *Casey v Arnott* (1876) 2 CPD 24; *Bree v Marescaux* (1881) 7 QBD 434, CA. But as the Brussels Convention art 16 para 1, the Lugano Convention art 16 para 1, and the Civil Jurisdiction and Judgments Act 1982 s 16(1) (as amended), (2), Sch 4 art 16(1) (as substituted) give exclusive jurisdiction to the court in many such cases, there will be comparatively few occasions upon which RSC Ord 11 r 1(1)(h) is relied on: see para 627 ante. As to the Brussels Convention see para 618 text and note 1 ante. As to the Lugano Convention see para 618 text and note 2 ante. As to the adaptation of the provisions of the Conventions by the Civil Jurisdiction and Judgments Act 1982 Sch 4, to a scheme applying as between parts of the United Kingdom, see para 619 ante. As to the construction of deeds and other instruments see generally DEEDS.

659. Debts secured on property. Leave may be given[1] to serve a writ out of the jurisdiction if the claim is made for a debt secured on immovable property or is made to assert, declare or determine proprietary or possessory rights, or rights of security, in or over movable property, or to obtain authority to dispose of movable property situated within the jurisdiction[2].

1   As to applications for leave see para 670 post.
2   RSC Ord 11 r 1(1)(i). See generally MORTGAGE.

660. Trusts. Leave may be given[1] to serve a writ out of the jurisdiction if the claim is brought to execute the trusts of a written instrument, being trusts that ought to be executed according to English law[2] and of which the person to be served is a trustee, or if the action is for any relief or remedy which might be obtained in any such action[3].

1   As to applications for leave see para 670 post.
2   As to the meaning of 'English law' see para 604 ante.
3   RSC Ord 11 r 1(1)(j). It is not necessary that there be some property which is subject to the trust instrument which is situated within the jurisdiction: cf *Winter v Winter* [1894] 1 Ch 421. See generally TRUSTS.

661. Administration actions. Leave may be given[1] to serve a writ out of the jurisdiction if the claim is made for the administration of the estate of a person who died domiciled[2] within the jurisdiction, or for any relief or remedy which might be obtained in any such action[3].

1 As to applications for leave see para 670 post.
2 The meaning of 'domicile' for these purposes is that contained in the Civil Jurisdiction and Judgments Act 1982 s 41: see para 652 ante and RSC Ord 11 r 1(4). See paras 631 note 9, 632 note 9, 635–638 ante.
3 RSC Ord 11 r 1(1)(k). As to administration of estates generally see EXECUTORS.

662. Probate actions. Leave may be given[1] to serve a writ out of the jurisdiction if the claim is brought in a probate action[2].

1 As to applications for leave see para 670 post.
2 RSC Ord 11 r 1(1)(l). 'Probate action' means a probate action within the meaning of Ord 76: Ord 11 r 1(1)(l). It does not include non-contentious probate proceedings: see Ord 76 r 1(2). As to probate actions see EXECUTORS vol 17 para 870 et seq.

663. Enforcement of judgments or awards. Leave may be given[1] to serve a writ out of the jurisdiction if the claim is brought to enforce any judgment or arbitral award[2].

1 As to applications for leave see para 670 post.
2 RSC Ord 11 r 1(1)(m). Where enforcement of a judgment by registration (see paras 1023–1065 post) is available, the personal jurisdiction of the English court over the judgment debtor is irrelevant. But where the judgment or award is required to be enforced by action, service out of the jurisdiction may be made under this head: see further para 997 et seq post. This head does not give jurisdiction for service where the only relief claimed is a Mareva injunction, because Mareva relief is not 'brought to enforce' a judgment; nor is it available if the judgment has not yet been given: *Mercedes-Benz AG v Leiduck* [1995] 3 All ER 929, [1995] 3 WLR 718, PC. As to arbitration awards generally see ARBITRATION.

664. Taxes and duties. Leave may be given[1] to serve a writ out of the jurisdiction if the action begun by the writ is brought against a defendant not domiciled[2] in Scotland or Northern Ireland in respect of a claim by the Commissioners of Inland Revenue for or in relation to any of the duties or taxes which have been, or are for the time being, placed under their care and management[3].

1 As to applications for leave see para 670 post.
2 'Domicile' in this provision means domicile as defined by the Civil Jurisdiction and Judgments Act 1982 ss 41–46 (as amended): RSC Ord 11 r 1(4). See paras 631 note 9, 632 note 9, 635–638 ante.
3 RSC Ord 11 r 1(1)(n). See generally CAPITAL GAINS TAXATION; INHERITANCE TAXATION; INCOME TAXATION.

665. Certain statutory claims. Leave may be given[1] to serve a writ out of the jurisdiction if the claim is made under one of a number of specified statutes, namely: (1) the Nuclear Installations Act 1965[2]; (2) social security legislation (in respect of contributions)[3]; (3) the Drug Trafficking Act 1994[4]; (4) the Financial Services Act 1986[5]; (6) the Banking Act 1987[6]; (7) Part VI of the Criminal Justice Act 1988[7]; or (8) the Immigration (Carriers' Liability) Act 1987[8].

1 As to applications for leave see para 670 post.
2 RSC Ord 11 r 1(1)(o). See generally FUEL AND ENERGY vol 19(2) para 1262 et seq.

3 RSC Ord 11 r 1(1)(o). The Order refers to the Social Security Act 1975 (repealed), but may be taken to refer to the corresponding provisions of the consolidating legislation: see the Social Security (Consequential Provisions) Act 1992 s 2.

4 RSC Ord 11 r 1(1)(q). The reference to the Drug Trafficking Act 1994 replaces a reference to the Drug Trafficking Offences Act 1986: see CRIMINAL LAW vol 11(2) para 1305 et seq.

5 RSC Ord 11 r 1(1)(r). See generally BANKING; BUILDING SOCIETIES; COMPANIES; FRIENDLY SOCIETIES.

6 RSC Ord 11 r 1(1)(r). See generally BANKING.

7 Ie the Criminal Justice Act 1988 Pt VI (ss 71–103) (as amended): RSC Ord 11 r 1(1)(s). See CRIMINAL LAW vol 11(2) para 1284 et seq.

8 RSC Ord 11 r 1(1)(u). See BRITISH NATIONALITY, IMMIGRATION AND RACE RELATIONS vol 4(2) para 79.

566. Claims relating to the European Agricultural Guidance and Guarantee Fund. Leave may be given[1] to serve a writ out of the jurisdiction if the claim is made for certain sums in respect of the financing of the European Agricultural Guidance and Guarantee Fund, agricultural levies, customs duties, value added tax and incidental interest and costs[2], where service is to be effected in a member state of the European Community[3].

1 As to applications for leave see para 670 post.

2 Ie a sum to which EC Council Directive 76/308 (OJ L73, 18.3.76, p 18) (as amended) applies. See further AGRICULTURE vol 1(2) para 1011.

3 RSC Ord 11 r 1(1)(p).

667. Money had and received; constructive trusteeship. Leave may be given[1] to serve a writ out of the jurisdiction if the claim is brought for money had and received or for an account or other relief against the defendant as constructive trustee, and the defendant's alleged liability arises out of acts committed, whether by himself or otherwise, within the jurisdiction[2].

1 As to applications for leave see para 670 post.

2 RSC Ord 11 r 1(1)(t). As long as some of the acts upon which liability is said to arise occurred within the jurisdiction, it is unnecessary for the actual receipt of money to have occurred within the jurisdiction: *ISC Technologies Ltd v Guerin* [1992] 2 Lloyd's Rep 430 (and see para 653 ante); *Polly Peck International plc v Nadir* (1992) Independent, 2 September. As to constructive trusts generally see TRUSTS vol 48 (Reissue) para 585 et seq. As to actions for money had and received see CONTRACT vol 9 para 676 et seq.

668. Documents other than writs of summons. Service out of the jurisdiction is permissible with the leave of the court[1] in the case of the following documents other than a writ of summons: (1) an originating summons[2], notice of motion or petition[3]; or (2) any summons, notice or order issued, given or made in any proceedings[4].

Application for leave to serve such documents is made in the ordinary way[5], and the ordinary rules[6] as to the mode of service out of the jurisdiction apply to them[7].

1 As to applications for leave see para 670 post.

2 An order granting leave to serve an originating summons out of the jurisdiction must limit the time within which the defendant to be served must acknowledge service: RSC Ord 11 r 9(6). In the case of an originating summons served out of the jurisdiction, references in the Rules of the Supreme Court to the time limited for acknowledgment of service are references to the time so limited by the order giving leave, or, if that time has been extended by or by virtue of the rules, to that time as so extended: RSC Ord 12 rr 5(b), 9(3).

3 See RSC Ord 11 r 9(1), applying Ord 11 r 1. This is expressed to be subject to Ord 73 r 7: see para 669 post.

4 See RSC Ord 11 r 9(4), which is expressed to be subject to Ord 73 r 7: see para 669 post. The provision of Ord 11 r 9(4) apply to service of judicial process, whether original or interlocutory, but not to informal notices sent for information or convenience: *Re Nathan, Newman & Co* (1887) 35 ChD 1; *Re King & Co's Trade-Mark* [1892] 2 Ch 462, CA. As to the service out of the jurisdiction of extra-judicia documents see the notice issued by the Lord Chancellor on 18 May 1931, cited in the Supreme Court Practice 1995 para 11/9/3.

5 Ie under RSC Ord 11 r 4(1)–(3) (see para 670 post), applied by Ord 11 r 9(5).

6 Ie RSC Ord 11 rr 5, 6, 8; and see PRACTICE AND PROCEDURE vol 37 paras 171, 194–195.

7 RSC Ord 11 r 9(7).

669. Documents in arbitration proceedings.

An originating summons or notice of originating motion under the Arbitration Act 1950, or the Arbitration Act 1979, or any order made on such a summons or motion, may be served out of the jurisdiction with the leave of the court, provided that the arbitration to which the summons, motion or order relates is governed by English law[1] or has been, or is to be, held within the jurisdiction[2]. Service out of the jurisdiction of an originating summons for leave to enforce an award is permissible with leave whether or not the arbitration is governed by English law[3]. In the case of an order giving leave to enforce an arbitration award as a judgment, service of the order out of the jurisdiction is permissible without leave[4].

1 As to the meaning of 'English law' see para 604 ante.

2 RSC Ord 73 r 7(1). If leave is given, the mode of service is as in the case of a writ: see Ord 11 rr 5, 6, 8 (see PRACTICE AND PROCEDURE vol 37 paras 171, 194–195), applied by Ord 73 r 7(3). The application for leave must be supported by an affidavit stating the grounds on which the application is made and showing in what place or country the person to be served is or probably may be found; and leave must not be granted unless it is made sufficiently to appear to the court that the case is a proper one for service out of the jurisdiction under the Order: Ord 73 r 7(3). Cf Ord 11 r 4(2); and para 671 post. As to arbitration generally see ARBITRATION.

3 RSC Ord 73 r 7(1A).

4 See RSC Ord 73 r 10(5).

670. Form of application and order for leave.

Every application for the grant of leave to serve a writ or other process[1] out of the jurisdiction[2] must be supported by an affidavit[3], which must state: (1) the grounds on which the application is made[4]; (2) that, in the deponent's belief, the plaintiff has a good cause of action[5]; and (3) in what place or country the defendant is or probably may be found[6]. Additionally, if the application is made in respect of the joining of a person as a necessary or proper party to the action[7], the affidavit must further state the grounds for the belief of the deponent that there is, between the plaintiff and the party who has been served, a real issue which the court may reasonably be asked to try[8].

The order granting leave to serve a writ or originating summons out of the jurisdiction must limit a time within which the defendant must acknowledge service[9].

1 RSC Ord 11 r 4(1) is also applied to the process referred to in para 668 ante: Ord 11 r 9(5)

2 Ie under RSC Ord 11 r 1(1): see para 650 et seq ante.

3 RSC Ord 11 r 4(1).

4 RSC Ord 11 r 4(1)(a). Although it is not essential to identify the particular head or heads of Ord 11 r 1(1) upon which the plaintiff relies, it is undoubtedly good practice to do so: *Newtherapeutics Ltd v Katz* [1991] Ch 226, [1991] 2 All ER 151. The plaintiff who appears to have advanced the claim to jurisdiction upon a particular ground should not be permitted at the hearing of the application to advance a different or additional ground which has not been foreshadowed: *Metall und Rohstoff AG v Donaldson Lufkin & Jenrette Inc* [1990] 1 QB 391, [1989] 3 All ER 14, CA; and see *Parker v Schuller* (1901) 17 TLR 299, CA. The affidavit must set out all the relevant facts and exhibit all the relevant documents on which the application is made, and since the application is made ex parte the affidavit must make a

full and frank disclosure (*Bloomfield v Serenyi* [1945] 2 All ER 646, CA, where the duty of the solicitor was considered); see also *Reynolds v Coleman* (1887) 36 ChD 453, CA; *The Hagen* [1908] P 189 at 201, CA; *Electric Furnace Co v Selas Corpn of America* [1987] RPC 23, CA; *Newtherapeutics Ltd v Katz* supra; otherwise the court may discharge any order it has made although the party may apply again (see *The Hagen* supra).

5 RSC Ord 11 r 4(1)(b). The affidavit should state the nature of the proposed cause of action and the relief or remedy sought: *Kinahan v Kinahan* (1890) 45 ChD 78; *Vaudrey v Nathan* [1928] WN 54, CA. This can conveniently be done by exhibiting a draft statement of claim settled by counsel. The facts relied on must enable the court to decide whether the case falls within one of the grounds of RSC Ord 11 r 1(1), giving the court jurisdiction to grant leave and also that it is a proper case for service out of the jurisdiction: *Great Australian Gold Mining Co v Martin* (1877) 5 ChD 1, CA; *Shearman v Findlay* (1883) 32 WR 122.

6 RSC Ord 11 r 4(1)(c). Leave is usually given to serve in a particular country; but substituted service in England upon a person who is abroad may be applied for and may be ordered: *Western Suburban and Notting Hill Permanent Benefit Building Society v Rucklidge* [1905] 2 Ch 472. The affidavit should also state whether or not the defendant is domiciled or ordinarily resident in Scotland or Northern Ireland. As to the significance of this requirement see para 672 post.

7 Ie under RSC Ord 11 r 1(1)(c): see para 654 ante.

8 RSC Ord 11 r 4(1)(d).

9 RSC Ord 11 rr 4(4), 9(6). The time depends on the place or country where the process is to be served. As to the time for acknowledging service of a writ or originating summons out of the jurisdiction see the Extra Jurisdiction Tables in the Supreme Court Practice 1995 vol 2 Pt 3C para 902.

671. Discretion to grant leave. Where, on an application for leave for service out of the jurisdiction, the court has determined that, on the material before it, it has jurisdiction to grant leave[1], nevertheless no leave may be granted unless it is made sufficiently to appear to the court that the case is a proper one for service out of the jurisdiction[2]. On this question it must be shown by the plaintiff that England is, clearly or distinctly, the most appropriate forum for the hearing of the dispute[3]; and if it is, the plaintiff must further show that he has, on the merits of the case he advances against the defendant, a serious issue to be tried[4].

1 Ie that the case falls within the requisite head of RSC Ord 11 r 1(1): see para 652 et seq ante.

2 RSC Ord 11 r 4(2).

3 *Spiliada Maritime Corpn v Cansulex Ltd* [1987] AC 460, [1986] 3 All ER 843, HL. This is a distinct and essential aspect of the statutory requirement that the case be a proper one for service out of the jurisdiction: *Seaconsar Far East Ltd v Bank Markazi Jomhouri Islami Iran* [1994] 1 AC 438, [1993] 4 All ER 456, HL. Earlier cases, which had suggested that this requirement did not strictly need to be satisfied if the plaintiff had an extremely strong claim on the merits are not reliable: see *Seaconsar Far East Ltd v Bank Markazi Jomhouri Islami Iran* supra at 456 and at 467. Upon the question whether the plaintiff has shown England to be, clearly or distinctly, the natural forum see the cases on stays of proceedings cited in para 1085 post, in which the same analysis is undertaken by the defendant who seeks a stay of English proceedings. The cases in which the concept of the natural forum has been developed differ only on the question of whether it is the defendant who must show a foreign court to be (in a stay application) the natural forum, or the plaintiff who must show England to be (in an application for leave to serve out of the jurisdiction) the natural forum. Although the fact that English law is the lex causae may be thought to be a good reason for considering England to be the natural forum, the court should not lightly hold that this follows from the fact that businessmen have expressly selected English law (but without a choice of forum) to govern their contract: *Spiliada Maritime Corpn v Cansulex Ltd* supra at 481–482, 859.

4 *Seaconsar Far East Ltd v Bank Markazi Jomhouri Islami Iran* [1994] 1 AC 438, [1993] 4 All ER 456, HL. This appears to mean that the claim is strong enough to enable the court to exercise its discretion, before it goes on to consider the exercise of discretion: see *Seaconsar Far East Ltd v Bank Markazi Jomhouri Islami Iran* supra at 456 and at 467.

672. Service in Scotland or Northern Ireland. Where an application is made[1] in England and Wales[2] for leave to serve a writ in Scotland or Northern Ireland, in addition to determining whether or not it has jurisdiction to grant such leave and whether in the ordinary way it would exercise its discretion to grant leave, the court must also consider whether there is a concurrent remedy there, and if there is, the court must have regard to the comparative cost and convenience of proceeding there or in England and Wales[3]. For this purpose, 'convenience' is to be given a wide meaning, as including, for example, where the parties and their witnesses live, where the relevant documents are, the possibility of double litigation, expedition or delay and the mode of enforcement[4]. Where relevant the court must have regard to the powers and jurisdiction of the sheriff court in Scotland or the county courts or courts of summary jurisdiction in Northern Ireland[5].

  1 Ie under RSC Ord 11 r 1: see paras 651–667 ante.
  2 As to the meaning of 'England and Wales' see para 604 ante.
  3 RSC Ord 11 r 4(3); but see para 673 post. These considerations may be sufficient to persuade the court to refuse leave: see *Lenders v Anderson* (1883) 12 QBD 50; *The Elton* [1891] P 265 at 269; *Witted v Galbraith* [1893] 1 QB 577, CA; *Williams v Cartwright* [1895] 1 QB 142 at 146, CA, per Lord Esher MR.
  4 See *Tozier v Hawkins* (1885) 15 QBD 680, CA; *Washburn & Moen etc Co v Cunard SS Co and J C Parker & Sons* (1889) 5 TLR 592; *Re Burland's Trade-Mark, Burland v Broxburn Oil Co* (1889) 41 ChD 542; *Re De Penny, De Penny v Christie* [1891] 2 Ch 63.
  5 RSC Ord 11 r 4(3).

673. Service out of the jurisdiction without leave. In certain cases, service out of the jurisdiction is permissible without the leave of the court[1].

If the court has jurisdiction to hear the claim by reason of the Civil Jurisdiction and Judgments Act 1982[2], no leave is required to serve the writ out of the jurisdiction[3]; indeed, the court has no power to grant leave even if it is mistakenly applied for[4]. Also, if the court has jurisdiction by virtue of any other enactment notwithstanding that the person against whom the claim is made is not within the jurisdiction or that the wrongful act, neglect or default giving rise to the claim did not take place within the jurisdiction, service out is permitted without leave[5].

  1 These cases, almost all of which owe their origins to international conventions to which the United Kingdom is party, are consequently very important.
  2 As to jurisdiction by reason of the Civil Jurisdiction and Judgments Act 1982, which contains the provisions of the Brussels and Lugano Conventions, as well as an analogous scheme for determining jurisdiction as between different parts of the United Kingdom, see paras 618–619 ante. As to the Brussels Convention see para 618 text and note 1 ante. As to the Lugano Convention see para 618 text and note 2 ante. The scheme referred to will usually determine whether a defendant domiciled in Scotland or Northern Ireland may be sued in the English courts, and if he is so liable, leave will not be required for service (see para 672 ante). It is expressly required that (1) there are no proceedings between the same parties in respect of the same cause of action in another contracting state or another part of the United Kingdom; and (2) either the defendant is domiciled in the United Kingdom or in another convention territory, or that art 16 or 17 of the Conventions or of the United Kingdom scheme applies to give the English court jurisdiction: RSC Ord 11 r 1(2)(a); and see paras 627–628, 633 ante. The effect is that jurisdiction which exists pursuant to the Conventions will entitle the writ to be served out of the jurisdiction without leave, but not where it is based on art 4 (see para 639 ante), for in such a case the conditions of RSC Ord 11 r 1(2)(a) are not satisfied. As to references to numbered articles 'of the Conventions' see para 618 note 5 ante.
    RSC Ord 11 r 1(2) uses the term 'Convention territory' rather than 'contracting state' to indicate that certain territories of contracting states were excluded from the Brussels Convention, but art 60 of that Convention, which specified the excluded territories, is now repealed (see the Civil Jurisdiction and Judgments Act 1982 (Amendment) Order 1990, SI 1990/2591).
  3 RSC Ord 11 r 1(2)(a). For the indorsement which must appear on the writ see RSC Ord 6 r 7.
  4 See RSC Ord 11 r 1(1); and *Agrafax Public Relations Ltd v United Scottish Society Inc* [1995] ILPr 753, CA.
  5 RSC Ord 11 r 1(2)(b). Excluded are the enactments listed in RSC Ord 11 r 1(1) (see para 652 et seq ante). It applies to the Civil Aviation Act 1982 ss 24 (as amended), 74(6), Sch 4 para 3 (as amended); and to the Protection of Trading Interests Act 1980 s 6(5) (see para 1014 post). It applies also to actions

brought under certain international conventions which have been given force in English law, and this is unaffected by the Brussels and Lugano Conventions, by reason of art 57 (see para 677 post), preserving the right to exercise jurisdiction provided for by another international Convention to which the United Kingdom is a party. As to the conventions in question see para 677 post.

674. Mode of service out of the jurisdiction. The general rules as to service of a writ of summons within the jurisdiction apply equally to the service of a writ[1] out of the jurisdiction, but this statement is subject to important modifications and to special rules regarding service abroad according to the country in which service is desired to be effected. In general, service abroad may be effected by personal service[2], by acceptance of service by a solicitor[3], by acknowledgment of service even if service has not been effected[4] or by substituted service[5]. Moreover, the parties to a contract which provides that the High Court is to have jurisdiction to hear and determine any action in respect of the contract may provide that service is to be effected in such manner or at such place, whether within or out of the jurisdiction, as is specified in the contract[6]. Every copy of a writ for service on a defendant, even if he is out of the jurisdiction, must be sealed with the seal of the court office out of which it is issued and the writ, served on the defendant must be accompanied by the appropriate form of acknowledgment of service[7].

A writ for service out of the jurisdiction need not be served personally on the defendant provided it is served on him in accordance with the law of the country of service[8], and it need not be served by the plaintiff or his agent if it is served by a specified method[9]. However, nothing in the provisions described above, or in any order or direction of the court made under them, authorises or requires the doing of anything in a country in which service is to be effected which is contrary to the law of that country[10].

The mode of service in particular countries to which somewhat different provisions apply is as follows:

(1) if the writ is to be served[11] on a defendant in any country which is a party to the Hague Convention[12], it may be served either (a) through the authority designated under the convention in respect of that country[13]; or (b) if the law of that country permits, through the judicial authority of that country[14] or through a British consular authority there[15];

(2) if the writ is to be served[16] on a defendant in any country with respect to which there subsists a civil procedure convention[17] (other than the Hague Convention) providing for service there of High Court process, the writ may be served either (a) through the judicial authorities of that country[18]; or (b) through a British consular authority there[19];

(3) if the writ is to be served[20] on a defendant in any country with respect to which no civil procedure convention subsists providing for service there of High Court process, the writ may be served either (a) through the government of that country, if it is willing to effect service[21]; or (b) through a British consular authority there, unless such service is contrary to the law of that country[22];

(4) if the writ is to be served in Scotland, Northern Ireland, the Isle of Man or the Channel Islands, any independent Commonwealth country, any associated state, any colony or the Republic of Ireland, then, unless the country concerned is a party to the Hague Convention[23], service must be effected in the ordinary way by the plaintiff or his agent and may not be effected through official channels[24].

A person wishing to serve a writ under head (1), (2) or (3) above must lodge in the Central Office a request for service of the writ by the appropriate method[25] together with a copy of the writ for each person to be served and one extra copy[26], and a translation of the writ in the official language of the country concerned[27]. The Senior Master must send the documents to the Parliamentary Under-Secretary of the Foreign and Commonwealth Office with a request that he arrange for service by the method indicated in the plaintiff's request for service or, where alternative methods are so indicated, by the most convenient of such methods[28].

An official certificate[29] stating that a writ as regards which these provisions have been complied with has been served on a person personally or in accordance with the law of the country of service, on a specified date, is evidence of the facts so stated[30].

1   The rules regulating the service of a writ of summons out of the jurisdiction apply equally to other originating processes (eg originating summonses, petitions, notices of motion and indeed any document for which leave to serve out of the jurisdiction has been granted under RSC Ord 11): Ord 11 r 9(7), applying Ord 11 rr 5, 6, 8. Those rules also apply to certain documents which may be served out of the jurisdiction without leave: see Ord 71 r 7(2), Ord 73 r 10(5); and para 673 ante.

2   RSC Ord 11 r 5(1), applying Ord 10 r 1(1) to such service. See PRACTICE AND PROCEDURE vol 37 para 150. Order 10 r 1(2), (3), which provide the alternative methods of service by post or by insertion through a letter box, are confined by their terms to service within the jurisdiction, and in any event they are not applied to service out of the jurisdiction by Ord 11 r 5(1).

3   RSC Ord 11 r 5(1), applying Ord 10 r 1(4); see PRACTICE AND PROCEDURE vol 37 para 154.

4   RSC Ord 11 r 5(1), applying Ord 10 r 1(5); see PRACTICE AND PROCEDURE vol 37 para 155.

5   RSC Ord 11 r 5(1), applying Ord 65 r 4; see PRACTICE AND PROCEDURE vol 37 para 153.

6   See RSC Ord 10 r 3(1); and see PRACTICE AND PROCEDURE vol 37 para 157. Leave to serve out of the jurisdiction must first be obtained under Ord 11 r 1(1) (see para 651 et seq ante) unless leave is not required by virtue of Ord 11 r 1(2) (see para 673 ante): Ord 10 r 3(2). See *Montgomery, Jones & Co v Liebenthal & Co* [1898] 1 QB 487, CA.

7   RSC Ord 11 r 5(1), applying Ord 10 r 1(6); see PRACTICE AND PROCEDURE vol 37 para 197.

8   RSC Ord 11 r 5(3)(a).

9   Ie a method provided in RSC Ord 11 rr 6, 7 (see the text and notes infra, and para 675 post): RSC Ord 11 r 5(3)(b).

10   RSC Ord 11 r 5(2).

11   Ie in accordance with the Rules of the Supreme Court: RSC Ord 11 r 6(2A).

12   'The Hague Convention' means the Convention on the Service Abroad of Judicial and Extrajudicial Documents in Civil or Commercial Matters (The Hague, 15 November 1965; TS 50 (1969); Cmnd 3986): RSC Ord 11 r 5(8). The Convention does not invalidate any bilateral civil procedure convention already in force. At the date at which this volume states the law, the following are convention countries: Antigua and Barbuda, Barbados, Belgium, Botswana, Canada, China, Cyprus, Czech Republic, Denmark, Egypt, Falkland Islands, Finland, France, Germany, Greece, Republic of Ireland, Israel, Italy, Japan, Latvia, Luxembourg, Malawi, The Netherlands (and Aruba), Norway, Pakistan, Portugal, Seychelles, Slovak Republic, Spain, Sweden, Switzerland, Turkey, United Kingdom (and dependencies), United States of America (and dependencies), and Venezuela.

13   RSC Ord 11 r 6(2A)(a).

14   RSC Ord 11 r 6(2A)(b)(i).

15   RSC Ord 11 r 6(2A)(b)(ii).

16   Ie in accordance with the Rules of the Supreme Court.

17   Countries with which such a bilateral civil procedure convention is in force providing for service of High Court process (some of which are also parties to the Hague Convention: see note 12 supra) include, at the date at which this volumes states the law, Austria, Belgium, Czechoslovakia, Denmark, Finland, France, Germany, Greece, Hungary, Iraq, Israel, Italy, The Netherlands, Norway, Poland, Portugal, Romania, Spain, Sweden and Turkey. Laos, Lebanon and Syria were included in the French Convention of 1922 and have accepted the continuation to them of the terms of that convention. Information as to the variations in the mode of service in these countries may be obtained from the Masters' Secretary's Department, Room 120, Royal Courts of Justice, Strand, London WC2A 2LL. This department deals with service out of the jurisdiction of process from every Division of the High Court, including district registry proceedings.

18   RSC Ord 11 r 6(2)(a).

19 RSC Ord 11 r 6(2)(b). This is subject to any provision of the convention as to the nationality of persons who may be so served: Ord 11 r 6(2)(b).

20 Ie in accordance with the Rules of the Supreme Court.

21 RSC Ord 11 r 6(3)(a).

22 RSC Ord 11 r 6(3)(b).

23 Ie unless the service is to be effected pursuant to RSC Ord 11 r 6(2A): see head (1) in the text.

24 See RSC Ord 11 r 6(1), which excludes service in those places from the operation of Ord 11 r 6. See also Ord 11 r 5(3)(b), which provides that a writ need not be served by the plaintiff or his agent if it is served by a method provided for by Ord 11 r 6 or 7. See *Gohoho v Guinea Press Ltd* [1963] 1 QB 948, [1962] 3 All ER 785, CA.

25 The request must include an undertaking to be responsible personally for all expenses incurred by the Secretary of State in respect of the service and to pay those expenses on demand: see RSC Ord 11 r 8.

26 RSC Ord 11 r 6(4).

27 RSC Ord 11 r 6(5). If there is more than one official language, the translation must be in the official language appropriate to the actual place of service: Ord 11 r 6(5). The translation must be certified as correct by the translator, who must state his name, address and qualifications for making the translation: Ord 11 r 6(6). There is no need to supply a translation if the official language is or includes English, or if the writ is to be served by a British consular authority on a British subject, unless service is to be under a civil procedure convention which requires a translation: Ord 11 r 6(5) proviso.

28 RSC Ord 11 r 6(7). This applies also to county court documents lodged for service under CCR Ord 8 r 48(5): RSC Ord 11 r 10.

29 The certificate must be by a British consular authority in the country of service, by the government or judicial authorities of that country or by any other authority designated in respect of that country under the Hague Convention: RSC Ord 11 r 5(5)(a)–(c).

30 RSC Ord 11 r 5(5). A document purporting to be such a certificate is deemed to be such a certificate until the contrary is proved: Ord 11 r 5(7). If the certificate states that it has not been possible to effect service, an order may be made for substituted service under Ord 65 r 4 (see PRACTICE AND PROCEDURE vol 37 para 153); see *Wilding v Bean* [1891] 1 QB 100, CA; *Porter v Freudenberg* [1915] 1 KB 857 at 889, CA. Substituted service by post may not be recognised in some countries. The kind of service ordered may be service by post to an address within the jurisdiction: *Western Suburban and Notting Hill Permanent Benefit Building Society v Rucklidge* [1905] 2 Ch 472.

675. Mode of service on foreign or Commonwealth state.

Where a person to whom leave has been granted[1] to serve a writ on a state[2] wishes to have the writ served on that state he must lodge in the Central Office a request for service to be arranged by the Secretary of State[3], a copy of the writ[4], and except where the official language of the state is or includes English, a translation of the writ in the official language or one of the official languages of that state[5]. The documents so lodged must be sent by the Senior Master to the Secretary of State with a request that he arrange for the writ to be served[6].

Where the Secretary of State has agreed a different method of service[7], the writ may be served either by the method agreed or as provided above[8].

An official certificate by the Secretary of State stating that a writ has been duly served on a specified date in accordance with such a request is evidence of that fact[9].

1 Ie under RSC Ord 11 r 1: see para 651 et seq ante.

2 Ie a state as defined in the State Immunity Act 1978 s 14: see PRACTICE AND PROCEDURE vol 37 para 239.

3 RSC Ord 11 r 7(1)(a). As to expenses see Ord 11 r 8; and para 674 note 25 ante.

4 RSC Ord 11 r 7(1)(b).

5 RSC Ord 11 r 7(1)(c). Order 11 r 6(6) (see para 674 note 27 ante), applies to the translation: Ord 11 r 7(2).

6 RSC Ord 11 r 7(3).

7 Ie under the State Immunity Act 1978 s 12(6): see PRACTICE AND PROCEDURE vol 37 para 165.

8 RSC Ord 11 r 7(4).

9 RSC Ord 11 r 5(6). A document purporting to be such a certificate is deemed to be such a certificate until the contrary is proved: Ord 11 r 5(7).

676. Service of foreign process in England and Wales. Service within England and Wales[1] of foreign process[2] may be effected where the Senior Master receives a written request for service either (1) from the Secretary of State for Foreign and Commonwealth Affairs with a recommendation by him that such service should be effected[3]; or (2) where the foreign court or tribunal is in a convention country[4], from a consular or other authority of that country[5]. The request must be accompanied by a translation of it in English, two copies of the process and, unless the foreign court or tribunal certifies that the person to be served understands the language of the process, two copies of a translation of the process[6]. The method of service is either personal service on the person to be served[7] or by the alternative method of service by insertion through the letter box of the defendant[8].

The process server[9] must send to the Senior Master a copy of the process and an affidavit, certificate or report proving due service or stating the reason why service could not be effected, as the case may be, and, if the court so directs, he must specify the costs incurred in effecting or attempting to effect service[10]. The Senior Master must send a certificate[11], together with the copy of the process, to the consular or other authority or the Secretary of State, as the case may be, stating (a) when and how the service was effected or the reason why it could not be effected[12]; and (b) where appropriate, the amount certified by the taxing master to be the costs of effecting or attempting to effect service[13].

1 As to the meaning of 'England and Wales' see para 604 ante.
2 Ie process in connection with civil or commercial proceedings in a foreign court or tribunal: RSC Ord 69 r 2. 'Process' includes a citation: Ord 69 r 1.
3 RSC Ord 69 r 2(a).
4 'Convention country' means a foreign country in relation to which there subsists a civil procedure convention providing for service in that country of process in the High Court, and includes a country which is a party to the Hague Convention: RSC Ord 69 r 1. As to the Hague Convention see para 674 note 12 ante. See also para 674 note 17 ante.
5 RSC Ord 69 r 2(b).
6 RSC Ord 69 r 3(1).
7 RSC Ord 69 r 3(2). This is expressed to be subject to any enactment providing for the manner of service of documents on corporate bodies: see eg the Companies Act 1985 s 725. Provision is made for substituted service under RSC Ord 65 r 4; but the Senior Master may make an order for substituted service on the basis of the affidavit, certificate or report of the process server (see note 9 infra), without an application being made by the Treasury Solicitor: RSC Ord 69 r 3(5).
8 RSC Ord 69 r 3(3), applying Ord 10 r 1(2)(b) (see PRACTICE AND PROCEDURE vol 37 para 152), except that service may be proved by affidavit, certificate or report.
9 'Process server' means the process server appointed by the Lord Chancellor for the purposes of RSC Ord 69 under Ord 69 r 4, or his authorised agent: Ord 69 r 1.
10 RSC Ord 69 r 3(4).
11 The certificate must be sealed with the seal of the Supreme Court for use out of the jurisdiction: RSC Ord 69 r 3(7).
12 RSC Ord 69 r 3(6)(a).
13 RSC Ord 69 r 3(6)(b).

(4) PARTICULAR INTERNATIONAL CONVENTIONS AFFECTING JURISDICTION AND THE RECOGNITION OF JUDGMENTS

677. International conventions affecting jurisdiction. The jurisdiction of the English court is sometimes excluded or limited by a statute implementing an international convention. If the convention in question contains particular provisions for the taking of jurisdiction, neither the Brussels Convention[1] nor the Lugano

Convention[2] prejudices the right of the plaintiff to take advantage of these particular conventional rules on jurisdiction[3]. Where the court has jurisdiction by reason of an enactment giving effect in English law to some other convention, service of the writ out of the jurisdiction will be available as of right[4]. Nor do the Brussels and Lugano Conventions prevent a court of a contracting state from assuming jurisdiction in accordance with some other convention, even where the defendant is domiciled in another Brussels or Lugano contracting state which is not a party to the other convention[5].

An action for damages against a carrier by air arising out of international carriage[6] must be brought at the option of the plaintiff in the territory of one of the high contracting parties to the Warsaw Convention[7], either before the court having jurisdiction where the carrier[8] is ordinarily resident[9] or has his principal place of business or has an establishment by which the contract of carriage was made, or before the court having jurisdiction at the place of destination of the flight[10].

Any legal proceedings arising out of the international carriage of goods by road may be brought only in the courts or tribunals of a contracting country[11] designated by agreement between the parties, or in the courts or tribunals of a country within whose territory (1) the defendant is ordinarily resident, or has his principal place of business, or the branch or agency through which the contract of carriage was made is situated; or (2) the place where the goods were taken over by the carrier or the place designated for delivery is situated[12].

As from a day to be appointed, legal proceedings arising out of the international carriage of passengers and their luggage by road may be brought in any court or tribunal designated by agreement between the parties, or in the country within whose territory is situated (a) the place where the defendant has his principal place of business, is habitually resident, or has the place of business through which the contract of carriage was made; or (b) the place where the loss or damage occurred; or (c) the place of departure or destination of the carriage, and in no other court[13].

Disputes arising out of membership of a liner conference must be settled by the prescribed conciliation procedure, and proceedings for remedies under national law must be stayed by the national courts in favour of the conciliation procedure[14].

Further Conventions apply to claims arising out of the international carriage of passengers by sea[15]; the international carriage of passengers and their luggage, and goods, by rail[16]; to claims for the recovery of air navigation charges[17]; to collisions at sea[18]; to oil pollution by ships[19], and to proceedings relating to the remuneration of officers or crew of ships or aircraft[20].

1 As to the Brussels Convention see para 618 text and note 1 ante.
2 As to the Lugano Convention see para 618 text and note 2 ante.
3 Brussels Convention art 57 para 1; Lugano Convention art 57 para 1. But the provisions of those Conventions as to lis alibi pendens (see para 645 ante) may still operate to prevent the exercise of such jurisdiction if the other convention contains no similar provision: Case C-406/92 *The Tatry (cargo owners) v The Maciej Rataj (owners)* [1994] ECR I-5439, [1995] All ER (EC) 229, ECJ.
4 RSC Ord 11 r 1(2)(b); see para 673 ante.
5 Brussels Convention art 57 para 2(a); Lugano Convention art 57 para 2, which further provide that the court must apply art 20 of the Brussels and Lugano Conventions (see para 645 ante). See also note 3 supra.
6 As to the meaning of 'international carriage' see AVIATION vol 2 (Reissue) paras 1541, 1585, 1605.
7 As to the Warsaw Convention of 1929, both unamended and as amended, see AVIATION vol 2 (Reissue) para 1528. For a list of the parties to the Warsaw Convention see the Carriage by Air (Parties to Convention) Order 1988, SI 1988/243.
8 This includes not only the 'contracting carrier' who made the contract of carriage but also the 'actual carrier' to whom part or all of the carriage was sub-contracted by the contracting carrier: Carriage by

Air (Supplementary Provisions) Act 1962 s 1(1), Schedule arts I, VII, VIII, implementing the Guadalajara Convention of 1961: see AVIATION vol 2 (Reissue) para 1539.

9 For the meaning of 'ordinarily resident' see para 704 post.

10 Carriage by Air Act 1961 s 1(1), Sch 1 art 28(1); and the Carriage by Air Acts (Application of Provisions) Order 1967, SI 1967/480, art 5, Sch 2 Pt B art 28(1): see AVIATION vol 2 (Reissue) paras 1545, 1588. The 1961 Act and the 1967 Order implement respectively the Warsaw Convention 1929 as amended at The Hague 1955, and the Warsaw Convention in its unamended form. As from a day to be appointed, a version of the Warsaw Convention as further amended at Montreal in 1975, will have effect as between the United Kingdom and other high contracting parties: see the Carriage by Air and Road Act 1979 s 1(1), Sch 1 Pt I; and AVIATION vol 2 (Reissue) paras 1528, 1605, 1607.

11 For a list of the parties to the convention see the Carriage of Goods by Road (Parties to Convention) Order 1967, SI 1967/1683 (amended by SI 1980/697).

12 Carriage of Goods by Road Act 1965 s 1, Schedule art 31 para 1. This Act implements the Geneva Convention on the Contract for the International Carriage of Goods by Road 1956 (Cmnd 2260); and see CARRIERS vol 5(1) (Reissue) para 566 et seq.

13 See the Carriage of Passengers by Road Act 1974 s 1(1), Schedule art 21 para 1, prospectively implementing the Geneva Convention on the contract for the international carriage of passengers and luggage 1973 (Cmnd 5622). At the date at which this volume states the law, the provisions of the 1974 Act giving effect to the Convention have not been brought into force: see s 14(5); and see CARRIERS vol 5(1) (Reissue) para 537 et seq.

14 See the Merchant Shipping (Liner Conferences) Act 1982 s 1(2), Schedule para 25. The 1982 Act implements the Geneva Convention on a Code of Conduct for Liner Conferences 1974.

15 Merchant Shipping Act 1979 s 14(1), which gives effect to the Athens Convention relating to the carriage of passengers and their luggage by sea 1974 (Cmnd 6326), reproduced in Sch 3 to the 1979 Act. See CARRIERS vol 5(1) (Reissue) para 420 et seq. See also the Carriage of Passengers and their Luggage by Sea (Interim Provisions) Order 1980, SI 1980/1092 (amended by SI 1987/670).

16 See the International Transport Conventions Act 1983 s 1 (as amended), which gives effect to the Berne Convention concerning international carriage by rail 1980 (Cmnd 8535, Cm 41). See CARRIERS vol 5(1) (Reissue) para 426 et seq.

17 See the Civil Aviation Act 1982 s 24, Sch 4 (both as amended), implementing the Eurocontrol Convention (ie the Brussels International Convention relating to co-operation for the safety of air navigation 1960 (Cmnd 1373); and AVIATION vol 2 (Reissue) para 1370 et seq, especially para 1381.

18 See the Supreme Court Act 1981 s 22, which is based on the Brussels International Convention on certain rules concerning civil jurisdiction in matters of collision 1952 (Cmnd 1128); and ADMIRALTY vol 1(1) (Reissue) para 307 et seq.

19 See the Merchant Shipping (Oil Pollution) Act 1971, (particularly s 13 (as amended)), giving effect to the Brussels Convention on civil liability for oil pollution damage 1969 (Cmnd 6183); and SHIPPING vol 43 para 1201.

20 See the Consular Relations Act 1968 s 4, and Orders in Council made thereunder, giving effect to a number of international agreements entered into by the United Kingdom; and see FOREIGN RELATIONS LAW vol 18 para 1594.

678. International conventions denying jurisdiction by certificate.

No court in England and Wales has jurisdiction to determine any claim or question certified under statutory powers by the Secretary of State to be a claim or question which under an international convention falls to be determined by the court of a foreign country[1].

1 See the Supreme Court Act 1981 s 23, in relation to the Rhine Navigation Convention: see ADMIRALTY vol 1(1) (Reissue) para 304 note 8; and the Nuclear Installations Act 1965 s 17(1): see FUEL AND ENERGY vol 19(2) (Reissue) para 1280.

679. International conventions and the recognition and enforcement of foreign judgments within their scope.

A judgment of a court or foreign country outside the United Kingdom in proceedings regulated by the terms of certain international conventions which have been given effect under the law of the United Kingdom will be recognised and enforced if the jurisdictional requirements of the convention in question are complied with. In the case of certain conventions, judgments given by foreign courts may be registered for enforcement in England and Wales[1]. Where the judgment is given in a contracting state to the Brussels Convention[2] or the Lugano Convention[3], then if both the foreign state and the United Kingdom are party to the particular convention, the conditions laid down in that particular convention for the recognition and enforcement of the judgment will apply. In any event, the provisions of the Brussels and Lugano Conventions themselves may also be applied to secure the enforcement of the judgment[4]. If the judgment is given by a court in a state to which the Foreign Judgments (Reciprocal Enforcement) Act 1933 applies, it would accord with principle if such a judgment were treated as one given by a court with jurisdiction pursuant to that Act[5].

1 See the Carriage of Goods by Road Act 1965 s 4; the Merchant Shipping (Oil Pollution) Act 1971 s 13 (as amended); the Carriage of Passengers by Road Act 1974 s 5 (not in force at the date at which this volume states the law); the Civil Aviation Act 1982 s 74A (as added); and the International Transport Conventions Act 1983 s 6. The scheme for registration is usually modelled on the Foreign Judgments (Reciprocal Enforcement) Act 1933: see para 1028 et seq post. As to the meaning of 'England and Wales' see para 604 ante.
2 As to the Brussels Convention see para 618 text and note 1 ante.
3 As to the Lugano Convention see para 618 text and note 2 ante.
4 Brussels Convention art 57 para 2; Lugano Convention art 57 para 5.
5 See Dicey and Morris *The Conflict of Laws* (12th Edn, 1993) 567.

3. DOMICILE AND RESIDENCE

(1) NATURE OF DOMICILE

680. Function and meaning of 'domicile'. Many questions concerning the personal status of an individual are governed by his personal law. The primary purpose of determining domicile is to identify this personal law. Domicile defines the legal relationship between an individual and a territory with a distinctive legal system which invokes that system as his personal law[1]. Domicile in the sense here examined is to be distinguished from the distinct concept used for the purposes of the Civil Jurisdiction and Judgments Acts 1982 and 1991[2].

A person is domiciled in that country in which he either has or is deemed by law to have his permanent home[3]. Every individual is regarded as belonging, at every stage in his life, to some community consisting of all persons domiciled in a particular country; the rules as to domicile are such that this legal idea may not correspond to social reality[4]. Although a person may have no permanent home, the law requires him to have a domicile[5]. He may have more than one home, but he may have only one domicile for any one purpose[6]. He may have his home in one country, but be deemed to be domiciled in another[7].

The relationship of domicile is between a person and a country, and never arises from membership of a group as distinguished from the country in which the group is domiciled; but the municipal law of the country of domicile may itself distinguish between classes of its subjects, and apply different rules according to the race, caste, creed or other characteristics of a particular person, so that even after the domicile has been ascertained it may also be necessary to inquire into the other characteristics of the individual before the particular rule applicable to his case can be known[8].

1 *Henderson v Henderson* [1967] P 77 at 79, [1965] 1 All ER 179 at 180–181. In many foreign legal systems, the personal law is the law of an individual's nationality, and English law is giving increasing weight to

nationality in matters of personal status: *Indyka v Indyka* [1969] 1 AC 33 at 80, 96–97, 111, [1967] 2 All ER 689 at 710–711, 721, 730, HL; and see paras 744, 789 post. For proposals for the reform of the law see *The Law of Domicile* (Law Com no 168).

2   See paras 634, 652 ante.

3   *Winans v A-G* [1904] AC 287 at 288, HL; *Whicker v Hume* (1858) 7 HL Cas 124 at 160; *Henderson v Henderson* [1967] P 77 at 79, [1965] 1 All ER 179 at 180–181. As to the domicile of a corporation see para 987 post. The difficulty of defining domicile is discussed in *Forbes v Forbes* (1854) Kay 341; *A-G v Lady Rowe* (1862) 1 H & C 31. The legal notion of domicile must be distinguished from the idea of residence, more or less permanent, which the word 'domicile' bears in some foreign systems and in common speech: *McMullen v Wadsworth* (1889) 14 App Cas 631, PC; *Le Mesurier v Le Mesurier* [1895] AC 517, PC.

4   *Udny v Udny* (1869) LR 1 Sc & Div 441 at 457, HL; *Bell v Kennedy* (1868) LR 1 Sc & Div 307 at 320, HL; *Indyka v Indyka* [1969] 1 AC 33 at 97, [1967] 2 All ER 689 at 721, HL.

5   *Re Craignish, Craignish v Hewitt* [1892] 3 Ch 180 at 192, CA; *Bell v Kennedy* (1868) LR 1 Sc & Div 307, HL; *Udny v Udny* (1869) LR 1 Sc & Div 441 at 453, HL.

6   *Somerville v Lord Somerville* (1801) 5 Ves 750; *Udny v Udny* (1869) LR 1 Sc & Div 441, HL; *Bell v Kennedy* (1868) LR 1 Sc & Div 307, HL; *Re Steer* (1858) 3 H & N 594 at 599; *Saccharin Corpn Ltd v Chemische Fabrik von Heyden AG* [1911] 2 KB 516 at 527, CA; *Garthwaite v Garthwaite* [1964] P 356 at 379, [1964] 2 All ER 233 at 236, CA. Contrast the rules as to nationality; an individual may have dual nationality or may be stateless: see FOREIGN RELATIONS LAW vol 18 para 1613 et seq.

7   See eg paras 695, 697–698 post.

8   *Abd-ul-Messih v Farra* (1888) 13 App Cas 431, PC; *Maltass v Maltass* (1844) 1 Rob Eccl 67; *Casdagli v Casdagli* [1919] AC 145 at 163, HL; *Re Askew, Marjoribanks v Askew* [1930] 2 Ch 259 at 270.

681. Area of domicile. Each person who has, or whom the law deems to have, his permanent home within the territorial limits of a single system of law is domiciled in the country over which the system extends; and he is domiciled in the whole of that country, even though his home may be fixed at a particular spot within it[1]. In federal states, some branches of law are within the competence of the federal authorities and for these purposes the whole federation will be subject to a single system of law, and an individual may be spoken of as domiciled in the federation as a whole[2]; other branches of law are within the competence of the states or provinces of the federation, and the individual will be domiciled in one state or province only.

1   *Re Capdevielle* (1864) 2 H & C 985 at 1018 per Pollock CB (dissenting).

2   See eg the Family Law Act 1975 (Aust) s 39(3)(b).

682. Law determining domicile. An English court must determine the question whether or not a domicile has been acquired for the purposes of an English choice of law rule solely by reference to the principles of English law[1]. It follows that a decision of the court of a foreign country that an individual is or is not domiciled in that country is immaterial, although this principle is subject to a statutory exception[2]. Similarly, in determining the domicile of an individual, the English court will disregard foreign legislation imposing restrictions on the acquisition of domicile in the foreign state[3].

1   *Re Annesley, Davidson v Annesley* [1926] Ch 692; *Re Martin, Loustalan v Loustalan* [1900] P 211 at 227, CA; *Re Askew, Marjoribanks v Askew* [1930] 2 Ch 259 at 266. As to the meaning of 'English law' see para 604 ante.

2   Ie the Family Law Act 1986 s 46(5): see para 746 post.

3   *Re Annesley, Davidson v Annesley* [1926] Ch 692. For cases where the possibility of a foreign domicile, despite local regulations, was recognised but without clear exposition of the principle see *Collier v Rivaz* (1841) 2 Curt 855; *Anderson v Laneuville* (1854) 9 Moo PCC 325; *Bremer v Freeman* (1857) 10 Moo PCC 306; *Hamilton v Dallas* (1875) 1 ChD 257.

683. Everyone has a domicile. Every person must have a personal law, and accordingly everyone must have a domicile. He receives at birth a domicile of origin which remains his domicile, wherever he goes, unless and until he acquires a new domicile (a domicile of choice) in accordance with the principles set out in the following paragraphs[1].

1 *Udny v Udny* (1869) LR 1 Sc & Div 441, HL; *Bell v Kennedy* (1868) LR 1 Sc & Div 307, HL. Some authorities list three types of domicile, the third being the domicile of dependence, that enjoyed by a dependent person, which for many purposes can be regarded as one of choice or quasi-choice: *Henderson v Henderson* [1967] P 77 at 79, 82, [1965] 1 All ER 179 at 180, 184.

(2) DETERMINATION OF DOMICILE OF ORIGIN AND OF CHOICE

(i) Domicile of Origin and of Choice

684. Description of domicile. The law attributes to everyone at birth a domicile which is called a domicile of origin. This domicile may be changed, and a new domicile, which is called a domicile of choice, acquired; but the two kinds of domicile differ in the following respects:

(1) the domicile of origin is received by operation of law at birth[1]; the domicile of choice is acquired later by the individual actually moving to another country and intending to remain there indefinitely;

(2) the domicile of origin is retained until the acquisition of a domicile of choice[2]; it cannot be divested, although it remains in abeyance during the continuance of a domicile of choice; the domicile of choice is lost by abandonment whereupon the domicile of origin will revive unless some other domicile is acquired[3]; the domicile of choice is destroyed when it is once lost, but may be acquired anew by fulfilling the same conditions as are required in the first instance[4];

(3) the domicile of origin is more durable than that of choice, in the sense that it is more difficult to establish a change of domicile when the domicile alleged to have been displaced is one of origin[5].

1 The domicile of origin is fixed at birth, not (as was sometimes suggested) on attaining majority: *Henderson v Henderson* [1967] P 77, [1965] 1 All ER 179; *Forbes v Forbes* (1854) Kay 341 at 353; *Udny v Udny* (1869) LR 1 Sc & Div 441 at 457, HL; *Firebrace v Firebrace* (1878) 4 PD 63 at 66 obiter; *Re Macreight, Paxton v Macreight* (1885) 30 ChD 165; *Re Craignish, Craignish v Hewitt* [1892] 3 Ch 180 at 184–185; *Harrison v Harrison* [1953] 1 WLR 865; *Re Flynn, Flynn v Flynn* [1968] 1 All ER 49 at 52, [1968] 1 WLR 103 at 108.
2 *Udny v Udny* (1869) LR 1 Sc & Div 441, HL; *Bell v Kennedy* (1868) LR 1 Sc & Div 307, HL; *Somerville v Lord Somerville* (1801) 5 Ves 750; *Munro v Munro* (1840) 7 Cl & Fin 842 at 876, HL; *Re Marrett, Chalmers v Wingfield* (1887) 36 ChD 400, CA.
3 See para 689 post.
4 *Fleming v Horniman* (1928) 138 LT 669.
5 See para 691 post.

685. How domicile of origin is fixed. The domicile of origin is determined by the domicile, at the time of the child's birth[1], of the person upon whom he is legally dependent. A legitimate child born in wedlock to a living father receives the domicile of the father at the time of the birth[2]; an illegitimate child receives the domicile of the mother[3]. A posthumous legitimate child receives the domicile of the mother[4]. The place of birth is immaterial[5], except that it may be presumed to be the domicile of a child about whose parentage nothing is known; similarly the domicile of origin of a foundling is the country in which he is found[6]. After adoption, the domicile of origin of the adopted child is fixed as if he had been born in wedlock to the adopters[7].

1 See para 684 note 1 ante.
2 *Udny v Udny* (1869) LR 1 Sc & Div 441, HL; *Somerville v Lord Somerville* (1801) 5 Ves 750; *Forbes v Forbes* (1854) Kay 341; *Henderson v Henderson* [1967] P 77, [1965] 1 All ER 179; *Re Clore (No 2), Official Solicitor v Clore* [1984] STC 609.
3 *Udny v Udny* (1869) LR 1 Sc & Div 441, HL; *Urquhart v Butterfield* (1887) 37 ChD 357 at 377 et seq, CA.
4 See Dicey and Morris *The Conflict of Laws* (12th Edn, 1993) 124–125.
5 *Somerville v Lord Somerville* (1801) 5 Ves 750 at 787; *Walcot v Botfield* (1854) Kay 534 at 544; *Peal v Peal* (1930) 46 TLR 645, also reported [1931] P 97, but not on this point; *Re Flynn, Flynn v Flynn* [1968] 1 All ER 49 at 52, [1968] 1 WLR 103 at 108.
6 Cf *Re McKenzie* (1951) 51 SR (NSW) 293.
7 See the Adoption Act 1976 s 39(1), by which a child is treated in law as having been born in wedlock to the adopters (or one of them): and CHILDREN vol 5(2) (Reissue) para 1090. Note particularly that citizenship is not determined by reference to the status conferred by adoption.

686. Change of domicile. Any person not legally dependent upon another may at any time change his existing domicile and acquire for himself a domicile of choice by the fact of residing in a country other than that of his domicile of origin with the intention of continuing to reside there indefinitely[1].

1 *Winans v A-G* [1904] AC 287, HL; *Marchioness of Huntly v Gaskell* [1906] AC 56, HL; *Udny v Udny* (1869) LR 1 Sc & Div 441, HL; *Bell v Kennedy* (1868) LR 1 Sc Div 307, HL; *Re Furse, Furse v IRC* [1980] 3 All ER 838; *Plummer v IRC* [1988] 1 All ER 97, [1988] 1 WLR 292.

687. Residence. In order to have acquired a domicile of choice in a country, an individual must have actually resided there[1]. It is not sufficient that he intended to reside there in the future, nor that he actually set out on a journey to the new country, only to die on the way there[2].

In this context, residence means no more than personal presence in a country other than casually or as a traveller[3]. It is immaterial that the residence is of brief duration[4], provided that it is accompanied by the required state of mind. Similarly, the motive for residence is immaterial except as evidence for the existence or non-existence of the necessary intention[5]. Illegal residence is insufficient[6].

1 *Bell v Kennedy* (1868) LR 1 Sc & Div 307 at 319, HL; *Brown v Smith* (1852) 15 Beav 444; *Harrison v Harrison* [1953] 1 WLR 865.
2 *Udny v Udny* (1869) LR 1 Sc & Div 441 at 449–450, 453–454, HL; *Re Raffenel's Goods* (1863) 3 Sw & Tr 49; *Bell v Kennedy* (1868) LR 1 Sc & Div 307 at 319, HL. Early dicta to the contrary would seem to be no longer good law: *Munroe v Douglas* (1820) 5 Madd 379 at 405; *Forbes v Forbes* (1854) Kay 341 at 353–354; and see *Lyall v Paton* (1856) 25 LJCh 746.
3 See further para 703 post. Cf *Plummer v IRC* [1988] 1 All ER 97, [1988] 1 WLR 292, suggesting that in cases of multiple residence, the test is where is the chief residence; cf Dicey and Morris *The Conflict of Laws* (12th Edn, 1993) 127.
4 *Bell v Kennedy* (1868) LR 1 Sc & Div 307 at 319, HL: *Fasbender v A-G* [1922] 2 Ch 850 at 857–858, CA; *Stone v Stone* [1959] 1 All ER 194, [1958] 1 WLR 1287.
5 *Re Cooke's Trusts* (1887) 56 LJCh 637; cf *Drexel v Drexel* [1916] 1 Ch 251.
6 *Puttick v A-G* [1980] Fam 1, [1979] 3 All ER 463; *Solomon v Solomon* (1912) 29 WN (NSW) 68; *Smith v Smith* 1962 (3) SA 930. Cf the Immigration Act 1971 s 33(2); and BRITISH NATIONALITY, IMMIGRATION AND RACE RELATIONS vol 4(2) (Reissue) para 11. It is uncertain whether the principle applies where the residence is in a foreign country and the illegality arises under the law of that country. As to the effect on domicile of possible or threatened deportation see para 696 post.

688. Intention to remain. In order to have acquired a domicile of choice, the individual must have had a certain state of mind, the *animus manendi*. He must have formed the intention of making his sole or principal permanent home in the country of residence, and of continuing to reside there indefinitely[1]. Residence alone, unaccompanied by this state of mind, is always insufficient[2].

The intention which must be shown is as to the quality of the residence; it is not necessary to show that the person concerned intended to change his domicile[3]. A person can change his domicile without changing his nationality; conversely a change of nationality does not necessarily involve a change of domicile[4].

An intention to reside in a country for a fixed period of time, or until some clearly foreseen and reasonably anticipated event happens, will not be sufficient[5], but if the proper conclusion from all the circumstances is that the individual intends to make his home in a country for an indefinite time, he will acquire a domicile of choice there notwithstanding a continuing emotional attachment to some other country or an intention to change his residence upon some vague or improbable contingency[6].

The individual need not intend, when he first arrives in the country where the domicile of choice is alleged to be acquired, to live there permanently. The intention may be, and often is, formed after the individual has resided there for some time. The acquisition of a domicile is complete as soon as the intention is formed[7]; no subsequent change of mind, or doubts arising as to the wisdom of the determination, can by themselves affect the domicile so acquired[8].

The individual must determine to settle in a particular country, and not necessarily at a particular place[9]; but the absence of a fixed residence is important as evidence, and may be sufficient to show that the individual has reached a final decision whether or not to reside in that country[10].

1 The rival merits of 'permanently' and 'indefinitely' in definitions of the *animus manendi* were discussed in *Gulbenkian v Gulbenkian* [1937] 4 All ER 618; both are used in the leading judgments and they are treated as synonymous in *Re Edwards, Edwards v Edwards* (1969) 113 Sol Jo 108. On the varieties of language see *Re Fuld's Estate (No 3), Hartley v Fuld* [1968] P 675 at 682–683.

2 *Udny v Udny* (1869) LR 1 Sc & Div 441, HL; *Winans v A-G* [1904] AC 287, HL; *Bowie (or Ramsay) v Liverpool Royal Infirmary* [1930] AC 588, HL; *Re Clore (No 2), Official Solicitor v Clore* [1984] STC 609; *Plummer v IRC* [1988] 1 All ER 97, [1988] 1 WLR 292.

3 *Qureshi v Qureshi* [1972] Fam 173 at 191, [1971] 1 All ER 325 at 338.

4 *Wahl v A-G* (1932) 147 LT 382, HL; *D'Etchegoyen v D'Etchegoyen* (1888) 13 PD 132; *Re Annesley, Davidson v Annesley* [1926] Ch 692 at 701; *Re Adams, Bank of Ireland Trustee Co Ltd v Adams, Hutchings and Parker* [1967] IR 424; *Re Fuld's Estate (No 3), Hartley v Fuld* [1968] P 675 at 683; *Qureshi v Qureshi* [1972] Fam 173 at 190, [1971] 1 All ER 325 at 337. Dicta in early cases, especially *Moorhouse v Lord* (1863) 10 HL Cas 272, that there must be an intent to cast off one's nationality, to 'become a Frenchman rather than an Englishman' or to 'change one's domicile' are no longer good law: *Udny v Udny* (1869) LR 1 Sc & Div 441 at 452, HL; *Douglas v Douglas* (1871) LR 12 Eq 617 at 644–645; *Re Fuld's Estate (No 3), Hartley v Fuld* supra at 683–684.

5 *Moorhouse v Lord* (1863) 10 HL Cas 272 at 285 (residence for health reasons); cf *Re James, James v James* (1908) 98 LT 438; *Pitt v Pitt* (1864) 4 Macq 627, HL (absence while settlement reached with creditors); *Aikman v Aikman* (1861) 3 Macq 854, HL; *Re Martin, Loustalan v Loustalan* [1900] P 211, CA (limitation period); *IRC v Bullock* [1976] 3 All ER 353, [1976] 1 WLR 1178, CA (Canadian-born taxpayer lived in England for 44 years but retained domicile of origin as intended to return to Canada if his wife predeceased him).

6 *Re Fuld's Estate (No 3), Hartley v Fuld* [1968] P 675 at 684–685; *Henderson v Henderson* [1967] P 77 at 80–81, [1965] 1 All ER 179 at 181; eg making one's fortune *(Bruce v Bruce* (1790) 2 Bos & P 229, HL; *Doucet v Geoghegan* (1878) 9 ChD 441, CA); the death of a mistress *(Anderson v Laneuville* (1854) 9 Moo PCC 325 at 334); 'panting for his native home' *(Stanley v Bernes* (1830) 3 Hag Ecc 373; *Re Capdevielle* (1864) 2 H & C 985; *A-G v Kent* (1862) 1 H & C 12); remote possibility of recall to active service abroad *(A-G v Pottinger* (1861) 6 H & N 733); 'vague and floating' ideas of residing elsewhere *(Re Marrett, Chalmers v Wingfield* (1887) 36 ChD 400, CA); *Re Furse, Furse v IRC* [1980] 3 All ER 838 (ill-defined onset of ill-health). See also *Pletinka v Pletinka (Boucher cited)* (1964) 109 Sol Jo 72 (intention to return to the Ukraine if it became independent was compatible with acquiring a domicile of choice in England).

7 *Udny v Udny* (1869) LR 1 Sc & Div 441 at 458, HL.

8   *Re Marrett, Chalmers v Wingfield* (1887) 36 ChD 400, CA; *Gulbenkian v Gulbenkian* [1937] 4 All ER 618.

9   *Bell v Kennedy* (1868) LR 1 Sc & Div 307 at 321, HL; *Aikman v Aikman* (1861) 3 Macq 854 at 881, HL; *Re Patience, Patience v Main* (1885) 29 ChD 976; *Re Eschmann* (1893) 9 TLR 426. Dicta to the contrary in *A-G v Dunn* (1840) 6 M & W 511 at 526 may simply reflect the politically fragmented condition of Italy at the time.

10   See *Re Patience, Patience v Main* (1885) 29 ChD 976.

689. Abandonment of domicile of choice. A domicile of choice can be lost by abandonment. This process is the exact converse of its acquisition. It is necessary for the person concerned to cease to reside in the country of domicile, and also to cease to have the intention to return to it as his permanent home[1]. Absence without the intention of abandonment is of no effect[2]; nor is intention without any actual change of residence[3]. Both the intention and the act must be demonstrated to be unequivocal, though the evidence necessary to establish abandonment is less than that required to establish acquisition[4].

It is never necessary to acquire another domicile of choice in order to abandon an earlier domicile of choice, but the individual may be said to have abandoned one domicile of choice and to have acquired another at the same time when either (1) the old is abandoned and the new is acquired by the same act; or (2) the individual, while already residing in the new domicile, forms an intention to settle there and to abandon the old domicile[5].

In every other case the domicile of origin revives to become again the actual domicile[6].

1   *Udny v Udny* (1869) LR 1 Sc & Div 441, HL; *Re Marrett, Chalmers v Wingfield* (1887) 36 ChD 400, CA; *Urquhart v Butterfield* (1887) 37 ChD 357, CA; *Re Bianchi's Goods* (1862) 3 Sw & Tr 16; *King v Foxwell* (1876) 3 ChD 518; *Fleming v Horniman* (1928) 138 LT 669. It is sufficient to show that the person has ceased to have all intention to return; he need not have formed any positive intention not to return: *Re Flynn, Flynn v Flynn* [1968] 1 All ER 49, [1968] 1 WLR 103; *Qureshi v Qureshi* [1972] Fam 173 at 191, [1971] 1 All ER 325 at 338; *Plummer v IRC* [1988] 1 All ER 97, [1988] 1 WLR 292.

2   *Craigie v Lewin* (1843) 3 Curt 435; *A-G v Pottinger* (1861) 6 H & N 733; *Bradford v Young* (1885) 29 ChD 617, CA; *Re Lloyd Evans, National Provincial Bank v Evans* [1947] Ch 695.

3   *Re Raffenel's Goods* (1863) 3 Sw & Tr 49; *Zanelli v Zanelli* (1948) 64 TLR 556, CA.

4   *Re Lloyd Evans, National Provincial Bank v Evans* [1947] Ch 695 at 701, 708; *Travers v Holley* [1953] P 246 at 252, [1951] 2 All ER 794 at 797, CA, per Jenkins LJ (dissenting); *Re Flynn, Flynn v Flynn* [1968] 1 All ER 49 at 58, [1968] 1 WLR 103 at 115.

5   See Dicey and Morris *The Conflict of Laws* (12th Edn, 1993) 145.

6   *Udny v Udny* (1869) LR 1 Sc & Div 441, HL; *King v Foxwell* (1876) 3 ChD 518; *Harrison v Harrison* [1953] 1 WLR 865; *Tee v Tee* [1973] 3 All ER 1105, [1974] 1 WLR 213, CA. It is questionable whether this revival rule applies where the domicile of origin is technical only and not 'bottomed in reality': *Re Flynn, Flynn v Flynn* [1968] 1 All ER 49 at 52, [1968] 1 WLR 103 at 108.

690. Married women. The domicile of a married woman, rather than being the same as her husband's by virtue only of marriage, must be ascertained by reference to the same factors as in the case of any other individual capable of having an independent domicile[1].

In considering the domicile of a married woman as at any date before 1 January 1974, it is necessary to apply the earlier rule, which stated that she acquired her husband's domicile on marriage and that during the existence of the marriage her domicile followed that of her husband[2]. This rule applied despite the existence of a decree of judicial separation[3], or of a decree of divorce not recognised as valid in England[4]. On the dissolution of the marriage by her husband's death, or by divorce, the wife became free to change her domicile[5], but until she did so she retained the domicile of the husband at the time the marriage was dissolved[6]. A void marriage had no effect upon a woman's domicile; but in the case of a voidable marriage she took her husband's domicile until the marriage was annulled[7]. A married woman who had her husband's domicile under these rules immediately before 1 January 1974 retained that domicile (as a domicile of choice if it was not also her domicile of origin) after that date until her domicile was changed under the rules governing changes in the domicile of independent persons[8].

1 Domicile and Matrimonial Proceedings Act 1973 s 1(1). Thus a married woman is not incapacitated by the fact of her marriage from acquiring a domicile of choice, and she may change her domicile independently of her husband. But see the text and notes infra for the position where a married woman's domicile has not been changed since before 1 January 1974 (the date when s 1 came into force).
2 See ibid s 1(1), which makes the new provision for determining the domicile of a married woman as at any time after the coming into force of the section. See *Re Daly's Settlement* (1858) 25 Beav 456; *Pitt v Pitt* (1864) 4 Macq 627 at 647, HL (and cf that case at 640); *Firebrace v Firebrace* (1878) 4 PD 63 at 67; *Harvey v Farnie* (1882) 8 App Cas 43, HL; *Lord Advocate v Jaffrey* [1921] 1 AC 146, HL; *H v H* [1928] P 206 at 212; and subsequent proceedings sub nom *Horn v Horn* (1929) 142 LT 93; *Herd v Herd* [1936] P 205, [1936] 2 All ER 1516; *Re Scullard, Smith v Brock* [1957] Ch 107, [1956] 3 All ER 898; *Garthwaite v Garthwaite* [1964] P 356, [1964] 2 All ER 233, CA.
3 *A-G for Alberta v Cook* [1926] AC 444, PC; *Garthwaite v Garthwaite* [1964] P 356 at 379, [1964] 2 All ER 233 at 236, CA; *H v H* [1928] P 206. See *Anghinelli v Anghinelli* [1918] P 247, CA.
4 *Garthwaite v Garthwaite* [1964] P 356, [1964] 2 All ER 233, CA.
5 Ie assuming she was not otherwise dependent. For the effect of her decision on the domicile of her children see para 701 post.
6 *Re Wallach, Weinschenk v Treasury Solicitor* [1950] 1 All ER 199; *Re Scullard, Smith v Brock* [1957] Ch 107, [1956] 3 All ER 898; and see *Re Cooke's Trusts* (1887) 56 LJCh 637; *Re Raffanel's Goods* (1863) 3 Sw & Tr 49.
7 *De Reneville v De Reneville* [1948] P 100, [1948] 1 All ER 56, CA.
8 See the Domicile and Matrimonial Proceedings Act 1973 s 1(2); *IRC v Duchess of Portland* [1982] Ch 314, [1982] 1 All ER 784; *Plummer v IRC* [1988] 1 All ER 97, [1988] 1 WLR 292.

(ii) Change of Domicile by Persons who are not Dependent

691. Proof of change of domicile. There is a presumption against a change of domicile. The burden of proving any change of domicile rests therefore upon the person alleging it[1]. A change of domicile is a serious matter, not to be lightly inferred, and it must be clearly and unequivocally proved[2]. Differing views have been expressed as to whether the standard of proof is the normal civil standard[3], or some higher standard[4].

The task of proving a change of domicile is particularly onerous when the domicile alleged to be displaced is one of origin as opposed to one of choice[5]. Similarly, a high degree of proof may be required to establish a change in domicile where the two countries are markedly dissimilar in language, climate or ethnic, cultural or religious background[6]. The court's caution in such cases in inferring changes of domicile is based on the observed infrequency of such changes, and there is no rule of law preventing the inference being drawn where the change of domicile is clearly established[7].

1 *Munro v Munro* (1840) 7 Cl & Fin 842 at 891, HL; *Aikman v Aikman* (1861) 3 Macq 854, HL; *Bell v Kennedy* (1868) LR 1 Sc & Div 307 at 316, HL; *The Lauderdale Peerage* (1885) 10 App Cas 692 at 739, HL; *Winans v A-G* [1904] AC 287, HL; *Rudd v Rudd* [1924] P 72; *A-G v Yule and Mercantile Bank of India*

(1931) 145 LT 9, CA; *IRC v Cohen* (1937) 21 Tax Cas 301; *Stransky v Stransky* [1954] P 428, [1954] 2 All ER 536.

2 *Re Fuld's Estate (No 3), Hartley v Fuld* [1968] P 675 at 685–686; *Re Flynn, Flynn v Flynn* [1968] 1 All ER 49 at 58, [1968] 1 WLR 103 at 115; *Re Edwards, Edwards v Edwards* (1969) 113 Sol Jo 108; *Moorhouse v Lord* (1863) 10 HL Cas 272 at 286; *Re Lloyd Evans, National Provincial Bank v Evans* [1947] Ch 695 at 707.

3 Ie the balance of probabilities: see *Re Fuld's Estate (No 3), Hartley v Fuld* [1968] P 675 at 685–686.

4 *Henderson v Henderson* [1967] P 77 at 80, [1965] 1 All ER 179 at 181, where the domicile alleged to have been displaced was one of origin; *Buswell v IRC* [1974] 2 All ER 520, [1974] 1 WLR 1631, CA.

5 *Winans v A-G* [1904] AC 287 at 291, HL; *Bowie (or Ramsay) v Liverpool Royal Infirmary* [1930] AC 588, HL; *Henderson v Henderson* [1967] P 77, [1965] 1 All ER 179; *Holden v Holden* [1968] NI 7; *Re Clore (No 2), Official Solicitor v Clore* [1984] STC 609; *Plummer v IRC* [1988] 1 All ER 97, [1988] 1 WLR 292.

6 *Whicker v Hume* (1858) 7 HL Cas 124 at 159; *Casdagli v Casdagli* [1919] AC 145 at 156–157, HL; *Henderson v Henderson* [1967] P 77 at 82, [1965] 1 All ER 179 at 183; *Qureshi v Qureshi* [1972] Fam 173 at 193, [1971] 1 All ER 325 at 339–340.

7 *Qureshi v Qureshi* [1972] Fam 173 at 193, [1971] 1 All ER 325 at 339–340, where Sir Jocelyn Simon P described the proposition in text and note 6 supra as 'not so much a proposition of law as an expression of common experience'. Early authorities suggesting that an Englishman could not acquire a domicile in a non-Christian country were overruled in *Casdagli v Casdagli* [1919] AC 145, HL.

692. Evidence of domicile. Any act, event or circumstance in the life of an individual may be evidence from which the state of his mind may be inferred with more or less precision; every aspect of his life, his actions and statements may be adduced. It is impossible to formulate any general rule by which the weight due to any particular piece of evidence may be determined. Not only does the strength of the evidence from which the intention may be inferred vary according to the inherent probability or improbability of an alleged change of domicile, but the importance of similar facts may differ absolutely in different cases. The age, character and general circumstances of the man himself and the climate, religion and customs of the country in which the domicile is alleged to have been acquired, are considerations which may cause the value of a particular fact to vary almost indefinitely[1].

The intention must be clearly and unequivocally proved[2], but it is unreasonable to require it to be proved by evidence which the person himself might not fairly be expected to have furnished if he had in fact formed the intention[3], and it is not necessary to prove any conscious deliberate decision at any particular moment[4].

Conduct subsequent to the time at which the state of mind has to be determined may be regarded[5].

1 *Drevon v Drevon* (1864) 34 LJCh 129 at 133; *Sharpe v Crispin* (1869) LR 1 P & D 611 at 619; *Re Fuld's Estate (No 3), Hartley v Fuld* [1968] P 675 at 682; *Re Flynn, Flynn v Flynn* [1968] 1 All ER 49 at 51, [1968] 1 WLR 103 at 107.

2 *Re Lloyd Evans, National Provincial Bank v Evans* [1947] Ch 695 at 707; *Travers v Holley* [1953] P 246 at 252, [1953] 2 All ER 794 at 797, CA, per Jenkins LJ (dissenting).

3 *Sharpe v Crispin* (1869) LR 1 P & D 611 at 619 (person of weak intellect).

4 *Gulbenkian v Gulbenkian* [1937] 4 All ER 618 at 627.

5 *Re Grove, Vaucher v Treasury Solicitor* (1888) 40 ChD 216, CA.

693. Direct and secondary evidence of intention. Direct evidence of intention is often not available, but a person whose domicile is in question may himself give evidence of his intentions, present or past. Evidence of this nature is to be accepted with considerable reserve, even if there is no suspicion that the witness is being untruthful[1].

Expressions of intention, written or oral, may be given in evidence[2], but such evidence must be carefully weighed in connection with the circumstances in which it occurred, and even if the expressions are clear and consistent they cannot prevail against a course of conduct leading to an opposite inference[3].

1 *Bell v Kennedy* (1868) LR 1 Sc & Div 307 at 313, HL; *Udny v Udny* (1869) LR 1 Sc & Div 441 at 444, HL; *Maxwell v Maclure* (1860) 2 LT 65; *Wilson v Wilson* (1872) LR 2 P & D 435 at 444; *D'Etchegoyen v D'Etchegoyen* (1888) 13 PD 132; *Re Craignish, Craignish v Hewitt* [1892] 3 Ch 180 at 190, CA; *Eleftheriou v Eleftheriou* [1964] CLY 511; *Qureshi v Qureshi* [1972] Fam 173 at 192, [1971] 1 All ER 325 at 339.

2 Hearsay evidence as to domicile may be admissible under the Civil Evidence Act 1968 ss 2, 9: see EVIDENCE vol 17 paras 55, 61. See also *Bryce v Bryce* [1933] P 83; *Scappaticci v A-G* [1955] P 47, [1955] 1 All ER 193n.

3 *Ross v Ellison (or Ross)* [1930] AC 1, HL; *Munro v Munro* (1840) 7 Cl & Fin 842, HL; *Anderson v Laneuville* (1854) 9 Moo PCC 325; *Hoskins v Matthews* (1856) 8 De GM & G 13 at 30; *Hodgson v De Beauchesne* (1858) 12 Moo PCC 285 at 325; *Re Steer* (1858) 3 H & N 594; *Drevon v Drevon* (1864) 34 LJCh 129; *Doucet v Geoghegan* (1878) 9 ChD 441 at 455, CA; *Re Annesley, Davidson v Annesley* [1926] Ch 692; *A-G v Yule and Mercantile Bank of India* (1931) 145 LT 9, CA; *Abraham v A-G* [1934] P 17; *Re Liddell-Grainger's Will Trusts, Dormer v Liddell-Grainger* [1936] 3 All ER 173; *Re Sillar, Hurley v Wimbush and Bavington* [1956] IR 344; *Re Fuld's Estate (No 3), Hartley v Fuld* [1968] P 675 at 692; *Re Flynn, Flynn v Flynn* [1968] 1 All ER 49 at 60, [1968] 1 WLR 103 at 117. See also *Tennekoon, Registration of Indian and Pakistani Residents Comr v Duraisamy* [1958] AC 354, [1958] 2 All ER 479, PC.

694. Residence as evidence.

Residence in a country, especially if it is continued for a long period, is evidence of an intention to remain there; in the absence of other evidence, residence alone may support the inference that a domicile has been acquired. Such cases will be rare, however, and, while residence is always material evidence, it is seldom decisive, for slight circumstances may serve to show the absence of a settled intention[1].

1 *Bruce v Bruce* (1790) 2 Bos & P 229n, HL; *Bempde v Johnstone* (1796) 3 Ves 198; *Stanley v Bernes* (1830) 3 Hag Ecc 373; *Hodgson v De Beauchesne* (1858) 12 Moo PCC 285; *King v Foxwell* (1876) 3 ChD 518; *Doucet v Geoghegan* (1878) 9 ChD 441, CA; *Re Patience, Patience v Main* (1885) 29 ChD 976; *Re Grove, Vaucher v Treasury Solicitor* (1888) 40 ChD 216, CA; *Winans v A-G* [1904] AC 287, HL; *Bowie (or Ramsay) v Liverpool Royal Infirmary* [1930] AC 588, HL; *Gulbenkian v Gulbenkian* [1937] 4 All ER 618.

695. Residence as a matter of duty.

A person may reside in a country as a result of his being under some duty, public or private. Examples include diplomats and other overseas servants of the Crown, members of the armed forces, employees of international organisations or of commercial undertakings with interests in several countries, and domestic servants attached to such persons. Such residence is likely to be temporary and may be in some measure involuntary. If it is not accompanied by any intention to make a permanent home in the country of residence, the person concerned will retain his former domicile[1].

Such a person may be held to have acquired a domicile of choice in the country of residence if the appropriate intention can be derived from all the circumstances[2]. Cogent evidence of such intention is required[3]. The fact that the public office is in the service of the country of residence, an alien country, is material[4].

1 *Maltass v Maltass* (1844) 1 Rob Eccl 67; *Gout v Zimmermann* (1847) 5 Notes of Cases 440 (diplomats); *Re Mitchell, ex p Cunningham* (1884) 13 QBD 418, CA; *A-G v Napier* (1851) 6 Exch 217; *Brown v Smith* (1852) 21 LJCh 356; *Yelverton v Yelverton* (1859) 1 Sw & Tr 574; *Firebrace v Firebrace* (1878) 4 PD 63; *Re Macreight, Paxton v Macreight* (1885) 30 ChD 165; *Cruickshanks v Cruickshanks* [1957] 1 All ER 889, [1957] 1 WLR 564 (members of armed forces); *A-G v Pottinger* (1861) 30 LJEx 284 (colonial governor); *A-G v Lady Rowe* (1862) 1 H & C 31 (colonial judge).

2 *Heath v Samson* (1851) 14 Beav 441; *A-G v Kent* (1862) 1 H & C 12 (diplomats); *Re Smith's Goods* (1850) 2 Rob Eccl 332 (colonial officer); *Donaldson (or Nichols) v Donaldson* [1949] P 363; *Stone v Stone* [1959] 1 All ER 194, [1958] 1 WLR 1287 (members of armed forces). The holder of a public office with duties in

England is not thereby prevented from acquiring a domicile abroad: *Hamilton v Dallas* (1875) 1 ChD 257 (peer of Parliament); *Horn v Horn* (1929) 142 LT 93 (army reservist). Appointment to an overseas post under the Crown will not by itself cause the revival of an English domicile of origin: *Sharpe v Crispin* (1869) LR 1 P & D 611; *Re Baron De Almeda, Sourdis v Keyser* (1902) 18 TLR 414, CA.

3 *Cruickshanks v Cruickshanks* [1957] 1 All ER 889 at 892, [1957] 1 WLR 564 at 568.

4 *Re Mitchell, ex p Cunningham* (1884) 13 QBD 418 at 423, CA; *Urquhart v Butterfield* (1887) 37 ChD 357 at 382, CA.

696. Persons liable to deportation. A person may be held to have acquired a domicile of choice in a country despite provisions in the local law as to aliens or immigration making his right to remain there precarious. The court will consider whether, despite the possibility of deportation, the individual has decided to make that country his permanent home, so far as it is within his power[1]. Similarly, a domicile once acquired will not necessarily be affected by the making of a deportation order[2], and may survive actual deportation if the individual intends to return[3].

1 *Boldrini v Boldrini and Martini* [1932] P 9, CA; *May v May and Lehmann* [1943] 2 All ER 146; *Zanelli v Zanelli* (1948) 64 TLR 556, CA; *Szechter (otherwise Karsov) v Szechter* [1971] P 286 at 294, [1970] 3 All ER 905 at 912. See, however, para 687 text and note 6 ante (illegal residence insufficient to establish domicile).

2 *Cruh v Cruh* [1945] 2 All ER 545.

3 *Thiele v Thiele* (1920) 150 LT Jo 387; *Cruh v Cruh* [1945] 2 All ER 545.

697. Residence by force of circumstances. Where a person resides in a country as a result of the pressure of circumstances, his residence will be in some measure involuntary. In such a case, where there is no intention to make a permanent home in the country of residence, the previous domicile will remain unchanged. The greater the pressure, the more likely it is that the individual will retain his earlier domicile[1].

Prisoners and persons under physical restraint fall into this class of persons. Political exiles and refugees are in a similar position, as are those escaping prosecution or the claims of their creditors. In such cases, strong evidence is required to show that a domicile has been acquired in the country of residence[2].

1 See Dicey and Morris *The Conflict of Laws* (12th Edn, 1993) 138–140.

2 *De Bonneval v De Bonneval* (1838) 1 Curt 856; *Charitable Donations Comrs v Devereux* (1842) 13 Sim 14 (refugees from the French revolution); *May v May and Lehmann* [1943] 2 All ER 146; *Re Lloyd Evans, National Provincial Bank v Evans* [1947] Ch 695 (refugees from German invaders); *Pitt v Pitt* (1864) 4 Macq 627, HL; *Udny v Udny* (1869) LR 1 Sc & Div 441, HL; *Briggs v Briggs* (1880) 5 PD 163 (avoiding creditors); *Re Martin, Loustalan v Loustalan* [1900] P 211, CA (escaping criminal prosecution).

698. Invalids. The acquisition of a domicile of choice is not necessarily prevented by the fact that residence has been established owing to reasons of health; but the state of health may be evidence to show that the intention to settle either does or does not exist. The question in these cases is not whether a person would prefer in different circumstances to live elsewhere, but what is his present intention with regard to his actual residence. If he has, however reluctantly, formed a fixed determination to make his home in the country of residence, a domicile is acquired[1]; but if he has not, then, even though he may expect to die there, no domicile is acquired[2].

1 *Hoskins v Matthews* (1856) 8 De GM & G 13 (court evenly divided); *Aitchison v Dixon* (1870) LR 10 Eq 589 (where a domicile was acquired).

2 *A-G v Fitzgerald* (1856) 3 Drew 610; *The Lauderdale Peerage* (1885) 10 App Cas 692 at 740, HL; *Gillis v Gillis* (1874) 8 IR Eq 597; *Re James, James v James* (1908) 98 LT 438; *Johnstone v Beattie* (1843) 10 Cl & Fin 42 at 139, HL.

699. Matrimonial home. Where a man has more than one place of residence, but establishes the home of his wife and family in one of them, this fact is important evidence that his domicile is in that place[1]. The evidence may, of course, be outweighed by other considerations[2].

1 *Forbes v Forbes* (1854) Kay 341; *Aitchison v Dixon* (1870) LR 10 Eq 589; *Platt v A-G of New South Wales* (1878) 3 App Cas 336, PC; *D'Etchegoyen v D'Etchegoyen* (1888) 13 PD 132; *A-G v Yule and Mercantile Bank of India* (1931) 145 LT 9, CA. See also *Haldane v Eckford* (1869) LR 8 Eq 631 (residence with grandchild).
2 *Douglas v Douglas* (1871) LR 12 Eq 617 at 647; *Wahl v A-G* (1932) 147 LT 382, HL; *IRC v Bullock* [1976] 3 All ER 353, [1976] 1 WLR 1178, CA.

700. Other evidence. Among the circumstances which have been regarded as throwing light on the question of intention are the following: (1) change of nationality[1], of religion[2], or of name[3]; (2) marriage to a person who is a native of the country of residence[4]; (3) the education, marriage or settlement in life of children[5]; (4) the purchase, sale or ownership of land[6], especially of family estates[7] or graves[8]; (5) attitude to the exercise of political rights in the country of residence[9]; and (6) the form and contents of wills or other documents[10]. All these factors take colour from their context, and none can be conclusive[11].

1 *Stanley v Bernes* (1830) 3 Hag Ecc 373; *D'Etchegoyen v D'Etchegoyen* (1888) 13 PD 132; *Wahl v A-G* (1932) 147 LT 382, HL; *Qureshi v Qureshi* [1972] Fam 173, [1971] 1 All ER 325; *Re Fuld's Estate (No 3), Hartley v Fuld* [1968] P 675, [1965] 3 All ER 776; *Re Flynn, Flynn v Flynn* [1968] 1 All ER 49, [1968] 1 WLR 103.
2 *Stanley v Bernes* (1830) 3 Hag Ecc 373.
3 *Drevon v Drevon* (1864) 34 LJCh 129 (spelling of Christian name); *Re Martin, Loustalan v Loustalan* [1900] P 211, CA (surname).
4 *Drevon v Drevon* (1864) 34 LJCh 129; *Doucet v Geoghegan* (1878) 9 ChD 441, CA; cf *Re Bethell, Bethell v Hildyard* (1888) 38 ChD 220; *Cramer v Cramer* [1987] 1 FLR 116, CA.
5 *Stevenson v Masson* (1873) LR 17 Eq 78; *President of United States of America v Drummond* (1864) 33 Beav 449.
6 Some sort of property transaction occurs in almost every case. Features of special importance may be the building of a house to a special personal design (*Re Flynn, Flynn v Flynn* [1968] 1 All ER 49, [1968] 1 WLR 103); the careful management and development of property (*Moorhouse v Lord* (1863) 10 HL Cas 272 at 288); or a preference for short leases of furnished houses or hotels (*Winans v A-G* [1904] AC 287, HL).
7 *Aitchison v Dixon* (1870) LR 10 Eq 589 (use of Scottish territorial distinctions); cf *Re Craignish, Craignish v Hewitt* [1892] 3 Ch 180 at 186.
8 *Stevenson v Masson* (1873) LR 17 Eq 78; *Re Patience, Patience v Main* (1885) 29 ChD 976 at 984; cf *Haldane v Eckford* (1869) LR 8 Eq 631.
9 *IRC v Bullock* [1976] 3 All ER 353, [1976] 1 WLR 1178, CA.
10 *Re Craignish, Craignish v Hewitt* [1892] 3 Ch 180, CA; *Drevon v Drevon* (1864) 34 LJCh 129; *Doucet v Geoghegan* (1878) 9 ChD 441, CA; *Ramsay-Fairfax (otherwise Scott-Gibson) v Ramsay-Fairfax* [1956] P 115, [1955] 2 All ER 709; affd [1956] P 115 at 126, [1955] 3 All ER 695, CA; *Qureshi v Qureshi* [1972] Fam 173, [1971] 1 All ER 325. As to statements in wills and documents as to the maker's domicile see para 693 ante.
11 See *Drevon v Drevon* (1864) 34 LJCh 129; and para 692 ante.

(iii) Dependent Persons

701. Children. A child first becomes capable of having an independent domicile when he attains the age of 16 or marries under that age[1]. Before 1 January 1974, he could not have an independent domicile while he remained a minor. This rule still applies in considering the domicile of any person as at any date before 1 January 1974[2].

The domicile of a dependent child (that is, a child who under either of the above rules cannot have an independent domicile) may in some cases be changed by the act of the person on whom he is dependent[3].

In the case of a legitimate dependent child whose parents are living together, his domicile follows any change in the domicile of his father[4]. It would seem that the same rule applies to legitimated and to adopted children, who are treated as if they had been born in wedlock to their adoptive parents[5]. After the father's death, the child's domicile will generally follow a change in the mother's domicile[6]. The exercise by the mother of her power to change the domicile of the child is only effectual where the change is for the benefit of the child[7]; and the power cannot be exercised where the child is a ward of court residing out of the jurisdiction by permission[8]. The power is not lost by the mother's remarriage[9].

Where the parents of a legitimate child are living apart, the child's domicile will be that of his mother if he has his home with his mother and has no home with his father or if, having once acquired his mother's domicile under this rule, he has not since had a home with his father[10]. Where a dependent child has his mother's domicile under these rules and she then dies, the child retains her last domicile until he has a home with his father (in which case he takes his father's domicile) or acquires an independent domicile of choice[11]. These rules also apply to adopted children[12], but do not affect any rule of law by which a child's domicile is regarded as being, by dependence, that of his mother[13].

The mother of an illegitimate child has the same power of changing his domicile when she changes her own as does the widowed mother of a legitimate child[14].

A guardian probably has no power to change the domicile of his ward[15].

On becoming capable of acquiring an independent domicile, the child retains his domicile of dependence, but may abandon it and acquire a domicile of choice at any time[16].

1 Domicile and Matrimonial Proceedings Act 1973 s 3(1). For the exceptional case in which a dependent child of separated parents changes his home and thereby changes his domicile see the text to notes 10–11 infra.
2 Ibid s 3(1).
3 *Somerville v Lord Somerville* (1801) 5 Ves 750 at 787; *Forbes v Forbes* (1854) Kay 341 at 353; *Re Macreight Paxton v Macreight* (1885) 30 ChD 165.
4 *Re Patten's Goods* (1860) 6 Jur NS 151; *Sharpe v Crispin* (1869) LR 1 P & D 611; *Firebrace v Firebrace* (1878) 4 PD 63; *D'Etchegoyen v D'Etchegoyen* (1888) 13 PD 132; *Gulbenkian v Gulbenkian* [1937] 4 All ER 618; *Henderson v Henderson* [1967] P 77, [1965] 1 All ER 179. As to the domicile of origin of a legitimate child see para 685 ante.
5 Adoption Act 1976 s 39(1), (5); and see para 685 ante.
6 *Potinger v Wightman* (1817) 3 Mer 67; *Johnstone v Beattie* (1843) 10 Cl & Fin 42 at 66, 138; *Re Beaumont* [1893] 3 Ch 490; *Hope v Hope* [1968] NI 1 at 5.
7 *Re Beaumont* [1893] 3 Ch 490 at 496–497; applied in *Re G* [1966] NZLR 1028, NZ SC.
8 *Johnstone v Beattie* (1843) 10 Cl & Fin 42 at 139.
9 *Re Beaumont* [1893] 3 Ch 490. See *Crumpton's Judicial Factor v Finch-Noyes* 1918 SC 378.
10 Domicile and Matrimonial Proceedings Act 1973 s 4(1), (2). These provisions do not apply so as to affect the domicile of any person as at a date before 1 January 1974.
11 Ibid s 4(3).
12 Adoption Act 1976 s 39(1), (5).
13 Domicile and Matrimonial Proceedings Act 1973 s 4(4). This effectively means illegitimate children see para 685 ante.
14 It is submitted that the grounds on which Stirling J based his decision in *Re Beaumont* [1893] 3 Ch 490 apply with equal force to the case of an illegitimate child. If such a child is legitimated, his domicile would appear to follow his father's.
15 See *Potinger v Wightman* (1817) 3 Mer 67; *Douglas v Douglas* (1871) LR 12 Eq 617 at 625; and Dicey and Morris *The Conflict of Laws* (12th Edn, 1993) 152.
16 *Henderson v Henderson* [1967] P 77, [1965] 1 All ER 179; *Harrison v Harrison* [1953] 1 WLR 865.

702. Persons suffering from mental disorder. The domicile of a person suffering from a mental disorder cannot be changed, either by his own act or by the act of the person having his custody[1]. There is a possible exception to this rule where the mental incapacity begins during childhood, when the child is incapable of an independent domicile, and is not succeeded by adult capacity; in these circumstances the domicile of a mentally disordered person continues to be governed by the rules applying to dependent children[2].

1 *Hepburn v Skirving* (1861) 9 WR 764; *Sharpe v Crispin* (1869) LR 1 P & D 611; *Urquhart v Butterfield* (1887) 37 ChD 357 at 383, CA. Cf *Bempde v Johnstone* (1796) 3 Ves 198 at 201. It is an open question what types of mental disorder attract this rule: see *Sharpe v Crispin* (1869) LR 1 P & D 611 at 618 ('ability to think and act for himself in the matter of domicile otherwise than as a minor child'). For the meaning of 'mental disorder' in the Mental Health Act 1983 see s 1(2); and MENTAL HEALTH vol 30 (Reissue) para 1202.
2 *Sharpe v Crispin* (1869) LR 1 P & D 611. Here, however, the intentions of the person concerned were also considered.

(3) RESIDENCE

703. Residence in general. The term 'residence' bears varying meanings according to its context[1], and great caution must be exercised before authorities on the meaning of 'residence' in such contexts as bankruptcy[2], taxation[3], or the old poor law provisions[4], are applied in other contexts. In particular, it is clear that some degree of permanence is required for the acquisition of residence in some contexts[5], but not, or to a lesser extent, in others[6].

Generally, 'residence' means physical presence other than casually or as a traveller[7]. In considering whether residence is established the court considers a man's whole environment, especially in relation to his wife and family, and not merely his physical situation[8]. In some cases, a person may be resident in England despite a temporary absence[9]; and he may be held to be resident in two or more countries[10]. It is possible to be resident in a country without owning or enjoying exclusive possession of any premises there[11].

1 See eg *Foreman v Beagley* [1969] 3 All ER 838 at 841, [1969] 1 WLR 1387 at 1392, CA.
2 See BANKRUPTCY vol 3(2) (Reissue) para 116.
3 See the leading cases of *Levene v IRC* [1928] AC 217, HL; and *IRC v Lysaght* [1928] AC 234, HL; and INCOME TAXATION vol 23 (Reissue) para 1252.
4 See eg *R v Norwood Overseers* (1867) LR 2 QB 457, applying the maxim *ubi uxor ibi domus* (a man's home is where his wife is).
5 See eg *Levene v IRC* [1928] AC 217 at 222, HL (taxation); *Fox v Stirk and Bristol Electoral Registration Officer* [1970] 2 QB 463, [1970] 3 All ER 7, CA (qualifications for entry on register of electors); *Brokelmann v Barr* [1971] 2 QB 602, [1971] 3 All ER 29, DC (relief from customs duty).
6 Eg *Bell v Kennedy* (1868) LR 1 Sc & Div 307 at 319, HL; *Fasbender v A-G* [1922] 2 Ch 850 at 857–858, CA; *Stone v Stone* [1959] 1 All ER 194, [1958] 1 WLR 1287 (acquisition of domicile of choice); *Armytage v Armytage* [1898] P 178; *Matalon v Matalon* [1952] P 233, [1952] 1 All ER 1025, CA; *Sinclair v Sinclair* [1968] P 189, [1967] 3 All ER 882, CA (judicial separation).
7 *Sinclair v Sinclair* [1968] P 189, [1967] 3 All ER 882, CA; *Manning v Manning* (1871) LR 2 P & D 223; *Armytage v Armytage* [1898] P 178; *Matalon v Matalon* [1952] P 233, [1952] 1 All ER 1025, CA (all cases of judicial separation).
8 *Sinclair v Sinclair* [1968] P 189 at 231–232, [1967] 3 All ER 882 at 898, CA.
9 *Sinclair v Sinclair* [1968] P 189 at 228–231, [1967] 3 All ER 882 at 896–898, CA; *Raeburn v Raeburn* (1928) 44 TLR 384; *Dasent v Dasent* (1850) 1 Rob Eccl 800 at 803 per Dr Lushington (all judicial separation);

Fox v Stirk and Bristol Electoral Registration Officer [1970] 2 QB 463 at 475, [1970] 3 All ER 7 at 12, CA (qualification for entry on register of electors).

10 *Sinclair v Sinclair* [1968] P 189 at 232, [1967] 3 All ER 882 at 899, CA; *Fox v Stirk and Bristol Electoral Registration Officer* [1970] 2 QB 463 at 475, [1970] 3 All ER 7 at 11, CA. For taxation purposes, residence may be 'multiple and manifold': *IRC v Lysaght* [1928] AC 234 at 245, HL.

11 See eg *Levene v IRC* [1928] AC 217, HL; *Matalon v Matalon* [1952] P 233, [1952] 1 All ER 1025, CA; *Stone v Stone* [1959] 1 All ER 194, [1958] 1 WLR 1287.

704. Ordinary residence. 'Ordinary residence' is residence adopted voluntarily and for settled purposes as part of the regular order of life for the time being, as opposed to such residence as is casual, temporary or unusual[1]. It is possible, in some contexts, for a person to be ordinarily resident in two or more places[2], but this would seem to be impossible in cases where ordinary residence is a basis for the court's jurisdiction[3].

Different views have been expressed on the question whether there is any difference between 'residence' and 'ordinary residence'[4]. It is clear that ordinary residence, like residence, can be changed in a day[5].

1 *Levene v IRC* [1928] AC 217, HL; *IRC v Lysaght* [1928] AC 234, HL; *Macrae v Macrae* [1949] P 397, [1949] 2 All ER 34, CA; *Hopkins v Hopkins* [1951] P 116, [1950] 2 All ER 1035; *Stransky v Stransky* [1954] P 428, [1954] 2 All ER 536; *Lewis v Lewis* [1956] 1 All ER 375, [1956] 1 WLR 200; *R v Barnet London Borough Council, ex p Shah* [1983] 2 AC 309, [1983] 1 All ER 226, HL. The fact that a person keeps a home available for immediate occupation in a country is evidence of ordinary residence there (*Stransky v Stransky* supra; *Lewis v Lewis* supra); but a home in this sense is not essential. A person who makes repeated attempts to enter the country but who is denied leave to enter cannot claim to be ordinarily resident: *R v Secretary of State for the Home Department, ex p Butta* [1994] Imm AR 197.

2 *Pittar v Richardson* (1917) 87 LJKB 59 at 61, DC (liability for military service).

3 See eg the Carriage by Air Act 1961 s 1(1), Sch 1 art 28(1); and AVIATION vol 2 (Reissue) para 1545.

4 For the view that there is a difference see *Levene v IRC* [1928] AC 217 at 232, HL; *IRC v Lysaght* [1928] AC 234 at 243, 248, HL; *Stransky v Stransky* [1954] P 428 at 437, [1954] 2 All ER 536 at 541. For the contrary view see *Levene v IRC* supra at 225; *Hopkins v Hopkins* [1951] P 116 at 121–122, [1950] 2 All ER 1035 at 1038–1039.

5 *Macrae v Macrae* [1949] P 397 at 403, [1949] 2 All ER 34 at 36, CA.

705. Habitual residence. 'Habitual residence' has been defined as a regular physical presence, enduring for some time[1]. In most contexts there will be no real distinction between 'habitual residence' and 'ordinary residence'[2]. In the law of continental European countries, where the term is more common, habitual residence is regarded as a matter of pure fact, in which the duration, continuity and durability of the residence are material[3]. In English law also, habitual residence is primarily a matter of fact[4]. It would seem possible to be habitually resident in two places, at least for certain purposes[5], and habitual residence may continue during periods of temporary absence[6].

In English law, too, special provision is made so that the habitual residence of a child is unaffected for one year by the unlawful removal of the child from the territory of his habitual residence[7].

1 *Cruse v Chittum (formerly Cruse)* [1974] 2 All ER 940. As a young child has habitual residence no element of intention can be required: see eg the Adoption Act 1976 s 17(2)(b).

2 *R v Barnet London Borough Council, ex p Shah* [1983] 2 AC 309, [1983] 1 All ER 226, HL; *Kapur v Kapur* [1984] FLR 920. Cf *Cruse v Chittum (formerly Cruse)* [1974] 2 All ER 940.

3 See Jurisdiction in Matrimonial Causes (Law Com no 48) para 42. Cf Dicey and Morris *The Conflict of Laws* (12th Edn, 1993) 161–162. For the need to weigh statements as to habitual residence by interested parties with care see *F v S (Wardship: Jurisdiction)* [1993] 2 FLR 686, CA.

4 *Re M (Minors) (Residence Order: Jurisdiction)* [1993] 1 FLR 495, CA; *Re M (A Minor) (Habitual Residence)* (1996) Times, 3 January, CA.

5 Cf para 704 text to note 2 ante; and *Re V (Abduction: Habitual Residence)* [1995] 2 FLR 992 (concurrent habitual residence in two countries impossible in context of Hague Child Abduction Convention).

6 *Oundjian v Oundjian* (1979) 1 FLR 198.

7 See the Family Law Act 1986 s 41 (as amended); and CHILDREN vol 5(2) (Reissue) para 1020.

4. FAMILY LAW

(1) MARRIAGE

(i) Formalities of Marriage

A. GENERAL PRINCIPLE OF VALIDITY

706. Lex loci governs. Subject to certain exceptions[1] the formal validity of a marriage is governed by the *lex loci celebrationis*, the law of the place where the marriage was celebrated[2]. Without exception, a marriage is formally valid if it complies with the formal requirements of the *lex loci celebrationis* or alternatively, it seems, with its conflict rules for the formal validity of the marriage[3], even though it does not comply with the formal requirements of the law of the parties' domicile or the conflict rules of that law for the formal validity of the marriage[4]; and in general[5] a marriage is invalid if it is invalid under the *lex loci celebrationis* for failure to comply with its rules for the formal validity of the marriage, even though it complies with those of the law of the domicile[6].

1 See paras 709–721 post.

2 *Berthiaume v Dastous* [1930] AC 79, PC; *Scrimshire v Scrimshire* (1752) 2 Hag Con 395; *Butler v Freeman* (1756) Amb 301; *Compton v Bearcroft* (1769) 2 Hag Con 444n; *Middleton v Janverin* (1802) 2 Hag Con 437; *Dalrymple v Dalrymple* (1811) 2 Hag Con 54; *Lady Herbert v Lord Herbert* (1819) 2 Hag Con 263; *Lacon v Higgins* (1822) 3 Stark 178; *Swift v Kelly* (1835) 3 Knapp 257, PC; *Kent v Burgess* (1840) 11 Sim 361; *Catherwood v Caslon* (1844) 13 M & W 261; *Ward and Codd v Dey* (1849) 1 Rob Eccl 759; *Simonin v Mallac* (1860) 2 Sw & Tr 67; *Brook v Brook* (1861) 9 HL Cas 193; *Rooker v Rooker* (1863) 3 Sw & Tr 526; *Re Alison's Trusts* (1874) 31 LT 638; *Lightbody v West* (1903) 19 TLR 319, CA; *Ogden v Ogden* [1908] P 46, CA; *Re Green, Noyes v Pitkin* (1909) 25 TLR 222; *Apt v Apt* [1948] P 83, [1947] 2 All ER 677, CA; *Kenward v Kenward* [1951] P 124, [1950] 2 All ER 297, CA; *Starkowski (otherwise Urbanski) v A-G* [1954] AC 155, [1953] 2 All ER 1272, HL; *Pilinski v Pilinska* [1955] 1 All ER 631, [1955] 1 WLR 329; *Lazarewicz (otherwise Fadanelli) v Lazarewicz* [1962] P 171, [1962] 2 All ER 5. As to the registration of foreign marriages celebrated under local law and of foreign marriage certificates see paras 722–723 post. As to proof of foreign marriages see EVIDENCE vol 17 paras 180–182. *McCabe v McCabe* [1994] 1 FCR 257, [1994] 1 FLR 410, CA, is not inconsistent with the proposition in the text, but involved the recognition as a valid marriage of an event held in Ghana, when both parties were in England and had appointed no proxies.

3 *Taczanowska (otherwise Roth) v Taczanowski* [1957] P 301 at 305, [1956] 3 All ER 457 at 460; on appeal [1957] P 301 at 318, [1957] 2 All ER 563 at 566, CA. In this case the evidence was that the marriage was invalid by the conflict rules of the *lex loci celebrationis*, but it is legitimate to infer from the fact of admission of such evidence that the marriage would have been held valid had it been recognised as such by those rules: see para 609 ante.

4 *Compton v Bearcroft* (1769) 2 Hag Con 444n; *Dalrymple v Dalrymple* (1811) 2 Hag Con 54; *Lady Herbert v Lord Herbert* (1819) 2 Hag Con 263; *Swift v Kelly* (1835) 3 Knapp 257 PC; *Ward and Codd v Dey* (1849) 1 Rob Eccl 759; *Simonin v Mallac* (1860) 2 Sw & Tr 67; *Rooker v Rooker and Newton* (1863) 3 Sw & Tr 526; *Lightbody v West* (1903) 19 TLR 319, CA; *Ogden v Ogden* [1908] P 46, CA; *Re Green, Noyes v Pitkin* (1909) 25 TLR 222; *Ramos v Ramos* (1911) 27 TLR 515; *Apt v Apt* [1948] P 83, [1947] 2 All ER 677, CA; *Starkowski (otherwise Urbanski) v A-G* [1954] AC 155, [1953] 2 All ER 1272, HL.

5 As to exceptions see paras 709–721 post.

6 *Scrimshire v Scrimshire* (1752) 2 Hag Con 395; *Middleton v Janverin* (1802) 2 Hag Con 437; *Lacon v Higgins* (1822) 3 Stark 178; *Kent v Burgess* (1840) 11 Sim 361; *Catherwood v Caslon* (1844) 13 M & W 261; *Re Alison's Trusts* (1874) 31 LT 638; *Berthiaume v Dastous* [1930] AC 79, PC; *Kenward v Kenward* [1951] P 124, [1950] 2 All ER 297, CA; *Pilinski v Pilinska* [1955] 1 All ER 631, [1955] 1 WLR 329; *Lazarewicz (otherwise Fadanelli) v Lazarewicz* [1962] P 171, [1962] 2 All ER 5.

707. Formalities of marriage. The *lex loci celebrationis* governs all the formalities surrounding the actual ceremony of marriage itself including such questions as whether a religious ceremony is necessary or sufficient[1], whether a marriage may be constituted *per verba de praesenti*, that is by an informal exchange of consent[2], or whether a marriage may be celebrated by proxy[3]. It also governs the validity of notices, publication of banns, and all formal preliminaries[4].

A requirement of parental consent to the marriage, whether imposed by English[5] or foreign law, is regarded as a matter of form[6].

1 *Re De Wilton, De Wilton v Montefiore* [1900] 2 Ch 481; *Berthiaume v Dastous* [1930] AC 79, PC; *Pilinski v Pilinska* [1955] 1 All ER 631, [1955] 1 WLR 329; *Lazarewicz (otherwise Fadanelli) v Lazarewicz* [1962] P 171, [1962] 2 All ER 5.

2 *Compton v Bearcroft* (1769) 2 Hag Con 444n; *Bell v Graham* (1859) 13 Moo PCC 242; *Beamish v Beamish* (1861) 9 HL Cas 274.

3 *Apt v Apt* [1948] P 83, [1947] 2 All ER 677, CA; *Ponticelli v Ponticelli (otherwise Giglio)* [1958] P 204, [1958] 1 All ER 357. Cf *McCabe v McCabe* [1994] 1 FCR 257, [1994] 1 FLR 410, CA (as to which see also para 706 note 2 ante).

4 As to these see the cases cited in para 706 note 2 ante.

5 *Compton v Bearcroft* (1769) 2 Hag Com 444n. As to the meaning of 'English law' see para 604 ante.

6 *Simonin v Mallac* (1860) 2 Sw & Tr 67; *Brook v Brook* (1861) 9 HL Cas 193 at 215, 217–218, 229; *Sottomayor v De Barros* (1877) 3 PD 1 at 7, CA; cf *Sottomayer v De Barros* (1879) 5 PD 94 at 102–103; *Ogden v Ogden* [1908] P 46, CA; *Chetti v Chetti* [1909] P 67 at 81–87; *Bliersbach v MacEwen* 1959 SC 43, 1959 SLT 81; *Lodge (otherwise Berkowitz) v Lodge* (1963) 107 Sol Jo 437. This proposition has been criticised on the ground that the requirement of parental consent should not be characterised in the abstract, since it varies in nature and effect under the laws of different countries and should in certain cases be treated as relating to legal capacity: see Dicey and Morris *The Conflict of Laws* (12th Edn, 1993) 645–646. However, in none of the above cases did the law imposing the requirement of parental consent provide that non-compliance rendered the marriage void ab initio: such a requirement might well relate to legal capacity.

708. Changes in the lex loci. Retrospective legislation in the place of celebration of the marriage curing the formal invalidity of the marriage will be recognised in England[1] even though at the time when the legislation takes effect both parties are domiciled in England[2].

1 As to the meaning of 'England' see para 604 ante.

2 *Starkowski (otherwise Urbanski) v A-G* [1954] AC 155, [1953] 2 All ER 1272, HL. The question as to whether such legislation would be recognised if one of the parties had entered into another marriage before it took effect was expressly reserved: *Starkowski (otherwise Urbanski) v A-G* supra at 168, 172, 176, 182, and at 1273, 1275, 1279, 1282 respectively. All laws passed by the legislatures of any of Her Majesty's possessions abroad establishing the validity of marriages contracted in those possessions are effective in all parts of Her Majesty's dominions, provided that, according to English conflict rules, both parties had capacity to contract the marriage: Colonial Marriages Act 1865 ss 1, 2. As to legal capacity to marry see paras 725–729 post. As to British possessions and dominions see COMMONWEALTH vol 6 (Reissue) paras 803–804.

B. EXCEPTIONS TO GENERAL PRINCIPLE

709. Compliance with lex loci impossible. Where the local forms are inapplicable[1] or where there is insuperable[2] difficulty in complying with them[3], a marriage is formally valid if celebrated in accordance with the English common law[4]. In such a case the marriage need not be celebrated in a church or chapel[5] or before a minister of religion[6] or in the presence of witnesses[7]; it is probably sufficient that the parties take each other for man and wife by an informal exchange of consent[8].

1   Local forms may be inapplicable by virtue of the principle that the English common law, or so much of it as is applicable in the circumstances, applies to British subjects in a settled colony and in countries where Her Majesty by capitulatory agreement exercises extra-territorial jurisdiction over British subjects. For cases in the former category see *Lautour v Teesdale* (1816) 8 Taunt 830; *Catterall v Catterall* (1847) 1 Rob Eccl 580; *Maclean v Cristall* (1849) 7 Notes of Cases, Supp xvii at xxv; *Countess of Limerick v Earl of Limerick* (1863) 4 Sw & Tr 252; *James v James and Smyth* (1881) 51 LJP 24. For cases in the latter category see *Phillips v Phillips* (1921) 38 TLR 150; *Watts (otherwise Carey) v Watts* (1922) 38 TLR 430; *Martin v Martin and May* (1928) 72 Sol Jo 612; *Doust v Doust* (1929) 168 LT Jo 113; *Matthews v Matthews* (1930) 99 LJP 142; *Wolfenden v Wolfenden* [1946] P 61, [1945] 2 All ER 539; *Penhas v Tan Soo Eng* [1953] AC 304, [1953] 2 WLR 459, PC. These cases are apparent but not real exceptions to the general rule: *Taczanowska (otherwise Roth) v Taczanowski* [1957] P 301 at 328–329, [1957] 2 All ER 563 at 574, CA; *Merker v Merker* [1963] P 283 at 294, [1962] 3 All ER 928 at 933.
2   Mere difficulty is insufficient: *Kent v Burgess* (1840) 11 Sim 361; *Starkowski v A-G* [1952] P 135 at 141, [1952] 1 All ER 495 at 496–497; on appeal [1952] P 302, [1952] 2 All ER 616, CA; [1954] AC 155, [1953] 2 All ER 1272, HL.
3   *Lord Cloncurry's Case* (1811) cited in 6 State Tr NS 87; *Ruding v Smith* (1821) 2 Hag Con 371; *Taczanowska (otherwise Roth) v Taczanowski* [1957] P 301 at 312–313, [1956] 3 All ER 457 at 465; on appeal [1957] P 301 at 324–325, 328–329, 332, [1957] 2 All ER 563 at 571, 574, 576, CA; *Kochanski v Kochanska* [1958] P 147 at 152, [1957] 3 All ER 142 at 144–145, disapproved on another point in *Preston (otherwise Putynski) v Preston (otherwise Putynska) (otherwise Basinska)* [1963] P 411, [1963] 2 All ER 405, CA; *Lazarewicz (otherwise Fadanelli) v Lazarewicz* [1962] P 171 at 177, [1962] 2 All ER 5 at 7–8; *Preston (otherwise Putynski) v Preston (otherwise Putynska) (otherwise Basinska)* [1963] P 141 at 155, [1962] 3 All ER 1057 at 1064; on appeal [1963] P 411, [1963] 2 All ER 405, CA; *Narewski v Narewski* (1966) 110 Sol Jo 466. The principle would presumably also apply where there was no lex loci, as in unclaimed deserted lands: see *Advocate-General of Bengal v Ranee Surnomoye Dossee* (1863) 2 Moo PCCNS 22 at 59; *Kochanski v Kochanska supra* at 152 and at 144. It applies to British subjects and aliens alike; the common law conception of marriage knows no distinction of race or nationality: *Taczanowska (otherwise Roth) v Taczanowski supra* at 326–327 and at 572–573; and see the cases cited supra.
4   See the cases cited in notes 1, 3 supra.
5   *Ruding v Smith* (1821) 2 Hag Con 371; *Smith v Maxwell* (1824) Ry & M 80; *Penhas v Tan Soo Eng* [1953] AC 304, [1953] 2 WLR 459, PC.
6   *Penhas v Tan Soo Eng* [1953] AC 304, [1953] 2 WLR 459, PC. In *R v Millis* (1844) 10 Cl & Fin 534, HL, and *Beamish v Beamish* (1861) 9 HL Cas 274, it was held that the presence of an episcopally ordained priest was essential to the validity of a common law marriage; but these decisions have since been confined to marriages celebrated in England and Ireland: *Wolfenden v Wolfenden* [1946] P 61, [1945] 2 All ER 539; approved on this point in *Apt v Apt* [1948] P 83 at 86, [1947] 2 All ER 677 at 679, CA; and in *Penhas v Tan Soo Eng supra* at 319 and at 464; and see the cases cited in notes 1, 3 supra and note 8 infra.
7   *Ussher v Ussher* [1912] 2 IR 445, 46 ILT 109.
8   Ie *per verba de praesenti*: see *Dalrymple v Dalrymple* (1811) 2 Hag Con 54 at 64–70; *Lautour v Teesdale* (1816) 8 Taunt 830 at 837; *Catterall v Catterall* (1847) 1 Rob Eccl 580 at 583; *Merker v Merker* [1963] P 283, [1962] 3 All ER 928; *Preston (otherwise Putynski) v Preston (otherwise Putynska) (otherwise Basinska)* [1963] P 411 at 436, [1963] 2 All ER 405 at 416, CA; and see also para 707 ante.

710. Marriages in merchant ships. It would seem that the formal validity of a marriage on board a merchant ship on the high seas is governed by the law of the country where the ship is registered[1]. In the case of a merchant ship registered in England the law applicable would seem to be the English common law[2].

1   This follows from the principle that the law of the flag governs transactions on board a vessel on the high seas: see SHIPPING.
2   The statutory formal requirements do not seem to apply to marriages at sea. For the common law requirements see para 709 ante. In *Du Moulin v Druitt* (1860) 13 ICLR 212 it was held that the presence of an episcopally ordained clergyman was necessary, but this is questionable: see para 709 note 6 ante. Dicey and Morris *The Conflict of Laws* (12th Edn, 1993) 649, suggests that the marriage is only valid if it is impracticable for the parties to wait until the ship has reached a port where sufficient facilities are available either by the lex loci or under the Foreign Marriage Act 1892 (see paras 713–721 post). This would bring the marriage into the same category as those in para 709 ante: cf *Culling v Culling* [1896] P 116. Marriages on board British warships are now governed by the Foreign Marriage Act 1892 s 22 (as substituted and amended): see para 712 post. As to the meaning of 'England' and 'English law' see para 604 ante.

711. Marriages in countries under belligerent occupation. A marriage in a country under belligerent occupation is formally valid if celebrated within the lines of the occupying forces, in accordance with the English common law[1], between parties of whom at least one[2] is a member of those forces[3] or of forces associated with them[4], unless both parties intended to subject themselves to the local law[5]. No distinction is made for this purpose between British subjects and aliens or between persons domiciled in England and persons domiciled elsewhere[6].

1 See para 709 ante.

2 The status of the other party seems to be immaterial: *Taczanowska (otherwise Roth) v Taczanowski* [1957] P 301 at 314, [1957] 2 All ER 563, CA; *Preston (otherwise Putynski) v Preston (otherwise Putynska) (otherwise Basinska)* [1963] P 411 at 425, 430, [1963] 2 All ER 405 at 410, 413, CA.

3 *Taczanowska (otherwise Roth) v Taczanowski* [1957] P 301 at 314, [1957] 2 All ER 563, CA; *Merker v Merker* [1963] P 283, [1962] 3 All ER 928; cf *Ruding v Smith* (1821) 2 Hag Con 371.

4 *Preston (otherwise Putynski) v Preston (otherwise Putynska) (otherwise Basinska)* [1963] P 411, [1963] 2 All ER 405, CA. The principle does not apply to the marriage of inmates of a displaced persons camp: *Preston (otherwise Putynski) v Preston (otherwise Putynska) (otherwise Basinska)* supra at 426–427, 434–435 and at 411, 415, CA, disapproving *Kochanski v Kochanska* [1958] P 147, [1957] 3 All ER 142. It may perhaps apply to members of an organised body of prisoners of war: *Merker v Merker* [1963] P 283, [1962] 3 All ER 928, explaining *Kochanski v Kochanska* supra.

5 *Lazarewicz (otherwise Fadanelli) v Lazarewicz* [1962] P 171, [1962] 2 All ER 5, approved in *Preston (otherwise Putynski) v Preston (otherwise Putynska) (otherwise Basinska)* [1963] P 411 at 432, [1963] 2 All ER 405 at 414, CA. The presumption is that the parties have not subjected themselves to the local law; it is a matter of intention in the limited sense that they may opt in: *Preston (otherwise Putynski) v Preston (otherwise Putynska) (otherwise Basinska)* supra at 433 and at 415, CA.

6 *Taczanowska (otherwise Roth) v Taczanowski* [1957] P 301 at 326, [1957] 2 All ER 563 at 572, CA. Apart from the *lex loci celebrationis*, the court will only refer to the English common law, and it will not refer to the law of the parties' domicile or nationality: *Taczanowska (otherwise Roth) v Taczanowski* supra at 326, 331 and at 572, 575; *Preston (otherwise Putynski) v Preston (otherwise Putynska) (otherwise Basinska)* [1963] P 141 at 152–153, [1962] 3 All ER 1057 at 1062–1063; on appeal [1963] P 411, [1963] 2 All ER 405, CA. The burden of proving that the marriage is valid under this exception to the general rule governing the formal validity of a marriage is on the party who asserts the exception: *Kochanski v Kochanska* [1958] P 147 at 151, [1957] 3 All ER 142 at 144; *Preston (otherwise Putynski) v Preston (otherwise Putynska) (otherwise Basinska)* supra at 153–154 and at 1063; on appeal [1963] P 411, [1963] 2 All ER 405, CA. As to the meaning of 'England' see para 604 ante.

712. Marriages by chaplains of Her Majesty's forces. A marriage solemnised in any foreign territory[1] by a chaplain serving with any part of the naval, military or air forces of Her Majesty[2] serving in that territory[3] or by a person authorised, either generally or in respect of the particular marriage, by the commanding officer of any part of those forces, is as valid in law as if the marriage had been solemnised in the United Kingdom[4] with a due observance of all forms required by law[5].

This provision applies only if at least one of the parties to the marriage is a person who is a member of the naval, military or air forces serving in the territory; or a person employed in that territory[6] in one of certain other prescribed capacities[7]; or a child[8] of any such person who has his home with that person in that territory; and provided that certain prescribed conditions as to (1) notification of absence of objection; and (2) solemnisation in the presence of witnesses, are complied with[9]. There is no requirement that either party must be a British subject[10].

A marriage solemnised under the above provisions must be registered[11]. In any legal proceedings touching upon the validity of the marriage, it is not necessary to prove the authority of the person by or before whom it was solemnised; nor may any evidence of his want of authority be given[12].

The above provisions do not apply to members of Dominion[13] forces other than members of those forces who are temporarily attached[14] to United Kingdom forces[15];

but any Dominion law which makes corresponding provisions as to forces of that Dominion country may be given effect by Order in Council as part of the law of the United Kingdom[16].

1   Ie a territory other than (1) any part of Her Majesty's dominions; or (2) any British protectorate; or (3) any other country or territory under Her Majesty's protection or suzerainty or in which Her Majesty has for the time being jurisdiction; but Her Majesty may by Order in Council direct that any British protectorate or any other country or territory within head (3) supra or any part of Her Majesty's dominions which has been occupied by a state at war with Her Majesty and in which facilities for marriage under local law have not been adequately restored may be treated as foreign territory: Foreign Marriage Act 1892 s 22(2) (s 22 substituted by the Foreign Marriage Act 1947 s 2). At the date at which this volume states the law, no Order in Council was in force for this purpose. Ships for the time being in the waters of a foreign territory are included in references to foreign territory: see the Foreign Marriage Act 1892 s 22(3) (as so substituted). Any Order in Council made under s 22 (as substituted) may be varied or revoked by a subsequent Order in Council; and any Order in Council under s 22 must be forthwith laid before each House of Parliament: s 22(6) (as so substituted).
2   This excludes a marriage solemnised by a chaplain of a foreign army corps which is not operating directly under British command: *Taczanowska (otherwise Roth) v Taczanowski* [1957] P 301 at 320, [1957] 2 All ER 563 at 568, CA.
3   This includes persons serving in ships in foreign waters: Foreign Marriage Act 1892 s 22(3) (as substituted: see note 1 supra). Provision for the solemnisation of marriages on Her Majesty's ships on foreign stations was formerly contained in s 12 (repealed by the Foreign Marriage Act 1947 s 4(1)). Banns of a marriage to be solemnised in England may be published on a British warship: Marriage Act 1949 s 14; see HUSBAND AND WIFE.
4   For the meaning of 'United Kingdom' see para 604 ante.
5   Foreign Marriage Act 1892 s 22(1) (as substituted: see note 1 supra). As to the position at common law regarding marriage within the British army abroad see *R v Brampton Inhabitants* (1808) 10 East 282; *Burn v Farrar* (1819) 2 Hag Con 369; *Waldegrave Peerage Case* (1837) 4 Cl & Fin 649, HL.
6   This includes persons employed in ships in foreign waters: Foreign Marriage Act 1892 s 22(3) (as substituted: see note 1 supra).
7   For this purpose, employment in a prescribed capacity is employment involving the performance of administrative, executive, judicial, clerical, typing, duplicating, machine operating, paper keeping, messengerial, professional, instructional, scientific, experimental, technical, industrial or labouring functions, if it is carried out by persons serving Her Majesty or otherwise employed in the territory where the marriage is solemnised, who are civilians subject to military, air force or naval law when not on active service by virtue of the Army Act 1955 Pt II (ss 24–143) (as amended), the Air Force Act 1955 Pt II (ss 24–143) (as amended), or the Naval Discipline Act 1957: Foreign Marriage (Armed Forces) Order 1964, SI 1964/1000, arts 1, 2 (both substituted by SI 1990/2592). As to the making of Orders in Council under the Foreign Marriage Act 1892 s 22 (as substituted) see note 1 supra.
8   For the purpose of determining whether one person is the child of another, it is immaterial whether the person's mother and father were at any time married to each other, and any person who is or was treated by another as a child of the family in relation to any marriage to which that other is or was a party must be regarded as his child: ibid s 22(1B) (s 22 as substituted: see note 1 supra; s 22(1A), (1B) added by the Foreign Marriage (Amendment) Act 1988 s 6).
9   Foreign Marriage Act 1892 s 22(1A) (as substituted and added: see note 8 supra). A certificate from the commander in the territory where the party is serving must be produced to the chaplain, stating that the commander has no objection and giving particulars of the party: see the Foreign Marriage (Armed Forces) Order 1964 arts 3(a), (b), 4. Certificates may be necessary in respect of each party: art 3(a) proviso. The marriage must be celebrated in the presence of not less than two witnesses: art 3(c). 'The commander in the territory' means, where a party to the marriage is a member of the naval forces or a person employed in any of the capacities mentioned in note 7 supra, the officer commanding the naval forces of Her Majesty in the territory; where a party to the marriage is a member of the military or air forces, it means the officer commanding the military or air forces of Her Majesty in the territory: art 4.
10 See *Taczanowska (otherwise Roth) v Taczanowski* [1957] P 301 at 319–320, [1957] 2 All ER 563 at 567–568, CA.
11 See the Foreign Marriage (Armed Forces) Order 1964 art 5, made under the Foreign Marriage Act 1892 s 22(4) (as substituted: see note 1 supra; amended by the Foreign Marriage (Amendment) Act 1988 s 7, Schedule); Registration of Births, Deaths and Marriages (Special Provisions) Act 1957 s 1; Service Departments Registers Order 1959, SI 1959/406 (amended by SI 1963/1624; and SI 1988/1295). See further REGISTRATION CONCERNING THE INDIVIDUAL.

12 Foreign Marriage Act 1892 s 22(5) (as substituted: see note 1 supra).
13 The Foreign Marriage Act 1947 s 3 refers to a Dominion, within the meaning of the Statute of Westminster 1931, namely, in effect, Canada, Australia and New Zealand: Foreign Marriage Act 1947 s 3(3) (amended by the Newfoundland (Consequential Provisions) Act 1950 s 1(2), Schedule Pt II (repealed)); and see COMMONWEALTH vol 6 (Reissue) paras 803, 805.
14 Ie under the Visiting Forces (British Commonwealth) Act 1933 s 4(2) (amended by the Defence (Transfer of Functions) (No 1) Order 1964, SI 1964/488): Foreign Marriage Act 1947 s 3(1) proviso: see ROYAL FORCES vol 41 para 314.
15 Ibid s 3(1).
16 Ibid s 3(2). Such provision has been made in relation to New Zealand and Australia: Foreign Marriage (Armed Forces) Order 1964 art 6, Sch 1 (substituted by SI 1965/137).

713. Marriages under the Foreign Marriage Act 1892. A marriage solemnised in the manner provided by the Foreign Marriage Act 1892[1] in any foreign[2] country or place, by or before a marriage officer[3], between parties of whom at least one is a United Kingdom national[4], is as valid as if it had been solemnised in the United Kingdom[5] with a due observance of all forms required by law[6], even though it may be invalid by the *lex loci celebrationis*[7].

1 The Foreign Marriage Act 1892 has been amended by the Foreign Marriage Act 1947 and by the Foreign Marriage (Amendment) Act 1988. See the Foreign Marriage (Armed Forces) Order 1964, SI 1964/1000 (amended by SI 1965/137; and SI 1990/2592) (as to which see para 712 ante); and the Foreign Marriage Order 1970, SI 1970/1539 (amended by SI 1990/598). The Acts do not apply to marriages of members of the royal family: Foreign Marriage Act 1892 s 23. Such marriages, wherever they take place, are governed by the Royal Marriages Act 1772: see *Sussex Peerage Case* (1844) 11 Cl & Fin 85, HL; and CONSTITUTIONAL LAW. As to marriages under the Foreign Marriage Act 1892 s 22 (as substituted and amended) see para 712 ante. By the Marriage of British Subjects (Facilities) Act 1915 and the Marriage of British Subjects (Facilities) Amendment Act 1916, provision is made for facilitating marriages between British subjects resident in the United Kingdom and British subjects resident in other parts of Her Majesty's dominions or in British Protectorates: see HUSBAND AND WIFE vol 22 para 950.
2 Ie presumably outside the Commonwealth, except in the case of British Protectorates and Protected States. See Dicey and Morris *The Conflict of Laws* (12th Edn, 1993) 653.
3 'Marriage officer' means a British ambassador (including a minister and a chargé d'affaires: Foreign Marriage Act 1892 s 24 (as amended: see note 4 infra)) residing in the country to whose government he is accredited, or any officer prescribed by marriage regulations as an officer for solemnising marriages in the official house of such an ambassador, or a British consul (ie a consul-general, consul, vice-consul, pro-consul and consular agent: s 24 (as so amended)), Governor, high commissioner, resident, consular or other officer, or any person appointed in pursuance of the marriage regulations to act in place of a high commissioner or resident, provided that he holds a marriage warrant signed by the Secretary of State, or any officer authorised by the marriage regulations to act as marriage officer without any marriage warrant: s 11(1), (2). As to the making of marriage regulations see s 21 (as amended). No marriage regulations for this purpose were in force at the date at which this volume states the law, and accordingly a marriage warrant is in every case necessary. The marriage regulations made for related purposes are contained in the Foreign Marriage Order 1970 (as amended).
  If a marriage warrant refers to the office without designating the name of any particular person holding it then, while the warrant is in force, the person for the time being holding or acting in that office is a marriage officer: Foreign Marriage Act 1892 s 11(3).
  A Secretary of State may by warrant under his hand vary or revoke any marriage warrant previously issued under the Foreign Marriage Act 1892: s 11(4).
4 For these purposes, 'United Kingdom national' means a person who is (1) a British citizen, a British Dependent Territories citizen, a British Overseas citizen or a British National (Overseas); or (2) a British subject under the British Nationality Act 1981; or (3) a British protected person within the meaning of that Act: Foreign Marriage Act 1892 ss 1(2), 24 (respectively added and amended by the Foreign Marriage (Amendment) Act 1988 s 1(2), (4), 7(2), Schedule). As to categories of citizenship see BRITISH NATIONALITY, IMMIGRATION AND RACE RELATIONS vol 4(2) (Reissue) paras 1–68.
5 For the meaning of 'United Kingdom' see para 604 ante.

6 Foreign Marriage Act 1892 s 1(1) (amended by the Foreign Marriage (Amendment) Act 1988 s 1). The marriage is thus formally valid, although not necessarily valid in other respects: Foreign Marriage Act 1892 s 23.

7 *Hay v Northcote* [1900] 2 Ch 262, where a marriage celebrated in accordance with the Consular Marriage Act 1849 (repealed and virtually re-enacted by the Foreign Marriage Act 1892) was held to be valid although it had been annulled by the court of the parties' domicile. The foreign nullity decree might now be recognised here: see para 745 et seq post; and *Merker v Merker* [1963] P 283 at 299–300, [1962] 3 All ER 928 at 936.

714. Notice of intended marriage. Where a marriage is intended to be solemnised under the Foreign Marriage Act 1892[1], one of the parties must sign a notice stating the name, surname, profession, condition and residence of each of the parties and whether each is or is not a minor, and give it to the marriage officer[2] within whose district[3] both parties have resided for not less than one week immediately preceding the notice, stating in the notice that they have so resided[4]. The marriage officer must file the notice in his registry, and, on payment of the proper fee[5], enter it in his book of notices, and keep a true copy of the notice posted up in some conspicuous place in his office[6] for 14 consecutive days before the marriage is solemnised[7]. If the marriage is not solemnised within three months of the date on which notice for it has been given to and entered by the marriage officer[8] the notice is void, and the marriage cannot be solemnised under it[9].

In special cases, where the Secretary of State is satisfied that for some good cause the requirements of the Act as to residence and notice cannot be complied with, and he is satisfied that the intended marriage is not clandestine and that adequate public notice has been given in the place or places where each of the parties resided not less than 15 days immediately preceding the giving of the notice, he may authorise the marriage officer to dispense with those requirements[10].

1 See para 713 ante.
2 For the meaning of 'marriage officer' see para 713 note 3 ante.
3 Ie the area within which the duties of his office are exercisable, or any such lesser area as is assigned by the marriage warrant or any other warrant of a Secretary of State, or is fixed by the marriage regulations: Foreign Marriage Act 1892 s 11(1). As to marriage warrants see para 713 note 3 ante. As to the making of marriage regulations see s 21 (as amended). No marriage regulations for this purpose were in force at the date at which this volume states the law. The marriage regulations made for related purposes are contained in the Foreign Marriage Order 1970, SI 1970/1539 (amended by SI 1990/598).
4 Foreign Marriage Act 1892 s 2. For a form of notice of marriage see the Foreign Marriage Order 1970 art 8, Schedule Form 1.
5 The proper fee is such as is fixed under the Consular Fees Act 1980, and the fee so fixed as respects a consul is the fee which may be taken by any marriage officer; the provisions of that Act relating to the levying, application and remission of and accounting for fees are the same when the marriage officer taking the fee is not a consul: Foreign Marriage Act 1892 s 20 (amended by the Consular Fees Act 1980 s 1(5)). The fees payable are now fixed by the Consular Fees Order 1995, SI 1995/1617; and the levying, application and remission of, and accounting for, fees are governed by the Consular Fees Regulations 1981, SI 1981/476 (made under s 1(3) of the Consular Fees Act 1980). At the date at which this volume states the law, the fee for receiving notice of an intended marriage is fixed at £35: Consular Fees Order 1995 art 3, Schedule para 25.
6 As to the office of a marriage officer see further para 719 note 5 post.
7 Foreign Marriage Act 1892 s 3(1). The book of notices and copy of the notice posted up must be open at all reasonable times, without fee, to the inspection of any person: s 3(2).
8 Ibid s 6(a). If, on a caveat being entered (see para 717 post), a statement has been transmitted to a Secretary of State, or if an appeal has been made to a Secretary of State (see para 716 post), the three months run from the date of the receipt from the Secretary of State of a decision directing the marriage to be solemnised: s 6(b).
9 Ibid s 6.
10 Foreign Marriage Order 1970 art 4(1). As to the oath before marriage in such circumstances see para 718 note 5 post.

715. Consents. The same consents are required, under the Foreign Marriage Act 1892[1], to a marriage of a party domiciled in England and Wales or in a country outside the United Kingdom[2] as would be required in respect of that party to a marriage solemnised in England and Wales on the authority of a superintendent registrar's certificate[3]. The same consents are required, under the Act, to the marriage of a party domiciled in Northern Ireland as would be required in respect of that party to a marriage solemnised there[4]. No consent is required to a marriage under the Act in respect of a party domiciled in Scotland[5]. Where by reason of the absence, inaccessibility or disability of a person whose consent is required that consent cannot be obtained, the requirement of obtaining the consent may be dispensed with by the Secretary of State, or, in such cases as may be prescribed by marriage regulations[6], the Registrar General for England and Wales[7].

A person whose consent is required may forbid the marriage by an entry to this effect in the marriage officer's book of notices of marriage[8]. The effect of such an entry is to render the notice void, and the marriage cannot be solemnised under it[9].

1 See para 713 ante.
2 For the meaning of 'United Kingdom', and as to England and Wales, see para 604 ante.
3 Foreign Marriage Act 1892 s 4(1) (s 4 substituted by the Foreign Marriage (Amendment) Act 1988 s 2(1)). As to the consents required by English domestic law see HUSBAND AND WIFE vol 22 para 953. The Foreign Marriage Act 1892 s 4 (as substituted) refers to the certificate of a superintendent registrar under the Marriage Act 1949 Pt III (ss 26–52): see HUSBAND AND WIFE.
4 Foreign Marriage Act 1892 s 4(2) (as substituted: see note 3 supra). Note, however, that consent may be dispensed with by order under Northern Ireland legislation, on application to a county court in Northern Ireland: see s 4(5) (as so substituted).
5 Ibid s 4(3) (as substituted: see note 3 supra).
6 As to the making of marriage regulations see ibid s 21 (as amended). No marriage regulations for this purpose were in force at the date at which this volume states the law. The marriage regulations made for related purposes are contained in the Foreign Marriage Order 1970, SI 1970/1539 (amended by SI 1990/598).
7 Foreign Marriage Act 1892 s 4(4) (as substituted: see note 3 supra). As to the office of Registrar General for England and Wales see REGISTRATION CONCERNING THE INDIVIDUAL vol 39 para 1067 et seq.
8 See ibid s 4(6) (as substituted: see note 3 supra). He must write the word 'forbidden' against the entry of the intended marriage in the book of notices and add his name and address and a statement of the capacity by virtue of which his consent is required: s 4(6) (as so substituted).
9 Ibid s 4(6) (as substituted: see note 3 supra).

716. Refusal of solemnisation of marriage. Before a marriage is solemnised in a foreign country under the Foreign Marriage Act 1892[1], the marriage officer[2] must be satisfied that (1) at least one of the parties is a United Kingdom national[3]; (2) the authorities of the foreign country will not object to the solemnisation of the marriage; (3) insufficient facilities exist for the marriage of the parties under the law of that country; and (4) the parties will be regarded as validly married by the law of the country in which each party is domiciled[4]. The marriage officer is not required to solemnise a marriage, or to allow it to be solemnised in his presence, if in his opinion its solemnisation would be inconsistent with international law or the comity of nations[5].

If the marriage officer refuses to solemnise the marriage of any person requiring it to be solemnised, or allow it to be solemnised in his presence, by reason of any of the provisions described above, that person has a right of appeal to a Secretary of State, who must give the marriage officer his decision on the appeal[6]. The marriage officer must forthwith inform the parties of, and conform to, the Secretary of State's decision[7].

1 See para 713 ante.
2 For the meaning of 'marriage officer' see para 713 note 3 ante (definition applied by the Foreign Marriage Order 1970, SI 1970/1539, art 2(1)).

3 For the meaning of 'United Kingdom national' see para 713 note 4 ante (definition as applied: see note 2 supra).
4 Foreign Marriage Order 1970 art 3(1) (amended by SI 1990/598).
5 Foreign Marriage Act 1892 s 19.
6 Ibid ss 5(3), 19 proviso; Foreign Marriage Order 1970 art 3(2).
7 Foreign Marriage Act 1892 s 5(4) (amended by the Foreign Marriage (Amendment) Act 1988 s 3(2)).

717. Objections. On payment of the proper fee[1] any person may enter with the marriage officer[2] a caveat, signed by him or on his behalf and stating his residence and the ground of his objection against the solemnisation of the marriage of any named person, and thereupon the marriage cannot be solemnised until either the marriage officer has examined the matter and is satisfied that the caveat ought not to obstruct solemnisation of the marriage, or the caveat has been withdrawn by the person entering it[3]. In a case of doubt the marriage officer may transmit a copy of the caveat with such statement respecting it as he thinks fit to the Secretary of State, who must refer it to the Registrar General for whichever part of the United Kingdom he considers appropriate[4]; and the Registrar General must give his decision in writing to the Secretary of State, who must communicate it to the marriage officer[5]. The marriage officer must forthwith inform the parties of, and conform to, the decision of the Registrar General[6].

1 As to the proper fee see para 714 note 5 ante. Although a fee was formerly payable on the receipt of a caveat, the Consular Fees Order 1995, SI 1995/1617, does not specify a fee.
2 For the meaning of 'marriage officer' see para 713 note 3 ante.
3 Foreign Marriage Act 1892 s 5(1).
4 Ie to the Registrar General for England and Wales, the Registrar General for Scotland or the Registrar General for Northern Ireland: ibid s 5(2) (amended by the Foreign Marriage (Amendment) Act 1988 s 3(1)). As to the office of Registrar General for England and Wales see REGISTRATION CONCERNING THE INDIVIDUAL vol 39 para 1067 et seq.
5 Ibid s 5(2) (as amended: see note 4 supra).
6 Ibid s 5(4) (amended by the Foreign Marriage (Amendment) Act 1988 s 3(2)).

718. Oath before marriage. Before a marriage is solemnised under the Foreign Marriage Act 1892[1], each of the parties must appear before the marriage officer[2] and make and subscribe an oath in a book kept by the officer for the purpose[3]: (1) that he or she believes that there is no impediment to the marriage by reason of kindred or alliance or otherwise[4]; (2) that they have both for the immediately preceding three weeks had their usual residence within the marriage officer's district[5]; and (3) where either party is under the age of 18 and domiciled in a country other than Scotland, (a) that any necessary consent has been obtained; or (b) that the necessity of obtaining consent has been dispensed with; or (c) if the party is domiciled in England and Wales or a country outside the United Kingdom[6], either that he or she is a widow or widower or that there is no person having authority to give such consent[7].

1 See para 713 ante.
2 For the meaning of 'marriage officer' see para 713 note 3 ante.
3 Foreign Marriage Act 1892 s 7.
4 Ibid s 7(a).
5 Ibid s 7(b). This part of the oath must be omitted in cases where, under the Foreign Marriage Order 1970, SI 1970/1539, art 4(1), the Secretary of State has authorised the marriage officer to dispense with

the requirements of the Foreign Marriage Act 1892 as to residence and notice (see para 714 text and note 10 ante): Foreign Marriage Order 1970 art 4(2).

6 For the meaning of 'United Kingdom', and as to England and Wales, see para 604 ante.

7 Foreign Marriage Act 1892 s 7(c) (substituted by the Foreign Marriage (Amendment) Act 1988 s 2(2)). For a form of oath see the Foreign Marriage Order 1970 art 8, Schedule Form 2. As to consents see para 715 ante.

719. Solemnisation of marriage. After the expiration of 14 days after notice of an intended marriage has been entered[1], if no lawful impediment to the marriage is shown to the satisfaction of the marriage officer[2] and the marriage has not been forbidden[3], it may be solemnised under the Foreign Marriage Act 1892[4]. It must be solemnised at the official house of the marriage officer[5], with open doors, between the hours of 8 am and 6 pm in the presence of two or more witnesses, either by the marriage officer or, if the parties so desire, by some other person in his presence, according to such form and ceremony as the parties see fit to adopt[6]. If a corresponding declaration is not otherwise included in the form adopted by the parties, each party must, in some part of the ceremony and in the presence of the marriage officer, declare that he or she knows of no lawful impediment to the marriage[7] and that he or she takes the other as lawful wedded wife or husband[8].

1 See para 714 ante.

2 See para 718 ante. For the meaning of 'marriage officer' see para 713 note 3 ante.

3 See para 715 ante.

4 Foreign Marriage Act 1892 s 8(1). The marriage officer is entitled to a proper fee: s 9(1). As to the proper fee see para 714 note 5 ante. At the date at which this volume states the law, the Consular Fees Order 1995, SI 1995/1617, art 3, Schedule para 26 specifies a fee of £70.

5 'Official house of the marriage officer' means the office at which the officer's business is transacted, and the official house of residence of that officer, and, in the case of any officer who is an officer for solemnising marriages in the official house of an ambassador, the ambassador's official house: Foreign Marriage Act 1892 s 24. Every place within the curtilage or precincts of the building which is for the time being used for the purpose of the marriage officer's office is part of his official house, and every place to which the public have ordinary access in that official house is deemed to be part of the office: Foreign Marriage Order 1970, SI 1970/1539, art 5. The certificate of a Secretary of State as to any house, office, chapel, or other place being, or being part of, the official house of a British ambassador or consul is conclusive: Foreign Marriage Act 1892 s 16(2).

6 Ibid s 8(2) (substituted by the Foreign Marriage (Amendment) Act 1988 s 4).

7 See the Foreign Marriage Act 1892 s 8(3) (substituted by the Foreign Marriage (Amendment) Act 1988 s 4).

8 See the Foreign Marriage Act 1892 s 8(4) (added by the Foreign Marriage (Amendment) Act 1988 s 4).

720. Registration and proof of marriage. The marriage officer[1] must forthwith register in duplicate a marriage solemnised under the Foreign Marriage Act 1892[2] in two marriage register books[3], according to the form provided by law for the registration of marriages in England[4], or as near to that form as the difference of circumstances permits[5]. In January of each year the marriage officer must forward to a Secretary of State, for transmission to the Registrar General for England and Wales, a certified copy of all the entries of marriage made in the register book during the preceding year, or if there has been no entry during that year, a certificate of that fact[6].

The marriage is proved by production of the official certificate of marriage[7]. After a marriage has been solemnised it is not necessary, in support of the marriage, to give any proof of the requisite residence of either of the parties prior to the marriage, or of the consent of any person whose consent was required by law, and evidence to the contrary may not be given in any legal proceeding touching the validity of the marriage[8]. Where a marriage purports to have been solemnised and registered under the Act in the official house of a British ambassador or consul[9], it is not necessary in support of the marriage to give any proof of the authority of the marriage officer by or before whom the marriage was solemnised and registered, and evidence of his want of authority[10] may not be given in any such proceeding[11].

1 For the meaning of 'marriage officer' see para 713 note 3 ante.
2 See para 719 ante.
3 The register books must be furnished to him from time to time by the Registrar General for England and Wales, through a Secretary of State: Foreign Marriage Act 1892 s 9(2) (amended by the Foreign Marriage (Amendment) Act 1988 s 5(1)).
4 As to the meaning of 'England' see para 604 ante.
5 Foreign Marriage Act 1892 s 9(2) (as amended: see note 3 supra). Every entry must be signed by the marriage officer (or by the person solemnising the marriage if other than that officer), by both parties and by two witnesses: s 9(3). Entries must be in regular order from the beginning to the end of the book, and the number of the entry in each duplicate must be the same: s 9(4). The marriage officer may ask the parties for the required particulars: s 9(5).
6 Ibid s 10(1) (amended by the Foreign Marriage (Amendment) Act 1988 s 5(1)). Every copy must be certified, and certificate given, under the marriage officer's hand and official seal: Foreign Marriage Act 1892 s 10(1) (as so amended). For a form of certificate see the Foreign Marriage Order 1970, SI 1970/1539, art 8, Schedule, Form 3. If either party is shown in a copy of a certificate received by the Registrar General for England and Wales to be from Scotland or Northern Ireland, that Registrar General must send a copy entry to the appropriate Registrar General in Scotland or Northern Ireland: art 6(1) (so numbered by SI 1990/598). The marriage officer must keep the duplicate books until they are filled, and then send one to the Secretary of State for transmission to the Registrar General for England and Wales: Foreign Marriage Act 1892 s 10(2) (amended by the Foreign Marriage (Amendment) Act 1988 s 5(1)).
   Where a marriage officer has no seal of office, reference to the official seal must be construed as reference to any seal ordinarily used by him, if authenticated by his signature with his official name and description: Foreign Marriage Act 1892 s 11(5).
7 The provisions and penalties of the Marriage Registration Acts relating to any registrar or register of marriages, or certified copies, extend to marriage officers and their registers and certified copies, so far as applicable: Foreign Marriage Act 1892 s 17. 'Marriage Registration Acts' means enactments for the time being in force in England and Wales relating to the registration of marriages: s 17 (definition added by the Foreign Marriage (Amendment) Act 1988 s 5(2)). Any books, notices or documents directed to be kept by a marriage officer are documents of such a public nature as to be admissible in evidence on mere production from his custody: Foreign Marriage Act 1892 s 16(1). See further HUSBAND AND WIFE; REGISTRATION CONCERNING THE INDIVIDUAL.
8 Ibid s 13(1). As to the requirements of residence see paras 714, 718 ante. As to the necessary consents see para 715 ante.
9 As to the meaning of 'ambassador', and for the meaning of 'consul', see para 713 note 3 ante.
10 Ie whether by reason of his not being duly authorised, or of any prohibitions or restrictions under the marriage regulations or otherwise: Foreign Marriage Act 1892 s 13(2).
11 Ibid s 13(2) (amended by the Foreign Marriage Act 1947 s 4). Cf *Watts (otherwise Carey) v Watts* (1922) 38 TLR 430.

721. Effect of non-compliance with the statutory requirements. The requirements of the Foreign Marriage Act 1892 as to notices[1], consents[2], the oath before marriage[3] and registration of the marriage[4] are directory only and not mandatory, so that a marriage solemnised under the Act may be valid even if these requirements have not been complied with[5]. On the other hand, the requirements of the Act as to the solemnisation of the marriage[6] are crucial, and they must be complied with in order for the marriage to be valid[7].

1 See para 714 ante.
2 See para 715 ante.
3 See para 718 ante.
4 See para 720 ante.

5 *Collett v Collett* [1968] P 482, [1967] 2 All ER 426.
6 See para 719 ante.
7 *Collett v Collett* [1968] P 482, [1967] 2 All ER 426.

C. MISCELLANEOUS PROVISIONS

722. Registration of foreign marriages celebrated under local law. If satisfied by personal attendance that a marriage between parties of whom one at least is a United Kingdom national[1] has been duly solemnised in accordance with the local law of a foreign country[2], a British consul[3] or person authorised to act as such may, on payment of the proper fee[4], register the marriage in accordance with the marriage regulations[5] as having been so solemnised[6], although registration gives it no more validity than it would otherwise have[7].

1 For the meaning of 'United Kingdom national' see para 713 note 4 ante.
2 Ie presumably outside the Commonwealth: see para 713 note 2 ante.
3 For the meaning of 'consul', see para 713 note 3 ante.
4 As to the proper fee see paras 714 note 5, 719 note 4 ante.
5 As to the making of marriage regulations see the Foreign Marriage Act 1892 s 21 (as amended). No marriage regulations for this purpose were in force at the date at which this volume states the law.
6 On registration the Foreign Marriage Act 1892 applies as if the marriage had been registered in pursuance of the Act (see para 720 ante): s 18(1).
7 Ibid s 18(1) (amended by the Foreign Marriage (Amendment) Act 1988 s 1(3)(a)).

723. Registration of foreign marriage certificates. In the case of marriages between parties of whom at least one is a United Kingdom national[1] solemnised in accordance with the local law of a foreign country[2], at which a British consul[3] or person authorised to act as British consul has not attended[4], provision may be made by Order in Council[5] for the transmission to the Registrar General for England and Wales[6], the Registrar General for Scotland or the Registrar General for Northern Ireland of certificates of such marriages issued in accordance with local law, for the issue by the Registrar General, on payment of a fee, of certified copies of such certificates, and for enabling such copies to be received in evidence[7].

Accordingly, where such a marriage has been so solemnised, a party to the marriage who is a United Kingdom national may produce a certified copy of the entry in the marriage register duly authenticated by the appropriate authority in that country or a marriage certificate issued by that authority, together with an English translation, to the British consul[8] for the district in which the marriage has been solemnised or has taken place[9]; and the consul must, on request, and on payment of the appropriate fee[10], if satisfied that the certificate has been duly issued and that the translation is a true one, transmit the certificate and translation, together with his own certificate as to the accuracy of the translation, to the appropriate Registrar General[11], who may issue a certified copy of any of these documents to any person[12], and a copy of a foreign marriage certificate so issued must be received in evidence without further proof to the same extent as if it were a certificate duly issued by the authorities of the foreign country in which the marriage was celebrated[13].

1 For the meaning of 'United Kingdom national' see para 713 note 4 ante.
2 Ie presumably outside the Commonwealth: see para 713 note 2 ante.
3 For the meaning of 'consul', see para 713 note 3 ante.
4 See text and notes 8–13 infra.
5 Any Order in Council may be varied or revoked by a subsequent Order in Council; and any such Order must be laid forthwith before each House of Parliament: Foreign Marriage Act 1892 s 18(3) (added by the Foreign Marriage Act 1947 s 6).
6 As to the office of Registrar General for England and Wales see REGISTRATION CONCERNING THE INDIVIDUAL vol 39 para 1067 et seq.
7 Foreign Marriage Act 1892 s 18(2) (added by the Foreign Marriage Act 1947 s 6).
8 In the absence of such an officer, the proper person is the appropriate consul of any other government which has undertaken consular representation in the district on behalf of Her Majesty's government in the United Kingdom: Foreign Marriage Order 1970, SI 1970/1539, art 7(1) (amended by SI 1990/598). For the meaning of 'United Kingdom' see para 604 ante.
9 Ibid art 7(1) (as amended: see note 8 supra).
10 As to the proper fee see para 714 note 5 ante. At the date at which this volume states the law, the fee is fixed at £40: Consular Fees Order 1995, SI 1995/1617, art 3, Schedule para 28.
11 Foreign Marriage Order 1970 art 7(1) (as amended: see note 8 supra). In the case of a certificate relating to a party shown to be from Scotland or Northern Ireland, the documents must be sent to the Registrar General for Scotland or Northern Ireland: art 7(1) (as so amended).
12 See ibid art 7(2).
13 Ibid art 7(3).

724. Certificate of no impediment to marriage. A British subject[1] who desires to be married in a foreign[2] country to a foreigner according to the law of that country may, if it is desired for the purpose of complying with the law of the foreign country to obtain a certificate that after proper notices have been given no legal impediment to the marriage has been shown to exist, give notice of the marriage (1) if he is resident in any part of the United Kingdom[3] other than Scotland, to a superintendent registrar of marriages[4]; or (2) if he is resident abroad, to the marriage officer[5], and apply to the registrar or marriage officer for such certificate[6]. After certain conditions[7] have been complied with, the registrar or marriage officer must give the certificate unless it is forbidden[8] or a caveat is in operation[9], or some legal impediment to the marriage is shown to exist[10].

Where arrangements have been made to the satisfaction of Her Majesty with any foreign country for the issue by the proper officers of that country, in the case of persons subject to the marriage law of that country proposing to marry British subjects in any part of the United Kingdom except Scotland, of certificates that, after proper notices have been given, no legal impediment has been shown to exist to the marriage, regulations may be made by Order in Council (1) requiring such a person to give notice of the fact that he is subject to the marriage law of that country to the person by whom or in whose presence the marriage is to be solemnised; and (2) forbidding any person to whom such notice is given to solemnise the marriage or to allow it to be solemnised until such a certificate is produced to him[11].

Her Majesty may by Order in Council make general regulations prescribing forms to be used for these purposes and making such other provisions as seem necessary or expedient, and may by Order in Council revoke, alter or add to any previous such Order in Council[12].

1 For the meaning of 'British subject' see the British Nationality Act 1981 s 51(1); and BRITISH NATIONALITY vol 4(2) (Reissue) paras 3, 52 note 6.
2 Ie presumably outside the Commonwealth: see para 713 note 2 ante.
3 For the meaning of 'United Kingdom' see para 604 ante.
4 See the Marriage with Foreigners Act 1906 s 4.

5 Ie a marriage officer for the time being under the Foreign Marriage Act 1892, including a person empowered under s 18 to register a foreign marriage celebrated under local law: Marriage with Foreigners Act 1906 s 4; and see paras 713 note 3, 722 ante.

6 Ibid s 1(1) (amended by the Marriage (Scotland) Act 1977 ss 28(1), 29(3), Sch 2). Fees may be charged as fixed under the Consular Fees Act 1980: Marriage with Foreigners Act 1906 s 1(4) (amended by the Consular Fees Act 1980 s 1(5)). The fees payable are now fixed by the Consular Fees Order 1995, SI 1995/1617; and the levying, application and remission of, and accounting for, fees are governed by the Consular Fees Regulations 1981, SI 1981/476 (made under s 1(3) of the Consular Fees Act 1980). At the date at which this volume states the law, the fee for receiving notice of an intended marriage is fixed at £35: Consular Fees Order 1995 art 3, Schedule para 25.

7 The conditions are as follows:
    (1) the applicant must sign a notice stating the name, surname, profession, condition, nationality and residence of each of the parties to the marriage, and whether each party is or is not a minor (Marriage with Foreigners Act 1906 s 1(1) (as amended: see note 6 supra), Schedule para 1);
    (2) the applicant must at the time of giving the notice make and subscribe, in a book to be kept by the registrar or marriage officer for the purpose, an oath (a) that he believes there to be no impediment to the marriage by reason of kindred or alliance or otherwise, and (b) that he has for three weeks immediately preceding had his usual residence within the district of the registrar or officer, and (c) if the applicant, not being a widow or widower, is under 18, that the consent of persons whose consent is required by law has been obtained (see note 8 infra), or that there is no person having authority to give such consent, as the case may be (Schedule para 2);
    (3) the registrar or officer must file every such notice and keep it with the archives of his office, and must forthwith enter in a book of notices kept for the purpose, and post up in some conspicuous place in his office, a copy of every such notice, and must keep it so posted for at least 21 days (Schedule para 3);
    (4) the book in which the notice is so entered, and the copy which is so posted, must be open at all reasonable times without fee to the inspection of any person (Schedule para 4).

8 Any person whose consent is required by law to marriages solemnised in England may forbid the certificate by writing the word 'forbidden' opposite the entry of the application in the book of notices, and by subscribing his name and residence and the character by reason of which he is authorised to forbid the certificate: ibid Schedule para 5.

9 Any person may enter with the registrar or officer a caveat against the granting of the certificate, signed by him or on his behalf, and stating his residence and the grounds of his objection: ibid Schedule para 6(a). The registrar or officer must examine into the matter of the caveat and decide whether it ought to obstruct the giving of the certificate or not, but he may if he thinks fit refer the matter to the Registrar General; if he decides the question himself, and decides that the caveat ought to obstruct the giving of the certificate, the applicant for the certificate may appeal to the Registrar General in manner provided by regulations: Schedule para 6(b). The caveat ceases to operate if it is withdrawn by the persons entering it or if it is decided by the registrar, the marriage officer or the Registrar General that it ought not to obstruct the giving of the certificate: Schedule para 6(c). As to the office of Registrar General for England and Wales see REGISTRATION CONCERNING THE INDIVIDUAL vol 39 para 1067 et seq.
    If a person enters a caveat on grounds which the registrar, the marriage officer or the Registrar General on appeal declares to be frivolous, that person is liable to pay as a debt to the applicant such sum as the registrar, the officer or the Registrar General considers to be proper compensation for the damage caused to the applicant by the entering of the caveat: s 1(3).

10 Ibid s 1(1) (as amended: see note 6 supra). At the date at which this volume states the law, the fee for the issue of the certificate is fixed at £35: Consular Fees Order 1995 Schedule para 27.

11 Marriage with Foreigners Act 1906 s 2(1) (amended by the Marriage (Scotland) Act 1977 ss 28(1), 29(3), Sch 2). At the date at which this volume states the law, no Order in Council making such regulations had been made. If a person knowingly acts in contravention of, or fails to comply with, any such regulations, he is guilty of an offence and liable on conviction on indictment to a fine or imprisonment for up to one year: Marriage with Foreigners Act 1906 s 2(2) (amended by virtue of the Criminal Law Act 1977 s 32(1)); Criminal Law Act 1967 ss 1(1), 8, Sch 1 List A Division II para 6(a) (repealed); Courts Act 1971 s 1(2), (3).
    Nothing in the Marriage with Foreigners Act 1906 s 2 relates to a marriage between two persons professing the Jewish religion solemnised according to Jewish usage in the presence of the secretary of a synagogue authorised by what is now the Marriage Act 1949 s 53(c) or the Marriages (Ireland) Act 1844 to register such a marriage, or a deputy appointed in writing under the hand of the secretary, and approved by the president for the time being of the London committee of deputies of the British Jews by writing under his hand: Marriage with Foreigners Act 1906 s 2(3).

12 Ibid s 3. At the date at which this volume states the law, no such Order in Council had been made.

(ii) Capacity to Marry

A. LEGAL CAPACITY

725. Capacity governed by domicile. Capacity to marry[1] is governed by the law of each party's antenuptial domicile[2]. Subject to certain exceptions[3], a marriage is valid as regards capacity if each of the parties has, under the law of his or her antenuptial domicile, capacity to marry the other[4], and, again subject to those exceptions, it is invalid if it is invalid under the law of either party's antenuptial domicile on the ground of that party's[5] incapacity[6].

As an exception to the above rule, a marriage celebrated in England between a party domiciled in England and a party domiciled elsewhere is valid if under English domestic law each of the parties has capacity to marry the other, even if the marriage is invalid under the law of the foreign domicile on the ground of incapacity[7].

A possible further exception to the above rule is that a marriage may be invalid if it is invalid under the *lex loci celebrationis* on the ground of either party's incapacity to marry the other[8].

1 'Capacity' here means legal capacity. As to the law governing the consent of the parties and their physical capacity see paras 730–731 post.
2 *Brook v Brook* (1858) 3 Sm & G 481; affd (1861) 9 HL Cas 193; *Mette v Mette* (1859) 1 Sw & Tr 416 at 423; *Sottomayor v De Barros* (1877) 3 PD 1, CA; *Re Paine, Re Williams, Griffith v Waterhouse* [1940] Ch 46 at 49–50; *R v Brentwood Superintendent Registrar of Marriages, ex p Arias* [1968] 2 QB 956 at 968, [1968] 3 All ER 279 at 282, DC; *Padolecchia v Padolecchia (otherwise Leis)* [1968] P 314 at 336, [1967] 3 All ER 863 at 873; *Szechter (otherwise Karsov) v Szechter* [1971] P 286 at 295, [1970] 3 All ER 905 at 912; Dicey and Morris *The Conflict of Laws* (12th Edn, 1993) 663, rule 70 (approved in *Re Paine, Re Williams, Griffith v Waterhouse* supra; *R v Brentwood Superintendent Registrar of Marriages, ex p Arias* supra; *Padolecchia v Padolecchia (otherwise Leis)* supra). The view that legal capacity to marry is generally governed by the law of the intended matrimonial home (see *Kenward v Kenward* [1951] P 124 at 144–146, [1950] 2 All ER 297 at 309–310, CA; *Ali v Ali* [1968] P 564 at 576, [1966] 1 All ER 664 at 668; *Radwan v Radwan (No 2)* [1973] Fam 35, [1972] 3 All ER 1026) is contrary to the weight of authority; see also, however, *Perrini v Perrini* [1979] Fam 84, [1979] 2 All ER 323.
3 In addition to the exceptions set out in this paragraph, there are three further exceptions: (1) that concerned with remarriage after a decree of divorce or nullity of marriage granted or entitled to recognition in England (see para 728 post); (2) that based on English public policy (see para 729 post); and (3) that of royal marriages (see CONSTITUTIONAL LAW). As to the meaning of 'England' and 'English' see para 604 ante.
4 *Re Bozzelli's Settlement, Husey-Hunt v Bozzelli* [1902] 1 Ch 751; *Re Green, Noyes v Pitkin* (1909) 25 TLR 222; *Vida v Vida* (1961) 105 Sol Jo 913; *Cheni (otherwise Rodriguez) v Cheni* [1965] P 85, [1962] 3 All ER 873; *Alhaji Mohamed v Knott* [1969] 1 QB 1, [1968] 2 All ER 563, DC; *Schwebel v Ungar (otherwise Schwebel)* [1964] 1 OR 430, 42 DLR (2d) 622, Ont CA; on appeal [1965] SCR 148, 48 DLR (2d) 644, Can SC.
5 In *Padolecchia v Padolecchia (otherwise Leis)* [1968] P 314 at 336, [1967] 3 All ER 863 at 873, and *Szechter (otherwise Karsov) v Szechter* [1971] P 286 at 295, [1970] 3 All ER 905 at 912, it was suggested that a marriage is invalid if either party is incapable of marrying the other by the law of either party's domicile; but it is submitted that a party's incapacity under the law of the country in which the other party only is domiciled can be relevant only in so far as it creates an incapacity in that other party; cf *Pugh v Pugh* [1951] P 482, [1951] 2 All ER 680; *Schwebel v Ungar (otherwise Schwebel* [1964] 1 OR 430, 42 DLR (2d) 622, Ont CA; on appeal [1965] SCR 148, 48 DLR (2d) 644, Can SC, approved in *Padolecchia v Padolecchia (otherwise Leis)* supra at 338–339 and at 874–875.
6 *Brook v Brook* (1858) 3 Sm & G 481; affd (1861) 9 HL Cas 193; *Mette v Mette* (1859) 1 Sw & Tr 416; *Chapman v Bradley* (1863) 33 Beav 61; affd 4 De GJ & s 71; *Shaw v Gould* (1868) LR 3 HL 55; *Sottomayor v De Barros* (1877) 3 PD 1, CA; *Re De Wilton, De Wilton v Montefiore* [1900] 2 Ch 481, 69 LJCh 717; *Re Paine, Re Williams, Griffith v Waterhouse* [1940] Ch 46, 108 LJCh 427; *Pugh v Pugh* [1951] P 482, [1951] 2 All ER 680; *R v Brentwood Superintendent Registrar of Marriages, ex p Arias* [1968] 2 QB 956, [1968] 3 All

ER 279, DC; *Padolecchia v Padolecchia (otherwise Leis)* [1968] P 314, [1967] 3 All ER 863; *Szechter (otherwise Karsov) v Szechter* [1971] P 286, [1970] 3 All ER 905.

7 *Sottomayer v De Barros* (1879) 5 PD 94; *Chetti v Chetti* [1909] P 67 at 81–88; *Ogden v Ogden* [1908] P 46 at 74–77, CA; *R v Brentwood Superintendent Registrar of Marriages, ex p Arias* [1968] 2 QB 956 at 968–969, [1968] 3 All ER 279 at 282–283, DC; cf *Ramos v Ramos* (1911) 27 TLR 515.

8 *Breen (otherwise Smith) v Breen* [1964] P 144, [1961] 3 All ER 225; cf *Pugh v Pugh* [1951] P 482 at 491–492, [1951] 2 All ER 680 at 687; *Padolecchia v Padolecchia (otherwise Leis)* [1968] P 314 at 335, [1967] 3 All ER 863 at 873; cf *Re Swan's Will* (1871) 2 VLR (IE & M) 47; *Frew (otherwise Reed) v Reed* (1969) 69 WWR 327, 6 DLR (3d) 617; and see Dicey and Morris *The Conflict of Laws* (12th Edn, 1993) 679, drawing a distinction in this connection between a marriage celebrated in England and a marriage celebrated in a foreign country.

726. Consanguinity and affinity. Subject to certain exceptions[1], a marriage is invalid if it is invalid under the law of either party's antenuptial domicile on the ground that it is within that law's prohibited degrees of consanguinity[2] or affinity[3]. If it is not within those prohibited degrees, it is, again subject to certain exceptions[4], valid as regards capacity notwithstanding that it is within the English prohibited degrees[5].

1 See para 725 note 3 ante.

2 *Sottomayor v De Barros* (1877) 3 PD 1, CA (foreign domicile); *Re De Wilton, De Wilton v Montefiore* [1900] 2 Ch 481 (English domicile); cf *Peal v Peal* [1931] P 97 (British subjects domiciled in India).

3 *Brook v Brook* (1858) 3 Sm & G 481; affd (1861) 9 HL Cas 193; *Mette v Mette* (1859) 1 Sw & Tr 416; *Chapman v Bradley* (1863) 33 Beav 61; affd 4 De G & Sm 71; *Re Paine, Re Williams, Griffith v Waterhouse* [1940] Ch 46, 108 LJCh 427 (all cases of invalidity under the law of English domicile). The Marriage (Enabling) Act 1960 s 1 (as amended) does not validate a marriage if either party is, at the time of the marriage, domiciled in a country outside Great Britain, and under the law of that country there cannot be a valid marriage between the parties: s 1(3). As to that Act and the English prohibited degrees see HUSBAND AND WIFE vol 22 paras 924–926. For the meaning of 'Great Britain' see para 604 ante. As to the meaning of 'English' see para 604 ante.

4 See para 725 note 3 ante.

5 *Re Bozzelli's Settlement, Husey-Hunt v Bozzelli* [1902] 1 Ch 751 (affinity); *Re Green, Noyes v Pitkin* (1909) 25 TLR 222 (affinity); *Cheni (otherwise Rodriguez) v Cheni* [1965] P 85, [1962] 3 All ER 873 (consanguinity).

727. Lack of age. The law governing capacity to marry governs the impediment of lack of age[1]. Subject to certain exceptions[2], a marriage is invalid if it is invalid under the law of either party's antenuptial domicile on this ground[3], and, again subject to certain exceptions[4], it is valid as regards capacity if it is valid under that law notwithstanding that one or both parties is below the English minimum age of marriage[5]. As a person domiciled in England has no capacity to marry any person who is below the English minimum age of marriage, a marriage to which either party is under 16 is void if either party is domiciled in England[6].

1 *Pugh v Pugh* [1951] P 482, [1951] 2 All ER 680; *Alhaji Mohamed v Knott* [1969] 1 QB 1, [1968] 2 All ER 563, DC; cf *Padolecchia v Padolecchia (otherwise Leis)* [1968] P 314 at 340, [1967] 3 All ER 863 at 875–876. As to the age of marriage under English domestic law see HUSBAND AND WIFE vol 22 para 916.

2 See para 725 note 3 ante.

3 *Pugh v Pugh* [1951] P 482, [1951] 2 All ER 680; *Padolecchia v Padolecchia (otherwise Leis)* [1968] P 314 at 340, [1967] 3 All ER 863 at 875–876.

4 See para 725 note 3 ante.

5 *Vida v Vida* (1961) 105 Sol Jo 913; *Alhaji Mohamed v Knott* [1969] 1 QB 1, [1968] 2 All ER 563, DC; cf the Domicile and Matrimonial Proceedings Act 1973 s 3(1), which impliedly recognises that parties may be validly married below the age of 16: see para 701 text and note 1 ante.

6 *Pugh v Pugh* [1951] P 482, [1951] 2 All ER 680.

728. Previous marriage. Subject to certain exceptions[1], a marriage is invalid if it is invalid under the law of either party's antenuptial domicile on the ground that he or she is a party to a prior subsisting marriage[2]. This principle is, however, set aside where a divorce or annulment has been granted by a court of civil jurisdiction in any part of the United Kingdom[3], or the validity of a divorce or annulment is recognised in that part, but the validity of such divorce or annulment is not recognised elsewhere[4]; in such a case, the fact that the divorce or annulment would not be recognised elsewhere does not preclude either party to the marriage from remarrying in that part of the United Kingdom or cause the remarriage of either party (wherever the remarriage takes place) to be treated as invalid in that part[5].

1 See para 725 note 3 ante.
2 *Shaw v Gould* (1868) LR 3 HL 55. This covers the position where a prior marriage is regarded as subsisting because a divorce or annulment is regarded by the law of the domicile of either party to the subsequent marriage as invalid. The strict application of this principle would, therefore, result in a situation in which a party to a divorce granted in or recognised in England could be unable to remarry because of the non-recognition of the divorce in the law of his or her domicile. The issue is the so-called 'incidental question', as to, essentially, whether priority is to be given to the rules relating to capacity to marry or to those governing the recognition of divorces and annulments. See Dicey and Morris *The Conflict of Laws* (12th Edn, 1993) 49–55; cf *Schwebel v Ungar (otherwise Schwebel)* [1964] 1 OR 430, 42 DLR (2d) 622, Ont CA; on appeal [1965] SCR 148, 48 DLR (2d) 644, Can SC.
3 'Part of the United Kingdom' means England and Wales, Scotland or Northern Ireland: Family Law Act 1986 s 54(1). Cf the definition of 'United Kingdom' set out in para 604 ante.
4 See note 2 supra; and para 744 et seq post.
5 Family Law Act 1986 s 50.

729. Public policy. The English court[1] will not recognise an incapacity to marry imposed by a foreign law if to do so would be contrary to English public policy[2]. Thus it will not recognise an incapacity to marry of a penal character[3], or certain types of incapacity to marry of a religious[4] or racial[5] character, at any rate if the marriage is celebrated in England[6]. A prohibition on remarriage following a divorce will be recognised if it is an integral part of the divorce proceedings by which alone both parties to the divorce can be released from their incapacity to contract a fresh marriage[7], but it may be disregarded on the ground of its penal character if it is imposed on the guilty party only[8].

Similarly, in an exceptional case[9] the English court will refuse to recognise a capacity to marry given by the law of the domicile if in the circumstances recognition would be unconscionable[10], as perhaps in the case of a marriage that is incestuous by English criminal law[11].

The court's discretion to refuse to recognise a foreign capacity or incapacity to marry on the ground of public policy is one to be most sparingly exercised[12].

1 As to the meaning of 'English' in relation to courts see para 604 ante.
2 See the cases cited in notes 3–4 infra; *Cheni (otherwise Rodriguez) v Cheni* [1965] P 85 at 98–99, [1962] 3 All ER 873 at 882–883; and see para 611 ante.
3 *Scott v A-G* (1886) 11 PD 128; as explained in *Warter v Warter* (1890) 15 PD 152.
4 *Sottomayer v De Barros* (1879) 5 PD 94 at 104 (incapacity under law of domicile of priest or monk); *Chetti v Chetti* [1909] P 67 (incapacity under Hindu caste rule); *Papadopoulos v Papadopoulos* [1930] P 55 (incapacity to marry otherwise than in accordance with rules of Greek Church); *Gray (otherwise Formosa) v Formosa* [1963] P 259, [1962] 3 All ER 419, CA (incapacity to marry otherwise than in Roman Catholic church; Maltese nullity decree based on this ground not recognised); followed in

Lepre v Lepre [1965] P 52, [1963] 2 All ER 49; *Re Meyer* [1971] P 298 at 309, [1971] 1 All ER 378 at 386–387.

5   *Sottomayer v De Barros* (1879) 5 PD 94 at 104 (colour bar).

6   Although such a limitation is consistent with the decided cases, on principle it should be unnecessary see Dicey and Morris *The Conflict of Laws* (12th Edn, 1993) 681–682.

7   *Warter v Warter* (1890) 15 PD 152; followed in *Le Mesurier (otherwise Gordon) v Le Mesurier* (1930) 46 TLR 203, 142 LT 496; distinguished in *Buckle v Buckle (otherwise Williams)* [1956] P 181, [1955] 3 All ER 641 (on the ground that the prohibition on remarriage within six months of decree absolute under the Indian Divorce Act 1869 s 57 did not apply where jurisdiction was taken by virtue of the Indian and Colonial Divorce Jurisdiction Acts 1926 and 1940 (both repealed). See para 728 ante.

8   *Scott v A-G* (1886) 11 PD 128; as explained in *Warter v Warter* (1890) 15 PD 152. In *R v Brentwood Superintendent Registrar of Marriages, ex p Arias* [1968] 2 QB 956 at 968–969, [1968] 3 All ER 279 at 282–283, DC, the court refused to disregard such an incapacity imposed by the law of a foreign country on the ground that both parties to the proposed remarriage were, and intended to remain, domiciled there.

9   The circumstances would have to be extreme: see paras 610–611 ante.

10   *Cheni (otherwise Rodriguez) v Cheni* [1965] P 85 at 98, [1962] 3 All ER 873 at 882; and see the cases cited in note 11 infra.

11   *Brook v Brook* (1861) 9 HL Cas 193 at 227–228; *Re Bozzelli's Settlement, Husey-Hunt v Bozzelli* [1902] 1 Ch 751 at 754–757; *Cheni (otherwise Rodriguez) v Cheni* [1965] P 85 at 97, [1962] 3 All ER 873 at 882 Cf *Alhaji Mohamed v Knott* [1969] 1 QB 1 at 16–17, [1968] 2 All ER 563 at 568, DC.

12   *Cheni (otherwise Rodriguez) v Cheni* [1965] P 85 at 98–99, [1962] 3 All ER 873 at 882–883; *R v Brentwood Superintendent Registrar of Marriages, ex p Arias* [1968] 2 QB 956 at 968–969, [1968] 3 All ER 279 at 282–283, DC; *Qureshi v Qureshi* [1972] Fam 173 at 201, [1971] 1 All ER 325 at 346. See paras 610–611 ante.

B. CONSENT OF PARTIES

730. Law governing consent of parties. The consent of the parties is a matter of the essential validity of a marriage[1]. Subject to certain exceptions[2], a marriage is invalid if it is invalid under the law of either party's antenuptial domicile on the ground of that party's lack of consent[3]. It is, possibly, also invalid if it is invalid under the *lex loci celebrationis* on the ground of either party's lack of consent[4]. Otherwise the marriage is probably valid in England so far as its validity relies upon the parties' consent, unless and until it is annulled by the English court on the ground of lack of consent under English domestic law[5].

1   *Szechter (otherwise Karsov) v Szechter* [1971] P 286 at 294–295, [1970] 3 All ER 905 at 912; cf *Apt v Apt* [1948] P 83 at 88, [1947] 2 All ER 677 at 679, CA.

2   See para 725 note 3 ante.

3   *Way v Way, Rowley v Rowley, Kenward v Kenward, Whitehead v Whitehead* [1950] P 71 at 78–79, [1949] 2 All ER 959 at 963; on appeal sub nom *Kenward v Kenward* [1951] P 124 at 133, [1950] 2 All ER 297 at 302, CA; *Szechter (otherwise Karsov) v Szechter* [1971] P 286 at 294–295, [1970] 3 All ER 905 at 912. In both of these cases the law of the domicile coincided with that of the place where the marriage was celebrated. See also, in respect of a marriage celebrated in England between a party domiciled in England and a party domiciled elsewhere, *Vervaeke v Smith* [1981] Fam 77, [1981] 1 All ER 55, Family Division and CA; affd, but not on this point, [1983] 1 AC 145, [1982] 2 All ER 144, HL.

4   See para 725 ante; *Parojcic (otherwise Ivetic) v Parojcic* [1959] 1 All ER 1 at 4, [1958] 1 WLR 1280 at 1283; cf *Cooper v Crane* [1891] P 369; *Valier v Valier (otherwise Davis)* (1925) 133 LT 830; *Hussein (otherwise Blitz) v Hussein* [1938] P 159, [1938] 2 All ER 344. In all of these cases the marriage was celebrated in England

5   In all of the cases cited in notes 3–4 supra, the law applied was effectively English domestic law. In *Szechter (otherwise Karsov) v Szechter* [1971] P 286 at 295, 298, [1970] 3 All ER 905 at 912, 915, English law was applied cumulatively with the law of the domicile; cf *Re Meyer* [1971] P 298 at 305–306, [1971] 1 All ER 378 at 383–384. See also *Mehta (otherwise Kohn) v Mehta* [1945] 2 All ER 690; *H v H* [1954] P 258, [1953] 2 All ER 1229; *Silver (otherwise Kraft) v Silver* [1955] 2 All ER 614, [1955] 1 WLR 728; *Kassim (otherwise Widmann) v Kassim (otherwise Hassim) (Carl and Dickson cited)* [1962] P 224, [1962] 3 All ER 426 *Buckland v Buckland (otherwise Camilleri)* [1968] P 296, [1967] 2 All ER 300. Before 1971 there was some doubt as to whether a lack of consent rendered a marriage void or voidable in English domestic law, but

the matter is clarified by the Matrimonial Causes Act 1973 s 12(c), which provides that lack of consent, whether in consequence of duress, mistake, unsoundness of mind or otherwise, renders a marriage voidable if it was celebrated after 31 July 1971. That Act does not affect the English conflict rules applicable to this question in so far as they refer to any foreign law: see s 14(1). For the English domestic rules applicable to lack of consent see ss 12(c)–(f), 13 (s 12(d) amended by the Mental Health Act 1983 s 148, Sch 4 para 34)); and see DIVORCE; HUSBAND AND WIFE.

C. PHYSICAL CAPACITY

731. Law governing physical capacity of parties. A marriage is invalid if it is invalid under the law of the petitioner's domicile at the date of the marriage on the ground of either party's incapacity or wilful refusal to consummate the marriage[1]. Otherwise it is probably valid in England so far as this aspect of validity is concerned unless and until it is annulled by the English court on one or other of these grounds under English domestic law[2].

1 *De Reneville v De Reneville* [1948] P 100, [1948] 1 All ER 56, CA (a decision on the jurisdiction of the English court to grant a nullity decree); cf *Ponticelli v Ponticelli (otherwise Giglio)* [1958] P 204, [1958] 1 All ER 357.
2 *Easterbrook v Easterbrook* [1944] P 10, [1944] 1 All ER 90; *Hutter v Hutter* [1944] P 95, [1944] 2 All ER 368; *Ross Smith v Ross Smith (otherwise Radford)* [1963] AC 280 at 306, 313, 322, [1962] 1 All ER 344 at 356, 361, 367, HL (suggesting that, had the court in that case taken jurisdiction over the voidable marriage, it would have applied the English grounds of nullity regardless of whether they existed under the law of the husband's domicile); *Magnier v Magnier* (1968) 112 Sol Jo 233. Contrast *Robert (otherwise De La Mare) v Robert* [1947] P 164 at 167–168, [1947] 2 All ER 22 at 24; *Addison (otherwise McAllister) v Addison* [1955] NI 1 at 30 (both cases favouring application of the *lex loci celebrationis*; overruled on the question of jurisdiction in *De Reneville v De Reneville* [1948] P 100 at 118, [1948] 1 All ER 56 at 63, CA; and *Ross Smith v Ross Smith (otherwise Radford)* supra at 306, 312, 348, and at 356, 369, 384, HL, respectively); *Ponticelli v Ponticelli (otherwise Giglio)* [1958] P 204 at 211–216, [1958] 1 All ER 357 at 360–363, following *Way v Way, Rowley v Rowley, Kenward v Kenward, Whitehead v Whitehead* [1950] P 71 at 80, [1949] 2 All ER 959 at 964; and not following *Robert (otherwise De La Mare) v Robert* supra, favouring application of the law of the husband's domicile; but in all of these cases there was no difference between the law which was applied and English law. As to the English domestic rules applicable to incapacity and wilful refusal to consummate a marriage see the Matrimonial Causes Act 1973 ss 12(a), (b), 13(1); and DIVORCE vol 13 para 539; HUSBAND AND WIFE vol 22 para 920.

(iii) Polygamous Marriages

732. Distinction between monogamous and polygamous marriage. The essential requirement of a monogamous marriage is that it must be the voluntary union for life of one man and one woman to the exclusion of all others[1]. A marriage is monogamous if it complies with this requirement, even though it can be dissolved by mutual consent or at the will of either party with merely formal conditions of official registration[2]. A marriage is polygamous if it is celebrated under a law[3] which permits the husband[4], during the subsistence of the marriage, without any change in his personal law[5], to take more than one wife, or to take concubines if concubinage has a recognised status under that law[6], whether or not he actually does so[7].

1 *Hyde v Hyde and Woodmansee* (1866) LR 1 P & D 130 at 133; *Re Bethell, Bethell v Hildyard* (1888) 38 ChD 220 at 234; *Brinkley v A-G* (1890) 15 PD 76 at 79–80; *R v Hammersmith Superintendent Registrar of Marriages, ex p Mir-Anwaruddin* [1917] 1 KB 634 at 657, 660, CA; *Nachimson v Nachimson* [1930] P 217 at 224, 227–228, 237–238, CA.
2 *Nachimson v Nachimson* [1930] P 217, CA.
3 See para 733 post.

4   A marriage in which the wife is allowed to have more than one husband (a polyandrous as opposed to a polygynous marriage) is also a polygamous marriage for this purpose.

5   Ie the law governing personal status. This is determined by the law of the domicile. Where this refers the matter of personal status to the religious law of the person concerned, his personal law will depend upon his religion. For the effect of a change in the husband's personal law see para 735 post.

6   *Lee v Lau* [1967] P 14, [1964] 2 All ER 248; cf *Re Bethell, Bethell v Hildyard* (1888) 38 ChD 220.

7   *Hyde v Hyde and Woodmansee* (1866) LR 1 P & D 130. The marriage is potentially polygamous until the husband has exercised his right to take more than one wife or to take further concubines; thereafter it is actually polygamous. Cf *Hussain v Hussain* [1983] Fam 26, [1982] 3 All ER 369, CA, considered in para 733 post. Note that, in relation to the question of the validity of a marriage, a marriage is void for polygamy where one of the parties is domiciled in England and Wales, but a potentially polygamous marriage is not polygamous for this purpose: see the Matrimonial Causes Act 1973 s 11 (as amended); and para 736 post.

733. Determination of nature of marriage. Whether a marriage is monogamous or polygamous in character depends upon the nature and incidents of the marriage according to the *lex loci celebrationis*[1]. Thus, a marriage is monogamous if celebrated in monogamous form in England[2] or elsewhere[3]. Subject to two exceptions, a marriage is polygamous if it is celebrated in polygamous form in a country permitting polygamy[4]. The first exception is that if neither party to a marriage has capacity under his or her personal law[5] to marry a second spouse, the marriage will be treated, at least for some purposes, as monogamous even though celebrated in polygamous form in a country permitting polygamy[6]. The second exception is that, as regards the question of the validity of a marriage where one of the parties is domiciled in England and Wales, it is not polygamous if at the time neither party was actually already married[7].

1   *Cheni (otherwise Rodriguez) v Cheni* [1965] P 85 at 90, [1962] 3 All ER 873 at 877; *Lee v Lau* [1967] P 14 at 20, [1964] 2 All ER 248 at 252; Dicey and Morris *The Conflict of Laws* (12th Edn, 1993) 689–690. Once the nature and incidents of the union have been ascertained according to local law, the monogamous or polygamous character of the marriage is a question of English law: *Lee v Lau* supra. For the effect of a change in the husband's personal law see para 735 post.

2   *Chetti v Chetti* [1909] P 67; *R v Hammersmith Superintendent Registrar of Marriages, ex p Mir-Anwaruddin* [1917] 1 KB 634, CA; *Hussein (otherwise Blitz) v Hussein* [1938] P 159, [1938] 2 All ER 344; *Srini Vasan (otherwise Clayton) v Srini Vasan* [1946] P 67, [1945] 2 All ER 21; *Baindail (otherwise Lawson) v Baindail* [1946] P 122, [1946] 1 All ER 342, CA; *Maher v Maher* [1951] P 342, [1951] 2 All ER 37; *Ohochuku v Ohochuku* [1960] 1 All ER 253, [1960] 1 WLR 183; *Russ (otherwise Geffers) v Russ (Russ otherwise De Waele intervening)* [1964] P 315, [1962] 3 All ER 193, CA; *Qureshi v Qureshi* [1972] Fam 173, [1971] 1 All ER 325; *Singh v Singh* [1971] P 226, [1971] 2 All ER 828, CA; *Hashmi v Hashmi* [1972] Fam 36, [1971] 3 All ER 1253. As to the meaning of 'England' see para 604 ante.

3   *Brinkley v A-G* (1890) 15 PD 76 (Japanese marriage); *Spivack v Spivack* (1930) 142 LT 492, DC (Jewish marriage in Poland); *Penhas v Tan Soo Eng* [1953] AC 304, [1953] 2 WLR 459, PC (composite marriage ceremony in Singapore).

4   *Re Bethell, Bethell v Hildyard* (1888) 38 ChD 220 (husband domiciled in England); *Risk (otherwise Yerburgh) v Risk* [1951] P 50, [1950] 2 All ER 973 (wife domiciled in England); *Ohochuku v Ohochuku* [1960] 1 All ER 253, [1960] 1 WLR 183 (the Nigerian marriage); *Sowa v Sowa* [1961] P 70 at 80, [1961] 1 All ER 687, CA.

5   As to personal law see para 732 note 5 ante.

6   *Hussain v Hussain* [1983] Fam 26, [1982] 3 All ER 369, CA, where for the purposes of the Matrimonial Causes Act 1973 s 11(d) (see para 736 note 6 post) a marriage celebrated in polygamous form in Pakistan was not polygamous because the right to take a second spouse did not extend to the wife, and the husband was domiciled in England and therefore unable, by his personal law, to take a further spouse (see s 11(b)).

7   See ibid s 11 (as amended); and para 736 text and note 6 post.

734. Marriages celebrated in England. A marriage celebrated in England[1] in accordance with the provisions of the Marriage Act 1949[2], whether in a register office[3] or in a registered building[4] or in approved premises[5] or otherwise[6], is monogamous, wherever the parties may be domiciled[7]. A marriage celebrated in England in polygamous form without a preceding civil ceremony[8] is a nullity[9].

1 As to the meaning of 'England' see para 604 ante.
2 As to the provisions of the Marriage Act 1949 see generally HUSBAND AND WIFE.
3 As to marriages in register offices and other places see ibid ss 45, 45A, 46 (s 45A as added, s 46 as amended); and HUSBAND AND WIFE.
4 As to marriages in registered buildings see ibid ss 41–44 (ss 41–43 as amended). See also the Sharing of Church Buildings Act 1969 s 6, Sch 1 (as amended); and ECCLESIASTICAL LAW; HUSBAND AND WIFE.
5 As to marriages in approved premises see the Marriage Act ss 46A, 46B (as added): and HUSBAND AND WIFE.
6 See eg ibid s 26(i)(dd) (as added); and the Marriage (Registrar General's Licence) Act 1970 s 9.
7 See the cases cited in para 733 note 4 ante.
8 A marriage solemnised in the presence of a superintendent registrar may lawfully be followed by a religious ceremony: Marriage Act 1949 s 46(1) (amended by the Marriage Act 1983 s 1(7), Sch 1 para 12). See also the Marriage (Registrar General's Licence) Act 1970 s 11(1). However, such a religious ceremony does not supersede or invalidate the civil ceremony and is not to be registered as a marriage: Marriage Act 1949 s 46(2) (amended by the Marriage Act 1983 Sch 1 para 12), applied by the Marriage (Registrar General's Licence) Act 1970 s 11(2).
9 *R v Bham* [1966] 1 QB 159, [1965] 3 All ER 124, CCA; *Qureshi v Qureshi* [1972] Fam 173 at 186, [1971] 1 All ER 325 at 333. This follows from the principle *locus regit actum* (the place governs the act): see para 706 ante.

735. Change in character of marriage. In determining the monogamous or polygamous character of a marriage, the possibility of a change of personal law[1] by the husband[2] and the possibility of a change in the substantive rules of the husband's personal law are disregarded unless and until they materialise[3]. When they do materialise, they may have a decisive effect upon the character of the marriage. Thus, a potentially polygamous marriage may be converted into a monogamous marriage by reason of subsequent events, as where the husband changes his religion to a monogamous religion[4], or his domicile to a country whose law prohibits polygamy[5], or where the *lex loci celebrationis* prohibits polygamy as a result of subsequent legislation[6], or prohibits it after the birth of a child[7], or where the parties subsequently go through a monogamous marriage ceremony[8]. It is uncertain whether a monogamous marriage can be converted into a potentially polygamous one by subsequent events[9].

1 As to personal law see para 732 note 5 ante.
2 See para 732 note 4 ante.
3 'After all, there are no marriages which are not potentially polygamous, in the sense that they may be rendered so by a change of domicile and religion on the part of the spouses': *Cheni (otherwise Rodriguez) v Cheni* [1965] P 85 at 90, [1962] 3 All ER 873 at 877 per Sir Jocelyn Simon P; approved in *A-G of Ceylon v Reid* [1965] AC 720 at 734, [1965] 1 All ER 812 at 817, PC; *Parkasho v Singh* [1968] P 233 at 244, [1967] 1 All ER 737 at 743, DC; and see *Mehta (otherwise Kohn) v Mehta* [1945] 2 All ER 690.
4 *Sinha Peerage Claim* (1939) 171 Lords Journals 350, [1946] 1 All ER 348n (Committee of Privileges); as explained in *Cheni (otherwise Rodriguez) v Cheni* [1965] P 85 at 90, [1962] 3 All ER 873 at 877–878; and in *Parkasho v Singh* [1968] P 233 at 243, 253, [1967] 1 All ER 737 at 742, 748, DC.
5 *Ali v Ali* [1968] P 564, [1966] 1 All ER 664; *Mirza v Mirza* (1966) 110 Sol Jo 708.
6 *Parkasho v Singh* [1968] P 233, [1967] 1 All ER 737, DC; cf *Cheni (otherwise Rodriguez) v Cheni* [1965] P 85 at 89, [1962] 3 All ER 873 at 876–877.
7 *Cheni (otherwise Rodriguez) v Cheni* [1965] P 85, [1962] 3 All ER 873.
8 *Ohochuku v Ohochuku* [1960] 1 All ER 253, [1960] 1 WLR 183; cf *Sowa v Sowa* [1961] P 70 at 82–83, [1961] 1 All ER 687 at 688, CA; *Cheni (otherwise Rodriguez) v Cheni* [1965] P 85 at 89, [1962] 3 All ER 873 at 876.
9 See *Cheni (otherwise Rodriguez) v Cheni* [1965] P 85 at 90, [1962] 3 All ER 873 at 877; *A-G of Ceylon v Reid* [1965] AC 720, [1965] 1 All ER 812, PC; cf *Mehta (otherwise Kohn) v Mehta* [1945] 2 All ER 690. For a discussion of this question see Dicey and Morris *The Conflict of Laws* (12th Edn, 1993) 693–695.

736. Capacity to contract polygamous marriage. Capacity to contract a polygamous marriage is governed by the law of each party's antenuptial domicile[1]. It has been held that the matter is governed by the law of the country of the parties' intended matrimonial residence[2], and it may be that capacity under that law would be accepted as an alternative to capacity under the law of the domicile[3]. Subject to that possibility, a person whose personal law[4] does not permit polygamy has no capacity to contract an actually polygamous marriage[5], and a polygamous marriage is void if entered into outside England and Wales and if at the time of the marriage either party is domiciled in England and Wales[6].

1 *Hussain v Hussain* [1983] Fam 26, [1982] 3 All ER 369, CA. See also *Re Ullee, Nawab Nazim of Bengal's Infants* (1885) 53 LT 711 at 712; *Re Bethell, Bethell v Hildyard* (1888) 38 ChD 220; *Risk (otherwise Yerburgh) v Risk* [1951] P 50, [1950] 2 All ER 973; *Ali v Ali* [1968] P 564, [1966] 1 All ER 664; *Mirza v Mirza* (1966) 110 Sol Jo 708; *Crowe v Kader* [1968] WAR 122 (potentially polygamous marriage in Penang between Muslim domiciled in Malaysia and woman domiciled in Australia held to be void). As to legal capacity see para 725 ante.
2 *Radwan v Radwan (No 2)* [1973] Fam 35, [1972] 3 All ER 1026; cf *Kenward v Kenward* [1951] P 124 at 145, [1950] 2 All ER 297 at 310, CA.
3 See Dicey and Morris *The Conflict of Laws* (12th Edn, 1993) 700.
4 As to personal law see para 732 note 5 ante.
5 See the cases cited in note 1 supra.
6 Matrimonial Causes Act 1973 s 11(d), which applies to marriages celebrated after 31 July 1971. For the purposes of s 11(d) a marriage is not polygamous if at its inception neither party has any spouse additional to the other: s 11 (amended by the Private International Law (Miscellaneous Provisions) Act 1995 s 8(2), Schedule para 2(1), (2)). See, however, *Hussain v Hussain* [1983] Fam 26, [1982] 3 All ER 369, CA; and para 733 ante on the question as to when a marriage will be regarded for this purpose as polygamous; and see the other cases cited in note 1 supra.

737. Recognition of polygamous marriages. A polygamous marriage which is valid under the *lex loci celebrationis* as regards form[1], and under the law of each party's antenuptial domicile as regards capacity[2], will be recognised in England[3] as a valid marriage unless there is some strong reason to the contrary[4]. During its subsistence the marriage will be held to constitute a bar to a subsequent marriage in England[5] or, probably, to a subsequent monogamous marriage elsewhere[6], and effect will be given to the legal consequences flowing from the marriage, such as the legitimacy of the children[7] and rights of succession to property[8]. The fact that the marriage was celebrated under a law permitting polygamy[9] does not preclude the English court from granting matrimonial relief or making a declaration concerning the validity of the marriage[10].

For the purpose of social security legislation, a polygamous marriage is to be treated as having the same consequences as a monogamous marriage for any day throughout which it is in fact monogamous[11].

1 See paras 706–707, 734 ante.
2 See para 736 ante.
3 As to the meaning of 'England' see para 604 ante.
4 Dicey and Morris *The Conflict of Laws* (12th Edn, 1993) 703, Rule 76, approved (under the number given in earlier editions of that text) in *Shahnaz v Rizwan* [1965] 1 QB 390 at 397, [1964] 2 All ER 993 at 995, and in *Alhaji Mohamed v Knott* [1969] 1 QB 1 at 13–14, [1968] 2 All ER 563 at 566–567, DC. There are now very few exceptions to the recognition for all purposes of a valid polygamous marriage: see notes 5, 8, 12 infra.
5 *Srini Vasan (otherwise Clayton) v Srini Vasan* [1946] P 67, [1945] 2 All ER 21; *Baindail (otherwise Lawson) v Baindail* [1946] P 122, [1946] 1 All ER 342, CA. On the other hand, a polygamous marriage is apparently not a sufficient first marriage to support an indictment for bigamy: *R v Sarwan Singh* [1962] 3 All ER 612, Quarter Sessions; cf *Harvey v Farnie* (1880) 6 PD 35 at 53, CA; *R v Naguib* [1917] 1 KB 359,

CCA; *Baindail (otherwise Lawson) v Baindail* supra at 130 and at 347, CA; *A-G of Ceylon v Reid* [1965] AC 720, [1965] 1 All ER 812, PC.

6 *Shahnaz v Rizwan* [1965] 1 QB 390 at 396–397, [1964] 2 All ER 993 at 995.

7 *Sinha Peerage Claim* (1939) 171 Lords Journals 350, [1946] 1 All ER 348n (Committee of Privileges); *Baindail (otherwise Lawson) v Bandail* [1946] P 122 at 128, [1946] 1 All ER 342 at 346, CA; *Lee v Lau* [1967] P 14 at 23, [1964] 2 All ER 248 at 254; cf *Hashmi v Hashmi* [1972] Fam 36, [1971] 3 All ER 1253.

8 *Sinha Peerage Claim* (1939) 171 Lords Journals 350, [1946] 1 All ER 348n (Committee of Privileges); *Baindail (otherwise Lawson) v Baindail* [1946] P 122 at 127–128, [1946] 1 All ER 342 at 346, CA; *Lee v Lau* [1967] P 14 at 23, [1964] 2 All ER 248 at 254. Cf *Cheang Thye Phin v Tan Ah Loy* [1920] AC 369, PC; *Khoo Hooi Leong v Khoo Hean Kwee* [1926] AC 529, PC; *Khoo Hooi Leong v Khoo Chong Yeok* [1930] AC 346, PC; *Bamgbose v Daniel* [1955] AC 107, [1954] 3 All ER 263, PC; *Coleman v Shang alias Quartey* [1961] AC 481, [1961] 2 All ER 406, PC. There is a possible exception to this in the case of the right to succeed as heir to real estate in England: *Sinha Peerage Claim* supra; and see para 788 post. See also *Re Sehota, Surjit Kaur v Gian Kaur* [1978] 3 All ER 385, [1978] 1 WLR 1506 (right to apply under the Inheritance (Provision for Family and Dependants) Act 1975); and EXECUTORS vol 17 para 1319 et seq.

9 Ie a marriage which is potentially or actually polygamous at its inception. A marriage which is monogamous at its inception is treated for the present purpose as always remaining monogamous: see para 735 ante.

o See paras 739–740 post. As to the meaning of 'English' in relation to courts see para 604 ante.

1 See the Social Security and Family Allowances (Polygamous Marriages) Regulations 1975, SI 1975/561 (amended by SI 1989/1642); Child Benefit (General) Regulations 1976, SI 1976/965, reg 12. Contrast *Imam Din v National Assistance Board* [1967] 2 QB 213, [1967] 1 All ER 750, DC (wife of a polygamous marriage, whether actually or potentially polygamous, may be a 'wife' within the meaning of the National Assistance Act 1948 s 42(1)).

738. Monogamous marriage celebrated under law permitting polygamy. A

marriage entered into outside England and Wales[1] on or after 8 January 1996[2] between parties neither of whom is already married, is not void under English law[3] on the ground that it is entered into under a law which permits polygamy and that either party is domiciled in England and Wales[4]. This is deemed also to apply to any marriage entered into before that date[5], except:

(1) a marriage a party to which has (also before that date) entered into a later marriage which (a) is valid apart from this provision[6] but would be void if the provision described above[7] applied to the earlier marriage[8], or (b) is valid by virtue of this provision[9]; and

(2) a marriage which has been annulled[10] before that date, whether by a decree granted in England and Wales or by an annulment obtained elsewhere and recognised in England and Wales at that date[11].

1 As to the meaning of 'England and Wales' see para 604 ante.

2 Ie the date on which the Private International Law (Miscellaneous Provisions) Act 1995 Pt II (ss 5–8) comes into force: s 16(2). Nothing in Pt II affects any law or custom relating to the marriage of members of the royal family: s 8(1).

3 As to the meaning of 'English law' see para 604 ante.

4 Private International Law (Miscellaneous Provisions) Act 1995 s 5(1). This does not, however, affect the determination of the validity of a marriage by reference to the law of another country to the extent that it falls to be so determined in accordance with the rules of private international law: s 5(2).

5 Ibid s 6(1). However, nothing in s 5, in its application to marriages entered into before 8 January 1996 (1) gives or affects any entitlement to an interest under the will or codicil of, or on the intestacy of, a person who died before that date, or under a settlement or other disposition of property made before that time (otherwise than by will or codicil); (2) gives or affects any entitlement to a benefit, allowance, pension or other payment payable before or in respect of a period before that date, or payable in respect of the death of a person before that date; (3) affects tax in respect of a period or event before that date; or (4) affects the succession to any dignity or title of honour: s 6(6).

6 Ie valid apart from ibid s 6.

7 Ie ibid s 5: see text and notes 1–4 supra.

8 Ibid s 6(2)(a).

9　Ie by virtue of ibid s 6: s 6(2)(b).

10　A marriage which has been declared invalid by a court of competent jurisdiction in any proceedings concerning either the validity of the marriage or any right dependent on its validity, is treated for this purpose as having been annulled: ibid s 6(5).

11　Ibid s 6(3). An annulment resulting from legal proceedings begun before 8 January 1996 must be treated for this purpose as having taken effect before that date: s 6(4). Section 6(5) (see note 10 supra) also applies for the purposes of s 6(4).

(2) MATRIMONIAL CAUSES

(i) Introduction; Polygamous Marriages

739. Jurisdiction. A court in England and Wales is not precluded from granting matrimonial relief or making a declaration concerning the validity of a marriage by reason only that either party to the marriage is, or during the subsistence of the marriage has been, married to more than one person[1]. 'Matrimonial relief' here means[2]: (1) any decree under Part I of the Matrimonial Causes Act 1973[3]; (2) an order for financial provision on the ground of failure to provide reasonable maintenance[4]; (3) an order for the alteration of a maintenance agreement[5]; (4) ancillary relief[6]; (5) an order under Part III of the Matrimonial and Family Proceedings Act 1984[7]; and (6) an order under Part I of the Domestic Proceedings and Magistrates' Courts Act 1978[8]. A 'declaration concerning the validity of a marriage' means any declaration under Part III of the Family Law Act 1986[9] involving a determination as to the validity of a marriage[10].

1　Matrimonial Causes Act 1973 s 47(1) (amended by the Private International Law (Miscellaneous Provisions) Act 1995 s 8(2), Schedule para 2(1), (3)(a)). The enactment of this provision effectively abolished the rule in *Hyde v Hyde and Woodmansee* (1866) LR 1 P & D 130. As to the validity and effect of polygamous marriages see paras 732–737 ante, 740 text and note 1 post. Provision may be made by rules of court for requiring notice of proceedings for matrimonial relief to be served on any additional spouse of a party to the marriage in question, and for conferring on any such additional spouse the right to be heard in any proceedings: Matrimonial Causes Act 1973 s 47(4) (substituted by the Private International Law (Miscellaneous Provisions) Act 1995 Schedule para 2(3)(b)). See the Family Proceedings Rules 1991, SI 1991/1247, r 3.11.

2　Matrimonial Causes Act 1973 s 47(2) (amended by the Domestic Proceedings and Magistrates' Courts Act 1978 s 89, Sch 2 para 39; and by the Matrimonial and Family Proceedings Act 1984 s 46(1), Sch 1 para 15).

3　Ie any decree under the Matrimonial Causes Act 1973 Pt I (ss 1–20) (as amended), namely, a decree of divorce, judicial separation, nullity of marriage, or presumption of death and dissolution of marriage (see paras 741–742, 751 post): s 47(2)(a).

4　Ie an order under ibid s 27 (as amended) (see para 755 post): s 47(2)(b).

5　Ie an order under ibid s 35 (see para 759 post) (as amended): s 47(2)(c).

6　Ie any order under any provision of the Matrimonial Causes Act 1973 which confers a power exercisable in connection with, or in with connection with proceedings for, any decree or order mentioned in heads (1)–(3) in the text: s 47(2)(d).

7　Ie an order under the Matrimonial and Family Proceedings Act 1984 Pt III (ss 12–27) (as amended), namely an order for financial relief for the parties to the marriage and the children of the family (see para 755 post) or an order relating to children (see para 774 et seq post): Matrimonial Causes Act 1973 s 47(2)(dd) (added by the Matrimonial and Family Proceedings Act 1984 s 46(1), Sch 1 para 15).

8　Ie an order under the Domestic Proceedings and Magistrates' Courts Act 1978 Pt I (ss 1–35) (as amended) (certain orders relating to financial relief and protection of parties) (see further para 757 post): Matrimonial Causes Act 1973 s 47(2)(e) (amended by the Domestic Proceedings and Magistrates' Courts Act 1978 s 89(2)(a), Sch 2 para 39).

9　Ie the Family Law Act 1986 Pt III (ss 55–67) (as amended).

10　Matrimonial Causes Act 1973 s 47(3) (substituted by the Family Law Act 1986 s 68, Sch 1 para 14).

740. Application to divorce and nullity of marriage. The statement of the law set out in the preceding paragraph does not mean that one wife of a valid polygamous marriage can obtain a divorce on the ground that the husband has committed adultery with another wife and that she finds it intolerable to live with him[1]. This is because both marriages are valid, and it is impossible to commit adultery with one's own spouse[2]. Nor does it mean that the second wife could obtain a decree of nullity on the ground of bigamy, for if each marriage was validly celebrated in polygamous form under a law permitting polygamy, and if the parties to each marriage had capacity to contract such a marriage by the law of their antenuptial domicile[3], the second marriage cannot be void for bigamy[4]. In the case of divorce petitions based on behaviour or desertion, the background of the parties[5] will be taken into account, and entry into a second marriage may be relevant to that extent[6].

On the other hand, if a Muslim domiciled in India marries a woman domiciled there in polygamous form in India, and subsequently goes through a ceremony with another woman in England[7], or subsequently acquires an English domicile and goes through a ceremony with another woman in India or elsewhere[8], the second wife could obtain a decree of nullity on the ground of bigamy.

1 Ie under the Matrimonial Causes Act 1973 s 1(2)(a): see DIVORCE.
2 See Rayden on Divorce (16th Edn) 197.
3 See paras 736–737 ante.
4 See the Matrimonial Causes Act 1973 s 11(b), which provides that a marriage is void if at the time of the marriage either party was already lawfully married and which, therefore, could hardly apply to such a case.
5 This includes Muslim law if it governed the inception of the marriage: *Quoraishi v Quoraishi* [1985] FLR 780, CA.
6 *Quoraishi v Quoraishi* [1985] FLR 780, CA.
7 *Baindail (otherwise Lawson) v Baindail* [1946] P 122, [1946] 1 All ER 342, CA. As to the meaning of 'England' see para 604 ante.
8 See the Matrimonial Causes Act 1973 s 11(d); and para 736 ante.

(ii) Divorce, Nullity of Marriage and Judicial Separation

A. JURISDICTION OF THE ENGLISH COURT

741. Divorce and judicial separation. The English court[1] has jurisdiction to entertain proceedings for divorce or for judicial separation if, and only if, either of the parties to the marriage is domiciled in England[2] on the date when the proceedings are begun or was habitually resident[3] in England throughout the period of one year ending with that date[4].

At any time when proceedings are pending which the court has jurisdiction to entertain[5], the court also has jurisdiction to entertain other proceedings, in respect of the same marriage, for divorce, judicial separation or nullity of marriage, notwithstanding that the court would not otherwise have such jurisdiction[6].

The exercise of the English court's jurisdiction in proceedings for divorce or judicial separation is subject to rules requiring or enabling the court to stay those proceedings in certain circumstances. These rules are considered elsewhere in this title[7].

1 In the Domicile and Matrimonial Proceedings Act 1973 Pt II (ss 5–6) (as amended), 'court' means the High Court and a divorce county court within the meaning of the Matrimonial and Family Proceed-

ings Act 1984 Pt V (ss 32–42) (as amended): Domicile and Matrimonial Proceedings Act 1973 s 5(1 (amended by the Matrimonial and Family Proceedings Act 1984 s 46(1), Sch 1 para 17). As to the meaning of 'English' in relation to courts see para 604 ante. See further COUNTY COURTS; DIVORCE
2 As to the meaning of 'England' see para 604 ante.
3 As to the meaning of 'habitually resident' see *Kapur v Kapur* [1984] FLR 920; and para 705 ante.
4 Domicile and Matrimonial Proceedings Act 1973 s 5(1)(a), (2).
5 Ie under ibid s 5(2), (3) or (5).
6 Ibid s 5(5).
7 See ibid s 5(6), Sch 1 (as amended); and paras 760–763 post.

742. Nullity of marriage. The English court[1] has jurisdiction to entertain proceed-ings for nullity of marriage if, and only if, either of the parties to the marriage (1) i: domiciled in England[2] on the date when the proceedings are begun; or (2) wa: habitually resident[3] in England throughout the period of one year ending with tha• date; or (3) died before that date and either was at death domiciled in England or hac been habitually resident in England throughout the period of one year ending with the date of death[4].

At any time when proceedings are pending which the court has jurisdiction tc entertain[5], the court also has jurisdiction to entertain other proceedings, in respect o| the same marriage, for divorce, judicial separation or nullity of marriage, notwith-standing that the court would not otherwise have such jurisdiction[6].

The exercise of the English court's jurisdiction in nullity proceedings is subject to rules enabling the court to stay those proceedings in certain circumstances. These rules are considered elsewhere in this title[7].

1 See para 741 note 1 ante.
2 As to the meaning of 'England' see para 604 ante.
3 As to the meaning of 'habitually resident' see *Kapur v Kapur* [1984] FLR 920; and para 705 ante.
4 Domicile and Matrimonial Proceedings Act 1973 s 5(3). The third ground of jurisdiction is intended to cover the rare case where a person with sufficient interest petitions for a decree that a marriage is void after the death of one or both parties to the marriage.
5 Ie under ibid s 5(2), (3) or (5).
6 Ibid s 5(5).
7 See ibid s 5(6), Sch 1 (as amended); and paras 760–763 post.

B. CHOICE OF LAW

743. Choice of law. Whenever it exercises jurisdiction in divorce or judicial separ-ation, the English court will apply English domestic law[1]. The grounds on which a decree may be pronounced are defined by statute, and a petition cannot be presented on any other ground[2].

In regard to the nullity of marriage, issues as to the formal validity of a marriage are governed by the *lex loci celebrationis*[3]; issues of legal capacity to marry are governed by the law of each party's antenuptial domicile[4]; issues of alleged want of consent by one party are governed by the law of either party's antenuptial domicile or, possibly, by the *lex loci celebrationis*[5]; and issues of alleged impotence or wilful refusal to consummate are governed by the law of the petitioner's domicile or, possibly, by English domestic law as the lex fori[6]. There seems to be no case in which a marriage alleged to be voidable under a foreign law has been annulled by the English court on a ground unknown to English law[7].

1 This was assumed to be the law in *Zanelli v Zanelli* (1948) 64 TLR 556, 92 Sol Jo 646, CA, and was subsequently confirmed by statute: see the Law Reform (Miscellaneous Provisions) Act 1949 s 1(4)

(repealed), successively re-enacted as the Matrimonial Causes Act 1950 s 18(2) (repealed); the Matrimonial Causes Act 1965 s 40(2) (repealed); and the Matrimonial Causes Act 1973 s 46(2) (repealed without replacement by the Domicile and Matrimonial Proceedings Act 1973 s 17(2), Sch 6; but this was not intended to alter the law as stated in the text: see *Jurisdiction in Matrimonial Causes* (Law Com no 48) paras 103–108).

2 See the Matrimonial Causes Act 1973 s 1 (divorce); s 17(1) (judicial separation); and DIVORCE.
3 See para 706 ante.
4 See para 725 ante.
5 See para 730 ante.
6 See para 731 ante.
7 See Dicey and Morris *The Conflict of Laws* (12th Edn, 1993) 724–725; and cf *Vervaeke (formerly Messina) v Smith* [1983] 1 AC 145, [1982] 2 All ER 144, HL.

C. RECOGNITION OF DIVORCES, ANNULMENTS AND LEGAL SEPARATIONS

(A) *Decrees granted in the British Islands*

744. Recognition of divorces, annulments and judicial separations granted in the British Islands. The validity of any divorce, annulment[1] or judicial separation granted by a court of civil jurisdiction in any part of the British Islands[2] is recognised throughout the United Kingdom[3] subject to certain specified grounds on which recognition may be refused[4]. However, no divorce or annulment obtained in any part of the British Islands is regarded as effective in any part of the United Kingdom[5] unless granted by a court of civil jurisdiction[6]. Where these provisions require or preclude the recognition of the validity of a divorce, annulment or judicial separation granted before 4 April 1988, they do not affect any property to which any person became entitled before that date, or affect the recognition of the validity of the divorce, annulment or separation if that matter has been decided by any competent court in the British Islands before that date[7].

A divorce obtained in any part of the British Islands before 1 January 1974 is to be recognised in all parts of the United Kingdom if it was recognised as valid under rules of law applicable before that date[8].

1 'Annulment' includes any decree or declaration of nullity of marriage, however expressed: Family Law Act 1986 s 54(1).
2 For the meaning of 'the British Islands' see para 604 ante.
3 For the meaning of 'United Kingdom' see para 604 ante.
4 Family Law Act 1986 s 44(2). As to the specified grounds see s 51; and para 749 post.
5 For the meaning of 'part of the United Kingdom' see para 728 note 3 ante.
6 Family Law Act 1986 s 44(1), which is expressed to be subject to s 52(4), (5)(a): see the text and note 8 infra.
7 Ibid s 52(2).
8 Ibid ss 52(4), (5)(a). The practical effect of these provisions, in this context, is to permit the recognition of those extra-judicial divorces which have been obtained in the British Islands before the relevant date, and which are recognised under the law of the parties' common domicile. See *Armitage v A-G* [1906] P 135; *Har-Shefi v Har-Shefi (No 2)* [1953] P 220, [1953] 2 All ER 373; *Qureshi v Qureshi* [1972] Fam 173, [1971] 1 All ER 325.

(B) *Decrees obtained outside the British Islands*

745. Introduction. The validity of an overseas divorce, annulment[1] or legal separation[2], is recognised in the United Kingdom if, and only if, it is entitled to recognition by virtue of the relevant provisions of the Family Law Act 1986[3] or any other enactment[4]. The provisions of the Act apply to overseas divorces, annulments and legal separations whenever obtained[5], but do not affect any property to which any person became entitled before 4 April 1988 or the recognition of the validity of the divorce, annulment or separation if that matter has been decided by any competent court in the British Islands before that date[6].

1   For the meaning of 'annulment' for these purposes see para 744 note 1 ante.
2   Ie a divorce, annulment or legal separation obtained in a country outside the British Islands. 'Country' includes a colony or other dependent territory of the United Kingdom; but for these purposes a person is to be treated as a national of such a territory only if it has a law of citizenship or nationality separate from that of the United Kingdom and he is a citizen or national of that territory under that law: Family Law Act 1986 s 54(2). For the meaning of 'United Kingdom' see para 604 ante. For the meaning of 'the British Islands' see para 604 ante.
3   Ie the Family Law Act 1986 ss 46–49: see paras 746–748 post.
4   Ibid s 45. The reference to other enactments seems to refer principally to decrees whose effect is also preserved by other provisions of the Act: see s 52(4), (5)(b)–(e). Under those provisions, certain divorces, annulments and legal separations are to be recognised in the United Kingdom whether or not they are entitled to recognition by virtue of the earlier provisions of the Act: s 52(4). They are: (1) overseas divorces recognised as valid under the Recognition of Divorces and Legal Separations Act 1971 (repealed) and not affected by the Domicile and Matrimonial Proceedings Act 1973 s 16(2) (repealed) (proceedings otherwise than in a court of law where both parties are resident in the United Kingdom); (2) divorces of which the decree was registered under the Indian and Colonial Divorce Jurisdiction Act 1926 s 1 (repealed); (3) divorces or annulments recognised as valid under the Matrimonial Causes (War Marriages) Act 1944 s 4 (repealed); and (4) overseas legal separations recognised as valid under the Recognition of Divorces and Legal Separations Act 1971 (repealed): Family Law Act 1986 s 52(5)(b)–(e).
     As to the grounds upon which recognition may be refused see s 51; and para 749 post.
5   Ibid s 52(1).
6   Ibid s 52(2).

746. Grounds for recognition; divorces etc obtained by means of proceedings.
The validity of an overseas divorce, annulment[1] or legal separation[2] obtained by means of proceedings[3] is to be recognised[4], subject to certain specified grounds on which recognition may be refused[5], if the divorce, annulment or legal separation is effective under the law of the country in which it was obtained[6] and, at the relevant date[7], either party to the marriage was habitually resident[8] in the country in which the divorce, annulment or legal separation was obtained, or was domiciled in that country[9], or was a national of that country[10].

Where there have been cross-proceedings, the validity of an overseas divorce, annulment or legal separation obtained either in the original proceedings or in the cross-proceedings is to be recognised in England and Wales if the requirements for recognition[11] are satisfied in relation to the date of the commencement either of the original proceedings or of the cross-proceedings, and the validity of the divorce, annulment or legal separation is otherwise entitled to recognition[12].

Where a legal separation, the validity of which is entitled to recognition, is converted, in the country in which it was obtained, into a divorce which is effective under the law of that country, the validity of the divorce is to be recognised whether or not it would itself be entitled to recognition under the above rules[13].

For the purpose of deciding whether an overseas divorce, annulment or legal separation obtained by means of proceedings is entitled to recognition by virtue of the provisions described above[14], any finding of fact[15] made (whether expressly or by implication) in the proceedings and on the basis of which jurisdiction was assumed is, where both parties to the marriage took part in the proceedings[16], conclusive evidence of the fact found, and, in any other case, sufficient proof of that fact unless the contrary is shown[17].

1 For the meaning of 'annulment' for these purposes see para 744 note 1 ante.
2 Ie one obtained outside the British Islands: Family Law Act 1986 s 45. For the meaning of 'the British Islands' see para 604 ante.
3 'Proceedings' means judicial or other proceedings: ibid s 54(1). It follows that certain divorces formerly categorised as extra-judicial are therefore capable of recognition under these provisions: see para 747 post.
4 Ibid s 46(1).
5 Ibid s 51; and see para 749 post.
6 Ibid s 46(1)(a); see the following cases under earlier legislation to the same effect: *Adams v Adams (A-G intervening)* [1971] P 188, [1970] 3 All ER 572; *M v R* (1971) Times, 6 December (judge's appointment unconstitutional); *Torok v Torok* [1973] 3 All ER 101, [1973] 1 WLR 1066 (as to decrees not yet effective in the foreign country); and see the statement of facts in *Woodland v Woodland (otherwise Belin)* [1928] P 169 (want of formal registration). As to the recognition of certain decrees of the then Southern Rhodesia see the Southern Rhodesia (Marriages, Matrimonial Causes and Adoptions) Order 1972, SI 1972/1718 (repealed).
7 Ie the date of the commencement of the proceedings: see the Family Law Act 1986 s 46(3)(a). Where in the case of an overseas annulment, the proceedings were commenced after the death of either party to the marriage, the relevant date in relation to that party is the date of death: s 46(4).
8 As to the meaning of 'habitually resident' see *Kapur v Kapur* [1984] FLR 920; and para 705 ante.
9 For this purpose a party is treated as domiciled in a country if he was domiciled there either according to the law of that country or according to the law of England and Wales: Family Law Act 1986 s 46(5). All parts of the proceedings must take place within a single country: *R v Secretary of State for the Home Department, ex p Fatima* [1986] AC 527, [1986] 2 All ER 32, HL, decided under the Recognition of Divorces and Legal Separations Act 1971 (repealed); *Berkovits v Grinberg (A-G intervening)* [1995] Fam 142, [1995] 2 All ER 681.
10 Family Law Act 1986 s 46(1)(b). As to the application of these rules in federal and composite states see s 49; and para 748 post.
11 Ie those of ibid s 46(1)(b).
12 Ibid s 47(1).
13 Ibid s 47(2).
14 Ie by virtue of ibid s 46 or s 47.
15 Ie a finding that either party to the marriage was habitually resident in the country in which the divorce, annulment or legal separation was obtained, or was under the law of that country domiciled there, or was a national of that country: ibid s 48(2).
16 A spouse who appears in the proceedings is treated as having taken part: ibid s 48(3); and see *Torok v Torok* [1973] 3 All ER 101 at 104, [1973] 1 WLR 1066 at 1069.
17 Family Law Act 1986 s 48(1).

747. Grounds for recognition: divorces etc obtained otherwise than by means of proceedings. Different, and more limited, grounds for recognition apply to divorces, annulments and separations obtained otherwise than by means of proceedings[1].

The validity of an overseas divorce, annulment[2] or legal separation[3] obtained otherwise than by means of proceedings is to be recognised, subject to certain specified grounds on which recognition may be refused[4], if (1) the divorce, annulment or legal separation is effective under the law of the country in which it was obtained; and (2) at the relevant date[5] (a) each party to the marriage was domiciled[6] in that country, or (b) either party to the marriage was domiciled in that country and the other party was domiciled in a country under whose law the divorce, annulment or legal separation is recognised as valid; and (3) neither party to the marriage was habitually resident[7] in the United Kingdom[8] throughout the period of one year immediately preceding that date[9].

Where a legal separation, the validity of which is entitled to recognition[10], is converted, in the country in which it was obtained, into a divorce which is effective under the law of that country, the validity of the divorce is to be recognised whether or not it would itself be entitled to recognition under the above rules[11].

1   The precise scope of 'proceedings', defined to include judicial and other proceedings (see the Family Law Act 1986 s 54(1); and para 746 note 3 ante), in this context remains unclear, but something more is required than mere acts by the parties which will be recognised as effective in the country in which they occur: see Dicey and Morris *The Conflict of Laws* (12th Edn, 1993) 742–744. So, a talak, by which under Islamic law a husband can divorce his wife by oral declaration, will not be regarded as involving proceedings (*Chaudhary v Chaudhary* [1985] Fam 19, [1984] 3 All ER 1017, CA), unless, as in Pakistan, some form of registration by a state body is required (*Quazi v Quazi* [1980] AC 744, [1979] 3 All ER 897, HL). Both the previously cited cases were decided under the similar but not identical provisions of the Recognition of Divorces and Legal Separations Act 1971 (repealed). A ghet, which in practice involves the officers of a rabbinical court, involves proceedings: *Berkovits v Grinberg (A-G intervening)* [1995] Fam 142, [1995] 2 All ER 681.
2   For the meaning of 'annulment' for these purposes see para 744 note 1 ante.
3   Ie one obtained outside the British Islands: Family Law Act 1986 s 45. All parts of the process must take place within a single country: *R v Secretary of State for the Home Department, ex p Fatima* [1986] AC 527, [1986] 2 All ER 32, HL, decided under the Recognition of Divorces and Legal Separations Act 1971 (repealed); *Berkovits v Grinberg (A-G intervening)* [1995] Fam 142, [1995] 2 All ER 681. For the meaning of 'the British Islands' see para 604 ante.
4   Ie subject to the Family Law Act 1986 s 51: see para 749 post.
5   Ie the date on which it was obtained: ibid s 46(3)(b). Where, in the case of an overseas annulment, the relevant date fell after the death of either party to the marriage, the relevant date in relation to that party is the date of death: s 46(4).
6   As to domicile for this purpose see para 746 note 9 ante.
7   As to the meaning of 'habitually resident' see *Kapur v Kapur* [1984] FLR 920; and para 705 ante.
8   For the meaning of 'United Kingdom' see para 604 ante.
9   Family Law Act 1986 s 46(2). As to the application of these rules in federal and composite states see s 49; and para 748 post.
10   Ie entitled to recognition by virtue of ibid s 46 or s 47(1) (cross-proceedings and divorce following legal separation).
11   Ibid s 47(2).

748. Application to federal and composite states. In relation to a country[1] comprising territories in which different systems of law are in force in matters of divorce, annulment[2] or legal separation, the provisions as to recognition are modified[3]. In the case of a divorce, annulment or legal separation obtained by proceedings, the recognition of the validity of which depends on the domicile or habitual residence of a party to the marriage[4], the relevant provisions[5] are to be read as if each territory were a separate country[6]. In the case of a divorce, annulment or legal separation obtained by proceedings, the recognition of the validity of which depends upon the nationality of a party to a marriage[7], the divorce, annulment or separation must be effective throughout the country and not merely in the territory in which it was granted[8]. In the case of a divorce, annulment or legal separation obtained otherwise than by means of proceedings, the recognition of the validity of which depends on the domicile of a party to the marriage[9], the relevant provisions[10] have effect as if each territory were a separate country[11].

1   As to the meaning of 'country' see para 745 note 2 ante.
2   For the meaning of 'annulment' for these purposes see para 744 note 1 ante.
3   See the Family Law Act 1986 s 49(1).
4   Ie on the satisfaction of the criteria in ibid s 46(1)(b)(i) or (ii): see para 746 ante.
5   Ie ibid ss 46(1), 47(2): see para 746 ante.
6   Ibid s 49(2).

7 Ie on the satisfaction of the criterion in ibid s 46(1)(b)(iii): see para 746 ante.
8 Ibid s 49(3), providing for a variant version of ss 46(1)(a), 47(2). The provisions of s 48(2) as to findings of fact by the foreign court are to be read as if each territory were a separate country: s 49(5).
9 Ie on the satisfaction of the criteria in ibid s 46(2)(b): see para 747 ante.
10 See ibid ss 47(2) (in the case of a legal separation: see para 746 ante), 51(3), (4) (see para 749 post); the text of s 49(4) refers to s 52(3), (4) but it is submitted that this is a drafting error and that the intention must have been to refer to s 51(3), (4).
11 Ibid s 49(4).

(C) *Refusal of Recognition*

749. Grounds for refusing recognition of divorces etc. Recognition of the validity of (1) a divorce, annulment[1] or judicial separation granted by a court of civil jurisdiction in any part of the British Islands[2], or (2) an overseas divorce, annulment or legal separation[3], may be refused in England and Wales if the divorce, annulment or separation was granted or obtained at a time when it was irreconcilable with a decision determining the question of the subsistence or validity of the marriage of the parties previously given by a court of civil jurisdiction in England and Wales or by a court elsewhere and recognised or entitled to be recognised in England and Wales[4].

Recognition of such a divorce or separation may also be so refused if it was granted or obtained at a time when, according to English law[5] (including its rules of private international law[6] and the provisions of the Family Law Act 1986[7]), there was no subsisting marriage between the parties[8].

Recognition[9] of the validity of an overseas divorce, annulment or legal separation obtained by means of proceedings[10] may be refused if (a) it was obtained without such steps having been taken for giving notice of the proceedings to a party to the marriage as, having regard to the nature of the proceedings and all the circumstances, should reasonably have been taken[11]; or (b) without a party to the marriage having been given, for any reason other than lack of notice, such opportunity to take part in the proceedings as, having regard to those matters, he should reasonably have been given[12]. In the case of a divorce, annulment or legal separation obtained otherwise than by means of proceedings[13], recognition may be refused if (i) there is no official[14] document certifying that the divorce, annulment or legal separation is effective under the law of the country in which it was obtained[15]; or (ii) where either party to the marriage was domiciled[16] in another country at the relevant date[17], there is no official document certifying that the divorce, annulment or legal separation is recognised as valid under the law of that other country[18].

Recognition of an overseas divorce, annulment or legal separation may also be refused if to grant it would be manifestly contrary to public policy[19].

The provisions as to recognition of divorces, annulments and legal separations do not require the recognition of any finding of fault made in divorce, annulment or separation proceedings, or of any maintenance, custody or other ancillary order made in any such proceedings[20].

1 For the meaning of 'annulment' for these purposes see para 744 note 1 ante.
2 For the meaning of 'the British Islands' see para 604 ante.
3 Ie one obtained outside the British Islands: Family Law Act 1986 s 45.
4 Ibid s 51(1). The provisions of s 51(1), (2) and (3) are subject to those of s 52 (see para 745 ante). Cf the common law rule as expressed in *Vervaeke (formerly Messina) v Smith* [1983] 1 AC 145, [1982] 2 All ER 144, HL. As to the meaning of 'England and Wales' see para 604 ante.
5 As to the meaning of 'English law' see para 604 ante.
6 As to the term 'private international law' see para 601 ante.
7 Ie the Family Law Act 1986 Pt II (ss 44–54).

8 Ibid s 51(2).
9 Ie by virtue of ibid s 45.
10 See ibid s 51(3)(a). As to the grounds for the recognition see para 746 ante.
11 Ibid s 51(3)(a)(i). Cf *Shaw v A-G* (1870) LR 2 P & D 156; *Rudd v Rudd* [1924] P 72; *Boettcher v Boettcher* (1949) 93 Sol Jo 237; *Maher v Maher* [1951] P 342, [1951] 2 All ER 37; *Igra v Igra* [1951] P 404, [1951] 2 TLR 670; *Arnold v Arnold* [1957] P 237, [1957] 1 All ER 570; *Wood v Wood* [1957] P 254 at 267, [1957] 2 All ER 14, CA; *Macalpine v Macalpine* [1958] P 35, [1957] 3 All ER 134; *Sabbagh v Sabbagh* [1985] FLR 29.
12 Family Law Act 1986 s 51(3)(a)(ii). Cf *Mitford v Mitford and von Kuhlmann* [1923] P 130; *Hack v Hack* (1976) 6 Fam Law 177; *Joyce v Joyce and O'Hare* [1979] Fam 93, [1979] 2 All ER 156; *Newmarch v Newmarch* [1978] Fam 79, [1978] 1 All ER 1; *Mamdani v Mamdani* [1984] FLR 699, CA; *Sabbagh v Sabbagh* [1985] FLR 29.
13 See the Family Law Act 1986 s 51(3)(b). As to these cases and the applicable grounds for recognition see para 747 ante.
14 'Official' in relation to a document certifying that a divorce, annulment or legal separation is effective or recognised as valid under the law of any country, means issued by a person or body appointed or recognised for the purpose under that law: ibid s 52(4).
15 Ibid s 51(3)(b)(i).
16 Ie either according to the law of that country in family matters or according to the law of England: ibid s 46(5), applied by s 51(4).
17 'Relevant date' has the same meaning as is given in para 747 note 5 ante: see ibid s 46(3)(b), applied by s 51(4).
18 Ibid s 51(3)(b)(ii).
19 Ibid s 51(3)(c). The discretion to refuse recognition on public policy grounds should be exercised with great caution: *Qureshi v Qureshi* [1972] Fam 173 at 201, [1971] 1 All ER 325 at 346; *Varanand v Varanand* (1964) 108 Sol Jo 693; *Chaudhary v Chaudhary* [1985] Fam 19, [1984] 3 All ER 1017, CA; *Eroglu v Eroglu* [1994] 2 FCR 525, [1994] 2 FLR 287. See also *Re Meyer* [1971] P 298, [1971] 1 All ER 378 (duress; racial discrimination); *Middleton v Middleton* [1967] P 62, [1966] 1 All ER 168 (false evidence); *Vardy v Smith (otherwise Vardy)* (1932) 48 TLR 661; affd 49 TLR 36, CA (want of authority by legal representatives); *Pemberton v Hughes* [1899] 1 Ch 781, CA (procedural defects); *Hornett v Hornett* [1971] P 255, [1971] 1 All ER 98 (resumption of cohabitation after decree); *Kendall v Kendall* [1977] Fam 208, [1977] 3 All ER 471 (wife deceived into signing petition for unwanted divorce containing false statements) and the nullity of marriage cases of *Mitford v Mitford and von Kuhlmann* [1923] P 130 at 137, 141–142; *Salvesen (or von Lorang) v Administrator of Austrian Property* [1927] AC 641, HL; *Merker v Merker* [1963] P 283, [1962] 3 All ER 928; *Gray (otherwise Formosa) v Formosa* [1963] P 259, [1962] 3 All ER 419, CA; *Lepre v Lepre* [1965] P 52, [1963] 2 All ER 49. In many of these cases, the reasons advanced for denying recognition (such as fraud or want of natural justice) are unavailable under the Family Law Act 1986 but the facts might attract the public policy ground. See, however, *Eroglu v Eroglu* supra.
20 Family Law Act 1986 s 51(5). Cf *Sabbagh v Sabbagh* [1985] FLR 29. As to foreign custody orders see para 779 post; and as to maintenance orders see paras 800–842 post.

(D) *Effect of Foreign Decrees*

750. Effect of foreign decrees. A foreign decree of divorce recognised in accordance with the principles considered in the preceding paragraphs[1] has the same effect upon the status of the parties as an English[2] decree of divorce. The English court will, however, recognise a condition in a foreign decree imposing a prohibition on remarriage by the parties within a period which has not yet elapsed[3]. A prohibition on remarriage affecting the guilty party only will be regarded as penal by the English court and treated as having no effect beyond the limits of the jurisdiction of the foreign court[4]. The recognition of a foreign decree does not require the revocation of maintenance orders made by the High Court[5] or by magistrates' courts; as in the case of an English decree, the courts have a discretion to discharge or vary an order or to continue it in its original form[6].

A foreign decree of nullity of marriage recognised in England operates as a universally binding judgment in rem determining status[7]. The English court will give effect to the retrospective operation of the decree, if any, under the law of the country in which it was pronounced[8], and any English proceedings for nullity of marriage must be dismissed on the ground that there is no marriage in existence to be annulled[9].

Where the validity of a divorce or annulment[10] is recognised in England and Wales (or was itself granted by a court of civil jurisdiction in England and Wales) the fact that the divorce or annulment would not be recognised elsewhere does not preclude either party to the marriage from remarrying in England and Wales or cause the remarriage of either party (wherever the remarriage takes place) to be treated as invalid in England and Wales[11].

 1 See para 745 et seq ante.
 2 As to the meaning of 'English' see para 604 ante.
 3 *Warter v Warter* (1890) 15 PD 152; *Le Mesurier (otherwise Gordon) v Le Mesurier* (1930) 99 LJP 33; *Boettcher v Boettcher* (1949) 93 Sol Jo 237. As to the position under the Indian and Colonial Divorce Jurisdiction Acts (repealed) see *Buckle v Buckle (otherwise Williams)* [1956] P 181, [1955] 3 All ER 641.
 4 *Scott v A-G* (1886) 11 PD 128, 50 JP 824.
 5 *Wood v Wood* [1957] P 254 at 295, [1957] 2 All ER 14 at 31, CA; cf *Pastre v Pastre* [1930] P 80.
 6 *Bragg v Bragg* [1925] P 20, DC; *Mezger v Mezger* [1937] P 19, [1936] 3 All ER 130, DC; *Kirk v Kirk* [1947] 2 All ER 118, 177 LT 151, DC; *Wood v Wood* [1957] P 254 at 267, [1957] 2 All ER 14, CA.
 7 *Salvesen (or von Lorang) v Administrator of Austrian Property* [1927] AC 641, HL; *Merker v Merker* [1963] P 283, [1962] 3 All ER 928.
 8 *Salvesen (or von Lorang) v Administrator of Austrian Property* [1927] AC 641, HL.
 9 *Turner v Thompson* (1888) 13 PD 37.
10 For the meaning of 'annulment' for this purpose see para 744 note 1 ante.
11 Family Law Act 1986 s 50. Cf *Perrini v Perrini* [1979] Fam 84, [1979] 2 All ER 323; *Lawrence v Lawrence* [1985] Fam 106, [1985] 2 All ER 733, CA. As to the meaning of 'England and Wales' see para 604 ante.

(iii) Presumption of Death and Dissolution of Marriage

751. Jurisdiction. The English court[1] has jurisdiction to entertain proceedings for death to be presumed and a marriage to be dissolved if and only if, the petitioner is domiciled in England and Wales[2] on the date when the proceedings are begun, or was habitually resident[3] in England throughout the period of one year ending with that date[4].

 1 For the meaning of 'court' see para 741 note 1 ante. As to the meaning of 'English' in relation to courts see para 604 ante.
 2 As to the meaning of 'England and Wales' see para 604 ante.
 3 As to the meaning of 'habitually resident' see *Kapur v Kapur* [1984] FLR 920; and para 705 ante.
 4 Domicile and Matrimonial Proceedings Act 1973 s 5(4).

752. Choice of law. Whenever it exercises jurisdiction, the English court will apply English domestic law[1].

 1 The repeal of the Matrimonial Causes Act 1973 s 19(5), by the Domicile and Matrimonial Proceedings Act 1973 s 17(2), Sch 6 was not intended to alter the law: see para 743 note 1 ante. As to the meaning of 'English' in relation to courts and law see para 604 ante.

753. Recognition of foreign decrees. A decree of presumption of death and dissolution of marriage, granted in circumstances in which the relationship between the parties and the country concerned was such that it corresponded to the circumstances in which the English court[1] would have jurisdiction[2], will be recognised in

England and Wales[3]. It would seem that the English court will not necessarily recognise a foreign decree of presumption of death which has no consequential effects in the law of the foreign country where the decree was granted[4].

1 As to the meaning of 'English' in relation to courts see para 604 ante.
2 See para 751 ante.
3 *Szemik v Gryla (otherwise Szemik) and Gryla* (1965) 109 Sol Jo 175.
4 Cf *Re Schulhof's Goods, Re Wolf's Goods* [1948] P 66, [1947] 2 All ER 841 (decree which did not vest property of deceased and was not linked with a vesting order). See also *Re Spenceley's Goods* [1892] P 255; *Re Dowds's Goods* [1948] P 256, [1948] LJR 1887; *Re Schulhof's Goods, Re Wolf's Goods* supra at 66–67, 841–842.

(iv) Declarations as to Status

754. Declarations as to status. The court[1] has power to make various declarations in relation to a marriage[2], namely: (1) that the marriage was at its inception a valid marriage[3]; (2) that the marriage subsisted on a date specified in the application[4]; (3) that the marriage did not subsist on a date so specified[5]; (4) that the validity of a divorce, annulment or legal separation obtained in any country outside England and Wales[6] in respect of the marriage is entitled to recognition[7]; (5) that the validity of a divorce, annulment or legal separation so obtained in respect of the marriage is not entitled to recognition[8]. Where on an application for such a declaration, the truth of the proposition to be declared is proved to the satisfaction of the court, the court must make that declaration unless to do so would manifestly be contrary to public policy[9]. A declaration binds the Crown and all other persons[10].

No court may make a declaration that a marriage was at its inception void, or that any person is or was illegitimate[11].

A court has jurisdiction to entertain an application[12] for such a declaration if, and only if, either of the parties to the marriage to which the application relates (a) is domiciled in England and Wales on the date of the application; or (b) has been habitually resident[13] in England and Wales throughout the period of one year ending with that date; or (c) died before that date and either (i) was at death domiciled in England and Wales; or (ii) had been habitually resident in England and Wales throughout the period of one year ending with the date of death[14]. The former power to make declarations under the inherent power of the High Court is excluded[15].

Any declaration under these provisions, and any application for such a declaration, must be in form prescribed by rules of court[16]. The court may direct that the whole or any part of proceedings is to be heard in camera, and an application for such a direction must be heard in camera unless the court otherwise directs[17].

The right to petition for jactitation of marriage[18] is abolished[19].

1 For this purpose 'the court' means the High Court or a county court: Family Law Act 1986 s 63.
2 The declaration sought should be specified in the application: ibid s 55(1). On dismissing an application, the court has no power to make any declaration for which an application has not been made: s 58(3). No declaration which may be applied for under the Family Law Act 1986 Pt III (ss 55–63) may be made otherwise than under that Part by any court: s 58(4).
   No proceedings under Pt III affect any final judgment or decree already pronounced or made by any court of competent jurisdiction: s 60(3).
3 Ibid s 55(1)(a).
4 Ibid s 55(1)(b).
5 Ibid s 55(1)(c).
6 As to the meaning of 'England and Wales' see para 604 ante.
7 Family Law Act 1986 s 55(1)(d).

8 Ibid s 55(1)(e).
9 Ibid s 58(1).
10 Ibid s 58(2). At any stage of the proceedings, the court may of its own motion, or on the application of any party, direct that all necessary papers in the matter be sent to the Attorney General: s 59(1). The Attorney General, whether or not he is sent papers, may intervene in the proceedings in such manner as he thinks necessary or expedient, and argue before the court any question in relation to the application which the court considers it necessary to have fully argued: s 59(2). Where the Attorney General incurs any costs in connection with any application for a declaration, the court may make such order as it considers just as to the payment of those costs by parties to the proceedings: s 59(3).
11 Ibid s 58(5). However, nothing in the Family Law Act 1986 affects the power of any court to grant a decree of nullity of marriage: s 58(6).
12 Where an application is made by any person other than a party to the marriage to which the application relates, the court must refuse to hear the application if it considers that the applicant does not have a sufficient interest in the determination of that application: ibid s 55(3).
13 As to the meaning of 'habitually resident' see *Kapur v Kapur* [1984] FLR 920; and para 705 ante.
14 Family Law Act 1986 s 55(2).
15 See ibid s 58(4).
16 Ibid s 60(1). Rules of court may make provision as to the information required to be given by any applicant for a declaration under Pt III, as to the persons who are to be parties to proceedings on an application under Pt III, and requiring notice of an application under Pt III to be served on the Attorney General and persons affected by any declaration applied for: s 60(2) (amended by the Family Law Reform Act 1987 s 33(1), Sch 2 para 96). As to the rules made for this purpose see the Family Proceedings Rules 1991, SI 1991/1247.
17 Ibid s 60(4).
18 Ie a declaration by the court that the respondent should be restrained from boasting that he or she is married to the petitioner when that is not true.
19 Family Law Act 1986 s 61.

(v) Financial Relief

755. Jurisdiction. The English court[1] has power to award maintenance pending suit to either party to proceedings for divorce, nullity of marriage or judicial separation[2]. This power may be exercised even though a substantial question which has been raised as to the court's jurisdiction over the principal proceedings awaits determination[3].

On granting a decree or at any time thereafter, the court has power to make orders for the payment by one party of a lump sum or sums or for periodical payments[4], the transfer or settlement of property, the variation of settlements made on the parties, or the extinction or reduction of the interest of either of the parties under any such settlement[5], orders for the sale of property[6], and orders for the transfer of certain tenancies[7]. The court has jurisdiction to make such orders whenever it has jurisdiction in the main suit[8], but will not exercise its powers when the order would be ineffectual or would infringe the authority of a foreign court[9].

Orders for periodical payments or for the payment of lump sums may be made in cases where there has been a failure by a party to a marriage to provide reasonable maintenance for the other party or certain children of the family[10]. The court has jurisdiction (1) if the applicant or the respondent is domiciled in England and Wales on the date of the application; or (2) if the applicant has been habitually resident[11] there throughout the period of one year ending with that date; or (3) if the respondent is resident there on that date[12].

Additionally, the court has jurisdiction if (a) if the respondent is domiciled as that term is defined in the Civil Jurisdiction and Judgments Act 1982[13] in England and Wales[14]; (b) if the respondent is so domiciled in any other part of the United Kingdom[15] or in another Brussels or Lugano contracting state[16] and the court is the court for the place where the maintenance creditor is so domiciled or habitually resident[17]; or (c) if the respondent enters an appearance otherwise than solely to contest the jurisdiction[18].

1   In the Matrimonial Causes Act 1973, 'court', except where the context otherwise requires, means the High Court or, where a county court has jurisdiction by virtue of the Matrimonial and Family Proceedings Act 1984 Pt V (ss 32–44) (as amended), a county court: Matrimonial Causes Act 197_ s 52(1) (definition amended by the Matrimonial and Family Proceedings Act 1984 s 46(1), Sch ▯ para 16). As to the meaning of 'English' in relation to courts see para 604 ante.
2   See the Matrimonial Causes Act 1973 s 22; and DIVORCE vol 13 para 791.
3   *Ronalds v Ronalds* (1875) LR 3 P & D 259. In *Inverclyde (otherwise Tripp) v Inverclyde* [1931] P 29, the petition for alimony fell with the main petition; but without argument on the point. See *Smith v Smith* [1923] P 128; *Johnstone v Johnstone* [1929] P 165, CA (payment of wife's costs in similar circumstances)
4   See the Matrimonial Causes Act 1973 s 23 (as amended); and DIVORCE vol 13 para 1052.
5   See ibid s 24; and DIVORCE vol 13 para 1052.
6   See ibid s 24A (as added and amended); and DIVORCE.
7   See the Matrimonial Homes Act 1983 s 7, Sch 1 (as amended); and DIVORCE.
8   *Nunneley v Nunneley and Marrian* (1890) 15 PD 186; *Forsyth v Forsyth* [1891] P 363; *Hunter v Hunter and Waddington* [1962] P 1, [1961] 2 All ER 121; *Cammell v Cammell* [1965] P 467, [1964] 3 All ER 255.
9   *Tallack v Tallack and Broekema* [1927] P 211; *Goff v Goff* [1934] P 107; *Wyler v Lyons* [1963] P 274, [1963] ▯ All ER 821.
10   See the Matrimonial Causes Act 1973 s 27(1) (substituted by the Domestic Proceedings and Magistrates Courts Act 1978 s 63). As to the children of the family to whom this provision applies see the Matrimonial Causes Act 1973 s 27(3) (substituted by the Matrimonial and Family Proceedings Act 1984 s 4); as to the variation of orders see the Matrimonial Causes Act 1973 s 31(1), (2) (s 31(1) amended by the Matrimonial and Family Proceedings Act 1984 s 6(2); s 31(2) amended by the Matrimonial Homes and Property Act 1981 s 8(2)). See also DIVORCE vol 13 para 656.
11   As to the meaning of 'habitually resident' see *Kapur v Kapur* [1984] FLR 920; and para 705 ante.
12   Matrimonial Causes Act 1973 s 27(2) (amended by the Domicile and Matrimonial Proceedings Act 1973 s 6(1)). These bases for jurisdiction are excluded if the court has jurisdiction under the Brussels Convention or the Lugano Convention, or the corresponding scheme in force within the United Kingdom: Brussels Convention art 3; Lugano Convention art 3; Civil Jurisdiction and Judgments Act 1982 s 16(1) (as amended), (2), Sch 4 art 3. As to the Brussels Convention see para 618 text and note 1 ante. As to the Lugano Convention see para 618 text and note 2 ante. As to the adaptation of the provisions of the Conventions by the Civil Jurisdiction and Judgments Act 1982 Sch 4, to a scheme applying as between parts of the United Kingdom, see para 619 ante.
13   See the Civil Jurisdiction and Judgments Act 1982 s 41 (as amended); and para 635 ante.
14   Brussels Convention art 2; Lugano Convention art 2; Civil Jurisdiction and Judgments Act 1982 Sch 4 art 2.
15   For the meaning of 'part of the United Kingdom' see para 619 note 4 ante.
16   For the meaning of 'Brussels contracting state' and 'Lugano contracting state' see para 618 notes 1–2 ante.
17   See the Brussels Convention art 5 para 2; the Lugano Convention art 5 para 2; the Civil Jurisdiction and Judgments Act 1982 Sch 4 art 5(2) (as amended); and para 643 ante.
18   Brussels Convention art 18; Lugano Convention art 18; Civil Jurisdiction and Judgments Act 1982 Sch 4 art 18; see para 630 ante.

756. Orders made after foreign decrees. The English court[1] has jurisdiction to make orders for financial relief[2] after the grant in an overseas country[3] of a divorce, annulment or legal separation which is entitled to recognition in England and Wales[4]. The court has jurisdiction if either party to the marriage (1) was domiciled in England and Wales on the date on which the divorce, annulment or legal separation took effect in the foreign country or on the date of the application for leave[5] to proceed with the application to the English court; or (2) if either party was habitually resident[6] in England and Wales throughout the period of one year ending with either of those dates; or (3) either party has, or both parties have, at the date of the application for leave, a beneficial interest in possession in a dwelling-house situated in England and Wales which was at some time during the marriage a matrimonial home of the parties[7].

If, however, the respondent is domiciled, as that term is defined in the Civil Jurisdiction and Judgments Act 1982[8], in a state, other than the United Kingdom[9], which is a party to the Brussels or Lugano Convention[10], jurisdiction exists only in accordance with the jurisdictional requirements of the applicable Convention[11].

Before making an order the court must be satisfied that it would be appropriate for a court in England and Wales to make such an order[12]. In particular, in considering whether or not to make an order, the court must have regard to[13]:

(a) the connection which the parties to the marriage have with England and Wales[14];

(b) the connection which they have with the country in which the marriage was dissolved or annulled or in which they were legally separated[15];

(c) the connection which they have with any other country outside England and Wales[16];

(d) any financial benefit which the applicant or a child of the family[17] has received, or is likely to receive, in consequence of the divorce, annulment or legal separation, by virtue of any agreement or the operation of the law of a country outside England and Wales[18];

(e) in a case where an order has been made by a court in a country outside England and Wales requiring the other party to the marriage to make any payment or transfer any property for the benefit of the applicant or a child of the family, the financial relief given by the order and the extent to which the order has been complied with or is likely to be complied with[19];

(f) any right which the applicant has, or has had, to apply for financial relief from the other party to the marriage under the law of any country outside England and Wales and if the applicant has omitted to exercise that right the reason for that omission[20];

(g) the availability in England and Wales of any property in respect of which an order under Part III of the Matrimonial and Family Proceedings Act 1984[21], in favour of the applicant, could be made[22];

(h) the extent to which any order made under Part III of that Act is likely to be enforceable[23];

(i) the length of time which has elapsed since the date of the divorce, annulment or legal separation[24].

1 'Court' means the High Court or, where a county court has jurisdiction by virtue of the Matrimonial and Family Proceedings Act 1984 Pt V (ss 32–42) (as amended), a county court: s 27. As to the meaning of 'English' in relation to courts see para 604 ante.

2 Ie an order under ibid s 17 (financial provision and property adjustment) or s 22 (powers in relation to tenancies of dwelling houses): see ss 12(4), 27.

3 'Overseas country' means a country outside the British Islands: ibid s 27. For the meaning of 'the British Islands' see para 604 ante.

4 See ibid s 12. As to the meaning of 'England and Wales' see para 604 ante.

5 The court will grant leave for an application to be made for the making of such an order only if there are substantial grounds for making the order: see ibid s 13(1). See *W v W (Financial Provision)* [1989] 1 FLR 22; *Holmes v Holmes* [1989] Fam 47, [1989] 3 All ER 786, CA; *Z v Z (Foreign Divorce: Financial Provision)* [1992] 2 FLR 291; *M v M (Financial Provision after Foreign Divorce)* [1994] 2 FCR 448, [1994] 1 FLR 399; *Hewitson v Hewitson* [1995] 1 All ER 472, [1995] 2 WLR 287, CA. Leave may be granted despite the existence of an order as to financial provision made in the overseas court, and may be granted on conditions: see the Matrimonial and Family Proceedings Act 1984 s 13(2), (3).

6 As to the meaning of 'habitually resident' see *Kapur v Kapur* [1984] FLR 920; and para 705 ante.

7 Ibid s 15(1).

8 See the Civil Jurisdiction and Judgments Act 1982 s 41 (as amended); and para 735 ante.

9　For the meaning of 'United Kingdom' see para 604 ante.
10　As to the Brussels and Lugano Conventions see para 618 ante.
11　See the Matrimonial and Family Proceedings Act 1984 s 15(2).
12　Ibid s 16(1).
13　Ibid s 16(2).
14　Ibid s 16(2)(a).
15　Ibid s 16(2)(b).
16　Ibid s 16(2)(c).
17　'Child of the family' has the same meaning as in para 759 note 4 post: see ibid s 27.
18　Ibid s 16(2)(d).
19　Ibid s 16(2)(e).
20　Ibid s 16(2)(f).
21　Ie ibid Pt III (ss 12–27) (as amended).
22　Ibid s 16(2)(g).
23　Ibid s 16(2)(h).
24　Ibid s 16(2)(i). See *Lamagni v Lamagni* [1995] 2 FLR 452, CA.

757. Magistrates' courts. Magistrates' courts have power under the Domestic Proceedings and Magistrates' Courts Act 1978 to make orders, including orders as to lump sums and periodical payments, in respect of maintenance. A magistrates' court has jurisdiction to make an order if the applicant or respondent ordinarily resides[1], at the date when the application is made, within the commission area[2] for which the court is appointed[3]. Jurisdiction is exercisable notwithstanding that any party to the proceedings is not domiciled in England and Wales[4]. Even if one of these conditions is satisfied, it must still be shown that the respondent is subject to the jurisdiction of the English courts[5].

A magistrates' court has jurisdiction if the respondent is domiciled, as that term is defined in the Civil Jurisdiction and Judgments Act 1982[6], in another part of the United Kingdom, or in another state which is a party to the Brussels or Lugano Convention[7], and the court is the court for the place where the maintenance creditor is so domiciled or habitually resident[8]; or the respondent enters an appearance otherwise than solely to contest the jurisdiction[9].

Provision in respect of claims for maintenance by persons outside the United Kingdom is made by the Maintenance Orders (Reciprocal Enforcement) Act 1972, which is considered elsewhere in this title[10].

1　For the meaning of 'ordinarily resided' see para 704 ante.
2　'Commission area has the same meaning as in the Justices of the Peace Act 1979 s 1 (as amended): Domestic Proceedings and Magistrates' Courts Act 1978 s 88(1) (amended by the Justices of the Peace Act 1979 s 71, Sch 2 para 31): see MAGISTRATES vol 29 para 207.
3　See the Domestic Proceedings and Magistrates' Courts Act 1978 s 30(1) (amended by the Magistrates' Courts Act 1980 s 154, Sch 7 para 163; the Family Law Act 1986 s 68(1), Sch 1 para 24; and the Police and Magistrates' Courts Act 1994 s 91(1), Sch 8 para 29). This is expressed to be subject to the Family Law Act 1986 s 2 (as substituted), and to the Magistrates' Courts Act 1980 s 70 (as amended).
4　Domestic Proceedings and Magistrates' Courts Act 1978 s 30(5).
5　*Berkley v Thompson* (1884) 10 App Cas 45, HL; *Forsyth v Forsyth* [1948] P 125, [1947] 2 All ER 623, CA; *Collister v Collister* [1972] 1 All ER 334, [1972] 1 WLR 54, DC. As to the meaning of 'English' in relation to courts see para 604 ante. Formerly, rules existed to establish the jurisdiction of English magistrates' courts where the applicant and respondent resided in different parts of the United Kingdom, so long as one of them resided in England and Wales: see the Domestic Proceedings and Magistrates' Courts Act 1978 s 30(3) (repealed). Jurisdiction of the courts of different parts of the United Kingdom is now to be determined in accordance with the Civil Jurisdiction and Judgments Act 1982 s 16, Sch 4 (both as amended), as to which see paras 619, 623 ante; and the text and notes infra. For the meaning of 'part of the United Kingdom' see para 619 note 4 ante.
6　See ibid s 41 (as amended); and paras 634–635 ante.
7　As to the Brussels and Lugano Conventions see para 618 ante.

8 See para 643 text and notes 1–3 ante.
9 See para 630 ante.
10 See the Maintenance Orders (Reciprocal Enforcement) Act 1972 Pt II (ss 25–39) (as amended); and paras 818–842 post.

758. Enforcement of foreign maintenance orders. The enforcement of foreign maintenance orders, including affiliation and certain other orders as well as those in matrimonial suits, is considered subsequently[1].

1 See paras 800–842 post.

759. Variation of maintenance agreements. The High Court, a divorce county court[1] or a magistrates' court has the power to vary or revoke any financial arrangements[2] in a maintenance agreement[3] in the light of changed circumstances or the need to make proper financial arrangements with respect to any child of the family[4]. The court has jurisdiction only where each party is either domiciled or resident in England and Wales[5]. The power of a magistrates' court to vary maintenance agreements in respect of periodical payments may only be exercised if both parties are resident in England and Wales, and at least one is resident in the commission area[6] for which the court was appointed[7]. These bases for jurisdiction are excluded if the respondent is domiciled, as that term is defined in the Civil Jurisdiction and Judgments Act 1982[8] in any other part of the United Kingdom[9] or in another state which is a party to the Brussels or Lugano Conventions[10].

The court also has jurisdiction (1) if the respondent is domiciled in England and Wales[11]; (2) if the respondent is so domiciled in any other part of the United Kingdom or in another state which is a party to the Brussels or Lugano Conventions and the court is the court for the place where the maintenance creditor is so domiciled or habitually resident[12]; or (3) if the respondent enters an appearance otherwise than solely to contest the jurisdiction[13].

1 Jurisdiction is conferred on county courts in this regard by the operation of the Matrimonial Causes Act 1952 s 52(1) (amended by the Matrimonial and Family Proceedings Act 1984 s 46(1), Sch 1 para 16), and the Matrimonial and Family Proceedings Act 1984 s 34.
2 For the meaning of 'financial arrangements' see the Matrimonial Causes Act 1973 s 34(2).
3 For the meaning of 'maintenance agreement' see ibid s 34(2).
4 See ibid s 35(1), (2) (s 35(2) amended by the Matrimonial and Family Proceedings Act 1984 Sch 1 para 13(a)). 'Child of the family' in relation to the parties to a marriage means (1) a child of both those parties, and (2) any other child (other than a child placed with those parties as foster parents by a local authority or voluntary organisation) treated by those parties as a child of their family: Matrimonial Causes Act 1973 s 52(1) (amended by the Children Act 1989 s 108(4), Sch 12 para 33).
5 Matrimonial Causes Act 1973 s 35(1).
6 Ie a commission area within the meaning of the Justices of the Peace Act 1979: see MAGISTRATES vol 29 para 207.
7 See the Matrimonial Causes Act 1973 s 35(3) (amended by the Matrimonial and Family Proceedings Act 1984 Sch 1 para 13(b)).
8 See the Civil Jurisdiction and Judgments Act 1982 s 41 (as amended); and paras 634–635 ante.
9 For the meaning of 'part of the United Kingdom' see para 619 note 4 ante.
10 Brussels Convention art 3; Lugano Convention art 3; Civil Jurisdiction and Judgments Act 1982 s 16(1) (as amended), (2), Sch 4 art 3. As to the Brussels and Lugano Conventions see para 618 ante; and As to the adaptation of the provisions of the Conventions by the Civil Jurisdiction and Judgments Act 1982 Sch 4, to a scheme applying as between parts of the United Kingdom, see para 619 ante.
11 See para 634 ante.

12 See para 643 text and notes 1–3 ante.
13 See para 630 ante.

(vi) Stay of Matrimonial Proceedings

760. Duty to furnish particulars of concurrent proceedings. While matrimonial proceedings[1] are pending in the English court[2] in respect of a marriage and the trial or first trial[3] in those proceedings has not begun, it is the duty of the petitioner, or of a respondent who has in his answer included a prayer for relief, to furnish in such manner and to such persons and on such occasions as may be prescribed[4], such particulars as may be prescribed[5] of any proceedings which he knows to be continuing in another jurisdiction[6] and which are in respect of that marriage or are capable of affecting its validity or subsistence[7].

1 'Matrimonial proceedings' means proceedings for divorce, judicial separation, nullity of marriage, a declaration as to the validity of the marriage of the petitioner, or a declaration as to the subsistence of such a marriage: Domicile and Matrimonial Proceedings Act 1973 s 5(6), Sch 1 paras 1, 2.

2 For the meaning of 'court' see para 741 note 1 ante. As to the meaning of 'English' in relation to courts see para 604 ante.

3 'The trial or first trial' does not include the separate trial of an issue as to jurisdiction only: Domicile and Matrimonial Proceedings Act 1973 Sch 1 para 4(1). Nor does it include a hearing relating to residence etc of children or ancillary relief: *Thyssen-Bornemisza v Thyssen-Bornemisza* [1986] Fam 1, [1985] 1 All ER 328, CA.

4 'Prescribed' means prescribed by rules of court: Domicile and Matrimonial Proceedings Act 1973 Sch 1 para 6. See the Family Proceedings Rules 1991, SI 1991/1247, rr 2.3, 2.15(4), App 2; and note 5 infra.

5 Unless otherwise directed every petition, other than a petition under ibid r 3.12, r 3.13, r 3.14 or r 3.15 (applications under the Family Law Act 1986 ss 55, 56 (as substituted), 57 for declarations as to marital status, parentage, legitimacy or legitimation, or adoption effected overseas), must state whether there are any proceedings continuing in any country outside England and Wales which relate to the marriage or are capable of affecting its validity or subsistence, and if so must state (1) particulars of the proceedings, including the court or tribunal before which they were begun; (2) the date they were begun; (3) the names of the parties; (4) the date or expected date of any trial in the proceedings; and (5) such other facts as may be relevant to the question whether the proceedings on the petition ought to be stayed under the Domicile and Matrimonial Proceedings Act 1973 Sch 1. Such proceedings include any which are not instituted in a court of law in that country if they are instituted before a tribunal or other authority having power under the law there to determine questions of status, and must be treated as continuing if they have been begun and not finally disposed of: Family Proceedings Rules 1991 r 2.3, App 2 para 1(j).

Where an answer to any petition contains a prayer for relief, that answer must contain the information mentioned supra to the extent that it has not been given by the petitioner: r 2.15(4).

Any party who makes a request for directions for trial must, if there has been a change in the information given under the provisions described supra, file a statement giving particulars of the change: r 2.27(4).

6 'Another jurisdiction' means any country outside England and Wales: Domicile and Matrimonial Proceedings Act 1973 Sch 1 para 3(1).

7 Ibid Sch 1 para 7.

761. Obligatory stays. Where before the beginning of the trial or first trial[1] in any proceedings for divorce[2] which are continuing in the court[3] it appears, on the application of a party to the marriage[4], that:

(1) proceedings in respect of the same marriage for divorce or nullity of marriage are continuing in a related jurisdiction[5]; and

(2) the parties to the marriage have resided together after its celebration[6]; and

(3) the place where they resided together when the English proceedings were begun, or, if they did not then reside together, where they last resided together before those proceedings were begun, is in that jurisdiction[7]; and

(4) either of the parties to the marriage was habitually resident[8] in that jurisdiction throughout the year ending with the date on which they last resided together before the date on which the English proceedings were begun[9],

the court must order the proceedings before it to be stayed[10].

The stay may be discharged on the application of any party to the proceedings if it appears to the court that the other proceedings by reference to which the stay was ordered are themselves stayed or concluded, or that a party to those other proceedings has delayed unreasonably in prosecuting them[11]. Where an obligatory stay, imposed under the above-mentioned duty, is discharged, the court may not, acting under that duty, again stay the proceedings[12].

1 For the meaning of 'the trial or first trial' see para 760 note 3 ante.
2 In the case of proceedings which are not only proceedings for divorce, the duty only applies to the proceedings so far as they are proceedings for divorce: see the Domicile and Matrimonial Proceedings Act 1973 s 5(6), Sch 1 para 8(2).
3 Proceedings are continuing in the court if they are pending and not stayed: ibid Sch 1 para 4(2).
4 An application for a stay under these provisions must be made to the district judge, who may either determine the application or refer it, or any question arising on it, to a judge for his decision as if it were an application for ancillary relief: Family Proceedings Rules 1991, SI 1991/1247, r 2.27(1). For the meaning of 'ancillary relief' see r 1.2(1).
5 Domicile and Matrimonial Proceedings Act 1973 s 5(6) Sch 1 para 8(1)(a). 'Related jurisdiction' means any of the following, namely: Scotland; Northern Ireland; Jersey, Guernsey (including Alderney and Sark) and the Isle of Man: Sch 1 para 3(2).
6 Ibid Sch 1 para 8(1)(b).
7 Ibid Sch 1 para 8(1)(c).
8 For the meaning of 'habitually resident' see para 705 ante.
9 Domicile and Matrimonial Proceedings Act 1973 Sch 1 para 8(1)(d).
10 Ibid Sch 1 para 8(1).
11 Ibid Sch 1 para 10(1). An application for the discharge of a stay may be made to the district judge, who may either determine the application or refer it, or any question arising on it, to a judge for his decision as if it were an application for ancillary relief: Family Proceedings Rules 1991 r 2.27(5).
12 Domicile and Matrimonial Proceedings Act 1973 Sch 1 para 10(2).

762. Discretionary stays. Without prejudice to any existing power to stay proceedings[1], where before the beginning of the trial or first trial[2] in any matrimonial proceedings[3] which are continuing in the court[4] it appears to the court that:

(1) any proceedings in respect of the marriage in question, or capable of affecting its validity or subsistence, are continuing in another jurisdiction[5]; and

(2) the balance of fairness, including convenience, as between the parties to the marriage, is such that it is appropriate for the proceedings in that jurisdiction to be disposed of before further steps are taken in the English proceedings or in those proceedings so far as they consist of a particular kind of matrimonial proceedings[6],

the court may, if it thinks fit, order the proceedings before it to be stayed or, as the case may be, to be stayed as far as they consist of proceedings of that kind[7].

In considering for this purpose the balance of fairness and convenience, the court must have regard to all factors appearing to be relevant, including the convenience of witnesses and any delay or expense which may result from the proceedings being stayed or not being stayed[8].

This discretionary power to order a stay may be exercised at any time after the beginning of the trial or first trial if the court declares by order that it is satisfied that a person has failed to perform his duty[9] to furnish particulars of proceedings continuing in a jurisdiction other than England[10].

A stay may be discharged on the application of any party to the proceedings if it appears to the court that the other proceedings by reference to which the stay was ordered are themselves stayed or concluded, or that a party in those other proceedings has delayed unreasonably in prosecuting them[11].

1 Domicile and Matrimonial Proceedings Act 1973 s 5(6)(b). As to these powers see paras 1084–1086 post.
2 As to the meaning of 'the trial or first trial' see para 760 note 3 ante.
3 For the meaning of 'matrimonial proceedings' see para 760 note 1 ante.
4 For the meaning of 'court' see para 741 note 1 ante. As to the meaning of 'continuing in the court' see para 761 note 3 ante.
5 Domicile and Matrimonial Proceedings Act 1973 s 5(6), Sch 1 para 9(1)(a). For the meaning of 'another jurisdiction' see para 760 note 6 ante.
6 Ibid Sch 1 para 9(1)(b).
7 Ibid Sch 1 para 9(1). The power may not be exercised in the case of any proceedings, so far as they are proceedings for divorce, while an application for an obligatory stay of those proceedings (see para 761 ante) is pending: Sch 1 para 9(3). An application for a stay under these provisions must be made to a judge: Family Proceedings Rules 1991, SI 1991/1247, r 2.27(2).
8 Domicile and Matrimonial Proceedings Act 1973 Sch 1 para 9(2). See *R v R (Divorce: Stay of Proceedings)* [1994] 2 FLR 1036; *T v T (Jurisdiction: Forum Conveniens)* [1995] 1 FCR 478, [1995] 2 FLR 660; *de Dampierre v de Dampierre* [1988] AC 92, [1987] 2 All ER 1, HL; and the earlier cases, which must be read in the light of that decision: *Shemshadfard v Shemshadfard* [1981] 1 All ER 726; *Gadd v Gadd* [1985] 1 All ER 58, [1984] 1 WLR 1435, CA; *Thyssen-Bornemisza v Thyssen-Bornemisza* [1986] Fam 1, [1985] 1 All ER 328, CA.
9 Ie his duty under the Domicile and Matrimonial Proceedings Act 1973 Sch 1 para 7: see para 760 ante.
10 See ibid Sch 1 para 9(4).
11 Ibid Sch 1 para 10(1). As to applications for the discharge of a stay see para 761 note 11 ante. Where, on giving directions for trial, it appears to a district judge from any information given in the required particulars (see para 760 note 5 ante) that any proceedings in respect of the marriage or capable of affecting its validity or subsistence are continuing in any country outside England and Wales, and he considers that the question whether the proceedings on the petition should be stayed under Sch 1 para 9 ought to be determined by the court, he must fix a date, time and place for consideration of the question by a judge, and notify the parties accordingly: Family Proceedings Rules 1991 r 2.27(3).

763. Effect of stay on ancillary orders. Where proceedings for divorce, judicial separation or nullity of marriage are stayed by reference to proceedings in a related jurisdiction[1] for divorce, judicial separation or nullity of marriage[2], then, without prejudice to any other effect of the stay[3], any relevant order[4] made in connection with the stayed proceedings ceases to have effect on the expiration of three months beginning with the date on which the stay was imposed, unless the stay is earlier removed or discharged[5] or the court orders otherwise so as to deal with circumstances needing to be dealt with urgently[6]. After imposing a stay, the English court has no power to make a relevant order, or a lump sum order[7] in connection with the stayed proceedings[8] unless the court considers that it is necessary to do so to deal with circumstances needing to be dealt with urgently[9].

If, when the stay is imposed, there is in force or there subsequently comes into force an order made in connection with the other proceedings which makes provision for periodical payments for a spouse or child or for certain other matters relating to a child[10], then, when the stay is imposed or, as the case may be, when the other court's order comes into force[11], any relevant order[12] of the English court in respect of the same subject matter ceases to have effect[13]. The English court may not make a similar order[14], and if the other order contains provisions for periodical payments for a child, the English court has no power to make a lump sum order for that child[15].

If proceedings are stayed so far as they consist of matrimonial proceedings[16] of a particular kind, but not so far as they consist of matrimonial proceedings of a different kind, the provisions described above do not apply; however, without prejudice to the effect of the stay apart from those provisions, the court does not have power to make a relevant order or a lump sum order in connection with the proceedings so far as they are stayed[17].

Nothing in the above provisions affects any power of the English court to vary or discharge a relevant order so far as it is in force[18], to enforce it for any period when it is or was in force[19], or to make a relevant order or a lump sum order in connection with proceedings which were but are no longer stayed[20].

1 For the meaning of 'related jurisdiction' see para 761 note 5 ante.
2 Ie in pursuance of the Domicile and Matrimonial Proceedings Act 1973 s 5(6), Sch 1 (as amended): see Sch 1 paras 8, 9; and paras 761–762 ante.
3 Ibid Sch 1 para 11(2).
4 'Relevant order' is defined by ibid Sch 1 para 11(1) (amended by the Children Act 1989 s 108(5), Sch 13 para 33), as follows:
    (1) an order under the Matrimonial Causes Act 1973 s 22 (existing order for maintenance of a spouse pending suit);
    (2) (a) an order mentioned in s 23(1)(d) or (e) (periodical payments for children), being an order made under s 23(1) or s 23(2)(a) (together with any related order made under s 24A(1) (as added) as to the sale of property: Domicile and Matrimonial Proceedings Act 1973 Sch 1 para 11(3A) (added by the Matrimonial Homes and Property Act 1981 s 8(3)); or (b) an order made in equivalent circumstances under the Children Act 1989 s 15(1), Sch 1 (as amended) and of a kind mentioned in Sch 1 para 1(2)(a) or (b);
    (3) an order under the Matrimonial Causes Act 1973 s 42(1)(a) (repealed with savings) (custody and education of children), or the Children Act 1989 s 8 (contact, residence, prohibited steps or specific issue orders); and
    (4) any order restraining a person from removing a child out of England and Wales or out of the care of another person.
5 Domicile and Matrimonial Proceedings Act 1973 Sch 1 para 11(2)(b).
6 See ibid Sch 1 para 11(2)(c).
7 'Lump sum order' means an order mentioned in the Matrimonial Causes Act 1973 s 23(1)(f), being an order made under s 23(1) or s 23(2)(a) or an order made in equivalent circumstances under the Children Act 1989 Sch 1 and of a kind mentioned in Sch 1 para 1(2)(c): Domicile and Matrimonial Proceedings Act 1973 Sch 1 para 11(1) (amended by the Children Act 1989 Sch 13 para 33).
8 Domicile and Matrimonial Proceedings Act 1973 Sch 1 para 11(2)(a).
9 Ibid Sch 1 para 11(2)(c).
10 Ie provision which could be made by an order under the Children Act 1989 s 8. See CHILDREN vol 5(2) (Reissue) para 770 et seq.
11 Domicile and Matrimonial Proceedings Act 1973 Sch 1 para 11(3) (amended by the Children Act 1989 Sch 13 para 33(1)).
12 See note 4 supra.
13 Domicile and Matrimonial Proceedings Act 1973 Sch 1 para 11(3)(a). Note, however, that the making by the other court of any of the orders referred to in the text has no effect on a previous order of the English court ordering a lump sum payment for a child, or restraining a person from removing a child out of the jurisdiction or out of the care of another person.
14 Ibid Sch 1 para 11(3)(b); and see note 13 supra.
15 Ibid Sch 1 para 11(3)(c); and see note 13 supra.
16 For the meaning of 'matrimonial proceedings' see para 760 note 1 ante. However, in ibid Sch 1 para 11(4) matrimonial proceedings do not include proceedings for a declaration: Sch 1 para 11(4).
17 Ibid Sch 1 para 11(4).
18 Ibid Sch 1 para 11(5)(a).
19 Ibid Sch 1 para 11(5)(b).
20 Ibid Sch 1 para 11(5)(c).

(3) ASSIGNMENT OF PROPERTY ON MARRIAGE

(i) Where there is no Marriage Contract or Settlement

764. Effect of marriage on movables. In the absence of any marriage contract or settlement and in the absence of any subsequent change of domicile, the rights of a husband and wife to each other's movables, whether possessed at the date of the marriage or acquired afterwards, are governed by the law of the parties' matrimonial domicile[1]. In the absence of special circumstances[2], this is presumed to be the husband's domicile at the date of the marriage[3].

1   *Sawer v Shute* (1792) 1 Anst 63; *Royal Bank of Scotland v Cuthbert* (1812) 1 Rose 462 at 481; as explained in *Selkrig v Davies* (1814) 2 Dow 230, HL; *M'Cormick v Garnett* (1854) 5 De GM & G 278; *Welch v Tennent* [1891] AC 639 at 644–645, HL; *Re Martin, Loustalan v Loustalan* [1900] P 211 at 233, CA; *Re Egerton's Will Trusts, Lloyds Bank Ltd v Egerton* [1956] Ch 593, [1956] 2 All ER 817.
2   Certain circumstances might lead the court to infer that the parties intend their proprietary rights to be regulated by another law, eg where parties without means agree before marrying to emigrate to another country immediately after the marriage, and do so: *Re Egerton's Will Trusts, Lloyds Bank Ltd v Egerton* [1956] Ch 593 at 604–605, [1956] 2 All ER 817 at 824.
3   See the cases cited in note 1 supra.

765. Change of domicile after marriage. The effect of a change of domicile after the date of the marriage on the rights of the parties to a marriage to each other's movables is unclear. Some authority suggests that the law of the new domicile governs all the rights of the parties to each other's movables[1], except in so far as proprietary rights have already vested in either spouse[2]. Other authority adopts a doctrine of immutability, whereby the property régime under which the parties were married applies notwithstanding a change in domicile[3].

1   *Lashley v Hog* (1804) 2 Coop temp Cott 449, HL; as explained and distinguished in *De Nicols v Curlier* [1900] AC 21 at 34, 36–37, 44, HL; cf *Re Mengel's Will Trusts, Westminster Bank Ltd v Mengel* [1962] Ch 791, [1962] 2 All ER 490, although in this case the point was not argued. However, *Lashley v Hog* supra can be explained as turning on the law of succession.
2   Cf *De Nicols v Curlier* [1900] AC 21, HL.
3   *De Nicols v Curlier* [1900] AC 21, HL, in which case, however, there was an implied contract. On the whole matter see Dicey and Morris *The Conflict of Laws* (12th Edn, 1993) 1081–1087.

766. Effect of marriage on immovables. In the absence of any marriage contract or settlement, the rights of husband and wife to each other's immovables are governed by the lex situs, that is the law of the country where the immovable is situated[1].

1   *Welch v Tennent* [1891] AC 639, HL; *Callwood v Callwood* [1960] AC 659 at 683, [1960] 2 All ER 1 at 10, PC; *Tezcan v Tezcan* (1992) 87 DLR (4th) 503, 38 RFL (3d) 142, BC CA. See also paras 924–927 post.

767. Married Women's Property Act 1882. The jurisdiction of the English court summarily to determine disputes between husband and wife as to the title to or possession of property[1] extends to movables and immovables situated abroad as well as in England[2], and the court may make an order under that jurisdiction even though the spouses are domiciled abroad and subject to a system of community of property[3].

1   Ie under the Married Women's Property Act 1882 s 17 (as amended): see HUSBAND AND WIFE vol 22 para 1027 et seq.

2 *Razelos v Razelos* [1969] 3 All ER 929, sub nom *Razelos v Razelos (No 2)* [1970] 1 WLR 392 (where at 936 and 403 the court assumed that its order relating to the foreign immovables would be recognised and enforced by the lex situs); for further proceedings see [1970] 1 All ER 386n, [1970] 1 WLR 390.
3 *Re Bettinson's Question* [1956] Ch 67, [1955] 3 All ER 296.

(ii) Where there is a Marriage Contract or Settlement

768. Contracts relating to movables. Where there is a marriage contract or settlement, the rights of the husband and wife to all movables within its terms, whether possessed at the date of the marriage or acquired afterwards, are governed by the proper law of the contract or settlement[1], even if the settlement is implied by law[2], and even if there is a change of domicile after the marriage[3].

1 *Feaubert v Turst* (1703) Prec Ch 207, 1 Bro Parl Cas 129, HL; *Anstruther v Adair* (1834) 2 My & K 513; *Este v Smyth* (1854) 18 Beav 112; *Duncan v Cannan* (1854) 18 Beav 128; *Watts v Shrimpton* (1855) 21 Beav 97; *Van Grutten v Digby* (1862) 31 Beav 561; *Chamberlain v Napier* (1880) 15 ChD 614; *Re Fitzgerald, Surman v Fitzgerald* [1904] 1 Ch 573, CA; *Duke of Marlborough v A-G* [1945] Ch 78, [1945] 1 All ER 165, CA. The proper law thus governs the material or essential validity of the settlement and its interpretation and effect: see the cases cited supra, and the cases cited in the notes to para 769 post. Contractual rights as to 'rights in property arising out of a matrimonial relationship' are not within the scope of the Rome Convention on the law applicable to contractual obligations as given effect in England by the Contracts (Applicable Law) Act 1990: s 2, Sch 1 art 1(2)(b); see para 844 et seq post.
2 *De Nicols v Curlier* [1900] AC 21, HL.
3 *De Nicols v Curlier* [1900] AC 21, HL; *Feaubert v Turst* (1703) Prec Ch 207, 1 Bro Parl Cas 129, HL; *Duncan v Cannan* (1854) 18 Beav 128. As to change in the terms of a contract after a change in domicile see *Duyvewaardt v Barber* (1992) 43 RFL (3d) 139, BC CA.

769. The proper law of a marriage contract or settlement. The most important factor in determining the proper law of a marriage contract or settlement relating to movables is the law of the matrimonial domicile[1], but this may be displaced by any sufficient indication[2] of an intention to contract with reference to some other law[3]. Such an intention may be apparent from an express stipulation in the settlement that another law is to apply[4]. Otherwise, it may be gathered from a consideration of the contract as a whole, taking into account circumstances such as the legal form of the settlement[5], the invalidity of certain provisions under the law of the matrimonial domicile[6], the character and situation of the property[7], the domicile and residence of the trustees of the settlement[8], the source of provision of property for the settlement[9], and the circumstances in which the settlement came to be made[10]. For the purpose of determining the proper law of the settlement, the contract must be considered as at the date of the settlement[11].

1 *De Nicols v Curlier* [1900] AC 21, HL; *Re Muspratt-Williams, Muspratt-Williams v Howe* (1901) 84 LT 191 at 192; *Re Bankes, Reynolds v Ellis* [1902] 2 Ch 333 at 343; *Re Fitzgerald, Surman v Fitzgerald* [1904] 1 Ch 573 at 587, 594, CA; *Re Hewitt's Settlement, Hewitt v Hewitt* [1915] 1 Ch 228 at 232; *Duke of Marlborough v A-G* [1945] Ch 78, [1945] 1 All ER 165, CA. As to the matrimonial domicile see para 764 ante.
2 For this purpose, all such evidence of the circumstances as is generally admissible for the purpose of construing a written contract is admissible to ascertain its proper law, and direct evidence of intention supplied after the date of the settlement is inadmissible: *Duke of Marlborough v A-G* [1945] Ch 78 at 88–89, [1945] 1 All ER 165 at 171, CA.
3 *Chamberlain v Napier* (1880) 15 ChD 614; *Re Barnard, Barnard v White* (1887) 56 LT 9; *Re Bankes, Reynolds v Ellis* [1902] 2 Ch 333; *Re Fitzgerald, Surman v Fitzgerald* [1904] 1 Ch 573, CA; *Re Mackenzie, Mackenzie v Edwards-Moss* [1911] 1 Ch 578 at 596; *Re Hewitt's Settlement, Hewitt v Hewitt* [1915] 1 Ch 228 at 232–233.

4   *Este v Smyth* (1854) 18 Beav 112 at 122; *Van Grutten v Digby* (1862) 31 Beav 561 at 568; *Re Fitzgerald, Surman v Fitzgerald* [1904] 1 Ch 573 at 587, CA; *Montgomery v Zarifi* (1918) 88 LJPC 20, HL; cf *Guépratte v Young* (1851) 4 De G & Sm 217; *Byam v Byam* (1854) 19 Beav 58; *Re Muspratt-Williams, Muspratt-Williams v Howe* (1901) 84 LT 191.

5   *Watts v Shrimpton* (1855) 21 Beav 97; *Re Barnard, Barnard v White* (1887) 56 LT 9; *Re Mégret, Tweedie v Maunder* [1901] 1 Ch 547; *Re Bankes, Reynolds v Ellis* [1902] 2 Ch 333; *Re Fitzgerald, Surman v Fitzgerald* [1904] 1 Ch 573, CA; *Re Mackenzie, Mackenzie v Edwards-Moss* [1911] 1 Ch 578; *Re Hewitt's Settlement, Hewitt v Hewitt* [1915] 1 Ch 228; *Duke of Marlborough v A-G* [1945] Ch 78, [1945] 1 All ER 165, CA; *Sawrey-Cookson v Sawrey-Cookson's Trustees* (1905) 8 F 157, Ct of Sess.

6   *Re Bankes, Reynolds v Ellis* [1902] 2 Ch 333; *Re Fitzgerald, Surman v Fitzgerald* [1904] 1 Ch 573, CA.

7   *Van Grutten v Digby* (1862) 31 Beav 561 at 567; *Watts v Shrimpton* (1855) 21 Beav 97; *Re Bankes, Reynolds v Ellis* [1902] 2 Ch 333; *Duke of Marlborough v A-G* [1945] Ch 78 at 85–86, [1945] 1 All ER 165 at 170, CA.

8   *Van Grutten v Digby* (1862) 31 Beav 561; *Re Cigala's Settlement Trusts* (1878) 7 ChD 351; *Re Mégret, Tweedie v Maunder* [1901] 1 Ch 547; *Re Hewitt's Settlement, Hewitt v Hewitt* [1915] 1 Ch 228; cf *Duke of Marlborough v A-G* [1945] Ch 78 at 84–87, [1945] 1 All ER 165 at 169–171, CA.

9   *Van Grutten v Digby* (1862) 31 Beav 561; *Re Mégret, Tweedie v Maunder* [1901] 1 Ch 547; *Re Bankes, Reynolds v Ellis* [1902] 2 Ch 333; *Re Fitzgerald, Surman v Fitzgerald* [1904] 1 Ch 573, CA; *Re Mackenzie, Mackenzie v Edwards-Moss* [1911] 1 Ch 578.

10   *Colliss v Hector* (1875) LR 19 Eq 334, where the settlement was held to be governed by English law, although the husband was a domiciled Turk, as the marriage had taken place on his express promise that the matrimonial domicile should be England; cf *Van Grutten v Digby* (1862) 31 Beav 561 at 567.

11   *Re Fitzgerald, Surman v Fitzgerald* [1904] 1 Ch 573 at 578, CA; *Re Hewitt's Settlement, Hewitt v Hewitt* [1915] 1 Ch 228; *Duke of Marlborough v A-G* [1945] Ch 78 at 85, [1945] 1 All ER 165 at 170, CA.

770. Capacity. Although it used to be thought that the capacity of the parties to enter into a marriage contract or settlement relating to movables was governed by the law of their respective domiciles[1], the better view seems to be that this capacity is governed by the proper law of the settlement[2].

1   See *Re Cooke's Trusts* (1887) 56 LJCh 637; *Cooper v Cooper* (1888) 13 App Cas 88, HL.

2   *Viditz v O'Hagan* [1900] 2 Ch 87, CA; explained in Dicey and Morris *The Conflict of Laws* (12th Edn, 1993) 1078–1079. The proper law here means the system of law with which the contract is most closely related, regardless of the parties' intention: see *Cooper v Cooper* (1888) 13 App Cas 88 at 108, HL. As to the proper law of marriage contracts or settlements generally see para 769 ante.

771. Formal validity. A marriage contract or settlement relating to movables is formally valid if it complies with the formal requirements either of the law of the place where it was executed[1] or of its proper law[2].

1   *Guépratte v Young* (1851) 4 De G & Sm 217.

2   *Watts v Shrimpton* (1855) 21 Beav 97; *Van Grutten v Digby* (1862) 31 Beav 561; *Re Barnard, Barnard v White* (1887) 56 LT 9; *Viditz v O'Hagan* [1899] 2 Ch 569; on appeal [1900] 2 Ch 87, CA; *Re Bankes, Reynolds v Ellis* [1902] 2 Ch 333. As to the proper law of marriage contracts or settlements generally see para 769 ante.

772. Contracts relating to immovables. Where there is a marriage contract or settlement relating to immovables, it seems that the rights of husband and wife to all English immovables within its terms[1], whether possessed at the date of the marriage or acquired afterwards, are governed by the proper law of the contract or settlement[2], even if the settlement is implied by law[3]. However, the settlement will only be operative as a conveyance if it conforms to the rules of English domestic law[4].

In so far as a marriage contract or settlement relates to foreign immovables, the rights of the parties to the marriage over such immovables are governed by the lex situs, that is the law of the country where the immovables are situated[5].

1 The question whether particular immovables are within the terms of the settlement is governed by its proper law: *Callwood v Callwood* [1960] AC 659, [1960] 2 All ER 1, PC.

2 As to the proper law of a marriage contract or settlement see para 769 ante.

3 *Re De Nicols, De Nicols v Curlier* [1900] 2 Ch 410; cf *Gray v Smith* (1889) 43 ChD 208, CA. See also *Chiwell v Carlyon* (1897) 14 SC 61 (Cape of Good Hope). This case originated in the Chancery Division (1897A No 2919), and raised the question as to what passed as the joint or community property under a joint will of spouses made while domiciled in South Africa; the spouses subsequently settled in England and the husband acquired land there; Stirling J submitted a question of law to the Cape Supreme Court, and accepted that court's opinion that where a couple had married in South Africa under the régime of community of goods, both being domiciled there at the time of the marriage, and had afterwards settled in England where the husband bought land, the land was subject to the community and was joint estate within the terms of the joint will.

  As regards contracts subject to English law, note the provisions of the Law of Property (Miscellaneous Provisions) Act 1989 s 2, which requires all dispositions of an interest in land (with certain exceptions, notably regarding the creation or operation of resulting, implied or constructive trusts), to be in writing.

4 *Re De Nicols, De Nicols v Curlier* [1900] 2 Ch 410 at 416; cf *Callwood v Callwood* [1960] AC 659 at 683, [1960] 2 All ER 1 at 10, PC (devolution of immovables).

5 *Re Fitzgerald, Surman v Fitzgerald* [1904] 1 Ch 573 at 588, CA; *Re Pearse's Settlement, Pearse v Pearse* [1909] 1 Ch 304. See also paras 924–927 post.

773. Variation of settlements. The English court[1] has jurisdiction to vary any antenuptial or post-nuptial settlement on or after granting a decree of divorce, nullity of marriage or judicial separation[2], even if the settlement is governed by foreign law and comprises property situated in a foreign country[3]. The jurisdiction will not be exercised if an order of the court would be ineffective in the foreign country[4], and in such a case the court may set aside service abroad on the foreign trustees of the settlement[5]. The court has similar powers in certain cases where the decree has been pronounced by a foreign court[6].

The English court[7] has jurisdiction to approve any arrangement varying or revoking all or any of the trusts on which property is held under any will, settlement or other disposition[8], even if the settlement is governed by foreign law[9]. The jurisdiction is unlimited[10], but where there are substantial foreign elements in the case the court will consider carefully whether it is proper for it to exercise the jurisdiction[11]. The jurisdiction may be exercised to convert an English settlement into a settlement governed by foreign law[12].

1 For the meaning of 'court' see para 755 note 1 ante. As to the meaning of 'English' in relation to courts see para 604 ante.

2 See the Matrimonial Causes Act 1973 s 24(1)(c).

3 *Nunneley v Nunneley and Marrian* (1890) 15 PD 186; *Forsyth v Forsyth* [1891] P 363; *Goff v Goff* [1934] P 107; cf *De Ricci v De Ricci* [1891] P 378; *Hunter v Hunter and Waddington* [1962] P 1, [1961] 2 All ER 121.

4 *Tallack v Tallack and Broekema* [1927] P 211; *Goff v Goff* [1934] P 107. Cf *Wyler v Lyons* [1963] P 274, [1963] 1 All ER 821; distinguished in *Razelos v Razelos* [1969] 3 All ER 929 at 936, sub nom *Razelos v Razelos (No 2)* [1970] 1 WLR 392 at 403–404; for further proceedings see [1970] 1 All ER 386n, [1970] 1 WLR 390.

5 *Goff v Goff* [1934] P 107.

6 See the Matrimonial and Family Proceedings Act 1984 Pt III (ss 12–27) (as amended), particularly s 17: see para 756 ante.

7 Ie the High Court or a county court: see the Variation of Trusts Act 1958 s 1(3) (as amended); and the County Courts Act 1984 s 23(b).

8 See the Variation of Trusts Act 1958 s 1(1); and TRUSTS vol 48 (Reissue) paras 923–924.

9 *Re Ker's Settlement Trusts* [1963] Ch 553, [1963] 1 All ER 801; *Re Paget's Settlement* [1965] 1 All ER 58, [1965] 1 WLR 1046.

10 *Re Ker's Settlement Trusts* [1963] Ch 553 at 556, [1963] 1 All ER 801 at 802–803; *Re Paget's Settlement* [1965] 1 All ER 58 at 60–61, [1965] 1 WLR 1046 at 1050.

11 *Re Paget's Settlement* [1965] 1 All ER 58, [1965] 1 WLR 1046.
12 *Re Seale's Marriage Settlement* [1961] Ch 574, [1961] 3 All ER 136; *Re Weston's Settlements, Weston v Weston* [1969] 1 Ch 223, [1968] 3 All ER 338, CA; *Re Windeatt's Will Trusts* [1969] 2 All ER 324, [1969] 1 WLR 692; *Re Whitehead's Will Trusts, Burke v Burke* [1971] 2 All ER 1334; [1971] 1 WLR 833; and see TRUSTS vol 48 (Reissue) para 923.

(4) ORDERS AS TO CHILDREN

774. Introductory. A court in England and Wales has jurisdiction to make certain orders as to children[1] if, and only if, certain requirements are satisfied[2]. The orders in question[3] are (1) contact, residence, specific issue or prohibited steps orders made under the Children Act 1989 other than an order varying or discharging such an order[4]; and (2) orders made in the exercise of the inherent jurisdiction of the High Court with respect to children so far as they give the care of a child to any person or provide for contact with, or the education of, a child; but excluding orders varying or revoking such an order[5].

1 'Child' in these provisions means a person who has not attained the age of 18: Family Law Act 1986 s 7(a) (s 7 substituted by the Children Act 1989 s 108(5), Sch 13 para 67).
2 See para 774 et seq post. As to the meaning of 'England and Wales' see para 604 ante.
3 Referred to as 'Part I orders', the reference being to the Family Law Act 1986 Pt I (ss 1–43) (as amended): s 1(1) (amended by the Children Act 1989 Sch 13 para 62).
4 Ie 'section 8 orders' made under the Children Act 1989 s 8 (see CHILDREN vol 5(2) (Reissue) para 770 et seq): Family Law Act 1986 s 1(1)(a) (substituted by the Children Act 1989 Sch 13 para 63(1)(a)).
5 Family Law Act 1986 s 1(1)(d) (substituted by the Children Act 1989 Sch 13 para 63(1)(b)). As to the exercise of the High Court's inherent jurisdiction see CHILDREN vol 5(2) (Reissue) para 747.
  'Part I order' also includes any order which would have been a custody order by virtue of the Family Law Act 1986 s 1 in any form in which it was in force at any time before its amendment by the Children Act 1989; and (with certain exceptions) excludes any order which would have been excluded from being a custody order by virtue of that section in any such form: Family Law Act 1986 s 1(3) (substituted by the Children Act 1989 Sch 13 para 63(3)). As to the duration and variation of orders see the Family Law Act 1986 s 6 (as amended); and CHILDREN vol 5(2) (Reissue) para 1014.

775. Matrimonial proceedings. A court in England and Wales has jurisdiction to make an order under the Children Act 1989[1] with respect to a child in or in connection with matrimonial proceedings[2] if, and only if[3] the matrimonial proceedings are proceedings in respect of the marriage of the parents of the child concerned[4], and:
  (1) the proceedings are for divorce or nullity of marriage, and are continuing[5]; or
  (2) they are proceedings for judicial separation, and are continuing, and the jurisdiction of the court is not excluded by virtue of the fact that after the grant of a decree of judicial separation, on the relevant date[6], proceedings for divorce or nullity in respect of the marriage are continuing in Scotland, Northern Ireland or a specified dependent territory[7]; or
  (3) the proceedings have been dismissed after the beginning of the trial but the order in respect of the child is being made forthwith, or the application for the order was made on or before the dismissal[8].
Where a court has jurisdiction to make an order in, or in connection with, matrimonial proceedings, but considers that it would be more appropriate for the matters relating to the child to be determined outside England and Wales, the court may direct that (for so long as the order making that direction remains in force) no such order may be made by any court in or in connection with those proceedings[9].

1 Ie a 'section 8 order': see para 774 text and note 4 ante.
2 'Matrimonial proceedings' means proceedings for divorce, nullity or judicial separation: Family Law
   Act 1986 s 7(b) (s 7 substituted by the Children Act 1989 Sch 13 para 67).
3 Family Law Act 1986 s 2(1) (s 2 substituted by the Children Act 1989 s 108(5), Sch 13 para 64).
4 Family Law Act 1986 s 2A(1) (s 2A added by the Children Act 1989 Sch 13 para 64).
5 Family Law Act 1986 s 2A(1)(a) (as added: see note 4 supra).
6 The relevant date is the date on which the application (or first application, if two or more are
   determined together) for the order was made, or if no such application was made, the date on which the
   court is considering whether to make the order: ibid s 7(c) (as substituted: see note 2 supra).
7 Ibid s 2A(1)(b), (2) (s 2A as added: see note 4 supra; s 2A(2) subsequently amended by the Family Law
   Act 1986 (Dependent Territories) Order 1991, SI 1991/1723, art 3(2), Sch 2, para 2). This exclusion
   does not apply where the court in Scotland, Northern Ireland or the dependent territory has made an
   order (1) directing that no Part I order (or equivalent) be made by any court; or (2) staying the
   proceedings before it in respect of the issues affecting the children: see the Family Law Act 1986 s 2A(3)
   (as added). 'Specified dependent territory' means a territory for the time being specified in the Family
   Law Act 1986 (Dependent Territories) Order 1991 Sch 1: Family Law Act 1986 s 42(1) (definition
   added by the Family Law Act 1986 (Dependent Territories) Order 1991 Sch 2 para 24(1)). At the date at
   which this volume states the law, that Schedule specifies the Isle of Man. As to 'Part I' orders see
   para 774 ante.
8 Family Law Act 1986 s 2A(1)(c) (as added: see note 4 supra).
9 Ibid s 2A(4) (as added: see note 4 supra).

776. Non-matrimonial cases. A court in England and Wales has jurisdiction to
make an order under the Children Act 1989[1] in a non-matrimonial case[2] if, and only if[3]
(1) on the relevant date[4] the child[5] concerned is habitually resident[6] in England and
Wales[7] or is present in England and Wales and is not habitually resident in any part of
the United Kingdom[8]; and (2) in either case the jurisdiction of the court is not
excluded by virtue of the fact that on the relevant date, matrimonial proceedings[9] are
continuing in a court in Scotland, Northern Ireland or a specified dependent territory[10]
in respect of the marriage of the parents of the child concerned[11].

1 Ie a 'section 8 order': see para 774 text and note 4 ante.
2 Ie where the condition in the Family Law Act 1986 s 2A (as added) (see para 775 ante) is not satisfied:
   s 2(2) (s 2 substituted by the Children Act 1989 s 108(5), Sch 13 para 64).
3 Family Law Act 1986 ss 2(2), 3(1) (s 2 as substituted: see note 2 supra; s 3(1) amended by the Children
   Act 1989 Sch 13 para 62).
4 For the meaning of 'the relevant date' see para 775 note 6 ante.
5 For the meaning of 'child' see para 774 note 1 ante.
6 As to the meaning of 'habitually resident' see *Kapur v Kapur* [1984] FLR 920; and para 705 ante.
7 Family Law Act 1986 s 3(1)(a).
8 Ibid s 3(1)(b) (amended by the Family Law Act 1986 (Dependent Territories) Order 1991, SI
   1991/1723, art 3(2), Sch 2 para 3). 'Part of the United Kingdom' means 'England and Wales, Scotland
   or Northern Ireland: Family Law Act 1986 s 42(1). For the meaning of 'United Kingdom' see para 604
   ante.
9 For the meaning of 'matrimonial proceedings' see para 775 note 2 ante.
10 As to specified dependent territories see para 775 note 7 ante.
11 Family Law Act 1986 s 3(1), (2) (s 3(2) amended by the Children Act 1989 Sch 13 para 65; and by the
   Family Law Act 1986 (Dependent Territories) Order 1991 Sch 2 para 3). This exclusion does not apply
   where the court in Scotland, Northern Ireland or the dependent territory has made an order (1)
   directing that no Part I order (or equivalent) be made by it; or (2) staying the proceedings before it in
   respect of the issues affecting the children: see the Family Law Act 1986 s 3(3) (amended by the Children
   Act 1989 Sch 13 para 62; and the Family Law Act 1986 (Dependent Territories) Order 1991 Sch 2
   para 3). As to 'Part I' orders see para 774 ante.

777. Inherent jurisdiction. A court in England and Wales has jurisdiction to make
orders in the exercise of the inherent jurisdiction of the High Court[1] with respect to
children[2] if, and only if, certain requirements as to residence or presence[3] are met or the

child concerned is present in England and Wales on the relevant date and the court considers that the immediate exercise of its powers is necessary for his protection[4].

1 Ie such orders as are mentioned in para 774 text and note 5 ante.
2 For the meaning of 'child' see para 774 note 1 ante.
3 Ie the requirements of the Family Law Act 1986 s 3 (as amended): see para 776 ante.
4 Ibid s 2(3) (substituted by the Children Act 1989 s 108(5), Sch 13 para 64).

778. Power of court to refuse application or stay proceedings. A court in England and Wales which has jurisdiction to make an order[1] may refuse an application for the order in any case where the matter in question has already been determined in proceedings outside England and Wales[2]. Where, at any stage of the proceedings on an application made to a court in England and Wales for such an order, or for the variation of such an order, it appears to the court (1) that proceedings with respect to the matters to which the application relates are continuing outside England and Wales; or (2) that it would be more appropriate for those matters to be determined in proceedings to be taken outside England and Wales, the court may stay the proceedings on the application[3].

1 Ie a 'Part I order': see para 774 text and notes 3, 5 ante.
2 Family Law Act 1986 s 5(1) (amended by the Children Act 1989 s 108(5), Sch 13 para 62).
3 Family Law Act 1986 s 5(2) (amended by the Children Act 1989 Sch 13 para 62). This is without prejudice to any other power the court may have to grant or remove a stay: Family Law Act 1986 s 5(4). The court may remove a stay granted under s 5(2) (as amended) if it appears to the court that there has been unreasonable delay in the taking or prosecution of the other proceedings referred to, or that those proceedings are stayed, sisted or concluded: s 5(3). In determining the most appropriate forum the child's welfare is an important, but not paramount, consideration: *Re S (A Minor) (Contact: Jurisdiction)* [1995] 2 FCR 162, [1995] 1 FLR 314.

779. Exercise of jurisdiction. In deciding any question as to the upbringing of a child[1], the child's welfare must be the court's paramount consideration[2].

The decisions of courts in other parts of the United Kingdom may be recognised and enforced in England and Wales[3], as may custody orders of courts in states party to the European Convention on the Recognition and Enforcement of Decisions Concerning Custody of Children and on the Restoration of Custody of Children[4]. Subject to that, the English court must make its own assessment as to the welfare of the child; relevant provisions of foreign law or orders made by foreign courts are to be given due weight but are not decisive[5].

To some extent, special considerations apply where there has been a kidnapping, that is where a minor has been brought to England in defiance of the order of a foreign court, or against the wishes of one or both parents and with some element of force or deception or secrecy[6]. In these cases the welfare of the child remains the paramount consideration, but in assessing it the court will take into account the kidnapper's conduct and its effect on the child[7]. The court may order the child's return to the foreign country to minimise the harmful consequences of a kidnapping and in some cases it will do so by way of a summary order without necessarily examining all the issues in the case: this prevents a kidnapper from gaining an advantage through the passing of time[8]. In dealing with these cases, the court will take into account the principles underlying the Hague Convention on the Civil Aspects of International Child Abduction[9], even where the Convention provisions do not apply as the foreign state concerned is not a party to it[10].

1 Ie a person under the age of 18: Children Act 1989 s 105(1).
2 Ibid s 1(1): see CHILDREN vol 5(2) (Reissue) para 809.
3 See para 780 post. For the meaning of 'United Kingdom' and 'England and Wales' see para 604 ante.
4 This Convention is given effect in English law by the Child Abduction and Custody Act 1985. See CHILDREN vol 5(2) (Reissue) para 996 et seq.
5 *J v C* [1970] AC 668 at 700–701, 720, [1969] 1 All ER 788 at 812, 828–829, HL; *Re B———'s Settlement, B——— v B———* [1940] Ch 54; *McKee v McKee* [1951] AC 352, [1951] 1 All ER 942, PC; *Re E (D) (an infant)* [1967] Ch 761, [1967] 2 All ER 881, CA; *Re B (S) (an infant)* [1968] Ch 204, [1967] 3 All ER 629. See also *Uhlig v Uhlig* (1916) 115 LT 647, CA (English public policy precluded order for removal of child to enemy jurisdiction).
6 *Re H (infants)* [1966] 1 All ER 886, [1966] 1 WLR 381 at 393, CA; *Re E (D) (an infant)* [1967] Ch 761, [1967] 2 All ER 881, CA. See also *Re P (GE) (an infant)* [1965] Ch 568 at 588, [1964] 3 All ER 977 at 984, CA; *Re T (infants)* [1968] Ch 704, [1968] 3 All ER 411; *Re S (M) (an infant)* [1971] Ch 621 at 624–625, [1971] 1 All ER 459 at 462; *Re F (A Minor) (Abduction: Custody Rights)* [1991] Fam 25, [1990] 3 All ER 97, CA. See also *Re T (an infant)* [1969] 3 All ER 998, [1969] 1 WLR 1608 (child almost of age).
7 *Re L (minors)* [1974] 1 All ER 913, [1974] 1 WLR 250, CA, applying *J v C* [1970] AC 668, [1969] 1 All ER 788, HL; *Re H (infants)* [1966] 1 All ER 886, [1966] 1 WLR 381 at 393, CA; *Re E (D) (an infant)* [1967] Ch 761, [1967] 2 All ER 881, CA. Cf *Re Kernot (an infant), Kernot v Kernot* [1965] Ch 217, [1964] 3 All ER 339.
8 *Re L (minors)* [1974] 1 All ER 913, [1974] 1 WLR 250, CA; *Re H (infants)* [1966] 1 All ER 886, [1966] 1 WLR 381 at 393, CA; *Re C (Minors) (Wardship: Jurisdiction* [1978] Fam 105, [1978] 2 All ER 230, CA; *Re F (A Minor) (Abduction: Custody Rights)* [1991] Fam 25, [1990] 3 All ER 97, CA; *Re M (Minors) (Abduction: Peremptory Return Order)* (1995) Times, 20 November.
9 This Convention is given effect in English law by the Child Abduction and Custody Act 1985: see CHILDREN vol 5(2) (Reissue) para 985 et seq.
10 *G v G (Minors)* [1991] 2 FLR 506, CA; *Re F (A Minor) (Abduction: Custody Rights)* [1991] Fam 25, [1990] 3 All ER 97, CA; *Re S (Minors) (Abduction)* [1993] 2 FCR 499, CA; *D v D (Child Abduction)* [1994] 1 FCR 654, CA; *Re M (Abduction: Non-Convention Country)* [1995] 1 FLR 89, CA; *Re M (Jurisdiction: Forum Conveniens)* [1995] 2 FLR 224, CA.

780. Recognition of orders. Where an order[1] made by a court in any part of the United Kingdom[2] or a specified dependent territory[3] is in force with respect to a child who has not attained the age of 16, the order is recognised in any other part of the United Kingdom (or, where the order was made in a dependent territory, in any part of the United Kingdom) as having the same effect in that part as if it had been made by the appropriate court in that part and as if that court had had jurisdiction to make it[4]. However, an order so recognised in a part of the United Kingdom will not be enforced there unless it has been registered[5] in that part of the United Kingdom and proceedings for enforcement[6] are taken[7].

1 Ie a 'Part I order': see para 774 text and notes 3, 5 ante.
2 For the meaning of 'part of the United Kingdom' see para 776 note 8 ante.
3 As to specified dependent territories see para 775 note 7 ante.
4 Family Law Act 1986 s 25(1) (amended by the Children Act 1989 s 108(5), Sch 13 para 62; and by the Family Law Act 1986 (Dependent Territories) Order 1991, SI 1991/1723, art 3(2), Sch 2 para 12). This does not extend to provisions in the order as to the means by which rights conferred by the order are to be enforced: Family Law Act 1986 s 25(2) (s 25(2), (3) amended by the Children Act 1989 Sch 13 para 62).
5 Ie under ibid s 27 (as amended): see CHILDREN vol 5(2) (Reissue) para 1016.
6 Ie under ibid s 29 (as amended): see CHILDREN vol 5(2) (Reissue) para 1017.
7 Ibid s 25(3) (as amended: see note 4 supra). A registered order becomes unenforceable if it is superseded by an order made by a court in England: *S v S (Custody: Jurisdiction)* [1995] 1 FLR 155.

781. Foreign guardians. The rights of a guardian appointed under the law of a foreign country will be recognised in England and Wales[1]. The jurisdiction of a foreign court to appoint a guardian will probably be recognised if it is exercised in circumstances corresponding to those in which the English court would claim inherent jurisdiction[2]. The foreign guardian cannot exercise any authority over the person or property of the ward as of right; the English court will respect his wishes if they are in accordance with the welfare of the child, which is always the paramount consideration[3].

1 As to the meaning of 'England and Wales' see para 604 ante.
2 As to the inherent jurisdiction see para 777 ante.
3 Children Act 1989 s 1(1) (see CHILDREN vol 5(2) (Reissue) para 809); *Stuart v Marquis of Bute* (1861) 9 HL Cas 440; *Re B——'s Settlement, B—— v B——* [1940] Ch 54. See also *McKee v McKee* [1951] AC 352 at 366, [1951] 1 All ER 942 at 949, PC; *Monaco v Monaco* (1937) 157 LTR 231. See also *Re S (Hospital Patient: Foreign Curator)* [1995] 3 WLR 596, where the jurisdiction of the English court (based on presence in England) regarding the care of a mentally incapacitated person was not displaced by the appointment of a guardian by the court of the state of his domicile).

782. Property of children. In deciding any question as to the administration of any property belonging to a child[1], the child's welfare must be the court's paramount consideration[2]. Property subject to the control of the court will not be paid over to the child's parent or guardian, even if payment would otherwise be proper, if to do so would be contrary to the child's interests[3]. Subject to this, the rights of a parent over the movable property of his minor child are governed by the law of their domicile[4], and the rights of a foreign guardian by the law under which he was appointed[5]. Under general principles, rights over the immovable property of minors are governed by the lex situs, namely the law of the country where the immovable is situated.

1 Ie a person under the age of 18: Children Act 1989 s 105(1).
2 Ibid s 1(1): see CHILDREN vol 5(2) (Reissue) para 809.
3 *Re Chatard's Settlement* [1899] 1 Ch 712. In the case of guardians appointed in Scotland note the effect of the Judicial Factors (Scotland) Act 1889 s 13.
4 *Gambier v Gambier* (1835) 7 Sim 263; *Re Chatard's Settlement* [1899] 1 Ch 712. See also *Re Brown's Trust* (1865) 12 LT 488; *Re Hellmann's Will* (1866) LR 2 Eq 363. These cases were decided at a time when parents and their minor children always had a common domicile, which is now not always the case: see paras 690, 701 ante. It is suggested that the law of the domicile of the child should govern.
5 *Re Crichton's Trust* (1855) 24 LTOS 267; *Mackie v Darling* (1871) LR 12 Eq 319; *Re Ferguson's Trusts* (1874) 22 WR 762; *Re Chatard's Settlement* [1899] 1 Ch 712 at 716.

(5) LEGITIMACY AND LEGITIMATION

783. Jurisdiction to grant declarations of parentage or legitimacy. The English court[1] has jurisdiction to grant a declaration that a named person is or was the parent of the applicant or that the applicant is the legitimate child of his parents[2] if the applicant is domiciled in England and Wales[3] on the date of the application or has been habitually resident[4] there throughout the period of one year ending with that date[5].

Where on an application for such a declaration the truth of the proposition to be declared is proved to the satisfaction of the court, the court must make that declaration unless to do so would manifestly be contrary to public policy[6]. A declaration binds the Crown and all other persons[7].

1 Ie the High Court or a county court: Family Law Act 1986 s 63.
2 See ibid s 56(1) (s 56 substituted by the Family Law Reform Act 1987 s 22); and CHILDREN vol 5(2) (Reissue) para 721.
3 As to the meaning of 'England and Wales' see para 604 ante.
4 As to the meaning of 'habitually resident' see *Kapur v Kapur* [1984] FLR 920; and para 705 ante.

5 Family Law Act 1986 s 56(3) (as substituted: see note 2 supra).
6 See ibid s 58(1); and CHILDREN vol 5(2) (Reissue) para 721.
7 Ibid s 58(2). At any stage of the proceedings, the court may, of its own motion or on the application of any party, direct that all necessary papers in the matter be sent to the Attorney General, who may, whether or not he is sent papers, intervene in the proceedings, and argue before the court any question in relation to the application which the court considers it necessary to have fully argued: see s 59; and CHILDREN vol 5(2) (Reissue) para 722.

784. Legitimacy. All persons born or conceived in lawful wedlock, no matter where, are prima facie legitimate in England and Wales[1]. This test of legitimacy may involve questions as to the validity of a marriage or divorce which will be decided by the English court on the principles already described[2].

A person may also be recognised by the English court as being legitimate if he is so regarded by the law of the domicile of each of his parents at the date of his birth[3], notwithstanding the lack of a valid marriage between those parents.

A person may also be recognised as legitimate if (1) he is the child of a void marriage[4] and, at the time of the insemination resulting in the birth, or, where there was no such insemination, the child's conception, or at the time of the celebration of the marriage if later, both or either of his parents reasonably believed that the marriage was valid[5]; and (2) his father was domiciled in England and Wales at the time of the birth or, if he died before the birth, was so domiciled immediately before his death[6]. It is immaterial that the belief that the marriage was valid was due to a mistake as to law[7]. It is presumed in respect of a child born after 4 April 1988[8] that, unless the contrary is shown, one of the parties did believe at the relevant date that the marriage was valid[9].

1 *Re Bozzelli's Settlement, Husey-Hunt v Bozelli* [1902] 1 Ch 751. As to the presumption of legitimacy see the Family Law Reform Act 1969 s 26; and CHILDREN vol 5(2) (Reissue) paras 708–709. As to the legitimacy of children of a polygamous marriage see para 737 ante.
2 See paras 706–738, 743–750 ante. See also *Shaw v Gould* (1868) LR 3 HL 55; *Brook v Brook* (1861) 9 HL Cas 193; *Re De Wilton, De Wilton v Montefiore* [1900] 2 Ch 481; *Re Stirling, Stirling v Stirling* [1908] 2 Ch 344; *Re Paine, Re Williams, Griffith v Waterhouse* [1940] Ch 46. *Hashmi v Hashmi* [1972] Fam 36, [1971] 3 All ER 1253, in so far as it suggests that it is sufficient if the marriage is recognised as valid by the law of the father's domicile, is inconsistent with *Shaw v Gould* supra, and appears to have been decided per incuriam.
3 *Re Bischoffsheim, Cassel v Grant* [1948] Ch 79, [1947] 2 All ER 830. It is submitted that the proposition in this case that this is the only test of legitimacy is untenable in the light of *Shaw v Gould* (1868) LR 3 HL 55. See also *Fenton v Livingstone* (1859) 3 Macq 497, HL.
4 A 'void marriage' means a marriage, not being voidable only, in respect of which the High Court has or had jurisdiction to grant a decree of nullity, or would have or would have had such jurisdiction if the parties were domiciled in England and Wales: Legitimacy Act 1976 s 10(1). As to the legitimacy of the children of a voidable marriage which was annulled on or before 31 July 1971, see the Matrimonial Causes Act 1973 s 16, Sch 1 para 12.
5 Legitimacy Act 1976 s 1(1) (amended by the Family Law Reform Act 1987 s 28(1)). This provision is retrospective as to status but not as to rights of succession: Legitimacy Act 1976 s 11(1), Sch 1 paras 3, 4(1).
6 Ibid s 1(2).
7 Ibid s 1(3) (s 1(3), (4) added by the Family Law Reform Act 1987 s 28(2)).
8 Ie the coming into force of the Family Law Reform Act 1987 s 28: Family Law Reform Act 1987 (Commencement No 1) Order 1988, SI 1988/425.
9 Legitimacy Act 1976 s 1(4) (as added: see note 7 supra).

785. Jurisdiction to grant declarations of legitimation. The English court[1] has jurisdiction to grant a declaration that the applicant has or has not become a legitimated person[2] if he is domiciled in England and Wales[3] on the date of the application or has been habitually resident[4] there throughout the period of one year ending with that date[5].

Where on an application for such a declaration the truth of the proposition to be declared is proved to the satisfaction of the court, the court must make that declaration unless to do so would manifestly be contrary to public policy[6]. A declaration binds the Crown and all other persons[7].

1 Ie the High Court or a county court: Family Law Act 1986 s 63.
2 'Legitimated person' means a person legitimated or recognised as legitimated under the Legitimacy Act 1976 s 2 or s 3; or under the Legitimacy Act 1926 s 1 or s 8 (repealed); or by a legitimation (whether or not by virtue of the subsequent marriage of his parents) recognised by the law of England and Wales and effected under the law of another country: Family Law Act 1986 s 56(5) (s 56 substituted by the Family Law Reform Act 1987 s 22).
3 As to the meaning of 'England and Wales' see para 604 ante.
4 As to the meaning of 'habitually resident' see *Kapur v Kapur* [1984] FLR 920; and para 705 ante.
5 Family Law Act 1986 s 56(2), (3) (as substituted: see note 2 supra).
6 See ibid s 58(1); and CHILDREN vol 5(2) (Reissue) para 721.
7 Ibid s 58(2). At any stage of the proceedings, the court may, of its own motion or on the application of any party, direct that all necessary papers in the matter be sent to the Attorney General, who may, whether or not he is sent papers, intervene in the proceedings, and argue before the court any question in relation to the application which the court considers it necessary to have fully argued: see s 59; and CHILDREN vol 5(2) (Reissue) para 722.

786. Legitimation at common law. Persons who are illegitimate at birth may be legitimated by subsequent events. At common law, if the father is domiciled both at the time of the child's birth and at the time of his subsequent marriage to the child's mother in a foreign country whose law permits legitimation by subsequent marriage, the child is recognised in England as having been legitimated[1]. A similar principle probably applies to legitimation by parental recognition[2]. If the child is legitimated by a foreign statute permitting legitimation by subsequent marriage, and his parents were married before the statute came into operation, it is probably sufficient if the father was domiciled in the foreign country at the time of the child's birth and at the time of the subsequent marriage; it is not necessary that he should have been domiciled there, or alive, when the statute came into operation[3].

1 *Re Goodman's Trusts* (1881) 17 ChD 266, CA; *Re Wright's Trusts* (1856) 2 K & J 595; *Re Grove, Vaucher v Treasury Solicitor* (1888) 40 ChD 216, CA.
2 *Re Luck's Settlement Trusts, Re Luck's Will Trusts, Walker v Luck* [1940] Ch 864, [1940] 3 All ER 307, CA.
3 *Re Hagerbaum, Bond v Pidding* [1933] IR 198; cf the British Nationality Act 1981 s 47(2).

787. Legitimation under the Legitimacy Act 1976. Where the parents of an illegitimate person marry one another and, at the time of the marriage, the father of the illegitimate person is domiciled in England and Wales[1], that person, if living, is deemed legitimate from the date of the marriage[2].

Where the parents of an illegitimate person marry one another and, at the time of the marriage, the father of the illegitimate person is domiciled in a foreign country by the law of which the illegitimate person became legitimated by virtue of that subsequent marriage, that person, if living, is recognised in England as having been so legitimated from 1 January 1927 or, if his father or mother was married to a third person when he was born, from 29 October 1959[3], or from the date of the marriage, whichever last happens, notwithstanding that his father was not at the time of that person's birth domiciled in a country in which legitimation by subsequent marriage was permitted by law[4]. This provision applies only to legitimation by subsequent marriage. It does not abrogate the common law rule described in the preceding paragraph[5]. Accordingly, if the father was domiciled in a foreign country whose law permits legitimation by subsequent marriage not only at the time of the marriage but also at the time of the child's birth, the child will be recognised as having been legitimated both at common law and under the Legitimacy Act 1976[6].

1 As to the meaning of 'England and Wales' see para 604 ante.
2 Legitimacy Act 1976 s 2.
3 Legitimacy Act 1976 s 11, Sch 1 para 1(1) (preserving the effect of the Legitimacy Act 1926 s 1 (repealed, but previously as amended by the Legitimacy Act 1959 ss 1, 6(3))).
4 Legitimacy Act 1976 ss 3, 11(1), Sch 1 para 1(1) (preserving the effect of the Legitimacy Act 1926 s 8(1) (repealed)).
5 See para 786 ante.
6 See *Re Askew, Marjoribanks v Askew* [1930] 2 Ch 259; *Re Hurll, Angelini v Dick* [1952] Ch 722, [1952] 2 All ER 322.

788. Succession by and to legitimated persons. A person who is recognised as having been legitimated at common law[1] or under the Legitimacy Act 1976[2] and any other person can succeed to property under English wills and intestacies and take property under English deeds as if the legitimated person[3] had been born legitimate[4]. This rule is subject to any contrary intention in the will or deed, and applies only where the testator or intestate dies, or the deed is executed, on or after 1 January 1976[5].

These rules are subject to minor exceptions as to titles of honour and property limited to devolve with such a title[6], and succession to the throne[7].

1 See para 784 ante.
2 See para 786 ante.
3 For the meaning of 'legitimated person' see para 785 note 2 ante.
4 See the Legitimacy Act 1976 ss 5(1), (3), 10(1).
5 See ibid s 5(1), 10(1), (3).
6 See ibid s 11(1), Sch 1 para 4(2), (3).
7 See ibid Sch 1 para 5.

(6) ADOPTION

789. Jurisdiction. The English court[1] has jurisdiction to make an adoption order when the applicant (or, in the case of an application by a married couple, at least one of the applicants) is domiciled in some part of the United Kingdom or the Isle of Man or one of the Channel Islands, and the child is in England when the application is made[2]. In addition, the High Court has jurisdiction when the above requirements, other than those as to the residence of the child, are satisfied, and the child is resident outside Great Britain[3].

In certain cases of international adoptions the Adoption Act 1976 confers an extended jurisdiction upon the High Court, giving effect to an international Convention on the adoption of children[4]. This extended jurisdiction does not apply where the applicant or applicants and the child are United Kingdom nationals[5] and are living in the United Kingdom[6].

1 Ie the Family Division of the High Court, or a county court or magistrates' court within whose district or area the child is, and certain other county courts: Adoption Act 1976 s 62(1), (2) (amended by the

Children (Allocation of Proceedings) (Amendment No 2) Order 1994, SI 1994/3138; and as from a day to be appointed by the Matrimonial and Family Proceedings Act 1984 s 46(1), Sch 1 para 20(a)).

2 Adoption Act 1976 ss 14(2), 15(2), 62(2) (as amended): see CHILDREN vol 5(2) (Reissue) para 1058 et seq. For the meaning of 'United Kingdom' see para 604 ante.

3 See ibid s 62(3). For the meaning of 'Great Britain' see para 604 ante.

4 Ie the Convention on the adoption of children, signed at The Hague on 15 November 1965 (see Cmnd 2613): Adoption Act 1976 ss 17, 72(1); and see CHILDREN vol 5(2) (Reissue) para 1085 et seq.

5 'United Kingdom national' for these purposes means a citizen of the United Kingdom and colonies satisfying such conditions, if any, as the Secretary of State may by order specify: ibid s 72(1). See also CHILDREN vol 5(2) (Reissue) para 1058 et seq; and BRITISH NATIONALITY vol 4(2) (Reissue) para 3.

6 See ss 17(2), 72(1) (definition of 'British territory': ie Great Britain, Northern Ireland, the Channel Islands, the Isle of Man and a colony, being a country designated for the purposes of any provision of the Act by order of the Secretary of State or, if no country is so designated, any of those countries); and the Convention Adoption (Miscellaneous Provisions) Order 1978, SI 1978/1432, art 5. See further CHILDREN vol 5(2) (Reissue) para 1086.

790. Relevance of foreign law. Before making an adoption order, the court must give first consideration to the need to safeguard and promote the welfare of the child[1]. In considering this, the court must examine the likelihood of the order being recognised in foreign countries with which the child is, or may be, connected. The countries are those in which the child is or may be domiciled, or of which he is a national, or in which he was at some recent date ordinarily resident[2]. Possible non-recognition of the order in those countries must be weighed against the advantages of making the order; in some cases the possibility of non-recognition will be ignored, as the welfare of the child clearly requires the making of the order[3].

1 See the Adoption Act 1976 s 6; and CHILDREN vol 5(2) (Reissue) para 1068.

2 *Re B (S) (an infant)* [1968] Ch 204, [1967] 3 All ER 629. As to ordinary residence see para 704 ante.

3 *Re B (S) (an infant)* [1968] Ch 204, [1967] 3 All ER 629, citing *Re R (Adoption)* [1966] 3 All ER 613, [1967] 1 WLR 34 (refugee never likely to return to his original country).

791. Recognition of adoptions granted in the British Isles. Adoption orders made in Scotland, Northern Ireland, the Channel Islands or the Isle of Man will be recognised in England and Wales[1].

1 See the Adoption Act 1976 s 38(1)(c); and CHILDREN vol 5(2) (Reissue) para 1089.

792. Recognition of foreign orders under the Adoption Act 1976. The Adoption Act 1976 empowers the Secretary of State to specify certain adoptions effected under the law of any country outside Great Britain as 'overseas adoptions' for the purposes of the Act[1].

A number of adoptions have now been designated as overseas adoptions for this purpose. They are adoptions of persons under 18 and who have not been married, effected in one of certain listed countries under the law in force in the relevant country[2].

1 Adoption Act 1976 ss 38(1)(d), 72(2); and see CHILDREN vol 5(2) (Reissue) para 1089 text and note 5. For the meaning of 'Great Britain' see para 604 ante. As to declarations concerning the validity of overseas adoptions, and as to determinations made in convention countries see CHILDREN vol 5(2) (Reissue) paras 1095 and 1103.

2 Adoption (Designation of Overseas Adoptions) Order 1973, SI 1973/19 (amended by SI 1993/690), which also makes provision for proof of overseas adoptions: see art 4. The 'law' of a country does not include customary or common law: art 3(3). The listed countries are (1) the following Commonwealth

countries and United Kingdom dependent territories: Australia, Bahamas, Barbados, Bermuda, Botswana, British Honduras, British Virgin Islands, Canada, Cayman Islands, Cyprus, Dominica, Fiji, Ghana, Gibraltar, Guyana, Hong Kong, Jamaica, Kenya, Lesotho, Malawi, Malaysia, Malta, Mauritius, Montserrat, New Zealand, Nigeria, Pitcairn, St Christopher, Nevis and Anguilla, St Vincent, Seychelles, Singapore, Southern Rhodesia, Sri Lanka, Swaziland, Tanzania, Tonga, Trinidad and Tobago, Uganda, Zambia: (art 3(2) Schedule Pt I); and (2) other countries and territories: Austria, Belgium, the People's Republic of China, Denmark (including Greenland and the Faroes), Finland, France (including Réunion, Martinique, Guadaloupe and French Guyana), Germany (the former Federal Republic and the former West Berlin), Greece, Iceland, Republic of Ireland, Israel, Italy, Luxembourg, Netherlands, Norway, Portugal, South Africa and South West Africa, Spain, Sweden, Switzerland, Turkey, the United States of America and the former Yugoslavia (art 3(2), Schedule Pt II (as so amended)).

793. Recognition of other foreign adoptions. A foreign adoption order not entitled to recognition under the rules previously discussed[1] will be recognised in England if it was made in the country in which the adopter was then domiciled[2]. It may also be a condition for recognition that the child should have been resident in the same country at the time of the order[3].

Such a foreign adoption may be refused recognition on the ground that its recognition would be contrary to English public policy[4].

1 See paras 791–792 ante.
2 *Re Valentine's Settlement, Valentine v Valentine* [1965] Ch 831, [1965] 2 All ER 226, CA; *Re G (Foreign Adoption: Consent)* [1995] 2 FLR 534. See the Adoption Act 1976 s 38(1)(e), by which an adoption recognised by the law of England and Wales and effected under the law of any other country is included in the meaning of adoption for the purpose of provisions affecting status.
3 This was required by Lord Denning MR in *Re Valentine's Settlement, Valentine v Valentine* [1965] Ch 831 at 843, [1965] 2 All ER 226 at 230–231, CA; but doubted by Dankwerts LJ at 846 and at 233.
4 *Re Valentine's Settlement, Valentine v Valentine* [1965] Ch 831, [1965] 2 All ER 226, CA; *Re Wilson, Grace v Lucas* [1954] Ch 733 at 741, [1954] 1 All ER 997 at 999–1000. As to public policy see para 611 ante.

794. Succession by and to adopted persons. A person whose adoption is recognised in England and Wales[1] (and any other person) can succeed to property as if the adopted person had been born to the adopter or adopters in wedlock and as if he were not the child of any other person[2]. This is however subject to any contrary intention in the deed or will and does not apply when the testator or intestate died or the deed was executed before 1 January 1976[3] or if the succession is governed by foreign law[4].

1 See paras 791–793 ante.
2 See the Adoption Act 1976 ss 38(1), 39, 42, Sch 2 para 6; and CHILDREN vol 5(2) (Reissue) paras 1092–1093.
3 See ibid ss 39(6), 42(1).
4 As to the circumstances in which this will be so see paras 958, 960–977 post.

(7) MAINTENANCE ORDERS

(i) Jurisdiction of the Court in England and Wales

795. Matrimonial suits. The jurisdiction of the divorce courts and of the magistrates' courts to make orders as to maintenance in matrimonial suits is discussed earlier in this title[1].

1 See paras 755–757 ante.

796. Financial provision for children. The power to make orders for periodical payments or for the payment of lump sums or the transfer of property to, or for the benefit of, a child[1] may be made if the respondent is served with process in England and Wales or elsewhere[2]; or if (1) the respondent is domiciled as that term is defined in the Civil Jurisdiction and Judgments Act 1982[3] in England and Wales[4]; or (2) the respondent is so domiciled in any other part of the United Kingdom[5] or in another Brussels or Lugano contracting state[6] and the child is so domiciled or habitually resident[7] in England and Wales[8]; or (3) if the respondent enters an appearance other than solely to contest the jurisdiction[9].

The court has the power to vary or revoke any financial arrangements in a maintenance agreement[10] in respect of a child if each of the parents is either domiciled or resident in England and Wales[11]; or if any of heads (1) to (3) above applies[12].

1   See the Children Act 1989 s 15(1), Sch 1 paras 1–9 (as amended). 'Child' generally means a person who has not attained the age of 18, but may in certain circumstances refer to a person who has attained that age and is in full-time education: see s 105(1), Sch 1 para 16.
2   See the Family Proceedings Rules 1991, SI 1991/1247, r 10.6; and *Re Dulles' Settlement* [1951] Ch 265, [1950] 2 All ER 1013, CA; *Re Dulles' Settlement (No 2)* [1951] Ch 842, [1951] 2 All ER 69, CA. These bases for jurisdiction are excluded if the court has jurisdiction under the Brussels Convention or the Lugano Convention, or the corresponding scheme in force within the United Kingdom: Brussels Convention art 3; Lugano Convention art 3; Civil Jurisdiction and Judgments Act 1982 s 16(1) (as amended), (2), Sch 4 art 3. As to the Brussels Convention see para 618 text and note 1 ante. As to the Lugano Convention see para 618 text and note 2 ante. As to the adaptation of the provisions of the Conventions by the Civil Jurisdiction and Judgments Act 1982 Sch 4, to a scheme applying as between parts of the United Kingdom, see para 619 ante.
3   See the Civil Jurisdiction and Judgments Act 1982 s 41 (as amended); and para 635 ante.
4   Brussels Convention art 2; Lugano Convention art 2; Civil Jurisdiction and Judgments Act 1982 Sch 4 art 2.
5   For the meaning of 'part of the United Kingdom' see para 619 note 4 ante.
6   For the meaning of 'Brussels contracting state' and 'Lugano contracting state' see para 618 notes 1–2 ante.
7   As to the meaning of 'habitually resident' see *Kapur v Kapur* [1984] FLR 920; and para 705 ante.
8   See the Brussels Convention art 5 para 2; the Lugano Convention art 5 para 2; the Civil Jurisdiction and Judgments Act 1982 Sch 4 art 5(2) (amended by SI 1993/603); and para 643 ante.
9   Brussels Convention art 18; Lugano Convention art 18; Civil Jurisdiction and Judgments Act 1982 Sch 4 art 18; and see para 630 ante.
10   For the meaning of 'maintenance agreement' see the Children Act 1989 Sch 1 para 10; and CHILDREN vol 5(2) (Reissue) para 858.
11   See ibid Sch 1 paras 10, 11; and CHILDREN vol 5(2) (Reissue) para 858. As to the exclusion of this basis for jurisdiction see note 2 supra.
12   See the text and notes 3–9 supra.

797. Contribution orders. A magistrates' court in England and Wales has power under various statutes, exerciseable at the instance of certain public bodies, to make a contribution order for the recovery of the cost of maintaining a child from certain persons[1]. A magistrates' court in England and Wales will also have jurisdiction where the respondent resides in Scotland or Northern Ireland[2], and in proceedings by or against a person resident in Scotland or Northern Ireland for the revocation, revival or variation of any of these orders[3]. The court will also have jurisdiction if the respondent is domiciled as that term is defined in the Civil Jurisdiction and Judgments Act 1982 in the United Kingdom[4]; or if the respondent enters an appearance otherwise than solely to contest the jurisdiction[5].

1   See the Children Act 1989 s 29(6), Sch 2 paras 21, 23; and the Children (Allocation of Proceedings) Order 1991, SI 1991/1677, art 3(1)(p); the National Assistance Act 1948 ss 42, 43 (both as amended); the Merchant Shipping Act 1995 s 40; and the Social Security Administration Act 1992 s 106.

2 Maintenance Orders Act 1950 s 4(1) (amended by the Supplementary Benefits Act 1976 s 35(2), Sch 7 para 8; the Child Care Act 1980 s 89(3), Sch 6; and the Social Security (Consequential Provisions) Act 1992 s 4, Sch 2 para 3(1)(a)); Merchant Shipping Act 1995 s 40(7).

3 Maintenance Orders Act 1950 s 4(2) (amended by the Supplementary Benefits Act 1976 s Sch 7 para 8; the Child Care Act 1980 Sch 6; and the Social Security (Consequential Provisions) Act 1992 Sch 2 para 3(2)); Merchant Shipping Act 1995 s 40(7). These bases for jurisdiction are excluded if the court has jurisdiction under the Brussels Convention or the Lugano Convention: Brussels Convention art 3; Lugano Convention art 3. As to the Brussels Convention see para 618 text and note 1 ante. As to the Lugano Convention see para 618 text and note 2 ante.

4 See the Brussels Convention art 2; Lugano Convention art 2; and para 643 ante. See also Dicey and Morris *The Conflict of Laws* (12th Edn, 1993) 844–845. For the meaning of 'United Kingdom' see para 604 ante.

5 Brussels Convention art 18; Lugano Convention art 18; and see para 630 ante.

798. Service of process. Where the jurisdiction of a court has been extended so that it may make a maintenance order against a person resident in another part of the United Kingdom[1], any summons or initial writ addressed to him in the proceedings may, if indorsed in the prescribed manner[2] by the appropriate indorsing authority in that part of the United Kingdom, be served there as if it had been issued or authorised to be served by the indorsing authority[3]. The appropriate indorsing authority is, in England and Wales a justice of the peace, in Scotland a sheriff, and in Northern Ireland a resident magistrate[4]. Service of a summons or writ under this power may be proved in the proceedings in which it is served by means of a declaration[5] before the appropriate indorsing authority[6].

This power of service does not authorise other than personal service, nor the execution in one part of the United Kingdom of a warrant for the arrest of a person who fails to appear in answer to any such process issued in another part of the United Kingdom[7].

1 Ie by virtue of, inter alia, (1) the Maintenance Orders Act 1950 Pt I (ss 1–15) (as amended); (2) the Domestic Proceedings and Magistrates' Courts Act 1978 ss 24(1), 30(3) (repealed); (3) the Children Act 1989 s 92, 93(2)(g), Sch 11 (as amended); and (4) the Civil Jurisdiction and Judgments Act 1982 s 16(1) (as amended), (2), Sch 4 art 5(2) (see para 643 ante): Maintenance Orders Act 1950 s 15 (amended by the Administration of Justice Act 1977 s 3, Sch 3 para 11; the Domestic Proceedings and Magistrates' Courts Act 1978 s 89(2)(a), Sch 2 para 12; the Courts and Legal Services Act 1990 s 116(2), Sch 16 para 34; and the Civil Jurisdiction and Judgments Act 1982 ss 16(5)). For the meaning of 'part of the United Kingdom' see para 619 note 4 ante.

2 See the Maintenance Orders Act 1950 s 15(2), Sch 2 Form 1.

3 Ibid s 15(1) (as amended), (2).

4 Ibid ss 15(2), 28(1).

5 The declaration must be in the form set out in ibid Sch 2 Form 2, or a form to the like effect: s 15(3).

6 Ibid s 15(3). As to proof of the declaration see s 26; and para 799 post.

7 See ibid s 15(4), (5); the Summary Jurisdiction (Process) Act 1881 s 4 (see MAGISTRATES vol 29 para 231) is excluded in these cases: Maintenance Orders Act 1950 s 15(5).

799. Proof of declarations and other documents. Any document purporting to be a declaration as to service of a process[1] or to be a certified copy, statutory declaration, affidavit, certificate, transcript or summary made for the purposes of the Maintenance Orders Act 1950 or rules under that Act, is deemed without further proof to be the document it purports to be and to have been made in the proper manner unless the contrary is shown[2].

1 Ie under the Maintenance Orders Act 1950 s 15 (as amended): see para 798 ante.

2 Ibid s 26(1).

(ii) Reciprocal Enforcement of Maintenance Orders

A. RECIPROCAL ENFORCEMENT AT COMMON LAW

800. Enforcement of orders. The order of a competent foreign court for period-ical payments by way of maintenance will be enforceable in England by an action in personam on the judgment debt if and only if the foreign order is final and conclusive[1]. If, as is frequently the case, the order is subject to variation in the light of changing circumstances, it will not be final and conclusive[2]. An action may still lie in England for accrued arrears, provided that variation by the foreign court cannot operate retrospec-tively[3]. Similar principles in the law of many foreign countries hinder the enforcement of English maintenance orders abroad.

Statutory provision has been made to overcome these difficulties by providing for reciprocal enforcement of orders between different parts of the United Kingdom[4] and between the United Kingdom and overseas countries[5]. Maintenance orders may also be enforced under the Brussels and Lugano Conventions[6]. Maintenance orders do not fall within the ambit of the Foreign Judgments (Reciprocal Enforcement) Act 1933[7].

1 For the meaning of 'final and conclusive' see *Nouvion v Freeman* (1889) 15 App Cas 1, HL; and para 1015 post.
2 *Harrop v Harrop* [1920] 3 KB 386; *Re Macartney, Macfarlane v Macartney* [1921] 1 Ch 522.
3 *Beatty v Beatty* [1924] 1 KB 807, CA.
4 See the Maintenance Orders Act 1950 Pt II (ss 16–25) (as amended); and paras 801–808 post.
5 See the Maintenance Orders (Facilities for Enforcement) Act 1920 (see paras 809–817 post) and the Maintenance Orders (Reciprocal Enforcement) Act 1972 (see paras 818–842 post).
6 See para 843 post.
7 See the Foreign Judgments (Reciprocal Enforcement) Act 1933 ss 1 (as amended), 11(2): see para 1028 et seq post.

B. RECIPROCAL ENFORCEMENT UNDER THE MAINTENANCE ORDERS ACT 1950

801. Orders registrable for enforcement. Various maintenance orders made by a court in any part of the United Kingdom[1] may be enforced in another part of the United Kingdom, if registered in accordance with the relevant statutory provisions[2] in a court of that other part of the United Kingdom[3]. The orders concerned are orders for alimony, maintenance or other payments made or deemed to be made by a court in England and Wales under any of the following enactments[4]:

(1) specified provisions of the Matrimonial Causes Act 1973[5];
(2) specified provisions of the Matrimonial and Family Proceedings Act 1984[6];
(3) Part I of the Domestic Proceedings and Magistrates' Courts Act 1978[7];
(4) specified provisions of the Children Act 1989[8];
(5) specified provisions of the National Assistance Act 1948[9];
(6) specified provisions of the Supplementary Benefits Act 1976[10]; or
(7) specified provisions of the Social Security Administration Act 1992[11].

Orders made in similar circumstances by courts in Scotland[12] and Northern Ireland[13] are similarly registrable.

1 'Part of the United Kingdom' means England (including Wales: Maintenance Orders Act 1950 s 28(1)), Scotland or Northern Ireland: s 28(2). Cf the definition of 'United Kingdom' set out in para 604 ante.
2 See para 802 post.
3 Maintenance Orders Act 1950 s 16(1).

4 Ibid s 16(2)(a) (amended by the Matrimonial Causes Act 1973 s 54, Sch 2 para 3(1)(a); the Supplementary Benefits Act 1976 s 35(2), Sch 7 para 13; the Domestic Proceedings and Magistrates' Courts Act 1978 s 89(2)(a), Sch 2 para 13; the Matrimonial and Family Proceedings Act 1984 s 46(1), Sch 1 para 1(a); the Social Security Act 1986 s 86, Sch 10 Pt II para 39; the Family Law Reform Act 1987 s 33, Sch 2 para 12, Sch 3 para 1, Sch 4; the Courts and Legal Services Act 1990 s 116, Sch 16 para 35; and the Social Security (Consequential Provisions) Act 1992 s 4, Sch 2 para 3(1)).

5 Ie the Matrimonial Causes Act 1973 ss 22, 23(1), (2), (4), 27 (as amended); and also the predecessor provisions (ie the Matrimonial Causes Act 1965 ss 15–17, 19–22, 30, 34–35 (repealed)): see further para 755 ante.

6 Ie the Matrimonial and Family Proceedings Act 1984 s 14 or s 17: see further para 756 ante.

7 Ie the Domestic Proceedings and Magistrates' Courts Act 1978 Pt I (ss 1–35) (as amended).

8 Ie the Children Act 1989 ss 15(1), 29(6), Sch 1 or Sch 2 para 23: see further paras 796–797 ante.

9 Ie the National Assistance Act 1948 s 43 (as amended): see further para 797 ante.

10 Ie the Supplementary Benefits Act 1976 s 18 (repealed).

11 Ie the Social Security Administration Act 1992 s 106: see further para 797 ante.

12 See the Maintenance Orders Act 1950 s 16(2)(b) (amended by the Social Work (Scotland) Act 1968 s 95(1), Sch 8 para 34; the Guardianship Act 1973 ss 14, 15(3), Sch 5 para 4; the Divorce (Scotland) Act 1976 s 12(1), Sch 1 para 1; the Supplementary Benefits Act 1976 Sch 7 para 13; the Administration of Justice Act 1977 s 3, Sch 3; the Civil Jurisdiction and Judgments Act 1982 s 54, Sch 14; the Social Security and Housing Benefits Act 1982 s 48(5), Sch 4; the Matrimonial and Family Proceedings Act 1984 Sch 1 para 1(b); the Family Law (Scotland) Act 1985 s 28(1), Sch 1 para 3; the Social Security Act 1986 Sch 10 para 39; and the Social Security (Consequential Provisions) Act 1992 Sch 2 para 3(1)).

13 See the Maintenance Orders Act 1950 s 16(2)(c) (amended by the Matrimonial Causes Act 1973 Sch 2 para 3(1)(a); the Social Security (Consequential Provisions) Act 1992 s 4, Sch 2 para 3(1); the Supplementary Benefits etc (Consequential Provisions) (Northern Ireland) Order 1977, SI 1977/2158; the Maintenance Orders (Northern Ireland Consequential Amendments) Order 1980, SI 1980/564; the Social Security Act 1986 Sch 10 para 39; the Matrimonial and Family Proceedings (Northern Ireland Consequential Amendments) Order 1989, SI 1989/678, art 2; and, as from a day to be appointed, the Children (Northern Ireland Consequential Amendments) Order 1995, SI 1995/756, arts 2, 15, Schedule).

802. Registration of orders. An application for the registration of a maintenance order must be made to the prescribed officer[1] of the court which made the order, except in the case of orders made by a magistrates' court in which case the application is to a justice or justices for the same place as that court[2]. An application must be made in the prescribed manner[3] by or on behalf of the person entitled to payments under the order[4]; but where sums are payable under an order of a magistrates' court to or through an officer of the court, that officer must, on the request of the person entitled, make application on that person's behalf[5].

If it appears that the person liable to make payments under the order resides in another part of the United Kingdom[6], and that it is convenient that the order should be enforceable there, the authority to whom application was made must send a certified copy of the order to the prescribed officer of the corresponding court in that part of the United Kingdom[7]. On receipt of the certified copy, that officer must register it in that court and give notice of the registration to the officer of the court which made the order[8], who must register the notice of registration[9]. The certified copy must be accompanied by an affidavit or statutory declaration by the applicant, or a certificate of the officer to or through whom payments are required to be made, as to the amount of any arrears due to the applicant[10].

1 See the Family Proceedings Rules 1991, SI 1991/1247, rr 1.2(1), 7.19(1), 7.20(1).

2 Maintenance Orders Act 1950 s 17(1).

3 See the Family Proceedings Rules 1991 rr 7.19, 7.20; the Maintenance Orders Act 1950 (Summary Jurisdiction) Rules 1950, SI 1950/2035, r 2 (amended by SI 1980/1895).

4 Maintenance Orders Act 1950 s 17(1), (2).

5 See ibid s 17(6). The person entitled is under the same liability for costs as if the application was made by him: s 17(6).

6 For the meaning of 'part of the United Kingdom' see para 801 note 1 ante.

7 Ibid s 17(2). In the case of an order made by a superior court, the certified copy is sent to the clerk of the Court of Session or the chief registrar of the Queen's Bench Division (Matrimonial) of the High Court of Justice in Northern Ireland: s 17(3)(a); Family Proceedings Rules 1991 rr 7.18, 7.19(2); but see r 7.19(6) as to county court orders. In any other case, the certified copy is sent to a court of summary jurisdiction in Northern Ireland or the sheriff court in Scotland within the area of which the defendant appears to be: Maintenance Orders Act 1950 s 17(3)(b).

8 Ibid s 17(4). For details as to the registers used, and of entries in the court minutes, see the Family Proceedings Rules 1991 rr 7.18, 7.19(3), (6); and the Maintenance Orders Act 1950 (Summary Jurisdiction) Rules 1950 r 2(4) (amended by SI 1980/1895).

9 Maintenance Orders Act 1950 s 17(5); and see note 8 supra.

10 See ibid s 20(1). The affidavit, declaration or certificate is evidence of the facts stated in it: s 20(2). As to arrears accrued before 1 January 1951 where enforcement is sought in Scotland see s 20(3).

803. Effect of registration. A maintenance order registered in a court in any part of the United Kingdom[1] may be enforced in that part of the United Kingdom in all respects as if it had been made by that court and as if that court had had jurisdiction to make it; and proceedings for or with respect to the enforcement of the order may be taken accordingly[2]. However, no court in England and Wales[3] in which an order is registered under Part II of the Maintenance Orders Act 1950[4] may enforce that order to the extent that it is for the time being registered in another court in England under Part I of the Maintenance Orders Act 1958[5]. No proceedings other than those provided for in the Maintenance Orders Act 1950 may be taken for or with respect to the enforcement of the order while it is so registered[6].

Every maintenance order registered in a magistrates' court in England and Wales is enforceable as if it were a magistrates' court maintenance order[7].

1 For the meaning of 'part of the United Kingdom' see para 801 note 1 ante.

2 Maintenance Orders Act 1950 s 18(1).

3 See para 801 note 1 ante.

4 Ie the Maintenance Orders Act 1950 Pt II (ss 16–25) (as amended).

5 Ie the Maintenance Orders Act 1958 Pt I (ss 1–5) (as amended): Maintenance Orders Act 1950 s 18(3A) (added by the Administration of Justice Act 1977 s 3, Sch 3 para 6; amended by the Civil Jurisdiction and Judgments Act 1982 s 37(1), Sch 11 paras 1, 5).

6 Maintenance Orders Act 1950 s 18(6). An order registered in a court of summary jurisdiction in England and Wales does not carry interest, but interest may be carried by orders registered in the High Court under the Maintenance Orders Act 1958 Pt I (as amended), or the Civil Jurisdiction and Judgments Act 1982 s 36: Maintenance Orders Act 1950 s 18(1A) (added by the Civil Jurisdiction and Judgments Act 1982 Sch 11 paras 1, 5).

7 Maintenance Orders Act 1950 s 18(2) (substituted by the Family Law Reform Act 1987 s 33(1), Sch 2 para 13; amended by the Maintenance Enforcement Act 1991 s 10, Sch 1 para 3). In relation to payment orders in this context the Magistrates' Courts Act 1980 ss 76, 93 (both as amended) are modified by the Maintenance Orders Act 1950 s 18(2ZA), (2ZB) (both added by the Maintenance Enforcement Act 1991 Sch 1 para 3). 'Magistrates' court maintenance order' means a maintenance order enforceable by a magistrates' court; and 'maintenance order' means any order specified by the Administration of Justice Act 1970 s 28, Sch 8 (as amended): Magistrates' Courts Act 1980 s 150(1) (definitions added by the Family Law Reform Act 1987 s 33(1), Sch 2 para 88); applied by the Maintenance Orders Act 1950 s 18(2) (as so substituted).

Any person under an obligation to make payments under a maintenance order registered in a court of summary jurisdiction in England and Wales must give notice of any change of address to the clerk of the court, and failure without reasonable excuse to do so is punishable on summary conviction with a fine not exceeding level 2 on the standard scale: Maintenance Orders Act 1950 s 18(2A) (added by the Matrimonial and Family Proceedings Act 1984 s 46(1), Sch 1 para 2; amended by the Statute Law (Repeals) Act 1993; and by the Matrimonial and Family Proceedings (Northern Ireland Consequential Amendments) Order 1989, SI 1989/678, art 42(1), Sch 2).

The 'standard scale' means the standard scale of maximum fines for summary offences as set out in the Criminal Justice Act 1982 s 37(2): Interpretation Act 1978 s 5, Sch 1 (amended by the Criminal Justice Act 1988 s 170(1), Sch 15 para 58(a)). See CRIMINAL LAW vol 11(2) (Reissue) para 808; and MAGIS-

TRATES. At the date at which this volume states the law, the standard scale is as follows: level 1, £200; level 2, £500; level 3, £1,000; level 4, £2,500; level 5, £5,000: Criminal Justice Act 1982 s 37(2) (substituted by the Criminal Justice Act 1991 s 17(1)). As to the determination of the amount of the fine actually imposed, as distinct from the level on the standard scale which it may not exceed, see the Criminal Justice Act 1991 s 18 (substituted by the Criminal Justice Act 1993 s 65); and MAGISTRATES.

804. Collection of sums payable. Where a maintenance order made in England and Wales[1] by a court of summary jurisdiction is registered in any court[2], any provision of the court by which sums payable under the order are required to be paid through or to any officer or person on behalf of the person entitled is of no effect so long as the order is registered[3].

Where a maintenance order is registered in a court of summary jurisdiction, the court must order that all payments to be made under the order, including arrears accrued before registration, are made through the collecting officer[4] of the court or the collecting officer of some other magistrates' court in England and Wales[5]. Such an order may be varied or revoked by a subsequent order[6].

Where payments under a maintenance order cease to be or become payable through or to any officer or person, the person liable to make the payments, until he is given the prescribed notice[7] to that effect, is deemed to comply with the maintenance order if he makes payments as he was required to do under that order and under any order as to payment of which he has had notice[8].

1 See para 801 note 1 ante.
2 Ie under the Maintenance Orders Act 1950 Pt II (ss 16–25) (as amended): see paras 802–803 ante.
3 Ibid ss 19(1), 28(1).
4 Ie the clerk to the justices of the court: Maintenance Orders Act 1950 s 28(1) (applying the Justices of the Peace Act 1979 s 29 (as amended)).
5 Maintenance Orders Act 1950 s 19(2) (amended by the Maintenance Enforcement Act 1991 s 11(1), Sch 2 para 4).
6 Maintenance Orders Act 1958 s 19(3) (substituted by the Maintenance Enforcement Act 1991 Sch 1 para 4).
7 See the Maintenance Orders Act 1950 (Summary Jurisdiction) Rules 1950, SI 1950/2035, r 13 (amended by SI 1980/1895).
8 Maintenance Orders Act 1950 s 19(4).

805. Discharge and variation of orders registered in superior courts. The registration of a maintenance order in a superior court[1] does not confer on that court any power to vary or discharge the order, or affect any jurisdiction of the court in which the order was made to vary or discharge the order[2]. Where a maintenance order made in Scotland is registered under certain statutory provisions[3], the person liable to make payments under the order may, on application made to that court in the prescribed manner[4], adduce any evidence on which he would be entitled to rely in proceedings before the court which made the order for the variation or discharge of the order[5]. The court before which the evidence is adduced must transmit a transcript or summary, signed by the deponent, to the court in Scotland, and in proceedings in that court for variation or discharge of the order the transcript or summary will be evidence of the facts stated in it[6].

1 Ie under the Maintenance Orders Act 1950 Pt II (ss 16–25) (as amended): see paras 802–803 ante.
2 Ibid s 21(1).
3 Ie under ibid Pt II (as amended); the Civil Jurisdiction and Judgments Act 1982 s 36; or the Maintenance Orders Act 1958 Pt I (ss 1–5) (as amended): see the Maintenance Orders Act 1950 s 21(2) (amended by the Civil Jurisdiction and Judgments Act 1982 s 36(6), Sch 12 Pt III para 1(3)).

4 See the Family Proceedings Rules 1991, SI 1991/1247, r 7.20(3) (which erroneously refers to the Maintenance Orders Act 1950 s 2(2) rather than s 21(2)); and the Maintenance Orders Act 1950 (Summary Jurisdiction) Rules 1950, SI 1950/2035, r 9A (added by SI 1980/1895).

5 Maintenance Orders Act 1950 s 21(2).

6 Ibid s 21(2), (3).

806. Discharge and variation of orders registered in inferior courts. Where a maintenance order is for the time being registered in a magistrates' court in England and Wales[1], or a court of summary jurisdiction in Northern Ireland or a sheriff court in Scotland, then, upon application[2] made by or on behalf of the person liable to make or entitled to periodical payments, that court may by order make such variation as it thinks fit in the rate of payments within the maximum rate, if any, authorised by the law of that part of the United Kingdom[3] in which the maintenance order was made[4].

If the court is satisfied that payment has not been made in accordance with the order, the court may vary it by exercising one of the following powers[5]: (1) power to order that payments be made directly to the clerk of the court or of any other magistrates' court in England and Wales[6]; (2) power to order that payments be made directly to such clerk, by a method of payment specified by statute[7]; or (3) power to make an attachment of earnings order[8]. In deciding which of these powers to exercise the court must have regard to any representations made by the person liable[9]. Where the court proposes to exercise its power under head (2) above and, having given the debtor[10] an opportunity of opening an account from which payments may be made in accordance with the method of payment proposed to be ordered, the court is satisfied that he has failed without reasonable excuse to do so, it may order that he open such an account[11].

Where a magistrates' court has made a maintenance order and payments under it are required to be made as indicated in head (2) above, an interested party[12] may apply in writing to the clerk of the court which made the order for the order to be varied[13]. On such an application the clerk may, after giving written notice to any other interested party[14] and allowing that party to make written representations within 14 days, vary the order to provide that payments are to be made in accordance with head (1) above[15]. If the clerk considers it inappropriate to exercise this power, he may refer the matter to the court which may vary the order by exercising one of its powers under heads (1) to (3) above[16]. In deciding which such power to exercise the court must have regard to any representations made by the debtor[17]. Where the court proposes to exercise its power under head (2) above and, having given the debtor an opportunity of opening an account from which payments may be made in accordance with the method of payment proposed to be ordered, the court is satisfied that he has failed without reasonable excuse to do so, it may order that he open such an account[18].

For the purposes of the variation of an order under the provisions described above a court in any part of the United Kingdom may take notice of the law in force in any other part of the United Kingdom[19].

Except as described above, no variation may be made in the rate of payments under an order which is registered in a court of summary jurisdiction, but this is without prejudice to the power of the court which made the order to discharge or vary it otherwise than in respect of the rate of payments[20].

The prescribed officer of any court by which an order is varied must give notice of the variation to the prescribed officer of any court in which the order is registered and, if it was made by another court, to the prescribed officer of that court[21].

Where a maintenance order is for the time being registered in a court of summary jurisdiction, the person liable to make or entitled to payments may, on application made in the prescribed manner[22] to the court which made the order or the court of registration, adduce in the prescribed manner evidence on which he would be entitled to rely in proceedings for the variation or discharge of the order[23]. The court which takes the evidence must transmit a transcript or summary of it, signed by the deponent, to the prescribed officer of the court of registration or the court which made the order, as the case may be; the transcript or summary is evidence of the facts stated in it in any proceedings for variation or discharge[24].

1 See para 801 note 1 ante.
2 For the procedure see the Maintenance Orders Act 1950 (Summary Jurisdiction) Rules 1950, SI 1950/2035, r 8.
3 For the meaning of 'part of the United Kingdom' see para 801 note 1 ante.
4 Maintenance Orders Act 1950 s 22(1) (amended by the Domestic Proceedings and Magistrates' Courts Act 1978 s 89, Sch 2 para 14). As to service of process see the Maintenance Orders Act 1950 s 15 (as amended), applied by s 22(3); and para 798 ante.
5 Ibid s 22(1A) (s 22(1A)–(1E) added by the Maintenance Enforcement Act 1991 s 10, Sch 1 para 5).
6 Maintenance Orders Act 1950 s 22(1B)(a) (as added: see note 5 supra).
7 Ie falling within the Magistrates' Courts Act 1980 s 59(6) (as substituted): Maintenance Orders Act 1950 s 22(1B)(b) (as added: see note 5 supra)
8 Ie an order under the Attachment of Earnings Act 1971 (see MAGISTRATES vol 29 para 432 et seq): Maintenance Orders Act 1950 s 22(1B)(c) (as added: see note 5 supra).
9 Ibid s 22(1C) (as added: see note 5 supra).
10 'Debtor' means the person required under a magistrates' court order to pay money periodically to another, and that other person is known as the 'creditor': Magistrates' Courts Act 1980 ss 59(1), 60(11) (ss 59, 60 substituted by the Maintenance Enforcement Act 1991 ss 2, 4 respectively; s 60(4)–(11) applied (in some cases with modifications) by the Maintenance Orders Act 1950 s 22(1E) (as added: see note 5 supra)).
11 Magistrates' Courts Act 1980 s 59(4) (as substituted: see note 10 supra), as applied and modified by the Maintenance Orders Act 1950 s 22(1D) (as added: see note 5 supra).
12 'Interested party' means the debtor or the creditor: Magistrates' Courts Act 1980 s 60(7) (as substituted, applied and modified: see note 10 supra).
13 Ibid s 60(4) (as substituted, applied and modified: see note 10 supra).
14 The clerk may proceed with an application notwithstanding that an interested party has not received written notice of it: ibid s 60(6) (as substituted and applied: see note 10 supra).
15 Ibid s 60(5) (as substituted, applied and modified: see note 10 supra).
16 Ibid s 60(8) (as substituted, applied and modified: see note 10 supra).
17 Ibid s 60(9) (s 60(9), (10) substituted for the purpose of its application to these provisions by the Maintenance Orders Act 1950 s 22(1E) (as added: see note 5 supra)).
18 Magistrates' Courts Act 1980 s 59(4) (substituted by the Maintenance Enforcement Act 1991 s 2), as applied and modified by the Magistrates' Courts Act 1980 s 60(10) (as substituted: see note 17 supra).
19 Maintenance Orders Act 1950 s 22(2).
20 Ibid s 22(4).
21 Ibid s 23(1) (s 23 substituted by the Administration of Justice Act 1977 s 3, Sch 3 para 8).; for the prescribed officers see the Family Proceedings Rules 1991, SI 1991/1247, rr 1.2(1), 7.19(4), 7.20(4); and the Maintenance Orders Act 1950 (Summary Jurisdiction) Rules 1950 rr 4, 10 (both amended by SI 1980/1895). An officer to whom such a notice is given must register the particulars in the manner prescribed by those rules: Maintenance Orders Act 1950 s 23(2) (as so substituted).
22 See the Maintenance Orders Act 1950 (Summary Jurisdiction) Rules 1950 rr 3, 8, 9.
23 Maintenance Orders Act 1950 s 22(5)(a).
24 Ibid s 22(5)(b). For proof of transcripts and summaries see s 26(1); and para 799 ante.

807. Cancellation of registration. At any time while a maintenance order is registered in any court[1], an application for the cancellation of the registration may be made in the prescribed manner to the prescribed officer of that court[2] by or on behalf of the person entitled to payments under the order, and on such an application that officer must, unless proceedings for variation of the order are pending in that court, cancel the registration, whereupon the order ceases to be registered in that court[3]. The prescribed officer must send notice of the cancellation to the prescribed officer of the court which made the order and of any court in which the order is registered[4]. On receipt of such a notice, the prescribed officer of the court which made the order must register particulars of the notice, and the prescribed officer of any court in which it is registered must register the notice and cancel the registration[5]. If the court of registration is a magistrates' court and has made an order for payment through a collecting officer[6], that officer must, if the person entitled to the payments so requests, make the application on behalf of that person[7].

Where an application is made by or on behalf of a person liable to make payments under a maintenance order registered in a magistrates' court in England and Wales or a court of summary jurisdiction in Northern Ireland or a sheriff court in Scotland, to the same authority to whom application for registration can be made[8], and it appears to that authority that the person liable under the order has ceased to reside in England and Wales[9], Northern Ireland or Scotland, as the case may be, that authority may cause a notice to that effect to be sent to the prescribed officer of the court of registration, who must cancel the registration, whereupon the order ceases to be registered in that court[10].

Orders for payment through collecting officers[11] cease to have effect on the cancellation of the registration of a maintenance order, but the person liable is deemed to comply with the maintenance order if he continues to make payments to the collecting officer until he receives notice of the cancellation[12]. The cancellation does not otherwise affect anything done in relation to the maintenance order while it was registered[13]. Similar provisions apply in respect of means of payment orders[14].

1 Ie under the Maintenance Orders Act 1950 Pt II (ss 16–25) (as amended): see paras 802–803 ante.
2 As to the prescribed manner and the prescribed officers see the Family Proceedings Rules 1991, SI 1991/1247, rr 7.19(5), 7.20(5); and the Maintenance Orders Act 1950 (Summary Jurisdiction) Rules 1950, SI 1950/2035, r 11 (amended by SI 1980/1895).
3 Maintenance Orders Act 1950 s 24(1).
4 Ie registered under the Maintenance Orders Act 1958 Pt I (ss 1–5) (as amended) or the Civil Jurisdiction and Judgments Act 1982 s 36: Maintenance Orders Act 1950 s 24(3) (amended by the Administration of Justice Act 1977 s 3, Sch 3 para 9; and the Civil Jurisdiction and Judgments Act 1982 s 36(6), Sch 12 Pt III para 1(4)); Maintenance Orders Act 1950 (Summary Jurisdiction) Rules 1950 r 6 (amended by SI 1980/1895).
5 Maintenance Orders Act 1950 s 24(3A) (added by the Administration of Justice Act 1977 Sch 3 para 9); Maintenance Orders Act 1950 (Summary Jurisdiction) Rules 1950 r 12A (added by SI 1980/1895).
6 As to such orders see para 804 ante.
7 See the Maintenance Orders Act 1950 s 24(6).
8 For these authorities see ibid s 17(1); and para 802 ante.
9 See para 801 note 1 ante.
10 Maintenance Orders Act 1950 s 24(2) (amended by the Administration of Justice Act 1977 Sch 3 para 9), to which text and notes 4–5 supra also apply. See also the Maintenance Orders Act 1950 (Summary Jurisdiction) Rules 1950 rr 5, 12 (amended by SI 1980/895).
11 See para 804 ante.
12 See the Maintenance Orders Act 1950 s 24(5).
13 Ibid s 24(4).
14 See ibid s 24(5A) (added by the Maintenance Enforcement Act 1991 s 10, Sch 1 para 6). 'Means of payment orders' here refers to orders made under the Maintenance Orders Act 1950 ss 18(2ZA) (as added), 22(1A) or (1E) (both as added), or the Magistrates' Courts Act 1980 s 59(6) (as substituted) (see paras 803, 806 ante): see the Maintenance Orders Act 1950 s 24(5A) (as so added).

808. Evidence of maintenance orders. For the purposes of the registration of maintenance orders under the Maintenance Orders Act 1950 for enforcement in other parts of the United Kingdom[1], the register of a magistrates' court, or any document purporting to be an extract from the register and to be certified by the clerk as a true extract, is admissible as evidence of the maintenance order registered in it[2]. A certificate purporting to be signed by the clerk of a magistrates' court, and stating that no minute or memorandum of an order cancelling the registration of, or varying, a maintenance order is entered in the register, is evidence that the registration of the order has not been cancelled or the order varied[3].

1 See paras 801–807 ante. For the meaning of 'part of the United Kingdom' see para 801 note 1 ante.
2 See the Magistrates' Courts Rules 1981, SI 1981/552, r 68.
3 See ibid r 69 (amended by SI 1989/384); and MAGISTRATES.

C. RECIPROCAL ENFORCEMENT UNDER THE MAINTENANCE ORDERS (FACILITIES FOR ENFORCEMENT) ACT 1920

809. Application of the Act. The Maintenance Orders (Facilities for Enforcement) Act 1920[1] provides for the reciprocal enforcement of maintenance orders[2] made in England and Wales[3] or Northern Ireland[4] and maintenance orders made in certain parts of Her Majesty's dominions outside the United Kingdom[5].

1 The Maintenance Orders (Facilities for Enforcement) Act 1920 (and the Maintenance Orders Act 1958 s 19: see note 5 infra) will be wholly repealed when the Maintenance Orders (Reciprocal Enforcement) Act 1972 s 22(2)(a), (c) is brought into force by order under s 49(2). At the date at which this volume states the law, no such order had been made.
2 For this purpose 'maintenance order' means an order (other than an order of affiliation) for the periodical payment of sums of money towards the maintenance of the wife or other dependants of the person against whom the order is made, and 'dependants' means such persons as that person is liable to maintain according to the law in force in that part of Her Majesty's dominions in which the maintenance order was made: Maintenance Orders (Facilities for Enforcement) Act 1920 s 10; *Harris v Harris* [1949] 2 All ER 318, DC; *Collister v Collister* [1972] 1 All ER 334, [1972] 1 WLR 54, DC.
3 As to England and Wales see para 604 ante.
4 See the Irish Free State (Consequential Adaptation of Enactments) Order 1923, SR & O 1923/405, by which references to Ireland in Acts passed prior to that instrument are taken to be references to Northern Ireland.
5 Her Majesty may by Order in Council extend the Maintenance Orders (Facilities for Enforcement) Act 1920 to any part of Her Majesty's dominions or to any British protectorate where reciprocal provisions have been made: s 12. As to Her Majesty's dominions and British protectorates see COMMONWEALTH vol 6 (Reissue) paras 803, 806. Such an Order in Council may be revoked or varied by a further Order in Council: Maintenance Orders Act 1958 s 19.
     At the date at which this volume states the law, the Maintenance Orders (Facilities for Enforcement) Act 1920 extends to Antigua and Barbuda, The Bahamas, Belize, Botswana, Brunei, certain parts of Canada (Newfoundland, Prince Edward Island, the Yukon Territory), Cayman Islands, Cyprus, Dominica, The Gambia, Grenada, Guernsey, Guyana, Jamaica, Jersey, Kiribati, Lesotho, Malawi, Malaysia, Mauritius, Montserrat, Nigeria, St Christopher and Nevis, St Lucia, St Vincent and the Grenadines, Seychelles, Sierra Leone, Solomon Islands, Sri Lanka, Swaziland, Tanzania, Trinidad and Tobago, Tuvalu, Uganda, Virgin Islands, Western Australia, and Zambia: Maintenance Orders (Facilities for Enforcement) Order 1959, SI 1959/377 (amended by the Pakistan Act 1973 s 4(4) (repealed); SI 1974/557, SI 1975/2188, SI 1979/166 and SI 1983/1124); and to Zimbabwe: Zimbabwe Act 1979 s 5(2) (as amended), Sch 2 para 3. As to Bangladesh see the Bangladesh Act 1973 s 1(1); and COMMONWEALTH vol 6 (Reissue) para 886.

810. Transmission of maintenance orders made in England and Wales.
Where a court in England and Wales[1] has made a maintenance order[2] and it is proved to the court that the person against whom the order was made is resident in any part of Her Majesty's dominions outside the United Kingdom to which the Maintenance Orders (Facilities for Enforcement) Act 1920 extends[3], the court must send to the Lord

Chancellor[4] for transmission to the Governor of that part a certified copy[5] of the order[6].

1 As to England and Wales see para 604 ante.
2 For the meaning of 'maintenance order' see para 809 note 2 ante.
3 See para 809 note 5 ante.
4 The functions formerly exercised by the Secretary of State under the Maintenance Orders (Facilities for Enforcement) Act 1920 were transferred to the Lord Chancellor by the Transfer of Functions (Magistrates Courts and Family Law) Order 1992, SI 1992/709, art 4(1), (2).
5 'Certified copy' means a copy certified by the proper officer of the court to be a true copy: Maintenance Orders (Facilities for Enforcement) Act 1920 s 10. In the case of a magistrates' court, the proper officer is the clerk: Home Office circular 469, 726/4 dated 15 June 1925, paras 4(a), 5(a).
6 Maintenance Orders (Facilities for Enforcement) Act 1920 s 2 (amended by virtue of the Transfer of Functions (Magistrates Courts and Family Law) Order 1992). As to the prospective repeal of the Act see para 809 note 1 ante. For the procedure in respect of High Court orders see the Family Proceedings Rules 1991, SI 1991/1247, rr 7.17(2)–(5). For the procedure in respect of magistrates' courts' orders see Home Office circular 469, 726/4 dated 15 June 1925, para 4.

811. Provisional orders made by magistrates' courts. Where an application is made to a magistrates' court in England and Wales[1] for a maintenance order[2] against a person, and it is proved that the person is resident in a part of Her Majesty's dominions outside the United Kingdom to which the Maintenance Orders (Facilities for Enforcement) Act 1920 extends[3], then if, in the absence of that person, the court is satisfied, after hearing the evidence[4], of the justice of the application, it may make any such order as it might have made if that person had been resident in England and Wales, had received reasonable notice of the hearing of the application, and had failed to appear at the hearing; but the order is provisional only and is of no effect unless and until it is confirmed by a competent court in the part of Her Majesty's dominions concerned[5].

Where an order is made the court must send to the Lord Chancellor[6] for transmission to the Governor of the part of Her Majesty's dominions concerned any depositions taken[7] and a certified copy[8] of the order, together with a statement of the grounds on which the making of the order might have been opposed if the person against whom it is made had been resident in England and Wales, had received reasonable notice of the hearing and had appeared at it, and such information as the court possesses for facilitating the identification of the person and ascertaining his whereabouts[9]. Where any provisional order has come for confirmation before a court in a part of the dominions to which the Act extends, and has been remitted to the magistrates' court which made it for the purpose of taking further evidence, that court or any other magistrates' court for the same commission area[10] must, after the prescribed notice, take evidence in the same way as on the original application. If it appears to the court that the order ought not to have been made, it may revoke[11] the order, but in any other case the depositions must be sent to the Lord Chancellor and dealt with as the original depositions[12].

The confirmation of the order does not affect the power of a magistrates' court to revoke or vary it, but a variation does not have effect until confirmed[13]. The applicant has the same right of appeal, if any, against a refusal to make a provisional order as he would have had if the person against whom the order is sought to be made had been resident in England and Wales and received reasonable notice of the date of the hearing of the application[14].

1 It is not necessary for the person against whom the order is sought to have been resident at any time within the United Kingdom, nor for the cause of complaint to have arisen there: *Collister v Collister* [1972] 1 All ER 334, [1972] 1 WLR 54, DC; cf para 757 ante. As to England and Wales see para 604 ante.

2 For the meaning of 'maintenance order' see para 809 note 2 ante.
3 See para 809 note 5 ante.
4 The evidence of any witness who is examined on such application must be put into writing, and the deposition must be read over to and signed by him: Maintenance Orders (Facilities for Enforcement) Act 1920 s 3(2). As to the prospective repeal of the Act see para 809 note 1 ante.
5 Ibid s 3(1) (amended by the Maintenance Orders (Reciprocal Enforcement) Act 1992 s 1(1), Sch 1 para 1(1), (2)). See the Maintenance Orders (Facilities for Enforcement) Rules 1922, SR & O 1922/1355 (amended by SI 1970/762; SI 1989/384; SI 1992/457; and SI 1993/617).
6 As to the transfer of functions to the Lord Chancellor see para 810 note 4 ante.
7 See note 4 supra.
8 For the meaning of 'certified copy' see para 810 note 5 ante.
9 Maintenance Orders (Facilities for Enforcement) Act 1920 s 3(3) (amended by the Maintenance Orders (Reciprocal Enforcement) Act 1992 Sch 1 para 1(3)); and by virtue of the Transfer of Functions (Magistrates Courts and Family Law) Order 1992); and see Home Office circular 469, 726/4 dated 15 June 1925, para 5.
10 Ie a commission area within the meaning of the Justices of the Peace Act 1979: see MAGISTRATES vol 29 para 207.
11 'Revoke' includes discharge: Maintenance Orders (Facilities for Enforcement) Act 1920 s 3(8) (added by the Maintenance Orders (Reciprocal Enforcement) Act 1992 Sch 1 para 1(7)).
12 Maintenance Orders (Facilities for Enforcement) Act 1920 s 3(4) (amended by the Domestic Proceedings and Magistrates' Courts Act 1978 s 89(2)(a), Sch 2 para 2; the Justices of the Peace Act 1979 s 71, Sch 2 para 1; and the Maintenance Orders (Reciprocal Enforcement) Act 1992 Sch 1 para 1(4)).
13 Maintenance Orders (Facilities for Enforcement) Act 1920 s 3(5) (amended by the Maintenance Orders (Reciprocal Enforcement) Act 1992 Sch 1 para 1(5); and by virtue of the Transfer of Functions (Magistrates Courts and Family Law) Order 1992). The varying or revoking order must be transmitted in the same manner as the original order, and a varying order is subject to the same confirmation as the original order: Maintenance Orders (Facilities for Enforcement) Act 1920 s 3(5) (as so amended).
14 Maintenance Orders (Facilities for Enforcement) Act 1920 s 3(6) (amended by the Maintenance Orders (Reciprocal Enforcement) Act 1992 Sch 1 para 1(6)).
  The Magistrates' Courts Act 1980 s 60(1) (as substituted) (revocation and variation of orders for periodical payment) is modified in its application to orders confirmed under the Maintenance Orders (Facilities for Enforcement) Act 1920 s 3: s 3(7) (added by the Maintenance Orders (Reciprocal Enforcement) Act 1992 Sch 1 para 1(7)).

812. Registration in England and Wales of overseas order.

Where a maintenance order[1] has been made against any person by a court in any part of Her Majesty's dominions outside the United Kingdom to which the Maintenance Orders (Facilities for Enforcement) Act 1920 extends[2] and a certified copy[3] has been transmitted by the Governor to the Lord Chancellor[4], the Lord Chancellor must send a copy of the order, if it was made by a court of superior jurisdiction, to the senior district judge, or, if the order was made by a court which was not a court of superior jurisdiction, to the clerk of the magistrates' court for the division or district where the defendant is living, for registration in the prescribed manner[5].

The registration of the order appears to be an administrative act initiated by the Lord Chancellor, and the party against whom the order to be registered was made has no right to be heard to show cause against the registration, nor does the fact that on registration the order becomes an order of the court give him the right to appeal either from the order itself or from its registration[6].

1 For the meaning of 'maintenance order' see para 809 note 2 ante.
2 See para 809 note 5 ante.
3 For the meaning of 'certified copy' see para 810 note 5 ante. As to proof of documents signed by officers of courts overseas see the Maintenance Orders (Facilities for Enforcement) Act 1920 s 8. As to the prospective repeal of the Act see para 809 note 1 ante.
4 As to the transfer of functions to the Lord Chancellor see para 810 note 4 ante.
5 Maintenance Orders (Facilities for Enforcement) Act 1920 s 1(1), (2) (s 1(1) amended by virtue of the Transfer of Functions (Magistrates Courts and Family Law) Order 1992, SI 1992/709; s 1(2) amended

by the Administration of Justice Act 1970 s 1(6), Sch 2 para 2); Supreme Court Act 1981 s 61, Sch 1. For the procedure see the Family Proceedings Rules 1991, SI 1991/1247, r 7.17; and the Maintenance Orders (Facilities for Enforcement) Rules 1922, SR & O 1922/1355, rr 1, 3. As to the distribution of business between divisions of the High Court see further COURTS vol 10 para 856 et seq.

6 *Pilcher v Pilcher* [1955] P 318 at 331, [1955] 2 All ER 644 at 652, DC. See para 817 note 5 post.

813. Confirmation by magistrates' courts of overseas provisional orders.
Where a maintenance order[1] has been made by a court in a part of Her Majesty's dominions outside the United Kingdom to which the Maintenance Orders (Facilities for Enforcement) Act 1920 extends[2] and:

(1) the order is provisional only and has no effect unless and until confirmed by a magistrates' court in England and Wales[3]; and

(2) a certified copy[4] of the order together with the depositions of witnesses[5] and a statement of the grounds on which the order might have been opposed has been transmitted to the Lord Chancellor[6] and it appears to him that the person against whom the order was made is resident in England and Wales,

he may send the documents to the clerk of the magistrates' court within whose area the defendant is living[7] with a requisition that a notice be served upon the person of the time and place of the hearing and informing him that he may attend to show cause why the order should not be confirmed[8].

It is open to the person on whom the notice is served to oppose the confirmation of the order on any grounds on which he might have opposed the making of the order in the original proceedings had he been a party to them, but on no other grounds[9]. If he fails to appear or, on appearing, fails to satisfy the court that the order should not be confirmed, the court may confirm the order with or without modification[10]. On confirming a provisional order, the court must, having regard to any representations by the person liable to make payments under the order[11], exercise one of the following powers[12]: (a) power to order that payments be made directly to the clerk of the court or of another magistrates' court[13]; (b) power to order that payments be made directly to such clerk, by a method of payment specified by statute[14]; and (c) power to make an attachment of earnings order[15]. Where the court proposes to exercise its power under head (2) above and, having given the debtor[16] an opportunity of opening an account from which payments may be made in accordance with the method of payment proposed to be ordered, the court is satisfied that he has failed without reasonable excuse to do so, it may order that he open such an account[17].

If the defendant satisfies the court at the hearing that for the purposes of any defence it is necessary to remit the case to the court which made the provisional order for the taking of further evidence, the magistrates' court may so remit the case and adjourn the proceedings for the purpose[18].

Where a provisional order has been confirmed, it may be varied or rescinded in like manner as if it had originally been made by the confirming court[19], which may remit the case to the court of origin for further evidence as necessary, and adjourn the proceedings for the purpose[20]. Where a provisional order has been confirmed, the person bound by it has the same right of appeal, if any, against the confirmation of the order as he would have had against the making of the order had the order been an order of the court confirming it[21].

1 For the meaning of 'maintenance order' see para 809 note 2 ante.
2 See para 809 note 5 ante.
3 As to England and Wales see para 604 ante.
4 For the meaning of 'certified copy' see para 810 note 5 ante.

5 Depositions taken in a court in a part of Her Majesty's dominions outside the United Kingdom to which the Maintenance Orders (Facilities for Enforcement) Act 1920 extends may be received in evidence before magistrates courts: s 9. As to the prospective repeal of the Act see para 809 note 1 ante.

6 As to the transfer of functions to the Lord Chancellor see para 810 note 4 ante.

7 See ibid s 10; and the Maintenance Orders (Facilities for Enforcement) Rules 1922, SR & O 1922/1355, rr 1–3 (as amended).

8 Maintenance Orders (Facilities for Enforcement) Act 1920 s 4(1) (amended by the Maintenance Orders (Reciprocal Enforcement) Act 1992 s 1, Sch 1 para 2(1), (2); and by virtue of the Transfer of Functions (Magistrates Courts and Family Law) Order 1992, SI 1992/709). A notice required to be served under the Maintenance Orders (Facilities for Enforcement) Act 1920 s 4 (as amended) may be served by post: s 4(2) (substituted by the Maintenance Orders (Reciprocal Enforcement) Act 1992 Sch 1 para 2(3)).

9 Maintenance Orders (Facilities for Enforcement) Act 1920 s 4(3) (amended by the Maintenance Orders (Reciprocal Enforcement) Act 1992 Sch 1 para 2(4)). The certificate of the court which made the provisional order, stating the grounds on which the order might have been opposed, is conclusive evidence that these grounds are available (Maintenance Orders (Facilities for Enforcement) Act 1920 s 4(3) (as so amended)), but the defendant may oppose the confirmation on grounds not included in the statement if they would have been available in the original proceedings (*Re Wheat* [1932] 2 KB 716, DC; *Harris v Harris* [1949] 2 All ER 318, DC).

10 Maintenance Orders (Facilities for Enforcement) Act 1920 s 4(4) (amended by the Maintenance Orders (Reciprocal Enforcement) Act 1992 Sch 1 para 2(5)). For the procedure after the hearing see the Maintenance Orders (Facilities for Enforcement) Rules 1922 r 4. For Home Office advice that fees are payable only on confirmation, that the order becomes effective from the date of confirmation, and that the order should be modified so as to make use of sterling see Home Office circular 469, 726/4 dated 15 June 1925, paras 7, 9.

11 Maintenance Orders (Facilities for Enforcement) Act 1920 s 4(5C) (s 4(5A)–(5D) added by the Maintenance Enforcement Act 1991 s 10, Sch 1 para 1).

12 Maintenance Orders (Facilities for Enforcement) Act 1920 s 4(5A) (as added: see note 11 supra).

13 Ibid s 4(5B)(a) (as added: see note 11 supra).

14 Ie falling within the Magistrates' Courts Act 1980 s 59(6) (as substituted): Maintenance Orders (Facilities for Enforcement) Act 1920 s 4(5B)(b) (as added: see note 11 supra).

15 Ibid s 4(5B)(c) (as added: see note 11 supra).

16 For the meaning of 'debtor' see para 806 note 10 ante.

17 Magistrates' Courts Act 1980 s 59(4) (substituted by the Maintenance Enforcement Act 1991 s 2), as applied and modified by the Maintenance Orders (Facilities for Enforcement) Act 1920 s 4(5D) (as added: see note 11 supra).

18 Maintenance Orders (Facilities for Enforcement) Act 1920 s 4(5) (amended by the Maintenance Orders (Reciprocal Enforcement) Act 1992 Sch 1 para 2(6)).

19 Maintenance Orders (Facilities for Enforcement) Act 1920 s 4(6) (substituted by the Maintenance Enforcement Act 1991 Sch 1 para 1(2)); see *Pilcher v Pilcher* [1955] P 318, [1955] 2 All ER 644, DC. The variation or revocation of an order by a magistrates' court must be in accordance with the Magistrates' Courts Act 1980 s 60 (substituted by the Maintenance Enforcement Act 1991 s 4), as modified: see the Maintenance Orders (Facilities for Enforcement) Act 1920 s 4(6A) (s 4(6A), (6B) added by the Maintenance Enforcement Act 1991 Sch 1 para 1(2); s 4(6A) amended by the Maintenance Orders (Reciprocal Enforcement) Act 1992 Sch 1 para 2(7)).

20 Maintenance Orders (Facilities for Enforcement) Act 1920 s 4(6B) (as added: see note 19 supra).

21 Ibid s 4(7). As to appeals against the making of a maintenance order see the Domestic Proceedings and Magistrates' Courts Act 1978 s 29 (as amended).

814. Variation and revocation of maintenance orders.

Where, on an application for the variation or revocation[1] of a relevant maintenance order[2], the respondent is residing in a part of Her Majesty's dominions outside the United Kingdom to which the Maintenance Orders (Facilities for Enforcement) Act 1920 extends[3], a magistrates' court in England and Wales[4] has jurisdiction to hear the application if it would have had jurisdiction had the respondent been residing in England and Wales[5]. Where the respondent to such an application does not appear at the time and place appointed for the hearing of the application by a magistrates' court in England and Wales, and the court is satisfied that he is residing in a part of Her Majesty's dominions outside the United Kingdom to which the Act extends, the court may proceed to hear and determine the application at the time and place appointed for the hearing or any adjourned hearing as if the respondent had so appeared⁶.

1 'Revocation' includes discharge: Maintenance Orders (Facilities for Enforcement) Act 1920 s 4A(6) (s 4A added by the Maintenance Orders (Reciprocal Enforcement) Act 1992 s 1(1), Sch 1 para 3).
2 Ie any maintenance order made by virtue of the Maintenance Orders (Facilities for Enforcement) Act 1920 s 3 (as amended) which has been confirmed as mentioned in s 3 (see para 811 ante), and any maintenance order confirmed under s 4 (as amended) (see para 813 ante): s 4A(1) (as added: see note 1 supra). For the meaning of 'maintenance order' see para 809 note 2 ante. As to the prospective repeal of the 1920 Act see para 809 note 1 ante.
3 See para 809 note 5 ante.
4 As to England and Wales see para 604 ante.
5 Maintenance Orders (Facilities for Enforcement) Act 1920 s 4A(2) (as added: see note 1 supra).
6 Ibid s 4A(4) (as added: see note 1 supra).

815. Application of the Magistrates' Courts Act 1980. The Magistrates' Courts Act 1980¹ applies to proceedings before magistrates' courts under the Maintenance Orders (Facilities for Enforcement) Act 1920². Proceedings for the making or confirmation of provisional maintenance orders by magistrates' courts are family proceedings for the purposes of the Magistrates' Courts Act 1980³.

1 The reference to the Magistrates' Courts Act 1980 replaces a reference to 'the Summary Jurisdiction Acts'.
2 See the Maintenance Orders (Facilities for Enforcement) Act 1920 s 7(1) (amended by the Justices of the Peace Act 1949 s 46(2), Sch 7 Pt II; so numbered by the Maintenance Orders (Reciprocal Enforcement) Act 1992 s 1(1), Sch 1 para 4). See generally MAGISTRATES. In particular, rules made under the Magistrates' Courts Act 1980 s 144 may include provision which falls within the Children Act 1989 s 93(2) (as amended) and which may be made in relation to relevant proceedings within s 93 (see CHILDREN vol 5(2) (Reissue) para 833): Maintenance Orders (Facilities for Enforcement) Act 1920 s 7(2) (added by the Maintenance Orders (Reciprocal Enforcement) Act 1992 Sch 1 para 4). As to the prospective repeal of the 1920 Act see para 809 note 1 ante.
3 Magistrates' Courts Act 1980 s 65(1)(a), (2) (amended by the Children Act 1989 s 92(11), Sch 11 para 8). Proceedings for the variation of any provision for the payment of money contained in a provisional order made or confirmed by a magistrates' court are not domestic proceedings: Magistrates' Courts Act 1980 s 65(1)(ii).

816. Payment and collection of money. Where a maintenance order¹ is registered in a magistrates' court², the court must order that payments due under the order are to be made to the clerk of the court³.

As regards an order which has been or is being so registered, or a provisional order which has been or is being confirmed⁴, where a magistrates' court orders that payments are to be made by a particular means⁵, the clerk must record on the copy of the order the means of payment ordered by the court and must notify in writing, as soon as practicable, the person liable⁶. Where the court orders payment to the clerk of that or another court of summary jurisdiction⁷, the clerk to whom payments are to be made must give to the person liable details of the account into which the payments should be made⁸. Where the clerk receives an application from an interested party⁹ for the variation of the means of payment, he must notify in writing, as soon as practicable, that party and (where practicable) any other interested party of the result of the application¹⁰.

Where an order has been registered or a provisional order confirmed, the clerk to whom payments are to be made must collect the monies due under the order as if it were a magistrates' court maintenance order¹¹, and may take proceedings in his own name for enforcing payment¹². He must send the monies collected to the court from which the order originally issued, or such other person or authority as that court directs[13].

1 For the meaning of 'maintenance order' see para 809 note 2 ante.
2 Ie under the Maintenance Orders (Facilities for Enforcement) Act 1920 s 1 (as amended): see para 812 ante.
3 Maintenance Orders (Facilities for Enforcement) Rules 1922, SR & O 1922/1355, r 5 (substituted by SI 1992/457).
4 Ie registered under the Maintenance Orders (Facilities for Enforcement) Act 1920 s 1 (as amended) (see para 812 ante), or confirmed under s 4 (as amended) (see para 813 ante): Maintenance Orders (Facilities for Enforcement) Rules 1922 r 5A(1) (r 5A added by SI 1992/457).
5 Ie under ibid r 5 (as substituted), or under the Maintenance Orders (Facilities for Enforcement) Act 1920 s 4(5A) or (6A) (both as added) or s 6(2) (as amended) (see paras 813 ante, 817 post).
6 See the Maintenance Orders (Facilities for Enforcement) Rules 1922 r 5A(2) (as added: see note 4 supra).
7 Ie by a method falling within the Magistrates' Courts Act 1980 s 59(6) (as substituted).
8 See the Maintenance Orders (Facilities for Enforcement) Rules 1922 r 5A(3) (as added: see note 4 supra).
9 Ie an application under the Magistrates' Courts Act 1980 s 60(4) (as substituted and modified by the Maintenance Orders (Facilities for Enforcement) Act 1920 s 4(6A) (as added)): see para 813 note 19 ante. For the meaning of 'interested party' see para 806 note 12 ante.
10 See the Maintenance Orders (Facilities for Enforcement) Rules 1922 r 5A(4) (as added: see note 4 supra).
11 For the meaning of 'magistrates' court maintenance order' see para 803 note 7 ante.
12 See the Maintenance Orders (Facilities for Enforcement) Rules 1922 r 6 (amended by SI 1970/762; SI 1989/384; and SI 1992/457).
13 See ibid r 6 (as amended: see note 12 supra).

817. Enforcement of orders registered or confirmed in England and Wales.
Where the order of an overseas court has been registered in England and Wales[1] under the statutory provisions[2], then from the date of registration[3] the order is of the same force and effect, and, subject to the special provisions of the Maintenance Orders (Facilities for Enforcement) Act 1920[4], all proceedings may be taken on the order, as if it had been originally obtained in the court in which it was registered; and the court has power to enforce the order accordingly[5].
If an order which has been registered in a magistrates' court or confirmed by such a court is of such a nature that, if made by the magistrates court, it would be enforceable in like manner as a magistrates' court maintenance order[6], the order is, subject to certain special provisions, so enforceable[7]. Subject to that, every such order is enforceable as if the order were for the payment of a civil debt recoverable summarily[8]. A warrant of distress or commitment issued by a magistrates' court for the purpose of enforcing an order so registered or confirmed may be executed in any part of the United Kingdom[9] in the same manner as if the warrant had been originally issued or subsequently indorsed by a magistrates' court having jurisdiction in the place where the warrant is executed[10].

1 As to the meaning of 'England and Wales' see para 604 ante.
2 See para 812 ante.
3 The view has been taken that a registered order has full retrospective effect from the date specified in it, or, if no date is specified, from the date of the order: Home Office circular 469, 726/4 dated 15 June 1925, para 7 (b).
4 Eg those provisions considered in the text and notes infra.
5 Maintenance Orders (Facilities for Enforcement) Act 1920 s 1(1). That provision is limited to enforcement and does not enable complaints to be maintained for the variation or discharge of registered orders: *Pilcher v Pilcher* [1955] P 318, [1955] 2 All ER 644, DC; *R v Rose, ex p McGibbon* (1959) 123 JP 374, DC. The court may, however, remit arrears due under the order: *Pilcher v Pilcher (No 2)* [1956] 1 All ER 463, [1956] 1 WLR 298, DC. As to the prospective repeal of the 1920 Act see para 809 note 1 ante.

6 Ie a magistrates' court maintenance order within the meaning of the Magistrates' Courts Act 1980 s 150(1) (definition as added): see para 803 note 7 ante.

7 The special provisions are modifications of Magistrates' Courts Act 1980 ss 76, 93 (both as amended) specified in the Maintenance Orders Act 1950 s 18(2ZA), (2ZB) (as added): Maintenance Orders (Facilities for Enforcement) Act 1920 s 6(2) proviso (amended by the Family Law Reform Act 1987 s 33(1), Sch 2 para 1; and by the Maintenance Enforcement Act 1991 s 10, Sch 1 para 2).

8 Maintenance Orders (Facilities for Enforcement) Act 1920 s 6(2). The court and its officers must take all such steps as may be prescribed for enforcing the order, and the clerk of the court to whom payments are directed to be made may take proceedings in his own name: s 6(1); Maintenance Orders (Facilities for Enforcement) Rules 1922, SR & O 1922/1355, r 6 (as amended); and see para 816 ante.

9 For the meaning of 'United Kingdom' see para 604 ante.

10 Maintenance Orders (Facilities for Enforcement) Act 1920 s 6(3).

D. RECIPROCAL ENFORCEMENT UNDER THE MAINTENANCE ORDERS (RECIPROCAL ENFORCEMENT) ACT 1972

(A) *Enforcement under Part I*

818. Application of the Act. If satisfied that reciprocal provision for the enforcement of maintenance orders[1] will be made in the country concerned, Her Majesty may provide by Order in Council for the designation of that country as a reciprocating country for the purposes of Part I of the Maintenance Orders (Reciprocal Enforcement) Act 1972[2]. The provisions of that Act may be applied with modifications and adaptations to other countries designated by Order in Council[3].

1 For the purposes of the Maintenance Orders (Reciprocal Enforcement) Act 1972 Pt I (ss 1–24) (as amended), 'maintenance order' means (1) an order (including an affiliation order or order consequent upon an affiliation order) which provides for the payment of a lump sum or the making of periodical payments towards the maintenance (including, in the case of a child, education: s 21(3)) of any person, being a person whom the person liable to make payments under the order is, according to the law applied in the place where the order was made, liable to maintain; and (2) an affiliation order or order consequent upon an affiliation order providing for the payment by the person adjudged, found or declared to be a child's father of expenses incidental to the child's birth or, where the child has died, of his funeral expenses: s 21(1) (amended by the Civil Jurisdiction and Judgments Act 1982 s 37(1), Sch 11 para 15). In the case of a maintenance order which has been varied, it means that order as varied: Maintenance Orders (Reciprocal Enforcement) Act 1972 s 21(1). 'Affiliation order' means an order, however described, adjudging, finding or declaring a person to be the father of a child, whether or not it also provides for the maintenance of the child: s 21(1).

In its application to particular countries, the Act may only extend to certain classes of maintenance orders falling within this definition: see note 2 infra.

2 See ibid s 1(1). Accordingly, 'reciprocating country' means a country designated as such by an Order in Council made under s 1: s 1(1). Where the designation of a country is as regards particular classes of maintenance order (see infra), the country is a reciprocating country only as regards maintenance of such classes: s 1(2).

Such an Order in Council may be varied or revoked by a subsequent Order in Council, which may contain such incidental, consequential and transitional provisions as seem expedient: s 45(1). An Order in Council is subject to annulment in pursuance of a resolution of either House of Parliament: s 45(2). It may designate a country as a reciprocating country as regards maintenance orders generally, or as regards maintenance orders other than those of any specified class, or as regards specified classes of orders only: see s 1(2)). It may contain special provisions as regards a reciprocating country to which the Maintenance Orders (Facilities for Enforcement) Act 1920 formerly applied: see the Maintenance Orders (Reciprocal Enforcement) Act 1972 s 24; see also s 23 as to maintenance orders registered under the 1920 Act. As to the replacement of the regime under the 1920 Act with that provided by the 1972 Act see para 809 note 1 ante.

The following countries are designated as reciprocating countries to various extents (see supra): Anguilla; the Australian States, the Australian Capital Territory, Norfolk Island and the Northern Territory; Barbados; Bermuda; the Canadian Provinces of Alberta, British Columbia, Manitoba, New

Brunswick, Nova Scotia, Ontario, Saskatchewan, and the Northwest Territories; the Falkland Islands and Dependencies; Fiji; Ghana; Gibraltar; Hong Kong; India; the Isle of Man; Kenya; Malta; Nauru; New Zealand; Papua New Guinea; St Helena; Singapore; South Africa; Tanzania (but excluding Zanzibar); the Turks and Caicos Islands; and Zimbabwe: see the Reciprocal Enforcement of Maintenance Orders (Designation of Reciprocating Countries) Order 1974, SI 1974/556 (amended by SI 1975/2187; SI 1979/115; and SI 1983/1125); the Reciprocal Enforcement of Maintenance Orders (Designation of Reciprocating Countries) Order 1979, SI 1979/115; and the Reciprocal Enforcement of Maintenance Orders (Designation of Reciprocating Countries) Order 1983, SI 1983/1125. There are also transitional provisions in art 4 in respect of maintenance orders and proceedings to which the Maintenance Orders (Facilities for Enforcement) Act 1920 (see paras 809–817 ante) applied before 8 May 1974.

3 See the Maintenance Orders (Reciprocal Enforcement) Act 1972 s 40. This power has been exercised in respect of (1) the Republic of Ireland: Recovery of Maintenance (Republic of Ireland) Order 1993, SI 1993/594 (and see for the procedure the Family Proceedings Rules 1991, SI 1991/1247, r 7.37 and the Magistrates' Courts (Reciprocal Enforcement of Maintenance Orders) (Republic of Ireland) Rules 1975, SI 1975/286 (amended by SI 1992/457; and SI 1993/617)); (2) the United States: Recovery of Maintenance (United States of America) Order 1993, SI 1993/591 (and see the Magistrates' Courts (Recovery Abroad of Maintenance) Rules 1975, SI 1975/488 (amended by SI 1980/1584; and SI 1993/617); and the Reciprocal Enforcement of Maintenance Orders (United States of America) Order 1995, SI 1995/2709; and the Magistrates' Courts (Reciprocal Enforcement of Maintenance Orders) (United States of America) Rules 1995, SI 1995/2802; and (3) a group of states party to the Hague Convention on Recognition and Enforcement of Decisions Relating to Maintenance Obligations 1973: Reciprocal Enforcement of Maintenance Orders (Hague Convention Countries) Order 1993, SI 1993/593 (amended by SI 1994/1902) (and see for the procedure the Family Proceedings Rules 1991 r 7.38; and the Magistrates' Courts (Reciprocal Enforcement of Maintenance Orders) (Hague Convention Countries) Rules 1980, SI 1980/108 (amended by SI 1986/1962; SI 1992/457; and SI 1993/617). The countries in the latter group are the Czech Republic; Denmark; Finland; France; Germany; Italy; Luxembourg; the Netherlands; Norway; Portugal; Slovakia; Sweden; Switzerland; and Turkey.

819. Transmission of English maintenance orders. Where the payer[1] under a maintenance order[2] made by a court in the United Kingdom[3] is residing or has assets in a reciprocating country[4], the payee[5] under the order may apply[6] for the order to be sent to that country for enforcement[7]. If the prescribed officer of the court is satisfied that the payer is residing or has assets in a reciprocating country, that officer must send specified documents to the Lord Chancellor[8], namely: (1) a certified copy[9] of the order[10]; (2) a certificate signed by the officer that the order is enforceable in the United Kingdom[11]; (3) a certificate of arrears[12] so signed[13]; (4) a statement giving such information as the officer possesses as to the whereabouts of the payer and the nature and location of his assets[14]; (5) a statement giving such information as the officer possesses for facilitating the identification of the payer[15]; and (6) where available, a photograph of the payer[16]. The Lord Chancellor must forward these documents to the responsible authority[17] in the reciprocating country if he is satisfied that the statement under head (4) above gives sufficient information to justify that being done[18].

The transmission of an order under these provisions does not affect the jurisdiction of the English court which made the order to enforce, vary or revoke it[19].

1 'Payer' means the person liable to make payments under the order: Maintenance Orders (Reciprocal Enforcement) Act 1972 s 21(1).
2 For the meaning of 'maintenance order' see para 818 note 1 ante. For the present purposes, a provisional order or an order made under ibid Pt II (ss 25–39) (as amended) (see paras 831–842 post) is excluded: s 2(2).
3 For the meaning of 'United Kingdom' see para 604 ante.
4 For the meaning of 'reciprocating country' see para 818 note 2 ante.
5 'Payee' means the person entitled to payments under the order: Maintenance Orders (Reciprocal Enforcement) Act 1972 s 21(1).

6 Every application must be made in the prescribed manner to the prescribed officer of the court which made the order: ibid s 2(3).

   'Prescribed' means prescribed by magistrates' courts rules under the Magistrates' Courts Act 1980 s 144 (as amended) or, as the case may be, by rules of court: Maintenance Orders (Reciprocal Enforcement) Act 1972 s 21(1) (definition amended by the Magistrates' Courts Act 1980 s 154, Sch 7 para 107). The prescribed officer, for any purpose of the Maintenance Orders (Reciprocal Enforcement) Act 1972 Pt I (ss 1–24) (as amended) in relation to a magistrates' court is the justices' clerk: Magistrates' Courts (Reciprocal Enforcement of Maintenance Orders) Rules 1974, SI 1974/668, r 3. As to the prescribed officer in other courts see the Family Proceedings Rules 1991, SI 1991/1247, rr 1.2, 7.31.

   As to the 'prescribed manner' for present purposes see the Magistrates' Courts (Reciprocal Enforcement of Maintenance Orders) Rules 1974 r 4 (amended by SI 1986/1962); and the Family Proceedings Rules 1991 r 7.31.
7 Maintenance Orders (Reciprocal Enforcement) Act 1972 s 2(1) (amended by the Civil Jurisdiction and Judgments Act 1982 s 37(1), Sch 11 para 9).
8 Maintenance Orders (Reciprocal Enforcement) Act 1972 s 2(4) (amended by virtue of the Transfer of Functions (Magistrates' Courts and Family Law) Order 1992, SI 1992/709). The functions formerly exercised by the Secretary of State under the Maintenance Orders (Reciprocal Enforcement) Act 1972 were transferred to the Lord Chancellor by the Transfer of Functions (Magistrates' Courts and Family Law) Order 1992 art 4(3).
9 'Certified copy', in relation to an order, means a copy of the order certified by the proper officer to be a true copy: Maintenance Orders (Reciprocal Enforcement) Act 1972 s 21(1).
10 Ibid s 2(4)(a).
11 Ibid s 2(4)(b).
12 'Certificate of arrears', in relation to a maintenance order, means a certificate that the sum specified is, to the best of the information or belief of the certifying officer, the amount of the arrears due under the order at the date of the certificate, or, as the case may be, that to the best of his information and belief there are no such arrears due at that date: ibid s 21(1).
13 Ibid s 2(4)(c).
14 Ibid s 2(4)(d) (amended by the Civil Jurisdiction and Judgments Act 1982 Sch 11 para 9).
15 Maintenance Orders (Reciprocal Enforcement) Act 1972 s 2(4)(e).
16 Ibid s 2(4)(f).
17 'Responsible authority' in relation to a reciprocating country means any person who in that country has functions similar to those of the Lord Chancellor under ibid Pt I (as amended): s 21(1) (amended by virtue of the Transfer of Functions (Magistrates' Courts and Family Law) Order 1992).
18 Maintenance Orders (Reciprocal Enforcement) Act 1972 s 2(4).
19 Ibid s 2(5). As to variation and revocation see para 821 post.

820. Provisional orders made by magistrates' courts. Where an application is made to a magistrates' court for a maintenance order[1] against a person residing in a reciprocating country[2], and the court would have jurisdiction to determine that application[3] if that person were residing in England and Wales[4] and received reasonable notice of the date of the hearing of the application, the court has jurisdiction to determine the application[5] and make a provisional maintenance order[6]. If the provisional order is confirmed by a court in a reciprocating country, it is to be treated for all purposes as if the court had made it in the form in which it was confirmed and as if it had never been a provisional order; accordingly, that court has jurisdiction to enforce, vary or revoke it[7].

Where a court makes a provisional order, the following documents must be sent to the Lord Chancellor[8], namely: (1) a certified copy[9] of the order[10]; (2) a document, authenticated in the prescribed manner[11], setting out or summarising the evidence given in the proceedings[12]; (3) a certificate signed by the prescribed officer[13] certifying that the grounds stated in it are the grounds on which the making of the order might have been opposed by the payer[14]; (4) a statement giving such information as was available to the court as to the whereabouts of the payer[15]; (5) a statement giving such information as the clerk possesses for facilitating the identification of the payer[16]; and

(6) where available, a photograph of the payer[17]. The Lord Chancellor must forward these documents to the responsible authority[18] in the reciprocating country in which the payer is residing if he is satisfied that the statement under head (4) above gives sufficient information to justify that being done[19].

No appeal lies from a provisional order made under these provisions[20].

1   For the meaning of 'maintenance order' see para 818 note 1 ante.
2   For the meaning of 'reciprocating country' see para 818 note 2 ante.
3   Ie under the Domestic Proceedings and Magistrates' Courts Act 1978 or the Children Act 1989.
4   As to the meaning of 'England and Wales' see para 604 ante.
5   Provisions requiring or enabling the transfer of proceedings from a magistrates' court to a county court or the High Court, or requiring or enabling a magistrates' court to refuse to make an order on the ground that the matter would be more conveniently dealt with by the High Court, are excluded: see the Maintenance Orders (Reciprocal Enforcement) Act 1972 s 3(4) (substituted by the Maintenance Orders (Reciprocal Enforcement) Act 1992 s 1(2), Sch 1 para 6(3)).
6   Maintenance Orders (Reciprocal Enforcement) Act 1972 s 3(1), (2) (s 3(1) substituted by the Maintenance Orders (Reciprocal Enforcement) Act 1992 Sch 1 para 6(2)). For the procedure see the Magistrates' Courts (Reciprocal Enforcement of Maintenance Orders) Rules 1974, SI 1974/668, rr 4A, 4C, Sch A1 (added by SI 1993/617). A 'provisional order' in this context is an order made by a court in the United Kingdom which is provisional only and of no effect unless and until it is confirmed, with or without alteration, by a competent court in the reciprocating country: Maintenance Orders (Reciprocal Enforcement) Act 1972 s 21(1). 'Court' includes any tribunal or person having power to make, confirm, enforce, vary or revoke a maintenance order: s 21(1).
7   Ibid s 3(6). As to revocation see para 821 post.
8   Ibid s 3(5) (amended by virtue of the Transfer of Functions (Magistrates' Courts and Family Law) Order 1992, SI 1992/709). As to the transfer of functions to the Lord Chancellor see para 819 note 8 ante.
9   For the meaning of 'certified copy' see para 819 note 9 ante.
10 Maintenance Orders (Reciprocal Enforcement) Act 1972 s 3(5)(a).
11 The document must be authenticated by a certificate signed by one of the justices before whom the evidence was given: Magistrates' Courts (Reciprocal Enforcement of Maintenance Orders) Rules 1974 r 5. For the meaning of 'prescribed' see para 819 note 6 ante.
12 Maintenance Orders (Reciprocal Enforcement) Act 1972 s 3(5)(b).
13 As to the prescribed officer see para 819 note 6 ante.
14 Maintenance Orders (Reciprocal Enforcement) Act 1972 s 3(5)(c). For the meaning of 'payer' see para 819 note 1 ante.
15 Ibid s 3(5)(d).
16 Ibid s 3(5)(e).
17 Ibid s 3(5)(f).
18 For the meaning of 'responsible authority' see para 819 note 17 ante.
19 Maintenance Orders (Reciprocal Enforcement) Act 1972 s 3(5) (as amended: see note 8 supra).
20 Ibid s 12(1).

821. Variation and revocation of orders made in England and Wales. Where an English court has made a maintenance order[1] which has been transmitted to a reciprocating country[2] for enforcement[3], or has made a provisional order[4] which has been confirmed in the reciprocating country[5], the court having power to vary the order may do so by way of provisional order subject to confirmation in the reciprocating country[6]. Where the court hearing an application[7] for variation proposes to grant it by increasing the rate of payment must do so by a provisional order unless either both the payer[8] and the payee[9] appear in the proceedings, or the applicant appears and process has been duly served on the other party[10].

Where a certified copy of a provisional order of the court of a reciprocating country, varying or revoking a maintenance order, is received by the English court, together with a duly authenticated document setting out or summarising the evidence[11] given at the proceedings at which the provisional order was made, the court may confirm or refuse to confirm the provisional order[12], and, in the case of a variation, may confirm it with or without alteration[13].

Where a maintenance order to which the provisions described above apply is varied by an order (including a provisional order which has been confirmed) made by a court in the United Kingdom, or by a competent court in a reciprocating country, the maintenance order has effect as from the date on which the variation is to take effect under the order[14]. Where such a maintenance order is revoked by an order made by a court in the United Kingdom or by a competent court in a reciprocating country (including a provisional order made by the court in the reciprocating country which has been confirmed by a court in the United Kingdom), the maintenance order must, as from the date on which the revocation is to take effect under the order, be deemed to have effect except as respects any arrears due at that date[15].

Before a maintenance order which is a provisional order is confirmed, if:

(1) the English court which made the order receives a duly authenticated document setting out or summarising evidence taken in a reciprocating country for the purpose of proceedings relating to the confirmation of the order; or

(2) the English court, in compliance with a request of a court in a reciprocating country takes evidence from a person residing in the United Kingdom for the purpose of such proceedings,

the court in the United Kingdom which made the order must consider that evidence and if, having done so it appears that the order ought not to have been made, that court (a) must in the prescribed manner give the person on whose application the maintenance order was made an opportunity to consider the evidence, to make representations and adduce further evidence, and (b) after considering all evidence and representations, may revoke the maintenance order[16].

1 For the meaning of 'maintenance order' see para 818 note 1 ante.

2 For the meaning of 'reciprocating country' see para 818 note 2 ante.

3 As to transmission for enforcement see para 819 ante.

4 For the meaning of 'provisional order' see para 820 note 6 ante.

5 See para 820 ante.

6 Maintenance Orders (Reciprocal Enforcement) Act 1972 s 5(1), (2). As to the court having power to vary an order see para 820 text and note 7 ante.

7 For the procedure on such an application see the Magistrates' Courts (Reciprocal Enforcement of Maintenance Orders) Rules 1974 SI 1974/668, rr 4A, 4C, Sch A1 (added by SI 1993/617).

8 For the meaning of 'payer' see para 819 note 1 ante.

9 For the meaning of 'payee' see para 819 note 5 ante.

10 Maintenance Orders (Reciprocal Enforcement) Act 1972 s 5(3).

The Magistrates' Courts Act 1980 s 60(1) (as substituted) (revocation and variation of orders for periodical payment) is modified in its application to orders to which the Maintenance Orders (Reciprocal Enforcement) Act 1972 s 5 (as amended) applies (see text and notes 1–6 supra): s 5(3A) (added by the Maintenance Orders (Reciprocal Enforcement) Act 1992 s 1(2), Sch 1 para 7(5)).

Where a court in the United Kingdom, under this provision, makes a provisional order varying a maintenance order, the prescribed officer must send in the prescribed manner to the court in the reciprocating country having power to confirm the provisional order, a certified copy of the provisional order, together with a document authenticated in the prescribed manner, setting out or summarising the evidence given in the proceedings: Maintenance Orders (Reciprocal Enforcement) Act 1972 s 5(4). For the meaning of 'prescribed' see para 819 note 6 ante; and see the Family Proceedings Rules 1991, SI 1991/1247, rr 7.32, 7.36; and the Magistrates' Courts (Reciprocal Enforcement of Maintenance Orders) Rules 1974 rr 5, 6. For the procedure where variation or revocation is by an order which is not a provisional order see the Family Proceedings Rules 1991 r 7.35; Magistrates' Courts (Reciprocal Enforcement of Maintenance Orders) Rules 1974 r 12(1), (2). As to the prescribed officer see para 819 note 6 ante.

11 The courts of the countries must be given the fullest possible information as to the evidence: see *Re McK* (1976) 126 NLJ 890.

12 For the purpose of determining whether the order should be confirmed, the court must proceed as if an application for the variation or revocation of the maintenance order had been made to it: Maintenance Orders (Reciprocal Enforcement) Act 1972 s 5(6).

13 Ibid s 5(5). For the procedure see the Family Proceedings Rules 1991 r 7.33; and the Magistrates' Courts (Reciprocal Enforcement of Maintenance Orders) Rules 1974 rr 4B, 4C, Sch A1 (added by SI 1993/617).

14 Maintenance Orders (Reciprocal Enforcement) Act 1972 s 5(7) (amended by the Domestic Proceedings and Magistrates' Courts Act 1978 s 54(a)). If the varying order was a provisional order, it takes effect as if made in the form in which it was confirmed, and as if it had never been a provisional order: Maintenance Orders (Reciprocal Enforcement) Act 1972 s 5(7) (as so amended).

15 Ibid s 5(8) (amended by the Domestic Proceedings and Magistrates' Courts Act 1978 s 54(b)).

16 See ibid s 5(9). For the procedure see the Magistrates' Courts (Reciprocal Enforcement of Maintenance Orders) Rules 1974 r 7.

822. Registration of maintenance orders made in reciprocating countries.

Where a court[1] in a reciprocating country[2] makes a maintenance order[3] other than a provisional order[4] which has not been confirmed, but including one which has been confirmed in some other reciprocating country[5], and a certified copy[6] of the order is received by the Lord Chancellor[7] from the responsible authority[8] in a reciprocating country then, if it appears to him that the payer[9] is residing or has assets in the United Kingdom[10], he must send the copy to the prescribed officer of the appropriate court[11]. That officer must register the order in the prescribed manner[12], unless, after taking such steps as he thinks fit to ascertain whether the payer is residing or has assets within the court's jurisdiction, he is satisfied that the payer is not residing and has no assets within that jurisdiction, in which case he must return the certified copy to the Lord Chancellor with such information as he possesses as to the payer's whereabouts and the nature and location of his assets[13].

1 See para 820 note 5 ante.
2 For the meaning of 'reciprocating country' see para 818 note 2 ante.
3 For the meaning of 'maintenance order' see para 818 note 1 ante.
4 For the meaning of 'provisional order' see para 820 note 6 ante.
5 Maintenance Orders (Reciprocal Enforcement) Act 1972 s 6(1).
6 For the meaning of 'certified copy' see para 819 note 9 ante. As to the proof of orders see para 829 post.
7 As to the transfer of functions to the Lord Chancellor see para 819 note 8 ante.
8 For the meaning of 'responsible authority' see para 819 note 17 ante.
9 For the meaning of 'payer' see para 819 note 1 ante.
10 For the meaning of 'United Kingdom' see para 604 ante.
11 Maintenance Orders (Reciprocal Enforcement) Act 1972 s 6(2) (amended by the Civil Jurisdiction and Judgments Act 1982 s 37(1), Sch 11 para 10; and by virtue of the Transfer of Functions (Magistrates' Courts and Family Law) Order 1992, SI 1992/709). 'Appropriate court' means (in England and Wales) a magistrates' court within the jurisdiction of which the person in question is residing or has assets: Maintenance Orders (Reciprocal Enforcement) Act 1972 s 21(1) (definition amended by the Civil Jurisdiction and Judgments Act 1982 Sch 11 paras 4, 15). For the meaning of 'prescribed', and as to the prescribed officer, see para 819 note 6 ante.

For the procedure where the payer appears not to be resident and to have no assets in the United Kingdom see para 827 post.

12 Maintenance Orders (Reciprocal Enforcement) Act 1972 s 6(3); and see the Magistrates' Courts (Reciprocal Enforcement of Maintenance Orders) Rules 1974, SI 1974/668, r 8. Where a justices' clerk registers such an order he must send written notice of registration to the Lord Chancellor: see r 13(1) (amended by virtue of SI 1992/709).

The court must order that payment of sums due shall be made to the clerk of the court, during such times and at such place as the clerk may direct: see the Magistrates' Courts (Reciprocal Enforcement of Maintenance Orders) Rules 1974 r 9(1) (substituted by SI 1992/457). As to the transmission of those payments by the clerk see r 9(1A) (added by SI 1992/457). Where it appears to the clerk to whom payments by way of periodical payments under any maintenance order are made that any sums payable under the order are in arrear he may and, if such sums are in arrear to an amount equal to four times the sum payable weekly under the order, he must, whether the payee requests him to do so or not, proceed in his own name for the recovery of the sums due, unless it appears to him that it is unreasonable in the circumstances to do so: r 9(2) (amended by SI 1986/1962; and SI 1992/457). The clerk must take reasonable steps to notify the person to whom payments are due under a registered order of the means of enforcement available in respect of it, including, in an appropriate case, the possibility of registration of the whole or a part of the order in the High Court under the Maintenance Orders Act 1958 Pt I (ss 1–5) (as amended): Magistrates' Courts (Reciprocal Enforcement of Maintenance Orders) Rules 1974 r 9A (added by SI 1986/1962). See further r 9B (added by SI 1992/457) as to the procedure where a particular means of payment is ordered, and where such means of payment is sought to be varied. As to the conversion of currency see the Maintenance Orders (Reciprocal Enforcement) Act 1972 s 16.

13 Ibid s 6(4). There is no hearing, and the payer has no right of objection or appeal. Cf *Pilcher v Pilcher* [1955] P 318 at 331, [1955] 2 All ER 644 at 652, DC (under the Maintenance Orders (Facilities for Enforcement) Act 1920).

823. Confirmation by magistrates' courts of provisional maintenance orders. Where a provisional maintenance order[1] has been made by a court[2] in a reciprocating country[3], and a certified copy[4] of the order with supporting documents[5] is received by the Lord Chancellor[6], then, if it appears to him that the payer is residing in the United Kingdom[7], he must send the copy and documents to the prescribed officer of the appropriate court[8]. That court must, if the payer establishes any ground on which he might have opposed the making of the order in the proceedings in which the provisional order was made, refuse to confirm the order, and, in any other case, confirm the order with or without such alterations as it thinks reasonable[9]. The statement from the court which made the provisional order as to the grounds on which the making of the order could have been opposed by the payer is conclusive evidence that the payer might have opposed the order on any of those grounds[10], but does not preclude the payer from relying on other defences which would have been open to him in the original proceedings[11]. On confirming a provisional order, a magistrates' court must exercise one of a number of powers[12], having regard to any representations by the payer under the order[13]: (1) power to order that payments be made directly to the clerk of the court or of another magistrates' court[14]; (2) power to order that payments be so made by a prescribed method[15]; and (3) power to make an attachment of earnings order[16]. Where the court proposes to exercise its power under head (2) above and, having given the debtor[17] an opportunity of opening an account from which payments may be made in accordance with the method of payment proposed to be ordered, the court is satisfied that he has failed without reasonable excuse to do so, it may order that he open such an account[18].

If the court confirms the provisional order, the prescribed officer must register the order in the prescribed manner in the court or, if the court refuses to confirm the order, return the certified copy of the order and the accompanying documents to the Lord Chancellor[19].

1 For the meaning of 'maintenance order' see para 818 note 1 ante. For the meaning of 'provisional order' see para 820 note 6 ante.
2 See para 820 note 5 ante.
3 For the meaning of 'reciprocating country' see para 818 note 2 ante.
4 For the meaning of 'certified copy' see para 819 note 9 ante.
5 Ie a duly authenticated document setting out or summarising the evidence given in the proceedings in which the order was made, and a statement of the grounds on which the making of the order might have been opposed by the payer: Maintenance Orders (Reciprocal Enforcement) Act 1972 s 7(2)(a), (b). For the meaning of 'payer' see para 819 note 1 ante.
6 As to the transfer of functions to the Lord Chancellor see para 819 note 8 ante.

7 For the meaning of 'United Kingdom' see para 604 ante.
8 Maintenance Orders (Reciprocal Enforcement) Act 1972 ss 7(1), (2). For the meaning of 'appropriate court' see para 822 note 11 ante. For the meaning of 'prescribed', and as to the prescribed officer, see para 819 note 6 ante. As to the procedure see the Magistrates' Courts (Reciprocal Enforcement of Maintenance Orders) Rules 1974, SI 1974/668, rr 4B, 4C, Sch A1 (added by SI 1993/617).
    If notice of proceedings for confirmation cannot be duly served on the payer, the officer by whom the certified copy was received must return it and the accompanying documents to the Lord Chancellor with a statement giving such information as he possesses as to the payer's whereabouts: Maintenance Orders (Reciprocal Enforcement) Act 1972 s 7(6) (amended by the Maintenance Orders (Reciprocal Enforcement) Act 1992 Sch 1 para 8(5); and by virtue of the Transfer of Functions (Magistrates' Courts and Family Law) Order 1992, SI 1992/709). As to the admissibility of the documents as evidence and proof of orders see para 829 post.
9 Maintenance Orders (Reciprocal Enforcement) Act 1972 s 7(2) (amended by the Maintenance Orders (Reciprocal Enforcement) Act 1992 s 1(2), Sch 1 para 8(2)). Where the order is confirmed, the clerk must give written notice to the court in the reciprocating country: Magistrates' Courts (Reciprocal Enforcement of Maintenance Orders) Rules 1974 r 12(4). The payer or payee has the same right of appeal as he would have from the decision of a magistrates' court to make, or refuse to make, a maintenance order: see the Maintenance Orders (Reciprocal Enforcement) Act 1972 s 12(2).
10 Ibid s 7(3) (amended by the Maintenance Orders (Reciprocal Enforcement) Act 1992 s 1, Sch 1 para 8(3)).
11 Cf *Re Wheat* [1932] 2 KB 716, DC; *Harris v Harris* [1949] 2 All ER 318, DC, both decisions being under the Maintenance Orders (Facilities for Enforcement) Act 1920.
12 Maintenance Orders (Reciprocal Enforcement) Act 1972 s 7(5A) (s 7(5A)–(5D) added by the Maintenance Enforcement Act 1991 s 10, Sch 1 para 12).
13 Maintenance Orders (Reciprocal Enforcement) Act 1972 s 7(5C) (as added: see note 12 supra).
14 Ibid s 7(5B)(a) (as added: see note 12 supra).
15 Ie under the Magistrates' Courts Act s 59(6) (as substituted): Maintenance Orders (Reciprocal Enforcement) Act 1972 s 7(5B)(b) (as added: see note 12 supra).
16 Ie an order under the Attachment of Earnings Act 1971 (see MAGISTRATES vol 29 para 432 et seq): Maintenance Orders (Reciprocal Enforcement) Act 1972 s 7(5B)(c) (as added: see note 12 supra).
17 For the meaning of 'debtor' see para 806 note 10 ante.
18 Magistrates' Courts Act 1980 s 59(4) (substituted by the Maintenance Enforcement Act 1991 s 2), as applied and modified by the Maintenance Orders (Facilities for Enforcement) Act 1972 s 7(5D) (as added: see note 12 supra).
19 Ibid s 7(5) (amended by virtue of the Transfer of Functions (Magistrates' Courts and Family Law) Order 1992). As to the registration procedure see the Magistrates' Courts (Reciprocal Enforcement of Maintenance Orders) Rules 1974 r 8(2), (3). As to written notice to the Lord Chancellor see r 13(1) (as amended): and para 822 note 12 ante.

824. Enforcement of registered orders.

A registered order[1] may be enforced as if it had been made by the registering court[2] and as if that court had had jurisdiction to make it, and proceedings for or with respect to the enforcement of any such order may be taken accordingly[3]. The order is enforceable as if it were a magistrates' court maintenance order[4], and the court and its officers must take all prescribed steps for enforcing or facilitating the enforcement of the order[5].

Sums of money payable under a registered order are payable in accordance with the order as from the date on which they are required to be paid under the provisions of the order[6], except that a court having power to confirm a provisional order[7] may specify a later date for this purpose[8].

In any proceedings for or with respect to the enforcement of a registered order a certificate of arrears sent to the prescribed officer of the court is evidence of the facts stated in it[9].

Any person obliged to make payments in pursuance of a registered order must give notice of change of address to the clerk of the registering court, and failure without reasonable excuse to do so is punishable on summary conviction with a fine not exceeding level 2 on the standard scale[10].

1 'Registered order' means an order for the time being registered in a court in the United Kingdom under the Maintenance Orders (Reciprocal Enforcement) Act 1972 Pt I (ss 1–24) (as amended): s 21(1). The provisions described in the text and notes infra do not apply to an order for the time being registered in the High Court under the Maintenance Orders Act 1958 Pt I (ss 1–5) (as amended): Maintenance Orders (Reciprocal Enforcement) Act 1972 s 8(2).
2 'Registering court' means the court in which for the time being a registered order is registered: ibid s 21(1).
3 Ibid s 8(1).
4 See ibid s 8(4) (substituted by the Family Law Reform Act 1987 s 33(1), Sch 2 para 45). For the meaning of 'magistrates' court maintenance order' see para 803 note 7 ante. In relation to payment orders in this context the Magistrates' Courts Act 1980 ss 76, 93 (both as amended) are modified by the Maintenance Orders (Reciprocal Enforcement) Act 1972 s 8(4A), (4B) (added by the Maintenance Enforcement Act 1991 s 10, Sch 1 para 13).
5 Maintenance Orders (Reciprocal Enforcement) Act 1972 s 8(5) (amended by the Civil Jurisdiction and Judgments Act 1982 s 37(1), Sch 11 para 11). For the meaning of 'prescribed' see para 819 note 6 ante. Payments under a registered order are to be made to the clerk of the registering court who may proceed in his own name for the recovery of arrears, and must so proceed if the arrears equal four times the sum payable weekly unless it appears to him unreasonable in the circumstances to do so: Magistrates' Courts (Reciprocal Enforcement of Maintenance Orders) Rules 1974, SI 1974/668, rr 9, 9A, 9B (amended by SI 1986/1962; SI 1992/457). As to transmission of sums by the clerk see r 9(1), (1A) (substituted by SI 1992/457).
6 Maintenance Orders (Reciprocal Enforcement) Act 1972 s 8(7) (amended by the Domestic Proceedings and Magistrates' Courts Act 1978 s 54(c)).
7 Ie under the Maintenance Orders (Reciprocal Enforcement) Act 1972 s 7 (as amended): see para 823 ante. For the meaning of 'provisional order' see para 820 note 6 ante.
8 See ibid s 8(8) (amended by the Domestic Proceedings and Magistrates' Courts Act 1978 s 54). In such a case a maintenance order registered under the Maintenance Orders (Reciprocal Enforcement) Act 1972 s 7 (as amended) is treated as if it had been made in the form in which it was confirmed and as if it had never been a provisional order: s 8(8) (as so amended).
9 Ibid s 8(6). For the meaning of 'certificate of arrears' see para 819 note 12 ante. As to the prescribed officer see para 819 note 6 ante.
10 Ibid s 8(3) (amended by the Domestic Proceedings and Magistrates' Courts Act 1978 s 89(2)(a), Sch 2 para 33; and subsequently by virtue of the Criminal Justice Act 1982 s 46). As to the standard scale see para 803 note 7 ante.

825. Variation and revocation of orders registered in England and Wales. The registering court[1], provided that either the payer[2] or the payee[3] is resident in the United Kingdom[4], has the like power to vary or revoke a registered order[5] on the application of the payer or payee as if that court had made the order and had had jurisdiction to make it[6]. These powers are not exercisable in relation to so much of a registered order as provides for the payment of a lump sum[7].

The court may vary a registered order by means of a provisional order[8], and must do so unless (1) both payer and payee are residing in the United Kingdom[9]; or (2) the application is made by the payee[10]; or (3) the variation is a reduction in the rate of payments made solely on the ground of a change in the financial circumstances of the payer since the order was made or confirmed, and the courts of the reciprocating country[11] in which the maintenance order in question was made do not have power under their own law to confirm a provisional order varying maintenance orders[12].

The court may revoke a registered order by means of a provisional order[13], and must do so unless both payer and payee are residing in the United Kingdom[14]. Unless both payer and payee are residing in the United Kingdom, the court considering an application for revocation must apply the law of the reciprocating country in which the registered order was made; but it may make a provisional order if it has reason to believe that the ground on which the application was made is a ground on which the order could be revoked under that law, even if it is not established that it is such a ground[15].

Where the registering court makes a provisional order varying or revoking a registered order, the prescribed officer[16] of the court must send, in prescribed manner, to the court in the reciprocating country, a certified copy[17] of the provisional order together with a document authenticated in the prescribed manner setting out or summarising the evidence given in the proceedings[18]. Where such a certified copy and document are received by the registering court, it may confirm the order either without alteration or with such alteration as it thinks reasonable, or refuse to confirm the order[19].

Where a registered order has been varied by an order (including a provisional order which has been confirmed) made by a court in the United Kingdom or a competent court in a reciprocating country, the variation takes effect from the date on which, under the provisions of the order, the variation was to take effect[20]. Where a registered order has been revoked by an order made by a court in the United Kingdom or a competent court in a reciprocating country (including a provisional order made by the United Kingdom court which has been confirmed by the competent court in a reciprocating country), the registered order ceases to have effect from the date when the revocation is to take effect under the order, except as regards any arrears due at that date[21].

1 For the meaning of 'registering court' see para 824 note 2 ante.
2 For the meaning of 'payer' see para 819 note 1 ante.
3 For the meaning of 'payee' see para 819 note 5 ante.
4 Maintenance Orders (Reciprocal Enforcement) Act 1972 s 9(1B) (added by the Civil Jurisdiction and Judgments Act 1982 s 37(1), Sch 11 para 12). For the meaning of 'United Kingdom' see para 604 ante.
5 For the meaning of 'registered order' see para 824 note 1 ante.
6 Maintenance Orders (Reciprocal Enforcement) Act 1972 s 9(1)(a). The Magistrates' Courts Act 1980 s 60(1) (as substituted) (revocation and variation of orders for periodical payment) is modified in its application to registered orders: see the Maintenance Orders (Reciprocal Enforcement) Act 1972 s 9(1ZA) (added by the Maintenance Enforcement Act 1991 s 10, Sch 1 para 14; amended by the Maintenance Orders (Reciprocal Enforcement) Act 1992 s 1(2), Sch 1 para 9). For the procedure see the Magistrates' Courts (Reciprocal Enforcement of Maintenance Orders) Rules 1974, SI 1974/668, rr 4A, 4C, 9B, 12(3), Sch A1 (rr 4A, 4C added by SI 1992/457; r 9B added by SI 1993/617).
7 Maintenance Orders (Reciprocal Enforcement) Act 1972 s 9(1A) (s 9(1A) added by the Civil Jurisdiction and Judgments Act 1982 Sch 11 para 4(1)).
8 Maintenance Orders (Reciprocal Enforcement) Act 1972 s 9(1)(b). For the meaning of 'provisional order' see para 820 note 6 ante.
9 Ibid s 9(2)(a).
10 Ibid s 9(2)(b).
11 For the meaning of 'reciprocating country' see para 818 note 2 ante.
12 See the Maintenance Orders (Reciprocal Enforcement) Act 1972 s 9(2)(c). For the procedure in connection with a provisional order see s 9(5); and see the Magistrates' Courts (Reciprocal Enforcement of Maintenance Orders) Rules 1974 rr 5, 6.
13 Maintenance Orders (Reciprocal Enforcement) Act 1972 s 9(1)(b).
14 Ibid s 9(3); and see note 12 supra.
15 See ibid s 9(4).
16 For the meaning of 'prescribed', and as to the prescribed officer, see para 819 note 6 ante.
17 For the meaning of 'certified copy' see para 819 note 9 ante.
18 Maintenance Orders (Reciprocal Enforcement) Act 1972 s 9(5).
19 Ibid s 9(6). For the purpose of determining whether a provisional order should be confirmed the court must proceed as if an application for the variation of the registered order had been made to it: s 9(7). The payer has the same right of appeal as he would have from the decision of a magistrates' court to make, or refuse to make, a maintenance order: s 12(3).
20 Ibid s 9(8) (amended by the Domestic Proceedings and Magistrates' Courts Act 1978 s 54(c)). Where the order was a provisional order, the variation takes effect as if the order had been made in the form in which it was confirmed and as if it had never been a provisional order: Maintenance Orders (Reciprocal

Enforcement) Act 1972 s 9(8). The prescribed officer must register, in prescribed manner, any order varying a registered order other than a provisional order which has not been confirmed: s 9(10); and see the Magistrates' Courts (Reciprocal Enforcement of Maintenance Orders) Rules 1974 r 8(2), (3).

21 Maintenance Orders (Reciprocal Enforcement) Act 1972 s 9(9) (amended by the Domestic Proceedings and Magistrates' Courts Act 1978 s 54(f)). As to the cancellation of the registration of the order on revocation see the Maintenance Orders (Reciprocal Enforcement) Act 1972 s 10(1); and para 826 post.

826. Cancellation of registration. Where a registered order[1] is revoked by:

(1) an order made by the registering court[2]; or

(2) a provisional order[3] made by that court which has been confirmed by a court in a reciprocating country[4] and notice of which has been received by the registering court; or

(3) an order made by a court in such a country and notice of which has been received by the registering court,

the prescribed officer[5] of the registering court must cancel the registration[6].

Where the prescribed officer is of opinion that the payer[7] is not residing within the jurisdiction of the court and has no assets within that jurisdiction against which the order can be effectively enforced, he must cancel the registration of the order and send a certified copy[8] of the order to the Lord Chancellor[9]. However, where the prescribed officer of a magistrates' court is of opinion that the payer is residing or has assets within the jurisdiction of another magistrates' court in the same part of the United Kingdom, he must transfer the order to that other court by sending the certified copy of it to the prescribed officer of the other court[10].

Where a certified copy of the order is received by the Lord Chancellor, and it appears to him that the payer is residing or has assets in the United Kingdom, he must transfer that order to the appropriate court[11] by sending the certified copy and related documents to the prescribed officer of that court, who must register it in that court in the prescribed manner[12].

Before registering an order an officer must take such steps as he thinks fit to ascertain whether the payer is residing or has assets in the jurisdiction of the court, and if he is then satisfied that the payer is not residing and has no assets in the jurisdiction, he must send the certified copy of the order to the Lord Chancellor[13].

If an officer of a court is required by any of the provisions described above to send to the Lord Chancellor or another prescribed officer a certified copy of the order, he must send with it a certificate of arrears[14] signed by him, a statement giving such information as he possesses as to the payer's whereabouts and the nature and location of his assets, and any relevant documents in his possession relating to the case[15].

1 For the meaning of 'registered order' see para 824 note 1 ante.
2 For the meaning of 'registering court' see para 824 note 2 ante.
3 For the meaning of 'provisional order' see para 820 note 6 ante.
4 For the meaning of 'reciprocating country' see para 818 note 2 ante.
5 For the meaning of 'prescribed', and as to the prescribed officer, see para 819 note 6 ante.
6 Maintenance Orders (Reciprocal Enforcement) Act 1972 s 10(1). However, any arrears due under the registered order when the registration is cancelled continue to be recoverable: see s 10(1). See also the Magistrates' Courts (Reciprocal Enforcement of Maintenance Orders) Rules 1974, SI 1974/668, r 14(1) (amended by SI 1975/2236).
7 For the meaning of 'payer' see para 819 note 1 ante.
8 For the meaning of 'certified copy' see para 819 note 9 ante.
9 Maintenance Orders (Reciprocal Enforcement) Act 1972 s 10(2) (s 10(2), (3), (5), (7) amended by the Civil Jurisdiction and Judgments Act 1982 s 37(1), Sch 11 para 13; s 10(2), (5), (6), (7) amended by virtue of the Transfer of Functions (Magistrates' Courts and Family Law) Order 1992, SI 1992/709). As to the transfer of functions to the Lord Chancellor see para 819 note 8 ante.

10 Maintenance Orders (Reciprocal Enforcement) Act 1972 s 10(3) (as amended: see note 9 supra). On such a transfer, the prescribed officer of the court to which the order is transferred must register it in that court in the prescribed manner: s 10(4); and see the Magistrates' Courts (Reciprocal Enforcement of Maintenance Orders) Rules 1974 rr 13(1), 14(2) (amended and added respectively by SI 1975/2236).
11 For the meaning of 'appropriate court' see para 822 note 11 ante.
12 Maintenance Orders (Reciprocal Enforcement) Act 1972 s 10(5) (as amended: see note 9 supra); and see the Magistrates' Courts (Reciprocal Enforcement of Maintenance Orders) Rules 1974 r 14(2) (as added: see note 10 supra).
13 Maintenance Orders (Reciprocal Enforcement) Act 1972 s 10(6) (as amended: see note 9 supra).
14 For the meaning of 'certificate of arrears' see para 819 note 12 ante.
15 Maintenance Orders (Reciprocal Enforcement) Act 1972 s 10(7) (as amended: see note 9 supra).

827. Payer not resident in the United Kingdom. If at any time it appears to the Lord Chancellor[1] that the payer[2] under a maintenance order[3], of which a certified copy[4] has been received by him from a reciprocating country[5], is not residing and has no assets in the United Kingdom[6], he must send certain documents to the responsible authority[7] in that country or (if he thinks it proper having regard to all the circumstances) to the responsible authority in another reciprocating country[8]. The documents in question are: (1) the certified copy of the order in question and a certified copy of any order varying that order[9]; (2) if the order has at any time been a registered order[10], a certificate of arrears[11] signed by the prescribed officer[12]; (3) a statement giving such information as the Lord Chancellor possesses as to the payer's whereabouts and the nature and location of his assets[13]; and (4) any other relevant documents in his possession relating to the case[14].

Where these documents are sent to the responsible authority in a reciprocating country other than that in which the order was made, the Lord Chancellor must inform the responsible authority in the reciprocating country in which the order was made of what he has done[15].

1 As to the transfer of functions to the Lord Chancellor see para 819 note 8 ante.
2 For the meaning of 'payer' see para 819 note 1 ante.
3 For the meaning of 'maintenance order' see para 818 note 1 ante.
4 For the meaning of 'certified copy' see para 819 note 9 ante.
5 For the meaning of 'reciprocating country' see para 818 note 2 ante.
6 For the meaning of 'United Kingdom' see para 604 ante.
7 For the meaning of 'responsible authority' see para 819 note 17 ante.
8 Maintenance Orders (Reciprocal Enforcement) Act 1972 s 11(1) (amended by the Civil Jurisdiction and Judgments Act 1982 s 37(1), Sch 11 para 14; and by virtue of the Transfer of Functions (Magistrates' Courts and Family Law) Order 1992, SI 1992/709).
9 Maintenance Orders (Reciprocal Enforcement) Act 1972 s 11(1)(a).
10 For the meaning of 'registered order' see para 824 note 1 ante.
11 For the meaning of 'certificate of arrears' see para 819 note 12 ante.
12 Maintenance Orders (Reciprocal Enforcement) Act 1972 s 11(1)(b). For the meaning of 'prescribed', and as to the prescribed officer, see para 819 note 6 ante.
13 Ibid s 11(1)(c) (as amended: see note 8 supra).
14 Ibid s 11(1)(d).
15 Ibid s 11(2).

828. Obtaining evidence. For the purposes of any proceedings under Part I of the Maintenance Orders (Reciprocal Enforcement) Act 1972[1] relating to a maintenance order[2] a court in the United Kingdom[3] may request a court in a reciprocating country[4] to take or provide evidence relating to such matters as may be specified in the request, and may remit the case to that court for that purpose[5].

Where a request is made by or on behalf of a court in a reciprocating country, for the purpose of any proceedings before it relating to a maintenance order, for the taking in the United Kingdom of evidence of a person residing there relating to matters specified in the request, such court in the United Kingdom as may be prescribed may take that evidence[6]. Evidence taken in compliance with such a request must be sent in the prescribed manner by the prescribed officer of the court to the court in the reciprocating country concerned[7].

Where any person, other than the payer[8] and the payee[9] under the maintenance order in question, is required to give evidence before a court in the United Kingdom, the court may order the payment of compensation for expense, trouble or loss of time properly incurred in or incidental to his appearance out of money provided by Parliament[10]. A person may be compelled by summons and arrest to give evidence[11].

1 Ie the Maintenance Orders (Reciprocal Enforcement) Act 1972 Pt I (ss 1–24) (as amended).
2 For the meaning of 'maintenance order' see para 818 note 1 ante.
3 For the meaning of 'United Kingdom' see para 604 ante.
4 For the meaning of 'reciprocating country' see para 818 note 2 ante.
5 Maintenance Orders (Reciprocal Enforcement) Act 1972 s 14(5). For the admissibility of such evidence in proceedings in England and Wales see para 829 post. For the procedure where the request is made by a magistrates' court see the Magistrates' Courts (Reciprocal Enforcement of Maintenance Orders) Rules 1974, SI 1974/668, r 11.
6 Maintenance Orders (Reciprocal Enforcement) Act 1972 s 14(1). For the meaning of 'prescribed' see para 819 note 6 ante. As to the prescribed court see the Family Proceedings Rules 1991, SI 1991/1247, r 7.34(1), (3); and the Magistrates' Courts (Reciprocal Enforcement of Maintenance Orders) Rules 1974 r 10(1), (2). After giving notice of the time and place where the evidence is to be taken to such persons and in such manner as it thinks fit, the court must take the evidence in such manner as may be prescribed: Maintenance Orders (Reciprocal Enforcement) Act 1972 s 14(1); Family Proceedings Rules 1991 r 7.34(2), (4); Magistrates' Courts (Reciprocal Enforcement of Maintenance Orders) Rules 1974 r 10(3)–(5).
7 Maintenance Orders (Reciprocal Enforcement) Act 1972 s 14(1). As to the prescribed officer see para 819 note 6 ante.
8 For the meaning of 'payer' see para 819 note 1 ante.
9 For the meaning of 'payee' see para 819 note 5 ante.
10 See the Maintenance Orders (Reciprocal Enforcement) Act 1972 s 14(2) (amended by the Northern Ireland (Modification of Enactments No 1) Order 1973, SI 1973/2163).
11 See the Maintenance Orders (Reciprocal Enforcement) Act 1972 s 14(3) (amended by the Magistrates' Courts Act 1980 s 154, Sch 7 para 105), applying the Magistrates' Courts Act 1980 s 97(1), (3), (4) (as amended) to the taking of evidence under the provisions described in the text and notes supra).

829. Admissibility of evidence and proof of orders. A statement contained in a duly authenticated[1] document which purports to:

(1) set out or summarise evidence given in proceedings in a court in a reciprocating country[2]; or

(2) set out or summarise evidence taken in such a country for the purpose of proceedings in a court in the United Kingdom[3] under Part I of the Maintenance Orders (Reciprocal Enforcement) Act 1972[4], whether in response to a request made by such a court or otherwise; or

(3) have been received in evidence in proceedings in such a country or to be a copy of a document so received,

is admissible in any proceedings in a court in the United Kingdom relating to a maintenance order[5] as evidence of the facts stated in it to the same extent as oral evidence of that fact is admissible in those proceedings[6].

Nothing in the provisions described above prejudices the admission in evidence of any document which would otherwise be admissible[7].

For the purposes of the Act, unless the contrary is shown, any order made by a court in a reciprocating country purporting to bear the seal of that court or be signed by any person in his capacity as a judge, magistrate or officer of that court, must be deemed without further proof to have been duly sealed or signed by that person[8]. The person by whom the order was signed must be deemed without further proof to have been a judge, magistrate or officer, as the case may be, of that court when he signed it and in the case of an officer to have been authorised to sign it[9]. A document purporting to be a certified copy[10] of an order made by a court in a reciprocating country must be deemed without further proof to be such a copy[11].

1   A document under head (1) or (2) in the text is duly authenticated if it purports to be certified by the judge, magistrate or other person before whom the evidence was given or, as the case may be, by whom it was taken, to be (a) the original document containing or recording or, as the case may be, summarising the evidence or (b) a true copy of that document: Maintenance Orders (Reciprocal Enforcement) Act 1972 s 13(2). A document under head (3) in the text is duly authenticated if it purports to be certified by a judge, magistrate or officer of the court in question to have been, or to be a true copy of a document which has been, received: s 13(3). It is not necessary in any such proceedings to prove the signature or official position of the person appearing to have given such a certificate: s 13(4).
2   For the meaning of 'reciprocating country' see para 818 note 2 ante.
3   For the meaning of 'United Kingdom' see para 604 ante.
4   Ie the Maintenance Orders (Reciprocal Enforcement) Act 1972 Pt I (ss 1–24) (as amended).
5   Ie a maintenance order to which ibid Pt I (as amended) applies. For the meaning of 'maintenance order' see para 818 note 1 ante.
6   Ibid s 13(1).
7   Ibid s 13(5).
8   Ibid s 15(a).
9   Ibid s 15(b).
10 For the meaning of 'certified copy' see para 819 note 9 ante.
11 Maintenance Orders (Reciprocal Enforcement) Act 1972 s 15(c).

830. Procedure. All proceedings in magistrates' courts under Part I of the Maintenance Orders (Reciprocal Enforcement) Act 1972[1] other than proceedings for the variation or enforcement of a maintenance order, are family proceedings for the purposes of the Magistrates' Courts Act 1980[2], although the court may order proceedings for the variation of an order, and any proceedings being heard with it, to be treated as family proceedings[3]. Magistrates' courts rules may be made with regard to certain matters under the 1972 Act[4].

1   Ie the Maintenance Orders (Reciprocal Enforcement) Act 1972 Pt I (ss 1–24) (as amended): see paras 818–829 ante.
2   Magistrates' Courts Act 1980 s 65(1)(f). As to domestic proceedings see MAGISTRATES vol 29 para 374.
3   See ibid s 65(2) (amended by the Children Act 1989 s 92(11), Sch 11 para 8).
4   See the Maintenance Orders (Reciprocal Enforcement) Act 1972 s 18(1) (amended by the Magistrates' Courts Act 1980 s 154, Sch 7 para 106). The matters with regard to which such rules may be made are:
    (1) the circumstances in which anything authorised or required to be done by the Maintenance Orders (Reciprocal Enforcement) Act 1972 Pt I (as amended) by, to or before a magistrates' court for a particular sessions area or by, to or before an officer of the court may be done by a court (or officer thereof) for another petty sessions area (s 18(1)(a));
    (2) the orders made, or other things done by a magistrates' court (or officer thereof), or by a court in a reciprocating country, notice of which is to be given to such persons as the rules may provide, and the manner of giving such notice (s 18(1)(b));
    (3) the cases and manner in which courts in reciprocating countries are to be informed of orders made or other things done by a magistrates' court (s 18(1)(c));
    (4) the cases and manner in which a justices' clerk may take evidence needed for the purpose of proceedings in a court in a reciprocating country relating to a maintenance order (s 18(1)(d));
    (5) the circumstances and manner in which cases may be remitted by magistrates' courts to courts in reciprocating countries (s 18(1)(e));
    (6) the circumstances and manner in which magistrates' courts may communicate with courts in reciprocating countries (s 18(1)(f)).

For the meaning of 'reciprocating country' see para 818 note 2 ante. For the meaning of 'maintenance order' see para 818 note 1 ante. As to petty sessions areas see MAGISTRATES vol 29 para 293 et seq.

For rules made or taking effect under this provision see the Magistrates' Courts (Reciprocal Enforcement of Maintenance Orders) Rules 1974, SI 1974/668 (amended by SI 1975/2236; SI 1979/170; SI 1983/1148; SI 1986/1962; SI 1992/457; and SI 1993/617); and the Magistrates' Courts (Reciprocal Enforcement of Maintenance Orders) (Hague Convention Countries) Rules 1980, SI 1980/108 (amended by SI 1986/1962; SI 1992/457; and SI 1993/617).

(B) *Enforcement under Part II*

831. Application of statutory provisions. Part II of the Maintenance Orders (Reciprocal Enforcement) Act 1972[1] contains provisions giving effect to an international convention[2] as to the reciprocal enforcement of claims for the recovery of maintenance. These provisions have effect in relation to countries outside the United Kingdom[3] declared by Order in Council to be Convention countries for the purposes of the provisions[4]. The provisions of the Act may be applied with modifications and adaptations to other countries designated by Order in Council[5].

  1 Ie the Maintenance Orders (Reciprocal Enforcement) Act 1972 Pt II (ss 25–39) (as amended): see the text and notes infra; and para 832 et seq post.
  2 Ie the United Nations Convention on the Recovery Abroad of Maintenance, done at New York on 20 June 1956 (Cmnd 4485): Maintenance Orders (Reciprocal Enforcement) Act 1972 s 25(2).
  3 For the meaning of 'United Kingdom' see para 604 ante.
  4 Maintenance Orders (Reciprocal Enforcement) Act 1972 s 25(1). Such countries are referred to in the Act as 'Convention countries': s 25(1). Such an Order in Council may be varied or revoked by a subsequent Order in Council, which may contain such incidental, consequential and transitional provisions as seem expedient: s 45(1). An Order in Council is subject to annulment in pursuance of a resolution of either House of Parliament: s 45(2).

     The following are declared to be Convention countries by Order in Council: Algeria, Austria, Barbados, Belgium, Brazil, Central African Republic, Chile, Czechoslovakia (but see infra), Denmark, Ecuador, Finland, France (including overseas territories), Germany, Greece, Guatemala, Haiti, Holy See, Hungary, Israel, Italy, Luxembourg, Monaco, Morocco, Netherlands, Niger, Norway, Pakistan, Philippines, Poland, Portugal, Spain, Sri Lanka, Suriname, Sweden, Switzerland, Tunisia, Turkey, and Upper Volta, and Yugoslavia (but see infra): Recovery Abroad of Maintenance (Convention Countries) Order 1975, SI 1975/423 (amended by SI 1978/279; and SI 1982/1530).

     Note, however, that the following countries, at the date at which this volume states the law, have ratified, acceded or succeeded to the Convention but have not been declared by Order in Council to be Convention countries: Argentina, Australia, Bosnia Herzegovina, China, Croatia, Cyprus, Czech Republic, Macedonia, Mexico, New Zealand, Romania, Slovak Republic, Slovenia.

     The following further countries, at the date at which this volume states the law, have signed, but not ratified, acceded to or succeeded to the Convention: Bolivia, Cambodia, Colombia, Cuba, Dominican Republic, El Salvador.
  5 See the Maintenance Orders (Reciprocal Enforcement) Act 1972 s 40; and the Recovery of Maintenance (United States of America) Order 1993, SI 1993/591.

832. Recovery of maintenance in Convention country. Where a person ('the applicant') in the United Kingdom[1] (1) claims to be entitled to recover maintenance in a Convention country[2] from a person subject to the jurisdiction of that country; or (2) seeks to vary any provision made in a Convention country for the payment by any other person who is subject to the jurisdiction of that country, he may apply[3] to the Lord Chancellor[4] to have his claim for recovery of maintenance or his application for variation transmitted to that country[5]. On receiving an application, the Lord Chancellor must transmit it, together with any accompanying documents, to the appropriate authority in the Convention country, unless he is satisfied that it is not made in good faith or that it does not comply with the requirements of the law applied by that country[6]. He may request the appropriate officer to obtain from the court of which he is an officer such information relating to the application as may be specified, and the court must furnish the Lord Chancellor with the information he requires[7].

1   For the meaning of 'United Kingdom' see para 604 ante.
2   For the meaning of 'Convention country' see para 831 note 4 ante.
3   An application must be made through the appropriate officer, who must assist the applicant in completing an application complying with the requirements of the law applied by the Convention country, and must send the application to the Lord Chancellor together with such other documents as may be required by that law: Maintenance Orders (Reciprocal Enforcement) Act 1972 s 26(3) (amended by virtue of the Transfer of Functions (Magistrates' Courts and Family Law) Order 1992, SI 1992/709). The appropriate officer is the clerk of the magistrates' court for the petty sessions area in which the applicant resides: Maintenance Orders (Reciprocal Enforcement) Act 1972 s 26(6). As to petty sessions areas see MAGISTRATES vol 29 para 293 et seq.
4   As to the transfer of functions to the Lord Chancellor see para 819 note 8 ante. For specific provision relating to the United States see the Maintenance Orders (Reciprocal Enforcement) Act 1972 s 26(3A) (added by the Recovery of Maintenance (United States of America) Order 1993, SI 1993/591); and the Magistrates' Courts (Recovery Abroad of Maintenance) Rules 1975, SI 1975/488, r 5A (added by SI 1979/1561).
5   Maintenance Orders (Reciprocal Enforcement) Act 1972 s 26(1), (2) (amended by virtue of the Transfer of Functions (Magistrates' Courts and Family Law) Order 1992).
6   Maintenance Orders (Reciprocal Enforcement) Act 1972 s 26(4) (as amended: see note 5 supra).
7   Ibid s 26(5) (as amended: see note 5 supra).

833. Recovery of maintenance in England and Wales by persons in Convention countries. Any application which is received by the Lord Chancellor from the appropriate authority in a Convention country[1] and is an application by a person in that country for the recovery of maintenance from another person who is for the time being residing in England and Wales[2], must be treated for the purposes of any enactment as if it were an application for a maintenance order[3] under a relevant Act[4], made at the time when the application was received by the Lord Chancellor[5].

On receipt of such an application the Lord Chancellor must send it, together with any accompanying documents, to the clerk of a magistrates' court for the petty sessions area where the respondent is residing[6]. If notice of the hearing of the application by a magistrates' court having jurisdiction to hear it cannot be duly served on the respondent, the clerk must return the application and accompanying documents to the Lord Chancellor with a statement giving such information as he possesses as to the whereabouts of the respondent[7]. If the clerk to whom the application is sent is satisfied that the respondent is residing within the petty sessions area for which another magistrates' court acts, he must send the application and accompanying documents to the clerk of the other court and inform the Lord Chancellor that he has done so[8].

Where a magistrates' court makes an order on such an application[9], the court must at the same time exercise one of the following powers[10]: (1) the power to order that payments under the order be made directly to the clerk of the court or of any other magistrates' court in England and Wales[11]; (2) the power to order that payments under the order be made to the clerk of that or any other magistrates' court in England and Wales by such method[12] as may be specified[13]; and (3) the power to make an attachment of earnings order[14]. In deciding which of these powers to exercise the court must have regard to any representations made by the person liable to make payments under the order[15]. Where the court proposes to exercise its power under head (2) above and, having given the debtor[16] an opportunity of opening an account from which payments may be made in accordance with the method of payment proposed to be ordered, the court is satisfied that he has failed without reasonable excuse to do so, it may order that he open such an account[17].

The clerk of the court must register the order in the court in the prescribed manner[18].

1 For the meaning of 'Convention country' see para 831 note 4 ante.
2 As to the meaning of 'England and Wales' see para 604 ante.
3 'Maintenance order' has the same meaning as is given in para 818 note 1 ante: Maintenance Orders (Reciprocal Enforcement) Act 1972 s 39 (definition added by the Maintenance Orders (Reciprocal Enforcement) Act 1992 s 1(2), Sch 1 para 19).
4 In the case of an application for maintenance for a child (or children) alone, the relevant Act is the Children Act 1989; in any other case, the relevant Act is the Domestic Proceedings and Magistrates' Courts Act 1978: Maintenance Orders (Reciprocal Enforcement) Act 1972 s 27A (ss 27A–27C added by the Maintenance Orders (Reciprocal Enforcement) Act 1992 Sch 1 para 13). 'Child' has the same meaning as in the Children Act 1989 s 15(1), Sch 1 (as amended): Maintenance Orders (Reciprocal Enforcement) Act 1972 s 27A(5) (as so added): see CHILDREN vol 5(2) (Reissue) para 849 et seq).
5 Ibid s 27A(1), (2) (as added: see note 4 supra).
6 Ibid s 27B(1) (as added: see note 4 supra). As to petty sessions areas see MAGISTRATES vol 29 para 293 et seq. As to the procedure to be followed by the clerk see the Magistrates' Courts (Recovery Abroad of Maintenance) Rules 1975, SI 1975/488, r 3A (added by SI 1993/617).
7 Maintenance Orders (Reciprocal Enforcement) Act 1972 s 27B(2) (as added: see note 4 supra). If the application is so returned, the Lord Chancellor must, unless he is satisfied that the respondent is not residing in the United Kingdom, take certain specified steps: see s 27B(3) (as so added). For the meaning of 'United Kingdom' see para 604 ante.
8 Ibid s 27B(4) (as added: see note 4 supra). If an application is sent to a clerk under this provision, he must proceed as if it had been sent to him under s 27B(1) (see text and note 6 supra): s 27B(5) (as so added).
9 Where the magistrates' court dismisses the application the clerk must send written notice to the Lord Chancellor, including a statement of reasons: Magistrates' Courts (Recovery Abroad of Maintenance) Rules 1975 r 4 (amended by SI 1993/617; and by virtue of SI 1992/709).
10 Maintenance Orders (Reciprocal Enforcement) Act 1972 s 27C(1), (3) (as added: see note 4 supra). Accordingly, the Magistrates' Courts Act 1980 s 59 (as substituted) does not apply: Maintenance Orders (Reciprocal Enforcement) Act 1972 s 27C(2) (as so added).
11 Ibid s 27C(4)(a) (as added: see note 4 supra).
12 Ie a method falling within the Magistrates' Courts Act 1980 s 59(6) (as substituted).
13 Maintenance Orders (Reciprocal Enforcement) Act 1972 s 27C(4)(b) (as added: see note 4 supra).
14 Ie an order under the Attachment of Earnings Act 1971 (see MAGISTRATES vol 29 para 432 et seq): Maintenance Orders (Reciprocal Enforcement) Act 1972 s 27C(4)(c) (as added: see note 4 supra).
15 Ibid s 27C(5) (as added: see note 4 supra).
16 For the meaning of 'debtor' see para 806 note 10 ante.
17 Magistrates' Courts Act 1980 s 59(4) (substituted by the Maintenance Enforcement Act 1991 s 2), as applied and modified by the Maintenance Orders (Facilities for Enforcement) Act 1972 s 27C(6) (as added: see note 4 supra).
18 Ibid s 27C(7) (as added: see note 4 supra); and see the Magistrates' Courts (Recovery Abroad of Maintenance) Rules 1975 rr 5(1), 6(1) (both amended by SI 1993/617). 'Prescribed' has the same meaning as is given in para 819 note 6 ante: Maintenance Orders (Reciprocal Enforcement) Act 1972 s 39.

834. Application by former spouse. Where an application for recovery of maintenance falls to be treated as if it were an application under the Domestic Proceedings and Magistrates' Courts Act 1978[1], and

(1) the applicant and respondent were formerly married[2];

(2) the marriage was dissolved or annulled in a country or territory outside the United Kingdom[3] by a divorce or annulment recognised as valid by the law of England and Wales[4];

(3) an order for the payment of maintenance for the benefit of the applicant or a child of the family[5] has, by reason of the divorce or annulment, been made by a court in a Convention country[6]; and

(4) where the order for the payment of maintenance was made by a court of a different country from that in which the divorce or annulment was obtained, either the applicant or the respondent was resident in the Convention country whose court made that order at the time the order was applied for[7],

any magistrates' court which would have jurisdiction under that Act[8] to hear the application if the parties were still married, has such jurisdiction notwithstanding the dissolution or annulment[9].

If the magistrates' court is satisfied that the respondent has failed to comply with the provisions of an order mentioned in head (3) above, it may make any order which it would have power to make under certain provisions of the 1978 Act[10]. The court may not make an order for periodical payments for the benefit of the applicant or any child of the family unless the order made in the Convention country makes such provision[11]. Nor may the court make an order for the payment of a lump sum for the benefit of the applicant or any child of the family unless the order made in the convention country makes provision for the payment of a lump sum to the applicant or that child[12].

1 Maintenance Orders (Reciprocal Enforcement) Act 1972 s 28A(1) (s 28A substituted, and ss 28B, 28C added, by the Maintenance Orders (Reciprocal Enforcement) Act 1992 s 1(2), Sch 1 para 13; s 28A previously added by the Domestic Proceedings and Magistrates' Courts Act 1978 s 58) As to applications to be treated as described in the text see para 833 text and note 4 ante. No provision of an order under the Children Act 1989 s 92, Sch 11 (as amended) requiring the transfer of proceedings from a magistrates' court to a county court or the High Court applies where an application is to be treated as an application for a maintenance order under that Act (see para 833 text and note 4 ante): Maintenance Orders (Reciprocal Enforcement) Act 1972 s 28B (as so added). For the meaning of 'maintenance order' see paras 818 note 1, 833 note 3 ante.
   Where s 28A (as so substituted) does not apply, the magistrates' court hearing an application which is to be treated as described in the text may make any order which it has power to make under the Domestic Proceedings and Magistrates' Courts Act 1978 s 2 or s 19(1) (as amended), and Pt I (ss 1–35) (as amended) of that Act is modified in such a case: see the Maintenance Orders (Reciprocal Enforcement) Act 1972 s 28 (substituted by the Maintenance Orders (Reciprocal Enforcement) Act 1992 Sch 1 para 13). But see para 838 note 14 post.
2 Maintenance Orders (Reciprocal Enforcement) Act 1972 s 28A(1)(a) (as substituted: see note 1 supra).
3 For the meaning of 'United Kingdom' see para 604 ante.
4 Maintenance Orders (Reciprocal Enforcement) Act 1972 s 28A(1)(b) (as substituted: see note 1 supra). As to the meaning of 'England and Wales' see para 604 ante. A divorce or annulment obtained in a country outside the United Kingdom is presumed to be recognised as valid under the law of England and Wales unless the contrary is proved: s 28A(7) (as so substituted).
5 'Child of the family' has the same meaning as in the Domestic Proceedings and Magistrates' Courts Act 1978 s 88(1) (as amended) (see CHILDREN vol 5(2) (Reissue) paras 813, 815 note 1): Maintenance Orders (Reciprocal Enforcement) Act 1972 s 28A(8) (as substituted: see note 1 supra).
6 Ibid s 28A(1)(c) (as substituted: see note 1 supra). For the meaning of 'Convention country' see para 831 note 4 ante.
7 Ibid s 28A(1)(d) (as substituted: see note 1 supra).
8 Ie under the Domestic Proceedings and Magistrates' Courts Act 1978 s 30 (as modified by the Maintenance Orders (Reciprocal Enforcement) Act 1972 s 28A(6) (as substituted: see note 1 supra)). But see para 838 note 14 post.
9 Ibid s 28A(2) (as substituted: see note 1 supra).
10 Ie under the Domestic Proceedings and Magistrates' Courts Act 1978 s 2 or s 19(1) (as amended): Maintenance Orders (Reciprocal Enforcement) Act 1972 s 28A(3) (as added: see note 1 supra).
11 Ibid s 28A(4) (as substituted: see note 1 supra).
12 Ibid s 28A(5) (as substituted: see note 1 supra).

835. Transfer of orders. Where the prescribed officer[1] of a registering court[2] is of opinion that the payer[3] under a registered order[4] has ceased to reside within the jurisdiction of the court, he must send a certified copy[5] of the order and the related documents[6] to the Lord Chancellor[7]. If the officer is of opinion that the payer has ceased to reside in the United Kingdom[8] he must send a notice to that effect to the Lord Chancellor[9]. Where the clerk of a registering magistrates' court is of opinion that the payer is residing within the jurisdiction of another magistrates' court in the same part of the United Kingdom, he must transfer the order to that other court by sending a certified copy of it and the related documents to the clerk of that other court, who must register the order in that court in the prescribed manner[10]. Where a certified copy of an order is received by the Lord Chancellor, and it appears to him that the payer is still residing in the United Kingdom, he must transfer the order to the appropriate court[11] by sending the copy and related documents to the prescribed officer of the appropriate court, who must register it in that court in the prescribed manner[12]. Where a certified copy of an order is received by the Lord Chancellor, and it appears to him that the payer is not residing in the United Kingdom, he must return the copy and the related documents to the registering court[13].

On registering an order, an officer must give notice of the registration in the prescribed manner to the prescribed officer of the court in which the order was registered immediately before registering it under the provisions described above[14], and the officer to whom such notice is given must cancel the previous registration[15].

Before registering an order as described above an officer of a court must take such steps as he thinks fit to ascertain whether the payer is residing within the jurisdiction of the court, and if after taking those steps he is satisfied that the payer is not so residing he must return the certified copy of the order and the related documents to the officer of the court (or, as the case may be, to the Lord Chancellor), from whom he received them, together with a statement giving such information as he possesses as to the whereabouts of the payer[16].

1   For the meaning of 'prescribed' see paras 819 note 6, 833 note 18 ante. In relation to a magistrates' court, the prescribed officer is the clerk to the justices: Magistrates' Courts (Recovery Abroad of Maintenance) Rules 1975, SI 1975/488, r 3.
2   'Registering court', in relation to a registered order (see note 4 infra), means the court in which that order is for the time being registered under the Maintenance Orders (Reciprocal Enforcement) Act 1972 Pt II (ss 25–39) (as amended): s 39.
3   'Payer', in relation to a registered order (see note 4 infra), means the person liable to make payments under the order: ibid s 32(8).
4   'Registered order' means an order which is for the time being registered in a court in the United Kingdom under ibid Pt II (as amended): s 39.
5   'Certified copy' has the same meaning as in para 819 note 9 ante: ibid s 32(8).
6   'Related documents' means (1) the application on which the order was made, (2) a certificate of arrears signed by the prescribed officer of the registering court, (3) a statement giving such information as he possesses as to the whereabouts of the payer, and (4) any relevant documents in his possession relating to the case: ibid s 32(8). 'Certificate of arrears' has the same meaning as in para 819 note 12 ante: s 32(8).
7   As to the transfer of functions to the Lord Chancellor see para 819 note 8 ante.
8   For the meaning of 'United Kingdom' see para 604 ante.
9   Maintenance Orders (Reciprocal Enforcement) Act 1972 s 32(1) (s 32(1), (3), (4), (5) amended by virtue of the Transfer of Functions (Magistrates' Courts and Family Law) Order 1992, SI 1992/709).
10   Maintenance Orders (Reciprocal Enforcement) Act 1972 s 32(2); and see the Magistrates' Courts (Recovery Abroad of Maintenance) Rules 1975 r 5(2), (3). See also text and note 16 infra. References to a part of the United Kingdom are to England and Wales, Scotland, or Northern Ireland: Maintenance Orders (Reciprocal Enforcement) Act 1972 s 47(2); and cf para 604 ante.
11   'The appropriate court' means a magistrates' court within the jurisdiction of which that person is residing: ibid s 32(8).
12   Ibid s 32(3) (as amended: see note 9 supra). See also text and note 16 infra.
13   Ibid s 32(5) (as amended: see note 9 supra).
14   Ibid s 32(6).
15   Ibid s 32(7).
16   Ibid s 32(4) (as amended: see note 9 supra).

836. Enforcement of registered orders. A registered order[1] which is registered in a court other than that in which it was made may be enforced as if the registering court[2] had made it and had had jurisdiction to do so, and proceedings relating to enforcement may be taken accordingly (but not otherwise)[3]. The order is enforceable as if it were a magistrates' court maintenance order[4], and the court and its officers must take all steps for enforcing it as may be prescribed[5]. In any proceedings for enforcement of an order which is for the time being registered in any court, a certificate of arrears[6] sent to the prescribed officer[7] is evidence of the facts stated in it[8].

1 For the meaning of 'registered order' see para 835 note 4 ante.
2 For the meaning of 'registering court' see para 835 note 2 ante.
3 Maintenance Orders (Reciprocal Enforcement) Act 1972 s 33(1). This does not apply to an order registered in the High Court under the Maintenance Orders Act 1958 Pt I (ss 1–5) (as amended): Maintenance Orders (Reciprocal Enforcement) Act 1972 s 33(2).
4 See ibid s 33(3), (3A) (s 33(3) substituted by the Family Law Reform Act 1987 s 33(1), Sch 2 para 50; s 33(3) subsequently amended, and s 33(3A) added, by the Maintenance Enforcement Act 1991 s 10, Sch 1 para 18). 'Magistrates' court maintenance order' has the same meaning as in the Magistrates' Courts Act 1980 s 150(1) (definition as added): Maintenance Orders (Reciprocal Enforcement) Act 1972 s 33(3) (as so substituted).
   The Magistrates' Courts Act 1980 ss 76, 93 (both as amended) (enforcement of judgment and complaint for arrears) are subject, in this regard, to the modifications made by the Maintenance Orders (Reciprocal Enforcement) Act 1972 s 8(4A), (4B) (as added) (see para 824 note 4 ante): s 33(3A) (as so added).
   The Maintenance Orders Act 1950 Pt II (ss 16–25) (as amended) (see para 801 et seq ante) does not apply to a registered order: Maintenance Orders (Reciprocal Enforcement) Act 1972 s 33(6).
5 Ibid s 33(4). For the meaning of 'prescribed' see paras 819 note 6, 833 note 18 ante.
6 Ie a certificate of arrears sent under ibid s 32 (as amended): see para 835 ante. For the meaning of 'certificate of arrears' see paras 819 note 12, 835 note 6 ante.
7 As to the prescribed officer see para 835 note 1 ante.
8 Maintenance Orders (Reciprocal Enforcement) Act 1972 s 33(5).

837. Variation and revocation of registered orders: general. Where a registered order[1] is registered in a court other than that in which it was made, the registering court[2] has the like power to vary or revoke[3] it as if that court had made it and had had jurisdiction to make it[4]. No court other than the registering court has power to vary or revoke a registered order[5]. Where a registering court revokes a registered order it must cancel the registration[6].

Where the Lord Chancellor[7] receives from the appropriate authority in a Convention country[8] an application by a person in that country for the variation of a registered order, he must, if the registering court is a magistrates' court, send the application, together with any accompanying documents, to the clerk of that court[9]. Where a court in a part of the United Kingdom[10] makes or refuses to make an order varying or revoking a registered order made by a court in another part of the United Kingdom, any person has the same right of appeal as if the registered order had been made by the first-mentioned court[11].

1 For the meaning of 'registered order' see para 835 note 4 ante.
2 For the meaning of 'registering court' see para 835 note 2 ante.
3 'Revoke' and 'revocation' include discharge: Maintenance Orders (Reciprocal Enforcement) Act 1972 s 39 (definition added by the Maintenance Orders (Reciprocal Enforcement) Act 1992 s 1(2), Sch 1 para 19).
4 Maintenance Orders (Reciprocal Enforcement) Act 1972 s 34(1) (amended by the Maintenance Enforcement Act 1991 s 10, Sch 1 para 19; and by the Maintenance Orders (Reciprocal Enforcement) Act 1992 Sch 1 para 15(1), (2)), which is expressed to be subject to the provisions described in para 838 post. The Magistrates' Courts Act 1980 s 60(1) (as substituted) is modified in its application to a

registered order: see the Maintenance Orders (Reciprocal Enforcement) Act 1972 s 34(3A) (added by the Maintenance Orders (Reciprocal Enforcement) Act 1992 Sch 1 para 15(3)).

5 Maintenance Orders (Reciprocal Enforcement) Act 1972 s 34(1) (as amended: see note 4 supra).

6 Ibid s 34(2).

7 As to the transfer of functions to the Lord Chancellor see para 819 note 8 ante.

8 For the meaning of 'Convention country' see para 831 note 4 ante.

9 Maintenance Orders (Reciprocal Enforcement) Act 1972 s 34(3) (amended by virtue of the Transfer of Functions (Magistrates' Courts and Family Law) Order 1992, SI 1992/709).

10 As to references to a part of the United Kingdom see para 835 note 10 ante.

11 Maintenance Orders (Reciprocal Enforcement) Act 1972 s 34(4).

838. Variation of registered orders by magistrates' courts. Where a registered order[1] is registered in a magistrates' court in England and Wales[2], and the court is satisfied that payment has not been made in accordance with the order, the power of the court to vary the order includes power to do one of the following[3]: (1) order that payments be made directly to the clerk of the court or of another magistrates' court[4]; (2) order that payments be so made by a prescribed method[5]; or (3) make an attachment of earnings order[6]. In deciding which of these powers to exercise, the court must have regard to any representations made by the debtor[7].

Where a registered order is registered in a magistrates' court in England and Wales and payments under it are required to be made as mentioned in head (2) above, an interested party[8] may apply in writing to the clerk of the court in which the order is registered for the order to be varied[9]. Where such an application has been made, the clerk, after giving written notice to any other interested party and allowing that party, within 14 days beginning with the date of the notice, an opportunity to make written representations, may vary the order to provide that payment is to be made as described in head (1) above[10]. The clerk may proceed with the application, however, notwithstanding that an interested party has not received written notice of it[11]. If the clerk considers it inappropriate to exercise his power to vary the order, he may refer the matter to the court which may vary the order by exercising one of its powers under heads (1) to (3) above[12].

Where the court proposes to exercise its power under head (2) above and, having given the debtor an opportunity of opening an account from which payments may be made in accordance with the method of payment proposed to be ordered, the court is satisfied that he has failed without reasonable excuse to do so, it may order that he open such an account[13].

A magistrates' court in England and Wales has jurisdiction to hear an application for the variation or revocation of a registered order registered in that court, made by the person against whom or on whose application the order was made, notwithstanding that the person by or against whom the application is made is residing outside England and Wales[14]. Where the respondent to an application for variation or revocation of an order registered in a magistrates' court in England and Wales does not appear at the time and place appointed for the hearing of the application, but the court is satisfied that he is residing outside England and Wales and that the prescribed[15] notice of the application and the time and place of the hearing has been given to him in the prescribed manner[16], the court may proceed to hear and determine the application at the time and place appointed for the hearing or any adjourned hearing as if the respondent had so appeared[17].

1 For the meaning of 'registered order' see para 835 note 4 ante.
2 Ie whether or not it is the court which made the order: Maintenance Orders (Reciprocal Enforcement) Act 1972 s 34A(1) (s 34A added by the Maintenance Enforcement Act 1991 s 10, Sch 1 para 19(2)). As to the meaning of 'England and Wales' see para 604 ante.
3 Maintenance Orders (Reciprocal Enforcement) Act 1972 s 34A(1), (2) (as added: see note 2 supra). The provisions described in this paragraph apply, in the circumstances set out in the text, in place of: (1) the Magistrates' Courts Act 1980 s 60(3)–(11) (as substituted); (2) the Domestic Proceedings and Magistrates' Courts Act 1978 s 20ZA (as added); and (3) the Children Act 1989 s 15(1) (as amended), Sch 1 para 6A (as added): Maintenance Orders (Reciprocal Enforcement) Act 1972 s 34A(1)(a)–(c) (as added: see note 2 supra). None of these powers apply in relation to an application under s 35 (as substituted): see text and notes 14–17 infra.
4 Ibid s 34A(3)(a) (as added: see note 2 supra).
5 Ie under the Magistrates' Courts Act s 59(6) (as substituted): Maintenance Orders (Reciprocal Enforcement) Act 1972 s 34A(3)(b) (as added: see note 2 supra).
6 Ie an order under the Attachment of Earnings Act 1971 (see MAGISTRATES vol 29 para 432 et seq): Maintenance Orders (Reciprocal Enforcement) Act 1972 s 34A(3)(c) (as added: see note 2 supra).
7 Ibid s 34A(9) (as added: see note 2 supra). 'Debtor' has the same meaning as in the Magistrates' Courts Act 1980 s 59 (as substituted) (see para 806 note 10 ante): Maintenance Orders (Reciprocal Enforcement) Act 1972 s 34A(11) (as so added).
8 'Interested party' means the debtor or the creditor: ibid s 34A(7) (as added: see note 2 supra). 'Creditor' has the same meaning as in the Magistrates' Courts Act 1980 s 59 (as substituted) (see para 806 note 10 ante): Maintenance Orders (Reciprocal Enforcement) Act 1972 s 34A(11) (as so added).
9 Ibid s 34A(4) (as added: see note 2 supra).
10 Ibid s 34A(5) (as added: see note 2 supra).
11 Ibid s 34A(6) (as added: see note 2 supra).
12 Ibid s 34A(8) (as added: see note 2 supra). In deciding which of these powers to exercise, the court must have regard to any representations made by the debtor: s 34A(9) (as so added).
13 Magistrates' Courts Act 1980 s 59(4) (substituted by the Maintenance Enforcement Act 1991 s 2), as applied and modified by the Maintenance Orders (Facilities for Enforcement) Act 1972 s 34A(10) (as added: see note 2 supra).
14 Ibid s 35(1) (s 35 substituted by the Maintenance Orders (Reciprocal Enforcement) Act 1992 s 1(2), Sch 1 para 16). This is notwithstanding anything in the Maintenance Orders (Facilities for Enforcement) Act 1972 s 28(2) (as substituted) or s 28A(6)(e) (as added) (see para 834 ante). None of the powers of the court or the clerk are available in relation to such an application: see s 35(2) (as so substituted).
15 For the meaning of 'prescribed' see paras 819 note 6, 833 note 18 ante.
16 See the Magistrates' Courts (Recovery Abroad of Maintenance) Rules 1975, SI 1975/488, r 8 (which refers to the corresponding provision of the Maintenance Orders (Reciprocal Enforcement) Act 1972 s 35 prior to its substitution).
17 Ibid s 35(3) (as substituted: see note 14 supra).

839. Obtaining evidence. A court in the United Kingdom[1], for the purpose of any proceedings in that court under Part II of the Maintenance Orders (Reciprocal Enforcement) Act 1972[2] arising out of an application received by the Lord Chancellor[3] from a Convention country[4], may request the Lord Chancellor to make to the appropriate authority or court in that country a request for the taking in that country of the evidence of a person residing there relating to matters connected with the application[5]. The request made by the court must give details of the application, state the name and address of the person whose evidence is to be taken, and specify the matters relating to which that person's evidence is required[6]. If the Lord Chancellor is satisfied that a request made to him contains sufficient information to enable the evidence of the person named in it, relating to the specified matters, to be taken by a court or person in the Convention country, he must transmit the request to the appropriate authority or court in that country[7].

1 For the meaning of 'United Kingdom' see para 604 ante.
2 Ie the Maintenance Orders (Reciprocal Enforcement) Act 1972 Pt II (ss 25–39) (as amended): see paras 831–838 ante.
3 As to the transfer of functions to the Lord Chancellor see para 819 note 8 ante.

4 For the meaning of 'Convention country' see para 831 note 4 ante.
5 Maintenance Orders (Reciprocal Enforcement) Act 1972 s 37(1) (amended by virtue of the Transfer of
   Functions (Magistrates' Courts and Family Law) Order 1992, SI 1992/709).
6 Maintenance Orders (Facilities for Enforcement) Act 1972 s 37(2).
7 Ibid s 37(3).

840. Admissibility of evidence. A statement contained in a duly authenticated[1] document which purports to:

(1) set out or summarise evidence given in proceedings in a court in a Convention country[2]; or

(2) set out or summarise evidence taken in such a country for the purpose of proceedings in a court in the United Kingdom[3] under Part II of the Maintenance Orders (Reciprocal Enforcement) Act 1972[4], whether in response to a request made by such a court or otherwise; or

(3) have been received in evidence in proceedings in such a country or to be a copy of a document so received, is admissible in specified proceedings[5] in a magistrates' court as evidence of the facts stated in it to the same extent as oral evidence of that fact is admissible in those proceedings[6].

Nothing in the provisions described above prejudices the admission in evidence of any document which would otherwise be admissible[7].

1 A document under head (1) or (2) in the text is duly authenticated if it purports to be certified by the judge, magistrate or other person before whom the evidence was given or, as the case may be, by whom it was taken, to be (a) the original document containing or recording or, as the case may be, summarising the evidence, or (b) a true copy of that document: Maintenance Orders (Reciprocal Enforcement) Act 1972 s 36(2). A document under head (3) in the text is duly authenticated if it purports to be certified by a judge, magistrate or officer of the court in question to have been, or to be a true copy of a document which has been, received: s 36(3). It is not necessary in any such proceedings to prove the signature or official position of the person appearing to have given such a certificate: s 36(4).
2 For the meaning of 'Convention country' see para 831 note 4 ante.
3 For the meaning of 'United Kingdom' see para 604 ante.
4 Ie the Maintenance Orders (Reciprocal Enforcement) Act 1972 Pt II (ss 25–39) (as amended).
5 Ie proceedings arising out of an application to which ibid s 27A(1) (as added) applies (see para 833 ante).
6 Ibid s 36(1) (amended by the Domestic Proceedings and Magistrates' Courts Act 1978 s 60(3); and the Maintenance Orders (Reciprocal Enforcement) Act 1992 s 1(2), Sch 1 para 17).
7 Maintenance Orders (Reciprocal Enforcement) Act 1972 s 36(5).

841. Taking evidence for court in Convention country. Where a request is made to the Lord Chancellor[1] by or on behalf of a court in a Convention country[2] to obtain the evidence of a person residing in the United Kingdom[3] relating to matters connected with an application[4], the Lord Chancellor must request such court, or such officer of a court, as he may determine to take the evidence of that person relating to such matters connected with the application as may be specified[5]. The court or officer receiving such a request from the Lord Chancellor has power to take the evidence and, after giving notice of the time and place at which it is to be taken to such persons and in such manner as it or he thinks fit, must take the evidence in such manner as may be prescribed[6]. The evidence so taken must be sent in the prescribed manner[7] by the prescribed officer[8] to the court in the Convention country concerned[9].

Where any person (other than the original applicant) is required to give evidence before a court in the United Kingdom, the court may order such payments, out of money provided by Parliament, as appear reasonably sufficient to compensate him for the expense, trouble or loss of time properly incurred in or incidental to his attendance[10]. A person may be compelled by summons and arrest to give evidence[11].

1 As to the transfer of functions to the Lord Chancellor see para 819 note 8 ante.
2 For the meaning of 'Convention country' see para 831 note 4 ante.
3 For the meaning of 'United Kingdom' see para 604 ante.
4 Ie an application under the Maintenance Orders (Reciprocal Enforcement) Act 1972 s 26 (as amended): see para 832 ante.
5 Ibid s 38(1) (s 38(1), (2) amended by virtue of the Transfer of Functions (Magistrates' Courts and Family Law) Order 1992, SI 1992/709).
6 See the Maintenance Orders (Reciprocal Enforcement) Act 1972 s 38(2) (as amended: see note 5 supra). For the meaning of 'prescribed' see paras 819 note 6, 833 note 18 ante. See the Magistrates' Courts (Recovery Abroad of Maintenance) Rules 1975, SI 1975/488, rr 9, 10.
7 See ibid r 11.
8 As to the prescribed officer see ibid rr 9–11; and para 819 note 6 ante.
9 Maintenance Orders (Reciprocal Enforcement) Act 1972 s 38(2).
10 Ibid s 38(3) (amended by the Northern Ireland (Modification of Enactments No 1) Order 1973, SI 1973/2163).
11 See the Maintenance Orders (Reciprocal Enforcement) Act 1972 s 38(4) (amended by the Magistrates' Courts Act 1980 s 154, Sch 7 para 109), applying the Magistrates' Courts Act 1980 s 97(1), (3), (4) (as amended) to the taking of evidence under the provisions described in the text and notes supra).

842. Magistrates' courts rules. Rules made under the Magistrates' Courts Act 1980[1] may make provision with respect to orders made or other things done by a magistrates' court or an officer of such a court by virtue of Part II of the Maintenance Orders (Reciprocal Enforcement) Act 1972[2], of which notice is required to be given to persons specified by such rules[3].

1 Ie under the Magistrates' Courts Act 1980 s 144 (as amended).
2 Ie the Maintenance Orders (Reciprocal Enforcement) Act 1972 Pt II (ss 25–39) (as amended).
3 See the Maintenance Orders (Reciprocal Enforcement) Act 1972 s 38A(1) (s 38A added by the Maintenance Orders (Reciprocal Enforcement) Act 1992 s 1(2), Sch 1 para 18). This is without prejudice to the generality of the power to make rules under the Magistrates' Courts Act 1980 s 144 (as amended): Maintenance Orders (Reciprocal Enforcement) Act 1972 s 38A(1) (as so added).
    Rules made under the Magistrates' Courts Act 1980 s 144 (as amended) may make provision, not covered by the Maintenance Orders (Reciprocal Enforcement) Act 1972 s 38A(1), for the purpose of giving effect to Pt II (as amended), which falls within the Children Act 1989 s 93(2) (as amended) and which may be made in relation to relevant proceedings within s 93 (see CHILDREN vol 5(2) (Reissue) para 833): Maintenance Orders (Reciprocal Enforcement) Act 1972 s 38A(2) (as so added).

E.   RECOGNITION AND ENFORCEMENT UNDER THE BRUSSELS AND
LUGANO CONVENTIONS

843. Provisions relating to recognition and enforcement of maintenance orders under the Brussels and Lugano Conventions. The function of transmitting to the appropriate court[1] an application under the Brussels or Lugano Convention[2] for the recognition or enforcement in the United Kingdom[3] of a maintenance order[4] must be discharged in England and Wales by the Lord Chancellor[5]. An application must be determined in the first instance by the prescribed officer[6] of that court[7]. Where on such an application the enforcement of the order is authorised to any extent, the order must to that extent be registered in the prescribed manner[8] in that court[9]. A maintenance order so registered is of the same force and effect, the registering court has the same powers as to enforcement, and proceedings relating to its enforcement may be taken, as if it had originally been made by the registering court[10].
    A maintenance order which is enforceable by a magistrates' court is enforceable as a magistrates' court maintenance order made by that court[11].
    The payer under a maintenance order so registered in a magistrates' court in England and Wales must give notice of any change of address to the clerk of that court[12].

Interest on arrears of sums payable under a maintenance order registered under the provisions described above in a magistrates' court in England and Wales is not recoverable in that court[13].

Sums payable in the United Kingdom under a maintenance order by virtue of registration under these provisions, including any arrears, must be paid in sterling[14]. When they are expressed in any other currency, they must be converted on the basis of the exchange rate prevailing on the date of registration[15].

1 'Appropriate court' means the magistrates' court having jurisdiction in the matter in accordance with art 32 of the Brussels and Lugano Conventions: Civil Jurisdiction and Judgments Act 1982 s 5(1). As to the Brussels and Lugano Conventions see paras 618 ante, 1040 post. As to references to numbered articles 'of the Conventions' see para 618 note 5 ante.
2 Ie under art 31 of the Conventions: see para 1049 post.
3 For the meaning of 'United Kingdom' see para 604 ante.
4 As to the meaning of 'maintenance order' see art 25 of the Conventions; and the Civil Jurisdiction and Judgments Act 1982 s 15(1).
5 Ibid s 5(1) (amended by the Civil Jurisdiction and Judgments Act 1991 s 3, Sch 3 para 2; and the Transfer of Functions (Magistrates' Courts and Family Law) Order 1992, SI 1992/709, art 4(7)).
6 Ie the justices' clerk: Magistrates' Courts (Civil Jurisdiction and Judgments Act 1982) Rules 1986, SI 1986/1962, r 3.
7 Civil Jurisdiction and Judgments Act 1982 s 5(2).
8 See the Magistrates' Courts (Civil Jurisdiction and Judgments Act 1982) Rules 1986 r 4.
9 Civil Jurisdiction and Judgments Act 1982 s 5(3).
10 Ibid s 5(4). This is subject to art 39 of the Conventions (see para 1052 post), to the Civil Jurisdiction and Judgments Act 1982 s 7 (see para 1048 post) and to any provision made by rules of court as to the manner in which and conditions subject to which an order so registered may be enforced: s 5(5).
11 Ibid s 5(5A) (added by the Family Law Reform Act 1987 s 33(1), Sch 2 para 89; amended by the Maintenance Enforcement Act 1991 s 10, Sch 1 para 21). 'Magistrates' court maintenance order' has the same meaning as in the Magistrates' Courts Act 1980 s 150(1) (definition as added): Civil Jurisdiction and Judgments Act 1982 s 5(5A) (as so added). The Magistrates' Courts Act 1980 ss 76, 93 (both as amended) (enforcement of judgment and complaint for arrears) are subject, in this regard, to the modifications made by the Civil Jurisdiction and Judgments Act 1982 s 5(5B), (5C) (added by the Maintenance Enforcement Act 1991 Sch 1 para 21).
12 Civil Jurisdiction and Judgments Act 1982 s 5(7). Failure without reasonable excuse to do so is an offence punishable on summary conviction with a fine not exceeding level 2 on the standard scale: s 5(7) (amended by virtue of the Criminal Justice Act 1982 s 46). As to the standard scale see para 803 note 7 ante.
13 Civil Jurisdiction and Judgments Act 1982 s 7(4). This is without prejudice, however, to the operation of the Maintenance Orders Act 1958 s 2A (as added) (recovery of interest on re-registration in the High Court): Civil Jurisdiction and Judgments Act 1982 s 7(4). Except in this regard, interest is only payable under s 7 (see para 1048 post): s 7(5).
14 Ibid s 8(1).
15 Ibid s 8(2). For this purpose a written certificate purporting to be signed by an officer of any bank in the United Kingdom, stating the exchange rate prevailing on a specified date, is evidence of the facts stated: s 8(3).

5. CONTRACTS

(1) INTRODUCTION

844. Determination of the governing law. In the case of most contracts made after 1 April 1991 the question of which law is to govern the obligations of the parties will be answered by the rules of the Rome Convention signed by the United Kingdom on 7 December 1981[1], which, subject to certain limitations, has force of law in the United Kingdom[2]. Accordingly, and save as expressly stated to the contrary, the law set out in the following paragraphs[3] is that derived from the Rome Convention (and referred to as 'the applicable law'). Those cases to which the Rome Convention does not extend[4] are governed by the rules of the common law, which have otherwise been replaced by the Rome Convention; the common law rules are set out subsequently[5].

At common law it was generally accepted that the 'law' which governed a contract as its proper law was the domestic law identified by the choice of law rules, and that there could be no renvoi from this to a different law[6]. Under the régime of the Rome Convention, the 'law' identified as applicable by that Convention means the domestic system of law so identified; no renvoi is permitted to the law of another country in order that this law should govern the contract ab initio[7].

1 Ie the Convention on the law applicable to contractual obligations opened for signature in Rome on 19 June 1980: see the Contracts (Applicable Law) Act 1990 s 1(a). Further supplementary Conventions have been made (1) on the accession to the Rome Convention of Greece ('the Luxembourg Convention', signed by the United Kingdom on 10 April 1984) (see the Contracts (Applicable Law) Act 1990 s 1(b)); and (2) on the accession to the Rome Convention of Spain and Portugal ('the Funchal Convention', signed by the United Kingdom on 18 May 1992) (see the Contracts (Applicable Law) Act 1990 s 1(d) (added by the Contracts (Applicable Law) Act 1990 (Amendment) Order 1994, SI 1994/1900, art 3)).

A Protocol ('the Brussels Protocol') on the interpretation of the Rome Convention by the European Court was signed by the United Kingdom in Brussels on 10 April 1984: see the Contracts (Applicable Law) Act 1990 s 1(c). At the date at which this volume states the law, the Brussels Protocol is not in force.

These Conventions and the Brussels Protocol are together referred to in the Act as 'the Conventions': s 1 (amended by the Contracts (Applicable Law) Act 1990 (Amendment) Order 1994 art 4). For convenience of reference, they are set out in the Contracts (Applicable Law) Act 1990 as follows (s 2(4) (amended by the Contracts (Applicable Law) Act 1990 (Amendment) Order 1994 arts 5, 6):

    (1) in Sch 1, the Rome Convention (as amended);
    (2) in Sch 2, the Luxembourg Convention;
    (3) in Sch 3, the Brussels Protocol; and
    (4) in Sch 3A (added by the Contracts (Applicable Law) Act 1990 (Amendment) Order 1994 art 9, Schedule), the Funchal Convention.

The Contracts (Applicable Law) Act 1990 came into force on 1 April 1991, except for ss 2(1) (in so far as it relates to the Brussels Protocol), 3(1), (2), (3)(b), which will come into force on a day to be appointed: s 7; Contracts (Applicable Law) Act 1990 (Commencement No 1) Order 1991, SI 1991/707.

Any member state may request the revision of the Rome Convention: see art 26.

2 Contracts (Applicable Law) Act 1990 s 2(1), which, however, is not in force in so far as it relates to the Brussels Protocol: see note 1 supra. The Rome Convention arts 7(1), 10(1)(e) do not have the force of law in the United Kingdom: Contracts (Applicable Law) Act 1990 s 2(2). The power to reserve the right not to apply those provisions, and to withdraw such reservation, is conferred by the Rome Convention art 22 paras 1, 3.

3 Ie paras 845–856 post.

4 The Rome Convention does not apply to contracts made on or before 1 April 1991: art 17; Contracts (Applicable Law) Act 1990 s 7; Contracts (Applicable Law) Act 1990 (Commencement No 1) Order. For contracts made after 1 April 1991 the Convention is nevertheless irrelevant to those contracts excluded from its scope by art 1(2) (see para 845 post). The Convention remains in force for ten years, and if there has been no denunciation, it is tacitly renewed every five years thereafter: see the Rome Convention art 30 (amended by the Contracts (Applicable Law) Act 1990 (Amendment) Order 1994).

5 See para 858 et seq post.

6 See *Re United Railways of the Havana and Regla Warehouses Ltd* [1960] Ch 52 at 96–97, 115, [1959] 1 All ER 214, CA; affd sub nom *Tomkinson v First Pennsylvania Banking and Trust Co* [1961] AC 1007, [1960] 2 All ER 332, HL; *Amin Rasheed Shipping Corpn v Kuwait Insurance Co* [1984] AC 50, [1983] 2 All ER 884, HL.

7 Rome Convention art 15. The parties themselves may nevertheless agree to change the applicable law: see para 846 post. As to the doctrine of renvoi generally see para 606 et seq ante.

(2) DETERMINATION AND APPLICATION OF GOVERNING LAW UNDER THE ROME CONVENTION

845. The sphere of application of the Rome Convention: date and subject matter. The Rome Convention applies only to contracts made after 1 April 1991[1]. It applies to contractual obligations[2] in any situation involving a choice between the laws of different countries[3]. For this purpose, where a state comprises several territorial units, each of which has its own rules of law in respect of contractual obligations, each territorial unit is considered as a country for the purpose of identifying the applicable law[4]. Conflicts of laws as between the laws of England and Wales, Scotland and Northern Ireland, are resolved by the rules of the Rome Convention[5].

The Convention does not apply to the following matters, even if they are contractual in nature[6]: (1) questions involving the status or legal capacity of natural persons[7]; (2) contractual obligations relating to wills and succession, rights in property arising out of a matrimonial relationship, rights and duties arising out of a family relationship, parentage, marriage or affinity, including maintenance obligations of children who are not legitimate[8]; (3) obligations arising under bills of exchange, cheques and promissory notes and other negotiable instruments to the extent that the obligations under such other negotiable instruments arise out of their negotiable character[9]; (4) arbitration agreements and agreements on the choice of court[10]; (5) questions governed by the law of companies and other bodies corporate or unincorporate such as the creation, by registration or otherwise, legal capacity, internal organisation or winding up of companies and other bodies corporate or unincorporate and the personal liability of officers and members as such for the obligations of the company or body[11]; (6) the question whether an agent is able to bind a principal, or an organ to bind a company or body corporate or unincorporate, to a third party[12]; (7) the constitution of trusts and the relationship between settlors, trustees and beneficiaries[13]; and (8) evidence and procedure[14].

The application of the Convention to contracts of insurance and reinsurance is dealt with separately[15].

In keeping with its being concerned with contractual obligations, the Convention does not apply to property rights, nor intellectual property[16], but it may not be easy to define in practice what is contractual and what is proprietary[17].

The Convention applies in modified form in relation to certain further species of contracts, most notably certain consumer contracts and contracts of employment; the particular special provisions applicable to these are discussed subsequently[18].

The Convention does not affect the application of provisions laying down choice of law rules contained in acts of the institutions of the European Community, or in national laws harmonised in implementation of such acts[21]; nor does it prejudice the application of international conventions to which a contracting state is or becomes a party[20].

1 Rome Convention art 17; Contracts (Applicable Law) Act 1990 s 7; Contracts (Applicable Law) Act 1990 (Commencement No 1) Order, SI 1991/707. As to the Rome Convention see para 844 note 1 ante).

2 It is thought that 'contractual obligations' refers to an autonomous or independent concept of 'contract' which is not necessarily co-terminous with the concept of contract in English law. See further para 894 text and notes 24–26 post. The Rome Convention requires courts to have regard to the international character of the rules, and to the desirability of achieving uniformity in their interpretation and application: see art 18. The Brussels Protocol, which, at the date at which this volume states the law, has not been given force of law in the United Kingdom (see para 844 note 1 ante), provides that if a court considers that a decision on a question is necessary to enable it to give judgment, a reference may be

made to the European Court for a preliminary ruling. As from a day to be appointed, an English court which does not make such a reference will nevertheless be bound to interpret the Rome Convention in accordance with principles laid down by, and any relevant decision of, the European Court (Contracts (Applicable Law) Act 1990 s 3(1)), and to take judicial notice of decisions or expressions of opinion by the European Court concerning any question as to the meaning or effect of any provision of the Rome Convention (Contracts (Applicable Law) Act 1990 s 3(2)). As to the meaning of 'European Court' see para 620 note 4 ante.

In ascertaining the meaning or effect of any provision of the Rome Convention, a court is permitted to have regard to the Official Report on the Rome Convention prepared by Professor Mario Giuliano and Professor Paul Lagarde (OJ C282, 31.10.80, p 1): Contracts (Applicable Law) Act 1990 s 3(3)(a). As from a day to be appointed, such a court will also be permitted to have regard to any official report on the Brussels Protocol which may be published in the Official Journal of the European Community: Contracts (Applicable Law) Act 1990 s 3(3)(b). As to the commencement of the Contracts (Applicable Law) Act 1990 see para 844 note 1 ante.

As to 'matters relating to a contract' within the meaning of the Brussels Convention, see particularly Case 34/82 *Peters v ZNAV* [1983] ECR 987, ECJ; and Case C-26/91 *Jakob Handte GmbH v Traitements Mécano-chimiques des Surfaces* [1992] ECR I-3967, ECJ; and see para 641 ante. Accordingly the law governing such an obligation will be that specified as applicable by the Rome Convention, notwithstanding that as a matter of English law they might be considered to be equitable obligations or as enforceable under the law of tort: see those cases, and the report on the Rome Convention supra, at pp 10–11. Thus the Rome Convention might be relevant to a case even if as a matter of domestic English law the claim made by the plaintiff would be seen as not being contractual.

3 Rome Convention art 1 para 1. Any law specified by the Convention must be applied whether or not it is the law of a contracting state: art 2.

4 Ibid art 19 para 1.

5 Contracts (Applicable Law) Act 1990 s 2(3); this provision applies notwithstanding the Rome Convention art 19 para 2, which provides that states are not bound to apply the rules of the Convention as between the different territorial units.

6 Ibid art 1 para 2.

7 Ibid art 1 para 2(a). This is expressed to be without prejudice to art 11 (see para 853 post). These matters will continue to be governed by the choice of law rules applicable to such questions under the law of the court seised.

8 Ibid art 1 para 2(b). In effect matters of family law are excluded from the Convention (see the Official Report on the Rome Convention at p 10), and are therefore governed by the choice of law rules applicable to such questions under the law of the court seised.

9 Rome Convention art 1 para 2(c). Obligations arising under such documents are excluded only if the document itself is regarded as a negotiable instrument under the law of the court seised. Contracts pursuant to which such documents are issued are not covered by the exclusion, nor are contracts for the sale and purchase of such instruments: see the Official Report on the Rome Convention at p 11.

10 Rome Convention art 1 para 2(d). The formal validity and effect of such agreements, as well as the question of whether they have actually been agreed to by the parties, are binding upon them, and can be enforced between them, are to be determined by the choice of law rules otherwise applicable under the law of the court seised. (In the United Kingdom this may require the proper law of the contract alleged to contain the agreement to be determined according to the traditional rules: see para 859 et seq post. Alternatively, it may be that such agreements are subject to the applicable law (as the law which governs the contract in which they are contained), as a matter of English private international law, even if this were not required to be so by force of the Rome Convention; see *Egon Oldendorff v Libera Corpn* [1995] 2 Lloyd's Rep 64). But once these matters have been determined, the existence of an agreed arbitration agreement or choice of court agreement may be taken into account as part of the exercise of determining the applicable law according to the Rome Convention art 3(1) (see the Official Report on the Rome Convention at p 12).

11 Rome Convention art 1 para 2(e). All those complex acts relating to the creation and to the winding-up of companies which fall within the scope of company law are excluded, but not acts or preliminary contracts between promoters with a view to forming a company (see the Official Report on the Rome Convention at p 12), and will be determined by the choice of law rules otherwise applicable under the law of the court seised. See para 983 et seq post. As to what constitutes 'internal organisation' see the report cited supra, at p 12.

12 Rome Convention art 1 para 2(f). The exclusion affects only the relationship between a principal and third party. Relations between agent and principal, and between agent and third party (if these may be seen as contractual) are not excluded (see the Official Report on the Rome Convention at p 13).

13 Rome Convention art 1 para 2(g); and see the Official Report on the Rome Convention at p 13; and paras 938–944 post.

14 Rome Convention art 1 para 2(h), which is expressed to be without prejudice to art 14; art 14 para 1 provides that the applicable law applies (and hence the exclusion does not apply) to burdens of proof and presumptions of law where these are part of the law of contract. Likewise, art 14 para 2 permits a contract to be proved according to the law of the forum, or according to any of the laws which, according to art 9, determine the formal validity of the contract. See paras 852, 1070, 1072, 1074 post.

15 The Rome Convention does not apply to insurance of risks within the European Community, but it does apply to reinsurance: see art 1 paras 3, 4; and paras 857–858 post.

16 See the Official Report on the Rome Convention at p 10.

17 Eg an action against a constructive trustee, such as an agent who has broken his fiduciary duties, may be seen as a proprietary action brought by the beneficiary of a constructive trust. On the other hand, it exists only because of, and arises directly out of, the contract of agency. It is wholly unclear whether such an action would be subject to the choice of law provisions of the Rome Convention. (The exclusion of certain aspects of agency from the scope of the Convention by art 1 para 2(f) is irrelevant to this question). Further, the Convention expressly applies to the assignment of debts, and imposes the applicable law upon claims relating to (1) the mutual obligations of assignor and assignee; and (2) the assignability of the debt and the relationship between assignee and debtor: art 12; and see also para 935 post. Under the traditional view of the common law the assignment of a debt (as distinct from the contract to assign it) is a proprietary matter. But it appears that, for the purposes of the Rome Convention, the question is to be treated as contractual (see para 935 post). Caution must be exercised before concluding that the issue is to be characterised as proprietary, and that accordingly the Rome Convention has no application. The question is not whether English law would characterise the issue as proprietary, but rather whether the Rome Convention sees it as contractual. Where a person (the creditor) has a contractual claim upon another, and a third party has a duty to satisfy the creditor or has done so in discharge of such a duty, the law governing the third person's duty determines whether he is entitled to exercise the creditor's rights against the debtor: see art 13.

18 See paras 855–856 post.

19 Rome Convention art 20.

20 Ibid art 21.

846. Express choice of applicable law. Under the Rome Convention[1] a contract is governed by the domestic system of law chosen by the parties[2]. Such choice must either be express[3], or be demonstrated with reasonable certainty by the terms of the contract or the circumstances of the case[4].

The parties may at any time agree to subject the contract to a new applicable law, but any variation by the parties of the law to be applied made after the conclusion of the contract must not prejudice its formal validity[5] or adversely affect the rights of third parties[6].

The fact that a foreign law has been chosen as the applicable law (whether or not accompanied by the choice of a foreign tribunal[7]) must not, where all the other elements relevant to the situation at the time of choice are connected with one country only, prejudice the application of rules of law of that country which may not be derogated from by contract ('the mandatory rules')[8].

It is open to the parties to agree, and open to a court to hold, that separate parts of a single contract are governed by different applicable laws[9].

1 For the meaning of 'the Rome Convention' see para 844 text and note 1 ante.

2 Rome Convention art 3 para 1. See the Official Report on the Rome Convention OJ C282, 31.10.80, p 1 at 15–18; and as to the consideration which may be given to that report see para 845 note 2 ante. Choice of law means the domestic law of the system chosen, as renvoi from that law is not permitted: see para 844 text and note 5 ante. As to the position in relation to countries with more than one legal system see para 845 text and notes 4–5 ante.

3 The question whether the choice is sufficiently express to satisfy the Convention will presumably be a question of fact for the trial court; although the common law authorities will not be decisive, they may well be persuasive: see para 860 post. See also *Egon Oldendorff v Libera Corpn (No 2)* (unreported, 16 November 1995).

4 Rome Convention art 3 para 1. Examples of non-express choice of law are a contract on a standard form such as a Lloyd's policy of marine insurance, or a contract where there is a previous course of dealing between the parties, where the applicable law is generally known: Official Report on the Rome Convention at p 1. The position under the Rome Convention where there is a choice of court clause would appear to be broadly similar to the position under the common law, where an express choice would be seen as a strong but not conclusive indication of the proper law: see eg *Compagnie Tunisienne de Navigation SA v Compagnie d'Armament Maritime SA* [1971] AC 572, HL; *The Komninos S* [1991] 1 Lloyd's Rep 370, CA. See also *Egon Oldendorff v Libera Corpn (No 2)* (unreported, 16 November 1995). The parties may also choose a law to govern only part of their contract: Rome Convention art 3 para 1.
5 Ie under ibid art 9: see para 852 post.
6 Ibid art 3 para 2. The choice of new applicable law is subject to the same restrictions (as to choice and manner of expression of that choice) as originally applied: Official Report on the Rome Convention at p 18. This effectively means that a 'floating' choice of law could be validly agreed to by the parties, according to which a contract is governed by a law to be chosen at any time (even though it might be argued that this did not amount to a clear or express choice of applicable law). For the contrasting view at common law see *Armar Shipping Co Ltd v Caisse Algérienne d'Assurance et de Réassurance, The Armar* [1981] 1 All ER 498, [1981] 1 WLR 207, CA; *The Mariannina* [1983] 1 Lloyd's Rep 12, CA. But once a choice has been made, pursuant to the clause, the Rome Convention art 3 para 1 or 2 will appear to give effect to the choice: see the Official Report on the Rome Convention supra at p 17–18.
7 On the question whether a choice of tribunal has been made see para 845 note 10 ante; and *Egon Oldendorff v Libera Corpn* [1995] 2 Lloyd's Rep 64.
8 Rome Convention art 3 para 3. It is uncertain what is meant by 'all other elements relevant to the situation at the time of choice'. It may mean that some connections between the transaction and the chosen law are for this purpose to be disregarded, but art 3 para 3 is intended to be construed as an exceptional provision (see the Official Report on the Rome Convention at p 18). 'Mandatory rules' may indicate either (1) those rules which cannot be evaded in a purely domestic context (such as the requirement for consideration), or (2) more narrowly, those which cannot be evaded by the choice of a foreign law, such as controls in the Unfair Contract Terms Act 1977 which are expressed by s 27 (as amended) (see para 860 post) to operate even if the contract in question is not governed by English law; but not the rule requiring consideration, which has no application if the contract is not subject to English law: see *Re Bonacina* [1912] 2 Ch 394. It is submitted that the Rome Convention art 3 para 3 relates to head (1) supra, as head (2) will fall under art 7 para 2: see para 848 post.
   Article 7 para 1, which would permit a court to give effect to the mandatory laws of another country with which the contract has merely a close connection, does not have the force of law in the United Kingdom: Contracts (Applicable Law) Act 1990 s 2(2).
9 See ibid arts 3 para 1, 4 para 1.

847. Applicable law where the law has not been so chosen. Where the parties do not make a choice of law[1], the contract will be governed by the law of the country with which it is most closely connected; nevertheless a severable part of the contract which has a closer connection with another country may, by way of exception, be governed by the law of that other country[2].

Except in the case of certain consumer contracts[3], it is presumed that the contract is most closely connected with the country where the party who is to effect the performance which is characteristic of the contract has, at the time of the conclusion of the contract, his habitual residence (or, in the case of a body corporate or unincorporate, its central administration); but if the contract is entered into in the course of that party's trade or profession, that country will instead be the country in which the principal place of business is situated (or where, under the terms of the contract, performance is to be made through a place of business other than the principal place of business, the country in which that other place of business is situated)[4].

To the extent that the subject matter of the contract is a right in, or a right to use, immovable property, it is presumed that the contract is most closely connected with the country where the immovable is situated[5].

Contracts for the carriage of goods (including single voyage charterparties) are not subject to the general presumption. If at the time the contract is concluded the carrier has his principal place of business in the country of loading, or of discharge, or of the consignor's principal place of business, this country is presumed to be the one with which the contract is most closely connected[6].

The party whose performance is characteristic of the contract will be, in simple cases, the party who is to provide the goods or services for payment from the other payment of the price is not the performance which is characteristic of the contract[7]. In more complex contractual arrangements it will be less easy to identify a characteristic performance[8]. If the characteristic performance cannot be determined, the general presumption does not apply[9]. All the presumptions set out above may be disregarded if it appears from the circumstances as a whole that the contract is more closely connected with another country[10].

1 Ie as described in para 846 ante.
2 Rome Convention art 4 para 1. For the meaning of 'the Rome Convention' see para 844 text and note 1 ante. For the official commentary on art 4 see the Official Report on the Rome Convention OJ C282, 31.10.80, p 1 at 19–23; and as to the consideration which may be given to that report see para 845 note 2 ante. The English court is permitted to take account of factors which supervened after the contract was concluded: see the Official Report on the Rome Convention supra at p 20. Contrast the position at common law: see para 861 post.
3 See the Rome Convention art 5: and para 855 post.
4 Ibid art 4 para 2.
5 Ibid art 4 para 3.
6 See ibid art 4 para 4.
7 See the Official Report on the Rome Convention at p 20, suggesting that the doctrine of the characteristic performance may be applied to contracts for the delivery of goods, for the right to use property, for the provision of services, and to contracts for transport, insurance, banking operations and security.
8 As between an issuing and a confirming bank, in relation to a letter of credit, the characteristic obligation is that of the confirming bank to give its confirmation and to honour the obligations thereby undertaken; it is not that of the issuing bank to indemnify the confirming bank, for this is merely consequential, not characteristic: *Bank of Baroda v Vysya Bank* [1994] 2 Lloyd's Rep 87.
9 Rome Convention art 4 para 5. The contract will then simply be governed by the law of the country with which it is most closely connected.
10 Ibid art 4 para 5. For an illustration of when art 4 para 5 may be applied see *Bank of Baroda v Vysya Bank* [1994] 2 Lloyd's Rep 87.

848. Limitations on the operation of the applicable law: mandatory rules of English law. Whatever the law governing a contract may be, rules of English law may still be applied where these are mandatory irrespective of the law otherwise applicable to the contract[1]. These mandatory rules of English law are generally referred to as 'overriding laws'[2]. Generally speaking it is presumed that an English statute has no application to a case unless English law is the lex causae, but if the statutory provision is drafted with sufficient clarity it may be construed as applicable whether or not English law is the lex causae[3]. Examples of such statutory provisions include the Carriage of Goods by Sea Act 1971, giving the force of law to the Hague-Visby Rules[4]; the provision in the Financial Services Act 1986, making unenforceable an investment agreement made through an unauthorised person[5]; and certain provisions dealing with employee and consumer protection[6].

1 Rome Convention art 7 para 2. For the meaning of 'the Rome Convention' see para 844 text and note 1 ante.
2 See generally Dicey and Morris *The Conflict of Laws* (12th Edn, 1993) 21.
3 See Dicey and Morris *The Conflict of Laws* (12th Edn, 1993) 21–25.
4 See the Carriage of Goods by Sea Act 1971 s 1(2), Schedule; and *The Hollandia* [1983] 1 AC 565, [1982] 3 All ER 1141, HL; although note that this case would be decided differently today in the light of the

Brussels Convention art 17. As to the Brussels Convention see para 618 text and note 1 ante. As to art 17 of the Brussels Convention see para 633 ante.
5 See the Financial Services Act 1986 s 5.
6 See paras 855–856 post. For further examples see Dicey and Morris *The Conflict of Laws* (12th Edn, 1993) 24–25.

849. Limitations on the operation of the applicable law: public policy of English law. The application of any rule of the applicable law[1] may be refused only if its application is manifestly[2] incompatible with the public policy of English law[3]. It is the application of the rule of the applicable law, rather than the law itself, which must give rise to the incompatibility[4]. The result may be to hold valid a contract otherwise unenforceable according to a provision of the applicable law which is offensive to English law[5], or to regard a contract valid and enforceable according to its applicable law as invalid and unenforceable by reason of some dominating requirement of English public policy[6].

1 For the meaning of 'applicable law' see para 844 ante.
2 'Manifestly' indicates that the court must have special reason for upholding an objection: Official Report on the Rome Convention OJ C282, 31.10.80, p 1 at 38. As to the consideration which may be given to that report see para 845 note 2 ante.
3 Rome Convention art 16. For the meaning of 'the Rome Convention' see para 844 text and note 1 ante. Thus while an English statute may be drafted so as to override a contract not governed by English law (see para 848 ante), a rule of the common law cannot have the same effect. For a discussion of the circumstances in which art 16 applies see Dicey and Morris *The Conflict of Laws* (12th Edn, 1993) 1277 et seq.
4 Official Report on the Rome Convention at p 38.
5 See *Wolff v Oxholm* (1817) 6 M & s 92, *Re Friedrich Krupp AG* [1917] 2 Ch 188, *Empresa Exportadora De Azucar v Industria Azucarera Nacional SA, The Playa Larga and the Marble Islands* [1983] 2 Lloyd's Rep 171, CA, *Oppenheimer v Cattermole* [1976] AC 249, [1975] 1 All ER 538, HL; *Williams & Humbert Ltd v W & H Trade Marks (Jersey) Ltd* [1986] AC 368, [1986] 1 All ER 129, HL; *Re Helbert Wagg & Co Ltd's Claim* [1956] Ch 323, [1956] 1 All ER 129.
6 *Kaufman v Gerson* [1904] 1 KB 591, CA; *Re Missouri SS Co* (1889) 42 ChD 321, CA; *Rousillon v Rousillon* (1880) 14 ChD 351; *Dynamit AG v Rio Tinto Co Ltd* [1918] AC 292, HL. Cf *Lemenda Trading Co Ltd v African Middle East Petroleum Co Ltd* [1988] QB 448, [1988] 1 All ER 513; *Trendtex Trading Corpn v Crédit Suisse* [1982] AC 679, [1981] 3 All ER 520, HL.

850. The effect of illegality under the law of the place of performance of the contractual obligation. Under the common law rules of the conflict of laws a contractual obligation will be unenforceable in the English courts where performance of that obligation would require an act which is illegal under the law of the place where it is to be performed (the *lex loci solutionis*)[1].

Such a provision does not in terms appear in the Rome Convention[2]. In consequence it may be stated that (1) where English law is the applicable law[3] of a contract, original illegality may make the contract wholly unenforceable, and supervening illegality may discharge it by frustration[4]; (2) where the applicable law acknowledges that a contract is illegal or void or discharged by reason of illegality according to the law of the place of performance, an English court will not enforce the contract[5]; but (3) it is as yet uncertain whether a contract which requires performance of an act which would be illegal under the law of the place where its performance is due, but the applicable law of which contract does not regard this fact as affecting the enforceability of the contract, would be enforceable in England[6].

1 See para 881 post. It is unclear whether this rule could be applied when (1) the proper law of the contract was not English, and (2) the proper law of the contract did not admit the illegality under the *lex*

loci solutionis as an excuse for non-performance, or a cause of the discharge of the contract; no case has been decided with this proposition as part of its ratio, and the dicta in the cases cited in para 881 post must therefore be read with caution.

2 For the meaning of 'the Rome Convention' see para 844 text and note 1 ante.

3 For the meaning of 'applicable law' see para 844 ante.

4 See the Rome Convention art 8 para 1, under which the existence and validity of a contract are governed by the law which is the applicable law if the contract is valid; as to the scope of the applicable law see art 10 para 1; and para 854 post.

5 This is the result on the basis that the Rome Convention does not affect the operation of the common law rules in the circumstances described in the text.

6 For a full discussion of this question see Dicey and Morris *The Conflict of Laws* (12th Edn, 1993) 1243–1247.

851. Formation of contract; disputes as to existence and validity. The existence and validity of a contract, or any term of a contract, must be determined by the law which would be the applicable law[1] if the contract were valid[2].

However, a party may rely on the law of the country in which he has his habitual residence[3] to establish that he did not consent if it appears from the circumstances that it would not be reasonable to determine the effect of his conduct in accordance with the applicable law[4].

1 For the meaning of 'applicable law' see para 844 ante.

2 Rome Convention art 8 para 1. This provision applies, inter alia, where one party disputes that he gave his consent to the choice of applicable law and contends that he is not therefore bound, or when it is contended by a party that a particular term, alleged to have been agreed to, is not part of the contract. The same principle applies if it is disputed whether the parties have consented to an express choice of law within the framework of art 3 (see para 846 ante): art 3 para 4. For the meaning of 'the Rome Convention' see para 844 text and note 1 ante. See also the Official Report on the Rome Convention OJ C282, 31.10.80, p 1 at 28.

   Although this rule is illogical, in that it conditionally assumes the existence of a contract in order to determine whether there is a contract, it is nevertheless clear, and is consistent with the previous common law on the point; the conditional assumption is made that the parties are bound as the first step in the argument. For the common law authorities see *Albeko Schihmaschinen AG v Kamborian Shoe Machine Co Ltd* (1961) 111 LJ 519; and *Compania Naviera Micro SA v Shipley International Inc, The Parouth* [1982] 2 Lloyd's Rep 351, CA; and see *Union Transport plc v Continental Lines SA* [1992] 1 All ER 161, [1992] 1 WLR 15, HL. Note, however, that disputes as to the existence or validity of a choice of court or an arbitration clause fall outside the scope of the Rome Convention (see art 1 para 2(d); and para 845 ante); as to the resolution of disputes on such a matter see paras 845 note 10 ante, 859 et seq post.

   If the contract is valid and enforceable notwithstanding the alleged illegality, the contract may still be held unenforceable in England on the ground that the illegality in question is such as to make the enforcement of the contract manifestly contrary to English public policy: see para 849 ante.

3 As to habitual residence see para 705 ante.

4 Rome Convention art 8 para 2. This is intended to cover, inter alia, the position where one party is silent as to the formation of the contract (such as where the applicable law provides that the effect of not communicating a response to an offer is acceptance of the offer, whereas the party acts in accordance with his own law where the effect would be rejection of the offer): see the Official Report on the Rome Convention at p 28. See *Egon Oldendorff v Libera Corpn* [1995] 2 Lloyd's Rep 64.

852. Formation of contract; disputes as to formal validity. A contract which is concluded between persons who are in the same country[1] is formally valid if it satisfies the formal requirements of its applicable law[2], or of the law of the country where it is concluded[3]. A contract which is concluded between persons who are in different countries is formally valid if it satisfies the formal requirements of its applicable law, or of the law of one of those countries[4]. An act intended to have legal effect relating to an existing or contemplated contract is formally valid if it satisfies the formal requirements of the law which is or would be the applicable law, or the law of the country where the act was done[5].

By way of exceptions to the general rule, (1) a consumer contract of a specified kind[6] is formally valid if and only if it is formally valid according to the law of the country in which the consumer has his habitual residence[7]; and (2) a contract the subject matter of which is a right in, or a right to use, immovable property is subject to the mandatory requirements of form of the law where the property is situated if by that law those requirements are imposed irrespective of the country where the contract is concluded or of the applicable law[8].

1 Where a contract is concluded by an agent, the country in which the agent acts is the country in which the person is for the purposes of this rule: Rome Convention art 9 para 3. For the meaning of 'the Rome Convention' see para 844 text and note 1 ante. See also the Official Report on the Rome Convention OJ C282, 31.10.80, p 1 at 28–32.
2 For the meaning of 'applicable law' see para 844 ante.
3 Rome Convention art 9 para 1. The same principle applies if it is disputed whether the parties have consented to an express choice of law within the framework of art 3 (see para 846 ante): art 3 para 4. For the meaning of 'the Rome Convention' see para 844 text and note 1 ante. See also the Official Report on the Rome Convention at pp 30–31.
4 Rome Convention art 9 para 2; and see note 3 supra.
5 Ibid art 9 para 4; and see note 3 supra.
6 Ie a consumer contract falling within ibid art 5 para 2: see para 855 post.
7 Ibid art 9 para 5. As to habitual residence see para 705 ante.
8 Ibid art 9 para 6. For the principal formal requirements of English law see the Law of Property (Miscellaneous Provisions) Act 1989 s 2. Compliance with these is presumably mandatory whenever the land in question is in England and Wales. The wording of the Rome Convention art 9 para 6 does not make it clear whether such a contract must comply with the general formality rules set out in text and notes 1–5 supra in addition to those of the place where the immovable is situated, or whether the formal requirements of the law of that place displace, rather than add to, the operation of the general rule.

853. Formation of contract; disputes as to contractual capacity. The capacity of an individual[1] to enter into a contract is governed by the law of the country with which the contract is most closely connected or by the law of his domicile (or residence)[2]. However, if a contract is concluded between persons who are in the same country, a natural person may invoke his own incapacity under the law of some other country[3] only if the other party was aware (or was unaware through negligence) of the incapacity at the time of conclusion of the contract[4].

1 For the capacity of corporations see para 988 post.
2 This general rule is derived from the common law authorities which continue to apply: see para 875 post. The Rome Convention does not apply to 'questions involving the status or legal capacity of natural persons, without prejudice to art 11 (see text and notes 3–4 infra): art 1(2)(a). For the meaning of 'the Rome Convention' see para 844 text and note 1 ante.
3 Ie some other country with which the contract is most closely connected or in which he is domiciled (or resident): see text and notes 1–2 supra.
4 See the Rome Convention art 11. The same principle applies if it is disputed whether the parties have consented to an express choice of law within the framework of art 3 (see para 846 ante): art 3 para 4. See also the Official Report on the Rome Convention OJ C282, 31.10.80, p 1 at 33–34.

854. Interpretation, performance, breach and discharge of contracts. The applicable law[1] of a contract applies in particular to[2]:
  (1) the interpretation of the contract[3];
  (2) the performance of the obligations arising from the contract[4];
  (3) the consequences of breach[5], including the assessment of damages[6] so far as this is governed by rules of law, and within the limits of the powers conferred on the court by its procedural law[7]; and

(4) the various ways of extinguishing obligations, and prescription and limitation of actions[8].

The provision which would have also held the applicable law to govern the consequences of nullity of the contract[9] does not have legal effect in the United Kingdom[10].

Although the text of the Rome Convention provides that the applicable law is to apply to these principal questions of interpretation, performance and non-performance, the operation of the applicable law is not confined to these issues[11].

1   For the meaning of 'applicable law' see para 844 ante.
2   Rome Convention art 10 para 1. For the meaning of 'the Rome Convention' see para 844 text and note 1 ante. The list set out in art 10 para 1 (heads (1)–(4) in the text), is not exhaustive: see the Official Report on the Rome Convention OJ C282, 31.10.80, p 1 at 32–33; and text and note 11 infra.
3   Rome Convention art 10 para 1(a); Official Report on the Rome Convention at p 32. It follows from this provision that if the applicable law permits matters occurring after the making of the contract to be taken into account in construing it, such matters are to be taken into account for the same purpose by an English court; contrast *James Miller and Partners Ltd v Whitworth Street Estates (Manchester) Ltd* [1970] AC 583, [1970] 1 All ER 796, HL.
4   Rome Convention art 10 para 1(b); Official Report on the Rome Convention at p 32. A distinction must be drawn between the substance of the obligation to perform and the manner of performance, reflecting the distinction at common law: see para 878 post.
    The substance of performance (as governed by the applicable law) will cover, inter alia, the standard of care in performance, the extent to which someone other than a contracting party may perform contractual obligations, conditions as to performance in relation to joint and several obligations, alternative obligations, divisible and indivisible obligations and pecuniary obligations: Official Report on the Rome Convention at p 32. In relation to the manner of performance, and also to the steps to be taken in the event of defective performance, regard must be had to the law of the place where performance takes place: Rome Convention art 10 para 2. This appears to indicate that a court may (but has a discretion whether to) apply the law of the place where performance was due to this question.
    The manner of performance, to which the *lex loci solutionis* (see para 850 ante) is relevant, will cover rules governing public holidays, rules for the inspection of goods, rules upon whether notes or coins may be delivered as lawful tender, and so on: Official Report supra at p 33.
5   The question whether the injured party may terminate the contract, or is excused from further performance, or must content himself with damages for breach, is a matter for the applicable law: Official Report on the Rome Convention at p 33.
6   In relation to the assessment of damages, matters such as the remoteness of damage, mitigation of losses, and fixed limits upon the amount of compensation, all of which may be subject to rules of law (as distinct from being questions of fact, which will be determined by the lex fori) will be governed by the applicable law: see the Official Report on the Rome Convention at p 33; and see *D'Almeida Araujo Lda v Sir Frederick Becker and Co Ltd* [1953] 2 QB 329; *Chaplin v Boys* [1971] AC 356, [1969] 2 All ER 1085, HL. The quantification of damages is a procedural matter for the lex fori: see para 1078 post.
7   Rome Convention art 10 para 1(c). It is unclear whether the availability of particular remedies, such as injunction and specific performance, remains a matter for the lex fori, or is now determined according to the applicable law. Whilst an English court will not grant a remedy unknown to it, it is uncertain whether an order for specific performance could be resisted or obtained on the sole ground that under the applicable law such a remedy would be unavailable or (as appropriate) available. In principle these matters could be seen as part of the contractual bargain made by the parties and subject to their governing law. On the other hand, the availability of remedies is in most systems of law a procedural matter (see para 1087 post); and the unspecific wording of art 10 may not be sufficient to have displaced this rule.
8   Ibid art 10 para 1(d). Cf the position at common law: para 884 post; particularly *Re United Railways of the Havana and Regla Warehouses Ltd* [1960] Ch 52, [1959] 1 All ER 214, CA; affd sub nom *Tomkinson v First Pennsylvania Banking and Trust Co* [1961] AC 1007, [1960] 2 All ER 332, HL. The Rome Convention effectively confirms the modern English statutory provision that matters of limitation and prescription are determined by the lex causae, here the applicable law, rather than by the law of the forum: see the Foreign Limitation Periods Act 1984; and para 1082 post. Note that under both the Rome Convention (see art 16; and para 849 ante) and the Foreign Limitation Periods Act s 2(1) this rule may be departed from if its application would be manifestly contrary to public policy.
9   Ie the Rome Convention art 10 para 1(e).
10 Contracts (Applicable Law) Act 1990 s 2(2). It is therefore unclear what law does apply to determine the consequences of the nullity of a contract. Harmony of result would appear to require that the applicable

law should still govern this question, notwithstanding s 2(2). The alternative would be that the recovery of sums due or returnable upon the nullity of a contract is governed by the law otherwise applicable to restitutionary obligations (as to which see para 858 post).

11   See the Official Report on the Rome Convention at p 32–33.

855. Applicable law in certain consumer contracts.

In the provisions described below a consumer contract is one the object of which is the supply of goods or services to a person ('the consumer') for a purpose which can be regarded as being outside his trade or profession, or a contract for the provision of credit for such an object[1]. The provisions described below do not apply in any event to a contract of carriage[2], or to a contract for the supply of services to a consumer where the services are to be supplied exclusively in a country other than that in which he has his habitual residence[3]. But they do apply to a contract which, for an inclusive price, provides for a combination of travel and accommodation[4].

Notwithstanding the rules regarding the express choice of applicable law[5], the choice of applicable law does not deprive the consumer of the protection afforded to him by the mandatory rules[6] of the law of the country in which he has his habitual residence[7] if (1) in that country the conclusion of the contract was preceded by a specific invitation addressed to him or by advertising, and he had taken in that country all the steps necessary on his behalf for the conclusion of the contract; or (2) the other party or his agent received the consumer's order in that country; or (3) the contract is for the sale of goods and the consumer travelled from that country to another country and there gave his order, provided that the consumer's journey was arranged by the seller for the purpose of inducing the consumer to buy[8].

In the absence of a choice of applicable law, notwithstanding the general provisions for determining the applicable law in the absence of choice[9], a consumer contract entered into in circumstances described in heads (1) to (3) above, will be governed by the law of the country in which the consumer has his habitual residence[10].

1   Rome Convention art 5 para 1. For the meaning of 'the Rome Convention' see para 844 text and note 1 ante. See also the Official Report on the Rome Convention OJ C282, 31.10.80, p 1 at 23–25. So the rule does not apply to traders, doctors, etc, who purchase equipment or obtain services for their trade or profession. If the purchaser acts partly within and partly outside his trade or profession the contract will fall within these special rules only if the purchaser acted primarily outside his trade or profession. But if the supplier did not know (and had no reason to know) that the purchaser was acting outside his trade or profession, the Rome Convention art 5 will be inapplicable: Official Report supra at p 23. It is not stated whether the supplier must be acting in the course of his trade or profession in making the supply, and the question remains open.

2   Rome Convention art 5 para 4(a). Such contracts are therefore governed by the general rules in arts 3, 4: see the Official Report on the Rome Convention at p 24.

3   Rome Convention art 5 para 4(b). Such a contract (eg a contract for the provision of holiday hotel services) is therefore governed by the general rules in arts 3, 4: see the Official Report on the Rome Convention at p 24.

4   Ie a package tour contract: Rome Convention art 5 para 5; Official Report on the Rome Convention at p 25. The Rome Convention art 5 para 5 will only apply if the general criteria for treating the contract as a consumer contract (art 5 paras 1, 2: see text and notes 1 supra, 7 infra) are satisfied: Official Report supra at p 25.

5   Ie the provisions of the Rome Convention art 3: see para 846 ante. For the meaning of 'applicable law' see para 844 ante.

6   For the meaning of 'mandatory rules' see para 846 ante.

7   As to habitual residence see para 705 ante.

8   Rome Convention art 5 para 2.

9   Ie the provisions of ibid art 4: see para 847 ante.

10   Ibid art 5 para 4.

856. Applicable law in individual contracts of employment. In a contract of employment[1], notwithstanding the rules regarding the express choice of applicable law[2], the choice of applicable law does not deprive the employee of the protection afforded to him by the mandatory rules[3] of the law which would have been applicable to the contract in the absence of choice[4]. In the absence of a choice of applicable law, notwithstanding the general provisions for determining the applicable law in the absence of choice[5], a contract of employment is governed:

(1) by the law of the country in which the employee habitually carries out his work in performance of the contract, even if he is temporarily employed in another country; or

(2) if he does not habitually carry out his work in any one country, by the law of the country in which the place of business through which he was engaged is situated,

unless it appears from the circumstances as a whole that the contract is more closely connected with another country, in which case the contract is governed by the law of that other country[6].

1 The Rome Convention does not define 'contract of employment'; it is consequently uncertain whether, in line with other terms in the Convention (eg 'contractual obligations': see para 845 note 2 ante), the term bears an autonomous meaning.
2 Ie the provisions of the Rome Convention art 3: see para 846 ante. For the meaning of 'the Rome Convention' see para 844 text and note 1 ante. For the meaning of 'applicable law' see para 844 ante.
3 For the meaning of 'mandatory rules' see para 846 ante. In this regard the mandatory rules will be those concerning employment protection, so long as they are regarded by the law in question as of mandatory application to the facts of the given case. See Dicey and Morris *The Conflict of Laws* (12th Edn, 1993) 1306–1309.
4 Rome Convention art 6 para 1. See also the Official Report on the Rome Convention OJ C282, 31.10.80, p 1 at 25–26. The choice of law is not ineffective, but in relation to the issues to which the mandatory rules apply, the provisions of those mandatory rules override the corresponding provisions of the chosen law (see the Official Report supra at p 25).
5 Ie the provisions of the Rome Convention art 4: see para 847 ante.
6 Ibid art 6 para 2. In relation to contracts of employment where the employee performs his duties in more than one country cf Case C-125/92 *Mulox IBC v Geels* [1993] ECR I-4075, ECJ, (a decision on the Brussels Convention); and see para 641 ante. As to the Brussels Convention see para 618 text and note 1 ante. As to the position where the employment appears not to be carried out within the jurisdiction of any country see Official Report on the Rome Convention at p 26; and cf *Sayers v International Drilling Co NV* [1971] 3 All ER 163, [1971] 1 WLR 1176, CA. For the problems which may arise in the application of this provision see Dicey and Morris *The Conflict of Laws* (12th Edn, 1993) 1310–1313.

(3) DETERMINATION OF GOVERNING LAW OF CONTRACTS OF INSURANCE

857. Applicable (or otherwise governing) law in contracts of insurance and reinsurance. The Rome Convention[1] does not apply to contracts of insurance which cover risks situated in the territories of the member states of the European Community[2], but it does apply to contracts of reinsurance[3]. In order to determine whether a risk is situated in those territories, the court must apply its internal law[4]. The law governing a contract of insurance of a risk which is not situated within such territories is accordingly that specified as applicable by the Rome Convention[5].

In relation to a contract of insurance other than life insurance or long term business[6], where the policyholder has his habitual residence[7] or central administration within the territory of the member state where the risk is situated[8], the law applicable to the contract is the law of that state, but if that law so allows, the parties may choose the law of another country[9]. Where the policyholder does not have his habitual residence or central administration within the territory of the member state where the risk is situated, the parties may choose to apply either the law of the member state where the risk is situated, or the law of the country where the policyholder has his habitual residence or central administration[10]. Where the policyholder carries on a business and the contract covers two or more risks relating to his business which are situated in different member states, the parties may choose to apply the law of any of those member states or the law of the country where the policyholder has his habitual residence or central administration[11]. Notwithstanding these restrictions, when the risks covered by the contract are limited to events occurring in a member state other than a state where the risk is situated, the parties may always choose the law of the former state[12].

Where the risk is situated in an EFTA state[13] and is of a class specified by statute[14], or is situated in a member state and is a large risk[15], the parties may choose any law[16].

Where the parties choose the law[17] their choice must be express or demonstrated with reasonable certainty by the terms of the contract or the circumstances of the case[18]. If this is not the case, or if a choice has not been made, the contract is governed by the law of the country with which it is most closely connected[19]; it is rebuttably presumed to be governed by the law of the member state where the risk is situated[20].

The fact that the parties have chosen a law does not, where all the other elements relevant to the situation at the time of the choice are connected with one member state only, prejudice the application of the mandatory rules[21] of that state[22].

The law applicable to a contract of long term insurance business not governed by the Rome Convention[23] is the law of the member state of the commitment[24], but if that law so allows, the parties may choose the law of another country[25].

Where the policyholder is an individual and has his habitual residence in a member state other than that of which he is a national, the parties may choose the law of the member state of which he is a national[26].

1 For the meaning of 'the Rome Convention' see para 844 text and note 1 ante.

2 Rome Convention art 1 para 3.

3 Ibid art 1 para 4; provided always that the contract was made after 1 April 1991: see para 844 ante. For contracts of reinsurance made prior to this date the common law choice of law rules, summarised in para 859 et seq post, will apply.

    As it is inconceivable that a contract of reinsurance may be a consumer contract, a choice of law which is express or which can be demonstrated with reasonable certainty by the terms of the contract will be effective: see art 3; and para 846 ante. Accordingly, in the absence of choice, the applicable law is determined as described in art 4 (see para 847 ante). It is thought that as regards the presumption in art 4 para 2 (contract presumed to be most closely connected with the country of residence of the party whose performance is characteristic of the contract: see para 847 ante) it is the obligation of the reinsurer which is characteristic of the contract; and therefore the place with which the contract is most closely connected is the place of business of the reinsurer (or that of the place of business through which performance is to be made).

4 Ibid art 3. In the United Kingdom, the internal law for this purpose is whichever is applicable of the following (Contracts (Applicable Law) Act 1990 s 2(1A) (added by the Insurance Companies (Amendment) Regulations 1993, SI 1993/174; substituted by the Friendly Societies (Amendment) Regulations 1993, SI 1993/2519)):

    (1) the Insurance Companies Act 1982 Sch 3A (as added and amended) (see text and notes 6–26 infra); or

    (2) the provisions of the Friendly Societies Act 1992 s 101, Sch 20 (as amended) (see para 858 post).

5 As stated in the text, the Rome Convention art 1 para 3 only excludes insurance contracts which cover risks situated within the territory of a member state of the European Community. As a contract of insurance may be a consumer contract (see para 855 ante), the general choice of law rules contained in arts 3, 4 (see paras 846–847 ante) are subject to the provisions of art 5 if the contract is a consumer contract. As regards the presumption in art 4 para 2, it is the performance of the insurer which is characteristic of the contract of insurance, and as the insurance will be entered into in the course of the insurer's business, it will initially be presumed that the principal place of business of the insurer is the country with which the contract is most closely connected: see para 847 text and notes 4, 7 ante.

6 As to life insurance and long term business see text and notes 23–26 infra.

7 As to habitual residence see para 705 ante.

8 If the policyholder is an individual, the risk is situated in the member state where he has his habitual residence; if the policyholder is not an individual, the risk is situated in the member state of that establishment of the policyholder to which the insurance is related: Insurance Companies Act 1982 s 96A(3)(d) (added by the Insurance Companies (Amendment) Regulations 1990, SI 1990/1333). But for buildings, or buildings and contents, insurance, the risk is situated in the member state in which the property is situated (Insurance Companies Act 1982 s 96A(3)(a) (as so added); for vehicle insurance, in the member state of registration (s 96A(3)(b) (as so added); and for travel or holiday insurance (where the length of the policy is four months or less), in the member state in which the policyholder took out the policy (s 96A(3)(c) (as so added).

9 Ibid s 94B (as added and amended), Sch 3A para 1(1) (Sch 3A added by the Insurance Companies (Amendment) Regulations 1993; renumbered Pt I (paras 1–5) by the Insurance Companies (Amendment) Regulations 1993)). Where a member state includes several territorial units, each having its own law concerning contractual obligations, each unit is considered as a country for the purpose of identifying the applicable law: Insurance Companies Act 1982 Sch 3A para 4(1) (as so added). The provisions of Pt I (paras 1–5) of that Schedule apply as between different parts of the United Kingdom: Sch 3A para 4(2) (as so added; amended by the Insurance Companies (Amendment) Regulations 1993).

Nothing in these provisions restricts the application of the rules of a part of the United Kingdom where they are mandatory, irrespective of the law otherwise applicable to the contract: Insurance Companies Act 1982 Sch 3A para 3(2) (as so added and amended).

Subject to the provisions of Sch 3A Pt I (as added and amended), a court in a part of the United Kingdom must act in accordance with the provisions of the Contracts (Applicable Law) Act 1990: Insurance Companies Act 1982 Sch 3A para 5(1) (as so added and amended). In particular the court must so act to ascertain what freedom of choice the parties have under a law of a part of the United Kingdom, and to determine whether mandatory rules of another member state should be applied where the law otherwise applicable is the law of a part of the United Kingdom: Sch 3A para 5(2) (as so added and amended).

10 Ibid Sch 3A para 1(2) (as added: see note 8 supra). However, where the member state in which the risk is situated grants greater freedom of choice of the law applicable to the contract, the parties may take advantage of that freedom: Sch 3A para 1(4) (as so added).

11 Ibid Sch 3A para 1(3) (as added: see note 8 supra). Schedule 3A para 1(4) (as so added) (see note 9 supra) also applies.

12 Ibid Sch 3A para 1(5) (as added: see note 8 supra).

13 For the meaning of 'EFTA state' see ibid s 96(1) (as amended).

14 Ie it falls within ibid Sch 2 class 4, 5, 6, 7, 11 or 12.

15 For the meaning of 'large risk' see ibid s 96B (added by the Insurance Companies (Amendment) Regulations 1990; amended by the Insurance Companies (Amendment) Regulations 1992, SI 1992/2890).

16 Insurance Companies Act 1982 Sch 3A para 1(6) (as added: see note 8 supra; substituted by the Insurance Companies (Third Insurance Directives) Regulations 1994, SI 1994/1696).

17 Ie under the Insurance Companies Act 1982 Sch 3A para 1 (as added): see text and notes 6–16 supra.

18 Ibid Sch 3A para 2(1) (as added: see note 8 supra).

19 Ibid Sch 3A para 2(2) (as added: see note 8 supra). This country must be one of those which would be applicable under Sch 3A para 1 (as so added): Sch 3A para 2(2) (as so added). A severable part of the contract which has a close connection with another country (being one of those would which would be so applicable) may by way of exception be governed by the law of that other country: Sch 3A para 2(3) (as so added).

20 Ibid Sch 3A para 2(4) (as added: see note 8 supra).

21 'Mandatory rules' means the rules from which the law of that state allows no derogation by contract: ibid Sch 3A para 3(1) (as added: see note 8 supra).

22 Ibid Sch 3A para 3(1) (as added: see note 8 supra).

23 There is no express provision analogous to that regarding general business (see note 8 supra), for determining where the risk in a contract of life or long term insurance is situated and consequently whether a contract is governed by the provisions of the Rome Convention. However, the law applicable to long term business is to be determined under the Insurance Companies Act 1982 Sch 3A Pt II (as added) if the policyholder is an individual habitually resident in a member state of the European Community, or if the policyholder is not an individual but the establishment of the policyholder to which the contract relates is situated in a member state: s 94B(1A) (added by the Insurance Companies (Amendment) Regulations 1993). Consequently, it is thought that, as regards the exclusion of the operation of the Rome Convention (see art 1 para 3), the risk is to be seen as being situated in a member state if the policyholder has his habitual residence or, as the case may be, the relevant place of establishment, in that state. Accordingly the governing law will not be determined by the Rome Convention. But if these conditions are not met, the applicable law will be determined by the Rome Convention if the contract was made after 1 April 1991, and by the rules of the common law if it was made on or before 1 April 1991.

24 'Commitment' means the commitment represented by insurance business falling within the classes set out in the Insurance Companies Act 1982 s 1, Sch 1 (long term business): s 96(1) (definition added by the Insurance Companies (Amendment) Regulations 1993). As to those classes see INSURANCE vol 25 (Reissue) para 18. 'State of the commitment', in relation to a commitment entered into at any date, means (1) where the policyholder is an individual, the state in which he had his habitual residence at that date; and (2) where the policyholder is not an individual, the state in which the establishment of the policyholder to which the commitment relates was situated at that date; 'member state of the commitment' must be construed accordingly: Insurance Companies Act 1982 s 96(1) (definition added by the Insurance Companies (Third Insurance Directives) Regulations 1994).

25 Insurance Companies Act 1982 Sch 3A para 6 (Sch 3A Pt II (paras 6–10) added by the Insurance Companies (Amendment) Regulations 1993). Nothing in the Insurance Companies Act 1982 Sch 3A Pt II restricts the application of the rules of a part of the United Kingdom in a situation where they are mandatory, irrespective of the law otherwise applicable to the contract: Sch 3A para 8 (as so added).

26 Ibid Sch 3A para 7 (as added: see note 25 supra). Where a member state includes several territorial units, each having its own law concerning contractual obligations, each unit is considered as a country for the purpose of identifying the applicable law: Sch 3A para 9(1) (as so added). The provisions of Pt II apply as between different parts of the United Kingdom: Sch 3A para 9(2) (as so added).

Subject to the provisions of Sch 3A Pt II (as added), a court in the United Kingdom must act in accordance with the provisions of the Contracts (Applicable Law) Act 1990: Insurance Companies Act 1982 Sch 3A para 10(1) (as so added). In particular the court must so act to determine what freedom of choice the parties have under a law of a part of the United Kingdom: Sch 3A para 10(2) (as so added).

858. Applicable (or otherwise governing) law in contracts of insurance entered into by Friendly Societies.

As has been stated, a contract of insurance is not governed by the Rome Convention[1] if the risk is situated in a member state of the European Community, and the court must apply its internal law to determine where the risk is situated[2].

Where a contract of general business[3] is made by a friendly society[4], covering risks situated in the United Kingdom[5] or another member state, the applicable law is determined according to the following provisions[6].

Where the person insured has his habitual residence[7] or central administration within the territory of the member state where the risk is situated[8], the law applicable to the contract is the law of that state, but if that law so allows, the parties may choose the law of another country[9]. Where the person insured does not have his habitual residence or central administration within the territory of the member state where the risk is situated, the parties may choose either the law of the member state where the risk is situated, or the law of the country where the person insured has his habitual residence or central administration[10]. Where the person insured carries on a business[11] and the contract covers two or more risks relating to his business which are situated in different member states, the parties may choose the law of any of those member states or the law of the country where the person insured has his habitual residence or central administration[12]. Notwithstanding these restrictions, where the risks covered by the contract are limited to events occurring in a member state other than a state in which the risk is situated, the parties may always choose the law of the former state[13].

Where the parties choose the law[14] their choice must be express or demonstrated with reasonable certainty by the terms of the contract or the circumstances of the case[15]. If this is not the case, or if a choice has not been made, the contract is governed by the law of the country with which it is most closely connected[16]; it is rebuttably presumed to be governed by the law of the member state where the risk is situated[17].

The fact that the parties have chosen a law does not, where all the other elements relevant to the situation at the time of the choice are connected with one member state only, prejudice the application of the mandatory rules[18] of that state[19].

Where a contract of long term business[20] is made by a friendly society, covering commitments or risks situated in the United Kingdom or another member state, the applicable law is determined according to the following provisions[21].

The law applicable to the contract is the law of the member state in which the commitment is situated[22], but if that law so allows, the parties may choose the law of another country[23].

Where the person who has entered into the contract is an individual and has his habitual residence in a member state other than that of which he is a national, the parties may choose the law of the member state of which he is a national[24].

1 For the meaning of 'the Rome Convention' see para 844 text and note 1 ante.
2 See para 857 text and notes 1–5, particularly note 4, ante.
3 For the meaning of 'general business' see FRIENDLY SOCIETIES vol 19(1) (Reissue) para 342 note 3.
4 For the meaning of 'friendly society' see FRIENDLY SOCIETIES vol 19(1) (Reissue) paras 102, 342 note 1.
5 For the meaning of 'United Kingdom' see para 604 ante.
6 Friendly Societies Act 1992 s 101(1) (s 101 substituted by the Friendly Societies (Amendment) Regulations 1993, SI 1993/2519). The provisions described in the text and notes 7–19 infra apply to a friendly society which is a directive society carrying on general business: see the Friendly Societies Act 1992 s 101(1)(a) (as so substituted), referring to societies to which s 37(3) applies; see also FRIENDLY SOCIETIES vol 19(1) (Reissue) para 352 note 4. In the case of other societies carrying on general business the provisions described are modified, by the omission of the words 'or central administration', and as otherwise indicated, by s 101(3) (as so substituted).
7 As to habitual residence see para 705 ante.
8 In relation to a directive society (ie one to which the Friendly Societies Act 1992 s 37(2) or (3) applies), if the person insured is an individual, a risk or commitment is situated in the member state (or EEA state) where he has his habitual residence; if the person insured is not an individual, the risk is situated in the member state (or EEA state) where the establishment of that person to which the contract relates is situated: Friendly Societies Act 1992 s 117(6) (substituted by the Friendly Societies (Amendment) Regulations 1993; amended by the Friendly Societies Act 1992 (Amendment) Regulations 1994, SI 1994/1984). In relation to any other contract of insurance with a friendly society, the member state in which the risk is situated is the state where the person who has entered into the contract has his habitual place of residence: Friendly Societies Act 1992 s 117(7). For the meaning of 'EEA state' see FRIENDLY SOCIETIES vol 19(1) (Reissue) para 128 note 8.
9 Ibid s 101(1) (as substituted: see note 6 supra), Sch 20 para 1(1) (amended by the Friendly Societies (Amendment) Regulations 1993). Where a member state includes several territorial units, each having its own law concerning contractual obligations, each unit is considered as a country for the purpose of identifying the applicable law: Friendly Societies Act 1992 Sch 20 para 4(1). The provisions of Pt I (paras 1–5) of that Schedule apply as between different parts of the United Kingdom: see Sch 20 para 4(2) (Sch 20 paras 1, 3–5 amended, and Pt I so numbered, by the Friendly Societies (Amendment) Regulations 1993).

Nothing in these provisions restricts the application of the rules of a part of the United Kingdom where they are mandatory, irrespective of the law otherwise applicable to the contract: Friendly Societies Act 1992 Sch 20 para 3(2) (as so amended).

Subject to the provisions of Sch 20 Pt I (as amended), a court in the United Kingdom must act in accordance with the provisions of the Contracts (Applicable Law) Act 1990: Friendly Societies Act 1992 Sch 20 para 5(1) (as so amended) (modified in the circumstances mentioned in note 6 supra, so as to require the court to apply the rules of private international law governing contractual obligations:

s 101(3) (as substituted: see note 6 supra)). In particular the court must so act to determine what freedom of choice the parties have under a law of a part of the United Kingdom, and to determine whether mandatory rules of another member state should be applied where the law otherwise applicable is the law of a part of the United Kingdom: see Sch 20 para 5(2) (as amended) (modified by s 101(3) (as so substituted)).

10 Ibid Sch 20 para 1(2) (as amended: see note 9 supra). However, where the member state in which the risk is situated grants greater freedom of choice as to the choice of law, the parties may take advantage of that freedom: Sch 20 para 1(4) (as so amended).

11 'Business' includes a trade or profession: ibid Sch 20 para 1(3).

12 Ibid Sch 20 para 1(3) (as amended: see note 9 supra). Sch 20 para 1(4) (as so amended) (see note 10 supra) also applies.

13 Ibid Sch 20 para 1(5) (as amended: see note 9 supra).

14 Ie under ibid Sch 20 para 1 (as amended): see text and notes 7–13 supra.

15 Ibid Sch 20 para 2(1).

16 See ibid Sch 20 para 2(2). This country must be one of those which would be applicable under Sch 20 para 1 (as amended): Sch 20 para 2(2). A severable part of the contract which has a close connection with another country (being one of those would which would be so applicable) may by way of exception be governed by the law of that other country: Sch 20 para 2(3).

17 Ibid Sch 20 para 2(4).

18 'Mandatory rules' means the rules from which the law of that state allows no derogation by contract: ibid Sch 20 para 3(1).

19 Ibid Sch 20 para 3(1).

20 For the meaning of 'long term business' see FRIENDLY SOCIETIES vol 19(1) (Reissue) para 342 note 3.

21 Friendly Societies Act 1992 s 101(2) (as substituted: see note 6 supra). The provisions described in the text and notes 22–24 infra apply to a friendly society which is a directive society carrying on long term business: see the Friendly Societies Act 1992 s 101(1)(a) (as so substituted), referring to societies to which s 37(2) applies; see also FRIENDLY SOCIETIES vol 19(1) (Reissue) para 352 note 4. In the case of other societies carrying on long term business the provisions described in the text and notes 7–19 supra apply, as modified: s 101(3) (as so substituted).

22 As to where a risk or commitment is situated see note 8 supra.

23 Friendly Societies Act 1992 Sch 20 para 6 (Sch 20 Pt II (paras 6–10) added by the Friendly Societies (Amendment) Regulations 1993). Nothing in the Friendly Societies Act 1992 Sch 20 Pt II restricts the application of the rules of a part of the United Kingdom in a situation where they are mandatory, irrespective of the law otherwise applicable to the contract: Sch 20 para 8 (as so added).

24 Ibid Sch 20 para 7 (as added: see note 23 supra). Where a member state includes several territorial units, each having its own law concerning contractual obligations, each unit is considered as a country for the purpose of identifying the applicable law: Sch 20 para 9(1) (as so added). The provisions of Pt II apply as between different parts of the United Kingdom: Sch 20 para 9(2) (as so added).

Subject to the provisions of Sch 20 Pt II (as so added), a court in the United Kingdom must act in accordance with the provisions of the Contracts (Applicable Law) Act 1990: Friendly Societies Act 1992 Sch 20 para 10(1) (as so added). In particular the court must so act to determine what freedom of choice the parties have under a law of a part of the United Kingdom: Sch 20 para 10(2) (as so added).

(4) DETERMINATION AND APPLICATION OF GOVERNING LAW UNDER COMMON LAW

(i) Determination of the Proper Law

859. Doctrine of the proper law. The Rome Convention has no application in relation to contracts made on or before 1 April 1991, or to certain types of contract whenever made[1]. In such cases the proper law of the contract governs most contractual issues[2]. The proper law may be determined in three ways: (1) by express selection by the parties[3]; or (2) by inferred selection from the circumstances[4]; or, failing either of these, (3) by judicial determination of the system of law with which the transaction has the closest and most real connection[5].

1 See paras 844–845 ante as to the application of the Rome Convention. For the meaning of 'the Rome Convention' see para 844 text and note 1 ante.

2 For a detailed examination of the law applicable to particular contractual issues see paras 871–889 post.

3 See para 860 post.

4 See paras 861–862 post.

5 See paras 863–865 post.

860. Express choice of the proper law. Where the parties have expressly stipulated that a contract is to be governed by a particular law, that law is the proper law of the contract[1]. The selection must be bona fide[2] and legal and there must be no reason for avoiding the choice on the grounds of public policy[3]. Where a law is expressly chosen to evade the provisions of the legal system with which the contract, objectively, is connected, that choice will probably be effective[4].

Express selection of a foreign law as the proper law of a contract does not prevent the application of the Unfair Contract Terms Act 1977 where (1) the term appears to the court or arbitrator to have been imposed wholly or mainly to evade the operation of that Act; or (2) one of the parties dealt as consumer, and was then habitually resident[5] in the United Kingdom[6] and the essential steps necessary for the making of the contract were taken there, whether by him or by others on his behalf[7]. Conversely, where the proper law of a contract is the law of some part of the United Kingdom only by choice of the parties (and would otherwise be the law of a country outside the United Kingdom) certain provisions of that Act do not operate as part of the applicable law[8].

If the parties have expressly selected as the proper law a legal system with which the contract has no real connection, effect will probably be given to their choice[9].

If the express choice of law clause is meaningless, then the court will disregard it and determine the proper law according to the inferred or implied intentions of the parties[10].

Where the parties choose the applicable law of arbitration under a contract, but not the seat, it may be inferred that the arbitration is to be conducted in the country of the applicable law[11].

1 *Vita Food Products Inc v Unus Shipping Co Ltd* [1939] AC 277 at 289–290, 292, [1939] 1 All ER 513 at 521, 522, PC; *Lloyd v Guibert* (1865) LR 1 QB 115 at 120, 121; *R v International Trustee for the Protection of Bondholders AG* [1937] AC 500 at 529, [1937] 2 All ER 164 at 166, HL; *Mount Albert Borough Council v Australasian Temperance and General Mutual Life Assurance Society Ltd* [1938] AC 224 at 240, [1937] 4 All ER 206 at 214, PC; *James Miller & Partners Ltd v Whitworth Street Estates (Manchester) Ltd* [1970] AC 583 at 603, [1970] 1 All ER 796 at 798, HL. Express choice of the proper law may be illustrated by *Pena Copper Mines Ltd v Rio Tinto Zinc Co Ltd* (1911) 105 LT 846, CA; *Perry v Equitable Life Assurance Society of the United States of America* (1929) 45 TLR 468; *Mackender v Feldia AG* [1967] 2 QB 590, [1966] 3 All ER 847, CA; *The Eleftheria* [1970] P 94, [1969] 2 All ER 641; *Compagnie D'Armement Maritime SA v Compagnie Tunisienne de Navigation SA* [1971] AC 572, [1970] 3 All ER 71, HL; *Acrow (Automation) Ltd v Rex Chainbelt Inc* [1971] 3 All ER 1175, [1971] 1 WLR 1676, CA; *Laertis Shipping Corpn v Exportadora Espanola de Cementos Portland SA* [1982] 1 Lloyd's Rep 613.

2 See *Golden Acres Ltd v Queensland Estates Pty Ltd* [1969] Qd R 378; affd on different grounds sub nom *Freehold Land Investments Ltd v Queensland Estates Pty Ltd* (1970) 123 CLR 418, Aust HC;

3 *Vita Food Products Inc v Unus Shipping Co Ltd* [1939] AC 277 at 290, [1939] 1 All ER 513 at 521, PC; *Tzortzis v Monark Line A/B* [1968] 1 All ER 949 at 951–952, [1968] 1 WLR 406 at 411, CA.

4 See Dicey and Morris *The Conflict of Laws* (11th Edn, 1987) 1172–1173. But see, contra, *Mynott v Barnard* (1939) 62 CLR 68 at 80, Aust HC; *Kay's Leasing Corpn Pty Ltd v Fletcher* (1964) 116 CLR 124 at 143–144, [1965] ALR 673 at 682–683, Aust HC; *Golden Acres Ltd v Queensland Estates Pty Ltd* [1969] Qd R 378 at 384–385. Where a statute in the forum expresses a policy applicable to the case before the court, then that statute may have to be applied irrespective of the proper law, whether or not expressly chosen by the parties: *English v Donnelly* 1958 SC 494; and see *Kay's Leasing Corpn Pty Ltd v Fletcher* supra; *Freehold Land Investments Ltd v Queensland Estates Pty Ltd* (1970) 123 CLR 418, Aust HC.

5 As to the meaning of 'habitually resident' see *Kapur v Kapur* [1984] FLR 920; and para 705 ante.

6 For the meaning of 'United Kingdom' see para 604 ante.
7 Unfair Contract Terms Act 1977 s 27(2).
8 Ibid s 27(1) (amended by the Contracts (Applicable Law) Act 1990 s 5, Sch 4 para 4).
9 See *Vita Food Products Inc v Unus Shipping Co Ltd* [1939] AC 277 at 290, [1939] 1 All ER 513 at 521, PC, suggesting that a real connection is not essential. See further Dicey and Morris *The Conflict of Laws* (11th Edn, 1987) 1174–1176. Although English law is often selected to govern contracts unconnected with England (see *Vita Food Products Inc v Unus Shipping Co Ltd* supra; and *British Controlled Oilfields Ltd v Stagg* (1921) 127 LT 209), frequently through the use of arbitration (see para 861 post) or choice of jurisdiction clauses, there has been support for the view that the courts are free, although not obliged, to strike down the choice of a law quite unconnected with the contract: see *Boissevain v Weil* [1949] 1 KB 482 at 490–491, [1949] 1 All ER 146 at 152–153, CA; affd [1950] AC 327, [1950] 1 All ER 728, HL; *Re Helbert Wagg & Co Ltd's Claim* [1956] Ch 323 at 341, [1956] 1 All ER 129 at 136; *The Fehmarn* [1958] 1 All ER 333 at 335, [1958] 1 WLR 159 at 162, CA; *Queensland Estates Pty Ltd v Collas* [1971] Qd R 75; and see *Kleinwort, Sons & Co v Ungarische Baumwolle Industrie AG* [1939] 2 KB 678 at 698, [1939] 3 All ER 38 at 45, CA; contrast *Vita Food Products Inc v Unus Shipping Co Ltd* supra; *Tzortzis v Monark Line AB* [1968] 1 All ER 949 at 951–952, [1968] 1 WLR 406 at 411, CA.
10 *Compagnie Tunisienne de Navigation SA v Compagnie D'Armement Maritime SA* [1969] 3 All ER 589, [1969] 1 WLR 1338, CA; revsd on a different interpretation of the clause in question sub nom *Compagnie D'Armement Maritime SA v Compagnie Tunisienne de Navigation SA* [1971] AC 572, [1970] 3 All ER 71, HL.
11 *Naviera Amazonica Peruana SA v Cia Internacional de Seguros del Peru* [1988] 1 Lloyd's Rep 116, CA.

861. Inferred choice of law. If the parties to a contract do not make an express choice of the proper law, the court will consider whether it can ascertain that there was an inferred or implied choice of law. If the parties agree that arbitration is to take place in a particular country, an English court will usually[1], although not always[2], conclude that the parties have impliedly chosen the law of the country of arbitration as the proper law[3]. Similarly, if the parties agree that the courts of a particular country are to have jurisdiction over the contract, there is a strong inference that the law of that country is to be the proper law[4]. Other factors from which the courts have been prepared to infer the intentions of the parties[5] as to the proper law are the legal terminology in which the contract is drafted[6], the form of the documents involved in the transaction[7], the currency in which payment is to be made[8], the use of a particular language[9], a connection with a preceding transaction[10], the nature and location of the subject matter of the contract[11], the residence[12] (but rarely the nationality[13]) of the parties, and the fact that one of the parties is a government[14].

1 *Hamlyn & Co v Talisker Distillery* [1894] AC 202, HL; *Spurrier v La Cloche* [1902] AC 446, PC; *Maritime Insurance Co Ltd v Assecuranz-Union Von 1865* (1935) 52 Ll L Rep 16; *Norske Atlas Insurance Co Ltd v London General Insurance Co Ltd* (1927) 43 TLR 541; *The Njegos* [1936] P 90 at 100; *Vita Food Products Inc v Unus Shipping Co Ltd* [1939] AC 277 at 290, [1939] 1 All ER 513 at 521, PC; *Tzortzis v Monark Line AB* [1968] 1 All ER 949, [1968] 1 WLR 406, CA; *Sayers v International Drilling Co NV* [1971] 3 All ER 163 at 168, [1971] 1 WLR 1176 at 1182–1183, CA.
2 *Compagnie D'Armement Maritime SA v Compagnie Tunisienne de Navigation SA* [1971] AC 572, [1970] 3 All ER 71, HL; *Bangladesh Chemical Industries Corpn v Henry Stephens Shipping Co Ltd, The SLS Everest* [1981] 2 Lloyd's Rep 389, CA.
3 In *James Miller & Partners Ltd v Whitworth Street Estates (Manchester) Ltd* [1970] AC 583, [1970] 1 All ER 796, HL, although the proper law of the contract was held to be English, the curial law to govern the arbitration was that of Scotland. See also *Don v Lippmann* (1837) 5 Cl & Fin 1 at 13, HL; *Hamlyn & Co v Talisker Distillery* [1894] AC 202, HL; *NV Kwik Hoo Tong Handel Maatschappij v James Finlay & Co Ltd* [1927] AC 604, HL; *Norske Atlas Insurance Co Ltd v London General Insurance Co Ltd* (1927) 43 TLR 541 at 542; and see ARBITRATION vol 2 (Reissue) paras 717–718. As to the effect of choosing the applicable law but not the seat of the arbitration see para 860 text and note 11 ante. The Rome Convention does not apply to arbitration agreements and choice of court agreements, whenever made: see para 845 ante.
4 *Hamlyn & Co v Talisker Distillery* [1894] AC 202 at 212–213, HL; *Royal Exchange Assurance Corpn v Sjoforsakrings Akt Vega* [1902] 2 KB 384 at 394, CA; *Kirchner & Co v Gruban* [1909] 1 Ch 413; *NV Kwik Hoo Tong Handel Maatschappij v James Finlay & Co Ltd* [1927] AC 604 at 608, HL; *Mackender v Feldia AG*

[1967] 2 QB 590, [1966] 3 All ER 847, CA; *Hellenic Steel Co v Svolamar Shipping Co Ltd, The Komninos S* [1991] 1 Lloyd's Rep 370, CA.

5 The intention must be that of both parties and not of one alone: *R v International Trustee for the Protection of Bondholders AG* [1937] AC 500 at 557, [1937] 2 All ER 164 at 180, HL; and see *Peninsular and Oriental Steam Navigation Co v Shand* (1865) 3 Moo PCCNS 272 at 292.

6 *The Leon XIII* (1883) 8 PD 121, CA; *Chatenay v Brazilian Submarine Telegraph Co Ltd* [1891] 1 QB 79 at 82, CA; *The Industrie* [1894] P 58, CA; *Spurrier v La Cloche* [1902] AC 446 at 450, PC; *R v International Trustee for the Protection of Bondholders AG* [1937] AC 500 at 553–554, [1937] 2 All ER 164 at 177–178, HL; *Re Pilkington's Will Trusts, Pilkington v Harrison* [1937] Ch 574, [1937] 3 All ER 213; *Rossano v Manufacturers' Life Insurance Co* [1963] 2 QB 352, [1962] 2 All ER 214; *James Miller & Partners Ltd v Whitworth Street Estates (Manchester) Ltd* [1970] AC 583 at 603, 608, 611–612, [1970] 1 All ER 796 at 798, 802, 805–806, HL; cf *Kadel Chajkin v Mitchell Cotts & Co (Middle East) Ltd and AS Motortramp* [1947] 2 All ER 786.

7 *Chamberlain v Napier* (1880) 15 ChD 614; *The Leon XIII* (1883) 8 PD 121, CA; *Re Barnard, Barnard v White* (1887) 56 LT 9; *Chartered Mercantile Bank of India, London and China v Netherlands India Steam Navigation Co Ltd* (1883) 10 QBD 521, CA; *Re Missouri SS Co* (1889) 42 ChD 321, CA; *South African Breweries Ltd v King* [1899] 2 Ch 173 at 179; *Royal Exchange Assurance Corpn v Sjoforsakrings Akt Vega* [1902] 2 KB 384, CA; *Re Hewitt's Settlement, Hewitt v Hewitt* [1915] 1 Ch 228; *The Adriatic* [1931] P 241; *Pick v Manufacturers Life Insurance Co* [1958] 2 Lloyd's Rep 93; *Rossano v Manufacturers' Life Insurance Co* [1963] 2 QB 352, [1962] 2 All ER 214; *James Miller & Partners Ltd v Whitworth Street Estates (Manchester) Ltd* [1970] AC 583, [1970] 1 All ER 796, HL; cf *NV Handel My J Smits Import-Export v English Exporters (London) Ltd* [1955] 2 Lloyd's Rep 69 at 72; affd [1955] 2 Lloyd's Rep 317, CA; *Compagnie D'Armement Maritime SA v Compagnie Tunisienne de Navigation SA* [1971] AC 572 at 583, [1970] 3 All ER 71 at 73–74, HL; *Armadora Occidental SA v Horace Mann Insurance Co* [1978] 1 All ER 407, [1977] 1 WLR 1098, CA; *Amin Rasheed Shipping Corpn v Kuwait Insurance Co, The Al Wahab* [1984] AC 50, [1983] 2 All ER 884, HL.

8 *R v International Trustee for the Protection of Bondholders AG* [1937] AC 500 at 553, [1937] 2 All ER 164 at 177, HL; *Keiner v Keiner* [1952] 1 All ER 643; *The Assunzione* [1954] P 150, [1954] 1 All ER 278, CA; *Rossano v Manufacturers' Life Insurance Co* [1963] 2 QB 352, [1962] 2 All ER 214; *Compagnie D'Armement Maritime SA v Compagnie Tunisienne de Navigation SA* [1971] AC 572 at 583, 593, [1970] 3 All ER 71 at 74, 82, HL; *Coast Lines Ltd v Hudig and Veder Chartering NV* [1972] 2 QB 34 at 47, 50, [1972] 1 All ER 451 at 458, 461, CA; cf *NV Handel My J Smits Import-Export v English Exporters (London) Ltd* [1955] 2 Lloyd's Rep 69 at 72; affd [1955] 2 Lloyd's Rep 317 at 323, CA; *Re Helbert Wagg & Co Ltd's Claim* [1956] Ch 323, [1956] 1 All ER 129; *Pick v Manufacturers Life Insurance Co* [1958] 2 Lloyd's Rep 93; *Sayers v International Drilling Co NV* [1971] 3 All ER 163 at 168, 171, [1971] 1 WLR 1176 at 1183, 1186, CA.

9 *The Leon XIII* (1883) 8 PD 121, CA; *Chatenay v Brazilian Submarine Telegraph Co Ltd* [1891] 1 QB 79, CA; *The Adriatic* [1931] P 241; *The Njegos* [1936] P 90; *St Pierre v South American Stores (Gath and Chaves) Ltd* [1937] 3 All ER 349, CA; but this is a factor of only minor importance: *The Industrie* [1894] P 58 at 72, CA; *The Metamorphosis* [1953] 1 All ER 723 at 727, [1953] 1 WLR 543 at 549; *NV Handel My J Smits Import-Export v English Exporters (London) Ltd* [1955] 2 Lloyd's Rep 317 at 323, CA; *Compagnie D'Armement Maritime SA v Compagnie Tunisienne de Navigation SA* [1971] AC 572 at 583, [1970] 3 All ER 71 at 74, 83, HL; *Sayers v International Drilling Co NV* [1971] 3 All ER 163 at 168–169, 171, [1971] 1 WLR 1176 at 1183–1184, 1186, CA; *Coast Lines Ltd v Hudig and Veder Chartering NV* [1972] 2 QB 34 at 47, 50, [1972] 1 All ER 451 at 458, 461, CA. See also *Amin Rasheed Shipping Corpn v Kuwait Insurance Co, The Al Wahab* [1984] AC 50, [1983] 2 All ER 884, HL.

10 *The Adriatic* [1931] P 241 at 247; *The Njegos* [1936] P 90; *R v International Trustee for the Protection of Bondholders AG* [1937] AC 500 at 554, 558, [1937] 2 All ER 164 at 178, 181, HL; cf *South African Breweries Ltd v King* [1899] 2 Ch 173 at 180; *The Metamorphosis* [1953] 1 All ER 723, [1953] 1 WLR 543.

11 *Lloyd v Guibert* (1865) LR 1 QB 115 at 122–123; *British South Africa Co v De Beers Consolidated Mines Ltd* [1910] 1 Ch 354 at 383; affd [1910] 2 Ch 502, CA; but revsd on another point sub nom *De Beers Consolidated Mines Ltd v British South Africa Co* [1912] AC 52, HL; cf *James Miller & Partners Ltd v Whitworth Street Estates (Manchester) Ltd* [1970] AC 583, [1970] 1 All ER 796, HL (contracts relating to land); *Re Missouri SS Co* (1889) 42 ChD 321 at 327, CA (contract of affreightment); cf *Kahler v Midland Bank Ltd* [1950] AC 24, [1949] 2 All ER 621, HL.

12 *Jacobs v Crédit Lyonnais* (1884) 12 QBD 589, CA; *Keiner v Keiner* [1952] 1 All ER 643; cf *South African Breweries Ltd v King* [1899] 2 Ch 173 at 178–179.

13 *Re Missouri SS Co* (1889) 42 ChD 321 at 328–329, CA; cf *Chartered Mercantile Bank of India, London and China v Netherlands India Steam Navigation Co Ltd* (1883) 10 QBD 521, CA; *Sayers v International Drilling Co NV* [1971] 3 All ER 163 at 168, [1971] 1 WLR 1176 at 1183, CA.

14 *R v International Trustee for the Protection of Bondholders AG* [1937] AC 500 at 531, 557, [1937] 2 All ER 164 at 168, 180, HL.

862. Inference from validity of the contract. In general, where a contract is, or any terms of it are, void or invalid under one system of law but good under another, the parties will be taken to have intended to contract with reference to that law by which the agreement would be valid[1]. This should not, however, be regarded as an irrebuttable presumption, but only used as a pointer to indicate the likely intentions of the parties[2].

1 *Peninsular and Oriental Steam Navigation Co v Shand* (1865) 3 Moo PCCNS 272; *Re Missouri SS Co* (1889) 42 ChD 321 at 341, CA; *Hamlyn & Co v Talisker Distillery* [1894] AC 202 at 208, 215, HL; *South African Breweries Ltd v King* [1899] 2 Ch 173 at 180–181; affd [1900] 1 Ch 273, CA; *British South Africa Co v De Beers Consolidated Mines Ltd* [1910] 1 Ch 354 at 383; affd [1910] 2 Ch 502, CA; but revsd on another point sub nom *De Beers Consolidated Mines Ltd v British South Africa Co* [1912] AC 52, HL; *Jones v Oceanic Steam Navigation Co Ltd* [1924] 2 KB 730 at 733; *NV Handel My J Smits Import-Export v English Exporters (London) Ltd* [1955] 2 Lloyd's Rep 317 at 324, CA; *Coast Lines Ltd v Hudig and Veder Chartering NV* [1972] 2 QB 34 at 44, 48, [1972] 1 All ER 451 at 456, 459, CA.
2 *South African Breweries Ltd v King* [1899] 2 Ch 173; affd [1900] 1 Ch 273, CA; *British South Africa Co v De Beers Consolidated Mines Ltd* [1910] 2 Ch 502 at 513, CA (see note 1 supra); *Maritime Insurance Co Ltd v Assecuranz-Union Von 1865* (1935) 52 Ll L Rep 16 at 19–20; *Sayers v International Drilling Co NV* [1971] 3 All ER 163 at 169, [1971] 1 WLR 1176 at 1184, CA; *Coast Lines Ltd v Hudig and Veder Chartering NV* [1972] 2 QB 34 at 50–51, [1972] 1 All ER 451 at 461, CA.

863. No express or inferred choice of law. Where the parties have not expressed a choice as to the proper law and no such choice can be inferred, the proper law of their contract is the system of law with which the transaction has the closest and most real connection[1]. In such a case the court does not seek to find some presumed or fictitious intention of the parties[2] but, rather, holds the contract to be governed by the law with which it is most closely connected, for that is what it is presumed that reasonable businessmen would have decided[3].

In determining with what system of law the transaction is most closely connected, the court should look at all the circumstances[4]. Whilst firm rules cannot be laid down[5], it is clear that the court will look at such factors as the place of contracting[6], the place of performance[7], the place of residence[8] or business[9] of the parties and the nature and subject matter[10] of the contract[11].

1 *Boissevain v Weil* [1949] 1 KB 482 at 490, [1949] 1 All ER 146 at 153, CA; affd [1950] AC 327, [1950] 1 All ER 728, HL; *The Assunzione* [1954] P 150, [1954] 1 All ER 278, CA; *Bonython v Commonwealth of Australia* [1951] AC 201 at 219, PC; *Re United Railways of the Havana and Regla Warehouses Ltd* [1960] Ch 52 at 91–92, 115, [1959] 1 All ER 214 at 233–234, 246, CA; affd sub nom *Tomkinson v First Pennsylvania Banking and Trust Co* [1961] AC 1007 at 1068, 1081–1082, [1960] 2 All ER 332 at 356, 364, HL; *Philipson-Stow v IRC* [1961] AC 727 at 760, [1960] 3 All ER 814 at 830, HL; *Rossano v Manufacturers' Life Insurance Co* [1963] 2 QB 352, [1962] 2 All ER 214; *Tzortzis v Monark Line AB* [1968] 1 All ER 949, [1968] 1 WLR 406, CA; *James Miller & Partners Ltd v Whitworth Street Estates (Manchester) Ltd* [1970] AC 583, [1970] 1 All ER 796, HL; *Compagnie D'Armement Maritime SA v Compagnie Tunisienne de Navigation SA* [1971] AC 572, [1970] 3 All ER 71, HL; *Sayers v International Drilling Co NV* [1971] 3 All ER 163 at 166, 168, [1971] 1 WLR 1176 at 1180–1181, 1183, CA; *Coast Lines Ltd v Hudig and Veder Chartering NV* [1972] 2 QB 34, [1972] 1 All ER 451, CA; *Offshore International SA v Banco Central SA* [1976] 3 All ER 749, [1977] 1 WLR 399; *Armadora Occidental SA v Horace Mann Insurance Co* [1978] 1 All ER 407, [1977] 1 WLR 1098, CA; *Armar Shipping Co Ltd v Caisse Algérienne d'Assurance et de Réassurance, The Armar* [1981] 1 All ER 498, [1981] 1 WLR 207, CA; *Power Curber International Ltd v National Bank of Kuwait SAK* [1981] 3 All ER 607, [1981] 1 WLR 1233, CA.
2 *The Assunzione* [1954] P 150 at 164, [1954] 1 All ER 278 at 282–283, CA. Older authorities support a more subjective approach, ie a search for the parties' presumed intentions: see *Lloyd v Guibert* (1865) LR 1 QB 115 at 120–123; *Hamlyn & Co v Talisker Distillery* [1894] AC 202 at 212, HL; *British South Africa Co v De Beers Consolidated Mines Ltd* [1910] 1 Ch 354 at 381; *R v International Trustee for the Protection of Bondholders AG* [1937] AC 500 at 529, [1937] 2 All ER 164 at 166, HL; *Vita Food Products Inc v Unus Shipping Co Ltd* [1939] AC 277 at 289–290, [1939] 1 All ER 513 at 521, PC.

3 *Mount Albert Borough Council v Australasian Temperance and General Mutual Life Assurance Society Ltd*
   [1938] AC 224 at 240, [1937] 4 All ER 206 at 214, PC; *The Assunzione* [1954] P 150 at 176–179, 186,
   [1954] 1 All ER 278 at 290–292, 295, CA; and see *The Njegos* [1936] P 90 at 102.
4 *Chartered Mercantile Bank of India, London and China v Netherlands India Steam Navigation Co Ltd* (1883) 10
   QBD 521 at 529, CA; and see *Kadel Chajkin v Mitchell Cotts & Co (Middle East) Ltd and AS Motortramp*
   [1947] 2 All ER 786; *The Assunzione* [1954] P 150, [1954] 1 All ER 278, CA; *Mauroux v Sociedade
   Commercial Abel Pereira Da Fonseca SARL* [1972] 2 All ER 1085 at 1089, [1972] 1 WLR 962 at 966; *BP
   Exploration Co (Libya) Ltd v Hunt* [1976] 3 All ER 879, [1976] 1 WLR 788.
5 *Jacobs v Crédit Lyonnais* (1884) 12 QBD 589 at 601, CA.
6 *Arnott v Redfern* (1825) 2 C & P 88; *Trimbey v Vignier* (1834) 1 Bing NC 151 at 159; *Scott v Pilkington*
   (1862) 2 B & S 11; *Peninsular and Oriental Steam Navigation Co v Shand* (1865) 3 Moo PCCNS 272; *Lloyd
   v Guibert* (1865) LR 1 QB 115 at 122; *Jacobs v Crédit Lyonnais* (1884) 12 QBD 589 at 596–597, 600, CA;
   Re Missouri SS Co (1889) 42 ChD 321 at 326, 338, CA; *Gibbs & Sons v Société Industrielle et Commerciale
   Des Métaux* (1890) 25 QBD 399, CA; *Chatenay v Brazilian Submarine Telegraph Co Ltd* [1891] 1 QB 79 at
   82, CA; *British South Africa Co v De Beers Consolidated Mines Ltd* [1910] 1 Ch 354 at 381; on appeal [1910]
   2 Ch 502 at 513, 515, CA; revsd on another point sub nom *De Beers Consolidated Mines Ltd v British South
   Africa Co* [1912] AC 52, HL; *The St Joseph* [1933] P 119; *Kahler v Midland Bank Ltd* [1950] AC 24, [1949]
   2 All ER 621, HL; *Zivnostenska Banka National Corpn v Frankman* [1950] AC 57, [1949] 2 All ER 671,
   HL; *Keiner v Keiner* [1952] 1 All ER 643; *Atlantic Underwriting Agencies Ltd v Compagnia Di Assicurazione
   di Milano SpA* [1979] 2 Lloyd's Rep 240; *Monterosso Shipping Co Ltd v International Transport Workers'
   Federation* [1982] 3 All ER 841, [1982] 2 Lloyd's Rep 120, CA. See also *Brinkibon Ltd v Stahag Stahl und
   Stahlwarenhandelsgesellschaft mbH* [1983] 2 AC 34, [1982] 1 All ER 293, HL.
7 *Lloyd v Guibert* (1865) LR 1 QB 115 at 122; *Rouquette v Overmann and Schou* (1875) LR 10 QB 525;
   Norden SS Co v Dempsey (1876) 1 CPD 654; *Jacobs v Crédit Lyonnais* (1884) 12 QBD 589 at 600, 602, CA;
   Re Missouri SS Co (1889) 42 ChD 321 at 341, CA; *Gibbs & Sons v Société Industrielle et Commerciale des
   Métaux* (1890) 25 QBD 399, CA; *Chatenay v Brazilian Submarine Telegraph Co Ltd* [1891] 1 QB 79 at
   82–83, CA; *Hamlyn & Co v Talisker Distillery* [1894] AC 202 at 207–208, HL; *Hansen v Dixon* (1906) 96
   LT 32; *Re Francke and Rasch* [1918] 1 Ch 470; *Ralli Bros v Compania Naviera Sota y Aznar* [1920] 1 KB 614
   at 630–631; affd [1920] 2 KB 287, CA; *Benaim & Co v Debono* [1924] AC 514 at 520, PC; *Adelaide Electric
   Supply Co Ltd v Prudential Assurance Co Ltd* [1934] AC 122 at 145, 151, HL; *Kremezi v Ridgway* [1949] 1
   All ER 662; *Keiner v Keiner* [1952] 1 All ER 643 at 644; *The Assunzione* [1954] P 150, [1954] 1 All ER
   278, CA; but see *Sayers v International Drilling Co NV* [1971] 3 All ER 163 at 171, [1971] 1 WLR 1176 at
   1187, CA.
8 *Jacobs v Crédit Lyonnais* (1884) 12 QBD 589, CA.
9 *Re Anglo-Austrian Bank* [1920] 1 Ch 69.
10 *British South Africa Co v De Beers Consolidated Mines Ltd* [1910] 1 Ch 354 at 383; affd [1910] 2 Ch 502,
   CA; but revsd on another point sub nom *De Beers Consolidated Mines Ltd v British South Africa Co* [1912]
   AC 52, HL.
11 *Re United Railways of the Havana and Regla Warehouses Ltd* [1960] Ch 52 at 91, [1959] 1 All ER 214 at 233,
   CA; affd sub nom *Tomkinson v First Pennsylvania Banking and Trust Co* [1961] AC 1007, [1960] 2 All ER
   332, HL.

864. Presumptions. There is authority in support of the view that the proper law of
a contract may be determined with the aid of presumptions[1] such as those in favour of
the law of the place of contracting[2], the law of the place of performance[3], the law of the
ship's flag in the case of contracts concerned with sea transport[4], or the law of the place
where the land is situated in contracts relating to immovables[5]; but there is more
modern authority to the effect that the relevant factors should be weighed without
reliance upon specific presumptions[6]. Despite the absence of presumptions, the law of
the place of performance is likely to be regarded as the proper law, that is the system of
law with which the contract is most closely connected, if the contract is made in one
country but is wholly to be performed by both parties in another[7]. Where performance
is to be made in more than one country, the significance of the place of performance
will be far less[8].

1 *R v International Trustee for the Protection of Bondholders AG* [1937] AC 500 at 529, [1937] 2 All ER 164 at
   166, HL; *Mount Albert Borough Council v Australasian Temperance and General Mutual Life Assurance Society
   Ltd* [1938] AC 224 at 240, [1937] 4 All ER 206 at 214, PC.

2 See para 863 note 6 ante.
3 See para 863 note 7 ante.
4 *Lloyd v Guibert* (1865) LR 1 QB 115; *The Karnak* (1869) LR 2 PC 505; *The Gaetano and Maria* (1882) 7 PD 137, CA; *The Stettin* (1889) 14 PD 142; *The August* [1891] P 328 (contracts made by masters during the voyage). The presumption was rarely effective in the case of contracts made before the voyage began: *Chartered Mercantile Bank of India, London and China v Netherlands India Steam Navigation Co Ltd* (1883) 10 QBD 521, CA; *The Industrie* [1894] P 58, CA; *The Adriatic* [1931] P 241; *The Njegos* [1936] P 90; *The Assunzione* [1954] P 150, [1954] 1 All ER 278, CA, although see at 189 and 297; *Coast Lines Ltd v Hudig and Veder Chartering NV* [1972] 2 QB 34 at 47–48, [1972] 1 All ER 451 at 458, CA. See also *The Patria* (1871) LR 3 A & E 436; *The San Roman* (1872) LR 3 A & E 583.
5 *Bank of Africa Ltd v Cohen* [1909] 2 Ch 129, CA (capacity); cf *Re Smith, Lawrence v Kitson* [1916] 2 Ch 206 (formalities); *Campbell v Dent* (1838) 2 Moo PCC 292; *Cood v Cood* (1863) 33 LJCh 273; *British South Africa Co v De Beers Consolidated Mines Ltd* [1910] 2 Ch 502, CA; revsd on other grounds sub nom *De Beers Consolidated Mines Ltd v British South Africa Co* [1912] AC 52, HL (essential validity).
6 *The Assunzione* [1954] P 150 at 176, [1954] 1 All ER 278 at 290, CA; *Coast Lines Ltd v Hudig and Veder Chartering NV* [1972] 2 QB 34 at 44, 47–48, 50, [1972] 1 All ER 451 at 455, 458, 461, CA; and see *Jacobs v Crédit Lyonnais* (1884) 12 QBD 589 at 601, CA; *Zivnostenska Banka National Corpn v Frankman* [1950] AC 57 at 85–86, [1949] 2 All ER 671 at 684, HL.
7 *Lloyd v Guibert* (1865) LR 1 QB 115 at 122–123; *The Assunzione* [1954] P 150 at 178, 184, [1954] 1 All ER 278 at 291, 294, CA; although even then it is not conclusive: *Zivnostenska Banka National Corpn v Frankman* [1950] AC 57 at 85–86, [1949] 2 All ER 671 at 684, HL.
8 *Jacobs v Crédit Lyonnais* (1884) 12 QBD 589, CA; *A V Pound & Co Ltd v M W Hardy & Co Inc* [1956] AC 588, [1956] 1 All ER 639, HL. Indeed it may be difficult to determine what is the place of performance: *Mauroux v Sociedade Commercial Abel Pereira da Fonseca SARL* [1972] 2 All ER 1085, [1972] 1 WLR 962.

865. System of law. The proposition that the proper law of the contract is the system of law with which the transaction has the closest and most real connection raises the distinction between the country and the system of law[1]. Despite earlier references to the country with which the transaction had to be connected[2], it seems now agreed that the connection should rather be with a 'system of law'[3], although it has been suggested that the two tests should be combined[4]. The connection with the country or system of law should be that of the transaction contemplated by the contract (that is, what is to be done under the contract), rather than of the technical forms of the contract itself[5].

1 See para 863 ante.
2 *Tomkinson v First Pennsylvania Banking and Trust Co* [1961] AC 1007 at 1068, [1960] 2 All ER 332 at 356, HL; *Philipson-Stow v IRC* [1961] AC 727 at 760, [1960] 3 All ER 814 at 830, HL; and see *Boissevain v Weil* [1949] 1 KB 482 at 490, [1949] 1 All ER 146 at 153, CA; affd [1950] AC 327, [1950] 1 All ER 728, HL; but see *Whitworth Street Estates (Manchester) Ltd v James Miller & Partners Ltd* [1969] 2 All ER 210 at 212, [1969] 1 WLR 377 at 380, CA; revsd sub nom *James Miller & Partners Ltd v Whitworth Street Estates (Manchester) Ltd* [1970] AC 583, [1970] 1 All ER 796, HL.
3 *Bonython v Commonwealth of Australia* [1951] AC 201 at 219, PC; *Tomkinson v First Pennsylvania Banking and Trust Co* [1961] AC 1007 at 1081, [1960] 2 All ER 332 at 364, HL; *Rossano v Manufacturers' Life Insurance Co* [1963] 2 QB 352 at 361, 368–369, [1962] 2 All ER 214 at 218, 223–224; *Tzortzis v Monark Line AB* [1968] 1 All ER 949 at 953, 954, [1968] 1 WLR 406 at 412, 414, CA; *Whitworth Street Estates (Manchester) Ltd v James Miller & Partners Ltd* [1969] 2 All ER 210 at 212, [1969] 1 WLR 377 at 380, CA; revsd sub nom *James Miller & Partners Ltd v Whitworth Street Estates (Manchester) Ltd* [1970] AC 583, [1970] 1 All ER 796, HL; *Compagnie D'Armement Maritime SA v Compagnie Tunisienne de Navigation SA* [1971] AC 572 at 603, [1970] 3 All ER 71 at 91, HL; *Sayers v International Drilling Co NV* [1971] 3 All ER 163 at 166, 168, 170 [1971] 1 WLR 1176 at 1180–1181, 1183, 1185, CA; *Coast Lines Ltd v Hudig and Veder Chartering NV* [1972] 2 QB 34 at 44, 46, [1972] 1 All ER 451 at 455, 457, CA; *Mauroux v Sociedade Commercial Abel Pereira Da Fonseca SARL* [1972] 2 All ER 1085 at 1088–1089, [1972] 1 WLR 962 at 966.
4 *James Miller & Partners Ltd v Whitworth Street Estates (Manchester) Ltd* [1970] AC 583 at 603–606, 614–615, [1970] 1 All ER 796 at 799–801, 808, HL; *Compagnie D'Armement Maritime SA v Compagnie Tunisienne de Navigation SA* [1971] AC 572 at 583, [1970] 3 All ER 71 at 74, HL; *Coast Lines Ltd v Hudig and Veder Chartering NV* [1972] 2 QB 34 at 50, [1972] 1 All ER 451 at 460–461, CA.
5 *Coast Lines Ltd v Hudig and Veder Chartering NV* [1972] 2 QB 34 at 46, [1972] 1 All ER 451 at 457–458, CA.

866. Time. The intention of the parties to a contract or the connection of the transaction with a country or system of law must be determined as at the time when the contract was made[1]. The subsequent conduct of the parties cannot be used as an aid to the interpretation of the contract[2] unless the parties have agreed to vary the original contract or have entered into a new contract collateral to it[3], or their later conduct amounts to an estoppel[4].

1 Nevertheless, effect will be given to later changes in the proper law as thus determined: *Rossano v Manufacturers' Life Insurance Co* [1963] 2 QB 352 at 362, [1962] 2 All ER 214 at 219; and see para 870 post.
2 *James Miller & Partners Ltd v Whitworth Street Estates (Manchester) Ltd* [1970] AC 583 at 603, 606, 611, 614–615, [1970] 1 All ER 796 at 798, 801, 805, 808, HL; *Compagnie D'Armement Maritime SA v Compagnie Tunisienne de Navigation SA* [1971] AC 572 at 593, 602–603, [1970] 3 All ER 71 at 82, 90, HL.
3 *James Miller & Partners Ltd v Whitworth Street Estates (Manchester) Ltd* [1970] AC 583 at 603, 614–615, [1970] 1 All ER 796 at 798, 808, HL; *Compagnie D'Armement Maritime SA v Compagnie Tunisienne de Navigation SA* [1971] AC 572 at 602–603, [1970] 3 All ER 71 at 90, HL.
4 *James Miller & Partners Ltd v Whitworth Street Estates (Manchester) Ltd* [1970] AC 583 at 611, 614–615, [1970] 1 All ER 796 at 805, 808, HL.

867. Determination of the proper law by statute. If a statute provides a general choice of law clause, then that must be applied as determining the proper law[1], as in the Bills of Exchange Act 1882[2] and the Uniform Laws on International Sales Act 1967[3], which expressly exclude the rules of the conflict of laws in relation to certain contractual issues. Other statutes limit the scope of their own application and provide choice of law rules for contractual issues covered by them, but leave unaffected the determination of the proper law in relation to issues outside the ambit of the statute. Thus, for example, the Carriage of Goods by Sea Act 1971 incorporates the Hague-Visby Rules into all contracts for the shipment of goods from a United Kingdom port, whatever may be the proper law of the contract, but the parties are free to determine what law is to govern all other contractual issues[4]. The Unfair Contract Terms Act 1977 provides that in prescribed circumstances its mandatory provisions may not be avoided by a choice of law clause[5].

1 *The Tagus* [1903] P 44 at 51.
2 See the Bills of Exchange Act 1882 s 72 (as amended); and BILLS OF EXCHANGE vol 4(1) (Reissue) para 489.
3 See the Uniform Laws on International Sales Act 1967 ss 1 (as amended), 2, Sch 1 art 2, Sch 2; and SALE OF GOODS vol 41 para 962.
4 See the Carriage of Goods by Sea Act 1971 s 1 (as amended); as to that Act, and the Hague-Visby Rules, see SHIPPING. See also *The Hollandia* [1983] 1 AC 565, [1982] 3 All ER 1141, HL. See, however, *Hellenic Steel Co v Svolamar Shipping Co Ltd, The Komninos S* [1991] 1 Lloyd's Rep 370, CA, where it was held that a contractual term referring disputes to the British courts did not extend the United Kingdom legislation giving effect to the Hague-Visby Rules to govern a contract which was not subject to the Rules.
5 See the Unfair Contract Terms Act 1977 s 27(2); and para 860 ante.

(ii) Scope of the Proper Law

868. Splitting of the contract. Whilst most contractual issues are governed by the proper law[1], the parties may agree that different contractual issues may be governed by different laws[2]. There is no authority against the courts' deciding that the objectively ascertained proper law is to vary according to the contractual issue involved[3]. However, the courts will not so decide readily or without good reason[4].

Apart from express or implied agreement to the contrary[5], the obligations of both parties to the contract will be governed by the same proper law[6].

1 See paras 871–889 post.
2 *Hamlyn & Co v Talisker Distillery* [1894] AC 202, HL; and see *Forsikringsaktieselskapet Vesta v Butcher* [1989] AC 852, [1989] 1 All ER 402, HL.
3 *Re Helbert Wagg & Co Ltd's Claim* [1956] Ch 323 at 340, [1956] 1 All ER 129 at 135; *Re United Railways of the Havana and Regla Warehouses Ltd* [1960] Ch 52 at 92, [1959] 1 All ER 214 at 234, CA; affd sub nom *Tomkinson v First Pennsylvania Banking and Trust Co* [1961] AC 1007, [1960] 2 All ER 332, HL.
4 *Kahler v Midland Bank Ltd* [1950] AC 24 at 42, [1949] 2 All ER 621 at 633, HL; but see *Chamberlain v Napier* (1880) 15 ChD 614; *British South Africa Co v De Beers Consolidated Mines Ltd* [1910] 1 Ch 354 at 383; revsd on another point [1912] AC 52, HL; *Sayers v International Drilling Co NV* [1971] 3 All ER 163 at 166–167, [1971] 1 WLR 1176 at 1180–1181, CA. The Uniform Laws on International Sales Act 1967 permits the parties to choose a law to govern some aspects of a contract different from that which will govern the remaining aspects: see para 867 ante; and SALE OF GOODS.
5 *Re Helbert Wagg & Co Ltd's Claim* [1956] Ch 323 at 340, [1956] 1 All ER 129 at 135.
6 *Zivnostenska Banka National Corpn v Frankman* [1950] AC 57 at 83, [1949] 2 All ER 671 at 683, HL; *Montreal Trust Co v Stanrock Uranium Mines Ltd* [1966] 1 OR 258 at 267–268, 270, 53 DLR (2d) 594 at 603, 606, Ont HC.

869. Renvoi. The proper law of the contract means the domestic rules of that legal system and not its rules of the conflict of laws. The doctrine of renvoi[1] has no place in the law of contract[2].

1 See paras 606–609 ante.
2 *Re United Railways of the Havana and Regla Warehouses Ltd* [1960] Ch 52 at 96–97, 115, [1959] 1 All ER 214 at 236, 246, CA; affd sub nom *Tomkinson v First Pennsylvania Banking and Trust Co* [1961] AC 1007, [1960] 2 All ER 332, HL; *Rosencrantz v Union Contractors Ltd and Thornton* (1960) 31 WWR 597 at 602, 23 DLR (2d) 473 at 478, BC SC; not following *Vita Food Products Inc v Unus Shipping Co Ltd* [1939] AC 277 at 292, [1939] 1 All ER 513 at 522, PC; *Amin Rasheed Shipping Corpn v Kuwait Insurance Co, The Al Wahab* [1984] AC 50 at 61–62, [1983] 2 All ER 884 at 888, HL, per Lord Diplock.

870. Incorporation by reference. Express selection of the proper law of the contract, which will generally govern the contract as a whole[1], must be distinguished from the incorporation into the contract of specific provisions of a foreign legal system to govern some particular issue[2], such as the obligation to make a ship seaworthy[3], the validity of an exemption clause[4] or even the validity of a choice of law clause[5].

The importance of the distinction between selection of the proper law and incorporation of a provision of foreign law into a contract by reference is most apparent where there is a change in foreign law between the date of the contract and of the proceedings. The proper law is normally that in force in the country in question from time to time, and effect will be given to any changes in that law before performance of the contract falls due[6], as where the requirement of legal tender is varied[7], or a debtor's obligations are varied by a moratorium[8], or there are changes in exchange control legislation[9], or where a gold value clause[10] or a contract of life insurance[11] is declared void retrospectively, or even where the sovereignty of a country changes[12]. However, where the provisions of a foreign law are incorporated they constitute terms of the contract as at the date of incorporation and are unaffected by subsequent changes, as where a statute, whose terms have been incorporated into a contract, has been repealed or amended[13].

1 But see para 868 ante.
2 *Re Suse and Sibeth, ex p Dever* (1887) 18 QBD 660, CA; *G E Dobell & Co v Rossmore SS Co Ltd* [1895] 2 QB 408, CA.
3 *G E Dobell & Co v Rossmore SS Co Ltd* [1895] 2 QB 408, CA; *Adamastos Shipping Co Ltd v Anglo-Saxon Petroleum Co Ltd* [1959] AC 133, [1958] 1 All ER 725, HL.
4 *Stafford Allen & Sons Ltd v Pacific Steam Navigation Co* [1956] 2 All ER 716, [1956] 1 WLR 629, CA.

5　*Ocean SS Co Ltd v Queensland State Wheat Board* [1941] 1 KB 402, [1941] 1 All ER 158, CA.
6　*Re Chesterman's Trusts, Mott v Browning* [1923] 2 Ch 466 at 478, CA; *Kahler v Midland Bank Ltd* [1950] AC 24 at 56, [1949] 2 All ER 621 at 641–642, HL; *Jabbour v Custodian of Israeli Absentee Property* [1954] 1 All ER 145 at 157, [1954] 1 WLR 139 at 157; *Re Helbert Wagg & Co Ltd's Claim* [1956] Ch 323 at 341–342, [1956] 1 All ER 129 at 135–136; *Rossano v Manufacturers' Life Insurance Co* [1963] 2 QB 352 at 362, [1962] 2 All ER 214 at 219.
7　*Re Chesterman's Trusts, Mott v Browning* [1923] 2 Ch 466, CA.
8　*Re Helbert Wagg & Co Ltd's Claim* [1956] Ch 323, [1956] 1 All ER 129.
9　*De Beéche v South American Stores Ltd and Chilian Stores Ltd* [1935] AC 148, HL; *Kahler v Midland Bank Ltd* [1950] AC 24, [1949] 2 All ER 621, HL; *Zivnostenska Banka National Corpn v Frankman* [1950] AC 57; [1949] 2 All ER 671, HL.
10　*R v International Trustee for the Protection of Bondholders AG* [1937] AC 500, [1937] 2 All ER 164, HL.
11　*Perry v Equitable Life Assurance Society of the United States of America* (1929) 45 TLR 468.
12　*Jabbour v Custodian of Israeli Absentee Property* [1954] 1 All ER 145, [1954] 1 WLR 139; and see *Banco de Bilbao v Sancha* [1938] 2 KB 176 at 195, [1938] 2 All ER 253 at 260, CA.
13　*Vita Food Products Inc v Unus Shipping Co Ltd* [1939] AC 277 at 286, [1939] 1 All ER 513 at 518–519, PC.

(iii) Formation of the Contract

871. Agreement between the parties. The question whether there has been agreement between the parties should be referred to the proper law of the contract[1]. This must be construed as the 'putative proper law', that is, what would be the proper law if the contract were validly created[2].

1　*Albeko Schuhmaschinen AG v Kamborian Shoe Machine Co Ltd* (1961) 111 L Jo 519; *Compania Naviera Micro SA v Shipley International Inc, The Parouth* [1982] 2 Lloyd's Rep 351, CA.
2　*Mackender v Feldia AG* [1967] 2 QB 590 at 602–603, [1966] 3 All ER 847 at 852–853, CA; Dicey and Morris *The Conflict of Laws* (11th Edn, 1987) 1199–1201. The Uniform Laws on International Sales Act 1967 permits the parties to select the law to govern the formation of a contract for sale of goods; see s 1 (as amended), Sch 1 art 4; and SALE OF GOODS.

872. Consideration. Although consideration is necessary for the creation of a valid contract under English law, the validity of a foreign contract may be upheld despite the absence of consideration[1]. Whether consideration is necessary should be determined by the putative proper law of the contract[2].

1　*Re Bonacina, Le Brasseur v Bonacina* [1912] 2 Ch 394, CA.
2　*Re Bonacina, Le Brasseur v Bonacina* [1912] 2 Ch 394 at 403–404, CA. As to the putative proper law see para 871 text and note 2 ante.

873. Privity of contract. The question whether a contract may confer rights or impose obligations on a third person who is not a party to it is to be determined by the proper law of the contract[1].

1　*Scott v Pilkington* (1862) 2 B & S 11; cf *Hartmann v Konig* (1933) 50 TLR 114, HL. The related issue of assignment of contractual rights is considered in para 935 post.

874. Reality of agreement. It appears that issues such as the effect of mistake, misrepresentation or duress should be referred to the proper law of the contract[1]. Where the effect of the vitiating factor may be to render the contract void, as in the case of a plea of non est factum[2], reference must be made to the putative proper law[3]; but if the contract would only be voidable, as with misrepresentation[4], non-disclosure under a contract of insurance[5] or duress, reference may be made to an expressly chosen proper law.

1   See *Mackender v Feldia AG* [1967] 2 QB 590, [1966] 3 All ER 847, CA.
2   As to the plea of non est factum see CONTRACT vol 9 para 284.
3   *Mackender v Feldia AG* [1967] 2 QB 590 at 598, [1966] 3 All ER 847 at 849–850, CA; and see *Compania Naviera Micro SA v Shipley International Inc, The Parouth* [1982] 2 Lloyd's Rep 351, CA. As to the putative proper law see para 871 text and note 2 ante.
4   See *British Controlled Oilfields Ltd v Stagg* (1921) 127 LT 209.
5   *Mackender v Feldia AG* [1967] 2 QB 590, [1966] 3 All ER 847, CA.

875. Capacity. The capacity of an individual[1] to enter into a contract is governed by the law of the country with which the contract is most closely connected or by the law of his domicile (or residence). If he has contractual capacity by either of those laws, the contract will be valid in point of capacity. If he does not have contractual capacity by either of these laws, the contract will not be valid and enforceable[2].

1   Note that the Rome Convention does not apply to 'questions involving the status or legal capacity of natural persons, without prejudice to art 11 (see para 853 ante): art 1(2)(a). For the meaning of 'the Rome Convention' see para 844 text and note 1 ante.
2   See Dicey and Morris *The Conflict of Laws* (11th Edn, 1987) 1202. This general rule does not refer to the 'proper law of the contract', which might otherwise have been expected, because it is believed that the parties are not competent to make an express choice of proper law and by so doing confer upon themselves a contractual capacity which they would not otherwise (that is, if the contract had been subject to the law with which it was most closely connected) have had. Hence a modified form of proper law will govern the question. However, there is little direct authority on the point at common law, and the proposition set out in the text is based primarily on principle (though see *Charron v Montreal Trust Co* [1958] OR 597, 15 DLR (2d) 240, Ont CA). Cases such as *Cooper v Cooper* (1888) 13 App Cas 88, HL, which hold that a lack of capacity to enter into a matrimonial settlement according to the law of the domicile is fatal to the validity of the contract without regard to its proper law are probably to be confined to matrimonial contracts, and treated as inapplicable to commercial contracts. Other dicta supporting the law of the domicile as the governing law (such as in *Sottomayor v De Barros* (1877) 3 PD 1 at 5, CA; (criticised in *Sottomayer v De Barros* (1879) 5 PD 94 at 100); *Re Cooke's Trusts* (1887) 56 LJCh 637 at 639; and *Guépratte v Young* (1851) 4 De G & Sm 217; *Stephens v M'Farland* (1845) 81 Eq R 444), are also to be confined to cases of matrimonial capacity.
    In the case of contracts relating to land, the law of the place where the land is situated is most likely to be the proper law of the contract, so that the law to govern capacity to enter into such a contract is almost certain to be the law of that place: *Bank of Africa Ltd v Cohen* [1909] 2 Ch 129, CA.

876. Formalities. A commercial contract is formally valid if it complies with the formal requirements of the law of the place of contracting[1]. Older authorities indicated that compliance with such formal requirements was mandatory[2]; but although there is no direct English authority on the point it is now generally agreed that compliance with the formal requirements of the proper law of the contract will suffice[3]. A contract which does not comply with the formal requirements of one or other of those laws is invalid in England.

In the case of an agreement for the sale of land, although the conveyance must comply with the formal requirements of the law of the place where the land is situated[4], the contract should be regarded as formally valid if it complies with the formal requirements of either the law of the place of contracting or the proper law[5].

A contract made abroad which conforms in every way to the formal requirements of the law of the place of contracting or the proper law of the contract may nevertheless not be enforceable in England and Wales if the English rules of procedure imperatively require the obligation to be proved in some particular way[6].

1 Ie on the basis of the maxim *locus regit actum* (the place governs the act); see *Guépratte v Young* (1851) 4 De G & Sm 217; but see para 875 note 2 ante.

2 *Trimbey v Vignier* (1834) 1 Bing NC 151 (indorsement of a negotiable instrument); *Alves v Hodgson* (1797) 7 Term Rep 241; *Clegg v Levy* (1812) 3 Camp 166; *Bristow v Sequeville* (1850) 5 Exch 275 (contracts void for lack of stamps required by the law of the place of contracting).

3 *Van Grutten v Digby* (1862) 31 Beav 561; *Re Bankes, Reynolds v Ellis* [1902] 2 Ch 333 (both marriage settlement cases); and see *Valery v Scott* (1876) 3 R 965, Ct of Sess; *Sharn Importing Ltd v Babchuk* [1971] 4 WWR 517, 21 DLR (3d) 349, BC SC; Dicey and Morris *The Conflict of Laws* (11th Edn, 1987) 1208–1209.

4 *Adams v Clutterbuck* (1883) 10 QBD 403.

5 *British Controlled Oilfields v Stagg* (1921) 127 LT 209; and see *Anthony v Popowich* [1949] 4 DLR 640, Man KB.

6 This is so in the cases of the Statutes of Frauds (1677) s 4 (as amended) which are binding by the lex fori: *Leroux v Brown* (1852) 12 CB 801 (valid French contract unenforceable in England owing to absence of note or memorandum required by the Statute of Frauds (1677)); and see *Britain v Rossiter* (1879) 11 QBD 123 at 128, CA; *Rochefoucauld v Boustead* [1897] 1 Ch 196 at 207, CA; *Morris v Baron & Co* [1918] AC 1 at 15, HL; *Nihalchand Navalchand v McMullan* [1934] 1 KB 171 at 176, CA; *Mahadervan v Mahadervan* [1964] P 233 at 241–242, [1962] 3 All ER 1108 at 1114–1115, DC; although cf the criticism of this rule in *Williams v Wheeler* (1860) 8 CBNS 299 at 316; *Gibson v Holland* (1865) LR 1 CP 1 at 8. See para 1072 post.

(iv) Essential Validity of the Contract

877. Essential validity. The essential validity[1] of a contract or any term of it is determined by the proper law of the contract, to which reference will be made on many issues which relate to the effects of the contract, such as: (1) the validity of an arbitration clause[2] or of an exemption or limitation clause[3]; (2) whether a defendant has a good excuse for non-performance of a contract[4]; (3) whether an agent has exceeded his authority[5]; (4) whether a carrier is liable for the loss of[6] or injury to[7] the goods carried or for delay in their delivery[8]; (5) whether the master of a ship is justified in selling the cargo at a port of distress[9]; and (6) whether a stipulation in a contract for a mortgage is void as being a clog on the equity of redemption[10].

1 Although illegality may be regarded as a question of essential validity, it is considered separately as it raises issues necessitating reference to legal systems other than the proper law: see paras 879–882 post.

2 *Hamlyn & Co v Talisker Distillery* [1894] AC 202, HL; *Spurrier v La Cloche* [1902] AC 446, PC.

3 *Peninsular and Oriental Steam Navigation Co v Shand* (1865) 3 Moo PCCNS 272; *Re Missouri SS Co* (1889) 42 ChD 321, CA; *Jones v Oceanic Steam Navigation Co Ltd* [1924] 2 KB 730; *Sayers v International Drilling Co NV* [1971] 3 All ER 163, [1971] 1 WLR 1176, CA. It was suggested by Lord Denning MR at 166–167, and at 1181, that where a contractual exemption clause exempts a party from liability in tort, the applicable law is the proper law of that issue, ie the law with which that particular issue has the closest connection, rather than the proper law of the contract (or tort) as a whole: see para 894 text and notes 19–23 post; and see *Coast Lines Ltd v Hudig and Veder Chartering NV* [1972] 2 QB 34, [1972] 1 All ER 451, CA; *Brodin v AR Seljan* 1973 SLT 198. As to the validity of exemption and limitation clauses see the Unfair Contract Terms Act 1977; and CONTRACT.

4 *Jacobs v Crédit Lyonnais* (1884) 12 QBD 589, CA.

5 *Mildred, Goyeneche & Co v Maspons y Hermano* (1883) 8 App Cas 874, HL; *Chatenay v Brazilian Submarine Telegraph Co Ltd* [1891] 1 QB 79, CA.

6 *Peninsular and Oriental Steam Navigation Co v Shand* (1865) 3 Moo PCCNS 272.

7 *De Cleremont & Co v Brasch & Co* (1885) 1 TLR 370, DC.

8 *The San Roman* (1872) LR 3 A & E 583.

9 *The August* [1891] P 328; *The Industrie* [1894] P 58, CA.

10 *British South Africa Co v De Beers Consolidated Mines Ltd* [1910] 2 Ch 502, CA; revsd on other grounds sub nom *De Beers Consolidated Mines Ltd v British South Africa Co* [1912] AC 52, HL.

878. Performance. Performance of the contract is a matter of substance to be governed by its proper law[1], and that law governs excuses for non-performance[2]. The substance of the obligation to perform the contract must be distinguished from the less important issues of the mode and manner of performance, which are governed by the law of the place of performance[3]. That law governs matters such as whether days of grace are allowed for the payment of a debt[4], or the date at which lay days begin to run[5], the hours during which delivery may be tendered (such as the meaning of 'usual business hours')[6], the time at which a ship may commence unloading its cargo[7], or whether an export licence is required[8].

In contracts involving monetary obligations the distinction between the substance of the obligation and the mode or manner of performance is seen from the fact that the law of the place of performance determines the currency in which a debt may be discharged[9], that is the money of payment, but the proper law will decide the money of account[10].

1 *Jacobs v Crédit Lyonnais* (1884) 12 QBD 589, CA; *Mount Albert Borough Council v Australasian Temperance and General Mutual Life Assurance Society Ltd* [1938] AC 224, [1937] 4 All ER 206, PC; *Bonython v Commonwealth of Australia* [1951] AC 201, PC. These last two cases reject the earlier suggestions that issues of the substance of performance should be referred to the law of the place of performance: *Chatenay v Brazilian Submarine Telegraph Co Ltd* [1891] 1 QB 79 at 83, CA; *Adelaide Electric Supply Co Ltd v Prudential Assurance Co Ltd* [1934] AC 122 at 151, HL; *M W Hardy & Co Inc v A V Pound & Co Ltd* [1955] 1 QB 499 at 512, [1955] 1 All ER 666 at 674, CA; affd sub nom *A V Pound & Co Ltd v M W Hardy & Co Inc* [1956] AC 588, [1956] 1 All ER 639, HL.
2 *Jacobs v Crédit Lyonnais* (1884) 12 QBD 589, CA; and see *Rouquette v Overmann and Schou* (1875) LR 10 QB 525.
3 *Jacobs v Crédit Lyonnais* (1884) 12 QBD 589 at 601, CA; *Auckland Corpn v Alliance Assurance Co Ltd* [1937] AC 587 at 606, [1937] 1 All ER 645 at 655–656, PC; *Mount Albert Borough Council v Australasian Temperance and General Mutual Life Assurance Society Ltd* [1938] AC 224 at 240, [1937] 4 All ER 206 at 214, PC; and see *Sharif v Azad* [1967] 1 QB 605 at 617, [1966] 3 All ER 785 at 789, CA.
4 *Rouquette v Overmann and Schou* (1875) LR 10 QB 525 at 535–536.
5 *Norden SS Co v Dempsey* (1876) 1 CPD 654, DC.
6 See Dicey and Morris *The Conflict of Laws* (11th Edn, 1987) 1237.
7 *Robertson v Jackson* (1845) 2 CB 412.
8 *A V Pound & Co Ltd v M W Hardy & Co Inc* [1956] AC 588, [1956] 1 All ER 639, HL. It is a question of substance, for the proper law, as to whether there is a contractual obligation to obtain such a licence: *A V Pound & Co Ltd v M W Hardy & Co Inc* supra.
9 *Auckland Corpn v Alliance Assurance Co Ltd* [1937] AC 587, [1937] 1 All ER 645, PC; *Mount Albert Borough Council v Australasian Temperance and General Mutual Life Assurance Society Ltd* [1938] AC 224 at 240–241, [1937] 4 All ER 206 at 215, PC.
10 The money of account is not, automatically, the currency of the country of the proper law: *The Alexandra I* [1971] 2 Lloyd's Rep 469 at 474; affd [1972] 1 Lloyd's Rep 399, CA. See also *Bonython v Commonwealth of Australia* [1951] AC 201, PC; cf *De Bueger v J Ballantyne & Co Ltd* [1938] AC 452, [1938] 1 All ER 701, PC; *W J Alan & Co Ltd v El Nasr Export and Import Co* [1972] 2 QB 189, [1972] 2 All ER 127, CA.

(v) Illegality of the Contract

879. Illegality by the proper law. A contract which by its proper law is void for illegality will not be enforced in England[1], even if the illegality is based on the revenue laws of the country of the proper law[2], and even though the contract might be valid under the law of the place of contracting[3].

1 *Heriz v Riera* (1840) 11 Sim 318; *De Beéche v South American Stores Ltd and Chilian Stores Ltd* [1935] AC 148, HL; *Kahler v Midland Bank Ltd* [1950] AC 24, [1949] 2 All ER 621, HL; *Zivnostenska Banka National Corpn v Frankman* [1950] AC 57, [1949] 2 All ER 671, HL; *Mackender v Feldia AG* [1967] 2 QB 590 at 601, [1966] 3 All ER 847 at 851, CA.
2 *Peter Buchanan Ltd and Macharg v McVey* [1955] AC 516n, [1954] IR 89. As to the general rule that the English court will not enforce a foreign revenue law see para 613 ante.
3 See *Royal Exchange Assurance Corpn v Sjoforsakrings Akt Vega* [1902] 2 KB 384 at 393–394, CA.

880. Illegality by the law of the place of contracting. It was suggested that a contract which is illegal by the law of the place of contracting is not enforceable in England[1]. Although there is no clear judicial authority on this issue, the better view appears to be that illegality by the law of the place of contracting does not render a contract unenforceable in England[2] because the place of contracting may be uncertain or fortuitous.

1   *Re Missouri SS Co* (1889) 42 ChD 321 at 336, CA; *The Torni* [1932] P 78 at 88, 91–92, CA; and see *Robinson v Bland* (1760) 1 Wm Bl 256 at 258–259; *Pattison v Mills* (1828) 1 Dow & Cl 342, HL; *Quarrier v Colston* (1842) 1 Ph 147; *Branley v South Eastern Rly Co* (1862) 12 CBNS 63 at 72; *Saxby v Fulton* [1909] 2 KB 208, CA.
2   *Vita Food Products Inc v Unus Shipping Co Ltd* [1939] AC 277 at 297–298, [1939] 1 All ER 513 at 525–526, PC; and see *Jones v Oceanic Steam Navigation Co Ltd* [1924] 2 KB 730; Dicey and Morris *The Conflict of Laws* (11th Edn, 1987) 1214–1215.

881. Illegality by the law of the place of performance. There is considerable authority in support of the proposition that a contract illegal by the law of the country where it is to be performed (the *lex loci solutionis*) will not be enforced in England[1]. However, it is not clear whether this alleged rule is applicable when English law is not the proper law of the contract, and does not admit the illegality under the law of the place of performance as an excuse for non performance, or a cause of the discharge of the contract[2]. In all the relevant cases either the contract was unenforceable because it offended against the public policy of English law[3], the lex fori, or the proper law of the contract was English law and the contract was invalidated by a rule of English domestic law[4].

The validity or enforceability of an English contract will not be affected if the law of the place of performance gives either or both of the parties an excuse for non-performance without rendering the contract illegal[5].

Whilst the effect of illegality under the law of the place of performance may be uncertain, there is no doubt that a contract is enforceable in England despite any illegality by the law of the country in which a party to it is resident or domiciled or of which he is a national, or where he has his place of business, provided the law of that country is not the proper law or the law of the place of performance[6].

Although some old authorities support the view that a contract made in England to do an act in violation of the revenue laws of the place of performance will be held valid in England[7], it is doubtful whether these now represent the position at common law[8]. The English court may refuse to enforce these contracts under the doctrine of public policy[9].

1   *Ralli Bros v Compania Naviera Sota y Aznar* [1920] 2 KB 287, CA; *Foster v Driscoll* [1929] 1 KB 470 at 520, CA; *De Beéche v South American Stores Ltd and Chilian Stores Ltd* [1935] AC 148 at 156, HL; *R v International Trustee for the Protection of Bondholders A G* [1937] AC 500 at 519, [1936] 3 All ER 407 at 428, CA; *Kleinwort Sons & Co v Ungarische Baumwolle Industrie A G* [1939] 2 KB 678 at 694, 697, 700, [1939] 3 All ER 38 at 42–43, 44–45, 47, CA; *Kahler v Midland Bank Ltd* [1950] AC 24 at 39, [1949] 2 All ER 621 at 631, HL; *Zivnostenska Banka National Corpn v Frankman* [1950] AC 57 [1949] 2 All ER 671, HL; *Mackender v Feldia A G* [1967] 2 QB 590 at 601, [1966] 3 All ER 847 at 851–852, CA; *Lemenda Trading Co Ltd v African Middle East Petroleum Co Ltd* [1988] QB 448, [1988] 1 All ER 513 (where public policy under both English law and the *lex loci solutionis* rendered the contract unenforceable); *Libyan Arab Foreign Bank v Bankers Trust Co* [1989] QB 728, [1989] 3 All ER 252; *Euro-Diam Ltd v Bathurst* [1990] 1 QB 1 at 30, [1988] 2 All ER 23, CA. But where the illegal acts of the plaintiff are committed in

circumstances which will not affront the public conscience, eg to avoid imminent danger to life, the contract may still be enforced against the defendant: *Howard v Shirlstar Container Transport Ltd* [1990] 3 All ER 366, [1990] 1 WLR 1292, CA.

2 See *Kahler v Midland Bank Ltd* [1950] AC 24 at 48, [1949] 2 All ER 621 at 636, HL, where Lord Reid limited the effect of illegality by the law of the place of performance to cases involving acts 'done in performance of an English contract'; and see Dicey and Morris *The Conflict of Laws* (11th Edn, 1987) 1219–1220; cf *Zivnostenska Banka National Corpn v Frankman* [1950] AC 57 at 79, [1949] 2 All ER 671 at 681, HL, where Lord Reid indicated that illegality by the law of the place of performance was fatal 'whatever be the proper law of the contract'.

3 Eg *Foster v Driscoll* [1929] 1 KB 470, CA.

4 Eg *Ralli Bros v Compania Naviera Sota y Aznar* [1920] 2 KB 287, CA; *Prodexport State Co for Foreign Trade v E D and F Man Ltd* [1973] QB 389, [1973] 1 All DR 355.

5 *Jacobs v Crédit Lyonnais* (1884) 12 QBD 589, CA; *Ralli Bros v Compania Naviera Sota y Aznar* [1920] 2 KB 287 at 292, 297, 301, CA; *R v International Trustee for the Protection of Bondholders AG* [1937] AC 500, [1936] 3 All ER 407, CA; revsd on another issue [1937] AC 500 at 528, [1937] 2 All ER 164, HL. The question whether an English contract is frustrated, in the English sense, by events occurring abroad is a matter of English domestic law: *Kursell v Timber Operators and Contractors Ltd* [1927] 1 KB 298, CA. Where neither party under an English contract is able to perform because both are prevented by vis major occurring abroad, neither party can maintain an action against the other: *Ford v Cotesworth* (1870) LR 5 QB 544; *Cunningham v Dunn* (1878) 3 CPD 443, CA.

6 *Kleinwort Sons & Co v Ungarische Baumwolle Industrie AG* [1939] 2 KB 678, [1939] 3 All ER 38, CA; and see *Trinidad Shipping and Trading Co Ltd v Alston & Co* [1920] AC 888, PC; *Kahler v Midland Bank Ltd* [1950] AC 24 at 48, [1949] 2 All ER 621 at 636, HL; *Rossano v Manufacturers' Life Insurance Co* [1963] 2 QB 352 at 371, [1962] 2 All ER 214 at 225; contrast *De Beéche v South American Stores Ltd and Chilian Stores Ltd* [1935] AC 148 at 158, HL.

7 *Holman v Johnson* (1775) 1 Cowp 341; *Boucher v Lawson* (1736) Lee temp Hard 85, 194; *Planché v Fletcher* (1779) 1 Doug KB 251; *Simeon v Bazett* (1813) 2 M & S 94; *Bazett v Meyer* (1814) 5 Taunt 824; *James v Catherwood* (1823) 3 Dow & Ry KB 190; *Sharp v Taylor* (1849) 2 Ph 801.

8 *Ralli Bros v Compania Naviera Sota y Aznar* [1920] 2 KB 287 at 300, CA; *Foster v Driscoll* [1929] 1 KB 470 at 515, CA; *Regazzoni v K C Sethia (1944) Ltd* [1958] AC 301 at 322, [1957] 3 All ER 286 at 292, HL.

9 See paras 611, 613 ante.

882. Illegality by the lex fori: English law. Whatever its proper law, a contract is illegal in England if it is illegal under an English statute having extra-territorial effect, such as exchange control legislation[1] or other revenue laws[2], or if it or any part of it is contrary to English ideas of public policy or morality[3]. An English court will not enforce foreign penal or revenue laws[4], but equally it will not enforce a contract whose object is to violate such penal or revenue laws[5] or exchange control legislation[6]. On the other hand, a contract which is void under its proper law for infringement of foreign exchange control legislation may be upheld as valid in England if that legislation is regarded as discriminatory[7].

A contract which is good by its proper law which would be void, rather than illegal, in England will be enforced in England. Thus a loan advanced for the purpose of gaming in a foreign country where gaming is not illegal may be recovered by action in this country[8]; but an action on a cheque payable in England and given for money so lent will not succeed, as in that case the transaction is governed by English law[9]. The general rule so far as foreign contracts contrary to Acts of Parliament are concerned is that a contract will be upheld unless it can be shown that the statute has extra-territorial effect and is applicable to foreign contracts[10].

1 *Boissevain v Weil* [1950] AC 327, [1950] 1 All ER 728, HL.

2 *Biggs v Lawrence* (1789) 3 Term Rep 454; *Clugas v Penaluna* (1791) 4 Term Rep 466; *Waymell v Reed* (1794) 5 Term Rep 599; *Lightfoot v Tenant* (1796) 1 Bos & P 551.

3 See paras 610–611 ante. See also *Lemenda Trading Co Ltd v African Middle East Petroleum Co Ltd* [1988] QB 448, [1988] 1 All ER 513 (where both English law and the *lex loci solutionis* had a public policy rendering the contract unenforceable).

4 See paras 612–613 ante.
5 *Regazzoni v K C Sethia (1944) Ltd* [1958] AC 301 at 322, 328–329, [1957] 3 All ER 286 at 292, 296–297, HL; *Re Emery's Investments Trusts, Emery v Emery* [1959] Ch 410, [1959] 1 All ER 577; cf *Pye Ltd v B G Transport Service Ltd* [1966] 2 Lloyd's Rep 300.
6 *Kahler v Midland Bank Ltd* [1950] AC 24 at 27, [1949] 2 All ER 621 at 624, HL; *Zivnostenska Banka National Corpn v Frankman* [1950] AC 57 at 72, [1949] 2 All ER 671 at 676, HL; *Re Helbert Wagg & Co Ltd's Claim* [1956] Ch 323 at 349, 351, [1956] 1 All ER 129 at 140, 141–142.
7 *Kahler v Midland Bank Ltd* [1950] AC 24 at 36, [1949] 2 All ER 621 at 629, HL; *Zivnostenska Banka National Corpn v Frankman* [1950] AC 57 at 72, [1949] 2 All ER 671 at 676, HL; *Re Helbert Wagg & Co Ltd's Claim* [1956] Ch 323 at 352, [1956] 1 All ER 129 at 142.
8 *Saxby v Fulton* [1909] 2 KB 208, CA; *Société Anonyme des Grands Etablissements de Touquet Paris-Plage v Baumgart* (1927) 96 LJKB 789; and see *Société des Hôtels Réunis (Société Anonyme) v Hawker* (1913) 29 TLR 578; affd (1914) 30 TLR 423, CA. As to whether a similar loan made in England is recoverable see BETTING vol 4(1) (Reissue) paras 27, 29, 39.
9 *Robinson v Bland* (1760) 1 Wm Bl 234 at 256; *Moulis v Owen* [1907] 1 KB 746, CA. See also BETTING vol 4(1) (Reissue) para 40.
10 See *Santos v Illidge* (1860) 8 CBNS 861, where a foreign contract for the sale of slaves was upheld in England because the statutory prohibition against such contracts (ie the Slave Trade Act 1824 s 2: see CRIMINAL LAW vol 11(1) (Reissue) para 345) did not apply to foreign contracts; but it is submitted that, although the principle stated in the text is correct, nonetheless a contract for the sale of slaves would not now be enforced in England, as it would be held contrary to public policy: see *Regazzoni v K C Sethia (1944) Ltd* [1956] 2 QB 490 at 524, [1956] 2 All ER 487 at 496, CA; affd [1958] AC 301, [1957] 3 All ER 286, HL.

(vi) Interpretation of the Contract

883. Interpretation. Uncertainty as to the meaning of any of the terms of a contract is a question of fact raising an issue of interpretation or construction[1]. As this may differ according to the legal system referred to, a choice of law rule is required. If the parties have expressly decided what law should govern issues of interpretation, then that law will be applied[2]. Failing such express choice, questions of interpretation will be referred to the rules of construction of the objectively ascertained proper law of the contract[3]. In a contract involving monetary obligations the proper law will decide, therefore, the meaning to be given to such phrases as payment in 'gold'[4], or 'pounds'[5]. If the rules of construction of the proper law ascribe a particular meaning to the phrase used by the parties then that construction must be applied[6]. If no such specific meaning may be ascribed by the proper law, as where the phrase is unknown to the proper law, then its rules of construction may permit the admission of evidence as to the meaning of the phrase in some foreign law[7].

1 This must be distinguished from the issue of the effect of the contract once interpreted, which is an issue of essential validity: *Chatenay v Brazilian Submarine Telegraph Co Ltd* [1891] 1 QB 79 at 85, CA; and see *Robertson v Brandes, Schönwald & Co* (1906) 8 F 815 at 819, Ct of Sess. As to essential validity see para 877 ante.
2 *Pena Copper Mines Ltd v Rio Tinto Co Ltd* (1911) 105 LT 846, CA; *Indian and General Investment Trust Ltd v Borax Consolidated Ltd* [1920] 1 KB 539 at 551; *St Pierre v South American Stores (Gath and Chaves) Ltd* [1937] 3 All ER 349 at 354, CA.
3 *The Industrie* [1894] P 58, CA; *Mowbray, Robinson & Co v Rosser* (1922) 91 LJKB 524, CA; *Equitable Trust Co of New York v Henderson* (1930) 47 TLR 90; and see *Korner v Witkowitzer* [1950] 2 KB 128 at 163, [1950] 1 All ER 558 at 576, CA; affd sub nom *Vitkovice Horni a Hutni Tezirstvo v Korner* [1951] AC 869, [1951] 2 All ER 334, HL.
4 *Feist v Société Intercommunale Belge d'Electricité* [1934] AC 161, HL; *New Brunswick Rly Co v British and French Trust Corpn Ltd* [1939] AC 1, [1938] 4 All ER 747, HL; and also *R v International Trustee for the Protection of Bondholders AG* [1937] AC 500, [1936] 3 All ER 407, CA; revsd on another point [1937] AC

500 at 528, [1937] 2 All ER 164, HL (construed as a gold value clause); *St Pierre v South American Stores (Cath and Chaves) Ltd* [1937] 3 All ER 349, CA; *Treseder-Griffin v Co-operative Insurance Society Ltd* [1956] 2 QB 127, [1956] 2 All ER 33, CA; *Campos v Kentucky and Indiana Terminal Railroad Co* [1962] 2 Lloyd's Rep 459 (construed as a mere statutory synonym of the unit of currency).

5   *Bonython v Commonwealth of Australia* [1951] AC 201, PC; *National Bank of Australasia Ltd v Scottish Union and National Insurance Co Ltd* [1952] AC 493, PC; and see *De Bueger v J Ballantyne & Co Ltd* [1938] AC 452, [1938] 1 All ER 701, PC. Where there is no doubt as to the country whose currency is intended, then the law of that country, and not the proper law, determines the meaning to be given to the units of currency mentioned: *Pyrmont Ltd v Schott* [1939] AC 145, [1938] 4 All ER 713, PC; and see *Ottoman Bank of Nicosia v Chakarian* [1938] AC 260, [1937] 4 All ER 570, PC. See also eg *W J Alan & Co Ltd v El Nasr Export and Import Co* [1972] 2 QB 189, [1972] 2 All ER 127, CA.

6   *Di Sora v Phillipps* (1863) 10 HL Cas 624 at 638.

7   See *Rowett, Leakey & Co v Scottish Provident Institution* [1927] 1 Ch 55, CA.

(vii) Discharge of the Contract

884. Discharge of contracts generally. The proper law of a contract determines whether or not it has been validly discharged[1], whether by performance[2], by accord and satisfaction[3], by impossibility of performance[4], by legislation[5], by the outbreak of war[6], by a moratorium[7], or by bankruptcy[8]. A discharge by some other law, such as the law of the place of performance or the lex situs of a debt, is not effective in England[9].

In the case of discharge of a debt by novation, where one debtor is discharged and replaced by another, the discharge of the original debtor is governed by the proper law of the original contract[10], whilst the obligation of the new debtor is governed by the system of law with which the entry of the new debtor is most closely connected[11].

1   *Ralli v Dennistoun* (1851) 6 Exch 483; *Perry v Equitable Life Assurance Society of the United States of America* (1929) 45 TLR 468; *R v International Trustee for the Protection of Bondholders AG* [1937] AC 500, [1937] 2 All ER 164, HL; *Tomkinson v First Pennsylvania Banking and Trust Co* [1961] AC 1007, [1960] 2 All ER 332, HL.

2   See para 878 ante.

3   *Ralli v Dennistoun* (1851) 6 Exch 483.

4   *Jacobs v Crédit Lyonnais* (1884) 12 QBD 589, CA.

5   *Employers' Liability Assurance Corpn Ltd v Sedgwick, Collins & Co Ltd* [1927] AC 95, HL; *Perry v Equitable Life Assurance Society of the United States of America* (1929) 45 TLR 468; *R v International Trustee for the Protection of Bondholders AG* [1937] AC 500, [1937] 2 All ER 164, HL; *Mount Albert Borough Council v Australasian Temperance and General Mutual Life Assurance Society Ltd* [1938] AC 224, [1937] 4 All ER 206, PC.

6   *Re Anglo-Austrian Bank* [1920] 1 Ch 69.

7   *Re Helbert Wagg & Co Ltd's Claim* [1956] Ch 323, [1956] 1 All ER 129; *National Bank of Greece and Athens SA v Metliss* [1958] AC 509, [1957] 3 All ER 608, HL; *Adams v National Bank of Greece SA* [1961] AC 255, [1960] 2 All ER 421, HL.

8   *Potter v Brown* (1804) 5 East 124; *Gardiner v Houghton* (1862) 2 B & S 743. For the exceptional case where the discharge takes effect under an Act of the United Kingdom Parliament see para 982 post.

9   *Jacobs v Crédit Lyonnais* (1884) 12 QBD 589, CA; *Gibbs & Sons v Société Industrielle et Commerciale des Métaux* (1890) 25 QBD 399, CA; *Mount Albert Borough Council v Australasian Temperance and General Mutual Life Assurance Society Ltd* [1938] AC 224, [1937] 4 All ER 206, PC; *National Bank of Greece and Athens SA v Metliss* [1958] AC 509, [1957] 3 All ER 608, HL; *Tomkinson v First Pennsylvania Banking and Trust Co* [1961] AC 1007, [1960] 2 All ER 332, HL.

10 *Re United Railways of the Havana and Regla Warehouses Ltd* [1960] Ch 52 at 84–85, [1959] 1 All ER 214 at 228–230, CA; affd sub nom *Tomkinson v First Pennsylvania Banking and Trust Co* [1961] AC 1007, [1960] 2 All ER 332, HL.

11 *Re United Railways of the Havana and Regla Warehouses Ltd* [1960] Ch 52 at 91, [1959] 1 All ER 214 at 233, CA; affd sub nom *Tomkinson v First Pennsylvania Banking and Trust Co* [1961] AC 1007, [1960] 2 All ER 332, HL. Where novation involves the substitution of a new debt between the same parties, the proper law of the original contract governs the discharge of the old debt: *Rozencrantz v Union Contractors Ltd and Thornton* (1960) 31 WWR 597, 23 DLR (2d) 473, BC SC.

885. Exceptional cases. The Bills of Exchange Act 1882 refers the question of the date of payment of a bill to the law of the place of performance[1]. Thus, if the law of that country postpones the date of maturity of a bill by a moratorium, payment cannot be enforced in England until the foreign moratorium is lifted[2].

The lex situs of the debt appears to govern the question of discharge in the case of the winding up in England of a foreign company dissolved by foreign governmental decree[3]; but this leaves the general rule of reference to the proper law unaffected[4].

1 Bills of Exchange Act 1882 s 72(5).
2 *Rouquette v Overmann and Schou* (1875) LR 10 QB 525; *Re Francke and Rasch* [1918] 1 Ch 470.
3 *Re Russian Bank for Foreign Trade* [1933] Ch 745; *Re Russo-Asiatic Bank, Re Russian Bank for Foreign Trade* [1934] Ch 720 at 736–738; *Re Banque des Marchands de Moscou (Koupetschesky), Royal Exchange Assurance v The Liquidator* [1952] 1 All ER 1269; *Re Banque des Marchands de Moscou (Koupetschesky)* [1954] 2 All ER 746, [1954] 1 WLR 1108. In these cases, the proper law was not considered as a possible alternative to the lex situs: *Re United Railways of the Havana and Regla Warehouses Ltd* [1960] Ch 52 at 88–90, [1959] 1 All ER 214 at 231–232, CA; affd sub nom *Tomkinson v First Pennsylvania Banking and Trust Co* [1961] AC 1007, [1960] 2 All ER 332, HL.
4 *Re United Railways of the Havana and Regla Warehouses Ltd* [1960] Ch 52 at 91, [1959] 1 All ER 214 at 233, CA; affd sub nom *Tomkinson v First Pennsylvania Banking and Trust Co* [1961] AC 1007, [1960] 2 All ER 332, HL. Discharge under a Bankruptcy Act of the United Kingdom Parliament is also an exceptional case: see para 982 post.

(viii) Remedies

886. Nature of the remedy. The nature of the remedy available to a plaintiff is determined by the lex fori as a matter of procedure[1], even though this may mean that a remedy unknown to the proper law of the contract is available[2]. An English court will not grant a remedy unknown to English law or not permitted in the circumstances[3], even though this may necessarily cause a claim, good by its proper law, to fail[4].

Other issues determined by the lex fori as procedural matters are the availability of a claim by way of counterclaim and the question whether a set-off can be raised[5], and the execution of a judgment[6].

1 *De La Vega v Vianna* (1830) 1 B & Ad 284; *Liverpool Marine Credit Co v Hunter* (1868) 3 Ch App 479 at 486; *Baschet v London Illustrated Standard Co* [1900] 1 Ch 73; *Chaplin v Boys* [1971] AC 356 at 378, 381–382, 394, [1969] 2 All ER 1085 at 1092–1093, 1095, 1106, HL: see para 1076 post. In *Richard West & Partners (Inverness) Ltd v Dick* [1969] 2 Ch 424, [1969] 1 All ER 943, CA, specific performance was granted in England of a contract for the sale of land in Scotland: see para 918 post.
2 See *Chaplin v Boys* [1971] AC 356, [1969] 2 All ER 1085, HL
3 Cf *Warner Bros Pictures Inc v Nelson* [1937] 1 KB 209, [1936] 3 All ER 160.
4 *Phrantzes v Argenti* [1960] 2 QB 19 at 34–36, [1960] 1 All ER 778 at 783–784.
5 See para 1079 post.
6 See para 1083 post.

887. Remoteness of damage. The law relating to damages is partly procedural and partly substantive[1]. The issue of remoteness of damage is a question of substance relating to the extent of the contractual obligation and is governed by the proper law of the contract[2].

1 *Chaplin v Boys* [1971] AC 356 at 379, [1969] 2 All ER 1085 at 1093, HL: see para 1077 post.
2 *D'Almeida Araujo Lda v Sir Frederick Becker & Co Ltd* [1953] 2 QB 329, [1953] 2 All ER 288; and see *Livesley v Horst* [1924] SCR 605, [1925] 1 DLR 159, Can SC; cf *Kremezi v Ridgway* [1949] 1 All ER 662 at 664; *NV Handel My J Smits Import-Export v English Exporters (London) Ltd* [1955] 2 Lloyd's Rep 69 at 72; affd [1955] 2 Lloyd's Rep 317, CA.

888. Measure of damages. The issue of measure or quantification of damages is a procedural issue to be governed by the lex fori[1]. However, it is well settled that an English court may give judgment expressed in a foreign currency or the sterling equivalent[2]. Where the currency for damages in the event of breach is not expressed or is unclear the court may order payment in the currency which best expresses the plaintiff's loss[3]. It appears that where it is necessary to convert a foreign currency into sterling for the purpose of enforcing a judgment, the date for determining the rate of exchange is the date on which the court authorises enforcement[4].

1 *D'Almeida Araujo Lda v Sir Frederick Becker & Co Ltd* [1953] 2 QB 329, [1953] 2 All ER 288; and see *Chaplin v Boys* [1971] AC 356 at 378, 381–382, 393–394, [1969] 2 All ER 1085 at 1092–1093, 1095, 1105–1106, HL.
2 *Miliangos v George Frank (Textiles) Ltd* [1976] AC 443, [1975] 3 All ER 801, HL; *MV Eleftherotria (Owners) v MV Despina R (Owners), The Despina R, Services Europe Atlantique Sud (SEAS) v Stockholms Rederiaktiebolag SVEA, The Folias* [1979] AC 685, [1979] 1 All ER 421, HL. See also *Schorsch Meier GmbH v Hennin* [1975] QB 416, [1975] 1 All ER 152, CA (court can give judgment for a debt expressed in a foreign currency); *Jugoslavenska Oceanska Plovidba v Castle Investment Co Inc* [1974] QB 292, [1973] 3 All ER 498, CA (arbitral award may be made in a foreign currency).
3 *MV Eleftherotria (Owners) v MV Despina R (Owners), The Despina R, Services Europe Atlantique Sud (SEAS) v Stockholms Rederiaktiebolag SVEA, The Folias* [1979] AC 685, [1979] 1 All ER 421, HL; *Société Française Bunge SA v Belcan NV, The Federal Huron* [1985] 3 All ER 378, [1985] 2 Lloyd's Rep 189.
4 *Miliangos v George Frank (Textiles) Ltd* [1976] AC 443, [1975] 3 All ER 801, HL.

889. Liability to pay interest. The liability to pay interest and the rate of interest[1] payable on a contractual debt are governed by the proper law of the contract[2]. The liability to pay interest as damages for non-payment of a contractual debt is also governed by the proper law of the contract, but in such a case the rate of interest is determined by the lex fori[3]. The proper law will normally, although not always[4], be the law of the country where the debt is to be paid or the loan repaid.

The proper law will also determine whether the interest is payable by reason of a term, express or implied, in the contract or by way of damages. In the case of the dishonour of a bill of exchange, the general rule is that whether interest is recoverable on dishonour depends upon the proper law of the contract between the drawer and the payee[5].

1 *Montreal Trust Co v Stanrock Uranium Mines Ltd* [1966] 1 OR 258, 53 DLR (2d) 594, Ont HC (payment of interest on interest).
2 *Arnott v Redfern* (1825) 2 C & P 88; *Shrichand & Co v Lacon* (1906) 22 TLR 245; *Mount Albert Borough Council v Australasian Temperance and General Mutual Life Assurance Society Ltd* [1938] AC 224, [1937] 4 All ER 206, PC.
3 *Miliangos v George Frank (Textiles) Ltd* [1976] AC 443, [1975] 3 All ER 801, HL. As to the rate of interest under English law see the Supreme Court Act 1981 s 35A (added by the Administration of Justice Act 1982 s 15(1), Sch 1).
4 *Mount Albert Borough Council v Australasian Temperance and General Mutual Life Assurance Society Ltd* [1938] AC 224, [1937] 4 All ER 206, PC.
5 *Allen v Kemble* (1848) 6 Moo PCC 314; *Gibbs v Fremont* (1853) 9 Exch 25.

(5) QUASI-CONTRACT AND RESTITUTION

890. Quasi-contractual or restitutionary claims. It would appear that claims for restitution arising in connection with a contract[1] are governed by the law applicable to that contract[2]. Otherwise, restitutionary claims are governed by the law of the country with which they have their closest and most real connection[3]. If the claim arises in relation to a transaction involving land, the applicable law is the law of the country where the land is situated[4]. It is not necessarily the case that because the defendant is subject to the jurisdiction of the English court, he is liable to the rules of English equity without consideration of the law which should govern his liability[5].

1   Although a claim for restitution upon breach of contract is clearly covered by the Rome Convention art 10 para 1(c), a claim for restitution consequent upon the nullity of a contract is not (the Rome Convention art 10 para 1(e) does not have the force of law in the United Kingdom: Contracts (Applicable Law) Act 1990 s 2(2): see para 854 text and notes 9–10 ante). For the meaning of 'the Rome Convention' see para 844 text and note 1 ante.

      The difficulties regarding restitutionary claims arise principally from the fact that the range of actions for restitution is very wide, and it is unrealistic to suppose that a single choice of law rule can comfortably govern all of them alike. There are very few authorities upon the choice of law rules as they apply to restitutionary claims.

2   See Dicey and Morris *The Conflict of Laws* (12th Edn, 1993) 1475; and cf *Fibrosa Spolka Akcyjna v Fairbairn Lawson Combe Barbour Ltd* [1943] AC 32, [1942] 2 All ER 122, HL. This principle does not contradict the Contracts (Applicable Law) Act 1990 s 2(2) (see note 1 supra), which does not prevent the development of a common law rule alongside the Rome Convention.

3   See *Chase Manhattan Bank NA v Israel-British Bank (London) Ltd* [1981] Ch 105, [1979] 3 All ER 1025; *El Ajou v Dollar Land Holdings plc* [1993] 3 All ER 717; revsd on other grounds: [1994] 2 All ER 685, CA; and especially *Arab Monetary Fund v Hashim* [1993] 1 Lloyd's Rep 543. This may be the place where the enrichment occurred: see eg *El Ajou v Dollar Land Holdings plc* supra. This analysis was accepted, but without deciding that it was correct, in *MacMillan Inc v Bishopsgate Investment Trust plc (No 3)* [1996] 1 All ER 585, CA.

4   *Batthyany v Walford* (1887) 36 ChD 269, CA.

5   Cf *El Ajou v Dollar Land Holdings plc* [1993] 3 All ER 717 (revsd on other grounds: [1994] 2 All ER 685, CA).

6. TORTS

(1) INTRODUCTORY

891. Jurisdiction in respect of tort claims. The rules on jurisdiction which apply in relation to tort claims no longer draw a sharp distinction between torts which took place in England and torts which took place outside[1]. The rules discussed in the following paragraphs, in respect of which the location of a tort is of central importance, are rules of choice of law, rather than of jurisdiction[2]. Accordingly, the English court has jurisdiction in respect of torts, whether English or foreign, whenever it has jurisdiction in personam over the defendant[3].

In cases to which the Brussels Convention[4], or the Lugano Convention[5] applies, the jurisdiction of the English court is determined according to whichever of the Conventions is applicable[6].

In cases in which the Brussels or Lugano Conventions authorise a court to apply its national laws of jurisdiction[7], or where the subject matter of the dispute means that the Conventions have no application[8], the jurisdiction of the court will be governed by the traditional common law principles of jurisdiction in personam[9]. By way of exception, there are special rules, discussed elsewhere, concerning torts in respect of foreign immovables[10].

1   As to the location of a tort see para 893 post.

2   *Chaplin v Boys* [1971] AC 356 at 385–387, [1969] 2 All ER 1085 at 1098–1100, HL. It had sometimes been suggested that the rules were rules of jurisdiction, or that the rule in *The Halley* (1868) LR 2 PC 193 was such: see *Boys v Chaplin* [1968] 2 QB 1 at 21, 38, [1968] 1 All ER 283 at, 287, 298, CA; on appeal sub

nom *Chaplin v Boys* supra at 375, 1090, HL. In the light of *Chaplin v Boys* this suggestion is now insupportable. See also *Metall und Rohstoff AG v Donaldson Lufkin & Jenrette Inc* [1990] 1 QB 391 at 446, [1989] 3 All ER 14 at 32, CA.

3 For general principles of jurisdiction in personam see para 615 et seq ante.
4 As to the Brussels Convention see para 618 text and note 1 ante. As to the application of the Brussels Convention see generally paras 618–647 ante.
5 As to the Lugano Convention see para 618 text and note 2 ante. As to the application of the Brussels Convention see generally paras 618–647 ante.
6 See para 642 ante.
7 Ie under art 4 of the Conventions: see para 639 ante. As to references to numbered articles 'of the Conventions' see para 618 note 5 ante.
8 See paras 625–626 ante.
9 See para 648 et seq ante.
10 See paras 914–915 post.

892. Choice of law for claims in tort: general. As from a day to be appointed, the rules of the common law for choice of law in tort[1] are largely, but not entirely, superseded by Part III of the Private International Law (Miscellaneous Provisions) Act 1995[2]. Accordingly it is necessary for choice of law purposes to distinguish between those claims which will continue to be governed by the rules of the common law and those which will be governed by the Act.

The claims which will continue to be governed by the common law are (1) claims which arise from acts or omissions which occur before the entry into force of the relevant provisions of the Act[3]; and (2) defamation claims[4]. All other tort claims and issues will be governed by the Act[5].

1 See paras 893–895 post.
2 Ie the Private International Law (Miscellaneous Provisions) Act 1995 Pt III (ss 9–15); Pt III comes into force on a day to be appointed under s 16(3). At the date at which this volume states the law, no such order had been made. The Act is based in large part on *Private International Law: Choice of Law in Tort and Delict* (Law Com no 193).
3 Private International Law (Miscellaneous Provisions) Act 1995 s 14(1).
   It is unclear whether this is meant to refer to a claim in which the act or omission of the defendant occurred before the commencement date, whenever the damage manifested itself, or only to a case in which the damage, together with the acts or omissions complained of, also occurred before the commencement date. On the footing that an act or omission will not give rise to a claim until the damage occurs, the latter might be thought to be arguably correct. But the natural construction of the Act would appear to require only that the act or omission of the defendant occur before the commencement date. Where a combination of acts and omissions is relied on, some occurring before and others after, the commencement date, it may be that the test is whether these occurred in substance before or after the commencement date. Such an approach would adopt the basis of the test used under the common law to identify the location of a tort: see para 893 post.
4 Ibid s 13(1): and see para 896 post.
5 See paras 897–901 post.

(2) TORTS NOT GOVERNED BY THE PRIVATE INTERNATIONAL LAW (MISCELLANEOUS PROVISIONS) ACT 1995

893. Location of the tort, and choice of law for torts committed in England. Where the Private International Law (Miscellaneous Provisions) Act 1995 does not apply[1], it is necessary first to determine whether the alleged tort occurred in England or overseas. If it is held to have occurred in England, all questions of liability arising out of it will be determined by English law alone[2]. There is no possibility of making an exception to the application of English law, as such a case is not governed by the 'double actionability' rule[3], which applies only to torts committed outside England[4].

Where the constituent elements of the tort did not all occur in a single jurisdiction, the general rule is that the tort occurred where in substance the cause of action arose[5]. Thus a claim alleging product liability arises where the article is purchased without warning as to its danger and is used, and not necessarily where it was manufactured[6]; negligent misrepresentation occurs where the careless advice is received and acted upon, and not necessarily where it is transmitted from[7], although a claim regarding the negligent production of accountancy advice may arise where the accountancy is performed, rather than where the information is relied upon[8]. A cause of action in defamation arises in the place into which, rather than the place from which, the defamatory material is communicated[9]; and a cause of action for inducing a breach of contract arises in the place where the breaches occurred and the damage was sustained, and not necessarily where the prior acts of inducement took place[10].

1 See para 892 ante.
2 *Szalatnay-Stacho v Fink* [1947] KB 1, CA; *Metall und Rohstoff AG v Donaldson Lufkin & Jenrette Inc* [1990] 1 QB 391 at 447, [1989] 3 All ER 14 at 32, CA.
3 See para 894 post.
4 *Metall und Rohstoff AG v Donaldson Lufkin & Jenrette Inc* [1990] 1 QB 391, [1989] 3 All ER 14, CA.
5 *Distillers Co (Biochemicals) Ltd v Thompson* [1971] AC 458, [1971] 1 All ER 694, PC; *Castree v E R Squibb & Sons Ltd* [1980] 2 All ER 589, [1980] 1 WLR 1248, CA; *Metall und Rohstoff AG v Donaldson Lufkin & Jenrette Inc* [1990] QB 391, [1989] 3 All ER 14, CA.
6 *Distillers Co (Biochemicals) Ltd v Thompson* [1971] AC 458, [1971] 1 All ER 694, PC; *Castree v E R Squibb & Sons Ltd* [1980] 2 All ER 589, [1980] 1 WLR 1248, CA.
7 *Diamond v Bank of London & Montreal* [1979] QB 333, [1979] 1 All ER 561, CA; *Cordoba Shipping Co Ltd v National State Bank, Elizabeth, New Jersey, The Albaforth* [1984] 2 Lloyd's Rep 91, CA.
8 *Voth v Manildra Flour Mills Pty Ltd* (1990) 171 CLR 538 at 568–569, Aust HC.
9 *Bata v Bata* [1948] WN 366, CA; *Shevill v Presse Alliance SA* [1992] 1 All ER 409, [1992] 2 WLR 1, CA; and the proceedings in the European Court: Case C-68/93 *Shevill v Presse Alliance SA* [1995] ECR I-415, [1995] 2 AC 18, [1995] All ER (EC) 289, ECJ.
10 *Metall und Rohstoff AG v Donaldson Lufkin & Jenrette Inc* [1990] 1 QB 391, [1989] 3 All ER 14, CA.

894. Choice of law for torts committed abroad. As a general rule, an act done abroad is actionable as a tort in England only if: (1) it would have been actionable as a tort if it had been done in England; and (2) it is actionable, though not necessarily as a tort, under the law of the foreign country[1]; this is known as the rule of 'double actionability'[2]. If both conditions are satisfied, it appears that the court will adopt English law to dispose of the case[3].

In order to satisfy the condition in head (1) above, the plaintiff must show that under the English domestic law of tort, he would have had a good cause of action in tort[4]. In particular, it must be established that he[5] must be able to sue, that no substantive defence would preclude his recovering damages or obtaining other relief[6], and that the defendant himself would be liable to the plaintiff[7]. To satisfy the condition in head (2) above, the plaintiff must establish that civil liability exists between the parties for the particular head of damages claimed[8]. A purely procedural defence to liability under that law will be disregarded[9], and it is not essential that the cause of action be classified under that law as lying in tort[10]. But if the only remedy available to the plaintiff in that country would be by way of criminal proceedings[11], or by claim from a statutory insurance fund in lieu of a civil claim[12], the second limb of the general rule will not have been satisfied.

The 'double actionability' rule has been said to be flexible, and may be departed from in an appropriate case on clear and satisfactory grounds a particular issue[13]: or even the entire question of liability if all, or virtually all, of the significant factors so indicate[14], may be governed instead by the law of the country which has the most significant relationship with the occurrence in question and with the parties[15]. Thus a plaintiff may recover even though the law of the place of the tort would have disallowed some or all of his claim[16]. Likewise, he may recover in respect of a tort actionable under the law of the place where it occurred even though the conduct would not have been actionable as a tort if it had occurred in England[17].

For this exception to apply, the connection between the case and the country whose law is to be denied application must be so weak that the law has no interest in being applied to the particular dispute, and another law should be applied instead[18].

As a matter of common law, a plaintiff who has sustained injury or suffered loss in circumstances which would entitle him to claim against a defendant for damages for tort or for breach of contract may proceed to bring an action on the contract if he so wishes, even though an action in tort would have failed under the rules set out in this paragraph[19]. It is less certain whether the reverse is true. As a matter of common law, the plaintiff may, if he wishes, frame his claim in tort rather than allege a breach of contract[20]. If the defendant wishes to set up a contractual term as a defence to the claim in tort, it is uncertain which law governs his ability to do so[21]. An exemption clause valid by the law of the place of the tort but invalid by the lex fori has been held to defeat the plaintiff's claim[22], but in another case, the entire issue was treated as governed solely by the proper law of the contract[23].

The coming into force of the Rome Convention on the law applicable to contractual obligations[24] may mean that the plaintiff no longer has this freedom to select between causes of action, for if a claim advanced by the plaintiff, even though framed in tort as a matter of English law, falls within the Convention definition of 'contractual obligation'[25], it is strongly arguable that the choice of law rule prescribed by that Convention, and not the common law rule of the conflict of laws, must be applied to both the claim and the defence[26].

1 It appears that it is for the defendant to plead and to establish the existence and application of a rule of law of the place where the alleged tort occurred which, he claims, furnishes him with a defence, rather than for it being for the plaintiff to adduce evidence of foreign law as part of his claim. The point is not established by English authority, but see Dicey and Morris *The Conflict of Laws* (12th Edn, 1993) 1514. For proof of foreign law see para 1093 post.

2 The rule is based on the formula in *Phillips v Eyre* (1870) LR 6 QB 1 at 28–29, as modified by *Chaplin v Boys* [1971] AC 356, [1969] 2 All ER 1085, HL; see especially the restatement by Lord Wilberforce at 389, 1102. The earlier diversity of judicial opinion was resolved in favour of this formulation by *Metall und Rohstoff v Donaldson Lufkin & Jenrette Inc* [1990] 1 QB 391 at 439–440, [1989] 3 All ER 14 at 27, CA; and *Red Sea Insurance Co Ltd v Bouygues SA* [1995] 1 AC 190, [1994] 3 All ER 749, PC. For the view that the lex fori plays a dominant role, see Lord Pearson in *Chaplin v Boys* supra at 398, 1109; and *Coupland v Arabian Gulf Petroleum Co* [1983] 2 All ER 434, [1983] 1 WLR 1136; affd [1983] 3 All ER 226, [1983] 1 WLR 1151, CA; but this view probably cannot stand with *Red Sea Insurance Co Ltd v Bouygues SA* supra: if both the lex fori and law of the place of the tort are liable to be displaced in an appropriate case, neither can be seen as dominant over the other.

  However, the rule is flexible, and may be departed from in the circumstances outlined below: see the text and notes 13–18 infra.

3 See *Chaplin v Boys* [1971] AC 356 at 387–389, [1969] 2 All ER 1085 at 1100–1102, HL, per Lord Wilberforce; *Coupland v Arabian Gulf Petroleum Co* [1983] 2 All ER 434, [1983] 1 WLR 1136; affd [1983] 3 All ER 226, [1983] 1 WLR 1151, CA.

4 *The Halley* (1868) LR 2 PC 193; *Chaplin v Boys* [1971] AC 356, [1969] 2 All ER 1085, HL; *Red Sea Insurance Co Ltd v Bouygues SA* [1995] 1 AC 190, [1994] 3 All ER 749, PC. It is insufficient to establish in English law the existence of a tort only approximately corresponding to the claim under the law of the place of the tort: the plaintiff must show that he could sue on the actual facts: *Def Lepp Music v Stuart-Brown* [1986] RPC 273. Thus an action cannot be brought in England to complain of the alleged infringement of a foreign copyright by acts done outside the United Kingdom, for this constitutes no tort under English law: see *Tyburn Productions Ltd v Conan Doyle* [1991] Ch 75, [1990] 1 All ER 909 (use

in film of characters Sherlock Holmes and Dr Watson allegedly infringing copyright under United States law): and see para 914 post. Nor yet does it appear sufficient that there would be some civil liability according to English law but not in tort: this follows from the wording of the general rule, which has been repeatedly approved in this form. But for a possible exception see text and note 17 infra.

5　This is particularly important where the plaintiff sues in a representative capacity under, eg the Fatal Accidents Act 1976 or the Law Reform (Miscellaneous Provisions) Act 1934: see Dicey and Morris *The Conflict of Laws* (12th Edn, 1993) 1519–1522.

6　Such as a defence of justification or privilege in defamation, or the English rules on remoteness of damage or contributory negligence.

7　*The Halley* (1868) LR 2 PC 193 (vicarious liability); *Armagas Ltd v Mundogas SA* [1986] AC 717 at 740, 752, 769, [1985] 3 All ER 795 at 810, 819, 831–832, CA; affd on other grounds [1986] AC 717, [1986] 2 All ER 385, HL (vicarious liability).

8　*Phillips v Eyre* (1870) LR 6 QB 1; *Chaplin v Boys* [1971] AC 356, [1969] 2 All ER 1085, HL; *Metall und Rohstoff v Donaldson Lufkin & Jenrette Inc* [1990] 1 QB 391, [1989] 3 All ER 14, CA; *Red Sea Insurance Co Ltd v Bouygues SA* [1995] 1 AC 190, [1994] 3 All ER 749, PC. For the requirement that the actual head of damages be recoverable see those cases and also *Mitchell v McCulloch* 1976 SLT 2, Ct of Sess. But quantification of the recoverable heads of damages is a matter for the lex fori alone: *Chaplin v Boys* supra, and for the questionable proposition that the existence of a statutory cap on damages is also a procedural matter for the lex fori alone see *Stevens v Head* (1993) 176 CLR 433, Aust HC. It is generally assumed that the reference to the 'law' of the place where the tort took place (ie the *lex loci delicti*) indicates a reference to the domestic law of the court within whose jurisdiction the alleged tort occurred: see Dicey and Morris *The Conflict of Laws* (12th Edn, 1993) 1515. This is open to question, on the ground that if the place of the tort constitutes the natural forum for the litigation, the law to be applied would on that account be the substantive law which would be applied by that court, whether or not this would be its own domestic law. Renvoi (as to which see paras 606–609 ante) is excluded by the Private International Law (Miscellaneous Provisions) Act 1995 s 9(4) (see para 897 post) from the torts to which that Act applies.

9　For procedure see paras 1066–1083 post.

10　This follows from the formulation of Lord Wilberforce in *Chaplin v Boys* [1971] AC 356 at 389, [1969] 2 All ER 1085 at 1102, HL.

11　*Chaplin v Boys* [1971] AC 356 esp at 377, 381, 388, [1969] 2 All ER 1085 esp at 1091, 1095, 1101, HL, overruling *Machado v Fontes* [1897] 2 QB 231, CA.

12　*Johnson v Coventry Churchill International Ltd* [1992] 3 All ER 14, 23.

13　*Chaplin v Boys* [1971] AC 356, [1969] 2 All ER 1085, HL (particular head of damages).

14　*Red Sea Insurance Co Ltd v Bouygues SA* [1995] 1 AC 190, [1994] 3 All ER 749, PC.

15　*Chaplin v Boys* [1971] AC 356, [1969] 2 All ER 1085, HL; *Johnson v Coventry Churchill International Ltd* [1992] 3 All ER 14; *Red Sea Insurance Co Ltd v Bouygues SA* [1995] 1 AC 190, [1994] 3 All ER 749, PC. However, see *Breavington v Godleman* (1988) 169 CLR 41, where the High Court of Australia refused to countenance a 'flexible' exception in relation to torts committed within Australia; *McKain v R W Miller & Co (South Australia) Pty Ltd* (1991) 174 CLR 1, Aust HC; *Stevens v Head* (1993) 176 CLR 433, Aust HC.

16　*Johnson v Coventry Churchill International Ltd* [1992] 3 All ER 14.

17　*Red Sea Insurance Co Ltd v Bouygues SA* [1995] 1 AC 190, [1994] 3 All ER 749, PC.

18　*Chaplin v Boys* [1971] AC 356 at 392, [1969] 2 All ER 1085 at 1104, HL. The relevant factors in this regard include the nature of the tort, the particular issues presenting themselves, the question whether there is any special relationship between the parties, the policy underlying the rule of law in question, and the question of which system of law, because of its relationship or contact with the occurrence or the parties, has the greatest concern with the issues: see generally *Chaplin v Boys* supra; the other cases cited in note 15 supra; and Dicey and Morris *The Conflict of Laws* (12th Edn, 1993) 1498–1503.

19　See *Matthews v Kuwait Bechtel Corpn* [1959] 2 QB 57, [1959] 2 All ER 345, CA.

20　As a matter of common law he was clearly entitled to do so: see *Coupland v Arabian Gulf Oil Co* [1983] 2 All ER 434, [1983] 1 WLR 1136; affd [1983] 3 All ER 226, [1983] 1 WLR 1151, CA.

21　It is thought that, in principle, the question whether the term of the contract is intrinsically valid should be governed by the law which governs the contract; if the term is valid, its admissibility as a defence to the claim in tort should be settled by the rule on double actionability.

22　*Canadian Pacific Rly Co v Parent* [1917] AC 195, PC (as there was accordingly no liability under the law of the place of the tort).

23　*Sayers v International Drilling Co NV* [1971] 3 All ER 163, [1971] 1 WLR 1176, CA. See also *Brodin v AR Seljan* 1973 SLT 198.

24　As to the Rome Convention see para 845 et seq ante; and for the meaning of 'the Rome Convention' see para 844 text and note 1 ante.

25 As to the meaning of 'contractual obligation' in the Rome Convention see para 845 note 2 ante.
26 This meaning may be wide enough to encompass and to govern, for example, claims made by an employee against an employer alleging negligence; the choice of law rule imposed by the Convention will accordingly displace the corresponding rule of the common law conflict of laws. In relation to torts to which the Private International Law (Miscellaneous Provisions) Act 1995 applies, the same result is brought about by s 14(2) (see para 901 notes 2, 4 post).

895. Maritime torts and torts in aircraft. If a claim is made in an English court in respect of a wrong done on a ship[1] or on a structure such as an oil rig in foreign territorial waters, the general rule requires that the conduct be such as would be actionable as a tort if it occurred in England, and actionable (though not necessarily as a tort) under the law of the state in whose waters it was committed[2]. If the wrong is done on a ship on the high seas, the general rule is still thought to apply, with the law of the place of the tort being the law of the flag of the ship[3]. But a claim in respect of damage caused by the collision of two ships on the high seas is governed by the general maritime law as administered in England as part of the common law of England[4].

There is no English authority on the law applicable to claims arising out of wrongs done in aircraft. The general rule as to foreign torts might be interpreted as treating the place of registration of the aircraft as the place of the tort, but in the circumstances, a court might properly conclude that the general rule was inapplicable[5].

1 For this purpose the flag of the ship is irrelevant: *The Mary Moxham* (1876) 1 PD 107, CA.
2 *The Halley* (1868) LR 2 PC 193; *Carr v Fracis Times & Co* [1902] AC 176, HL; *Yorke v British and Continental SS Co Ltd* (1945) 78 Ll L Rep 181, CA; *Mackinnon v Iberia Shipping Co Ltd* 1955 SC 20, [1954] 2 Lloyd's Rep 372.
3 See *R v Anderson* (1868) LR 1 CCR 161 at 168; *R v Carr* (1882) 10 QBD 76, CCR; *The Esso Malaysia* [1975] QB 198. As to the problem arising if a tort is alleged on the high seas between persons on ships of different countries see Dicey and Morris *The Conflict of Laws* (12th Edn, 1993) 1536.
4 *Chartered Mercantile Bank of India, London and China v Netherlands India Steam Navigation Co Ltd* (1883) 10 QBD 521, CA; *The Leon* (1881) 6 PD 148; *The Waziristan* [1953] 2 All ER 1213; and see generally ADMIRALTY vol 1(1) (Reissue) para 303. This is so, even if they fly the same flag: *Chartered Mercantile Bank of India, London and China v Netherlands India Steam Navigation Co Ltd* supra.
5 See Dicey and Morris *The Conflict of Laws* (12th Edn, 1993) 1541–1542. For the exceptions to the general rule see para 894 notes 13–18 ante.

896. Choice of law in defamation claims. The Private International Law (Miscellaneous Provisions) Act 1995[1] has no application to issues arising in any defamation claim[2]. Liability in respect of such claims, whenever arising, will therefore be governed by English domestic law if the alleged tort occurred in England, or by the common law choice of law rules described previously[3] if the alleged tort was committed overseas. As has been stated, the tort of defamation is committed in the place into which the defamatory material is communicated[4].

For the purpose of the exclusion of defamation claims from the operation of the Act, 'defamation claim' means (1) any claim under the law of any part of the United Kingdom[5] for libel or slander or for slander of title, slander of goods or other malicious falsehood[6]; and (2) any claim under the law of any other country corresponding to or otherwise in the nature of a claim mentioned in head (1) above[7].

1 Ie the Private International Law (Miscellaneous Provisions) Act 1995 Pt III (ss 9–16), in force as from a day to be appointed: see para 892 note 2 ante.
2 Ibid s 13(1).
3 See paras 893–894 ante.
4 See the cases cited in para 893 note 9 ante.

5 For the meaning of 'United Kingdom' see para 604 ante.

6 Private International Law (Miscellaneous Provisions) Act 1995 s 13(2)(a). See generally LIBEL AND SLANDER. In Scotland this includes claims for verbal injury: s 13(2)(a).

7 Ibid s 13(2)(b). It is unclear to what extent this formulation encompasses other types of claim dealing with protection of reputation or self-esteem, more or less analogous to defamation, but which would not succeed under English law. Examples may be found in a defamation claim brought by an organ of government (*Derbyshire County Council v Times Newspapers Ltd* [1993] AC 534, [1993] 1 All ER 1011, HL), or a head of state, or a claim for compensation for causing embarrassment to such a plaintiff, or for breach of privacy in the acquisition of information, none of which give rise to an action in tort in English law. There is little guidance in *Private International Law: Choice of Law in Tort and Delict* (Law Com no 193), but see para 3.28. For the view that the Act as drafted is intended to be confined to liability for statements, see the speech of the Lord Chancellor in the debate in the House of Lords: 562 HL Official Report col 1416. In principle, and in line with this intention, a claim founded on the communication (though not necessarily to a third party) of prejudicial information is likely to fall within the definition, but a claim concerned with the wrongful acquisition of such information would not appear to do so.

(3) TORTS GOVERNED BY THE PRIVATE INTERNATIONAL LAW (MISCELLANEOUS PROVISIONS) ACT 1995

897. Scope of the Act. As from a day to be appointed, Part III of the Private International Law (Miscellaneous Provisions) Act 1995[1] applies for choosing the law ('the applicable law') to be used for determining issues relating to tort[2]. It applies to events occurring in the forum[3] as well as to events occurring in any other country[4], but it has no application to acts or omissions giving rise to a claim which occurred before the commencement of Part III of the Act[5], nor to defamation claims[6].

The applicable law must be used (excluding its choice of law rules[7]) for determining the issues arising in a claim, including in particular the question whether an actionable tort has occurred[8].

In relation to claims to which the Act applies, the rules of the common law, in so far as they:

(1) require actionability under both the law of the forum and the law of another country for the purpose of determining whether a tort is actionable (the 'double actionability rule')[9]; or

(2) allow, as an exception to the double actionability rule, for the law of a single country to be applied for the purpose of determining the issues or any of them arising in the case in question[10],

are abolished[11].

1 Ie the Private International Law (Miscellaneous Provisions) Act 1995 Pt III (ss 9–15). At the date at which this volume states the law, Pt III had not been brought into force: see para 892 note 2 ante.

2 Ibid s 9(1). For the purpose of private international law the characterisation of issues arising in a claim as issues relating to tort is a matter for the courts of the forum: s 9(2). 'Issues relating to tort' is not defined. Thus it is not expressly stated whether the rules in the Act will apply to any or all of the following issues: (1) capacity; (2) vicarious liability; (3) defences and immunities; (4) some or all aspects of the law of damages; (5) limitations on recovery; (6) limitation of actions; (7) transmission of claims on death and the survival of actions; (8) wrongful death; (9) intra-family immunities; (10) contribution and indemnity; (11) contractual defences to claims in tort; (12) direct actions by a third party against an insurer; and (13) claims against a constructive trustee on the ground of his wrongful assistance in another's fraudulent breach of trust.

The matters in heads (1)–(5) supra are regarded as matters relating to tort: see *Private International Law: Choice of Law in Tort and Delict* (Law Com no 193) paras 3.34, 3.35–3.36 3.37, 3.38, 3.39 (but note, to contrary effect with regard to head (5), the decision of the High Court of Australia in *Stevens v Head* (1993) 176 CLR 433). Matters in head (6) supra are governed by the law which governs liability for the tort: Foreign Limitation Periods Act 1984 s 1: see para 1082 post. The silence as to heads (7), (9), (10),

(11), (12) supra is deliberate: see *Private International Law: Choice of Law in Tort and Delict* (Law Com no 193) paras 3.41–3.43, 3.45–3.46, 3.49–3.50, 3.51. As to head (8) supra see *Private International Law: Choice of Law in Tort and Delict* (Law Com no 193) para 3.44. With regard to head (10), it was stated by the Law Commission that such a claim for contribution was a restitutionary one, separate and distinct from the law of tort, and was for that reason intended to be omitted from the legislation: see *Private International Law: Choice of Law in Tort and Delict* (Law Com no 193) para 3.47. It has been held that a claim for contribution is governed exclusively by the Civil Liability (Contribution) Act 1978, which applies in an English court without regard to the identity of the law chosen to determine the liabilities of the defendants to the plaintiff, or otherwise inter se: see *Arab Monetary Fund v Hashim (No 9)* [1994] TLR 502. No provision was made regarding head (13) supra in the Private International Law (Miscellaneous Provisions) Act 1995. But it was held in *Arab Monetary Fund v Hashim (No 9)* supra that where the conduct took place in a foreign country, the 'double actionability' rule (see para 894 ante) governed whether a claim based on it could be brought in England. It is thought that the use of that rule does not ipso facto render this issue of liability an issue in tort, and that the result of that case is therefore unaffected by the Private International Law (Miscellaneous Provisions) Act 1995.

3 'Forum' means, as the case may be, England and Wales, Scotland or Northern Ireland: see ibid s 9(7).
4 Ibid s 9(6).
5 Ibid s 14(1): see paras 892–895 ante.
6 Ibid ss 9(3), 13(1): see paras 892, 896 ante.
7 Ibid s 9(5). It may, however, be argued that, since the Act permits exceptions where circumstances demonstrate a close link between the tort and the law of another country (see para 899 post), an exception could be made to s 9(5) if it would be substantially more appropriate to apply the choice of law rules of the applicable law. See the comments of the Lord Chancellor in the Report of the Special Public Bill Committee (1 March 1995): *Private International Law (Miscellaneous Provisions) Bill [HL]: Proceedings of the Special Public Bill Committee* (HL Paper (1994–95) no 36, Part II col 25.
8 Private International Law (Miscellaneous Provisions) Act 1995 s 9(4).
9 See para 894 text and notes 1–12 ante.
10 See para 894 text and notes 13–18 ante.
11 Private International Law (Miscellaneous Provisions) Act 1995 s 10. The effect is that it will no longer be necessary for the plaintiff to prove that the conduct complained of would have constituted a tort according to English domestic law unless English law is that selected by the Act for application to the case.

898. General choice of law rule.

The general rule is that the applicable law[1] is that of the country in which the events constituting the tort in question occurred[2]. But where elements of those events occur in different countries, the applicable law under the general rule is as follows[3]:

(1) for a cause of action in respect of personal injury[4] caused to an individual, or death resulting from personal injury, the law of the country where the individual was when he sustained the injury[5];

(2) for a cause of action in respect of damage to property, the law of the country where the property was when it was damaged[6]; and

(3) in any other case, the law of the country in which the most significant elements of the events constituting the tort occurred[7].

1 For the meaning of 'applicable law' see para 897 ante.
2 Private International Law (Miscellaneous Provisions) Act 1995 s 11(1). At the date at which this volume states the law, Pt III (ss 9–15) of the Act had not been brought into force: see para 892 note 2 ante.
3 Ibid s 11(2).
4 'Personal injury' includes disease or any impairment of physical or mental condition: ibid s 11(3).
5 Ibid s 11(2)(a).
6 Ibid s 11(2)(b).
7 Ibid s 11(2)(c). Apart from the cases of personal injury, death or damage to property, it may be anticipated that the cases which held that a tort was committed where in substance the cause of action arose (see para 893 ante) may offer guidance as to the application of the new general rule.

899. Displacement of the general rule. If it appears, in all the circumstances, from a comparison of (1) the significance of the factors which connect a tort with the country whose law is the applicable law[1] under the general rule[2]; and (2) the significance of factors connecting the tort with another country, that it is substantially more appropriate for the applicable law for the determination of issues arising in the case, or any of the issues, to be the law of the other country, the general rule is displaced and the applicable law for determining those issues or that issue, as the case may be, is the law of that other country[3].

The factors which may be taken into account as connecting a tort with a country for this purpose include[4], in particular, factors relating to the parties, to any events which constitute the tort in question, or to any of the circumstances or consequences of those events[5].

1 For the meaning of 'applicable law' see para 897 ante.
2 As to the general rule see para 898 ante.
3 Private International Law (Miscellaneous Provisions) Act 1995 s 12(1). At the date at which this volume states the law, Pt III (ss 9–15) of the Act had not been brought into force: see para 892 note 2 ante.
4 Ibid s 12(2).
5 The word 'include' indicates that the list is not exhaustive, and that (for example) the fact that the courts of the country whose law is selected by the general rule would apply the law of another country may indicate that the law of that other country should be applied in the interests of preventing 'forum shopping': see para 897 note 7 ante.
    Although the Act expressly provides that the applicable law is to be determined in relation to the specific issue or issues in question, it is unclear whether a court may also take into account under these provisions the fact that claims arising out of the same transaction between different parties would be governed by a different law. Although as between a single plaintiff and the defendant there may be no sufficient justification for departure from the general rule, it may be that when the identity of other plaintiffs having claims arising out of the same facts is concerned, this perception may be altered: see *Private International Law: Choice of Law in Tort and Delict* (Law Com no 193) para 3.53, where it is suggested that in a case of multiple actual parties the choice of applicable law should be made 'separately for each pair of opponents'.

900. Issues still to be governed by English law. Nothing in Part III of the Private International Law (Miscellaneous Provisions) Act 1995[1] authorises a court to apply the law of a country outside the forum[2] for determining issues arising in any claim where to do so would either conflict with the principles of public policy[3], or give effect to a penal, revenue or other public law which would not otherwise be enforceable under the law of the forum[4]. The Act does not affect rules of evidence, pleading or practice, and does not authorise questions of procedure in any proceedings to be determined otherwise than in accordance with the law of the forum[5]. Any rule of law which applies notwithstanding the rules of private international law, or which modifies the rules of private international law, is not prejudiced by Part III of the Act[6].

1 Ie the Private International Law (Miscellaneous Provisions) Act 1995 Pt III (ss 9–15). At the date at which this volume states the law, Pt III had not been brought into force: see para 892 note 2 ante.
2 For the meaning of 'forum' see para 897 note 3 ante.
3 Private International Law (Miscellaneous Provisions) Act 1995 s 14(3)(a)(i). As to public policy see para 611 ante.
4 Ibid s 14(3)(a)(ii). As to penal and revenue laws see paras 612–613 ante.
5 Ibid s 14(3)(b). As to procedure see paras 1066–1083 post.
6 Ibid s 14(4). This provision relates to provisions of English law which are 'mandatory' or 'overriding' in the manner in which they apply to a case litigated in the English courts notwithstanding that the issues in the case are not otherwise governed by English law.

901. Maritime torts and torts in aircraft. Part III of the Private International Law (Miscellaneous Provisions) Act 1995[1] has no effect on any rule of law except the 'double actionability' rule (and the exceptions thereto) specifically abolished by the Act[2]. Accordingly, since the Act makes no express provision for torts committed at sea, whether in territorial waters or on the high seas, or for torts committed in aircraft, the general rule of the Act[3] will apply to these torts if it can be said that they were previously governed by the double actionability rule. However, if the position is rather that torts committed on ships and in aircraft were governed not by the double actionability rule but by special rules of the conflict of laws, these special rules will continue to govern after the Act is in force[4].

1   Ie the Private International Law (Miscellaneous Provisions) Act 1995 Pt III (ss 9–15). At the date at which this volume states the law, Pt III had not been brought into force: see para 892 note 2 ante.
2   Ibid s 14(2). As to the 'double actionability' rule and its exceptions see para 894 ante.
3   As to the general rule of the Private International Law (Miscellaneous Provisions) Act 1995 see para 898 ante.
4   For the proposition that the peculiar rules applicable to torts committed on the high seas (whether on board ships or by collision) are preserved by this section, see the comments of the Lord Chancellor in the Report of the Special Public Bill Committee (1 March 1995): *Private International Law (Miscellaneous Provisions) Bill [HL]: Proceedings of the Special Public Bill Committee* (HL Paper (1994–95) no 36, Part II col 27. However, this interpretation cannot clearly be derived from the words of the Act. The true position at common law may have been that maritime and aerial torts were governed by the rule of double actionability with exceptions and, if so, s 14(2) will not have the effect suggested by the Lord Chancellor.

7. PROPERTY

(1) CLASSIFICATION AND LOCATION

(i) Classification of Property

902. Classification and terminology. For the purposes of the English rules of the conflict of laws, property is classified as movable or immovable[1]. Whether property is movable or immovable is determined by the lex situs, the law of the place where the property is situated[2]. These rules apply to choses in action as well as to choses in possession[3].

1   See the cases cited in note 2 infra. This system of classification applies even in cases in which the domestic law of the foreign country concerned makes use of the English domestic classification of property as realty or personalty: see *Macdonald v Macdonald* 1932 SC (HL) 79 at 84; *Re Cutcliffe's Will Trusts, Brewer v Cutcliffe* [1940] Ch 565, [1940] 2 All ER 297; and, to the contrary effect, *Re Hoyles, Row v Jagg* [1911] 1 Ch 179 at 183, 185, CA.
2   *Drummond v Drummond* (1799) 6 Bro Parl Cas 601, HL; *Johnstone v Baker* (1817) 4 Madd 474n; *Dowager Duchess of Buccleuch and Queensbury v Hoare* (1819) 4 Madd 467; *Elliott v Lord Minto* (1821) 6 Madd 16; *Trotter v Trotter* (1828) 4 Bli NS 502, HL; *Jerningham v Herbert* (1829) 4 Russ 388; *Allen v Anderson* (1846) 5 Hare 163; *Cust v Goring* (1854) 18 Beav 383 (all cases on Scottish heritable bonds); *Freke v Lord Carbery* (1873) LR 16 Eq 461; *Re Fitzgerald, Surman v Fitzgerald* [1904] 1 Ch 573, CA; *Re Hoyles, Row v Jagg* [1911] 1 Ch 179, CA; *Re Berchtold, Berchtold v Capron* [1923] 1 Ch 192; *Re Cutcliffe's Will Trusts, Brewer v Cutcliffe* [1940] Ch 565, [1940] 2 All ER 297. As to the location of property see paras 907–913 post.
3   See eg *Re Hoyles, Row v Jagg* [1911] 1 Ch 179 at 183, CA (immovables); *Re Anziani, Herbert v Christopherson* [1930] 1 Ch 407 at 424 (movables); and, for a general analysis see *Haque v Haque (No 2)* (1965) 114 CLR 98 at 107, [1966] ALR 553 at 555, Aust HC. Choses in action which are classified as movables are sometimes described as 'intangible movables': cf *Haque v Haque (No 2)* supra at 107 and at 555: 'physical mobility is not a quality of the conceptual'. The term 'intangible movable' is not used in this title.

903. Interests in land. All estates, interests and charges in or over English[1] land are classified as immovables[2]. This applies to freehold[3] and leasehold[4] interests, to freehold land subject to a trust for sale but remaining unsold[5], to rentcharges[6], mineral rights[7] and to the interest of a mortgagee[8]. For this purpose the distinction between realty and personalty is wholly immaterial[9].

1 Interests in land in a country outside England and Wales are classified by the law of that country: see para 902 ante. As to the meaning of 'England and Wales' see para 604 ante.
2 See *Re Hoyles, Row v Jagg* [1911] 1 Ch 179 at 183, 186, CA.
3 See eg *Freke v Lord Carbery* (1873) LR 16 Eq 461 at 466.
4 *Freke v Lord Carbery* (1873) LR 16 Eq 461; *Duncan v Lawson* (1889) 41 ChD 394; *Pepin v Bruyère* [1902] 1 Ch 24, CA. See also *Re Gentili's Goods* (1875) LR 9 Eq 541; *De Fogassieras v Duport* (1881) 11 LR Ir 123.
5 *Re Berchtold, Berchtold v Capron* [1923] 1 Ch 192. See also *Murray v Champernowne* [1901] 2 IR 232.
6 *Chatfield v Berchtoldt* (1872) 7 Ch App 192. See also *Whitaker v Forbes* (1875) LR 10 CP 583; affd 1 CPD 51, CA (Australian land).
7 *Re Trepca Mines Ltd* [1960] 3 All ER 304n, [1960] 1 WLR 1273, CA.
8 *Re Hoyles, Row v Jagg* [1911] 1 Ch 179, CA. Commonwealth courts, in cases concerning land within their jurisdictions, are divided as to the correctness of the principle in this case: see the authorities reviewed in *Haque v Haque (No 2)* (1965) 114 CLR 98, [1966] ALR 553, Aust HC, where it was held that the interest of an unpaid vendor of land could be equated with that of a mortgagee and was therefore, in the court's view, movable; and *Re Greenfield* [1985] 2 NZLR 662, NZ CA.
9 See eg *Re Berchtold, Berchtold v Capron* [1923] 1 Ch 192 at 200.

904. Proceeds of sale of immovables. The proceeds of sale of land will normally fall to be treated as movables. An interest in partnership land is immovable property, but a right to claim in the distribution of partnership assets, or to payment out of the assets of the value of a share in the partnership, is movable[1].

The above principle is subject to certain qualifications. The proceeds, situated in England and Wales[2], of sale of English settled land are, by virtue of statute[3], immovable property for the purposes of disposition, transmission and devolution[4]. Also, the rights of persons interested in the proceeds of sale of immovable property are governed by the law of the country where the immovable is situated, even if the proceeds are removed from that country[5].

1 *Haque v Haque (No 2)* (1965) 114 CLR 98 at 122, 130, [1966] ALR 553 at 565–566, 571, Aust HC. The treatment of the proceeds of the sale of partnership land as personalty for certain purposes (eg *Forbes v Steven, Mackenzie v Forbes* (1870) LR 10 Eq 178; *Re Stokes, Stokes v Ducroz* (1890) 62 LT 176 (both as to legacy duty)) is not relevant to the question whether these proceeds are movables or immovables: *Re Berchtold, Berchtold v Capron* [1923] 1 Ch 192 at 206; *Haque v Haque (No 2)* supra at 149 and at 583–584.
2 See *Earl of Midleton v Baron Cottesloe* [1949] AC 418, [1949] 1 All ER 841, HL (effect of Settled Land Act 1882 as part of Irish law). As to the meaning of 'England and Wales' see para 604 ante.
3 Settled Land Act 1925 s 75(5) (replacing the Settled Land Act 1882 s 22(5)): see SETTLEMENTS vol 42 para 825.
4 *Re Cutcliffe's Will Trusts, Brewer v Cutcliffe* [1940] Ch 565, [1940] 2 All ER 297. However, they are not immovables for fiscal purposes: *Earl of Midleton v Baron Cottesloe* [1949] AC 418, [1949] 1 All ER 841, HL (death duty). See *Chatfield v Berchtoldt* (1872) 7 Ch App 192.
5 *Hanson v Walker* (1829) 7 LJOS Ch 135; *Waterhouse v Stansfield* (1851) 9 Hare 234; *Re Peat's Trusts* (1869) LR 7 Eq 302; *Grimwood v Bartels* (1877) 46 LJCh 788; *Murray v Champernowne* [1901] 2 IR 232; *Re Rea, Rea v Rea* [1902] 1 IR 451. Cf *Re Piercy, Whitwham v Piercy* [1895] 1 Ch 83; *Philipson-Stow v IRC* [1961] AC 727 at 744–745, [1960] 3 All ER 814 at 820, HL.

905. Other property associated with land. The law of the place of the land in question will determine whether property associated with it, such as title deeds, fixtures or growing crops, is to be regarded as movable or immovable property[1]. Growing crops on English land, if *fructus industriales*[2], may be treated as movables; crops which have been harvested, and so severed from the land, are movables[3].

1 See para 902 ante.
2 Ie the product of human labour, as opposed to *fructus naturales*.
3 The reported cases deal with similar, but distinct, questions: whether a contract was for the sale of goods for the purposes of the Statute of Frauds (1677) (eg *Evans v Roberts* (1826) 5 B & C 829) and the definition of personal chattels for the purposes of the Bills of Sale Acts (eg *Stephenson v Thompson* [1924] 2 KB 240, CA). See *Saunders (Inspector of Taxes) v Pilcher* [1949] 2 All ER 1097, CA; and AGRICULTURE vol 1(2) (Reissue) paras 706–707; BILLS OF SALE vol 4(1) (Reissue) para 643.

906. Chattels. Unless classified under the rules stated previously as immovable[1], all interests in chattels situated in England and Wales[2] are classified as movable property; this applies to choses in action as well as to choses in possession[3].

1 Eg 'chattels real', leasehold land (see para 903 ante), fixtures, etc (see para 905 ante).
2 As to the meaning of 'England and Wales' see para 604 ante.
3 See *Re Hoyles, Row v Jagg* [1911] 1 Ch 179 at 186, CA.

(ii) Location of Property

907. Location of property in general. The location of property is a matter for English law[1]. It is possible for property to be regarded as having different locations for different purposes. So far as corporeal property is concerned, the general rule is that the property is situated where it is to be found[2]. Choses in action are treated as having a situs[3] in accordance with the principles stated in the following paragraphs.

1 See *Rossano v Manufacturers' Life Insurance Co* [1963] 2 QB 352 at 379–380, [1962] 2 All ER 214 at 230. As to the meaning of 'English law' see para 604 ante.
2 As to ships on the high seas see para 913 post.
3 See *English, Scottish and Australian Bank Ltd v IRC* [1932] AC 238, HL; and CHOSES IN ACTION vol 6 (Reissue) para 2.

908. Simple contract debts. A debt arising out of a simple contract is deemed to be situated in the place in which it is properly recoverable by action[1], that is, in general, the country in which the debtor is resident[2] or, in cases falling within the Brussels and Lugano Conventions[3], domiciled[4]. The debtor may be resident in a number of countries; in such a case the situs of the debt is the place where payment would be made in the normal course of commercial usage, for example, in the case of a debt due from a bank to a customer, at the branch where the account is kept[5], in the case of a debt due under a policy of insurance, at the place where the policy money is made payable by the policy[6], and similarly with a debt due under a sterling bill issued by a foreign government[7]. If the debtor is not resident in England and Wales, the mere fact that the debt can be recovered by action in England and Wales from the debtor out of the jurisdiction does not make the debt locally situated in England and Wales[8]; nor does a stipulation for payment in England and Wales[9].

1 Until a debt is payable and recoverable it has no situs: *Re Helbert Wagg & Co Ltd's Claim* [1956] Ch 323 at 339–340, [1956] 1 All ER 129 at 135. Cf *Kwok Chi Leung Karl v Comr of Estate Duty* [1988] 1 WLR 1035, PC (non-negotiable promissory note had a situs for estate duty purposes).
2 *Re Maudslay, Sons and Field, Maudslay v Maudslay, Sons and Field* [1900] 1 Ch 602; *Payne v R* [1902] AC 552, PC; *Swiss Bank Corpn v Boehmische Industrial Bank* [1923] 1 KB 673 at 678, CA; *English, Scottish and Australian Bank Ltd v IRC* [1932] AC 238, HL; *Re Russian Bank for Foreign Trade* [1933] Ch 745; *Re Banque des Marchands de Moscou (Koupetschesky), Royal Exchange Assurance v The Liquidator* [1952] 1 All ER 1269.

3 As to the Brussels and Lugano Conventions see para 618 text and notes 1–2 ante.
4 See paras 634–639 ante.
5 *Martin v Nadel* [1906] 2 KB 26, CA; *R v Lovitt* [1912] AC 212 at 218–219, PC; *Clare & Co v Dresdner Bank* [1915] 2 KB 576; *Joachimson v Swiss Bank Corpn* [1921] 3 KB 110, CA; *Swiss Bank Corpn v Boehmische Industrial Bank* [1923] 1 KB 673, CA; *Richardson v Richardson* [1927] P 228; *Arab Bank Ltd v Barclays Bank (Dominion, Colonial and Overseas)* [1954] AC 495, [1954] 2 All ER 226, HL.
6 *New York Life Insurance Co v Public Trustee* [1924] 2 Ch 101, CA; *Jabbour v Custodian of Israeli Absentee Property* [1954] 1 All ER 145, [1954] 1 WLR 139; *Rossano v Manufacturers' Life Insurance Co* [1963] 2 QB 352, [1962] 2 All ER 214.
7 *Re Russo-Asiatic Bank, Re Russian Bank for Foreign Trade* [1934] Ch 720.
8 *Re Banque des Marchands de Moscou (Koupetschesky)* [1954] 2 All ER 746, [1954] 1 WLR 1108, following *Deutsche Bank und Disconto Gesellschaft v Banque des Marchands de Moscou* (1938) 158 LT 364, CA.
9 *Re Helbert Wagg & Co Ltd's Claim* [1956] Ch 323, [1956] 1 All ER 129, following *Deutsche Bank und Disconto Gesellschaft v Banque des Marchands de Moscou* (1938) 158 LT 364, CA.

909. Specialty debts. A debt due on a specialty, which has a species of corporeal existence in the sealed instrument[1], is located where that instrument is situated[2]. This rule has been applied to mortgage debts[3] and to bonds issued by overseas governments under statutory authority[4].

1 There is no longer a requirement that a deed be executed under seal: see the Law of Property (Miscellaneous Provisions) Act 1989 s 1. For the proposition that deeds to which that Act applies are specialties whether or not they are executed under seal see Dicey and Morris *The Conflict of Laws* (12th Edn, 1993) 928.
2 *Stamps Comr v Hope* [1891] AC 476, PC; approving *Gurney v Rawlins* (1836) 2 M & W 87; *Toronto General Trusts Corpn v R* [1919] AC 679, PC; *Royal Trust Co v A-G for Alberta* [1930] AC 144, PC.
3 *Toronto General Trusts Corpn v R* [1919] AC 679, PC.
4 *Royal Trust Co v A-G for Alberta* [1930] AC 144, PC. As to United Kingdom government stock see para 911 post.

910. Securities transferable by delivery. Negotiable instruments and all bonds and securities transferable by delivery[1] are located where the instrument or document is to be found[2].

1 Ie not requiring transfer on a register: cf para 911 post.
2 *A-G v Bouwens* (1838) 4 M & W 171; *A-G v Glendining* (1904) 92 LT 87; *Winans v A-G (No 2)* [1910] AC 27, HL; *Re Clark, McKecknie v Clark* [1904] 1 Ch 294.

911. Location where title dependent on registration. Where title to a chose in action, such as a share in a company or United Kingdom government stock, depends upon registration, the chose in action is situated in the place at which the appropriate register is kept[1].

1 *A-G v Higgins* (1857) 2 H & N 339; *New York Breweries Co Ltd v A-G* [1899] AC 62, HL; *IRC v Maple & Co (Paris) Ltd* [1908] AC 22, HL; *Brassard v Smith* [1925] AC 371, PC; *Baelz v Public Trustee* [1926] Ch 863; *London and South American Investment Trust Ltd v British Tobacco Co (Australia) Ltd* [1927] 1 Ch 107; *Erie Beach Co Ltd v A-G for Ontario* [1930] AC 161, PC; *R v Williams* [1942] AC 541, [1942] 2 All ER 95, PC. Letters of allotment of shares fall within the same principle: *Young v Phillips (Inspector of Taxes)* [1984] STC 520, 58 TC 232.

912. Interests under a trust. Where the terms of a trust give a beneficiary a beneficial interest in property, the situs of the interest will be the same as that of the property[1]. Where the trust creates merely a right of action against the trustees, that chose in action will be located where it can be enforced against the trustees, normally where they reside[2].

1 *Re Berchtold, Berchtold v Capron* [1923] 1 Ch 192; *Philipson-Stow v IRC* [1961] AC 727 at 762, [1960] 3 All ER 814 at 831, HL; and see the analysis in *Haque v Haque (No 2)* (1965) 114 CLR 98 at 107, [1966] ALR 553 at 555, Aust HC.
2 *Re Cigala's Settlement Trusts* (1878) 7 ChD 351; *Lord Sudeley v A-G* [1897] AC 11, HL; *Re Smyth, Leach v Leach* [1898] 1 Ch 89; *A-G v Johnson* [1907] 2 KB 885; *Favorke v Steinkopff* [1922] 1 Ch 174; *Stamp Duties (Queensland) Comr v Livingston* [1965] AC 694, [1964] 3 All ER 692, PC.

913. Ships. A ship within the limits of territorial waters is treated as situated where it is actually located[1]. It would seem that a ship on the high seas may be treated as situated at her port of registry[2].

1 *Trustees Executors and Agency Co Ltd v IRC* [1973] Ch 254, [1973] 1 All ER 563.
2 *Trustees Executors and Agency Co Ltd v IRC* [1973] Ch 254 at 263, [1973] 1 All ER 563 at 568. See also *Compania Naviera Vascongado v SS Cristina* [1938] AC 485 at 509, [1938] 1 All ER 719 at 733, HL; *The Jupiter* [1924] P 236 at 239, CA.

(2) JURISDICTION REGARDING FOREIGN IMMOVABLES

(i) General Rules relating to Foreign Immovables

914. Jurisdiction with respect to immovables. The English court[1] has jurisdiction, regardless of domicile, in civil or commercial matters within the scope of the Brussels or Lugano Convention[2], or the corresponding scheme for determining jurisdiction as between parts of the United Kingdom[3] in proceedings which have as their object rights in rem in immovable property or tenancies of immovable property situated in England and Wales[4]. In any other case falling within the Conventions and the scheme referred to above, the English court has no jurisdiction, subject to one exception[5], to entertain such proceedings[6].

Subject to the Brussels and Lugano Conventions and the scheme referred to above, and to certain exceptions considered below[7], the jurisdiction of the English court to entertain proceedings for trespass[8] to, or any other tort affecting, immovable property[9] extends to cases in which the property in question is situated outside England and Wales unless the proceedings are principally concerned with a question of the title to, or right to possession of, that property[10]. The origin of this rule lies in the distinction between local actions, in which there is a necessary connection between the facts and a particular locality, and transitory actions, where there is no such necessary connection. The English court had no jurisdiction in respect of local actions where the relevant locality was outside England[11]. It remains the case that the English court cannot entertain any action for a declaration as to title to foreign immovables[12], or for possession of such immovables[13], or for injunctions having a similar effect[14]. The same rule applies to other proceedings the primary question in which is one of title to foreign immovables, such as an action for an account of the proceeds of foreign land, title to which is in dispute[15], for the enforcement of covenants for quiet enjoyment of foreign land[16], or for the partition of such land[17].

Where the proceedings are not principally concerned with the title to or possession of immovables, the usual rules as to jurisdiction in personam apply[18]. This applies to actions brought by the owners of foreign immovables damaged by a ship, and there is jurisdiction to enforce a maritime lien based on damage by a ship to foreign immovables by an admiralty action in rem against the ship[19].

1 As to the meaning of 'English' in relation to courts see para 604 ante.
2 As to the Brussels and Lugano Conventions see para 618 text and notes 1–2 ante.
3 As to the adaptation of the provisions of the Brussels and Lugano Conventions by the Civil Jurisdiction and Judgments Act 1982 s 16 (as amended), Sch 4, to a scheme applying as between parts of the United Kingdom, see para 619 ante. As to the interpretation of the scheme by reference to decisions under the Conventions see para 623 ante.
4 See para 627 ante.
5 As to the exception see para 627 text and note 9 ante.
6 Ie the courts for the contracting state or part of the United Kingdom in question have exclusive jurisdiction: see para 627 ante.
7 See paras 915–923, 1090 post.
8 This includes proceedings in respect of conspiracy to commit a trespass: see *Hesperides Hotels Ltd v Muftizade* [1979] AC 508, [1978] 2 All ER 1168, HL.
9 This includes rights arising under foreign intellectual property laws: *Tyburn Productions Ltd v Conan Doyle* [1991] Ch 75, [1990] 1 All ER 909. It does not include chattels: *Hesperides Hotels Ltd v Muftizade* [1979] AC 508, [1978] 2 All ER 1168, HL (chattel contents of a hotel).
10 Civil Jurisdiction and Judgments Act 1982 s 30 (amended by the Civil Jurisdiction and Judgments Act 1991 s 3, Sch 2 para 13), which qualifies the rule in *British South Africa Co v Companhia de Moçambique* [1893] AC 602, HL. It would seem that jurisdiction cannot be created by agreement between the parties; see *The Tolten* [1946] P 135 at 166, [1946] 2 All ER 372 at 388, CA; cf *The M Moxham* (1876) 1 PD 107 at 109, CA; *Re Duke of Wellington, Glentanar v Wellington* [1948] Ch 118, CA; and see *Razelos v Razelos* [1969] 3 All ER 929 at 935, sub nom *Razelos v Razelos (No 2)* [1970] 1 WLR 392 at 403; for further proceedings see [1970] 1 All ER 386n, [1970] 1 WLR 390.
11 The pre-Judicature Acts rules as to local venue made use of the distinction between local and transitory actions, but neither those rules nor their abolition in 1875, by virtue of the Supreme Court of Judicature Act 1875 (repealed), affected the jurisdiction of the English court. See, for an exhaustive discussion, *British South Africa Co v Companhia de Moçambique* [1893] AC 602 at 617–629, HL. The scope of this principle, which formerly barred any action whatever in the English courts in respect of any tort affecting foreign land, was narrowed by the Civil Jurisdiction and Judgments Act 1982 s 30 (as amended) into the principle set out in the text and note 10 supra.
12 *Companhia de Moçambique v British South Africa Co* [1892] 2 QB 358, DC (claims for declaration and injunction abandoned on appeal at 385, CA; for the text of the injunction sought see 66 LT 775); *Inglis v Commonwealth Trading Bank of Australia* (1972) 20 FLR 30.
13 *Roberdeau v Rous* (1738) 1 Atk 543.
14 See note 10 supra.
15 *Re Hawthorne, Graham v Massey* (1883) 23 ChD 743.
16 See *Black Point Syndicate Ltd v Eastern Concession Ltd* (1898) 79 LT 658 (where the existence of jurisdiction was doubted).
17 *Cartwright v Pettus* (1675) 2 Cas in Ch 214; cf to the contrary *Tulloch v Hartley* (1841) 1 Y & C Ch Cas 114, sed quaere.
18 See para 915 et seq post.
19 *The Tolten* [1946] P 135, [1946] 2 All ER 372, CA; and see ADMIRALTY vol 1(1) (Reissue) para 319.

(ii) Equitable Jurisdiction in Personam

A. GENERAL PRINCIPLES

915. Jurisdiction in personam. The rule that the English court[1] has no jurisdiction to entertain proceedings principally concerned with a question of title to, or the right to possession of, immovable property situated outside England and Wales[2] is subject not only to the provisions of the Brussels and Lugano Conventions[3] but also to certain principles governing the exercise of jurisdiction in personam. The English court exercises a jurisdiction in personam in cases involving foreign immovables against persons subject to its jurisdiction where there exists between the parties a personal

obligation or equity arising out of contract, or trust, or from fraud or other unconscionable conduct[4]. This principle does not give jurisdiction to determine title to
foreign immovables where there is no personal obligation between the parties[5], or only
some equity which depends for its existence on the lex situs of the immovable, namely
the law of the country where it is situated[6].

1 As to the meaning of 'English' in relation to courts see para 604 ante.
2 See para 914 ante.
3 As to the Brussels and Lugano Conventions see para 618 text and notes 1–2 ante. See also para 903 ante.
4 *Archer v Preston* (prior to 1682) 1 Eq Cas Abr 133, pl 3, cited in *Arglasse v Muschamp* (1682) 1 Vern 76;
   Foster v Vassall (1747) 3 Atk 587; *Penn v Lord Baltimore* (1750) 1 Ves Sen 444; *Lord Cranstown v Johnston*
   (1796) 3 Ves 170; *Lord Portarlington v Soulby* (1834) 3 My & K 104 at 108; *Ewing v Orr Ewing* (1883) 9 App
   Cas 34, HL; *British South Africa Co v Companhia de Moçambique* [1893] AC 602 at 626–627, HL;
   Deschamps v Miller [1908] 1 Ch 856; *Richard West & Partners (Inverness) Ltd v Dick* [1969] 2 Ch 424, [1969]
   1 All ER 289; affd [1969] 2 Ch 424 at 433, [1969] 1 All ER 943, CA; *Razelos v Razelos* [1969] 3 All ER
   929, sub nom *Razelos v Razelos (No 2)* [1970] 1 WLR 392 (for further proceedings see [1970] 1 All ER
   386n, [1970] 1 WLR 390); *Cook Industries Inc v Galliher* [1979] Ch 439, [1978] 3 All ER 945; *Chellaram v
   Chellaram* [1985] Ch 409, [1985] 1 All ER 1043; and see generally the cases cited in paras 916–922 post.
   Cf *Companhia de Moçambique v British South Africa Co* [1892] 2 QB 358 at 404–405, CA.
5 *Re Hawthorne, Graham v Massey* (1883) 23 ChD 743; *Companhia de Moçambique v British South Africa Co*
   [1892] 2 QB 358 at 364, 366, DC; *Deschamps v Miller* [1908] 1 Ch 856. Cf Case C–294/92 *Webb v Webb*
   [1994] ECR I–1717, [1994] QB 696, [1994] 3 All ER 911, ECJ.
6 *Deschamps v Miller* [1908] 1 Ch 856 at 863. For further restrictions on this jurisdiction see paras 916–917
   post.

916. Jurisdiction in respect of third persons. The English court[1] will not grant
relief in order to enforce English principles of equity against third persons who have
acquired a good title by the lex situs of the immovables[2], or, in the absence of privity
between the parties, to impose on a foreign immovable a burden other than that which
the local law requires it to bear[3].

Thus where the claim is not recognised by the lex situs this principle will defeat a
claim by legatees to marshal against the heir of foreign land[4], by an unpaid vendor of
foreign land to enforce a lien against the land in the hands of a subsequent purchaser[5],
or by a beneficiary under a marriage settlement to enforce a claim against the land in the
hands of a mortgagee[6]. Similarly, a purchaser under a contract for the sale of foreign
land has no power to claim relief against a person who subsequently gained a good title
by the lex situs, even where that person took with notice of the contract[7].

The English court will exercise its equitable jurisdiction against third parties who are
affected by equities under the lex situs of the immovables itself. Thus where an English
company takes a foreign immovable under an express obligation to satisfy another's
equitable claim out of it, the court can exercise jurisdiction and enforce the claim by
restraining the company and its directors from applying the proceeds of the foreign
land without making proper provision for satisfying the claim[8].

1 As to the meaning of 'English' in relation to courts see para 604 ante.
2 *Martin v Martin* (1831) 2 Russ & M 507; *Waterhouse v Stansfield* (1851) 9 Hare 234; subsequent
   proceedings (1852) 10 Hare 254; *Norris v Chambres* (1861) 29 Beav 246; affd (1861) 3 De GF & J 583;
   Hicks v Powell (1869) 4 Ch App 741.
3 *Harrison v Harrison* (1873) 8 Ch App 342; *Re Hewit, Lawson v Duncan* [1891] 3 Ch 568; and see para 917
   note 3 post.
4 *Harrison v Harrison* (1873) 8 Ch App 342.
5 *Norris v Chambres* (1861) 29 Beav 246; affd (1861) 3 De GF & J 583.
6 *Martin v Martin* (1831) 2 Russ & M 507; cf *Deschamps v Miller* [1908] 1 Ch 856.
7 *Norton v Florence Land and Public Works Co* (1877) 7 ChD 332.
8 *Mercantile Investment and General Trust Co v River Plate Trust, Loan and Agency Co* [1892] 2 Ch 303.

917. Exercise of jurisdiction. Equitable remedies are in the discretion of the court, and an English court[1] will act upon its own principles in deciding whether to grant relief. Accordingly, the effect of laches or acquiescence as a bar to specific performance is a matter for English law[2].

It is uncertain to what extent the English court will grant relief to a party so as to enforce rights which would not be recognised by the lex situs of the immovables[3]. The English court will not act so as to prevent a person from enjoying what a judgment of the local court has declared him to be entitled to[4]; nor will it act where to do so would be useless, and where it would be impossible for the decree to be carried into effect[5]. Jurisdiction will not be exercised (and a fortiori the taking or continuance of proceedings in foreign courts will not be restrained by injunction[6]) where, on the whole, the question can be more conveniently decided in the local courts than in England[7].

1 As to the meaning of 'English' in relation to courts see para 604 ante.
2 *Cood v Cood* (1863) 33 Beav 314.
3 See *Richard West & Partners (Inverness) Ltd v Dick* [1969] 2 Ch 424, [1969] 1 All ER 289; affd [1969] 2 Ch 424 at 433, [1969] 1 All ER 943, CA. For the view that English law will prevail see *Re Courtney, ex p Pollard* (1840) Mont & Ch 239, especially at 251 (but cf at 250); *Coote v Jecks* (1872) LR 13 Eq 597; *Re Scheibler, ex p Holthausen* (1874) 9 Ch App 722; *British South Africa Co v De Beers Consolidated Mines Ltd* [1910] 1 Ch 354 at 387; *Re Anchor Line (Henderson Bros) Ltd* [1937] Ch 483, [1937] 2 All ER 823. For the contrary view see *Bent v Young* (1838) 9 Sim 180; *Waterhouse v Stansfield* (1852) 10 Hare 254; *Norris v Chambres* (1861) 29 Beav 246 at 255; affd (1861) 3 De GF & J 583; *Hicks v Powell* (1869) 4 Ch App 741.
4 *White v Hall* (1806) 12 Ves 321.
5 *Mercantile Investment and General Trust Co v River Plate Trust, Loan and Agency Co* [1892] 2 Ch 303; *Grey v Manitoba and North Western Rly Co of Canada* [1897] AC 254, PC; *Richard West & Partners (Inverness) Ltd v Dick* [1969] 2 Ch 424, [1969] 1 All ER 289; affd [1969] 2 Ch 424 at 433, [1969] 1 All ER 943, CA.
6 As to restraining actions in foreign courts concerning immovables see *Beckford v Kemble* (1822) 1 Sim & St 7; *Booth v Leycester* (1837) 1 Keen 579; *Bunbury v Bunbury* (1839) 1 Beav 318; affd (1839) 8 LJCh 297 at 302; *Jones v Geddes* (1845) 1 Ph 724; *Hope v Carnegie* (1866) 1 Ch App 320; *Hearn v Glanville* (1883) 48 LT 356; and generally paras 1084–1087 post.
7 See *Cookney v Anderson* (1863) 1 De GJ & Sm 365; *Blake v Blake* (1870) 18 WR 944; *Matthaei v Galitzin* (1874) LR 18 Eq 340; *Doss v Secretary of State for India in Council* (1875) LR 19 Eq 509; all as explained in *Companhia de Moçambique v British South Africa Co* [1892] 2 QB 358 at 367, DC. See also *Norton v Florence Land and Public Works Co* (1877) 7 ChD 332 (where proceedings had been commenced abroad). For special cases as to proceedings against the Crown see *Re Holmes* (1861) 2 John & H 527; *Doss v Secretary of State for India in Council* supra; and CROWN PROCEEDINGS vol 11 (Supp) para 12.

B. APPLICATION OF PRINCIPLES

918. Contract. Under the principle stated previously[1], the English court[2] may exercise jurisdiction in an action on a contract relating to foreign immovables[3]. It may order specific performance[4] of any such contract[5] which the lex situs of the immovables in question allows to be carried into effect[5].

1 See para 915 ante.
2 As to the meaning of 'English' in relation to courts see para 604 ante.
3 *St Pierre v South American Stores (Gath and Chaves) Ltd* [1936] 1 KB 382, CA (rent); *Buenos Ayres and Ensenada Port Rly Co v Northern Rly Co of Buenos Ayres* (1877) 2 QBD 210 (rent and share of cost of works on foreign land). Cf Case C–294/92 *Webb v Webb* [1994] ECR I-1717, [1994] QB 696, [1994] 3 All ER 911, ECJ.
4 For the principles upon which the court will act in granting equitable remedies see para 917 ante.
5 *Penn v Lord Baltimore* (1750) 1 Ves Sen 444; *Jackson v Petrie* (1804) 10 Ves 164; *Re Courtney, ex p Pollard* (1840) Mont & Ch 239 at 250–252; *Cood v Cood* (1863) 33 Beav 314; *Richard West & Partners (Inverness) Ltd v Dick* [1969] 2 Ch 424, [1969] 1 All ER 289; affd [1969] 2 Ch 424 at 433, [1969] 1 All ER 943, CA. See *White v Hall* (1806) 12 Ves 321; *Lord Portarlington v Soulby* (1834) 3 My & K 104 at 108; *Ewing v Orr Ewing* (1883) 9 App Cas 34 at 40, HL; *British South Africa Co v Companhia de Moçambique* [1893] AC 602 at 626, HL; *Duder v Amsterdamsch Trustees Kantoor* [1902] 2 Ch 132.
5 See para 917 ante.

919. Trusts. Under the principle stated previously[1], the English court[2] may exercise jurisdiction to enforce a trust relating to foreign immovables[3], including jurisdiction to decide whether or not a valid trust exists[4].

1 See para 915 ante.
2 As to the meaning of 'English' in relation to courts see para 604 ante.
3 *Earl of Kildare v Eustace* (1686) 1 Vern 419; *Clarke v Earl of Ormonde* (1821) Jac 108 at 125; *Harrison v Gurney* (1821) 2 Jac & W 563; *Jenney v Mackintosh* (1886) 33 ChD 595; *Re Clinton, Clinton v Clinton* (1903) 88 LT 17; and see *Ewing v Orr Ewing* (1883) 9 App Cas 34 at 40, HL; *British South Africa Co v Companhia de Moçambique* [1893] AC 602 at 626, HL.
4 *Re Clinton, Clinton v Clinton* (1903) 88 LT 17; *Chellaram v Chellaram* [1985] Ch 409, [1985] 1 All ER 1043. As to the recognition of trusts see paras 938–944 post. The English court has power to make vesting orders relating to property in any part of Her Majesty's dominions except Scotland: Trustee Act 1925 s 56. For the procedure in respect of applications under that Act where land or investments are situated in Scotland see *Practice Note* (1945) 61 TLR 319.

920. Fraud and inequitable dealing. Under the principle stated previously[1], the English court[2] has jurisdiction to grant relief in cases of fraud or inequitable dealing with regard to foreign immovables[3], including power to set aside, or otherwise relieve against, a conveyance of foreign immovables procured by fraud[4].

A creditor who, under his own execution, purchases foreign land belonging to his debtor, will be compelled by the court to hold it as security for the debt, and therefore subject to a right of redemption[5].

1 See para 915 ante.
2 As to the meaning of 'English' in relation to courts see para 604 ante.
3 *Arglasse v Muschamp* (1682) 1 Vern 76; *Angus v Angus* (1737) West *temp* Hard 23; *Lord Cranstown v Johnston* (1796) 3 Ves 170; *White v Hall* (1806) 12 Ves 321; *Jones v Geddes* (1845) 1 Ph 724; *Lord Portarlington v Soulby* (1834) 3 My & K 104 at 108; *British South Africa Co v Companhia de Moçambique* [1893] AC 602 at 626, HL; *Razelos v Razelos* [1969] 3 All ER 929, sub nom *Razelos v Razelos (No 2)* [1970] 1 WLR 392 (for further proceedings see [1970] 1 All ER 386n, [1970] 1 WLR 390); *Cook Industries Inc v Galliher* [1979] Ch 439, [1978] 3 All ER 945.
4 *Arglasse v Muschamp* (1682) 1 Vern 76; *Angus v Angus* (1737) West *temp* Hard 23. For the principles upon which the court grants relief see para 917 ante.
5 *Lord Cranstown v Johnston* (1796) 3 Ves 170. It is otherwise if the local court ordered a judicial sale: see *White v Hall* (1806) 12 Ves 321; and para 917 ante.

921. Mortgages of foreign immovables. Where a legal or equitable mortgage of foreign immovables has been validly made according to English law[1], the English court, acting under the principle stated previously[2], may exercise jurisdiction to make orders for foreclosure[3] or for redemption[4], and will compel the mortgagor to pay off the mortgage debt out of the proceeds of the sale of the land[5]. Where an order for redemption has been made in England an injunction will be granted against a mortgagee who brings a foreclosure action in the local courts, and vice versa[6].

The English court will decree the specific performance[7] of a contract governed by English law to grant a mortgage of foreign land, and the contract will be interpreted as requiring a mortgage which contains such equities and rights of redemption as are usually found in an English mortgage[8].

1 As to the meaning of 'English law' see para 604 ante.
2 See para 915 ante.

3   *Toller v Carteret* (1705) 2 Vern 494; *Earl of Derby v Duke of Atholl* (1749) 1 Ves Sen 202 at 204; *Lord Portarlington v Soulby* (1834) 3 My & K 104 at 108; *Norris v Chambres* (1861) 29 Beav 246 at 255; affd (1861) 3 De GF & J 583; *Paget v Ede* (1874) LR 18 Eq 118; *Re Hawthorne, Graham v Massey* (1883) 23 ChD 743 at 747–748. See also *Bawtree v Great North-West Central Rly Co* (1898) 14 TLR 448, CA. For the position where the local law does not permit foreclosure, cf para 917 text to note 3 ante. The court cannot order the sale of foreign land: *Grey v Manitoba and North Western Rly Co of Canada* [1897] AC 254, PC; and see para 917 text to note 6 ante.

4   *Beckford v Kemble* (1822) 1 Sim & St 7.

5   *Earl of Derby v Duke of Atholl* (1749) 1 Ves Sen 202 at 204; *Re Courtney, ex p Pollard* (1840) Mont & Ch 239. See *Norton v Florence Land and Public Works Co* (1877) 7 ChD 332; *Mercantile Investment and General Trust Co v River Plate Trust, Loan and Agency Co* [1892] 2 Ch 303; *Re Anchor Line (Henderson Bros) Ltd* [1937] Ch 483, [1937] 2 All ER 823 (effect on property in Scotland of what is now the Insolvency Act 1986 s 185). As to accounts and receivers see para 922 post. For the position where local law would not recognise the plaintiff's rights see para 917 text to note 3 ante.

6   *Beckford v Kemble* (1822) 1 Sim & St 7; and see para 917 text to note 6 ante.

7   For the principles on which the court will act see para 917 ante.

8   *British South Africa Co v De Beers Consolidated Mines Ltd* [1910] 2 Ch 502, CA; revsd on other grounds sub nom *De Beers Consolidated Mines Ltd v British South Africa Co* [1912] AC 52, HL; *Re Smith, Lawrence v Kitson* [1916] 2 Ch 206 (order made against deceased debtor's personal representatives).

922. Accounts and receivers. The English court[1] may exercise jurisdiction under the principle stated previously[2] to order an account of the rents and profits of a foreign immovable against any person liable to account in respect of them[3], and in a suitable case a receiver will be appointed[4]. The English court cannot put the receiver in possession of foreign immovables, but any party to the action in which the order is made who prevents the necessary steps being taken to enable the receiver to take possession according to the lex situs is guilty of contempt of court[5]. It is not contempt for any other person to take proceedings in the local court for possession before the receiver can take proceedings[6].

1   As to the meaning of 'English' in relation to courts see para 604 ante.

2   See para 915 ante.

3   *Cartwright v Pettus* (1675) 2 Cas in Ch 214 (see sub nom *Carteret v Petty* (1676) 2 Swan 323n); *Scott v Nesbitt* (1808) 14 Ves 438; *Beattie v Johnstone* (1848) 8 Hare 169 at 177; *Hendrick v Wood* (1861) 30 LJCh 583; *Paget v Ede* (1874) LR 18 Eq 118 at 126.

4   *Harrison v Gurney* (1821) 2 Jac & W 563; *Clarke v Earl of Ormonde* (1821) Jac 108 at 116, 121; *Houlditch v Marquess of Donegall* (1834) 2 Cl & Fin 470, HL; *Paget v Ede* (1874) LR 18 Eq 118 at 126; *Mercantile Investment and General Trust Co v River Plate Trust, Loan and Agency Co* [1892] 2 Ch 303; *Re Maudslay, Sons and Field, Maudslay v Maudslay, Sons and Field* [1900] 1 Ch 602 at 611; *Duder v Amsterdamsch Trustees Kantoor* [1902] 2 Ch 132. For the principles on which the court exercises its jurisdiction see para 917 ante. See also COMPANIES vol 7(2) (Reissue) para 1189.

5   *Re Maudslay, Sons and Field, Maudslay v Maudslay, Sons and Field* [1900] 1 Ch 602 at 611.

6   *Re Maudslay, Sons and Field, Maudslay v Maudslay, Sons and Field* [1900] 1 Ch 602.

(iii) Administration of Estates and Trusts

923. Administration of estates and trusts. Where the English court[1] has jurisdiction to administer a trust or the estate of a deceased person[2], and the property includes both movable or immovable property in England and immovable property abroad, the court has jurisdiction to determine questions of title to the foreign immovables for the purposes of the administration[3].

1   As to the meaning of 'English' in relation to courts see para 604 ante.

2   See para 954 post.

3   *Bunbury v Bunbury* (1839) 1 Beav 318; *Earl Nelson v Lord Bridport* (1845) 8 Beav 547; *Hope v Carnegie* (1866) 1 Ch App 320; *Ewing v Orr Ewing* (1883) 9 App Cas 34, HL; *Re Piercy, Whitwham v Piercy* [1895] 1

Ch 83; *Re Moses, Moses v Valentine* [1908] 2 Ch 235; *Re Stirling, Stirling v Stirling* [1908] 2 Ch 344; *Re Pearse's Settlement, Pearse v Pearse* [1909] 1 Ch 304; *Re Hoyles, Row v Jagg* [1911] 1 Ch 179, CA; *Re Ross, Ross v Waterfield* [1930] 1 Ch 377; *Re Duke of Wellington, Glentanar v Wellington* [1948] Ch 118, [1947] 2 All ER 854 at 864, CA; and see *British South Africa Co v Companhia de Moçambique* [1893] AC 602 at 626, HL.

(3) IMMOVABLES: CHOICE OF LAW

924. In general. As a general rule[1], all questions concerning rights over immovables are governed by the lex situs, namely the law of the country where the immovable is situated[2]. This principle is based upon obvious considerations of convenience and expediency. Any other rule might be ineffective, because in the last resort land can only be dealt with in a manner which the lex situs allows.

The general rule applies not only to immovables situated in England but also to immovables situated abroad, so far as the English court has jurisdiction to deal with them[3]. In the latter case, there is general agreement among text book writers[4], and some support from decided cases[5], that the lex situs means, not the domestic law of the situs, but whatever system of domestic law the courts of the situs would apply. In other words, there is a strong case for applying the doctrine of total renvoi[6] to cases concerning title to foreign immovables, for the application of the domestic law of the situs might be ineffective if the courts of the situs would apply some other law.

1 For exceptions see paras 772, 860–864 ante, 964, 966, 974–975 post.
2 See the cases cited in paras 925–927, 956, 961, 969 post.
3 See paras 915–923 ante.
4 See eg Dicey and Morris *The Conflict of Laws* (12th Edn, 1993) 960; Cheshire and North *Private International Law* (12th Edn) 72, 786,
5 *Re Ross, Ross v Waterfield* [1930] 1 Ch 377; *Re Duke of Wellington, Glentanar v Wellington* [1947] Ch 506, [1947] 2 All ER 854; affd [1948] Ch 118, [1947] 2 All ER 854 at 864, CA.
6 See paras 606–609 ante.

925. Capacity. All questions of capacity to assign[1] or acquire an immovable are governed by the lex situs of the immovable[2].

1 As to assignment by will see para 962 post.
2 *Bank of Africa Ltd v Cohen* [1909] 2 Ch 129, CA; criticised in Dicey and Morris *The Conflict of Laws* (12th Edn, 1993) 962.

926. Formalities. An assignment of an immovable must comply in point of form with the lex situs of the immovable[1], and accordingly a conveyance of English land must comply with the formalities prescribed by English law[2]. An assignment which does not satisfy the formal requirements of the lex situs may give rise to an equity recognised by and enforceable in the English court[3].

The formal validity of a contract relating to immovables is subject to the rules of the Rome Convention[4]. However, a contract the subject matter of which is a right in immovable property or a right to use immovable property is subject to the mandatory requirements of form of the law of the country where the property is situated if by that law those requirements are imposed irrespective of the country where the contract is concluded and irrespective of the law governing the contract[5].

A rule of the lex situs declaring a valid assignment or contract relating to immovables inadmissible in evidence will be ignored in England, procedural questions being governed by the lex fori[6].

1   *Waterhouse v Stansfield* (1852) 10 Hare 254; *Adams v Clutterbuck* (1883) 10 QBD 403. As to the formal validity of wills of immovables see paras 963–964 post.
2   *Re Hernando, Hernando v Sawtell* (1884) 27 ChD 284 at 293, 296; cf *Coppin v Coppin* (1725) 2 P Wms 291 (will). As to the meaning of 'English law' see para 604 ante.
3   As to the jurisdiction to enforce such equities and the principles upon which it is exercised see paras 915–917 ante.
4   See the Rome Convention art 9; and para 852 ante. For the meaning of 'the Rome Convention' see para 844 text and note 1 ante. Note that the Rome Convention only applies in respect of contracts made after 1 April 1991: see para 844 ante. As to the position in relation to contracts to which the Rome Convention does not apply see para 876 ante.
5   Rome Convention art 9 para 6.
6   *Hicks v Powell* (1869) 4 Ch App 741 at 746. See paras 1070–1071 post; and cf para 1072 post.

927. Material or essential validity. The material or essential validity of an assignment of immovable property is governed by the lex situs of the immovable[1]. This principle applies to such matters as the nature and incidents of the estates created in the immovable[2] and restraints on alienation[3]. In the case of immovables subject to a trust, the construction, effects and administration of the trust are governed by the applicable law as determined under the Hague Convention on the Law Applicable to Trusts and Their Recognition[4]; this includes restrictions upon the duration of the trust, and upon the power to accumulate the income of the trust[5].

1   See the cases cited in notes 2–3 infra; and para 969 post (wills of immovables).
2   See *Earl Nelson v Lord Bridport* (1845) 8 Beav 547; *Re Miller, Bailie v Miller* [1914] 1 Ch 511.
3   *Waterhouse v Stansfield* (1852) 10 Hare 254 at 259.
4   See the Recognition of Trusts Act 1987 s 1(1), Schedule art 8. As to the Hague Convention referred to in the text see para 938 et seq post.
5   Recognition of Trusts Act 1987 art 8(f).

928. Sums charged upon immovables. Where a sum of money is charged upon an immovable, the question as to which currency provides the unit of account by reference to which the amount of the debt is to be measured[1] is one of construction[2]. Prima facie the money of account will be the currency of the country in which the immovables are situated, but in every case the intention of the parties is the governing consideration[3].

The same principle applies to the rate of interest payable. The rate will be that fixed by the lex situs of the immovable[4], unless a contrary intention appears[5]. Where the sum is charged partly upon land in England and partly upon land elsewhere, the English rate will apply[6].

1   As to money of account, and of payment, and the effect of changing rates of exchange see MONEY vol 32 paras 103–105. See also DAMAGES vol 12 para 1201. Cf para 878 text and notes 9–10 ante.
2   *Phipps v Earl of Anglesea* (1721) 1 P Wms 696 (marriage settlement and will); *Lansdowne v Lansdowne* (1820) 2 Bli 60, HL (settlement); *Cope v Cope* (1846) 15 Sim 118 (marriage settlement); *Macrae v Goodman* (1846) 5 Moo PCC 315 (mortgage). For other cases on wills see para 968 post.
3   *Lansdowne v Lansdowne* (1820) 2 Bli 60 at 88, HL; *Northern Bank Ltd v Edwards* [1985] IR 284.
4   *Balfour v Cooper* (1883) 23 ChD 472, CA. See, to the contrary, *Stapleton v Conway* (1750) 1 Ves Sen 427.
5   *Phipps v Earl of Anglesea* (1721) 1 P Wms 696 although the rate was there fixed by consent; and see the cases on wills cited in para 968 note 7 post.
6   *Young v Lord Waterpark* (1842) 13 Sim 199; as explained in *Balfour v Cooper* (1883) 23 ChD 472, CA.

929. Lapse of time. The effect of lapse of time upon the existence or enforcement of any right in respect of immovables is governed by the lex situs of the immovables[1].

Accordingly where by the lex situs a person's title to immovables is extinguished, the English court[2] will look upon it as extinguished[3]. A similar principle applies where an action for the recovery of land is statute-barred by the lex situs[4]. Where the English court has jurisdiction to pronounce upon or enforce rights in respect of foreign immovables[5], it will only hold a right barred by lapse of time if it is so barred by the lex situs[6].

1 Cf the rule as to limitation of actions in other contexts: see para 1082 post.
2 As to the meaning of 'English' in relation to courts see para 604 ante.
3 *Beckford v Wade* (1805) 17 Ves 87, PC (prescriptive title after possession for a stated period).
4 See the Foreign Limitation Periods Act 1984 s 1: para 1082 post. Cf *Re Peat's Trusts* (1869) LR 7 Eq 302 (English action for proceeds of foreign land barred by foreign statute of limitations barred in England).
5 For the circumstances in which such jurisdiction exists see paras 914–923 ante.
6 *Pitt v Lord Dacre* (1876) 3 ChD 295 (land in Jamaica; English statute of limitations inapplicable); cf *Colonial Investment and Loan Co v Martin* [1928] SCR 440, [1928] 3 DLR 784, Can SC; Dicey and Morris *The Conflict of Laws* (12th Edn, 1993) 963. If the action in England is for an equitable remedy, eg specific performance, the defence of laches may be available: see para 917 ante.

(4) MOVABLES: CHOICE OF LAW

930. Assignments of choses in possession. The validity and effect of an assignment[1] of a chose in possession[2] are governed by the lex situs of the chose[3]. Accordingly, an assignment will be recognised in England as giving a good title if, and only if, it has that effect in the lex situs[4]; an assignee regarded by the lex situs as bound by prior rights will be similarly bound in the view of the English court[5]. It is immaterial that the former owner of the chose, whose title is defeated by an assignment taking place abroad, never consented to the chose being in the relevant foreign country, or was the victim of a theft[6]. If the property is in England, the validity and effect of the assignment will be governed by English law[7], but not all rules of English domestic law are applicable to assignments taking place abroad[8].

1 This part of the title is concerned with particular assignments. As to assignment on marriage see paras 764–773 ante; as to bankruptcy see paras 979, 981 post; and as to succession see paras 956–977 post. As to the recognition of foreign judgments in rem see paras 1019–1020 post.
2 As to documents of title see para 934 post. As to choses in action see para 935 post.
3 As to the location of property see paras 907–913 ante. As to the effect of a change of situs see para 931 post.
4 *Inglis v Usherwood* (1801) 1 East 515; *Cammell v Sewell* (1860) 5 H & N 728; *Castrique v Imrie* (1870) LR 4 HL 414 at 429; *City Bank v Barrow* (1880) 5 App Cas 664, HL; *Alcock v Smith* [1892] 1 Ch 238 at 268, CA; *Inglis v Robertson* [1898] AC 616, HL; *Embiricos v Anglo-Austrian Bank* [1905] 1 KB 677 at 683, CA; *Re Korvine's Trust, Levashoff v Block* [1921] 1 Ch 343 at 348; *Re Anziani, Herbert v Christopherson* [1930] 1 Ch 407 at 420; *Bank voor Handel en Scheepvaart NV v Slatford* [1953] 1 QB 248 at 257, [1951] 2 All ER 779 at 786; *Winkworth v Christie Manson and Woods Ltd* [1980] Ch 496, [1980] 1 All ER 1121. The principle in the text is illustrated by the recognition in England of sales ordered or confirmed by the courts of the situs: *Cammell v Sewell* supra; *Minna Craig SS Co v Chartered Mercantile Bank of India, London and China* [1897] 1 QB 460, CA.
5 See *Hooper v Gumm, McLellan v Gumm* (1867) 2 Ch App 282. As to pledges see para 932 post.
6 *Winkworth v Christie Manson and Woods Ltd* [1980] Ch 496, [1980] 1 All ER 1121.
7 *Re Korvine's Trust, Levashoff v Block* [1921] 1 Ch 343 (donatio mortis causa). Cf *Re Craven's Estate, Lloyds Bank v Cockburn* [1937] Ch 423, [1937] 3 All ER 33 (same question treated as one of administration of estates).
8 *Dulaney v Merry & Son* [1901] 1 KB 536; *Re Pilkington's Will Trusts, Pilkington v Harrison* [1937] Ch 574, [1937] 3 All ER 213 (registration under the Deeds of Arrangement Act 1914).

931. Change of location. A change in the location of a chose in possession does not itself affect title to the chose[1]. Thus, if the new lex situs does not recognise the validity or effect of an assignment which took place before the change of location, the English court will nevertheless apply the old lex situs to those questions[2]. Nevertheless, the validity and effect of an assignment made after the change of location will be governed, under the principle already stated[3], by the new lex situs; in appropriate cases a good title acquired under the old lex situs will be defeated[4].

1 *Cammell v Sewell* (1860) 5 H & N 728 at 742–743; *Winkworth v Christie Manson and Woods Ltd* [1980] Ch 496, [1980] 1 All ER 1121.
2 Eg where the new lex situs does not recognise a reservation of title valid under the old lex situs: see Dicey and Morris *The Conflict of Laws* (12th Edn, 1993) 972–976; *Simpson v Fogo* (1863) 1 Hem & M 195; *Hooper v Gumm, McLellan v Gumm* (1867) 2 Ch App 282; *Industrial Acceptance Corpn Ltd v LaFlamme* [1950] OR 311, [1950] 2 DLR 822; *Century Credit Corpn v Richard* [1962] OR 815, 34 DLR (2d) 291, Ont CA.
3 See para 930 ante.
4 Eg rules of the new lex situs as to sales in market overt, sales by mercantile agents and judicial sales: see *Cammell v Sewell* (1860) 5 H & N 728 at 744; *Alcock v Smith* [1892] 1 Ch 238 at 267, CA; *Embiricos v Anglo-Austrian Bank* [1905] 1 KB 677, CA; *Mehta v Sutton* (1913) 108 LT 214; affd (1913) 109 LT 529, CA; *Winkworth v Christie Manson and Woods Ltd* [1980] Ch 496, [1980] 1 All ER 1121.

932. Pledges. The validity and effect of a pledge are governed by the lex situs of the property pledged[1]. The relative rights of pledgor and pledgee are governed by the proper law of their transaction, which will determine, for example, whether the pledgee may redeliver the goods to the pledgor in certain circumstances without losing his security[2].

1 *City Bank v Barrow* (1880) 5 App Cas 664, HL; *Inglis v Robertson* [1898] AC 616, HL; cf *North Western Bank Ltd v Poynter, Son and Macdonalds* [1895] AC 56, HL.
2 *North Western Bank Ltd v Poynter, Son and Macdonalds* [1895] AC 56, HL; see *Inglis v Robertson* [1898] AC 616 at 626–627, HL. For the effect of later transactions see *North Western Bank Ltd v Poynter, Son and Macdonalds* supra at 67.

933. Stoppage in transit. The lex situs of the property determines the existence of a right of stoppage in transit and the manner of its exercise[1].

1 *Inglis v Usherwood* (1801) 1 East 515. See AVIATION vol 2 (Reissue) para 1576; CARRIERS vol 5(1) (Reissue) para 491 et seq; SALE OF GOODS vol 41 para 842 et seq.

934. Assignment of negotiable instruments and documents of title. Negotiable instruments and documents of title to movables, such as bills of lading, are regarded as corporeal movables, the assignment of which is governed by rules different from those affecting bare choses in action[1].

The validity and effect of an assignment of a negotiable instrument or document of title are governed by the law of the country in which the assignment takes place[2]. This will be the lex situs of the instrument or document, and the rule just stated accords with the general principle governing assignments of movables[3].

1 As to the assignment of bare choses in action see para 935 post. The Rome Convention does not apply to obligations arising under bills of exchange, cheques and promissory notes and other negotiable instruments to the extent that the obligations under such other negotiable instruments arise out of their negotiable character: art 1 para 2(c); see para 845 text and note 9 ante. For the meaning of 'the Rome Convention' see para 844 text and note 1 ante.
2 *Alcock v Smith* [1892] 1 Ch 238 at 255, CA; *Inglis v Robertson* [1898] AC 616, HL; *Embiricos v Anglo-Austrian Bank* [1905] 1 KB 677, CA; cf *North Western Bank Ltd v Poynter, Son and Macdonalds*

[1895] AC 56, HL; as explained in *Inglis v Robertson* supra at 626–627, HL. As to bills of exchange, and the effect of the Bills of Exchange Act 1882 s 72 (as amended), see BILLS OF EXCHANGE vol 4(1) (Reissue) paras 488–492, 496; and Dicey and Morris *The Conflict of Laws* (12th Edn, 1993) 1442–1444.
3 See para 930 ante.

935. Assignment of bare choses in action. The mutual obligations of assignor and assignee under a voluntary assignment of a right against another person ('the debtor') are governed by the law which applies to the contract between the assignor and assignee[1]. The law governing the right to which the assignment relates determines its assignability[2], the relationship between the assignee and the debtor, the conditions under which the assignment can be invoked against the debtor and any question whether the debtor's obligations have been discharged[3].

1 Rome Convention art 12 para 1. For the meaning of 'the Rome Convention' see para 844 text and note 1 ante. Note that the Rome Convention does not apply to contracts made on or before 1 April 1991: see para 844 ante; and note 2 infra.
2 Cf *Campbell Connelly & Co Ltd v Noble* [1963] 1 All ER 237 at 239, [1963] 1 WLR 252 at 255; *Compania Colombiana de Seguros v Pacific Steam Navigation Co* [1965] 1 QB 101 at 128–129, [1964] 1 All ER 216 at 235; and *Macmillan Inc v Bishopsgate Investment Trust plc (No 3)* [1995] 3 All ER 747, [1995] 1 WLR 978; on appeal [1996] 1 All ER 585, CA.
3 Rome Convention art 12 para 2.

(5) GOVERNMENTAL SEIZURE OF PROPERTY

936. Effect of foreign decrees. A decree of a foreign government[1] which purports to seize private property situated[2] in the territory controlled by that government[3] will be recognised in England as having deprived the owner of his interest in the property to the extent provided in the decree[4], even if the owner is not a national of the foreign state[5], and even if the property is later brought to England[6]. On the other hand, such a decree will not be recognised in England as having any effect on the ownership of property situated outside the territory controlled by the foreign government at the time of the decree, even if the owner is a national of the foreign state[7]. However, if the foreign government is in possession or control of the property, the owner cannot recover it by legal process in England, because his action would be stayed if the foreign government pleaded sovereign immunity[8].

The rules stated above apply to immovables and to chattels and choses in action. With regard to contractual rights, the applicable law of the contract[9] giving rise to the debt will govern the various ways of extinguishing obligations under the contract[10]. Although there is no authority on the point, this would seem to include the extinguishing of contractual obligations by a foreign governmental decree.

1 The principles set out in the text and notes infra formerly applied to Governments recognised either de jure or de facto by Her Majesty's Government in the United Kingdom, but it is no longer the practice of Her Majesty's Government to accord recognition to foreign governments (although it will continue to recognise foreign states): see (1980) 51 BYIL 367–368; and Dicey and Morris *The Conflict of Laws* (12th Edn, 1993) 992–993. Whether a body purporting to be a government will be so treated by the English court depends on a number of factors: whether it is the constitutional government of the State; the degree, nature and stability of its administrative control over the territory of the State; the existence, extent and nature of any dealings between it and Her Majesty's Government; and, in marginal cases, the extent of international recognition it enjoys as the government of the State: *Republic of Somalia v Woodhouse Drake & Carey (Suisse) SA, The Mary* [1993] QB 54, [1993] 1 All ER 371. See FOREIGN RELATIONS LAW vol 18 para 1425 et seq; and see *Carl Zeiss Stiftung v Rayner & Keeler Ltd (No 2)* [1967] 1 AC 853, [1966] 2 All ER 536, HL; *GUR Corpn v Trust Bank of Africa* [1987] QB 599, [1986] 3 All ER

449, DC. Under the former recognition practice, the doctrine of the retroactive effect of recognition might render it immaterial that recognition was not granted until after the decree was made: *Aksionairnoye Obschestvo A M Luther v James Sagor & Co* [1921] 3 KB 532, CA; cf *Gdynia Ameryka Linie Zeglugowe Spolka Akcyjina v Boguslawski* [1953] AC 11, [1952] 2 All ER 470, HL; *Civil Air Transport Inc v Central Air Transport Corpn* [1953] AC 70, [1952] 2 All ER 733, PC.

2   As to the location of property see paras 907–913 ante.

3   Where there are two governments claiming to represent the same state, the competence of each is limited to the area under its effective control: *Banco de Bilbao v Sancha* [1938] 2 KB 176, [1938] 2 All ER 253, CA; *The Arantzazu Mendi* [1939] AC 256, [1939] 1 All ER 719, HL; see also *Bank of Ethiopia v National Bank of Egypt and Liguori* [1937] Ch 513, [1937] 3 All ER 8.

4   *Aksionairnoye Obschestvo A M Luther v James Sagor & Co* [1921] 3 KB 532, CA; *Russian Commercial and Industrial Bank v Comptoir d'Escompte de Mulhouse* [1925] AC 112 at 124, HL; *Princess Paley Olga v Weisz* [1929] 1 KB 718, CA; *Re Banque des Marchands de Moscou (Koupetschesky), Royal Exchange Assurance Co v The Liquidator* [1952] 1 All ER 1269; *Jabbour v Custodian of Israeli Absentee Property* [1954] 1 All ER 145 at 153–154, [1954] 1 WLR 139 at 152; *Re Banque des Marchands de Moscou (Koupetschesky)* [1954] 2 All ER 746, [1954] 1 WLR 1108; *Re Helbert Wagg & Co Ltd's Claim* [1956] Ch 323 at 344–345, [1956] 1 All ER 129 at 138.

5   *Perry v Equitable Life Assurance Society of United States of America* (1929) 45 TLR 468; *Re Banque des Marchands de Moscou (Koupetschesky), Royal Exchange Assurance Co v The Liquidator* [1952] 1 All ER 1269; *Re Helbert Wagg & Co Ltd's Claim* [1956] Ch 323 at 344–349, [1956] 1 All ER 129 at 138–140, not following *The Rose Mary* [1953] 1 WLR 246, Aden SC.

6   *Aksionairnoye Obschestvo A M Luther v James Sagor & Co* [1921] 3 KB 532, CA; *Princess Paley Olga v Weisz* [1929] 1 KB 718, CA.

7   *Folliott v Ogden* (1789) 1 Hy Bl 124; affd sub nom *Ogden v Folliott* (1790) 3 Term Rep 726; *Lecouturier v Rey* [1910] AC 262, HL; *The Jupiter (No 3)* [1927] P 122 at 144; affd [1927] P 250, CA; *Employers' Liability Assurance Corpn Ltd v Sedgwick, Collins & Co Ltd* [1927] AC 95 at 102, HL; *Re Russian Bank for Foreign Trade* [1933] Ch 745 at 767; *Government of the Republic of Spain v National Bank of Scotland* 1939 SC 413; *Frankfurther v W L Exner Ltd* [1947] Ch 629; *Novello & Co Ltd v Hinrichsen Edition Ltd* [1951] Ch 595, [1951] 1 All ER 779; affd on other grounds [1951] Ch 1026, [1951] 2 All ER 457, CA; *Bank voor Handel en Scheepvaart NV v Slatford* [1953] 1 QB 248, [1951] 2 All ER 779; not following *Lorentzen v Lydden & Co Ltd* [1942] 2 KB 202; *Williams & Humbert Ltd v W & H Trade Marks (Jersey) Ltd* [1986] AC 368, [1986] 1 All ER 129, HL.

8   *Compania Naviera Vascongado v SS Cristina* [1938] AC 485, [1938] 1 All ER 719, HL; *The Arantzazu Mendi* [1939] AC 256, [1939] 1 All ER 719, HL.

9   Ie the applicable law determined in accordance with the Rome Convention: see para 845 et seq ante. For the meaning of 'the Rome Convention' see para 844 text and note 1 ante. Note that the Rome Convention does not apply to contracts made on or before 1 April 1991: see para 844 et seq ante. With regard to contracts to which the Convention does not apply, reference to the proper law of the contract may be necessary: see *Perry v Equitable Life Assurance Society of United States of America* (1929) 45 TLR 468; *Re Helbert Wagg & Co Ltd's Claim* [1956] Ch 323, [1956] 1 All ER 129; and paras 859–868 ante.

10 See the Rome Convention art 10 para 1(c); and para 854 ante. Note, however, the public policy provision contained in art 16: para 849 ante.

937. Penal decrees. The English court[1] will not enforce a foreign penal law[2]. Hence, if the foreign governmental decree which purports to expropriate private property is penal, that is an additional reason for not giving it extra-territorial effect[3]. If the property is in England at the time of the action, it may also be a reason for not recognising its effect on property situated within the territory controlled by the foreign government at the time of the decree[4].

It is impossible to define precisely what decrees are likely to be treated as penal, but it seems that one which is directed against the property of a particular individual[5] or of a particular company[6] or of persons of a particular race[7] or of a particular alien nationality[8] may be so treated. A decree is not necessarily penal merely because no compensation, or inadequate compensation, is payable to the owner under it[9]. In general, the English court is not concerned with the political merits or demerits of the decree. Thus it will not give an extra-territorial effect to a decree requisitioning private property merely because the foreign government was an ally of the United Kingdom during a war and the object of the decree was to prevent the property from falling into enemy hands[10].

1 As to the meaning of 'English' in relation to courts see para 604 ante.
2 See para 612 ante.
3 *Banco de Vizcaya v Don Alfonso de Borbon y Austria* [1935] 1 KB 140.
4 *Folliott v Ogden* (1789) 1 Hy Bl 124; affd sub nom *Ogden v Folliott* (1790) 3 Term Rep 726; *The Rose Mary* [1953] 1 WLR 246, Aden SC; as explained in *Re Helbert Wagg & Co Ltd's Claim* [1956] Ch 323 at 346, [1956] 1 All ER 129 at 139.
5 *Banco de Vizcaya v Don Alfonso de Borbon y Austria* [1935] 1 KB 140.
6 *The Rose Mary* [1953] 1 WLR 246, Aden SC; as explained in *Re Helbert Wagg & Co Ltd's Claim* [1956] Ch 323 at 346, [1956] 1 All ER 129 at 139.
7 *Frankfurther v W L Exner Ltd* [1947] Ch 629; *Novello & Co Ltd v Hinrichsen Edition Ltd* [1951] Ch 595, [1951] 1 All ER 779; affd [1951] Ch 1026, [1951] 2 All ER 457, CA.
8 *Wolff v Oxholm* (1817) 6 M & S 92; *Re Fried Krupp AG* [1917] 2 Ch 188; *Re Helbert Wagg & Co Ltd's Claim* [1956] Ch 323 at 345–346, [1956] 1 All ER 129 at 138–139.
9 *Aksionairnoye Obschestvo A M Luther v James Sagor & Co* [1921] 3 KB 532, CA; *Princess Paley Olga v Weisz* [1929] 1 KB 718, CA; *Bank voor Handel en Scheepvaart NV v Slatford* [1953] 1 QB 248 at 258, 260–263, [1951] 2 All ER 779 at 787, 788–790; *Re Helbert Wagg & Co Ltd's Claim* [1956] Ch 323 at 349, [1956] 1 All ER 129 at 140. Cf *AS Tallina Laevauhisus v Estonian State SS Line* (1947) 80 Ll L Rep 99 at 111, CA.
10 *Bank voor Handel en Scheepvaart NV v Slatford* [1953] 1 QB 248, [1951] 2 All ER 779; not following *Lorentzen v Lydden & Co Ltd* [1942] 2 KB 202.

(6) RECOGNITION OF TRUSTS

938. Introduction. The Recognition of Trusts Act 1987 gives effect in the United Kingdom to most of the Hague Convention on the law applicable to trusts and on their recognition[1]. The Act binds the Crown[2]. The Act may be extended by Order in Council[3] to the Isle of Man, any of the Channel Islands or any colony[4].

1 Ie the Convention on the law applicable to trusts and on their recognition, signed by the United Kingdom on 10 January 1986; see art 1. The provisions of the Convention which have the force of law in the United Kingdom are set out in the Recognition of Trusts Act 1987 s 1(1), Schedule. Articles 13, 19–21 are not included.
2 Recognition of Trusts Act 1987 s 3(3).
3 Such an Order in Council may modify the Act and contain supplementary provisions: see s 2(3). An Order in Council is subject to annulment in pursuance of a resolution of either House of Parliament: s 2(4).
4 Ibid s 2(2); and see the Recognition of Trusts Act 1987 (Overseas Territories) Order 1989, SI 1989/673, which provides for the application of the Recognition of Trusts Act 1987, with modifications, to Bermuda, British Antarctic Territory, the Falkland Islands, St Helena and Dependencies, South Georgia and the South Sandwich Islands, Akrotiri and Dhekelia, and the Virgin Islands.

939. General provisions. The Hague Convention[1] applies to trusts[2] regardless of the date on which they were created[3]. However, this is not to be construed as affecting the law to be applied in relation to anything done or omitted before 1 August 1987[4]. The provisions of the Convention may be disregarded when their application would be manifestly incompatible with public policy[5].

1 As to the Hague Convention see para 938 ante.
2 For the meaning of 'trust' see para 940 post.

3 Recognition of Trusts Act 1987 s 1(1), Schedule art 22.
4 Recognition of Trusts Act 1987 s 1(5); Recognition of Trusts Act 1987 (Commencement) Order 1987, SI 1987/1177.
5 Recognition of Trusts Act 1987 Schedule art 18.

940. Scope of the Convention. In the Hague Convention[1], the term 'trust' refers to the legal relationship created, inter vivos or on death, by a person, the settlor, when assets have been placed under the control of a trustee for the benefit of a beneficiary or for a specified purpose[2]. A trust has the following characteristics: (1) the assets constitute a separate fund and are not a part of the trustee's own estate; (2) title to the trust assets stands in the name of the trustee or in the name of another person on behalf of the trustee; and (3) the trustee has the power and the duty, in respect of which he is accountable, to manage, employ or dispose of the assets in accordance with the terms of the trust and the special duties imposed upon him by law[3]. The reservation by the settlor of certain rights and powers, and the fact that the trustee may himself have rights as a beneficiary, are not necessarily inconsistent with the existence of a trust[4]. The Convention applies only to trusts created voluntarily and evidenced in writing[5]. In the United Kingdom[6], however, the provisions of the Convention, so far as applicable[7], have effect also in relation to any other trusts of property arising under the law of any part of the United Kingdom or by virtue of a judicial decision whether in the United Kingdom or elsewhere[8]. The Convention does not apply to preliminary issues relating to the validity of wills or of other acts by virtue of which assets are transferred to the trustee[9], nor the extent that the applicable law[10] does not provide for trusts or the category of trusts involved[11].

1 As to the Hague Convention and its application see paras 938–939 ante.
2 Recognition of Trusts Act 1987 s 1(1), Schedule art 1.
3 Ibid Schedule art 2(a)–(c).
4 Ibid Schedule art 2.
5 Ibid Schedule art 3.
6 For the meaning of 'United Kingdom' see para 604 ante.
7 For a discussion of the trusts to which this may apply see Dicey and Morris *The Conflict of Laws* (12th Edn, 1993) 1089.
8 Recognition of Trusts Act 1987 s 1(2).
9 Ibid Schedule art 4.
10 Ie the law specified by ibid Schedule Ch II (arts 6–10) as the applicable law (see para 941 post): Schedule art 5
11 Ibid Schedule art 5.

941. Applicable law. A trust[1] is governed by the law[2] chosen by the settlor; the choice must be express or be implied in the terms of the instrument creating or the writing evidencing the trust, interpreted, if necessary, in the light of the circumstances of the case[3]. Where no applicable law has been chosen (or where the chosen law does not provide for trusts or the category of trust involved[4]), a trust is governed by the law with which it is most closely connected[5]. In ascertaining the law with which a trust is most closely connected reference is to be made in particular to: (1) the place of administration of the trust designated by the settlor; (2) the situs of the assets of the trust; (3) the place of residence or business of the trustee; and (4) the objects of the trust and the places where they are to be fulfilled[6].

The Hague Convention does not prevent the application of provisions of the law designated by the conflicts rules of the forum, in so far as those provisions cannot be derogated from by voluntary act[7], relating in particular to: (a) the protection of minors and incapable parties; (b) the personal and proprietary effects of marriage; (c) succession rights, testate and intestate, especially the indefeasible shares of spouses and relatives; (d) the transfer of title property and security interests in property; (e) the protection of creditors in matters of insolvency; (f) the protection, in other respects, of third parties acting in good faith[8]. Nor does the Convention prevent the application of those provisions of the law of the forum which must be applied even to international situations, irrespective of rules of conflict of laws[9].

The Rome Convention on the law applicable to contractual obligations[10] does not apply to the constitution of trusts or the relationship between settlors, trustees and beneficiaries[11].

1 For the meaning of 'trust' see para 940 ante.
2 In the Hague Convention 'law' means the rules of law in force in a state other than its rules of conflict of laws: Recognition of Trusts Act 1987 s 1(1), Schedule, art 17. As to the Hague Convention and its application see para 938–939 ante. The reference to a state includes a reference to any country or territory (whether or not a party to the Convention and whether or not forming part of the United Kingdom) which has its own system of law: Recognition of Trusts Act 1987 s 1(4). For the meaning of 'United Kingdom' see para 604 ante.
3 Ibid Schedule art 6.
4 Ibid Schedule art 6.
5 Ibid Schedule art 7.
6 Ibid Schedule art 7(a)–(d).
7 Ibid s 1(3), Schedule art 15. These may be referred to as the 'mandatory rules'.
8 Ibid s 1(3), Schedule art 15(a)–(f).
9 Ibid s 1(3), Schedule art 16.
10 As to the Rome Convention see para 844 ante.
11 Rome Convention art 1 para 2(g); see para 845 text and note 13 ante.

942. Scope of the applicable law. Under the Hague Convention[1], the applicable law[2] governs the validity of the trust[3], its construction, its effects and the administration of the trust[4]. In particular it governs: (1) the appointment, resignation and removal of trustees, the capacity to act as a trustee, and the devolution of the office of trustee; (2) the rights and duties of trustees among themselves; (3) the right of trustees to delegate in whole or in part the discharge of their duties or the exercise of their powers; (4) the power of trustees to administer or to dispose of trust assets, to create security interests in the trust assets, or to acquire new assets; (5) the powers of investment of trustees; (6) restrictions upon the duration of the trust, and upon the power to accumulate the income of the trust; (7) the relationships between the trustees and the beneficiaries including the personal liability of the trustees to the beneficiaries; (8) the variation or termination of the trust; (9) the distribution of the trust assets; and (10) the duty of trustees to account for their administration[5]. A severable aspect of the trust, particularly matters of administration, may be governed by a different law[6]. The law applicable to the validity of the trust determines whether that law or the law governing a severable aspect of the trust may be replaced by another law[7].

1 As to the Hague Convention and its application see paras 938–939 ante.
2 Ie the law as determined in accordance with the Recognition of Trusts Act 1987 s 1(1), Schedule arts 6, 7: see para 941 ante.
3 For the meaning of 'trust' see para 940 ante.
4 Recognition of Trusts Act 1987 Schedule art 8.
5 Ibid Schedule art 8(a)–(j).
6 Ibid Schedule art 9. The English courts will not lightly treat different parts of the trust property as governed by different laws; cf *Re Fitzgerald* [1904] 1 Ch 573, CA. The administration of a trust will normally be governed by the applicable law rather than some other law: cf *Chellaram v Chellaram* [1985] Ch 409, [1985] 1 All ER 1043.

7 Recognition of Trusts Act 1987 Schedule art 10. Cf *Re Fitzgerald* [1904] 1 Ch 573, CA; *Re Hewitt's Settlement* [1915] 1 Ch 228; *Duke of Marlborough v A-G* [1945] Ch 78, [1945] 1 All ER 165, CA.

943. Trusts not within the scope of the Hague Convention. There is little authority on the conflict of laws rules applicable to a trust which is not within the scope of the Hague Convention[1]. The applicable principles appear to be very similar to those applying under the Convention; thus the trust is governed by the law chosen by the settlor or, in the absence of such a choice, by the law with which the trust is most closely connected[1].

1 Eg a trust created orally in the Irish Republic. As to the Hague Convention and its scope see paras 938–940 ante.
2 *A-G v Campbell* (1872) LR 5 HL 524; *Duke of Marlborough v A-G* [1945] Ch 78, [1945] 1 All ER 165, CA; *Iveagh v IRC* [1954] Ch 364, [1954] 1 All ER 609; *Chellaram v Chellaram* [1985] Ch 409, [1985] 1 All ER 1043; *Revenue Comrs v Pelly* [1940] IR 122.

944. Recognition of trusts. A trust[1] created in accordance with the law applicable under the Hague Convention[2] is to be recognised as a trust[3]. Such recognition implies, as a minimum, that the trust property constitutes a separate fund, that the trustee may sue and be sued in his capacity as trustee, and that he may appear or act in this capacity before a notary or any person acting in an official capacity[4].

In so far as the law applicable to the trust requires or provides, such recognition implies in particular[5]:

(1) that personal creditors of the trustee have no recourse against the trust assets[6];
(2) that the trust assets do not form part of the trustee's estate upon his insolvency or bankruptcy[7];
(3) that the trust assets do not form part of the matrimonial property of the trustee or his spouse nor part of the trustee's estate upon his death[8];
(4) that the trust assets may be recovered when the trustee, in breach of trust, has mingled trust assets with his own property or has alienated trust assets[9].

A trustee desiring to register assets, movable or immovable, or documents of title to them, is entitled, in so far as this is not prohibited by or inconsistent with the law of the state where registration is sought, to do so in his capacity as trustee or in such other way that the existence of the trust is disclosed[10].

The Convention does not prevent the application of rules of law more favourable to the recognition of trusts[11].

If recognition of a trust is prevented by the application of mandatory rules of the law designated by the conflicts rules of the forum[12], the court must try to give effect to the objects of the trust by other means[13].

1 For the meaning of 'trust' see para 940 ante.
2 As to the Hague Convention and its application see paras 938–939 ante. As to the determination of the applicable law see para 941 ante.
3 Recognition of Trusts Act 1987 s 1(1), Schedule art 11 1st para.
4 Ibid Schedule art 11 2nd para.
5 Ibid Schedule art 11 3rd para.
6 Ibid Schedule art 11(a).
7 Ibid Schedule art 11(b).
8 Ibid Schedule art 11(c).
9 Ibid Schedule art 11(d). However, the rights and obligations of any third party holder of the assets remain subject to the law determined by the choice of law rules of the forum: Schedule art 11(d).
10 Ibid Schedule art 12.

11 Ibid Schedule art 14.
12 Ie the provisions set out in para 941 text and notes 6–7 ante.
13 Recognition of Trusts Act 1987 s 1(3), Schedule art 15.

8. SUCCESSION

(1) ADMINISTRATION OF ESTATES

(i) Law governing Administration

945. Choice of law. The administration of a deceased person's assets is governed by the law of the country from which the personal representative derives his authority to collect them[1]. Thus irrespective of whether the administration is principal or ancillary[2], assets administered by an English personal representative[3] must be administered according to English law[4], and assets administered by a foreign personal representative[5] must be administered according to the law of that foreign country[6].

A personal representative who has collected assets in a foreign country under a grant obtained there is thus entitled to hold them against a personal representative under an English grant[7], and a personal representative under an English grant is not accountable in his capacity as personal representative for assets received by him under a foreign grant[8].

1 *Preston v Melville* (1841) 8 Cl & Fin 1, HL; *Blackwood v R* (1882) 8 App Cas 82, PC; *Re Kloebe, Kannreuther v Geiselbrecht* (1884) 28 ChD 175; *Ewing v Orr Ewing* (1885) 10 App Cas 453, HL; *Re Lorillard, Griffiths v Catforth* [1922] 2 Ch 638, CA; *Re Wilks, Keefer v Wilks* [1935] Ch 645; *Re Kehr, Martin v Foges* [1952] Ch 26, [1951] 2 All ER 812.
2 Principal administration is administration of the deceased's assets under the authority of the country of the deceased's domicile; ancillary administration is administration under the authority of some other country.
3 Ie a person administering the assets under the authority of English domestic law, either by virtue of entitlement to an English grant of probate as an executor, or by virtue of an English grant of letters of administration. For present purposes, an English personal representative includes a personal representative acting under a grant resealed in England pursuant to the Colonial Probates Act 1892 or under a Scottish confirmation or Northern Irish grant of representation recognised by virtue of the Administration of Estates Act 1971 s 1. As to these Acts see EXECUTORS vol 17 para 1027 et seq.
4 See the cases cited in note 1 supra; and paras 949–951 post.
5 Ie a person administering the assets under the authority of the law of a foreign country, in some cases by virtue of a grant from the courts of that country, but not in all cases: see eg *Re Achillopoulos, Johnson v Mavromichali* [1928] Ch 433.
6 *Huthwaite v Phaire* (1840) 1 Man & G 159; *Cook v Gregson* (1854) 2 Drew 286 (assets prematurely transmitted to another country directed to be administered according to the law of the country in which they were collected).
7 *Currie v Bircham* (1822) 1 Dow & Ry KB 35; *Jauncy v Sealey* (1686) 1 Vern 397. There is an exception to this in the case of an administration action: see para 947 post.
8 See Dicey and Morris *The Conflict of Laws* (12th Edn, 1993) 1012. There is an exception to this in the case of an administration action: see para 947 post.

946. Administration and succession distinguished. Administration does not include the distribution to beneficiaries of the deceased's net assets after payment of all debts, duties and expenses[1]: this is a matter of succession, which is governed by separate rules[2]. The rules of English domestic law relating to the order of payment of debts[3], and the power to postpone sale of assets[4] and to make payments out of the estate for the maintenance or advancement of minor beneficiaries[5], are rules of administration; the rules of English law which determine the order of application of assets in payment of debts or legacies are rules of succession[6].

1 *Re Wilks, Keefer v Wilks* [1935] Ch 645 at 648.
2 See paras 954–977 post.
3 *Re Kloebe, Kannreuther v Geiselbrecht* (1884) 28 ChD 175; *Re Lorillard, Griffiths v Catforth* [1922] 2 Ch 638, CA.
4 *Re Wilks, Keefer v Wilks* [1935] Ch 645.
5 *Re Kehr, Martin v Foges* [1952] Ch 26, [1951] 2 All ER 812.
6 *Re Hewit, Lawson v Duncan* [1891] 3 Ch 568.

947. Administration actions. An order of the English court[1] for the judicial administration of a deceased person's estate will normally extend to all his assets, wherever situated[2]. The court will require all claims to be proved in the administration, and may restrain English creditors from proceeding against the estate in foreign courts[3]. The order does not make a foreign personal representative outside the jurisdiction accountable for his administration except with regard to those of the deceased's assets which he has brought to England before so appropriating them as to take them out of the deceased's estate[4]. If he is personally within the jurisdiction, he is also accountable under the order, in his capacity as trustee of the will, for the ultimate distribution to beneficiaries of the deceased's net assets wherever situated[5].

1 As to the meaning of 'English' in relation to courts see para 604 ante.
2 *Ewing v Orr Ewing* (1883) 9 App Cas 34, HL; subsequent proceedings (1885) 10 App Cas 453, HL.
3 *Bunbury v Bunbury* (1839) 8 LJCh 297; *Graham v Maxwell* (1849) 1 Mac & G 71; *Carron Iron Co v Maclaren* (1855) 5 HL Cas 416; *Maclaren v Stainton, Maclaren v Carron Co* (1855) 26 LJCh 332; *Re Boyse, Crofton v Crofton* (1880) 15 ChD 591; *Hope v Carnegie* (1866) 1 Ch App 320; *Baillie v Baillie* (1867) LR 5 Eq 175; *Re Low, Bland v Low* [1894] 1 Ch 147, CA; and see paras 1084–1086 post.
4 *Lowe v Farlie* (1817) 2 Madd 101; *Logan v Fairlie* (1825) 2 Sim & St 284; revsd on another point (1835) 1 My & Cr 59; *Sandilands v Innes* (1829) 3 Sim 263; *Tyler v Bell* (1837) 2 My & Cr 89; *Bond v Graham* (1842) 1 Hare 482; *Hervey v Fitzpatrick* (1854) Kay 421. In such a case the English personal representative must be a party to the action: see the cases cited supra; and RSC Ord 85 r 3(1).
5 *Ewing v Orr Ewing* (1883) 9 App Cas 34, HL; subsequent proceedings (1885) 10 App Cas 453, HL.

(ii) Position of English Personal Representatives

948. Effect of English grant. An English grant of representation[1] vests in the personal representative all the deceased's movable and immovable estate[2] which at the date of his death is situated in England[3]. It does not vest in him assets outside England[4], that matter being governed by the law of the country where they are situated[5]. However, where such foreign assets are brought into England before any person has acquired a title to them under their lex situs, they will vest in the English personal representative by virtue of his grant[6].

1 As to the English court's jurisdiction to make a grant, the types of grant which may be obtained, and the law, practice and procedure for obtaining a grant see generally EXECUTORS vol 17. As to the meaning of 'English' in relation to courts see para 604 ante.
2 This is subject to certain exceptions in the case of certain kinds of property, eg settled land, joint property, and property subject to a power of appointment, as to which see generally EXECUTORS vol 17 para 1071.
3 *A-G v Dimond* (1831) 1 Cr & J 356; *A-G v Hope* (1834) 1 Cr M & R 530, HL; *Blackwood v R* (1882) 8 App Cas 82, PC; *Re Fitzpatrick, Bennett v Bennett* [1952] Ch 86, [1951] 2 All ER 949.
4 See the cases cited in note 3 supra.

5 See para 945 ante. If the deceased died domiciled in England, the English personal representative has at most a 'generally recognised claim' to a local grant: *Blackwood v R* (1882) 8 App Cas 82 at 92, PC.

6 *Whyte v Rose* (1842) 3 QB 493 at 506, Ex Ch. A personal representative's title under the lex situs to assets which have been reduced into his possession before they are brought to England will be recognised in England: see para 952 post.

949. Collection of assets. An English personal representative is entitled to seek to collect assets of the deceased which are situated in another country, and he is accountable in England for all such assets as he may collect in his capacity as the English personal representative[1]. If the deceased died domiciled in England, and there are insufficient assets in England to meet his debts, the personal representative may be under a duty to seek to collect foreign assets[2]. If there are sufficient assets in England to pay the debts, he is under no duty to collect specifically bequeathed movables situated abroad, and he is entitled simply to assent to their vesting in the legatee and to leave him to bear any foreign duty in respect of them[3] and the cost of their transport to England[4].

1 *Dowdale's Case* (1605) 6 Co Rep 46b; *Atkins v Smith* (1740) 2 Atk 63; *Whyte v Rose* (1842) 3 QB 493, Ex Ch; *Re Scott, Scott v Scott* [1916] 2 Ch 268, CA. He is not accountable in England in his capacity as foreign personal representative, except in an administration action: see paras 945, 947 ante. As to the meaning of 'England' and 'English' see para 604 ante.

2 *Re Fitzpatrick, Bennett v Bennett* [1952] Ch 86 at 87–88, [1951] 2 All ER 949.

3 *Re Scott, Scott v Scott* [1915] 1 Ch 592, CA.

4 *Re Fitzpatrick, Bennett v Bennett* [1952] Ch 86, [1951] 2 All ER 949.

950. Payment of debts. Wherever they have been collected, assets which have come into the hands of an English personal representative in his capacity as such are available for all the deceased's debts, wherever they have been incurred, without distinction between English and foreign creditors[1]. The English personal representative must follow the order of priority prescribed by English law[2], although where foreign creditors have, as such, received a preference in respect of assets in their own country, he may be required to adjust the order of priority so that they do not receive payment before English creditors have been paid a proportionate amount[3]. An English ancillary personal representative need not advertise for foreign claims[4].

1 *Re Kloebe, Kannreuther v Geiselbrecht* (1884) 28 ChD 175.

2 *Re Kloebe, Kannreuther v Geiselbrecht* (1884) 28 ChD 175; *Re Bowes, Earl of Strathmore v Vane* [1889] WN 53; on appeal [1889] WN 138, CA; *Re Doetsch, Matheson v Ludwig* [1896] 2 Ch 836; *Re Smith, Smith v Smith* [1913] 2 Ch 216; *Re Lorillard, Griffiths v Catforth* [1922] 2 Ch 638, CA. See also EXECUTORS vol 17 para 1128.

3 *Re Kloebe, Kannreuther v Geiselbrecht* (1884) 28 ChD 175 at 177; cf *Carron Iron Co v Maclaren* (1855) 5 HL Cas 416 at 457–458.

4 *Re Achillopoulos, Johnson v Mavromichali* [1928] Ch 433 at 445; cf *Re Holden, Isaacson v Holden* [1935] WN 52. As to the distinction between principal and ancillary administration see para 945 note 2 ante.

951. Distribution and remission of net assets. Where the principal administration of a deceased person's estate is in England, the English personal representative will normally carry out the distribution to beneficiaries of the deceased's net assets[1]. Where the English administration is ancillary, he is not bound to remit the net assets for this purpose to the principal administrator[2]. If it thinks fit[3] the court may authorise him to do so[4], but it may instead direct him to carry out the distribution himself[5].

An English personal representative acting as attorney for the principal administrator will normally be justified in making a remission of the net assets to the principal administrator[6], or, in appropriate circumstances, to a third person upon the former's instructions[7]; but he ought not to make such a remission without first seeking the court's directions if it appears that the remission might alter the ultimate destination of the assets, as where the principal administrator would use them to pay debts which by English domestic law are statute-barred[8] or would distribute them in accordance with a will which by English conflict rules has been revoked[9]. In such a case the court has a discretionary power to restrain him from making the remission[10].

1   This will be done in accordance with rules of succession. For the rules of succession of English domestic law see the Administration of Estates Act 1925; and generally, EXECUTORS. For the English choice of law rules for succession see paras 956–977 post. As to the meaning of 'England' and 'English' see para 604 ante.

2   *Re Manifold, Slater v Chryssaffinis* [1962] Ch 1 at 12, [1961] 1 All ER 710 at 715–716. As to the distinction between principal and ancillary administration see para 945 note 2 ante.

3   *Ewing v Orr Ewing* (1885) 10 App Cas 453 at 514, HL.

4   *Preston v Melville* (1841) 8 Cl & Fin 1 at 14–15; *Eames v Hacon* (1881) 18 ChD 347, CA; *Re Achillopoulos, Johnson v Mavromichali* [1928] Ch 433.

5   *Enohin v Wylie* (1862) 10 HL Cas 1 at 19, 24; *Re Lorillard, Griffiths v Catforth* [1922] 2 Ch 638, CA; *Re Manifold, Slater v Chryssaffinis* [1962] Ch 1, [1961] 1 All ER 710.

6   *Eames v Hacon* (1881) 18 ChD 347, CA; *Re Achillopoulos, Johnson v Mavromichali* [1928] Ch 433; *Re Manifold, Slater v Chryssaffinis* [1962] Ch 1, [1961] 1 All ER 710; *Re Weiss's Estate* [1962] P 136 at 144, [1962] 1 All ER 308 at 312.

7   *Re Weiss's Estate* [1962] P 136, [1962] 1 All ER 308. Payment to such a third person will be proper only if he has no notice of any limitation upon his principal's power so to instruct him and has no reason to believe that the effect of compliance with those instructions will be to deprive creditors or beneficiaries of their respective entitlements or otherwise to cause loss to the estate; otherwise he should seek the court's directions: *Re Weiss's Estate* supra at 144–145 and at 313.

8   *Re Lorillard, Griffiths v Catforth* [1922] 2 Ch 638, CA.

9   *Re Manifold, Slater v Chryssaffinis* [1962] Ch 1, [1961] 1 All ER 710.

10   *Re Lorillard, Griffiths v Catforth* [1922] 2 Ch 638, CA; *Re Manifold, Slater v Chryssaffinis* [1962] Ch 1, [1961] 1 All ER 710; *Re Weiss's Estate* [1962] P 136 at 143–144, [1962] 1 All ER 308 at 312–313.

(iii) Position of Foreign Personal Representatives

952. Actions by foreign personal representatives. As in general an English grant of representation is necessary to enable a personal representative to make title to and administer the property of a deceased person in England, a foreign personal representative cannot sue in England in his capacity as such[1]; although he can sue in his personal capacity, as where he has obtained a judgment against a debtor of the estate in the foreign country[2]. He can also enforce his title under the lex situs to assets of the deceased which he has reduced into his possession, even if the assets have later been brought to England[3].

1   *Carter and Crost's Case* (1585) Godb 33; *Tourton v Flower* (1735) 3 P Wms 369; *Whyte v Rose* (1842) 3 QB 493 at 507–508, Ex Ch; *Eames v Hacon* (1881) 18 ChD 347 at 353–354, CA; *Finnegan v Cementation Co Ltd* [1953] 1 QB 688, [1953] 1 All ER 1130, CA. This is subject to an exception in the case of the recovery of money payable in England in respect of a life insurance policy effected by a person who died domiciled outside the United Kingdom: Revenue Act 1884 s 11 (amended by the Revenue Act 1889 s 19); *Haas v Atlas Assurance Co Ltd* [1913] 2 KB 209; *Re Loir's Policies* [1916] WN 87.

2   *Vanquelin v Bouard* (1863) 15 CBNS 341; *Re Macnichol, Macnichol v Macnichol* (1874) LR 19 Eq 81.

3   *Currie v Bircham* (1822) 1 Dow & Ry KB 35; *Vanquelin v Bouard* (1863) 15 CBNS 341; *Re Macnichol, Macnichol v Macnichol* (1874) LR 19 Eq 81. It is an open question whether the foreign personal representative's title under the lex situs would be recognised where there has been no reduction into possession: *Whyte v Rose* (1842) 3 QB 493 at 506, Ex Ch; and see Dicey and Morris *The Conflict of Laws* (12th Edn, 1993) 1011. See para 948 ante.

953. Actions against foreign personal representatives. A foreign personal representative cannot be made liable in England for acts done or assets received by him by virtue of his authority as foreign personal representative[1]. As in general only executors or administrators acting under the authority of English law may administer a deceased's assets situated in England[2], a foreign personal representative who is not an executor or administrator under English law will be liable as an executor de son tort[3] if he intermeddles with the assets of the deceased in England[4].

  1   *Degazon v Barclays Bank International* [1988] 1 FTLR 17, CA. See para 945 ante. This is subject to an exception in the case of administration actions: see para 947 ante.
  2   See para 952 ante.
  3   As to executors de son tort see EXECUTORS vol 17 para 753 et seq
  4   *New York Breweries Co Ltd v A-G* [1899] AC 62, HL; *IRC v Stype Investments (Jersey) Ltd, Re Clore* [1982] Ch 456, CA.

(2) BENEFICIAL DISTRIBUTION

(i) Jurisdiction

954. Jurisdiction of English court. The English court[1] has jurisdiction to determine any question with regard to the succession[2] to a deceased person's estate, irrespective of his domicile, wherever it has exercised jurisdiction to make a grant of representation[3]. The jurisdiction extends to all the deceased's movables and immovables, wherever situated[4]. The court will not, however, make any order with regard to the beneficial distribution of the estate unless there is before the court some person recognised by it as authorised to deal with the property in question[5].

  1   As to the meaning of 'English' in relation to courts see para 604 ante.
  2   Ie the beneficial distribution of the net estate, after payment of all debts, duties and expenses. Questions of administration must be distinguished: see para 946 ante.
  3   *Bremer v Freeman* (1857) 10 Moo PCC 306; *Enohin v Wylie* (1862) 10 HL Cas 1; *Doglioni v Crispin* (1866) LR 1 HL 301; *Ewing v Orr Ewing* (1883) 9 App Cas 34, HL; subsequent proceedings (1885) 10 App Cas 453, HL; *Re Trufort, Trafford v Blanc* (1887) 36 ChD 600; *Re Bonnefoi, Surrey v Perrin* [1912] P 233, CA; *Re Ross, Ross v Waterfield* [1930] 1 Ch 377; cf *Stirling-Maxwell v Cartwright* (1879) 11 ChD 522, CA. It also has jurisdiction wherever it has resealed a grant made in a country to which the Colonial Probates Act 1892 has been applied or has treated a Scottish confirmation or Northern Irish grant of representation as an English grant pursuant to the Administration of Estates Act 1971 s 1. As to these Acts see EXECUTORS vol 17 para 1027 et seq.
  4   For cases concerning domicile abroad and movables abroad see the cases cited in note 3 supra. For cases involving domicile in England and movables abroad see *Hope v Carnegie* (1866) 1 Ch App 320; *Re Duke of Wellington, Glentanar v Wellington* [1948] Ch 118, [1947] 2 All ER 854 at 864, CA. For a case involving domicile abroad and immovables abroad see *Ewing v Orr Ewing* (1883) 9 App Cas 34, HL; subsequent proceedings (1885) 10 App Cas 453, HL; *Re Ross, Ross v Waterfield* [1930] 1 Ch 377. For cases involving domicile in England and immovables abroad see *Hope v Carnegie* supra; *Re Piercy, Whitwham v Piercy* [1895] 1 Ch 83; *Re Moses, Moses v Valentine* [1908] 2 Ch 235; *Re Hoyles, Row v Jagg* [1911] 1 Ch 179, CA; *Re Duke of Wellington, Glentanar v Wellington* supra. Cf *Re Stirling, Stirling v Stirling* [1908] 2 Ch 344; *Jubert v Church Comrs for England* 1952 SC 160. For the distinction between movables and immovables see paras 902–906 ante.
  5   A foreign grant of representation is not sufficient (except in the case of a Scottish confirmation or Northern Irish grant of representation): *A-G v Hope* (1834) 1 Cr M & R 530 at 540, 562–564, HL; *Enohin v Wylie* (1862) 10 HL Cas 1 at 14, 19; *Vanquelin v Bouard* (1863) 15 CBNS 341; *Ewing v Orr Ewing* (1883) 9 App Cas 34 at 38–39, 46, HL. Cf *Re Lorillard, Griffiths v Catforth* [1922] 2 Ch 638, CA; RSC Ord 85 r 3(1); and see paras 952–953 ante.

955. Jurisdiction of foreign courts. The English court[1] will follow the decision of the court of the domicile of the deceased at the date of his death upon any question with regard to the succession to his movables, wherever situated². It will follow the decision of the court of the country where his immovables are situated upon any question with regard to the succession to those immovables³.

1   As to the meaning of 'English' in relation to courts see para 604 ante.
2   *Larpent v Sindry* (1828) 1 Hag Ecc 382; *Moore v Budd* (1832) 4 Hag Ecc 346; *Enohin v Wylie* (1862) 10 HL Cas 1; *Re Cosnahan's Goods* (1866) LR 1 P & D 183; *Doglioni v Crispin* (1866) LR 1 HL 301; *Re Smith's Goods* (1868) 16 WR 1130; *Miller v James* (1872) LR 3 P & D 4; *Ewing v Orr Ewing* (1883) 9 App Cas 34, HL; subsequent proceedings (1885) 10 App Cas 453, HL; *Re Trufort, Trafford v Blanc* (1887) 36 ChD 600; *Re Yahuda's Estate* [1956] P 388, [1956] 2 All ER 262. It is otherwise if the foreign decision is contrary to English public policy: *Re Askew, Marjoribanks v Askew* [1930] 2 Ch 259 at 275.
3   This follows from the principle that the English court will recognise a judgment in rem given by the court of a foreign country with regard to immovable property situated within that country: see para 1021 post. Cf *Re Trepca Mines Ltd* [1960] 3 All ER 304n, [1960] 1 WLR 1273, CA.

(ii) Choice of Law

A. GENERAL

956. The law governing succession. Subject to certain exceptions¹, the succession to the movables of a deceased person is governed by the law of his domicile at the date of his death². Again subject to certain exceptions³, the succession to his immovables is governed by the lex situs, that is the law of the place where the immovable is situated⁴.

1   See paras 962 note 2, 964, 966, 971–972, 974–977 post.
2   For general statements of this rule see *Pipon v Pipon* (1744) Amb 25 at 27; *Somerville v Lord Somerville* (1801) 5 Ves 750 at 786; *Re Ewin* (1830) 1 Cr & J 151 at 156; *De Bonneval v De Bonneval* (1838) 1 Curt 856 at 858–859; *Preston v Melville* (1841) 8 Cl & Fin 1 at 12, HL; *Bremer v Freeman* (1857) 10 Moo PCC 306 at 359; *Whicker v Hume* (1858) 7 HL Cas 124 at 165; *Enohin v Wylie* (1862) 10 HL Cas 1 at 13, 19; *Doglioni v Crispin* (1866) LR 1 HL 301 at 314; *Ewing v Orr Ewing* (1883) 9 App Cas 34 at 39, HL; subsequent proceedings (1885) 10 App Cas 453 at 502, HL; *Re Trufort, Trafford v Blanc* (1887) 36 ChD 600 at 610–611; *Duncan v Lawson* (1889) 41 ChD 394 at 397; *Re Barnett's Trusts* [1902] 1 Ch 847 at 855–856; *Re Bonnefoi, Surrey v Perrin* [1912] P 233 at 237, CA; *Re Berchtold, Berchtold v Capron* [1923] 1 Ch 192 at 199; *Re Ross, Ross v Waterfield* [1930] 1 Ch 377 at 387; *Re Duke of Wellington, Glentanar v Wellington* [1947] Ch 506 at 513, [1947] 2 All ER 854 at 857; affd [1948] Ch 118, [1947] 2 All ER 854 at 864, CA; *Re Maldonado, State of Spain v Treasury Solicitor* [1954] P 223 at 226, [1953] 2 All ER 300 at 302; affd [1954] P 223 at 245–246, 250, [1953] 2 All ER 1579 at 1584, 1586, CA; *Philipson-Stow v IRC* [1961] AC 727 at 748, 761–762, [1960] 3 All ER 814 at 822, 830–831, HL; *Re Collens, Royal Bank of Canada (London) Ltd v Krogh* [1986] Ch 505 at 509, [1986] 1 All ER 611 at 613–614. As to succession by and to legitimated and adopted persons see paras 788, 794 ante.
3   See paras 964, 966, 971, 974–975 post.
4   *Brodie v Barry* (1813) 2 Ves & B 127 at 131; *Duncan v Lawson* (1889) 41 ChD 394 at 397; *Pepin v Bruyère* [1902] 1 Ch 24 at 26, CA; *Re Miller, Bailie v Miller* [1914] 1 Ch 511 at 519; *Re Berchtold, Berchtold v Capron* [1923] 1 Ch 192 at 199; *Re Ross, Ross v Waterfield* [1930] 1 Ch 377 at 404–405; *Re Duke of Wellington, Glentanar v Wellington* [1947] Ch 506 at 513, [1947] 2 All ER 854 at 857–858; affd [1948] Ch 118, [1947] 2 All ER 854 at 864, CA; *Philipson-Stow v IRC* [1961] AC 727 at 744, 748, 761–762, [1960] 3 All ER 814 at 820, 822–823, 830–831, HL.

957. Renvoi. The English court¹ generally² applies the doctrine of total renvoi to questions of succession³. Thus in arriving at a decision it considers itself to be a court sitting in the country where the deceased was domiciled at the date of his death or the property is situated, as the case may be, and it decides the question as such a court would have decided it⁴.

1 As to the meaning of 'English' in relation to courts see para 604 ante.
2 In innumerable succession cases the English court has applied the domestic rules of the foreign law without any reference to its conflict rules, but these can mostly be explained by the fact that no one was concerned to argue that renvoi applied: see Dicey and Morris *The Conflict of Laws* (12th Edn, 1993) 79. Renvoi is excluded from many cases falling within the Wills Act 1963, and presumably it does not apply to the construction of wills, which depends on the law intended by the testator: see paras 964, 966, 975 post.
3 See the cases cited in note 4 infra. As to the renvoi doctrine see paras 606–609 ante.
4 For reference to conflict rules of the law of the domicile see *Collier v Rivaz* (1841) 2 Curt 855; *Frere v Frere* (1847) 5 Notes of Cases 593; *Re Trufort, Trafford v Blanc* (1887) 36 ChD 600; *Re Brown-Séquard* (1894) 70 LT 811; *Re Johnson, Roberts v A-G* [1903] 1 Ch 821; disapproved on another point in *Casdagli v Casdagli* [1918] P 89, CA; on appeal [1919] AC 145, HL; *Re Annesley, Davidson v Annesley* [1926] Ch 692: *Re Ross, Ross v Waterfield* [1930] 1 Ch 377; *Re O'Keefe, Poingdestre v Sherman* [1940] Ch 124, [1940] 1 All ER 216; *Re Fuld's Estate (No 3), Hartley v Fuld* [1968] P 675, [1965] 3 All ER 776. Cf *Enohin v Wylie* (1862) 10 HL Cas 1; *Abd-ul-Messih v Farra* (1888) 13 App Cas 431 at 444–445, PC. For reference to conflict rules of the law of the place where the immovable is situated see *Re Ross, Ross v Waterfield* supra; *Re Duke of Wellington, Glentanar v Wellington* [1947] Ch 506, [1947] 2 All ER 854; on appeal [1948] Ch 118, [1947] 2 All ER 854 at 864, CA. For reference to conflict rules of the law of the place where the will is made see *Re Lacroix's Goods* (1877) 2 PD 94, decided under the Wills Act 1861 (repealed).

958. The time factor. In the case of succession to movables the English court[1] generally disregards changes in the law of the domicile, whether or not retrospective, made after the death of the deceased[2]. These changes are taken into account, however, in the case of succession to immovables[3].

In determining for the purposes of the Wills Act 1963[4] whether a will complied with the formal requirements of a particular law, in the case of succession both to movables and immovables, the court must have regard to the law as it was at the time of execution of the will, but not so as to prevent account being taken of a retrospective alteration in the law, provided that this validates the will[5].

1 As to the meaning of 'English' in relation to courts see para 604 ante.
2 *Lynch v Paraguay Provisional Government* (1871) LR 2 P & D 268; followed in *Re Aganoor's Trusts* (1895) 64 LJCh 521; applied in *Re Marshall, Barclays Bank Ltd v Marshall* [1957] Ch 507, [1957] 3 All ER 172, CA; approved in *Adams v National Bank of Greece SA* [1961] AC 255, [1960] 2 All ER 421, HL; criticised by Dicey and Morris *The Conflict of Laws* (12th Edn, 1993) 60, 62: cf para 708 ante.
3 *Earl Nelson v Lord Bridport* (1845) 8 Beav 547.
4 As to the Wills Act 1963 see para 964 post.
5 Ibid s 6(3). For the meaning of 'will' in that Act see para 964 note 2 post.

959. Effect of grant of representation. So long as a grant of letters of administration by the English court[1] remains unrevoked, it is conclusive evidence that the deceased died intestate, having left no effective will[2]. So long as a grant of probate by the English court remains unrevoked, it is conclusive evidence that the instrument proved is the last will of the testator[3]. It is conclusive as to the testator's capacity and as to the formal validity of the will[4], but it is not conclusive as to the testator's domicile[5] or as to the material or essential validity[6] or construction[7] of the will[8].

1 As to the meaning of 'English' in relation to courts see para 604 ante.
2 *Tourton v Flower* (1735) 3 P Wms 369.
3 *Thornton v Curling* (1824) 8 Sim 310; *Whicker v Hume* (1858) 7 HL Cas 124.
4 *Thornton v Curling* (1824) 8 Sim 310; *Whicker v Hume* (1858) 7 HL Cas 124.
5 *Bradford v Young* (1884) 26 ChD 656; on appeal (1885) 29 ChD 617, CA; *Concha v Concha* (1886) 11 App Cas 541, HL.
6 *Thornton v Curling* (1824) 8 Sim 310; *Whicker v Hume* (1858) 7 HL Cas 124; *Concha v Concha* (1886) 11 App Cas 541 at 554–555, 572, HL; *Pouey v Hordern* [1900] 1 Ch 492.

7 *Bradford v Young* (1884) 26 ChD 656; on appeal (1885) 29 ChD 617, CA; *Concha v Concha* (1886) 11 App Cas 541 at 562, HL.
8 The principle is one of English domestic law: see eg *Re Barrance, Barrance v Ellis* [1910] 2 Ch 419; and see further EXECUTORS vol 17 para 765.

B. INTESTATE SUCCESSION

960. Intestate succession to movables. The succession to an intestate's movables, wherever situated, is governed by the law of his domicile at the date of his death[1]. This law has been applied to all questions of succession[2], including the distribution of the deceased's choses in action[3], the applicability of the doctrine of election[4], the entitlement to a proportion of the estate of his widow[5] and illegitimate children[6], and the ascertainment of his next of kin[7].

If the movables pass to a foreign state by way of a right of succession under the law of the domicile, by which the state claims as the deceased's *ultimus heres*[8], the English court will recognise and give effect to this right[9]. However, if the state claims the property as bona vacantia or under a *jus regale*[10], the claim is not governed by the law of the domicile, for it has nothing to do with the rules governing succession[11]. Accordingly, where there is no one who is entitled by the law of the domicile to take the deceased's movables in England by way of succession, the Crown has an absolute right to take them[12].

1 *Pipon v Pipon* (1744) Amb 25; *Thorne v Watkins* (1750) 2 Ves Sen 35; *Bruce v Bruce* (1790) 6 Bro Parl Cas 566, HL; *Hog v Lashley* (1792) 6 Bro Parl Cas 577, HL; *Balfour v Scott* (1793) 6 Bro Parl Cas 550, HL; *Bempde v Johnstone* (1796) 3 Ves 198; *Somerville v Lord Somerville* (1801) 5 Ves 750; *Re Ewin* (1830) 1 Cr & J 151 at 156; *De Bonneval v De Bonneval* (1838) 1 Curt 856 at 858; *Craigie v Lewin* (1843) 3 Curt 435 at 450; *Enohin v Wylie* (1862) 10 HL Cas 1; *Doglioni v Crispin* (1866) LR 1 HL 301; *Blackwood v R* (1882) 8 App Cas 82, PC; *Re Trufort, Trafford v Blanc* (1887) 36 ChD 600 at 609–611; *Abd-ul-Messih v Farra* (1888) 13 App Cas 431 at 438, PC; *Duncan v Lawson* (1889) 41 ChD 394 at 397; *Re Barnett's Trusts* [1902] 1 Ch 847; *Re O'Keefe, Poingdestre v Sherman* [1940] Ch 124, [1940] 1 All ER 216; *Re Maldonado, State of Spain v Treasury Solicitor* [1954] P 223 at 233, [1953] 2 All ER 1579, CA.
2 See the cases cited in note 1 supra.
3 *Pipon v Pipon* (1744) Amb 25; *Thorne v Watkins* (1750) 2 Ves Sen 35.
4 *Balfour v Scott* (1793) 6 Bro Parl Cas 550, HL.
5 *Re Rea, Rea v Rea* [1902] 1 IR 451; *Re Collens, Royal Bank of Canada (London) Ltd v Krogh* [1986] Ch 505, [1986] 1 All ER 611.
6 *Doglioni v Crispin* (1866) LR 1 HL 301.
7 *Bruce v Bruce* (1790) 6 Bro Parl Cas 566, HL; *Bempde v Johnstone* (1796) 3 Ves 198; *Somerville v Lord Somerville* (1801) 5 Ves 750; *Enohin v Wylie* (1862) 10 HL Cas 1; *Re O'Keefe, Poingdestre v Sherman* [1940] Ch 124, [1940] 1 All ER 216.
8 Ie the ultimate heir of the deceased.
9 *Re Maldonado, State of Spain v Treasury Solicitor* [1954] P 223 at 233, [1953] 2 All ER 1579, CA.
10 Ie a royal title.
11 *Re Barnett's Trusts* [1902] 1 Ch 847; *Re Musurus's Estate* [1936] 2 All ER 1666.
12 *Re Barnett's Trusts* [1902] 1 Ch 847; *Re Musurus's Estate* [1936] 2 All ER 1666; Administration of Estates Act 1925 s 46(1)(vi). See also CONSTITUTIONAL LAW; and EXECUTORS vol 17 para 1399.

961. Intestate succession to immovables. All questions of succession to an intestate's immovables are governed by the lex situs[1].

1 *Balfour v Scott* (1793) 6 Bro Parl Cas 550, HL; *Drummond v Drummond* (1799) 6 Bro Parl Cas 601, HL; *Brodie v Barry* (1813) 2 Ves & B 127; *Dundas v Dundas* (1830) 2 Dow & Cl 349, HL; *Doe d Birtwhistle v Vardill* (1835) 2 Cl & Fin 571, HL; subsequent proceedings sub nom *Birtwhistle v Vardill* (1840) 7 Cl & Fin 895, HL; *Freke v Lord Carbery* (1873) LR 16 Eq 461; *Re Gentili's Goods* (1875) IR 9 Eq 541;

De Fogassieras v Duport (1881) 11 LR Ir 123; Duncan v Lawson (1889) 41 ChD 394; Re Rea, Rea v Rea [1902] 1 IR 451; Pepin v Bruyère [1902] 1 Ch 24, CA; Re Berchtold, Berchtold v Capron [1923] 1 Ch 192; Re Cutcliffe's Will Trusts, Brewer v Cutcliffe [1940] Ch 565, [1940] 2 All ER 297; Re Collens, Royal Bank of Canada (London) Ltd v Krogh [1986] Ch 505, [1986] 1 All ER 611.

C. TESTATE SUCCESSION

962. Capacity. The personal capacity[1] of a testator to make a will of movables is governed by the law of his domicile[2]. No distinction is drawn for this purpose between lack of capacity due to immaturity or status and incapacity arising from ill health[3].

A beneficiary under a will has capacity to receive a legacy if he has capacity either by the law of his domicile or by the law of the testator's domicile[4].

The lex situs governs capacity both to make a will of immovables and to take under such a will[5].

1   This is a different question from the question of proprietary incapacity, in which the incapacity generally arises from the nature of the bequest or devise, and which is best regarded as a question of material or essential validity: see para 969 post. The question of personal capacity concerns restrictions which attach to the person rather than the property of the testator, eg physical and mental capacity, capacity of minors and married women.
2   Re Maraver's Goods (1828) 1 Hag Ecc 498; Re Guttierez's Goods (1869) 38 LJP & M 48; Re Fuld's Estate (No 3), Hartley v Fuld [1968] P 675 at 696, [1965] 3 All ER 776 at 780. It is uncertain whether, where there has been a change of domicile after execution, the domicile at the date of execution or at the date of death governs. Re Lewal's Settlement Trusts, Gould v Lewal [1918] 2 Ch 391 (a case on the exercise of a power of appointment by will) seems to support the former, but only to a very limited degree, as it was not a case of a change of domicile.
3   Re Fuld's Estate (No 3), Hartley v Fuld [1968] P 675 at 696, [1965] 3 All ER 776 at 780. While the question of undue influence is part of the substantive law of wills and is governed by the law of the domicile, the English rule of knowledge and approval is evidentiary and applicable in an English court as part of the lex fori: Re Fuld's Estate (No 3), Hartley v Fuld supra at 697–698 and at 781.
4   Re Hellmann's Will (1866) LR 2 Eq 363; cf Leslie v Baillie (1843) 2 Y & C Ch Cas 91; Donohoe v Donohoe (1887) 19 LR Ir 349; Re Schnapper [1928] Ch 420.
5   Philipson-Stow v IRC [1961] AC 727 at 743, [1960] 3 All ER 814 at 819, HL; and see Bank of Africa Ltd v Cohen [1909] 2 Ch 129, CA (a case on capacity to transfer immovables inter vivos).

963. Formal validity at common law. A will of movables is valid in point of form at common law[1] if its execution complied with the formalities prescribed by the law of the testator's domicile at the date of his death[2]. Compliance with either the internal law of the domicile or the internal law of any system of law referred to by the domicile is sufficient[3]. In determining whether a document is a valid testamentary disposition the court will have regard to the law of only one country at a time[4].

A will of immovables is valid in point of form at common law if its execution complied with the formal requirements of the lex situs[5]. Compliance with any system of law referred to by the lex situs is probably sufficient[6].

1   The common law rules regarding the formal validity of wills have survived the Wills Act 1963. The Act repealed the Wills Act 1861 (Wills Act 1963 s 7(3)), but did not abolish the common law rules. Renvoi is applicable under the common law rules, but not under the Wills Act 1963: see paras 957 ante, 964 post.
2   Bremer v Freeman (1857) 10 Moo PC 306; Hare v Nasmyth (1823) 2 Add 25, HL; Stanley v Bernes (1830) 3 Hag Ecc 373; De Bonneval v De Bonneval (1838) 1 Curt 856; Collier v Rivaz (1841) 2 Curt 855; Craigie v Lewin (1843) 3 Curt 435; Maltass v Maltass (1844) 1 Rob Eccl 67; Croker v Marquis of Hertford (1844) 4 Moo PCC 339; Frere v Frere (1847) 5 Notes of Cases 593; Whicker v Hume (1858) 7 HL Cas 124; Crookenden v Fuller (1859) 29 LJP & M 1 (corrected on another point in Re Alexander's Goods (1860) 29 LJPM & A 93); Laneuville v Anderson (1860) 2 Sw & Tr 24; De Fogassieras v Duport (1881) 11 LR Ir 123;

Abd-ul-Messih v Farra (1888) 13 App Cas 431, PC: *Re Martin, Loustalan v Loustalan* [1900] P 211, CA; *Re Manifold, Slater v Chryssaffinis* [1962] Ch 1, [1961] 1 All ER 710.

3   *Collier v Rivaz* (1841) 2 Curt 855; *Maltass v Maltass* (1844) 1 Rob Eccl 67; *Frere v Frere* (1847) 5 Notes of Cases 593; cf *Re Lacroix's Goods* (1877) 2 PD 94 (a decision under the Wills Act 1861 (repealed)); see also para 957 ante. As to renvoi generally see paras 606–609 ante. It seems clear that the rule is one of alternative reference to the internal and conflict rules of the law of the domicile; both in *Collier v Rivaz* supra, and in *Re Lacroix's Goods* supra, it was necessary to have recourse both to the internal rules and the conflict rules of the foreign law in order to admit all the testamentary documents to probate; and there seems to be no case in which a will complying with the internal law of the law of the domicile has been held formally invalid for non-compliance with the formal requirements of a system of law referred to by its conflict rules. Cf *Re Manifold, Slater v Chryssaffinis* [1962] Ch 1 at 16, [1961] 1 All ER 710 at 718.

4   *Pechell v Hilderley* (1869) LR 1 P & D 673, a decision under the Wills Act 1861 (repealed) (will, invalid by English and Italian law, confirmed by codicil executed in accordance with Italian law but invalidated by that law as being annexed to an invalid will: held that the two laws could not be combined to validate the codicil or the will by construing the codicil as a valid English codicil validating the invalid will by republication).

5   *Coppin v Coppin* (1725) 2 P Wms 291; *Re Gentili's Goods* (1875) IR 9 Eq 541; *De Fogassieras v Duport* (1881) 11 LR Ir 123; *Pepin v Bruyère* [1902] 1 Ch 24, CA; *Philipson-Stow v IRC* [1961] AC 727 at 743, [1960] 3 All ER 814 at 819, HL.

6   This follows from the general application of renvoi in all cases governed by the lex situs: see *Bank of Africa Ltd v Cohen* [1909] 2 Ch 129 at 146–147, CA; and paras 609, 924, 957 ante.

964. Formal validity under the Wills Act 1963. By virtue of the Wills Act 1963[1] a will[2] of movables or immovables will be treated as properly executed if its execution conformed to the internal law[3] in force in the territory where it was executed, or where, at the time of its execution or of the testator's death, he was domiciled or had his habitual residence[4], or in a state of which, at either of those times, he was a national[5]. In addition, a will of immovables will be treated as properly executed if its execution conformed to the internal law in force in the territory where the property was situated[6].

A will of movables or immovables executed on board a vessel[7] or aircraft will be treated as properly executed if its execution satisfies either one of the laws indicated above or the internal law in force in the territory with which, having regard to its registration, if any, and other relevant circumstances, the vessel or aircraft may be taken to have been most closely connected[8].

1   The Wills Act 1963, which repeals the Wills Act 1861 (Lord Kingsdown's Act), applies to the will of a testator dying on or after 1 January 1964, whenever the will was made, although the repeal of the Act of 1861 does not invalidate a will made before 1 January 1964: Wills Act 1963 s 7(3), (4). Under the 1861 Act a will of personalty made outside the United Kingdom by a British subject was valid in point of form if made in accordance with the forms required either by the law of the place of execution, or by the law of the testator's domicile at the date of execution, or by the law then in force in that part of the British dominions where he had his domicile of origin: Wills Act 1861 s 1 (repealed). A will of personalty made within the United Kingdom by a British subject was valid in point of form if made in accordance with the forms required by the law of the place of execution: s 2 (repealed). The Wills Act 1963 extends to Northern Ireland: s 7(5) (amended by the Northern Ireland Constitution Act 1973 s 41(1), Sch 6 Pt I).

2   'Will' includes any testamentary instrument or act; and 'testator' must be construed accordingly: Wills Act 1963 s 6(1). There is no requirement that each such instrument should conform to the same law. However, the principle of *Pechell v Hilderley* (1869) LR 1 P & D 673 (see para 963 note 4 ante) would still seem to apply.

3   'Internal law' in relation to any territory or state means the law which would apply in a case where no question of the law in force in any other territory or state arose; and 'state' means a territory or group of territories having its own law of nationality: Wills Act 1963 s 6(1). The Act thus excludes renvoi from cases falling within its ambit.

4   For the meaning of 'habitual residence' see para 705 ante.

5   Wills Act 1963 s 1; *Re Kanani, Engledow v Davidson* (1978) 122 Sol Jo 611. Where there are two or more systems of internal law relating to formal validity of wills, the system to be applied is the one indicated by

any rule in force throughout the territory or state: Wills Act 1963 s 6(2)(a). If there is no such rule, it is the system with which the testator was most closely connected at the relevant time, namely the date of his death where the matter is to be determined by circumstances prevailing at his death, and the time of execution of the will in any other case: s 6(2)(b).

6 Ibid s 2(1)(b). For the additional rules under the Wills Act 1963 for the revocation of wills and the exercise of powers of appointment see paras 971, 974 post.

7 References to vessels in the Wills Act 1963 or activities or places connected with them are extended to include hovercraft or activities or places connected with hovercraft: see the Hovercraft (Application of Enactments) Order 1972, SI 1972/971, art 4, Sch 1 Pt A.

8 Wills Act 1963 s 2(1)(a).

965. Characterisation of special formal requirements. Where a law in force outside the United Kingdom[1] falls to be applied in relation to a will[2], any requirement of that law whereby special formalities are to be observed by testators[3] answering a particular description, or witnesses to the execution of a will are to possess certain qualifications, is treated, notwithstanding any rule of that law to the contrary, as a formal requirement only[4].

1 For the meaning of 'United Kingdom' see para 604 ante.
2 For the meaning of 'will' see para 964 note 2 ante.
3 For the meaning of 'testator' see para 964 note 2 ante.
4 Wills Act 1963 s 3. This provision operates irrespective of whether the application of the foreign law is in pursuance of the Act: s 3.

966. Construction. The construction[1] of a will is governed by the law intended by the testator[2]. In the case of a will of movables, this is presumed to be the law of the testator's domicile at the date of execution of the will[3], but this presumption is rebutted by any sufficient indication that the testator intended his will to be construed according to the law of another country[4]. The testator's intention may be expressed in the will[5], or it may be implied from circumstances such as his use of a particular language[6], or of expressions known only to a particular law[7].

Prima facie, a will of immovables must be construed according to the law of the testator's domicile at the date of execution of the will[8], but this presumption may be rebutted by any sufficient indication that the testator intended to refer to some other law[9], as where he uses the technical language of the country where the immovables are situated[10]. When construing a will of immovables in accordance with the law of the testator's domicile, the court will construe it so as to enable its dispositions to operate to the fullest extent that they are allowed to do so by the lex situs[11].

Under the Wills Act 1963 the construction of a will[12] of movables or immovables cannot be altered by reason of any change in the testator's[13] domicile after the execution of the will[14].

1 Ie all questions concerning the meaning and interpretation of the will. The question of construction must be distinguished from the question of status: *Re Fergusson's Will* [1902] 1 Ch 483 at 487 (meaning of gift to 'next of kin' a matter of construction; legitimacy of those entitled a matter of status). It must also be distinguished from the question of material or essential validity (see para 969 post): the former determines the testator's intention, while the latter determines the effect to be given to that intention: see *Baring v Ashburton* (1886) 54 LT 463 (construction governed by the law of the domicile; essential validity by the lex situs); *Philipson-Stow v IRC* [1961] AC 727 at 761, [1960] 3 All ER 814 at 830, HL. The question whether a legacy is given in satisfaction of a previous obligation is one of construction (*Campbell v Campbell* (1866) LR 1 Eq 383); so too is the question of applicability of the cy-près doctrine to a charitable bequest (*Re De Noailles, Clouston v Tufnell* (1916) 114 LT 1089); so too is the question of destination of lapsed legacies (*Anstruther v Chalmer* (1826) 2 Sim 1; *Re Cunnington, Healing v Webb* [1924] 1 Ch 68; cf *Yates v Thomson* (1835) 3 Cl & Fin 544 at 570, HL). As to construction of wills in English domestic law see WILLS vol 50 para 370 et seq.

2   *Bradford v Young* (1885) 29 ChD 617 at 624, CA; *Philipson-Stow v IRC* [1961] AC 727 at 760–761, [1960] 3 All ER 814 at 830, HL; cf *Enohin v Wylie* (1862) 10 HL Cas 1 at 24; *Di Sora v Phillipps* (1863) 10 HL Cas 624 (a case of contract).

3   'A person's meaning can only be gathered from assuming that he intended to use words in the sense affixed to them by the law of the country he belonged to at the time of framing his instrument': *Yates v Thomson* (1835) 3 Cl & Fin 544 at 588, HL, per Lord Brougham; *Trotter v Trotter* (1828) 4 Bli NS 502, HL; *Bernal v Bernal* (1838) 3 My & Cr 559; *Enohin v Wylie* (1862) 10 HL Cas 1; *Ewing v Orr Ewing* (1883) 9 App Cas 34 at 43, HL; *Bradford v Young* (1885) 29 ChD 617, CA; *Re Cliff's Trusts* [1892] 2 Ch 229 at 232; *Re Fergusson's Will* [1902] 1 Ch 483; *Re Manners, Manners v Manners* [1923] 1 Ch 220; *Re Cunnington, Healing v Webb* [1924] 1 Ch 68; *Philipson-Stow v IRC* [1961] AC 727 at 761, [1960] 3 All ER 814 at 830, HL; *Re Sillar, Hurley v Wimbush and Bavington* [1956] IR 344.

4   *Bradford v Young* (1885) 29 ChD 617, CA; *Re Cunnington, Healing v Webb* [1924] 1 Ch 68. See also *Re Price, Tomlin v Latter* [1900] 1 Ch 442 at 452; *Re D'Este's Settlement Trusts, Poulter v D'Este* [1903] 1 Ch 898 at 905 (both cases on exercise by will of a power of appointment), approving Dicey's statement (see now the slightly amended text in Dicey and Morris *The Conflict of Laws* (12th Edn, 1993) 1039–1040) that the maxim that the terms of a will should be construed with reference to the law of the testator's domicile 'is a mere canon of interpretation [now 'merely a rebuttable presumption'] which should not be adhered to when there is any reason, from the nature of the will, or otherwise, to suppose that the testator wrote it with reference to the law of some other country'.

5   *Raphael v Boehm, Cockburn v Raphael* (1852) 22 LJCh 299 (express reference to the law of inheritance in Great Britain); cf *Re Price, Tomlin v Latter* [1900] 1 Ch 442 (exercise by will of power of appointment).

6   However, the fact that the will is written in a language other than that of the domicile is not, of itself a sufficient indication that it should be construed according to the law of the country in whose language it is written: *Reynolds v Kortright* (1854) 18 Beav 417 (English domicile; Spanish language); *Baring v Ashburton* (1886) 54 LT 463 (English domicile; French language); *Re Bonnefoi, Surrey v Perrin* [1912] P 233, CA (Italian domicile; English language); *Re Manners, Manners v Manners* [1923] 1 Ch 220 (English domicile; Spanish language). The fact that a will by a domiciled Frenchman was made in England in English form chiefly benefiting English legatees was held not to be a sufficient indication that the testator intended his will to be construed according to English law: *Re Cunnington, Healing v Webb* [1924] 1 Ch 68. See para 967 post.

7   *Studd v Cook* (1883) 8 App Cas 577, HL (will of immovables); cf *Re Cliff's Trusts* [1892] 2 Ch 229; *Trotter v Trotter* (1828) 4 Bli NS 502, HL; contrast *Bradford v Young* (1885) 29 ChD 617, CA, where the presence of a few technical expressions was held to be insufficient indication of an intention that the will should be construed according to the law of the country to which the expressions belonged.

8   *Trotter v Trotter* (1828) 4 Bli NS 502, HL; *Maxwell v Maxwell* (1852) 2 De GM & G 705; *Studd v Cook* (1883) 8 App Cas 577, HL; *Bradford v Young* (1885) 29 ChD 617 at 623, CA; *Baring v Ashburton* (1886) 54 LT 463; *Philipson-Stow v IRC* [1961] AC 727 at 761, [1960] 3 All ER 814 at 830, 831, HL.

9   *Yates v Thomson* (1835) 3 Cl & Fin 544 at 588, HL.

10   Cf *Bradford v Young* (1885) 29 ChD 617 at 623, CA. The effect may be that, in so far as a will disposes of both movables and immovables, it is to be construed according to two different laws.

11   *Studd v Cook* (1883) 8 App Cas 577 at 591, HL. Cf *Re Miller, Bailie v Miller* [1914] 1 Ch 511, where the question was one of essential validity rather than construction.

12   For the meaning of 'will' see para 964 note 2 ante.

13   For the meaning of 'testator' see para 964 note 2 ante.

14   Wills Act 1963 s 4. Cf para 958 ante.

967. Wills in foreign languages. Where probate has been granted of a foreign will or copy will, accompanied by an English translation, or of an English translation, accompanied by the original or copy will[1], the court may refer to the original or copy will for the purpose of deciding questions of construction[2]. Where the will is to be construed according to English law[3], the court will only look at the effect of the language in which it is written in order to ascertain what are the equivalent expressions in English[4]; and even where it is to be construed according to the law of the country in whose language it is written, the court will not refer to that law for the meaning of words which are not subject to any technical rules of construction under that law[5].

1   As to probate of foreign wills and translations of such wills see EXECUTORS vol 17 para 830.

2   *Re Cliff's Trusts* [1892] 2 Ch 229, correcting the report in *L'Fit v L'Batt* (1718) 1 P Wms 526; *Re Manners, Manners v Manners* [1923] 1 Ch 220.

3 As to the meaning of 'English law' see para 604 ante.
4 *Reynolds v Kortright* (1854) 18 Beav 417 at 426; cf *Baring v Ashburton* (1886) 54 LT 463.
5 *Bernal v Bernal* (1838) 3 My & Cr 559 at 580.

968. Certain English principles of construction.
Where a will is construed according to English law, certain principles of construction govern gifts of debts, the currency of payment of legacies, and devises of estates of immovables.

Debts, other than specialty and judgment debts, are usually to be regarded as situated where the debtor is resident, so that a gift of all the testator's property in a particular country passes debts due from persons resident there[1].

Prima facie, a legacy is to be paid in the currency of the testator's domicile[2], but where a currency is expressly indicated the legacy must be paid in that currency[3], and where the testator makes a separate distribution of property in different countries, charging legacies on each, those legacies must be paid respectively in the currency of the country in which the property on which they are charged is situated[4]. Where the legacy is payable in the currency of a foreign country, its value must be computed according to the value of the currency in that country, irrespective of the rate of exchange, and without any deduction for the cost of remittance[5]; but where such a legacy is payable out of assets in England, its value must be computed according to the rate of exchange, and not according to the actual value in the foreign country itself[6]. The date for ascertaining the value of the legacy is the date on which it becomes due, that is, one year from the death of the testator[7].

The lex situs normally determines what passes under a general devise of a foreign immovable estate, so that this law will decide whether the devise includes livestock or other movables necessary for the work of the estate[8].

1 *Nisbett v Murray* (1799) 5 Ves 149; *Earl of Tyrone v Marquis of Waterford* (1860) 1 De GF &J 613; *Guthrie v Walrond* (1883) 22 ChD 573; *Re Clark, McKechnie v Clark* [1904] 1 Ch 294. As to the locality of a debt see further paras 908–909 ante.
2 *Wallis v Brightwell* (1722) 2 P Wms 88; *Saunders v Drake* (1742) 2 Atk 465; *Pierson v Garnet* (1786) 2 Bro CC 38; *Malcolm v Martin* (1790) 3 Bro CC 50; *Holmes v Holmes* (1830) 1 Russ & M 660.
3 *Raymond v Brodbelt* (1800) 5 Ves 199. Where a different currency is expressly indicated with regard to some legacies, and none is indicated with regard to others, the latter are payable in the currency of the domicile: *Saunders v Drake* (1742) 2 Atk 465; *Pierson v Garnet* (1786) 2 Bro CC 38; *Malcolm v Martin* (1790) 3 Bro CC 50; *Cockerell v Barber* (1810) 16 Ves 461 at 465.
4 *Saunders v Drake* (1742) 2 Atk 465 at 466; *Pierson v Garnet* (1786) 2 Bro CC 38 at 47. However, the mere fact that the testator owns properties in different countries does not exclude the currency of the domicile: *Saunders v Drake* supra. As to legacies charged on immovables see para 928 ante.
5 *Cockerell v Barber* (1810) 16 Ves 461.
6 *Campbell v Graham* (1831) 1 Russ & M 453; on appeal sub nom *Campbell v Sandford* (1834) 2 Cl & Fin 429 at 450, HL.
7 *Re Eighmie, Colbourne v Wilks* [1935] Ch 524. Thereafter, unless a contrary intention appears on the face of the will, a legacy in the currency of a foreign country carries interest at the local rate: *Saunders v Drake* (1742) 2 Atk 465; *Raymond v Brodbelt* (1800) 5 Ves 199; but see *Malcolm v Martin* (1790) 3 Bro CC 50, where English interest was given. The true rule is perhaps that interest must be given according to the rate of the country in which the fund is situated: see *Malcolm v Martin* supra at 54n; cf *Raymond v Brodbelt* supra, which was apparently decided on this principle. See also *Bourke v Ricketts* (1804) 10 Ves 330, where there were two funds, and legatees preferring to take payments out of the English fund were held to be entitled only to English interest. For the English rate of interest see RSC Ord 44 r 10; and EXECUTORS vol 17 para 1255.
8 *Lushington v Sewell* (1827) 1 Sim 435; *Stewart v Garnett* (1830) 3 Sim 398, both cases of estates in the West Indies.

969. Material or essential validity.
The material or essential validity of a will of movables is governed by the law of the testator's domicile at the date of his death[1]. This

law has been applied to such questions as whether the testator is bound to leave a part of his movable estate, *legitima portio* or legitim[2], to his widow or children[3], whether a gift of movables to an attesting witness[4], to a charity[5], or for superstitious uses[6] is valid.

The material or essential validity of a will of immovables is governed by the lex situs[7]. This law has been applied to such questions as whether the testator is bound to leave a part of his immovable estate to his widow or children[8], or whether a gift of immovables to a charity is valid[9], and to questions concerning the nature and incidents of the estates created in the immovables[10].

1 *Whicker v Hume* (1858) 7 HL Cas 124; *Re Priest, Belfield v Duncan* [1944] Ch 58, [1944] 1 All ER 51; *Philipson-Stow v IRC* [1961] AC 727, [1960] 3 All ER 814, HL; *Re Levick's Will Trust, Ffennell v IRC* [1963] 1 All ER 95, [1963] 1 WLR 311.
2 Legitim, in Scottish law, is the children's share of the father's movable property which he cannot otherwise dispose of by will. *Legitima portio* in some continental European systems means much the same thing.
3 *Thornton v Curling* (1824) 8 Sim 310; *Campbell v Beaufoy* (1859) John 320; *Re Trufort, Trafford v Blanc* (1887) 36 ChD 600: *Re Groos, Groos v Groos* [1915] 1 Ch 572; *Bartlett v Bartlett* [1925] AC 377, PC; *Re Annesley, Davidson v Annesley* [1926] Ch 692; *Re Ross, Ross v Waterfield* [1930] 1 Ch 377; *Re Adams, Bank of Ireland Trustee Co Ltd v Adams* [1967] IR 424. These cases are better regarded as raising a question of material or essential validity rather than one of capacity, as the restriction under the law of the domicile attached in each case to the property rather than the person of the testator: see para 962 ante. Analogous rights exist under English law by virtue of the English court's power to award reasonable financial provision out of the estate of a deceased person. The court's jurisdiction is limited to cases where the deceased died domiciled in England and Wales, whether the property is movable or immovable: Inheritance (Provision for Family and Dependants) Act 1975 s 1. The burden of proving an English domicile lies on the applicant: *Mastaka v Midland Bank Executor and Trustee Co Ltd* [1941] Ch 192, [1941] 1 All ER 236. As to family provision see further EXECUTORS vol 17 para 1318 et seq.
4 *Re Priest, Belfield v Duncan* [1944] Ch 58, [1944] 1 All ER 51. See now the Wills Act 1968, validating gifts to supernumerary attesting witnesses; and generally see WILLS.
5 *Macdonald v Macdonald* (1872) LR 14 Eq 60 (marshalling in favour of a charity).
6 *Re Elliott, Elliott v Johnson* (1891) 39 WR 297. As to superstitious uses see CHARITIES vol 5(2) (Reissue) paras 56–57.
7 *Philipson-Stow v IRC* [1961] AC 727, [1960] 3 All ER 814, HL; *Re Levick's Will Trusts, Ffennell v IRC* [1963] 1 All ER 95, [1963] 1 WLR 311.
8 *Re Hernando, Hernando v Sawtell* (1884) 27 ChD 284; *Bartlett v Bartlett* [1925] AC 377, PC; *Re Ross, Ross v Waterfield* [1930] 1 Ch 377.
9 *Whicker v Hume* (1858) 7 HL Cas 124; *Duncan v Lawson* (1889) 41 ChD 394; *Re Hoyles, Row v Jagg* [1911] 1 Ch 179; *Re Grassi, Stubberfield v Grassi* [1905] 1 Ch 584.
10 *Earl Nelson v Lord Bridport* (1846) 8 Beav 547 (change in nature of estate from entailed to absolute interest); *Re Moses, Moses v Valentine* [1908] 2 Ch 235 (right to enjoy lease in specie); *Re Miller, Bailie v Miller* [1914] 1 Ch 511 (disposability of entailed interest). See para 927 ante.

970. Election. The question whether a beneficiary under a will must elect between taking a benefit given to him by the will and taking a benefit to which he is entitled outside the will, but which is given to another person by the will, is one of material or essential validity[1]. Thus, where the benefit under the will consists of movables, the question whether the beneficiary is put to his election is governed by the law of the testator's domicile at the date of his death, irrespective of the lex situs of any immovables which may constitute the benefit outside the will[2]. Where the benefit under the will consists of immovables, the question of election is governed by the lex situs of those immovables, again irrespective of the lex situs of any immovables which may constitute the benefit outside the will and irrespective of the law of the testator's domicile[3].

The heir to an entailed interest in English immovables is not put to his election between those immovables and any benefit given him by the will[4].

1 Cf *Re Mengel's Will Trusts, Westminster Bank Ltd v Mengel* [1962] Ch 791 at 797, [1962] 2 All ER 490 at 492. The doctrine of election has nothing to do with intention, and, consequently, nothing to do with construction of the testator's will: *Re Mengel's Will Trusts, Westminster Bank Ltd v Mengel* supra at 800 and at 495, not following *Re Allen's Estate, Prescott v Allen and Beaumont* [1945] 2 All ER 264. As to the application of the doctrine of election in English law see EQUITY vol 16 (Reissue) para 842 et seq.

2 *Re Ogilvie, Ogilvie v Ogilvie* [1918] 1 Ch 492 at 498; *Re Mengel's Will Trusts, Westminster Bank Ltd v Mengel* [1962] Ch 791, [1962] 2 All ER 490. For cases illustrating this principle see also *Balfour v Scott* (1793) 6 Bro Parl Cas 550, HL; *Brodie v Barry* (1813) 2 Ves & B 127; *Trotter v Trotter* (1828) 4 Bli NS 502, HL; *Dundas v Dundas* (1830) 2 Dow & Cl 349, HL; *Allen v Anderson* (1846) 5 Hare 163; *Maxwell v Maxwell* (1852) 2 De GM & G 705; *Harrison v Harrison* (1873) 8 Ch App 342; *Baring v Ashburton* (1886) 54 LT 463; *Brown v Gregson* [1920] AC 860, HL, where a rule of the lex situs preventing a beneficiary from giving up foreign immovables taken outside the will exonerated him from the duty to elect under Scottish domestic law.

3 For cases illustrating this principle see *Johnson v Telford* (1830) 1 Russ & M 244; *Maxwell v Maxwell* (1852) 2 De GM & G 705; *Dewar v Maitland* (1866) LR 2 Eq 834; *Orrell v Orrell* (1871) 6 Ch App 302.

4 This is a special rule for the heir to English land. A distinction has been drawn between the heir to English immovables and the heir to foreign immovables. The heir to English immovables can take both the immovables and the benefits given him by the will: *Hearle v Greenbank* (1749) 1 Ves Sen 298; *Re De Virte, Vaiani v De Virte* [1915] 1 Ch 920; cf *Boughton v Boughton* (1750) 2 Ves Sen 12 (election imposed by express condition). On the other hand, the heir to foreign immovables is put to his election: *Brodie v Barry* (1813) 2 Ves & B 127; *Dundas v Dundas* (1830) 2 Dow & Cl 349, HL; *Dewar v Maitland* (1866) LR 2 Eq 834; *Orrell v Orrell* (1871) 6 Ch App 302; *Harrison v Harrison* (1873) 8 Ch App 342; *Re Ogilvie, Ogilvie v Ogilvie* [1918] 1 Ch 492. Descent to the heir was abolished except in the case of entailed interests (Administration of Estates Act 1925 s 45), so that it is now only the heir to an entailed interest in English immovables who can claim the benefit of this rule. In all other cases of succession to English immovables following an ineffective disposition by will the immovables pass to the persons entitled on intestacy, who have no beneficial interest in the property until an assent or conveyance is made in their favour: *Stamp Duties Comr (Queensland) v Livingston* [1965] AC 694, [1964] 3 All ER 692, PC; *Lall v Lall* [1965] 3 All ER 330, [1965] 1 WLR 1249. Accordingly, as the testator cannot be said to have purported to dispose of property belonging to them, they cannot be put to an election. As to election see further EQUITY vol 16 (Reissue) para 842 et seq; and as to descent to the heir and succession on intestacy see EXECUTORS vol 17 para 1369 et seq

971. Testamentary revocation. The question whether a will is revoked by a later will or codicil containing an express revocation clause is governed by the law governing the validity of the later instrument[1]. So far as its formal validity is concerned, it will be treated as properly executed if its execution complied with the choice of law rules previously set out[2], or, in so far as it revokes a will or any provision of a will which is formally valid under the Wills Act 1963, if its execution conformed to any law by reference to which the revoked will or provision would be so treated[3].

Other testamentary modes of revocation[4] are probably governed by the law of the testator's domicile in the case of movables[5] and by the lex situs in the case of immovables[6].

1 *Cottrell v Cottrell* (1872) LR 2 P & D 397; *Re Manifold, Slater v Chryssaffinis* [1962] Ch 1, [1961] 1 All ER 710. This depends on the choice of law rules for wills of movables so far as the instrument purports to revoke a will of movables, and on the choice of law rules for wills of immovables so far as it purports to revoke a will of immovables. The question of validity must be distinguished from the question of construction of the revocation clause, which is governed, prima facie, by the law of the testator's domicile: *Re Wayland's Estate* [1951] 2 All ER 1041; *Re Manifold, Slater v Chryssaffinis* supra (revocation clause in will dealing with property in one country does not necessarily revoke will dealing with property in another country). The question whether a later will impliedly revokes an earlier will is similarly one of construction, governed, prima facie, by the law of the testator's domicile. As to construction see para 966 ante.

2 See paras 963–964 ante.

3 Wills Act 1963 s 2(1)(c).

4 Eg by destruction of the will.
5 *Velasco v Coney* [1934] P 143 (a case on the exercise of a power of appointment by will). As to whether this is the domicile at the date of revocation or at the date of death see Dicey and Morris *The Conflict of Laws* (12th Edn, 1993) 1049–1050.
6 This would seem to follow from principle: see para 956 ante.

972. Revocation by subsequent marriage. The question whether marriage revokes a previous will of movables[1] is governed by the law of the testator's domicile at the date of the marriage[2]. A subsequent change of domicile is immaterial[3].

The question whether marriage revokes a previous will of immovables is governed by the lex situs[4].

1 See the Wills Act 1837 s 18 (substituted by the Administration of Justice Act 1982 s 18(1)). The rule of English law which makes a will null and void on marriage is part of matrimonial law and not of testamentary law: *Re Martin, Loustalan v Loustalan* [1900] P 211 at 240, CA. As to English domestic law see WILLS vol 50 para 278 et seq
2 *Re Reid's Goods* (1866) LR 1 P & D 74; *Re Martin, Loustalan v Loustalan* [1900] P 211, CA; *Re Groos's Estate* [1904] P 269; *Re Von Faber's Goods* (1904) 20 TLR 640; *Westerman's Executor v Schwab* (1905) 8 F 132, Ct of Sess.
3 *Re Reid's Goods* (1866) LR 1 P & D 74; *Re Groos's Estate* [1904] P 269.
4 *Re Earl of Caithness* (1891) 7 TLR 354; cf *Re Martin, Loustalan v Loustalan* [1900] P 211 at 234, CA. However, to the contrary see Dicey and Morris *The Conflict of Laws* (12th Edn, 1993) 1051, citing *Davies v Davies* (1915) 31 WLR 396 at 399, 24 DLR 737 at 740 (Alta); and *Re Howard* (1924) 54 OLR 109 at 119, [1924] 1 DLR 1062 at 1071.

D. TESTAMENTARY EXERCISE OF POWER OF APPOINTMENT

973. Capacity. A testator has capacity to exercise by will a power of appointment over movables if he has capacity to make the will by the law of his domicile, even though he has no capacity by the law governing the instrument of creation[1].

The capacity of a testator to exercise by will a power of appointment over immovables is governed by the lex situs[2].

1 *Re Lewal's Settlement Trusts, Gould v Lewal* [1918] 2 Ch 391, where, however, the instrument of creation provided that the donee might exercise the power 'by will or codicil executed in such manner as to be valid according to the law of her domicile': see at 396. Capacity by the law governing the instrument of creation is probably also sufficient wherever the law of the domicile does not govern the essential validity of the appointment, as to which see para 976 post. The point arose, but did not have to be decided, in *Re Langley's Settlement Trusts, Lloyds Bank Ltd v Langley* [1961] 1 All ER 78, [1961] 1 WLR 41; on appeal [1962] Ch 541, [1961] 3 All ER 803, CA (power of withdrawal from fund). As to capacity to make a will see para 962 ante. As to the law governing marriage settlements see paras 768–769 ante. As to powers generally see POWERS.
2 See para 962 ante.

974. Formal validity. A will exercising a power of appointment will be treated as properly executed if its execution complied with the choice of law rules previously set out[1] or conformed to the law governing the essential validity of the power[2]. In so far as it exercises the power it will not be treated as improperly executed by reason only that its execution was not in accordance with any formal requirements contained in the instrument creating the power[3].

1 See paras 963–964 ante. Compliance with the formal requirements of the law of the testator's domicile was a way of satisfying the common law rule for the formal validity of the exercise of a power: *D'Huart v*

Harkness (1865) 34 Beav 324; *Re Price, Tomlin v Latter* [1900] 1 Ch 442; *Re Wilkinson's Settlement, Butler v Wilkinson* [1917] 1 Ch 620.
2   Wills Act 1963 s 2(1)(d), confirming the rule at common law: *Tatnall v Hankey* (1838) 2 Moo PCC 342; *Re Alexander's Goods* (1860) 29 LJPM & A 93; *Re Hallyburton's Goods* (1866) LR 1 P & D 90; *Re Huber's Goods* [1896] P 209; *Re Tréfond's Goods* [1899] P 247; *Murphy v Deichler* [1909] AC 446, HL; *Re Baker's Settlement Trusts, Hunt v Baker* [1908] WN 161.
3   Wills Act 1963 s 2(2).

975. Construction. The question whether a will exercises a power of appointment will be determined, prima facie, by the law of the testator's domicile at the date of execution of the will[1]. If there is a sufficient indication that he intended the will to be construed in accordance with the law governing the instrument of creation[2], or if powers of appointment are unknown to the law of the testator's domicile[3], the question will be determined by the law governing the instrument of creation[4].

1   *Re Price, Tomlin v Latter* [1900] 1 Ch 442 at 452; *Re D'Este's Settlement Trusts, Poulter v D'Este* [1903] 1 Ch 898 at 905; *Re Simpson, Coutts & Co v Church Missionary Society* [1916] 1 Ch 502; *Re McMorran, Mercantile Bank of India Ltd v Perkins* [1958] Ch 624, [1958] 1 All ER 186; *Durie's Trustees v Osborne* 1960 SC 444. For the rule of English domestic law see the Wills Act 1837 s 27 (as amended); and POWERS vol 36 para 895.
2   *Re Price, Tomlin v Latter* [1900] 1 Ch 442.
3   *Re Price, Tomlin v Latter* [1900] 1 Ch 442; *Re Baker's Settlement Trusts, Hunt v Baker* [1908] WN 161; *Re Simpson, Coutts & Co v Church Missionary Society* [1916] 1 Ch 502; *Re Wilkinson's Settlement, Butler v Wilkinson* [1917] 1 Ch 620; *Re Lewal's Settlement Trusts, Gould v Lewal* [1918] 2 Ch 391; *Re Strong, Strong v Meissner* (1925) 95 LJCh 22; *Re Waite's Settlement Trusts, Westminster Bank Ltd v Brouard* [1958] Ch 100, [1957] 1 All ER 629; *Re Fenston's Settlement, Max-Muller v Simonsen* [1971] 3 All ER 1092 at 1095–1096, [1971] 1 WLR 1640 at 1644–1645; cf *Re McMorran, Mercantile Bank of India Ltd v Perkins* [1958] Ch 624, [1958] 1 All ER 186. Two cases to the contrary, *Re D'Este's Settlement Trusts, Poulter v D'Este* [1903] 1 Ch 898; *Re Scholefield, Scholefield v St John* [1905] 2 Ch 408, have not been followed.
4   In a case where the power arises under an English settlement, and powers of appointment are unknown to the law of the testator's domicile, the court must first interpret the words of the will according to the law governing construction of the will (as to which see para 966 ante) in order to ascertain the testator's intention with regard to the property subject to the power, and it must then decide as a matter of English law whether the power has been exercised: *Re Fenston's Settlement, Max-Muller v Simonsen* [1971] 3 All ER 1092 at 1095, [1971] 1 WLR 1640 at 1644.

976. Material or essential validity. The material or essential validity of the exercise by will of a power of appointment over movables is governed by the law governing the instrument of creation[1], unless it is the exercise of a general power by which the testator has blended the appointed movables into one mass with his own estate, in which case the material or essential validity of the appointment is governed by the law of the testator's domicile at the date of his death[2].

The material or essential validity of an appointment of immovables by will is governed by the lex situs[3].

1   *Pouey v Hordern* [1900] 1 Ch 492 (special power); *Re Mégret, Tweedie v Maunder* [1901] 1 Ch 547 (general power). The reason is that the testator has not disposed by will of his own property; he has only nominated the persons whose names are to be inserted in the settlement creating the power: *Re Pryce, Lawford v Pryce* [1911] 2 Ch 286 at 296, CA.
2   *Re Pryce, Lawford v Pryce* [1911] 2 Ch 286, CA; *Re Khan's Settlement, Coutts & Co v Senior Dowager Begum of Bhopal* [1966] Ch 567, [1966] 1 All ER 160, not following *Re Waite's Settlement Trusts, Westminster Bank Ltd v Brouard* [1958] Ch 100, [1957] 1 All ER 629; cf *Pouey v Hordern* [1900] 1 Ch 492 at 495. The reason is that by his disposition the testator has shown an intention that the movables subject to the power should be treated as being and deemed to be part of his free estate: see *Re Pryce, Lawford v Pryce* supra; *Re Khan's Settlement, Coutts & Co v Senior Dowager Begum of Bhopal* supra; and see further POWERS vol 36 para 914.
3   *Re Hernando, Hernando v Sawtell* (1884) 27 ChD 284.

977. Revocation. The question of the revocation of the exercise by will of a power of appointment is governed by the choice of law rules previously set out[1].

1 See paras 971–972 ante; and see *Velasco v Coney* [1934] P 143. By English domestic law, a will exercising a power of appointment is not revoked by the subsequent marriage of the testator if the appointed property would not pass to his executor or administrator or the persons entitled on intestacy in default of appointment: Wills Act 1837 s 18(2) (substituted by the Administration of Justice Act 1982 s 18(1)).

9. BANKRUPTCY AND CORPORATIONS

(1) BANKRUPTCY

978. Bankruptcy jurisdiction of English court. The English court[1] has jurisdiction to adjudicate bankrupt[2] any debtor who: (1) is domiciled in England and Wales on the day on which the petition is presented[3]; or (2) is personally present in England and Wales on the day on which the petition is presented[4]; or (3) has been ordinarily resident or has had a place of residence in England and Wales at any time in the period of three years ending with the day on which the petition is presented[5]; or (4) has carried on business in England and Wales, personally or by means of an agent or manager, at any time within the period of three years ending with the day on which the petition is presented[6]; or (5) was a member of a firm or partnership which has carried on business in England and Wales as such or by means of an agent or manager at any time within the period of three years ending with the day on which the petition is presented[7]. However, if the debtor is, for the time being, bound by a voluntary arrangement proposed by the debtor and approved pursuant to the statutory scheme, there is no specific jurisdictional requirement to be satisfied, for in accepting the voluntary arrangement the debtor has submitted to the jurisdiction of the English court in relation to it[8].

The fact that the court has jurisdiction to adjudicate the debtor bankrupt does not mean that it is obliged to exercise that jurisdiction or to hear the petition: it may dismiss the petition or stay the proceedings[9]. Under previous bankruptcy law[10] it was relevant to the exercise of a similar discretion that the debtor possessed no assets within the jurisdiction[11], or had already been made bankrupt in a foreign country[12], or (more generally) that it was in the circumstances not equitable that the bankruptcy should proceed[13]; and such factors are presumed to continue to be relevant. As bankruptcy is excluded from the Brussels and Lugano Conventions and the relevant provisions of the Civil Jurisdiction and Judgments Act 1982[14], the court is entitled to stay its proceedings on the ground of forum non conveniens if it considers it appropriate so to do[15].

If the debtor is subject to the jurisdiction of the English court, an order may be made for service of the petition on him in such manner as the court directs[16]. Substituted service may be ordered if the court is satisfied that prompt personal service cannot be made[17]. An order may be made for the public examination of any debtor who is subject to the bankruptcy jurisdiction of the English court[18]; but the power to order the private examination of any other person[19] is probably limited to those who are present in England and liable to be served with the summons.

1 Ie the High Court and the county courts: Insolvency Act 1986 s 373(1).
2 The jurisdictional rules are established by the Insolvency Act 1986 (repealing the Bankruptcy Act 1914), and govern the presentation of a petition by creditor or debtor. See generally BANKRUPTCY AND INSOLVENCY.

3 Insolvency Act 1986 s 265(1)(a). Domicile in this context has the meaning ascribed to it at common law, and not that in the Civil Jurisdiction and Judgments Act 1982 s 41: see paras 680–702 ante.

4 Insolvency Act 1986 s 265(1)(b). This ground will also apply to a petition presented by the debtor himself.

5 Ibid s 265(1)(c)(i). For the meaning of 'ordinary residence' see para 704 ante. See also *Re Hecquard, ex p Hecquard* (1889) 24 QBD 71, CA; *Re Nordenfelt* [1895] 1 QB 151, CA; *Re Brauch (a debtor), ex p Britannic Securities and Investments Ltd* [1978] Ch 316, CA.

6 Insolvency Act 1986 s 265(1)(c)(ii), (2)(b). A person still carries on business if he gives up the business and goes abroad leaving unpaid trading debts behind him: *Re A Debtor (No 784 of 1991)* [1992] Ch 554, [1992] 3 All ER 376; cf *Theophile v Solicitor General* [1950] AC 186, [1950] 1 All ER 405, HL.

7 Insolvency Act 1986 s 265(1)(c)(ii), (2)(a).

8 See ibid s 264(1)(c). A voluntary arrangement means such a scheme approved by the court pursuant to the provisions of Pt VIII (ss 252–263) of the Act: see s 253(1). The petition in such a case may be presented by a creditor or other person (other than the debtor); and if presented by a creditor who is also a person bound by a voluntary arrangement the presentor may elect the capacity in which the presentation of the petition is made: ss 264(1)(c), 266(1).

9 Ibid s 266(3).

10 Ie the Bankruptcy Act 1914 (repealed).

11 *Re Behrends* (1865) 12 LT 149; *Re Robinson, ex p Robinson* (1883) 22 ChD 816, CA; *Re Hecquard, ex p Hecquard* (1889) 24 QBD 71, CA.

12 The fact that a debtor has been made bankrupt in a foreign country does not deprive the court of jurisdiction to adjudicate him bankrupt in England, and English law does not recognise the principle of 'unity of bankruptcy' according to which all creditors must have recourse to a single court. This was the position under the old law, and nothing in the Insolvency Act 1986 is expressed to alter the position. But the fact that he has been made bankrupt overseas, especially if coupled with the fact that there are no assets in England, may be a strong reason for the court to exercise its discretion by declining jurisdiction. Cf *Re McCulloch, ex p McCulloch* (1880) 14 ChD 716, CA; *Re Robinson, ex p Robinson* (1883) 22 ChD 816, CA; *Re Artola Hermanos* (1890) 24 QBD 640, CA.

13 *Re McCulloch, ex p McCulloch* (1880) 14 ChD 716, CA; *Re Betts, ex p Official Receiver* [1901] 2 KB 39; *Re a Debtor (No 737 of 1928)* [1929] 1 Ch 362, CA.

14 Civil Jurisdiction and Judgments Act 1982 s 18(3)(ba) (added by the Insolvency Act 1985 s 235, Sch 8 para 36; amended by the Insolvency Act 1986 s 429, Sch 14); Brussels Convention art 1 para 2; Lugano Convention art 1 para 2. See also Case 133/78 *Gourdain v Nadler* [1979] ECR 733, ECJ; and para 626 ante. As to the Brussels Convention see para 618 text and note 1 ante. As to the Lugano Convention see para 618 text and note 2 ante.

15 See the Civil Jurisdiction and Judgments Act 1982 s 49 (amended by the Civil Jurisdiction and Judgments Act 1991 s 3, Sch 2 para 24); and para 1085 post.

16 Insolvency Rules 1986, SI 1986/1925, r 12.12(2). RSC Ord 11 does not apply in bankruptcy proceedings: Insolvency Rules 1986 r 12.12(1); *Re Busytoday Ltd, Popely v Lewis* [1992] 4 All ER 61, [1992] 1 WLR 683. A statutory demand (see the Insolvency Act 1986 s 268) is not a document issued by the court, and leave to serve it out of the jurisdiction is not required: *Practice Direction (Bankruptcy 1/88)* [1988] 2 All ER 126, [1988] 1 WLR 461.

17 Insolvency Rules 1986 r 6.14(2); and see *Re Urquhart, ex p Urquhart* (1890) 24 QBD 723, CA; *Re a Debtor (No 419 of 1939)* [1939] 3 All ER 429, CA.

18 See, eg, Insolvency Act 1986 s 290; *Re Seagull Manufacturing Co Ltd (in liquidation)* [1993] Ch 345, [1993] 2 All ER 980, CA. The same is probably true in relation to the private examination of the bankrupt: see the Insolvency Act 1986 s 366(1)(a).

19 See ibid s 366(1)(c); and *Re Tucker (RC) (a bankrupt), ex p Tucker (KR)* [1990] Ch 148, [1988] 1 All ER 603, CA; *Re Tucker (a bankrupt) (No 2), ex p the Trustee v Langton Investment SA* [1988] 2 All ER 339, [1988] 1 WLR 497; *Re Seagull Manufacturing Co Ltd (in liquidation)* [1993] Ch 345, [1993] 2 All ER 980, CA.

979. Effect of an English bankruptcy on debtor's property. The assignment of a bankrupt's property to the trustee in bankruptcy under the Insolvency Act 1986 operates to transfer title to all the debtor's property, whether movable or immovable, and whether situated in England and Wales or elsewhere[1].

Although an English court[2] may consider that a transfer of foreign land has been effectively made, it may in practice be difficult for the trustee to enforce his title in the foreign jurisdiction. Even so, if the debtor is personally present within the jurisdiction, the court may be able to order him to act to support the trustee's obtaining an effective title to the land in a foreign jurisdiction[3]. Further, any court in the United Kingdom is obliged to assist another such court in insolvency matters upon request; and a request to a Scottish or Northern Irish court for assistance could enable an English trustee to obtain an effective title to property in Scotland or Northern Ireland[4]. A similar scheme exists under which the Secretary of State can designate other countries for the purposes of mutual assistance in insolvency matters[5].

A court may restrain a creditor from taking proceedings abroad to recover a debt due from a bankrupt debtor in order to preserve the principle of equal distribution among creditors. If the creditor has claimed in the English bankruptcy he may be so restrained[6]; if he is resident in England he may likewise be restrained[7]. It is unclear to what extent the courts retain a power to compel a creditor who has satisfied his claim against the debtor abroad to pool those assets for the benefit of creditors generally; but it is thought that the power has survived the Insolvency Act 1986[8]. Such a creditor will not be allowed to prove under the English bankruptcy unless he brings the assets into hotchpot[9]. If he chooses not to prove in the English bankruptcy he may still be ordered to pool the assets as if he were subject to the restraining jurisdiction of the English court[10].

1 See the Insolvency Act 1986 ss 283 (as amended), 306, 436. In other words, the assignment of property to the trustee is universal, and the Act, to the extent that it operates to transfer foreign land to the trustee, claims to have a wider effect than would be acknowledged by an English court as the consequence of a foreign bankruptcy (see para 982 post). The property must be that of the debtor, and it will be assigned subject to such charges and burdens as are recognised by the lex situs: *Re Somes, ex p De Lemos* (1896) 3 Mans 131; *Galbraith v Grimshaw* [1910] AC 508, HL; *Re Sykes, Cloghran Stud Farm Co v The Trustee* (1932) 101 LJCh 298, DC; *Re Doyle, ex p Brien v Doyle* (1993) 112 ALR 653; cf *Murphy's Trustee v Aitken* 1983 SLT 78, Ct of Sess.
2 As to the meaning of 'English' in relation to courts see para 604 ante.
3 If the foreign court follows the same approach as the English conflict of laws, this will be the case: see Dicey and Morris *The Conflict of Laws* (12th Edn, 1993) 1164.
4 See the Insolvency Act 1986 s 426 (as amended); and BANKRUPTCY AND INSOLVENCY vol 3(2) (Reissue) para 713.
5 Ibid s 426(4), (11); and the Co-operation of Insolvency Courts (Designation of Relevant Countries and Territories) Order 1986, SI 1986/2123; and see para 994 post.
6 *Re Tait & Co, ex p Tait* (1872) LR 13 Eq 311. Cf *Barclays Bank plc v Homan* [1993] BCLC 680.
7 *Re Distin, ex p Ormiston* (1871) 24 LT 197.
8 See *Re Paramount Airways Ltd (in administration)* [1993] Ch 223, [1992] 3 All ER 1, CA.
9 *Re Morton, ex p Robertson* (1875) LR 20 Eq 733; *Banco de Portugal v Waddell* (1880) 5 App Cas 161, HL.
10 See the cases in notes 6–7 supra.

980. Choice of law in an English bankruptcy.

The court will administer the property of a bankrupt in accordance with English law as the lex fori[1]. A creditor may prove for any debt due to him from the bankrupt, no matter whether the debt is governed by English law or foreign law[2]. Of course, it may be necessary to refer to foreign law in order to discover whether a debt governed by a foreign proper law is valid by that law. But, subject to this, a foreigner proving for a foreign debt stands in the same position as an English creditor proving for an English debt[3]. The English court will apply its own rules designed to secure equality as between creditors of the same class, and will compel a creditor who seeks to prove in the English bankruptcy[4] or who is subject to the jurisdiction of the English court[5] to bring into the common pool any debt or dividend recovered by him abroad[6].

The Insolvency Act 1986 contains particular rules as to the effect of bankruptcy on antecedent transactions, such as the effect of a fraudulent preference, or of a transaction at an undervalue[7]. These permit a court to reopen and reverse a transaction entered into by the bankrupt with another person[8]. Although there is no territorial restriction upon who the other person may be, and no express restriction upon the nature or locus of the transaction, if a claim is made under these provisions, it must be shown that there is sufficient connection between the defendant (against whom an order is sought) and England to make it just and convenient in all the circumstances to make the order despite the foreign element[9]. If the defendant is outside the jurisdiction, the service on him of the proceedings will require the leave of the court; and the grant of leave will depend on, inter alia, the strength or otherwise of the connection of the defendant with England[10].

1 *Re Melbourn, ex p Melbourn* (1870) 6 Ch App 64; *Thurburn v Steward* (1871) LR 3 PC 478; *Re Scheibler, ex p Holthausen* (1874) 9 Ch App 722; *Re Kloebe, Kannreuther v Geiselbrecht* (1884) 28 ChD 175; *Re Doetsch, Matheson v Ludwig* [1896] 2 Ch 836.
2 *Re Melbourn, ex p Melbourn* (1870) 6 Ch App 64; *Re Kloebe, Kannreuther v Geiselbrecht* (1884) 28 ChD 175.
3 *Re Scheibler, ex p Holthausen* (1874) 9 Ch App 722; *Re Wiskemann, ex p Trustee* (1923) 92 LJCh 349.
4 *Selkrig v Davies* (1814) 2 Dow 230 at 249, HL; *Re Morton, ex p Robertson* (1875) LR 20 Eq 733; *Banco de Portugal v Waddell* (1880) 5 App Cas 161, HL.
5 *Sill v Worswick* (1791) 1 Hy Bl 665; *Hunter v Potts* (1791) 4 Term Rep 182; *Phillips v Hunter* (1795) 2 Hy Bl 402.
6 Ie except in pursuance of a judgment in rem given by a foreign court: *Minna Craig SS Co v Chartered Mercantile Bank of India, London and China* [1897] 1 QB 460, CA.
7 See the Insolvency Act 1986 ss 339–342 (as amended), 423–425; and generally BANKRUPTCY AND INSOLVENCY vol 3(2) (Reissue) para 644 et seq.
8 See ibid ss 339, 340, 423.
9 *Re Paramount Airways Ltd (in administration)* [1993] Ch 223, [1992] 3 All ER 1, CA.
10 Insolvency Rules 1986 r 12.12 (see para 978 text and note 16 ante); *Re Paramount Airways Ltd (in administration)* [1993] Ch 223, [1992] 3 All ER 1, CA; *Re Busytoday Ltd, Popely v Lewis* [1992] 4 All ER 61, [1992] 1 WLR 683; *Re Tucker (a bankrupt) (No 2), ex p the Trustee v Langton Investment SA* [1988] 2 All ER 339, [1988] 1 WLR 497.

981. Discharge by reason of an English order. An order of discharge under an English bankruptcy discharges the debtor from all debts provable in the bankruptcy, irrespective of the law which governs the contract giving rise to the debt[1], because it operates as a release from all debts provable in bankruptcy[2]. In addition, a discharge in accordance with the law which governs the contract or debt is a valid discharge in England[3], and the same principle may apply to a voluntary arrangement[4] under the Insolvency Act 1986[5].

1 *Royal Bank of Scotland v Cuthbert* (1813) 1 Rose 462; *Gill v Barron* (1868) LR 2 PC 157; *Ellis v M'Henry* (1871) LR 6 CP 228.
2 Insolvency Act 1986 s 281(1); and BANKRUPTCY AND INSOLVENCY vol 3(2) (Reissue) para 630.
3 See paras 854 ante, 982 post.
4 See para 978 note 8 ante.
5 See the Insolvency Act 1986 ss 260, 261; and Dicey and Morris *The Conflict of Laws* (12th Edn, 1993) 1172.

982. Effect in England of foreign bankruptcies. An English court may not question the jurisdiction of a Scottish or Northern Irish court to adjudicate a debtor bankrupt[1]. They will recognise that the courts of a foreign country have jurisdiction over a debtor if he was domiciled in that country at the time of presentation of the petition[2], or if he submitted to the jurisdiction of the court by presenting the petition himself[3] or by appearing in the proceedings[4]. It is possible that further grounds of jurisdictional competence may be recognised as sufficient by the court[5].

An assignment of a bankrupt's property in Scotland[6] or Northern Ireland[7] operates to transfer to the assignee title to of all the debtor's property, whether movable or immovable and wherever situated[8]. The property of the debtor vests in the assignee subject to any charges which are recognised as affecting it by the lex situs[9]. By contrast, an assignment of a bankrupt's property in any other foreign country which is recognised as jurisdictionally competent[10] operates to transfer to the assignee title to the movable (but not to the immovable) property of the debtor situated in England[11]. This depends upon the foreign bankruptcy being intended to operate with extra-territorial effect[12]; and the assignment is in any event subject to such charges as bound the movables in the hands of the bankrupt[13]. Once there has been such a foreign adjudication, there may still be an English bankruptcy; but if the effect of the foreign adjudication is that there remains no property of the debtor in England, the court is likely to exercise its discretion against the making of such an order[14].

In the event of successive foreign bankruptcies, if under each of these an English court would recognise that there had been an assignment of the movable property of the debtor in England, the earlier in time will prevail[15]. The English bankruptcy rules relating to the vesting of property in the trustee where there are successive bankruptcies[16] do not apply if the first bankruptcy takes place in England and the second in a foreign country[17].

A discharge from any debt or liability under the bankruptcy law of a foreign country outside the United Kingdom[18] is a discharge therefrom in England if (but only if) it operates as a discharge under the law which governs the contract[19]. Even if the court which makes the order was one which was recognised as having bankruptcy jurisdiction[20], the effect of any discharge is a matter for the law which governs the contract[21].

1   See the Insolvency Act 1986 s 426(1); but this does not require a court to enforce an order made in a Scottish or Northern Irish bankruptcy in relation to property in England.
2   *Re Blithman* (1866) LR 2 Eq 23; *Re Hayward, Hayward v Hayward* [1897] 1 Ch 905.
3   *Re Davidson's Settlement Trusts* (1873) LR 15 Eq 383; *Re Lawson's Trusts* [1896] 1 Ch 175; *Re Burke, King v Terry* (1919) 54 LJo 430.
4   *Re Anderson* [1911] 1 KB 896; *Re Craig, Catling v Esson* (1916) 86 LJCh 62.
5   The question is not one regulated by statute, and authorities under the common law are few. But the courts may well recognise the bankruptcy jurisdiction of a court in whose jurisdiction the debtor carried on business.
6   Under the Bankruptcy (Scotland) Act 1985.
7   Under the Insolvency (Northern Ireland) Order 1989.
8   Ie whether in England and Wales, Scotland, Northern Ireland or elsewhere. The obligation contained in the Insolvency Act 1986 s 426 requiring the rendering of mutual judicial assistance will mean that a Scottish or Northern Irish trustee may easily obtain an effective title to property in England and Wales.
9   See *Murphy's Trustee v Aitken* 1983 SLT 78; and *Galbraith v Grimshaw* [1910] AC 508, HL.
10   See text and notes 2–5 supra.
11   *Solomons v Ross* (1764) 1 Hy Bl 131n; *Re Blithman* (1866) LR 2 Eq 23; *Re Davidson's Settlement Trusts* (1873) LR 15 Eq 383; *Re Anderson* [1911] 1 KB 896; *Re Craig, Catling v Esson* (1917) 86 LJCh 62; *Re Burke, King v Terry* (1919) 54 LJo 430. In relation to immovables situated in England, no assignment will take place, but an English court may authorise the appointment of a receiver of the rents and profits of such immovables: *Re Levy's Trusts* (1885) 30 ChD 119; *Re Osborn, ex p Trustee* [1931–32] B & CR 189. If the country has been designated as one for the purposes of mutual assistance (see para 979 note 5 ante), such a result may the more easily be achieved.
12   See the cases cited in note 11 supra.
13   *Solomons v Ross* (1764) 1 Hy Bl 131n; *Galbraith v Grimshaw* [1910] AC 508, HL.
14   See para 978 ante.
15   *Geddes v Mowat* (1824) 1 Gl & J 414; *Re O'Reardon* (1873) 9 Ch App 74; *Re Anderson* [1911] 1 KB 896; *Re Temple* [1947] Ch 345.

16 Insolvency Act 1986 ss 334, 335 (as amended): see BANKRUPTCY AND INSOLVENCY vol 3(2) (Reissue) paras 595–596.
17 *Re Temple, ex p Official Receiver v Official Assignee of Bombay* [1947] Ch 345, [1947] 1 All ER 592. See also *Re Anderson* [1911] 1 KB 896; on contemporaneous English and foreign bankruptcies see *Re Macfadyen & Co, ex p Vizianagaram Co Ltd* [1908] 1 KB 675.
18 A Scottish or Northern Irish discharge is effective in England. This is said to follow from the fact that it derives its effect in each case from an Act of the United Kingdom Parliament.
19 See generally paras 844–857 ante; *Gibbs & Sons v Société Industrielle et Commerciale des Métaux* (1890) 25 QBD 399, CA.
20 See text and notes 2–5 supra.
21 See *Burrows v Jemino* (1726) 2 Stra 733; *Potter v Brown* (1804) 5 East 124; *Ellis v M'Henry* (1871) LR 6 CP 228; *International Harvester Co Ltd v Zarbok* [1918] 3 WWR 38; *Smith v Buchanan* (1800) 1 East 6; *Bartley v Hodges* (1861) 1 B & S 375; *Gibbs & Sons v Société Industrielle et Commerciale des Métaux* (1890) 25 QBD 399, CA; *National Bank of Greece and Athens SA v Metliss* [1958] AC 509, [1957] 3 All ER 608, HL. But a discharge from a liability which does not derive from a contract appears to be a good discharge in England provided that the foreign court had (bankruptcy) jurisdiction to make the order: *Phillips v Eyre* (1870) LR 6 QB 1.

(2) CORPORATIONS

(i) Status, Domicile and Powers

983. Recognition of foreign corporations. English law recognises the existence of a corporation duly created in a foreign country, and will allow it to sue and be sued in England in its corporate capacity[1]. It follows that whether a corporation has continued in existence, or has been dissolved, is likewise governed by the law of its place of incorporation[2].

The law of the place of incorporation determines who are entitled to act on behalf of the corporation[3], and also the extent of an individual member's liability for the corporation's debts[4]. The English court is reluctant to interfere in domestic issues between members of a foreign corporation, especially where the exercise of discretionary powers is in issue[5]. Nevertheless, all matters such as these, which are part of the internal management of the corporation, must in principle be governed by the law of the place of incorporation.

The same principle has been extended to permit an international organisation (which as such has no legal personality, and hence no capacity to sue or be sued in England[6]) which has incorporated itself under the domestic law of a foreign country to be recognised as a corporation[7]; and to an international organisation recognised by a number of foreign states but whose proper law is public international law[8]. It has been further extended, by analogy, to recognise the legal personality created under the law of a foreign country of other corporate bodies[9].

1 *Henriques v General Privileged Dutch Co Trading to West Indies* (1728) 2 Ld Raym 1532; *Newby v von Oppen and Colt's Patent Firearms Manufacturing Co* (1872) LR 7 QB 293; *Lazard Bros & Co v Midland Bank Ltd* [1933] AC 289 at 297, HL. Whether a partnership or other entity is a corporation depends on the law of the country where it is formed: *Von Hellfeld v Rechnitzer and Mayer Frères & Co* [1914] 1 Ch 748, CA.
2 See para 986 post. See also, on the law of the place of incorporation the Foreign Corporations Act 1991; and para 984 post. Note that the Rome Convention on the Law Applicable to contractual obligations has no application to questions governed by the law of companies and other bodies corporate or unincorporate such as the creation by registration or otherwise, legal capacity, internal organisation or winding-up of companies and other bodies corporate or unincorporate and the personal liability of officers and members as such for the obligations of the company or body': Rome Convention art 1

para 2(e). The common law rules, as set out here, will continue to govern these issues. For the meaning of 'the Rome Convention' see para 844 text and note 1 ante.

3 *Bank of Ethiopia v National Bank of Egypt and Liguori* [1937] Ch 513, [1937] 3 All ER 8; *Banco de Bilbao v Sancha* [1938] 2 KB 176, [1938] 2 All ER 253, CA; *Carl Zeiss Stiftung v Rayner & Keeler Ltd (No 2)* [1967] 1 AC 853 at 919, 972, [1966] 2 All ER 536 at 556, 588, HL; *Damon Compania Naviera SA v Hapag-Lloyd International SA, The Blankenstein, The Bartenstein, The Birkenstein* [1985] 1 All ER 475, [1985] 1 WLR 435, CA.

4 *Risdon Iron and Locomotive Works v Furness* [1906] 1 KB 49, CA; *J H Rayner (Mincing Lane) Ltd v Department of Trade and Industry* [1990] 2 AC 418, sub nom *Maclaine Watson & Co Ltd v Department of Trade and Industry* [1989] 3 All ER 523, HL; *Kutchera v Buckingham International Holdings* [1988] IR 61; cf *Bateman v Service* (1881) 6 App Cas 386, PC.

5 See *Sudlow v Dutch Rhenish Rly Co* (1855) 21 Beav 43; *Re Schintz, Schintz v Warr* [1926] Ch 710, CA; *Pergamon Press Ltd v Maxwell* [1970] 2 All ER 809, [1970] 1 WLR 1167. Contrast *Pickering v Stephenson* (1872) LR 14 Eq 322, where the court restrained by injunction the application of a foreign corporation's funds in an ultra vires transaction.

6 *J H Rayner (Mincing Lane) Ltd v Department of Trade and Industry* [1990] 2 AC 418, sub nom *Maclaine Watson & Co Ltd v Department of Trade and Industry* [1989] 3 All ER 523, HL.

7 *Arab Monetary Fund v Hashim (No 3)* [1991] 2 AC 114, [1991] 1 All ER 871, HL.

8 *Westland Helicopters Ltd v Arab Organisation for Industrialisation* [1995] 2 All ER 387.

9 *Bumper Development Corpn v Metropolitan Police Comr (Union of India, claimants)* [1991] 4 All ER 638, [1991] 1 WLR 1362, CA. See also para 1069 post.

984. Recognition under the Foreign Corporations Act 1991. If at any time (1) any question arises whether a body which purports to have, or as the case may be appears to have, lost corporate status under the laws of a territory which is not at that time a recognised state[1] should or should not be regarded as having legal personality as a body corporate under the law of any part of the United Kingdom[2]; and (2) it appears that the laws of that territory are at that time applied by a settled court system in that territory[3], that question and any other material question[4] relating to the body must be determined (and account must be taken of those laws) as if that territory were a recognised state[5].

Any registration or other thing done before 25 September 1991[6] is valid if it would have been valid before that date had the provisions described above then been in force[7].

1 A 'recognised state' is a territory which is recognised by Her Majesty's Government in the United Kingdom as a state: Foreign Corporations Act 1991 s 1(2)(a). The laws of a territory which is so recognised are taken to include the laws of any part of the territory which are acknowledged by the federal or other central government of the territory as a whole: s 1(2)(b). As to the recognition of foreign states see Dicey and Morris *The Conflict of Laws* (12th Edn, 1993) 1109; and FOREIGN RELATIONS LAW.

2 Foreign Corporations Act 1991 s 1(1)(a). For the meaning of 'United Kingdom' see para 604 ante.

3 Ibid s 1(1)(b).

4 A material question is a question, whether as to capacity, constitution or otherwise, which in the case of a body corporate falls to be determined by reference to the laws of the territory under which the body is incorporated: ibid s 1(2)(c).

5 Ibid s 1(1).

6 Ie the day on which the Foreign Corporations Act 1991 came into force: see s 2(3).

7 Ibid s 1(3).

985. Amalgamation. If a foreign corporation is amalgamated with another foreign corporation under the law of the place of incorporation, the new entity will be recognised in England. If that law provides for the new corporation to succeed to the assets and liabilities of its predecessors, it will be recognised in England as having done so[1]. However, the law of the place of incorporation cannot discharge the new company from the liabilities of the old unless it happens to be the applicable law of the contract giving rise to those liabilities[2].

1 *National Bank of Greece and Athens SA v Metliss* [1958] AC 509, [1957] 3 All ER 608, HL; *Steel Authority of India Ltd v Hind Metals Inc* [1984] 1 Lloyd's Rep 405; cf *RKO Pictures Inc v Cannon Screen Entertainment Ltd* [1990] BCLC 364. For certain procedural consequences of amalgamation see *Toprak Enerji Sanayi AS v Sale Tilney Technology plc* [1994] 3 All ER 483, [1994] 1 WLR 840; not followed in *Industrie Chimiche Italia Centrale v Alexander Tsarrilis & Sons Maritime Co, The Choko Star* [1996] 1 All ER 114.
2 *Adams v National Bank of Greece SA* [1961] AC 255, [1960] 2 All ER 421, HL. As to the discharge of contracts see para 854 ante.

986. Dissolution. English law[1] will similarly recognise that a foreign corporation has been dissolved under the law of its place of incorporation, for the will of the sovereign authority which created it can also destroy it[2]. If, according to that law, the corporation is in the process of being wound up, it can still sue and be sued in England[3]; but if this process has ended and the corporation has been dissolved it is dead in the eyes of English law[4]. Neither it nor its unincorporated English branch can sue or be sued in the English courts[5]. Whether the corporation has been so dissolved is a question of fact depending on the evidence of the foreign law concerned[6].

Many of the cases on these points were concerned with the effect of legislation of the USSR passed after the Revolution of 1917, dissolving banking and insurance companies and confiscating their property. At first it was held that these decrees declaring banking and insurance to be state monopolies did not have the effect of dissolving the Russian companies formerly engaged in those activities, but merely of winding them up; and they were allowed to sue and be sued in England[7]. However, from 1932 onwards it was consistently held, in the light of more reliable evidence as to the legal effect of the decrees, that the Russian banks and insurance companies in question were in fact dissolved in or about December 1917 or January 1918[8].

1 As to the meaning of 'English law' see para 604 ante.
2 *Lazard Bros & Co v Midland Bank Ltd* [1933] AC 289 at 297, HL. See also the Foreign Corporations Act 1991; and para 984 ante.
3 *Russian Commercial and Industrial Bank v Comptoir D'Escompte de Mulhouse* [1925] AC 112, HL; *Banque Internationale de Commerce de Petrograd v Goukassow* [1925] AC 150, HL; *Employers' Liability Assurance Corpn Ltd v Sedgwick Collins & Co Ltd* [1927] AC 95, HL; *First Russian Insurance Co v London and Lancashire Insurance Co Ltd* [1928] Ch 922.
4 *Russian and English Bank v Baring Bros & Co Ltd* [1932] 1 Ch 435; *Lazard Bros & Co v Midland Bank* [1933] AC 289, HL. However, it will be briefly revived by the making of an English winding up order: see para 991 post.
5 *Russian and English Bank v Baring Bros & Co Ltd* [1932] 1 Ch 435; *Deutsche Bank und Disconto Gesellschaft v Banque des Marshands de Moscou* (1932) 158 LT 364, CA; *Lazard Bros & Co v Midland Bank Ltd* [1933] AC 289, HL.
6 *Lazard Bros & Co v Midland Bank Ltd* [1933] AC 289, HL; *Re Russo-Asiatic Bank* [1934] Ch 720.
7 See the cases cited in note 3 supra.
8 See the cases cited in note 5 supra.

987. Domicile of corporations. A corporation is domiciled in the country under the law of which it is incorporated[1]. Thus a company formed under the Companies Act 1985 has an English domicile if registered in England, and a Scottish domicile if registered in Scotland[2]. Unlike an individual, it cannot change its domicile, even if it carries on business elsewhere[3]. Most of the reasons for attributing a domicile to individuals (for example, legitimacy, legitimation, marriage, divorce and succession on death) are inapplicable to corporations; but statutes occasionally refer to the domicile of corporations, thus making it necessary to decide where they are domiciled[4].

1 *Gasque v IRC* [1940] 2 KB 80; *Carl Zeiss Stiftung v Rayner & Keeler Ltd (No 3)* [1970] Ch 506 at 544, [1969] 3 All ER 897 at 914.

2 See further COMPANIES vol 7(1) para 91.

3 *Gasque v IRC* [1940] 2 KB 80; *Carl Zeiss Stiftung v Rayner & Keeler Ltd (No 3)* [1970] Ch 506 at 544; [1969] 3 All ER 897 at 914. This does not prevent a corporation being dissolved in the country in which is incorporated, and 'reincorporating' in another country.

4 The Civil Jurisdiction and Judgments Act 1982 s 42 contains rules for determining the 'domicile' of a corporation, but only for the purposes of the jurisdictional rules of that Act: see para 636 ante.

988. Powers of foreign corporations. The powers of a foreign corporation are defined and governed by its constitution as interpreted by the law of its place of incorporation[1]. Its powers in relation to a particular transaction may also be limited by the law of the country which governs the transaction in question. But it does not follow that if the transaction is ultra vires the corporation, it must be void. The effect of this lack of capacity on the validity of the transaction is a matter for the law which governs the transaction in question[2].

1 *Risdon Iron and Locomotive Works v Furness* [1906] 1 KB 49, CA; *Janred Properties Ltd v Ente Nazionale Italiano per il Turismo* [1989] 2 All ER 444, CA; *J H Rayner (Mincing Lane) Ltd v Department of Trade and Industry* [1990] 2 AC 418, sub nom *Maclaine Watson & Co Ltd v Department of Trade and Industry* [1989] 3 All ER 523, HL. But the company may be estopped from reliance upon the incapacity under the law of its place of incorporation, at least if the particular transaction is governed by English law: *Janred v Ente Nazionale Italiano per il Turismo* supra.

2 See *The Saudi Prince* [1982] 2 Lloyd's Rep 255; *Janred Properties v Ente Nazionale Italiano per il Turismo* [1989] 2 All ER 444, CA.

(ii) Jurisdiction over Corporations

989. Substantive rules of jurisdiction. In principle a corporation, English or foreign, may be a defendant to an action in the English courts in the same way as any other defendant having (or recognised as having) legal personality; and the jurisdictional rules applicable to commercial disputes in general will apply to companies as well[1]. But in civil or commercial proceedings which have as their object the validity of the constitution, the nullity or the dissolution of companies or other legal persons or associations of natural persons, or the decisions of their organs, the contracting state in which the company has its seat has exclusive jurisdiction[2]. It follows that many questions, including those relating to the internal management of a company, may not come before an English court if the company in question has its seat in a contracting state[3].

1 See para 615 et seq ante.

2 See para 628 text and note 3 ante.

3 See the Civil Jurisdiction and Judgments Act 1982 s 43; and para 636 ante. Note, however, that the Brussels and Lugano Conventions (as to which see para 618 text and notes 1-2 ante), and hence their limitations on jurisdiction, have no application to bankruptcy, proceedings relating to the winding-up of insolvent companies or other legal persons, judicial arrangements, compositions and analogous proceedings: see para 626 ante.

990. Service of process on corporations. If a corporation is present within England and Wales at the time of service of a writ, the corporation may be served with the writ[1]. But it is not always a straightforward matter to determine whether a corporation is present within the jurisdiction.

In relation to a company registered in England and Wales under the Companies Act 1985, or under any other Act to which the Companies Act 1985 applies[2], the company is deemed, wherever it carries on business, to be present in England and Wales by virtue of its incorporation and registration under that Act[3], and service of a writ may be made by leaving it at (or posting it to) the registered office of the company in England and Wales[4]. If it is registered in Scotland but has a place of business in England and Wales, service of the writ, addressed to the manager or head officer there, may be made at that place[5].

A company incorporated outside the United Kingdom but having established a place of business in Great Britain (an 'oversea company'[6]), must file with the Registrar of Companies the name and address of a person resident in Great Britain authorised to accept service on behalf of the company[7]. Service may then be made on this person[8]. If the company has failed to comply with this obligation, or if the persons whose names and addresses are registered are dead, or refuse service, or cannot be served, a writ may be served by leaving it at, or posting it to, any place of business established by the company in Great Britain[9].

If, therefore, a foreign corporation carries on business in England without complying with the requirements of registration of a person authorised to accept service, it may be served at a place of business established by it within the jurisdiction. A corporation can be treated as having a place of business in England, and therefore as being amenable to English jurisdiction[10], if it carries on business[11] in England for a substantial period of time[12] at some fixed and definite place[13]. The business must be that of the corporation[14], not that of an agent who acts for it in England[15]. The cause of action need not be in respect of a transaction effected through the corporation's place of business in England: it may be quite independent[16].

In cases for which provision is not otherwise made by any enactment, service may be effected by leaving a copy of the document with the chairman, president, secretary, treasurer or other similar officer of the corporation[17].

1 See para 615 text and note 4 ante.
2 See the Companies Act 1985 ss 675–678; and COMPANIES.
3 This follows from the requirement that a company registered under the Acts referred to in the text have a registered office which fixes the country of registration: see the Companies Act 1985 ss 2(1), (2), 287(1) (as substituted). There is no equivalent position for unregistered companies, and, in theory at least, the presence of such a company within the jurisdiction cannot be presumed from the fact of its incorporation. It is thought, however, that the problem of an unregistered company incorporated, but not otherwise present, in England and Wales, is unlikely to arise.
4 Ibid s 725(1).
5 Ibid s 725(2).
6 See ibid s 744.
7 Ibid s 691(1)(b)(ii).
8 Ibid s 695(1) (amended by the Oversea Companies and Credit and Financial Institutions (Branch Disclosure) Regulations 1992, SI 1992/3179, reg 3(1), Sch 2 paras 1, 9). Service may also be effected in this way if the company no longer has an established place of business in Great Britain: see *Rome v Punjab National Bank (No 2)* [1990] 1 All ER 58, [1989] 1 WLR 1211, CA.
9 Companies Act 1985 s 695(2).
10 *Newby v von Oppen and Colt's Patent Firearms Manufacturing Co* (1872) LR 7 QB 293; *Lhoneux Limon & Co v Hong Kong and Shanghai Banking Corpn* (1886) 33 ChD 446; *Haggin v Comptoir D'Escompte de Paris* (1889) 23 QBD 519, CA.
11 The activity need not be the principal, or even a major, part of the activity of the corporation: *South India Shipping Corpn Ltd v Export-Import Bank of Korea* [1985] 2 All ER 219, [1985] 1 WLR 585, CA.
12 Nine days has been held sufficient in special circumstances, as where a foreign manufacturer of motor cars occupied a stand at an exhibition in London: *Dunlop Pneumatic Tyre Co Ltd v AG für Motor und Motorfahrzeugbau vorm Cudell & Co* [1902] 1 KB 342, CA. But this may be open for reconsideration in the light of *Adams v Cape Industries plc* [1990] Ch 433, [1991] 1 All ER 929, CA ('more than a minimal period of time'), which, however, concerned the establishment of a place of business in a foreign jurisdiction.

13 *Saccharin Corpn Ltd v Chemische Fabrik von Heyden AG* [1911] 2 KB 516 at 523, 525–526, CA; *The Theodohos* [1977] 2 Lloyd's Rep 428; cf *Littauer Glove Corpn v F W Millington (1920) Ltd* (1928) 44 TLR 746; *Okura & Co Ltd v Forsbacka Jernverks A/B* [1914] 1 KB 715, CA.

14 *La Bourgogne* [1899] P 1, CA; affd sub nom *Compagnie Générale Trans-Atlantique v Thomas Law & Co, La Bourgogne* [1899] AC 431, HL; *Saccharin Corpn Ltd v Chemische Fabrik von Heyden AG* [1911] 2 KB 516, CA; *Thames and Mersey Marine Insurance Co v Società di Navigazione a Vapore del Lloyd Austriaco* (1914) 111 LT 97, CA; *The World Harmony* [1967] P 341, [1965] 2 All ER 139.

15 *Walter Nutter & Co v Messageries Maritimes de France* (1885) 54 LJQB 527; *The Princesse Clémentine* [1897] P 18; *Allison v Independent Press Cable Association of Australasia Ltd* (1911) 28 TLR 128, CA; *Okura & Co Ltd v Forsbacka Jernverks AB* [1914] 1 KB 715, CA; *The Lalandia* [1933] P 56; *Donovan v North German Lloyd ss Co* [1933] IR 33; *The Holstein* [1936] 2 All ER 1660; cf *Sfeir & Co v National Insurance Co of New Zealand Ltd* [1964] 1 Lloyd's Rep 330; *Vogel v R & A Kohnstamm Ltd* [1973] QB 133, [1971] 2 All ER 1428. It will not matter that the agent carries on his own business there as well as his principal's: *Adams v Cape Industries plc* [1990] Ch 433, [1991] 1 All ER 929, CA. The distinction between the two may not always be easy to draw, but it is unlikely that a company will be held to carry on business within the jurisdiction unless contracts are made here to which it is bound: see *Adams v Cape Industries plc* supra.

16 *Haggin v Comptoir D'Escompte de Paris* (1889) 23 QBD 519, CA; *Compagnie Générale Trans-Atlantique v Thomas Law & Co, La Bourgogne* [1899] AC 431, HL; *Logan v Bank of Scotland* [1904] 2 KB 495 at 499, CA; *Actiesselskabet Dampskib Hercules v Grand Trunk Pacific Rly Co* [1912] 1 KB 222, CA.

17 See RSC Ord 65 r 3(1). But this does not apply to a foreign corporation alleged to be carrying on business within the jurisdiction, which must be served in accordance with the rules previously set out. As to who is a chairman etc or other similar officer, contrast *Dunlop Pneumatic Tyre Co Ltd v A G Cudell & Co* [1902] 1 KB 342, CA (a motor car salesman at an exhibition is such an officer) with *Mackereth v Glasgow and South Western Rly Co* (1873) LR 8 Exch 149 (a railway booking clerk is not).

(iii) Winding up

991. Jurisdiction of English court. The High Court has jurisdiction to wind up any company registered in England and Wales[1], whether the company is solvent or insolvent[2], and even though it was formed solely to carry on business abroad. It has no jurisdiction to wind up a company registered in Scotland[3], but may wind up one incorporated in Northern Ireland provided that it has a principal place of business in England[4].

It also has jurisdiction to wind up an unregistered company (the definition of which includes a company incorporated outside Great Britain[5]), if there is a sufficient connection between the company and England and there are persons who could benefit from the making of a winding-up order[6], and provided that the company is insolvent; if the company is solvent, it may be wound up by the English court only if the company does not have its seat in a contracting state to the Brussels or Lugano Conventions[7]. The grounds upon which an unregistered company may be wound up are that (1) the company is dissolved[8] or has ceased to carry on business, or is carrying on business only for the purpose of winding up its affairs; or (2) the company is unable to pay its debts; or (3) the court is of the opinion that it is just and equitable that the company be wound up[9].

The court has jurisdiction to wind up an insolvent company which has been dissolved under the law of its place of incorporation; the company is brought back to life for this one purpose[10], and the fact that its assets will already have vested in the Crown as bona vacantia is overridden by the making of the order[11].

The court also has jurisdiction to wind up an unregistered solvent company if it has its seat in England and Wales[12]; but if such a company is incorporated in a Brussels or Lugano contracting state[13], and that state regards the company as having its seat within its jurisdiction, the two courts will each have jurisdiction to wind the company up, and the English court must decline jurisdiction if the courts of the other state are seised of a winding-up application first[14].

1   Insolvency Act 1986 s 117(1). As to the jurisdiction of the county court see s 117(2). The making of the order is a matter of discretion; see also *Re Harrods (Buenos Aires) Ltd (No 2)* [1992] Ch 72, [1991] 4 All ER 348, CA.
2   The Brussels and Lugano Conventions confer exclusive jurisdiction in matters relating to (inter alia) the dissolution of companies on the courts of the country where the body corporate has its seat; the Conventions do not apply to proceedings relating to the winding up of insolvent companies: see arts 1 para 2, 16 para 2 of the Conventions; and paras 626, 628 ante. As to the Brussels Convention see para 618 text and note 1 ante. As to the Lugano Convention see para 618 text and note 2 ante. As to references to numbered articles 'of the Conventions' see para 618 note 5 ante. As to where a corporation has its seat for these purposes see para 636 ante.
3   The express provision in the Insolvency Act 1986 s 117(1) does not extend to Scotland.
4   See *Re A Company (No 007946 of 1993)* [1994] 1 All ER 1007, where the definition of 'unregistered company' in the Insolvency Act 1986 s 220 (as amended) was held to extend to a private company incorporated in Northern Ireland.
5   See ibid s 220 (as amended). See also *Re Matheson Bros Ltd* (1884) 27 ChD 225; *Re Commercial Bank of South Australia* (1886) 33 ChD 174; and *Re A Company (No 007946 of 1993)* [1994] 1 All ER 1007. But the Insolvency Act 1986 s 220 does not allow the winding-up of an international organisation as such: *Re International Tin Council* [1989] Ch 309, [1988] 3 All ER 257, CA.
6   See the Insolvency Act 1986 s 221 (as amended); *Banque des Marchands de Moscou (Koupetschesky) v Kindersley* [1951] Ch 112, [1950] 2 All ER 549, CA; *Re A Company (No 00359 of 1987)* [1988] Ch 210, [1987] 3 All ER 137. It is irrelevant that the company had no place of business in England (*Banque des Marchands de Moscou (Koupetschesky) v Kindersley* supra; *Re Compania Merabello San Nicholas SA* [1973] Ch 75, [1972] 3 All ER 448); and it is no longer a necessity that the company have assets in England (*Re A Company (No 00359 of 1987)* supra; approved obiter in *Re Paramount Airways Ltd (in administration)* [1993] Ch 223, [1992] 3 All ER 1, CA). There must be a sufficient connection with England to justify the order, and there must be persons who could benefit from the order. The latter is a matter of common sense, the former a matter of discretion for the trial judge. See, for further illustration of the necessary connection, *Re A Company (No 003102 of 1991), ex p Nyckeln Finance Co Ltd* [1991] BCLC 539; *Re Real Estate Development Co* [1991] BCLC 210; *Re Wallace Smith & Co Ltd* [1992] BCLC 970; *Re Wallace Smith Group Ltd* [1992] BCLC 989. For the former view that it was necessary for assets to be within the jurisdiction see *Banque des Marchands de Moscou (Koupetschesky) v Kindersley* supra; *Re Compania Merabello San Nicholas SA* supra; and *Re Eloc Electro-Optieck and Communicatie BV* [1982] Ch 43, [1981] 2 All ER 1111.
7   See note 2 supra.
8   Or has been dissolved: *Re Family Endowment Society* (1870) 5 Ch App 118; *Re Russian and English Bank* [1932] 1 Ch 663; *Banque des Marchands de Moscou (Koupetschesky) v Kindersley* [1951] Ch 112, [1950] 2 All ER 549, CA.
9   Insolvency Act 1986 s 221(5).
10 See ibid ss 221(5), 225. For the position prior to this legislation see *Re Russian and English Bank* [1932] 1 Ch 663; *Re Tea Trading Co, K & C Popoff Bros* [1933] Ch 647; *Re Russian Bank for Foreign Trade* [1933] Ch 745; *Russian and English Bank and Florance Montefiore Guedalla v Baring Bros & Co Ltd* [1936] AC 405, [1936] 1 All ER 505, HL; *Banque des Marchands de Moscou (Koupetschesky) v Kindersley* [1951] Ch 112, [1950] 2 All ER 549, CA; *Re Azoff-Don Commercial Bank* [1954] Ch 315, [1954] 1 All ER 947.
11 *Re Azoff-Don Commercial Bank* [1954] Ch 315, [1954] 1 All ER 947; *Re Banque Industrielle de Moscou* [1952] Ch 919, [1952] 2 All ER 532; *Russian and English Bank and Florance Montefiore Guedalla v Baring Bros & Co Ltd* [1936] AC 405, [1936] 1 All ER 505, HL.
12 See note 2 supra; and paras 626, 628, 636 ante.
13 For the meaning of 'Brussels contracting state' and 'Lugano contracting state' see para 618 notes 1–2 ante.
14 Brussels Convention art 23; Lugano Convention art 23: see para 629 ante.

992. Scope and effect of an English winding-up order. The winding up of a company under the Insolvency Act 1986[1] impresses the property of the company with a trust for its application for the benefit of the persons interested in the winding-up[2]. The liquidator must take into his custody all the assets to which the company is or appears to be entitled[3], although the court may provide in its order that he is not to act without a direction from the court except for the purpose of getting in English assets and settling a list of English creditors[4]. But as the winding-up is a liquidation of the company, as distinct from its purely English affairs, assets collected in may be applied in discharge of English and non-English liabilities[5]; if there is a contemporaneous foreign liquidation, efforts must be made to secure equal treatment of all claimants rather than reserve English assets for English creditors[6].

Once a winding-up order has been made, no action may be brought against the company without the leave of the court[7]. Whilst this only applies to proceedings in the United Kingdom, a claimant subject to the personal jurisdiction of the court may be restrained from commencing proceedings against a company in such circumstances, to obtain an inequitable share of the assets overseas[8]. Similarly, attachment, sequestration, distress or execution put into force against the assets of the company after the commencement of the winding-up is void[9]. This does not apply to executions, etc, overseas, but a claimant subject to the personal jurisdiction of the court may be required to surrender the fruits of his foreign execution for the general benefit of all the creditors[10].

The territorial scope of certain other provisions of the Insolvency Act 1986 is less clear. The court has jurisdiction to order the public examination of a director of an English company in compulsory liquidation[11], even though the director is resident outside the jurisdiction[12]; and there is discretion as to the manner of service of the notice on him[13]. The provision can also be invoked against a director of a foreign company wound up in an English court[14]. It is also possible for a liquidator to seek an order that a transaction be set aside on the ground that it was entered into with another person at an undervalue[15]. The court will exercise its discretion in favour of making such an order only if the connections with England are sufficiently strong for this to be appropriate[16].

If a foreign company is being wound up in England and also in its country of incorporation, and there remain surplus assets in the hands of the liquidator after the creditors have been paid, these will be normally be handed over to the foreign liquidator[17].

---

1 An unregistered company may be wound up under the Insolvency Act 1986 Pt IV (ss 73–218) (as amended): s 221(1).

2 *Re Oriental Inland Steam Co, ex p Scinde Rly Co* (1874) 9 Ch App 557; Dicey and Morris *The Conflict of Laws* (12th Edn, 1993) 1130.

3 Insolvency Act 1986 s 144(1).

4 *Re Hibernian Merchants Ltd* [1958] Ch 76, [1957] 3 All ER 97; *Re International Tin Council* [1989] Ch 309, [1988] 3 All ER 257, CA.

5 *Re Azoff-Don Commercial Bank* [1954] Ch 315, [1954] 1 All ER 947; *Re Vocalion (Foreign) Ltd* [1932] 2 Ch 196; *Re Bank of Credit and Commerce International SA* [1992] BCLC 570; *Re Bank of Credit and Commerce International SA (No 2)* [1992] BCLC 579. This presupposes that the foreign claims are valid according to their governing law.

6 See *Re Bank of Credit and Commerce International SA* [1992] BCLC 570 at 577; Dicey and Morris *The Conflict of Laws* (12th Edn, 1993) 1131–1132; and para 994 post.

7 See the Insolvency Act 1986 s 130(2). Between the presentation of the petition and the making of the order the position is governed by s 126(1): see COMPANIES.

8 *Re Vocalion (Foreign) Ltd* [1932] 2 Ch 196; *Re North Carolina Estate Co* (1889) 5 TLR 328; but a secured creditor will not be impeded in the enforcement of his security: *Minna Craig SS Co v Chartered etc Bank* [1897] 1 QB 55; 460, CA.

9 Insolvency Act 1986 s 128(1).

10 *Re Oriental Inland Steam Co, ex p Scinde Rly Co* (1874) 9 Ch App 557; *Re Vocalion (Foreign) Ltd* [1932] 2 Ch 196.

11 Ie under the Insolvency Act 1986 s 132.

12 *Re Seagull Manufacturing Co Ltd (in liquidation)* [1993] Ch 345, [1993] 2 All ER 980, CA; cf *Re Tucker (RC) (a bankrupt), ex p Tucker (KR)* [1990] Ch 148, [1988] 1 All ER 603, CA.
13 Insolvency Rules 1986, SI 1986/1925, r 12.12; *Re Seagull Manufacturing Co Ltd (in liquidation)* [1993] Ch 345, [1993] 2 All ER 980, CA; *Re Busytoday Ltd, Popely v Lewis* [1992] 4 All ER 61, [1992] 1 WLR 683.
14 See the Insolvency Act 1986 ss 221(1), 229(1); *Re Busytoday Ltd, Popely v Lewis* [1992] 4 All ER 61, [1992] 1 WLR 683; and para 991 text and notes 4–5 ante.
15 Insolvency Act 1986 s 238. See also s 239; *Re Paramount Airways Ltd (in administration)* [1993] Ch 223, [1992] 3 All ER 1, CA; *Barclays Bank plc v Homan* [1993] BCLC 680.
16 *Re Paramount Airways Ltd (in administration)* [1993] Ch 223, [1992] 3 All ER 1, CA.
17 *Re Commercial Bank of South Australia* (1886) 33 ChD 174; *Re Vocalion (Foreign) Ltd* [1932] 2 Ch 196.

993. Scope and effect of a foreign winding-up order. Since the law of the place of incorporation determines who is entitled to act on behalf of a company[1], it appears to follow that a liquidator of a company appointed under the law of the place of incorporation will be recognised by the English courts[2]. It is open to the courts to recognise the authority of a liquidator appointed under another law[3].

1 See para 983 ante.
2 *Bank of Ethiopia v National Bank of Egypt and Ligouri* [1937] Ch 513; *Baden Delvaux and Lecuit v Société Générale pour Favoriser le Développement du Commerce et de l'Industrie en France SA* [1983] BCLC 325; *Felixstowe Dock and Rly Co v United States Lines Inc* [1989] QB 360, [1988] 2 All ER 77.
3 See, for a possible analogy, *Re A Company (No 00359 of 1987)* [1988] Ch 210, [1987] 3 All ER 137; *Re A Company (No 003102 of 1991), ex p Nyckeln Finance Co Ltd* [1991] BCLC 539.

994. Multi-national insolvencies: judicial co-operation. It is clear that the insolvency of a company may have important ramifications in other jurisdictions. Although there was a considerable degree of flexibility at common law[1], the Insolvency Act 1986 creates a more formal statutory framework for inter-state co-operation in the winding-up of insolvent companies[2].

Accordingly, courts in the United Kingdom have a statutory obligation to assist each other in matters of winding-up[3]. In relation to countries outside the United Kingdom, the Secretary of State may designate countries as those to which assistance is also to be extended[4]. The courts of such a country may make a request to the English court for assistance, and the English court may give assistance by applying English insolvency law, or the provisions of the insolvency law of the foreign country[5]. But the request must be made by a foreign court: a foreign liquidator may not himself apply directly to the English court[6].

In the particular context of foreign legal procedures for the rescue and re-organisation of companies which are close to insolvency, the English courts have a discretion to act in compliance with and in support of those rescue procedures[7]; but the discretion may be exercised against doing so in a particular case where there is a risk of substantial prejudice to an applicant who has invoked the jurisdiction of the English court[8].

1 Ie both in the immediate context of insolvency, and in other contexts (such as the general application of the Evidence (Proceedings in Other Jurisdictions) Act 1975: see EVIDENCE vol 17 para 326 et seq). It appears that there is no reason in principle why an English liquidator may not seek assistance from the courts (or otherwise under the law) of a foreign country, but his power to do so will be subject to the control of the English court: see *Re Bank of Credit and Commerce International SA* [1992] BCLC 570; *Re Bank of Credit and Commerce International SA (No 3)* [1993] BCLC 106; *Re Maxwell Communications Corpn plc (No 2)* [1994] 1 All ER 737, [1993] 1 WLR 1402; *Barclays Bank v Homan* [1993] BCLC 680.
2 See the Insolvency Act 1986 s 426 (as amended); and the text and notes infra.
3 Ibid s 426(4).
4 See ibid s 426(4), (11); and see the Co-operation of Insolvency Courts (Designation of Relevant Countries and Territories) Order 1986, SI 1986/2123.

5 See the Insolvency Act 1986 s 426(5). See *Re Bank of Credit and Commerce International SA (No 9)* [1994] 3 All ER 764. Insolvency law under English law, in this context, means any provision made by or under the Insolvency Act 1986, and certain provisions of the Company Directors Disqualification Act 1989: Insolvency Act 1986 s 426(10)(a)–(c) (as amended). See also the Companies Act 1989 s 183; and COMPANIES. In relation to the law of a foreign country, insolvency law means so much of that foreign law as corresponds to the English law on insolvency: Insolvency Act 1986 s 426(10)(d). The assistance to be provided, if any, is discretionary: *Re Bank of Credit and Commerce International SA (No 9)* supra.

6 See *Re Dallhold Estates (UK) Pty Ltd* [1992] BCLC 621, [1992] BCC 394; *Re Bank of Credit and Commerce International SA (No 9)* [1994] 3 All ER 764; *Re Wallace Smith & Co Ltd* [1992] BCLC 970.

7 *Felixstowe Dock and Rly Co v United States Lines Inc* [1989] QB 360, [1988] 2 All ER 77: the court declined to lift a Mareva injunction to permit assets to be repatriated to the United States for use in the reconstruction of a company under Chapter 11 of the United States Bankruptcy Code. Cf *Banque Indosuez SA v Ferromet Resources Inc* [1993] BCLC 112; *Barclays Bank v Homan* [1993] BCLC 680. The Insolvency Act 1986 Pt II (ss 8–27) permits the making of an administration order in relation to a company created and registered under the Companies Act 1985 (or its predecessors).

8 *Felixstowe Dock and Rly Co v United States Lines Inc* [1989] QB 360, [1988] 2 All ER 77.

995. Receivership. A receiver appointed under the law of any other part of the United Kingdom[1] in respect of the property of a corporation, and in consequence of the corporation having created a charge which, as created, was a floating charge, may exercise his powers in England and Wales[2]. A receiver appointed otherwise than under the law of another part of the United Kingdom in respect of the property of the corporation, and in consequence of the corporation having created a charge which, as created, was a floating charge, may exercise his powers in England if he is so authorised by the law of the place of incorporation[3].

1 For the meaning of 'Great Britain' see para 604 ante.
2 Administration of Justice Act 1977 s 7; Insolvency Act 1986 s 72.
3 As the law of the place of incorporation determines who may act on behalf of the corporation; see para 983 ante; and see *Cretanor Maritime Co Ltd v Irish Maritime Management Ltd* [1978] 1 WLR 966. For the law in relation to floating charges and the registration thereof see COMPANIES.

10. FOREIGN AND UNITED KINGDOM JUDGMENTS

(1) SCHEMES FOR ENFORCEMENT

996. Enforcement under statute and at common law. The procedural mechanism according to which a foreign judgment is given effect in England will depend upon many different factors, such as the nationality of the court which gave judgment, the subject matter of the action, the date at which the proceedings were commenced or the judgment was handed down, and the nature of the order made by the foreign court. In short, it may be possible to bring an action at common law upon the foreign judgment[1], or to take advantage of the various statutory schemes which provide for the registration of the judgment[2], and in particular for the registration of judgments from the Commonwealth and from the countries of western Europe. These alternatives are not, in general, mutually exclusive. The recognition and enforcement of United Kingdom judgments is governed by statute[3].

1   See paras 997–1018 post.
2   See paras 1023 et seq post.
3   See paras 1060 et seq post.

(2) ENFORCEMENT OF FOREIGN JUDGMENTS BY ACTION AT COMMON LAW

(i) Recognition and Enforcement of Foreign Judgments in Personam

997. Actions on foreign judgments. Subject to certain qualifications[1], a judgment in personam of a foreign court[2] of competent jurisdiction[3] is capable of recognition and enforcement in England[4]. Apart from statute[5], it will not be enforced directly by execution or any other process, but will be regarded as creating a debt between the parties to it[6], the debtor's liability arising on an implied promise to pay the amount of the foreign judgment[7]. The debt so created is a simple contract debt[8] and not a specialty debt, and is subject to the appropriate limitation period[9]. It is immaterial that the debtor dies before judgment is given by the foreign court, and that the judgment is pronounced against his personal representative[10].

1   See para 1007 et seq post.
2   *Robinson v Bland* (1760) 2 Burr 1077 at 1083 (court of honour); *Gage v Bulkeley* (1744) 3 Atk 215 (political court); cf *Waldron v Coombe* (1810) 3 Taunt 162 (vice-consul's certificate as to sale of damaged goods); *Price v Dewhurst* (1837) 8 Sim 279; on appeal (1838) 4 My & Cr 76 (executors' court); *Berliner Industriebank AG v Jost* [1971] 2 QB 463, [1971] 1 All ER 1513, CA (ascertainment of debt in bankruptcy proceedings). As to the recognition and enforcement of foreign arbitration awards see ARBITRATION vol 2 (Reissue) paras 714–717.
3   See paras 999–1006 post.
4   See the text and notes infra. A foreign judgment must be recognised by the English court if it is to be enforced in England. As to the conditions of recognition see paras 999–1011 post. There may be recognition without enforcement of a foreign judgment in personam, eg where it is relied upon as a defence to an action brought in England (as to which see paras 1017–1018 post).
5   See para 1023 et seq post.
6   *Walker v Witter* (1778) 1 Doug KB 1; *Russell v Smyth* (1842) 9 M & W 810; *Williams v Jones* (1845) 13 M & W 628 at 633–634; *Godard v Gray* (1870) LR 6 QB 139 at 148–150; *Schibsby v Westenholz* (1870) LR 6 QB 155 at 159; *Grant v Easton* (1883) 13 QBD 302, CA.
7   *Grant v Easton* (1883) 13 QBD 302 at 303, CA. The plaintiff in England must be the successful party abroad or his assignee: *Barber v Mexican Land and Colonisation Co Ltd* (1899) 16 TLR 127; cf *Carl Zeiss Stiftung v Rayner & Keeler Ltd (No 2)* [1967] 1 AC 853, [1966] 2 All ER 536, HL.
8   *Dupleix v De Roven* (1705) 2 Vern 540; *Grant v Easton* (1883) 13 QBD 302, CA.
9   *Re Flynn (No 2), Flynn v Flynn* [1969] 2 Ch 403, [1969] 2 All ER 557; *Berliner Industriebank AG v Jost* [1971] 2 QB 463, [1971] 2 All ER 1513, CA; cf *Bouchet v Simmons* (1895) 11 TLR 227, CA. The appropriate period is six years: Limitation Act 1980 s 24(1); see also LIMITATION OF ACTIONS.
10   *Re Flynn (No 2), Flynn v Flynn* [1969] 2 Ch 403, [1969] 2 All ER 557.

998. Judgment barring proceedings on the underlying cause of action. No proceedings may be brought by a person[1] in England and Wales[2] upon a cause of action[3] upon which judgment has been given in his favour in proceedings between the same parties or their privies[4] in a court in another part of the United Kingdom[5] or in a court of an overseas country[6] unless the judgment is not enforceable[7] or entitled to recognition in England and Wales[8]. The provision does not provide, in terms, that the underlying cause of action merges in the foreign judgment, and it is not therefore subject to the technical aspects of the law of merger[9]. The barring of the cause of action is to be seen as a matter of procedure, and it may therefore be lifted or set aside by the court in circumstances in which it would be inequitable or unjust to deprive a party of the right to sue on the underlying claim[10].

1   As to the meaning of 'person' see para 624 note 3 ante.
2   As to the meaning of 'England and Wales' see para 604 ante.
3   As to whether the causes of action are the same see *Black v Yates* [1992] QB 526, [1991] 4 All ER 722; *Republic of India v India SS Co Ltd, The Indian Endurance* [1993] AC 410, [1993] 1 All ER 998, HL; *Republic of India v India SS Co Ltd (No 2)* [1994] 2 Lloyd's Rep 331.
4   As to who is privy to the judgment see *Carl Zeiss Stiftung v Rayner & Keeler Ltd (No 2)* [1967] 1 AC 853, [1966] 2 All ER 536, HL; *House of Spring Gardens Ltd v Waite* [1991] 1 QB 241, [1990] 2 All ER 990, CA.
5   For the meaning of 'part of the United Kingdom' see para 619 note 4 ante.
6   'Overseas country' means any country or territory outside the United Kingdom: Civil Jurisdiction and Judgments Act 1982 s 50.
7   Whether by action at common law or by registration under the appropriate statutory scheme.
8   Civil Jurisdiction and Judgments Act 1982 s 34. This alters the rule of the common law, which provided that there was no merger of the cause of action in the judgment, although it was possible that an estoppel might bar further proceedings in respect of the same cause of action: see *Carl Zeiss Stiftung v Rayner & Keeler Ltd (No 2)* [1967] 1 AC 853, [1966] 2 All ER 536, HL. Although the Foreign Judgments (Reciprocal Enforcement) Act 1933 s 6 provides that no action may be brought on a foreign judgment which is registrable under Pt I (ss 1–7) (as amended) of the Act, it is not provided in that Act that no action can be brought on the underlying cause of action. The Civil Jurisdiction and Judgments Act 1982 s 34 now applies to such a judgment. The judgment of an English court of record extinguishes the original cause of action: *King v Hoare* (1844) 13 M & W 494 at 504; and see JUDGMENTS vol 26 para 550.
9   See *Republic of India v India SS Co Ltd, The Indian Endurance* [1993] AC 410, [1993] 1 All ER 998, HL.
10 For example by reason of estoppel or waiver: *Republic of India v India SS Co Ltd, The Indian Endurance* [1993] AC 410, [1993] 1 All ER 998, HL; and see *Republic of India v India SS Co Ltd (No 2)* [1994] 2 Lloyd's Rep 331.

(ii) International Jurisdictional Competence of the Foreign Court

999. In general. It is a precondition to the recognition or enforcement in England of a foreign judgment in personam that the foreign court should have had international jurisdiction according to English rules of the conflict of laws[1].

1   *Buchanan v Rucker* (1808) 9 East 192 at 194; *Sirdar Gurdyal Singh v Rajah of Faridkote* [1894] AC 670 at 683–684, PC; and see paras 1000–1005 post.

1000. Presence of defendant in foreign country. A foreign court has jurisdiction to pronounce a judgment in personam which is capable of recognition and enforcement in England if, at the date of the commencement of the proceedings[1], the defendant was present[2] in the country[3] of the foreign court.

Where the defendant is a corporation, the foreign court will probably be treated as having jurisdiction over the corporation only if either (1) it has established and maintained at its own expense (whether as owner or lessee) a fixed place of business of its own in the foreign country, and for more than a minimal period of time has carried on its own business at or from such premises by its servants or agents; or (2) a representative of the corporation has for more than a minimal period of time been carrying on the corporation's business in the other country at or from some fixed place of business. In either case presence can only be established if it can fairly be said that the corporation's business (whether or not together with the representative's own business) has been transacted at or from the fixed place of business[4]. This is likely to be the case only where the local agent or representative has authority to enter into contracts on behalf of the corporation without submitting them to the corporation for approval[5].

It is not permissible to argue that a corporation is present merely because it is part of a larger economic grouping, another member of which is present within the jurisdiction of the foreign court[6].

1 This probably means the date of service of process on him: *Adams v Cape Industries plc* [1990] Ch 433 at 518, [1991] 1 All ER 929 at 1003, CA.
2 *Adams v Cape Industries plc* [1990] Ch 433, [1991] 1 All ER 929, CA; and see *Carrick v Hancock* (1895) 12 TLR 59. The reasoning was said in *Adams v Cape Industries plc* supra to follow from the fact that the defendant, when present, is liable to observe the summons to court of the local sovereign. It is unclear whether a defendant who was resident but not present at the particular date within the foreign country is similarly liable: *Adams v Cape Industries plc* supra (although if he elects to appear in the proceedings he will submit, and the point will become academic). See also *Emanuel v Symon* [1908] 1 KB 302 at 309, CA; *Rousillon v Rousillon* (1880) 14 ChD 351 at 371; *Schibsby v Westenholz* (1870) LR 6 QB 155 at 161; cf the Administration of Justice Act 1920 s 9(2)(b); the Foreign Judgments (Reciprocal Enforcement) Act 1933 s 4(2)(a)(iv); and see paras 1024, 1034 post.
3 In a country where there are federal and state courts, it is probably sufficient that a defendant is present somewhere within the federation if sued in a federal court, but he must be within the state if sued in a state court: *Adams v Cape Industries plc* [1990] Ch 433 at 550–557, [1991] 1 All ER 929 at 1031–1042, CA.
4 *Adams v Cape Industries plc* [1990] Ch 433 at 530–531, [1991] 1 All ER 929 at 1014–1015, CA. See also *Littauer Glove Corpn v F W Millington (1920) Ltd* (1928) 44 TLR 746; *Sfeir & Co v National Insurance Co of New Zealand Ltd* [1964] 1 Lloyd's Rep 330 (in which registration was sought under the Administration of Justice Act 1920); *Vogel v R and A Kohnstamm Ltd* [1973] QB 133, [1971] 2 All ER 1428. Assistance is to be derived from those cases in which the English court has said that process may issue to foreign companies on the footing that such foreign companies are in England: see eg *Okura & Co Ltd v Forsbacka Jernverks Aktiebolag* [1914] 1 KB 715, CA (Swedish company not in England by virtue of working through, but not by, an English agent); *Adams v Cape Industries plc* supra at 528 and at 1012. As to this see para 990 ante. Cf the Administration of Justice Act 1920 s 9(2)(b); the Foreign Judgments (Reciprocal Enforcement) Act 1933 s 4(2)(a)(iv), (v); and paras 1024, 1034 post.
5 *F & K Jabbour v Custodian of Israeli Absentee Property* [1954] 1 All ER 145, [1954] 1 WLR 139. It is not clear whether compliance with this condition will be required if the corporation is a non-trading corporation: see *Adams v Cape Industries plc* [1990] Ch 433 at 524, [1991] 1 All ER 929 at 1009, CA.
6 See *Adams v Cape Industries plc* [1990] Ch 433 at 532–539, [1991] 1 All ER 929 at 1016–1022, CA.

1001. Actual submission. A foreign court has jurisdiction to pronounce a judgment in personam capable of recognition and enforcement in England if the defendant submitted or agreed to submit to the jurisdiction of the foreign court[1].

There is clearly submission where the defendant, in his character as plaintiff in the foreign action, himself selected the forum where the judgment was given against him, whether this took the form of dismissal of his claim[2] or of judgment against him in respect of a counterclaim, cross-action or costs[3].

The defendant may also be held to have submitted where he voluntarily appeared in the foreign action[4]. But if the purpose of the appearance was any or all of the following, namely: (1) to contest the jurisdiction of the court; (2) to seek dismissal or a stay of proceedings on the ground that the dispute should be submitted to arbitration or to the determination of the courts of another country; or (3) to protect or obtain the release of property seized or threatened with seizure, then the appearance will not amount to a submission[5]. It appears that it is the purpose of the appearance, rather than the form which it actually took, which is the determining factor, and if the defendant was in effect constrained by local procedure to enter a defence on the merits at the same time as the challenge to the jurisdiction, he will be entitled to argue that he did not submit. But if the entry of a defence on the merits was not required at the same time as the challenge to the jurisdiction, it is open to a court to conclude that, by entering it, he did submit to the jurisdiction of the foreign court[6].

1   *Emanuel v Symon* [1908] 1 KB 302 at 309, CA. Cf the Administration of Justice Act 1920 s 9(2)(b); the Foreign Judgments (Reciprocal Enforcement) Act 1933 s 4(2)(a)(i)–(iii) (as amended); and see the cases cited in notes 2–6 infra; and paras 1024, 1034 post.
2   As to which see para 1018 post.
3   *Schibsby v Westenholz* (1870) LR 6 QB 155 at 161, citing *General Steam Navigation Co v Guillou* (1843) 11 M & W 877 at 894; *Emanuel v Symon* [1908] 1 KB 302 at 309, CA; cf *Novelli v Rossi* (1831) 2 B & Ad 757; Foreign Judgments (Reciprocal Enforcement) Act 1933 s 4(2)(a)(ii); and para 1034 post.
4   *De Cosse Brissac v Rathbone* (1861) 6 H & N 301; as explained in *Schibsby v Westenholz* (1870) LR 6 QB 155 at 162; *Rousillon v Rousillon* (1880) 14 ChD 351 at 371; *Sirdar Gurdyal Singh v Rajah of Faridkote* [1894] AC 670 at 683–684, PC; *Emanuel v Symon* [1908] 1 KB 302, CA; *Harris v Taylor* [1915] 2 KB 580, CA; as explained in *Re Dulles' Settlement (No 2), Dulles v Vidler* [1951] Ch 842 at 851, [1951] 2 All ER 69 at 72–73 CA. The same principle will apply where the defendant suffers judgment in default of appearance, but then appeals on the merits of the case: *SA Consortium General Textiles v Sun & Sand Agencies Ltd* [1978] QB 279, [1978] 2 All ER 339, CA. It may be otherwise if the application is confined to an attempt to have the judgment set aside purely on jurisdictional grounds: *SA Consortium General Textiles v Sun & Sand Agencies Ltd* supra.
5   See the Civil Jurisdiction and Judgments Act 1982 s 33(1), reversing the principle in *Henry v Geopresco International* Ltd [1976] QB 726, [1975] 2 All ER 702, CA. Cf Case 150/80 *Elefanten Schuh GmbH v Jacqmain* [1981] ECR 1671, [1982] 3 CMLR 1, ECJ (a case on the Brussels Convention art 18, as to which see para 630 ante); *Marc Rich & Co AG v Società Italiana Impianti PA, The Atlantic Emperor (No 2)* [1992] 1 Lloyd's Rep 624, CA.
6   *Marc Rich & Co AG v Società Italiana Impianti PA, The Atlantic Emperor (No 2)* [1992] 1 Lloyd's Rep 624, CA; cf *Ngcobo v Thor Chemical Holdings Ltd* (1995) Times, 10 November, CA (service of defence as waiver of challenge to jurisdiction of English court).

1002. Agreement to submit. The jurisdiction of the foreign court will be recognised where the defendant has agreed to submit to its jurisdiction, in particular where he is a party to a contract which provides that all disputes between the parties are to be referred to the exclusive, or to the non-exclusive, jurisdiction of that court[1]. The foreign court similarly has jurisdiction where the defendant has agreed to accept service of process in the foreign country[2]. Thus, where the defendant has taken shares in a foreign company whose articles of association or statutes provide that all disputes are to be submitted to the jurisdiction of a foreign court and that every shareholder must elect a domicile at a particular place for service of process, and which declare his domicile to be in a certain place in default of such election, then in the event of such default he is deemed to have agreed to submit to the jurisdiction of the court where that place is situated[3].

The defendant is similarly bound by a statute enacted in the country where the company is incorporated which makes specific provision for service of process on the particular company and for execution of judgment against its members[4], but, as only a clear agreement to submit can give the foreign court jurisdiction, a mere general provision in the foreign law that the shareholder is deemed to have elected a domicile in the foreign country is insufficient to found jurisdiction[5].

1   *Feyerick v Hubbard* (1902) 71 LJKB 509; *Jeannot v Fuerst* (1909) 100 LT 816. As to the English court's power to stay proceedings brought in England in breach of such an agreement (or its duty to dismiss those brought in violation of a clause validated by the Brussels or Lugano Conventions) see paras 633 ante, 1088–1090 post. Whether the agreement was one which encompassed the actual claim brought is a matter of construction for the English court, which will have to interpret the agreement according to its proper law: see para 1088 post.
2   *Copin v Adamson* (1874) LR 9 Exch 345; affd (1875) 1 ExD 17, CA; *Emanuel v Symon* [1908] 1 KB 302 at 308–309, 314, CA; cf *Vallée v Dumergue* (1849) 4 Exch 290.
3   *Copin v Adamson* (1874) LR 9 Exch 345; affd (1875) 1 ExD 17, CA; *Emanuel v Symon* [1908] 1 KB 302 at 308–309, 314, CA; cf *Vallée v Dumergue* (1849) 4 Exch 290.
4   *Bank of Australasia v Harding* (1850) 9 CB 661; *Bank of Australasia v Nias* (1851) 16 QB 717; *Kelsall v Marshall* (1856) 1 CBNS 241.

5   *Meeus v Thellusson* (1853) 8 Exch 638; *Copin v Adamson* (1874) LR 9 Exch 345 (the second replication: on appeal (1875) 1 ExD 17 at 19, CA, the point was reserved); *Emanuel v Symon* [1908] 1 KB 302 at 308–309, CA.

1003. Agreement to submit not to be implied.

1003. Agreement to submit not to be implied. It has been said that an agreement to submit to the jurisdiction of a foreign court will not be implied by the English court[1]. Thus, it has refused to imply such an agreement from an agreement that a contract is to be governed by the law of a foreign country[2], or from the fact that the defendant was a member of a partnership firm which carried on business in the foreign country[3], or from the fact that the cause of action arose in the foreign country at a time when the defendant was present there[4]. Nevertheless, the proper interpretation of these cases may be that the court was unwilling to make the implication in the particular case, as distinct from a broader holding that it was generally impossible to imply an agreement to submit[5].

1   *Vogel v R and A Kohnstamm Ltd* [1973] QB 133 at 144–147, [1971] 2 All ER 1428 at 1438–1440, citing *Sirdar Gurdyal Singh v Rajah of Faridkote* [1894] AC 670 at 686, PC; and *Emanuel v Symon* [1908] 1 KB 302 at 305, 313–314, CA; not following *Blohn v Desser* [1962] 2 QB 116, [1961] 3 All ER 1; and distinguishing *Sfeir & Co v National Insurance Co of New Zealand Ltd* [1964] 1 Lloyd's Rep 330; *New Hampshire Insurance Co v Strabag Bau AG* [1992] 1 Lloyd's Rep 361, CA.
2   *Dunbee Ltd v Gilman & Co (Australia) Pty Ltd* [1968] 2 Lloyd's Rep 394, NSW CA.
3   *Emanuel v Symon* [1908] 1 KB 302, CA; contra *Blohn v Desser* [1962] 2 QB 116, [1961] 3 All ER 1; not followed in *Vogel v R and A Kohnstamm Ltd* [1973] QB 133, [1971] 2 All ER 1428.
4   *Sirdar Gurdyal Singh v Rajah of Faridkote* [1894] AC 670, PC; *Emanuel v Symon* [1908] 1 KB 302, CA.
5   Cf *Adams v Cape Industries plc* [1990] Ch 433 at 465–466, [1991] 1 All ER 929 at 954–955; affd on other grounds at [1990] Ch 503, [1991] 1 All ER 987, CA; but see also *New Hampshire Insurance Co v Strabag Bau AG* [1992] 1 Lloyd's Rep 361, CA.

1004. Lack of international jurisdiction by reason of choice of court or arbitration clause.

1004. Lack of international jurisdiction by reason of choice of court or arbitration clause. Despite the fact that the principles outlined previously may lead to the provisional conclusion that a court did have international jurisdiction[1], a judgment given by a court of an overseas country[2] must not be recognised or enforced in the United Kingdom[3] if the proceedings were brought contrary to an agreement under which the dispute in question was to be settled otherwise than by proceedings in the courts of that country[4]. But if the defendant agreed to the bringing of the proceedings in that court, or if he counterclaimed in the proceedings or otherwise submitted to the jurisdiction of the court, he will lose the protection of this provision[5]. The United Kingdom court is not bound by any decision of the overseas court on the matter[6].

1   See paras 999–1003 ante.
2   For the meaning of 'overseas country' see para 998 note 6 ante.
3   For the meaning of 'United Kingdom' see para 604 ante.
4   Civil Jurisdiction and Judgments Act 1982 s 32(1)(a). Both a choice of court agreement and an arbitration agreement would fall within the ambit of this provision. Section 32(1) does not apply where the agreement was illegal, void or unenforceable or incapable of being performed for reasons not attributable to the fault of the party bringing the proceedings in which the judgment was given: s 32(2).
5   Ibid s 32(1)(b), (c); *Marc Rich & Co AG v Società Italiana Impianti PA (No 2)* [1992] 1 Lloyd's Rep 624, CA.
6   Civil Jurisdiction and Judgments Act 1982 s 32(3), which also applies in relation to decisions of the foreign court on matters mentioned in s 32(2) (see note 4 supra). See also *Tracomin SA v Sudan Oil Seeds Co Ltd* [1983] 1 All ER 404, [1983] 1 WLR 662; affd [1983] 3 All ER 137, [1983] 1 WLR 1026, CA.

1005. Other possible bases of international jurisdiction.

1005. Other possible bases of international jurisdiction. Notwithstanding dicta in several cases to the effect that the courts of a foreign country have jurisdiction over a national of that country[1], it is doubtful whether this is sufficient by itself to give a foreign court jurisdiction[2].

Certain dicta also suggest that the courts of a foreign country have jurisdiction over a person domiciled in that country[3], but it has not yet been clearly held that this is a sufficient basis of jurisdiction[4].

The mere fact that a foreign court has assumed jurisdiction in circumstances in which, mutatis mutandis, the English court would have assumed jurisdiction[5] is insufficient to give the foreign court jurisdiction for the purpose of recognition or enforcement of a foreign judgment in personam[6].

The possession by the defendant of property, whether movable or immovable, in the country of the foreign court is an insufficient basis of jurisdiction[7]. The mere fact that the defendant was present in the foreign country at the time when the cause of action arose is also insufficient to give the foreign court jurisdiction[8].

It has been held that a judgment in personam which is ancillary to a divorce decree pronounced in a country forming part of the Commonwealth may be enforced in England even though, at the date of the commencement of the proceedings, the defendant was neither resident nor present in the country where the decree was pronounced and did not submit to the jurisdiction[9].

1 *Douglas v Forrest* (1828) 4 Bing 686; *General Steam Navigation Co v Guillou* (1843) 11 M & W 877 at 894; *Schibsby v Westenholz* (1870) LR 6 QB 155 at 161; *Rousillon v Rousillon* (1880) 14 ChD 351 at 371; *Emanuel v Symon* [1908] 1 KB 302 at 309, CA; *Gavin Gibson & Co Ltd v Gibson* [1913] 3 KB 379 at 388; *Harris v Taylor* [1915] 2 KB 580 at 591, CA; *Forsyth v Forsyth* [1948] P 125 at 132, [1947] 2 All ER 623 at 624, CA; cf *Société Coopérative Sidmetal v Titan International Ltd* [1966] 1 QB 828 at 843, [1965] 3 All ER 494 at 501.
2 *Blohn v Desser* [1962] 2 QB 116 at 123, [1961] 3 All ER 1 at 4; *Rossano v Manufacturers' Life Insurance Co* [1963] 2 QB 352 at 382–383, [1962] 2 All ER 214 at 232; *Vogel v R and A Kohnstamm Ltd* [1973] QB 133 at 141, [1971] 2 All ER 1428 at 1435; *Rainford v Newell-Roberts* [1962] IR 95.
3 *Turnbull v Walker* (1892) 67 LT 767 at 769; *Emanuel v Symon* [1908] 1 KB 302 at 308, 314, CA; *Jaffir v Williams* (1908) 25 TLR 12 at 13; *Gavin Gibson & Co Ltd v Gibson* [1913] 3 KB 379 at 385.
4 See Dicey and Morris *The Conflict of Laws* (12th Edn, 1993) 486.
5 *Travers v Holley* [1953] P 246, [1953] 2 All ER 794, CA (recognition of foreign divorce decree).
6 *Schibsby v Westenholz* (1870) LR 6 QB 155 at 159; *Turnbull v Walker* (1892) 67 LT 767; *Re Trepca Mines Ltd* [1960] 1 WLR 1273 at 1280–1282, CA (not following on this point *Re Dulles' Settlement (No 2), Dulles v Vidler* [1951] Ch 842 at 851, [1951] 2 All ER 69 at 73, CA); *Société Coopérative Sidmetal v Titan International Ltd* [1966] 1 QB 828, [1965] 3 All ER 494. But the Supreme Court of Canada has held, in effect, that this is a sufficient basis for the recognition of a judgment at common law, and the question may therefore be open to re-examination in an English court in an appropriate case: see *Morguard Investments Ltd v De Savoye* [1990] 3 SCR 1077.
7 *Emanuel v Symon* [1908] 1 KB 302, CA; cf *Schibsby v Westenholz* (1870) LR 6 QB 155 at 163; *Rousillon v Rousillon* (1880) 14 ChD 351 at 371; *Sirdar Gurdyal Singh v Rajah of Faridkote* [1894] AC 670 at 685, PC; disapproving on this point *Becquet v MacCarthy* (1831) 2 B & Ad 951.
8 *Sirdar Gurdyal Singh v Rajah of Faridkote* [1894] AC 670, PC; disapproving on this point *Schibsby v Westenholz* (1870) LR 6 QB 155 at 163; but cf *Morguard Investments Ltd v De Savoye* [1990] SCR 1077, Can SC.
9 *Phillips v Batho* [1913] 3 KB 25, but this is questionable: the reasoning in this case was undermined by the decision in *Jacobs v Jacobs and Ceen* [1950] P 146, [1950] 1 All ER 96, and the decision was not followed in *Redhead v Redhead and Crothers* [1926] NZLR 131 (costs). For criticism of *Phillips v Batho* supra see Dicey and Morris *The Conflict of Laws* (12th edn, 1993) 489.

1006. International jurisdiction, but lack of internal competence. Provided that the foreign court had jurisdiction to pronounce a judgment in personam according to the English conflict of laws rules previously mentioned[1], it is probably immaterial to the recognition or enforcement of the foreign judgment in England that the court lacked competence by the law of its own country[2]. If, however, the evidence is that the foreign judgment is not merely voidable or irregular according to the law under which it was pronounced (and therefore valid until such time as further proceedings are brought to annul it or have it set aside), but rather is a complete nullity, it is probable that it will not be recognised in England[3].

1   See paras 999–1004 ante.
2   *Vanquelin v Bouard* (1863) 15 CBNS 341; approved in *Pemberton v Hughes* [1899] 1 Ch 781 at 791, CA.
3   Cf *SA Consortium General Textiles v Sun & Sand Agencies Ltd* [1978] QB 279, [1978] 2 All ER 339, CA; and the Foreign Judgments (Reciprocal Enforcement) Act 1933 s 2(1) proviso (b): see para 1030 post.

(iii) Conclusiveness of Foreign Judgments in Personam

1007. Foreign judgment generally conclusive. Subject to certain exceptions[1], a judgment in personam of a foreign court of competent jurisdiction[2] which is final and conclusive[3] on the merits[4] is conclusive in England between parties and privies as to any issue upon which it adjudicates[5]. It is not impeachable or examinable on the merits, whether for error of fact[6] or of law[7].

It has, however, been held that a foreign judgment will not be recognised if it shows on its face a perverse and deliberate refusal to apply generally accepted doctrines of private international law[8]. In the interests of international comity English courts will recognise the validity of the decisions of foreign arbitration tribunals whose competence is derived from international law or practice[9].

Although every presumption is to be made in favour of a foreign judgment, and the burden of proof lies on the party who seeks to impeach it[10], such a judgment may be impeached on the ground that it was obtained by fraud[11], or that its recognition or enforcement would be contrary to public policy[12], or that it was obtained in proceedings which were contrary to natural or substantial justice[13].

Where there are two competing foreign judgments, each of which is pronounced by a court of competent jurisdiction, both being final and not open to challenge, the earlier in time will prevail[14].

1   See paras 1008–1010 post.
2   See paras 999–1006 ante.
3   For the meaning of final and conclusive see para 1015 post.
4   A foreign action may be taken as having been heard and decided on the merits if the foreign court held that it had jurisdiction to adjudicate on an issue raised in the cause of action to which the particular set of facts gave rise and its judgment on that cause of action could not be varied, reopened or set aside by that court or by any other court of co-ordinate jurisdiction, notwithstanding that it might be subject to appeal to a court of higher jurisdiction: see *DSV Silo- und Verwaltungsgesellschaft mbH v Sennar (Owners), The Sennar* [1985] 2 All ER 104, [1985] 1 WLR 490, HL.
5   *Godard v Gray* (1870) LR 6 QB 139; *Henderson v Henderson* (1844) 6 QB 288; *Ricardo v Garcias* (1845) 12 Cl & Fin 368, HL; *Bank of Australasia v Harding* (1850) 9 CB 661; *Bank of Australasia v Nias* (1851) 16 QB 717; *Cammell v Sewell* (1858) 3 H & N 617 at 647; *De Cosse Brissac v Rathbone* (1861) 6 H & N 301; *Scott v Pilkington* (1862) 2 B & s 11; *Vanquelin v Bouard* (1863) 15 CBNS 341; *Ellis v M'Henry* (1871) LR 6 CP 228 at 238–239; *Carl Zeiss Stiftung v Rayner & Keeler Ltd (No 2)* [1967] 1 AC 853 at 917–918, 925–927, 966–967, [1966] 2 All ER 536 at 555, 560, 584–585, HL; *Vervaeke (formerly Messina) v Smith* [1983] 1 AC 145, [1982] 2 All ER 144, HL; *Tracomin SA v Sudan Oil Seeds Co Ltd* [1983] 1 All ER 404, [1983] 1 WLR 662; affd [1983] 3 All ER 137, [1983] 1 WLR 1026, CA; *DSV Silo- und Verwaltungsgesellschaft mbH v Sennar (Owners), The Sennar* [1985] 2 All ER 104, [1985] 1 WLR 490, HL; *E D & F Man (Sugar) Ltd v Yani Haryanto (No 2)* [1991] 1 Lloyd's Rep 429, CA; *House of Spring Gardens Ltd v Waite* [1991] 1 QB 241, [1990] 2 All ER 990, CA; *Black v Yates* [1992] QB 526, [1991] 4 All ER 772. The doctrine of issue estoppel is to be applied to foreign judgments with caution: *Carl Zeiss Stiftung v Rayner & Keeler Ltd (No 2)* supra at 918, 925–926, 967, and at 555, 560, 585, HL. Cf the Foreign Judgments (Reciprocal Enforcement) Act 1933 s 8; and see generally ESTOPPEL. Even if there is not the basis for an estoppel, it may be an abuse of the process of the court for the matter to be re-litigated: *House of Spring Gardens Ltd v Waite* supra; *Owens Bank Ltd v Etoile Commerciale SA* [1995] 1 WLR 44, PC.

6 *Henderson v Henderson* (1844) 6 QB 288; *De Cosse Brissac v Rathbone* (1861) 6 H & N 301 (the third plea).
   It seems that the discovery of fresh evidence after the date of the foreign judgment is immaterial: *De
   Cosse Brissac v Rathbone* supra (the fifth plea), but this is questionable: see Dicey and Morris *The Conflict
   of Laws* (12th edn, 1993) 501.
7 *Godard v Gray* (1870) LR 6 QB 139; *Scott v Pilkington* (1862) 2 B & S 11; *De Cosse Brissac v Rathbone*
   (1861) 6 H & N 301 (the third plea). It is immaterial that the judgment was a default judgment: *Russell v
   Smyth* (1842) 9 M & W 810.
8 *Simpson v Fogo* (1863) 1 Hem & M 195 (judgment in rem); as explained in *Carl Zeiss Stiftung v Rayner &
   Keeler Ltd (No 2)* [1967] 1 AC 853 at 922, [1966] 2 All ER 536 at 557–558, HL. *Simpson v Fogo* supra has,
   however, been doubted: see *Aksionairnoye Obschestvo A M Luther v James Sagor & Co* [1921] 3 KB 532 at
   558, CA; *Carl Zeiss Stiftung v Rayner & Keeler Ltd (No 2)* supra at 917–918, 922, 978, and at 555, 557, 592,
   HL; and see Dicey and Morris *The Conflict of Laws* (12th edn) 499–500. Cf *Banco Atlantico SA v British
   Bank of the Middle East* [1990] 2 Lloyd's Rep 504, CA.
9 *Dallal v Bank Mellat* [1986] QB 441, [1986] 1 All ER 239.
10 *Alivon v Furnival* (1834) 1 Cr M & R 277; *Robertson v Struth* (1844) 5 QB 941; *Henderson v Henderson*
   (1844) 6 QB 288; *Bank of Australasia v Nias* (1851) 16 QB 717; *Taylor v Ford* (1873) 29 LT 392.
11 See para 1008 post.
12 See para 1009 post.
13 See para 1010 post.
14 *Showlag v Mansour* [1995] 1 AC 431, [1994] 2 All ER 129, PC.

1008. Judgment obtained by fraud. A foreign judgment which has been obtained
by fraud will not be recognised or enforced in England[1]. The judgment is impeachable
whether the fraud was on the part of the court[2] or on the part of the successful party[3]. It
is immaterial that the fraud has already been investigated by the foreign court, although
in such a case the plea of fraud may involve a retrial in England of the matters
adjudicated upon by the foreign court[4]; and it is immaterial that the unsuccessful party
in the foreign proceedings refrained from raising the plea of fraud in those proceedings
although the facts were known to him at all material times[5]. If, however, the allegation
of fraud has been made in fresh proceedings before the foreign court by way of an
application to have the judgment set aside, the English court may hold the applicant to
be estopped from challenging the judgment of the court which he elected to seise, or
may find it to be an abuse of the process of the court for the allegation of fraud to be
relitigated in England[6].

1 *Ochsenbein v Papelier* (1873) 8 Ch App 695; *Abouloff v Oppenheimer & Co* (1882) 10 QBD 295, CA;
   Manger etc (Syndics under Bankruptcy of Rodrigues et Cie) v Cash (1889) 5 TLR 271, DC; *Vadala v Lawes*
   (1890) 25 QBD 310, CA; *Ellerman Lines Ltd v Read* [1928] 2 KB 144, CA (judgment in rem); *Syal v
   Heyward* [1948] 2 KB 443, [1948] 2 All ER 576, CA (a case on the Foreign Judgments (Reciprocal
   Enforcement) Act 1933); *Jet Holdings Ltd v Patel* [1990] 1 QB 335, [1989] 2 All ER 648, CA; *House of
   Spring Gardens Ltd v Waite* [1991] 1 QB 241, [1990] 2 All ER 990, CA; *Owens Bank Ltd v Bracco* [1992] 2
   AC 443, [1992] 2 All ER 193, HL (a case under the Administration of Justice Act 1920, although the
   authority of this decision in relation to fraud at common law is not beyond argument: *Owens Bank Ltd v
   Etoile Commerciale SA* [1995] 1 WLR 44, PC). See also *Bowles v Orr* (1835) 1 Y & C Ex 464; *Bank of
   Australasia v Nias* (1851) 16 QB 717 at 735; *Cammell v Sewell* (1858) 3 H & N 617 at 646 (judgment in
   rem); *Godard v Gray* (1870) LR 6 QB 139 at 149; *Castrique v Imrie* (1870) LR 4 HL, 414 at 433 (judgment
   in rem). Cf the Administration of Justice Act 1920 s 9(2)(d); Foreign Judgments (Reciprocal Enforcement) Act 1933 s 4(1)(a)(iv); and paras 1024, 1034 post. As to the rejection in Australia of English
   authorities see *Keele v Findley* (1991) 21 NSWLR 444, NSW SC. The plaintiff will not be given leave to
   sign summary judgment under RSC Ord 14 in the face of affidavit evidence that the judgment has been
   obtained by fraud: *Manger etc (Syndics under Bankruptcy of Rodrigues et Cie) v Cash* supra; *Codd v Delap*
   (1905) 92 LT 510, HL. As to judgments obtained by fraud see generally *Duchess of Kingston's Case* (1776)
   1 Leach 146, 2 Smith LC (13th Edn) 644, 717; and see ESTOPPEL vol 16 (Reissue) para 974 et seq.
2 *Price v Dewhurst* (1837) 8 Sim 279 (court interested in subject matter of dispute).
3 See the cases cited in note 1 supra.
4 *Abouloff v Oppenheimer & Co* (1882) 10 QBD 295, CA; *Vadala v Lawes* (1890) 25 QBD 310, CA; *Jet
   Holdings Inc v Patel* [1990] 1 QB 335, [1989] 2 All ER 648, CA; *Owens Bank Ltd v Bracco* [1992] 2 AC 443,
   [1992] 2 All ER 193, HL (a case on the Administration of Justice Act 1920).

5 *Syal v Heyward* [1948] 2 KB 443, [1948] 2 All ER 576, CA (a case on the Foreign Judgments (Reciprocal Enforcement) Act 1933, applying *Vadala v Lawes* (1890) 25 QBD 310, CA); *Owens Bank Ltd v Bracco* [1992] 2 AC 443, [1992] 2 All ER 193, HL.
6 *House of Spring Gardens Ltd v Waite* [1991] 1 QB 241, [1990] 2 All ER 990, CA; *Owens Bank Ltd v Etoile Commerciale SA* [1995] 1 WLR 44, PC.

1009. Judgment contrary to public policy. A foreign judgment will not be recognised or enforced in England if its recognition or, as the case may be, enforcement, would be contrary to public policy[1]. It has been held that if the foreign court has itself considered the public policy issue in the course of the proceedings, or if public policy in the country of the foreign court is held to be substantially the same in relevant respects as that in England, the conclusion of the foreign court may bar the re-opening of the issue in the English court[2].

It would be contrary to public policy to recognise a judgment which is irreconcilable with the prior decision of the English court in an action between the same parties or their privies[3].

1 *Re Macartney, Mafarlane v Macartney* [1921] 1 Ch 522 (posthumous affiliation order not limited to the child's minority; the order was also held to be unenforceable on the ground that it was not final and conclusive; distinguished in *Phrantzes v Argenti* [1960] 2 QB 19 at 31–33, [1960] 1 All ER 778 at 781–782); cf *Mayo-Perrott v Mayo-Perrott* [1958] IR 336; Administration of Justice Act 1920 s 9(2)(f); Foreign Judgments (Reciprocal Enforcement) Act 1933 s 4(1)(a)(v). As to what is final and conclusive see para 1015 post. See also *Dalmia Dairy Industries v National Bank of Pakistan*: (1977) 121 Sol Jo 442, CA (enforcement in England of an award arising out of agreement between nationals of states now at war but friendly to England not precluded). As to public policy generally see para 611 ante.
2 *Israel Discount Bank of New York v Hadjipateras* [1983] 3 All ER 129, [1984] 1 WLR 137, CA. It is not certain, however, that this will always be the case, as the foreign court will have made an assessment of its own public policy in relation to the underlying cause of action, as distinct from English public policy in relation to the enforcement: see Dicey and Morris *The Conflict of Laws* (12th Edn, 1993) 512–513.
3 *Vervaeke (formerly Messina) v Smith* [1983] 1 AC 145, [1982] 2 All ER 144, HL; *E D & F Man (Sugar) Ltd v Haryanto (No 2)* [1991] 1 Lloyd's Rep 429, CA.

1010. Proceedings contrary to natural or substantial justice. A foreign judgment can be impeached if the proceedings in which the judgment was obtained were contrary to natural or substantial justice[1]. Proceedings are not regarded as having been contrary to natural or substantial justice merely because the foreign court admitted evidence which was inadmissible under English law[2], or excluded evidence which was admissible under English law[3], nor because of a mere procedural irregularity (or departure from the standards of corresponding English procedure) on the part of the foreign court[4], provided that the unsuccessful party was given an opportunity to present his case[5]. The objection that the foreign proceedings were contrary to natural or substantial justice may be taken in England even though it could have been or was taken before the foreign court[6].

At first sight, lack of notice of the foreign proceedings is not a ground on which objection can be taken in England to a foreign judgment if the defendant was resident in the foreign country at the date when the proceedings were commenced[7], or if he voluntarily appeared in the proceedings[8], at any rate if the law of the foreign country with regard to notice was complied with, as in those circumstances it may be argued that any notice is sufficient which is in accordance with the law of the foreign country[9]. If the defendant agreed to submit to the jurisdiction of the foreign court[10] he may be said to have agreed to submit to the foreign court's rules of procedure, and to be bound by its judgment even though he may not have had notice of the proceedings[11]. It is nevertheless open to the defendant to argue that, notwithstanding the above, there was a breach of the rules of natural justice in the manner in which the proceedings against him were conducted in the foreign court[12].

1   *Buchanan v Rucker* (1808) 9 East 192; *Price v Dewhurst* (1837) 8 Sim 279; *Henderson v Henderson* (1844) 6 QB 288 at 298; *Sheehy v Professional Life-Assurance Co* (1857) 2 CBNS 211; *Crawley v Isaacs* (1867) 16 LT 529; *Liverpool Marine Credit Co v Hunter* (1867) LR 4 Eq 62 at 68; on appeal (1868) 3 Ch App 479; *Pemberton v Hughes* [1899] 1 Ch 781 at 790, CA (foreign divorce decree); *Robinson v Fenner* [1913] 3 KB 835; *Bergerem v Marsh* (1921) 91 LJKB 80; *Richardson v Army, Navy and General Assurance Association Ltd* (1925) 21 Ll L Rep 345; *Jacobson v Frachon* (1927) 138 LT 386, CA; *Adams v Cape Industries plc* [1990] Ch 433, [1991] 1 All ER 929, CA. It is not clear from that case whether there is a formal distinction between natural and substantial justice.
2   *De Cosse Brissac v Rathbone* (1861) 6 H & N 301 (the sixth plea).
3   *Scarpetta v Lowenfeld* (1911) 27 TLR 509 (exclusion of personal evidence of the parties to the proceedings); *Robinson v Fenner* [1913] 3 KB 835 (exclusion of evidence of fraud by a third party tendered as relieving defendant from a promise to pay).
4   *Pemberton v Hughes* [1899] 1 Ch 781, CA (foreign divorce decree).
5   *Jacobson v Frachon* (1927) 138 LT 386 at 390, 392, CA (judgment founded on biased and erroneous evidence); and see the cases cited in note 1 supra.
6   *Jet Holdings Inc v Patel* [1990] 1 QB 335, [1989] 2 All ER 648, CA. An objection founded upon lack of notice or lack of an opportunity to be heard may be taken de novo in England, but in other cases it is necessary to examine the entirety of the foreign procedure before concluding that it operated in violation of English conceptions of natural or substantial justice: *Adams v Cape Industries plc* [1990] Ch 433, [1991] 1 All ER 929, CA.
7   See para 1000 ante.
8   See para 1001 ante.
9   See Dicey and Morris *The Conflict of Laws* (12th edn, 1993) 515–516.
10 See para 1002 ante.
11 *Vallée v Dumergue* (1849) 4 Exch 290; *Bank of Australasia v Harding* (1850) 9 CB 661; *Bank of Australasia v Nias* (1851) 16 QB 717; *Copin v Adamson* (1875) 1 ExD 17, CA; *Feyerick v Hubbard* (1902) 71 LJKB 509; *Jeannot v Fuerst* (1909) 25 TLR 424. Cf the Administration of Justice Act 1920 s 9(2); the Foreign Judgments (Reciprocal Enforcement) Act 1933 s 4(1)(a)(iii); and paras 1024, 1034 post.
12 See *Adams v Cape Industries plc* [1990] Ch 433 at 570, [1991] 1 All ER 929 at 1052–1053, CA.

1011. Injunction. The English court has jurisdiction to grant an injunction to restrain anyone subject to its jurisdiction from enforcing a judgment in the foreign court[1]. If such a person has committed a breach of contract, or has acted in breach of some fiduciary duty, or has in any way violated the principles of equity and conscience in obtaining the foreign judgment, it may restrain him personally from seeking to enforce that judgment in the foreign court[2]. However, although in theory such an injunction does not seek to interfere with the foreign court, as, in issuing it, the English court is exercising its jurisdiction in personam[3], nevertheless a court will be very slow to restrain a judgment creditor from seeking to enforce his judgment in a court which may be presumed to have its own procedures to prevent improper behaviour of the part of the judgment creditor[4].

1   *Ellerman Lines Ltd v Read* [1928] 2 KB 144, CA (judgment in rem).
2   *Ellerman Lines Ltd v Read* [1928] 2 KB 144 at 155, CA. See also *Tracomin SA v Sudan Oil Seeds Co Ltd* [1983] 3 All ER 137, [1983] 1 WLR 1026, CA; *Tracomin SA v Sudan Oil Seeds Co Ltd (No 2)* [1983] 3 All ER 140, [1983] 1 WLR 1026, CA.
3   *Ellerman Lines Ltd v Read* [1928] 2 KB 144 at 151–152, 155, CA.
4   *E D & F Man (Sugar) Ltd v Haryanto (No 2)* [1991] 1 Lloyd's Rep 429, CA; see also *Zeeland Navigation Co Ltd v Banque Worms* (14 December 1995, unreported).

(iv) Enforcement of Foreign Judgments in Personam

1012. Conditions of enforcement in England. A foreign judgment in personam given by a court of competent jurisdiction[1] is enforceable by action in England[2] provided that (1) it is for a definite sum of money[3], other than a sum payable in respect of taxes, penalties or multiple damages[4]; and (2) it is final and conclusive[5].

1 See paras 999–1006 ante.
2 It may, however, be impeached on the grounds set out in paras 1008–1010 ante.
3 See para 1013 post.
4 See para 1014 post.
5 See para 1015 post.

1013. Judgment must be for definite sum. To be enforceable by action upon the judgment at common law, the foreign judgment must be for a definite sum[1]. An order for the payment of costs is therefore not enforceable until the costs have been taxed[2]. A sum is sufficiently certain for this purpose if it can be ascertained by a simple arithmetical process[3].

The decree in equity of a foreign court can be sued upon in England, provided it orders the payment of an ascertained sum by one party to the other, as, for example, a balance due on a dissolution of partnership[4], or in connection with a trust or an executorship[5].

1 *Sadler v Robins* (1808) 1 Camp 253; *Hall v Odber* (1809) 11 East 118 at 123; *Henley v Soper* (1828) 8 B & C 16; *Henderson v Henderson* (1844) 6 QB 288; *Beatty v Beatty* [1924] 1 KB 807, CA.
2 Cf *Sadler v Robins* (1808) 1 Camp 253. A final order for costs in a foreign divorce suit is enforceable in England: *Russell v Smyth* (1842) 9 M & W 810.
3 *Beatty v Beatty* [1924] 1 KB 807, CA.
4 *Henley v Soper* (1828) 8 B & C 16.
5 *Henderson v Henderson* (1844) 6 QB 288.

1014. Judgment must not be for taxes or penalties, or for multiple damages. As the English court will not entertain an action for the enforcement, either directly or indirectly, of a foreign penal or revenue law[1], it will not enforce a foreign judgment ordering the payment of taxes[2] or penalties[3]. A judgment which enforces both civil and criminal liability is severable, and that part of it which awards a sum of money as damages is enforceable in England[4].

Proceedings may not be brought to enforce a judgment which was given for multiple damages[5], that is, one in which the foreign court arrived at its conclusion by doubling, trebling or otherwise multiplying a sum assessed as compensation for the loss or damage sustained by the judgment creditor[6]. The rule is not limited to denying enforcement of the balance over the compensatory amount: the judgment is unenforceable in respect of the entire sum[7].

1 See paras 612–613 ante.
2 *Government of India, Ministry of Finance (Revenue Division) v Taylor* [1955] AC 491 at 514, [1955] 1 All ER 292 at 301, HL; *Rossano v Manufacturers' Life Insurance Co* [1963] 2 QB 352 at 376–378, [1962] 2 All ER 214 at 228–229; cf *Brokaw v Seatrain UK Ltd* [1971] 2 QB 476, [1971] 2 All ER 98, CA.
3 *Huntingdon v Attrill* [1893] AC 150, PC; *United States of America v Inkley* [1989] QB 255, [1988] 3 All ER 144, CA. But an order for exemplary damages is, as a matter of common law at least, probably enforceable and is not (in this sense) penal: *SA Consortium General Textiles v Sun & Sand Agencies Ltd* [1978] QB 279, [1978] 2 All ER 339, CA.
4 *Raulin v Fischer* [1911] 2 KB 93 (French order for compensation to 'partie civile'); *Black v Yates* [1992] QB 526, [1991] 4 All ER 722.

5 Protection of Trading Interests Act 1980 s 5(1), (2)(a).
6 Ibid s 5(3). A qualified right to certain victims of such a judgment to bring an action to recover the excess element if it has been compelled to pay it is given by s 6.
7 See ibid s 5(1), which prohibits proceedings for 'any sum payable under such a judgment'.

1015. Judgment must be final and conclusive. In order to be enforceable, a judgment must finally and conclusively determine the rights and liabilities of the parties to it so as to be res judicata in the country where it has been pronounced[1].

A judgment is not final and conclusive if the court which has pronounced it has power to rescind or vary it subsequently[2]. Consequently no judgment of a foreign court in proceedings of an executive nature, in which the defendant is precluded from raising all available defences, and which may be rendered null and void by subsequent plenary proceedings in the same court, will be enforced by the English court[3]. The same is true of an interlocutory order for payment of money into court[4] and of an order for payment of costs to one party on his undertaking to repay them in the event of his failing upon appeal[5]. A judgment for maintenance or similar periodical payments may be final and conclusive as regards payments already due, if the foreign court has no power to vary or remit arrears[6]. A judgment may be final and conclusive even before it can be enforced by execution in the foreign country[7].

The judgment must be final in the particular court in which it was pronounced[8], but it does not cease to be final merely because it may be the subject of an appeal to a higher court, or because an appeal is actually pending[9], unless a stay of execution has been granted in the foreign country pending the hearing of the appeal[10]. Where no such stay has been granted, the judgment may be enforced in England[11], but in a proper case the English court may order a stay of the English proceedings pending an appeal[12].

1 *Nouvion v Freeman* (1889) 15 App Cas 1, HL; *Plummer v Woodburne* (1825) 4 B & C 625; *Paul v Roy* (1852) 15 Beav 433; *Patrick v Shedden* (1853) 2 E & B 14; *Frayes v Worms* (1861) 10 CBNS 149; *Re Macartney, Macfarlane v Macartney* [1921] 1 Ch 522 at 531–532; *Blohn v Desser* [1962] 2 QB 116, [1961] 3 All ER 1; *Carl Zeiss Stiftung v Rayner & Keeler Ltd (No 2)* [1967] 1 AC 853 at 918–919, 936, 969–970, [1966] 2 All ER 536 at 555, 566, 587, HL; *Berliner Industriebank AG v Jost* [1971] 2 QB 463 at 470–471, [1971] 2 All ER 1513 at 1518, CA. The onus of proof that the judgment is final and conclusive lies on the party asserting this fact: *Carl Zeiss Stiftung v Rayner & Keeler Ltd (No 2)* supra at 927, 970, and at 560, 587.
   Where a foreign court order is made without a hearing on the merits, requiring production of documents in breach of a bank's duty of confidentiality to its customer, that order is not treated as being analogous to a foreign judgment, and an injunction may be granted restraining compliance with it: *X AG v A Bank* [1983] 2 All ER 464, [1983] 2 Lloyd's Rep 535.
2 *Nouvion v Freeman* (1889) 15 App Cas 1, HL; *Re Macartney, Macfarlane v Macartney* [1921] 1 Ch 522 at 531–532; *Blohn v Desser* [1962] 2 QB 116, [1961] 3 All ER 1; cf *Charm Maritime Inc v Kyriakou and Mathias* [1987] 1 Lloyd's Rep 433, CA. However, a default judgment can be final and conclusive, even though it may be set aside by the court which pronounced it: *Vanquelin v Bouard* (1863) 15 CBNS 341 at 367–368; and see Dicey and Morris *The Conflict of Laws* (12th edn, 1993) 463–464.
3 *Nouvion v Freeman* (1889) 15 App Cas 1, HL; cf *Blohn v Desser* [1962] 2 QB 116, [1961] 3 All ER 1 (Austrian judgment against partner as member of firm not enforceable against partner personally without further Austrian proceedings in which personal defences would be available).
4 *Paul v Roy* (1852) 15 Beav 433.
5 *Patrick v Shedden* (1853) 2 E & B 14.
6 *Beatty v Beatty* [1924] 1 KB 807, CA. If the judgment is capable of variation in respect of arrears as well as future payments, it is unenforceable at common law in England: *Harrop v Harrop* [1920] 3 KB 386; *Re Macartney, Macfarlane v Macartney* [1921] 1 Ch 522; cf *Bailey v Bailey* (1884) 13 QBD 855, CA; *Robins v Robins* [1907] 2 KB 13. As to the reciprocal enforcement of maintenance orders by statute see paras 800–843 ante.
7 *Berliner Industriebank AG v Jost* [1971] 2 QB 463, [1971] 2 All ER 1513, CA (unconditional ascertainment of debt in German bankruptcy proceedings carrying with it the right to levy execution on after-acquired property only after the termination of the bankruptcy proceedings).
8 *Beatty v Beatty* [1924] 1 KB 807 at 816, CA.

9 *Scott v Pilkington* (1862) 2 B & S 11; *Beatty v Beatty* [1924] 1 KB 807 at 815–816, CA; *Colt Industries Inc v Sarlie (No 2)* [1966] 3 All ER 85, [1966] 1 WLR 1287, CA. Contrast the Administration of Justice Act 1920 s 9(2)(e); Foreign Judgments (Reciprocal Enforcement) Act 1933 ss 1(3), 5(1); and paras 1024, 1034 post.

10 *Berliner Industriebank AG v Jost* [1971] 2 QB 463 at 470–471, [1971] 2 All ER 1513 at 1518, CA; approving *Colt Industries Inc v Sarlie (No 2)* [1966] 3 All ER 85 at 88, [1966] 1 WLR 1287 at 1293.

11 *Scott v Pilkington* (1862) 2 B & S 11; *Colt Industries Inc v Sarlie (No 2)* [1966] 3 All ER 85, [1966] 1 WLR 1287, CA.

12 *Scott v Pilkington* (1862) 2 B & S 11; *Nouvion v Freeman* (1889) 15 App Cas 1 at 13, HL; cf *Colt Industries Inc v Sarlie (No 2)* [1966] 3 All ER 85, [1966] 1 WLR 1287, CA.

1016. Proceedings in England. An action on a foreign judgment is usually begun by a writ indorsed with a statement of claim for the amount of the judgment debt and costs, and summary judgment may be given for the plaintiff[1]. In the action for enforcement the plaintiff may claim the amount of the judgment in the foreign currency in which it was rendered, the date for conversion into sterling being the date of payment[2].

A foreign judgment in personam cannot be enforced in England by an action in rem[3].

1 *Grant v Easton* (1888) 13 QBD 302, CA; cf *Codd v Delap* (1905) 92 LT 510, HL. The proceedings are therefore largely formal unless the defendant can set up a credible defence to enforcement. Costs will not normally be awarded if the foreign judgment is capable of registration under the Administration of Justice Act 1920: see s 9(5); and para 1026 post. No action may be brought at all on a judgment which is registrable under the Foreign Judgments (Reciprocal Enforcement) Act 1933: s 6.

2 Ie the date when the court authorises enforcement of the judgment in terms of sterling: *Miliangos v George Frank (Textiles) Ltd* [1976] AC 443, [1975] 3 All ER 801, HL; and see para 888 ante.

3 *The City of Mecca* (1881) 6 PD 106, CA; *The Sylt* [1991] 1 Lloyd's Rep 240.

(v) Foreign Judgments in Personam as Defences

1017. Pleading foreign judgment in defence. The judgment of a foreign court of competent jurisdiction[1] is in general a good defence[2] to an action brought in England by the successful party in respect of the same cause of action whether the judgment was in favour of the defendant[3] or (for a lesser sum than he had claimed) for the plaintiff[4].

1 See paras 999–1006 ante. In order to use the foreign judgment against the party who was plaintiff in the foreign court it is necessary to regard the foreign court as jurisdictionally competent, for the plaintiff in those proceedings must be taken to have submitted to its jurisdiction.

2 It may, however, be impeached on the grounds set out in paras 1008–1010 ante.

3 *Plummer v Woodburne* (1825) 4 B & C 625; *Ricardo v Garcias* (1845) 12 Cl & Fin 368; *Société Générale de Paris v Dreyfus Bros* (1887) 37 ChD 215, CA; *Jacobson v Frachon* (1927) 138 LT 386, CA; *DSV Silo- und Verwaltungsgesellschaft mbH v Sennar (Owners), The Sennar* [1985] 2 All ER 104, [1985] 1 WLR 490, HL.

4 See the Civil Jurisdiction and Judgments Act 1982 s 34. But as to the possibility that proceedings may nevertheless still be brought see *Republic of India v India SS Co Ltd, The Indian Endurance* [1993] AC 410, [1993] 1 All ER 998, HL; *Republic of India v India SS Co Ltd (No 2)* [1994] 2 Lloyd's Rep 331; and see para 998 ante.

1018. Judgment in favour of defendant. In order to be a good defence to an action in England on the original cause of action, a foreign judgment must be final and conclusive[1] between the parties[2]. The judgment must also have been pronounced upon the merits of the case[3], and for this purpose a determination of a foreign court wholly or partly by reference to a foreign statute of limitation is a determination on the merits[4]. The judgment must, however, be in respect of the same cause of action[5], and a plaintiff who has unsuccessfully attempted to obtain rescission of a contract in a foreign court will not be debarred from bringing an action for damages for breach of the same contract in an English court[6]. A foreign judgment in personam is a bar to proceedings in rem in England in respect of the same subject matter[7].

In the exercise of its discretion, the English court will not grant leave to serve the writ out of the jurisdiction in a case where the plaintiff's cause of action depends wholly upon the law of a foreign country, the courts of which have already decided that no cause of action exists[8]. In the converse situation, the English court will restrain a plaintiff from proceeding with an action abroad after the English court has given judgment against him in an action on the same question[9].

  1 *Plummer v Woodburne* (1825) 4 B & C 625; *Frayes v Worms* (1861) 10 CBNS 149; *Carl Zeiss Stiftung v Rayner & Keeler Ltd (No 2)* [1967] 1 AC 853, [1966] 2 All ER 536, HL; and see para 1015 ante.
  2 There must be identity of parties (or their privies): *Carl Zeiss Stiftung v Rayner & Keeler Ltd (No 2)* [1967] 1 AC 853 at 900, 911, 928–929, 936–937, 944–946, [1966] 2 All ER 536 at 550, 561, 566–567, 571–572, HL; *House of Spring Gardens Ltd v Waite* [1991] 1 QB 241, [1990] 2 All ER 990, CA.
  3 *Re Low, Bland v Low* [1894] 1 Ch 147 at 162, CA; *Carl Zeiss Stiftung v Rayner & Keeler Ltd (No 2)* [1967] 1 AC 853 at 927, 969, [1966] 2 All ER 536 at 560, 586–587, HL; *DSV Silo- und Verwaltungsgesellschaft mbH v Sennar (Owners), The Sennar* [1985] 2 All ER 104, [1985] 1 WLR 490, HL; *Vervaeke (formerly Messina) v Smith* [1983] 1 AC 145, [1982] 2 All ER 144, HL; *Tracomin SA v Sudan Oil Seeds Co Ltd* [1983] 1 All ER 404, [1983] 1 WLR 662; affd [1983] 3 All ER 137, [1983] 1 WLR 1026; *E D & F Man (Sugar) Ltd v Yani Haryanto (No 2)* [1991] 1 Lloyd's Rep 429, CA. A judgment by consent or in default may be a judgment on the merits: *Re South American and Mexican Co, ex p Bank of England* [1895] 1 Ch 37, CA.
  4 See the Foreign Limitation Periods Act 1984 s 3; and para 1082 post.
  5 *Callandar v Dittrich* (1842) 4 Man & G 68; cf *Carl Zeiss Stiftung v Rayner & Keeler Ltd (No 2)* [1967] 1 AC 853, [1966] 2 All ER 536, HL.
  6 *Callandar v Dittrich* (1842) 4 Man & G 68.
  7 *The Griefswald* (1859) Sw 430 at 435. The rule that money paid under pressure of legal process cannot be recovered applies to legal process in a foreign country: *Clydesdale Bank Ltd v Schröder & Co* [1913] 2 KB 1.
     It is arguable that a foreign judgment cannot be relied upon as a defence in English proceedings if it was not given until after those proceedings began, but the matter is far from settled: *Bell v Holmes* [1956] 3 All ER 449, [1956] 1 WLR 1359; *Morrison Rose & Partners v Hillman* [1961] 2 All ER 891, [1961] 2 QB 266, CA; *E I du Pont de Nemours v Agnew (No 2)* [1988] 2 Lloyd's Rep 240, CA. But see also *The Delta, The Erminia Foscolo* (1876) 1 PD 393; *Houstoun v Marquis of Sligo* (1885) 29 ChD 448 at 454, CA; cf *Mutrie v Binney* (1887) 35 ChD 614, CA; and see ESTOPPEL vol 16 (Reissue) para 966.
  8 See *Société Générale de Paris v Dreyfus Bros* (1887) 37 ChD 215 at 225, CA.
  9 *Booth v Leycester* (1837) 1 Keen 579 at 580; and see para 1092 post. See also *E D & F Man (Sugar) Ltd v Yani Haryanto (No 2)* [1991] 1 Lloyd's Rep 429, CA; *Zeeland Navigation Co Ltd v Banque Worms* (14 December 1995, unreported).

(vi) Foreign Judgments in Rem

1019. In general. A judgment in rem may be defined as the judgment of a court of competent jurisdiction when it determines the status of a person or thing, or the disposition of a thing, as distinct from the particular interest that a party to the litigation has in it[1]. Thus the judgment in rem vests in a person the possession of or property in a thing or decrees the sale of a thing in satisfaction of a claim against the thing itself, or is a judgment as to the status of a person[2].

A judgment in rem pronounced by a court of competent jurisdiction is conclusive and binding in England, not only between parties and privies, as in the case of a judgment in personam[3], but against all the world[4].

1 *Castrique v Imrie* (1870) LR 4 HL 414 at 427 et seq; *Lazarus-Barlow v Regent Estates Co Ltd* [1949] 2 KB 465 at 475, [1949] 2 All ER 118 at 122, CA.
2 *Fracis Times & Co v Carr* (1900) 82 LT 698 at 701–702, CA; revsd on other grounds sub nom *Carr v Fracis Times & Co* [1902] AC 176, HL. A further type of judgment in rem is a judgment ordering movables to be sold by way of administration. As to administration in bankruptcy see BANKRUPTCY AND INSOLVENCY; as to administration on death see EXECUTORS.
3 See para 1018 text and note 2 ante.
4 *Castrique v Imrie* (1870) LR 4 HL 414; *Castrique v Behrens* (1861) 3 E & E 709; *Messina v Petrcocchino* (1872) LR 4 PC 144; *Meyer v Ralli* (1876) 1 CPD 358; *The City of Mecca* (1879) 5 PD 28; revsd on other grounds (1881) 6 PD 106, CA; *Re Trufort, Trafford v Blanc* (1887) 36 ChD 600; *Ballantyne v Mackinnon* [1896] 2 QB 455 at 462, CA; *Minna Craig SS Co v Chartered Mercantile Bank of India, London and China* [1897] 1 QB 460, CA; *Bater v Bater* [1906] P 209, CA; *Salvesen (or von Lorang) v Administrator of Austrian Property* [1927] AC 641, HL.

1020. Judgments in rem relating to movables. A foreign judgment in rem relating to movables will be recognised and enforced in England if the movables were situated in the foreign country at the time of the proceedings[1]. The judgment need not be an actual adjudication as to the status of the thing itself[2]. A decision as to right or title will of course be conclusive, but so also will any disposition by the court by way of sale, transfer or otherwise[3], as, for example, where an Admiralty court orders the sale of a ship to satisfy a maritime lien[4], or a prize court orders the sale of goods because they have been adjudged lawful prize[5]. In such a case the foreign court can give a bona fide purchaser a title which cannot be impeached in England, even though by English law, but for the foreign judgment, some other person would have been regarded as owner of the thing sold or as having preferential rights over it[6].

It seems that a foreign judgment in rem relating to movables can be enforced in England by an action in rem[7].

1 *Castrique v Imrie* (1870) LR 4 HL 414; *Meyer v Ralli* (1876) 1 CPD 358; *The City of Mecca* (1879) 5 PD 28; revsd on other grounds (1881) 6 PD 106, CA; *Re Trufort, Trafford v Blanc* (1887) 36 ChD 600; *Minna Craig SS Co v Chartered Mercantile Bank of India, London and China* [1897] 1 QB 460, CA. Cf the Foreign Judgments (Reciprocal Enforcement) Act 1933 s 4(2)(b); and para 1034 post.
2 *Castrique v Imrie* (1870) LR 4 HL 414 at 428.
3 *Castrique v Imrie* (1870) LR 4 HL 414 at 428.
4 *Minna Craig SS Co v Chartered Mercantile Bank of India, London and China* [1897] 1 QB 460, CA; and see SHIPPING vol 43 para 1131 et seq.
5 *Stringer v English and Scottish Marine Insurance Co* (1870) LR 5 QB 599, Ex Ch; *Castrique v Imrie* (1870) LR 4 HL 414 at 428; and see PRIZE.
6 See *Cammell v Sewell* (1860) 5 H & N 728; *Alcock v Smith* [1892] 1 Ch 238, CA.
7 *The City of Mecca* (1879) 5 PD 28; revsd on other grounds (1881) 6 PD 106, CA; *The Despina GK* [1983] QB 214, [1983] 1 All ER 1.

1021. Judgments in rem relating to immovables. A foreign judgment in rem relating to immovables will be recognised in England if the immovables are situated in the foreign country[1].

1 See paras 924–927 ante.

1022. Judgments relating to personal status. The rules relating to the recognition of foreign judgments affecting personal status are set out elsewhere in this title[1].

1 As to divorce, nullity and legal separation see paras 744–750 ante. As to the presumption of death and dissolution of marriage see para 753 ante.

(3) ENFORCEMENT OF FOREIGN JUDGMENTS BY REGISTRATION PURSUANT TO STATUTE

(i) Enforcement of Foreign Judgments by Registration under the Administration of Justice Act 1920

1023. Application of the Administration of Justice Act 1920. Under statutory provisions currently in force[1], where a judgment[2] has been obtained in a superior court in any part of Her Majesty's dominions outside the United Kingdom[3] to which the provisions extend[4], the judgment creditor[5] may apply to the High Court in England, at any time within 12 months after the date of the judgment, or such longer period as may be allowed by the court, to have the judgment registered in the court[6]. The court may order the judgment to be registered if it thinks, in all the circumstances, that it is just and convenient that the judgment should be enforced in the United Kingdom[7].

1 These provisions are, however, liable to be superseded. Where an Order in Council makes the Foreign Judgments (Reciprocal Enforcement) Act 1933 Pt I (ss 1–7) (as to which see paras 1028–1039 post) operative in relation to any part of Her Majesty's dominions, the Administration of Justice Act 1920 Pt II (ss 9–14) (as amended) ceases to have effect in relation to that part of such dominions: Foreign Judgments (Reciprocal Enforcement) Act 1933 s 7(2). As a result, the Administration of Justice Act 1920 Pt II can now only apply to those territories to which it applied at the date (10 November 1933) of the Reciprocal Enforcement of Judgments (General Application to His Majesty's Dominions, etc) Order 1933, SR & O 1933/1073: see the Foreign Judgments (Reciprocal Enforcement) Act 1933 s 7(1); and para 1028 post. See also note 4 infra. As to Her Majesty's dominions see COMMONWEALTH vol 6 (Reissue) para 803.

2 'Judgment' means any judgment or order given or made by a court in any civil proceedings whereby any sum of money is made payable, and includes an award in proceedings on an arbitration if, in pursuance of the law in force in the place where it was made, the award has become enforceable in the same manner as a judgment: Administration of Justice Act 1920 s 12(1). It does not include, for instance, an order setting aside an assignment of property: *Platt v Platt* 1958 SC 95. As to the enforcement of foreign arbitral awards see ARBITRATION vol 2 (Reissue) paras 714–717. As to the enforcement of foreign maintenance orders see paras 800–843 ante.

3 A number of the territories to which the Administration of Justice Act 1920 was extended have ceased to be parts of Her Majesty's dominions on, for example, becoming republics within the Commonwealth. It is customary in such cases for United Kingdom legislation to provide for existing law to be applied as regards the new republic, and this ensures that existing orders remain in force.

4 The Administration of Justice Act 1920 Pt II (as amended) might be extended by Order in Council to any part of Her Majesty's dominions outside the United Kingdom, including protectorates and mandated territories: see ss 13, 14. Orders were made extending the Act to various territories. The various orders were consolidated, pursuant to the Administration of Justice Act 1920 s 14(3) (added by the Civil Jurisdiction and Judgments Act 1982 s 35(3)), under the Reciprocal Enforcement of Judgments (Administration of Justice Act 1920, Part II) (Consolidation) Order 1984, SI 1984/129 (amended by the Judgments (Administration of Justice Act 1920, Part II) (Amendment) Order 1985, SI 1985/1994 and by the Reciprocal Enforcement of Foreign Judgments (Australia) Order 1994, SI 1994/1901). Accordingly the Administration of Justice Act 1920 Pt II now extends to the following territories: Anguilla, Antigua and Barbuda, Bahamas, Barbados, Belize, Bermuda, Botswana, British Indian Ocean Territory, British Virgin Islands, Cayman Islands, Christmas Island, Cocos (Keeling) Islands, Cyprus, Dominica, Falkland Islands, Fiji, Gambia, Ghana, Gibraltar, Grenada, Guyana, Hong Kong, Jamaica, Kenya, Kiribati, Lesotho, Malawi, Malaysia, Malta, Mauritius, Montserrat, Newfoundland, New Zealand, Nigeria, Norfolk Island, Papua New Guinea, St Christopher and Nevis, St Helena, St Lucia, St Vincent and the Grenadines, Seychelles, Sierra Leone, Singapore, Solomon Islands, Sovereign Base Areas of Akrotiri and Dhekalia in Cyprus, Sri Lanka, Swaziland, Tanzania, Trinidad and Tobago, Turks and Caicos Islands, Tuvalu, Uganda, Zambia, and Zimbabwe.

5 'Judgment creditor' means the person by whom the judgment was obtained, and includes the successors and assigns of that person: Administration of Justice Act 1920 s 12(1).
6 Ibid s 9(1). Application is made ex parte or by originating summons to a judge or master, and must be supported by an affidavit: see RSC Ord 71 rr 1–3.
7 Administration of Justice Act 1920 s 9(1).

1024. Restrictions on registration. No judgment[1] may be ordered to be registered[2] if (1) the court by which the judgment was given acted without jurisdiction[3]; or (2) the judgment debtor[4], being a person who was neither carrying on business nor ordinarily resident[5] within the jurisdiction of the court by which the judgment was given, did not voluntarily appear or otherwise submit or agree to submit to the jurisdiction of that court[6]; or (3) the judgment debtor, being the defendant in the proceedings, was not duly served with the process of the court by which the judgment was given and did not appear, notwithstanding that he was ordinarily resident or was carrying on business within the jurisdiction of that court, or agreed to submit to its jurisdiction[7]; or (4) the judgment was obtained by fraud[8]; or (5) the judgment debtor satisfies the court to which the application is made, either that an appeal is pending or that he is entitled and intends to appeal against the judgment[9]; or (6) the judgment was in respect of a cause of action which for reasons of public policy[10], or for some other similar reason, could not have been entertained by the registering court to which application is made[11]. Furthermore, registration is within the discretion of the English court and is only allowed if the court thinks it just and convenient that the judgment should be enforced in the United Kingdom[12].

The judgment debtor may apply to set aside the registration[13], notice of which must be served upon him[14].

A judgment to which the Protection of Trading Interests Act 1980 applies[15] may not be registered under the Administration of Justice Act 1920[16].

1 For the meaning of 'judgment' see para 1023 note 2 ante.
2 Ie under the Administration of Justice Act 1920 s 9: see para 1023 ante.
3 Ibid s 9(2)(a). Cf para 999 et seq ante.
4 'Judgment debtor' means the person against whom the judgment was given, and includes the person against whom it is enforceable in the place where it was given: ibid s 12(1).
5 For the meaning of 'ordinarily resident' see para 704 ante.
6 Administration of Justice Act 1920 s 9(2)(b); *Sfeir & Co v National Insurance Co of New Zealand Ltd* [1964] 1 Lloyd's Rep 330.
7 Administration of Justice Act 1920 s 9(2)(c).
8 Ibid s 9(2)(d). The defence of fraud is in terms identical with that applicable to an action upon a foreign judgment at common law: *Owens Bank Ltd v Bracco* [1992] 2 AC 443, [1992] 2 All ER 193, HL; see para 1008 ante.
9 Administration of Justice Act 1920 s 9(2)(e).
10 Cf para 1009 ante.
11 Administration of Justice Act 1920 s 9(2)(f).
12 Ibid s 9(1); and see para 1023 text and note 7 ante. As it is not expressly provided in the Act that a judgment for a foreign penalty or tax is excluded from registration, the exclusion of such a judgment could be accommodated within this provision.
13 See RSC Ord 71 r 9.
14 See RSC Ord 71 r 7(1), (2). As to the contents of the notice see Ord 71 r 7(3).
15 Ie to which the Protection of Trading Interests Act 1980 s 5 applies. That provision applies to any judgment given by a court of an overseas country which is (1) a judgment for multiple damages (see para 1014 ante); (2) a judgment based on a provision or rule of law specified by order; or (3) a judgment on a claim for contribution in respect of damages awarded by a judgment falling within head (1) or (2) supra: s 5(2)(a)–(c). At the date at which this volume states the law, no order had been made for the purposes of head (2) supra. As to the power to make such orders see also s 5(3), (4).
16 Ibid s 5(1).

1025. Effect of registration. From the date of its registration a judgment[1] registered under the foregoing provisions[2] has the same force and effect, and proceedings may be taken on it, as if it had been a judgment originally obtained or entered on the date of registration in the registering court[3]. That court has the same control and jurisdiction over the judgment as it has over similar judgments given by itself, but only in so far as relates to execution[4]. The reasonable costs of, and incidental to, registration[5] are recoverable as if they were sums payable under the judgment[6].

1 For the meaning of 'judgment' see para 1023 note 2 ante.
2 See paras 1023–1024 ante.
3 Administration of Justice Act 1920 s 9(3)(a).
4 Ibid s 9(3)(b).
5 These include the costs of obtaining a certified copy of the judgment from the court by which the judgment was given, and of the application for registration: ibid s 9(3)(c).
6 Ibid s 9(3)(c). As to execution see RSC Ord 71 r 10. As to the power to make rules of court see the Administration of Justice Act 1920 ss 9(4), 11.

1026. Action on judgment. If an action is brought in any court in the United Kingdom[1] on any judgment[2] which might be ordered to be registered under the foregoing provisions[3], the plaintiff will not be entitled to the costs of the action unless an application for registration has been refused or unless the court otherwise orders[4].

1 For the meaning of 'United Kingdom' see para 604 ante.
2 For the meaning of 'judgment' see para 1023 note 2 ante.
3 See paras 1023–1024 ante.
4 Administration of Justice Act 1920 s 9(5). No action may be brought on the underlying cause of action in any event: see the Civil Jurisdiction and Judgments Act 1982 s 34; and para 998 ante.

1027. Certificates of judgments. Where a judgment[1] has been obtained in the High Court in England against any person, then on an application made by the judgment creditor[2] and on proof that the judgment debtor[3] is resident in some part of Her Majesty's dominions outside the United Kingdom[4] to which the foregoing provisions[5] apply, the court must issue to the judgment creditor a certified copy of the judgment[6].

1 For the meaning of 'judgment' see para 1023 note 2 ante.
2 For the meaning of 'judgment creditor' see para 1023 note 5 ante.
3 For the meaning of 'judgment debtor' see para 1024 note 4 ante.
4 For the meaning of 'United Kingdom' see para 604 ante.
5 See paras 1023–1024 ante.
6 Administration of Justice Act 1920 s 10 (substituted by the Civil Jurisdiction and Judgments Act 1982 s 35(2)). Application for the certificate is made ex parte to a master on affidavit: see RSC Ord 71 r 13(1), (2). As to the certificate see Ord 71 r 13(4).

(ii) Enforcement of Foreign Judgments by Registration under the Foreign Judgments (Reciprocal Enforcement) Act 1933

1028. Application of the Foreign Judgments (Reciprocal Enforcement) Act 1933. The principle whereby foreign judgments are registered on a reciprocal basis is applied in the Foreign Judgments (Reciprocal Enforcement) Act 1933[1], under which, where a foreign country will give substantial reciprocity of treatment as respects the enforcement of judgments[2] given in courts of the United Kingdom[3], an Order in Council may direct that (1) Part I of the Act[4] is to extend to that country[5]; (2) such courts of that country as may be specified are to be recognised for the purposes of the Act[6]; and (3) judgments of any such recognised court, or of any specified class, are to be judgments to which the Act applies[7]. Any such Order in Council may be varied or revoked[8].

The Act also provides for its own extension, by Order in Council, to Her Majesty's dominions[9] outside the United Kingdom, and to judgments obtained in the courts of those jurisdictions[10]. This power has been exercised[11], with the effect that no new Orders may be made under Part II of the Administration of Justice Act 1920[12]. A further Order in Council is required to bring into effect the enforcement machinery of the 1933 Act in relation to any particular part of Her Majesty's dominions[13]. When such a further Order is made, the corresponding Order made pursuant to the Act of 1920 ceases to have effect[14].

Part I of the Act of 1933 has also been extended, with modifications, to certain other foreign judgments by the Carriage of Goods by Road Act 1965[15], the Nuclear Installations Act 1965[16], the Carriage of Passengers by Road Act 1974[17], the International Transport Conventions Act 1983[18], and the Merchant Shipping Act 1995[19], but only in relation to proceedings under those Acts.

Rules of court may make provision with respect to various matters connected with the registration of judgments under the Foreign Judgments (Reciprocal Enforcement) Act 1933[20].

1 The Foreign Judgments (Reciprocal Enforcement) Act 1933 was variously amended by the Civil Jurisdiction and Judgments Act 1982 s 35(1), Sch 10 in order to extend its application from superior courts to recognised courts, and to include within its scope judgments providing for interim payments and certain arbitration awards.
2 For the meaning of 'judgment' see para 1029 post.
3 Reciprocity must be found to exist between the courts of that country or any particular class of courts and the similar courts of the United Kingdom: Foreign Judgments (Reciprocal Enforcement) Act 1933 s 1(1) (substituted by the Civil Jurisdiction and Judgments Act 1982 Sch 10 para 1(1), (2)). In the Foreign Judgments (Reciprocal Enforcement) Act 1933 (except s 10 (as substituted) (see para 1037 post)), 'court' includes a tribunal: s 11(1) (definition added by the Civil Jurisdiction and Judgments Act 1982 Sch 10 para 5(1), (2)). As to the continued entitlement of courts identified by Orders in Council made prior to this amendment see the Foreign Judgments (Reciprocal Enforcement) Act 1933 s 1(5) (added by the Civil Jurisdiction and Judgments Act 1982 Sch 10 para 1(3)). For the meaning of 'United Kingdom' see para 604 ante.
4 Ie the Foreign Judgments (Reciprocal Enforcement) Act 1933 Pt I (ss 1–7) (as amended).
5 Ibid s 1(1)(a) (as substituted: see note 3 supra). The following Orders in Council have been made under this provision: the Reciprocal Enforcement of Foreign Judgments (France) Order in Council 1936, SR & O 1936/609; the Reciprocal Enforcement of Foreign Judgments (Belgium) Order in Council 1936, SR & O 1936/1169; the Reciprocal Enforcement of Foreign Judgments (Pakistan) Order 1958, SI 1958/141 (and see also the Pakistan Act 1990 Sch para 8); the Reciprocal Enforcement of Foreign Judgments (India) Order 1958, SI 1958/425; Reciprocal Enforcement of Foreign Judgments (Germany) Order 1961, SI 1961/1199; Reciprocal Enforcement of Foreign Judgments (Norway) Order 1962, SI 1962/636; Reciprocal Enforcement of Foreign Judgments (Austria) Order 1962, SI 1962/1339; Reciprocal Enforcement of Foreign Judgments (The Netherlands) Order 1969, SI 1969/1063 (amended by SI 1977/2149); Reciprocal Enforcement of Foreign Judgments (Israel) Order 1971, SI 1971/1039; Reciprocal Enforcement of Foreign Judgments (Guernsey) Order 1973, SI 1973/610; Reciprocal Enforcement of Foreign Judgments (Isle of Man) Order 1973, SI 1973/611; Reciprocal Enforcement of Foreign Judgments (Jersey) Order 1973, SI 1973/612; Reciprocal Enforcement of Foreign Judgments (Italy) Order 1973, SI 1973/1894; Reciprocal Enforcement of Foreign Judgments (Tonga) Order 1980, SI 1980/1523; Reciprocal Enforcement of Foreign Judgments (Suriname) Order 1981, SI 1981/735; Reciprocal Enforcement of Foreign Judgments (Canada) Order 1987, SI 1987/468 (amended by SI 1987/2211; SI 1988/1304; SI 1988/1853; SI 1989/987; SI 1991/1724; SI 1992/1731;

and SI 1995/2708); Reciprocal Enforcement of Foreign Judgments (Australia) Order 1994, SI 1994/1901.

The Orders in Council in respect of Belgium, Germany, France, Italy and The Netherlands are for most purposes superseded by the provisions of the Brussels Convention, and those in respect of Austria and Norway by the provisions of the Lugano Convention: Brussels Convention art 55; Lugano Convention art 55; and see para 618 text and note 10 ante. As to the relevant provisions of those Conventions see para 1040 et seq post.

6 Foreign Judgments (Reciprocal Enforcement) Act 1933 s 1(1)(b) (as substituted: see note 3 supra).

7 Ibid s 1(1)(c) (as substituted: see note 3 supra).

8 Ibid s 1(4).

9 The reference to Her Majesty's dominions includes a reference to British protectorates: see ibid s 7(3). As to Her Majesty's dominions and British protectorates see COMMONWEALTH vol 6 (Reissue) paras 803, 806.

10 Ibid s 7(1).

11 See the Reciprocal Enforcement of Judgments (General Application to His Majesty's Dominions etc) Order 1933, SR & O 1933/1073.

12 Foreign Judgments (Reciprocal Enforcement) Act 1933 s 7(1). As to the Administration of Justice Act 1920 Pt II (ss 9–14) see paras 1023–1027 ante.

13 *Yukon Consolidated Gold Corpn Ltd v Clark* [1938] 2 KB 241, [1938] 1 All ER 366, CA; and see note 5 supra.

14 Foreign Judgments (Reciprocal Enforcement) Act 1933 s 7(2). Part I will apply to an existing judgment given by a court of a country to which, by such an Order, that Part is newly extended provided that the judgment is registered within 12 months of the date when it was given or within such longer period as the High Court may allow: see the Administration of Justice Act 1956 s 51(b).

   A judgment registered or dealt with under the Administration of Justice Act 1920 Pt II or attendant provisions before an Order implementing the Foreign Judgments (Reciprocal Enforcement) Act 1933 comes into operation will, once that Order comes into operation, be treated as falling within the scope of the latter Act and its attendant provisions: Administration of Justice Act 1956 s 51(c).

15 Carriage of Goods by Road Act 1965 s 4 (judgments of foreign courts under the Convention to which the Act gives effect): the Foreign Judgments (Reciprocal Enforcement) Act 1933 s 4(2), (3) does not apply.

16 Nuclear Installations Act 1965 s 17(4) (certain judgments certified as determined under an international agreement): the Foreign Judgments (Reciprocal Enforcement) Act 1933 s 4(1)(a)(ii), (2), (3) does not apply.

17 Carriage of Passengers by Road Act 1974 s 5(1), (2) (certain judgments to enforce claims arising out of international carriage of passengers by road): the Foreign Judgments (Reciprocal Enforcement) Act 1933 s 4(2), (3) does not apply.

18 International Transport Conventions Act 1983 s 6 (certain judgments to enforce a claim for the death of or personal injury to a passenger by rail in international carriage): the Foreign Judgments (Reciprocal Enforcement) Act 1933 s 4(2), (3) does not apply.

19 Merchant Shipping Act 1995 ss 166(4), 177(4), (5) (certain judgments relating to liability in respect of oil pollution): in each case the Foreign Judgments (Reciprocal Enforcement) Act 1933 s 4(2), (3) does not apply.

20 See ibid s 3(1) (amended by the Supreme Court Act 1981 ss 152(1), 153(4), Sch 5). Such rules have effect subject to the provisions of the Orders mentioned in note 5 supra, for which there is otherwise no power to make rules of court: Foreign Judgments (Reciprocal Enforcement) Act 1933 s 3(2).

1029. Judgments to which the statutory provisions apply. The Foreign Judgments (Reciprocal Enforcement) Act 1933 applies to judgments, defined as judgments or orders made by a recognised[1] court[2] in civil proceedings, or in criminal proceedings for the payment of a sum of money in respect of compensation or damages to an injured party[3]. The judgment must be for a sum of money, not being a tax, fine or penalty[4], or for multiple damages[5]. It must be final and conclusive[6] as between the judgment debtor[7] and the judgment creditor[8], or require the making of an interim payment[9]. It must have been pronounced after the commencement of the Order in Council extending the Act to the foreign country concerned[10], and must have been pronounced, or the final appeal disposed of, within six years before the application for registration[11].

The Act does not, however, apply to a judgment of a recognised court which is: (1) a judgment given on appeal from a court which is not a recognised court; or (2) a judgment or other instrument which is regarded for the purposes of enforcement as a judgment of that court but was given or made in another country; or (3) a judgment given by that court in proceedings founded on a judgment of a court in another country and having as their objective the enforcement of that judgment[12].

1 As to the recognition of courts see para 1028 text and note 6 ante.
2 For the meaning of 'court' see para 1028 note 3 ante.
3 Foreign Judgments (Reciprocal Enforcement) Act 1933 s 11(1).
4 Ibid s 1(2)(b) (s 1(2) substituted by the Civil Jurisdiction and Judgments Act 1982 s 35(1), Sch 10 para 1(2)).
5 Protection of Trading Interests Act 1980 s 5: see paras 1014 ante, 1030 note 15 post.
6 For the meaning of 'final and conclusive' see para 1015 ante. For this purpose a judgment may be held to be final and conclusive even if an appeal is pending or may be initiated in courts of the country of the original court: Foreign Judgments (Reciprocal Enforcement) Act 1933 s 1(3). 'Country of the original court' means the country in which the original court is situated; 'original court' means the court by which the judgment was given; 'appeal' includes any proceeding for discharging or setting aside a judgment, for a new trial or for a stay of execution: s 11(1).
7 'Judgment debtor' means the person against whom the judgment was given, and includes any person against whom it is enforceable under the law of the original court: Foreign Judgments (Reciprocal Enforcement) Act 1933 s 11(1).
8 'Judgment creditor' means the person in whose favour the judgment was given, and includes any person in whom the rights under it have become vested by succession or assignment or otherwise: ibid s 11(1).
9 Ibid s 1(2)(a) (as substituted: see note 4 supra).
10 Ibid s 1(2)(c) (as substituted: see note 4 supra).
11 Ibid s 2(1). 'Registration' means registration under Pt I (ss 1–7) (as amended), and 'register' and 'registered' must be construed accordingly: s 11(1).
12 Ibid s 1(2A) (added by the Civil Jurisdiction and Judgments Act 1982 Sch 10 para 1).

1030. Registration. Application for registration[1] of a judgment[2] is made by the judgment creditor[3] to the High Court[4]. The judgment may not be registered if it has been wholly satisfied[5], or if it is not capable of being enforced by execution in the country in which it was pronounced[6]. On proof of these and other prescribed matters[7] the court must order the judgment to be registered[8].

If it appears to the court that the judgment deals with different matters, the judgment may be registered only in respect of those of its provisions which could be registered if they were the subject of separate judgments[9]. If the sum payable under the judgment is expressed in foreign currency, registration may take place in that currency[10]. If the judgment has been partially satisfied, it is registered in respect of the balance remaining payable at the date of registration[11]. In addition to the sums due under the judgment, including any interest which by the law of the original court[12] becomes due under the judgment up to the date of registration[13], the judgment must be registered for the reasonable costs of and incidental to registration, including the cost of obtaining a certified copy of the foreign judgment[14].

A judgment to which the Protection of Trading Interests Act 1980 applies may not be registered under the Foreign Judgments (Reciprocal Enforcement) Act 1933[15].

1 For the meaning of 'registration' and cognate expressions see para 1029 note 11 ante.
2 For the meaning of 'judgment' see para 1029 text and notes 1–3 ante.
3 For the meaning of 'judgment creditor' see para 1029 note 8 ante.
4 Foreign Judgments (Reciprocal Enforcement) Act 1933 s 2(1). Application may be made ex parte to a Queen's Bench judge in chambers or master (RSC Ord 71 r 1) who may order an originating summons to be issued (Ord 71 r 2).

5   Foreign Judgments (Reciprocal Enforcement) Act 1933 s 2(1) proviso (a).
6   Ibid s 2(1) proviso (b). See *Re a Debtor (No 11 of 1939), Debtor v Creditor and Official Receiver* [1939] 2 All ER 400, CA (enforceability by execution at the time of registration is alone relevant, and it is immaterial that the judgment may later become unenforceable). Whether a judgment is enforceable by execution must be determined in accordance with any provision for the purpose in the Order in Council relevant to the judgment (see para 1028 ante): RSC Ord 71 r 11.
7   See RSC Ord 71 r 3.
8   Foreign Judgments (Reciprocal Enforcement) Act 1933 s 2(1). The court has no discretion to refuse registration. Contrast the position under the Administration of Justice Act 1920: see para 1024 text and note 12 ante. As to the procedure see RSC Ord 71 rr 4–8.
9   See the Foreign Judgments (Reciprocal Enforcement) Act 1933 s 2(5).
10   The provision to the contrary contained in ibid s 2(3) was repealed by the Administration of Justice Act 1977 ss 4, 32(4), Sch 5 Pt I.
11   Foreign Judgments (Reciprocal Enforcement) Act 1933 s 2(4).
12   For the meaning of 'original court' see para 1029 note 6 ante.
13   Any question as to interest payable is determined in accordance with any provisions for the purpose in the Order in Council relevant to the judgment: RSC Ord 71 r 11.
14   Foreign Judgments (Reciprocal Enforcement) Act 1933 s 2(6).
15   Protection of Trading Interests Act 1980 s 5(1): see para 1024 text and notes 15–16 ante.

1031. Effect of registration. For the purposes of execution, a registered[1] judgment[2] has the same force and effect, and proceedings may be taken on it, and the sum carries interest, and the High Court has the same control over execution, as if the judgment had been one originally given by the High Court and entered on the date of registration[3]. No execution may issue so long as it is competent for application to be made to have the registration set aside or, where such an application is made, until after it has been finally determined[4]. The period within which such an application may be made must be stated in the order for registration[5].

1   For the meaning of 'registered' see para 1029 note 11 ante.
2   For the meaning of 'judgment' see para 1029 text and notes 1–3 ante.
3   Foreign Judgments (Reciprocal Enforcement) Act 1933 s 2(2).
4   Ibid s 2(2) proviso; RSC Ord 71 r 10(1), (2). As to the issue of execution see generally RSC Ord 71 r 10.
5   RSC Ord 71 r 5(3).

1032. Non-registration of registrable judgment. If a foreign judgment[1] is one which may be registered under the Foreign Judgments (Reciprocal Enforcement) Act 1933[2], no proceedings for the recovery of the sum payable under it can be entertained in any court in the United Kingdom otherwise than by way of registration of the judgment[3]; nor may proceedings subsequently be brought on the original cause of action[4]. If, however, the judgment is not entitled to be registered, it is still possible to seek to enforce it by action at common law under the rules set out elsewhere in this title[5].

1   For the meaning of 'judgment' see para 1029 text and notes 1–3 ante.
2   See para 1029 ante.
3   Foreign Judgments (Reciprocal Enforcement) Act 1933 s 6. See *Re a Judgment Debtor (No 2176 of 1938)* [1939] Ch 601, [1939] 1 All ER 1, CA.
4   See the Civil Jurisdiction and Judgments Act 1982 s 34; and para 998 ante.
5   See paras 997–1018 ante. However, many of the reasons why the judgment is incapable of registration under the Act (see para 1029 ante), or which will lead to the registration being set aside (see para 1033 post), are also defences to an action on the judgment at common law, so in practice there will be few instances in which this freedom has any value.

1033. Setting aside registration. An order for the registration[1] of a foreign judgment[2] must be set aside on the application[3] of any party against whom the registered judgment may be enforced if the registering court[4] is satisfied (1) that the judgment is not one to which Part I of the Foreign Judgments (Reciprocal Enforcement) Act 1933[5] applies or that it was registered in contravention of the provisions of that Part[6]; or (2) that the courts[7] of the country of the original court[8] had no jurisdiction in the circumstances of the case[9]; or (3) that the judgment debtor[10], being the defendant in the proceedings in the original court, did not receive notice of those proceedings in sufficient time to enable him to defend and did not appear[11]; or (4) that the judgment was obtained by fraud[12]; or (5) that enforcement would be contrary to English public policy[13]; or (6) that the rights under the judgment are not vested in the person who applied for registration[14].

Registration of a foreign judgment may be set aside if the registering court is satisfied that, prior to the date of the judgment in the original court, the matter in dispute had been the subject of a final and conclusive judgment of a court having jurisdiction in the matter[15].

1   For the meaning of 'registration' see para 1029 note 11 ante.
2   For the meaning of 'judgment' see para 1029 text and notes 1–3 ante.
3   The application must be made to a judge of Queen's Bench Division in chambers, or to a master (RSC Ord 71 r 1) by summons supported by affidavit: Ord 71 r 9(1). An issue between the judgment creditor and judgment debtor may be ordered to be tried as if it were an issue in an action: Ord 71 r 9(2).
4   'Registering court' means the court to which an application to register the judgment is made: Foreign Judgments (Reciprocal Enforcement) Act 1933 s 11(1).
5   Ie the Foreign Judgments (Reciprocal Enforcement) Act 1933 Pt I (ss 1–7) (as amended): see para 1029 ante.
6   Ibid s 4(1)(a)(i).
7   For the meaning of 'court' see para 1028 note 3 ante.
8   For the meaning of 'country of the original court' see para 1029 note 6 ante.
9   Foreign Judgments (Reciprocal Enforcement) Act 1933 s 4(1)(a)(ii). The foreign court is deemed not to have had jurisdiction in the cases mentioned in para 1035 post and, subject to that, is deemed to have had jurisdiction in the cases mentioned in para 1034 post.
10   For the meaning of 'judgment debtor' see para 1029 note 7 ante.
11   Foreign Judgments (Reciprocal Enforcement) Act 1933 s 4(1)(a)(iii). This is so notwithstanding that process may have been duly served on him in accordance with the law of the country of the foreign court: s 4(1)(a)(iii). See *Re a Debtor (No 11 of 1939), Debtor v Creditor and Official Receiver* [1939] 2 All ER 400, CA.
12   Foreign Judgments (Reciprocal Enforcement) Act 1933 s 4(1)(a)(iv); see *Syal v Heyward* [1948] 2 KB 443, [1948] 2 All ER 576, CA. Fraud will have the same meaning as in relation to a judgment enforced by action at common law: cf *Owens Bank Ltd v Bracco* [1992] 2 AC 443, [1991] 4 All ER 833, HL (the reasoning in which case appears to be applicable to the meaning of fraud under the Foreign Judgments (Reciprocal Enforcement) Act 1933); and see para 1008 ante.
13   Ibid s 4(1)(a)(v); cf para 1009 ante.
14   Ibid s 4(1)(a)(vi).
15   Ibid s 4(1)(b); and see, as to the circumstances in which a court is deemed to have jurisdiction, para 1034 post.

1034. Circumstances in which a foreign court is deemed to have jurisdiction.

For the purposes of an application to set aside the registration[1] of a foreign judgment[2], and subject to the rules set out in the next paragraph, a foreign court[3] is deemed to have had jurisdiction in an action in personam[4] if the judgment debtor[5] who was a defendant in that court (1) submitted to the jurisdiction of that court by voluntarily appearing in the proceedings[6]; or (2) had, before the commencement of the proceedings, agreed in respect of the subject matter of the proceedings to submit to the jurisdiction of that court or of the courts of the country of that court[7]; or (3) was, when the proceedings were instituted, resident in, or, being a body corporate, had its principal place of business in, the country of that court[8]; or (4) had an office or place of business in the country of that court, and the proceedings were in respect of a transaction effected through or at that office or place[9]. The foreign court is so deemed to have had jurisdiction if the judgment debtor was plaintiff in or counterclaimed in the proceedings in that court[10].

In an action of which the subject matter was immovable property, or in an action in rem of which the subject matter was movable property, the foreign court is deemed to have jurisdiction if, at the time of the proceedings, the property in question was situated in the country of that court[11].

In the case of a judgment given in an action other than such kinds of action as are mentioned above, the foreign court is deemed to have jurisdiction if its jurisdiction either is recognised by the law of England[12].

1 For the meaning of 'registration' see para 1029 note 11 ante.
2 See para 1033 ante. For the meaning of 'judgment' see para 1029 text and notes 1–3 ante.
3 Ie the 'original court', for the meaning of which see para 1029 note 6 ante.
4 'Action in personam' does not include any matrimonial cause or any proceedings in connection with matrimonial matters, administration of the estates of deceased persons, bankruptcy, winding up, lunacy proceedings or guardianship of minors: Foreign Judgments (Reciprocal Enforcement) Act 1933 s 11(2).
5 For the meaning of 'judgment debtor' see para 1029 note 7 ante.
6 Foreign Judgments (Reciprocal Enforcement) Act 1933 s 4(2)(a)(i) (amended by the Civil Jurisdiction and Judgments Act 1982 s 54, Sch 14). As to when appearance is deemed not to constitute submission see the Civil Jurisdiction and Judgments Act 1982 s 33(1); as to provisions unaffected by this provision see s 33(2) (amended by the Civil Jurisdiction and Judgments Act 1991 Sch 2 para 15); and for transitional provisions see the Civil Jurisdiction and Judgments Act 1982 s 53, Sch 13 para 9. See also para 1001 ante.
7 Foreign Judgments (Reciprocal Enforcement) Act 1933 s 4(2)(a)(iii).
8 Ibid s 4(2)(a)(iv). Note that mere presence is not sufficient to satisfy the jurisdictional requirement for registration under the Act; and cf *Adams v Cape Industries plc* [1990] Ch 433, [1991] 1 All ER 929, CA; and see para 1000 ante.
9 Foreign Judgments (Reciprocal Enforcement) Act 1933 s 4(2)(a)(v).
10 Ibid s 4(2)(a)(ii).
11 Ibid s 4(2)(b).
12 Ibid s 4(2).

1035. Circumstances in which a foreign court has no jurisdiction. For the purposes of an application to set aside the registration[1] of a foreign judgment[2], the courts of the country of the original court[3] are deemed not to have had jurisdiction (1) if the subject matter of the proceedings was immovable property situated outside the foreign country in question; or (2) if the judgment debtor[4], being a defendant in the original proceedings, was a person who, under the rules of public international law, was entitled to immunity from the jurisdiction of the courts of the country of the foreign court[5] and did not submit to the jurisdiction of that court[6]. A court is also deemed to have no jurisdiction where the proceedings were brought before it in breach of an agreement for the settlement of disputes[7].

1 For the meaning of 'registration' see para 1029 note 11 ante.
2 See para 1033 ante. For the meaning of 'judgment' see para 1029 text and notes 1–3 ante.
3 For the meaning of 'country of the original court' see para 1029 note 6 ante.
4 For the meaning of 'judgment debtor' see para 1029 note 7 ante.
5 See para 616 ante.
6 Foreign Judgments (Reciprocal Enforcement) Act 1933 s 4(3) (amended by the Civil Jurisdiction and Judgments Act 1982 s 54, Sch 14).
7 See the Civil Jurisdiction and Judgments Act 1982 s 32(1); and para 1004 ante.

1036. Court's powers on application to set aside. If an applicant for the setting aside of the registration[1] of a foreign judgment[2] satisfies the registering court[3] either that an appeal[4] is pending or that he is entitled to appeal and intends to appeal against the judgment, the court may, if it thinks fit, on such terms as it may think just, either set aside the registration or adjourn the application until after the expiration of such period as appears to it to be reasonably sufficient to enable the applicant to take the necessary steps to have the appeal disposed of by the competent tribunal[5]. If the registration is set aside under this power, or if it is set aside solely for the reason that, at the date of the application for registration, the judgment was not enforceable by execution in the foreign country[6], the setting aside of the registration does not prejudice a further application for registration when the appeal is disposed of or if and when the judgment becomes enforceable by execution in that country[7]. Where the registration is set aside solely for the reason that the judgment, although partly satisfied at the date of the application for registration, was registered for the whole sum payable under it, then, on the application of the judgment creditor[8], the judgment must be registered for the balance remaining payable at that date[9].

1 For the meaning of 'registration' see para 1029 note 11 ante.
2 See para 1033 ante. For the meaning of 'judgment' see para 1029 text and notes 1–3 ante.
3 For the meaning of 'registering court' see para 1033 note 4 ante.
4 For the meaning of 'appeal' see para 1029 note 6 ante.
5 Foreign Judgments (Reciprocal Enforcement) Act 1933 s 5(1); *SA Consortium General Textiles v Sun and Sand Agencies Ltd* [1978] QB 279, [1978] 2 All ER 339, CA.
6 See para 1030 note 6 ante.
7 Foreign Judgments (Reciprocal Enforcement) Act 1933 s 5(2).
8 For the meaning of 'judgment creditor' see para 1029 note 8 ante.
9 Foreign Judgments (Reciprocal Enforcement) Act 1933 s 5(3).

1037. Certificates of judgments. Rules[1] may be made enabling any judgment creditor[2] who wishes to secure the enforcement of a judgment[3] in a foreign country to which Part I of the Foreign Judgments (Reciprocal Enforcement) Act 1933[4] extends[5] to obtain a copy of the judgment and a certificate giving particulars relating to the judgment and the proceedings in which it was given[6].

1 'Rules' means, in relation to judgments given by a court, rules of court, and in relation to judgments given by any other tribunal, rules or regulations made by the authority having power to make rules or regulations regulating the procedure of that tribunal: Foreign Judgments (Reciprocal Enforcement) Act 1933 s 10(3) (s 10 substituted by the Civil Jurisdiction and Judgments Act 1982 s 35(1), Sch 10 para 3). See note 6 infra.
2 For the meaning of 'judgment creditor' see para 1029 note 8 ante.
3 For the meaning of 'judgment' see para 1029 text and notes 1–3 ante. These provisions apply to any judgment given by a court or tribunal in the United Kingdom under which a sum of money is payable, not being a sum payable in respect of taxes or other charges of a like nature or in respect of a fine or other penalty: Foreign Judgments (Reciprocal Enforcement) Act 1933 s 10(2) (as substituted: see note 1 supra).
4 Ie the Foreign Judgments (Reciprocal Enforcement) Act 1933 Pt I (ss 1–7) (as amended).
5 See para 1028 ante.
6 Foreign Judgments (Reciprocal Enforcement) Act 1933 s 10(1) (as substituted: see note 1 supra). As to applications for obtaining a copy of a High Court judgment see RSC Ord 71 r 13; as to applications for obtaining a copy of a county court judgment see CCR Ord 35.

1038. Recognition of foreign judgments. A judgment[1] to which Part I of the Foreign Judgments (Reciprocal Enforcement) Act 1933[2] applies or would have applied if a sum of money had been payable under it, whether it can be registered[3] or not, and whether, if it can be registered, it is registered or not, must be recognised in any court in the United Kingdom[4] as conclusive between the parties in all proceedings founded on the same cause of action and may be relied on by way of defence or counterclaim in any such proceedings[5]. This provision does not apply where a judgment has been registered and the registration has been set aside on some ground other than that a sum of money was not payable under it, or that it had been wholly or partly satisfied, or that at the date of the application for registration the judgment could not be enforced by execution in the country of the original court[6]; nor does it apply in the case of a judgment not actually registered if it is shown (whether the judgment could have been registered or not) that, if it had been registered, the registration would have been set aside on grounds other than those set out above[7].

Nothing in the provisions described above prevents any court in the United Kingdom recognising any judgment as conclusive of any matter of law or fact if it would have been so recognised before the passing of the Act[8].

1 For the meaning of 'judgment' see para 1029 text and notes 1–3 ante.
2 Ie the Foreign Judgments (Reciprocal Enforcement) Act 1933 Pt I (ss 1–7) (as amended).
3 For the meaning of 'registered' see para 1029 note 11 ante.
4 For the meaning of 'United Kingdom' see para 604 ante.
5 Foreign Judgments (Reciprocal Enforcement) Act 1933 s 8(1). That provision does not apply to judgments of marital status: *Maples (formerly Melamud) v Maples, Maples v Melamud* [1988] Fam 14, [1987] 3 All ER 188. A foreign judgment dismissing a plaintiff's claim on the ground that it is statute-barred will prevent a further action in England in respect of the same cause of action: *Black-Clawson International Ltd v Papierwerke Waldhof-Aschaffenburg AG* [1975] AC 591, [1975] 1 All ER 810, HL; approving *Harris v Quine* (1869) LR 4 QB 653 (decided at common law); but see also the Foreign Limitation Periods Act 1984 s 3; and para 1082 post. Where there are two competing foreign judgments, each of which is pronounced by a court of competent jurisdiction and is final and not open to challenge, the earlier in time will prevail: *Showlag v Mansour* [1995] 1 AC 431, [1994] 2 All ER 129, PC; but as this rule is part of the doctrine of res judicata there may, in rare cases, be circumstances in which the party holding the earlier judgment may be estopped from relying on it: *Showlag v Mansour* supra at 134.
6 Foreign Judgments (Reciprocal Enforcement) Act 1933 s 8(2)(a). As to the grounds for setting aside registration see para 1033 ante. For the meaning of 'country of the original court' see para 1029 note 6 ante.
7 Ibid s 8(2)(b).
8 Ibid s 8(3).

1039. Power to make foreign judgments unenforceable. If it appears to Her Majesty that the treatment in respect of recognition and enforcement accorded by the courts[1] of any foreign country to judgments given in the courts of the United Kingdom[2] is substantially less favourable[3] than that accorded by the courts of the United Kingdom to judgments of the courts of that country, Her Majesty may by Order in Council provide that, except in so far as the Order in Council otherwise provides, no proceedings are to be entertained in any court in the United Kingdom for the recovery of any sum alleged to be payable under a judgment of a court of that country[4]. Such an Order in Council may be varied or revoked by a subsequent Order in Council[5].

1 For the meaning of 'court' see para 1028 note 3 ante.
2 For the meaning of 'United Kingdom' see para 604 ante.
3 Cf the term 'substantial reciprocity of treatment' as used in the Foreign Judgments (Reciprocal Enforcement) Act 1933 s 1: see para 1028 ante.
4 Ibid s 9(1), (2) (s 9(1) amended by the Civil Jurisdiction and Judgments Act 1982 s 35(1), Sch 10 para 2). At the date at which this volume states the law, no such Order in Council had been made.
5 Foreign Judgments (Reciprocal Enforcement) Act 1933 s 9(3).

(iii) Recognition and Enforcement under the Brussels and Lugano Conventions

A. APPLICATION OF THE BRUSSELS AND LUGANO CONVENTIONS

1040. In general. The rules for the recognition and enforcement of judgments from the courts of member states of the European Community, and of the courts of the member states of the European Free Trade Association, are governed to a very large extent by the Brussels and Lugano Conventions[1].

In order that one or other of the Conventions may govern the question of recognition and enforcement, it is necessary (1) that the judgment fall within the scope of the Convention as concerns its subject matter[2]; (2) that the judgment was obtained, or the proceedings which gave rise to it were instituted, on a date which allows it to fall within the scope of the Convention[3]; and (3) that the judgment be given by a court[4]. If the judgment creditor is able to satisfy the court on these points, the defendant will thereafter be entitled to advance limited grounds of objection based upon (a) the jurisdiction of the court which gave the judgment[5]; or (b) certain substantial or procedural objections[6]. In general, however, it is not open to a judgment debtor to allege that the court which gave judgment violated the jurisdictional provisions of the Convention[7]. Nor, in general, is it of any relevance as a ground to oppose recognition or enforcement of the judgment that the judgment debtor had no connection, domiciliary or otherwise, with any contracting state to either of the Conventions[8].

The provisions for recognition and enforcement of judgments under the Conventions are not confined to money judgments or to final judgments[9].

1 As to the Brussels Convention, and the states as between which it operates, see para 618 text and note 1 ante. As to the Lugano Convention, and the states as between which it operates, see para 618 text and note 2 ante. See paras 1041–1059 post. For provisions relating to the interpretation of the Conventions see paras 620–622 ante.
2 See para 1041 post.
3 See para 1042 post.
4 See para 1043 post. As to the application of the Conventions to authentic instruments and court settlements see para 1044 post.
5 See para 1045 post.
6 See para 1046 post.
7 See para 1045 post.
8 See para 1045 post.
9 See paras 1043–1044 post.

1041. Subject matter of the judgment. The Brussels and Lugano Conventions[1] are expressed to apply in civil and commercial matters. They are expressed to be inapplicable to revenue, customs or administrative matters. They are also excluded from application to (1) the status or legal capacity of natural persons, rights in property arising out of a matrimonial relationship, wills and succession; (2) bankruptcy, proceedings relating to the winding-up of insolvent companies or other legal persons, judicial arrangements, compositions and analogous proceedings; (3) social security; and (4) arbitration[2].

It is open to the court in which recognition or enforcement is sought to examine for itself whether the subject matter of the judgment falls within the scope of the Convention[3]. To this extent the court called upon to grant recognition will be entitled to examine a matter upon which the jurisdiction of the original court may have been founded[4].

If the judgment is found by the court not to fall within the scope of the Conventions, an alternative method of enforcement must be sought[5].

1 As to the Brussels and Lugano Conventions see paras 618, 1040 ante.
2 Brussels Convention art 1; Lugano Convention art 1. See para 626 ante.
3 Case 29/76 *LTU Lufttransportunternehmen GmbH & Co KG v Eurocontrol* [1976] ECR 1541, ECJ; Case 9/77 *Bavaria Fluggesellschaft Schwabe & Co KG and Germanair Bedarsluftfahrt GmbH & Co KG v Eurocontrol* [1977] ECR 1517, ECJ; Case 145/86 *Hoffman v Krieg* [1988] ECR 645, ECJ.
4 Cf the Brussels Convention art 28, 1st para; Lugano Convention art 28, 1st para; and para 1045 post. It is unclear whether a judgment from another contracting state determining that (for example) a contract contained no valid or binding arbitration clause may be re-examined, or whether (by contrast) it must be treated as a judgment which does fall within the scope of the Conventions. The case law of the European Court suggests that the court called upon to recognise the judgment is entitled to re-examine this matter for itself, but the position is not wholly free from doubt: see the cases cited in note 3 supra; and see also Case C-190/89 *Marc Rich & Co AG v Società Italiana Impianti PA* [1991] ECR I-3855, ECJ; *Marc Rich & Co AG v Società Italiana Impianti PA (No 2)* [1992] 1 Lloyd's Rep 624, CA. The duty to recognise the judgment in such a case has been held to be beyond doubt, but this cannot be determinative: *The Heidberg* [1994] 2 Lloyd's Rep 287, obiter. As to the duty to have regard to the judgments of the European Court and other contracting states see paras 620–621 ante. As to the meaning of 'European Court' see para 620 note 4 ante.
5 See paras 997–1039 ante.

1042. Date of the judgment to be enforced. The basic principle of the Brussels and Lugano Conventions[1] is that the recognition and enforcement of judgments in England will be governed by the particular Convention if that Convention was in force in the state in which judgment was given on the date on which the proceedings in that state were instituted[2]. In such a case the court which exercised jurisdiction will have done so, or should have done so, in accordance with the jurisdictional provisions of the Convention[3].

If the particular Convention (1) was not in force in the state from which the judgment originated on the date upon which proceedings were instituted; but (2) had come into force in that state prior to the date upon which judgment was given, then recognition or enforcement may be obtained under the scheme of the Convention if the jurisdiction of the court which gave judgment was founded upon rules which accorded with the jurisdictional rules of the Convention, or, alternatively, was based upon a Convention in force between the states on the date upon which the proceedings were instituted[4].

1 As to the Brussels and Lugano Conventions see paras 618, 1040 ante.
2 Brussels Convention art 54, 1st para; Lugano Convention art 54, 1st para.
3 See generally para 618 et seq ante.
4 Brussels Convention art 54, 2nd para; Lugano Convention art 54, 2nd para. In such a case the court called upon to recognise the judgment must necessarily examine for itself whether the jurisdiction of the court which gave judgment corresponded with the jurisdictional provisions of the Convention because, ex hypothesi, the court which gave judgment will not have done so itself. It is unclear, however, whether it is the jurisdictional rule relied on, or simply the actual exercise of jurisdiction in the individual case, which must be examined, but it is thought that the latter would be the more consistent with principle.

1043. Meaning of 'judgment' for the purposes of the Conventions. The Brussels and Lugano Conventions[1] extend their provisions for recognition and enforcement to any judgment given by a court or tribunal in a contracting state[2], whatever the judgment may be called, including a decree, order, decision or writ of execution, as well as the determination of costs or expenses by an officer of the court[3].

Three particular forms of order are, nevertheless, excluded from this definition. First, as the Conventions have been held to have no application to proceedings to enforce the judgments of a non-contracting state, it appears that a judgment from a court of a contracting state which declares that the judgment of a non-contracting state is locally enforceable is not within the scope of the Conventions[4]. Secondly, the Conventions probably exclude directions given by a national court as to the conduct of proceedings before it, such as orders relating to the taking of evidence[5]. Thirdly, they exclude orders which are not, of their nature, of a kind obtained after enquiry in adversarial proceedings[6].

1 As to the Brussels and Lugano Conventions see paras 618, 1040 ante.
2 For the meaning of 'contracting state' see para 618 note 3 ante.
3 Brussels Convention art 25; Lugano Convention art 25. The Conventions therefore extend beyond final judgments for a fixed sum of money: contrast the position at common law or under the Foreign Judgments (Reciprocal Enforcement) Act 1933: see paras 1013, 1030–1033 ante. The extent to which they apply to orders made by a tribunal presumably depends upon whether the body concerned is exercising judicial functions: art 25 of the Conventions would probably apply to such of a tribunal's orders as may be seen as judgments (eg those of an industrial tribunal). The effect of art 1, however, is that orders made by an arbitral tribunal are excluded, as are orders made by a national court as supervisory authority over an arbitration: see para 1041 ante. As to references to numbered articles 'of the Conventions' see para 618 note 5 ante. The definition of 'judgment' given in art 25 of the Conventions is applied for the purposes of the Civil Jurisdiction and Judgments Act 1982 by s 15(1). 'Judgment' in art 25 of the Conventions refers to judicial decisions actually given by a court or tribunal in a contracting state, deciding on its own authority on the issues between the parties: Case C-414/92 *Solo Kleinmotoren GmbH v Boch* [1994] ECR I-2237, ECJ.
4 Case C-129/92 *Owens Bank Ltd v Bracco* [1994] ECR I-117, [1994] QB 509, [1994] 1 All ER 336, ECJ. But if the judgment of the non-contracting state were used only as evidence in relation to the underlying cause of action, which is prosecuted de novo in a contracting state, it is thought that the later judgment would fall within the scope of the Conventions and within art 25.
5 See the report of Professor Peter Schlosser on the Accession Convention (OJ C59, 5.3.79, p 71 at 126). Cf the Civil Jurisdiction and Judgments Act 1982 s 25(7); and see *CFEM Façades SA v Bovis Construction Ltd* [1992] ILPr 561.
6 Case 125/79 *Denilauler v Snc Couchet Frères* [1980] ECR 1553, [1981] 1 CMLR 62, ECJ; *EMI Records Ltd v Modern Music Karl-Ulrich Walterbach GmbH* [1992] QB 115, [1992] 1 All ER 616. Thus a Mareva injunction obtained ex parte, or a corresponding order from a court in a contracting state, does not as such qualify as a judgment. It is arguable (although the issue has not yet arisen for decision) that such an order made by a court and maintained by it after an inter partes hearing will qualify as a judgment on the basis that if the order is maintained or re-imposed after a hearing inter partes, it is difficult to see that it can be objected to on the grounds set out in *Denilauler v Snc Couchet Frères* supra. But it would be different if any burden of proof on the applicant was greater on the application inter partes by reason of the order having already been made ex parte: see Case C-123/91 *Minalmet GmbH v Branden's Ltd* [1992] ECR I-5661, ECJ.

1044. Authentic instruments and court settlements. A document which has been formally drawn up or registered as an authentic instrument[1] and is enforceable in one contracting state[2] must, in another contracting state, be declared enforceable there, on application made as if for enforcement of a foreign judgment[3]; such an application may be refused only if enforcement of the instrument is contrary to public policy in the state addressed[4].

A settlement approved by a court in the course of proceedings and enforceable in the state in which it was concluded is enforceable in the state addressed under the same conditions as authentic instruments[5].

Her Majesty may by Order in Council[6] provide that any provision of the Civil Jurisdiction and Judgments Act 1982, or any other statutory provision, relating to the recognition or enforcement of judgments to which the Brussels or Lugano Convention applies, is to apply with specified modifications[7] to authentic instruments and settlements as if they were judgments[8].

1   The instrument produced must satisfy the conditions necessary to establish its authenticity in the state of origin: Brussels Convention art 50, 2nd para; Lugano Convention art 50, 2nd para. As to the Brussels and Lugano Conventions see paras 618, 1040 ante.

2   For the meaning of 'contracting state' see para 618 note 3 ante.

3   Ie application made in accordance with the procedures described in paras 1049–1059 post. The provisions of Title III, Section 3 (arts 46–49) of the Conventions (see para 1049 text and note 11 post) apply as appropriate: Brussels Convention art 50, 3rd para; Lugano Convention art 50, 3rd para. For the meaning of 'judgment' for these purposes see para 1043 ante.

4   Brussels Convention art 50, 1st para; Lugano Convention art 50, 1st para.

5   Brussels Convention art 51; Lugano Convention art 51. The irreconcilability of a settlement with a judgment under art 27 of the Conventions (see para 1046 post) does not preclude a challenge to the recognition of a judgment: Case C-414/92 *Solo Kleinmotoren GmbH v Boch* [1994] ECR I-2237, ECJ.

6   Such an Order in Council is subject to annulment in pursuance of a resolution of either House of Parliament: Civil Jurisdiction and Judgments Act 1982 s 13(3).

7   An Order in Council may make different provision in relation to different descriptions of documents and settlements: ibid s 13(2).

8   Ibid s 13(1) (amended by the Civil Jurisdiction and Judgments Act 1991 s 3, Sch 2 para 8).

     The provisions of the Civil Jurisdiction and Judgments Act 1982 are applied in relation to authentic instruments and court settlements by the Civil Jurisdiction and Judgments (Authentic Instruments and Court Settlements) Order 1993, SI 1993/604, arts 2–8:

     (1)   in relation to authentic instruments and court settlements which are not maintenance orders, the Civil Jurisdiction and Judgments Act 1982 ss 4 (as amended) (with a modification), 6(1) (as amended), (2), 7(1)–(3), (5) (see paras 1048–1049, 1051 post);

     (2)   in relation to authentic instruments and court settlements which are maintenance orders, ss 5 (as amended) (with a modification), 6(3), 7(1), (2), (4), (5), 8;

     (3)   in relation to authentic instruments and court settlements, ss 11 (with a modification relating to authentic instruments), 15(2), (3), 48;

     (4)   in relation to authentic instruments, s 12 (as amended) (with a modification);

     (5)   in relation to authentic instruments and court settlements, the disapplication of s 18 by s 18(7).

B. RECOGNITION AND ENFORCEMENT

1045. Objections to recognition based on the jurisdiction of the court of the state in which judgment was obtained. If a judgment[1] falls within the scope of the Brussels and Lugano Conventions[2], the defendant may challenge the original exercise of jurisdiction by that court, and call upon the court asked to recognise the judgment to re-examine and to decide for itself whether the court giving judgment had jurisdiction to do so[3]. The grounds upon which he may do so are exhaustively set out in the Conventions[4].

The defendant may object on the ground that the court which gave judgment took jurisdiction in violation of the provisions giving exclusive jurisdiction to the courts of another contracting state[5], or in violation of the particular jurisdictional provisions which apply to insurance[6] and to consumer contracts[7]. Subject to one further exception relating to both Conventions[8], and one relating only to the Lugano Convention[9], the jurisdiction of the original court may not be reviewed, and, in particular, the test of public policy[10] may not be applied to the rules relating to jurisdiction[11].

The exception relating to both Conventions is that if:

     (1)   the defendant is domiciled or habitually resident in a non-contracting state[12]; and

(2) he was not domiciled in any contracting state according to its law[13]; and

(3) the claim against him fell outside the scope of the exclusive jurisdiction provisions of the Conventions[14]; and

(4) the jurisdiction of the court which gave judgment could only have been founded upon specified jurisdictional provisions[15]; and

(5) there exists a convention between the state addressed and the non-contracting state in which the defendant is domiciled or habitually resident, according to the terms of which the state addressed is obliged not to recognise the judgment[16],

then the judgment may be denied recognition or enforcement according to that convention[17].

1 For the meaning of 'judgment' for these purposes see para 1043 ante.

2 As to the Brussels and Lugano Conventions see paras 618, 1040 ante.

3 In its examination of the grounds of jurisdiction, the court or authority is bound by the findings of fact on which the court of the state of origin based its jurisdiction: Brussels Convention art 28, 2nd para; Lugano Convention art 28, 3rd para.

4 See the Brussels Convention art 28; the Lugano Convention art 28; and the text and notes infra.

5 Ie the provisions of Title II, Section 5 (art 16) of the Conventions: Brussels Conventions art 28, 1st para; Lugano Convention art 28, 1st para. See paras 627–628 ante. As to references to numbered articles 'of the Conventions' see para 618 note 5 ante.

6 Ie the provisions of Title II, Section 3 (arts 7–12) of the Conventions: Brussels Conventions art 28, 1st para; Lugano Convention art 28, 1st para. See para 631 ante. It is thought that a judgment from a court before which the defendant entered an appearance does not violate the jurisdictional rules governing insurance contracts: see para 631 note 1 ante.

7 Ie the provisions of Title II, Section 3 (arts 13–15) of the Conventions: Brussels Conventions art 28, 1st para; Lugano Convention art 28, 1st para. See para 632 ante. It is thought that a judgment from a court before which the defendant entered an appearance does not violate the jurisdictional rules governing consumer contracts: see para 632 note 1 ante.

8 See art 59 of the Conventions; and text and notes 12–17 infra.

9 Recognition or enforcement may be refused if (1) the ground of jurisdiction on which the judgment is based differs from that resulting from the Lugano Convention, and recognition or enforcement is sought against a party who is domiciled in a contracting state which is not a member of the European Community, unless it may otherwise be recognised or enforced under any rule of law in the state addressed (Lugano Convention art 54B para 3); or (2) the state addressed is not a party to any other convention affecting recognition or enforcement and the person against whom recognition or enforcement is sought is domiciled in that state, unless the judgment may otherwise be recognised or enforced under any rule of law in the state addressed (art 57 para 4).

10 Ie the test referred to in art 27 para 1 of the Conventions: see para 1046 post.

11 Brussels Convention art 28, 3rd para; Lugano Convention art 28, 4th para.

12 As to these provisions see the Brussels Convention art 59 and the Lugano Convention art 59. This does not apply in certain cases of claims to property within the jurisdiction of the court which gave judgment: Brussels Convention art 59, 2nd para; Lugano Convention art 59, 2nd para. As to domicile in a non-contracting state see the Civil Jurisdiction and Judgments Act 1982 s 41(7).

13 Ie the case falls within art 4 of the Conventions: see para 639 ante.

14 Ie the case is not, by virtue of art 4 of the Conventions, one within art 16 of the Conventions: see paras 627–628 ante.

15 Ie jurisdictional provisions, which may not be applied in the courts of one contracting state against persons domiciled in another, as are mentioned in art 3 of the Conventions: see para 634 note 11 ante.

16 Her Majesty may by Order in Council declare a provision of a convention entered into by the United Kingdom to be a provision whereby the United Kingdom has assumed an obligation of this kind: Civil Jurisdiction and Judgments Act 1982 s 9(2). See the Reciprocal Enforcement of Foreign Judgments (Canada) Order 1987, SI 1987/468 (amended by SI 1987/2211; SI 1988/1304; SI 1988/1853; SI 1989/987; SI 1991/1724; SI 1992/1731; and SI 1995/2708); Reciprocal Enforcement of Foreign Judgments (Australia) Order 1994, SI 1994/1901.

17 Brussels Convention art 59; Lugano Convention art 59.

1046. Non-jurisdictional objections to recognition of a judgment. The Brussels and Lugano Conventions[1] provide that under no circumstances may a judgment[2] be reviewed as to its substance[3], although a judgment may be denied recognition on any of five alternative non-jurisdictional grounds[4], as described below.

(1) A judgment must not be recognised if to recognise it would be contrary to English public policy[5]. The term 'public policy' is to be given a narrow interpretation, although its precise content is likely to be a matter for the national law of the court seised[6]. Although it is open to an English court to find that a judgment was (or may have been) procured by fraud[7], the court is not thereby entitled to find that to recognise it would, on that ground alone, be contrary to public policy, for procedures may exist in the state where the judgment originated for the allegation of fraud to be investigated, and, if there are adequate local remedies, recognition may well be found, notwithstanding the allegation of fraud, not to infringe public policy[8].

(2) A judgment must not be recognised if it was given in default of appearance and the defendant was not duly served with the document which instituted the proceedings or with an equivalent document in sufficient time to enable him to arrange for his defence[9]. Whether a defendant has appeared before the foreign court must be determined by the procedural law of that court[10]. Whether service was duly made upon him is to be determined by reference to the law of the court in which judgment was obtained, and whose document it was[11], and not by the law of the place in which service was actually made (unless the law of the state of origin regards service as duly made if it complies with the law of the state in which it is actually effected[12]). Whether any irregularity in service can be cured is likewise a matter for the law of the state whose document it was[13]. The fact that the defendant may have known of the irregularly-served document is irrelevant[14]. Whether service was made timeously is a matter of fact to be assessed by the court called upon to recognise the judgment; it is not decisive that the court which gave judgment reached the conclusion that the defendant had been served in good time. In making the assessment, the court called upon to consider whether service was timeously made is entitled to consider whether the manner of effecting service should affect the amount of time which the defendant should have been allowed[15]; but the length of time is only that needed to prevent a judgment from being entered in default of appearance[16]. The fact that the defendant would have been entitled, under the law of the court which gave judgment, to apply to have the judgment set aside does not affect the default character of the judgment[17]. If such an application is made, but is unsuccessful, the judgment may still be treated as a default judgment if the defendant was under a procedural handicap by reason of its having been entered[18].

(3) A judgment will not be recognised if it is irreconcilable with a judgment given in a dispute between the same parties in the state in which recognition is sought[19]. The test of irreconcilability is whether the legal consequences are mutually exclusive[20].

(4) A judgment will not be recognised if the court which gave it, in order to arrive at its judgment, decided, in a way that conflicts with a rule of the private international law of the state in which recognition is sought, a preliminary question concerning the status or legal capacity of natural persons, rights in property arising out of a matrimonial relationship, wills or succession, unless the same result would have been reached by applying the rules of private international law of that state[21].

(5) A judgment will not be recognised if it is irreconcilable with an earlier judgment given in a non-contracting state involving the same cause of action and between the same parties, provided that this latter judgment fulfils the conditions necessary for recognition in the state in which recognition is sought[22].

1 As to the Brussels and Lugano Conventions see paras 618, 1040 ante.
2 For the meaning of 'judgment' for these purposes see para 1043 ante.
3 Brussels Convention art 29; Lugano Convention art 29.
4 Brussels Convention art 27; Lugano Convention art 27.
5 Brussels Convention art 27 para 1; Lugano Convention art 27 para 1.
6 Its precise content in England is a matter of English law. There is, however, support for the view that the term is to be interpreted narrowly: see *Interdesco SA v Nullifire Ltd* [1992] 1 Lloyd's Rep 180; *Société d'Informatique Service Réalisation Organisation (SISRO) v Ampersand Software BV* [1994] ILPr 55, CA.
7 See para 1008 ante.
8 See the cases cited in note 6 supra; see also the report of Professor Peter Schlosser on the Accession Convention (OJ C59, 5.3.79, p 71 at 128).
9 Brussels Convention art 27 para 2; Lugano Convention art 27 para 2. As to what constitutes a 'document which instituted the proceedings' see Case C-474/93 *Firma Hengst Import BV v Campese* [1995] ILPr 587, ECJ.
10 Matters of procedure are determined by the law of the court seised with the procedural question: see Case 129/83 *Zelger v Salinitri (No 2)* [1984] ECR 2397, [1985] 3 CMLR 366, ECJ. As to the position in English law see RSC Ord 12 r 10.
11 Case C-305/88 *Isabelle Lancray SA v Peters und Sickert KG* [1990] ECR I-2725, ECJ; Case C-123/91 *Minalmet GmbH v Brandeis Ltd* [1992] ECR I-5661, ECJ.
12 Case C-123/91 *Minalmet GmbH v Brandeis Ltd* [1992] ECR I-5661, ECJ.
13 *Isabelle Lancray SA v Peters und Sickert KG* [1990] ECR I-2725, ECJ.
14 See the cases cited in note 11 supra.
15 Case 166/80 *Klomps v Michel* [1981] ECR 1593, ECJ; Case 288/81 *Pendy Plastic Products v Pluspunkt* [1982] ECR 2723, ECJ.
16 See the cases cited in note 15 supra.
17 Case C-123/91 *Minalmet GmbH v Brandeis Ltd* [1992] ECR I-5661, ECJ.
18 Case C-123/91 *Minalmet GmbH v Brandeis Ltd* [1992] ECR I-5661, ECJ; see also Case 49/84 *Debaecker and Plouvier v Bouwman* [1985] ECR 1779, ECJ.
19 Brussels Convention art 27 para 3; Lugano Convention art 27 para 3. Such instances should be rare, since most occasions when they might arise would be forestalled by the operation of art 21 of the Conventions: see para 645 ante. An enforceable settlement between the parties (see para 1044 ante) does not constitute a judgment for the purposes of this provision: Case C-414/92 *Solo Kleinmotoren GmbH v Boch* [1994] ECR I-2237, ECJ.
20 Case 145/86 *Hoffman v Krieg* [1988] ECR 645, ECJ; see also *Macaulay v Macaulay* [1991] 1 All ER 865, [1991] 1 WLR 179; *Gascoine v Pyrah* [1994] ILPr 82, CA. It does not appear that the local judgment is required to have been given first, and it is not clear what the consequences would be if, execution having been commenced upon a judgment of a contracting state, an irreconcilable judgment were subsequently handed down in the state in which recognition is sought. If the judgment of the contracting state were irreconcilable with a judgment which fell outside the scope of the Conventions, it would not be recognised, for to require recognition in such circumstances would be to undermine art 1 of the Convention: see in particular Case 145/86 *Hoffman v Krieg* supra; Case C-190/89 *Marc Rich & Co AG v Società Italiana Impianti PA* [1991] ECR I-3855, ECJ. For the meaning of 'contracting state' see para 618 note 3 ante.
21 Brussels Convention art 27 para 4; Lugano Convention art 27 para 4. See also Case 145/86 *Hoffman v Krieg* [1988] ECR 645, ECJ.
22 Brussels Convention art 27 para 5; Lugano Convention art 27 para 5. The non-contracting state judgment must have been given, and it is probable that it must already have met the criteria for recognition, when the question of recognition of the contracting state judgment arises. It is not clear what is the precise moment at which the question of recognition will be held to arise, but it may be that it is the date of the judgment in the court which made its order, rather than the (later) date of the proceedings in the English court. As no procedure is required for the recognition of a judgment (see para 1048 post) it is arguable that the obligation to grant recognition to the judgment of the contracting state arises as soon as it is handed down by the court. Nevertheless, at the date at which this volume states the law, the position remains unclear, especially where the judgment is itself subject to an appeal. The

problem created when judgments from two contracting states conflict has no textual, or otherwise obvious, solution: see the Report on the Lugano Convention by Mr P Jenard and Mr G Möller (OJ C 189, 28.7.90, p 57 at 79).

1047. Effect of a pending appeal upon the obligation to recognise a judgment. A court of a contracting state[1] in which recognition is sought of a judgment[2] is sought of a judgment given in another contracting state may stay the proceedings if an ordinary appeal has been lodged against the judgment and (in the case of a judgment given in the Republic of Ireland or the United Kingdom) if enforcement is suspended in the state of origin by reason of an appeal[3].

1 For the meaning of 'contracting state' see para 618 note 3 ante.
2 For the meaning of 'judgment' for these purposes see para 1043 ante.
3 Brussels Convention art 30; Lugano Convention art 30. As to the Brussels and Lugano Conventions see paras 618, 1040 ante.

1048. Procedure for, and effect of, recognition of the judgment. The Brussels and Lugano Conventions[1] provide that a judgment[2] given in a contracting state[3] must be recognised in the other contracting states without any special procedure being required[4], but an interested party who raises the question of recognition of a judgment may apply for a decision that the judgment be recognised[5]. If the outcome of proceedings in a court of a contracting state depends on the determination of an incidental question of recognition, that court has jurisdiction over that question[6].

The recognition of the judgment is intended to confer upon it the same authority and effectiveness as is accorded to it in the state in which it was given[7]. When recognised, however, a judgment may be used to found an issue or cause of action estoppel, for the doctrine of res judicata applies equally to judgments entitled to recognition under the Conventions[8].

In the United Kingdom where an applicant for registration of a judgment[9] shows that the judgment provides for the payment of a sum of money and that under the law of the contracting state in which the judgment was given interest is recoverable on it from a particular date or time, the rate of interest and that date or time must be registered with the judgment, and the debt resulting from the registration carries interest in accordance with the registered particulars[10].

1 As to the Brussels and Lugano Conventions see paras 618, 1040 ante.
2 For the meaning of 'judgment' for these purposes see para 1043 ante.
3 For the meaning of 'contracting state' see para 618 note 3 ante.
4 Brussels Convention art 26, 1st para; Lugano Convention art 26, 1st para.
5 Brussels Convention art 26, 2nd para; Lugano Convention art 26, 2nd para. The application must be in accordance with Title III (ss 2, 3) of the Conventions: see RSC Ord 71 r 35; and paras 1049–1059 post. As to references to numbered articles 'of the Conventions' see para 618 note 5 ante.
6 Brussels Convention art 26, 3rd para; Lugano Convention art 26, 3rd para.
7 Case 145/86 *Hoffman v Krieg* [1988] ECR 645, ECJ. See also the report of Mr P Jenard on the 1968 Convention and the 1971 Protocol (OJ C59, 5.3.79, p 1, 66). It is, however, unclear how this may affect the position of a third party. If the judgment given by a court is one which, according to the law of that state, is binding on a third party who was not party to the proceedings, it is not clear whether it must likewise be recognised as against him in England. As a matter of English common law, such a judgment could not be binding on the third party unless he were privy to one of the parties: see para 1007 note 5 ante. But cf the report of Professor Peter Schlosser on the Accession Convention (OJ C59, 5.3.79, p 71 at 127–128), concerning a judgment against a debtor which is also binding upon a surety. The obligation to give the judgment the effect it has under the law of the court which handed it down would suggest that it should be recognised; however, a judgment given in default of the appearance of the third

party should be denied recognition: see para 1046 text and notes 9–18 ante. It is suggested, therefore, that even if the judgment is, according to the law of the court which rendered it, binding upon certain third parties, the protection afforded by the provisions dealing with default judgments may render it not liable to be recognised as against such third parties.

8　*Berkeley Administration Inc v McClelland* [1995] ILPr 201, CA.
9　Ie under the Civil Jurisdiction and Judgments Act 1982 s 4 (as amended) or s 5 (as amended): see paras 843 ante, 1049 post.
10　Ibid s 7(1). Such judgments may carry interest only as provided by s 7, with an exception made by s 7(4) relating to maintenance orders (see para 843 note 13 ante). Rules of court may make provision as to the manner in which and the periods by reference to which interest is to be calculated and paid, including provision for interest to cease to accrue from a prescribed date: s 7(2). At the date at which this volume states the law, no rules of court had been made for this purpose.

1049. Enforcement of judgments which qualify for recognition: application for registration. A judgment[1] given in a contracting state[2] and enforceable there is enforceable in England and Wales when, on the application of any interested party, it has been registered for enforcement there[3]. If the judgment has been given for several matters, but enforcement cannot be authorised for all of them, enforcement may be authorised for some of them[4].

A judgment, other than a maintenance order[5], which is the subject of such an application for enforcement in England and Wales must, to the extent that enforcement is authorised by the appropriate court[6], be registered in the prescribed manner in that court[7]. A judgment so registered is, for the purposes of its enforcement, of the same force and effect, the registering court has the same powers as to enforcement, and proceedings relating to its enforcement may be taken, as if it had originally been made by the registering court and had, where relevant, been entered[8].

The application is made to the High Court judge in chambers, or to a master[9]. It is made ex parte[10], and must be supported by an affidavit[11].

The court must give its decision without delay[12]. The application may be refused only for one of the reasons specified by the Conventions as a reason for non-recognition of a judgment[13]. Under no circumstances may a foreign judgment be reviewed as to its substance[14].

If the court makes an order for registration, notice of registration must be served on the other party[15], who has a right of appeal[16].

1　For the meaning of 'judgment' for these purposes see para 1043 ante.
2　For the meaning of 'contracting state' see para 618 note 3 ante.
3　Brussels Convention art 31; Lugano Convention art 31. As to the Brussels and Lugano Conventions see paras 618, 1040 ante.
4　Brussels Convention art 42, 1st para; Lugano Convention art 42, 1st para; cf *Raulin v Fischer* [1911] 2 KB 93. An applicant may request partial enforcement of a judgment: Brussels Convention art 42, 2nd para; Lugano Convention art 42, 2nd para.
5　As to the registration of maintenance orders under the Civil Jurisdiction and Judgments Act 1982 see para 843 ante.
6　'Appropriate court' means the court to which the application is made in pursuance of art 32 of the Conventions, ie the High Court: Civil Jurisdiction and Judgments Act 1982 s 4(1). As to references to numbered articles 'of the Conventions' see para 618 note 5 ante.
7　Ibid s 4(1) (amended by the Civil Jurisdiction and Judgments Act 1991 s 3, Sch 2 para 2). Where a judgment is so registered, the reasonable costs or expenses of or incidental to its registration are recoverable as if they were sums recoverable under the judgment: Civil Jurisdiction and Judgments Act 1982 s 4(2). Such costs or expenses carry interest as if they were the subject of an order for the payment of costs or expenses made by the registering court on the date of registration: s 7(3). For the prescribed manner of registration see RSC Ord 71 r 25 et seq.
8　Civil Jurisdiction and Judgments Act 1982 s 4(3). This is subject to art 39 of the Conventions (see para 1052 post), to the Civil Jurisdiction and Judgments Act 1982 s 7 (see para 1048 ante) and to any

provision made by rules of court as to the manner in which and conditions subject to which a judgment so registered may be enforced: s 4(4).

9 Brussels Convention arts 32, 33; Lugano Convention arts 32, 33; RSC Ord 71 rr 26–27.
10 Brussels Convention art 34, 1st para; Lugano Convention art 34, 1st para; RSC Ord 71 r 27.
11 Brussels Convention arts 46, 47; Lugano Convention arts 46, 47; RSC Ord 71 r 28. The court may, if the prescribed documents are not produced, specify a time for production, accept equivalent documents or, if it considers that it already has sufficient information before it, dispense with their production, and may also require a translation of documents: Brussels Convention art 48; Lugano Convention art 48; RSC Ord 71 r 28(1)(iv), (2). No other formality may be required in respect of documents: Brussels Convention art 49; Lugano Convention art 49. The original or a copy of any such document is evidence in the United Kingdom of any matter to which it relates: Civil Jurisdiction and Judgments Act 1982 s 11(1)(b).
12 Brussels Convention art 34, 1st para; Lugano Convention art 34, 1st para.
13 Brussels Convention art 34, 2nd para; Lugano Convention art 34, 2nd para: see arts 27, 28 of the Conventions; and paras 1045–1046 ante.
14 Brussels Convention art 34, 3rd para; Lugano Convention art 34, 3rd para.
15 Brussels Convention art 35; Lugano Convention art 35; RSC Ord 71 rr 30, 32. Note that art 35 of the Conventions provides for the decision to be brought 'to the notice of the applicant'; it is conceived that this should refer rather to the party against whom enforcement is sought, who was not entitled to be heard on the application, but who subsequently has a right of appeal (see text and note 16 infra).
16 Brussels Convention art 36; Lugano Convention art 36; RSC Ord 71 r 33; and see para 1050 post.

1050. Appeal by respondent against order for registration. An appeal against the registration of a judgment[1] is made by summons to a judge[2]. The appellant has one month from the date on which the notice of registration was served upon him (or two months if he is not domiciled in the United Kingdom) to appeal against the order for registration[3].

1 For the meaning of 'judgment' for these purposes see para 1043 ante.
2 Brussels Convention art 37 para 1; Lugano Convention art 37 para 1; RSC Ord 71 r 33(1). As to the Brussels and Lugano Conventions see paras 618, 1040 ante.
3 Brussels Convention art 36; Lugano Convention art 36; RSC Ord 71 r 33(2), (3). As to the meaning of 'domicile' see para 634 ante. The grounds of appeal are not specified in the Conventions, but they must be taken to be the same as the grounds on which the court might have refused registration, and upon which the appellant would have had no previous opportunity to make submissions: see para 1049 text and notes 10, 15 ante. Thus the grounds of appeal would be that (1) the judgment does not fall within the scope of the Convention (see para 1041 ante); or (2) that one or more of the specific grounds upon which its recognition may be opposed are applicable (see paras 1043–1046 ante).

1051. Further appeal. After the determination of the appeal by the judgment debtor against registration[1], the unsuccessful party may make a single further appeal upon a point of law[2].

1 See para 1050 ante.
2 Brussels Convention art 37 para 2; Lugano Convention art 37 para 2. As to the Brussels and Lugano Conventions see paras 618, 1040 ante. In the United Kingdom, the appeal may be to the Court of Appeal or the House of Lords: see the Civil Jurisdiction and Judgments Act 1982 s 6 (amended by the Civil Jurisdiction and Judgments Act 1991 s 3, Sch 2 para 3).

1052. Measures pending the determination of the appeal. If the judgment debtor appeals against the order for registration[1], he is entitled to apply to the court for a stay of the proceedings on the ground that (1) an appeal has been lodged against the judgment; or (2) the time for lodging such an appeal has not yet expired[2]. The court may also make enforcement conditional upon the provision of security[3].

Until the determination of the appeal, no measures of execution, other than protective measures, may be taken against the judgment debtor, but the decision to authorise enforcement carries with it the power to proceed to any such protective measures[4].

1 See para 1050 ante.
2 Brussels Convention art 38, 1st para; Lugano Convention art 38, 1st para. As to the Brussels and Lugano Conventions see paras 618, 1040 ante. It is not clear whether a court can order a stay on the ground that an appeal is pending in the state of origin of the judgment, even though there are no longer proceedings in relation to enforcement in the English court, all appeals having been determined: see *Société d'Informatique Service Réalisation Organisation (SISRO) v Ampersand Software BV* [1994] ILPr 55, CA; and see the proceedings in the European Court, Case C-432/93 *Société d'Information Service Réalisation Organisation (SISRO) v Ampersand Software BV* [1995] All ER (EC) 783, ECJ. Any form of appeal available in the United Kingdom is treated as an appeal for this purpose: Brussels Convention art 38, 2nd para; Lugano Convention art 38, 2nd para. A decision of a court to lift or refuse a stay cannot be contested by appeal on point of law under art 37 para 2 (see para 1051 ante), and therefore the court does not have jurisdiction to impose or reimpose a stay in these circumstances under art 38: Case C-432/93 *Société d' Information Service Réalisation Organisation (SISRO) v Ampersand Software BV* supra.
3 Brussels Convention art 38, 3rd para; Lugano Convention art 38, 3rd para: see *Petereit v Babcock International Ltd* [1990] 2 All ER 135, [1990] 1 WLR 350; *Société d'Informatique Service Réalisation Organisation (SISRO) v Ampersand Software BV* [1994] ILPr 55, CA.
4 Brussels Convention art 39; Lugano Convention art 39; RSC Ord 71 r 34.

1053. Appeal by applicant for registration against refusal to order registration. If the court refused to make an order for registration of the judgment[1], the applicant may within one month appeal to the High Court against the refusal[2]. The party against whom enforcement is sought must be summoned to appear before the court[3].

1 See para 1049 ante.
2 Brussels Convention art 40 para 1; Lugano Convention art 40 para 1; RSC Ord 71 r 33. As to the Brussels and Lugano Conventions see paras 618, 1040 ante.
3 Brussels Convention art 40 para 2; Lugano Convention art 40 para 2; it is provided that if he fails to appear, the provisions set out at para 645 text and note 5 ante apply.

1054. Further appeal. After the determination of an appeal by the applicant against the refusal to authorise registration of a judgment[1], the unsuccessful party may make a single further appeal upon a point of law[2].

1 See para 1053 ante.
2 Brussels Convention art 41; Lugano Convention art 41 (as to which see paras 618, 1040 ante); Civil Jurisdiction and Judgments Act 1982 s 6. In the United Kingdom, the appeal may be to the Court of Appeal or the House of Lords: see s 6 (amended by the Civil Jurisdiction and Judgments Act 1991 s 3, Sch 2 para 3).

C. MISCELLANEOUS PROVISIONS

1055. Periodic payments by way of penalty. A foreign judgment[1] which orders a periodic payment by way of a penalty is enforceable in the state in which enforcement is sought only if the amount of the payment has been finally determined by the courts of the state of origin[2].

1 For the meaning of 'judgment' for these purposes see para 1043 ante.
2 Brussels Convention art 43; Lugano Convention art 43. As to the Brussels and Lugano Conventions see paras 618, 1040 ante.

1056. Legal aid. An applicant who, in the state of origin, has benefited from complete or partial legal aid or exemption from costs or expenses, is entitled in relation to an application for enforcement of a foreign judgment[1] to benefit from the most favourable legal aid or the most extensive exemption from costs provided for by the law of the state addressed[2].

1   For the meaning of 'judgment' for these purposes see para 1043 ante.
2   Brussels Convention art 44, 1st para; Lugano Convention art 44, 1st para. As to the Brussels and Lugano Conventions see paras 618, 1040 ante. Article 44, 2nd para of the Conventions contains an exception relating to the enforcement of decisions given by an administrative authority in Denmark or Iceland in respect of a maintenance order. The Lord Chancellor has power, by regulations, to modify legal aid provisions so as to give effect to international agreements or to facilitate the enforcement of judgments under such agreements: Legal Aid Act 1988 s 34(4). As to the availability of legal aid in proceedings in England and Wales see LEGAL AID.

1057. Security for enforcement. No security, bond or deposit, however described, may be required of a party who in one contracting state[1] applies for enforcement of a judgment[2] given in another contracting state on the ground that he is a foreign national or that he is not domiciled or resident in the state in which enforcement is sought[3].

1   For the meaning of 'contracting state' see para 618 note 3 ante.
2   For the meaning of 'judgment' for these purposes see para 1043 ante.
3   Brussels Convention art 45; Lugano Convention art 45. As to the Brussels and Lugano Conventions see paras 618, 1040 ante.

1058. Proof of admissibility of judgments and documents. For the purposes of the Brussels and Lugano Conventions[1], a document, duly authenticated[2], purporting to be a copy of a judgment[3] given by a court of a contracting state[4] other than the United Kingdom[5] must be deemed without further proof to be a true copy, unless the contrary is shown[6].

1   As to the Brussels and Lugano Conventions see paras 618, 1040 ante.
2   A document purporting to be a copy of a judgment given by any such court as is mentioned in the text is duly authenticated for this purpose if it purports to bear the seal of that court or to be certified by any person in his capacity as judge or officer of that court to be a true copy of a judgment given by that court: Civil Jurisdiction and Judgments Act 1982 s 11(2).
3   For the meaning of 'judgment' for these purposes see para 1043 ante.
4   For the meaning of 'contracting state' see para 618 note 3 ante.
5   For the meaning of 'United Kingdom' see para 604 ante.
6   Civil Jurisdiction and Judgments Act 1982 s 11(1)(a) (s 11(1) amended by the Civil Jurisdiction and Judgments Act 1991 s 3, Sch 2 para 6). See also para 1049 note 11 ante. Nothing in the Civil Jurisdiction and Judgments Act 1982 s 11 prejudices the admission in evidence of any document which is admissible apart from that section: s 11(3).

1059. Copies of and certificates as to United Kingdom judgments. Provision may be made by rules of court to enable any interested party wishing to secure under the Brussels or Lugano Convention[1] the recognition in another contracting state[2] of a judgment[3] given by a court in the United Kingdom[4] to obtain a copy of the judgment and a certificate giving particulars relating to the judgment and the proceedings in which it was given[5].

1   As to the Brussels and Lugano Conventions see paras 618, 1040 ante.
2   For the meaning of 'contracting state' see para 618 note 3 ante.
3   For the meaning of 'judgment' for these purposes see para 1043 ante.

4 For the meaning of 'United Kingdom' see para 604 ante.
5 Civil Jurisdiction and Judgments Act 1982 s 12. See RSC Ord 71 r 36; CCR Ord 35 r 3; and the Magistrates' Courts (Civil Jurisdiction and Judgments Act 1982) Rules 1986, SI 1986/1962, r 12.

(4) ENFORCEMENT OF UNITED KINGDOM JUDGMENTS

1060. Enforcement of United Kingdom judgments by registration: money and non-money provisions. The rules and procedure governing the recognition in England of both money and non-money provisions in other United Kingdom judgments have been simplified, and are now contained in statute[1].

Subject to certain exceptions[2], an interested party who wishes to secure the enforcement in another part of the United Kingdom[3] of any money provisions[4] or non-money provisions[5] contained in a judgment[6] may apply for a certificate (in the case of money provisions)[7] or a certified copy of the relevant judgment (in the case of non-money provisions)[8] to the proper officer of the original court[9]. The original court is (1) in relation to any judgment or order (however named) given or made by a court of law in the United Kingdom, the court by which the judgment or order was given or made[10]; (2) in relation to a judgment or order not included in head (1) above which has been entered in England and Wales or Northern Ireland in the High Court or a county court, the court in which the judgment or order is entered[11]; (3) in relation to any award or order made by a tribunal in any part of the United Kingdom which is enforceable in that part without an order of a court of law, the tribunal by which the award or order was made[12]; (4) in relation to an arbitration award which has become enforceable in the part of the United Kingdom in which it was given in the same manner as a judgment given by a court of law in that part, the court which gave the judgment or made the order by virtue of which that award has thereby become enforceable[13].

With the exception of an order relating to fines for contempt of court and forfeiture of recognisances which is enforceable in the same manner as a judgment of the High Court in England and Wales[14], the enforcement provisions described above do not apply to: (a) a judgment given in proceedings in a magistrates' court in England and Wales or Northern Ireland[15]; or (b) a judgment given in proceedings other than civil proceedings[16]; or (c) certain judgments given in exercise of jurisdiction in relation to insolvency law[17]; or (d) a judgment given in proceedings relating to the obtaining of title to administer the estate of a deceased person[18]. Nor do they apply as respects (e) the enforcement in Scotland of orders made by the High Court or a county court in England and Wales under or for the purposes of Part VI of the Criminal Justice Act 1988[19] or the Drug Trafficking Act 1994[20]; or (f) as respects the enforcement in England and Wales of orders made by the Court of Session under or for the purposes of the Criminal Justice (Scotland) Act 1987[21].

The enforcement provisions described above do not apply to as much of any judgment[22] as (i) is an order[23] for whose enforcement in another part of the United Kingdom provision is made under Part II of the Maintenance Orders Act 1950[24]; or (ii) concerns the status or legal capacity of an individual[25]; or (iii) relates to the management of the affairs of a person not capable of managing his own affairs[26]; or (iv) is a provisional (including protective) measure other than an order for the making of an interim payment[27]. Nor do they apply to a judgment of a court outside the United Kingdom which falls to be treated for the purposes of its enforcement as a judgment of a court of law in the United Kingdom by virtue of its registration under certain specified statutory provisions[28].

No judgment to which these provisions apply and which does not fall within one of the exceptions described above, other than an arbitration award which has become enforceable in the part of the United Kingdom in which it was given in the same manner as a judgment given by a court of law in that part[29], may be enforced in another part of the United Kingdom except by registration under the Civil Jurisdiction and Judgments Act 1982[30].

1 See the Civil Jurisdiction and Judgments Act 1982 ss 18 (as amended), 19. It is not possible to enforce a judgment to which the statutory scheme applies by any other method: s 18(8): see text and note 30 infra. As to arbitration awards see para 1064 text and note 8 post.
2 See ibid s 18(3) (as amended), (4A) (as substituted), (5), (6) (as amended), (7).
3 For the meaning of 'United Kingdom' see para 604 ante.
4 'Money provision' means a provision for the payment of one or more sums of money: Civil Jurisdiction and Judgments Act 1982 s 18(1)(a), Sch 6 para 1.
5 'Non-money provision' means a provision for any relief or remedy not requiring payment of a sum of money: ibid s 18(1)(b), Sch 7 para 1.
6 For these purposes 'judgment' means any judgment to which ibid s 18 applies (see text and notes 10–13 infra), and references to the giving of a judgment must be construed accordingly: Sch 6 para 1; Sch 7 para 1; and see text and note 28 infra.
7 Ibid Sch 6 para 2(1).
8 Ibid Sch 7 para 2(1).
9 Ibid Sch 6 para 2(2); Sch 7 para 2(2).
10 Ibid s 18(2)(a); Sch 6 para 2(2)(a); Sch 7 para 2(2)(a).
11 Ibid s 18(2)(b); Sch 6 para 2(2)(b); Sch 7 para 2(2)(b).
12 Ibid s 18(2)(d); Sch 6 para 2(2)(d); Sch 7 para 2(2)(d).
13 Ibid s 18(2)(e); Sch 6 para 2(2)(e); Sch 7 para 2(2)(e).
14 Ie by virtue of the Contempt of Court Act 1981 s 16 (as amended) or the Supreme Court Act 1981 s 140: Civil Jurisdiction and Judgments Act 1982 s 18(4)(b).
15 Ibid s 18(3)(a).
16 Ibid s 18(3)(b).
17 Ie within the meaning of the Insolvency Act 1986 s 426: Civil Jurisdiction and Judgments Act s 18(3)(ba) (added by the Insolvency Act 1985 s 235(1), Sch 8; amended by the Insolvency Act 1986 s 439(2), Sch 14).
18 Civil Jurisdiction and Judgments Act 1982 s 18(3) (amended by the Insolvency Act 1985 s 235(3), Sch 10 Pt IV).
19 Ie the Criminal Justice Act 1988 Pt VI (ss 71–103) (as amended): Civil Jurisdiction and Judgments Act 1982 s 18(4A)(a) (s 18(4A) added by the Drug Trafficking Offences Act 1986 s 39(4); substituted by the Drug Trafficking Act 1994 s 65(1), Sch 1 para 6).
20 Civil Jurisdiction and Judgments Act 1982 s 18(4A)(a) (as added and substituted: see note 19 supra).
21 Ibid s 18(4A)(b) (as added and amended: see note 19 supra).
22 Except where otherwise stated references to a judgment to which ibid s 18 applies are to such a judgment exclusive of such provisions: s 18(5).
23 Ie an order to which the Maintenance Orders Act 1950 s 16 (as amended) applies: Civil Jurisdiction and Judgments Act 1982 s 18(5)(a).
24 Ie the Maintenance Orders Act 1950 Pt III (ss 16–25) (as amended): Civil Jurisdiction and Judgments Act 1982 s 18(5)(a).
25 Ibid s 18(5)(b). A decree of judicial separation or of separation and any order which is a Part I order for the purposes of the Family Law Act 1986 are within this provision, though without prejudice to its generality: Civil Jurisdiction and Judgments Act 1982 s 18(6)(a), (b) (substituted by the Courts and Legal Services Act 1990 s 116, Sch 16 para 41).
26 Civil Jurisdiction and Judgments Act 1982 s 18(5)(c).
27 Ibid s 18(5)(d).
28 Ie the Administration of Justice Act 1920 Pt II (ss 9–14) (as amended) (see paras 1023–1027 ante); the Foreign Judgments (Reciprocal Enforcement) Act 1933 Pt I (ss 1–7) (as amended) (see paras 1028–1039 ante); the Maintenance Orders (Reciprocal Enforcement) Act 1972 Pt II (ss 1–24) (as amended) (see paras 818–830 ante); and the Civil Jurisdiction and Judgments Act 1982 ss 4, 5 (both as amended) (see paras 843, 1049 ante): s 18(7).
29 Ie an award of the kind described in ibid s 18(2)(e); see the text to note 13 supra.
30 Ie under ibid Sch 6 or Sch 7: s 18(8).

1061. Registration of certificates: money provisions. Provided that (1) either the time for bringing an appeal against a judgment[1] has expired and no such appeal has been brought within that time[2] or, such an appeal having been brought within that time, it has been finally disposed of[3]; and (2) enforcement of the judgment is not for the time being stayed or suspended[4], and the time available for its enforcement has not expired[5], the proper officer[6] must issue to the applicant, on a relevant application[7], a certificate in the prescribed[8] form which (a) states the sum or aggregate of the sums (including any costs or expenses)[9] payable under the money provisions[10] contained in the judgment, the rate of interest[11], if any, payable thereon and the date or time from which any such interest began to accrue[12]; and (b) states that the conditions set out in heads (1) and (2) above are satisfied in relation to the judgment[13]; and contains such other particulars as may be prescribed[14]. More than one certificate may be issued under these provisions (simultaneously or at different times) in respect of the same judgment[15].

Where a certificate has been issued under the provisions described above in any part of the United Kingdom[16], any interested party may, within six months from the date of its issue, apply in the prescribed manner to the proper officer of the superior court[17] in any other part of the United Kingdom for the certificate to be registered in that court[18], and that officer must register the certificate in that court in the prescribed manner[19]. Subject to the provisions described below, and to any provision made by rules of court as to the manner in which and the conditions subject to which a certificate registered under these provisions may be enforced[20], a certificate registered under these provisions is, for the purposes of its enforcement, of the same force and effect, and the registering court has in relation to its enforcement the same powers, and proceedings for or with respect to its enforcement may be taken, as if the certificate had been a judgment originally given in the registering court and had (where relevant) been entered[21].

Where a certificate is registered under these provisions, the reasonable costs or expenses of and incidental to the obtaining of the certificate and its registration are recoverable as if they were costs or expenses stated in the certificate to be payable under a money provision contained in the original judgment[22]. These sums carry interest as if they were the subject of an order for costs or expenses made by the registering court on the date of registration of the certificate[23].

Subject to certain provisions[24], the debt resulting from the registration of the certificate, apart from the reasonable costs or expenses mentioned above, carries interest at the rate, if any, stated in the certificate from the date or time so stated[25]. Rules of court may provide as to the manner in which, and the periods by reference to which, any interest so payable is to be calculated and paid, including provision for such interest to cease to accrue as from a prescribed date[26]. Except as provided above, sums payable by virtue of the registration of a certificate do not carry interest[27].

1 As to the meaning of 'judgment' see para 1060 note 6 ante.
2 Civil Jurisdiction and Judgments Act 1982 s 18(1)(a), Sch 6 para 3(a)(i).
3 Ibid Sch 6 para 3(a)(ii).
4 As to stays and suspension of enforcement see para 1063 post.
5 Civil Jurisdiction and Judgments Act 1982 Sch 6 para 3(b).
6 Ie the proper officer of the original court: see para 1060 ante.
7 Ie an application under the Civil Jurisdiction and Judgments Act 1982 Sch 6 para 2: see para 1060 text and notes 9–13 ante.
8 'Prescribed' means prescribed by rules of court: ibid Sch 6 para 1. For the relevant rules of court see RSC Ord 71 rr 25, 37, 39; and CCR Ord 35 rr 4–5.
9 As to these see text and notes 21–22 infra.

10 For the meaning of 'money provisions' see para 1060 note 4 ante.
11 As to interest see text and notes 23–27 infra.
12 Civil Jurisdiction and Judgments Act 1982 Sch 6 para 4(1)(a).
13 Ibid Sch 6 para 4(1)(b).
14 Ibid Sch 6 para 4(1); and see note 7 supra.
15 Ibid Sch 6 para 4(2).
16 For the meaning of 'United Kingdom' see para 604 ante.
17 'Superior court' means, in relation to England and Wales or Northern Ireland, the High Court and, in
    relation to Scotland, the Court of Session: Civil Jurisdiction and Judgments Act 1982 Sch 6 para 5(2);
    Sch 7 para 5(2).
18 Ibid Sch 6 para 5(1).
19 Ibid Sch 6 para 5(3).
20 Ibid Sch 6 para 6(2).
21 Ibid Sch 6 para 6(1).
22 Ibid Sch 6 para 7.
23 Ibid Sch 6 para 8(3).
24 Ie the provisions in ibid Sch 6 para 8(2): see text and note 26 infra.
25 Ibid Sch 6 para 8(1).
26 Ibid Sch 6 para 8(2); and see note 8 supra.
27 Ibid Sch 6 para 8(4).

1062. Registration of certified copy of judgment containing non-money provisions. Provided that (1) either the time for bringing an appeal against a judgment[1] containing non-money provisions[2] has expired and no such appeal has been brought within that time[3] or, such an appeal having been brought within that time, it has been finally disposed of[4]; and (2) enforcement of the judgment is not for the time being stayed or suspended[5], and the time available for its enforcement has not expired[6], the proper officer must issue to the applicant, on a relevant application[7], a certified copy of the judgment (including any money provisions or excepted provisions[8] which it may contain)[9] and a certificate stating that the conditions in heads (1) and (2) above are satisfied in relation to the judgment[10]. More than one certified copy of the same judgment, and more than one certificate in respect of the same judgment, may be issued (simultaneously or at different times) under these provisions[11].

Where a certified copy of a judgment has been issued under the above provisions in any part of the United Kingdom[12], any interested party may apply in the manner prescribed by rules of court to the superior court[13] in any other part of the United Kingdom for the judgment to be registered in that court[14]. An application under these provisions for the registration of a judgment must be accompanied by (a) a certified copy of the judgment issued under these provisions[15]; and (b) the certificate issued in respect of the judgment by the proper officer of the original court[16] not more than six months before the date of the application[17]. A judgment must not be registered under these provisions by the superior court in any part of the United Kingdom if compliance with the non-money provisions contained in it would involve a breach of the law of that part of the United Kingdom[18]. Except when to do so would involve such a breach, where an application under these provisions is duly made to a superior court, the court must order the whole of the judgment, as set out in the certified copy, to be registered in that court in the prescribed manner[19].

Subject to provisions described below, and to any provision made by rules of court as to the manner in which and the conditions subject to which the non-money provisions contained in a judgment registered under these provisions may be enforced[20], the non-money provisions contained in a judgment registered under these provisions are, for the purposes of its enforcement, of the same force and effect, and the registering court has in relation to its enforcement the same powers, and proceedings for or with respect to its enforcement may be taken, as if the judgment containing them had been originally given in the registering court and had (where relevant) been entered[21].

Where a judgment is registered under these provisions, the reasonable costs or expenses of and incidental to (i) the obtaining of the certified copy of the judgment, together with the certificate from the proper officer of the original court stating that certain conditions concerning appeals and the staying or suspension of enforcement have been satisfied[22]; and (ii) the registration of the judgment[23], are recoverable as if on the date of registration there had also been registered in the original court a certificate[24] in respect of the judgment and as if those costs or expenses were costs or expenses stated in that certificate to be payable under a money provision contained in the judgment[25]. All such reasonable costs and expenses carry interest as if they were the subject of an order for costs or expenses made by the registering court on the date of registration of the judgment[26].

1 For the meaning of 'judgment' see para 1060 note 5 ante.
2 For the meaning of 'non-money provision' see para 1060 note 5 ante.
3 Civil Jurisdiction and Judgments Act 1982 s 18(1)(b), Sch 7 para 3(a)(i).
4 Ibid Sch 7 para 3(a)(ii).
5 As to stays and suspension of enforcement see para 1063 post.
6 Civil Jurisdiction and Judgments Act 1982 Sch 7 para 3(b).
7 Ie an application under ibid Sch 7 para 2 (a)–(e), (as to which see para 1060 text and notes 9–12 ante): Sch 7 para 4(1).
8 'Excepted provision' means any provision of a judgment which is excepted from the application of ibid s 18 by s 18(5) (see para 1060 text and notes 22–27 ante): Sch 7 para 4(2).
9 Ibid Sch 7 para 4(1)(a).
10 Ibid Sch 7 para 4(1)(b).
11 Ibid Sch 7 para 4(3).
12 For the meaning of 'United Kingdom' see para 604 ante.
13 For the meaning of 'superior court' see para 1061 note 17 ante.
14 Civil Jurisdiction and Judgments Act 1982 Sch 7 para 5(1). See RSC Ord 71 r 38; and CCR Ord 35 r 6.
15 Civil Jurisdiction and Judgments Act 1982 Sch 7 para 5(3)(a).
16 Ie the certificate stating that the conditions concerning appeals and the staying or suspension of enforcement are satisfied in relation to the judgment: see text and notes 2–4 supra.
17 Civil Jurisdiction and Judgments Act 1982 Sch 7 para 5(3)(b).
18 Ibid Sch 7 para 5(5).
19 Ibid Sch 7 para 5(4).
20 Ibid Sch 7 para 6(2).
21 Ibid Sch 7 para 6(1).
22 As to these conditions see note 8 supra.
23 Civil Jurisdiction and Judgments Act 1982 Sch 7 para 7(1)(a)–(b).
24 Ie a certificate under ibid Sch 6: see para 1061 ante.
25 Ibid Sch 7 para 7(1).
26 Ibid Sch 7 para 7(2).

1063. Staying of enforcement and setting aside of registration: money and non-money provisions. Where a certificate[1] in respect of a judgment[2] (in the case of money provisions)[3], or a judgment (in the case of non-money provisions)[4], has been registered[5], the registering court may, if it is satisfied that any person against whom it is sought to enforce the certificate or judgment is entitled and intends to apply under the law of that part of the United Kingdom[6] in which the judgment was given for any remedy which would result in the setting aside of the judgment, stay[7] proceedings for the enforcement of the judgment, on such terms as it thinks fit, for such period as appears to the court to be reasonably sufficient to enable the application to be disposed of[8].

Where the certificate or judgment has been registered, the registering court (1) must set aside the registration if, on an application made by any interested party, it is satisfied that the registration was contrary to the relevant statutory provisions⁹; and (2) may set aside the registration if, on an application made by any interested party, it is satisfied that the matter in dispute in the proceedings in which the judgment in question was given had previously been the subject of a judgment by another court or tribunal having jurisdiction in the matter¹⁰.

1 As to certificates in respect of money provisions in a judgment see the Civil Jurisdiction and Judgments Act 1982 s 18(1)(a), Sch 6; and para 1061 ante.
2 For the meaning of 'judgment' see para 1060 note 6 ante.
3 See the Civil Jurisdiction and Judgments Act 1982 Sch 6; and para 1061 ante.
4 See ibid s 18(1)(b), Sch 7; and para 1062 ante.
5 Ie registered in the superior court in a part of the United Kingdom other than that in which it was obtained: see ibid Sch 6 para 5, Sch 7 para 5; and see paras 1061–1062 ante. For the meaning of 'superior court' see para 1061 note 17 ante.
6 For the meaning of 'United Kingdom' see para 604 ante.
7 Or, in Scotland, sist: Civil Jurisdiction and Judgments Act 1982 Sch 6 para 9; Sch 7 para 8.
8 Ibid Sch 6 para 9; Sch 7 para 8.
9 Ie ibid Sch 6 or, as appropriate, Sch 7.
10 Ibid Sch 6 para 10; Sch 7 para 9.

1064. Recognition of United Kingdom judgments. Subject to certain¹ exceptions, no judgment² to which Part II of the Civil Jurisdiction and Judgments Act³ applies may be refused recognition in another part of the United Kingdom⁴ solely on the ground that, in relation to that judgment, the court which gave it was not a court of competent jurisdiction according to the rules of private international law in force in that other part⁵.

This provision does not, however, apply⁶ to (1) any award or order made by a tribunal in any part of the United Kingdom which is enforceable in that part without an order of a court of law⁷; or (2) an arbitration award which has become enforceable in the part of the United Kingdom in which it was given in the same manner as a judgment given by a court of law in that part⁸; or (3) an order which is enforceable in the same manner as a judgment of the High Court of England and Wales by virtue of certain statutory provisions⁹.

1 As to which see the text and notes 6–9 infra.
2 For the meaning of 'judgment' see para 1060 note 6 ante.
3 Ie the Civil Jurisdiction and Judgments Act 1982 Pt II (ss 16–19) (as amended).
4 For the meaning of 'United Kingdom' see para 604 ante.
5 Civil Jurisdiction and Judgments Act 1982 s 19(1).
6 Ibid s 19(2)(1).
7 Ie an award within the definition in ibid s 18(2)(d): s 19(3)(b).
8 Ie an award within the definition in ibid s 18(2)(e): s 19(3)(b).
9 Ie an order enforceable by virtue of the Contempt of Court Act 1981 s 16 (as amended) or the Supreme Court Act 1981 s 140 (relating to fines for contempt of court and forfeiture of recognisances): Civil Jurisdiction and Judgments Act 1982 ss 18(4), 19(3).

(5) ENFORCEMENT OF COMMUNITY JUDGMENTS

1065. Enforcement of European Community judgments. The High Court¹ must, upon application² duly made for the purpose by the person entitled to enforce it, forthwith register³ (1) any community judgment⁴ to which the Secretary of State⁵ has appended an order for enforcement[6]; or (2) any Euratom inspection order[7]. Rules of court require notice to be given of the registration of a Community judgment or Euratom inspection order to the persons against whom the judgment was given or the order was made[8]. Where it appears that a Community judgment under which a sum of money is payable has been partly satisfied at the date of the application for its registration, the judgment must be registered only in respect of the balance remaining payable at that date[9]. Where, after the date of registration of a Community judgment under which a sum of money is payable, it is shown that at that date the judgment had been partly or wholly satisfied, the registration must be varied or cancelled accordingly with effect from that date[10].

A Community judgment registered in accordance with the provisions described above has, for all purposes of execution, the same force and effect, and proceedings may be taken on the judgment, and any sum payable under the judgment carries interest, as if the judgment had been a judgment or order given or made by the High Court on the date of registration[11]. An order of the European Court that enforcement of a registered Community judgment be suspended must, on production to the High Court, be registered forthwith and is of the same effect as if the order had been an order made by the High Court on the date of its registration staying[12] the execution of the judgment for the same period and on the same conditions as are stated in the order of the European Court; and no steps to enforce the judgment may thereafter be taken while such an order remains in force[13].

Upon registration of a Euratom inspection order in accordance with the provisions described above, the High Court may make such order as it thinks fit against any person for the purpose of ensuring that effect is given to the Euratom inspection order[14].

1 The 'High Court' means in England and Wales and in Northern Ireland the High Court and in Scotland the Court of Session: European Communities (Enforcement of Community Judgments) Order 1972, SI 1972/1590, art 2(1). The functions assigned to the High Court under that Order may be exercised by a judge in chambers or a master of the Queen's Bench Division: RSC Ord 71 r 16.

2 Such an application is made ex parte: RSC Ord 71 r 17. It must be supported by an affidavit exhibiting (1) the Community judgment (see note 4 infra) and the order for its enforcement (see note 6 infra), or, as the case may be, the Euratom inspection order (see note 7 infra), or in either case a duly authenticated copy thereof; and (2) where the Community judgment or Euratom inspection order is not in English, a translation into English certified by a notary public or authenticated by affidavit: RSC Ord 71 r 18(1). Where the application is for registration of a Community judgment under which a sum of money is payable, the affidavit must also state, so far as is known, the name, occupation and last known place of abode of the judgment debtor, and that, to the best of the deponent's knowledge and belief, the European Court has not suspended enforcement of the judgment (see text and notes 12–13 infra) and the judgment is unsatisfied (or, if appropriate, the amount to which it remains unsatisfied): RSC Ord 71 r 18(2). For the meaning of 'European Court' see para 620 note 4 ante.

3 There must be kept in the Central Office a register of Community judgments and Euratom inspection orders, including particulars of any execution issued on a judgment so registered: RSC Ord 71 r 19.

4 'Community judgment' means any decision, judgment or order which is enforceable under or in accordance with the EC Treaty art 187 or 192, the Euratom Treaty art 18, 159 or 164 or the ECSC Treaty art 44 or 92: European Communities (Enforcement of Community Judgments) Order 1972 art 2(1).

5 'Secretary of State' means one of Her Majesty's Principal Secretaries of State: Interpretation Act 1978 s 5, Sch 1.

6 An 'order for enforcement' means an order by or under the authority of the Secretary of State that the Community judgment to which it is appended is to be registered for enforcement in the United Kingdom: European Communities (Enforcement of Community Judgments) Order 1972 art 2(1).

7 Ibid art 3(1). A 'Euratom inspection order' means an order made by or in the exercise of the functions of the President of the European Court or by the Commission of the European Communities under the Euratom Treaty art 81: European Communities (Enforcement of Community Judgments) Order 1972 art 2(1).

8 Ibid art 3(3). As to notice of registration see RSC Ord 71 r 20. Execution may not issue without the leave of the court on a Community judgment under which a sum of money is payable until 28 days after notice of registration or, as the case may be, until any application made within that period for variation or cancellation of the registration has been determined: RSC Ord 71 r 21.
9 European Communities (Enforcement of Community Judgments) Order 1972 art 3(4).
10 Ibid art 3(5). An application for variation or cancellation of registration on this ground must be made by summons supported by affidavit: RSC Ord 71 r 22.
11 European Communities (Enforcement of Community Judgments) Order 1972 art 4.
12 Or, in Scotland, sisting: ibid art 5.
13 Ibid art 5. An application for registration in the High Court of an order of the European Court suspending enforcement of a registered Community judgment may be made ex parte by lodging a copy of the order in the Central Office: RSC Ord 71 r 23.
14 European Communities (Enforcement of Community Judgments) Order 1972 art 6. In case of urgency, an application for ensuring that effect is given to a Euratom inspection order may be made ex parte on affidavit, but otherwise must be made by motion or summons: RSC Ord 71 r 24.

11. PROCEDURE

(1) SUBSTANCE AND PROCEDURE

1066. Lex fori governs procedure. Whereas matters of substantive law are governed by the lex causae, namely the law applicable under the English rules for the choice of law, all matters of procedure are governed by the lex fori, namely the law of the country in which the action is brought[1]. It is not always easy to classify rules of law into those which are substantive and those which are procedural, but, generally speaking, it may be said that substantive rules give or define the right which it is sought to enforce and procedural rules govern the mode of proceeding or machinery by which the right is enforced[2]. Whether an issue is a procedural or substantive one is one of authority rather than principle. The following paragraphs deal with matters raising questions of procedure.

1 *Melan v Duke de Fitzjames* (1797) 1 Bos & P 138 at 142; *British Linen Co v Drummond* (1830) 10 B & C 903; *De la Vega v Vianna* (1830) 1 B & Ad 284; *Trimbey v Vignier* (1834) 1 Bing NC 151 at 159; *Huber v Steiner* (1835) 2 Bing NC 202; *Don v Lippmann* (1837) 5 Cl & Fin 1 at 13, HL; *General Steam Navigation Co v Guillou* (1843) 11 M & W 877 at 895; *Leroux v Brown* (1852) 12 CB 801; *Chaplin v Boys* [1971] AC 356 at 378–379, 381–383, 392–395, [1969] 2 All ER 1085 at 1092–1093, 1095–1096, 1104–1106, HL; cf *James Miller & Partners Ltd v Whitworth Street Estates (Manchester) Ltd* [1970] AC 583 at 606–607, 616, [1970] 1 All ER 796 at 801, 809–810, HL (law governing arbitration procedure). See also *Re Fuld's Estate (No 3), Hartley v Fuld* [1968] P 675 at 695, [1965] 3 All ER 776 at 779.
2 *Poyser v Minors* (1881) 7 QBD 329 at 333, CA; and see *Re Shoesmith* [1938] 2 KB 637, [1938] 3 All ER 186, CA.

1067. Service of process. Matters relating to the service of originating process are procedural and are determined by the lex fori[1].

1 *Dobson v Festi, Rasini & Co* [1891] 2 QB 92, CA. See generally PRACTICE AND PROCEDURE vol 37 para 145–195. As to the lex fori see para 1066 ante.

1068. Mode of trial and time for appealing. All matters relating to the mode of trial of an action, such as whether there is a right to trial by jury, are for the lex fori[1]. The period within which an appeal against judgment in an action may be entered is also governed by the lex fori[2].

1 *Don v Lippmann* (1837) 5 Cl & Fin 1 at 14–15, HL; *General Steam Navigation Co v Guillou* (1843) 11 M & W 877 at 895. As to the evidence admissible at the trial see paras 1070–1073 post. As to the lex fori see para 1066 ante.
2 *Lopez v Burslem* (1843) 4 Moo PCC 300.

1069. Parties. Rules determining whether a person is capable of suing or being sued, such as a rule relating to the question whether an action may be brought in the name of a dead man[1], or a rule relating to the question of whether an action may be brought by or against a dissolved corporation[2], or an international organisation[3], or a state[4], or an inanimate object[5], are procedural and are thus governed by the lex fori[6].

The question whether a party may sue or be sued in a representative capacity is sometimes a matter for the lex causae, and in other cases a matter for the lex fori. The lex causae will determine whether a trustee in bankruptcy[7], liquidator[8], receiver[9], administrator of enemy property[10], or curator of a mentally disordered person[11] may sue or be sued; and if under that law he may, the lex fori will acknowledge his title. But the lex fori alone governs in the cases of administrators of deceased persons, whose foreign appointment is ineffective in England and Wales[12], and curators of disappeared persons[13]; and in England and Wales such persons may neither sue nor be sued. English courts will not recognise a judicial administrator's right to sue in a person's absence[14].

Rules determining whether a party to a particular action before the court is the proper plaintiff or the proper defendant are sometimes procedural and sometimes substantive[15]. Thus, a rule relating to the question whether an assignee of a chose in action may bring an action in his own name is regarded as procedural where the rule is not intended to have extra-territorial effect[16], and as substantive in other cases[17]. Similarly, a rule which regards the defendant as being liable, but makes his liability dependent upon other persons being sued first, is procedural[18], whereas a rule which regards him as not being liable at all unless other persons are sued first is substantive[19]. Again, an action may be available in England and Wales against a defendant for breach of an obligation governed by a foreign law, which, by reason of the particular circumstances, although valid and subsisting, is not actionable at all by the foreign procedural law[20].

1 *Banque Internationale de Commerce de Petrograd v Goukassow* [1923] 2 KB 682 at 691, CA; revsd on the facts [1925] AC 150, HL.
2 *Banque Internationale de Commerce de Petrograd v Goukassow* [1923] 2 KB 682, CA; revsd on the facts [1925] AC 150, HL; *Lazard Bros & Co v Banque Industrielle de Moscou* [1932] 1 KB 617, CA; affd sub nom *Lazard Bros & Co v Midland Bank Ltd* [1933] AC 289, HL; *Russian and English Bank v Baring Bros & Co Ltd* [1932] 1 Ch 435, CA. Cf *Toprak Enerji Sanayi AS v Sale Tilney Technology plc* [1994] 3 All ER 483, [1994] 1 WLR 840 on the application of this rule where one company merges with another, and is then dissolved; not followed in *Industrie Chimiche Italia Centrale v Alexander Tsavrilis & Sons Maritime Co, The Choko Star* [1996] 1 All ER 114. As to the law governing the question of whether a corporation has been dissolved see para 986 ante.
3 *J H Rayner (Mincing Lane) Ltd v Department of Trade and Industry* [1990] 2 AC 418, sub nom *Maclaine Watson & Co Ltd v Department of Trade and Industry* [1989] 3 All ER 523, HL. But the lex fori may recognise legal personality arising under a foreign law and so permit the party to sue: *Arab Monetary Fund v Hashim (No 3)* [1991] 2 AC 114, [1991] 1 All ER 871, HL; *Westland Helicopters Ltd v Arab Organisation for Industrialisation* [1995] QB 282, [1995] 2 All ER 387 (proper law of the organisation was public international law established by governing treaty).
4 See generally the State Immunity Act 1978; and FOREIGN RELATIONS LAW.
5 But the lex fori may recognise legal personality arising under a foreign law: *Bumper Development Corpn v Metropolitan Police Comr* [1991] 4 All ER 638, [1991] 1 WLR 1362, CA (Hindu temple).
6 See para 1066 ante; and see generally PRACTICE AND PROCEDURE vol 37 paras 215–217. The lex fori may recognise legal personality arising under another law, and having done so, permit such a person to sue or be sued as such.

7 *Smith v Buchanan* (1800) 1 East 6 at 11; *Macaulay v Guaranty Trust of New York* (1927) 44 TLR 99; *Kamouh v Associated Electrical Industries International Ltd* [1980] QB 199 at 206, [1979] 2 WLR 795 at 800. See also para 982 ante.

8 *Bank of Ethiopia v National Bank of Egypt and Ligouri* [1937] Ch 513; *Kamouh v Associated Electrical Industries International Ltd* [1980] QB 199 at 206, [1979] 2 WLR 795 at 800. See also para 993 ante.

9 *Schemmer v Property Resources Ltd* [1975] Ch 273, [1974] 3 All ER 451; *Kamouh v Associated Electrical Industries International Ltd* [1980] QB 199 at 206, [1979] 2 WLR 795 at 800. Cf *Perry v Zissis* [1977] 1 Lloyd's Rep 607 at 615, CA.

10 *Lepage v São Paulo Copper Estates Ltd* [1917] WN 216.

11 *Didisheim v London and Westminster Bank Ltd* [1900] 2 Ch 15, CA; *Kamouh v Associated Electrical Industries International Ltd* [1980] QB 199 at 206, [1979] 2 WLR 795 at 800.

12 See *New York Breweries Co Ltd v A-G* [1899] AC 62; *Kamouh v Associated Electrical Industries International Ltd* [1980] QB 199 at 206, [1979] 2 WLR 795 at 800; and see para 952 ante.

13 *Kamouh v Associated Electrical Industries International Ltd* [1980] QB 199, [1979] 2 WLR 795.

14 *Kamouh v Associated Electrical Industries International Ltd* [1980] QB 199, [1979] 2 WLR 795.

15 See text and notes 16–20 infra. A person cannot enforce a right which has vested not in him but in someone else under the lex causae: *Ross v Bhagvat Sinhjee* (1891) 19 R 31, Ct of Sess; cf *Hartmann v Konig* (1933) 50 TLR 114, HL. Similarly a person cannot be liable if, by the lex causae, the liability falls not on him but on someone else: *General Steam Navigation Co v Guillou* (1843) 11 M & W 877; *Armagas Ltd v Mundogas SA* [1986] AC 717, [1985] 3 All ER 795, CA; affd on other grounds [1986] AC 717 at 773, [1986] 2 All ER 385, HL. Cf *The Mary Moxham* (1876) 1 PD 107, CA.

16 *Jeffery v M'Taggart* (1817) 6 M & s 126; *Barber v Mexican Land and Colonization Co Ltd* (1899) 16 TLR 127.

17 *Innes v Dunlop* (1800) 8 Term Rep 595; *O'Callaghan v Marchioness Thomond* (1810) 3 Taunt 82; cf *Trimbey v Vignier* (1834) 1 Bing NC 151. See, however, *Wolff v Oxholm* (1817) 6 M & s 92 at 99 (where English law was both the lex fori and the lex causae). The question whether a trustee in bankruptcy may sue in his own name is substantive: *Alivon v Furnival* (1834) 1 Cr M & R 277.

18 *General Steam Navigation Co v Guillou* (1843) 11 M & W 877; *Bullock v Caird* (1875) LR 10 QB 276; *Re Doetsch, Matheson v Ludwig* [1896] 2 Ch 836; *Johnson Mathey & Wallace Ltd v Alloush* (1984) 135 NLJ 1012, CA.

19 *General Steam Navigation Co v Guillou* (1843) 11 M & W 877; *The Mary Moxham* (1876) 1 PD 107, CA.

20 See *Hansen v Dixon* (1906) 96 LT 32 (action for breach of promise of marriage made in Denmark, the promise being valid in Denmark, but in the particular circumstances of the case not enforceable there); and as to statutes of limitation see para 1082 post.

1070. Evidence in general. Questions of evidence are, in general, matters of procedure for the lex fori[1]. Thus while the question of the facts to be proved in an action is substantive and is to be determined by the lex causae[2], the question of proof of those facts is determined by the lex fori[3]. A contract may be proved by any mode of proof recognised by the law of England and Wales or by any of the laws pursuant to which its formal validity may be established[4].

1 *Yates v Thomson* (1835) 3 Cl & Fin 544, HL; *Bain v Whitehaven and Furness Junction Rly Co* (1850) 3 HL Cas 1; see *Mahadervan v Mahadervan* [1964] P 233 at 243, [1962] 3 All ER 1108 at 1115, DC; *Dubai Bank v Galadari (No 5)* (1990) Times, 26 June; and see paras 774–775. As to the lex fori see para 1066 ante.

2 *The Gaetano and Maria* (1882) 7 PD 137 especially at 149, CA. As to the lex causae see para 1066 ante.

3 See paras 1071–1075 post. As to proof of foreign marriages, proof of foreign judgments, proof of foreign documents, and the taking of evidence for foreign courts, see generally EVIDENCE. As to proof of foreign law see paras 1093–1094 post.

4 See the Rome Convention arts 9, 14 para 2; and paras 845 text and note 14, 852 ante. For the meaning of 'the Rome Convention' see para 844 text and note 1 ante.

1071. Admissibility of evidence. Questions relating to the admissibility of evidence are governed by the lex fori[1]. Thus a document which is inadmissible by the lex causae[2] for want of a stamp may nevertheless be admissible in England[3], provided that, by the lex causae, the absence of the stamp does not render the document wholly null and void[4]; and a document which is admissible by the lex causae may nevertheless be inadmissible in England[5].

The admissibility of extrinsic evidence adduced to interpret a document is a question of construction for the lex causae[6]; but the admissibility of extrinsic evidence to add to, vary or contradict its terms is, it seems, a question of evidence, governed by the lex fori[7].

1 *Yates v Thomson* (1835) 3 Cl & Fin 544, HL; *Bain v Whitehaven and Furness Junction Rly Co* (1850) 3 HL Cas 1. As to the lex fori see para 1066 ante.
2 As to the lex causae see para 1066 ante.
3 *Bristow v Sequeville* (1850) 5 Exch 275; see also *James v Catherwood* (1823) 3 Dow & Ry KB 190; *Wynne v Jackson* (1826) 2 Russ 351.
4 *Alves v Hodgson* (1797) 7 Term Rep 241; *Clegg v Levy* (1812) 3 Camp 166; *Bristow v Sequeville* (1850) 5 Exch 275 at 279; but see *James v Catherwood* (1823) 3 Dow & Ry KB 190.
5 *Appleton v Lord Braybrook* (1817) 6 M & s 34; *Brown v Thornton* (1837) 6 Ad & El 185; *Finlay v Finlay and Rudall* (1862) 31 LJPM & A 149; cf *Abbott v Abbott and Godoy* (1860) 4 Sw & Tr 254.
6 *St Pierre v South American Stores (Gath and Chaves) Ltd* [1937] 1 All ER 206 at 209–210; affd [1937] 3 All ER 349, CA. In the case of a contract the lex causae will be the law identified by the Rome Convention: see art 10 para 1; and para 850 ante. For the meaning of 'the Rome Convention' see para 844 text and note 1 ante.
7 *Korner v Witkowitzer* [1950] 2 KB 128 at 162–163, [1950] 1 All ER 558 at 576, CA; on appeal sub nom *Vitkovice Horni a Hutni Tezirstvo v Korner* [1951] AC 869, [1951] 2 All ER 334, HL. Cf the Rome Convention art 14 para 2; and para 845 text and note 14 ante.

1072. Requirement of written evidence. The rule of English law that no action can be brought on a contract of guarantee unless the agreement or some note or memorandum of it is in writing[1] is a rule of procedure, and it may render a contract unenforceable in England even if it is valid by its proper law[2]; but if it may be proved under the foreign law which governs its formal validity without the need for writing, the lack of writing will be irrelevant[3].

1 See the Statute of Frauds (1677) s 4 (amended by the Law Reform (Enforcement of Contracts) Act 1954 s 1): see CONTRACT vol 9 para 218. The analogous rule concerning contracts for the disposition of an interest in land (Law of Property Act 1925 s 40(1)) has been replaced by the Law of Property (Miscellaneous Provisions) Act 1989 s 2, by virtue of which a contract for the sale or other disposition of an interest in land can only be made in writing and only by incorporating all the terms of the agreement in one document or, where the contracts are exchanged, in each document. See also SALE OF LAND vol 42 para 27.
2 *Leroux v Brown* (1852) 12 CB 801; cf *Acebal v Levy* (1834) 10 Bing 376. *Leroux v Brown* supra, has been approved in *Jones v Victoria Graving Dock Co* (1877) 2 QBD 314 at 323, CA; *Britain v Rossiter* (1879) 11 QBD 123 at 128, CA; *Maddison v Alderson* (1883) 8 App Cas 467 at 474, 488, HL; *Rochefoucauld v Boustead* [1897] 1 Ch 196 at 207, CA; *Morris v Baron & Co* [1918] AC 1 at 15–16, HL; cf *G & H Montage GmbH v Irvani* [1990] 2 All ER 225, [1990] 1 WLR 667, CA. But it was doubted in *Williams v Wheeler* (1860) 8 CBNS 299 at 316; *Gibson v Holland* (1865) LR 1 CP 1 at 8; *Rawley v Rawley* (1876) 1 QBD 460 at 461, CA. See also *Re De Nicols, De Nicols v Curlier* [1900] 2 Ch 410; and para 772 note 3 ante.
3 See the Rome Convention arts 9, 14 para 2; and paras 845 text and note 14, 852 ante. For the meaning of 'the Rome Convention' see para 844 text and note 1 ante.

1073. Witnesses. Questions such as whether a witness is competent[1] or whether he can claim privilege[2] are matters for the lex fori[3].

1 *Bain v Whitehaven and Furness Junction Rly Co* (1850) 3 HL Cas 1 at 19.
2 *United States of America v McRae* (1867) 3 Ch App 79.
3 As to the lex fori see para 1066 ante.

1074. Burden of proof. Questions relating to the burden of proof, including the standard of proof[1], are questions of evidence for the lex fori[2].

1 *Wiedemann v Walpole* [1891] 2 QB 534, CA (corroboration).
2 *The Roberta* (1937) 58 Ll L Rep 159 at 177; *Re Fuld's Estate (No 3), Hartley v Fuld* [1968] P 675 at 696–698, [1965] 3 All ER 776 at 780–781; and see EVIDENCE vol 17 para 13–19. As to the exception which applies in relation to contracts see the Rome Convention art 14(1); and para 845 note 14 ante. As to the lex fori see para 1066 ante.

1075. Presumptions. Irrebuttable presumptions of law, such as the English presumption of survivorship[1], are matters of substance for the lex causae[2]. It is uncertain whether rebuttable presumptions of law, such as the English presumption of marriage[3], are matters of substance, and so governed by the lex causae, or matters of procedure, and so governed by the lex fori[4]. Nor is it certain whether the operation of an estoppel is a matter of evidence for the lex fori or a matter governed by the lex causae[5].

1 See the Law of Property Act 1925 s 184; and see EXECUTORS vol 17 para 856.
2 *Re Cohn* [1945] Ch 5. As to the distinction between rebuttable and irrebuttable presumptions of law see EVIDENCE vol 17 paras 111–121. As to the lex causae see para 1066 ante.
3 *Piers v Piers* (1849) 2 HL Cas 331: *Re Shephard, George v Thyer* [1904] 1 Ch 456; and see HUSBAND AND WIFE vol 22 paras 992–993.
4 *Hill v Hibbit* (1870) 25 LT 183; *De Thoren v A-G* (1876) 1 App Cas 686, HL; *Re Shephard, George v Thyer* [1904] 1 Ch 456; *Mahadervan v Mahadervan* [1964] P 233 at 242–243, [1962] 3 All ER 1108 at 1115, DC; *Radwan v Radwan (No 2)* [1973] Fam 35 at 42–43, [1972] 3 All ER 1026 at 1030. As to the lex fori see para 1066 ante.
5 *Low v Bouverie* [1891] 3 Ch 82 at 105, CA; *Carl Zeiss Stiftung v Rayner & Keeler Ltd (No 2)* [1967] 1 AC 853 at 919, [1966] 2 All ER 536 at 554, HL; *Vervaeke (formerly Messina) v Smith* [1983] 1 AC 146 at 162, [1982] 2 All ER 145 at 156, HL; *Janred Properties Ltd v Ente Nazionale Italiano per il Turismo* [1989] 2 All ER 444, CA.

1076. Interlocutory procedural matters. Certain procedural matters, being of an interlocutory character, are governed by the lex fori[1]. For instance, the High Court may, by interlocutory order made either unconditionally or on such terms and conditions as the court thinks just[2], grant an injunction or appoint a receiver in all cases in which it appears to the court to be just and convenient to do so[3], and the power of the High Court under this provision to grant an interlocutory injunction restraining a party to any proceedings from removing from the jurisdiction of the High Court, or otherwise dealing with, assets located within that jurisdiction, is exercisable in cases where that party is, as well as in cases where he is not, domiciled, resident or present within that jurisdiction[4].

The High Court also has power to grant interim relief[5] where (1) proceedings have been or are to be commenced in a Brussels or Lugano Contracting State[6] other than the United Kingdom[7] or in a part of the United Kingdom other than that in which the High Court in question exercises jurisdiction[8]; and (2) they are or will be proceedings whose subject matter is within the scope of the Brussels Convention[9] whether or not that or any other Convention has effect in relation to the proceedings[10]. Nevertheless, on an application for any interim relief under this provision[11] the court may refuse to grant that relief if, in its opinion, the fact that the court has no jurisdiction apart from this provision in relation to the subject matter of the proceedings in question makes it inexpedient for the court to grant it[12]. Her Majesty may by Order in Council[13] extend the power to grant interim relief conferred by this provision so as to make it exercisable in relation to (a) proceedings commenced or to be commenced otherwise than in a Brussels or Lugano Contracting State[14]; and (b) proceedings whose subject matter is not within the scope of the Brussels Convention[15]; and (c) arbitration proceedings[16]. Such an Order in Council may (i) confer power to grant only specified descriptions of interim relief[17]; (ii) make different provision for different classes of proceedings, for proceedings pending in different countries or courts outside the United Kingdom or in different parts of the United Kingdom, and for other different circumstances[18]; and (iii) impose conditions or restrictions on the exercise of any power conferred by the Order[19].

Where, on the application of a defendant[20] to an action or other proceeding in the High Court, it appears to the court that one of certain conditions obtains[21], then if, having regard to all the circumstances of the case, the court thinks it is just to do so, it may order the plaintiff[22] to give such security for the defendant's costs of the action or other proceeding as it thinks just[23].

1 As to the lex fori see para 1066 ante.
2 Supreme Court Act 1981 s 37(2).
3 Ibid s 37(1).
4 Ibid s 37(3).
5 In this provision 'interim relief' means interim relief of any kind which the High Court has power to grant in proceedings relating to matters within its jurisdiction, other than (1) a warrant for the arrest of property; or (2) provision for obtaining evidence: Civil Jurisdiction and Judgments Act 1982 s 25(7). As to the granting of interim relief see *Nippon Yusen Kaisha v Karageorgis* [1975] 3 All ER 282, [1975] 1 WLR 1093, CA; *Mareva Compania Naviera SA v International Bulkcarriers SA* [1980]1 All ER 213n, [1975] 2 Lloyd's Rep 509, CA; *Babanaft International Co SA v Bassatne* [1990] Ch 13, [1989] 1 All ER 433, CA; *Republic of Haiti v Duvalier* [1990] 1 QB 202, [1989] 1 All ER 456; *Derby & Co Ltd v Weldon* [1990] Ch 48, [1989] 1 All ER 469, CA; *Derby & Co Ltd v Weldon (Nos 3 and 4)* [1990] Ch 65, [1989] 1 All ER 1002, CA.
6 For the meaning of 'Brussels contracting state' and 'Lugano contracting state' see para 618 notes 1–2 ante.
7 For the meaning of 'United Kingdom' see para 604 ante.
8 Civil Jurisdiction and Judgments Act 1982 s 25(1)(a) (s 25(1) amended by the Civil Jurisdiction and Judgments Act 1991 s 3, Sch 2 para 11).
9 Ie the Brussels Convention art 1: see para 626 ante. As to the Brussels Convention see para 618 text and note 1 ante.
10 Civil Jurisdiction and Judgments Act 1982 s 25(1)(b) (as amended: see note 8 supra).
11 Ie ibid s 25(1) (as amended: see note 8 infra).
12 Ibid s 25(2).
13 Any such Order in Council is subject to annulment in pursuance of a resolution of either House of Parliament: ibid s 25(6).
14 Ibid s 25(3)(a) (amended by the Civil Jurisdiction and Judgments Act 1991 Sch 2 para 11).
15 Civil Jurisdiction and Judgments Act 1982 s 25(3)(b).
16 Ibid s 25(3)(c). An Order in Council which confers power to grant interim relief in relation to arbitration proceedings may provide for the repeal of any provision of the Arbitration Act 1950 s 12(6) (see ARBITRATION vol 2 (Reissue) para 677) to the extent that it is superseded by the provisions of the Order: Civil Jurisdiction and Judgments Act 1982 s 25(5).
17 Ibid s 25(4)(a).
18 Ibid s 25(4)(b).
19 Ibid s 25(4)(c).
20 References in RSC Ord 23 r 1(1)–(2) to a plaintiff and a defendant are construed as references to the person (howsoever described on the record) who is in the position of plaintiff or defendant, as the case may be, in the proceeding in question, including a proceeding on the counterclaim: Ord 23 r 1(3).
21 Ie where it appears to the court that (1) that the plaintiff is ordinarily resident out of the jurisdiction; or (2) that the plaintiff (not being a plaintiff who is suing in a representative capacity) is a nominal plaintiff who is suing for the benefit of some other person and that there is reason to believe that he will be unable to pay the costs of the defendant if ordered to do so; or (3) subject to head (2) supra, that the plaintiff's address is not stated in the writ or other originating process or is incorrectly stated therein; or (4) that the plaintiff has changed his address during the course of the proceedings with a view to evading the consequences of the litigation: RSC Ord 23 r 1 (1)(a)–(d). The court will not require a plaintiff to give security by reason only of head (3) supra if he satisfies the court that the failure to state his address or the misstatement thereof was made innocently and without intention to deceive: Ord 23 r 1(2). The English court should not order security for costs under head (1) supra where the plaintiff is an individual

who is a national of and resident in another Brussels contracting state: *Fitzgerald v Williams, O'Regan v Williams* (1996) Times, 3 January, CA.

22 See note 20 supra.

23 RSC Ord 23 r 1. See also Case C-398/92 *Firma Mund & Fester v Firma Hatrex International Transport* [1994] ECR I-467, ECJ; *Fitzgerald v Williams, O'Regan v Williams* (1996) Times, 3 January, CA; and PRACTICE AND PROCEDURE vol 37 paras 298–309.

1077. Nature of remedy. All matters relating to the nature of the plaintiff's remedy, such as whether the plaintiff is entitled to an injunction or to an order for specific performance or for an account of profits, are for the lex fori[1]. A plaintiff bringing an action in England to enforce a foreign right will not be defeated merely because English remedies are greater or less than, or otherwise different from, those in the foreign country[2]; but his action will fail if the machinery by way of remedies in England is so different from that in the foreign country as to make the right sought to be enforced an essentially different right[3]. In relation to a contract to which the Rome Convention applies[4], the consequences of breach (which will include the remedies available) are governed by the law which governs the contract[5].

1　*Liverpool Marine Credit Co v Hunter* (1868) 3 Ch App 479 at 486; *Baschet v London Illustrated Standard Co* [1900] 1 Ch 73; *Chaplin v Boys* [1971] AC 356 at 394, [1969] 2 All ER 1085 at 1106, HL. As to injunctions see INJUNCTIONS vol 24 paras 415–540. As to specific performance see SPECIFIC PER-FORMANCE. As to the lex fori see para 1066 ante.

2　*Phrantzes v Argenti* [1960] 2 QB 19 at 35, [1960] 1 All ER 778 at 784.

3　*Phrantzes v Argenti* [1960] 2 QB 19 at 35–36, [1960] 1 All ER 778 at 784; cf *Shahnaz v Rizwan* [1965] 1 QB 390, [1964] 2 All ER 993.

4　For the meaning of 'the Rome Convention' see para 844 text and note 1 ante. As to that convention see para 844 et seq ante).

5　See the Rome Convention art 10 para 1; and para 854 ante.

1078. Damages. The assessment of damages for breach of a contract to which the Rome Convention[1] applies is a matter for the law which governs the contract[2], and there is no separate role for the lex fori. Otherwise there remains a distinction between remoteness of damage, which is a question of substance governed by the lex causae[3], and the measure or quantification of damages, which is a question of procedure governed by the lex fori[4]. Remoteness of damage includes such questions as whether the plaintiff can recover only for reasonably foreseeable kinds of loss[5], or for particular heads of damage, such as damages for pain and suffering[6]. The measure or quantification of damages includes such matters as the determination of the money value to be put on any particular item of loss for which the defendant is liable[7], and the manner in which provision is made for future or prospective losses[8].

Damages may be awarded in sterling or in a foreign currency[9]. The latter course may be followed if the foreign currency is that in which the loss was felt or borne by the plaintiff[10]. Such an order has been made in the case of a liquidated debt expressed in a foreign currency[11], damages for breach of contract[12], damages for tort[13], and for restitution upon the frustration of a contract[14]. If the latter is ordered, the sum will be converted into sterling at the date upon which the court authorises enforcement[15], unless statute provides otherwise.

The liability to pay interest and the rate of interest payable upon a contractual debt are matters of substance and are governed by the law which governs the contract[16]. The interest rate should be that which applies to the currency in question[17].

1　For the meaning of 'the Rome Convention' see para 844 text and note 1 ante. As to that convention see para 844 et seq ante).

2   As to the applicable law see the Rome Convention arts 3–6, 12.
3   As to the 'lex causae' see para 1066 ante.
4   *J D'Almeida Araujo Lda v Sir Frederick Becker & Co Ltd* [1953] 2 QB 329 at 333–338, [1953] 2 All ER 288 at 290–293; *Chaplin v Boys* [1971] AC 356 at 379, 381–382, 392–395, [1969] 2 All ER 1085 at 1093, 1095, 1105–1106, HL. See also *Breavington v Godleman* (1988) 169 CLR 41, Aust HC; cf *Stevens v Head* (1993) 176 CLR 433, Aust HC. As to the lex fori see para 1066 ante.
5   *J D'Almeida Araujo Lda v Sir Frederick Becker & Co Ltd* [1953] 2 QB 329, [1953] 2 All ER 288.
6   *Chaplin v Boys* [1971] AC 356 at 379, 392–393, 395, [1969] 2 All ER 1085 at 1093, 1104–1106, HL; contra at 382–383, and at 1095–1096; and see, in the court below, sub nom *Boys v Chaplin* [1968] 2 QB 1 at 20, 41, [1968] 1 All ER 283 at 286–287, 299, CA; contra at 32 and at 294. See also *Kendrick v Burnett* (1897) 25 R 82, Ct of Sess; *Naftalin v London, Midland and Scottish Rly Co* 1933 SC 259; *M'Elroy v M'Allister* 1949 SC 110; *MacKinnon v Iberia Shipping Co Ltd* 1955 SC 20.
7   *Kohnke v Karger* [1951] 2 KB 670, [1951] 2 All ER 179; *Chaplin v Boys* [1971] AC 356 at 379, 381–382, 392–394, [1969] 2 All ER 1085 at 1093, 1095–1096, 1105–1106, HL. But cf *Stevens v Head* (1993) 176 CLR 433, Aust HC.
8   *Kohnke v Karger* [1951] 2 KB 670, [1951] 2 All ER 179; *Chaplin v Boys* [1971] AC 356 at 393–394, [1969] 2 All ER 1085 at 1105–1106, HL; and, as to circumstances in which these damages may be awarded, see the Supreme Court Act 1981 s 32A (added by the Administration of Justice Act 1982 s 6).
9   *Miliangos v George Frank (Textiles) Ltd* [1976] AC 443, [1975] 3 All ER 801, HL.
10 *MV Eleftherotria (Owners) v MV Despina R (Owners), The Despina R, Services Europe Atlantique Sud (SEAS) v Stockholms Rederiaktiebolag SVEA, The Folias* [1979] AC 685, [1979] 1 All ER 421, HL.
11 *Miliangos v George Frank (Textiles) Ltd* [1976] AC 443, [1975] 3 All ER 801, HL.
12 *MV Eleftherotria (Owners) v MV Despina R (Owners), The Despina R, Services Europe Atlantique Sud (SEAS) v Stockholms Rederiaktiebolag SVEA, The Folias* [1979] AC 685, [1979] 1 All ER 421, HL (so far as it relates to the *Despina R*).
13 *MV Eleftherotria (Owners) v MV Despina R (Owners), The Despina R; Services Europe Atlantique Sud v Stockholms Rederaktiebolag Svea, The Folias* [1979] AC 685, [1979] 1 All ER 421, HL (so far as it relates to the *Folias*).
14 *BP Exploration Co (Libya) Ltd v Hunt (No 2)* [1982] 1 All ER 925 at 970, [1979] 1 WLR 783 at 840; affd [1982] 1 All ER 925 at 978, [1981] 1 WLR 232, CA; affd [1983] 2 AC 352, [1982] 1 All ER 925, 986, HL.
15 *Miliangos v George Frank (Textiles) Ltd* [1976] AC 443 at 463, 468–469, 497–498, 501, [1975] 3 All ER 801 at 809, 813–814, 838, 841, HL; *Re Lines Bros Ltd* [1983] Ch 1, [1982] 2 All ER 183, CA.
16 As to which see the Rome Convention art 10(1)(b); and para 854 ante.
17 *Shell Tankers (UK) Ltd v Astro Comino Armadora SA, The Pacific Colocotronis* [1981] 2 Lloyd's Rep 40, CA. But the judgment will itself carry interest at the English rate: *Practice Direction* [1976] 1 All ER 669, [1976] 1 WLR 83. However, on the coming into force of the Private International Law (Miscellaneous Provisions) Act 1995 Pt I (ss 1–4), the court may order the interest rate applicable to the judgment debt to be such rate as it thinks fit: Administration of Justice Act 1970 s 44A(1) (added by the Private International Law (Miscellaneous Provisions) Act 1995 s 1(1) as from a day to be appointed).

1079. Set-off and counterclaim. Whether the defendant's counterclaim[1] may be tried together with the plaintiff's claim is a matter of procedure to be determined by the lex fori[2]. But the question whether a set-off has the effect of discharging or extinguishing the plaintiff's claim (in whole or in part) is one of substance, and is governed by the lex causae[3].

The question whether a counterclaim may be made in an action is for the lex fori[4].

1   Ie the defendant's claim against a plaintiff which he seeks to set off against the plaintiff's claim against him.
2   *Meyer v Dresser* (1864) 16 CBNS 646; *Maspons y Hermano v Mildred* (1882) 9 QBD 530, CA. As to the lex fori see para 1066 ante.
3   *MacFarlane v Norris* (1862) 2 B & S 783; *Rouquette v Overmann and Schou* (1875) LR 10 QB 525 at 540–541, explaining *Allen v Kemble* (1848) 6 Moo PCC 314. See generally SET-OFF AND COUNTER-CLAIM vol 42 para 401–513. As to the lex causae see para 1066 ante.
4   *South African Republic v La Compagnie Franco-Belge du Chemin de Fer du Nord* [1897] 2 Ch 487, CA.

1080. Priorities. Questions of priorities among claimants upon a limited fund, such as creditors in a bankruptcy, winding up or administration[1], are procedural and are determined by the lex fori[2], which also governs the priority of claims against a ship in admiralty proceedings[3].

Not all questions of priorities are governed by the lex fori. Thus the priority of competing assignments of a debt is probably governed by the law governing the contract to which the assignment relates[4]; and it seems that the priority of claims against immovables is governed by the lex situs, namely the law of the place where they are situated[5].

1   *Pardo v Bingham* (1868) LR 6 Eq 485; *Re Melbourn, ex p Melbourn* (1870) 6 Ch App 64; *Re Kloebe, Kannreuther v Geiselbrecht* (1884) 28 ChD 175, reviewing *Cook v Gregson* (1854) 2 Drew 286; and see para 980 ante.
2   As to the lex fori see para 1066 ante.
3   *Bankers Trust International Ltd v Todd Shipyards Corpn (The Halcyon Isle)* [1981] AC 221, [1980] 3 All ER 197, PC. See also *The Jonathan Goodhue* (1859) Sw 524; *The Tagus* [1903] P 44; *The Colorado* [1923] P 102, CA; *The Zigurds* [1932] P 113; revsd on another point [1933] P 87, CA; affd sub nom *Smith v Zigurds (Owners)* [1934] AC 209, HL. It may be that there had been a failure here to distinguish between the lex fori and the lex loci. As to the priority of such claims generally see also SHIPPING.
4   See para 935 ante.
5   *Norton v Florence Land and Public Works Co* (1877) 7 ChD 332.

1081. Gaming and wagering contracts. In so far as the Gaming Act 1845 enacts that no suit is to be brought or maintained to recover any sum of money or valuable thing alleged to have been won upon any wager[1], it is a statute affecting procedure, and therefore no action lies in England for money won upon a wager in a foreign country, even though the wager is lawful by its proper law[2].

1   Gaming Act 1845 s 18 (as amended). Cf the Gaming Act 1892 s 1; and see BETTING vol 4(1) (Reissue) paras 15–22.
2   *Moulis v Owen* [1907] 1 KB 746 at 753, CA; *Hill v William Hill (Park Lane) Ltd* [1949] AC 530 at 579, [1949] 2 All ER 452 at 481–482, HL. This principle is unaffected by the Rome Convention, which does not apply to matters of procedure: see the Rome Convention art 1 para 2(h): see para 845 text and note 14 ante. As to the enforceability generally of loans made abroad for the purpose of betting or gaming see *Saxby v Fulton* [1909] 2 KB 208, CA; and para 882 ante. See also BETTING vol 4(1) (Reissue) para 29.

1082. Limitation of actions. Subject to certain exceptions[1], where in any action or proceedings in a court in England and Wales the law[2] of any other country falls (in accordance with rules of private international law applicable by any such court) to be taken into account in the determination of any matter, (1) the law of that other country relating to limitation applies in respect of that matter for the purposes of the action or proceedings; and (2) unless both the law of England and Wales and the law of some other country fall to be taken into account in the matter being determined[3], the law of England and Wales relating to limitation does not so apply[4].

In any case, however, in which the provisions described above would conflict[5] to any extent with public policy, they do not apply to the extent that such conflict would result[6]; the application of those provisions in relation to any action or proceedings conflicts with public policy to the extent that their application would cause undue hardship to a person who is, or might be, a party to the action or proceedings[7]. Where, under a foreign limitation law which is applicable[8] for the purposes of any action or proceedings, a limitation period is or may be extended or interrupted in respect of the absence of a party to the action or proceedings from any specified jurisdiction or country, so much of that law as provides for the extension or interruption must be disregarded for those purposes[9].

Where a court in any country outside England and Wales has determined any matter wholly or partly by reference to the law of that or any other country (including England and Wales) relating to limitation[10], then, for the purposes of the law relating to the effect to be given in England and Wales to that determination, that court must, to the extent that it has so determined the matter, be deemed to have determined it on its merits[11].

The provisions described above apply to any action or proceedings by or against the Crown[12] as they apply to actions and proceedings to which the Crown is not a party[13].

1   As to which see text and notes 5–13 infra.
2   'Law' in relation to any country does not include rules of private international law applicable to the courts of that country or, in the case of England and Wales, the Foreign Limitation Periods Act 1984: s 1(5). As to the background to the Act see *Classification of Limitation in Private International Law* (Law Com No 114).
3   Foreign Limitation Periods Act 1984 s 1(2).
4   Ibid s 1(1). As to the meaning of law relating to limitation see note 10 infra. The law of England and Wales determines for the purposes of any law applicable under s 1(1)(a) (ie head (1) in the text) whether, and the time at which, proceedings have been commenced in respect of any matter: s 1(3). The Limitation Act 1980 s 35 (see LIMITATION OF ACTIONS vol 28 para 651) applies to time limits applicable under the Foreign Limitation Periods Act 1984 s 1(1)(a): s 1(3). A court in England and Wales, in exercising under s 1(1)(a) any discretion conferred by the law of any other country, must so far as practicable exercise that discretion in the manner in which it is exercised in comparable cases by the courts of that other country: s 1(4). As to the application of the Act to arbitration see s 5; and LIMITATION OF ACTIONS vol 28 para 619.
5   Ie under ibid s 2(2) or otherwise.
6   Ibid s 2(1).
7   Ibid s 2(2). See *Jones v Trollope Colls Cementation Overseas Ltd* (1990) Times, 26 January, CA; *Hellenic Steel Co v Svolamar Shipping Co Ltd, The Komninos S* [1990] 1 Lloyd's Rep 541, DC; and cf *Arab Monetary Fund v Hashim* [1993] 1 Lloyd's Rep 543 at 592–593. In such a case it is likely that the limitation period fixed by English law applies instead.
8   Ie under the Foreign Limitation Periods Act 1984 s 1(1)(a).
9   Ibid s 2(3).
10   Subject to ibid s 4(3), references to the law of any country (including England and Wales) relating to limitation are construed as references to so much of the relevant law of that country as makes provision with respect to a limitation period applicable to the bringing of proceedings in respect of that matter in the courts of that country and include (1) references to so much of that law as relates to, and to the effect of, the application, extension, reduction or interruption of that period; and (2) a reference, where under that law there is no limitation period which is so applicable, to the rule that such proceedings may be brought within an indefinite period: s 4(1). 'Relevant law' in relation to any country means the procedural and substantive law applicable, apart from any rules of private international law, by the courts of that country: s 4(2).

    References to the law of England and Wales relating to limitation do not include the rules by virtue of which a court may, in the exercise of any discretion, refuse equitable relief on the grounds of acquiescence or otherwise: s 4(3). However, in applying those rules to a case in relation to which the law of any country outside England and Wales is applicable by virtue of s 1(1)(a) (not being a law that provides for a limitation period that has expired), a court in England and Wales must have regard, in particular, to the provisions of the law that is so applicable: s 4(3).
11   Ibid s 3.
12   This includes any action or proceedings by or against (1) Her Majesty in right of the Duchy of Lancaster; (2) any government department or any officer of the Crown as such or any person acting on behalf of the Crown; and (3) the Duke of Cornwall: ibid s 6(2).
13   Ibid s 6(1). As to actions or proceedings by or against the Crown see LIMITATION OF ACTIONS vol 28 para 603.

1083. Method of enforcement. All matters relating to process generally, including mesne process and execution after judgment, are determined by the lex fori[1]. This law, therefore, governs such questions as whether a judgment debtor can be arrested for non-payment of the debt[2], or whether a writ *ne exeat regno* can be granted against a defendant[3].

1 *Flack v Holm* (1820) 1 Jac & W 405; *De la Vega v Vianna* (1830) 1 B & Ad 284; *Liverpool Marine Credit Co v Hunter* (1868) 3 Ch App 479 at 486. As to the lex fori see para 1066 ante.
2 *De la Vega v Vianna* (1830) 1 B & Ad 284. Cf *Talleyrand v Boulanger* (1797) 3 Ves 447; as explained in *Liverpool Marine Credit Co v Hunter* (1868) 3 Ch App 479 at 486; *Brettillot v Sandos* (1837) 4 Scott 201.
3 *Flack v Holm* (1820) 1 Jac & W 405; *Grant v Grant* (1827) 3 Russ 598.

(2) DISCRETIONARY STAY OF PROCEEDINGS

1084. General principle. The question whether an English court has or may exercise jurisdiction in a particular case is dealt with elsewhere in this title[1]. Even when the court may exercise such jurisdiction, it still has a discretion[2] to act in the interests of justice by ordering a stay of proceedings which have been commenced before it[3]. This power is to be distinguished from the issuing of an injunction to restrain a party who has brought, or who threatens to bring, proceedings before a foreign court[4], and from the putting of a party to his election as to which of two sets of proceedings that he has commenced will be pursued[5]. The power to order a stay[6] is in all cases discretionary and will be exercised in the interests of justice[7].

Where a stay is sought on the ground that the parties have by contract agreed that the courts of a foreign country are to have jurisdiction over a dispute, and it is argued that the bringing of proceedings in England is a breach of that contract, the discretion is guided by separate considerations[8].

Special considerations apply when the court has jurisdiction by reason of the provisions of the Brussels[9] or Lugano[10] Conventions, which put limitations upon the inherent power of the court to stay its proceedings[11]. In particular, if the court in favour of which it would wish to stay its proceedings is that of another contracting state to one of the Conventions, it has no power to do so apart from the express provisions on this point of the Conventions[12].

The power of the court to grant interim relief pending trial or pending the determination of an appeal extends to a case where the issue to be tried or which is the subject of the appeal relates to the jurisdiction of the court to entertain the proceedings, or the proceedings involve the reference of any matter to the European Court[13] under the 1971 Protocol[14]. This does not restrict any such powers as the court has apart from this provision[15]. The High Court also has power to grant injunctions and other means of interim relief in cases where proceedings within the scope of the Brussels Convention[16] or any other Convention have been, or are to be, brought in a Brussels or Lugano contracting state or in another part of the United Kingdom[17].

1 See para 615 et seq ante.
2 Supreme Court Act 1981 s 49(3); Civil Jurisdiction and Judgments Act 1982 s 49 (amended by the Civil Jurisdiction and Judgments Act 1991 s 3, Sch 2 para 24).
3 See *Spiliada Maritime Corpn v Cansulex Ltd* [1987] AC 460, [1986] 3 All ER 843, HL. As to the operation of the principle contained in this decision see the cases cited in paras 1085–1089 post.
4 As to which see para 1092 post.
5 As to which see para 1087 post.
6 As to circumstances in which a court will stay its proceedings see paras 1085–1091 post.
7 *Spiliada Maritime Corpn v Cansulex Ltd* [1987] AC 460, [1986] 3 All ER 843, HL.
8 See paras 1088–1089 post.
9 As to the Brussels Convention see para 618 text and note 1 ante.
10 As to the Lugano Convention see para 618 text and note 2 ante.

11 See para 1090 post.
12 See the Brussels Convention art 22; the Lugano Convention art 22; and para 1090 post.
13 As to the meaning of 'European Court' see para 620 note 4 ante.
14 Civil Jurisdiction and Judgments Act 1982 s 24(1). For the meaning of 'the 1971 Protocol' see para 618 note 1 ante.
15 Ibid s 24(3).
16 As defined in the Civil Jurisdiction and Judgments Act 1982: see para 1050 ante.
17 See ibid s 25 (as amended); and para 1076 ante.

1085. Stay of proceedings: forum non conveniens. The court has power at any stage of the proceedings[1] to order a stay on the ground of forum non conveniens where to do so is not inconsistent with the Brussels or Lugano Convention[2]. As a general rule the party seeking the stay (usually the defendant) must establish that there exists another forum to whose jurisdiction he is amenable, and which is clearly or distinctly more appropriate than England for the trial of the action. If the defendant fails to establish this, a stay on this ground will not be granted; if the defendant succeeds in establishing it, the plaintiff will nevertheless be permitted to proceed in England, and the action will not be stayed, if in the interests of justice the action should be permitted to proceed[3].

In determining whether there is another forum clearly or distinctly more appropriate than England for the trial of the action, the court is entitled to take into account all factors connected to the parties, the claim or the action, including the residence of the parties[4]; the factual connections between the dispute and the courts, such as the place where the relevant events occurred and the residence of the witnesses[5]; the law which will be applied to resolve the dispute[6]; the possibility of a lis alibi pendens or other related proceedings[7]; and the question whether other persons may become parties to the litigation[8]. The question of which factors are relevant, and the weight to be accorded to each of them (which will vary from case to case)[9], is essentially one for the discretion of the trial judge[10], with whose assessment an appellate court will be reluctant to interfere[11].

In determining whether, even though the forum conveniens lies elsewhere, the interests of justice nevertheless favour allowing the plaintiff to proceed in England[12] (the burden of proof lying in this instance with the plaintiff[13]), the general permit the plaintiff to allege that the quality of justice, or some individual aspect of it, available to him in the foreign forum would be inferior[14]. If, however, the plaintiff clearly[15] establishes that he would not obtain a fair hearing in the foreign court[16], or that a time bar would mean the case would not be heard at all in the foreign court (except where the plaintiff has culpably failed to issue proceedings to save limitation in the foreign forum)[17], or that the costs of the action in the foreign court would deprive him of the fruits of his victory[18], or that he would lose in the foreign court despite the fact that he would win in England[19], it may still be proper for the court to permit the English proceedings to continue, although the question remains a discretionary one. The availability of legal aid in another jurisdiction is generally not, however, a relevant consideration[20].

1 Where the court has jurisdiction over the dispute, the application for a stay should be made as soon as possible: *Mansour v Mansour* [1990] FCR 17, CA. If the application is dismissed, it is permissible to reapply for a stay at a later date if changing circumstances justify it: *Owens Bank Ltd v Bracco* [1992] 2 AC 443 at 474, [1991] 4 All ER 833, CA; affd on other grounds [1992] 2 AC 443 at 474, [1992] 2 All ER 193, HL. An application for a stay is not a challenge to the jurisdiction under RSC Ord 12 r 8: *Astro Exito Navegacion SA v WT Hsu, The Messiniaki Tolmi* [1984] 1 Lloyd's Rep 266, CA; *Bankers Trust Co v Galadari* [1987] QB 222, [1986] 2 Lloyd's Rep 446, CA. But if, after making such an application, the

applicant elects to take a step in the proceedings which is inconsistent with his plea that the court should decline jurisdiction, he may forfeit the right to apply for the stay: *Ngcobo v Thor Chemicals Holdings Ltd* (1995) Times, 10 November, CA.

2   See the Civil Jurisdiction and Judgments Act 1982 s 49 (amended by the Civil Jurisdiction and Judgments Act 1991 s 3, Sch 2 para 24). As to the Brussels and Lugano Conventions see paras 618, 1040 ante, 1090 post. As to grounds for a stay other than the ground of forum non conveniens see para 1086 post.

3   *Spiliada Maritime Corpn v Cansulex Ltd* [1987] AC 460, [1986] 3 All ER 843, HL; applied in *Bank of Credit & Commerce Hong Kong Ltd (in liquidation) v Sonali Bank* [1995] 1 Lloyd's Rep 227. The statement of principle given in *Spiliada Maritime Corpn v Cansulex Ltd* supra supersedes earlier House of Lords decisions such as those in *The Atlantic Star* [1974] AC 436, [1973] 2 All ER 175, HL; *MacShannon v Rockware Glass Ltd* [1978] AC 795, [1978] 1 All ER 625, HL; *The Abidin Daver* [1984] AC 398, [1984] 1 All ER 470, HL. It is, however, clear from these decisions that the principles apply in identical fashion to admiralty actions in rem.

4   *Spiliada Maritime Corpn v Cansulex Ltd* [1987] AC 460 at 478, 481–482, [1986] 3 All ER 843 at 856, 858–859, HL.

5   But if they are expert witnesses they may be expected to be able to travel: *Spiliada Maritime Corpn v Cansulex Ltd* [1987] AC 460 at 469, [1986] 3 All ER 843 at 849 (citing Staughton J, whose judgment at first instance is unreported); and this factor may be of greater significance in jurisdictions which place greater reliance upon the oral testimony of witnesses.

6   *Trendtex Trading Corpn v Credit Suisse* [1982] AC 679, [1981] 3 All ER 520, HL; cf *Charm Maritime Inc v Kyriakou* [1987] 1 Lloyd's Rep 433, CA; *Crédit Chimique v James Scott Engineering Group Ltd* (1982) SLT 131.

7   *The El Amria* [1981] 2 Lloyd's Rep 119, CA; *The Abidin Daver* [1984] AC 398 at 411–412, [1984] 1 All ER 470 at 476–477, HL; *Cleveland Museum of Art v Capricorn International SA* [1990] 2 Lloyd's Rep 166, CA; *Meadows Indemnity Co Ltd v Insurance Corpn of Ireland plc* [1989] 2 Lloyd's Rep 298, CA.

8   Cf *First National Bank of Boston v Union Bank of Switzerland* [1990] 1 Lloyd's Rep 32, CA; *New Hampshire Insurance Co v Strabag Bau AG* [1992] 1 Lloyd's Rep 361, CA; *Kinnear v Falconfilms NV* [1994] 3 All ER 42.

9   *Spiliada Maritime Corpn v Cansulex Ltd* [1987] AC 460 at 481, [1986] 3 All ER 843 at 858, HL.

10   *Spiliada Maritime Corpn v Cansulex Ltd* [1987] AC 460 at 465, [1986] 3 All ER 843 at 846, HL.

11   *Spiliada Maritime Corpn v Cansulex Ltd* [1987] AC 460 at 465, [1986] 3 All ER 843 at 846, HL.

12   *Spiliada Maritime Corpn v Cansulex Ltd* [1987] AC 460 at 465, 478, [1986] 3 All ER 843 at 846, 856, HL.

13   *Spiliada Maritime Corpn v Cansulex Ltd* [1987] AC 460 at 478, [1986] 3 All ER 843 at 856, HL.

14   *The Abidin Daver* [1984] AC 398, [1984] 1 All ER 470, HL; *Muduroglu Ltd v TC Ziraat Bankasi* [1986] QB 1225, [1986] 3 All ER 682, CA; *Spiliada Maritime Corpn v Cansulex Ltd* [1987] AC 460 at 482–483, [1986] 3 All ER 843 at 859–860, HL. But if there has been very similar litigation on a similarly difficult topic, the interests of justice may require that this expertise be reused by permitting the English action to proceed: the 'Cambridgeshire' factor (referring to one of the vessels in the case). See *Spiliada Maritime Corpn v Cansulex Ltd* supra at 465, 484–486, and at 846, 861–862, HL.

15   *The Abidin Daver* [1984] AC 398 at 410, [1984] 1 All ER 470 at 475, HL.

16   Cf *Purcell v Khayat* (1987) Times, 23 November.

17   *Spiliada Maritime Corpn v Cansulex Ltd* [1987] AC 460 at 483–484, [1986] 3 All ER 843 at 860–861, HL; *The Pioneer Container, KH Enterprise (cargo owners) v Pioneer Container (owners)* [1994] 2 AC 324 at 347, [1994] 2 All ER 250 at 267–268, PC.

18   *The Vishva Ajay* [1989] 2 Lloyd's Rep 558; *Roneleigh Ltd v MII Exports Inc* [1989] 1 WLR 619, CA; *The Al Battani* [1993] 2 Lloyd's Rep 219; *Agrafax Public Relations Ltd v United Scottish Society Inc* [1995] ILPr 753, CA.

19   *Banco Atlantico SA v The British Bank of the Middle East* [1990] 2 Lloyd's Rep 504, CA; *Britannia Steamship Insurance Association Ltd v Ausonia Assicurazioni SpA* [1984] 2 Lloyd's Rep 98, CA; although these decisions may depend on the conclusion that the foreign court, in finding for the defendant, would be acting contrary to generally accepted principles of private international law. Cf *The Hamburg Star* [1994] 1 Lloyd's Rep 399 at 410.

20   *Connelly v RTZ Corpn plc* 37 LS Gaz R 24, 139 Sol Jo 213, CA.

1086. Stay of proceedings: abuse of process. It is open to an English court to stay proceedings which have been brought, even if there is no other forum in which they could be brought, if they amount to an abuse of the process of the court, or if they are vexatious or harassing to the defendant[1].

1 *The Christiansborg* (1885) 10 PD 141, CA; *Re Norton's Settlement, Norton v Norton* [1908] 1 Ch 471, CA. See also RSC Ord 18 r 19.

1087. Plaintiff put to his election. Where a plaintiff has commenced proceedings which are substantially identical in two courts, he may be put to his election and required to discontinue those with which he elects not to proceed[1].

1 *Peruvian Guano Co v Bockwoldt* (1883) 23 ChD 225, CA; *Australian Commercial Research & Development Ltd v ANZ McCaughan Merchant Bank Ltd* [1989] 3 All ER 65. This involves the dismissal of proceedings, rather than merely a stay: *Australian Commercial Research & Development Ltd v ANZ McCaughan Merchant Bank Ltd* supra. Cf *Advanced Portfolio Technologies Inc v Ainsworth* (1995) Times, 15 November, where the court would not order a stay of English proceedings but would restrain a plaintiff from proceeding in a foreign jurisdiction (see para 1092 post).

1088. Stay of proceedings: breach of jurisdiction clause. A court has power[1] to stay proceedings brought in England in breach of a provision in a contract, known as a jurisdiction clause, that such disputes are to be referred to the exclusive jurisdiction of that foreign court[2]. This power will be exercised on the defendant's application unless the plaintiff establishes that it is just and proper to allow the English action to proceed; the burden of proof is on the plaintiff, who must establish a strong case before being allowed to break his contract[3]. But where the jurisdiction clause confers jurisdiction upon the courts of another contracting state to the Brussels or Lugano Conventions[4], the court will be deprived of jurisdiction altogether[5], and the proceedings should be dismissed as being without jurisdiction, rather than stayed[6]. If, however, the defendant agrees to appear, he waives the breach, and his submission confers jurisdiction upon the court[7].

A stay will not be granted if the foreign jurisdiction clause contravenes a statutory provision forbidding ouster of the jurisdiction of the English court in a certain type of case[8], nor where the term, or the entire contract, is void or otherwise unenforceable[9]. Nor will a stay be granted where the court on which the contract purports to confer jurisdiction is no longer the same as that contemplated by the parties at the time of the making of the contract[10]. In the context of the Brussels or Lugano Conventions, it is less clear that these arguments may be deployed to resist the enforcement of the clause[11].

It is for the proper law of the contract[12] to determine whether a foreign jurisdiction clause provides for the exclusive jurisdiction of the courts of a country or merely that the parties, as where a 'non-exclusive jurisdiction' clause is used, will not object to the exercise of jurisdiction by those courts[13]. The burden of proving that the clause purports to confer exclusive jurisdiction over the dispute in question, or obliges the plaintiff to sue in the nominated court, is on the defendant who relies on it[14]. If, on its proper construction, the clause gives non-exclusive jurisdiction to the foreign court, an application for a stay will be determined in accordance with the general principle governing stays on the ground of forum non conveniens[15].

1 See the Supreme Court Act 1981 s 49(3). The court also has an inherent jurisdiction to stay the proceedings: see *Racecourse Betting Control Board v Secretary for Air* [1944] Ch 114 at 126, [1944] 1 All ER 60 at 65, CA; *The Fehmarn* [1958] 1 All ER 333 at 336–337, [1958] 1 WLR 159 at 163–164, CA; *Evans Marshall & Co Ltd v Bertola SA* [1973] 1 All ER 992, [1973] 1 WLR 349 at 362.
2 *Law v Garrett* (1878) 8 ChD 26, CA; *Austrian Lloyd SS Co v Gresham Life Assurance Society Ltd* [1903] 1 KB 249, CA; *Kirchner & Co v Gruban* [1909] 1 Ch 413; *The Cap Blanco* [1913] P 130, CA; *The Athenée*

(1922) 11 Ll L Rep 6, CA; *The Media* (1931) 41 Ll L Rep 80; *The Vestris* (1932) 43 Ll L Rep 86; *The Fehmarn* [1958] 1 All ER 333, [1958] 1 WLR 159, CA; *The Eleftheria* [1970] P 94, [1969] 2 All ER 641; *The Makefjell* [1976] 2 Lloyd's Rep 29, CA; *Carvalho v Hull Blyth (Angola) Ltd* [1979] 3 All ER 280, [1979] 1 WLR 1228, CA; *The El Amria* [1981] 2 Lloyd's Rep 119, CA; *DSV Silo- und Verwaltungsgesellschaft mbH v Sennar (Owners), The Sennar* [1985] 2 All ER 104, [1985] 1 WLR 490, HL; *British Aerospace plc v Dee Howard Corpn* [1993] 1 Lloyd's Rep 368; *The Pioneer Container, KH Enterprise (cargo owners) v Pioneer Container (owners)* [1994] 2 AC 324 at 347, [1994] 2 All ER 250 at 267, PC.

The English court also has power to restrain proceedings abroad begun in breach of a clause in a contract conferring exclusive jurisdiction on English courts: *Mike Trading and Transport Ltd v R Pagnan & Fratelli, The Lisboa* [1980] 2 Lloyds Rep 546, CA (injunction refused notwithstanding that proceedings might be in breach of such a clause).

3 It is insufficient for him to establish merely that England is the natural forum for the proceedings, for it is more natural for the court to uphold a contract freely entered into: *The Fehmarn* [1957] 2 All ER 707 at 710, [1957] 1 WLR 815 at 819–820; *The Eleftheria* [1970] P 94 at 99, [1969] 2 All ER 641 at 645; *Evans Marshall & Co Ltd v Bertola SA* [1973] 1 All ER 992 at 1001; on appeal [1973] 1 WLR 349 at 362–363, 375, CA; *The Kislovodsk* [1980] 1 Lloyd's Rep 183; *The El Amria* [1981] 2 Lloyd's Rep 119, CA; *DSV Silo- und Verwaltungsgesellschaft mbH v Sennar (Owners), The Sennar* [1985] 2 All ER 104, [1985] 1 WLR 490, HL; *The Pioneer Container, K H Enterprise (cargo owners) v Pioneer Container (owners)* [1994] 2 AC 324, [1994] 2 All ER 250, PC; *British Aerospace plc v Dee Howard Corpn* [1993] 1 Lloyd's Rep 368.

4 See para 1084 notes 9–10 ante.

5 Ie by virtue of the Brussels Convention art 17; Lugano Convention art 17. As to the Brussels and Lugano Conventions see para 618 text and notes 1–2 ante.

6 See para 633 ante.

7 See the Brussels Convention art 18; Lugano Convention art 18; and para 630 note 6 ante.

8 *The Hollandia* [1983] 1 AC 565, [1982] 3 All ER 1141, HL. But note that this case 'would be decided differently today by reason of the Brussels Convention art 17. As to the operation of the general principle see also, for example, the Employment Protection (Consolidation) Act 1978 s 140 (as amended); and EMPLOYMENT vol 16 (Reissue) para 69.

9 *Re Jogia* [1988] 2 All ER 328 at 335, [1988] 1 WLR 484 at 492, *The Emre II* [1989] 2 Lloyd's Rep 182; *Mackender v Feldia AG* [1967] 2 QB 590, [1966] 3 All ER 847, CA. See further *The Hollandia* [1983] 1 AC 565, [1982] 3 All ER 1141, HL (foreign jurisdiction clause held void as amounting to lower limitation of liability under bill of lading than permitted by the Hague-Visby rules). See also, however, *The Benarty, R A Lister & Co Ltd v E G Thomson (Shipping) Ltd* [1985] QB 325, [1984] 3 All ER 961, CA (foreign jurisdiction clause valid where reduced limit of liability under bill of lading was provided for by foreign statute expressly preserved by Hague-Visby rules).

10 *Carvalho v Hull Blyth (Angola) Ltd* [1979] 3 All ER 280, [1979] 1 WLR 1228, CA.

11 See para 633 text and notes 15–18 ante.

12 Ie the law which governs the contract as it is determined by the rules of the common law: see para 859 et seq ante.

13 See *Evans Marshall & Co Ltd v Bertola SA* [1973] 1 WLR 349 at 361; citing *Hoerler (Trading as C F Mumm) v Hanover Caoutchouc Gutta Percha and Telegraph Works* (1893) 10 TLR 22; on appeal (1893) 10 TLR 103, CA; *Sohio Supply Co v Gatoil (USA) Inc* [1989] 1 Lloyd's Rep 588, CA; *S & W Berisford plc v New Hampshire Insurance Co* [1990] 2 QB 631 at 637, [1990] 3 WLR 688 at 693; overruled on other grounds: *Re Harrods (Buenos Aires) Ltd* [1992] Ch 72, [1991] 4 All ER 334, CA; *Continental Bank NA v Aeakos Compania Naviera SA* [1994] 2 All ER 540, [1994] 1 WLR 588, CA. There is a clear tendency to construe ambiguous clauses in favour of exclusive jurisdiction, especially where the nominated court would in the absence of a clause still have had jurisdiction. The Rome Convention excludes agreements on choice of law from its scope: art 1(2)(d); and see para 845 note 10 ante. For the meaning of 'the Rome Convention' see para 844 text and note 1 ante. This law should in principle determine who is to be bound by the agreement; but for a case in which English law rather than the proper law was applied see *The Pioneer Container, KH Enterprise (cargo owners) v Pioneer Container (owners)* [1994] 2 AC 324, [1994] 2 All ER 250, PC (bailor bound by clause agreed between bailee and sub-bailee, whose contract was governed by Chinese law).

14 *DSV Silo- und Verwaltungsgesellschaft mbH v Sennar (Owners), The Sennar (No 2)* [1984] 2 Lloyd's Rep 142; affd [1985] 2 All ER 104, [1985] 1 WLR 490, HL; *Evans Marshall & Co Ltd v Bertola SA* [1973] 1 WLR 349 at 361. In relation to the scope of the clause and the actions which will be subject to it see *Harbour Assurance Co (UK) Ltd v Kansa General International Insurance Co Ltd* [1993] QB 701, [1993] 3 All ER 897, CA.

15 As to which see para 1085 ante. But it will follow from the clause that there is a court to whose jurisdiction the defendant is amenable.

1089. Breach of jurisdiction clause: relevant considerations. In exercising its discretion to grant or refuse a stay[1], the court will consider all the circumstances of the case, including in particular[2] (1) in what country the evidence on the issues of fact is situated, or more readily available, and the effect of that on the relative convenience and expense of trial as between the English and foreign courts; (2) whether the law of the foreign court applies and, if so, whether it differs from English law in any material respects; (3) with what country either party is connected, and how closely; (4) whether the defendant genuinely desires trial in the foreign country, or is only seeking procedural advantages[3]; and (5) whether the plaintiff would be (a) prejudiced by having to sue in the foreign court because he would be deprived of security for his claim; or (b) unable to enforce any judgment obtained; or (c) faced by a time-bar not applicable in England; or (d) for political, racial, religious or other reasons, unlikely to get a fair trial[4]. Although these matters are similar to those taken into account on an application for a stay on the ground of forum non conveniens[5], the two tests are separate and may not be elided[6], for the presumption here is strong that a stay should be granted.

1 The discretion should be exercised in favour of granting a stay unless strong cause is shown for not doing so: *The Eleftheria* [1970] P 94 at 99–100, [1969] 2 All ER 641 at 645.
2 *The Eleftheria* [1970] P 94, [1969] 2 All ER 641; *Aratra Potato Co Ltd v Egyptian Navigation Co, The El Amria* [1981] 2 Lloyd's Rep 119, CA; *The Pioneer Container, KH Enterprise (cargo owners) v Pioneer Container (owners)* [1994] 2 AC 324, [1994] 2 All ER 250, PC.
3 Delay in applying for a stay will be taken into account: *The Vestris* (1932) 43 Ll L Rep 86.
4 *The Eleftheria* [1970] P 94 at 99–100, [1969] 2 All ER 641 at 645.
5 As to which see para 1085 ante.
6 See *Aratra Potato Co Ltd v Egyptian Navigation Co, The El Amria* [1981] 2 Lloyd's Rep 119, CA; *British Aerospace plc v Dee Howard Corpn* [1993] 1 Lloyd's Rep 368; *The Pioneer Container, KH Enterprise (cargo owners) v Pioneer Container (owners)* [1994] 2 AC 324, [1994] 2 All ER 250, PC. *Cf Hamed El Chiaty & Co (t/a Travco Nile Cruise Lines) v Thomas Cook Group Ltd, The Nile Rhapsody* [1992] 2 Lloyd's Rep 399 at 401; affd on other grounds [1994] 1 Lloyd's Rep 382, CA.

1090. Stay of proceedings: effects of Brussels and Lugano Conventions. The principles described previously[1] are applicable in modified form to discrete kinds of cases to which the Brussels and Lugano Conventions[2] apply.

The doctrine of forum non conveniens does not apply as between the contracting states to the Conventions[3]. The court may not, therefore, apply that doctrine as a general procedural principle in order to order a stay of proceedings on the ground that the natural forum is a court in another contracting state to one of the Conventions[4].

In cases where the natural forum is in a non-contracting state, the Conventions will not disapply the procedural principle of forum non conveniens, even though the English court has jurisdiction according to the rules of the Conventions, and this jurisdiction has been regularly invoked by the plaintiff. A stay may accordingly be ordered[5].

The Conventions confer a power, exercisable on limited and narrowly defined grounds, to stay proceedings in favour of the courts of another contracting state. If there are proceedings in a related action in the courts of another contracting state, any court other than the court first seised is permitted to stay its proceedings while the related proceedings are pending at first instance in the other court[6]. It is probable that, when the court seised first has reached its decision, the other court will lift the stay and proceed with its hearing[7].

The Conventions also confer a limited power on the court to dismiss the proceedings if (1) the two actions are related; and (2) the court first seised has jurisdiction over both actions; and (3) its law permits the actions to be consolidated[8].

In a case where a jurisdiction agreement giving jurisdiction to the courts of another contracting state has been broken, the Conventions, by giving the nominated court exclusive jurisdiction, oblige the other court to decline jurisdiction (and the other court therefore has no power simply to stay proceedings) if the clause conforms to the formal and other requirements[9] of either Convention and confers jurisdiction on the courts of a contracting state[10].

On the other hand, where the chosen court is in a non-contracting state, the power of a court to exercise its procedural power to stay its proceedings is unaffected by the Conventions, even though, but for the jurisdiction agreement, the court would have jurisdiction over the defendant according to the rules of the Conventions; accordingly, a stay may be ordered in favour of the courts of the nominated state[11].

If there are proceedings between the same parties in respect of the same cause of action in two contracting states, the court seised second has no jurisdiction once the jurisdiction of the court first seised is established; when the jurisdiction of the court first seised has been established, the court seised second must declare that it has no jurisdiction[12].

1 See paras 1084–1089 ante.
2 As to the Brussels and Lugano Conventions see para 618 notes 1–2 ante.
3 *Re Harrods (Buenos Aires) Ltd* [1992] Ch 72, [1991] 4 All ER 334, CA; *The Po* [1991] 2 Lloyd's Rep 206, CA. See also Dicey and Morris *The Conflict of Laws* (12th Edn, 1993) 401–402. For the meaning of 'contracting state' see para 618 note 3 ante.
4 As a court which stays its proceedings remains seised of them (see *ROFA Sport Management AG v DHL International (UK) Ltd* [1989] 2 All ER 743, [1989] 1 WLR 902, CA), the other court, being the court seised second, would not have jurisdiction in any event: see para 645 ante. It is possible, however, that the court retains a power to stay proceedings on the ground that they are an abuse of the process of the court, because the remedy is in such a case part of national procedural law, which the Conventions are not intended to affect: see Case C-365/88 *Kongress Agentur Hagen GmbH v Zeehaghe BV* [1990] ECR I-1845, ECJ.
5 *Re Harrods (Buenos Aires) Ltd* [1992] Ch 72, [1991] 4 All ER 334, CA. The European Court may, however, take the view that once a plaintiff has lawfully invoked jurisdiction in accordance with the Convention, the court is bound in law to hear the case, and has no discretion to decline to do so. A reference was made to the European Court in *Re Harrods (Buenos Aires) Ltd* supra, but the case was settled and the reference withdrawn.
   As between the courts of England and Scotland the common law principle of forum non conveniens applies, and the statutory mechanism found in the Convention is not applicable: Civil Jurisdiction and Judgments Act 1982 s 2, Sch 4. But as to doubt on this point see *Foxen v Scotsman Publications Ltd* (1994) Times, 17 February; not followed in *Cumming v Scottish Daily Record and Sunday Mail Ltd* (1995) Times, 8 June.
6 Brussels Convention art 22, 1st para; Lugano Convention art 22, 1st para.
7 This remedy is discretionary, but in the interests of judicial efficiency, and to reduce the risk of irreconcilable judgments, the court seised second should incline towards granting one or the other species of relief: Case C-406/92 *The Tatry (cargo owners) v The Maciej Rataj (owners)* [1994] ECR I-5439, [1995] All ER (EC) 229, ECJ. See also *The Linda* [1988] 1 Lloyd's Rep 175; *The Nordglimt* [1988] QB 183; [1988] 2 All ER 531; *The Maciej Rataj* [1992] 2 Lloyd's Rep 552, CA. Article 22 of the Conventions applies to cases where the court seised second does have jurisdiction to hear the case brought before it (as distinct from the case where the court seised second has no jurisdiction at all by reason of art 21: see para 645 ante).
8 Brussels Convention art 22, 2nd and 3rd paras; Lugano Convention art 22, 2nd and 3rd paras. As to the use of this power see the cases relating to the staying of proceedings cited in note 7 supra.
9 Ie the formal requirements of art 17 of the Conventions: see para 633 ante.
10 See the Brussels Convention art 17; Lugano Convention art 17; and para 633 ante. Article 17 of the Conventions gives the nominated court exclusive jurisdiction, but if the defendant does not object to the breach of the jurisdiction clause, the court will acquire jurisdiction by the entry of an appearance,

pursuant to art 18: Case 150/80 *Elefanten Schuh GmbH v Jacqmain* [1981] ECR 1671, [1982] 3 CMLR 1, ECJ. The court seised will determine whether the dispute in question falls within the scope of the clause as a matter of construction: Case C-214/89 *Powell Duffryn plc v Petereit* [1992] ECR I-1745, ECJ.
11 *Re Harrods (Buenos Aires) Ltd* [1992] Ch 72, [1991] 4 All ER 334, CA; *The Nile Rhapsody* [1992] 2 Lloyds Rep 399; affd [1994] 1 Lloyd's Rep 382, CA.
12 See the Brussels Convention art 21; Lugano Convention art 21; and para 645 ante.

1091. Matrimonial proceedings. Where matrimonial proceedings are pending in respect of the same marriage both in England and Wales and in another jurisdiction, the English court, in addition to its inherent power to order a stay, has the power, and in some cases the duty, to order a stay in respect of the English proceedings under the provisions of the Domicile and Matrimonial Proceedings Act 1973[1].

1 See paras 760–763 ante.

(3) INJUNCTION TO RESTRAIN FOREIGN PROCEEDINGS

1092. Injunction to restrain foreign proceedings. If the court has jurisdiction[1] over a person ('the respondent') who has commenced, or who threatens to commence[2], proceedings against a party ('the applicant') in a foreign court, the court may issue an injunction to restrain the respondent from continuing with or commencing such foreign proceedings. The general basis upon which the court will restrain the respondent will be that it is inequitable for the respondent so to act[3]. The injunction is directed at the respondent and not to the judge in the foreign court[4], but the power to order an injunction is exercised with great caution[5].

The jurisdiction of the court over the respondent must be established in accordance with the normal principles of jurisdiction in personam[6]. Thus it must be lawful for him to be served with process of the English court, and if the respondent has a defence to the assertion of jurisdiction over him he will be entitled, on application[7], to have service of process set aside[8].

If the court has jurisdiction over the respondent, it will order an injunction if in all the circumstances of the case it is equitable so to do[9]. The categories of case in which the court will act are not fixed[10], but the ground most commonly resorted to is that it is oppressive or vexatious for the respondent to continue the proceedings against the applicant[11]; and the court will generally also require it to be shown that England constitutes the natural forum for the litigation of the respondent's claim against the applicant[12]. The jurisdiction will be exercised sparingly[13]; but if the applicant can establish that the foreign proceedings constitute the breach of an exclusive jurisdiction clause, the court may be prepared to grant an injunction on that ground alone[14].

1 See para 615 et seq ante.
2 The court will normally require the challenge first to be brought in the foreign court itself: *Arab Monetary Fund v Hashim (No 6)* (1992) Times, 24 July; *Pan American World Airways Inc v Andrews* 1992 SLT 268, Ct of Sess; *Barclays Bank plc v Homan* [1993] BCLC 680, CA; *Bank of Tokyo v Karoon (Note)* [1987] AC 45 at 63, [1986] 3 All ER 468, CA; *Amchem Products Inc v Workers' Compensation Board* [1993] 1 SCR 897 at 931, Can SC. It will also normally expect any threat to sue, which is relied on as the ground for application, to be immediate: *Petromin SA v Secnav Marine Ltd* [1995] 1 Lloyd's Rep 603.
3 *Carron Iron Co v Maclaren* (1855) 5 HLC 416 at 439; *Société Nationale Industrielle Aérospatiale v Lee Kui Jak* [1987] AC 871, 892, [1987] 3 All ER 510, PC; *Advanced Portfolio Technologies Inc v Ainsworth* (1995) Times, 15 November; and see *Castanho v Brown & Root (UK) Ltd* [1981] AC 557 at 573, [1981] 1 All ER 143, HL

4 *Lord Portarlington v Soulby* (1834) 3 My & K 104; *Carron Iron Co v Maclaren* (1855) 5 HL Cas 416; *Earl of Oxford's case* (1615) 1 Rep Ch 1; *Lett v Lett* [1906] 1 IR 618; *Bushby v Munday* (1821) 5 Madd 297.

5 *Settlement Corpn v Hochschild* [1966] Ch 10, [1965] 3 All ER 486; *Castanho v Brown & Root (UK) Ltd* [1981] AC 557, [1981] 1 All ER 143, HL; *British Airways Board v Laker Airways Ltd* [1985] AC 58, [1984] 3 All ER 39, HL; *Société Nationale Industrielle Aérospatiale v Lee Kui Jak* [1987] AC 871, [1987] 3 All ER 510, PC.

6 See para 615 et seq ante.

7 Under RSC Ord 12 r 8: see para 617 ante.

8 However, the Brussels and Lugano Conventions (as to which see para 618 et seq ante) may deprive the court of a jurisdiction which, but for those Conventions, it would have had. For instance, if the respondent is domiciled in a contracting state, the personal jurisdiction of the court over him may not be established in accordance with the rules of art 3 of the applicable Convention, and it will be insufficient that he is present within the jurisdiction of the court: see para 634 text and note 11 ante. It is open to question whether the court may restrain a respondent over whom it has jurisdiction from taking proceedings in the courts of another contracting state. This was considered not to be a relevant objection in *Continental Bank NA v Aeakos Compania Naviera SA* [1994] 2 All ER 540, [1994] 1 WLR 588, CA. See also *Aggeliki Charis Compania Maritima SA v Pagnan SpA, The Angelic Grace* [1995] 1 Lloyd's Rep 87, CA. There is nothing express in the Conventions to suggest that the court may not so act, but it can be argued that art 21 of the Conventions (as to which see para 645 ante) deprives the court of jurisdiction to make such an order.

9 See the cases cited in note 12 infra.

10 See the cases cited in notes 3 supra, 11 infra. Eg the court has jurisdiction to restrain a respondent from litigating in a foreign court matters which he could have raised in earlier English proceedings, but at the date at which this volume states the law, no injunction of the kind has been issued: see *Zeeland Navigation Co Ltd v Banque Worms* (14 December 1995, unreported).

11 *British Airways Board v Laker Airways Ltd* [1985] AC 58, [1984] 3 All ER 39, HL; *South Carolina Insurance Co v Assurantie Maatschappij 'de Zeven Provincien' NV* [1987] AC 24, [1986] 3 All ER 487, HL; *Société Nationale Industrielle Aérospatiale v Lee Kui Jak* [1987] AC 871, [1987] 3 All ER 510, PC; *Cohen v Rothfield* [1919] 1 KB 410, CA; *Settlement Corpn v Hochschild* [1966] Ch 10 [1965] 3 All ER 486; and see *Smith Kline & French Laboratories Ltd v Bloch* [1983] 2 All ER 72, [1983] 1 WLR 730, CA; *Midland Bank plc v Laker Airways Ltd* [1986] QB 689, [1986] 1 All ER 526, CA; *Bank of Tokyo v Karoon (Note)* [1987] AC 45, [1986] 3 All ER 468, CA; *E I du Pont de Nemours & Co and Endo Laboratories Inc v Agnew (No 2)* [1988] 2 Lloyd's Rep 240, CA; *Sohio Supply Co v Gatoil (USA) Inc* [1989] 1 Lloyd's Rep 588, CA; *Arab Monetary Fund v Hashim (No 6)* (1992) Times, 24 July; *Barclays Bank plc v Homan* [1993] BCLC 680, CA; *Amchem Products Inc v Workers' Compensation Board* [1993] 1 SCR 897, Can SC. In making this assessment, the consequences of ordering the injunction must be compared with the possible effect of not doing so. Where the failure to restrain the respondent would be to expose the applicant to the need to undertake further expensive litigation, covering the same issues, in order to obtain a contribution, this may constitute evidence of oppression: *Société Nationale Industrielle Aérospatiale v Lee Kui Jak* supra. So too might the procedures inherent in the foreign proceedings: *Midland Bank plc v Laker Airways Ltd* supra. It is clear from *Société Nationale Industrielle Aérospatiale v Lee Kui Jak* supra, that the test is more demanding than that applied when a defendant seeks a stay of domestic proceedings, and that suggestions to the contrary in *Castanho v Brown & Root (UK) Ltd* [1981] AC 557, [1981] 1 All ER 143, HL, are not good law. See also *Barclays Bank plc v Homan* supra. An injunction to protect the jurisdiction of the court may be granted, but see *South Carolina Insurance Co v Assurantie Maatschappij 'de Zeven Provincien' NV* supra; *X AG v A Bank* [1983] 2 All ER 464, [1983] 2 Lloyd's Rep 535; *National Mutual Holdings Pty Ltd v Sentry Corpn* (1989) 87 ALR 539, Aust Fed Ct; cf *Barclays Bank plc v Homan* supra.

12 *Société Nationale Industrielle Aérospatiale v Lee Kui Jak* [1987] AC 871, [1987] 3 All ER 510, PC. If the respondent would be unable in England to prosecute the claim which he has commenced in the foreign court, it is unclear whether this condition needs to be satisfied, but in principle it should be sufficient that England is the natural forum for the dispute between the parties: see *British Airways Board v Laker Airways Ltd* [1985] AC 58, [1984] 3 All ER 39, HL; cf *Midland Bank plc v Laker Airways Ltd* [1986] QB 689, [1986] 1 All ER 526, CA; *Société Nationale Industrielle Aérospatiale v Lee Kui Jak* [1987] AC 871, [1987] 3 All ER 510, PC.

13 See cases cited in note 5 supra.

14 *Sohio Supply Co v Gatoil (USA) Inc* [1989] 1 Lloyd's Rep 588, CA; *Continental Bank NA v Aeakos Compania Naviera SA* [1994] 2 All ER 540, [1994] 1 WLR 588, CA; see also *Aggeliki Charis Compania Maritima SA v Pagnan SpA, The Angelic Grace* [1995] 1 Lloyd's Rep 87, CA. Cf *British Airways Board v Laker Airways Ltd* [1985] AC 58, [1984] 3 All ER 39, HL; cf *Doherty v Allman* (1878) 3 App Cas 709.

(4) PROOF OF FOREIGN LAW

1093. Need for proof. Subject to certain exceptions[1], foreign law is a question of fact[2] which must be specifically pleaded by the party relying upon it[3], and must be proved to the court[4]. The English court cannot generally take judicial notice of foreign law[5], and it presumes that this is the same as English law unless the contrary is proved[6]. Thus, the onus of proof of foreign law lies on the party relying on it[7]. Where, for the purpose of disposing of any action or other matter which is being tried by a judge with a jury in any court in England or Wales, it is necessary to ascertain the law of any other country which is applicable to the facts of the case, any question as to the effect of the evidence given with respect to that law shall, instead of being submitted to the jury, be decided by the judge alone[8].

This rule does not apply in the case of an appellate court which has jurisdiction to hear appeals from several countries. Thus, the House of Lords[9] takes judicial notice of the law of Scotland and Northern Ireland so far as it is material to the issues raised by the record in all cases that come before it[10]; and, similarly, the Judicial Committee of the Privy Council takes judicial notice of the law of the particular country from which appeal is made to it[11].

A statutory exception to the rule is provided by the British Law Ascertainment Act 1859, by which a court in any part of Her Majesty's dominions may, if of the opinion that it is necessary or expedient for the proper disposal of any action, state a case for the opinion of a superior court in any other part of Her Majesty's dominions[12] upon the law applicable to the facts stated in the case[13]. The European Convention on Information on Foreign Law permits the judicial authority of a contracting state to make a request for information[14].

1 See text and notes 9–14 infra.
2 *Mostyn v Fabrigas* (1774) 1 Cowp 161 at 174; *Guaranty Trust Co of New York v Hannay & Co* [1918] 2 KB 623 at 667, CA; *Bankers and Shippers Insurance Co of New York v Liverpool Marine and General Insurance Co Ltd* (1925) 24 Ll L Rep 85 at 88, HL; *Ottoman Bank of Nicosia v Chakarian* [1938] AC 260 at 279, [1937] 4 All ER 570 at 581, PC. As to the powers of an appellate court to review a finding of a lower court as to foreign law see *Parkasho v Singh* [1968] P 233 at 250–254, [1967] 1 All ER 737 at 746–749, DC.
3 *Ascherberg, Hopwood and Crew Ltd v Casa Musicale Sonzogno (Di Piero, Ostale Societa in Nome Collettivo)* [1971] 3 All ER 38, [1971] 1 WLR 1128, CA.
4 *Fremoult v Dedire* (1718) 1 P Wms 429; *Mostyn v Fabrigas* (1774) 1 Cowp 161; *Earl Nelson v Lord Bridport* (1845) 8 Beav 527; *Lloyd v Guibert* (1865) LR 1 QB 115 at 129. Foreign law need not be proved if it is admitted: see eg *Moulis v Owen* [1907] 1 KB 746, CA; and the court can, in exceptional circumstances and with the consent of the parties, decide a question of foreign law without proof: *Beatty v Beatty* [1924] 1 KB 807 at 814–815, CA; *Jabbour v Custodian of Israeli Absentee Property* [1954] 1 All ER 145 at 153, [1954] 1 WLR 139 at 147–148. Evidence may also be given as to how a discretion in the foreign law would be exercised: *National Mutual Holdings Pty Ltd v Sentry Corpn* (1989) 87 ALR 539.
5 As to the exceptions to this see text and notes 9–14 infra; and see also the cases cited in note 4 supra.
6 *The Parchim* [1918] AC 157 at 161, PC; *Dynamit AG v Rio Tinto Co* [1918] AC 292 at 295, HL; *The Colorado* [1923] P 102 at 111, CA; *Sedgwick Collins & Co Ltd v Highton* (1929) 34 Ll L Rep 448 at 457; *The Torni* [1932] P 78 at 91, CA; *Hartmann v Konig* (1933) 50 TLR 114 at 117, HL; *Casey v Casey* [1949] P 420 at 430, [1949] 2 All ER 110 at 116, CA.
7 *Brown v Gracey* (1821) 1 Dow & Ry NP 41; *Smith v Gould* (1842) 4 Moo PCC 21; *Nouvelle Banque de l'Union v Ayton* (1891) 7 TLR 377, CA.
8 Administration of Justice Act 1920 s 15; Supreme Court Act 1981 s 69(5); County Courts Act 1984 s 68.
9 *Cooper v Cooper* (1888) 13 App Cas 88 at 104, HL, per Lord Watson. As to the jurisdiction of the House of Lords see COURTS vol 10 para 741 et seq.
10 *Douglas v Brown* (1831) 2 Dow & Cl 171, HL; *De Thoren v A-G* (1876) 1 App Cas 686, HL; *Cooper v Cooper* (1888) 13 App Cas 88, HL; *Lyell v Kennedy* (1889) 14 App Cas 437, HL; *Elliot v Joicey* [1935] AC 209 at 213, 236, HL; *MacShannon v Rockware Glass Ltd* [1978] AC 795, [1978] 1 All ER 625, HL.

11 *Sumboochunder Chowdry v Naraini Dibeh and Ramkishor* (1835) 3 Knapp 55, PC; *Cameron v Kyte* (1835) 3 Knapp 332, PC.
12 The British Law Ascertainment Act 1859 also applies to certain Commonwealth countries which are no longer part of Her Majesty's dominions: see EVIDENCE vol 17 para 96.
13 British Law Ascertainment Act 1859 s 1; *Topham v Duke of Portland* (1863) 1 De GJ & Sm 517; *Phosphate Sewage Co v Molleson* (1876) 1 App Cas 780 at 787, HL.
14 Ie the European Convention on Information on Foreign Law (1969): TS No 117 (1969) (Cmnd 4229). The contracting states are the members of the Council of Europe. The competent authority in the United Kingdom is the Legal and Executive branch of the Foreign Office.

1094. Mode of proof. The English court will not, in general[1], make its own researches into foreign law[2]. Foreign law must be proved by properly qualified witnesses[3]. In civil proceedings a person who is suitably qualified to do so on account of his knowledge or experience is competent to give expert evidence as to the law of any country or territory outside the United Kingdom, or on any part of the United Kingdom other than England and Wales, irrespective of whether he has acted or is entitled to act as a legal practitioner there[4]. If his evidence is uncontradicted, the court will normally accept it[5], unless it is obviously unreliable or extravagant[6]. Where the witness puts in materials as part of his evidence, the court is entitled to examine those materials[7], and where there is a conflict of evidence as to the interpretation to be placed upon the materials, the court must scrutinise them and form its own conclusion on them[8].

Because foreign law is a question of fact, the court will not at common law act upon a previous English decision on foreign law[9], although this rule has been altered by statute in the case of civil proceedings[10], so that previous findings or decisions of certain courts[11] which are reported or recorded in citable form[12], whether in civil or criminal proceedings, can be adduced in evidence in civil proceedings[13]. If such findings or decisions are so adduced, the law of the country, territory or part with respect to that matter must be taken to be in accordance with them unless the contrary is proved[14], except where they conflict on the point[15].

1 As to the exceptions to this rule see para 1091 ante; and as to proof of colonial and other statutes see the Evidence (Colonial Statutes) Act 1907. See also EVIDENCE vol 17 para 159.
2 *Di Sora v Phillipps* (1863) 10 HL Cas 624 at 640; *Bumper Development Corpn v Metropolitan Police Comr* [1991] 4 All ER 638, [1991] 1 WLR 1362, CA.
3 *Sussex Peerage Case* (1844) 11 Cl & Fin 85 at 115, HL; *Baron de Bode's Case* (1845) 8 QB 208 at 246–247; *Earl Nelson v Lord Bridport* (1845) 8 Beav 527 at 536; *Castrique v Imrie* (1870) LR 4 HL 414 at 430; *Bumper Development Corpn v Metropolitan Police Comr* [1991] 4 All ER 638, [1991] 1 WLR 1362, CA. As to the competency of witnesses see EVIDENCE vol 17 para 231 et seq.
4 Civil Evidence Act 1972 s 4(1); *Practice Direction* [1972] 3 All ER 912, [1972] 1 WLR 1433; *Associated Shipping Services Ltd v Department of Private Affairs of HH Sheikh Zayed Bin Sultan Al-Nahayan* (1990) Financial Times, 31 July. See also EVIDENCE vol 17 para 93.
5 *Buerger v New York Life Assurance Co* (1927) 96 LJKB 930 at 940, CA; *F Koechlin & Cie v Kestenbaum Bros* [1927] 1 KB 616 at 622; on appeal [1927] 1 KB 889 at 895, CA; *Re Banque des Marchands & Moscou (Koupetschesky)* [1958] Ch 182, [1957] 3 All ER 182; *Rossano v Manufacturers' Life Insurance Co Ltd* [1963] 2 QB 352 at 381, [1962] 2 All ER 214 at 231; *Sharif v Azad* [1967] 1 QB 605 at 616, [1966] 3 All ER 785 at 788; and see EVIDENCE vol 17 para 94.
6 *Buerger v New York Life Assurance Co* (1927) 96 LJKB 930 at 941, CA; *A S Tallinna Laevauhisus v Estonian State SS Line* (1947) 80 Ll L Rep 99 at 108; *Re Valentine's Settlement, Valentine v Valentine* [1965] Ch 831 at 855, [1965] 2 All ER 226 at 238, CA; *Associated Shipping Services Ltd v Department of HH Sheikh Zayed Bin Sultan Al-Nahayan* (1990) Financial Times, 31 July.
7 *Earl Nelson v Lord Bridport* (1845) 8 Beav 527 at 541; *Concha v Murrietta, De Mora v Concha* (1889) 40 ChD 543, CA; *Lazard Bros & Co v Midland Bank Ltd* [1933] AC 289 at 298, HL; and see EVIDENCE vol 17 para 94.
8 *Dalrymple v Dalrymple* (1811) 2 Hag Con 54; *Trimbey v Vignier* (1834) 1 Bing NC 151; *Earl Nelson v Lord Bridport* (1845) 8 Beav 527; *Bremer v Freeman* (1857) 10 Moo PCC 306; *Concha v Murrieta, De Mora v*

Concha (1889) 40 ChD 543, CA; *Guaranty Trust Co of New York v Hannay & Co* [1918] 2 KB 623, CA; *Buerger v New York Life Assurance Co* (1927) 96 LJKB 930, CA; *Re Duke of Wellington, Glentanar v Wellington* [1947] Ch 506, [1947] 2 All ER 854; *Re Fuld's Estate (No 3), Hartley v Fuld* [1968] P 675 at 700–703; *Qureshi v Qureshi* [1972] Fam 173 at 195–197, [1971] 1 All ER 325 at 341–343; *Bumper Development Corpn v Metropolitan Police Comr* [1991] 4 All ER 638, [1991] 1 WLR 1362, CA; and see EVIDENCE vol 17 para 94.

9 *Lazard Bros & Co v Midland Bank Ltd* [1933] AC 289, HL.

10 Civil Evidence Act 1972 s 4(2).

11 The finding or decision must have been made in proceedings at first instance in the High Court, Crown Court, quarter sessions (now abolished) or the Lancaster or Durham Chancery Court (now abolished), or by any court hearing an appeal from any of the foregoing, or by the Privy Council (whether to Her Majesty in Council or to the Judicial Committee as such) when hearing an appeal from any court outside the United Kingdom: Civil Evidence Act 1972 s 4(4).

12 Ie which are reported or recorded in writing in a report, transcript or other document which, if the question in relation to the determination of which they are cited had been a question as to the law of England and Wales, could be cited as an authority in legal proceedings in England and Wales: see ibid s 4(2), (5).

13 Ibid s 4(2)(a). Notice must be given to every other party to the proceedings in accordance with rules of court: s 4(3). The appropriate rule is RSC Ord 38 r 7.

14 See the Civil Evidence Act 1972 s 4(2)(b).

15 Ibid s 4(2) proviso, disapplying s 4(2) in the case of a finding or decision which conflicts with another finding or decision on the same question adduced by virtue of s 4(2) in the same proceedings.

INDEX

Compulsory Acquisition of Land

COMPENSATION—*continued*
  compulsory acquisition—*continued*
    general vesting declaration. *See under* VESTING
      DECLARATION
    increase or decrease in value due to scheme
      underlying. *See* statutory disregard *below*
    interest—
      general vesting declaration, under, 177
      survey, damage by, 92n[9]
    Lands Tribunal. *See* LANDS TRIBUNAL
    leases and short tenancies—
      delivery of possession, 184
      interests entitled, 182
      notice requiring possession, need for, 183
    market value. *See* market value *below*
    mistakes and omissions, 133, 134
    negative equity cases, 195
    offers by claimant or acquiring authority, 199
    payment on account, 92n[9]
    persons entitled, 197
    planning permission—
      assumed. *See* assumed permission *above*
      potential value generally, 242–244
    principle of equivalence, 233
    reinstatement value. *See* reinstatement value
      below
    rentcharge, release from, 192
    severance. *See* severance *below*
    small sums—
      £20 or less, 167
      £200 or less, payment to trustees, 166
    statutory disregard of scheme. *See* statutory
      disregard *below*
    survey, damage caused by, 92
    unconditional offers, 199
    tenant's entitlement, 180n[5]
    value of land less than mortgage debt, 195
    withdrawal of notice to treat, 120
  development charge, and, 261n[2]
  development plan, effect on potential value. *See*
    under assumed permission *above*
  disturbance—
    meaning, 295n[2]
    agricultural holding, 305, 306
    assessment, 295
    date for assessment, 295
    entitlement, 295
    expense of finding new premises and remov-
      ing goods, 296
    goodwill, 297
    interest charges incurred by, 296
    loss of profits, 297
    new premises, expenses as to, 296
    owner not in occupation, 295
    persons entitled, 295
    re-establishment of business not practicable,
      298
    rehousing, disregard, 295
    removal of fixtures, furniture and goods, 296

COMPENSATION—*continued*
  disturbance—*continued*
    short tenancies—
      agricultural holdings, 305, 306
      counter-notice requiring acquisition of
        whole, 306
      date of assessment, 300
      goodwill and loss of profits, 303
      home loss payment, 308–310
      loss of value of unexpired term, 302
      nature of compensation, 301
      notice of entry compensation, right to opt
        for, 305
      re-establishment impracticable, 303
      rehousing, disregard, 301
      removal expenses, 303
      service of notice to quit instead of notice
        requiring possession, 304
      statutory provisions, 300
    tenants—
      generally, 299
      short tenancies. *See* short tenancies *supra*
  illegal land use or works, 240
  injurious affection—
    advance payments and interest, 358
    breach of restrictive covenants, 355
    claims, 358
    construction or user of works, by, 356
    damage not otherwise actionable, 355
    easements, obstruction of, 355
    extension of rights. *See* noise etc *below*
    noise, vibration etc, extension of rights. *See*
      noise etc *below*
    persons entitled, 354
    severance, in addition to, 292
    statutory provision for compensation, 353,
      354
    subsequent acquisition of adjacent land, 277
    value of land, 357
    works and uses not giving rise to, 355
  injurious works—
    acquisition of land to mitigate effects, 349, 350
    act of God or of third parties, 335
    caravans etc affected by, 338
    execution of works to mitigate effects, 351
    expenses of persons moving temporarily, 352
    highways, acquisition of land to mitigate
      effects, 349
    injurious affection. *See* injurious affection
      above
    mitigation of effects generally, 336
    negligence, 335
    nuisance clause, 335
    power to execute, 335
    sound-proofing buildings. *See under* SOUND-
      PROOFING
    standard of care, 335
    statutory power, 335
    third party's actions, by, 335
  interest (payment)—
    in advance, 138
    on account, 125
    power to award, 226
    rate of, 125n[5]

References are to paragraph numbers; superior figures refer to notes

References are to paragraph numbers; superior figures refer to notes

References are to paragraph numbers; superior figures refer to notes

References are to paragraph numbers; superior figures refer to notes

References are to paragraph numbers; superior figures refer to notes

References are to paragraph numbers; superior figures refer to notes

References are to paragraph numbers; superior figures refer to notes

References are to paragraph numbers; superior figures refer to notes

References are to paragraph numbers; superior figures refer to notes

Confidence and Data Protection

References are to paragraph numbers; superior figures refer to notes

References are to paragraph numbers; superior figures refer to notes

References are to paragraph numbers; superior figures refer to notes

References are to paragraph numbers; superior figures refer to notes

PUBLIC INTEREST
  bank, disclosure by, 456
  confidence, limits of obligation, 416
  defence in breach of confidence action, 485
  doctor's duty of confidence, and, 441
  governmental confidences, and, 434, 435
  journalists and confidential material, 472
  non-disclosure obligations, duration of, 421
  police documents, 473
  public interest immunity, scope of, 499
PUBLIC UTILITY UNDERTAKER
  confidence, obligations of, 435
PUBLISHER
  material acquired in breach of confidence, 466
RECEIVER
  confidentiality, 469
REGISTRAR
  data protection. *See* DATA PROTECTION REGIS-
    TRAR
REGISTRATION
  computer bureaux. *See under* DATA PROTEC-
    TION
  data users. *See under* DATA PROTECTION
REGULATIONS
  power to make, personal files, access to, 538n[3]
REHABILITATION OF OFFENDERS
  disclosure of information, 478
RELEASE
  obligation of confidence, from, 423
REMUNERATION
  data protection exemption, 534
REQUEST
  personal data, for, 525
SCIENTIST
  health professional, as, 452
SEARCH WARRANT
  data protection, as to, 522, 523
SEIZURE
  data protection, as to, 522, 523
SERVICE (DOCUMENTS)
  Data Protection Registrar, by, 510n[2]
SETTLEMENT (LEGAL PROCEEDINGS)
  confidentiality of documents, 479
SOCIAL SERVICES
  personal files. *See* PERSONAL FILES
SOCIAL WORK
  data protection exemption, 531
SOCIAL WORKER
  disclosure of information to police, 474n[3]
SOLICITOR
  compromises and settlements, negotiated by, 479
  confidence, duty of, 455
  deceased client, obligation of confidence, 426
SPOUSE
  confidence, obligations of, 431
  disclosure of risk of AIDS or HIV, 443

STATISTICS
  data protection exemption of information held for, 535
STOCKBROKER
  confidence, duty of, 458
SUB-CONTRACTOR
  confidence, duty of, 463
SUBJECT MATTER
  confidence, of, 417
  confidential, restriction of disclosure in liti-gation, 500
SURVEYOR
  confidence, duty of, 458
TAX
  data protection exemption, 530
TEACHER
  confidence, duty of, 468
TELEVISION
  filming patients, consent and confidentiality, 444
  material acquired in breach of confidence, 466
TENANT
  personal files, access to. *See* PERSONAL FILES
THIRD PARTY
  breach of confidence, liability, 484
  confidence, creation of obligation, 420
  purchase of confidential information without notice, 428
TORT
  obligations of confidence and, 405
TRADE
  payrolls and accounts, data protection exemp-tion, 534
TRADE MARK AGENT
  confidence, duty of, 465
TRADE SECRET
  confidence, obligations of, 407
  form of, 417
  injunction restraining disclosure, 491, 492
  know-how as, 412
  restraint of trade, duration of terms in, 421
  restriction of disclosure in litigation, 500
TRESPASS TO GOODS
  confidence, obligations of, 407
TRIBUNAL
  data protection. *See* DATA PROTECTION TRI-BUNAL
VALUE
  confidential material, of, 413
VENEREAL DISEASE
  confidentiality relating to patients, 442
WARDSHIP
  disclosure of confidential information, 474n[9]
WITNESS
  Data Protection Tribunal, 519

References are to paragraph numbers; superior figures refer to notes

Conflict of Laws

References are to paragraph numbers; superior figures refer to notes

References are to paragraph numbers; superior figures refer to notes

References are to paragraph numbers; superior figures refer to notes

LEGITIMACY
conflict of laws, 783, 784
LEGITIMATION
conflict of laws. *See under* CONFLICT OF LAWS
LIMITATION OF ACTIONS
governing law, 1082
LUGANO CONVENTION
jurisdictional provisions. *See* CONFLICT OF LAWS (Convention jurisdiction)
recognition provisions. *See under* FOREIGN JUDGMENT
MAGISTRATES' COURT
financial relief in matrimonial proceedings, conflict of laws, 757
MAINTENANCE AGREEMENT
jurisdiction to vary, 759
MAINTENANCE ORDER
meaning. See under WORDS AND PHRASES *post*
certificate of arrears: meaning, 819n[12]
collecting officer: meaning, 804n[4]
enforcement—
  Brussels and Lugano Conventions, under, 843
  common law, at, 800
  proof of declarations etc, 799
  reciprocal. *See* reciprocal enforcement *below*
  service of process, 798
jurisdiction—
  children, as to, 796
  contribution orders, 797
  matrimonial suits, 795
New York Convention countries. *See* reciprocal enforcement (1972 Act Pt II, under) *below*
proof of declarations and other documents, 799
reciprocal enforcement—
  common law, 800
  1920 Act, under—
    application of legislation, 809
    certified copies, 810n[5]
    confirmation of overseas provisional orders, 813
    dominions and protectorates within scope of, 809n[5]
    effect of registration or confirmation of orders, 817
    Magistrates' Courts Act 1980, application of, 815
    maintenance order: meaning, 809n[2]
    payment and collection of money, 816
    provisional orders in magistrates' courts, 811
    registration of overseas orders, 812
    transmission of orders made in England and Wales, 810
    variation and revocation of orders, 814
  1950 Act, under—
    cancellation of registration, 807
    change of address, 803n[7]
    collection of sums payable, 804
    discharge and variation of orders, 805, 806
    effect of registration, 803
    evidence of orders, 808

MAINTENANCE ORDER—*continued*
reciprocal enforcement—*continued*
  1950 Act, under—*continued*
    inferior courts, discharge etc of orders registered in, 806
    maintenance order: meaning, 803n[7]
    orders registrable, 801
    registration of orders, 802, 803
    superior courts, discharge etc of orders registered in, 805
  1972 Act Pt I, under—
    admissibility of evidence, 829
    application of legislation, 818
    cancellation of registration, 826
    confirmation of overseas provisional orders, 823
    evidence, 828, 829
    family proceedings, as, 830
    Hague Convention countries, 818n[3]
    magistrates' courts rules, 830n[4]
    maintenance order: meaning, 818n[1]
    payer not resident in UK, 827
    payment of sums due, 822n[12]
    proof of orders, 829
    provisional orders by magistrates' courts, 820
    reciprocating countries, 818n[2]
    registered orders, enforcement of, 824
    registration of orders made in reciprocating countries, 822
    responsible authority, 819n[17]
    transmission of English orders, 819
    variation and revocation of English orders, 821
    variation and revocation of registered orders, 825
    witnesses, 828
  1972 Act Pt II, under—
    admissibility of evidence, 840
    application of legislation, 831
    attachment of earnings order, 833n[14]
    court in Convention country, evidence for, 841
    enforcement of registered orders, 836
    evidence, 839–841
    former spouse, application by, 834
    magistrates' courts rules, 842
    maintenance order: meaning, 833n[3]
    New York Convention countries, 831n[4]
    recovery from Convention country, 832
    recovery from England and Wales, 833
    registering court: meaning, 835n[2]
    registration, 835
    transfer of orders, 835
    variation and revocation of registered orders, 837, 838
  reciprocating countries. *See* reciprocal enforcement (1972 Act Pt I, under) *above*
  registration—
    Brussels and Lugano Conventions, under, 843
    cancellation—
      1950 Act, under, 807
      1972 Act Pt I, under, 826

SUBJECT MATTER
  Brussels and Lugano Convention jurisdiction by
    reference to, 626
SUCCESSION
  conflict of laws. *See under* CONFLICT OF LAWS
SUMMONS
  service out of jurisdiction, 668
TENANCY AGREEMENT
  jurisdiction under Brussels and Lugano Conven-
    tions, 627
THIRD PARTY
  English court's equitable jurisdiction as to for-
    eign immovables, 916
  recognition of judgments under Brussels and
    Lugano Conventions, effect of, 1048n[7]
TORT
  conflict of laws. *See under* CONFLICT OF LAWS
  jurisdiction under Brussels and Lugano Conven-
    tions, 642
  service of writ out of jurisdiction, 656
TRANSLATION
  documents for service abroad, 674n[27]
TRIAL
  mode of, governed by lex fori, 1068
TRUST
  domicile under Brussels and Lugano Conven-
    tions, 637

TRUST—*continued*
  equitable jurisdiction as to foreign immovables,
    919
  location of interests under, 912
  recognition of. *See under* CONFLICT OF LAWS
    (trusts)
  service of writ out of jurisdiction, 660
TRUSTEE IN BANKRUPTCY
  foreign land, title to, 979
VESSEL
  will executed on, 964
VOLUNTARY ARRANGEMENT
    (INDIVIDUAL)
  bankruptcy jurisdiction, effect on, 978
WARSAW CONVENTION
  jurisdiction, effect on, 677
WILL (TESTAMENT)
  conflict of laws. *See under* CONFLICT OF LAWS
WINDING UP
  conflict of laws. *See under* CONFLICT OF LAWS
WITNESS
  governing law, 1073
WRIT OF SUMMONS IN ACTION
  service out of jurisdiction. *See* SERVICE OUT OF
    JURISDICTION

Words and Phrases

Words in parentheses indicate the context in which the word or phrase is used

accessible personal information, 539
Accession Convention (civil jurisdiction and judg-
    ments), 618n[1]
accrual rate (interest), 138n[4]
acquiring authority—
  (compensation), 106n[7], 120n[5]
  (compulsory acquisition), 34n[2]
  (compulsory purchase), 92n[5]
  (local inquiry), 43n[8]
  (vesting declaration), 168n[1]
acquisition, compulsory (land), 1
action area, 247n[2]
actual carrier, 677n[8]
additional development, 263
administration—
  ancillary, 945n[2]
  principal, 945n[2]
aerodrome, 337n[1]
affected area (agricultural unit), 90n[13]
affiliation order (reciprocal enforcement), 818n[1]
agricultural holding (land compensation), 185n[3]
agricultural land (notice to treat), 106n[3]

agricultural unit—
  (blight notice), 90n[4]
  (land compensation), 106n[6]
agriculture (land compensation), 106n[3]
AIDS, 443
alterations—
  (public works), 361n[9]
  runway or apron, 361n[10]
amenity, 112n[5]
ancillary administration, 945n[2]
annual value, 362n[11]
annulment (marriage), 744n[1]
another jurisdiction (matrimonial proceedings),
    760n[6]
appropriate—
  authority (blight notice), 90n[6]
  court—
    (foreign judgment), 1049n[6]
    (maintenance order), 822n[11], 835n[11], 843n[1]
  health professional, 542n[4]
  highway authority, 337n[3]
  minister (aquisition of land), 41n[5]
assessor (compulsory purchase inquiry), 46

References are to paragraph numbers; superior figures refer to notes

References are to paragraph numbers; superior figures refer to notes

local enactment, 271n[3]
local housing authority, 290n[4]
local planning authority, 244n[8]
local social services authority, 539n[9]
long tenancy which is about to expire, 170n[6]
Lugano contracting states, 618n[2]
Lugano Convention (civil jurisdiction and judgments), 618n[2]
lump sum order, 763n[7]
Luxembourg Convention (contract), 844n[1]
magistrates' court maintenance order (1950 Act), 803n[7]
maintenance order—
  (1920 Act), 809n[2]
  (1950 Act), 803n[7]
  (1972 Act), 818n[1]
  registered, 824n[1]
mandatory rules (applicable law), 846, 857n[21], 858n[18]
manufacturing (compulsory purchase), 110
market value, 278
marriage—
  declaration concerning the validity of, 739
  monogamous, 732
  polygamous, 732
  void, 783n[4]
marriage officer—
  (marriages abroad), 713n[3]
  official house of, 719n[5]
Marriage Registration Acts, 720n[7]
material question (foreign corporation), 984n[4]
matrimonial proceedings, 760n[1]
matrimonial relief (conflict of laws), 739
matter relating to a contract (jurisdiction), 641
matter relating to tort (jurisdiction), 642
meeting, pre-inquiry (compulsory purchase), 45n[1]
mesne profits, 133n[7]
minor tenancy, 170n[5]
money provision, 1060n[4]
national, United Kingdom (foreign marriage), 713n[4]
National Trust, 38n[8]
necessary (free speech), 434n[12]
necessary for prevention of crime, 472
necessary in the interests of justice, 472
necessary or proper party, 654n[6]
nominee purchaser, 363n[10]
non-disclosure provisions, 529n[7]
non-money provision, 1060n[4]
notice—
  blight, 90
  objection to severance, of, 172
  purchase, 88
  quit, to, 288n[7]
  response, 88
  treat, to, 100, 120n[4]
numbered article (Brussels and Lugano Conventions), 618n[5]
obligation—
  contractual (Rome Convention), 845n[2]
  in question (jurisdiction), 641

officer—
  collecting (magistrates' court), 804n[4]
  marriage, 713n[3]
official—
  address (corporation or association), 636n[5]
  body (compulsory purchase), 44n[3]
  case (compulsory purchase), 44n[7]
  house of the marriage officer, 719n[5]
  representation (compulsory purchase), 44n[3]
open space (acquisition), 29n[4]
opencast planning permission, 83n[3]
order, compulsory purchase, 34n[1]
order for enforcement (Community judgment), 1065n[6]
ordinary residence, 704
original court (conflict of laws), 1029n[6]
other relevant land (agricultural unit), 106n[8]
outline application, 243n[4]
outline statement (compulsory purchase), 45n[13]
oversea company, 990
overseas country, 756n[3], 998n[6]
overseas divorce, annulment or legal separation, 745n[2]
owner—
  (land acquisition), 37n[3], 92n[7]
  (premises), 290n[5]
owner-occupier, 330n[3]
owner's interest—
  (farm loss payment), 311n[1]
  (home loss payment), 310n[4]
park, 112n[3]
part of the United Kingdom (jurisdiction), 619n[4], 720n[3]
Part I order (children), 774n[3,5]
partial renvoi, 606n[5]
participating tenant (compensation), 363n[9]
parties—
  directly concerned (interest in land), 253n[3]
  necessary or proper, 654n[6]
payee (maintenance order), 819n[5]
payer (maintenance order), 819n[1], 835n[3]
payment into court (compensation), 98n[6], 124
pensions, 534n[7]
pensions (data protection), 534n[7]
permitted development value, 89n[7]
person (Interpretation Act 1978), 624n[3]
person aggrieved—
  (compulsory purchase order), 85n[1]
  (Lands Tribunal), 231n[1]
person under disability (land acquisition by agreement), 96n[8]
personal data, 502
personal information, 538n[1]
personal representative—
  English, 945n[3]
  foreign, 945n[5]
persons directly concerned (opencast coal), 83n[3]
physical factors, 360n[2]
planned range of uses (development plan), 250n[5]

References are to paragraph numbers; superior figures refer to notes